*Less managing. More teaching. Greater learning.*

# INSTRUCTORS...

Would you like your **students** to show up for class **more prepared**?
*(Let's face it, class is much more fun if everyone is engaged and prepared...)*

Want an **easy way to assign** homework online and track student **progress**?
*(Less time grading means more time teaching...)*

Want an **instant view** of student or class performance relative to learning objectives? *(No more wondering if students understand...)*

Need to **collect data and generate reports** required for administration or accreditation? *(Say goodbye to manually tracking student learning outcomes...)*

Want to **record and post your lectures** for students to view online?

## With **McGraw-Hill's *Connect*™ Plus Accounting**,

### INSTRUCTORS GET:

- Simple **assignment management**, allowing you to spend more time teaching.
- **Auto-graded** assignments, quizzes, and tests.
- **Detailed Visual Reporting** where student and section results can be viewed and analyzed.
- Sophisticated **online testing** capability.
- A **filtering and reporting** function that allows you to easily assign and report on materials that are correlated to accreditation standards, learning outcomes, and Bloom's taxonomy.
- An easy-to-use **lecture capture** tool.
- The option to **upload course documents** for student access.

Want an online, **searchable version** of your textbook?

Wish your textbook could be **available online** while you're doing your assignments?

### Connect™ Plus Accounting eBook

If you choose to use *Connect™ Plus Accounting*, you have an affordable and searchable online version of your book integrated with your other online tools.

### Connect™ Plus Accounting eBook offers features like:

- Topic search
- Direct links from assignments
- Adjustable text size
- Jump to page number
- Print by section

Want to get more **value** from your textbook purchase?

Think learning accounting should be a bit more **interesting**?

### Check out the STUDENT RESOURCES section under the *Connect™* Library tab.

Here you'll find a wealth of resources designed to help you achieve your goals in the course. You'll find things like **quizzes, PowerPoints, and Internet activities** to help you study. Every student has different needs, so explore the STUDENT RESOURCES to find the materials best suited to you.

Sixth Edition

# Fundamental Managerial
# Accounting Concepts

**Thomas P. Edmonds**
University of Alabama–Birmingham

**Bor-Yi Tsay**
University of Alabama–Birmingham

**Philip R. Olds**
Virginia Commonwealth University

McGraw-Hill
Irwin

**McGraw-Hill**
**Irwin**

FUNDAMENTAL MANAGERIAL ACCOUNTING CONCEPTS
Published by McGraw-Hill/Irwin, a business unit of The McGraw-Hill Companies, Inc., 1221
Avenue of the Americas, New York, NY, 10020. Copyright © 2011, 2009, 2008, 2006, 2003, 2000 by
The McGraw-Hill Companies, Inc. All rights reserved. No part of this publication may be reproduced
or distributed in any form or by any means, or stored in a database or retrieval system, without the
prior written consent of The McGraw-Hill Companies, Inc., including, but not limited to, in any
network or other electronic storage or transmission, or broadcast for distance learning.

Some ancillaries, including electronic and print components, may not be available to customers
outside the United States.

This book is printed on acid-free paper.

3 4 5 6 7 8 9 0 DOW/DOW 1 0 9 8 7 6 5 4 3 2

ISBN   978-0-07-811089-4
MHID   0-07-811089-0

Vice president and editor-in-chief:  *Brent Gordon*
Editorial director:  *Stewart Mattson*
Publisher:  *Tim Vertovec*
Sponsoring editor:  *Donna Dillon*
Director of development:  *Ann Torbert*
Development editor II:  *Katie Jones*
Vice president and director of marketing:  *Robin J. Zwettler*
Marketing manager:  *Kathleen Klehr*
Vice president of editing, design, and production:  *Sesha Bolisetty*
Lead project manager:  *Pat Frederickson*
Senior buyer:  *Carol A. Bielski*
Designer:  *Pam Verros*
Senior photo research coordinator:  *Jeremy Cheshareck*
Photo researcher:  *Robin Sand*
Senior media project manager:  *Greg Bates*
Typeface:  *10.5/12 Times LT Standard*
Compositor:  *Aptara®, Inc.*
Printer:  *R. R. Donnelley*

**Library of Congress Cataloging-in-Publication Data**

Edmonds, Thomas P.
    Fundamental managerial accounting concepts / Thomas P. Edmonds, Bor-Yi Tsay,
Philip R. Olds.—6th ed.
        p. cm.
    Includes index.
    ISBN-13: 978-0-07-811089-4 (alk. paper)
    ISBN-10: 0-07-811089-0 (alk. paper)
    1. Managerial accounting.  I. Tsay, Bor-Yi.  II. Olds, Philip R.  III. Title.
HF5657.4.E35 2011
658.15'11—dc22

                                                                        2010026306

www.mhhe.com

This book is dedicated to our students whose questions have so frequently caused us to reevaluate our method of presentation that they have, in fact, become major contributors to the development of this text.

Our goal in writing this text is to teach students managerial accounting concepts that will improve their ability to make sound business decisions. The text differs from traditional managerial accounting books in the following ways:

## WE EMPHASIZE THE DEVELOPMENT OF DECISION-MAKING SKILLS

Notice that the table of contents places decision making up front. Procedural topics like manufacturing cost flow, job-order, and process costing are placed at the end of our text while traditional books discuss these topics early. We put decision making front and center because we believe it is important. Beyond placement we introduce topics within a decision-making context. For example, in Chapter 2 we introduce "cost behavior" within the context of operating leverage. We focus on how cost behavior affects decisions such as "am I sure enough that volume will be high that I want to employ a fixed cost structure or do I want to reduce operating leverage risk by building a variable cost structure?" Further, notice that Chapter 3 is written around a realistic business scenario where a management team is using CVP data to evaluate decision alternatives. Indeed, all chapters are written in a narrative style with content focused on decision-making scenarios. This makes the text easy to read and interesting as well as informative.

## WE EMPLOY A STEP-WISE LEARNING MODEL

We believe students learn better if concepts are isolated and introduced progressively in a step-wise fashion. For example, understanding cost behavior is essential to comprehending the need for allocation and an understanding of allocation is essential for comprehending the concept of relevance. Likewise, understanding cost behavior and allocation is critical to comprehending the purpose and function of the manufacturing overhead account. This step-wise learning approach also explains the way chapters are arranged in the text. We provide thorough coverage of basic concepts before students are expected to use those concepts. Traditional texts fail to recognize the importance of this learning principle.

## WE PLACE GREATER EMPHASIS ON SERVICE COMPANIES

For example, our budgeting chapter uses a merchandising business while most traditional texts use a manufacturing company. Using a service company is not only more relevant but also simplifies the learning environment thereby making it easier for students to focus on budgeting concepts rather than procedural details. This is only one example of our efforts to place greater emphasis on service companies.

"Crisp chapters that cover the material without wasted pages, emphasis on decision making, and coverage of accountability."

ANNE WILLIAMS, GATEWAY COMMUNITY COLLEGE

"This book is excellent for the non-accounting major because it is user-oriented. This book actually interests non-accounting majors. I have seen many students actually get excited about what they are learning because they can relate the information to the real world."

JACQUELINE BURKE, HOFSTRA UNIVERSITY

"Few other books have succeeded in elucidating so many critical managerial accounting concepts in such a clear and concise way. This textbook focuses on teaching students the strategy, to master a vital and challenging subject."

RONALD ZHAO, MONMOUTH UNIVERSITY

"I like that the authors used service companies for the budgeting process."

ALANA FERGUSON, MOTT COMMUNITY COLLEGE

## WE PROVIDE EXTENSIVE COVERAGE OF CORPORATE GOVERNANCE

The accounting scandals of Enron, MCI WorldCom, HealthSouth, and others led to the enactment of the Sarbanes-Oxley Act (SOX). SOX places significant pressure on managerial accountants to identify and eliminate fraudulent reporting. This text not only provides coverage of appropriate content but also provides a framework for emphasizing ethics throughout the text. We encourage you to review the content on page 5 in Chapter 1. Further, look at Exercises 16 and 17, and Problem 26 to see how students are challenged to apply the new content. Also, notice that a corporate governance case is included in the Analyze, Think, and Communicate (ATC) section of end-of-chapter materials for every chapter in the text. Specifically, look at ATC Problem 5 in each chapter.

Tom Edmonds • Bor-Yi Tsay • Phil Olds

**Required**

Assume that you are Maytag's vice president of human relations. Write a letter to the employees who are affected by the restructuring. The letter should explain why it was necessary for the company to undertake the restructuring. Your explanation should refer to the ideas discussed in the section "Emerging Trends in Managerial Accounting" of this chapter (see Appendix A).

**ATC 1-5   Ethical Dilemma   *Product cost versus selling and administrative expense***

Emma Emerson is a proud woman with a problem. Her daughter has been accepted into a prestigious law school. While Ms. Emerson beams with pride, she is worried sick about how to pay for the school; she is a single parent who has worked hard to support herself and her three children. She had to go heavily into debt to finance her own education. Even though she now has a good job, family needs have continued to outpace her income and her debt burden is staggering. She knows she will be unable to borrow the money needed for her daughter's law school.

Ms. Emerson is the chief financial officer (CFO) of a small manufacturing company. She has just accepted a new job offer. Indeed, she has not yet told her employer that she will be leaving in a month. She is concerned that her year-end incentive bonus may be affected if her boss learns of her plans to leave. She plans to inform the company immediately after receiving the bonus. She knows her behavior is less than honorable, but she believes that she has been underpaid for a long time. Her boss, a relative of the company's owner, makes twice what she makes and does half the work. Why should she care about leaving with a little extra cash? Indeed, she is considering an opportunity to boost the bonus.

## Thomas P. Edmonds

Thomas P. Edmonds, Ph.D., holds the Friends and Alumni Professorship in the Department of Accounting at the University of Alabama at Birmingham (UAB). He has been actively involved in teaching accounting principles throughout his academic career. Dr. Edmonds has coordinated the accounting principles courses at the University of Houston and UAB. He currently teaches introductory accounting in mass sections and in UAB's distance learning program. He has received five prestigious teaching awards including the Alabama Society of CPAs Outstanding Educator Award, the UAB President's Excellence in Teaching Award, and the distinguished Ellen Gregg Ingalls Award for excellence in classroom teaching. He has written numerous articles that have appeared in many publications including *Issues in Accounting,* the *Journal of Accounting Education, Advances in Accounting Education, Accounting Education: A Journal of Theory, Practice and Research,* the *Accounting Review, Advances in Accounting,* the *Journal of Accountancy, Management Accounting,* the *Journal of Commercial Bank Lending,* the *Banker's Magazine,* and the *Journal of Accounting, Auditing, and Finance.* Dr. Edmonds is a member of the editorial board for *Advances in Accounting: Teaching and Curriculum Innovations* and *Issues in Accounting Education.* He has published five textbooks, five practice problems (including two computerized problems), and a variety of supplemental materials including study guides, work papers, and solutions manuals. Dr. Edmonds's writing is influenced by a wide range of business experience. He is a successful entrepreneur. He has worked as a management accountant for Refrigerated Transport, a trucking company. Dr. Edmonds also worked in the not-for-profit sector as a commercial lending officer for the Federal Home Loan Bank. In addition, he has acted as a consultant to major corporations including First City Bank of Houston (now Citi Bank), AmSouth Bank in Birmingham (now Wachovia Bank), Texaco, and Cortland Chemicals. Dr. Edmonds began his academic training at Young Harris Community College in Young Harris, Georgia. He received a B.B.A. degree with a major in finance from Georgia State University in Atlanta, Georgia. He obtained an M.B.A. degree with a concentration in finance from St. Mary's University in San Antonio, Texas. His Ph.D. degree with a major in accounting was awarded by Georgia State University. Dr. Edmonds's work experience and academic training have enabled him to bring a unique user perspective to this textbook.

## Bor-Yi Tsay

Bor-Yi Tsay, Ph.D., CPA, is Professor of Accounting at the University of Alabama at Birmingham (UAB) where he has taught since 1986. He has taught principles of accounting courses at the University of Houston and UAB. Currently, he teaches an undergraduate cost accounting course and an MBA accounting analysis course. Dr. Tsay received the 1996 Loudell Ellis Robinson Excellence in Teaching Award. He has also received numerous awards for his writing and publications including John L. Rhoads Manuscripts Award, John Pugsley Manuscripts Award, Van Pelt Manuscripts Award, and three certificates of merit from the Institute of Management Accountants. His articles have appeared in *Journal of Accounting Education, Management Accounting, Journal of Managerial Issues, CPA Journal, CMA Magazine, Journal of Systems Management,* and *Journal of Medical Systems.* He currently serves as a member of the board of the Birmingham Chapter, Institute of Management Accountants. He is also a member of the American Institute of Certified Public Accountants and Alabama Society of Certified Public Accountants. Dr. Tsay received a B.S. in agricultural economics from National Taiwan University, an M.B.A. with a concentration in accounting from Eastern Washington University, and a Ph.D. in accounting from the University of Houston.

## Philip R. Olds

Professor Olds is Associate Professor of Accounting at Virginia Commonwealth University (VCU). He serves as the coordinator of the introduction to accounting courses at VCU. Professor Olds received his A.S. degree from Brunswick Junior College in Brunswick, Georgia (now Costal Georgia Community College). He received a B.B.A. in accounting from Georgia Southern College (now Georgia Southern University) and his M.P.A. and Ph.D. degrees are from Georgia State University. After graduating from Georgia Southern, he worked as an auditor with the U.S. Department of Labor in Atlanta, Georgia. A CPA in Virginia, Professor Olds has published articles in various professional journals and presented papers at national and regional conferences. He also served as the faculty adviser to the VCU chapter of Beta Alpha Psi for five years. In 1989, he was recognized with an Outstanding Faculty Vice-President Award by the national Beta Alpha Psi organization.

## PRINCIPAL FEATURES

### Isolating Concepts

How do you promote student understanding of concepts? We believe new concepts should be isolated and introduced individually in decision-making contexts. For example, we do not include a chapter covering cost terminology (usually Chapter 2 in traditional approaches). We believe introducing a plethora of detached cost terms in a single chapter is ineffective, as students have no conceptual framework for the new vocabulary.

### Interrelationships between Concepts

Although introducing concepts in isolation enhances student comprehension of them, students must ultimately understand how business concepts interrelate. The text is designed to build knowledge progressively, leading students to integrate the concepts they have learned independently. For example, see how the concept of relevance is compared on page 255 of Chapter 6 to the concept of cost behavior (which is explained in Chapter 2) and how the definitions of direct costs are contrasted on page 154 of Chapter 4 with the earlier introduced concepts of cost behavior. Also, Chapters 1 through 12 include a comprehensive problem designed to integrate concepts across chapters. The problem builds in each successive chapter with the same company experiencing new conditions that require the application of concepts across chapters.

### Context-Sensitive Nature of Terminology

Students can be confused when they discover the exact same cost can be classified as fixed, variable, direct, indirect, relevant, or not relevant. For example, the cost of a store manager's salary is fixed regardless of the number of customers that shop in the store. The cost of store manager salaries, however, is variable relative to the number of stores a company operates. The salary costs are directly traceable to particular stores but not to particular sales made in a store. The salary cost is relevant when deciding whether to eliminate a given store but not relevant to deciding whether to eliminate a department within a store. Students must learn to identify the circumstances that determine the classification of costs. The chapter material, exercises, and problems in this text are designed to encourage students to analyze the decision-making context rather than to memorize definitions. Exercise 2-1A and ATC 4-1 in Chapters 2 and Chapter 4 respectively, illustrate how the text teaches students to interpret different decision-making environments.

## Corporate Governance
Accountants have always recognized the importance of ethical conduct. However, the enactment of Sarbanes-Oxley (SOX) has signaled the need for educators to expand the subject of ethics to a broader concept of corporate governance. We focus our expanded coverage on four specific areas including:

- Quality of Earnings—We explain how financial statements can be manipulated.
- The Statement of Ethical Professional Practice for Management Accountants—Our coverage focuses on the policies and practices promulgated by the Institute of Management Accountants.
- The Fraud Triangle—We discuss the three common features of criminal and ethical misconduct including opportunity, pressure, and rationalization.
- Specified Features of Sarbanes-Oxley (SOX)—We cover four key provisions of SOX that that are applicable to managerial accountants.

Corporate governance is introduced in Chapter 1. This chapter includes four exercises, two problems, and one case that relate to the subject. Thereafter a corporate governance case is included in every chapter, thereby enabling continuing coverage of this critically important topic.

"Given the current economic environment, [Edmonds'] extensive coverage of corporate governance is critical to accounting."

PATRICK STEGMAN, COLLEGE OF LAKE COUNTY

## Information Overload
The table of contents reflects our efforts to address the information overload problem. We believe existing managerial textbooks include significantly more material than can be digested by the typical managerial accounting student. In contrast with traditional texts that normally have between 18 and 20 chapters, we have limited this text to 14 chapters.

"I believe the Excel templates are a very strong asset for the text as they introduce the students to the skills needed to design spreadsheets to solve business problems."

JOHN SNEED, JACKSONVILLE STATE UNIVERSITY

## Excel Spreadsheets
Spreadsheet applications are essential to contemporary accounting practice. Students must recognize the power of spreadsheet software and know how accounting data are presented in spreadsheets. We discuss Microsoft Excel spreadsheet applications where appropriate throughout the text. In most instances, the text illustrates actual spreadsheets. End-of-chapter materials include problems students can complete using spreadsheet software. A sample of the logo used to identify problems suitable for Excel spreadsheet solutions is shown here.

## Real World Examples

The Edmonds' text provides a variety of thought-provoking, real-world examples of managerial accounting as an essential part of the management process.

## The Curious Accountant

Each chapter opens with a short vignette that sets the stage and helps pique student interest. These vignettes pose a question about a real-world accounting issue related to the topic of the chapter. The answer to the question appears in a separate sidebar a few pages further into the chapter.

### The Curious Accountant

In the first course of accounting, you learned how retailers, such as Sears, account for the cost of equipment that lasts more than one year. Recall that the equipment was recorded as an asset when purchased, and then it was depreciated over its expected useful life. The depreciation charge reduced the company's assets and increased its expenses. This approach was justified under the matching principle, which seeks to recognize costs as expenses in the same period that the cost (resource) is used to generate revenue.

Is depreciation always shown as an expense on the income statement? The answer may surprise you. Consider the following scenario. Schwinn manufactures the bicycles that it sells to Sears. In order to produce the bicycles, Schwinn had to purchase a robotic machine that it expects can be used to produce 50,000 bicycles.

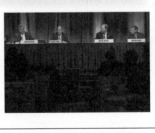

### Answers to The Curious Accountant

As you have seen, accounting for depreciation related to manufacturing assets is different from accounting for depreciation for nonmanufacturing assets. Depreciation on the checkout equipment at Sears is recorded as depreciation expense. Depreciation on manufacturing equipment at Schwinn is considered a product cost. It is included first as a part of the cost of inventory and eventually as a part of the expense, cost of goods sold. Recording depreciation on manufacturing equipment as an inventory cost is simply another example of the matching principle, because the cost does not become an expense until revenue from the product sale is recognized.

## Focus on International Issues

These boxed inserts expose students to international issues in accounting.

### FOCUS ON INTERNATIONAL ISSUES

**FINANCIAL ACCOUNTING VERSUS MANAGERIAL ACCOUNTING—AN INTERNATIONAL PERSPECTIVE**

This chapter has already explained some of the conceptual differences between financial and managerial accounting, but these differences have implications for international businesses as well. With respect to financial accounting, publicly traded companies in most countries must follow the generally accepted accounting principles (GAAP) for their country, but these rules can vary from country to country. Generally, companies that are audited under the auditing standards of the United States follow the standards established by the Financial Accounting Standards Board. Most companies located outside of the United States follow the standards established by the International Accounting Standards Board. For example, the United States is one of very few countries whose GAAP allow the use of the LIFO inventory cost flow assumption.

## Check Yourself

These short question/answer features occur at the end of each main topic and ask students to stop and think about the material just covered. The answer is then given to provide immediate feedback before students go on to a new topic.

### ✓ CHECK YOURSELF 1.1

All boxes of General Mills' Total Raisin Bran cereal are priced at exactly the same amount in your local grocery store. Does this mean that the actual cost of making each box of cereal was exactly the same?

**Answer** No, making each box would not cost exactly the same amount. For example, some boxes contain slightly more or less cereal than other boxes. Accordingly, some boxes cost slightly more or less to make than others do. General Mills uses average cost rather than actual cost to develop its pricing strategy.

"I especially like the Check Yourself and A Look Back/A Look Forward features because they help students to review and refresh topics as they progress through the chapter."

ANNA L. LUSHER,
SLIPPERY ROCK UNIVERSITY

"The Curious Accountant, the real world examples, and the Check Yourself boxes are unique features."

RONALD REED,
UNIVERSITY OF NORTHERN COLORADO

## REALITY BYTES

Unethical behavior occurs in all types of organizations. In its *2007 National Government Ethics Survey,* the Ethics Resource Center reported its findings on the occurrences and ratings of unethical behavior in local, state, and federal governments.

Fifty-seven percent of those surveyed reported having observed unethical conduct during the past year. Unethical conduct was reported most often by those in local governments (63%) and least often at the federal level (52%). The definition of ethical misconduct used in the study was quite broad, ranging from behavior such as an individual putting his or her personal interest ahead of the interest of the organization, to sexual harassment, to taking bribes. The more egregious offences, such as discrimination or taking bribes, were reported much less often than activities such as lying to customers, vendors, or the public.

Once observed, unethical behavior often was not reported. For example, only 25 percent of observed incidents of the alteration of financial records were reported to supervisors or whistleblower hotlines, and only 54 percent of observed bribes were reported.

The survey also found that only 18 percent of government entities have ethics and compliance programs in place that could be considered well-implemented. However, where well-implemented programs do exist, observed unethical misconduct is less likely to occur and more likely to be reported. In these entities only 36 percent of respondents said they had observed misconduct (compared to 57 percent overall), and when they did observe misconduct, 75 percent said they reported it.

## Reality Bytes

Real-world applications related to specific chapter topics are introduced through this feature. *Reality Bytes* may offer survey results, graphics, quotations from business leaders, and other supplemental topics that enhance opportunities for students to connect the text material to actual accounting practice.

### Name and Type of Company Used as Main Chapter Example

| Chapter Title | Company Used as Main Chapter Example | Company Logo | Type of Company |
|---|---|---|---|
| 1. Management Accounting and Corporate Governance | Patillo Manufacturing Company | PATILLO | Manufactures ceramic pottery |
| 2. Cost Behavior, Operating Leverage, and Profitability Analysis | Star Productions, Inc. (SPI) | | Promotes rock concerts |
| 3. Analysis of Cost, Volume, and Pricing to Increase Profitability | Bright Day Distributors | BRIGHT DAY | Sells nonprescription health food supplements |
| 4. Cost Accumulation, Tracing, and Allocation | In Style, Inc. (ISI) | STYLE | Retail clothing store |
| 5. Cost Management in an Automated Business Environment: ABC, ABM, and TQM | Unterman Shirt Company | Unterman Shirt Company | Produces dress and casual shirts |
| 6. Relevant Information for Special Decisions | Premier Office Products | PREMIER | Manufactures printers |
| 7. Planning for Profit and Cost Control | Hampton Hams (HH) | | Sells cured hams nationwide through retail outlets |
| 8. Performance Evaluation | Melrose Manufacturing Company | | Makes small, high-quality statues used in award ceremonies |
| 9. Responsibility Accounting | Panther Holding Company | | Furniture Manufacturing Division |
| 10. Planning for Capital Investments | EZ Rentals | | Rents computers, monitors, and projection equipment |
| 11. Product Costing in Service and Manufacturing Entities | Ventra Manufacturing Company | | Constructs mahogany jewelry boxes |
| 12. Job-Order, Process, and Hybrid Costing Systems | Benchmore Boat Company | | Manufactures boats |
| | Janis Juice Company | JANIS | Makes fruit juice |

## Chapter Focus Company

Each chapter introduces important managerial accounting topics within the context of a realistic company. Students see the impact of managerial accounting decisions on the company as they work through the chapter. When the Focus Company is presented in the chapter, its logo is shown so the students see its application to the text topics.

> "I like the book a great deal. I especially like how the text opens with an interesting 'big picture' question, covers more detailed information in the middle, then goes back to the 'big picture' (in more detail) at the end."
>
> STEVE BUCCHEIT, TEXAS TECH UNIVERSITY

### A Look Back <<

*Managerial accounting* focuses on the information needs of *internal* users, while *financial accounting* focuses on the information needs of *external* users. Managerial accounting uses economic, operating, and nonfinancial, as well as financial, data. Managerial accounting information is local (pertains to the company's subunits), is limited by cost/benefit considerations, is more concerned with relevance and timeliness, and is future oriented. Financial accounting information, on the other hand, is more global than managerial accounting... company. Financial... by objectivity, is focu...

### A Look Forward >>

In addition to distinguishing costs by product versus SG&A classification, other classifications can be used to facilitate managerial decision making. In the next chapter, costs are classified according to the *behavior* they exhibit when the number of units of product increases or decreases (volume of activity changes). You will learn to distinguish between costs that vary with activity volume changes versus costs that remain fixed with activity volume changes. You will learn not only to recognize *cost behavior* but also how to use such recognition to evaluate business risk and opportunity.

## A Look Back/A Look Forward

Students need a roadmap to make sense of where the chapter topics fit into the "whole" picture. *A Look Back* reviews the chapter material and *A Look Forward* introduces students to what is to come.

> "By following one company through several situations as the chapter progresses, more of a 'real world' decision-making process is obtained."
>
> ALEECIA HIBBETS, UNIVERSITY OF LOUISIANA AT MONROE

Regardless of the instructional approach, there is no shortcut to learning accounting. Students must practice to master basic accounting concepts. The text includes an ample supply of practice materials, exercises, and problems.

## Self-Study Review Problem

These representative example problems include a detailed, worked-out solution and provide another level of support for students before they work problems on their own. These review problems are included as iPod animated audio presentations.

"End of chapter exercise and problem materials are varied and first rate."

DARLENE COARTS, UNIVERSITY OF NORTHERN IOWA

## Exercise Series A & B and Problem Series A & B

There are two sets of problems and exercises, Series A and B. Instructors can assign one set for homework and use the set for in-class work.

## Check Figures

The figures provide a quick reference for students to check their progress in solving the problem. These are included for all problems in Series A.

## Excel

Many exercises and problems can be solved using the Excel™ spreadsheet templates located at the text's Online Learning Center. A logo appears in the margins next to these exercises and problems for easy identification.

"A lot of good exercises and problems at the end of each chapter."

CHUO-HSUAN LEE, SUNY PLATTSBURGH

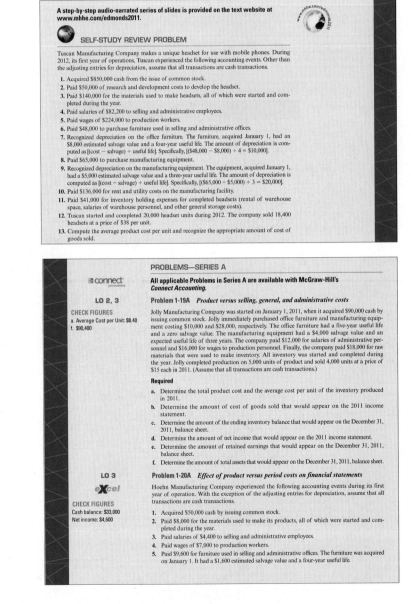

A step-by-step audio-narrated series of slides is provided on the text website at www.mhhe.com/edmonds2011.

### SELF-STUDY REVIEW PROBLEM

Tuscan Manufacturing Company makes a unique headset for use with mobile phones. During 2012, its first year of operations, Tuscan experienced the following accounting events. Other than the adjusting entries for depreciation, assume that all transactions are cash transactions.

1. Acquired $850,000 cash from the issue of common stock.
2. Paid $50,000 of research and development costs to develop the headset.
3. Paid $140,000 for the materials used to make headsets, all of which were started and completed during the year.
4. Paid salaries of $82,200 to selling and administrative employees.
5. Paid wages of $224,000 to production workers.
6. Paid $48,000 to purchase furniture used in selling and administrative offices.
7. Recognized depreciation on the office furniture. The furniture, acquired January 1, had an $8,000 estimated salvage value and a four-year useful life. The amount of depreciation is computed as [(cost − salvage) ÷ useful life]. Specifically, [($48,000 − $8,000) ÷ 4 = $10,000].
8. Paid $65,000 to purchase manufacturing equipment.
9. Recognized depreciation on the manufacturing equipment. The equipment, acquired January 1, had a $5,000 estimated salvage value and a three-year useful life. The amount of depreciation is computed as [(cost − salvage) ÷ useful life]. Specifically, [($65,000 − $5,000) ÷ 3 = $20,000].
10. Paid $136,000 for rent and utility costs on the manufacturing facility.
11. Paid $41,000 for inventory holding expenses for completed headsets (rental of warehouse space, salaries of warehouse personnel, and other general storage costs).
12. Tuscan started and completed 20,000 headset units during 2012. The company sold 18,400 headsets at a price of $38 per unit.
13. Compute the average product cost per unit and recognize the appropriate amount of cost of goods sold.

### PROBLEMS—SERIES A

All applicable Problems in Series A are available with McGraw-Hill's *Connect Accounting.*

LO 2, 3

**CHECK FIGURES**
a. Average Cost per Unit: $8.40
f. $90,400

**Problem 1-19A** *Product versus selling, general, and administrative costs*

Jolly Manufacturing Company was started on January 1, 2011, when it acquired $90,000 cash by issuing common stock. Jolly immediately purchased office furniture and manufacturing equipment costing $10,000 and $28,000, respectively. The office furniture had a five-year useful life and a zero salvage value. The manufacturing equipment had a $4,000 salvage value and an expected useful life of three years. The company paid $12,000 for salaries of administrative personnel and $16,000 for wages to production personnel. Finally, the company paid $18,000 for raw materials that were used to make inventory. All inventory was started and completed during the year. Jolly completed production on 5,000 units of product and sold 4,000 units at a price of $15 each in 2011. (Assume that all transactions are cash transactions.)

**Required**

a. Determine the total product cost and the average cost per unit of the inventory produced in 2011.
b. Determine the amount of cost of goods sold that would appear on the 2011 income statement.
c. Determine the amount of the ending inventory balance that would appear on the December 31, 2011, balance sheet.
d. Determine the amount of net income that would appear on the 2011 income statement.
e. Determine the amount of retained earnings that would appear on the December 31, 2011, balance sheet.
f. Determine the amount of total assets that would appear on the December 31, 2011, balance sheet.

LO 3

**CHECK FIGURES**
Cash balance: $33,000
Net income: $4,600

**Problem 1-20A** *Effect of product versus period costs on financial statements*

Hoehn Manufacturing Company experienced the following accounting events during its first year of operation. With the exception of the adjusting entries for depreciation, assume that all transactions are cash transactions.

1. Acquired $50,000 cash by issuing common stock.
2. Paid $8,000 for the materials used to make its products, all of which were started and completed during the year.
3. Paid salaries of $4,400 to selling and administrative employees.
4. Paid wages of $7,000 to production workers.
5. Paid $9,600 for furniture used in selling and administrative offices. The furniture was acquired on January 1. It had a $1,600 estimated salvage value and a four-year useful life.

## Analyze, Think, Communicate (ATC)

Each chapter includes an innovative section called Analyze, Think, Communicate (ATC). This section contains:

- **Writing Assignments**

- **Group Exercises**

- **Ethics Cases**

- **Internet Assignments**

- **Real Company Examples**

### ANALYZE, THINK, COMMUNICATE

**ATC 1-1  Business Applications Case  *Financial versus managerial accounting***

The following information was taken from the 2008 and 2009 Form 10-Ks for Dell, Inc.

| | Fiscal Year Ended | |
| --- | --- | --- |
| | January 30, 2009 | February 1, 2008 |
| Number of regular employees | 76,500 | 82,700 |
| Number of temporary employees | 2,400 | 5,500 |
| Revenues (in millions) | $61,101 | $61,133 |
| Properties owned or leased in the U.S. | 7.4 million square feet | 8.2 million square feet |
| Properties owned or leased outside the U.S. | 9.4 million square feet | 9.7 million square feet |
| Total assets (in millions) | $26,500 | $27,561 |
| Gross margin (in millions) | $10,957 | $11,671 |

**Required**

a. Explain whether each line of information in the table above would best be described as being primarily financial accounting or managerial accounting in nature.

b. Provide some additional examples of managerial and financial accounting information that could apply to Dell.

c. If you analyze only the data you identified as financial in nature, does it appear that Dell's 2009 fiscal year was better or worse than its 2008 fiscal year? Explain.

d. If you analyze only the data you identified as managerial in nature, does it appear that Dell's 2009 fiscal year was better or worse than its 2008 fiscal year? Explain.

**ATC 1-2  Group Assignment  *Product versus upstream and downstream costs***

Victor Holt, the accounting manager of Sexton, Inc., gathered the following information for 2011. Some of it can be used to construct an income statement for 2011. Ignore items that do not appear on an income statement. Some computation may be required. For example, the cost of manufacturing equipment would not appear on the income statement. However, the cost of manufacturing equipment is needed to compute the amount of depreciation. All units of product were started and completed in 2011.

1. Issued $864,000 of common stock.
2. Paid engineers in the product design department $10,000 for salaries that were accrued at the end of the previous year.
3. Incurred advertising expenses of $70,000.
4. Paid $720,000 for materials used to manufacture the company's product.
5. Incurred utility costs of $160,000. These costs were allocated to different departments on the basis of square footage of floor space. Mr. Holt identified three departments and determined the square footage of floor space for each department to be as shown in the table below.

| Department | Square Footage |
| --- | --- |
| Research and development | 10,000 |
| Manufacturing | 60,000 |
| Selling and administrative | 30,000 |
| Total | 100,000 |

## Mastering Excel and Using Excel

The Excel applications are used to make students comfortable with this analytical tool and to show its use in accounting.

**ATC 1-7  Spreadsheet Assignment  *Mastering Excel***

Mantooth Manufacturing Company experienced the following accounting events during its first year of operation. With the exception of the adjusting entries for depreciation, assume that all transactions are cash transactions.

1. Acquired $50,000 by issuing common stock.
2. Paid $8,000 for the materials used to make its products, all of which were started and completed during the year.
3. Paid salaries of $4,400 to selling and administrative employees.
4. Paid wages of $7,000 to production workers.
5. Paid $9,600 for furniture used in selling and administrative offices. The furniture was acquired on January 1. It had a $1,600 estimated salvage value and a four-year useful life.
6. Paid $13,000 for manufacturing equipment. The equipment was acquired on January 1. It had a $1,000 estimated salvage value and a three-year useful life.
7. Sold inventory to customers for $25,000 that had cost $14,000 to make.

Construct a spreadsheet of the financial statements model as shown here:

> "The students also seem to like the ATC group assignments. These work very well as an in-class activity."

CASSIE BRADLEY, DALTON STATE COLLEGE

> "The innovative end-of-chapter materials are especially on target as an aid to improving student critical thinking and writing skills. The Excel spreadsheet applications are also excellent real-world activities."

DAN R. WARD, UNIVERSITY OF LOUISIANA, LAFAYETTE

> "I really appreciate the Analyze, Think and Communicate section, especially since we emphasize use of information and communicating results to management."

LISA BANKS, CHARLES S. MOTT COMMUNITY COLLEGE

## WHAT'S NEW THIS EDITION?

We thank our reviewers and focus group participants for their suggestions for the sixth edition. Many of these suggestions motivated the changes described below:

### Chapter 1 Management Accounting and Corporate Governance

- Updated Exhibits
- Updated Curious Accountant
- New Reality Bytes
- Updated exercises, problems, and cases

### Chapter 2 Cost Behavior, Operating Leverage, and Profitability Analysis

- Expanded discussion of fixed cost risk avoidance
- Rewrote the content related to mixed costs
- Revised content related to cost averaging
- New Curious Accountant
- New Focus on International Issues
- Updated exercises, problems, and cases

### Chapter 3 Analysis of Cost, Volume, and Pricing to Increase Profitability

- Rewrote the content related to multiproduct CVP analysis
- Rewrote the content related to CVP limitations
- Added new content regarding the relationship between cost structure and the break-even point
- Revised the introduction to the contribution margin ration method
- Enhanced readability by adding several transition sentences
- New Curious Accountant
- New Focus on International Issues
- New Reality Bytes
- Updated exercises, problems, and cases

### Chapter 4 Cost Accumulation, Tracing, and Allocation

- Updated Curious Accountant
- New Reality Bytes
- New Focus on International Issues
- Updated exercises, problems, and cases

### Chapter 5 Cost Management in an Automated Business Environment: ABC, ABM and TQM (Previously Chapter 6)

- This chapter was relocated because of its natural connection to the allocation concepts covered in Chapter 4
- Updated Curious Accountant
- Updated Focus on International Issues
- New Reality Bytes
- Updated exercises, problems, and cases

## Chapter 6 Relevant Information for Special Decisions (Previously Chapter 5)

- This chapter was relocated because of changes described in the previous chapter
- Revised the chapter opening for greater clarity
- Undated Curious Accountant
- Updated exercises, problems, and cases

## Chapter 7 Planning for Profit and Cost Control

- Updated Curious Accountant
- Updated exercises, problems, and cases

## Chapter 8 Performance Evaluation

- Consolidated and rewrote the sections of material covering the fixed cost variances to enhance clarity
- Reorganized the learning objectives to be consistent with the revised fixed cost variance material
- Updated Curious Accountant
- New Reality Bytes
- Updated exercises, problems, and cases

## Chapter 9 Responsibility Accounting

- Updated Curious Accountant
- Updated exercises, problems, and cases

## Chapter 10 Planning for Capital Investments

- Updated Curious Accountant
- Updated Reality Bytes
- Updated exercises, problems, and cases

## Chapter 11 Product Costing in Service and Manufacturing Entities

- Updated Exhibit 11.1 and 11.6 for clarification
- New Curious Accountant
- Updated Reality Bytes
- Updated exercises, problems, and cases

## Chapter 12 Job-Order, Process, and Hybrid Costing Systems

- New Curious Accountant
- Updated Reality Bytes
- Updated exercises, problems, and cases

## Chapter 13 Financial Statement Analysis

- New Curious Accountant
- Updated exercises, problems, and cases

## Chapter 14 Statement of Cash Flows

- Rewrote chapter to provide balanced coverage of the direct and indirect methods of reporting cash flow from operating activities
- Rearranged end-of-chapter material to allow independent coverage of the direct or indirect method
- New Curious Accountant, Reality Bytes, and Focus on International Issues
- New exercises, problems, and cases

## ● McGRAW-HILL's *CONNECT*™ *ACCOUNTING*

**Less Managing.
More Teaching.
Greater Learning.**

McGraw-Hill's *Connect*™ *Accounting* is an online assignment and assessment solution that connects students with the tools and resources they'll need to achieve success.

McGraw-Hill's *Connect*™ *Accounting* helps prepare students for their future by enabling faster learning, more efficient studying, and higher retention of knowledge.

*Connect*™ *Accounting* offers a number of powerful tools and features to make managing assignments easier, so instructors can spend more time teaching. With *Connect*™ *Accounting,* students can engage with their coursework anytime and anywhere, making the learning process more accessible and efficient. *Connect*™ *Accounting* offers you the features described below.

### Simple Assignment Management

With *Connect*™ *Accounting,* creating assignments is easier than ever, so you can spend more time teaching and less time managing. The assignment management function enables you to:

- Create and deliver assignments easily with selectable end-of-chapter questions and test bank items.
- Streamline lesson planning, student progress reporting, and assignment grading to make classroom management more efficient than ever.
- Go paperless with the eBook and online submission and grading of student assignments.

### Smart Grading

When it comes to studying, time is precious. *Connect*™ *Accounting* helps students learn more efficiently by providing feedback and practice material when they need it, where they need it. When it comes to teaching, your time also is precious. The grading function enables you to:

- Have assignments scored automatically, giving students immediate feedback on their work and side-by-side comparisons with correct answers.

- Access and review each response; manually change grades or leave comments for students to review.
- Reinforce classroom concepts with practice tests and instant quizzes.

### Instructor Library

The *Connect*™ *Accounting* Instructor Library is your repository for additional resources to improve student engagement in and out of class. You can select and use any asset that enhances your lecture. The *Connect*™ *Accounting* Instructor Library for Edmonds 6e includes:

- *eBook*
- *PowerPoint files*
- *Instructor's and Solutions Manuals*
- *Test Bank*
- *Excel Spreadsheet Solutions*

### Student Library

The *Connect*™ *Accounting* Student Library is the place for students to access additional resources. The Student Library provides:

- Quick access to lectures, practice materials, eBook, and more.
- Instant practice material and study questions, easily accessible on the go.

### Student Progress Tracking

*Connect*™ *Accounting* keeps instructors informed about how each student, section, and class is performing, allowing for more productive use of lecture and office hours. The progress-tracking function enables you to:

- View scored work immediately and track individual or group performance with assignment and grade reports.
- Access an instant view of student or class performance relative to learning objectives.
- Collect data and generate reports required by many accreditation organizations, such as AACSB and AICPA.

## Tegrity Lecture Capture

Increase the attention paid to lecture discussion by decreasing the attention paid to note taking. For a minimal charge Tegrity Lecture Capture offers new ways for students to focus on the in-class discussion, knowing they can revisit important topics later. Tegrity Lecture Capture enables you to:

- Record and distribute your lecture with a click of a button.
- Record and index PowerPoint presentations and anything shown on your computer so it is easily searchable, frame by frame.
- Offer access to lectures anytime and anywhere by computer, iPod, or mobile device.
- Increase intent listening and class participation by easing students' concerns about note-taking. Tegrity Lecture Capture will make it more likely you will see students' faces, not the tops of their heads.

## McGraw-Hill's *Connect™ Plus Accounting*

McGraw-Hill's reinvents the textbook learning experience for the modern student with *Connect™ Plus Accounting*. A seamless integration of an eBook and *Connect™ Accounting*, *Connect™ Plus Accounting* provides all of the *Connect™ Accounting* features plus the following:

- An integrated eBook, allowing for anytime, anywhere access to the textbook.
- Dynamic links between the problems or questions you assign to your students and the location in the eBook where that problem or question is covered.
- A powerful search function to pinpoint and connect key concepts in a snap.

In short, *Connect™ Accounting* offers you and your students powerful tools and features that optimize your time and energies, enabling you to focus on course content, teaching, and student learning. *Connect™ Accounting* also offers a wealth of content resources for both instructors and students. This state-of-the-art, thoroughly tested system supports you in preparing students for the world that awaits.

For more information about *Connect™ Accounting*, go to **www.mcgrawhillconnect.com,** or contact your local McGraw-Hill representative.

### Online Learning Center (OLC)
*www.mhhe.com/edmonds2011*

More and more students are studying online. That's why we offer an Online Learning Center (OLC) that follows **Fundamental Managerial Accounting Concepts** chapter by chapter. The OLC includes the following:

- Excel Spreadsheets
- Spreadsheet Tips
- Interactive Quizzes
- PowerPoint Slides
- Additional Check Figures
- Links to Professional Resources

### CourseSmart.com

CourseSmart is a new way to find and buy eTextbooks. At Course-

Smart you can save up to 40 percent off the cost of a printed textbook, reduce your impact on the environment, and gain access to powerful web tools for learning. CourseSmart has the largest selection of eTextbooks available anywhere, offering thousands of the most commonly adopted textbooks from a wide variety of higher education publishers. Course-Smart eTextbooks are available in one standard online reader with full text search, notes and highlighting, and email tools for sharing notes between classmates.

### iPod® Content

Harness the power of one of the most popular technology tools students use today— the Apple iPod. Our innovative approach allows students to download audio and video presentations right into their iPod and take learning materials with them wherever they go. Students can visit the Online Learning Center at **www.mhhe.com/edmonds2011** to download our iPod content. For each chapter of the book they will be able to download narrated lecture presentations, managerial accounting videos, and self-quizzes. It makes review and study time as easy as putting on earphones.

## TEGRITY CAMPUS: LECTURES 24/7

Tegrity Campus is a service that makes class

time available 24/7 by automatically capturing every lecture in a searchable format for students to review when they study and complete assignments. With a

simple one-click start-and-stop process, you capture all computer screens and corresponding audio. Students can replay any part of any class with easy-to-use browser-based viewing on a PC or Mac.

Educators know that the more students can see, hear, and experience class resources, the better they learn. In fact, studies prove it. With Tegrity Campus, students quickly recall key moments by using Tegrity Campus's unique search feature. This search helps students efficiently find what they need, when they need it, across an entire semester of class recordings. Help turn all your students' study time into learning moments immediately supported by your lecture.

To learn more about Tegrity watch a 2-minute Flash demo at **http://tegritycampus.mhhe.com.**

## ASSURANCE OF LEARNING READY

Many educational institutions today are focused on the notion of *assurance of learning,* an important element of some accreditation standards. Edmonds **Fundamental Managerial Accounting Concepts 6e** is designed specifically to support your assurance of learning initiatives with a simple, yet powerful solution.

Each test bank question for **Fundamental Managerial Accounting Concepts** maps to a specific chapter learning outcome/objective listed in the text. You can use our test bank software, EZ Test and EZ Test Online, or in *Connect*™ Accounting to easily query for learning outcomes/objectives that directly relate to those objectives for your course. You can then use the reporting features of EZ Test and *Connect*™ Accounting to aggregate student results in similar fashion, making the collection and presentation of assurance of learning data simple and easy.

### Online Course Management

No matter what online course management system you use (WebCT, BlackBoard, or eCollege), we have a course content ePack available for your course. Our new ePacks are specifically designed to make it easy for students to navigate and access content online. They are easier than ever to install on the latest version of the course management system available today.

Don't forget that you can count on the highest level of service from McGraw-Hill. Our online Digital Learning Consultants are ready to assist you with your online course needs. They provide training and will answer any questions you have throughout the life of your adoption.

# SUPPLEMENTS FOR INSTRUCTORS

## Instructor's Resource CD-ROM

**ISBN-10: 0077318110    ISBN-13: 9780077318116**

This CD includes electronic versions of the Instructor's Manual, Solutions Manual, Test Bank, computerized Test Bank, as well as PowerPoint slides, video clips, all exhibits in the text in PowerPoint, and spreadsheet templates with solutions. This CD-ROM makes it easy for instructors to create their own multimedia presentations.

## Instructor's Manual

This comprehensive manual includes step-by-step, explicit instructions on how the text can be used to implement alternative teaching methods. It also provides guidance for instructors who use the traditional lecture method. The guide includes lesson plans and demonstration problems with student work papers, as well as solutions. It was prepared by Sue Cullers of Tarleton State University.

## Solutions Manual

Prepared by the authors, the manual contains complete solutions to all the text's end-of-chapter exercises, problems, and cases.

## Test Bank

This test bank in Microsoft Word format contains multiple-choice questions, essay, and short problems. Each test item is coded for level of difficulty, learning objective, AACSB, AICPA, and Bloom's Taxonomy. In addition to an expansive array of traditional test questions, the test bank includes new types of questions that focus exclusively on how business events affect financial statements.

## Managerial Accounting Video Library

**ISBN-10: 0072376171    ISBN-13: 9780072376173**

These short videos, developed by Dallas County Community College, provide an impetus for class discussion, focusing on the preparation, analysis, and use of accounting information for business decision making.

"This is the book you would like to adopt because it helps your students to succeed in your course."

NASHWA GEORGE, MONTCLAIR STATE UNIVERSITY

## PowerPoint® Presentation

These slides can serve as interactive class discussions and cover key concepts in each chapter.

## AACSB STATEMENT

The McGraw-Hill Companies is a proud corporate member of AACSB International. Understanding the importance and value of AACSB accreditation, **Edmonds Fundamental Managerial Accounting Concepts 6e** recognizes the curricula guidelines detailed in the AACSB standards for business accreditation by connecting selected questions in the test bank to the six general knowledge and skill guidelines in the AACSB standards.

The statements contained in **Fundamental Managerial Accounting Concepts 6e** are provided only as a guide for the users of this textbook. The AACSB leaves content coverage and assessment within the purview of individual schools, the mission of the school, and the faculty. While **Fundamental Managerial Accounting Concepts 6e** and the teaching package make no claim of any specific AACSB qualification or evaluation, we have within **Fundamental Managerial Accounting Concepts 6e** labeled selected questions according to the six general knowledge and skills areas.

## McGRAW-HILL CUSTOMER CARE CONTACT INFORMATION

At McGraw-Hill, we understand that getting the most from new technology can be challenging. That's why our services don't stop after you purchase our products. You can contact our Product Specialists 24 hours a day to get product-training online. Or you can search our knowledge bank of Frequently Asked Questions on our support website. For Customer Support, visit **www.mhhe.com/support.** One of our Technical Support Analysts will be able to assist you in a timely fashion.

## McGraw-Hill's *Connect™ Plus Accounting*

This integrates all of the text's multimedia resources. With just one access code, students can obtain state-of-the-art study aids, including McGraw-Hill's *Connect™ Accounting* and an online version of the text.

## McGraw-Hill's *Connect™ Accounting*

This web-based software duplicates problem structures directly from the end-of-chapter material in the textbook. It uses algorithms to provide a limitless supply of self-graded practice for students. It shows students where they made errors. All applicable Exercises and Problems in Series A are available with McGraw-Hill's *Connect™ Accounting.*

## Study Guide

This proactive guide incorporates many of the accounting skills essential to student success. Each chapter contains a review and explanation of the chapter's learning objectives, as well as multiple-choice problems and short exercises. Unique to this Study Guide is a series of articulation problems that require students to indicate how accounting events affect the elements of financial statements.

## Working Papers

This study aid contains forms that help students organize their solutions to homework exercises and problems and is available through our custom database program, Create. Ask your McGraw-Hill representative for more information.

## Excel Templates

These templates allow students to develop spreadsheet skills to solve selected assignments identified by an icon in the end-of-chapter material.

## Narrated PowerPoint Slides

**(Available on the Online Learning Center (OLC))**
These PowerPoint slides cover key chapter topics in an audio-narrated presentation sure to help students learn.

## Online Learning Center (OLC)

*www.mhhe.com/ edmonds2011*
See page xviii for details.

Special thanks to the talented people who prepared the supplements. These take a great deal of time and effort to write and we appreciate their efforts. Diana Benyaminy of Hofstra University prepared the Test Bank and Online Quizzes. LuAnn Bean of Florida Institute of Technology prepared the PowerPoint presentations and accuracy checked the Instructor's Manual. Sue Cullers of Tarleton State University prepared the Instructor's Manual. Jack Terry of ComSource Associates prepared the Excel templates. We also thank our accuracy checkers, Ilene Persoff of CW Post Campus/Long Island University and Beth Woods of Accuracy Counts, for checking the text manuscript and solutions manual. We also thank our supplement accuracy checker Angela Sandberg, of Jacksonville State University.

We are deeply indebted to our sponsoring editor, Donna Dillion. Her direction and guidance have added clarity and quality to the text. We especially appreciate the efforts of our developmental editor, Katie Jones. Katie has coordinated the exchange of ideas among our class testers, reviewers, and error checkers; she has done far more than simply pass along ideas. Our editors have certainly facilitated our efforts to prepare a book that will facilitate a meaningful understanding of accounting. Even so, their contributions are to no avail unless the text reaches its intended audience. We are most grateful to Kathleen Klehr and the sales staff for providing the informative marketing that has so accurately communicated the unique features of the concepts approach to accounting educators. Many others at McGraw-Hill/Irwin at a moment's notice redirected their attention to focus their efforts on the development of this text. We extend our sincere appreciation to Pat Frederickson, Stewart Mattson, Tim Vertovec, Carol Bielski, Pam Verros, Jeremy Cheshareck, Greg Bates, and Allison Souter. We deeply appreciate the long hours that you committed to the formation of a high-quality text.

**Thomas P. Edmonds • Bor-Yi Tsay • Philip R. Olds**

We express our sincere thanks to the following individuals who provided extensive reviews for the sixth edition:

## Reviewers

Lisa Banks, *Mott Community College*
Cassie Bradley, *Dalton State College*
Amy Browning, *Ivy Tech Community College*
Steve Buchheit, *Texas Tech University*
Alan Campbell, *Troy University-Montgomery Campus*
Julie Chenier, *Louisiana State University*
Darlene Coarts, *University of Northern Iowa*
Alana Ferguson, *Mott Community College*
Richard Griffin, *The University of Tennessee at Marin*
Chuo-Hsuan Lee, *SUNY Plattsburgh*

Jeanette Maier-Lytle, *University of Southern Indiana*
Mary Malina, *University of Colorado Denver*
Michael Meyer, *Ohio University*
Arabian Morgan, *Orange Coast College*
Lisa Murawa, *Mott Community College*
Letitia Pleis, *Metropolitan State College of Denverw*
Patrick Stegman, *College of Lake County*
Scott Wandler, *University of New Orleans*
Anne Williams, *Gateway Community College*
Ronald Zhao, *Monmouth University*

## Our appreciation to those who reviewed previous editions

Jed Ashley, *Grossmont College*
James Bates, *Mountain Empire Community College*
Frank Beigbeder, *Rancho Santiago College*
Daniel Benco, *Southeastern Oklahoma University*
Dorcas Berg, *Wingate College*
Ashton Bishop, *James Madison University*
Amy Bourne, *Tarrant County College*

Jacqueline Burke, *Hofstra University*
Dennis Caplan, *Iowa State University*
Eric Carlsen, *Kean University*
Chiaho Chang, *Montclair State University*
Chak-Tong Chau, *University of Houston—Downtown*
Sue Counte, *Jefferson College*
Rich Criscione, *Morehead State University*

Jill D'Aquila, *Iona College*
David Deeds, *University of Northern Iowa*
Naman Desai, *Florida State University—Tallahassee*
Walt Doehring, *Genesee Community College*
Patricia Douglas, *Loyola Marymount University*
Jan Duffy, *Iowa State University*
Dean Edmiston, *Emporia State University*
Robert Elmore, *Tennessee Technological University*
Terry Elliot, *Morehead State University*
James Emig, *Villanova University*
Robert Fahnestock, *University of West Florida*
Jeffrey Galbreath, *Greenfield Community College*
William Geary, *College of William and Mary*
Nashwa George, *Montclair State University*
John Goetz, *University of Texas Arlington*
Dinah Gottschalk, *James Madison University*
Donald Gribbin, *Southern Illinois University*
Judith Harris, *Nova Southeastern University*
Larry Hegstad, *Pacific Lutheran University*
Aleecia Hibbets, *University of Louisiana at Monroe*
Lyle Hicks, *Danville Area Community College*
Jay Holmen, *University of Wisconsin at Eau Claire*
Fred Jex, *Macomb Community College*
Robyn Jarnagin, *Montana State University—Bozeman*
Shondra Johnson, *Bradley University*
Sheila Johnston, *University of Louisville, Louisville*
Marrk Kaiser, *SUNY at Plattsburg*
Thomas Klammer, *University of North Texas*
Lawrence Klein, *Bentley College*
Mehmet Kocakulah, *University of Southern Indiana*
Lynn Krausse, *Bakersfield College*
Robert Landry, *Massassoit Community College*
Chor Lau, *California State University at Los Angeles*
Mark Lawrence, *University of Alabama at Birmingham*
Minwoo Lee, *Western Kentucky University*
Deborah Lee, *Northeastern State University*
Elliott Levy, *Bentley College*
Bruce Lindsey, *Genesee Community College*
Philip Little, *Western Carolina University*
Julie Lockhart, *Western Washington University*
Cathy Lumbattis, *Southern Illinois University*
Anna L. Lusher, *Slippery Rock University*
Nancy Lynch, *West Virginia University—Morgantown*
Suneel Maheshwari, *Marshall University*
Lois Mahoney, *University of Central Florida*
David McIntyre, *Clemson University*

Pat McMahon, *Palm Beach Community College*
Florence McGovern, *Bergen Community College*
Brian McGuire, *University of Southern Indiana*
Pam Meyer, *University of Louisiana at Lafayette*
John Moore, *Virginia State University*
Michelle Moshier, *SUNY at Albany*
Irvin Nelson, *Utah State University*
Bruce Neumann, *University of Colorado*
Hossein Nouri, *College of New Jersey*
Ashton Oravetz, *Tyler Junior College*
Chei Paik, *George Washington University*
Thomas Phillips, *Louisiana Tech University*
Marjorie Platt, *Northeastern University*
Emil Radosevich, *Albuquerque TVI Community College*
Ronald Reed, *University of Northern Colorado*
Roy Regel, *University of Montana at Missoula*
Jane Reimers, *Florida State University*
Celia Renner, *Boise State University*
Gary Reynolds, *Ozark Technical Community College*
Diane Riordan, *James Madison University*
Tom Robinson, *University of Alaska*
Luther Ross, *Central Piedmont Community College*
Harold Royer, *Miami-Dade College*
Nancy Ruhe, *West Virginia University, Morgantown*
Charles Russo, *Bloomsburg University of Pennsylvania*
Marilyn Salter, *University of Central Florida*
Angela Sandberg, *Jacksonville State University*
Kathryn Savage, *Northern Arizona University*
John Shaver, *Louisiana Tech University*
Bob Smith, *Florida State University*
Walter Smith, *Siena College*
John Sneed, *Jacksonville State University*
John Stancil, *Florida Southern College*
Scott Steinkamp, *College of Lake County*
Scott Stroher, *Glendale Community College*
Holly Sudano, *Florida State University*
Bill Talbot, *Montgomery College*
Pavani Tallapally, *Slippery Rock University*
Suneel Udpa, *St. Mary's College*
Michael VanBreda, *Southern Methodist University*
Sharon T. Walters, *Morehead State University*
Dan Ward, *University of Louisiana, Lafayette*
Sean Wright, *DeVry Institute of Technology, Phoenix*
Allan Young, *DeVry Institute of Technology, Atlanta*
Nan Zhou, *Binghamton University*

Many others have contributed directly or indirectly to the development of the text. Participants in workshops and focus groups have provided useful feedback. Colleagues and friends have extended encouragement and support. Among these individuals our sincere appreciation is extended to Lowell Broom, Samford University; Bill Schwartz, Home School of Technology Management; Ed Spede, Virginia Commonwealth University; Doug Cloud, Pepperdine University—Malibu; Charles Bailey, University of Memphis; Bob Holtfreter, Central Washington University; Kimberly Temme, Maryville University; Beth Vogel, Mount Mary College; Robert Minnear, Emory University; Shirish Seth, California State University at Fullerton; Richard Emery, Linfield College; Gail Hoover, Rockhurst; Bruce Robertson, Lock Haven University; Jeannie Folk, College of Dupage; Marvelyn Burnette, Wichita State University; Ron Mannino, University of Massachusetts; John Reisch, Florida Atlantic University; Rosalie Hallbaurer, Florida International University; Lynne H. Shoaf, Belmont Abbey College; Jayne Maas, Towson University; Ahmed Goma, Manhattan College; John Rude, Bloomsburg University; Jack Paul, Lehigh University; Terri Gutierrez, University of Northern Colorado; Khondkar Karim, Monmouth University; Carol Lawrence, University of Richmond; Jeffrey Power, Saint Mary's University; Joanne Sheridan, Montana State University; and George Dow.

Tom Edmonds/Bor-Yi Tsay/Phil Olds

# Brief Contents

# Contents

## Chapter 3   Analysis of Cost, Volume, and Pricing to Increase Profitability   106

# Chapter 4    Cost Accumulation, Tracing, and Allocation    150

# Chapter 5    Cost Management in an Automated Business Environment: ABC, ABM, and TQM    202

# Chapter 6   Relevant Information for Special Decisions   252

## Chapter 9 Responsibility Accounting 398

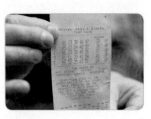

## Chapter 10 Planning for Capital Investments 442

## Chapter 11 Product Costing in Service and Manufacturing Entities 484

## Chapter 12 Job-Order, Process, and Hybrid Costing Systems 534

# Chapter 13    Financial Statement Analysis    586

# Chapter 14    Statement of Cash Flows    636

## CHAPTER 1

# Management Accounting and Corporate Governance

## LEARNING OBJECTIVES

**After you have mastered the material in this chapter, you will be able to:**

**1** Distinguish between managerial and financial accounting.

**2** Identify the cost components of a product made by a manufacturing company: the cost of materials, labor, and overhead.

**3** Explain the effects on financial statements of product costs versus general, selling, and administrative costs.

**4** Distinguish product costs from upstream and downstream costs.

**5** Explain how product costing differs in service, merchandising, and manufacturing companies.

**6** Show how just-in-time inventory can increase profitability.

**7** Identify the key components of corporate governance.

**8** Identify emerging trends in accounting (Appendix A).

## CHAPTER OPENING

Andy Grove, Senior Advisor to Executive Management of **Intel Corporation**, is credited with the motto "Only the paranoid survive." Mr. Grove describes a wide variety of concerns that make him paranoid. Specifically, he declares:

> I worry about products getting screwed up, and I worry about products getting introduced prematurely. I worry about factories not performing well, and I worry about having too many factories. I worry about hiring the right people, and I worry about morale slacking off. And, of course, I worry about competitors. I worry about other people figuring out how to do what we do better or cheaper, and displacing us with our customers.

Do Intel's historically-based financial statements contain the information Mr. Grove needs? No. **Financial accounting** is not designed to satisfy all the information needs of business managers. Its scope is limited to the needs of external users such as investors and creditors. The field of accounting designed to meet the needs of internal users is called **managerial accounting.**

# The Curious Accountant

In the first course of accounting, you learned how retailers, such as **Sears**, account for the cost of equipment that lasts more than one year. Recall that the equipment was recorded as an asset when purchased, and then it was depreciated over its expected useful life. The depreciation charge reduced the company's assets and increased its expenses. This approach was justified under the matching principle, which seeks to recognize costs as expenses in the same period that the cost (resource) is used to generate revenue.

Is depreciation always shown as an expense on the income statement? The answer may surprise you. Consider the following scenario. **Schwinn** manufactures the bicycles that it sells to Sears. In order to produce the bicycles, Schwinn had to purchase a robotic machine that it expects can be used to produce 50,000 bicycles.

Do you think Schwinn should account for depreciation on its manufacturing equipment the same way Sears accounts for depreciation on its registers at the checkout counters? If not, how should Schwinn account for its depreciation? Remember the matching principle when thinking of your answer. (Answer on page 12.)

# DIFFERENCES BETWEEN MANAGERIAL AND FINANCIAL ACCOUNTING

Distinguish between managerial and financial accounting.

While the information needs of internal and external users overlap, the needs of managers generally differ from those of investors or creditors. Some distinguishing characteristics are discussed in the following section.

## Users and Types of Information

Financial accounting provides information used primarily by investors, creditors, and others *outside* a business. In contrast, managerial accounting focuses on information used by executives, managers, and employees who work *inside* the business. These two user groups need different types of information.

Internal users need information to *plan, direct,* and *control* business operations. The nature of information needed is related to an employee's job level. Lower level employees use nonfinancial information such as work schedules, store hours, and customer service policies. Moving up the organizational ladder, financial information becomes increasingly important. Middle managers use a blend of financial and nonfinancial information, while senior executives concentrate on financial data. To a lesser degree, senior executives also use general economic data and nonfinancial operating information. For example, an executive may consider the growth rate of the economy before deciding to expand the company's workforce.

External users (investors and creditors) have greater needs for general economic information than do internal users. For example, an investor debating whether to purchase stock versus bond securities might be more interested in government tax policy than financial statement data. Exhibit 1.1 summarizes the information needs of different user groups.

## Level of Aggregation

External users generally desire *global information* that reflects the performance of a company as a whole. For example, an investor is not so much interested in the performance of a particular Sears store as she is in the performance of Sears Roebuck Company versus that of JC Penney Company. In contrast, internal users focus on detailed information about specific subunits of the company. To meet the needs of the different user groups, financial accounting data are more aggregated than managerial accounting data.

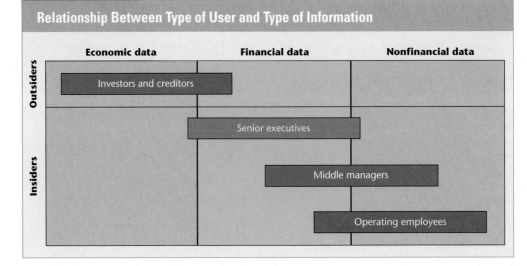

**EXHIBIT 1.1**

**Relationship Between Type of User and Type of Information**

## Regulation

Financial accounting is designed to generate information for the general public. In an effort to protect the public interest, Congress established the **Securities and Exchange Commission (SEC)** and gave it authority to regulate public financial reporting practices. The SEC has delegated much of its authority for developing accounting rules to the private sector **Financial Accounting Standards Board (FASB),** thereby allowing the accounting profession considerable influence over financial accounting reports. The FASB supports a broad base of pronouncements and practices known as **generally accepted accounting principles (GAAP).** GAAP severely restricts the accounting procedures and practices permitted in published financial statements.

Beyond financial statement data, much of the information generated by management accounting systems is proprietary information not available to the public. Since this information is not distributed to the public, it need not be regulated to protect the public interest. Management accounting is restricted only by the **value-added principle.** Management accountants are free to engage in any information gathering and reporting activity so long as the activity adds value in excess of its cost. For example, management accountants are free to provide forecasted information to internal users. In contrast, financial accounting as prescribed by GAAP does not permit forecasting.

## Information Characteristics

While financial accounting is characterized by its objectivity, reliability, consistency, and historical nature, managerial accounting is more concerned with relevance and timeliness. Managerial accounting uses more estimates and fewer facts than financial accounting. Financial accounting reports what happened yesterday; managerial accounting reports what is expected to happen tomorrow.

## Time Horizon and Reporting Frequency

Financial accounting information is reported periodically, normally at the end of a year. Management cannot wait until the end of the year to discover problems. Planning, controlling, and directing require immediate attention. Managerial accounting information is delivered on a continuous basis.

Exhibit 1.2 summarizes significant differences between financial and managerial accounting.

## PRODUCT COSTING IN MANUFACTURING COMPANIES

A major focus for managerial accountants is determining **product cost.**[1] Managers need to know the cost of their products for a variety of reasons. For example, **cost-plus pricing** is a common business practice.[2] **Product costing** is also used to control business operations. It is useful in answering questions such as: Are costs higher or lower than expected? Who is responsible for the variances between expected and actual costs? What actions can be taken to control the variances?

**LO 2**

Identify the cost components of a product made by a manufacturing company: the cost of materials, labor, and overhead.

### Components of Product Cost

A company normally incurs three types of costs when making products. Specifically, the company must pay for (1) the *materials* used to make the products, (2) the *labor*

---

[1]This text uses the term *product* in a generic sense to mean both goods and services.
[2]Other pricing strategies will be introduced in subsequent chapters.

### EXHIBIT 1.2

#### Comparative Features of Managerial versus Financial Accounting Information

| Features | Managerial Accounting | Financial Accounting |
|---|---|---|
| Users | Insiders including executives, managers, and operators | Outsiders including investors, creditors, government agencies, analysts, and reporters |
| Information type | Economic and physical data as well as financial data | Financial data |
| Level of aggregation | Local information on subunits of the organization | Global information on the company as a whole |
| Regulation | No regulation, limited only by the value-added principle | Regulation by SEC, FASB, and other determiners of GAAP |
| Information characteristics | Estimates that promote relevance and enable timeliness | Factual information that is characterized by objectivity, reliability, consistency, and accuracy |
| Time horizon | Past, present, and future | Past only, historically based |
| Reporting frequency | Continuous reporting | Delayed with emphasis on annual reports |

expended by the employees who transform the materials into products, and (3) the **overhead** (other resources such as utilities and equipment consumed in the process of making the products). If the company stores its products, the costs of the materials, labor, and overhead used in making the products are maintained in an inventory account until the products are sold. For a detailed explanation of how product costs flow through the financial statements, refer to the following example of Tabor Manufacturing Company.

## Tabor Manufacturing Company

Tabor Manufacturing Company makes wooden tables. The company spent $1,000 cash to build four tables: $390 for materials, $470 for a carpenter's labor, and $140 for tools used in making the tables. How much is Tabor's expense? The answer is zero. The $1,000 cash has been converted into products (four tables). The cash payments for materials, labor, and tools (overhead) were *asset exchange* transactions. One asset (cash) decreased while another asset (tables) increased. Tabor will not recognize any expense until the tables are sold; in the meantime, the cost of the tables is held in an asset account called **Finished Goods Inventory.** Exhibit 1.3 illustrates how cash is transformed into inventory.

## Average Cost per Unit

How much did each table made by Tabor cost? The *actual* cost of each of the four tables likely differs. The carpenter probably spent a little more time on some of the tables than others. Material and tool usage probably varied from table to table. Determining the exact cost of each table is virtually impossible. Minute details such as a second of labor time cannot be effectively measured. Even if Tabor could determine the exact cost of each table, the information would be of little use. Minor differences in the cost per table would make no difference in pricing or other decisions management needs to make. Accountants therefore normally calculate cost per unit as an *average*. In the case of Tabor Manufacturing, the **average cost** per table is $250 ($1,000 ÷ 4 units). Unless otherwise stated, assume *cost per unit* means *average cost per unit*.

## EXHIBIT 1.3

### Transforming the Asset Cash Into the Asset Finished Goods Inventory

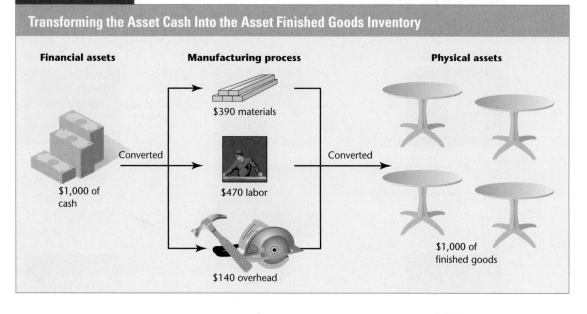

**Financial assets**     **Manufacturing process**     **Physical assets**

$390 materials

$1,000 of cash   Converted   $470 labor   Converted

$140 overhead

$1,000 of finished goods

## ✓ CHECK YOURSELF 1.1

All boxes of **General Mills'** Total Raisin Bran cereal are priced at exactly the same amount in your local grocery store. Does this mean that the actual cost of making each box of cereal was exactly the same?

**Answer** No, making each box would not cost exactly the same amount. For example, some boxes contain slightly more or less cereal than other boxes. Accordingly, some boxes cost slightly more or less to make than others do. General Mills uses average cost rather than actual cost to develop its pricing strategy.

## Costs Can Be Assets or Expenses

It might seem odd that wages paid to production workers are recorded as inventory instead of being expensed. Remember, however, that expenses are assets used in the process of *earning revenue*. The cash paid to production workers is not used to produce revenue. Instead, the cash is used to produce inventory. Revenue will be earned when the inventory is used (sold). So long as the inventory remains on hand, all product costs (materials, labor, and overhead) remain in an inventory account.

When a table is sold, the average cost of the table is transferred from the Inventory account to the Cost of Goods Sold (expense) account. If some tables remain unsold at the end of the accounting period, part of the *product costs* is reported as an asset (inventory) on the balance sheet while the other part is reported as an expense (cost of goods sold) on the income statement.

Costs that are not classified as product costs are normally expensed in the period in which they are incurred. These costs include *general operating costs, selling and administrative costs, interest costs,* and the *cost of income taxes.*

To illustrate, return to the Tabor Manufacturing example. Recall that Tabor made four tables at an average cost per unit of $250. Assume Tabor pays an employee who sells three of the tables a $200 sales commission. The sales commission is expensed immediately. The total product cost for the three tables (3 tables × $250 each = $750) is expensed on the income statement as cost of goods sold. The portion of the total

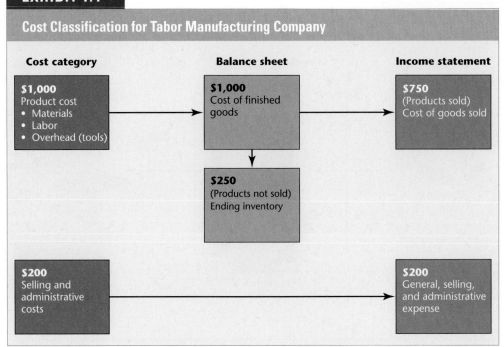

**EXHIBIT 1.4**

**Cost Classification for Tabor Manufacturing Company**

| Cost category | Balance sheet | Income statement |
|---|---|---|
| **$1,000** Product cost • Materials • Labor • Overhead (tools) | **$1,000** Cost of finished goods | **$750** (Products sold) Cost of goods sold |
| | **$250** (Products not sold) Ending inventory | |
| **$200** Selling and administrative costs | | **$200** General, selling, and administrative expense |

product cost remaining in inventory is $250 (1 table × $250). Exhibit 1.4 shows the relationship between the costs incurred and the expenses recognized for Tabor Manufacturing Company.

## Effect of Product Costs on Financial Statements

Explain the effects on financial statements of product costs versus general, selling, and administrative costs.

We illustrate accounting for product costs in manufacturing companies with Patillo Manufacturing Company, a producer of ceramic pottery. Patillo, started on January 1, 2013, experienced the following accounting events during its first year of operations.[3] *Assume that all transactions except 6, 8, and 10 are cash transactions.*

1. Acquired $15,000 cash by issuing common stock.
2. Paid $2,000 for materials that were used to make products. All products started were completed during the period.
3. Paid $1,200 for salaries of selling and administrative employees.
4. Paid $3,000 for wages of production workers.
5. Paid $2,800 for furniture used in selling and administrative offices.
6. Recognized depreciation on the office furniture purchased in Event 5. The furniture was acquired on January 1, had a $400 estimated salvage value, and a four-year useful life. The annual depreciation charge is $600 [($2,800 − $400) ÷ 4].
7. Paid $4,500 for manufacturing equipment.
8. Recognized depreciation on the equipment purchased in Event 7. The equipment was acquired on January 1, had a $1,500 estimated salvage value, and a three-year useful life. The annual depreciation charge is $1,000 [($4,500 − $1,500) ÷ 3].
9. Sold inventory to customers for $7,500 cash.
10. The inventory sold in Event 9 cost $4,000 to make.

[3]This illustration assumes that all inventory started during the period was completed during the period. Patillo therefore uses only one inventory account, Finished Goods Inventory. Many manufacturing companies normally have three categories of inventory on hand at the end of an accounting period: Raw Materials Inventory, Work in Process Inventory (inventory of partially completed units), and Finished Goods Inventory. Chapter 11 discusses these inventories in greater detail.

## EXHIBIT 1.5

### Effect of Product versus Selling and Administrative Costs on Financial Statements

| Event No. | Cash | + | Inventory | + | Office Furn.* | + | Manuf. Equip.* | = | Com. Stk. | + | Ret. Earn. | Rev. | − | Exp. | = | Net Inc. |
|---|---|---|---|---|---|---|---|---|---|---|---|---|---|---|---|---|
| 1 | 15,000 | | | | | | | = | 15,000 | | | | | | | |
| 2 | (2,000) | + | 2,000 | | | | | | | | | | | | | |
| 3 | (1,200) | | | | | | | = | | | (1,200) | | − | 1,200 | = | (1,200) |
| 4 | (3,000) | + | 3,000 | | | | | | | | | | | | | |
| 5 | (2,800) | + | | | 2,800 | | | | | | | | | | | |
| 6 | | | | | (600) | | | = | | | (600) | | − | 600 | = | (600) |
| 7 | (4,500) | + | | | | | 4,500 | | | | | | | | | |
| 8 | | | 1,000 | + | | | (1,000) | | | | | | | | | |
| 9 | 7,500 | | | | | | | = | | | 7,500 | 7,500 | | | = | 7,500 |
| 10 | | | (4,000) | | | | | = | | | (4,000) | | − | 4,000 | = | (4,000) |
| Totals | 9,000 | + | 2,000 | + | 2,200 | + | 3,500 | = | 15,000 | + | 1,700 | 7,500 | − | 5,800 | = | 1,700 |

*Negative amounts in these columns represent accumulated depreciation.

The effects of these transactions on the balance sheet and income statement are shown in Exhibit 1.5. Study each row in this exhibit, paying particular attention to how similar costs such as salaries for selling and administrative personnel and wages for production workers have radically different effects on the financial statements. The example illustrates the three elements of product costs, materials (Event 2), labor (Event 4), and overhead (Event 8). These events are discussed in more detail below.

### Materials Costs (Event 2)

Materials used to make products are usually called **raw materials.** The cost of raw materials is first recorded in an asset account (Inventory). The cost is then transferred from the Inventory account to the Cost of Goods Sold account at the time the goods are sold. Remember that materials cost is only one component of total manufacturing costs. When inventory is sold, the combined cost of materials, labor, and overhead is expensed as *cost of goods sold*. The costs of materials that can be easily and conveniently traced to products are called **direct raw materials** costs.

### Labor Costs (Event 4)

The salaries paid to selling and administrative employees (Event 3) and the wages paid to production workers (Event 4) are accounted for differently. Salaries paid to selling and administrative employees are expensed immediately, but the cost of production wages is added to inventory. Production wages are expensed as part of cost of goods sold at the time the inventory is sold. Labor costs that can be easily and conveniently traced to products are called **direct labor** costs. The cost flow of wages for production employees versus salaries for selling and administrative personnel is shown in Exhibit 1.6.

### Overhead Costs (Event 8)

Although depreciation cost totaled $1,600 ($600 on office furniture and $1,000 on manufacturing equipment), only the $600 of depreciation on the office furniture is expensed directly on the income statement. The depreciation on the manufacturing equipment is split between the income statement (cost of goods sold) and the balance sheet (inventory). The depreciation cost flow for the manufacturing equipment versus the office furniture is shown in Exhibit 1.7.

**EXHIBIT 1.6**

**Flow of Labor Costs**

**Labor costs** → **Balance sheet** → **Income statement**

Production wages → Inventory → Cost of goods sold

Selling and administrative salaries → Salaries expense

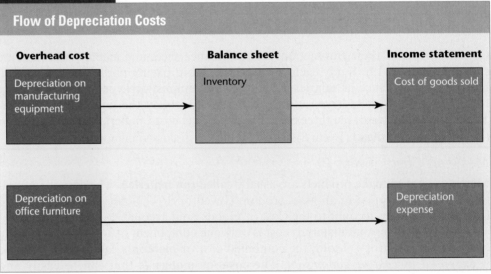

**EXHIBIT 1.7**

**Flow of Depreciation Costs**

**Overhead cost** → **Balance sheet** → **Income statement**

Depreciation on manufacturing equipment → Inventory → Cost of goods sold

Depreciation on office furniture → Depreciation expense

**Total Product Cost.**  A summary of Patillo Manufacturing's total product cost is shown in Exhibit 1.8.

*Financial Statements*

The income statement and balance sheet for Patillo Manufacturing are displayed in Exhibit 1.9.

**Product Costs.**  The $4,000 cost of goods sold reported on the income statement includes a portion of the materials, labor, and overhead costs incurred by Patillo during the year. Similarly, the $2,000 of finished goods inventory on the balance sheet includes materials, labor, and overhead costs. These product costs will be recognized as expense in the next accounting period when the goods are sold. Initially classifying a cost as a product cost delays, but does not eliminate, its recognition as an expense. All product costs are ultimately recognized as expense (cost of goods sold).

**Selling, General, and Administrative Costs.**  Selling, general, and administrative costs (SG&A) are normally expensed *in the period* in which they are incurred. Because of this recognition pattern, nonproduct expenses are sometimes called **period costs.** In Patillo's

## EXHIBIT 1.8

### Schedule of Inventory Costs

| | |
|---|---|
| Materials | $2,000 |
| Labor | 3,000 |
| Manufacturing overhead* | 1,000 |
| Total product costs | 6,000 |
| Less: Cost of goods sold | (4,000) |
| Ending inventory balance | $2,000 |

*Depreciation [($4,500 − $1,500) ÷ 3]

## EXHIBIT 1.9

### PATILLO MANUFACTURING COMPANY
### Financial Statements

#### Income Statement for 2013

| | |
|---|---|
| Sales revenue | $ 7,500 |
| Cost of goods sold | (4,000) |
| Gross margin | 3,500 |
| SG&A expenses | |
| Salaries expense | (1,200) |
| Depreciation expense—office furniture | (600) |
| Net income | $ 1,700 |

#### Balance Sheet as of December 31, 2013

| | | |
|---|---|---|
| Cash | | $ 9,000 |
| Finished goods inventory | | 2,000 |
| Office furniture | $2,800 | |
| Accumulated depreciation | (600) | |
| Book value | | 2,200 |
| Manufacturing equipment | 4,500 | |
| Accumulated depreciation | (1,000) | |
| Book value | | 3,500 |
| Total assets | | $16,700 |
| Stockholders' equity | | |
| Common stock | | $15,000 |
| Retained earnings | | 1,700 |
| Total stockholders' equity | | $16,700 |

case, the salaries expense for selling and administrative employees and the depreciation on office furniture are period costs reported directly on the income statement.

## Overhead Costs: A Closer Look

Costs such as depreciation on manufacturing equipment cannot be easily traced to products. Suppose that Patillo Manufacturing makes both tables and chairs. What part of the depreciation is caused by manufacturing tables versus manufacturing chairs? Similarly, suppose a production supervisor oversees employees who work on both tables and chairs. How much of the supervisor's salary relates to tables and how much to chairs? Likewise, the cost of glue used in the production department would be difficult to trace to tables versus chairs. You could count the drops of glue used on each product, but the information would not be useful enough to merit the time and money spent collecting the data.

Costs that cannot be traced to products and services in a *cost-effective* manner are called **indirect costs.** The indirect costs incurred to make products are called **manufacturing overhead.** Some of the items commonly included in manufacturing overhead are indirect materials, indirect labor, factory utilities, rent of manufacturing facilities, and depreciation on manufacturing assets.

✓ **CHECK YOURSELF 1.2**

Lawson Manufacturing Company paid production workers wages of $100,000. It incurred materials costs of $120,000 and manufacturing overhead costs of $160,000. Selling and administrative salaries were $80,000. Lawson started and completed 1,000 units of product and sold 800 of these units. The company sets sales prices at $220 above the average per unit production cost. Based on this information alone, determine the amount of gross margin and net income. What is Lawson's pricing strategy called?

**Answer**   Total product cost is $380,000 ($100,000 labor + $120,000 materials + $160,000 overhead). Cost per unit is $380 ($380,000 ÷ 1,000 units). The sales price per unit is $600 ($380 + $220). Cost of goods sold is $304,000 ($380 × 800 units). Sales revenue is $480,000 ($600 × 800 units). Gross margin is $176,000 ($480,000 revenue − $304,000 cost of goods sold). Net income is $96,000 ($176,000 gross margin − $80,000 selling and administrative salaries). Lawson's pricing strategy is called *cost-plus* pricing.

### EXHIBIT 1.10

**Cost Allocation**

Allocation rate
$120 ÷ 8 = $15
per labor hour

$15 × 2 hours → $30

$15 × 6 hours → $90

Since indirect costs cannot be effectively traced to products, they are normally assigned to products using **cost allocation,** a process of dividing a total cost into parts and assigning the parts to relevant cost objects. To illustrate, suppose that production workers spend an eight-hour day making a chair and a table. The chair requires two hours to complete and the table requires six hours. Now suppose that $120 of utilities cost is consumed during the day. How much of the $120 should be assigned to each piece of furniture? The utility cost cannot be directly traced to each specific piece of furniture, but the piece of furniture that required more labor also likely consumed more of the utility cost. Using this line of reasoning, it is rational to allocate the utility cost to the two pieces of furniture based on *direct labor hours* at a rate of $15 per hour ($120 ÷ 8 hours). The chair would be assigned $30 ($15 per hour × 2 hours) of the utility cost and the table would be assigned the remaining $90 ($15 × 6 hours) of utility cost. The allocation of the utility cost is shown in Exhibit 1.10.

We discuss the details of cost allocation in a later chapter. For now, recognize that overhead costs are normally allocated to products rather than traced directly to them.

### Manufacturing Product Cost Summary

As explained, the cost of a product made by a manufacturing company is normally composed of three categories: direct materials, direct labor, and manufacturing overhead. Relevant information about these three cost components is summarized in Exhibit 1.11.

## *Answers to* The Curious Accountant

As you have seen, accounting for depreciation related to manufacturing assets is different from accounting for depreciation for nonmanufacturing assets. Depreciation on the checkout equipment at **Sears** is recorded as depreciation expense. Depreciation on manufacturing equipment at **Schwinn** is considered a product cost. It is included first as a part of the cost of inventory and eventually as a part of the expense, cost of goods sold. Recording depreciation on manufacturing equipment as an inventory cost is simply another example of the matching principle, because the cost does not become an expense until revenue from the product sale is recognized.

**EXHIBIT 1.11**

## Components of Manufacturing Product Cost

**Component 1—Direct Raw Materials**
Sometimes called *raw materials*. In addition to basic resources such as wood or metals, it can include manufactured parts. For example, engines, glass, and car tires can be considered as raw materials for an automotive manufacturer. If the amount of a material in a product is known, it can usually be classified as a direct material. The cost of direct materials can be easily traced to specific products.

**Component 2—Direct Labor**
The cost of wages paid to factory workers involved in hands-on contact with the products being manufactured. If the amount of time employees worked on a product can be determined, this cost can usually be classified as direct labor. Like direct materials, labor costs must be easily traced to a specific product in order to be classified as a direct cost.

**Component 3—Manufacturing Overhead**
Costs that cannot be easily traced to specific products. Accordingly, these costs are called indirect costs. They can include but are not limited to the following:

1. Indirect materials such as glue, nails, paper, and oil. Indeed, note that indirect materials used in the production process may not appear in the finished product. An example is a chemical solvent used to clean products during the production process but not a component material found in the final product.

2. Indirect labor such as the cost of salaries paid to production supervisors, inspectors, and maintenance personnel.

3. Rental cost for manufacturing facilities and equipment.

4. Utility costs.

5. Depreciation.

6. Security.

7. The cost of preparing equipment for the manufacturing process (i.e., setup costs).

8. Maintenance cost for the manufacturing facility and equipment.

## UPSTREAM AND DOWNSTREAM COSTS

Most companies incur product-related costs before and after, as well as during, the manufacturing process. For example, Ford Motor Company incurs significant research and development costs prior to mass producing a new car model. These **upstream costs** occur before the manufacturing process begins. Similarly, companies normally incur significant costs after the manufacturing process is complete. Examples of **downstream costs** include transportation, advertising, sales commissions, and bad debts. While upstream and downstream costs are not considered to be product costs for financial reporting purposes, profitability analysis requires that they be considered in cost-plus pricing decisions. To be profitable, a company must recover the total cost of developing, producing, and delivering its products to customers.

Distinguish product costs from upstream and downstream costs.

## PRODUCT COSTING IN SERVICE AND MERCHANDISING COMPANIES

Companies are frequently classified as being service, merchandising, or manufacturing businesses. As the name implies, service organizations provide services, rather than physical products, to consumers. For example, St. Jude Children's Hospital provides treatment programs aimed at healing patient diseases. Other common service providers include public accountants, lawyers, restaurants, dry cleaning establishments, and lawn care companies. Merchandising businesses are sometimes called retail or wholesale companies; they sell goods other companies make. The Home Depot, Inc., Costco Wholesale Corporation,

Explain how product costing differs in service, merchandising, and manufacturing companies.

and **Best Buy Co., Inc.**, are merchandising companies. Manufacturing companies make the goods they sell to their customers. **Toyota Motor Corporation**, **Texaco, Inc.**, and **American Standard Companies, Inc.**, are manufacturing businesses.

How do manufacturing companies differ from service and merchandising businesses? Do service and merchandising companies incur materials, labor, and overhead costs? Yes. For example, **Ernst & Young**, a large accounting firm, must pay employees (labor costs), use office supplies (material costs), and incur utilities, depreciation, and so on (overhead costs) in the process of conducting audits. *The primary difference between manufacturing entities and service companies is that the products provided by service companies are consumed immediately.* In contrast, products made by manufacturing companies can be held in the form of inventory until they are sold to consumers. Similarly, most labor and overhead costs incurred by merchandising companies result from providing assistance to customers. These costs are normally treated as selling, general, and administrative expenses rather than accumulated in inventory accounts. Indeed, merchandising companies are often viewed as service companies rather than considered a separate business category.

The important point to remember is that all business managers are expected to control costs, improve quality, and increase productivity. Like managers of manufacturing companies, managers of service and merchandising businesses can benefit from the analysis of the cost of satisfying their customers. For example, **Wendy's**, a service company, can benefit from knowing how much a hamburger costs in the same manner that **Bayer Corporation**, a manufacturing company, benefits from knowing the cost of a bottle of aspirin.

---

### ✓ CHECK YOURSELF 1.3

The cost of making a **Burger King** hamburger includes the cost of materials, labor, and overhead. Does this mean that Burger King is a manufacturing company?

**Answer**   No, Burger King is not a manufacturing company. It is a service company because its products are consumed immediately. In contrast, there may be a considerable delay between the time the product of a manufacturing company is made and the time it is consumed. For example, it could be several months between the time **Ford Motor Company** makes an Explorer and the time the Explorer is ultimately sold to a customer. The primary difference between service and manufacturing companies is that manufacturing companies have inventories of products and service companies do not.

---

## JUST-IN-TIME INVENTORY

Show how just-in-time inventory can increase profitability.

Companies attempt to minimize the amount of inventory they maintain because of the high cost of holding it. Many **inventory holding costs** are obvious: financing, warehouse space, supervision, theft, damage, and obsolescence. Other costs are hidden: diminished motivation, sloppy work, inattentive attitudes, and increased production time.

Many businesses have been able to simultaneously reduce their inventory holding costs and increase customer satisfaction by making products available **just in time (JIT)** for customer consumption. For example, hamburgers that are cooked to order are fresher and more individualized than those that are prepared in advance and stored until a customer orders one. Many fast-food restaurants have discovered that JIT systems lead not only to greater customer satisfaction but also to lower costs through reduced waste.

### Just-in-Time Illustration

To illustrate the benefits of a JIT system, consider Paula Elliot, a student at a large urban university. She helps support herself by selling flowers. Three days each week,

Paula drives to a florist, purchases 25 single-stem roses, returns to the school, and sells the flowers to individuals from a location on a local street corner. She pays $2 per rose and sells each one for $3. Some days she does not have enough flowers to meet customer demand. Other days, she must discard one or two unsold flowers; she believes quality is important and refuses to sell flowers that are not fresh. During May, she purchased 300 roses and sold 280. She calculated her driving cost to be $45. Exhibit 1.12 displays Paula's May income statement.

After studying just-in-time inventory systems in her managerial accounting class, Paula decided to apply the concepts to her small business. She *reengineered* her distribution system by purchasing her flowers from a florist within walking distance of her sales location. She had considered purchasing from this florist earlier but had rejected the idea because the florist's regular selling price of $2.25 per rose was too high. After learning about *most-favored customer status,* she developed a strategy to get a price reduction. By guaranteeing that she would buy at least 30 roses per week, she was able to convince the local florist to match her current cost of $2.00 per rose. The local florist agreed that she could make purchases in batches of any size so long as the total amounted to at least 30 per week. Under this arrangement, Paula was able to buy roses *just in time* to meet customer demand. Each day she purchased a small number of flowers. When she ran out, she simply returned to the florist for additional ones.

At **Ford Motor Company**'s plant in Valencia, Spain, suppliers feed parts such as these bumpers just in time and in the right order directly to the assembly line.

The JIT system also enabled Paula to eliminate the cost of the *nonvalue-added activity* of driving to her former florist. Customer satisfaction actually improved because no one was ever turned away because of the lack of inventory. In June, Paula was able to buy and sell 310 roses with no waste and no driving expense. The June income statement is shown in Exhibit 1.13.

Paula was ecstatic about her $115 increase in profitability ($310 in June − $195 in May = $115 increase), but she was puzzled about the exact reasons for the change. She had saved $40 (20 flowers × $2 each) by avoiding waste and eliminated $45 of driving expenses. These two factors explained only $85 ($40 waste + $45 driving expense) of the $115 increase. What had caused the remaining $30 ($115 − $85) increase in profitability? Paula asked her accounting professor to help her identify the remaining $30 difference.

The professor explained that May sales had suffered from *lost opportunities*. Recall that under the earlier inventory system, Paula had to turn away some prospective customers because she sold out of flowers before all customers were served. Sales increased from 280 roses in May to 310 roses in June. A likely explanation for the 30 unit difference (310 − 280) is that customers who would have purchased flowers in May were unable to do so because of a lack of availability. May's sales suffered from the lost opportunity to earn a gross margin of $1 per flower on 30 roses, a $30 **opportunity cost.** This opportunity cost is the missing link in explaining the profitability difference between May and June. The total $115 difference consists of (1) $40 savings from waste elimination, (2) $45 savings from eliminating driving expense, and (3) opportunity cost of $30. The subject of opportunity cost has widespread application and is discussed in more depth in subsequent chapters of the text.

## EXHIBIT 1.12

### Income Statement for May

| | |
|---|---|
| Sales revenue (280 units × $3 per unit) | $840 |
| Cost of goods sold (280 units × $2 per unit) | (560) |
| Gross margin | 280 |
| Driving expense | (45) |
| Excess inventory waste (20 units × 2) | (40) |
| Net income | $195 |

## EXHIBIT 1.13

### Income Statement for June

| | |
|---|---|
| Sales revenue (310 units × $3 per unit) | $930 |
| Cost of goods sold (310 units × $2 per unit) | (620) |
| Gross margin | 310 |
| Driving expense | 0 |
| Net income | $310 |

✓ **CHECK YOURSELF 1.4**

A strike at a General Motors brake plant caused an almost immediate shutdown of many of the company's assembly plants. What could have caused such a rapid and widespread shutdown?

**Answer**    A rapid and widespread shutdown could have occurred because General Motors uses a just-in-time inventory system. With a just-in-time inventory system, there is no stockpile of inventory to draw on when strikes or other forces disrupt inventory deliveries. This illustrates a potential negative effect of using a just-in-time inventory system.

## CORPORATE GOVERNANCE

**LO 7**

Identify the key components of corporate governance.

Corporate governance is the set of relationships between the board of directors, management, shareholders, auditors, and other stakeholders that determine how a company is operated. Until recently, corporations were generally free to govern themselves. However, several high-profile scandals have motivated governmental authorities to enact legislation designed to influence corporate governance. This section of the chapter examines the factors affecting corporate governance. We examine the motives and means of management corruption. Further, we introduce the mechanisms for self control including codes of ethics and internal controls. Finally, we discuss recent legislation designed to influence managerial responsibility for financial reporting.

Management accountants are at the forefront of corporate governance. They are the guardians of the information used to report on the financial condition of their companies. The information they prepare and analyze is used by the board of directors and company executives to formulate the company's operating strategy. Indeed, management accountants constitute the intelligence function of corporate governance. Scandals usually begin with schemes to manipulate a company's financial reports and end when the falsification is so great it becomes obvious the reports no longer represent reality. The appropriate management of the information function is a highly effective force against corrupt governance. It is little wonder why recent legislation requires the chief financial officer along with the chief executive officer to personally certify that the company's annual report does not contain false statements nor omit significant facts.

### The Motive to Manipulate

Many managers are judged on their company's financial statements or the company's stock price which is determined, in part, by the financial statements. Managers are rewarded for strong financial statements with promotions, pay raises, bonuses, and stock options. Weak financials can result in a manager being passed over for promotions, demoted, or even fired. It is little wonder that some executives are tempted to manipulate financial statements.

To illustrate implications of statement manipulation, consider the events experienced by Marion Manufacturing Company (MMC) during its first year of operations. All transactions are cash transactions.

1.  MMC was started when it acquired $12,000 from issuing common stock.
2.  MMC incurred $4,000 of costs to design its product and plan the manufacturing process.
3.  MMC incurred specifically identifiable product costs (materials, labor, and overhead) of $8,000 to make 1,000 units of product, resulting in a cost per unit of $8 ($8,000 ÷ 1,000 units).
4.  MMC sold 700 units of inventory for $18 each.

## EXHIBIT 1.14

### Financial Statements Under Alternative Cost Classification Scenarios

| Income Statements | Scenario 1 | Scenario 2 |
|---|---|---|
| Sales revenue (700 × $18) | $12,600 | $12,600 |
| Cost of goods sold | (5,600)[1] | (8,400)[3] |
| Gross margin | 7,000 | 4,200 |
| Selling and administrative expense | (4,000) | 0 |
| Net income | $ 3,000 | $ 4,200 |

| Balance Sheets | | |
|---|---|---|
| Assets | | |
|   Cash | $12,600 | $12,600 |
|   Inventory | 2,400[2] | 3,600[4] |
| Total assets | $15,000 | $16,200 |
| Stockholders' equity | | |
|   Common stock | $12,000 | $12,000 |
|   Retained earnings | 3,000 | 4,200 |
| Total stockholders' equity | $15,000 | $16,200 |

[1] 700 units × $8 per unit = $5,600
[2] 300 units × $8 per unit = $2,400
[3] [$5,600 + ($4,000 × .70)] = $8,400
[4] [$2,400 + ($4,000 × .30)] = $3,600

Exhibit 1.14 displays a balance sheet and income statement prepared under the following two scenarios.

**Scenario 1:** The $4,000 of design and planning costs are classified as selling and administrative expenses.

**Scenario 2:** The $4,000 of design and planning costs are classified as product costs, meaning they are first accumulated in the Inventory account and then expensed when the goods are sold. Given that MMC made 1,000 units and sold 700 units of inventory, 70% (700 ÷ 1,000) of the design cost has passed through the Inventory account into the Cost of Goods Sold account, leaving 30% (300 ÷ 1,000) remaining in the Inventory account.

### Statement Differences

Comparing the financial statements prepared under Scenario 1 with those prepared under Scenario 2 reveals the following.

1. There are no selling and administrative expenses under Scenario 2. The design cost was treated as a product cost and placed into the Inventory account rather than being expensed.

2. Cost of goods sold is $2,800 ($4,000 design cost × .70) higher under Scenario 2.

3. Net income is $1,200 higher under Scenario 2 ($4,000 understated expense − $2,800 overstated cost of goods sold).

4. Ending inventory is $1,200 ($4,000 design cost × .30) higher under Scenario 2.

### Practical Implications

The financial statement differences shown in Exhibit 1.14 are *timing differences*. When MMC sells the remaining 300 units of inventory, the $1,200 of design and planning costs included in inventory under Scenario 2 will be expensed through cost of goods sold. In other words, once the entire inventory is sold, total expenses and retained earnings will be the same under both scenarios. Initially recording cost in an inventory account only delays eventual expense recognition. However, the temporary effects on the financial statements can influence the (1) availability of financing, (2) motivations of management, and (3) timing of income tax payments.

**Availability of Financing.**   The willingness of creditors and investors to provide capital to a business is influenced by their expectations of the business's future financial performance. In general, more favorable financial statements enhance a company's ability to obtain financing from creditors or investors.

**Management Motivation.**   Financial statement results might affect executive compensation. For example, assume that Marion Manufacturing adopted a management incentive plan that provides a bonus pool equal to 10 percent of net income. In Scenario 1, managers would receive $300 ($3,000 × 0.10). In Scenario 2, however, managers would receive $420 ($4,200 × 0.10). Do not be deceived by the small numbers used for convenience in the example. We could illustrate with millions of dollars just as well as with hundreds of dollars. Managers would clearly favor Scenario 2. In fact, managers might be tempted to misclassify costs to manipulate the content of financial statements.

**Income Tax Considerations.**   Since income tax expense is calculated as a designated percentage of taxable income, managers seek to minimize taxes by reporting the minimum amount of taxable income. Scenario 1 in Exhibit 1.14 depicts the most favorable tax condition. In other words, with respect to taxes, managers prefer to classify costs as expenses rather than assets. The Internal Revenue Service is responsible for enforcing the proper classification of costs. Disagreements between the Internal Revenue Service and taxpayers are ultimately settled in federal courts.

## Statement of Ethical Professional Practice

The preceding discussion provides some insight into conflicts of interest management accountants might face. It is tempting to misclassify a cost if doing so will significantly increase a manager's bonus. Management accountants must be prepared not only to make difficult choices between legitimate alternatives but also to face conflicts of a more troubling nature, such as pressure to:

1. Undertake duties they have not been trained to perform competently.
2. Disclose confidential information.
3. Compromise their integrity through falsification, embezzlement, bribery, and so on.
4. Issue biased, misleading, or incomplete reports.

To provide management accountants with guidance for ethical conduct the Institute of Management Accountants (IMA) issued a *Statement of Ethical Professional Practice,* which is shown in Exhibit 1.15. Management accountants are also frequently required to abide by organizational codes of ethics. Failure to adhere to professional and organizational ethical standards can lead to personal disgrace, loss of employment, or imprisonment.

## The Fraud Triangle

Unfortunately, it takes more than a code of conduct to stop fraud. People frequently engage in activities that they know are unethical or even criminal. The auditing profession has determined that the following three elements are typically present when fraud occurs:

1. The availability of an *opportunity.*
2. The existence of some form of *pressure* leading to an incentive.
3. The capacity to *rationalize.*

## EXHIBIT 1.15

### Statement of Ethical Professional Practice

Members of IMA shall behave ethically. A commitment to ethical professional practice includes overarching principles that express our values, and standards that guide our conduct. IMA's overarching ethical principles include: Honesty, Fairness, Objectivity, and Responsibility. Members shall act in accordance with these principles and shall encourage others within their organizations to adhere to them. A member's failure to comply with the following standards may result in disciplinary action.

**Competence** Each member has a responsibility to
- Maintain an appropriate level of professional expertise by continually developing knowledge and skills.
- Perform professional duties in accordance with relevant laws, regulations, and technical standards.
- Provide decision support information and recommendations that are accurate, clear, concise, and timely.
- Recognize and communicate professional limitations or other constraints that would preclude responsible judgment or successful performance of an activity.

**Confidentiality** Each member has a responsibility to
- Keep information confidential except when disclosure is authorized or legally required.
- Inform all relevant parties regarding appropriate use of confidential information. Monitor subordinates' activities to ensure compliance.
- Refrain from using confidential information for unethical or illegal advantage.

**Integrity** Each member has a responsibility to
- Mitigate actual conflicts of interest and avoid apparent conflicts of interest. Advise all parties of any potential conflicts.
- Refrain from engaging in any conduct that would prejudice carrying out duties ethically.
- Abstain from engaging in or supporting any activity that might discredit the profession.

**Credibility** Each member has a responsibility to
- Communicate information fairly and objectively.
- Disclose all relevant information that could reasonably be expected to influence an intended user's understanding of the reports, analyses, or recommendations.
- Disclose delays or deficiencies in information, timeliness, processing, or internal controls in conformance with organization policy and/or applicable law.

**Resolution of Ethical Conflict** In applying these standards, you may encounter problems identifying unethical behavior or resolving an ethical conflict. When faced with ethical issues, follow your organization's established policies on the resolution of such conflict. If these policies do not resolve the ethical conflict, consider the following courses of action:
- Discuss the issue with your immediate supervisor except when it appears that the supervisor is involved. In that case, present the issue to the next level. If you cannot achieve a satisfactory resolution, submit the issue to the next management level. Communication of such problems to authorities or individuals not employed or engaged by the organization is not considered appropriate, unless you believe there is a clear violation of the law.
- Clarify relevant ethical issues by initiating a confidential discussion with an IMA Ethics Counselor or other impartial advisor to obtain a better understanding of possible courses of action.
- Consult your own attorney as to legal obligations and rights concerning the ethical conflict.

The three elements are frequently arranged in the shape of a triangle as shown in Exhibit 1.16.

*Opportunity* is shown at the head of the triangle because without opportunity fraud could not exist. The most effective way to reduce opportunities for ethical or criminal misconduct is to implement an effective set of internal controls. *Internal controls* are policies and procedures that a business implements to reduce opportunities for fraud and to ensure that its objectives will be accomplished. Specific controls are tailored to meet the individual needs of particular businesses. For example, banks use elaborate vaults to protect cash and safety deposit boxes, but universities have little use for this type of equipment. Even so, many of the same procedures are used by a wide variety of businesses.

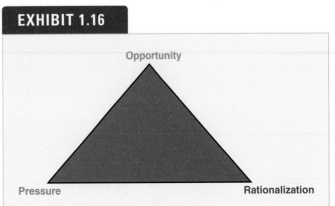

## EXHIBIT 1.16

Opportunity

Pressure

Rationalization

# REALITY BYTES

Unethical behavior occurs in all types of organizations. In its *2007 National Government Ethics Survey,* the Ethics Resource Center reported its findings on the occurrences and reporting of unethical behavior in local, state, and federal governments.

Fifty-seven percent of those surveyed reported having observed unethical conduct during the past year. Unethical conduct was reported most often by those in local governments (63%) and least often at the federal level (52%). The definition of ethical misconduct used in the study was quite broad, ranging from behavior such as an individual putting his or her personal interest ahead of the interest of the organization, to sexual harassment, to taking bribes. The more egregious offences, such as discrimination or taking bribes, were reported much less often than activities such as lying to customers, vendors, or the public.

Once observed, unethical behavior often was not reported. For example, only 25 percent of observed incidents of the alteration of financial records were reported to supervisors or whistleblower hotlines, and only 54 percent of observed bribes were reported.

The survey also found that only 18 percent of government entities have ethics and compliance programs in place that could be considered well-implemented. However, where well-implemented programs do exist, observed unethical misconduct is less likely to occur and more likely to be reported. In these entities only 36 percent of respondents said they had observed misconduct (compared to 57 percent overall), and when they did observe misconduct, 75 percent said they reported it.

For the complete *2007 National Government Ethics Survey,* go to www.ethics.org.

Exhibit 1.17 contains a summary of many of the internal control policies and procedures that have gained widespread acceptance.

Only a few employees turn to the dark side even when internal control is weak and opportunities abound. So, what causes one person to commit fraud and another to remain honest? The second element of the fraud triangle recognizes *pressure* as a key ingredient of misconduct. A manager who is told to either make the numbers or be fired is more likely to cheat than one who is told to tell it like it is. Pressure can come from a variety of sources, including:

- Personal vices such as drug addiction, gambling, and promiscuity.
- Intimidation from superiors.
- Personal debt from credit cards, consumer loans, mortgage loans or, poor investments.
- Family expectations to provide a standard of living that is beyond one's capabilities.
- Business failure caused by poor decision making or temporary factors such as a poor economy.
- Loyalty or trying to be agreeable.

The third and final element of the fraud triangle is *rationalization*. Few individuals think of themselves as evil. They develop rationalizations to justify their misconduct. Common rationalizations include the following:

- Everybody does it.
- They are not paying me enough. I'm only taking what I deserve.
- I'm only borrowing the money. I'll pay it back.
- The company can afford it. Look what they are paying the officers.
- I'm taking what my family needs to live like everyone else.

**EXHIBIT 1.17**

**Common Internal Control Practices**

| Internal Control Practice | Explanation |
|---|---|
| Separating duties | Separating the duties necessary to complete a task and assigning the separated duties to two or more employees reduces the opportunity for either employee to defraud the company. It would require collusion between the two employees in order to make payment for a fabricated expense. |
| Hiring competent personnel | Cheap labor is not a bargain if the employees are incompetent. Employees should be properly trained and have a record that attests to personal integrity. |
| Bonding employees | Employees in positions of trust should be bonded through insurance policies that protect a company from losses caused by employee dishonesty. |
| Requiring extended absences | Forcing extended absences (such as vacations) creates an opportunity for the temporary replacement employee to check the work of the absent employees. Fraud is difficult to cover up if you are not present to do so. |
| Establishing clear lines of authority and responsibility | Employees tend to be more zealous in supporting company policies when they have clear authority to exercise enforcement. Further, they take their work more seriously when they realize that they cannot shirk responsibility. |
| Using prenumbered documents | Missing documents become apparent when there are gaps in a recorded sequence of numbers. For example, a stolen check would become apparent if a check register omits a check number. |
| Establishing physical controls | Keeping money in a safe; holding inventory in locked warehouses; and bolting computers to a desk are examples of using physical controls designed to protect assets. |
| Performing evaluations at regular intervals | Knowing that inventory will be counted on a regular basis encourages the inventory control manager to maintain documents that support the actual balance of inventory on hand. Similarly verifying the mileage on a car will encourage employees to use company-owned vehicles for legitimate business purposes. Regular evaluations and examinations are strong deterrents to the inappropriate utilization of company-owned assets. |

Most people are able to resist pressure and the tendency to rationalize ethical or legal misconduct. However, some people will yield to temptation. What can companies do to protect themselves from unscrupulous characters? The answer lies in personal integrity. The best indicator of personal integrity is past performance. Accordingly companies must exercise due care in performing appropriate background investigations before hiring people to fill positions of trust.

## Sarbanes-Oxley Act of 2002

In spite of ethics training and accounting controls, fraud and its devastating consequences persist. Enron, WorldCom, and HealthSouth are examples of massive scandals that destroyed or crippled major U.S. corporations in recent years. These high-profile cases led government officials to conclude that the force of law would be necessary to restore and maintain confidence in the capital markets. The **Sarbanes-Oxley (SOX) Act,** which became effective July 30, 2002, provides the muscle that Congress hopes will deter future fiascos. SOX affects four groups including: management, boards of directors, external auditors, and the Public Company Accounting Oversight Board (PCAOB). In

# FOCUS ON INTERNATIONAL ISSUES

## FINANCIAL ACCOUNTING VERSUS MANAGERIAL ACCOUNTING—AN INTERNATIONAL PERSPECTIVE

This chapter has already explained some of the conceptual differences between financial and managerial accounting, but these differences have implications for international businesses as well. With respect to financial accounting, publicly traded companies in most countries must follow the generally accepted accounting principles (GAAP) for their country, but these rules can vary from country to country. Generally, companies that are audited under the auditing standards of the United States follow the standards established by the Financial Accounting Standards Board. Most companies located outside of the United States follow the standards established by the International Accounting Standards Board. For example, the United States is one of very few countries whose GAAP allow the use of the LIFO inventory cost flow assumption.

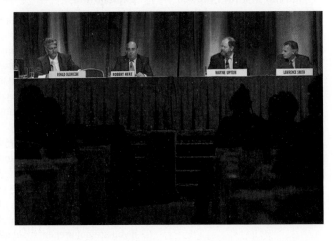

Conversely, most of the managerial accounting concepts introduced in this course can be used by businesses in any country. For example, *activity-based costing (ABC)* is a topic addressed in Chapter 6 and is used by many companies in the United States. Meanwhile, a study published in *Accountancy Ireland** found that approximately one-third of the companies surveyed in Ireland, the United Kingdom, and New Zealand were also either using ABC, or were considering adopting it.

*Bernard Pierce, "Activity-Based Costing; the Irish Experience: True Innovation or Passing Fad?" *Accountancy Ireland,* October 2004, pp. 28–31.

---

this text, we focus on how SOX affects corporate management. While extensive coverage of SOX is beyond the scope of this text, all management accountants should be aware of the following:

■ SOX holds the chief executive officer (CEO) and the chief financial officer (CFO) responsible for the establishment and enforcement of a strong set of internal controls. Along with its annual report, companies are required to report on the effectiveness of their internal controls. Also, the company's external auditors are required to attest to the accuracy of the internal controls report.

■ SOX charges the CEO and the CFO with the ultimate responsibility for the accuracy of the company's financial statements and the accompanying notes. Even though lower-level managers will likely prepare the annual report, the CEO and CFO are required to certify that they have reviewed the report and that, to their knowledge, the report does not contain false statements or significant omissions. An intentional misrepresentation is punishable by a fine of up to $5 million and imprisonment of up to 20 years.

■ SOX requires management to establish a code of ethics and to file reports on the code in the company's annual 10K report filed with the Securities and Exchange Commission.

■ SOX demands that management establish a hotline and other mechanisms for the anonymous reporting of fraudulent activities. Further, SOX prohibits companies from punishing whistleblowers, employees who legally report corporate misconduct.

The accounting profession and government authorities are becoming increasingly intolerant of unethical conduct and illegal activity. A single mistake can jeopardize an accountant's career. A person guilty of white-collar crime loses the opportunity for white-collar employment. Second chances are rarely granted.

# A Look Back

*Managerial accounting* focuses on the information needs of *internal* users, while *financial accounting* focuses on the information needs of *external* users. Managerial accounting uses economic, operating, and nonfinancial, as well as financial, data. Managerial accounting information is local (pertains to the company's subunits), is limited by cost/benefit considerations, is more concerned with relevance and timeliness, and is future oriented. Financial accounting information, on the other hand, is more global than managerial accounting information. It supplies information that applies to the whole company. Financial accounting is regulated by numerous authorities, is characterized by objectivity, is focused on reliability and accuracy, and is historical in nature.

Both managerial and financial accounting are concerned with product costing. Financial accountants need product cost information to determine the amount of inventory reported on the balance sheet and the amount of cost of goods sold reported on the income statement. Managerial accountants need to know the cost of products for pricing decisions and for control and evaluation purposes. When determining unit product costs, managers use the average cost per unit. Determining the actual cost of each product requires an unreasonable amount of time and record keeping and it makes no difference in product pricing and product cost control decisions.

*Product costs* are the costs incurred to make products: the costs of direct materials, direct labor, and overhead. *Overhead costs* are product costs that cannot be cost effectively traced to a product; therefore, they are assigned to products using *cost allocation*. Overhead costs include indirect materials, indirect labor, depreciation, rent, and utilities for manufacturing facilities. Product costs are first accumulated in an asset account (Inventory). They are expensed as cost of goods sold in the period the inventory is sold. The difference between sales revenue and cost of goods sold is called *gross margin*.

*Selling, general, and administrative costs* are classified separately from product costs. They are subtracted from gross margin to determine net income. Selling, general, and administrative costs can be divided into two categories. Costs incurred before the manufacturing process begins (research and development costs) are *upstream costs*. Costs incurred after manufacturing is complete (transportation) are *downstream costs*.

Service companies, like manufacturing companies, incur materials, labor, and overhead costs, but the products provided by service companies are consumed immediately. Therefore, service company product costs are not accumulated in an Inventory account.

A *code of ethical conduct* is needed in the accounting profession because accountants hold positions of trust and face conflicts of interest. In recognition of the temptations that accountants face, the IMA has issued a *Statement of Ethical Professional Practice,* which provides accountants guidance in resisting temptations and in making difficult decisions.

Emerging trends such as *just-in-time inventory* and *activity-based management* are methods that many companies have used to reengineer their production and delivery systems to eliminate waste, reduce errors, and minimize costs. Activity-based management seeks to eliminate or reduce *nonvalue-added activities* and to create new *value-added activities*. Just-in-time inventory seeks to reduce inventory holding costs and to lower prices for customers by making inventory available just in time for customer consumption.

# A Look Forward >>

In addition to distinguishing costs by product versus SG&A classification, other classifications can be used to facilitate managerial decision making. In the next chapter, costs are classified according to the *behavior* they exhibit when the number of units of product increases or decreases (volume of activity changes). You will learn to distinguish between costs that vary with activity volume changes versus costs that remain fixed with activity volume changes. You will learn not only to recognize *cost behavior* but also how to use such recognition to evaluate business risk and opportunity.

## APPENDIX A

LO 8

Identify emerging trends in accounting.

### Emerging Trends in Managerial Accounting

Global competition has forced many companies to reengineer their production and delivery systems to eliminate waste, reduce errors, and minimize costs. A key ingredient of successful **reengineering** is benchmarking. **Benchmarking** involves identifying the **best practices** used by world-class competitors. By studying and mimicking these practices, a company uses benchmarking to implement highly effective and efficient operating methods. Best practices employed by world-class companies include total quality management (TQM), activity-based management (ABM), and value-added assessment.

#### Total Quality Management

To promote effective and efficient operations, many companies practice **total quality management (TQM).** TQM is a two-dimensional management philosophy using (1) a systematic problem-solving philosophy that encourages frontline workers to achieve *zero defects* and (2) an organizational commitment to achieving *customer satisfaction.* A key component of TQM is **continuous improvement,** an ongoing process through which employees strive to eliminate waste, reduce response time, minimize defects, and simplify the design and delivery of products and services to customers.

#### Activity-Based Management

Simple changes in perspective can have dramatic results. For example, imagine how realizing the world is round instead of flat changed the nature of travel. A recent change in perspective developing in management accounting is the realization that an organization cannot manage *costs.* Instead, it manages the *activities* that cause costs to be incurred. **Activities** represent the measures an organization takes to accomplish its goals.

The primary goal of all organizations is to provide products (goods and services) their customers *value.* The sequence of activities used to provide products is called a **value chain. Activity-based management** assesses the value chain to create new or refine existing **value-added activities** and to eliminate or reduce *nonvalue-added activities.* A value-added activity is any unit of work that contributes to a product's ability to satisfy customer needs. For example, cooking is an activity that adds value to food served to a hungry customer. **Nonvalue-added activities** are tasks undertaken that do not contribute to a product's ability to satisfy customer needs. Waiting for the oven to preheat so that food can be cooked does not add value. Most customers value cooked food, but they do not value waiting for it.

To illustrate, consider the value-added activities undertaken by a pizza restaurant. Begin with a customer who is hungry for pizza; certain activities must occur to satisfy that hunger. These activities are pictured in Exhibit 1.18. At a minimum, the restaurant must conduct research and development (devise a recipe), obtain raw materials (acquire the ingredients), manufacture the product (combine and bake the ingredients), market the product (advertise its availability), and deliver the product (transfer the pizza to the customer).

**EXHIBIT 1.18**

**Value Chain**

| Conducting research and development | Obtaining materials | Manufacturing | Marketing | Delivering |

Businesses gain competitive advantages by adding activities that satisfy customer needs. For example, **Domino's Pizza** grew briskly by recognizing the value customers placed on the convenience of home pizza delivery. Alternatively, **Little Caesar's** has been highly successful by satisfying customers who value low prices. Other restaurants capitalize on customer values pertaining to taste, ambience, or location. Businesses can also gain competitive advantages by identifying and eliminating nonvalue-added activities, providing products of comparable quality at lower cost than competitors.

## Value Chain Analysis Across Companies

Comprehensive value chain analysis extends from obtaining raw materials to the ultimate disposition of finished products. It encompasses the activities performed not only by a particular organization but also by that organization's suppliers and those who service its finished products. For example, **PepsiCo** must be concerned with the activities of the company that supplies the containers for its soft drinks as well as the retail companies that sell its products. If cans of Pepsi fail to open properly, the customer is more likely to blame PepsiCo than the supplier of the cans. Comprehensive value chain analysis can lead to identifying and eliminating nonvalue-added activities that occur between companies. For example, container producers could be encouraged to build manufacturing facilities near Pepsi's bottling factories, eliminating the nonvalue-added activity of transporting empty containers from the manufacturer to the bottling facility. The resulting cost savings benefits customers by reducing costs without affecting quality.

**A step-by-step audio-narrated series of slides is provided on the text website at www.mhhe.com/edmonds2011.**

### SELF-STUDY REVIEW PROBLEM

Tuscan Manufacturing Company makes a unique headset for use with mobile phones. During 2012, its first year of operations, Tuscan experienced the following accounting events. Other than the adjusting entries for depreciation, assume that all transactions are cash transactions.

1. Acquired $850,000 cash from the issue of common stock.
2. Paid $50,000 of research and development costs to develop the headset.
3. Paid $140,000 for the materials used to make headsets, all of which were started and completed during the year.
4. Paid salaries of $82,200 to selling and administrative employees.
5. Paid wages of $224,000 to production workers.
6. Paid $48,000 to purchase furniture used in selling and administrative offices.
7. Recognized depreciation on the office furniture. The furniture, acquired January 1, had an $8,000 estimated salvage value and a four-year useful life. The amount of depreciation is computed as [(cost − salvage) ÷ useful life]. Specifically, [($48,000 − $8,000) ÷ 4 = $10,000].
8. Paid $65,000 to purchase manufacturing equipment.
9. Recognized depreciation on the manufacturing equipment. The equipment, acquired January 1, had a $5,000 estimated salvage value and a three-year useful life. The amount of depreciation is computed as [(cost − salvage) ÷ useful life]. Specifically, [($65,000 − $5,000) ÷ 3 = $20,000].
10. Paid $136,000 for rent and utility costs on the manufacturing facility.
11. Paid $41,000 for inventory holding expenses for completed headsets (rental of warehouse space, salaries of warehouse personnel, and other general storage costs).
12. Tuscan started and completed 20,000 headset units during 2012. The company sold 18,400 headsets at a price of $38 per unit.
13. Compute the average product cost per unit and recognize the appropriate amount of cost of goods sold.

**Required**

a. Show how these events affect the balance sheet and income statement by recording them in a horizontal financial statements model.

b. Prepare a formal income statement for the year.

c. Distinguish between the product costs and the upstream and downstream costs that Tuscan incurred.

d. The company president believes that Tuscan could save money by buying the inventory that it currently makes. The warehouse supervisor said that would not be possible because the purchase price of $27 per unit was above the $26 average cost per unit of making the product. Assuming that the purchased inventory would be available on demand, explain how the company president could be correct and why the warehouse supervisor could be biased in his assessment of the option to buy the inventory.

## Solution to Requirement a

| Event No. | | Assets | | | | = | Equity | | | | Rev. | − | Exp. | = | Net Inc. |
|---|---|---|---|---|---|---|---|---|---|---|---|---|---|---|---|
| | Cash | Inventory | + | Office Furn.* | + | Manuf. Equip.* = | Com. Stk. | + | Ret. Earn. | | Rev. | − | Exp. | = | Net Inc. |
| 1 | 850,000 | | | | | | 850,000 | | | | | | | | |
| 2 | (50,000) | | | | | | | | (50,000) | | | − | 50,000 | | (50,000) |
| 3 | (140,000) | 140,000 | | | | | | | | | | | | | |
| 4 | (82,200) | | | | | | | | (82,200) | | | − | 82,200 | | (82,200) |
| 5 | (224,000) | 224,000 | | | | | | | | | | | | | |
| 6 | (48,000) | | | 48,000 | | | | | | | | | | | |
| 7 | | | | (10,000) | | | | | (10,000) | | | − | 10,000 | | (10,000) |
| 8 | (65,000) | | | | | 65,000 | | | | | | | | | |
| 9 | | 20,000 | | | | (20,000) | | | | | | | | | |
| 10 | (136,000) | 136,000 | | | | | | | | | | | | | |
| 11 | (41,000) | | | | | | | | (41,000) | | | − | 41,000 | | (41,000) |
| 12 | 699,200 | | | | | | | | 699,200 | | 699,200 | | | | 699,200 |
| 13 | | (478,400) | | | | | | | (478,400) | | | − | 478,400 | | (478,400) |
| Totals | 763,000 | + 41,600 | + | 38,000 | + | 45,000 = | 850,000 | + | 37,600 | | 699,200 | − | 661,600 | = | 37,600 |

*Negative amounts in these columns represent accumulated depreciation.

The average cost per unit of product is determined by dividing the total product cost by the number of headsets produced. Specifically, ($140,000 + $224,000 + $20,000 + $136,000) ÷ 20,000 = $26. Cost of goods sold is $478,400 ($26 × 18,400).

## Solution to Requirement b

**TUSCAN MANUFACTURING COMPANY**
**Income Statement**
**For the Year Ended December 31, 2012**

| | |
|---|---:|
| Sales revenue (18,400 units × $38) | $699,200 |
| Cost of goods sold (18,400 × $26) | (478,400) |
| Gross margin | 220,800 |
| R&D expenses | (50,000) |
| Selling and admin. salaries expense | (82,200) |
| Admin. depreciation expense | (10,000) |
| Inventory holding expense | (41,000) |
| Net income | $ 37,600 |

## Solution to Requirement c

Inventory product costs for manufacturing companies focus on the costs necessary to make the product. The cost of research and development (Event 2) occurs before the inventory is made and is therefore an upstream cost, not an inventory (product) cost. The inventory holding costs (Event 11) are incurred after the inventory has been made and are therefore downstream costs, not product costs. Selling costs (included in Events 4 and 7) are normally incurred after products have been made and are therefore usually classified as downstream costs. Administrative costs (also included in Events 4 and 7) are not related to making products and are therefore not classified as product costs. Administrative costs may be incurred before, during, or after products are made, so they may be classified as either upstream or downstream costs. Only the costs of materials, labor, and overhead that are actually incurred for the purpose of making goods (Events 3, 5, 9, and 10) are classified as product costs.

## Solution to Requirement d

Since the merchandise would be available on demand, Tuscan could operate a just-in-time inventory system thereby eliminating the inventory holding expense. Since the additional cost to purchase is $1 per unit ($27 − $26), it would cost Tuscan an additional $20,000 ($1 × 20,000 units) to purchase its product. However, the company would save $41,000 of inventory holding expense. The warehouse supervisor could be biased by the fact that his job would be lost if the company purchased its products and thereby could eliminate the need for warehousing inventory. If Tuscan does not maintain inventory, it would not need a warehouse supervisor.

## KEY TERMS

| | | |
|---|---|---|
| Activities 24 | Finished Goods Inventory 6 | Raw materials 9 |
| Activity-based management (ABM) 23 | Generally accepted accounting principles (GAAP) 5 | Reengineering 24 |
| Average cost 26 | Indirect costs 11 | Sarbanes-Oxley Act of 2002 21 |
| Benchmarking 24 | Inventory holding costs 14 | Securities and Exchange Commission (SEC) 5 |
| Best practices 24 | Just in time (JIT) 14 | |
| Continuous improvement 24 | Managerial accounting 2 | Selling, general, and administrative costs (SG&A) 10 |
| Cost allocation 12 | Manufacturing overhead 11 | |
| Cost-plus pricing 5 | Nonvalue-added activities 15 | Total quality management (TQM) 24 |
| Direct labor 9 | | |
| Direct raw materials 9 | Opportunity cost 15 | Upstream costs 13 |
| Downstream costs 14 | Overhead 6 | Value-added activity 24 |
| Financial accounting 2 | Period costs 10 | Value-added principle 5 |
| Financial Accounting Standards Board (FASB) 5 | Product costs 5 | Value chain 24 |
| | Product costing 5 | |

## QUESTIONS

1. What are some differences between financial and managerial accounting?

2. What does the value-added principle mean as it applies to managerial accounting information? Give an example of value-added information that may be included in managerial accounting reports but is not shown in publicly reported financial statements.

3. What are the two dimensions of a total quality management (TQM) program? Why is TQM being used in business practice? (Appendix A)

4. How does product costing used in financial accounting differ from product costing used in managerial accounting?

5. What does the statement "costs can be assets or expenses" mean?

6. Why are the salaries of production workers accumulated in an inventory account instead of being expensed on the income statement?

7. How do product costs affect the financial statements? How does the classification of product cost (as an asset vs. an expense) affect net income?

8. What is an indirect cost? Provide examples of product costs that would be classified as indirect.

9. How does a product cost differ from a selling, general, and administrative cost? Give examples of each.

10. Why is cost classification important to managers?

11. What is cost allocation? Give an example of a cost that needs to be allocated.

12. How has the Institute of Management Accountants responded to the need for high standards of ethical conduct in the accounting profession?

13. What are some of the common ethical conflicts that accountants encounter?

14. What costs should be considered in determining the sales price of a product?

15. What is a just-in-time (JIT) inventory system? Name some inventory costs that can be eliminated or reduced by its use.

16. What does the term *reengineering* mean? Name some reengineering practices. (Appendix A)

17. What does the term *activity-based management* mean? (Appendix A)

18. What is a value chain? (Appendix A)

19. What do the terms *value-added activity* and *nonvalue-added activity* mean? Provide an example of each type of activity. (Appendix A)

## MULTIPLE-CHOICE QUESTIONS

**Multiple-choice questions are provided on the text website at www.mhhe.com/edmonds2011.**

## EXERCISES—SERIES A

**All applicable Exercises in Series A are available with McGraw-Hill's *Connect Accounting*.**

**LO 1**

**Exercise 1-1A** *Identifying financial versus managerial accounting items*

**Required**

Indicate whether each of the following items is representative of managerial or of financial accounting.

a. Information is provided to outsiders including investors, creditors, government agencies, analysts, and reporters.

b. Information is regulated by the SEC, FASB, and other sources of GAAP.

c. Information is based on estimates that are bounded by relevance and timeliness.

d. Information is historically based and usually reported annually.

e. Information is local and pertains to subunits of the organization.

f. Information includes economic and nonfinancial data as well as financial data.

g. Information is global and pertains to the company as a whole.

h. Information is provided to insiders including executives, managers, and employees.

i. Information is factual and is characterized by objectivity, reliability, consistency, and accuracy.

j. Information is reported continuously and has a current or future orientation.

**LO 2, 3**

**Exercise 1-2A** *Identifying product versus general, selling, and administrative costs*

**Required**

Indicate whether each of the following costs should be classified as a product cost or as a selling, general, and administrative cost.

a. Salaries of employees working in the accounting department.

b. Commissions paid to sales staff.

c. Interest on the mortgage for the company's corporate headquarters.

d. Indirect labor used to manufacture inventory.

e. Attorney's fees paid to protect the company from frivolous lawsuits.

**f.** Research and development costs incurred to create new drugs for a pharmaceutical company.

**g.** The cost of secretarial supplies used in a doctor's office.

**h.** Depreciation on the office furniture of the company president.

**i.** Direct materials used in a manufacturing company.

**j.** Indirect materials used in a manufacturing company.

## Exercise 1-3A   *Classifying Costs: Product or SG&A/Asset or Expense*                LO 2, 3

**Required**

Use the following format to classify each cost as a product cost or a selling, general, and administrative (SG&A) cost. Also indicate whether the cost would be recorded as an asset or an expense. The first item is shown as an example.

| Cost Category | Product/SG&A | Asset/Expense |
|---|---|---|
| Research and development costs | SG&A | Expense |
| Cost to set up manufacturing equipment | | |
| Utilities used in manufacturing facility | | |
| Cars for sales staff | | |
| Distributions to stockholders | | |
| General office supplies | | |
| Raw materials used in the manufacturing process | | |
| Cost to rent office equipment | | |
| Wages of production workers | | |
| Advertising costs | | |
| Promotion costs | | |
| Production supplies | | |
| Depreciation on administration building | | |
| Depreciation on manufacturing equipment | | |

## Exercise 1-4A   *Identifying effect of product versus selling, general, and*                LO 3
*administrative costs on financial statements*

**Required**

Nailry Corporation recognized accrued compensation cost. Use the following model to show how this event would affect the company's financial statement under the following two assumptions: (1) the compensation is for office personnel and (2) the compensation is for production workers. Use pluses or minuses to show the effect on each element. If an element is not affected, indicate so by placing the letters NA under the appropriate heading.

| | Assets | = | Liab. | + | Equity | Rev. | − | Exp. | = | Net Inc. |
|---|---|---|---|---|---|---|---|---|---|---|
| 1. | | | | | | | | | | |
| 2. | | | | | | | | | | |

## Exercise 1-5A   *Identify effect of product versus selling, general, and administrative*                LO 3
*costs on financial statements*

**Required**

Engle Industries recognized the annual cost of depreciation on its December 31, 2012, financial statements. Using the following horizontal financial statements model, indicate how this event affected the company's financial statements under the following two assumptions: (1) the depreciation was on office furniture and (2) the depreciation was on manufacturing equipment. Indicate whether the event increases (I), decreases (D), or has no affect (NA) on each element of the financial statements. (Note: Show accumulated depreciation as a decrease in the book value of the appropriate asset account.)

| Event No. | Assets | | | | Equity | | | | |
|---|---|---|---|---|---|---|---|---|---|
| | Cash + | Inventory + | Manuf. Equip. + | Office Furn. = | Com. Stk. + | Ret. Ear. | Rev. − | Exp. = | Net Inc. |
| 1. | | | | | | | | | |
| 2. | | | | | | | | | |

**LO 2**

### Exercise 1-6A   *Identifying product costs in a manufacturing company*

Tiffany Crissler was talking to another accounting student, Bill Tyrone. Upon discovering that the accounting department offered an upper-level course in cost measurement, Tiffany remarked to Bill, "How difficult can it be? My parents own a toy store. All you have to do to figure out how much something costs is look at the invoice. Surely you don't need an entire course to teach you how to read an invoice."

**Required**

a. Identify the three main components of product cost for a manufacturing entity.

b. Explain why measuring product cost for a manufacturing entity is more complex than measuring product cost for a retail toy store.

c. Assume that Tiffany's parents rent a store for $7,500 per month. Different types of toys use different amounts of store space. For example, displaying a bicycle requires more store space than displaying a deck of cards. Also, some toys remain on the shelf longer than others. Fad toys sell rapidly, but traditional toys sell more slowly. Under these circumstances, how would you determine the amount of rental cost required to display each type of toy? Identify two other costs incurred by a toy store that may be difficult to allocate to individual toys.

**LO 3**

### Exercise 1-7A   *Identifying product versus selling, general, and administrative costs*

A review of the accounting records of Rayford Manufacturing indicated that the company incurred the following payroll costs during the month of September.

1. Salary of the company president—$32,000.
2. Salary of the vice president of manufacturing—$16,000.
3. Salary of the chief financial officer—$18,800.
4. Salary of the vice president of marketing—$15,600.
5. Salaries of middle managers (department heads, production supervisors) in manufacturing plant—$196,000.
6. Wages of production workers—$938,000.
7. Salaries of administrative secretaries—$112,000.
8. Salaries of engineers and other personnel responsible for maintaining production equipment—$178,000.
9. Commissions paid to sales staff—$252,000.

**Required**

a. What amount of payroll cost would be classified as selling, general, and administrative expense?

b. Assuming that Rayford made 4,000 units of product and sold 3,600 of them during the month of September, determine the amount of payroll cost that would be included in cost of goods sold.

**LO 2, 3**

### Exercise 1-8A   *Recording product versus selling, general, and administrative costs in a financial statements model*

Pappas Manufacturing experienced the following events during its first accounting period.

1. Recognized depreciation on manufacturing equipment.
2. Recognized depreciation on office furniture.

3. Recognized revenue from cash sale of products.
4. Recognized cost of goods sold from sale referenced in Event 3.
5. Acquired cash by issuing common stock.
6. Paid cash to purchase raw materials that were used to make products.
7. Paid wages to production workers.
8. Paid salaries to administrative staff.

## Required

Use the following horizontal financial statements model to show how each event affects the balance sheet and income statement. Indicate whether the event increases (I), decreases (D), or has no effect (NA) on each element of the financial statements. The first transaction has been recorded as an example. (*Note:* Show accumulated depreciation as a decrease in the book value of the appropriate asset account.)

| Event No. | Cash | + | Inventory | + | Manuf. Equip. | + | Office Furn. | = | Com. Stk. | + | Ret. Ear. | Rev. | − | Exp. | = | Net Inc. |
|-----------|------|---|-----------|---|---------------|---|--------------|---|-----------|---|-----------|------|---|------|---|----------|
| 1. | NA | | I | | D | | NA | | NA | | NA | NA | | NA | | NA |

**Assets** spans Cash, Inventory, Manuf. Equip., Office Furn. **Equity** spans Com. Stk., Ret. Ear.

## Exercise 1-9A  Allocating product costs between ending inventory and cost of goods sold

LO 2

Howle Manufacturing Company began operations on January 1. During the year, it started and completed 1,700 units of product. The company incurred the following costs.

1. Raw materials purchased and used—$3,150.
2. Wages of production workers—$3,530.
3. Salaries of administrative and sales personnel—$1,995.
4. Depreciation on manufacturing equipment—$4,370.
5. Depreciation on administrative equipment—$1,835.

Howle sold 1,020 units of product.

## Required

a. Determine the total product cost for the year.
b. Determine the total cost of the ending inventory.
c. Determine the total of cost of goods sold.

## Exercise 1-10A  Financial statement effects for manufacturing versus service organizations

LO 3

The following financial statements model shows the effects of recognizing depreciation in two different circumstances. One circumstance represents recognizing depreciation on a machine used in a factory. The other circumstance recognizes depreciation on computers used in a consulting firm. The effects of each event have been recorded using the letter (I) to represent increase, (D) for decrease, and (NA) for no effect.

| Event No. | Cash | + | Inventory | + | Equip. | = | Com. Stk. | + | Ret. Ear. | Rev. | − | Exp. | = | Net Inc. |
|-----------|------|---|-----------|---|--------|---|-----------|---|-----------|------|---|------|---|----------|
| 1. | NA | | NA | | D | | NA | | D | NA | | I | | D |
| 2. | NA | | I | | D | | NA | | NA | NA | | NA | | NA |

**Assets** spans Cash, Inventory, Equip. **Equity** spans Com. Stk., Ret. Ear.

**Required**

a.  Identify the event that represents depreciation on the computers.

b.  Explain why recognizing depreciation on equipment used in a manufacturing company affects financial statements differently from recognizing depreciation on equipment used in a service organization.

**LO 3**

### Exercise 1-11A   *Identifying the effect of product versus selling, general, and administrative cost on the income statement*

Each of the following events describes acquiring an asset that requires a year-end adjusting entry.

1.  Paid $14,000 cash on January 1 to purchase computer equipment to be used for administrative purposes. The equipment had an estimated expected useful life of four years and a $2,000 salvage value.

2.  Paid $14,000 cash on January 1 to purchase manufacturing equipment. The equipment had an estimated expected useful life of four years and a $2,000 salvage value.

3.  Paid $12,000 cash in advance on May 1 for a one-year rental contract on administrative offices.

4.  Paid $12,000 cash in advance on May 1 for a one-year rental contract on manufacturing facilities.

5.  Paid $2,000 cash to purchase supplies to be used by the marketing department. At the end of the year, $400 of supplies was still on hand.

6.  Paid $2,000 cash to purchase supplies to be used in the manufacturing process. At the end of the year, $400 of supplies was still on hand.

**Required**

Explain how the adjusting entry affects the amount of net income shown on the year-end financial statements. Assume a December 31 annual closing date. The first event has been recorded as an example. Assume that any products that have been made have not been sold.

| | Net Income |
| --- | --- |
| **Event No.** | **Amount of Change** |
| 1.  Adjusting entry | $(3,000) |

**LO 4**

### Exercise 1-12A   *Upstream and downstream costs*

During 2011, Gallo Manufacturing Company incurred $90,000,000 of research and development (R&D) costs to create a long-life battery to use in computers. In accordance with FASB standards, the entire R&D cost was recognized as an expense in 2011. Manufacturing costs (direct materials, direct labor, and overhead) are expected to be $260 per unit. Packaging, shipping, and sales commissions are expected to be $50 per unit. Gallo expects to sell 2,000,000 batteries before new research renders the battery design technologically obsolete. During 2011, Gallo made 440,000 batteries and sold 400,000 of them.

**Required**

a.  Identify the upstream and downstream costs.

b.  Determine the 2011 amount of cost of goods sold and the ending inventory balance.

c.  Determine the sales price assuming that Gallo desires to earn a profit margin that is equal to 25 percent of the *total cost* of developing, making, and distributing the batteries.

d.  Prepare an income statement for 2011. Use the sales price developed in Requirement *c.*

e.  Why would Gallo price the batteries at a level that would generate a loss for the 2011 accounting period?

**LO 6**

### Exercise 1-13A   *Identify the effect of a just-in-time inventory system on financial statements*

After reviewing the financial statements of Bearden Company, Todd Howard concluded that the company was a service company. Mr. Howard based his conclusion on the fact that Bearden's financial statements displayed no inventory accounts.

**Required**

Explain how Bearden's implementation of a 100 percent effective just-in-time inventory system could have led Mr. Howard to a false conclusion regarding the nature of Bearden's business.

### Exercise 1-14A   *Using JIT to minimize waste and lost opportunity*

**LO 6**

Anne Kyser, a teacher at Hewitt Middle School, is in charge of ordering the T-shirts to be sold for the school's annual fund-raising project. The T-shirts are printed with a special Hewitt School logo. In some years, the supply of T-shirts has been insufficient to satisfy the number of sales orders. In other years, T-shirts have been left over. Excess T-shirts are normally donated to some charitable organization. T-shirts cost the school $8 each and are normally sold for $14 each. Ms. Kyser has decided to order 800 shirts.

**Required**

a.  If the school receives actual sales orders for 725 shirts, what amount of profit will the school earn? What is the cost of waste due to excess inventory?

b.  If the school receives actual sales orders for 825 shirts, what amount of profit will the school earn? What amount of opportunity cost will the school incur?

c.  Explain how a JIT inventory system could maximize profitability by eliminating waste and opportunity cost.

### Exercise 1-15A   *Using JIT to minimize holding costs*

**LO 6**

Lee Pet Supplies purchases its inventory from a variety of suppliers, some of which require a six-week lead time before delivering the goods. To ensure that she has a sufficient supply of goods on hand, Ms. Polk, the owner, must maintain a large supply of inventory. The cost of this inventory averages $21,000. She usually finances the purchase of inventory and pays a 9 percent annual finance charge. Ms. Polk's accountant has suggested that she establish a relationship with a single large distributor who can satisfy all of her orders within a two-week time period. Given this quick turnaround time, she will be able to reduce her average inventory balance to $4,000. Ms. Polk also believes that she could save $2,500 per year by reducing phone bills, insurance, and warehouse rental space costs associated with ordering and maintaining the larger level of inventory.

**Required**

a.  Is the new inventory system available to Ms. Polk a pure or approximate just-in-time system?

b.  Based on the information provided, how much of Ms. Polk's inventory holding cost could be eliminated by taking the accountant's advice?

### Exercise 1-16A   *Applications of the Sarbanes-Oxley Act*

**LO 7**

The CFO of the Rigney Microscope Corporation intentionally misclassified a downstream transportation expense in the amount of $67,500,000 as a product cost in an accounting period when the company made 12,000 microscopes and sold 7,000 microscopes. Rigney rewards its officers with bonuses that are based on net earnings.

**Required**

a.  Indicate whether the elements on the financial statements (i.e., assets, liabilities, equity, revenue, expense, and net income) would be overstated or understated as a result of the misclassification of the upstream research and development expense. Determine the amount of the overstatement or understatement for each element.

b.  Based on the provisions of the Sarbanes-Oxley Act, what is the maximum penalty that the CFO could face for deliberately missrepresenting the financial statements?

### Exercise 1-17A   *Professional conduct and code of ethics*

**LO 7**

In February 2006 former senator Warren Rudman of New Hampshire completed a 17-month investigation of an $11 billion accounting scandal at Fannie Mae (a major enterprise involved in home mortgage financing), The Rudman investigation concluded that Fannie Mae's CFO and controller used an accounting gimmick to manipulate financial statements in order to meet earnings-per-share (EPS) targets. Meeting the EPS targets triggered bonus payments for the executives. Fannie Mae's problems continued after 2006, and on September 8, 2008, it went into conservatorship under the control of the Federal Housing Financing Agency. The primary executives at the time of the Rudman investigation were replaced, and the enterprise reported a $59.8 billion loss in 2008.

**Required**

Review the principles of ethical professional practice shown in Exhibit 1.15. Identify and comment on which of the ethical principles the CFO and controller violated.

**LO 8**

### Exercise 1-18A   *Value chain analysis ( Appendix )*

Sonic Company manufactures and sells high-quality audio speakers. The speakers are encased in solid walnut cabinets supplied by Moore Cabinet, Inc. Moore packages the speakers in durable moisture-proof boxes and ships them by truck to Sonic manufacturing facility, which is located 50 miles from the cabinet factory.

**Required**

Identify the nonvalue-added activities that occur between the companies described in the preceding scenario. Provide a logical explanation as to how these nonvalue-added activities could be eliminated.

## PROBLEMS—SERIES A

**All applicable Problems in Series A are available with McGraw-Hill's *Connect Accounting.***

**LO 2, 3**

CHECK FIGURES
a. Average Cost per Unit: $8.40
f. $90,400

### Problem 1-19A   *Product versus selling, general, and administrative costs*

Jolly Manufacturing Company was started on January 1, 2011, when it acquired $90,000 cash by issuing common stock. Jolly immediately purchased office furniture and manufacturing equipment costing $10,000 and $28,000, respectively. The office furniture had a five-year useful life and a zero salvage value. The manufacturing equipment had a $4,000 salvage value and an expected useful life of three years. The company paid $12,000 for salaries of administrative personnel and $16,000 for wages to production personnel. Finally, the company paid $18,000 for raw materials that were used to make inventory. All inventory was started and completed during the year. Jolly completed production on 5,000 units of product and sold 4,000 units at a price of $15 each in 2011. (Assume that all transactions are cash transactions.)

**Required**

a. Determine the total product cost and the average cost per unit of the inventory produced in 2011.

b. Determine the amount of cost of goods sold that would appear on the 2011 income statement.

c. Determine the amount of the ending inventory balance that would appear on the December 31, 2011, balance sheet.

d. Determine the amount of net income that would appear on the 2011 income statement.

e. Determine the amount of retained earnings that would appear on the December 31, 2011, balance sheet.

f. Determine the amount of total assets that would appear on the December 31, 2011, balance sheet.

**LO 3**

eXcel

CHECK FIGURES
Cash balance: $33,000
Net income: $4,600

### Problem 1-20A   *Effect of product versus period costs on financial statements*

Hoehn Manufacturing Company experienced the following accounting events during its first year of operation. With the exception of the adjusting entries for depreciation, assume that all transactions are cash transactions.

1. Acquired $50,000 cash by issuing common stock.

2. Paid $8,000 for the materials used to make its products, all of which were started and completed during the year.

3. Paid salaries of $4,400 to selling and administrative employees.

4. Paid wages of $7,000 to production workers.

5. Paid $9,600 for furniture used in selling and administrative offices. The furniture was acquired on January 1. It had a $1,600 estimated salvage value and a four-year useful life.

6. Paid $13,000 for manufacturing equipment. The equipment was acquired on January 1. It had a $1,000 estimated salvage value and a three-year useful life.

7. Sold inventory to customers for $25,000 that had cost $14,000 to make.

**Required**

Explain how these events would affect the balance sheet and income statement by recording them in a horizontal financial statements model as indicated here. The first event is recorded as an example.

| | Financial Statements Model | | | | | | | | |
|---|---|---|---|---|---|---|---|---|---|
| | **Assets** | | | | **Equity** | | | | |
| Event No. | Cash | + Inventory | + Manuf. Equip.* | + Office Furn.* | = Com. Stk. | + Ret. Ear. | Rev. | − Exp. | = Net Inc. |
| 1. | 50,000 | | | | 50,000 | | | | |

*Record accumulated depreciation as negative amounts in these columns.

## Problem 1-21A  *Product versus selling, general, and administrative costs*

LO 2, 3

The following transactions pertain to 2012, the first-year operations of Hall Company. All inventory was started and completed during 2012. Assume that all transactions are cash transactions.

CHECK FIGURES
Net income: $36
Total assets: $4,036

1. Acquired $4,000 cash by issuing common stock.
2. Paid $720 for materials used to produce inventory.
3. Paid $1,800 to production workers.
4. Paid $540 rental fee for production equipment.
5. Paid $180 to administrative employees.
6. Paid $144 rental fee for administrative office equipment.
7. Produced 300 units of inventory of which 200 units were sold at a price of $12 each.

**Required**

Prepare an income statement and a balance sheet.

## Problem 1-22A  *Service versus manufacturing companies*

LO 2, 3, 5

Goree Company began operations on January 1, 2011, by issuing common stock for $30,000 cash. During 2011, Goree received $40,000 cash from revenue and incurred costs that required $60,000 of cash payments.

**Required**

Prepare an income statement and a balance sheet for Goree Company for 2011, under each of the following independent scenarios.

a. Goree is a promoter of rock concerts. The $60,000 was paid to provide a rock concert that produced the revenue.

CHECK FIGURES
a. Net loss: $20,000
b. Total assets: $55,500
c. Net income: $11,000

b. Goree is in the car rental business. The $60,000 was paid to purchase automobiles. The automobiles were purchased on January 1, 2011, have four-year useful lives, with no expected salvage value. Goree uses straight-line depreciation. The revenue was generated by leasing the automobiles.

c. Goree is a manufacturing company. The $60,000 was paid to purchase the following items:

(1) Paid $8,000 cash to purchase materials that were used to make products during the year.

(2) Paid $20,000 cash for wages of factory workers who made products during the year.

(3) Paid $2,000 cash for salaries of sales and administrative employees.

(4) Paid $30,000 cash to purchase manufacturing equipment. The equipment was used solely to make products. It had a three-year life and a $6,000 salvage value. The company uses straightline depreciation.

(5) During 2011, Goree started and completed 2,000 units of product. The revenue was earned when Goree sold 1,500 units of product to its customers.

1800

**d.** Refer to Requirement *c*. Could Goree determine the actual cost of making the 907th unit of product? How likely is it that the actual cost of the 907th unit of product was exactly the same as the cost of producing the 908th unit of product? Explain why management may be more interested in average cost than in actual cost.

### Problem 1-23A   *Importance of cost classification*

Cooke Manufacturing Company (CMC) was started when it acquired $40,000 by issuing common stock. During the first year of operations, the company incurred specifically identifiable product costs (materials, labor, and overhead) amounting to $24,000. CMC also incurred $16,000 of engineering design and planning costs. There was a debate regarding how the design and planning costs should be classified. Advocates of Option 1 believe that the costs should be classified as general, selling, and administrative costs. Advocates of Option 2 believe it is more appropriate to classify the design and planning costs as product costs. During the year, CMC made 4,000 units of product and sold 3,000 units at a price of $24 each. All transactions were cash transactions.

**Required**

**a.** Prepare an income statement and a balance sheet under each of the two options.

**b.** Identify the option that results in financial statements that are more likely to leave a favorable impression on investors and creditors.

**c.** Assume that CMC provides an incentive bonus to the company president equal to 13 percent of net income. Compute the amount of the bonus under each of the two options. Identify the option that provides the president with the higher bonus.

**d.** Assume a 35 percent income tax rate. Determine the amount of income tax expense under each of the two options. Identify the option that minimizes the amount of the company's income tax expense.

**e.** Comment on the conflict of interest between the company president as determined in Requirement *c* and the owners of the company as indicated in Requirement *d*. Describe an incentive compensation plan that would avoid a conflict of interest between the president and the owners.

### Problem 1-24A   *Using JIT to reduce inventory holding costs*

Burt Manufacturing Company obtains its raw materials from a variety of suppliers. Burt's strategy is to obtain the best price by letting the suppliers know that it buys from the lowest bidder. Approximately four years ago, unexpected increased demand resulted in materials shortages. Burt was unable to find the materials it needed even though it was willing to pay premium prices. Because of the lack of raw materials, Burt was forced to close its manufacturing facility for two weeks. Its president vowed that her company would never again be at the mercy of its suppliers. She immediately ordered her purchasing agent to perpetually maintain a one-month supply of raw materials. Compliance with the president's orders resulted in a raw materials inventory amounting to approximately $1,600,000. Warehouse rental and personnel costs to maintain the inventory amounted to $8,000 per month. Burt has a line of credit with a local bank that calls for a 12 percent annual rate of interest. Assume that Burt finances the raw materials inventory with the line of credit.

**Required**

**a.** Based on the information provided, determine the annual holding cost of the raw materials inventory.

**b.** Explain how a JIT system could reduce Burt's inventory holding cost.

**c.** Explain how most-favored customer status could enable Burt to establish a JIT inventory system without risking the raw materials shortages experienced in the past.

### Problem 1-25A   *Using JIT to minimize waste and lost opportunity*

CMA Review, Inc., provides review courses twice each year for students studying to take the CMA exam. The cost of textbooks is included in the registration fee. Text material requires constant updating and is useful for only one course. To minimize printing costs and ensure availability of books on the first day of class, CMA Review has books printed and delivered to its offices two weeks in advance of the first class. To ensure that enough books are available, CMA Review normally orders 10 percent more than expected enrollment. Usually there is an oversupply and books are thrown away. However, demand occasionally exceeds expectations by more than 10 percent and there are too few books available for student use. CMA Review has been forced to turn away students because of a lack of textbooks. CMA Review expects to enroll approximately 100 students per course. The tuition fee is $800 per student. The cost of teachers is $25,000 per course, textbooks cost $60 each, and other operating expenses are estimated to be $35,000 per course.

### Required

a. Prepare an income statement, assuming that 95 students enroll in a course. Determine the cost of waste associated with unused books.

b. Prepare an income statement, assuming that 115 students attempt to enroll in the course. Note that five students are turned away because of too few textbooks. Determine the amount of lost profit resulting from the inability to serve the five additional students.

c. Suppose that textbooks can be produced through a high-speed copying process that permits delivery *just in time* for class to start. The cost of books made using this process, however, is $65 each. Assume that all books must be made using the same production process. In other words, CMA Review cannot order some of the books using the regular copy process and the rest using the high-speed process. Prepare an income statement under the JIT system assuming that 95 students enroll in a course. Compare the income statement under JIT with the income statement prepared in Requirement *a.* Comment on how the JIT system would affect profitability.

d. Assume the same facts as in Requirement *c* with respect to a JIT system that enables immediate delivery of books at a cost of $65 each. Prepare an income statement under the JIT system, assuming that 115 students enroll in a course. Compare the income statement under JIT with the income statement prepared in Requirement *b.* Comment on how the JIT system would affect profitability.

e. Discuss the possible effect of the JIT system on the level of customer satisfaction.

## Problem 1-26A    *Internal control procedures*

**LO 7**

Adam Kimble is a model employee. He has not missed a day of work in the last five years. He even forfeits his vacation time to make sure that things run smoothly. Adam literally does the work of two people. He started out working as the purchasing agent in charge of buying raw materials for a small manufacturing company. Approximately five years ago the inventory control agent in the receiving department resigned. Adam agreed to assume the duties of the control agent until a replacement could be hired. After all, Adam said that he knew what was supposed to be delivered to the company because as the purchasing agent he had been the person who placed orders for the inventory purchases. Adam did such a good job that the company never got around to hiring a replacement. Adam received the employee of the year award five out of the last six years. Adam is also very active in his community. He works with underprivileged children. His weekends are always filled with community service. Indeed, his commitment to social consciousness is described by some people as bordering on fanatical.

    Adam recently had a serious heart attack. People said that he had overworked himself. His hospital room was filled with flowers and a steady stream of friends visited him. So, people were in shock when Adam was charged with embezzlement. Ultimately, it was revealed that while Adam was in the hospital his replacement discovered that Adam had been purchasing excess quantities of raw materials. He then sold the extra materials and kept the money for himself. This became apparent when the companies to whom Adam had been selling the excess materials called to place new orders. It was difficult to determine the extent of the embezzlement. After the accounting department paid for Adam's excess purchases, he would remove the paid voucher forms from the accounting files and destroy them. Since the forms were not numbered, it was impossible to determine how many of the paid forms were missing. At his trial, Adam's only explanation was: "I did it for the children. They needed the money far more than the company needed it."

### Required

a. If the internal control procedures shown in Exhibit 1.17 had been followed, this embezzlement could have been avoided. Name the internal control procedures that were violated in this case.

b. Identify the specific components of the fraud triangle that were present in this case.

**LO 8**

## Problem 1-27A    *Value chain analysis (Appendix)*

Jensen Company invented a new process for manufacturing ice cream. The ingredients are mixed in high-tech machinery that forms the product into small round beads. Like a bag of balls, the ice cream beads are surrounded by air pockets in packages. This design has numerous advantages. First, each bite of ice cream melts rapidly when placed in a person's mouth, creating a more fla-vorful sensation when compared to ordinary ice cream. Also, the air pockets mean that a typical serving includes a smaller amount of ice cream. This not only reduces materials cost but also provides the consumer with a low-calorie snack. A cup appears full of ice cream, but it is really half full of air. The consumer eats only half the ingredients that are contained in a typical cup of blended ice cream. Finally, the texture of the ice cream makes scooping it out of a large con-tainer a very easy task. The frustration of trying to get a spoon into a rock-solid package of blended ice cream has been eliminated. Jensen Company named the new product Sonic Cream.

Like many other ice cream producers, Jensen Company purchases its raw materials from a food wholesaler. The ingredients are mixed in Jensen's manufacturing plant. The packages of finished product are distributed to privately owned franchise ice cream shops that sell Sonic Cream directly to the public.

Jensen provides national advertising and is responsible for all research and development costs associated with making new flavors of Sonic Cream.

### Required

a. Based on the information provided, draw a comprehensive value chain for Jensen Company that includes its suppliers and customers.

b. Identify the place in the chain where Jensen Company is exercising its opportunity to create added value beyond that currently being provided by its competitors.

## EXERCISES—SERIES B

**LO 1**

### Exercise 1-1B    *Financial versus managerial accounting items*

### Required

Indicate whether each of the following items is representative of financial or managerial accounting.

a. Condensed financial information sent to current investors at the end of each quarter.

b. Audited financial statements submitted to bankers when applying for a line of credit.

c. A weekly cash budget used by the treasurer to determine whether cash on hand is excessive.

d. Monthly sales reports used by the vice president of marketing to help allocate funds.

e. Divisional profit reports used by the company president to determine bonuses for divisional vice presidents.

f. Financial results used by stockbrokers to evaluate a company's profitability.

g. Quarterly budgets used by management to determine future borrowing needs.

h. Financial statements prepared in accordance with generally accepted accounting principles.

i. Annual financial reports submitted to the SEC in compliance with federal securities laws.

j. Projected budget information used to make logistical decisions.

**LO 2, 3**

### Exercise 1-2B    *Identifying product versus selling, general, and administrative costs*

### Required

Indicate whether each of the following costs should be classified as a product cost or as a general, selling, and administrative cost.

a. The salary of the cell phone manufacturing plant manager.

b. The depreciation on administrative buildings.

c. The depreciation on the company treasurer's computer.

d. The fabric used in making a customized sofa for a customer.

e. The salary of an engineer who maintains all manufacturing plant equipment.

f. Wages paid to workers in a manufacturing plant.

g.  The salary of the receptionist working in the sales department.

h.  Supplies used in the sales department.

i.  Wages of janitors who clean the factory floor.

j.  The salary of the company president.

## Exercise 1-3B    *Classifying costs: product or period / asset or expense*          LO 2, 3

**Required**

Use the following format to classify each cost as a product cost or a selling, general, and administrative (SG&A) cost. Also indicate whether the cost would be recorded as an asset or an expense. The first cost item is shown as an example.

| Cost Category | Product/ SG&A | Asset/ Expense |
|---|---|---|
| Supplies used in the plant manager's office | Product | Asset |
| Purchase of computers for the accounting department | | |
| Depreciation on computers used in factory | | |
| Natural gas used in the factory | | |
| Cost of television commercials | | |
| Wages of factory workers | | |
| Paper and ink cartridges used in the cashier's office | | |
| Raw material used to make products | | |
| Lubricant used to maintain factory equipment | | |
| Cost of a delivery truck | | |
| Cash dividend to stockholders | | |
| Cost of merchandise shipped to customers | | |
| Depreciation on vehicles used by salespeople | | |
| Wages of administrative building security guards | | |

## Exercise 1-4B    *Effect of product versus selling, general, and administrative costs on financial statements*          LO 3

**Required**

Pedigo Plastics Company accrued a tax liability for $4,000. Use the following horizontal financial statements model to show the effect of this accrual under the following two assumptions: (1) the tax is on administrative buildings, or (2) the tax is on production equipment. Use plus signs and/or minus signs to show the effect on each element. If an element is not affected, indicate so by placing the letters NA under the appropriate heading.

| | Assets | = | Liab. | + | Equity | Rev. | − | Exp. | = | Net Inc. |
|---|---|---|---|---|---|---|---|---|---|---|
| 1. | | | | | | | | | | |
| 2. | | | | | | | | | | |

## Exercise 1-5B    *Effect of product versus selling, general, and administrative cost on financial statements*          LO 3

**Required**

Stanley Corporation recognized the annual expiration of insurance on December 31, 2012. Using the following horizontal financial statements model shown, indicate how this event affected the company's financial statements under the following two assumptions: (1) the insurance was for office equipment, or (2) the insurance was for manufacturing equipment. Indicate whether the event increases (I), decreases (D), or does not affect (NA) each element of the financial statements.

| Event No. | | Assets | | | | Equity | | | | | |
|---|---|---|---|---|---|---|---|---|---|---|---|
| | Cash | + | Prepaid Insurance | + | Inventory | = | Com. Stk. | + | Ret. Ear. | Rev. − Exp. = Net Inc. |
| 1. | | | | | | | | | | |
| 2. | | | | | | | | | | |

## LO 2

### Exercise 1-6B   *Product costs in a manufacturing company*

Because friends and neighbors frequently praise her baking skills, Martha Plott plans to start a new business baking cakes for customers. She wonders how to determine the cost of her cakes.

**Required**

a.  Identify and give examples of the three components of product cost incurred in producing cakes.

b.  Explain why measuring product cost for a bakery is more complex than measuring product cost for a retail store.

c.  Assume that Martha decides to bake cakes for her customers at her home. Consequently, she will avoid the cost of renting a bakery. However, her home utility bills will increase. She also plans to offer different types of cakes for which baking time will vary. Cakes mixed with ice cream will require freezing, and other cakes will need refrigeration. Some can cool at room temperature. Under these circumstances, how can Martha estimate the amount of utility cost required to produce a given cake? Identify two costs other than utility cost that she will incur that could be difficult to measure.

## LO 3

### Exercise 1-7B   *Product versus selling, general, and administrative costs*

In reviewing Laxton Company's September accounting records, Mitchell Hinz, the chief accountant, noted the following depreciation costs.

1.  Factory buildings—$25,000.
2.  Computers used in manufacturing—$4,000.
3.  A building used to display finished products—$8,000.
4.  Trucks used to deliver merchandise to customers—$14,000.
5.  Forklifts used in the factory—$22,000.
6.  Furniture used in the president's office—$9,000.
7.  Elevators in administrative buildings—$6,000.
8.  Factory machinery—$9,000.

**Required**

a.  What amount of depreciation cost would be classified as selling, general, and administrative expense?

b.  Assume that Laxton manufactured 3,000 units of product and sold 2,000 units of product during the month of September. Determine the amount of depreciation cost that would be included in cost of goods sold.

## LO 2, 3

### Exercise 1-8B   *Recording product versus selling, general, and administrative costs in a financial statements model*

Reid Electronics Company experienced the following events during its first accounting period.

1.  Received $120,000 cash by issuing common stock.
2.  Paid $18,000 cash for wages to production workers.
3.  Paid $9,000 for salaries to administrative staff.
4.  Purchased for cash and used $9,000 of raw materials.
5.  Recognized $1,000 of depreciation on administrative offices.
6.  Recognized $1,500 of depreciation on manufacturing equipment.

7. Recognized $48,000 of sales revenue from cash sales of products.
8. Recognized $30,000 of cost of goods sold from the sale referenced in Event 7.

**Required**

Use a horizontal financial statements model to show how each event affects the balance sheet and income statement. Indicate whether the event increases (I), decreases (D), or does not affect (NA) each element of the financial statements. The first transaction is shown as an example. (*Note:* Show accumulated depreciation as a decrease in the book value of the appropriate asset account.)

| Event No. | Assets | | | | Equity | | | | |
|---|---|---|---|---|---|---|---|---|---|
| | Cash + | Inventory + | Manuf. Equip. + | Adm. Offices = | Com. Stk. + | Ret. Ear. | Rev. − | Exp. = | Net Inc. |
| 1. | I | NA | NA | NA | I | NA | NA | NA | NA |

## Exercise 1-9B   Allocating product costs between ending inventory and cost of goods sold

**LO 2**

Ryan Manufacturing Company began operations on January 1. During January, it started and completed 3,000 units of product. The company incurred the following costs:

1. Raw materials purchased and used—$5,000.
2. Wages of production workers—$4,000.
3. Salaries of administrative and sales personnel—$2,000.
4. Depreciation on manufacturing equipment—$3,000.
5. Depreciation on administrative equipment—$2,400.

Ryan sold 2,500 units of product.

**Required**

a. Determine the total product cost.
b. Determine the total cost of the ending inventory.
c. Determine the total of cost of goods sold.

## Exercise 1-10B   Financial statement effects for manufacturing versus service organizations

**LO 3**

The following horizontal financial statements model shows the effects of recording the expiration of insurance in two different circumstances. One circumstance represents the expiration of insurance on a factory building. The other circumstance represents the expiration of insurance on an administrative building. The effects of each event have been recorded using the letters (I) for increase, (D) for decrease, and (NA) for no effect.

| Event No. | Assets | | | Equity | | | | |
|---|---|---|---|---|---|---|---|---|
| | Cash + | Prepaid Insurance + | Inventory = | Com. Stk. + | Ret. Ear. | Rev. − | Exp. = | Net Inc. |
| 1. | NA | D | I | NA | NA | NA | NA | NA |
| 2. | NA | D | NA | NA | D | NA | I | D |

**Required**

a. Identify the event that represents the expiration of insurance on the factory building.
b. Explain why recognizing the expiration of insurance on a factory building affects financial statements differently than recognizing the expiration of insurance on an administrative building.

**LO 3**

### Exercise 1-11B  *Effect of product versus selling, general, and administrative cost on the income statement*

Each of the following asset acquisitions requires a year-end adjusting entry.

1. Paid $80,000 cash on January 1 to purchase a hamburger franchise that had an estimated expected useful life of 10 years and no salvage value.
2. Paid $80,000 cash on January 1 to purchase a patent to manufacture a special product. The patent had an estimated expected useful life of 10 years.
3. Paid $10,000 cash on April 1 for a one-year insurance policy on the administrative building.
4. Paid $10,000 cash on April 1 for a one-year insurance policy on the manufacturing building.
5. Paid $5,400 cash to purchase office supplies for the accounting department. At the end of the year, $1,000 of office supplies was still on hand.
6. Paid $5,400 cash to purchase factory supplies. At the end of the year, $500 of factory supplies was still on hand.

**Required**

Explain how the adjusting entry affects the amount of net income reported in the annual financial statements. The first event is shown as an example. Assume that any products that have been made have not been sold.

| Event No. | Net Income Amount of Change |
|---|---|
| 1. Adjusting Entry | (8,000) |

**LO 4**

### Exercise 1-12B  *Upstream and downstream costs*

During 2011 Jada Pharmaceutical Company incurred $50,000,000 of research and development (R&D) costs to develop a new hay fever drug called Allergone. In accordance with FASB standards, the entire R&D cost was recognized as expense in 2011. Manufacturing costs (direct materials, direct labor, and overhead) to produce Allergone are expected to be $40 per unit. Packaging, shipping, and sales commissions are expected to be $5 per unit. Jada expects to sell 5,000,000 units of Allergone before developing a new drug to replace it in the market. During 2011, Jada produced 800,000 units of Allergone and sold 500,000 of them.

**Required**

a. Identify the upstream and downstream costs.
b. Determine the 2011 amount of cost of goods sold and the December 31, 2011, ending inventory balance.
c. Determine the unit sales price Jada should establish assuming it desires to earn a profit margin equal to 40 percent of the *total cost* of developing, manufacturing, and distributing Allergone.
d. Prepare an income statement for 2011 using the sales price from Requirement *c*.
e. Why would Jada price Allergone at a level that would generate a loss for 2011?

**LO 6**

### Exercise 1-13B  *Effect of a just-in-time inventory system on financial statements*

In reviewing Kopplin Company's financial statements for the past two years, Nancy Martin, a bank loan officer, noticed that the company's inventory level had increased significantly while sales revenue had remained constant. Such a trend typically indicates increasing inventory carrying costs and slowing cash inflows. Ms. Martin concluded that the bank should deny Kopplin's credit line application.

**Required**

Explain how implementing an effective just-in-time inventory system would affect Kopplin's financial statements and possibly reverse Ms. Martin's decision about its credit line application.

## Exercise 1-14B  *Using JIT to minimize waste and lost opportunity*

**LO 6**

May Motz is the editor-in-chief of her school's yearbook. The school has 1,000 students and 60 faculty and staff members. The firm engaged to print copies of the yearbook charges the school $13 per book and requires a 10-day lead time for delivery. May and her editors plan to order 800 copies to sell at the school fair for $20 each.

### Required

**a.** If the school sells 700 yearbooks, what amount of profit will it earn? What is the cost of waste due to excess inventory?

**b.** If 150 buyers are turned away after all yearbooks have been sold, what amount of profit will the school earn? What amount of opportunity cost will the school incur?

**c.** How could May use a JIT inventory system to maximize profits by eliminating waste and opportunity cost?

## Exercise 1-15B  *Using JIT to minimize holding costs*

**LO 6**

Olivia's Beauty Salon purchases inventory supplies from a variety of vendors, some of which require a four-week lead time before delivering inventory purchases. To ensure that she will not run out of supplies, Olivia Stear, the owner, maintains a large inventory. The average cost of inventory on hand is $9,000. Ms. Stear usually finances inventory purchases with a line of credit that has a 12 percent annual interest charge. Her accountant has suggested that she purchase all inventory from a single large distributor that can satisfy all of her orders within a three-day period. With such prompt delivery, Ms. Stear would be able to reduce her average inventory balance to $2,000. She also believes that she could save $1,000 per year through reduced phone bills, insurance costs, and warehouse rental costs associated with ordering and maintaining the higher level of inventory.

### Required

**a.** Is the inventory system the accountant suggested to Ms. Stear a pure or approximate just-in-time system?

**b.** Based on the information provided, how much inventory holding cost could Ms. Stear eliminate by taking the accountant's advice?

## Exercise 1-16B  *The fraud triangle*

**LO 7**

The accounting records of Rice Manufacturing Company (RMC) revealed that the company incurred $3 million of materials, $5 million of production labor, $4 million of manufacturing overhead, and $6 million of selling, general, and administrative expense during 2011. It was discovered that RMC's chief financial officer (CFO) included $2.6 million dollars of upstream research and development expense in the manufacturing overhead account when it should have been classified as selling, general, and administrative expense. RMC made 5,000 units of product and sold 4,000 units of product in 2011.

### Required

**a.** Indicate whether the elements on the 2011 financial statements (i.e., assets, liabilities, equity, revenue, expense, and net income) would be overstated or understated as a result of the misclassification of the upstream research and development expense. Determine the amount of the overstatement or understatement for each element.

**b.** Speculate as to what would cause the CFO to intentionally misclassify the research and development expense. (Hint: Review the chapter material regarding the fraud triangle.)

## Exercise 1-17B  *Applications of the Sarbanes-Oxley Act*

**LO 7**

Greg Madrid, a HealthSouth billing clerk, filed a suit under the False Claims Act charging that HealthSouth purchased computer equipment from a company owned by Richard Scrushy's parents at prices two and three times the normal price. At the time, Richard Scrushy was the CEO of HealthSouth. The overcharges inflated HealthSouth's expense ratios that the government used when calculating a Medicare reimbursement rate. As a result, the government was overcharged for services provided by HealthSouth. While refusing to recognize any wrongdoing, HealthSouth agreed to pay an $8 million settlement related to the lawsuit brought by the whistleblower.

**Required**

Explain how the provisions of Sarbanes-Oxley would provide protection to a whistleblower such as Greg Madrid.

**LO 10**

### Exercise 1-18B   *Value chain analysis (Appendix)*

Fastidious Vincent washed his hair at home and then went to a barbershop for a haircut. The barber explained that shop policy is to shampoo each customer's hair before cutting, regardless of how recently it had been washed. Somewhat annoyed, Vincent submitted to the shampoo, after which the barber cut his hair with great skill. After the haircut, the barber dried his hair and complimented Vincent on his appearance. He added, "That will be $18; $3 for the shampoo and $15 for the cut and dry." Vincent did not tip the barber.

**Required**

Identify the nonvalue-added activity described. How could the barber modify this nonvalue-added activity?

## PROBLEMS—SERIES B

**LO 2, 3**

### Problem 1-19B   *Product versus selling, general, and administrative costs*

Garcin Manufacturing Company was started on January 1, 2011, when it acquired $180,000 cash by issuing common stock. Garcin immediately purchased office furniture and manufacturing equipment costing $20,000 and $38,000, respectively. The office furniture had a four-year useful life and a zero salvage value. The manufacturing equipment had a $2,000 salvage value and an expected useful life of six years. The company paid $14,000 for salaries of administrative personnel and $18,000 for wages of production personnel. Finally, the company paid $24,000 for raw materials that were used to make inventory. All inventory was started and completed during the year. Garcin completed production on 8,000 units of product and sold 6,000 units at a price of $14 each in 2011. (Assume that all transactions are cash transactions.)

**Required**

a.  Determine the total product cost and the average cost per unit of the inventory produced in 2011.

b.  Determine the amount of cost of goods sold that would appear on the 2011 income statement.

c.  Determine the amount of the ending inventory balance that would appear on the December 31, 2011, balance sheet.

d.  Determine the amount of net income that would appear on the 2011 income statement.

e.  Determine the amount of retained earnings that would appear on the December 31, 2011, balance sheet.

f.  Determine the amount of total assets that would appear on the December 31, 2011, balance sheet.

**LO 2, 3**

### Problem 1-20B   *Effect of product versus selling, general, and administrative costs on financial statements*

Windsor Company experienced the following accounting events during its first year of operation. With the exception of the adjusting entries for depreciation, all transactions were cash transactions.

1.  Acquired $80,000 cash by issuing common stock.

2.  Paid $15,000 for the materials used to make its products. All products started were completed during the period.

3.  Paid salaries of $6,000 to selling and administrative employees.

4.  Paid wages of $9,000 to production workers.

5.  Paid $12,000 for furniture used in selling and administrative offices. The furniture was acquired on January 1. It had a $1,500 estimated salvage value and a seven-year useful life.

**6.** Paid $22,000 for manufacturing equipment. The equipment was acquired on January 1. It had a $2,000 estimated salvage value and a five-year useful life.

**7.** Sold inventory to customers for $43,000 that had cost $25,000 to make.

**Required**

Explain how these events would affect the balance sheet and income statement by recording them in a horizontal financial statements model as indicated here. The first event is recorded as an example.

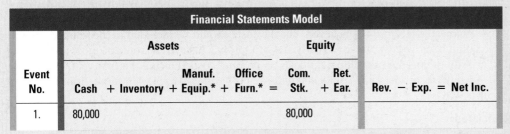

*Record accumulated depreciation as negative amounts in these columns.

## Problem 1-21B  *Product versus selling, general, and administrative costs*    LO 2, 3

The following transactions pertain to 2012, the first year of operations of Jardine Company. All inventory was started and completed during the accounting period. All transactions were cash transactions.

**1.** Acquired $56,000 of contributed capital from its owners.
**2.** Paid $9,600 for materials used to produce inventory.
**3.** Paid $4,400 to production workers.
**4.** Paid $5,000 rental fee for production equipment.
**5.** Paid $1,500 to administrative employees.
**6.** Paid $3,200 rental fee for administrative office equipment.
**7.** Produced 1,900 units of inventory of which 1,500 units were sold at a price of $17.40 each.

**Required**

Prepare an income statement and a balance sheet.

## Problem 1-22B  *Service versus manufacturing companies*    LO 2, 3, 5

Knoll Company began operations on January 1, 2012, by issuing common stock for $94,000 cash. During 2012, Knoll received $77,000 cash from revenue and incurred costs that required $90,000 of cash payments.

**Required**

Prepare an income statement and a balance sheet for Knoll Company for 2012, under each of the following independent scenarios.

**a.** Knoll is an employment agency. The $90,000 was paid for employee salaries and advertising.
**b.** Knoll is a trucking company. The $90,000 was paid to purchase two trucks. The trucks were purchased on January 1, 2012, had five-year useful lives and no expected salvage value. Knoll uses straight-line depreciation.
**c.** Knoll is a manufacturing company. The $90,000 was paid to purchase the following items:
   **(1)** Paid $18,000 cash to purchase materials used to make products during the year.
   **(2)** Paid $28,000 cash for wages to production workers who make products during the year.
   **(3)** Paid $4,000 cash for salaries of sales and administrative employees.
   **(4)** Paid $40,000 cash to purchase manufacturing equipment. The equipment was used solely for the purpose of making products. It had a six-year life and a $4,000 salvage value. The company uses straight-line depreciation.
   **(5)** During 2012, Knoll started and completed 2,600 units of product. The revenue was earned when Knoll sold 2,200 units of product to its customers.

**d.** Refer to Requirement *c*. Could Knoll determine the actual cost of making the 500th unit of product? How likely is it that the actual cost of the 500th unit of product was exactly the same as the cost of producing the 501st unit of product? Explain why management may be more interested in average cost than in actual cost.

**LO 2, 3, 7**

### Problem 1-23B   *Importance of cost classification*

Livy Company was started when it acquired $70,000 by issuing common stock. During the first year of operations, the company incurred specifically identifiable product costs (materials, labor, and overhead) amounting to $40,000. Livy also incurred $20,000 of product development costs. There was a debate regarding how the product development costs should be classified. Advocates of Option 1 believed that the costs should be included in the selling, general, and administrative cost category. Advocates of Option 2 believed it would be more appropriate to classify the product development costs as product costs. During the first year, Livy made 10,000 units of product and sold 8,000 units at a price of $14 each. All transactions were cash transactions.

**Required**

**a.** Prepare an income statement and a balance sheet under each of the two options.

**b.** Identify the option that results in financial statements that are more likely to leave a favorable impression on investors and creditors.

**c.** Assume that Livy provides an incentive bonus to the company president that is equal to 8 percent of net income. Compute the amount of the bonus under each of the two options. Identify the option that provides the president with the higher bonus.

**d.** Assume a 35 percent income tax rate. Determine the amount of income tax expense under each of the two options. Identify the option that minimizes the amount of the company's income tax expense.

**e.** Comment on the conflict of interest between the company president as determined in Requirement *c* and the stockholders of the company as indicated in Requirement *d*. Describe an incentive compensation plan that would avoid conflicts between the interests of the president and the owners.

**LO 6**

### Problem 1-24B   *Using JIT to reduce inventory holding costs*

Olsen Automobile Dealership, Inc. (OAD), buys and sells a variety of cars made by Great Motor Corporation. OAD maintains about 30 new cars in its parking lot for customers' selection; the cost of this inventory is approximately $400,000. Additionally, OAD hires security guards to protect the inventory from theft and a maintenance crew to keep the facilities attractive. The total payroll cost for the guards and maintenance crew amounts to $75,000 per year. OAD has a line of credit with a local bank that calls for a 15 percent annual rate of interest. Recently, Neil Tanner, the president of OAD, learned that a competitor in town, Pardoe Dealership, has been attracting some of OAD's usual customers because Pardoe could offer them lower prices. Mr. Tanner also discovered that Pardoe carries no inventory at all but shows customers a catalog of cars as well as pertinent information from online computer databases. Pardoe promises to deliver any car that a customer identifies within three working days.

**Required**

**a.** Based on the information provided, determine OAD's annual inventory holding cost.

**b.** Name the inventory system that Pardoe uses and explain how the system enables Pardoe to sell at reduced prices.

**LO 6**

### Problem 1-25B   *Using JIT to minimize waste and lost opportunity*

Mark's Hamburger is a small fast-food shop in a busy shopping center that operates only during lunch hours. Mark Haygood, the owner and manager of the shop, is confused. On some days, he does not have enough hamburgers to satisfy customer demand. On other days, he has more hamburgers than he can sell. When he has excess hamburgers, he has no choice but to dump them. Usually, Mr. Haygood prepares about 160 hamburgers before the busy lunch hour. The product cost per hamburger is approximately $0.75; the sales price is $3.00 each. Mr. Haygood pays general, selling, and administrative expenses that include daily rent of $60 and daily wages of $40.

**Required**

a. Prepare an income statement based on sales of 100 hamburgers per day. Determine the cost of wasted hamburgers if 160 hamburgers were prepared in advance.

b. Prepare an income statement assuming that 200 customers attempt to buy a hamburger. Since Mr. Haygood has prepared only 160 hamburgers, he must reject 40 customer orders because of insufficient supply. Determine the amount of lost profit.

c. Suppose that hamburgers can be prepared quickly after each customer orders. However, Mr. Haygood must hire an additional part-time employee at a cost of approximately $20 per day. The per unit cost of each hamburger remains at $0.75. Prepare an income statement under the JIT system assuming that 100 hamburgers are sold. Compare the income statement under JIT with the income statement prepared in Requirement *a.* Comment on how the JIT system would affect profitability.

d. Assume the same facts as in Requirement *c* with respect to a JIT system that requires additional labor costing $20 per day. Prepare an income statement under the JIT system, assuming that 200 hamburgers are sold. Compare the income statement under JIT with the income statement prepared in Requirement *b.* Comment on how the JIT system would affect profitability.

e. Explain how the JIT system might be able to improve customer satisfaction as well as profitability.

## Problem 1-26B    *The fraud triangle, ethics, and the Sarbanes-Oxley Act*

**LO 7**

The CEO and the CFO of Automation Company were both aware that the company's controller was reporting fraudulent revenues. Upper level executives are paid very large bonuses when the company meets the earnings goals established in the company's budgets. While the CEO had pushed the CFO and controller to "make the numbers," he had not told him to "make up the numbers." Besides, he could plead ignorance if the fraud was ever discovered. The CFO knew he should prohibit the fraudulent reporting but also knew the importance of making the numbers established in the budget. He told himself that it wasn't just for his bonus but for the stockholders as well. If the actual earnings were below the budgeted target numbers, the stock price would drop and the shareholders would suffer. Besides, he believed that the actual revenues would increase dramatically in the near future and they could cover for the fraudulent revenue by underreporting these future revenues. He concluded that no one would get hurt and everything would be straightened out in the near future.

**Required**

a. Explain why the internal control practice of separation of duties failed to prevent the fraudulent reporting.

b. Identify and discuss the elements of the fraud triangle that motivated the fraud.

c. Explain how the provisions of the Sarbanes-Oxley Act would serve to deter this type of fraudulent reporting.

d. Review the statement of ethical professional practice shown in Exhibit 1.15. Identify and comment on which of the ethical principles were violated by the CFO.

## Problem 1-27B    *Value chain analysis (Appendix)*

**LO 8**

Ellen Milan visited her personal physician for treatment of flu symptoms. She was greeted by the receptionist, who gave her personal history and insurance forms to complete. She needed no instructions; she completed these same forms every time she visited the doctor. After completing the forms, Ms. Milan waited for 30 minutes before being ushered into the patient room. After waiting there for an additional 15 minutes, Dr. Heape entered the room. The doctor ushered Ms. Milan into the hallway where he weighed her and called her weight out to the nurse for recording. Ms. Milan had gained 10 pounds since her last visit, and the doctor suggested that she consider going on a diet. Dr. Heape then took her temperature and asked her to return to the patient room. Ten minutes later, he returned to take a throat culture and draw blood. She waited another 15 minutes for the test results. Finally, the doctor returned and told Ms. Milan that she had strep throat and bronchitis. Dr. Heape prescribed an antibiotic and told her to get at least two days of bed rest. Ms. Milan was then ushered to the accounting department to settle her bill. The accounting clerk asked her several questions; the answers to most of them were on the forms that she had completed when she first arrived at the office. Finally, Ms. Milan paid her required copayment and left the office. Three weeks later, she received a bill indicating that she had not paid the copayment. She called the accounting department, and after a search of the records, the clerk verified that the bill had, in fact, been paid. The clerk apologized for the inconvenience and inquired as to whether Ms. Milan's health had improved.

**Required**

a.  Identify at least three value-added and three nonvalue-added activities suggested in this scenario.

b.  Provide logical suggestions for how to eliminate the nonvalue-added activities.

## ANALYZE, THINK, COMMUNICATE

### ATC 1-1    Business Applications Case    *Financial versus managerial accounting*

The following information was taken from the 2008 and 2009 Form 10-Ks for Dell, Inc.

| | **Fiscal Year Ended** | |
| --- | --- | --- |
| | **January 30, 2009** | **February 1, 2008** |
| Number of regular employees | 76,500 | 82,700 |
| Number of temporary employees | 2,400 | 5,500 |
| Revenues (in millions) | $61,101 | $61,133 |
| Properties owned or leased in the U.S. | 7.4 million square feet | 8.2 million square feet |
| Properties owned or leased outside the U.S. | 9.4 million square feet | 9.7 million square feet |
| Total assets (in millions) | $26,500 | $27,561 |
| Cross margin (in millions) | $10,957 | $11,671 |

**Required**

a.  Explain whether each line of information in the table above would best be described as being primarily financial accounting or managerial accounting in nature.

b.  Provide some additional examples of managerial and financial accounting information that could apply to Dell.

c.  If you analyze only the data you identified as financial in nature, does it appear that Dell's 2009 fiscal year was better or worse than its 2008 fiscal year? Explain.

d.  If you analyze only the data you identified as managerial in nature, does it appear that Dell's 2009 fiscal year was better or worse than its 2008 fiscal year? Explain.

### ATC 1-2    Group Assignment    *Product versus upstream and downstream costs*

Victor Holt, the accounting manager of Sexton, Inc., gathered the following information for 2011. Some of it can be used to construct an income statement for 2011. Ignore items that do not appear on an income statement. Some computation may be required. For example, the cost of manufacturing equipment would not appear on the income statement. However, the cost of manufacturing equipment is needed to compute the amount of depreciation. All units of product were started and completed in 2011.

1.  Issued $864,000 of common stock.

2.  Paid engineers in the product design department $10,000 for salaries that were accrued at the end of the previous year.

3.  Incurred advertising expenses of $70,000.

4.  Paid $720,000 for materials used to manufacture the company's product.

5.  Incurred utility costs of $160,000. These costs were allocated to different departments on the basis of square footage of floor space. Mr. Holt identified three departments and determined the square footage of floor space for each department to be as shown in the table below.

| Department | Square Footage |
| --- | --- |
| Research and development | 10,000 |
| Manufacturing | 60,000 |
| Selling and administrative | 30,000 |
| Total | 100,000 |

6. Paid $880,000 for wages of production workers.

7. Paid cash of $658,000 for salaries of administrative personnel. There was $16,000 of accrued salaries owed to administrative personnel at the end of 2011. There was no beginning balance in the Salaries Payable account for administrative personnel.

8. Purchased manufacturing equipment two years ago at a cost of $10,000,000. The equipment had an eight-year useful life and a $2,000,000 salvage value.

9. Paid $390,000 cash to engineers in the product design department.

10. Paid a $258,000 cash dividend to owners.

11. Paid $80,000 to set up manufacturing equipment for production.

12. Paid a one-time $186,000 restructuring cost to redesign the production process to implement a just-in-time inventory system.

13. Prepaid the premium on a new insurance policy covering nonmanufacturing employees. The policy cost $72,000 and had a one-year term with an effective starting date of May 1. Four employees work in the research and development department and eight employees in the selling and administrative department. Assume a December 31 closing date.

14. Made 69,400 units of product and sold 60,000 units at a price of $70 each.

### Required

a. Divide the class into groups of four or five students per group, and then organize the groups into three sections. Assign Task 1 to the first section of groups, Task 2 to the second section of groups, and Task 3 to the third section of groups.

### Group Tasks

(1) Identify the items that are classified as product costs and determine the amount of cost of goods sold reported on the 2011 income statement.

(2) Identify the items that are classified as upstream costs and determine the amount of upstream cost expensed on the 2011 income statement.

(3) Identify the items that are classified as downstream costs and determine the amount of downstream cost expensed on the 2011 income statement.

b. Have the class construct an income statement in the following manner. Select a member of one of the groups assigned the first group task identifying the product costs. Have that person go to the board and list the costs included in the determination of cost of goods sold. Anyone in the other groups who disagrees with one of the classifications provided by the person at the board should voice an objection and explain why the item should be classified differently. The instructor should lead the class to a consensus on the disputed items. After the amount of cost of goods sold is determined, the student at the board constructs the part of the income statement showing the determination of gross margin. The exercise continues in a similar fashion with representatives from the other sections explaining the composition of the upstream and downstream costs. These items are added to the income statement started by the first group representative. The final result is a completed income statement.

---

### ATC 1-3    Research Assignment    *Identifying product costs at Snap-on Inc.*

Use the 2008 Form 10-K for Snap-on Inc. to complete the requirements below. To obtain the Form 10-K you can use either use the EDGAR system following the instructions in Appendix A, or it can be found under "Corporate Information" on the company's corporate website; www.snapon.com. Read carefully the following portions of the document:

■  "Products and Services" on page 5.
   "Consolidated Statement of Earnings" on page 55.
   The following parts of Note 1 on page 60:
   • "Shipping and handling"
   • "Advertising and promotion"
■  "Note 4: Inventories" on page 66.
■  "Note 5: Property and equipment" on page 67.

**Required**

a. Does the level of detail that Snap-on provides regarding costs incurred to manufacture its products suggests the company's financial statements are designed primarily to meet the needs of external or internal users?

b. Does Snap-on treat shipping and handling costs as product or period costs?

c. Does Snap-on treat advertising and promotion costs as product or period costs?

d. In the first accounting course you learned about a class of inventory called merchandise inventory. What categories of inventory does Snap-on report in its annual report?

e. What is the cost of the land owned by Snap-on? What is the cost of its machinery and equipment?

### ATC 1-4   Writing Assignment   *Emerging practices in managerial accounting*

An annual report of the Maytag Corporation contained the following excerpt:

> *The Company announced the restructuring of its major appliance operations in an effort to strengthen its position in the industry and to deliver improved performance to both customers and shareowners. This included the consolidation of two separate organizational units into a single operation responsible for all activities associated with the manufacture and distribution of the Company's brands of major appliances and the closing of a cooking products plant in Indianapolis, Indiana, with transfer of that production to an existing plant in Cleveland, Tennessee.*

The restructuring cost Maytag $40 million and disrupted the lives of many of the company's employees.

**Required**

Assume that you are Maytag's vice president of human relations. Write a letter to the employees who are affected by the restructuring. The letter should explain why it was necessary for the company to undertake the restructuring. Your explanation should refer to the ideas discussed in the section "Emerging Trends in Managerial Accounting" of this chapter (see Appendix A).

### ATC 1-5   Ethical Dilemma   *Product cost versus selling and administrative expense*

Emma Emerson is a proud woman with a problem. Her daughter has been accepted into a prestigious law school. While Ms. Emerson beams with pride, she is worried sick about how to pay for the school; she is a single parent who has worked hard to support herself and her three children. She had to go heavily into debt to finance her own education. Even though she now has a good job, family needs have continued to outpace her income and her debt burden is staggering. She knows she will be unable to borrow the money needed for her daughter's law school.

Ms. Emerson is the chief financial officer (CFO) of a small manufacturing company. She has just accepted a new job offer. Indeed, she has not yet told her employer that she will be leaving in a month. She is concerned that her year-end incentive bonus may be affected if her boss learns of her plans to leave. She plans to inform the company immediately after receiving the bonus. She knows her behavior is less than honorable, but she believes that she has been underpaid for a long time. Her boss, a relative of the company's owner, makes twice what she makes and does half the work. Why should she care about leaving with a little extra cash? Indeed, she is considering an opportunity to boost the bonus.

Ms. Emerson's bonus is based on a percentage of net income. Her company recently introduced a new product line that required substantial production start-up costs. Ms. Emerson is fully aware that GAAP requires these costs to be expensed in the current accounting period, but no one else in the company has the technical expertise to know exactly how the costs should be treated. She is considering misclassifying the start-up costs as product costs. If the costs are misclassified, net income will be significantly higher, resulting in a nice boost in her incentive bonus. By the time the auditors discover the misclassification, Ms. Emerson will have moved on to her new job. If the matter is brought to the attention of her new employer, she will simply plead ignorance. Considering her daughter's needs, Ms. Emerson decides to classify the start-up costs as product costs.

**Required**

a. Based on this information, indicate whether Ms. Emerson believes the number of units of product sold will be equal to, less than, or greater than, the number of units made. Write a brief paragraph explaining the logic that supports your answer.

b. Explain how the misclassification could mislead an investor or creditor regarding the company's financial condition.

c. Explain how the misclassification could affect income taxes.

d. Identify the specific components of the fraud triangle that were present in this case.

e. Review the Statement of Ethical Professional Practice shown in Exhibit 1.15 and identify at least two ethical principles that Ms. Emerson's misclassification of the start-up costs violated.

f. Describe the maximum penalty that could be imposed under the Sarbanes-Oxley Act for the actions Ms. Emerson has taken.

g. Comment on how proper internal controls could have prevented fraudulent reporting in this case.

## ATC 1-6   Spreadsheet Assignment   *Using Excel*

The following transactions pertain to 2011, the first year of operations of the Barlett Company. All inventory was started and completed during 2011. Assume that all transactions are cash transactions.

1. Acquired $2,000 cash by issuing common stock.
2. Paid $400 for materials used to produce inventory.
3. Paid $600 to production workers.
4. Paid $200 rental fee for production equipment.
5. Paid $160 to administrative employees.
6. Paid $80 rental fee for administrative office equipment.
7. Produced 300 units of inventory of which 200 units were sold at a price of $7.00 each.

### Required

Construct a spreadsheet that includes the income statement and balance sheet.

## ATC 1-7   Spreadsheet Assignment   *Mastering Excel*

Mantooth Manufacturing Company experienced the following accounting events during its first year of operation. With the exception of the adjusting entries for depreciation, assume that all transactions are cash transactions.

1. Acquired $50,000 by issuing common stock.
2. Paid $8,000 for the materials used to make its products, all of which were started and completed during the year.
3. Paid salaries of $4,400 to selling and administrative employees.
4. Paid wages of $7,000 to production workers.
5. Paid $9,600 for furniture used in selling and administrative offices. The furniture was acquired on January 1. It had a $1,600 estimated salvage value and a four-year useful life.
6. Paid $13,000 for manufacturing equipment. The equipment was acquired on January 1. It had a $1,000 estimated salvage value and a three-year useful life.
7. Sold inventory to customers for $25,000 that had cost $14,000 to make.

Construct a spreadsheet of the financial statements model as shown here:

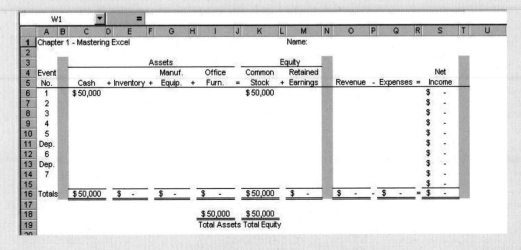

## Required

Place formulas in row 16 to automatically add the columns. Also add formulas in column S to calculate net income after each event, and add formulas in row 18 to compute total assets and equity. Notice that you must enter the events since only the first one is shown as an example.

## Spreadsheet Tips

1. The column widths are set by choosing Format, then Column, and then Width.
2. The shading in columns B, N, and T is added by highlighting a column and choosing Format, then Cells, and then clicking on the tab titled Patterns and choosing a color.
3. The sum function is an easy way to add a column or row. For example, the formula in cell C16 is =SUM(C6:C15).
4. As an example of the formulas in column S (net income), the formula in cell S7 is =O7−Q7.
5. If you find that some of the columns are too far to the right to appear on your screen, you can set the zoom level to show the entire spreadsheet. The zoom is set by choosing View, then Zoom, and then clicking on Custom and typing 100 percent in the box. The shortcut method to set the zoom is to click in the box on the right side of the top tool bar that appears immediately below the menu.

## COMPREHENSIVE PROBLEM

Magnificent Modems, Inc., makes modem cards that are used in notebook computers. The company completed the following transactions during 2010. All purchases and sales were made with cash.

1. Acquired $750,000 of cash from the owners.
2. Purchased $270,000 of manufacturing equipment. The equipment has a $30,000 salvage value and a four-year useful life. Label the purchase of the equipment as **Event 2a** and the recognition of depreciation as **Event 2b.**
3. The company started and completed 5,000 modems. Direct materials purchased and used amounted to $40 per unit.
4. Direct labor costs amounted to $25 per unit.
5. The cost of manufacturing supplies used amounted to $4 per unit.
6. The company paid $50,000 to rent the manufacturing facility.
7. Magnificent sold all 5,000 units at a cash price of $120 per unit. Label the recognition of the sale as **Event 7a** and the cost of goods sold as **Event 7b.** (Hint: It will be necessary to determine the manufacturing costs in order to record the cost of goods sold.)
8. The sales staff was paid a $6 per unit sales commission.
9. Paid $39,000 to purchase equipment for administrative offices. The equipment was expected to have a $3,000 salvage value and a three-year useful life. Label the purchase of the equipment as **Event 9a** and the recognition of depreciation as **Event 9b.**
10. Administrative expenses consisting of office rental and salaries amounted to $71,950.

## Required

a. Record the transaction data for Magnificent Modems, Inc., in the financial statements like the one shown below. The first transaction is recorded as an example.

| Event No. | Assets | | | | | | | = | Equity | | | | | | | | |
| | Cash | + | Inventory | + | Manuf. Equip.* | + | Office Equip.* | = | Com. Sock. | + | Ret. Ear. | | Rev. | − | Exp. | = | Net Inc. |
|---|---|---|---|---|---|---|---|---|---|---|---|---|---|---|---|---|---|
| 1. | 750,000 | | | | | | | | 750,000 | | | | | | | | |
| Ck. Fig. | 544,050 | + | 0 | + | 210,000 | + | 27,000 | = | 750,000 | + | 31,050 | | 600,000 | − | 568,950 | = | 31,050 |

*Negative amounts in these columns represent accumulated depreciation.

**b.** Use the following forms to prepare an income statement and balance sheet.

### MAGNIFICENT MODEMS, INC.
#### Income Statement
#### For the Period Ended December 31, 2011

| | |
|---|---|
| Sales | |
| Cost of goods sold | |
| Gross margin | |
| Sales commission | |
| Depreciation expense | |
| Administrative expense | |
| Net income | $31,050 |

### MAGNIFICENT MODEMS, INC.
#### Balance Sheet
#### As of December 31, 2011

| Assets: | |
|---|---|
| Cash | |
| Manufacturing equipment, net of acc. depreciation | |
| Office equipment, net of acc. depreciation | |
| Finished goods inventory | |
| Total assets | $781,050 |
| Equity | |
| Common stock | |
| Retained earnings | |
| Total stockholder's equity | $781,050 |

## CHAPTER 2

# Cost Behavior, Operating Leverage, and Profitability Analysis

## LEARNING OBJECTIVES

**After you have mastered the material in this chapter, you will be able to:**

1 Identify and describe fixed, variable, and mixed cost behavior.

2 Demonstrate the effects of operating leverage on profitability.

3 Prepare an income statement using the contribution margin approach.

4 Calculate the magnitude of operating leverage.

5 Demonstrate how the relevant range and decision context affect cost behavior.

6 Select an appropriate time period for calculating the average cost per unit.

7 Use the high-low method, scattergraphs, and regression analysis to estimate fixed and variable costs.

## CHAPTER OPENING

Three college students are planning a vacation. One of them suggests inviting a fourth person along, remarking that four can travel for the same cost as three. Certainly, some costs will be the same whether three or four people go on the trip. For example, the hotel room costs $800 per week, regardless of whether three or four people stay in the room. In accounting terms the cost of the hotel room is a **fixed cost.** The total amount of a fixed cost does not change when volume changes. The total hotel room cost is $800 whether 1, 2, 3, or 4 people use the room. In contrast, some costs vary in direct proportion with changes in volume. When volume increases, total variable cost increases; when volume decreases, total variable cost decreases. For example, the cost of tickets to a theme park is a **variable cost.** The total cost of tickets increases proportionately with each vacationer who goes to the theme park. Cost behavior (fixed versus variable) can significantly impact profitability. This chapter explains cost behavior and ways it can be used to increase profitability.

# The Curious Accountant

*News flash!* On April 29, 2009, Eastman Kodak, Inc., announced that its first quarter's revenues decreased 29 percent compared to the same quarter in 2008, yet its earnings had decreased by 213 percent. On May 4, 2009, Walt Disney announced that a decrease in revenue of 7 percent for the just-ended quarter would cause its earnings to decrease 46 percent compared to the same quarter in 2008. On April 12, 2009, Apple computer reported that its revenue for the quarter had increased by 9 percent compared to the previous year, but its earnings increased by 15 percent.

Can you explain why such relatively small changes in these companies' revenues resulted in such relatively large changes in their earnings or losses? In other words, if a company's sales increase 10 percent, why do its earnings not also increase 10 percent? (Answer on page 60.)

Identify and describe fixed, variable, and mixed cost behavior.

# FIXED COST BEHAVIOR

How much more will it cost to send one additional employee to a sales meeting? If more people buy our products, can we charge less? If sales increase by 10 percent, how will profits be affected? Managers seeking answers to such questions must consider **cost behavior.** Knowing how costs behave relative to the level of business activity enables managers to more effectively plan and control costs. To illustrate, consider the entertainment company Star Productions, Inc. (SPI).

SPI specializes in promoting rock concerts. It is considering paying a band $48,000 to play a concert. Obviously, SPI must sell enough tickets to cover this cost. In this example, the relevant activity base is the number of tickets sold. The cost of the band is a fixed cost because it does not change regardless of the number of tickets sold. Exhibit 2.1 illustrates the fixed cost behavior pattern, showing the *total cost* and the *cost per unit* at three different levels of activity.

*Total* versus *per-unit* fixed costs behave differently. The total cost for the band remains constant (fixed) at $48,000. In contrast, fixed cost per unit decreases as volume (number of tickets sold) increases. The term *fixed cost* is consistent with the behavior of *total cost.* Total fixed cost remains constant (fixed) when activity changes. However, there is a contradiction between the term *fixed cost per unit* and the *per-unit behavior pattern of a fixed cost.* Fixed cost per unit is *not* fixed. It changes with the number of tickets sold. This contradiction in terminology can cause untold confusion. Study carefully the fixed cost behavior patterns in Exhibit 2.2.

## EXHIBIT 2.1

### Fixed Cost Behavior

| | | | |
|---|---|---|---|
| Number of tickets sold (a) | 2,700 | 3,000 | 3,300 |
| Total cost of band (b) | $48,000 | $48,000 | $48,000 |
| Cost per ticket sold (b ÷ a) | $17.78 | $16.00 | $14.55 |

## EXHIBIT 2.2

### Fixed Cost Behavior

| | When Activity Increases | When Activity Decreases |
|---|---|---|
| **Total** fixed cost | Remains constant | Remains constant |
| Fixed cost **per unit** | Decreases | Increases |

The fixed cost data in Exhibit 2.1 help SPI's management decide whether to sponsor the concert. For example, the information influences potential pricing choices. The per-unit costs represent the minimum ticket prices required to cover the fixed cost at various levels of activity. SPI could compare these per-unit costs to the prices of competing entertainment events (such as the prices of movies, sporting events, or theater tickets). If the price is not competitive, tickets will not sell and the concert will lose money. Management must also consider the number of tickets to be sold. The volume data in Exhibit 2.1 can be compared to the band's track record of ticket sales at previous concerts. A proper analysis of these data can reduce the risk of undertaking an unprofitable venture.

## OPERATING LEVERAGE

Demonstrate the effects of operating leverage on profitability.

Heavy objects can be moved with little effort using *physical* leverage. Business managers apply **operating leverage** to magnify small changes in revenue into dramatic changes in profitability. The *lever* managers use to achieve disproportionate changes between revenue and profitability is fixed costs. The leverage relationships between revenue, fixed costs, and profitability are displayed in Exhibit 2.3.

When all costs are fixed, every sales dollar contributes one dollar toward the potential profitability of a project. Once sales dollars cover fixed costs, each

## EXHIBIT 2.3

### Operating Leverage

| Small percentage change in revenue | Dramatic percentage change in profitability |
|---|---|

**Fixed costs**

# FOCUS ON INTERNATIONAL ISSUES

### FIXED COSTS BRING INTERNATIONAL INTRIGUE INTO THE AUTOMOBILE INDUSTRY

The major advantage of fixed costs is that as output increases, cost per unit decreases. Of course fixed costs can be a disadvantage if output is falling. Due to the nature of the industry automobile manufacturers have high fixed costs. It takes a lot of land, buildings, and machinery to mass produce cars and trucks.

In 2007 the worldwide production of autos was 73.3 million units;* in 2008 it had fallen to 70.5 million units due to the global recession. Not surprisingly, this had an adverse effect on companies that were already struggling, such as **GM**, **Ford**, and **Chrysler**, but it also affected the strongest company in the industry, Toyota. In its fiscal year ended March 31, 2008, Toyota produced 8.5 million vehicles and had a profit of $17.1 billion. In its fiscal year ended March 31, 2009, the company's output had fallen to 7.1 million vehicles, and it had a *net loss* of $4.0 billion.

A company with high fixed costs suffers on two fronts during a recession. First, the lower production causes its cost per unit to rise. Second, the weak economy puts pressure on it, and its competitors, to lower prices, or at least not to raise them. In **Toyota**'s case, this meant that a company that had been reporting growing profits for many years suddenly had a significant loss.

*Sources of data: International Organization of Motor Vehicle Manufactures and Toyota's annual reports.

additional sales dollar represents pure profit. As a result, a small change in sales volume can significantly affect profitability. To illustrate, assume SPI estimates it will sell 3,000 tickets for $18 each. A 10 percent difference in actual sales volume will produce a 90 percent difference in profitability. Examine the data in Exhibit 2.4 to verify this result.[1]

## EXHIBIT 2.4

### Effect of Operating Leverage on Profitability

| | | | | | |
|---|---|---|---|---|---|
| Number of tickets sold | 2,700 | ⇐ −10% ⇐ | 3,000 | ⇒ +10% ⇒ | 3,300 |
| Sales revenue ($18 per ticket) | $48,600 | | $54,000 | | $59,400 |
| Cost of band (fixed cost) | (48,000) | | (48,000) | | (48,000) |
| Gross margin | $   600 | ⇐ −90% ⇐ | $ 6,000 | ⇒ +90% ⇒ | $11,400 |

## Calculating Percentage Change

The percentages in Exhibit 2.4 are computed as follows:

$$\text{(Alternative measure} - \text{Base measure)} \div \text{Base measure} = \% \text{ change}$$

*The base measure is the starting point.* To illustrate, compute the percentage change in gross margin when moving from 3,000 units (base measure) to 3,300 units (the alternative measure).

$$\text{(Alternative measure} - \text{Base measure)} \div \text{Base measure} = \% \text{ change}$$

$$(\$11,400 - \$6,000) \div \$6,000 = 90\%$$

[1]Do not confuse operating leverage with financial leverage. Companies employ *financial leverage* when they use debt to profit from investing money at a higher rate of return than the rate they pay on borrowed money. Companies employ *operating leverage* when they use proportionately more fixed costs than variable costs to magnify the effect on earnings of changes in revenues.

The percentage *decline* in profitability is similarly computed:

(**Alternative measure** − **Base measure**) ÷ **Base measure** = **% change**

($600 − $6,000) ÷ $6,000 = (90%)

### Risk and Reward Assessment

*Risk* refers to the possibility that sacrifices may exceed benefits. A fixed cost represents a commitment to an economic sacrifice. It represents the ultimate risk of undertaking a particular business project. If SPI pays the band but nobody buys a ticket, the company will lose $48,000. SPI can avoid this risk by substituting *variable costs* for the *fixed cost*.

## VARIABLE COST BEHAVIOR

Identify and describe fixed, variable, and mixed cost behavior.

To illustrate variable cost behavior, assume SPI arranges to pay the band $16 per ticket sold instead of a fixed $48,000. Exhibit 2.5 shows the total cost of the band and the cost per ticket sold at three different levels of activity.

### EXHIBIT 2.5

**Variable Cost Behavior**

| | | | |
|---|---|---|---|
| Number of tickets sold (a) | 2,700 | 3,000 | 3,300 |
| Total cost of band (b) | $43,200 | $48,000 | $52,800 |
| Cost per ticket sold (b ÷ a) | $16 | $16 | $16 |

Since SPI will pay the band $16 for each ticket sold, the *total* variable cost increases in direct proportion to the number of tickets sold. If SPI sells one ticket, total band cost will be $16 (1 × $16); if SPI sells two tickets, total band cost will be $32 (2 × $16); and so on. The total cost of the band increases proportionately as ticket sales move from 2,700 to 3,000 to 3,300. The variable cost *per ticket* remains $16, however, regardless of whether the number of tickets sold is 1, 2, 3, or 3,000. The behavior of variable cost *per unit* is contradictory to the word *variable*. Variable cost per unit remains *constant* regardless of how many tickets are sold. Study carefully the variable cost behavior patterns in Exhibit 2.6.

### EXHIBIT 2.6

**Variable Cost Behavior**

| | **When Activity Increases** | **When Activity Decreases** |
|---|---|---|
| **Total** variable cost | Increases proportionately | Decreases proportionately |
| Variable cost **per unit** | Remains constant | Remains constant |

### Risk and Reward Assessment

Shifting the cost structure from fixed to variable enables SPI to avoid the fixed-cost risk. Recall that under the fixed cost structure, SPI was locked into a $48,000 cost for the band regardless of how many tickets are sold. If no tickets are sold, SPI will have to report a $48,000 loss on its income statement. The risk of incurring this loss is eliminated by the variable cost structure that requires SPI to only pay the band $16 per ticket sold. If SPI sells zero tickets then the cost of the band is zero. For each ticket sold, SPI earns a $2 profit ($18 ticket sales price − $16 fee paid to band).

Shifting the cost structure from fixed to variable reduces not only the level of risk but also the potential for profits. Managers cannot avoid the risk of fixed costs without also sacrificing the benefits. Variable costs do not offer operating leverage. Exhibit 2.7 shows

**LO 2**

Demonstrate the effects of operating leverage on profitability.

## EXHIBIT 2.7

### Variable Cost Eliminates Operating Leverage

| | | | | | |
|---|---|---|---|---|---|
| Number of tickets sold | 2,700 | ⇐ −10% ⇐ | 3,000 | ⇒ +10% ⇒ | 3,300 |
| Sales revenue ($18 per ticket) | $48,600 | | $54,000 | | $59,400 |
| Cost of band ($16 variable cost) | (43,200) | | (48,000) | | (52,800) |
| Gross margin | $ 5,400 | ⇐ −10% ⇐ | $ 6,000 | ⇒ +10% ⇒ | $ 6,600 |

that a variable cost structure produces a proportional relationship between sales and profitability. A 10 percent increase or decrease in sales results in a corresponding 10 percent increase or decrease in profitability. While the variable cost structure reduces risk, Exhibit 2.7 demonstrates that it also limits the opportunity to benefit from operating leverage.

The risk versus reward trade-off of cost structure is widespread in business practice. For example, borrowing money to buy an office building may require a company to commit to a fixed monthly principal and interest payment. If the company's revenue stream unexpectedly declines, the company still has to make its monthly payment. Indeed, many companies are forced into bankruptcy because they cannot satisfy their fixed debt commitments. Many companies avoid these fixed cost risks by renting their office space instead of purchasing buildings. If revenue dips, the company simply reduces the amount of office space it rents, thereby reducing its rental cost. Other real-world examples of fixed-cost risk avoidance include using temporary employees instead of hiring for permanent positions and paying a variable retainer fee to an independent law firm instead of creating a legal department within the company. These examples demonstrate the widespread applicability of the trade-offs associated with cost structure. Managers continually apply professional judgment to assess the risks of locking in costs with the opportunities provided by operating leverage.

### ✓ CHECK YOURSELF 2.1

Suppose that you are sponsoring a political rally at which Ralph Nader will speak. You estimate that approximately 2,000 people will buy tickets to hear Mr. Nader's speech. The tickets are expected to be priced at $12 each. Would you prefer a contract that agrees to pay Mr. Nader $10,000 or one that agrees to pay him $5 per ticket purchased?

**Answer**   Your answer would depend on how certain you are that 2,000 people will purchase tickets. If it were likely that many more than 2,000 tickets would be sold, you would be better off with a fixed cost structure, agreeing to pay Mr. Nader a flat fee of $10,000. If attendance numbers are highly uncertain, you would be better off with a variable cost structure thereby guaranteeing a lower cost if fewer people buy tickets.

## EFFECT OF COST STRUCTURE ON PROFIT STABILITY

The preceding discussion suggests that companies with higher levels of fixed costs are more likely to experience earnings volatility. To illustrate, suppose three companies produce and sell the same product. Each company sells 10 units for $10 each. Furthermore, each company incurs costs of $60 in the process of making and selling its products. However, the companies operate under radically different **cost structures.** The entire $60 of cost incurred by Company A is fixed. Company B incurs $30 of fixed cost and $30 of variable cost ($3 per unit). All $60 of cost incurred by Company C is variable ($6 per unit). Exhibit 2.8 displays income statements for the three companies.

**LO 2**

Demonstrate the effects of operating leverage on profitability.

**EXHIBIT 2.8**

**Income Statements**

|  | Company Name | | |
|---|---|---|---|
|  | **A** | **B** | **C** |
| Variable cost per unit (a) | $ 0 | $ 3 | $ 6 |
| Sales revenue (10 units × $10) | $100 | $100 | $100 |
| Variable cost (10 units × a) | 0 | (30) | (60) |
| Fixed cost | (60) | (30) | 0 |
| Net income | $ 40 | $ 40 | $ 40 |

**EXHIBIT 2.9**

**Income Statements**

|  | Company Name | | |
|---|---|---|---|
|  | **A** | **B** | **C** |
| Variable cost per unit (a) | $ 0 | $ 3 | $ 6 |
| Sales revenue (11 units × $10) | $110 | $110 | $110 |
| Variable cost (11 units × a) | 0 | (33) | (66) |
| Fixed cost | (60) | (30) | 0 |
| Net income | $ 50 | $ 47 | $ 44 |

When sales change, the amount of the corresponding change in net income is directly influenced by the company's cost structure. The more fixed cost, the greater the fluctuation in net income. To illustrate, assume sales increase by one unit; the resulting income statements are displayed in Exhibit 2.9.

Company A, with the highest level of fixed costs, experienced a $10 ($50 − $40) increase in profitability; Company C, with the lowest level of fixed cost (zero), had only a $4 ($44 − $40) increase in profitability. Company B, with a 50/50 mix of fixed and variable cost, had a mid-range $7 ($47 − $40) increase in net income. The effect of fixed cost on volatility applies to decreases as well as increases in sales volume. To illustrate, assume sales decrease by one unit (from 10 to 9 units). The resulting income statements are displayed in Exhibit 2.10.

Company A again experiences the largest variance in earnings ($10 decrease). Company B had a moderate decline of $7, and Company C had the least volatility with only a $4 decline.

What cost structure is the best? Should a manager use fixed or variable costs? The answer depends on sales volume expectations. A manager who expects revenues to increase should use a fixed cost structure. On the other hand, if future sales growth is uncertain or if the manager believes revenue is likely to decline, a variable cost structure makes more sense.

**EXHIBIT 2.10**

**Income Statements**

|  | Company Name | | |
|---|---|---|---|
|  | **A** | **B** | **C** |
| Variable cost per unit (a) | $ 0 | $ 3 | $ 6 |
| Sales revenue (9 units × $10) | $90 | $90 | $90 |
| Variable cost (9 units × a) | 0 | (27) | (54) |
| Fixed cost | (60) | (30) | 0 |
| Net income | $30 | $33 | $36 |

## Answers to The Curious Accountant

The explanation for how a company's earnings can rise faster, as a percentage, than its revenue rises is operating leverage, and operating leverage is due entirely to fixed costs. As the chapter explains, when a company's output goes up, its fixed cost per unit goes down. As long as it can keep prices about the same, this lower unit cost will result in higher profit per unit sold. In real-world companies, the relationship between changing sales levels and changing earnings levels can be very complex, but the existence of fixed costs helps to explain why a 9 percent rise in revenue can cause a 15 percent rise in net earnings. Chapter 3 will investigate the relationships among an entity's cost structure, output level, pricing strategy, and profits earned in more depth.

# AN INCOME STATEMENT UNDER THE CONTRIBUTION MARGIN APPROACH

The impact of cost structure on profitability is so significant that managerial accountants frequently construct income statements that classify costs according to their behavior patterns. Such income statements first subtract variable costs from revenue; the resulting subtotal is called the **contribution margin.** The contribution margin represents the amount available to cover fixed expenses and thereafter to provide company profits. Net income is computed by subtracting the fixed costs from the contribution margin. A contribution margin style income statement cannot be used for public reporting (GAAP prohibits its use in external financial reports), but it is widely used for internal reporting purposes. Exhibit 2.11 illustrates income statements prepared using the contribution margin approach.

**LO 3**

Prepare an income statement using the contribution margin approach.

**EXHIBIT 2.11**

**Income Statements**

| | Company Name | |
| --- | --- | --- |
| | **Bragg** | **Biltmore** |
| Variable cost per unit (a) | $ 6 | $ 12 |
| Sales revenue (10 units × $20) | $200 | $200 |
| Variable cost (10 units × a) | (60) | (120) |
| Contribution margin | 140 | 80 |
| Fixed cost | (120) | (60) |
| Net income | $ 20 | $ 20 |

# USING FIXED COST TO PROVIDE A COMPETITIVE OPERATING ADVANTAGE

Mary MaHall and John Strike have established tutoring companies to support themselves while they attend college. Both Ms. MaHall and Mr. Strike function as owner/managers; they each hire other students to actually provide the tutoring services. Ms. MaHall pays her tutors salaries; her labor costs are fixed at $16,000 per year regardless of the number of hours of tutoring performed. Mr. Strike pays his employees $8 per hour; his labor is therefore a variable cost. Both businesses currently provide 2,000 hours of tutoring services at a price of $11 per hour. As shown in Exhibit 2.12, both companies currently produce the same profit.

Suppose Ms. MaHall adopts a strategy to win over Mr. Strike's customers by reducing the price of tutoring services from $11 per hour to $7 per hour. If Ms. MaHall

**LO 2**

Demonstrate the effects of operating leverage on profitability.

## EXHIBIT 2.12

| Comparative Profitability at 2,000 Hours of Tutoring | | | | |
|---|---|---|---|---|
| | | **MaHall** | | **Strike** |
| Number of hours of tutoring provided | | 2,000 | | 2,000 |
| Service revenue ($11 per hour) | | $22,000 | | $22,000 |
| Cost of tutors | Fixed | (16,000) | Variable ($8 × 2,000) | (16,000) |
| Net income | | $ 6,000 | | $ 6,000 |

succeeds, her company's income will double as shown in Exhibit 2.13. Mr. Strike is in a vulnerable position because if he matches MaHall's price cut he will lose $1 ($7 new per-hour price − $8 cost per hour for tutor) for each hour of tutoring service that his company provides.

## EXHIBIT 2.13

| MaHall's Profitability at 4,000 Hours of Tutoring | | |
|---|---|---|
| | | **MaHall** |
| Number of hours of tutoring provided | | 4,000 |
| Service revenue ($7 per hour) | | $28,000 |
| Cost of tutors | Fixed | (16,000) |
| Net income (loss) | | $12,000 |

Is Mr. Strike's business doomed? Not necessarily; Ms. MaHall's operating leverage strategy only works if volume increases. If Mr. Strike matches Ms. MaHall's price, thereby maintaining the existing sales volume levels between the two companies, both companies incur losses. Exhibit 2.14 verifies this conclusion. Under these circumstances, Ms. MaHall would be forced to raise her price or to face the same negative consequences that she is attempting to force on Mr. Strike.

## EXHIBIT 2.14

| Comparative Profitability at 2,000 Hours of Tutoring | | | | |
|---|---|---|---|---|
| | | **MaHall** | | **Strike** |
| Number of hours of tutoring provided | | 2,000 | | 2,000 |
| Service revenue ($7 per hour) | | $14,000 | | $14,000 |
| Cost of tutors | Fixed | (16,000) | Variable ($8 × 2,000) | (16,000) |
| Net income (loss) | | $(2,000) | | $(2,000) |

# MEASURING OPERATING LEVERAGE USING CONTRIBUTION MARGIN

**LO 4**

Calculate the magnitude of operating leverage.

A contribution margin income statement allows managers to easily measure operating leverage. The magnitude of operating leverage can be determined as follows:

$$\text{Magnitude of operating leverage} = \frac{\text{Contribution margin}}{\text{Net income}}$$

Applying this formula to the income statement data reported for Bragg Company and Biltmore Company in Exhibit 2.11 produces the following measures.

**Bragg Company:**

$$\text{Magnitude of operating leverage} = \frac{\$140}{\$20} = 7$$

**Biltmore Company:**

$$\text{Magnitude of operating leverage} = \frac{\$80}{\$20} = 4$$

The computations show that Bragg is more highly leveraged than Biltmore. Bragg's change in profitability will be seven times greater than a given percentage change in revenue. In contrast, Biltmore's profits change by only four times the percentage change in revenue. For example, a 10 percent increase in revenue produces a 70 percent increase (10 percent × 7) in profitability for Bragg Company and a 40 percent increase (10 percent × 4) in profitability for Biltmore Company. The income statements in Exhibits 2.15 and 2.16 confirm these expectations.

## EXHIBIT 2.15

### Comparative Income Statements for Bragg Company

| | | | |
|---|---|---|---|
| Units (a) | 10 | | 11 |
| Sales revenue ($20 × a) | $200 | ⇒ +10% ⇒ | $220 |
| Variable cost ($6 × a) | (60) | | (66) |
| Contribution margin | 140 | | 154 |
| Fixed cost | (120) | | (120) |
| Net income | $ 20 | ⇒ +70% ⇒ | $ 34 |

## EXHIBIT 2.16

### Comparative Income Statements for Biltmore Company

| | | | |
|---|---|---|---|
| Units (a) | 10 | | 11 |
| Sales revenue ($20 × a) | $200 | ⇒ +10% ⇒ | $220 |
| Variable cost ($12 × a) | (120) | | (132) |
| Contribution margin | 80 | | 88 |
| Fixed cost | (60) | | (60) |
| Net income | $ 20 | ⇒ +40% ⇒ | $ 28 |

Operating leverage itself is neither good nor bad; it represents a strategy that can work to a company's advantage or disadvantage, depending on how it is used. The next section explains how managers can use operating leverage to create a competitive business advantage.

## ✓ CHECK YOURSELF 2.3

Boeing Company's 2001 10K annual report filed with the Securities and Exchange Commission refers to "higher commercial airlines segment margins." Is Boeing referring to gross margins or contribution margins?

**Answer**  Since the data come from the company's external annual report, the reference must be to gross margins (revenue − cost of goods sold), a product cost measure. The contribution margin (revenue − variable cost) is a measure used in internal reporting.

## COST BEHAVIOR SUMMARIZED

The term *fixed* refers to the behavior of *total* fixed cost. The cost *per unit* of a fixed cost *varies inversely* with changes in the level of activity. As activity increases, fixed cost per unit decreases. As activity decreases, fixed cost per unit increases. These relationships are graphed in Exhibit 2.17.

LO 1

Identify and describe fixed, variable, and mixed cost behavior.

**EXHIBIT 2.17**

**Graphical Presentation of Fixed Cost Behavior**

Total Fixed Cost          Fixed Cost per Unit

**EXHIBIT 2.18**

**Graphical Presentation of Variable Cost Behavior**

Total Variable Cost          Variable Cost per Unit

**EXHIBIT 2.19**

**Fixed and Variable Cost Behavior**

| When Activity Level Changes | Total Cost | Cost per Unit |
|---|---|---|
| Fixed costs | Remains constant | Changes *inversely* |
| Variable costs | Changes in direct proportion | Remains constant |

The term *variable* refers to the behavior of *total* variable cost. Total variable cost increases or decreases proportionately with changes in the volume of activity. In contrast, variable cost *per unit* remains *fixed* at all levels of activity. These relationships are graphed in Exhibit 2.18.

The relationships between fixed and variable costs are summarized in the chart in Exhibit 2.19. Study these relationships thoroughly.

## Mixed Costs (Semivariable Costs)

**Mixed costs (semivariable costs)** include both fixed and variable components. For example, suppose Star Productions, Inc., has to pay for janitorial services. The charge for these services includes a base fee of $1,000 plus $20 per hour required to do a cleanup. The $1,000 base fee is fixed. It is the same no matter how many hours it takes to accomplish the cleanup. In contrast, the $20 hourly cost is a variable cost because the total cost increases with each additional hour it takes to complete the cleanup. Since the total janitorial cost is composed of fixed and variable components, it is frequently called a mixed cost. It may also be called a semivariable cost.

Given the $1,000 base plus $20 per hour cost components, the total janitorial cost for any cleanup can be easily computed as shown below:

Total cost = Fixed cost + (Variable cost per hour × Number of hours)

If 60 hours are required to accomplish a cleanup, the total mixed cost is:

Total cost = $1,000 + ($20 × 60) = $2,200

If 90 hours are required to accomplish a cleanup, the total mixed cost is:

Total cost = $1,000 + ($20 × 90) = $2,800

Exhibit 2.20 illustrates a variety of mixed costs businesses commonly encounter.

## EXHIBIT 2.20

### Examples of Mixed Costs

| Type of Cost | Fixed Cost Component(s) | Variable Cost Component(s) |
|---|---|---|
| Cost of sales staff | Monthly salary | Bonus based on sales volume |
| Truck rental | Monthly rental fee | Cost of gas, tires, and maintenance |
| Legal fees | Monthly retainer | Reimbursements to attorney for out-of-pocket costs (copying, postage, travel, filing fees) |
| Outpatient service cost | Salaries of doctors and nurses, depreciation of facility, utilities | Medical supplies such as bandages, sterilization solution, and paper products |
| Phone services | Monthly connection fee | Per-minute usage fee |
| LP gas utility cost | Container rental fee | Cost of gas consumed |
| Cable TV services | Monthly fee | Pay-per-view charges |
| Training cost | Instructor salary, facility cost | Textbooks, supplies |
| Shipping and handling | Salaries of employees who process packages | Boxes, packing supplies, tape, and other shipping supplies, postage |
| Inventory holding cost | Depreciation on inventory warehouse, salaries of employees managing inventory | Delivery costs, interest on funds borrowed to finance inventory, cost of supplies |

## The Relevant Range

Suppose SPI, the rock concert promoter mentioned earlier, must pay $5,000 to rent a concert hall with a seating capacity of 4,000 people. Is the cost of the concert hall fixed or variable? Since total cost remains unchanged regardless of whether one ticket, 4,000 tickets, or any number in between is sold, the cost is fixed relative to ticket sales. However, what if demand for tickets is significantly more than 4,000? In that case, SPI might rent a larger concert hall at a higher cost. In other words, *the cost is fixed only for a designated range of activity (1 to 4,000).*

A similar circumstance affects many variable costs. For example, a supplier may offer a volume discount to buyers who purchase more than a specified number of products. The point is that descriptions of cost behavior pertain to a specified range of activity. The range of activity over which the definitions of fixed and variable costs are valid is commonly called the **relevant range.**

**LO 5**

Demonstrate how the relevant range and decision context affect cost behavior.

## Context-Sensitive Definitions of Fixed and Variable

The behavior pattern of a particular cost may be either fixed or variable, depending on the context. For example, the cost of the band was fixed at $48,000 when SPI was considering hiring it to play a single concert. Regardless of how many tickets SPI sold, the total band cost was $48,000. However, the band cost becomes variable if SPI decides to hire it to perform at a series of concerts. The total cost and the cost per concert for one, two, three, four, or five concerts are shown in Exhibit 2.21.

In this context, the total cost of hiring the band increases proportionately with the number of concerts while cost per concert remains constant. The band cost is therefore variable. The same cost can behave as either a fixed cost or a variable cost, depending on the **activity base.** When identifying a cost as fixed or variable, first ask, fixed or variable *relative to what activity base?* The cost of the band is fixed relative to *the number of tickets sold for a specific concert;* it is variable relative to *the number of concerts produced.*

**EXHIBIT 2.21**

**Cost Behavior Relative to Number of Concerts**

| | 1 | 2 | 3 | 4 | 5 |
|---|---|---|---|---|---|
| Number of concerts (a) | 1 | 2 | 3 | 4 | 5 |
| Cost per concert (b) | $48,000 | $48,000 | $ 48,000 | $ 48,000 | $ 48,000 |
| Total cost (a × b) | $48,000 | $96,000 | $144,000 | $192,000 | $240,000 |

✓ **CHECK YOURSELF 2.4**

Is the compensation cost for managers of Pizza Hut Restaurants a fixed cost or a variable cost?

**Answer**   The answer depends on the context. For example, since a store manager's salary remains unchanged regardless of how many customers enter a particular restaurant, it can be classified as a fixed cost relative to the number of customers at a particular restaurant. However, the more restaurants that Pizza Hut operates, the higher the total managers' compensation cost will be. Accordingly, managers' salary cost would be classified as a variable cost relative to the number of restaurants opened.

## COST AVERAGING

**LO 6**

Select an appropriate time period for calculating the average cost per unit.

Lake Resorts, Inc. (LRI), offers water skiing lessons for guests. Since the demand for lessons is seasonal (guests buy more lessons in July than in December), LRI has chosen to rent (rather than own) the necessary equipment (boats, skis, ropes, life jackets) only when it is needed. LRI's accountant has collected the following data pertaining to providing ski lessons:

1.   The daily fee to rent equipment is $80.
2.   Instructors are paid $15 per lesson hour.
3.   Fuel costs are $2 per lesson hour.
4.   Lessons take one hour each.
5.   LRI can provide up to 20 lessons in one day.

During a recent weekend, LRI provided 2 lessons on Friday, 10 on Saturday, and 20 on Sunday. Exhibit 2.22 shows the total cost per day and average cost per lesson for each of the three days. Since equipment rental cost is fixed relative to the number of lessons provided, the cost per lesson declines as the number of lessons increases. This explains why the cost per lesson is significantly lower on Sunday than Friday.

Assume LRI uses a cost-plus pricing strategy. The cost per lesson figures shown in Exhibit 2.22 are not useful in determining the price to charge customers. For example, it makes no sense to charge more for lessons on days like Friday when demand is low. Indeed, many businesses lower prices on days when demand is low in order to stimulate business.

The pricing problem can be solved by averaging the costs over a longer span of time. To illustrate, assume LRI uses the

**EXHIBIT 2.22**

**Analysis of Total and Unit Cost**

| | | | |
|---|---|---|---|
| Number of Lessons (a) | 2 | 10 | 20 |
| Cost of equipment rental | $ 80 | $ 80 | $ 80 |
| Cost of instruction (a × $15) | 30 | 150 | 300 |
| Cost of fuel (a × $2) | 4 | 20 | 40 |
| Total cost (b) | $114 | $250 | $420 |
| Cost per lesson (b ÷ a) | $ 57 | $ 25 | $ 21 |

# REALITY BYTES

Alice is a business student who works part time at Costco Wholesale Corporation to help pay for her college expenses. She is currently taking a managerial accounting course and has heard her instructor refer to depreciation as a fixed cost. However, as a requirement for her first accounting course, Alice reviewed Costco's financial statements for 2006, 2007, and 2008. The depreciation expense increased about 21 percent over these three years. She is not sure why depreciation expense would be considered a fixed cost.

Alice's accounting instructor reminded her that when an accountant says a cost is fixed, he or she means the cost is fixed in relation to one particular factor. A cost that is fixed in relation to one factor can be variable when compared to some other factor. For example, the depreciation for a retailer may be fixed relative to the number of customers who visit a particular store, but variable relative to the number of stores the company opens. In fact, Costco's depreciation increased from 2006 to 2008 mainly because the company built and opened additional stores.

Alice's instructor suggested that Costco's depreciation expense would be more stable if analyzed on a per store basis, rather than in total. Being curious, Alice prepared the following table, where costs are in thousands. Over the three years, she noted that total depreciation expense increased 21.1 percent, while depreciation per store increased only 11.8 percent. Although the costs on a per store basis were more stable than the total depreciation costs, they still were not fixed, so she asked her instructor for further explanation.

| Fiscal year | Total Depreciation Expense | Average Depreciation Expense per Store |
|---|---|---|
| 2006 | $515,285 | $1,125.1 |
| 2007 | 566,385 | 1,160.6 |
| 2008 | 653,082 | 1,275.6 |

The instructor suggested Costco's average per store depreciation costs were increasing because the equipment and buildings purchased for the new stores (opened from 2006 to 2008) probably cost more than those purchased for the older stores and Costco's new stores are often bigger than its older stores. This would raise the average depreciation expense per store. The instructor also reminded her that in the real world very few costs are perfectly fixed or perfectly variable.

weekly average instead of a daily average. Further, assume that the costs for the week include the following:

| | |
|---|---|
| Equipment rental (7 days × $80 per day) | $ 560 |
| Cost of instruction ($15 × 50 lessons) | 750 |
| Cost of fuel ($2 × 50 lessons) | 100 |
| Total | $1,410 |
| Average cost per lesson | $1,410/50 lessons = $28.20 |

If LRI desires to earn a profit of $10 per lesson, the company will set the price at $38.20 ($28.20 weekly average cost per lesson + $10.00 profit) per lesson regardless of the day of the week that a lesson is administered. On slow days the daily profit margin is less than $10 per lesson. Indeed, on Friday, when only two lessons are provided, LRI incurs a loss of $18.80 per lesson ($38.20 price per lesson − $57 daily average cost per lesson). This loss is offset on busy days when the daily profit margin exceeds the $10 weekly average. For example, on Sunday, when 20 lessons are administered, the profit margin is $17.20 per lesson ($38.20 price per lesson − $21 daily average cost per lesson). The differences in the daily profit margins average out over the course of the week. As a result, LRI is able to charge the same price per lesson regardless of the daily demand and still attain an average profit margin of $10 per lesson for the week.

The need for a weekly average occurs because the number of lessons per day fluctuates radically, thereby causing significant differences in the cost per lesson when calculated on a daily basis. A similar problem occurs if the number of lessons per week fluctuates radically from week to week. For example, the demand for skiing lessons may increase significantly during the week of July 4th or other holidays. Similarly, the demand for lessons may taper off toward the end of the summer. In this case, it will be necessary to expand the time frame for which the average is calculated, perhaps over the summer months or even several seasons.

Distortions can occur when the time period is too long as well as too short. For example, the price of fuel and equipment rental changes over time. If older costs are mixed with newer costs, the average does not represent current conditions. Choosing the best time frame for calculating the average cost of a product or service requires thoughtful analysis and judgment.

## USE OF ESTIMATES IN REAL-WORLD PROBLEMS

**LO 7**

Use the high-low method, scattergraphs, and regression analysis to estimate fixed and variable costs.

Imagine trying to classify as fixed or variable all the different costs incurred by a large company such as Delta Airlines. Record keeping would be horrendous. Further complications would arise because some costs are mixed costs. Consider the cost Delta incurs to use airport facilities. An airport may charge Delta a flat annual rental fee for terminal space plus a charge each time a plane takes off or lands. The flat rental fee is a fixed cost while the charge per flight is variable. The total facilities cost is mixed.

To minimize the record-keeping difficulties involved in identifying actual fixed and variable costs, many companies make decisions using estimated rather than actual costs. Several techniques exist to divide total cost into estimated fixed and variable components.

### High-Low Method of Estimating Fixed and Variable Costs

The management of Rainy Day Books (RDB) wants to expand operations. To help evaluate the risks involved in opening an additional store, the company president wants to know the amount of fixed cost a new store will likely incur. Suppose RDB's accountant decides to use the **high-low method** to supply the president with the requested information. The estimated amount of fixed cost for the new store would be developed in the following four steps.

**Step 1**  *Assemble sales volume and cost history for an existing store.* Assuming the new store would operate with roughly the same cost structure, the accountant can use the historical data to estimate the fixed cost likely to be incurred by the new store. To illustrate, assume the accounting data set for the existing store is displayed in Exhibit 2.23.

**Step 2**  *Select the high and low points in the data set.* In this example, the month with the lowest number of units sold does not correspond to the month with the lowest total cost. The lowest point in units sold occurred in May; the lowest total cost occurred in March. Because the total cost depends on the *number of units sold,* May should be

## EXHIBIT 2.23

### Cost Data

| Month | Units Sold | Total Cost |
|---|---|---|
| January | 30,000 | $450,000 |
| February | 14,000 | 300,000 |
| March | 12,000 | 150,000 |
| April | 25,000 | 440,000 |
| May | 10,000 | 180,000 |
| June | 11,000 | 240,000 |
| July | 20,000 | 350,000 |
| August | 18,000 | 400,000 |
| September | 17,000 | 360,000 |
| October | 16,000 | 320,000 |
| November | 27,000 | 490,000 |
| December | 34,000 | 540,000 |

classified as the low point. The high point in sales volume occurred in December. The units sold and cost data for the December and May high and low points follow:

|  | Units Sold | Total Cost |
|---|---|---|
| High (December) | 34,000 | $540,000 |
| Low (May) | 10,000 | $180,000 |

**Step 3**  ***Determine the estimated variable cost per unit.*** The variable cost per unit is determined by dividing the difference in the total cost by the difference in the number of units sold. In this case, the variable cost per unit is as follows:

$$\frac{\text{Variable}}{\text{cost per unit}} = \frac{\text{Difference in total cost}}{\text{Difference in volume}} = \frac{(\$540{,}000 - \$180{,}000)}{(34{,}000 - 10{,}000)} = \frac{\$360{,}000}{24{,}000} = \$15$$

**Step 4**  ***Determine the estimated total fixed cost.*** The total fixed cost can now be determined by subtracting the variable cost from the total cost using either the high point or the low point. Either point yields the same result. Computations using the high point follow:

$$\text{Fixed cost} + \text{Variable cost} = \text{Total cost}$$

$$\text{Fixed cost} = \text{Total cost} - \text{Variable cost}$$

$$\text{Fixed cost} = \$540{,}000 - (\$15 \times 34{,}000 \text{ units})$$

$$\text{Fixed cost} = \$30{,}000$$

Once determined, the *total* fixed cost and variable cost *per unit* estimates can be used to predict expected total cost at any volume of activity as follows:

$$\text{Total cost} = \text{Fixed cost} + (\text{Variable cost per unit} \times \text{Number of units})$$

If 22,000 books are sold, the total estimated cost is:

$$\text{Total cost} = \$30{,}000 + (\$15 \times 22{,}000) = \$360{,}000$$

If 32,000 books are sold, the total estimated cost is:

$$\text{Total cost} = \$30{,}000 + (\$15 \times 32{,}000) = \$510{,}000$$

Although 12 data points are available, the high-low method uses only 2 of them to estimate the amounts of fixed and variable costs. If either or both of these points is not representative of the true relationship between fixed and variable costs, the estimates produced by the high-low method will be inaccurate. *The chief advantage of the high-low method is its simplicity; the chief disadvantage is its vulnerability to inaccuracy.* RDB's accountant decides to test the accuracy of the high-low method results.

## Scattergraph Method of Estimating Fixed and Variable Costs

Scattergraphs are sometimes used as an estimation technique for dividing total cost into fixed and variable cost components. To assess the accuracy of the high-low estimate of fixed cost, RDB's accountant constructs a **scattergraph.** The horizontal axis is labeled with the number of books sold and the vertical axis with total costs. The 12 data points are plotted on the graph, and a line is drawn through the high and low points in the data set. The result is shown in Exhibit 2.24.

After studying the scattergraph in Exhibit 2.24, the accountant is certain that the high and low points are not representative of the data set. Most of the data points are above the high-low line. As shown in the second scattergraph in Exhibit 2.25, the line should be shifted upward to reflect the influence of the other data points.

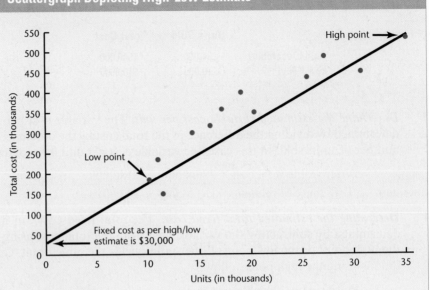

**EXHIBIT 2.24**

**Scattergraph Depicting High-Low Estimate**

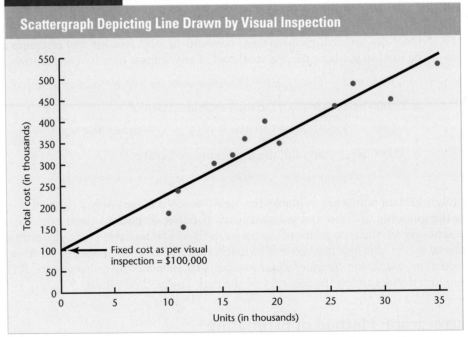

**EXHIBIT 2.25**

**Scattergraph Depicting Line Drawn by Visual Inspection**

The graph in Exhibit 2.25 is identical to the graph in Exhibit 2.24 except the straight line is plotted through the center of the entire data set rather than just the high and low points. The new line, a **visual fit line,** is drawn to visually minimize the total distance between the data points and the line. Usually, half of the data points are above and half below a visual fit line. The estimated variable cost per unit is measured by the slope (steepness) of the visual fit line. The fixed cost is the point (the *intercept*) where the visual fit line intersects the vertical axis (the total cost line).

The intercept in Exhibit 2.25 provides a fixed cost estimate of $100,000. Although RDB's president had only asked for the amount of fixed cost, the variable cost can be easily determined by subtracting the fixed cost from the total cost at any point along

# FOCUS ON **INTERNATIONAL ISSUES**

## ANOTHER REASON FIXED COSTS AREN'T ALWAYS FIXED

Suppose that a company is renting a facility at an annual rental rate that does not change for the next five years *no matter what.* Is this a fixed cost? By now, you are aware that the proper response is to ask fixed in relation to what? Is the rental cost of this facility fixed in relation to the activity at this facility? The answer seems to be yes, but it might be "not necessarily."

Consider the **Exxon Mobil Corporation**. If Exxon Mobil rents facilities in a country in the eastern hemisphere, Malaysia for example, the annual rental fee may be stated and paid in the local currency. In Malaysia, this is the ringgit. Even though Exxon Mobil may be paying the same number of ringgit in rent each year, Exxon Mobil's rental cost in U.S. dollars could vary greatly over time. Such potential foreign currency exchange fluctuations cause companies to enter very complex hedging arrangements to add stability to transactions that must be paid in foreign currencies.

Exxon Mobil was founded and has its headquarters in the United States. It does much business in the United States. Furthermore, it is listed on the New York Stock Exchange and prepares its financial statements in U.S. dollars. However, it does much more business and has many more assets in countries outside the United States. Consider the following table from Exxon Mobil's 2008 financial statements. Before a multinational company can determine whether a cost is fixed, it must determine the applicable currency.

| Geographical Area | Earnings* | Percentage of Total | Total Assets* | Percentage of Total |
|---|---|---|---|---|
| United States | $ 8,616 | 19% | $ 46,240 | 25% |
| Non-United States | 37,894 | 81 | 139,094 | 75 |
| Totals | $46,510 | 100% | $185,334 | 100% |

*Amounts in millions.

the visual fit line. For example, at 15,000 units, total cost is $300,000. Variable cost is determined as follows:

$$\text{Fixed cost} + \text{Variable cost} = \text{Total cost}$$

$$\text{Variable cost} = \text{Total cost} - \text{Fixed cost}$$

$$\text{Variable cost} = \$300,000 - \$100,000$$

$$\text{Variable cost} = \$200,000$$

Variable cost per unit is $13.3333, calculated by dividing the total variable cost by the number of units ($200,000 ÷ 15,000 units = $13.3333 per unit).

As with the high-low method these *total* fixed cost and variable cost *per unit* estimates can be used to predict expected total cost at any volume of activity as follows:

$$\text{Total cost} = \text{Fixed cost} + (\text{Variable cost per unit} \times \text{Number of units})$$

If 22,000 books are sold, the total estimated cost is:

$$\text{Total cost} = \$100,000 + (\$13.3333 \times 22,000) = \$393,333$$

If 32,000 books are sold, the total estimated cost is:

$$\text{Total cost} = \$100,000 + (\$13.3333 \times 32,000) = \$526,666$$

Clearly, the visual fit scattergraph approach produces different estimates of total cost than the high-low method provides. Remember, both approaches produce estimates about anticipated future costs. Accuracy cannot be determined until actual costs are incurred. Accountants must exercise judgment in deciding which method is the best approach for the particular circumstances under consideration.

## Regression Method of Cost Estimation

Since the scattergraph is drawn by simple visual inspection, it is subject to human error. A better fit can be obtained using a statistical procedure known as **least-squares regression.**[2] Many of today's spreadsheet programs include a regression procedure. For example, the regression estimates shown in Exhibit 2.26 were generated in an *Excel* spreadsheet by performing the following functions.

### EXHIBIT 2.26

**Excel Spreadsheet Showing the Results of Least-Squares Regression**

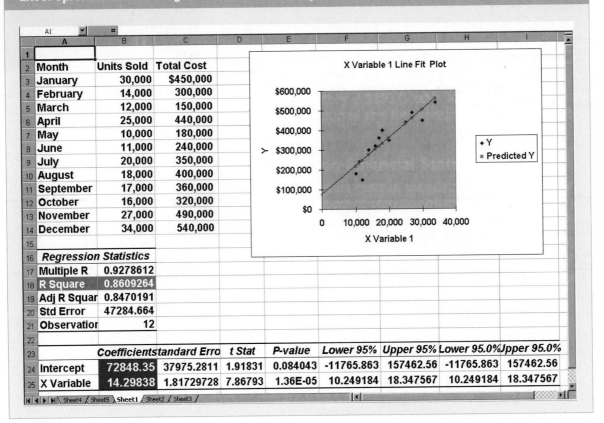

| | A | B | C |
|---|---|---|---|
| 2 | Month | Units Sold | Total Cost |
| 3 | January | 30,000 | $450,000 |
| 4 | February | 14,000 | 300,000 |
| 5 | March | 12,000 | 150,000 |
| 6 | April | 25,000 | 440,000 |
| 7 | May | 10,000 | 180,000 |
| 8 | June | 11,000 | 240,000 |
| 9 | July | 20,000 | 350,000 |
| 10 | August | 18,000 | 400,000 |
| 11 | September | 17,000 | 360,000 |
| 12 | October | 16,000 | 320,000 |
| 13 | November | 27,000 | 490,000 |
| 14 | December | 34,000 | 540,000 |
| 15 | | | |
| 16 | *Regression Statistics* | | |
| 17 | Multiple R | 0.9278612 | |
| 18 | R Square | 0.8609264 | |
| 19 | Adj R Squar | 0.8470191 | |
| 20 | Std Error | 47284.664 | |
| 21 | Observatior | 12 | |

| | Coefficients | standard Erro | t Stat | P-value | Lower 95% | Upper 95% | Lower 95.0% | Upper 95.0% |
|---|---|---|---|---|---|---|---|---|
| 24 Intercept | 72848.35 | 37975.2811 | 1.91831 | 0.084043 | -11765.863 | 157462.56 | -11765.863 | 157462.56 |
| 25 X Variable | 14.29838 | 1.81729728 | 7.86793 | 1.36E-05 | 10.249184 | 18.347567 | 10.249184 | 18.347567 |

---

[2]Although the least-squares regression is a more accurate method than the high-low method and the visual scattergraph method, the three methods follow the same logical reasoning. Basically, the procedure locates a straight line on a coordinate with the $Y$ axis representing the cost in dollars and the $X$ axis representing the cost driver. In the examples shown in this chapter, the measurement of production in units is used as the cost driver and appears on the $X$ axis. The basic regression model can be explained in the following equation:

$$Y = a + bX$$

Where

$a$ = total fixed cost, or the $Y$ intercept of the regression line
$b$ = variable cost per unit of $X$, or the slope of the regression line
$X$ = independent variable
$Y$ = dependent variable

1. Enter the data in spreadsheet columns[3] (see columns B and C, rows 3 through 14 in Exhibit 2.26).
2. Click the *Data* tab.
3. Click *Data Analysis*.[4]
4. Click *Regression* and then *OK*.
5. Define data ranges and click *Line Fit Plot*.
6. Click *OK*.

### Cost Estimates

The regression function returns a fixed cost estimate of $72,848 and a variable cost estimate of $14.30 per unit. These estimates are highlighted in blue in the spreadsheet shown in Exhibit 2.26. As with the high-low and visual fit scattergraph methods, the *total* fixed cost and variable cost *per unit* estimates computed using regression can be used to predict expected total cost at any volume of activity as follows:

$$\text{Total cost} = \text{Fixed cost} + (\text{Variable cost per unit} \times \text{Number of units})$$

If 22,000 books are sold, the total estimated cost is:

$$\text{Total cost} = \$72,848 + (\$14.30 \times 22,000) = \$387,448$$

If 32,000 books are sold, the total estimated cost is:

$$\text{Total cost} = \$72,848 + (\$14.30 \times 32,000) = \$530,448$$

As with the high-low method, **regression analysis** can be skewed by data points that are not representative of the complete data set. Here also, such outliers can be identified using visual fit scattergraphs. Again, management accountants must use common sense when interpreting the cost estimates. Choosing among the high-low method, visual fit scattergraphs, or regression analysis requires judgment. All three methods may be used to evaluate the consistency of the results.

### Regression Statistics

An advantage of the regression method is that it provides statistics that give insight as to the reliability of the cost estimates. The R Square ($R^2$), highlighted in red in Exhibit 2.26, is the most commonly used measure of reliability. The **$R^2$ statistic** represents the percentage of change in the dependent variable (total cost) that is explained by a change in the independent variable (units sold). In the case of Rainy Day Books, the $R^2$ suggests that 86% of the change in the total monthly cost of operating a new store is caused by a change in the number of books sold. In other words, some factors other than the number of books sold also affect total costs. For example, the weight and size of the books, as well as the number sold, may affect shipping costs.

The $R^2$ values vary between zero and 100 percent. Higher $R^2$ values suggest that the independent variable more strongly influences the dependent variable. For Rainy Day Books, the relatively high $R^2$ of 86% suggests that the number of books sold will significantly affect the total cost of operating a new store.

## Multiple Regression Analysis

As discussed above, Rainy Day Books' dependent variable (total cost) is influenced by more factors than the single independent variable (units sold). **Multiple regression analysis** is a statistical tool that permits analysis of how a number of independent variables

[3]Statistical reliability requires an information set that includes more than 30 data points. The illustration shown here has been limited in size to simplify the demonstration.

[4]If the data tab does not contain a data analysis option, it is likely that the statistical functions have not been activated in your program. You will need to consult the *Excel* user manual or help routine for instructions to activate the statistical functions.

simultaneously affect a dependent variable. Multiple regression analysis can improve the accuracy of fixed and variable cost estimates. A trial and error process using multiple regression analysis is frequently used to assess the relative importance of a variety of independent variables. The regression analysis is performed repeatedly, dropping and adding independent variables, until an acceptable level of accuracy is achieved.

## << A Look Back

To plan and control business operations effectively, managers need to understand how different costs behave in relation to changes in the volume of activity. Total *fixed cost* remains constant when activity changes. Fixed cost per unit decreases with increases in activity and increases with decreases in activity. In contrast, total *variable cost* increases proportionately with increases in activity and decreases proportionately with decreases in activity. Variable cost per unit remains constant regardless of activity levels. The definitions of fixed and variable costs have meaning only within the context of a specified range of activity (the relevant range) for a defined period of time. In addition, cost behavior depends on the relevant volume measure (a store manager's salary is fixed relative to the number of customers visiting a particular store but is variable relative to the number of stores operated). A mixed cost has both fixed and variable cost components.

Fixed costs allow companies to take advantage of *operating leverage*. With operating leverage, each additional sale decreases the cost per unit. This principle allows a small percentage change in volume of revenue to cause a significantly larger percentage change in profits. The *magnitude of operating leverage* can be determined by dividing the contribution margin by net income. When all costs are fixed and revenues have covered fixed costs, each additional dollar of revenue represents pure profit. Having a fixed cost structure (employing operating leverage) offers a company both risks and rewards. If sales volume increases, costs do not increase, allowing profits to soar. Alternatively, if sales volume decreases, costs do not decrease and profits decline significantly more than revenues. Companies with high variable costs in relation to fixed costs do not experience as great a level of operating leverage. Their costs increase or decrease in proportion to changes in revenue. These companies face less risk but fail to reap disproportionately higher profits when volume soars.

Under the contribution margin approach, variable costs are subtracted from revenue to determine the *contribution margin*. Fixed costs are then subtracted from the contribution margin to determine net income. The contribution margin represents the amount available to pay fixed costs and provide a profit. Although not permitted by GAAP for external reporting, many companies use the contribution margin format for internal reporting purposes.

*Cost per unit* is an average cost that is easier to compute than the actual cost of each unit and is more relevant to decision making than actual cost. Accountants must use judgment when choosing the time span from which to draw data for computing the average cost per unit. Distortions can result from using either too long or too short a time span.

Fixed and variable costs can be estimated using such tools as the *high-low method, scattergraphs* and regression analysis. The high-low method and scattergraphs are easy to use. Regression analysis is more accurate.

## >> A Look Forward

The next chapter will show you how changes in cost, volume, and pricing affect profitability. You will learn to determine the number of units of product that must be produced and sold in order to break even (the number of units that will produce an amount of revenue that is exactly equal to total cost). You will learn to establish the price of a product using a cost-plus pricing approach and to establish the cost of a product using a target-pricing approach. Finally, the chapter will show you how to use a break-even chart to examine potential profitability over a range of operating activity and how to use a technique known as *sensitivity analysis* to examine how simultaneous changes in sales price, volume, fixed costs, and variable costs affect profitability.

**A step-by-step audio-narrated series of slides is provided on the text website at www.mhhe.com/edmonds2011.**

## SELF-STUDY REVIEW PROBLEM

Mensa Mountaineering Company (MMC) provides guided mountain climbing expeditions in the Rocky Mountains. Its only major expense is guide salaries; it pays each guide $4,800 per climbing expedition. MMC charges its customers $1,500 per expedition and expects to take five climbers on each expedition.

### Part 1

Base your answers on the preceding information.

**Required**

a. Determine the total cost of guide salaries and the cost of guide salaries per climber assuming that four, five, or six climbers are included in a trip. Relative to the number of climbers in a single expedition, is the cost of guides a fixed or a variable cost?

b. Relative to the number of expeditions, is the cost of guides a fixed or a variable cost?

c. Determine the profit of an expedition assuming that five climbers are included in the trip.

d. Determine the profit assuming a 20 percent increase (six climbers total) in expedition revenue. What is the percentage change in profitability?

e. Determine the profit assuming a 20 percent decrease (four climbers total) in expedition revenue. What is the percentage change in profitability?

f. Explain why a 20 percent shift in revenue produces more than a 20 percent shift in profitability. What term describes this phenomenon?

### Part 2

Assume that the guides offer to make the climbs for a percentage of expedition fees. Specifically, MMC will pay guides $960 per climber on the expedition. Assume also that the expedition fee charged to climbers remains at $1,500 per climber.

**Required**

g. Determine the total cost of guide salaries and the cost of guide salaries per climber assuming that four, five, or six climbers are included in a trip. Relative to the number of climbers in a single expedition, is the cost of guides a fixed or a variable cost?

h. Relative to the number of expeditions, is the cost of guides a fixed or a variable cost?

i. Determine the profit of an expedition assuming that five climbers are included in the trip.

j. Determine the profit assuming a 20 percent increase (six climbers total) in expedition revenue. What is the percentage change in profitability?

k. Determine the profit assuming a 20 percent decrease (four climbers total) in expedition revenue. What is the percentage change in profitability?

l. Explain why a 20 percent shift in revenue does not produce more than a 20 percent shift in profitability.

### Solution to Part 1, Requirement a

| Number of climbers (a) | 4 | 5 | 6 |
|---|---|---|---|
| Total cost of guide salaries (b) | $4,800 | $4,800 | $4,800 |
| Cost per climber (b ÷ a) | 1,200 | 960 | 800 |

Since the total cost remains constant (fixed) regardless of the number of climbers on a particular expedition, the cost is classified as fixed. Note that the cost per climber decreases as the number of climbers increases. This is the *per-unit* behavior pattern of a fixed cost.

### Solution to Part 1, Requirement b

Since the total cost of guide salaries changes proportionately each time the number of expeditions increases or decreases, the cost of salaries is variable relative to the number of expeditions.

### Solution to Part 1, Requirements c, d, and e

| Number of Climbers | 4 | Percentage Change | 5 | Percentage Change | 6 |
|---|---|---|---|---|---|
| Revenue ($1,500 per climber) | $6,000 | ⇐ (20%) ⇐ | $7,500 | ⇒ +20% ⇒ | $9,000 |
| Cost of guide salaries (fixed) | 4,800 | | 4,800 | | 4,800 |
| Net income | $1,200 | ⇐ (55.6%) ⇐ | $2,700 | ⇒ +55.6% ⇒ | $4,200 |

Percentage change in revenue: ±$1,500 ÷ $7,500 = ±20%
Percentage change in profit: ±$1,500 ÷ $2,700 = ±55.6%

### Solution to Part 1, Requirement f

Since the cost of guide salaries remains fixed while volume (number of climbers) changes, the change in net income, measured in absolute dollars, exactly matches the change in revenue. More specifically, each time MMC increases the number of climbers by one, revenue and net income increase by $1,500. Since the base figure for net income ($2,700) is lower than the base figure for revenue ($7,500), the percentage change in net income ($1,500 ÷ $2,700 = 55.6%) is higher than percentage change in revenue ($1,500 ÷ $7,500). This phenomenon is called *operating leverage*.

### Solution for Part 2, Requirement g

| Number of climbers (a) | 4 | 5 | 6 |
|---|---|---|---|
| Per climber cost of guide salaries (b) | $ 960 | $ 960 | $ 960 |
| Cost per climber (b × a) | 3,840 | 4,800 | 5,760 |

Since the total cost changes in proportion to changes in the number of climbers, the cost is classified as variable. Note that the cost per climber remains constant (stays the same) as the number of climbers increases or decreases. This is the *per-unit* behavior pattern of a variable cost.

### Solution for Part 2, Requirement h

Since the total cost of guide salaries changes proportionately with changes in the number of expeditions, the cost of salaries is also variable relative to the number of expeditions.

### Solution for Part 2, Requirements i, j, and k

| Number of Climbers | 4 | Percentage Change | 5 | Percentage Change | 6 |
|---|---|---|---|---|---|
| Revenue ($1,500 per climber) | $6,000 | ⇐ (20%) ⇐ | $7,500 | ⇒ +20% ⇒ | $9,000 |
| Cost of guide salaries (variable) | 3,840 | | 4,800 | | 5,760 |
| Net income | $2,160 | ⇐ (20%) ⇐ | $2,700 | ⇒ +20% ⇒ | $3,240 |

Percentage change in revenue: ±$1,500 ÷ $7,500 = ±20%
Percentage change in profit: ±$540 ÷ $2,700 = ±20%

### Solution for Part 2, Requirement l

Since the cost of guide salaries changes when volume (number of climbers) changes, the change in net income is proportionate to the change in revenue. More specifically, each time the number of climbers increases by one, revenue increases by $1,500 and net income increases by $540 ($1,500 − $960). Accordingly, the percentage change in net income will always equal the percentage change in revenue. This means that there is no operating leverage when all costs are variable.

## KEY TERMS

| | | |
|---|---|---|
| Activity base 65 | High-low method 68 | $R^2$ statistic 73 |
| Contribution margin 61 | Least-squares regression 72 | Regression analysis 73 |
| Cost averaging 66 | Mixed costs (semivariable | Relevant range 65 |
| Cost behavior 54 | costs) 64 | Scattergraph 69 |
| Cost structure 59 | Multiple regression analysis 73 | Variable cost 54 |
| Fixed cost 54 | Operating leverage 56 | Visual fit line 70 |

## QUESTIONS

1. Define *fixed cost* and *variable cost* and give an example of each.

2. How can knowing cost behavior relative to volume fluctuations affect decision making?

3. Define the term *operating leverage* and explain how it affects profits.

4. How is operating leverage calculated?

5. Explain the limitations of using operating leverage to predict profitability.

6. If volume is increasing, would a company benefit more from a pure variable or a pure fixed cost structure? Which cost structure would be advantageous if volume is decreasing?

7. When are economies of scale possible? In what types of businesses would you most likely find economies of scale?

8. Explain the risk and rewards to a company that result from having fixed costs.

9. Are companies with predominately fixed cost structures likely to be more profitable?

10. How is the relevant range of activity related to fixed and variable cost? Give an example of how the definitions of these costs become invalid when volume is outside the relevant range.

11. Sam's Garage is trying to determine the cost of providing an oil change. Why would the average cost of this service be more relevant information than the actual cost for each customer?

12. When would the high-low method be appropriate for estimating variable and fixed costs? When would least-squares regression be the most desirable?

13. Which cost structure has the greater risk? Explain.

14. The president of Bright Corporation tells you that he sees a dim future for his company. He feels that his hands are tied because fixed costs are too high. He says that fixed costs do not change and therefore the situation is hopeless. Do you agree? Explain.

15. All costs are variable because if a business ceases operations, its costs fall to zero. Do you agree with the statement? Explain.

16. Because of seasonal fluctuations, Norel Corporation has a problem determining the unit cost of the products it produces. For example, high heating costs during the winter months causes per-unit cost to be higher than per-unit cost in the summer months even when the same number of units of product is produced. Suggest several ways that Norel can improve the computation of per-unit costs.

17. Verna Salsbury tells you that she thinks the terms fixed cost and variable cost are confusing. She notes that fixed cost per unit changes when the number of units changes. Furthermore, variable cost per unit remains fixed regardless of how many units are produced. She concludes that the terminology seems to be backward. Explain why the terminology appears to be contradictory.

 ## MULTIPLE-CHOICE QUESTIONS

**Multiple-choice questions are provided on the text website at www.mhhe.com/edmonds2011.**

## EXERCISES—SERIES A

**All applicable Exercises in Series A are available with McGraw-Hill's *Connect Accounting.***

### Exercise 2-1A   *Identifying cost behavior*

**LO 1**

Deer Valley Kitchen, a fast-food restaurant company, operates a chain of restaurants across the nation. Each restaurant employs eight people; one is a manager paid a salary plus a bonus equal to 3 percent of sales. Other employees, two cooks, one dishwasher, and four waitresses, are paid salaries. Each manager is budgeted $3,000 per month for advertising costs.

**Required**

Classify each of the following costs incurred by Deer Valley Kitchen as fixed, variable, or mixed:

a. Cooks' salaries at a particular location relative to the number of customers.
b. Cost of supplies (cups, plates, spoons, etc.) relative to the number of customers.
c. Manager's compensation relative to the number of customers.
d. Waitresses' salaries relative to the number of restaurants.
e. Advertising costs relative to the number of customers for a particular restaurant.
f. Rental costs relative to the number of restaurants.

**LO 1**

### Exercise 2-2A    *Identifying cost behavior*

At the various activity levels shown, Ambrose Company incurred the following costs:

| | Units sold | 20 | 40 | 60 | 80 | 100 |
|---|---|---|---|---|---|---|
| a. | Depreciation cost per unit | $ 240.00 | $ 120.00 | $ 80.00 | $ 60.00 | $ 48.00 |
| b. | Total rent cost | 3,200.00 | 3,200.00 | 3,200.00 | 3,200.00 | 3,200.00 |
| c. | Total cost of shopping bags | 2.00 | 4.00 | 6.00 | 8.00 | 10.00 |
| d. | Cost per unit of merchandise sold | 90.00 | 90.00 | 90.00 | 90.00 | 90.00 |
| e. | Rental cost per unit of merchandise sold | 36.00 | 18.00 | 12.00 | 9.00 | 7.20 |
| f. | Total phone expense | 80.00 | 100.00 | 120.00 | 140.00 | 160.00 |
| g. | Cost per unit of supplies | 1.00 | 1.00 | 1.00 | 1.00 | 1.00 |
| h. | Total insurance cost | 480.00 | 480.00 | 480.00 | 480.00 | 480.00 |
| i. | Total salary cost | 1,200.00 | 1,600.00 | 2,000.00 | 2,400.00 | 2,800.00 |
| j. | Total cost of goods sold | 1,800.00 | 3,600.00 | 5,400.00 | 7,200.00 | 9,000.00 |

**Required**

Identify each of these costs as fixed, variable, or mixed.

**LO 1**

### Exercise 2-3A    *Determining fixed cost per unit*

Henke Corporation incurs the following annual fixed costs:

| Item | Cost |
|---|---|
| Depreciation | $ 50,000 |
| Officers' salaries | 120,000 |
| Long-term lease | 51,000 |
| Property taxes | 9,000 |

**Required**

Determine the total fixed cost per unit of production, assuming that Henke produces 4,000, 4,500, or 5,000 units.

**LO 1**

### Exercise 2-4A    *Determining total variable cost*

The following variable production costs apply to goods made by Watson Manufacturing Corporation:

| Item | Cost per Unit |
|---|---|
| Materials | $5.00 |
| Labor | 2.50 |
| Variable overhead | 0.25 |
| Total | $7.75 |

**Required**

Determine the total variable production cost, assuming that Watson makes 5,000, 15,000, or 25,000 units.

## Exercise 2-5A   *Fixed versus variable cost behavior*

LO 1

Robbins Company's cost and production data for two recent months included the following:

|  | March | April |
|---|---|---|
| Production (units) | 100 | 250 |
| Rent | $1,500 | $1,500 |
| Utilities | $ 450 | $1,125 |

**Required**

a. Separately calculate the rental cost per unit and the utilities cost per unit for both March and April.
b. Identify which cost is variable and which is fixed. Explain your answer.

## Exercise 2-6A   *Fixed versus variable cost behavior*

LO 1

Lovvern Trophies makes and sells trophies it distributes to little league ballplayers. The company normally produces and sells between 8,000 and 14,000 trophies per year. The following cost data apply to various activity levels:     7000

| Number of trophies | 8,000 | 10,000 | 12,000 | 14,000 |
|---|---|---|---|---|
| **Total costs incurred** | | | | |
| Fixed | $42,000 | | | |
| Variable | 42,000 | | | |
| Total costs | $84,000 | | | |
| **Cost per unit** | | | | |
| Fixed | $ 6.00 | | | |
| Variable | 6.00 | | | |
| Total cost per trophy | $ 12.00 | | | |

**Required**

a. Complete the preceding table by filling in the missing amounts for the levels of activity shown in the first row of the table. Round all cost per unit figures to the nearest whole penny.
b. Explain why the total cost per trophy decreases as the number of trophies increases.

## Exercise 2-7A   *Fixed versus variable cost behavior*

LO 1

Harrell Entertainment sponsors rock concerts. The company is considering a contract to hire a band at a cost of $75,000 per concert.

**Required**

a. What are the total band cost and the cost per person if concert attendance is 2,000, 2,500, 3,000, 3,500, or 4,000?
b. Is the cost of hiring the band a fixed or a variable cost?
c. Draw a graph and plot total cost and cost per unit if attendance is 2,000, 2,500, 3,000, 3,500, or 4,000.
d. Identify Harrell's major business risks and explain how they can be minimized.

## Exercise 2-8A   *Fixed versus variable cost behavior*

LO 1, 2

Harrell Entertainment sells souvenir T-shirts at each rock concert that it sponsors. The shirts cost $9 each. Any excess shirts can be returned to the manufacturer for a full refund of the purchase price. The sales price is $15 per shirt.

**Required**

a. What are the total cost of shirts and cost per shirt if sales amount to 2,000, 2,500, 3,000, 3,500, or 4,000?

b. Is the cost of T-shirts a fixed or a variable cost?

c. Draw a graph and plot total cost and cost per shirt if sales amount to 2,000, 2,500, 3,000, 3,500, or 4,000.

d. Comment on Harrell's likelihood of incurring a loss due to its operating activities.

**LO 1**

## Exercise 2-9A    *Graphing fixed cost behavior*

The following graph setups depict the dollar amount of fixed cost on the vertical axes and the level of activity on the horizontal axes:

**Required**

a. Draw a line that depicts the relationship between total fixed cost and the level of activity.

b. Draw a line that depicts the relationship between fixed cost per unit and the level of activity.

**LO 1**

## Exercise 2-10A    *Graphing variable cost behavior*

The following graph setups depict the dollar amount of variable cost on the vertical axes and the level of activity on the horizontal axes:

**Required**

a. Draw a line that depicts the relationship between total variable cost and the level of activity.

b. Draw a line that depicts the relationship between variable cost per unit and the level of activity.

**LO 1**

## Exercise 2-11A    *Mixed cost at different levels of activity*

Omar Corporation paid one of its sales representatives $4,300 during the month of March. The rep is paid a base salary plus $15 per unit of product sold. During March, the rep sold 200 units.

**Required**

Calculate the total monthly cost of the sales representative's salary for each of the following months:

| Month | April | May | June | July |
|---|---|---|---|---|
| Number of units sold | 240 | 150 | 250 | 160 |
| Total variable cost | | | | |
| Total fixed cost | | | | |
| Total salary cost | | | | |

### Exercise 2-12A    *Using fixed cost as a competitive business strategy*

LO 1, 2, 3

The following income statements illustrate different cost structures for two competing companies:

| Income Statements | | |
|---|---|---|
| **Company Name** | | |
| | Hank | Rank |
| Number of customers (a) | 80 | 80 |
| Sales revenue (a × $250) | $20,000 | $20,000 |
| Variable cost (a × $175) | N/A | (14,000) |
| Variable cost (a × $0) | 0 | N/A |
| Contribution margin | 20,000 | 6,000 |
| Fixed cost | (14,000) | 0 |
| Net income | $ 6,000 | $ 6,000 |

**Required**

a.  Reconstruct Hank's income statement, assuming that it serves 160 customers when it lures 80 customers away from Rank by lowering the sales price to $150 per customer.

b.  Reconstruct Rank's income statement, assuming that it serves 160 customers when it lures 80 customers away from Hank by lowering the sales price to $150 per customer.

c.  Explain why the price-cutting strategy increased Hank Company's profits but caused a net loss for Rank Company.

### Exercise 2-13A    *Using contribution margin format income statement to measure the magnitude of operating leverage*

LO 3, 4

The following income statement was drawn from the records of Ulrich Company, a merchandising firm:

| ULRICH COMPANY<br>Income Statement<br>For the Year Ended December 31, 2011 | |
|---|---|
| Sales revenue (4,000 units × $150) | $600,000 |
| Cost of goods sold (4,000 units × $80) | (320,000) |
| Gross margin | 280,000 |
| Sales commissions (10% of sales) | (60,000) |
| Administrative salaries expense | (90,000) |
| Advertising expense | (40,000) |
| Depreciation expense | (50,000) |
| Shipping and handling expenses (4,000 units × $1) | (4,000) |
| Net income | $ 36,000 |

**Required**

a. Reconstruct the income statement using the contribution margin format.

b. Calculate the magnitude of operating leverage.

c. Use the measure of operating leverage to determine the amount of net income Ulrich will earn if sales increase by 10 percent.

**LO 4**

### Exercise 2-14A   *Assessing the magnitude of operating leverage*

The following income statement applies to Stuart Company for the current year:

| Income Statement | |
| --- | --- |
| Sales revenue (400 units × $25) | $10,000 |
| Variable cost (400 units × $10) | (4,000) |
| Contribution margin | 6,000 |
| Fixed costs | (3,500) |
| Net income | $ 2,500 |

**Required**

a. Use the contribution margin approach to calculate the magnitude of operating leverage.

b. Use the operating leverage measure computed in Requirement *a* to determine the amount of net income that Stuart Company will earn if it experiences a 10 percent increase in revenue. The sales price per unit is not affected.

c. Verify your answer to Requirement *b* by constructing an income statement based on a 10 percent increase in sales revenue. The sales price is not affected. Calculate the percentage change in net income for the two income statements.

**LO 6**

### Exercise 2-15A   *Averaging costs*

Getaway Camps, Inc., leases the land on which it builds camp sites. Getaway is considering opening a new site on land that requires $3,000 of rental payment per month. The variable cost of providing service is expected to be $7 per camper. The following chart shows the number of campers Getaway expects for the first year of operation of the new site:

| Jan. | Feb. | Mar. | Apr. | May | June | July | Aug. | Sept. | Oct. | Nov. | Dec. | Total |
| --- | --- | --- | --- | --- | --- | --- | --- | --- | --- | --- | --- | --- |
| 120 | 250 | 200 | 200 | 300 | 500 | 650 | 650 | 350 | 380 | 100 | 300 | 4,000 |

**Required**

Assuming that Getaway wants to earn $8 per camper, determine the price it should charge for a camp site in February and August.

**LO 7**

### Exercise 2-16A   *Estimating fixed and variable costs using the high-low method*

Knox Boat Company makes inexpensive aluminum fishing boats. Production is seasonal, with considerable activity occurring in the spring and summer. Sales and production tend to decline in the fall and winter months. During 2011, the high point in activity occurred in June when it produced 200 boats at a total cost of $140,000. The low point in production occurred in January when it produced 40 boats at a total cost of $44,000.

**Required**

a. Use the high-low method to estimate the amount of fixed cost incurred each month by Knox Boat Company.

b. Determine the total estimated cost if 100 boats are made.

c. Comment on the strengths and weaknesses of the high-low method.

d. Explain how a visual fit scattergraph could be used to improve accuracy.

## PROBLEMS—SERIES A

**All applicable Problems in Series A are available with McGraw-Hill's Connect Accounting.**

**Problem 2-17A**   *Identifying cost behavior*

**LO 1**

**Required**

Identify the following costs as fixed or variable:

Costs related to plane trips between Seattle, Washington, and Orlando, Florida, follow. Pilots are paid on a per-trip basis.

  **a.** Pilots' salaries relative to the number of trips flown.
  **b.** Depreciation relative to the number of planes in service.
  **c.** Cost of refreshments relative to the number of passengers.
  **d.** Pilots' salaries relative to the number of passengers on a particular trip.
  **e.** Cost of a maintenance check relative to the number of passengers on a particular trip.
  **f.** Fuel costs relative to the number of trips.

First Federal Bank operates several branch offices in grocery stores. Each branch employs a supervisor and two tellers.

  **g.** Tellers' salaries relative to the number of tellers in a particular district.
  **h.** Supplies cost relative to the number of transactions processed in a particular branch.
  **i.** Tellers' salaries relative to the number of customers served at a particular branch.
  **j.** Supervisors' salaries relative to the number of branches operated.
  **k.** Supervisors' salaries relative to the number of customers served in a particular branch.
  **l.** Facility rental costs relative to the size of customer deposits.

Costs related to operating a fast-food restaurant follow.

  **m.** Depreciation of equipment relative to the number of restaurants.
  **n.** Building rental cost relative to the number of customers served in a particular restaurant.
  **o.** Manager's salary of a particular store relative to the number of employees.
  **p.** Food cost relative to the number of customers.
  **q.** Utility cost relative to the number of restaurants in operation.
  **r.** Company president's salary relative to the number of restaurants in operation.
  **s.** Land costs relative to the number of hamburgers sold at a particular restaurant.
  **t.** Depreciation of equipment relative to the number of customers served at a particular restaurant.

**Problem 2-18A**   *Cost behavior and averaging*

**LO 1, 6**

**eXcel**

Carlia Weaver has decided to start Carlia Cleaning, a residential housecleaning service company. She is able to rent cleaning equipment at a cost of $750 per month. Labor costs are expected to be $75 per house cleaned and supplies are expected to cost $6 per house.

**Required**

  **a.** Determine the total expected cost of equipment rental and the average expected cost of equipment rental per house cleaned, assuming that Carlia Cleaning cleans 10, 20, or 30 houses during one month. Is the cost of equipment a fixed or a variable cost?
  **b.** Determine the total expected cost of labor and the average expected cost of labor per house cleaned, assuming that Carlia Cleaning cleans 10, 20, or 30 houses during one month. Is the cost of labor a fixed or a variable cost?
  **c.** Determine the total expected cost of supplies and the average expected cost of supplies per house cleaned, assuming that Carlia Cleaning cleans 10, 20, or 30 houses during one month. Is the cost of supplies a fixed or a variable cost?
  **d.** Determine the total expected cost of cleaning houses, assuming that Carlia Cleaning cleans 10, 20, or 30 houses during one month.

**CHECK FIGURES**
c. Total supplies cost for cleaning 30 houses: $180
d. Total cost for 20 houses: $2,370

e. Determine the average expected cost per house, assuming that Carlia Cleaning cleans 10, 20, or 30 houses during one month. Why does the cost per unit decrease as the number of houses increases?

f. If Ms. Weaver tells you that she prices her services at 25 percent above cost, would you assume that she means average or actual cost? Why?

### Problem 2-19A    *Context-sensitive nature of cost behavior classifications*

Pacific Bank's start-up division establishes new branch banks. Each branch opens with three tellers. Total teller cost per branch is $90,000 per year. The three tellers combined can process up to 90,000 customer transactions per year. If a branch does not attain a volume of at least 60,000 transactions during its first year of operations, it is closed. If the demand for services exceeds 90,000 transactions, an additional teller is hired, and the branch is transferred from the start-up division to regular operations.

**Required**

a. What is the relevant range of activity for new branch banks?

b. Determine the amount of teller cost in total and the average teller cost per transaction for a branch that processes 60,000, 70,000, 80,000, or 90,000 transactions. In this case (the activity base is the number of transactions for a specific branch), is the teller cost a fixed or a variable cost?

c. Determine the amount of teller cost in total and the average teller cost per branch for Pacific Bank, assuming that the start-up division operates 10, 15, or 25 branches. In this case (the activity base is the number of branches), is the teller cost a fixed or a variable cost?

### Problem 2-20A    *Context-sensitive nature of cost behavior classifications*

Susan Hicks operates a sales booth in computer software trade shows, selling an accounting software package, *Dollar System.* She purchases the package from a software manufacturer for $175 each. Booth space at the convention hall costs $10,000 per show.

**Required**

a. Sales at past trade shows have ranged between 200 and 400 software packages per show. Determine the average cost of sales per unit if Ms. Hicks sells 200, 250, 300, 350, or 400 units of *Dollar System* at a trade show. Use the following chart to organize your answer. Is the cost of booth space fixed or variable?

| | Sales Volume in Units (a) | | | | |
|---|---|---|---|---|---|
| | 200 | 250 | 300 | 350 | 400 |
| Total cost of software (a × $175) | $35,000 | | | | |
| Total cost of booth rental | 10,000 | | | | |
| Total cost of sales (b) | $45,000 | | | | |
| Average cost per unit (b ÷ a) | $225.00 | | | | |

b. If Ms. Hicks wants to earn a $50 profit on each package of software she sells at a trade show, what price must she charge at sales volumes of 200, 250, 300, 350, or 400 units?

c. Record the total cost of booth space if Ms. Hicks attends one, two, three, four, or five trade shows. Record your answers in the following chart. Is the cost of booth space fixed or variable relative to the number of shows attended?

| | Number of Trade Shows Attended | | | | |
|---|---|---|---|---|---|
| | 1 | 2 | 3 | 4 | 5 |
| Total cost of booth rental | $10,000 | | | | |

d.  Ms. Hicks provides decorative shopping bags to customers who purchase software packages. Some customers take the bags; others do not. Some customers stuff more than one software package into a single bag. The number of bags varies in relation to the number of units sold, but the relationship is not proportional. Assume that Ms. Hicks uses $30 of bags for every 50 software packages sold. What is the additional cost per unit sold? Is the cost fixed or variable?

## Problem 2-21A  *Effects of operating leverage on profitability*

LO 1, 2

Webster Training Services (WTS) provides instruction on the use of computer software for the employees of its corporate clients. It offers courses in the clients' offices on the clients' equipment. The only major expense WTS incurs is instructor salaries; it pays instructors $5,000 per course taught. WTS recently agreed to offer a course of instruction to the employees of Chambers Incorporated at a price of $400 per student. Chambers estimated that 20 students would attend the course.

**CHECK FIGURES**
Part 1, b: $2,200
Part 2, h: $3,000 & 10%
Part 3, k: cost per student for 22 students: $25

Base your answers on the preceding information.

### Part 1:

**Required**

a.  Relative to the number of students in a single course, is the cost of instruction a fixed or a variable cost?

b.  Determine the profit, assuming that 20 students attend the course.

c.  Determine the profit, assuming a 10 percent increase in enrollment (i.e., enrollment increases to 22 students). What is the percentage change in profitability?

d.  Determine the profit, assuming a 10 percent decrease in enrollment (i.e., enrollment decreases to 18 students). What is the percentage change in profitability?

e.  Explain why a 10 percent shift in enrollment produces more than a 10 percent shift in profitability. Use the term that identifies this phenomenon.

### Part 2:

The instructor has offered to teach the course for a percentage of tuition fees. Specifically, she wants $250 per person attending the class. Assume that the tuition fee remains at $400 per student.

**Required**

f.  Is the cost of instruction a fixed or a variable cost?

g.  Determine the profit, assuming that 20 students take the course.

h.  Determine the profit, assuming a 10 percent increase in enrollment (i.e., enrollment increases to 22 students). What is the percentage change in profitability?

i.  Determine the profit, assuming a 10 percent decrease in enrollment (i.e., enrollment decreases to 18 students). What is the percentage change in profitability?

j.  Explain why a 10 percent shift in enrollment produces a proportional 20 percent shift in profitability.

### Part 3:

WTS sells a workbook with printed material unique to each course to each student who attends the course. Any workbooks that are not sold must be destroyed. Prior to the first class, WTS printed 20 copies of the books based on the client's estimate of the number of people who would attend the course. Each workbook costs $25 and is sold to course participants for $40. This cost includes a royalty fee paid to the author and the cost of duplication.

**Required**

k.  Calculate the workbook cost in total and per student, assuming that 18, 20, or 22 students attempt to attend the course.

l.  Classify the cost of workbooks as fixed or variable relative to the number of students attending the course.

m.  Discuss the risk of holding inventory as it applies to the workbooks.

n.  Explain how a just-in-time inventory system can reduce the cost and risk of holding inventory.

**CHECK FIGURES**
a. Eastern NI: $810
b. NI: $2,610

**Problem 2-22A**   *Effects of fixed and variable cost behavior on the risk and rewards of business opportunities*

Eastern and Western Universities offer executive training courses to corporate clients. Eastern pays its instructors $5,310 per course taught. Western pays its instructors $295 per student enrolled in the class. Both universities charge executives a $340 tuition fee per course attended.

**Required**

a. Prepare income statements for Eastern and Western, assuming that 18 students attend a course.

b. Eastern University embarks on a strategy to entice students from Western University by lowering its tuition to $220 per course. Prepare an income statement for Eastern assuming that the university is successful and enrolls 36 students in its course.

c. Western University embarks on a strategy to entice students from Eastern University by lowering its tuition to $220 per course. Prepare an income statement for Western, assuming that the university is successful and enrolls 36 students in its course.

d. Explain why the strategy described in Requirement *b* produced a profit but the same strategy described in Requirement *c* produced a loss.

e. Prepare income statements for Eastern and Western Universities, assuming that 15 students attend a course, and assuming that both universities charge executives a $340 tuition fee per course attended.

f. It is always better to have fixed rather than variable cost. Explain why this statement is false.

g. It is always better to have variable rather than fixed cost. Explain why this statement is false.

**LO 4**

**Problem 2-23A**   *Analyzing operating leverage*

Justin Zinder is a venture capitalist facing two alternative investment opportunities. He intends to invest $1 million in a start-up firm. He is nervous, however, about future economic volatility. He asks you to analyze the following financial data for the past year's operations of the two firms he is considering and give him some business advice.

| | Company Name | |
| --- | --- | --- |
| | **Ensley** | **Kelley** |
| Variable cost per unit (a) | $ 21.00 | $ 10.50 |
| Sales revenue (8,000 units × $28) | $224,000 | $224,000 |
| Variable cost (8,000 units × a) | (168,000) | (84,000) |
| Contribution margin | $ 56,000 | $140,000 |
| Fixed cost | (25,000) | (109,000) |
| Net income | $ 31,000 | $ 31,000 |

**CHECK FIGURES**
b. % of change for Kelley: 45.16
c. % of change for Ensley: (18.06)

**Required**

a. Use the contribution margin approach to compute the operating leverage for each firm.

b. If the economy expands in coming years, Ensley and Kelley will both enjoy a 10 percent per year increase in sales, assuming that the selling price remains unchanged. Compute the change in net income for each firm in dollar amount and in percentage. (*Note:* Since the number of units increases, both revenue and variable cost will increase.)

c. If the economy contracts in coming years, Ensley and Kelley will both suffer a 10 percent decrease in sales volume, assuming that the selling price remains unchanged. Compute the change in net income for each firm in dollar amount and in percentage. (*Note:* Since the number of units decreases, both total revenue and total variable cost will decrease.)

d. Write a memo to Justin Zinder with your analyses and advice.

**LO 6**

**Problem 2-24A**   *Selecting the appropriate time period for cost averaging*

Trinkle Cinemas is considering a contract to rent a movie for $1,800 per day. The contract requires a minimum one-week rental period. Estimated attendance is as follows:

| Monday | Tuesday | Wednesday | Thursday | Friday | Saturday | Sunday |
|--------|---------|-----------|----------|--------|----------|--------|
| 450 | 300 | 200 | 550 | 1,000 | 1,000 | 500 |

**CHECK FIGURES**
a. Monday: $4.00
b. Friday: $4.30

**Required**

a. Determine the average cost per person of the movie rental contract separately for each day.

b. Suppose that Trinkle chooses to price movie tickets at cost as computed in Requirement *a* plus $2.50. What price would it charge per ticket on each day of the week?

c. Use weekly averaging to determine a reasonable price to charge for movie tickets.

d. Comment on why weekly averaging may be more useful to business managers than daily averaging.

## Problem 2-25A    *Identifying relevant issues for cost averaging*

**LO 6**

Cliff Corporation, offers mountain-climbing expeditions for its customers, providing food, equipment, and guides. Climbs normally require one week to complete. The company's accountant is reviewing historical cost data to establish a pricing strategy for the coming year. The accountant has prepared the following table showing cost data for the most recent climb, the company's average cost per year, and the five-year average cost.

|  | Span of Time | | |
|--|--------------|--|--|
|  | **Recent Climb** | **One Year** | **Five Years** |
| Total cost of climbs (a) | $4,800 | $266,000 | $1,125,000 |
| Number of climbers (b) | 10 | 560 | 2,500 |
| Cost per climber (a ÷ b) | $480 | $475 | $450 |

**Required**

Write a memo that explains the potential advantages and disadvantages of using each of the per-unit cost figures as a basis for establishing a price to charge climbers during the coming year. What other factors must be considered in developing a pricing strategy?

## Problem 2-26A    *Estimating fixed and variable cost*

**LO 7**

Newteh Computer Services, Inc., has been in business for six months. The following are basic operating data for that period.

**CHECK FIGURE**
b. FC = $1,540

|  | Month | | | | | |
|--|-------|--|--|--|--|--|
|  | **July** | **Aug.** | **Sept.** | **Oct.** | **Nov.** | **Dec.** |
| Service hours | 120 | 136 | 260 | 420 | 320 | 330 |
| Revenue | $6,000 | $6,800 | $13,000 | $21,000 | $16,000 | $16,500 |
| Operating costs | $4,300 | $5,300 | $ 7,100 | $11,200 | $ 9,100 | $10,600 |

**Required**

a. What is the average service revenue per hour for the six-month time period?

b. Use the high-low method to estimate the total monthly fixed cost and the variable cost per hour.

c. Determine the average contribution margin per hour.

d. Use the scattergraph method to estimate the total monthly fixed cost and the variable cost per hour.

e. Compare the results of the two methods and comment on the difference.

## Problem 2-27A    *Estimating fixed and variable cost*

**LO 7**

Nabil Woodcraft Company (NWC) manufactures "antique" wooden cabinets to house modern radio and CD players. NWC began operations in January of last year. Paul Nabil, the owner, asks for your assistance. He believes that he needs to better understand the cost of the cabinets for pricing purposes. You have collected the following data concerning actual production over the past year:

**CHECK FIGURE**
c. VC/unit: $5

| Month | Number of Cabinets Produced | Total Cost |
|---|---|---|
| January | 800 | $21,000 |
| February | 3,600 | 32,500 |
| March | 1,960 | 29,500 |
| April | 600 | 18,600 |
| May | 1,600 | 29,000 |
| June | 1,300 | 27,000 |
| July | 1,100 | 25,600 |
| August | 1,800 | 31,000 |
| September | 2,280 | 32,000 |
| October | 2,940 | 31,500 |
| November | 3,280 | 32,000 |
| December | 400 | 16,500 |

**Required**

a. To understand the department's cost behavior, you decide to plot the points on graph paper and sketch a total cost line.

   (1) Enter the number of units and their costs in increasing order.

   (2) Plot the points on the graph.

   (3) Sketch a graph so the line "splits" all of the points (half of the points appear above and half below the line).

   (4) Using the line you just sketched, visually estimate the total cost to produce 2,000 units.

b. Using the high-low method, compute the total cost equation for the preceding data.

   (1) Compute the variable cost per unit.

   (2) Compute total fixed costs.

   (3) Sketch a line between the high and low points on your graph.

   (4) Calculate the total cost assuming 2,000 cabinets are made.

c. Comment on which method you believe is better.

**LO 7**

**CHECK FIGURES**
b. VC/hr: $15.19
FC: $1,142

**Problem 2-28A   Estimating fixed and variable cost using the regression method**

Latif and Koehler Tax Services Company has 31 branch offices in the nation. Each office has about three to six professional accountants and one to two secretaries. In a busy season, the office manager, who is also a professional accountant, can hire temporary employees for support work such as document filing and typing. Josh Lane, the president, is wondering whether he should expand his business by opening more offices. One of the factors that he is considering is how to estimate office support costs. Vineeta Riley, the accountant, collected the following cost data for all 31 offices:

| Branch | Professional Hours | Support Costs | Branch | Professional Hours | Support Costs |
|---|---|---|---|---|---|
| A1 | 225 | $4,241 | F2 | 165 | $3,856 |
| A2 | 113 | 3,435 | G1 | 358 | 5,936 |
| A3 | 387 | 6,398 | G2 | 471 | 8,615 |
| A4 | 412 | 6,502 | G3 | 492 | 9,639 |
| B1 | 258 | 4,140 | G4 | 328 | 5,968 |
| B2 | 146 | 3,368 | G5 | 359 | 7,115 |
| B3 | 275 | 3,820 | G6 | 174 | 3,287 |
| D1 | 364 | 6,396 | H1 | 394 | 7,515 |
| D2 | 190 | 3,946 | H2 | 386 | 7,374 |
| D3 | 484 | 8,189 | I2 | 279 | 5,376 |
| D4 | 251 | 4,506 | I5 | 314 | 5,784 |
| D5 | 377 | 6,744 | J2 | 283 | 5,426 |
| E1 | 264 | 4,645 | J3 | 198 | 4,418 |
| E2 | 169 | 6,073 | J4 | 226 | 4,506 |
| E3 | 338 | 6,290 | J5 | 341 | 6,488 |
| F1 | 437 | 9,113 | | | |

**Required**

a. The company uses the number of professional hours as the cost driver for office support costs. Use an algebraic equation to describe how total office support costs can be estimated.

b. Use a spreadsheet program to perform a regression analysis. Use office support costs as the dependent variable ($Y$) and the professional hours as the independent variable ($X$). Determine the total fixed cost per office and variable cost per professional hour.

c. Identify the $R^2$ statistic provided by the Excel program and explain what it means.

d. Mr. Lane plans to open a new branch office in a Chicago suburb. He expects that the monthly professional hours will be 3,000. Estimate the total office support cost for Mr. Lane. What portion of the total cost is fixed and what portion is variable?

e. Explain how multiple regression analysis could be used to improve the accuracy of the cost estimates.

# EXERCISES—SERIES B

### Exercise 2-1B   *Identifying cost behavior*                                      LO 1

Parker Copies Company provides professional copying services to customers through the 35 copy stores it operates in the southwestern United States. Each store employs a manager and four assistants. The manager earns $4,000 per month plus a bonus of 3 percent of sales. The assistants earn hourly wages. Each copy store costs $3,000 per month to lease. The company spends $5,000 per month on corporate-level advertising and promotion.

**Required**

Classify each of the following costs incurred by Parker Copies as fixed, variable, or mixed:

a. Lease cost relative to the number of stores.
b. Advertising and promotion costs relative to the number of copies a particular store makes.
c. Lease cost relative to the number of copies made for customers.
d. Assistants' wages relative to the number of copies made for customers.
e. Store manager's salary relative to the number of copies made for customers.
f. Cost of paper relative to the number of copies made for customers.

### Exercise 2-2B   *Identifying cost behavior*                                      LO 1

At the various sales levels shown, Kukreja Company incurred the following costs:

| | Units sold | 50 | 100 | 150 | 200 | 250 |
|---|---|---|---|---|---|---|
| a. | Total insurance cost | $ 500.00 | $ 500.00 | $ 500.00 | $ 500.00 | $ 500.00 |
| b. | Total salary cost | 1,500.00 | 2,000.00 | 2,500.00 | 3,000.00 | 3,500.00 |
| c. | Cost per unit of merchandise sold | 8.00 | 8.00 | 8.00 | 8.00 | 8.00 |
| d. | Total cost of goods sold | 4,000.00 | 8,000.00 | 12,000.00 | 16,000.00 | 20,000.00 |
| e. | Depreciation cost per unit | 30.00 | 15.00 | 10.00 | 7.50 | 6.00 |
| f. | Total rent cost | 600.00 | 600.00 | 600.00 | 600.00 | 600.00 |
| g. | Total shipping cost | 40.00 | 80.00 | 120.00 | 160.00 | 200.00 |
| h. | Rent cost per unit of merchandise sold | 12.00 | 6.00 | 4.00 | 3.00 | 2.40 |
| i. | Total utility cost | 200.00 | 300.00 | 400.00 | 500.00 | 600.00 |
| j. | Supplies cost per unit | 4.00 | 4.00 | 4.00 | 4.00 | 4.00 |

**Required**

Identify each of these costs as fixed, variable, or mixed.

**LO 1**

### Exercise 2-3B   *Determining fixed cost per unit*

Miranda Corporation incurs the following annual fixed production costs:

| Item | Cost |
|---|---|
| Insurance cost | $ 50,000 |
| Patent amortization cost | 400,000 |
| Depreciation cost | 250,000 |
| Property tax cost | 100,000 |

**Required**

Determine the total fixed production cost per unit if Miranda produces 10,000, 20,000, or 50,000 units.

**LO 1**

### Exercise 2-4B   *Determining total variable cost*

The following variable manufacturing costs apply to goods produced by King Manufacturing Corporation:

| Item | Cost per Unit |
|---|---|
| Materials | $2.80 |
| Labor | 2.40 |
| Variable overhead | 2.00 |
| Total | $7.20 |

**Required**

Determine the total variable manufacturing cost if King produces 4,000, 6,000, or 8,000 units.

**LO 1**

### Exercise 2-5B   *Fixed versus variable cost behavior*

Griffin Company's production and total cost data for two recent months follow:

| | January | February |
|---|---|---|
| Units produced | 1,000 | 500 |
| Total depreciation cost | $4,000 | $4,000 |
| Total factory supplies cost | $2,000 | $1,000 |

**Required**

a. Separately calculate the depreciation cost per unit and the factory supplies cost per unit for both January and February.
b. Identify which cost is variable and which is fixed. Explain your answer.

**LO 1**

### Exercise 2-6B   *Fixed versus variable cost behavior*

Satcher Chairs Corporation produces ergonomically designed chairs favored by architects. The company normally produces and sells from 4,000 to 10,000 chairs per year. The following cost data apply to various production activity levels:

| Number of Chairs | 4,000 | 6,000 | 8,000 | 10,000 |
|---|---|---|---|---|
| Total costs incurred | | | | |
| Fixed | $ 84,000 | | | |
| Variable | 60,000 | | | |
| Total costs | $144,000 | | | |
| Per-unit chair cost | | | | |
| Fixed | $ 21.00 | | | |
| Variable | 15.00 | | | |
| Total cost per chair | $ 36.00 | | | |

**Required**

a. Complete the preceding table by filling in the missing amounts for the levels of activity shown in the first row of the table.

b. Explain why the total cost per chair decreases as the number of chairs increases.

## Exercise 2-7B    *Fixed versus variable cost behavior*    LO 1, 2

Dennis Owen needs extra money quickly to help cover some unexpected school expenses. Mr. Owen has learned fortune-telling skills through his long friendship with Joel Allman, who tells fortunes during the day at the city market. Mr. Allman has agreed to let Mr. Owen use his booth to tell fortunes during the evening for a rent of $50 per night.

**Required**

a. What is the booth rental cost both in total and per customer if the number of customers is 5, 10, 15, 20, or 25?

b. Is the cost of renting the fortune-telling booth fixed or variable relative to the number of customers?

c. Draw two graphs. On one, plot total booth rental cost for 5, 10, 15, 20, and 25 customers; on the other, plot booth rental cost per customer for 5, 10, 15, 20, or 25 customers.

d. Mr. Owen has little money. What major business risks would he take by renting the fortune-telling booth? How could he minimize those risks?

## Exercise 2-8B    *Fixed versus variable cost behavior*    LO 1, 2

In the evenings, Dennis Owen works telling fortunes using his friend Joel Allman's booth at the city market. Mr. Allman pays the booth rental, so Mr. Owen has no rental cost. As a courtesy, Mr. Owen provides each customer a soft drink. The drinks cost him $0.50 per customer.

**Required**

a. What is the soft drink cost both in total and per customer if the number of customers is 5, 10, 15, 20, or 25?

b. Is the soft drink cost fixed or variable?

c. Draw two graphs. On one, plot total soft drink cost for 5, 10, 15, 20, and 25 customers; on the other, plot soft drink cost per customer for 5, 10, 15, 20, and 25 customers.

d. Comment on the likelihood that Mr. Owen will incur a loss on this business venture.

## Exercise 2-9B    *Graphing fixed cost behavior*    LO 1

Saeed Computers leases space in a mall at a monthly rental cost of $3,000. The following graph setups depict rental cost on the vertical axes and activity level on the horizontal axes:

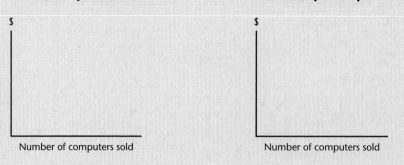

**Required**

a. Draw a line that depicts the relationship between the total monthly rental cost and the number of computers sold.

b. Draw a line that depicts the relationship between rental cost per computer and the number of computers sold.

**LO 1**

### Exercise 2-10B    *Graphing variable cost behavior*

Dubovsky Computers purchases computers from a manufacturer for $500 per computer. The following graph setups depict product cost on the vertical axes and activity level on the horizontal axes:

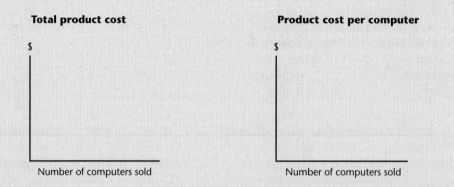

**Required**

a. Draw a line that depicts the relationship between total product cost and the number of computers sold.

b. Draw a line that depicts the relationship between cost per computer and the number of computers sold.

**LO 1**

### Exercise 2-11B    *Mixed cost at different levels of activity*

Blackwell Hats Corporation uses workers in Indonesia to manually weave straw hats. The company pays the workers a daily base wage plus $0.25 per completed hat. On Monday, workers produced 100 hats for which the company paid wages of $70.

**Required**

Calculate the total cost of the workers' wages for each of the following days:

| Day | Monday | Tuesday | Wednesday | Thursday |
|---|---|---|---|---|
| Number of hats woven | 100 | 120 | 160 | 80 |
| Total variable cost | | | | |
| Total fixed cost | | | | |
| Total wages cost | | | | |

**Exercise 2-12B**    *Effect of cost structure on projected profits*    **LO 1, 2**

Bland and Strand compete in the same market. The following budgeted income statements illustrate their cost structures:

| Income Statements | | |
|---|---|---|
| | **Company** | |
| | **Bland** | **Strand** |
| Number of customers (a) | 100 | 100 |
| Sales revenue (a × $100) | $10,000 | $10,000 |
| Variable cost (a × $64) | NA | (6,400) |
| Contribution margin | 10,000 | 3,600 |
| Fixed costs | (6,400) | N/A |
| Net income | $ 3,600 | $ 3,600 |

**Required**

a. Assume that Bland can lure all 100 customers away from Strand by lowering its sales price to $60 per customer. Reconstruct Bland's income statement based on 200 customers.

b. Assume that Strand can lure all 100 customers away from Bland by lowering its sales price to $60 per customer. Reconstruct Strand's income statement based on 200 customers.

c. Why does the price-cutting strategy increase Bland's profits but result in a net loss for Strand?

**Exercise 2-13B**    *Using a contribution margin format income statement to measure    **LO 3, 4**
the magnitude of operating leverage*

Willig Company, a merchandising firm, reported the following operating results:

| Income Statements | |
|---|---|
| Sales revenue (4,000 units × $75) | $ 300,000 |
| Cost of goods sold (4,000 units × $45) | (180,000) |
| Gross margin | 120,000 |
| Sales commissions (10% of sales revenue) | (30,000) |
| Administrative salaries expense | (25,000) |
| Advertising expense | (31,000) |
| Depreciation expense | (24,000) |
| Shipping and handling expense (4,000 units × $1) | (4,000) |
| Net income | $ 6,000 |

**Required**

a. Reconstruct the income statement using the contribution margin format.

b. Calculate the magnitude of operating leverage.

c. Use the measure of operating leverage to determine the amount of net income that Willig will earn if sales revenue increases by 10 percent.

**Exercise 2-14B**    *Assessing the magnitude of operating leverage*    **LO 4**

The following budgeted income statement applies to Biggio Company:

| Income Statement | |
|---|---|
| Sales Revenue (1,000 units × $90) | $ 90,000 |
| Variable Cost (1,000 units × $50) | (50,000) |
| Contribution margin | 40,000 |
| Fixed Costs | (30,000) |
| Net Income | $ 10,000 |

**Required**

a. Use the contribution margin approach to calculate the magnitude of operating leverage.

b. Use the operating leverage measure computed in Requirement *a* to determine the amount of net income that Biggio Company will earn if sales volume increases by 10 percent. Assume the sales price per unit remains unchanged at $90.

c. Verify your answer to Requirement *b* by constructing an alternative income statement based on a 10 percent increase in sales volume. The sales price per unit remains unchanged at $90. Calculate the percentage change in net income for the two income statements.

**LO 6**

### Exercise 2-15B  *Averaging costs*

Nuttall Entertainment Company operates a movie theater that has monthly fixed expenses of $5,000. In addition, the company pays film distributors $1.00 per ticket sold. The following chart shows the number of tickets Nuttall expects to sell in the coming year:

| Jan. | Feb. | Mar. | Apr. | May | June | July | Aug. | Sept. | Oct. | Nov. | Dec. | Total |
|------|------|------|------|------|------|------|------|-------|------|------|------|-------|
| 2,000 | 1,600 | 3,200 | 3,400 | 3,200 | 4,200 | 4,700 | 4,000 | 5,000 | 3,100 | 3,000 | 2,600 | 40,000 |

**Required**

Assume that Nuttall wants to earn $3.00 per movie patron. What price should it charge for a ticket in January and in September?

**LO 7**

### Exercise 2-16B  *Estimating fixed and variable costs using the high-low method*

Conry Ice Cream Company produces various ice cream products for which demand is highly seasonal. The company sells more ice cream in warmer months and less in colder ones. Last year, the high point in production activity occurred in August when Conry produced 50,000 gallons of ice cream at a total cost of $42,000. The low point in production activity occurred in February when the company produced 20,000 gallons of ice cream at a total cost of $33,000.

**Required**

a. Use the high-low method to estimate the amount of fixed cost per month incurred by Conry Ice Cream Company.

b. Determine the total estimated monthly cost when 40,000 gallons of ice cream are produced.

c. What factors could cause the estimate determined in Requirement *b* to be inaccurate?

d. Explain how regression analysis could be used to improve accuracy. Your explanation should include a discussion of the $R^2$ statistic as well as the potential impact of multiple regression analysis.

## PROBLEMS—SERIES B

**LO 1**

### Problem 2-17B  *Identifying cost behavior*

**Required**

Identify the following costs as fixed or variable:

Costs related to operating a retail gasoline company.

a. Depreciation of equipment relative to the number of stations.

b. Cashiers' wages relative to the number of customers served in a station.

c. Salary of a manager of a particular station relative to the number of employees.

d. Gasoline cost relative to the number of customers.

e. Utility cost relative to the number of stations in operation.

f. The company's cost of national TV commercials relative to the number of stations in operation.

g. Depreciation of equipment relative to the number of customers served at a station.

h. Property and real estate taxes relative to the amount of gasoline sold at a particular station.

Costs related to shuttle bus trips between John F. Kennedy International Airport and downtown New York. Each bus driver receives a specific salary per month. A manager schedules bus trips and supervises drivers, and a secretary receives phone calls.

 **i.** Fuel costs relative to the number of passengers on a particular trip.

 **j.** Drivers' salaries relative to the number of trips driven.

 **k.** Office staff salaries relative to the number of passengers on a particular trip.

 **l.** Depreciation relative to the number of buses in service.

 **m.** A driver's salary relative to the number of passengers on a particular trip.

 **n.** Fuel costs relative to the number of trips.

Suzy's Barbershop operates several stores in shopping centers. Each store employs a supervisor and three barbers. Each barber receives a specific salary per month plus a 10 percent commission based on the service revenues he or she has generated.

 **o.** Store rental costs relative to the number of customers.

 **p.** Barbers' commissions relative to the number of customers.

 **q.** Supervisory salaries relative to the number of customers served in a particular store.

 **r.** Barbers' salaries relative to the number of barbers in a particular district.

 **s.** Supplies cost relative to the number of hair services provided in a particular store.

 **t.** Barbers' salaries relative to the number of customers served at a particular store.

## Problem 2-18B  *Cost behavior and averaging*                                    LO 1, 6

Andy Posey asks you to analyze the operating cost of his lawn services business. He has bought the needed equipment with a cash payment of $45,000. Upon your recommendation, he agrees to adopt straight-line depreciation. The equipment has an expected life of three years and no salvage value. Mr. Posey pays his workers $30 per lawn service. Material costs, including fertilizer, pesticide, and supplies, are expected to be $6 per lawn service.

### Required

 **a.** Determine the total cost of equipment depreciation and the average cost of equipment depreciation per lawn service, assuming that Mr. Posey provides 20, 25, or 30 lawn services during one month. Is the cost of equipment a fixed or a variable cost?

 **b.** Determine the total expected cost of labor and the average expected cost of labor per lawn service, assuming that Mr. Posey provides 20, 25, or 30 lawn services during one month. Is the cost of labor a fixed or a variable cost?

 **c.** Determine the total expected cost of materials and the average expected cost of materials per lawn service, assuming that Mr. Posey provides 20, 25, or 30 lawn services during one month. Is the cost of fertilizer, pesticide, and supplies a fixed or a variable cost?

 **d.** Determine the total expected cost per lawn service, assuming that Mr. Posey provides 20, 25, or 30 lawn services during one month.

 **e.** Determine the average expected cost per lawn service, assuming that Mr. Posey provides 20, 25, or 30 lawn services during one month. Why does the cost per unit decrease as the number of lawn services increases?

 **f.** If Mr. Posey tells you that he prices his services at 30 percent above cost, would you assume that he means average or actual cost? Why?

## Problem 2-19B  *Context-sensitive nature of cost behavior classifications*        LO 1

Warren and Carter Tax Services' Development Department is responsible for establishing new community branches. Each branch opens with two tax accountants. Total cost of payroll per branch is $108,000 per year. Together the two accountants can process up to 2,500 simple tax returns per year. The firm's policy requires closing branches that do not reach the quota of 1,500 tax returns per year. On the other hand, the firm hires an additional accountant for a branch and elevates it to the status of a regular operation if the customer demand for services exceeds 2,500 tax returns.

### Required

 **a.** What is the relevant range of activity for a new branch established by the Development Department?

b. Determine the amount of payroll cost in total and the average payroll cost per transaction for a branch that processes 1,500, 2,000, or 2,500 tax returns. In this case (the activity base is the number of tax returns for a specific branch), is the payroll cost a fixed or a variable cost?

c. Determine the amount of payroll cost in total and the average payroll cost per branch for Warren and Carter Tax Services, assuming that the Development Department operates 20, 30, or 40 branches. In this case (the activity base is the number of branches), is the payroll cost a fixed or a variable cost?

LO 1

## Problem 2-20B  *Context-sensitive nature of cost behavior classifications*

Kevin Munden sells a newly developed camera, Sharp Vision. He purchases the cameras from the manufacturer for $70 each and rents a store in a shopping mall for $5,000 per month.

### Required

a. Determine the average cost of sales per unit if Mr. Munden sells 100, 200, 300, 400, or 500 units of Sharp Vision per month. Use the following chart to organize your answer.

|  | Sales Volume in Units (a) | | | | |
|---|---|---|---|---|---|
|  | 100 | 200 | 300 | 400 | 500 |
| Total cost of cameras (a × $70) | $ 7,000 | | | | |
| Total cost of store rental | 5,000 | | | | |
| Total cost of sales (b) | $12,000 | | | | |
| Average cost per unit (b ÷ a) | $120.00 | | | | |

b. If Mr. Munden wants to make a gross profit of $20 on each camera he sells, what price should he charge at sales volumes of 100, 200, 300, 400, or 500 units?

c. Record the total cost of store rental if Mr. Munden opens a camera store at one, two, three, four, or five shopping malls. Record your answers in the following chart. Is the cost of store rental fixed or variable relative to the number of stores opened?

|  | Shopping Malls | | | | |
|---|---|---|---|---|---|
|  | 1 | 2 | 3 | 4 | 5 |
| Total cost of store rental | $5,000 | | | | |

d. Mr. Munden provides decorative ornaments to customers who purchase cameras. Some customers take the ornaments, others do not, and some take more than one. The number of ornaments varies in relation to the number of cameras sold, but the relationship is not proportional. Assume that, on average, Mr. Munden gives away $150 worth of ornaments for every 100 cameras sold. What is the additional cost per camera sold? Is the cost fixed or variable?

LO 1, 2

## Problem 2-21B  *Effects of operating leverage on profitability*

CPAs R Us conducts CPA review courses. Public universities that permit free use of a classroom support the classes. The only major expense incurred by CPAs R Us is the salary of instructors, which is $6,000 per course taught. The company recently planned to offer a review course in Houston for $320 per candidate; it estimated that 50 candidates would attend the course.

Complete these requirements based on the preceding information.

### Part 1:

### Required

a. Relative to the number of CPA candidates in a single course, is the cost of instruction a fixed or a variable cost?

b. Determine the profit, assuming that 50 candidates attend the course.

**c.** Determine the profit, assuming a 10 percent increase in enrollment (i.e., enrollment increases to 55 students). What is the percentage change in profitability?

**d.** Determine the profit, assuming a 10 percent decrease in enrollment (i.e., enrollment decreases to 45 students). What is the percentage change in profitability?

**e.** Explain why a 10 percent shift in enrollment produces more than a 10 percent shift in profitability. Use the term that identifies this phenomenon.

## Part 2:

The instructor has offered to teach the course for a percentage of tuition fees. Specifically, he wants $120 per candidate attending the class. Assume that the tuition fee remains at $320 per candidate.

### Required

**f.** Is the cost of instruction a fixed or a variable cost?

**g.** Determine the profit, assuming that 50 candidates take the course.

**h.** Determine the profit, assuming a 10 percent increase in enrollment (i.e., enrollment increases to 55 students). What is the percentage change in profitability?

**i.** Determine the profit, assuming a 10 percent decrease in enrollment (i.e., enrollment decreases to 45 students). What is the percentage change in profitability?

**j.** Explain why a 10 percent shift in enrollment produces a proportional 10 percent shift in profitability.

## Part 3:

CPAs R Us sells a workbook to each student who attends the course. The workbook contains printed material unique to each course. Workbooks that are not sold must be destroyed. Prior to the first class, CPAs R Us printed 50 copies of the books based on the estimated number of people who would attend the course. Each workbook costs $40 and is sold for $50. This cost includes a royalty fee paid to the author and the cost of duplication.

### Required

**k.** Calculate the total cost and the cost per candidate of the workbooks, assuming that 45, 50, or 55 candidates attempt to attend the course.

**l.** Classify the cost of workbooks as fixed or variable relative to the number of candidates attending the course.

**m.** Discuss the risk of holding inventory as it applies to the workbooks.

**n.** Explain how a just-in-time inventory system can reduce the cost and risk of holding inventory.

## Problem 2-22B   *Effects of fixed and variable cost behavior on the risk and rewards of business opportunities*

**LO 2**

Beach Club and Mountain Club are competing health and recreation clubs in Chicago. They both offer tennis training clinics to adults. Beach pays its coaches $9,000 per season. Mountain pays its coaches $300 per student enrolled in the clinic per season. Both clubs charge a tuition fee of $432 per season.

### Required

**a.** Prepare income statements for Beach and Mountain, assuming that 30 students per season attend each clinic.

**b.** The ambitious new director of Beach Club tries to increase his market share by reducing the club's tuition per student to $250 per clinic. Prepare an income statement for Beach, assuming that the club attracts all of Mountain's customers and therefore is able to enroll 60 students in its clinics.

**c.** Independent of Requirement *b,* Mountain Club tries to lure Beach's students by lowering its price to $210 per student. Prepare an income statement for Mountain, assuming that the club succeeds in enrolling 60 students in its clinics.

**d.** Explain why the strategy described in Requirement *b* produced a profit while the same strategy described in Requirement *c* produced a loss.

e. Prepare an income statement for Beach Club and Mountain Club, assuming that 18 students attend a clinic at the original $432 tuition price.

f. It is always better to have fixed rather than variable cost. Explain why this statement is false.

g. It is always better to have variable rather than fixed cost. Explain why this statement is false.

**LO 5, 6**

### Problem 2-23B   *Analysis of operating leverage*

Rachel Geer has invested in two start-up companies. At the end of the first year, she asks you to evaluate their operating performance. The following operating data apply to the first year:

|  | Company Name | |
|---|---|---|
|  | Ander | Sander |
| Variable cost per unit (a) | $12 | $6 |
| Sales revenue (25,000 units × $16) | $400,000 | $400,000 |
| Variable cost (25,000 units × a) | (300,000) | (150,000) |
| Contribution margin | 100,000 | 250,000 |
| Fixed cost | (50,000) | (200,000) |
| Net income | $ 50,000 | $ 50,000 |

**Required**

a. Use the contribution margin approach to compute the operating leverage for each firm.

b. If the economy expands in the coming year, Ander and Sander will both enjoy a 10 percent per year increase in sales volume, assuming that the selling price remains unchanged. (*Note:* Since the number of units increases, both revenue and variable cost will increase.) Compute the change in net income for each firm in dollar amount and in percentage.

c. If the economy contracts in the following year, Ander and Sander will both suffer a 10 percent decrease in sales volume, assuming that the selling price remains unchanged. (*Note:* Since the number of units decreases, both revenue and variable cost decrease.) Compute the change in net income for each firm in both dollar amount and percentage.

d. Write a memo to Rachel Geer with your evaluation and recommendations.

**LO 6**

### Problem 2-24B   *Selecting the appropriate time period for cost averaging*

The Vaughan Amusement Park is considering signing a contract to hire a circus at a cost of $2,400 per day. The contract requires a minimum performance period of one week. Estimated circus attendance is as follows:

| Monday | Tuesday | Wednesday | Thursday | Friday | Saturday | Sunday |
|---|---|---|---|---|---|---|
| 500 | 450 | 450 | 600 | 950 | 1,500 | 1,400 |

**Required**

a. For each day, determine the average cost of the circus contract per person attending.

b. Suppose that the park prices circus tickets at cost as computed in Requirement *a* plus $1.60. What would be the price per ticket charged on each day of the week?

c. Use weekly averaging to determine a reasonable price to charge for the circus tickets.

d. Comment on why weekly averaging may be more useful to business managers than daily averaging.

**LO 5**

### Problem 2-25B   *Identifying relevant issues for cost averaging*

Sahara Tours, Inc., organizes adventure tours for people interested in visiting a desert environment. A desert tour generally lasts three days. Sahara provides food, equipment, and guides. Larry Jobaria, the president of Sahara Tours, needs to set prices for the coming year. He has available the company's past cost data in the following table:

### Span of Time

| | Recent Tour | One Year | Ten Years |
|---|---|---|---|
| Total cost of tours (a) | $8,000 | $390,000 | $2,700,000 |
| Number of tourists (b) | 32 | 1,500 | 12,000 |
| Cost per tourist (a ÷ b) | $ 250 | $ 260 | $ 225 |

**Required**

Write a memo to Mr. Jobaria explaining the potential advantages and disadvantages of using each of the different per-tourist cost figures as a basis for establishing a price to charge tourists during the coming year. What other factors must Mr. Jobaria consider in developing a pricing strategy?

### Problem 2-26B   *Estimating fixed and variable costs*                                    LO 7

Hanno Legal Services provides legal advice to clients. The following data apply to the first six months of operation:

### Month

| | Jan. | Feb. | Mar. | Apr. | May | June |
|---|---|---|---|---|---|---|
| Service hours | 60 | 80 | 120 | 160 | 180 | 200 |
| Revenue | $4,800 | $6,400 | $9,600 | $12,800 | $14,400 | $16,000 |
| Operating costs | 6,200 | 7,100 | 8,380 | 8,500 | 8,761 | 9,700 |

**Required**

a. What is the average service revenue per hour for the six-month time period?
b. Use the high-low method to estimate the total monthly fixed cost and the variable cost per hour.
c. Determine the average contribution margin per hour.
d. Use the scattergraph method to estimate the total monthly fixed cost and the variable cost per hour.
e. Compare the results of the two methods and comment on any differences.

### Problem 2-27B   *Estimating fixed and variable cost*                                     LO 7

Vicardo Frames Company, which manufactures ornate frames for original art work, began operations in January 2011. Sam Waits, the owner, asks for your assistance. He believes that he needs to better understand the cost of the frames for pricing purposes. You have collected the following data concerning actual production over the past year:

| Month | Number of Frames Produced | Total Cost |
|---|---|---|
| January | 1,600 | $42,000 |
| February | 7,200 | 65,000 |
| March | 3,920 | 59,000 |
| April | 1,200 | 37,200 |
| May | 3,200 | 58,000 |
| June | 2,600 | 54,000 |
| July | 2,200 | 51,200 |
| August | 3,600 | 62,000 |
| September | 4,560 | 64,000 |
| October | 5,880 | 63,000 |
| November | 6,560 | 64,000 |
| December | 800 | 33,000 |

**Required**

a. To understand the department's cost behavior, you decide to plot the points on graph paper and sketch a total cost line.

   **(1)** Enter the number of units and their costs in increasing order.

   **(2)** Plot the points on the graph.

   **(3)** Sketch a graph so the line "splits" all of the points (half of the points appear above and half appear below the line).

   **(4)** Using the line you just sketched, visually estimate the total cost to produce 4,000 units.

b. Using the high-low method, compute the total cost equation for the preceding data.

   **(1)** Compute the variable cost per unit.

   **(2)** Compute total fixed costs.

   **(3)** Sketch a line between the high and low points on your graph.

   **(4)** Using the high-low method, estimate the total cost to produce 4,000 units.

c. Name a third method that could be used to determine the fixed and variable cost estimate and comment on the advantages of your suggested approach.

**LO 7**

**Problem 2-28B**  *Estimating fixed and variable cost using the regression method*

Ray Rogers, the production manager of Martin Construction Components, is trying to figure out the cost behavior of his factory supplies cost. The company uses machine hours as the cost driver. Victor Hoover, the assistant manager, collected the following cost data for the last 32 weeks:

| Week No. | Machine Hours | Supplies Costs | Week No. | Machine Hours | Supplies Costs |
|---|---|---|---|---|---|
| 1 | 86 | $3,819 | 17 | 64 | $3,856 |
| 2 | 72 | 3,610 | 18 | 88 | 4,279 |
| 3 | 79 | 3,916 | 19 | 129 | 5,633 |
| 4 | 62 | 2,915 | 20 | 137 | 5,298 |
| 5 | 91 | 4,327 | 21 | 144 | 6,721 |
| 6 | 42 | 2,214 | 22 | 37 | 2,448 |
| 7 | 37 | 2,106 | 23 | 56 | 3,528 |
| 8 | 33 | 2,390 | 24 | 49 | 2,837 |
| 9 | 23 | 2,107 | 25 | 12 | 1,359 |
| 10 | 96 | 4,868 | 26 | 57 | 3,296 |
| 11 | 94 | 5,021 | 27 | 54 | 3,472 |
| 12 | 91 | 4,811 | 28 | 65 | 3,264 |
| 13 | 72 | 3,580 | 29 | 77 | 3,925 |
| 14 | 60 | 2,800 | 30 | 85 | 4,002 |
| 15 | 48 | 2,269 | 31 | 92 | 4,583 |
| 16 | 53 | 2,748 | 32 | 82 | 3,523 |

**Required**

a. The company uses the number of machine hours as the cost driver for factory supplies costs. Use an algebraic equation to describe how total factory supplies costs can be estimated.

b. Use a spreadsheet program to perform a regression analysis. Use factory supplies costs as the dependent variable ($Y$) and the machine hours as the independent variable ($X$). Determine the total fixed cost per week and variable cost per machine hour.

c. Identify the $R^2$ statistic provided by the Excel program and explain what it means.

d. Identify a potential weakness of regression analysis and explain what can be done to minimize it.

e. Determine the estimated total cost of factory supplies, if machine hour usage amounts to 100 hours for the next week. What portion of the total cost is fixed and what portion is variable?

# ANALYZE, THINK, COMMUNICATE

### ATC 2-1    Business Applications    *Operating leverage*

#### Description of Business for Amazon.com, Inc.

Amazon.com opened its virtual doors on the World Wide Web in July 1995 and we offer Earth's Biggest Selection. We seek to be Earth's most customer-centric company for three primary customer sets: consumer customers, seller customers and developer customers. In addition, we generate revenue through co-branded credit card agreements and other marketing and promotional services, such as online advertising.

| Amazon.com | 2008 | 2007 |
|---|---|---|
| Operating revenue | $19,166 | $14,835 |
| Operating earnings | 842 | 655 |

#### Description of Business for CSX, Inc.

CSX Corporations ("CSX") together with its subsidiaries (the "Company"), based in Jacksonville, Florida, is one of the nation's leading transportation suppliers. The Company's rail and inter-modal businesses provide rail-based transportation services including traditional rail service and the transport of intermodal containers and trailers.

| CSX, Inc. | 2008 | 2007 |
|---|---|---|
| Operating revenue | $11,255 | $10,030 |
| Operating earnings | 2,768 | 2,260 |

#### Required

a.  Determine which company appears to have the higher operating leverage.

b.  Write a paragraph or two explaining why the company you identified in Requirement *a* might be expected to have the higher operating leverage.

c.  If revenues for both companies declined, which company do you think would likely experience the greater decline in operating earnings? Explain your answer.

### ATC 2-2    Group Assignment    *Operating leverage*

The Parent Teacher Association (PTA) of Meadow High School is planning a fund-raising campaign. The PTA is considering the possibility of hiring Eric Logan, a world-renowned investment counselor, to address the public. Tickets would sell for $28 each. The school has agreed to let the PTA use Harville Auditorium at no cost. Mr. Logan is willing to accept one of two compensation arrangements. He will sign an agreement to receive a fixed fee of $10,000 regardless of the number of tickets sold. Alternatively, he will accept payment of $20 per ticket sold. In communities similar to that in which Meadow is located, Mr. Logan has drawn an audience of approximately 500 people.

#### Required

a.  In front of the class, present a statement showing the expected net income assuming 500 people buy tickets.

b.  The instructor will divide the class into groups and then organize the groups into four sections. The instructor will assign one of the following tasks to each section of groups.

#### Group Tasks

(1) Assume the PTA pays Mr. Logan a fixed fee of $10,000. Determine the amount of net income that the PTA will earn if ticket sales are 10 percent higher than expected. Calculate the percentage change in net income.

(2) Assume that the PTA pays Mr. Logan a fixed fee of $10,000. Determine the amount of net income that the PTA will earn if ticket sales are 10 percent lower than expected. Calculate the percentage change in net income.

**(3)** Assume that the PTA pays Mr. Logan $20 per ticket sold. Determine the amount of net income that the PTA will earn if ticket sales are 10 percent higher than expected. Calculate the percentage change in net income.

**(4)** Assume that the PTA pays Mr. Logan $20 per ticket sold. Determine the amount of net income that the PTA will earn if ticket sales are 10 percent lower than expected. Calculate the percentage change in net income.

**c.** Have each group select a spokesperson. Have one of the spokespersons in each section of groups go to the board and present the results of the analysis conducted in Requirement *b*. Resolve any discrepancies in the computations presented at the board and those developed by the other groups.

**d.** Draw conclusions regarding the risks and rewards associated with operating leverage. At a minimum, answer the following questions:

**(1)** Which type of cost structure (fixed or variable) produces the higher growth potential in profitability for a company?

**(2)** Which type of cost structure (fixed or variable) faces the higher risk of declining profitability for a company?

**(3)** Under what circumstances should a company seek to establish a fixed cost structure?

**(4)** Under what circumstances should a company seek to establish a variable cost structure?

### ATC 2-3  Research Assignment  *Fixed versus variable cost*

Use the 2008 Form 10-K for Black & Decker Corp. (B&D) (not StanleyBlack & Decker) to complete the requirements below. To obtain the Form 10-K you can use either use the EDGAR system following the instructions in Appendix A, or it can be found under "Investor Relations" on the company's corporate website at www.bdk.com. Be sure to read carefully the following portions of the document:

■  "General Development of the Business" on page 1.
■  "Consolidated Statement of Earnings" on page 36.

**Required**

**a.** Calculate the percentage decrease in B&D's sales and its "operating income" from 2007 to 2008.

**b.** Would fixed costs or variable costs be more likely to explain why B&D's operating earnings decreased by a bigger percentage than its sales?

**c.** On page 42, B&D reported that it incurred product development costs of $146.0 million in 2008. If this cost is thought of in the context of the number of units of products sold, should it be considered as primarily fixed or variable in nature?

**d.** If the product development costs are thought of in the context of the number of new products developed, should they be considered as primarily fixed or variable in nature?

### ATC 2-4  Writing Assignment  *Cost averaging*

Candice Sterling is a veterinarian. She has always been concerned for the pets of low-income families. These families love their pets but frequently do not have the means to provide them proper veterinary care. Dr. Sterling decides to open a part-time veterinary practice in a low-income neighborhood. She plans to volunteer her services free of charge two days per week. Clients will be charged only for the actual costs of materials and overhead. Dr. Sterling leases a small space for $300 per month. Utilities and other miscellaneous costs are expected to be approximately $180 per month. She estimates the variable cost of materials to be approximately $10 per pet served. A friend of Dr. Sterling who runs a similar type of clinic in another area of town indicates that she should expect to treat the following number of pets during her first year of operation.

| Jan. | Feb. | Mar. | Apr. | May | June | July | Aug. | Sept. | Oct. | Nov. | Dec. |
|------|------|------|------|-----|------|------|------|-------|------|------|------|
| 18 | 26 | 28 | 36 | 42 | 54 | 63 | 82 | 42 | 24 | 20 | 15 |

Dr. Sterling's friend has noticed that visits increase significantly in the summer because children who are out of school tend to bring their pets to the vet more often. Business tapers off during the winter and reaches a low point in December when people spend what little money they have on Christmas presents for their children. After looking at the data, Dr. Sterling becomes concerned that the people in the neighborhood will not be able to afford pet care during some months of operation even if it is offered at cost. For example, the cost of providing services in December would be approximately $42 per pet treated ($480 overhead ÷ 15 pets = $32 per pet, plus $10 materials cost). She is willing to provide her services free of charge, but she realizes that she cannot afford to subsidize the practice further by personally paying for the costs of materials and overhead in the months of low activity. She decides to discuss the matter with her accountant to find a way to cut costs even more. Her accountant tells her that her problem is cost *measurement* rather than cost *cutting*.

### Required

Assume that you are Dr. Sterling's accountant. Write a memo describing a pricing strategy that resolves the apparent problem of high costs during months of low volume. Recommend in your memo the price to charge per pet treated during the month of December.

### ATC 2-5   Ethical Dilemma   *Profitability versus social conscience (effects of cost behavior)*

Advances in biological technology have enabled two research companies, Bio Labs, Inc., and Scientific Associates, to develop an insect-resistant corn seed. Neither company is financially strong enough to develop the distribution channels necessary to bring the product to world markets. World Agra Distributors, Inc., has negotiated contracts with both companies for the exclusive right to market their seed. Bio Labs signed an agreement to receive an annual royalty of $1,000,000. In contrast, Scientific Associates chose an agreement that provides for a royalty of $0.50 per pound of seed sold. Both agreements have a 10-year term. During 2011, World Agra sold approximately 1,600,000 pounds of the Bio Labs, Inc., seed and 2,400,000 pounds of the Scientific Associates seed. Both types of seed were sold for $1.25 per pound. By the end of 2011, it was apparent that the seed developed by Scientific Associates was superior. Although insect infestation was virtually nonexistent for both types of seed, the seed developed by Scientific Associates produced corn that was sweeter and had consistently higher yields.

World Agra Distributors' chief financial officer, Roger Weatherstone, recently retired. To the astonishment of the annual planning committee, Mr. Weatherstone's replacement, Ray Borrough, adamantly recommended that the marketing department develop a major advertising campaign to promote the seed developed by Bio Labs, Inc. The planning committee reluctantly approved the recommendation. A $100,000 ad campaign was launched; the ads emphasized the ability of the Bio Labs seed to avoid insect infestation. The campaign was silent with respect to taste or crop yield. It did not mention the seed developed by Scientific Associates. World Agra's sales staff was instructed to push the Bio Labs seed and to sell the Scientific Associates seed only on customer demand. Although total sales remained relatively constant during 2012, sales of the Scientific Associates seed fell to approximately 1,300,000 pounds while sales of the Bio Labs, Inc., seed rose to 2,700,000 pounds.

### Required

a. Determine the amount of increase or decrease in profitability experienced by World Agra in 2012 as a result of promoting Bio Labs seed. Support your answer with appropriate commentary.

b. Did World Agra's customers in particular and society in general benefit or suffer from the decision to promote the Bio Labs seed?

c. Review the standards of ethical conduct in Exhibit 1.15 of Chapter 1 and comment on whether Mr. Borrough's recommendation violated any of the standards in the code of ethical conduct.

d. Comment on your belief regarding the adequacy of the Standards of Ethical Conduct for Managerial Accountants to direct the conduct of management accountants.

e. Are the actions of Ray Borrough in violation of the provisions of Sarbanes-Oxley that were described in Chapter 1? Explain your answer.

### ATC 2-6   Spreadsheet Assignment   *Using Excel*

Charlie Stork rented a truck for his business on two previous occasions. Since he will soon be renting a truck again, he would like to analyze his bills and determine how the rental fee is calculated. His two bills for truck rental show that on September 1, he drove 1,000 miles and the bill was $1,500, and on December 5, he drove 600 miles and the bill was $1,380.

## Required

Construct a spreadsheet to calculate the variable and fixed costs of this mixed cost that will allow Mr. Stork to predict his cost if he drives the truck 700 miles. The cells that show as numbers should all be formulas except C5, C6, E5, E6, and C18. Constructing the spreadsheet in this manner will allow you to change numbers in these five cells to recalculate variable cost, fixed cost, or predicted total cost.

```
ch02-working.xls
        A         B           C    D    E        F         G        H
 1  Chapter 2 - Working with Excel                 Name:
 2
 3                          Rental          Miles
 4                          Cost            Driven
 5          High          $ 1,500          1,000
 6          Low             1,380            600
 7          Difference    $   120            400
 8
 9          Variable cost per mile =       Change in Total Cost/Change in Miles
10          Variable cost per mile =       $  0.30  per mile
11
12          Fixed cost =        Total Cost - Variable Cost
13          Fixed cost =        $ 1,200
14
15
16          Predicted Cost =    $ 1,200 + $  0.30  per mile  x  Predicted Mileage
17
18          If predicted mileage is:    700
19
20          Predicted Cost =    $ 1,410
21
```

## Spreadsheet Tip

1. To format cells to show dollar signs, commas, or both, choose Format, then Cells, then click on the tab titled Numbers, and choose Accounting.

### ATC 2-7    Spreadsheet Assignment    *Mastering Excel*

Siwa Company makes and sells a decorative ceramic statue. Each statue costs $50 to manufacture and sells for $75. Siwa spends $3 to ship the statue to customers and pays salespersons a $2 commission for each statue sold. The remaining annual expenses of operation are administrative salaries, $70,000; advertising, $20,000; and rent, $30,000. Siwa plans to sell 9,000 statues in the coming year.

```
     A  B           C           D   E   F  G   H      I       J      K
 1  Chapter 2 - Mastering Excel                     Name:
 2
 3
 4     Contribution Margin Format Income Statement
 5
 6     Sales Revenue          ( 9,000  x  $75 )               $675,000
 7     Variable Expenses
 8         Cost of Goods Sold ( 9,000  x  $50 )  $450,000
 9         Sales Commissions  ( 9,000  x  $ 2 )    18,000
10         Shipping Expenses  ( 9,000  x  $ 3 )    27,000      495,000
11     Contribution Margin                                    $180,000
12     Fixed Expenses
13         Administrative Salaries            $ 70,000
14         Advertising                          20,000
15         Rent                                 30,000        120,000
16     Net Income                                           $  60,000
17
18
19     Operating Leverage                                       3.00
20
```

**Required**

Construct a spreadsheet that shows a contribution margin format income statement and that calculates operating leverage. Place formulas in the spreadsheet to allow changes to any of the preceding information to be automatically reflected in the income statement and operating leverage.

## COMPREHENSIVE PROBLEM

Use the same transaction data for Magnificent Modems, Inc., as was used in Chapter 1 (see page 52).

**Required**

a. Based on these data, identify each cost incurred by the company as (1) fixed versus variable relative to the number of units produced and sold; and (2) product versus selling, general, and administrative (S,G,&A). The solution for the first item is shown as an example.

| Cost Item | Fixed | Variable | Product | S,G,&A |
|---|---|---|---|---|
| Depreciation on manufacturing equipment | X | | X | |
| Direct materials | | | | |
| Direct labor | | | | |
| Production supplies | | | | |
| Rent on manufacturing facility | | | | |
| Sales commissions | | | | |
| Depreciation on administrative equipment | | | | |
| Administrative costs (rent and salaries) | | | | |

b. Replace the question marks in the following table to indicate the product cost per unit assuming levels of production of 5,000, 6,000, 7,000, and 8,000.

| | | | | |
|---|---|---|---|---|
| Cost of goods sold | $455,000 | ? | ? | ? |
| Divided by number of units | 5,000 | 6,000 | 7,000 | 8,000 |
| Cost per unit | $ 91 | ? | ? | ? |

## CHAPTER 3

# Analysis of Cost, Volume, and Pricing to Increase Profitability

## LEARNING OBJECTIVES

**After you have mastered the material in this chapter, you will be able to:**

1 Use the equation method to determine the break-even point.

2 Use the contribution margin per unit method to determine the break-even point.

3 Use the contribution margin ratio method to determine the break-even point.

4 Determine the sales volume required to attain a desired profit.

5 Set selling prices by using cost-plus, prestige, and target costing.

6 Explain cost-volume-profit relationships.

7 Draw and interpret a cost-volume-profit graph.

8 Calculate and interpret the margin of safety.

9 Conduct sensitivity analysis for cost-volume-profit relationships.

10 Perform multiproduct cost-volume-profit analysis.

## CHAPTER OPENING

The president of Bright Day Distributors recently completed a managerial accounting course. He was particularly struck by the operating leverage concept. His instructor had demonstrated how a small percentage increase in sales volume could produce a significantly higher percentage increase in profitability. Unfortunately, the discussion had been limited to the effects of changes in sales volume. In practice, changes in sales volume are often related to changes in sales price. For example, reducing selling prices often leads to increases in sales volume. Sales volume may also change in response to cost changes such as increasing the advertising budget. Furthermore, significant changes in sales volume could redefine the relevant range, changing the fixed and variable costs. Bright Day's president realized that understanding operating leverage was only one piece of understanding how to manage a business. He also needed to understand how changes in prices, costs, and volume affect profitability. Bright Day's president is interested in **cost-volume-profit (CVP) analysis.**

# The Curious Accountant

At a meeting in November 2009, **InterContinental Hotels Group (IHG)** reminded its franchisees that they had until February 1, 2010, to complete renovations of their properties and install new corporate logos. If they did not comply by the deadline, they would no longer be allowed to call themselves Holiday Inns. IHC itself owns only 17 hotels, but it is the global franchisor of 4,400 hotels. These hotels operate under several brand names including **Holiday Inn, Holiday Inn Express**, and **Crown Plaza Hotels**, but most of its franchisees operate under the Holiday Inn name. At the time of the meeting, 300 of the 2,700 Holiday Inns in North America had not even started the process of renovation and were likely to lose their franchise rights.

In February, 2009, **American Express** began offering some of its cardholders a $300 gift card if they would pay off their account balances and close their accounts. Remember that this is the same company that spends millions each year trying to attract new customers.

Why would a company like IHG that earns most of its revenues, and profits, from franchise fees collected from hotels it does not even own threaten to force 300 of them to take down their Holiday Inn signs? Would this not reduce IHG's revenues without significantly reducing its costs? At a time when the economy was slow and hotel occupancy was down, why would IHC take such action? Why would American Express pay some of its customers to leave? (Answers on page 115.)

# DETERMINING THE BREAK-EVEN POINT

Bright Day Distributors sells nonprescription health food supplements including vitamins, herbs, and natural hormones in the northwestern United States. Bright Day recently obtained the rights to distribute the new herb mixture Delatine. Recent scientific research found that Delatine delayed aging in laboratory animals. The researchers hypothesized that the substance would have a similar effect on humans. Their theory could not be confirmed because of the relatively long human life span. The news media reported the research findings; as stories turned up on television and radio news, talk shows, and in magazines, demand for Delatine increased.

Bright Day plans to sell the Delatine at a price of $36 per bottle. Delatine costs $24 per bottle. Bright Day's management team suspects that enthusiasm for Delatine will abate quickly as the news media shift to other subjects. To attract customers immediately, the product managers consider television advertising. The marketing manager suggests running a campaign of several hundred cable channel ads at an estimated cost of $60,000.

Bright Day's first concern is whether it can sell enough units to cover its costs. The president made this position clear when he said, "We don't want to lose money on this product. We have to sell at least enough units to break-even." In accounting terms, the **break-even point** is where profit (income) equals zero. So how many bottles of Delatine must be sold to produce a profit of zero? The break-even point is commonly computed using either the *equation method,* the *contribution margin per unit method,* or the *contribution margin ratio method.* All three of these approaches produce the same result. They are merely different ways to arrive at the same conclusion.

## Equation Method

**LO 1**

Use the equation method to determine the break-even point.

The **equation method** begins by expressing the income statement as follows:

$$\text{Sales} - \text{Variable costs} - \text{Fixed costs} = \text{Profit (Net income)}$$

As previously stated, profit at the break-even point is zero. Therefore, the break-even point for Delatine is computed as follows:

$$\text{Sales} - \text{Variable costs} - \text{Fixed costs} = \text{Profit}$$
$$\$36N - \$24N - \$60,000 = \$0$$
$$\$12N = \$60,000$$
$$N = \$60,000 \div \$12$$
$$N = 5,000 \text{ Units}$$

Where:

$N$ = Number of units
$36 = Sales price per unit
$24 = Variable cost per unit
$60,000 = Fixed costs

---

## ✓ CHECK YOURSELF 3.1

B-Shoc is an independent musician who is considering whether to independently produce and sell a CD. B-Shoc estimates fixed costs of $5,400 and variable costs of $2.00 per unit. The expected selling price is $8.00 per CD. Use the equation method to determine B-Shoc's break-even point.

**Answer**

$$\text{Sales} - \text{Variable costs} - \text{Fixed costs} = \text{Profit}$$

$$\$8N - \$2N - \$5,400 = \$0$$

$$\$6N = \$5,400$$

$$N = \$5,400 \div \$6$$

$$N = 900 \text{ Units (CDs)}$$

Where:

N = Number of units
$8 = Sales price per unit
$2 = Variable cost per unit
$5,400 = Fixed costs

## Contribution Margin per Unit Method

Recall that the *total contribution margin* is the amount of sales minus total variable cost. The **contribution margin per unit** is the sales price per unit minus the variable cost per unit. Therefore, the contribution margin per unit for Delatine is:

Use the contribution margin per unit method to determine the break-even point.

| Sales price per unit | $36 |
|---|---|
| Less: Variable cost per unit | (24) |
| Contribution margin per unit | $12 |

For every bottle of Delatine it sells, Bright Day earns a $12 contribution margin. In other words, every time Bright Day sells a bottle of Delatine, it receives enough money to pay $24 to cover the variable cost of the bottle of Delatine and still has $12 left to go toward paying the fixed cost. Bright Day will reach the break-even point when it sells enough bottles of Delatine to cover its fixed costs. Therefore the break-even point can be determined as follows:

$$\text{Break-even point in units} = \frac{\text{Fixed costs}}{\text{Contribution margin per unit}}$$

$$\text{Break-even point in units} = \frac{\$60,000}{\$12}$$

$$\textbf{Break-even point in units} = \textbf{5,000 Units}$$

This result is the same as that determined under the equation method. Indeed, the contribution margin per unit method formula is an abbreviated version of the income statement formula used in the equation method. In other words both methods are simply different derivations of the same formula. The proof is provided in the footnote below.[1]

[1]The formula for the *contribution margin per unit method* is (where N is the number of units at the break-even point):

**N = Fixed costs ÷ Contribution margin per unit**

The income statement formula for the *equation method* produces the same result as shown below (where N is the number of units at the break-even point):

Sales − Variable costs − Fixed costs = Profit
Sales price per unit (N) − Variable cost per unit (N) − Fixed costs = Profit
Contribution margin per unit (N) − Fixed costs = Profit
Contribution margin per unit (N) − Fixed costs = 0
Contribution margin per unit (N) = Fixed costs
**N = Fixed costs ÷ Contribution margin per unit**

Both the *equation method* and the *contribution margin per unit method* yield the amount of break-even sales measured *in units*. To determine the amount of break-even sales measured *in dollars,* multiply the number of units times the sales price per unit. For Delatine the break-even point measured in dollars is $180,000 (5,000 units × $36 per unit). The following income statement confirms this result:

| | |
|---|---:|
| Sales revenue (5,000 units × $36) | $180,000 |
| Total variable expenses (5,000 units × $24) | (120,000) |
| Total contribution margin (5,000 units × $12) | 60,000 |
| Fixed expenses | (60,000) |
| Net income | $      0 |

## Contribution Margin Ratio Method

Use the contribution margin ratio method to determine the break-even point.

The equation method and the contribution margin per unit method produce a break-even point measured *in units.* The break-even point expressed *in dollars* can be determined using the contribution margin ratio method. We begin by determining the **contribution margin ratio,** which is defined as follows.

$$\text{Contribution margin ratio} = \text{Contribution margin} \div \text{Sales}$$

The ratio can be computed using the total amount of the contribution margin and sales or by using per unit amounts. Either approach will yield the same result, as shown here.

Using total dollar values:

$$\text{Contribution margin ratio} = \text{Contribution margin in dollars} \div \text{Sales in dollars}$$

$$\text{Contribution margin ratio} = \$60,000 \div \$180,000 = .3333333$$

Using per unit values:

$$\text{Contribution margin ratio} = \text{Contribution margin per unit} \div \text{Sales price per unit}$$

$$\text{Contribution margin ratio} = \$12 \div \$36 = .3333333$$

Using the *contribution margin ratio method* the break-even point in dollars is computed by dividing the fixed cost by the contribution margin ratio. The computations for Bright Day follow.

$$\text{Break-even point in dollars} = \frac{\text{Fixed costs}}{\text{Contribution margin ratio}}$$

$$\text{Break-even point in dollars} = \frac{\$60,000}{.333333}$$

$$\text{Break-even point in dollars} = \$180,000 \text{ Sales revenue}$$

The break-even volume measured in units can be determined by dividing the total sales revenue by the sales price per unit as follows:

$$\text{Break-even point} = \$180,000 \text{ Sales revenue} \div \$36 = 5,000 \text{ Units}$$

The *contribution margin ratio method* yields the same results as the *contribution margin per unit method* and the *equation method.* The results are the same because all three methods are merely different derivations of the income statement formula.

# DETERMINING THE SALES VOLUME NECESSARY TO REACH A DESIRED PROFIT

Bright Day's president decides the ad campaign should produce a $40,000 profit. He asks the accountant to determine the sales volume that is required to achieve this level of profitability. Using the *equation method,* the sales volume in units required to attain the desired profit is computed as follows:

Determine the sales volume required to attain a desired profit.

$$\text{Sales} - \text{Variable costs} - \text{Fixed costs} = \text{Profit}$$

$$\$36N - \$24N - \$60,000 = \$40,000$$

$$\$12N = \$60,000 + \$40,000$$

$$N = \$100,000 \div \$12$$

$$N = 8,333 \text{ Units}$$

Where:

N = Number of units

$36 = Sales price per unit

$24 = Variable cost per unit

$60,000 = Fixed costs

$40,000 = Desired profit

The accountant used the *contribution margin per unit method* to confirm these computations as follows:

$$\text{Sales volume in units} = \frac{\text{Fixed costs} + \text{Desired profit}}{\text{Contribution margin per unit}}$$

$$= \frac{\$60,000 + \$40,000}{\$12} = 8,333.33 \text{ Units}$$

The required volume in sales dollars is this number of units multiplied by the sales price per unit (8,333.33 units × $36 = $300,000). The following income statement confirms this result; all amounts are rounded to the nearest whole dollar.

| | |
|---|---|
| Sales revenue (8,333.33 units × $36) | $300,000 |
| Total variable expenses (8,333.33 units × $24) | (200,000) |
| Total contribution margin (8,333.33 units × $12) | 100,000 |
| Fixed expenses | (60,000) |
| Net income | $ 40,000 |

In practice, the company will not sell partial bottles of Delatine. The accountant rounds 8,333.33 bottles to whole units. For planning and decision making, managers frequently make decisions using approximate data. Accuracy is desirable, but it is not as important as relevance. Do not be concerned when computations do not produce whole numbers. Rounding and approximation are common characteristics of managerial accounting data.

## ✓ CHECK YOURSELF 3.2

VolTech Company manufactures small engines that it sells for $130 each. Variable costs are $70 per unit. Fixed costs are expected to be $100,000. The management team has established a target profit of $188,000. Use the contribution margin per unit method to determine how many engines VolTech must sell to attain the target profit. Use the contribution margin ratio method to determine the amount of sales volume in dollars required to attain the desired profit.

**Answer**

**Contribution margin per unit approach:**

$$\text{Sales volume in units} = \frac{\text{Fixed costs} + \text{Desired profit}}{\text{Contribution margin per unit}} = \frac{\$100,000 + \$188,000}{\$130 - \$70} = 4,800 \text{ Units}$$

**Contribution margin ratio approach:**

$$\text{Sales volume in \$} = \frac{\text{Fixed costs} + \text{Desired profit}}{\text{Contribution margin ratio}} = \frac{\$100,000 + \$188,000}{(\$60 \div \$130)} = \$624,000$$

**Proof that the two approaches produce the same result:**

Sales price × No. units = Sales in dollars

$130 × 4,800 Units = $624,000

## ASSESSING THE PRICING STRATEGY

Set selling prices by using cost-plus, prestige, and target costing.

After reviewing the accountant's computations, the president asked the marketing manager, "What are our chances of reaching a sales volume of 8,334 units?" The manager replied, "Slim to none." She observed that no Bright Day product has ever sold more than 4,000 bottles when initially offered. Further, she feels the $36 price is too high. She asked who set the $36 price and how it was established.

The accountant explained that the price was established using a **cost-plus pricing** strategy. The normal policy is to price products at variable cost plus 50 percent of the variable cost. In this case the variable cost was $24, resulting in a price of $36 [$24 + ($24 × .5)] The accountant knew the price was high but expected Delatine to sell anyway. Indeed, he supported his position by referencing a strategy known as **prestige pricing.** Many people will pay a premium to be the first to use a new product. Similarly, people will pay more for a product with a prestigious brand name. The accountant noted that the widespread news coverage coupled with Bright Day's brand identity makes Delatine a prime product for prestige pricing.

The marketing manager recognized the accountant's arguments, but contended that news coverage will fade rapidly, competitors will enter the market, and therefore, Delatine cannot support a $36 price for an extended period of time. As an alternative, she suggested they use a strategy known as target costing. **Target costing** begins by determining the market price at which a product will sell. This becomes the target price. The focus then shifts to developing the product at a cost that will enable the company to be profitable while selling the product at the target price.

Market research indicates that Delatine could sustain long-term sales at a price of $28 per bottle. At this price, the new contribution margin becomes a mere $4 ($28 Sales price − $24 Variable cost per unit). Lowering the contribution margin per unit will dramatically increase the sales volume necessary to attain the desired profit. Using the *equation method,* the sales volume in units required to attain the desired profit when the sales price per unit is reduced to $28 is as follows:

Sales − Variable costs − Fixed costs = Profit

$28N − $24N − $60,000 = $40,000

$4N = $60,000 + $40,000

N = $100,000 ÷ $4

N = 25,000 Units

Where:

N = Number of units

$28 = Sales price per unit

$24 = Variable cost per unit

$60,000 = Fixed costs

$40,000 = Desired profit

The accountant used the *contribution margin per unit method* to confirm these computations as follows:

$$\text{Sales volume in units} = \frac{\textbf{Fixed costs} + \textbf{Desired profit}}{\textbf{Contribution margin per unit}}$$

$$= \frac{\$60,000 + \$40,000}{\$4} = 25,000 \text{ Units}$$

The required sales volume *in dollars* is $700,000 (25,000 units × $28 per bottle). The following income statement confirms these results.

| | |
|---|---|
| Sales revenue (25,000 units × $28) | $700,000 |
| Total variable expenses (25,000 units × $24) | (600,000) |
| Total contribution margin (25,000 units × $4) | 100,000 |
| Fixed expenses | (60,000) |
| Net income | $ 40,000 |

The marketing manager recognized that it would be impossible to sell 25,000 bottles of Delatine. She noted that this is where target costing enters the picture. Delatine must be made at a cost that will enable the company to earn the desired profit of $40,000 while selling at a price of $28 per bottle. Clearly, the cost structure must change, and the marketing manager has some suggestions for making the necessary changes.

## ASSESSING THE EFFECTS OF CHANGES IN VARIABLE COSTS

The previously discussed $24 cost is for a bottle of 100 capsules, each containing 90 milligrams (mg) of pure Delatine. The manufacturer is willing to provide Delatine to Bright Day in two alternative package sizes: (1) a bottle costing $12 that contains 100 capsules of 30 mg strength pure Delatine and (2) a bottle costing $3 that contains 100 capsules containing 5 mg of Delatine mixed with a vitamin C compound. The 5 mg dosage is the minimum required to permit a package label to indicate the product contains Delatine. The marketing manager observes that either option would enable Bright Day to sell Delatine at a price customers would be willing to pay.

Explain cost-volume-profit relationships.

The president vehemently rejected the second option, calling it a blatant attempt to deceive customers by suggesting they were buying Delatine when in fact they were getting vitamin C. *He considered the idea unethical and dangerous.* He vowed that he would not be seen on the six o'clock news trying to defend a fast buck scheme while his company's reputation went up in smoke. After calming down, he agreed that the first option had merit. The appropriate dosage for Delatine was uncertain; customers who wanted 90 mg per day could take three capsules instead of one. He asked the accountant, "What's the effect on the bottom line?"

The variable cost changes from $24 to $12 per bottle. The contribution margin per unit increases from $4 per bottle ($28 sales price − $24 variable cost per bottle) to $16 per bottle ($28 sales price − $12 variable cost per bottle). The significant increase in contribution margin per unit dramatically decreases the sales volume necessary to attain the target profit.

# FOCUS ON INTERNATIONAL ISSUES

## COST-VOLUME-PROFIT ANALYSIS AT A GERMAN CHEMICAL COMPANY

The greater the percentage of a company's total costs that are fixed, the more sensitive the company's earnings are to changes in revenue or volume. Operating leverage, the relationship between the changes in revenue and changes in earnings, introduced earlier, applies to companies throughout the world, large or small.

Large chemical manufacturers have significant fixed costs. It takes a lot of buildings and equipment to produce chemicals. **BASF** claims to be the largest chemical company in the world. It has its headquarters in Ludwigshafen, Germany. From 2004 through 2006 BASF's revenues increased 40.2 percent, but its earnings increased 60.4 percent. In other words, its earnings grew one and one-half times faster than its revenues.

Studying BASF offers insight into a true global enterprise. Though headquartered in Germany, it has manufacturing facilities at 150 locations throughout the world. Only 21 percent of its 2006 revenue came from sales within Germany, which was 1 percent less than the revenue it earned in the United States. Although its financial statements are presented in euros and prepared in accordance with international financial accounting standards, its stock is traded on the New York Stock Exchange as well as on the Frankfurt Stock Exchange.

Using the *equation method,* the sales volume in units required to attain the desired profit when the variable cost per unit is reduced to \$12 per bottle is as follows:

$$\text{Sales} - \text{Variable costs} - \text{Fixed costs} = \text{Profit}$$

$$\$28N - \$12N - \$60{,}000 = \$40{,}000$$

$$\$16N = \$60{,}000 + \$40{,}000$$

$$N = \$100{,}000 \div \$16$$

$$N = 6{,}250 \text{ Units}$$

Where:

$N$ = Number of units

\$28 = Sales price per unit

\$12 = Variable cost per unit

\$60,000 = Fixed costs

\$40,000 = Desired profit

The accountant used the *contribution margin per unit method* to confirm these computations as follows:

$$\text{Sales volume in units} = \frac{\text{Fixed costs} + \text{Desired profit}}{\text{Contribution margin per unit}}$$

$$= \frac{\$60{,}000 + \$40{,}000}{\$16} = 6{,}250 \text{ Units}$$

The required sales volume in sales dollars is \$175,000 (6,250 units × \$28 per bottle). The following income statement confirms these amounts.

| | |
|---|---|
| Sales revenue (6,250 units × $28) | $175,000 |
| Total variable expenses (6,250 units × $12) | (75,000) |
| Total contribution margin (6,250 units × $16) | 100,000 |
| Fixed expenses | (60,000) |
| Net income | $ 40,000 |

Although the drop in required sales from 25,000 units to 6,250 was significant, the marketing manager was still uneasy about the company's ability to sell 6,250 bottles of Delatine. She observed again that no other Bright Day product had produced sales of that magnitude. The accountant suggested reducing projected fixed costs by advertising on radio rather than television. While gathering cost data for the potential television ad campaign, the accountant had consulted radio ad executives who had assured him radio ads could equal the TV audience exposure at about half the cost. Even though the TV ads would likely be more effective, he argued that since radio advertising costs would be half those of TV, the desired profit could be attained at a significantly lower volume of sales. The company president was impressed with the possibilities. He asked the accountant to determine the required sales volume if advertising costs were $30,000 instead of $60,000.

## Answers to The Curious Accountant

InterContinental Hotel Group (IHG) obviously believed that the revenue it lost from dropping some hotels that did not meet its new image standards would be more than offset by the fees it received from new franchisees. If the Holiday Inn brand was perceived as a low-quality lodging choice because of a few unattractive properties, new franchisees may not be eager to sign on. Also, existing hotels can charge higher prices if the brand is perceived as more upscale. Since IHG gets a piece of these higher fees, it was willing to eliminate some units in order to, it hopes, improve overall profitability. It would be more difficult for IHG to initiate a marketing campaign based on the quality of Holiday Inns if several of its franchisees were perceived poorly.

American Express (AMEX) was trying to get rid of a small percentage of customers who had relatively large account balances, but who were not using their cards very often. AMEX could receive at least two benefits if these customers left. First, the company could avoid the higher-than-average default risk associated with them. Second, AMEX could avoid the costs of servicing the accounts of these infrequent card users. These costs occur even though the customers do not generate much revenue for the company.

IHC and American Express made their decisions by focusing on multiple factors, not just revenues and not just cost. Their decisions were based on an analysis of the interactions of costs, revenues, and the volume of revenues that would be generated as cost and pricing strategies were altered. Traditionally accountants refer to the topics covered in this chapter as cost-volume-profit analysis, but more accurately it could be called *price*-cost-volume-profit analysis.

Sources: "Hotels Risk Losing Holiday Inn Brand," *The Wall Street Journal*, November 13, 2009, p. B-3, and "AmEx Encourages Cardholders to Leave," *The Wall Street Journal*, February 24, 2009, p. D-2.

## ASSESSING THE EFFECTS OF CHANGES IN FIXED COSTS

Explain cost-volume-profit relationships.

Changing the fixed costs from $60,000 to $30,000 will dramatically reduce the sales level required to earn the target profit. Using the *equation method* the sales volume in units required to attain the desired profit when fixed costs are reduced to $30,000 is as follows.

$$\text{Sales} - \text{Variable costs} - \text{Fixed costs} = \text{Profit}$$

$$\$28N - \$12N - \$30,000 = \$40,000$$

$$\$16N = \$30,000 + \$40,000$$

$$N = \$70,000 \div \$16$$

$$N = 4,375 \text{ Units}$$

Where:

N = Number of units

$28 = Sales price per unit

$12 = Variable cost per unit

$30,000 = Fixed costs

$40,000 = Desired profit

The accountant used the *contribution margin per unit method* to confirm these computations as follows.

$$\text{Sales volume in units} = \frac{\text{Fixed costs} + \text{Desired profit}}{\text{Contribution margin per unit}}$$

$$= \frac{\$30,000 + \$40,000}{\$16} = 4,375 \text{ units}$$

The required sales volume in sales dollars is $122,500 (4,375 units × $28). The following income statement confirms these amounts.

| | |
|---|---|
| Sales revenue (4,375 units × $28) | $122,500 |
| Total variable expenses (4,375 units × $12) | (52,500) |
| Total contribution margin (4,375 units × $16) | 70,000 |
| Fixed expenses | (30,000) |
| Net income | $ 40,000 |

The marketing manager supported using radio instead of television ads. Obviously, she could not guarantee any specific sales volume, but she felt confident that sales projections within a range of 4,000 to 5,000 units were reasonable.

### The Effect of Cost Structure on the Break-Even Point

Reducing fixed cost from $60,000 to $30,000 also significantly reduces the break-even point. This conclusion is confirmed by computing the break-even point before and after the reduction of the fixed cost as follows:

$$\text{Break-even point} = \text{Fixed costs} \div \text{Contribution margin per unit}$$

$$\text{Break-even point before fixed cost reduction} = \$60,000 \div \$16 = 3,750 \text{ units}$$

$$\text{Break-even point after fixed cost reduction} = \$30,000 \div \$16 = 1,875 \text{ units}$$

The lower break-even point is consistent with the conclusion reached in Chapter 2 regarding operating leverage. Recall that higher risk exists for companies with high fixed cost structures while variable cost structures limit risk. It follows that companies with high fixed cost structures will have higher break-even points than companies with low fixed cost structures. A high break-even point suggests that a company must attain a high sales volume or face operating losses. Indeed, failure to attain the required sales volume will result in leveraged losses. In other words, operating leverage will cause any change in sales revenue to have a disproportionately larger impact on net income.

## USING THE COST-VOLUME-PROFIT GRAPH

To visually analyze the revised projections, Bright Day's accountant prepared a cost-volume-profit (CVP) graph that pictured CVP relationships over a range of sales activity from zero to 6,000 units. The accountant followed the steps below to produce the CVP graph (sometimes called a *break-even chart*) shown in Exhibit 3.1. The graph is drawn under the following assumptions.

**LO 7**

Draw and interpret a cost-volume-profit graph.

- The contribution margin is $16 (sales price $28 − variable cost $12 per bottle).
- The fixed cost is $30,000.
- The desired profit is $40,000.

### Procedures for Drawing the CVP Graph

1. *Draw and label the axes:* The horizontal axis represents activity (expressed in units) and the vertical axis represents dollars.
2. *Draw the fixed-cost line:* Total fixed costs are constant for all levels of activity. Draw a horizontal line representing the amount of fixed costs across the graph at $30,000, the fixed-cost level.
3. *Draw the total cost line:* The total cost line representing the combination of fixed and variable costs is a diagonal line that rises as it moves from left to right. To draw the line, plot one point of the total cost line at the intersection of the fixed-cost line and the vertical axis. In this case, plot the first point at the zero level of activity and $30,000 (fixed cost). Next, select an arbitrary activity level. In this case we assume

**EXHIBIT 3.1**

**Cost-Volume-Profit Graph**

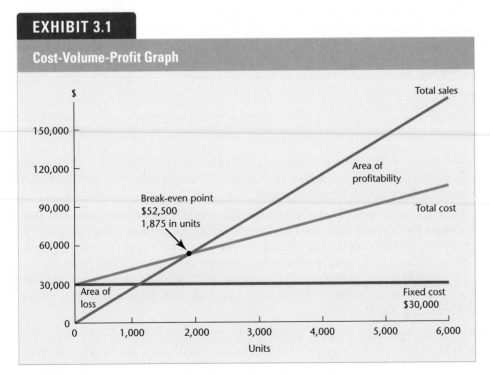

# REALITY BYTES

The relationship among the costs to produce goods, the volume of goods produced, the price charged for those goods, and the profit earned is relevant to all industries, but perhaps no industry demonstrates the effects of these relationships more dramatically than automobile manufacturing. First, the automobile industry is characterized by having a lot of fixed production-costs for things such as buildings, equipment, research, and development, but also financing costs associated with borrowed funds, such as the interest expense bonds. Second, the industry is globally competitive, and companies in the United States are often at a cost disadvantage. Some of this cost disadvantage comes from obvious sources, such as having to pay higher wages than do companies in countries such as South Korea. Finally, for many customers, price and quality are more important than brand loyalty.

Over the past decades, domestic auto makers, and in particular General Motors (GM), have used different strategies to try to deal with the issues mentioned above. Early on it had a dominant market share. As long as it produced more cars than its competitors, its fixed cost per car was lower, resulting in better profits. In the 1980s, however, foreign manufactures began increasing their market share and decreasing GM's. As its relative levels of production fell, its fixed cost per unit increased. In response, GM and others tried to regain market share by lowering prices, largely through rebates. Unfortunately this did not work, so the lower prices, combined with the higher relative fixed costs, seriously eroded profits.

These problems reached a crisis in 2008 and 2009 when GM and Chrysler sought financial help from the government and entered expedited bankruptcy proceedings.

What did GM and Chrysler hope to achieve? Primarily they needed to lower their costs, especially their fixed costs. As a result of bankruptcy proceedings, they were able to greatly reduce interest and principal payments on their outstanding bonds (fixed costs), reduce the number of brands (fixed costs), shut down some plants (fixed costs), reduce health care costs to retirees (fixed costs), and reduce the number of dealers. While reducing the number of dealers did reduce some cost to the companies, it also reduced price competition among the dealers, which had the potential of allowing the companies to charge more for their cars. All of these changes, it was hoped, would allow the companies to return to profitability.

However, before a company can be profitable, it must break even. At one time GM's break-even point was estimated at around 16 million vehicles per year. GM's CEO until 2000, Rick Wagoner, had implemented changes that reduced the company's break-even point to 12 million units. On March 29, 2009, as a condition of receiving government support, the administration of President Barack Obama asked Mr. Wagoner to resign as GM's CEO. Perhaps lost by many in the news coverage of Mr. Wagoner's resignation were reports by several news organizations that officials at the U.S. Treasury Department would ask the new leadership at GM to take steps to reduce the company's break-even point to 10 million units.

It would be a major achievement if GM can reduce its break even from 16 million units to 10 million units in the span of a few years. This may not be enough, however. In 2008 GM sold only 8.8 million units, and its sales in the first quarter of 2009 were even lower than the same quarter of 2008. Furthermore, it should be remembered that the objective of businesses is not simply to break even, but to make a profit.

6,000 units. At this volume, the total cost is $102,000 [(6,000 units × $12) + $30,000 fixed cost]. Plot a point at the coordinates of 6,000 units and $102,000. Draw a straight line through these two points.

4. *Draw the sales line:* Draw the revenue line using a procedure similar to that described for drawing the total cost line. Select some arbitrary level of activity and multiply that volume by the sales price per unit. Plot the result on the graph and draw a line from the origin (zero units, zero revenue) through this point. For example, at a volume of 6,000 units, the revenue is $168,000 (6,000 units × $28). Plot a point at the coordinates of 6,000 units and $168,000. Draw a line from the origin through the plotted point.

Trace these steps to the graph in Exhibit 3.1. After analyzing the graph, the president concludes that the sales volume of 4,375 units is well above the break-even point of 1,875 units. Still he wonders if the level of safety could be measured and compared with other investment opportunities.

# CALCULATING THE MARGIN OF SAFETY

The final meeting of Bright Day's management team focused on the reliability of the data used to construct the CVP chart. The accountant called attention to the sales volume figures in the area of profitability. Recall that Bright Day must sell 4,375 bottles of Delatine to earn the desired profit. In dollars, budgeted sales are $122,500 (4,375 bottles × $28 per bottle). The accountant highlighted the large gap between these budgeted sales and break-even sales. The amount of this gap, called the *margin of safety,* can be measured in units or in sales dollars as shown here.

Calculate and interpret the margin of safety.

|  | In Units | In Dollars |
|---|---|---|
| Budgeted sales | 4,375 | $122,500 |
| Break-even sales | (1,875) | (52,500) |
| Margin of safety | 2,500 | $ 70,000 |

The **margin of safety** measures the cushion between budgeted sales and the break-even point. It quantifies the amount by which actual sales can fall short of expectations before the company will begin to incur losses.

To help compare diverse products or companies of different sizes, the margin of safety can be expressed as a percentage. Divide the margin of safety by the budgeted sales volume[2] as shown here.

$$\text{Margin of safety} = \frac{\text{Budgeted sales} - \text{Break-even sales}}{\text{Budgeted sales}}$$

$$\text{Margin of safety} = \frac{\$122,500 - \$52,500}{\$122,500} = 57.14\%$$

This analysis suggests actual sales would have to fall short of expected sales by more than 57 percent before Bright Day would experience a loss on Delatine. The large margin of safety suggests the proposed radio advertising program to market bottles of 30mg Delatine capsules has minimal risk. As a result, the project team recommends that Delatine be added to the company's line of products. The steps Bright Day's project team experienced to arrive at this decision are summarized in Exhibit 3.2.

## ✓ CHECK YOURSELF 3.3

Suppose that Bright Day is considering the possibility of selling a protein supplement that will cost Bright Day $5 per bottle. Bright Day believes that it can sell 4,000 bottles of the supplement for $25 per bottle. Fixed costs associated with selling the supplement are expected to be $42,000. Does the supplement have a wider margin of safety than Delatine?

**Answer**   Calculate the break-even point for the protein supplement.

$$\text{Break-even volume in units} = \frac{\text{Fixed costs}}{\text{Contribution margin per unit}} = \frac{\$42,000}{\$25 - \$5} = 2,100 \text{ Units}$$

Calculate the margin of safety. Note that the margin of safety expressed as a percentage can be calculated using the number of units or sales dollars. Using either units or dollars yields the same percentage.

$$\text{Margin of safety} = \frac{\text{Budgeted sales} - \text{Break-even sales}}{\text{Budgeted sales}} = \frac{4,000 - 2,100}{4,000} = 47.5\%$$

The margin of safety for Delatine (57.14 percent) exceeds that for the protein supplement (47.5 percent). This suggests that Bright Day is less likely to incur losses selling Delatine than selling the supplement.

[2]The margin of safety percentage can be based on actual as well as budgeted sales. For example, an analyst could compare the margins of safety of two companies under current operating conditions by substituting actual sales for budgeted sales in the computation, as follows: [(Actual sales − Break-even sales) ÷ Actual sales].

## EXHIBIT 3.2

### Recap of Delatine Decision Process

Management considers a new product named Delatine. Delatine has a projected sales price of $36 and variable cost of $24 per bottle. Fixed cost is projected to be $60,000. The break-even point is 5,000 units [$60,000 ÷ ($36 − $24) = 5,000].

Management desires to earn a $40,000 profit on Delatine. The sales volume required to earn the desired profit is 8,334 units [($60,000 + $40,000) ÷ ($36 − $24) = 8,334].

The marketing manager advocates a target pricing approach that lowers the proposed selling price to $28 per bottle. The sales volume required to earn a $40,000 profit increases to 25,000 units [($60,000 + $40,000) ÷ ($28 − $24) = 25,000].

Target costing is employed to reengineer the product, thereby reducing variable cost to $12 per bottle. The sales volume required to earn a $40,000 profit decreases to 6,250 units [($60,000 + $40,000) ÷ ($28 − $12) = 6,250].

Target costing is applied further to reduce fixed cost to $30,000. The sales volume required to earn a $40,000 profit decreases to 4,375 units [($30,000 + $40,000) ÷ ($28 − $12) = 4,375]. The new break-even point is 1,875 units [$30,000 ÷ ($28 − $12) = 1,875].

In view of a 57.14% margin of safety [(4,375 − 1,875) ÷ 4,375 = .5714], management decides to add Delatine to its product line.

# PERFORMING SENSITIVITY ANALYSIS USING SPREADSHEET SOFTWARE

While useful, the margin of safety offers only a one dimensional measure of risk—change in sales volume. Profitability is affected by multidimensional forces. Fixed or variable costs, as well as sales volume, could differ from expectations. Exhibit 3.3 uses data pertaining to Bright Day's proposed project for marketing Delatine to illustrate an Excel spreadsheet showing the sensitivity of profits to simultaneous changes in fixed cost, variable cost, and sales volume. Recall the accountant estimated the radio ad campaign would cost $30,000. The spreadsheet projects profitability if advertising costs are as low as $20,000 or as high as $40,000. The effects of potential simultaneous changes in variable cost and sales volume are similarly projected.

Conduct sensitivity analysis for cost-volume-profit relationships.

The range of scenarios illustrated in the spreadsheet represents only a few of the many alternatives management can analyze with a few quick keystrokes. The spreadsheet program recalculates profitability figures instantly when one of the variables changes. If the president asks what would happen if Bright Day sold 10,000 units, the accountant merely substitutes the new number for one of the existing sales volume figures, and revised profitability numbers are instantly available. By changing the variables, management can get a real feel for the sensitivity of profits to changes in cost and volume. Investigating a multitude of what-if possibilities involving simultaneous changes in fixed cost, variable cost, and volume is called **sensitivity analysis.**

After reviewing the spreadsheet analysis, Bright Day's management team is convinced it should undertake radio advertising for Delatine. Only under the most dire circumstances (if actual sales are significantly below expectations while costs are well above expectations) will the company incur a loss.

**EXHIBIT 3.3**

**Spreadsheet Report to Facilitate "What-If" Analysis**

| If Fixed Cost is | While Variable Cost is | And Sales Volume is 2,000 | 3,000 | 4,000 | 5,000 | 6,000 |
|---|---|---|---|---|---|---|
| | | Then Profitability Will Be | | | | |
| $ 20,000 | 11 | $14,000 | $31,000 | $48,000 | $65,000 | $82,000 |
| 20,000 | 12 | 12,000 | 28,000 | 44,000 | 60,000 | 76,000 |
| 20,000 | 13 | 10,000 | 25,000 | 40,000 | 55,000 | 70,000 |
| 30,000 | 11 | 4,000 | 21,000 | 38,000 | 55,000 | 72,000 |
| 30,000 | 12 | 2,000 | 18,000 | 34,000 | 50,000 | 66,000 |
| 30,000 | 13 | - | 15,000 | 30,000 | 45,000 | 60,000 |
| 40,000 | 11 | (6,000) | 11,000 | 28,000 | 45,000 | 62,000 |
| 40,000 | 12 | (8,000) | 8,000 | 24,000 | 40,000 | 56,000 |
| 40,000 | 13 | (10,000) | 5,000 | 20,000 | 35,000 | 50,000 |

Selling Price = $ 28.00

# ASSESSING THE EFFECT OF SIMULTANEOUS CHANGES IN CVP VARIABLES

When spreadsheet software is not available, the effects of simultaneous changes in CVP variables can be examined using the equation method. To illustrate several possible scenarios, assume Bright Day has developed the budgeted income statement in Exhibit 3.4.

---

## EXHIBIT 3.4

**Budgeted Income Statement**

| | |
|---|---:|
| Sales revenue (4,375 units × $28 sale price) | $122,500 |
| Total variable expenses (4,375 units × $12 cost per bottle) | (52,500) |
| Total contribution margin (4,375 units × $16) | 70,000 |
| Fixed expenses | (30,000) |
| Net income | $ 40,000 |

---

## A Decrease in Sales Price Accompanied by an Increase in Sales Volume

The marketing manager believes reducing the sales price per bottle to $25 will increase sales volume by 625 units. The expected sales volume would become 5,000 (4,375 + 625). Variable cost per unit is expected to remain at $12. Should Bright Day reduce the price? Compare the projected profit without these changes ($40,000) with the projected profit if the sales price is $25 and volume increases to 5,000 units.

$$\text{Sales} - \text{Variable costs} - \text{Fixed costs} = \text{Profit}$$

$$(\$25 \times 5{,}000 \text{ units}) - (\$12 \times 5{,}000) - \$30{,}000 = \text{Profit}$$

$$\$35{,}000 = \text{Profit}$$

Since budgeted income falls from $40,000 to $35,000, Bright Day should not reduce the sales price.

## An Increase in Fixed Cost Accompanied by an Increase in Sales Volume

Return to the budgeted income statement in Exhibit 3.4. If the company buys an additional $12,000 of advertising, management believes sales can increase to 6,000 units. The sales price remains at $28 and variable cost per unit at $12. Should Bright Day incur the additional advertising cost, increasing fixed costs to $42,000 and sales volume to 6,000 units? The expected profit would be:

$$\text{Sales} - \text{Variable costs} - \text{Fixed costs} = \text{Profit}$$

$$(\$28 \times 6{,}000 \text{ units}) - (\$12 \times 6{,}000) - \$42{,}000 = \text{Profit}$$

$$\$54{,}000 = \text{Profit}$$

Since budgeted income increases from $40,000 to $54,000, Bright Day should seek to increase sales through additional advertising.

## A Simultaneous Reduction in Sales Price, Fixed Costs, Variable Costs, and Sales Volume

Return again to the budgeted income statement in Exhibit 3.4. Suppose Bright Day negotiates a $4 reduction in the cost of a bottle of Delatine. The management team considers passing some of the savings on to customers by reducing the sales price to $25 per bottle. Furthermore, the team believes it could reduce advertising costs by $8,000 and still achieve sales of 4,200 units. Should Bright Day adopt this plan to reduce prices and advertising costs?

The contribution margin would increase to $17 per bottle ($25 revised selling price − $8 revised variable cost per bottle) and fixed cost would fall to $22,000 ($30,000 − $8,000). Based on a sales volume of 4,200 units, the expected profit is:

$$Sales - Variable\ costs - Fixed\ costs = Profit$$

$$(\$25 \times 4{,}200\ units) - (\$8 \times 4{,}200) - \$22{,}000 = Profit$$

$$\$49{,}400 = Profit$$

Because budgeted income increases from $40,000 to $49,400, Bright Day should proceed with the revised operating strategy.

Many other possible scenarios could be considered. The contribution approach can be used to analyze independent or simultaneous changes in the CVP variables.

## MULTIPRODUCT COST-VOLUME-PROFIT ANALYSIS

To this point we have simplified our discussion of CVP by assuming a company sells only one product. In the real world, most companies sell many products. Each product has an independent impact on the profitability of the company. Calculating the break-even point requires an analyst to consider the simultaneous impact of the contribution margins of all products. This impact can be easily measured by computing the weighted average contribution margin.

To illustrate we assume that Bright Day's management team is examining its annual Vitamin C Sales Days event. The sales event focuses on two products. One product is labeled Synthetic C; the other is called Organic C. The sales price, variable cost, and contribution margin for each bottle of each product is shown here.

**LO 10**

Perform multiproduct cost-volume-profit analysis.

|  | Synthetic C | Organic C |
|---|---|---|
| Sales price | $7 | $9 |
| Variable cost | 5 | 6 |
| Contribution margin | $2 | $3 |

Due to its lower cost, Synthetic C has consistently outsold the Organic C. Indeed, Synthetic C historically accounts for approximately 80 percent of the total sales; with Organic C making up the remaining 20 percent. The fixed costs for the annual sales event are expected to be $2,112. These fixed costs are largely composed of advertising and training expenses. Based on this information the management team begins its examination by determining the break-even point.

### Determining the Break-Even Point

The first step in determining the break-even point is to compute the *weighted average contribution margin per unit.* The weighted average depends on each product's proportionate share of the total sales. In accounting terms, the relative proportions in which a company's products are sold is called the **sales mix.** The expected sales mix for the annual sales event is 80 percent for Synthetic C and 20 percent for Organic C. In other words, the two products in the event have an 80/20 sales mix. Base on this sales mix, the weighted average contribution margin per bottle is computed as follows.

|  | Contribution Margin | Times Proportionate Share | Weighted Average |
|---|---|---|---|
| Synthetic C | $2 | × .8 | $1.60 |
| Organic C | 3 | × .2 | .60 |
| Weighted average contribution margin |  |  | $2.20 |

Using the per unit contribution margin approach, the break-even point in total units can be determined by dividing the fixed cost by the weighted average contribution margin as follows.

Break-even point = Fixed costs ÷ Weighted average contribution margin per unit

Break-even point = $2,112 ÷ $2.20 = 960 Total units

The 960 units represent the total number of bottles of both products combined. To determine the number of bottles of each product, multiply the total number of bottles times the proportionate share of the sales mix as follows.

Break-even point = Total units × Proportionate share of sales mix

Break-even point for Synthetic C = 960 bottles × .8 share of sales mix = 768 Bottles

Break-even point for Organic C = 960 bottles × .2 share of sales mix = 192 Bottles

The following income statement confirms that these sales volume figures constitute the break-even point.

| | |
|---|---:|
| Sales of Synthetic C (768 bottles × $7) | $5,376 |
| Sales of Organic C (192 bottles × $9) | 1,728 |
| Total sales | 7,104 |
| Variable cost of Synthetic C (768 bottles × $5) | (3,840) |
| Variable cost of Organic C (192 bottles × $6) | (1,152) |
| Contribution margin | 2,112 |
| Fixed cost | (2,112) |
| Net income | $ 0 |

## Determining the Sales Volume Necessary to Reach a Desired Profit

Suppose Bright Day's president wants to know the number of bottles of each product that must be sold to earn a profit of $264 from the sales event. This information can be easily determined by adding the amount of the desired profit to the amount of fixed cost and then dividing the total by the weighted average contribution margin per unit. The computations are as follows.

$$\text{Sales volume in units} = \frac{\text{Fixed cost} + \text{Desired profit}}{\text{Weighted average contribution margin per unit}}$$

$$= \frac{\$2,112 + \$264}{\$2.20} = 1,080 \text{ Total units}$$

The 1,080 units represent the total number of bottles of both products combined. To determine the number of bottles of each product, multiply the total number of bottles times the proportionate share of the sales mix as follows.

Break-even point = Total units × Proportionate share of sales mix

Break-even point for Synthetic C = 1,080 bottles × .8 share of sales mix = 864 Bottles

Break-even point for Organic C = 1,080 bottles × .2 share of sales mix = 216 Bottles

The following income statement confirms that these sales volume figures constitute the sales volumes necessary to earn a desired profit of $264.

| | |
|---|---|
| Sales of Synthetic C (864 bottles × $7) | $6,048 |
| Sales of Organic C (216 bottles × $9) | 1,944 |
| Total sales | 7,992 |
| Variable cost of Synthetic C (864 bottles × $5) | (4,320) |
| Variable cost of Organic C (216 bottles × $6) | (1,296) |
| Contribution margin | 2,376 |
| Fixed cost | (2,112) |
| Net income | $ 264 |

## Managing the Sales Mix

Bright Day's president asks the management team to consider possibilities for increasing profitability. The team first considers the possibility of increasing the total number of bottles of vitamins sold. The marketing manager is pessimistic about this possibility. She notes that there are only so many people buying vitamin C. Trying to convince the same number of customers to purchase more bottles of the vitamin is not likely. The accountant notes that it is not necessary to sell more bottles of vitamins. Indeed, he argues that profitability can be increased even if sales volume remains flat. His solution is to change the sales mix.

Since Organic C has a higher contribution margin, shifting customers from Synthetic C to Organic C will increase profitability. The accountant demonstrates his point by computing the level of profitability assuming the sales mix shifts from an 80/20 split to a 60/40 mix. The income statement for a total sales volume of 1,080 bottles under a 60/40 sales mix is developed as follows.

The 1,080 units represent the total number of bottles of both products combined. To determine the number of bottles of each product using the 60/40 sales mix, multiply the total number of bottles times the proportionate share of the sales mix as follows.

Break-even point = Total units × Proportionate share of sales mix

Break-even point for Synthetic C = 1,080 bottles × .6 share of sales mix = 648 Bottles

Break-even point for Organic C = 1,080 bottles × .4 share of sales mix = 432 Bottles

The following income statement confirms that revised sales mix produces a higher net income. Indeed, in this case net income increases from $264 to $480 given the same total sales volume of 1,080 total bottles of vitamin C.

| | |
|---|---|
| Sales of Synthetic C (648 bottles × $7) | $4,536 |
| Sales of Organic C (432 bottles × $9) | 3,888 |
| Total sales | 8,424 |
| Variable cost of Synthetic C (648 bottles × $5) | (3,240) |
| Variable cost of Organic C (432 bottles × $6) | (2,592) |
| Contribution margin | 2,592 |
| Fixed cost | (2,112) |
| Net income | $ 480 |

The president is very impressed with this potential increase in profitability. His immediate response is to ask, how do we change the sales mix? A number of possibilities are examined, including slanting the advertising to emphasize Organic C and training the sales staff to promote the product. After careful consideration the team implements the most promising ideas. Ultimately, the team would compare the expected income statement with actual results to evaluate and fine tune the strategy. Variance analysis and performance evaluation are important subjects that will be covered in coming chapters.

It is important to note that the sales mix affects all aspects of CVP analysis. For example, the new break-even point for a sales mix of 60/40 is computed as discussed here. The first step is to compute the weighted average contribution margin per unit as follows.

|  | Contribution Margin | Times Proportionate Share | Weighted Average |
|---|---|---|---|
| Synthetic C | $2 | × .6 | $1.20 |
| Organic C | 3 | × .4 | 1.20 |
| Weighted average contribution margin |  |  | $2.40 |

Using the per unit contribution margin approach, the break-even point in total units can be determined by dividing the fixed cost by the weighted average contribution margin as follows:

Break-even point = Fixed costs ÷ Weighted average contribution margin per unit

Break-even point = $2,112 ÷ $2.40 = 880 Total units

Note that the break-even point is 80 units less (960 units − 880 units) than when the sales mix was 80/20. This demonstrates that shifting the sales mix not only increases net income but also reduces the break-even point. The 880 units represent the total number of bottles of both products combined that must be sold under an 60/40 sales mix for the company to break even. To determine the number of bottles of each product, multiply the total number of bottles times the proportionate share of the sales mix as follows:

Break-even point = Total units × Proportionate share of sales mix

Break-even point for Synthetic C = 880 bottles × .6 share of sales mix = 528 Bottles

Break-even point for Organic C = 880 bottles × .4 share of sales mix = 352 Bottles

The following income statement confirms that these sales volume figures constitute the break-even point.

| | |
|---|---|
| Sales of Synthetic C (528 bottles × $7) | $3,696 |
| Sales of Organic C (352 bottles × $9) | 3,168 |
| Total sales | 6,864 |
| Variable cost of Synthetic C (528 bottles × $5) | (2,640) |
| Variable cost of Organic C (352 bottles × $6) | (2,112) |
| Contribution margin | 2,112 |
| Fixed cost | (2,112) |
| Net income | $    0 |

The contribution margin per unit formula can be used to determine the number of units required to attain a target profit. Simply add the desired profit to the fixed costs and then divide by the weighted average contribution margin per unit. The resulting formula is:

$$\text{Sales volume in units} = \frac{\text{Fixed costs} + \text{Desired profit}}{\text{Weighted average contribution margin per unit}}$$

# COST-VOLUME-PROFIT LIMITATIONS

CVP is limited by a number of underlying assumptions. These assumptions include:

1.  The selling price is constant. It does not increase or decrease regardless of changes in sales volume.
2.  Costs are linear.
    a.  The variable cost per unit is constant and moves in direct proportion with changes in sales volume.
    b.  Total fixed costs do not change with changes in sales volume.
    c.  Efficiency and productivity are constant.
3.  The sales mix in multiproduct companies is constant.
4.  Inventory levels in manufacturing companies are constant.
5.  All CVP variables are within the relevant range.

Violating these assumptions will produce inaccuracies in CVP analysis. Unfortunately some violations are unavoidable in practice. For example, some companies may offer a discounted sales price for large orders, thereby violating the first assumption. Similarly, managers may desire to analyze operations at levels of sales volume that are outside the relevant range. Fortunately, many violations are insignificant. Further, accountants can make appropriate adjustments if serious violations are unavoidable. The widespread use of CVP in the real world suggests that the benefits of the analysis exceed the minor inaccuracies that inevitably occur. Even so, accountants must remain vigilant to avoid inaccuracies in the advice they render.

# A Look Back <<

Profitability is affected by changes in sales price, costs, and the volume of activity. The relationship among these variables is examined using *cost-volume-profit (CVP) analysis.* The *contribution margin,* determined by subtracting variable costs from the sales price, is a useful variable in CVP analysis. The *contribution margin per unit* is the amount each unit sold provides to cover fixed costs. Once fixed costs have been covered, each additional unit sold increases net income by the amount of the per-unit contribution margin.

The *break-even point* (the point where total revenue equals total cost) can be determined by the equation method, the contribution margin method, or the contribution margin ratio method. All three methods produce the same result because all three methods are derivations of the income statement formula:

**Sales − Variable costs − Fixed costs = Profit**

Beyond determining the break-even point, all three methods can also be used to assess the effects in other CVP relationships.

Many methods are available to determine the prices at which products should sell. In *cost-plus pricing,* the sales price per unit is determined by adding a percentage markup to the cost per unit. In contrast, *target costing* begins with an estimated market price customers would be willing to pay for the product and then develops the product at a cost that will enable the company to earn its desired profit.

A *break-even graph* can depict cost-volume-profit relationships for a product over a range of sales activity. The horizontal axis represents volume of activity and the vertical axis represents dollars. Lines for fixed costs, total costs, and sales are drawn based on the sales price per unit, variable cost per unit, and fixed costs. The graph can be used to determine the break-even point in units and sales dollars.

The *margin of safety* is the number of units or the amount of sales dollars by which actual sales can fall below expected sales before a loss is incurred. The margin of safety can also be expressed as a percentage to permit comparing different size companies. The margin of safety can be computed as a percentage by dividing the difference between budgeted sales and break-even sales by the amount of budgeted sales.

Spreadsheet software as well as the contribution margin approach can be used to conduct sensitivity analysis of cost-volume-profit relationships. *Sensitivity analysis* predicts the effect on profitability of different scenarios of fixed costs, variable costs, and sales volumes. The effects of simultaneous changes in all three variables can be assessed.

Cost-volume-profit analysis is built upon certain simplifying assumptions. The analysis assumes true linearity among the CVP variables and a constant level of inventory. Although these assumptions are not literally valid in actual practice, CVP analysis nevertheless provides managers with helpful insights for decision making.

# >> A Look Forward

The next chapter introduces a new cost classification scheme. Specifically, you will learn how to classify costs as being either direct or indirect costs. Direct costs are directly traceable to cost objects. Cost objects are items for which management needs to determine their cost. For example, a manager may need to determine the cost of making a product, providing a service, or operating a department. In these cases the cost object is the product, the service or the department. Indirect costs are those costs that cannot be directly traced to a cost object. The chapter will discuss the techniques such as cost tracing and cost allocation which are used to assign indirect costs to various objects.

www.mhhe.com/edmonds2011

**A step-by-step audio-narrated series of slides is provided on the text website at www.mhhe.com/edmonds2011.**

## SELF-STUDY REVIEW PROBLEM

Sharp Company makes and sells pencil sharpeners. The variable cost of each sharpener is $20. The sharpeners are sold for $30 each. Fixed operating expenses amount to $40,000.

### Required

a. Determine the break-even point in units and sales dollars.

b. Determine the sales volume in units and dollars that is required to attain a profit of $12,000. Verify your answer by preparing an income statement using the contribution margin format.

c. Determine the margin of safety between sales required to attain a profit of $12,000 and break-even sales.

d. Prepare a break-even graph using the cost and price assumptions outlined above.

### Solution to Requirement a

| Formula for Computing Break-even Point in Units |
| --- |
| Sales − Variable costs − Fixed costs = Profit |
| Sales price per unit (N) − Variable cost per unit (N) − Fixed costs = Profit |
| Contribution margin per unit (N) − Fixed costs = Profit |
| N = (Fixed costs + Profit) ÷ Contribution profit per unit |
| N = ($40,000 + 0) ÷ ($30 − $20) = 4,000 Units |

### Break-even Point in Sales Dollars

| | |
|---|---:|
| Sales price | $ 30 |
| × Number of units | 4,000 |
| Sales volume in dollars | $120,000 |

## Solution to Requirement b

### Formula for Computing Unit Sales Required to Attain Desired Profit

Sales − Variable costs − Fixed costs = Profit
Sales price per unit (N) − Variable cost per unit (N) − Fixed costs = Profit
Contribution margin per unit (N) − Fixed costs = Profit
N = (Fixed costs + Profit) ÷ Contribution profit per unit
N = ($40,000 + 12,000) ÷ ($30 − $20) = 5,200 Units

### Sales Dollars Required to Attain Desired Profit

| | |
|---|---:|
| Sales price | $ 30 |
| × Number of units | 5,200 |
| Sales volume in dollars | $156,000 |

### Income Statement

| | |
|---|---:|
| Sales volume in units (a) | 5,200 |
| Sales revenue (a × $30) | $156,000 |
| Variable costs (a × $20) | (104,000) |
| Contribution margin | 52,000 |
| Fixed costs | (40,000) |
| Net income | $ 12,000 |

## Solution to Requirement c

| Margin of Safety Computations | Units | Dollars |
|---|---:|---:|
| Budgeted sales | 5,200 | $156,000 |
| Break-even sales | (4,000) | (120,000) |
| Margin of safety | 1,200 | $ 36,000 |

### Percentage Computation

$$\frac{\text{Margin of safety in \$}}{\text{Budgeted sales}} = \frac{\$36,000}{\$156,000} = 23.08\%$$

**Solution to Requirement d**

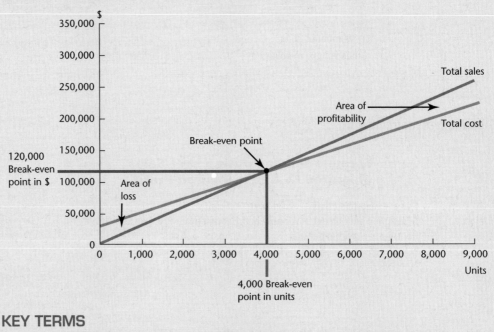

## KEY TERMS

Break-even point  108
Contribution margin per
   unit  109
Contribution margin ratio  110
Cost-plus pricing  112

Cost-volume-profit (CVP)
   analysis  107
Equation method  108
Margin of safety  119
Prestige pricing  112

Sales mix  123
Sensitivity analysis  121
Target costing  112

## QUESTIONS

1. What does the term *break-even point* mean? Name the two ways it can be measured.

2. How does a contribution margin income statement differ from the income statement used in financial reporting?

3. In what three ways can the contribution margin be useful in cost-volume-profit analysis?

4. If Company A has a projected margin of safety of 22 percent while Company B has a margin of safety of 52 percent, which company is at greater risk when actual sales are less than budgeted?

5. What variables affect profitability? Name two methods for determining profitability when simultaneous changes occur in these variables.

6. When would the customer be willing to pay a premium price for a product or service? What pricing strategy would be appropriate under these circumstances?

7. What are three alternative approaches to determine the break-even point? What do the results of these approaches show?

8. What is the equation method for determining the break-even point? Explain how the results of this method differ from those of the contribution margin approach.

9. If a company is trying to find the break-even point for multiple products that sell simultaneously, what consideration must be taken into account?

10. What assumptions are inherent in cost-volume-profit analysis? Since these assumptions are usually not wholly valid, why do managers still use the analysis in decision making?

11. Mary Hartwell and Jane Jamail, college roommates, are considering the joint purchase of a computer that they can share to prepare class assignments. Ms. Hartwell wants a particular model that costs $2,000; Ms. Jamail prefers a more economical model that costs $1,500. In fact, Ms. Jamail is adamant about her position, refusing to contribute more than $750 toward the purchase. If Ms. Hartwell is also adamant about her position, should she accept Ms. Jamail's $750 offer and apply that amount toward the purchase of the more expensive computer?

12. How would the algebraic formula used to compute the break-even point under the equation method be changed to solve for a desired target profit?

13. Setting the sales price is easy: Enter cost information and desired profit data into

one of the cost-volume-profit formulas, and the appropriate sales price can be computed mathematically. Do you agree with this line of reasoning? Explain.

**14.** What is the relationship between cost-volume-profit analysis and the relevant range?

## MULTIPLE-CHOICE QUESTIONS

**Multiple-choice questions are provided on the text website at www.mhhe.com/edmonds2011.**

## EXERCISES—SERIES A

**All applicable Exercises in Series A are available with McGraw-Hill's** *Connect Accounting.*

### Exercise 3-1A   *Equation method*     LO 1

Adair Corporation produces products that it sells for $12 each. Variable costs per unit are $5, and annual fixed costs are $140,000. Adair desires to earn a profit of $21,000.

**Required**

a. Use the equation method to determine the break-even point in units and dollars.

b. Determine the sales volume in units and dollars required to earn the desired profit.

### Exercise 3-2A   *Per-unit contribution margin approach*     LO 2

Connor Corporation sells products for $25 each that have variable costs of $13 per unit. Connor's annual fixed cost is $264,000.

**Required**

Use the per-unit contribution margin approach to determine the break-even point in units and dollars.

### Exercise 3-3A   *Contribution margin ratio*     LO 3

Garcia Company incurs annual fixed costs of $60,000. Variable costs for Garcia's product are $22.75 per unit, and the sales price is $35.00 per unit. Garcia desires to earn an annual profit of $45,000.

**Required**

Use the contribution margin ratio approach to determine the sales volume in dollars and units required to earn the desired profit.

### Exercise 3-4A   *Cost structure, risk, and the break-even point*     LO 1, 4, 6

Kennedy Company produces a product that sells for $37 per unit and has a variable cost of $22 per unit. Kennedy incurs annual fixed costs of $75,000.

**Required**

a. Determine the sales volume in units and dollars required to break even.

b. Calculate the break-even point assuming fixed costs increase to $120,000.

c. Explain how a fixed cost structure affects risk and the break-even point.

### Exercise 3-5A   *Target costing*     LO 5

Mote Enterprises produces a product with fixed costs of $36,000 and variable cost of $2.50 per unit. The company desires to earn a $20,000 profit and believes it can sell 10,000 units of the product.

**Required**

a. Based on this information, determine the target sales price.

b. Assume a competitor is currently selling a similar product for $6.80 per unit. Explain how Mote can use target costing to maintain its desired profitability.

**LO 6**

### Exercise 3-6A  *Determining variable cost from incomplete cost data*

Laya Corporation produced 200,000 watches that it sold for $16 each during 2012. The company determined that fixed manufacturing cost per unit was $7 per watch. The company reported an $800,000 gross margin on its 2012 financial statements.

**Required**

Determine the variable cost per unit, the total variable, and the total contribution margin.

**LO 2, 4**

### Exercise 3-7A  *Contribution margin per unit approach for break-even and desired profit*

Information concerning a product produced by Salter Company appears here:

| | |
|---|---|
| Sales price per unit | $175 |
| Variable cost per unit | $75 |
| Total annual fixed manufacturing and operating costs | $600,000 |

**Required**

Determine the following:

a.  Contribution margin per unit.
b.  Number of units that Salter must sell to break even.
c.  Sales level in units that Salter must reach to earn a profit of $200,000.

**LO 6**

### Exercise 3-8A  *Changing sales price*

Pettigrew Company produces a product that has a variable cost of $13 per unit; the product sells for $28 per unit. The company's annual fixed costs total $375,000; it had net income of $75,000 in the previous year. In an effort to increase the company's market share, management is considering lowering the selling price to $25 per unit.

**Required**

If Pettigrew desires to maintain net income of $75,000, how many additional units must it sell to justify the price decline?

**LO 4, 6**

### Exercise 3-9A  *Simultaneous change in sales price and desired profit*

Use the cost data presented in Exercise 3-8A but assume that in addition to increasing its market share by lowering its selling price to $25, Pettigrew desires to increase its net income by $36,000.

**Required**

Determine the number of units the company must sell to earn the desired income.

**LO 1, 7**

### Exercise 3-10A  *Components of break-even graph*

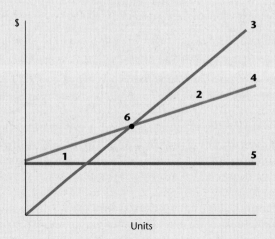

Units

**Required**

Match the numbers shown in the graph with the following items.

a. Fixed cost line          d. Area of profit
b. Total cost line          e. Revenue line
c. Break-even point         f. Area of loss

## Exercise 3-11A  *Evaluating simultaneous changes in fixed and variable costs*          LO 6

Naylor Company currently produces and sells 6,400 units annually of a product that has a variable cost of $18 per unit and annual fixed costs of $161,400. The company currently earns a $69,000 annual profit. Assume that Naylor has the opportunity to invest in new labor-saving production equipment that will enable the company to reduce variable costs to $16 per unit. The investment would cause fixed costs to increase by $9,000 because of additional depreciation cost.

**Required**

a. Use the equation method to determine the sales price per unit under existing conditions (current equipment is used).
b. Prepare a contribution margin income statement, assuming that Naylor invests in the new production equipment. Recommend whether Naylor should invest in the new equipment.

## Exercise 3-12A  *Margin of safety*          LO 8

Jensen Company makes a product that sells for $38 per unit. The company pays $16 per unit for the variable costs of the product and incurs annual fixed costs of $176,000. Jensen expects to sell 21,000 units of product.

**Required**

Determine Jensen's margin of safety expressed as a percentage.

## Exercise 3-13A  *Cost-volume-profit relationship*          LO 1, 2, 4, 6

Feskin Corporation is a manufacturing company that makes small electric motors it sells for $36 per unit. The variable costs of production are $22 per motor, and annual fixed costs of production are $196,000.

**Required**

a. How many units of product must Feskin make and sell to break even?
b. How many units of product must Feskin make and sell to earn a $56,000 profit?
c. The marketing manager believes that sales would increase dramatically if the price were reduced to $34 per unit. How many units of product must Feskin make and sell to earn a $56,000 profit, if the sales price is set at $34 per unit?

## Exercise 3-14A  *Complexities of CVP Analysis in Multinational Companies*          LO 6

Pinero Barrels, Inc. (PBI), manufactures oak barrels for the wine industry at its facility in the United States. One of the raw materials used for some of its barrels is French oak lumber. The company fabricates the oak lumber into the appropriate-sized staves and assembles these staves, along with other components, into barrels. In January 2009, the company signed a contract to buy oak lumber from a French supplier for the coming two years. The contract calls for PBI to pay the supplier in euros (€), although all other costs that PBI incurs are paid for in dollars. A summary of the production cost for one barrel, based on the expected production level, follows:

| Variable costs: | |
|---|---|
| French oak | $100* |
| All other variable costs | 150 |
| Fixed costs: | 50 |

*Based on the exchange rate at the time the contract with the French supplier was signed. The cost of lumber in euros was €77.50 as of January 2009.

The exchange rate between the dollar and the euro was $1.33 = €1.00 in January 2009 when the contract was signed. By September 2009, the exchange rate had changed to $1.48 = €1.00.

**Required**

a. CVP analysis is based on several assumptions. Explain which of these assumptions would be violated as a result of PBI having to pay for one of its raw materials in euros while its other costs and revenues are priced in dollars.

b. What effect, if any, would the change in the exchange rate have on PBI's variable cost per unit for September versus January 2009?

c. What effect, if any, would the change in the exchange rate have on PBI's contribution margin per unit for September versus January 2009?

d. What effect, if any, would the change in the exchange rate have on PBI's fixed cost per unit for September versus January 2009?

**LO 5**

### Exercise 3-15A    *Target costing*

The marketing manager of Ross Corporation has determined that a market exists for a telephone with a sales price of $19 per unit. The production manager estimates the annual fixed costs of producing between 40,000 and 80,000 telephones would be $344,000.

**Required**

Assume that Ross desires to earn a $116,000 profit from the phone sales. How much can Ross afford to spend on variable cost per unit if production and sales equal 46,000 phones?

**LO 10**

### Exercise 3-16A    *Multiple product break-even analysis*

Eaton Company manufactures two products. The budgeted per-unit contribution margin for each product follows:

|  | Super | Supreme |
|---|---|---|
| Sales price | $100 | $125 |
| Variable cost per unit | (65) | (74) |
| Contribution margin per unit | $ 35 | $ 51 |

Eaton expects to incur annual fixed costs of $145,160. The relative sales mix of the products is 80 percent for Super and 20 percent for Supreme.

**Required**

a. Determine the total number of products (units of Super and Supreme combined) Eaton must sell to break even.

b. How many units each of Super and Supreme must Eaton sell to break even?

## PROBLEMS—SERIES A

**All applicable Problems in Series A are available with McGraw-Hill's *Connect Accounting.***

**LO 1, 2, 3**

### Problem 3-17A    *Determining the break-even point and preparing a contribution margin income statement*

Inman Manufacturing Company makes a product that it sells for $60 per unit. The company incurs variable manufacturing costs of $24 per unit. Variable selling expenses are $12 per unit, annual fixed manufacturing costs are $189,000, and fixed selling and administrative costs are $141,000 per year.

**Required**

Determine the break-even point in units and dollars using each of the following approaches:

a. Equation method.

b. Contribution margin per unit.

**CHECK FIGURE**
a. 13,750 units

c. Contribution margin ratio.

d. Confirm your results by preparing a contribution margin income statement for the break-even sales volume.

## Problem 3-18A  *Determining the break-even point and preparing a break-even graph*

LO 1, 2, 3, 7

Whitaker Company is considering the production of a new product. The expected variable cost is $48.75 per unit. Annual fixed costs are expected to be $650,000. The anticipated sales price is $65 each.

**CHECK FIGURE**
a. $2,600,000

### Required

Determine the break-even point in units and dollars using each of the following:

a. Equation method.

b. Contribution margin per unit approach.

c. Contribution margin ratio approach.

d. Prepare a break-even graph to illustrate the cost-volume-profit relationships.

## Problem 3-19A  *Effect of converting variable to fixed costs*

LO 2, 4, 6

Yule Manufacturing Company reported the following data regarding a product it manufactures and sells. The sales price is $42.

**CHECK FIGURE**
b. 19,000 units

| | |
|---|---|
| Variable costs | |
| Manufacturing | $18 per unit |
| Selling | 6 per unit |
| Fixed costs | |
| Manufacturing | $150,000 per year |
| Selling and administrative | 66,000 per year |

### Required

a. Use the per-unit contribution margin approach to determine the break-even point in units and dollars.

b. Use the per-unit contribution margin approach to determine the level of sales in units and dollars required to obtain a profit of $126,000.

c. Suppose that variable selling costs could be eliminated by employing a salaried sales force. If the company could sell 20,000 units, how much could it pay in salaries for salespeople and still have a profit of $126,000? (*Hint:* Use the equation method.)

## Problem 3-20A  *Analyzing change in sales price using the contribution margin ratio*

LO 3, 6

Hugh Company reported the following data regarding the product it sells:

**CHECK FIGURE**
c. 9,000 units

| | |
|---|---|
| Sales price | $40 |
| Contribution margin ratio | 15% |
| Fixed costs | $144,000 |

### Required

Use the contribution margin ratio approach and consider each requirement separately.

a. What is the break-even point in dollars? In units?

b. To obtain a profit of $36,000, what must the sales be in dollars? In units?

c. If the sales price increases to $50 and variable costs do not change, what is the new break-even point in dollars? In units?

LO 1, 6

CHECK FIGURE
a. 8,000 units

## Problem 3-21A    *Analyzing sales price and fixed cost using the equation method*

Tainan Company is considering adding a new product. The cost accountant has provided the following data.

| | |
|---|---|
| Expected variable cost of manufacturing | $47 per unit |
| Expected annual fixed manufacturing costs | $78,000 |

The administrative vice president has provided the following estimates.

| | |
|---|---|
| Expected sales commission | $3 per unit |
| Expected annual fixed administrative costs | $42,000 |

The manager has decided that any new product must at least break even in the first year.

### Required

Use the equation method and consider each requirement separately.

a.  If the sales price is set at $65, how many units must Tainan sell to break even?

b.  Tainan estimates that sales will probably be 10,000 units. What sales price per unit will allow the company to break even?

c.  Tainan has decided to advertise the product heavily and has set the sales price at $66. If sales are 9,000 units, how much can the company spend on advertising and still break even?

LO 8

CHECK FIGURES
b. NI:
    Skin Cream $60,000
    Bath Oil    $60,000
    Color Gel   $40,000

## Problem 3-22A    *Margin of safety and operating leverage*

Santiago Company is considering the addition of a new product to its cosmetics line. The company has three distinctly different options: a skin cream, a bath oil, or a hair coloring gel. Relevant information and budgeted annual income statements for each of the products follow.

| **Relevant Information** | | | |
|---|---|---|---|
| | **Skin Cream** | **Bath Oil** | **Color Gel** |
| Budgeted sales in units (a) | 50,000 | 90,000 | 30,000 |
| Expected sales price (b) | $7.00 | $4.00 | $13.00 |
| Variable costs per unit (c) | $4.00 | $1.50 | $9.00 |
| Income statements | | | |
| Sales revenue (a × b) | $350,000 | $360,000 | $390,000 |
| Variable costs (a × c) | (200,000) | (135,000) | (270,000) |
| Contribution margin | 150,000 | 225,000 | 120,000 |
| Fixed costs | (120,000) | (210,000) | (104,000) |
| Net income | $ 30,000 | $ 15,000 | $ 16,000 |

### Required

a.  Determine the margin of safety as a percentage for each product.

b.  Prepare revised income statements for each product, assuming a 20 percent increase in the budgeted sales volume.

c.  For each product, determine the percentage change in net income that results from the 20 percent increase in sales. Which product has the highest operating leverage?

d.  Assuming that management is pessimistic and risk averse, which product should the company add to its cosmetic line? Explain your answer.

e.  Assuming that management is optimistic and risk aggressive, which product should the company add to its cosmetics line? Explain your answer.

LO 2, 4, 6, 7, 8

## Problem 3-23A    *Comprehensive CVP analysis*

Borysko Company makes and sells products with variable costs of $47 each. Borysko incurs annual fixed costs of $22,400. The current sales price is $63.

**Required**

The following requirements are interdependent. For example, the $4,800 desired profit introduced in Requirement *c* also applies to subsequent requirements. Likewise, the $55 sales price introduced in Requirement *d* applies to the subsequent requirements.

a. Determine the contribution margin per unit.

b. Determine the break-even point in units and in dollars. Confirm your answer by preparing an income statement using the contribution margin format.

c. Suppose that Borysko desires to earn a $4,800 profit. Determine the sales volume in units and dollars required to earn the desired profit. Confirm your answer by preparing an income statement using the contribution margin format.

d. If the sales price drops to $55 per unit, what level of sales is required to earn the desired profit? Express your answer in units and dollars. Confirm your answer by preparing an income statement using the contribution margin format.

e. If fixed costs drop to $16,800, what level of sales is required to earn the desired profit? Express your answer in units and dollars. Confirm your answer by preparing an income statement using the contribution margin format.

f. If variable cost drops to $39 per unit, what level of sales is required to earn the desired profit? Express your answer in units and dollars. Confirm your answer by preparing an income statement using the contribution margin format.

g. Assume that Borysko concludes that it can sell 1,350 units of product for $55 each. Recall that variable costs are $39 each and fixed costs are $16,800. Compute the margin of safety in units and dollars and as a percentage.

h. Draw a break-even graph using the cost and price assumptions described in Requirement *g*.

## Problem 3-24A   *Assessing simultaneous changes in CVP relationships*

**LO 6, 7, 8, 9**

Braun Corporation sells hammocks; variable costs are $75 each, and the hammocks are sold for $125 each. Braun incurs $240,000 of fixed operating expenses annually.

**Required**

a. Determine the sales volume in units and dollars required to attain a $60,000 profit. Verify your answer by preparing an income statement using the contribution margin format.

b. Braun is considering implementing a quality improvement program. The program will require a $10 increase in the variable cost per unit. To inform its customers of the quality improvements, the company plans to spend an additional $10,000 for advertising. Assuming that the improvement program will increase sales to a level that is 4,000 units above the amount computed in Requirement *a,* should Braun proceed with plans to improve product quality? Support your answer by preparing a budgeted income statement.

c. Determine the new break-even point in units and sales dollars as well as the margin of safety percentage, assuming that the quality improvement program is implemented.

d. Prepare a break-even graph using the cost and price assumptions outlined in Requirement *c.*

## Problem 3-25A   *Determining the break-even point and margin of safety for a company with multiple products*

**LO 10**

*eXcel*

Tottori Company produces two products. Budgeted annual income statements for the two products are provided here:

| | Power | | | Lite | | | Total | |
|---|---|---|---|---|---|---|---|---|
| | Budgeted Number | Per Unit | Budgeted Amount | Budgeted Number | Per Unit | Budgeted Amount | Budgeted Number | Budgeted Amount |
| Sales | 160 | @ $500 = | $80,000 | 640 | @ $450 = | $288,000 | 800 | $368,000 |
| Variable cost | 160 | @ 320 = | (51,200) | 640 | @ 330 = | (211,200) | 800 | (262,400) |
| Contribution margin | 160 | @ 180 = | 28,800 | 640 | @ 120 = | 76,800 | 800 | 105,600 |
| Fixed cost | | | (12,000) | | | (54,000) | | (66,000) |
| Net income | | | $16,800 | | | $ 22,800 | | $ 39,600 |

**Required**

a. Based on budgeted sales, determine the relative sales mix between the two products.
b. Determine the weighted-average contribution margin per unit.
c. Calculate the break-even point in total number of units.
d. Determine the number of units of each product Tottori must sell to break even.
e. Verify the break-even point by preparing an income statement for each product as well as an income statement for the combined products.
f. Determine the margin of safety based on the combined sales of the two products.

## EXERCISES—SERIES B

**LO 1**

### Exercise 3-1B   *Equation method*

Jade Corporation manufactures products that it sells for $57 each. Variable costs are $32 per unit, and annual fixed costs are $750,000. Jade desires to earn a profit of $200,000.

**Required**

a. Use the equation method to determine the break-even point in units and dollars.
b. Determine the sales volume in units and dollars required to earn the desired profit.

**LO 2**

### Exercise 3-2B   *Per-unit contribution margin approach*

Kemeth Corporation manufactures products that have variable costs of $43 per unit. Its fixed cost amounts to $84,000. It sells the products for $78 each.

**Required**

Use the per-unit contribution margin approach to determine the break-even point in units and dollars.

**LO 3**

### Exercise 3-3B   *Contribution margin ratio*

Lambert Company incurs annual fixed costs of $960,000. Variable costs for Lambert's product are $36 per-unit, and the sales price is $60 per unit. Lambert desires to earn a profit of $240,000.

**Required**

Use the contribution margin ratio approach to determine the sales volume in dollars and units required to earn the desired profit.

**LO 4, 6**

### Exercise 3-4B   *Cost structure, risk, and the break-even point*

Wava Company manufactures a product that sells for $125 per unit. It incurs fixed costs of $198,000. Variable cost for its product is $81 per unit.

**Required**

a. Determine the sales volume in units and dollars required to earn the desired profit.
b. Calculate the break-even point assuming fixed costs increase to $308,000.
c. Explain how a fixed cost structure affects risk and the break-even point.

**LO 5**

### Exercise 3-5B   *Prestige pricing*

Weng Company is considering the production and sale of a new product with fixed costs of $35,000 and variable cost of $4 per unit. Based on its normal profit margins, Weng desires to earn a $40,000 profit and believes it can sell 5,000 units of the product.

**Required**

a. Based on this information determine the target sales price.
b. Explain how prestige pricing could be used to increase profitability.

**Exercise 3-6B   *Determining variable cost from incomplete data***                    **LO 6**

Sohail Corporation produced 80,000 tires and sold them for $100 each during 2011. The company determined that fixed manufacturing cost per unit was $25 per tire. The company reported gross profit of $1,440,000 on its 2011 financial statements.

**Required**

Determine the variable cost per unit, the total variable cost, and the total contribution margin.

**Exercise 3-7B   *Contribution margin per unit approach for break-even and***          **LO 2, 4**
                      ***desired profit***

Information concerning a product produced by Agar Company appears here:

| | |
|---|---:|
| Sales price per unit | $420 |
| Variable cost per unit | $270 |
| Total fixed manufacturing and operating costs | $750,000 |

**Required**

Determine the following:

a.  Contribution margin per unit.
b.  Number of units Agar must sell to break even.
c.  Sales level in units that Agar must reach in order to earn a profit of $150,000.

**Exercise 3-8B   *Changing sales price***                                             **LO 6**

Mendez Company manufactures a product that has a variable cost of $30 per unit. The company's fixed costs total $750,000. Mendez had net income of $90,000 in the previous year. Its product sells for $50 per unit. In an effort to increase the company's market share, management is considering lowering the product's selling price to $46 per unit.

**Required**

If Mendez desires to maintain net income of $90,000, how many additional units must it sell in order to justify the price decline?

**Exercise 3-9B   *Simultaneous change in sales price and desired profit***            **LO 4, 6**

Use the cost data presented in Exercise 3-8B but assume that in addition to increasing its market share by lowering its selling price to $46, Mendez desires to increase its net income by $42,000.

**Required**

Determine the number of units that Mendez must sell to earn the desired income.

**Exercise 3-10B   *Components of break-even graph***                                  **LO 1, 7**

Jimmy, a 10-year-old boy, wants to sell lemonade on a hot summer day. He hopes to make enough money to buy a new iPod. Sam, his elder brother, tries to help him compute his prospect of doing so. The following is the relevant information:

| | |
|---|---|
| Variable costs | |
|    Lemonade | $0.30 per cup |
|    Paper cups | $0.10 per cup |
| Fixed costs | |
|    Table and chair | $36.00 |
| Price | $1.00 per cup |

The following graph depicts the dollar amount of cost or revenue on the vertical axis and the number of lemonade cups sold on the horizontal axis.

**Required**

a. Draw a line that depicts the total cost.

b. Draw a line that depicts the total revenue.

c. Identify the break-even point.

d. Identify the area representing profit.

e. Identify the area representing loss.

**LO 6**

### Exercise 3-11B  *Evaluating simultaneous changes in fixed and variable costs*

Kasmira Company currently produces and sells 10,000 units of a telephone per year that has a variable cost of $13 per unit and a fixed cost of $380,000. The company currently earns a $120,000 annual profit. Assume that Kasmira has the opportunity to invest in a new machine that will enable the company to reduce variable costs to $10 per unit. The investment would cause fixed costs to increase by $15,000.

**Required**

a. Use the equation method to determine the sales price per unit under existing conditions (current machine is used).

b. Prepare a contribution margin income statement assuming Kasmira invests in the new technology. Recommend whether Kasmira should invest in the new technology.

**LO 8**

### Exercise 3-12B  *Margin of safety*

Conway Company manufactures scanners that sell for $250 each. The company pays $130 per unit for the variable costs of the product and incurs fixed costs of $3,600,000. Conway expects to sell 54,000 scanners.

**Required**

Determine Conway's margin of safety expressed as a percentage.

**LO 1, 2, 4, 6**

### Exercise 3-13B  *Cost-volume-profit relationship*

Dalton Corporation manufactures faucets. The variable costs of production are $27 per faucet. Fixed costs of production are $600,000. Dalton sells the faucets for a price of $52 per unit.

**Required**

a. How many faucets must Dalton make and sell to break even?

b. How many faucets must Dalton make and sell to earn a $180,000 profit?

c. The marketing manager believes that sales would increase dramatically if the price were reduced to $47 per unit. How many faucets must Dalton make and sell to earn a $180,000 profit, assuming the sales price is set at $47 per unit?

**LO 6**

### Exercise 3-14B  *Complexities of CVP analysis in multinational companies*

Castillo Wood Products (CWP) manufactures disposable chopsticks for the restaurant industry at its highly automated production facility in China. The main raw material used to produce the chopsticks is wood that is purchased in bulk from suppliers in the United States. In September

2007, the company signed a contract to buy wood from a U.S. supplier for the coming two years. The contract calls for CWP to pay the supplier in dollars, although all other costs CWP incurs are paid for in Chinese Renminbi (¥). A summary of the production costs for a box of 1,000 sets of chopsticks, based on the expected production level, follows:

| Variable costs: | |
| --- | --- |
| Wood | ¥6,000* |
| All other variable costs | 600 |
| Fixed costs: | 5,400 |

*Based on the exchange rate at the time the contract with the U.S. supplier was signed. The cost of wood in dollars was $50 as of January 2007.

The exchange rate between the yen and the dollar was ¥100 = $13.24 in September 2007 when the contract was signed. By September 2009, the exchange rate had changed to ¥100 = $14.65. (Exchange rates are rounded to the nearest cent.)

**Required**

a. CVP analysis is based on several assumptions. Explain which of these assumptions would be violated as a result of CWP having to pay for one of its raw materials in dollars while its other costs and revenues are priced in yen.

b. What effect, if any, would the change in the exchange rate have on CWP's variable cost per unit for September 2007 versus September 2009?

c. What effect, if any, would the change in the exchange rate have on CWP's contribution margin per unit for September 2007 versus September 2009?

d. What effect, if any, would the change in the exchange rate have on CWP's fixed cost per unit for September 2007 versus September 2009?

## Exercise 3-15B    *Target costing*                                                   LO 5

After substantial marketing research, Ewing Corporation management believes that it can make and sell a new battery with a prolonged life for laptop computers. Management expects the market demand for its new battery to be 12,000 units per year if the battery is priced at $90 per unit. A team of engineers and accountants determines that the fixed costs of producing 8,000 units to 16,000 units is $480,000.

**Required**

Assume that Ewing desires to earn a $240,000 profit from the battery sales. How much can it afford to spend on the variable cost per unit if production and sales equal 12,000 batteries?

## Exercise 3-16B    *Multiple product break-even analysis*                            LO 10

Harvey Company makes two products. The budgeted per-unit contribution margin for each product follows:

| | Deluxe | Luxury |
| --- | --- | --- |
| Sales price | $48 | $75 |
| Variable cost per unit | 33 | 40 |
| Contribution margin per unit | $15 | $35 |

Harvey expects to incur fixed costs of $115,000. The relative sales mix of the products is 60 percent for Deluxe and 40 percent for Luxury.

**Required**

a. Determine the total number of products (units of Deluxe and Luxury combined) Harvey must sell to break even.

b. How many units each of Deluxe and Luxury must Harvey sell to break even?

## PROBLEMS—SERIES B

**LO 1, 2, 3**

### Problem 3-17B  *Determining the break-even point and preparing a contribution margin income statement*

Nickolas Company manufactures radio and cassette players and sells them for $100 each. According to the company's records, the variable costs, including direct labor and direct materials, are $50. Factory depreciation and other fixed manufacturing costs are $192,000 per year. Nickolas pays its salespeople a commission of $18 per unit. Annual fixed selling and administrative costs are $128,000.

**Required**

Determine the break-even point in units and dollars, using each of the following:

**a.** Equation method.

**b.** Contribution margin per unit approach.

**c.** Contribution margin ratio approach.

**d.** Confirm your results by preparing a contribution margin income statement for the break-even point sales volume.

**LO 1, 2, 3, 7**

### Problem 3-18B  *Determining the break-even point and preparing a break-even graph*

Executive officers of Vaclar Company are assessing the profitability of a potential new product. They expect that the variable cost of making the product will be $54 per unit and fixed manufacturing cost will be $720,000. The executive officers plan to sell the product for $72 per unit.

**Required**

Determine the break-even point in units and dollars using each of the following approaches:

**a.** Contribution margin per unit.

**b.** Equation method.

**c.** Contribution margin ratio.

**d.** Prepare a break-even graph to illustrate the cost-volume-profit relationships.

**LO 2, 3, 4, 6**

### Problem 3-19B  *Effect of converting variable to fixed costs*

Souta Company manufactures and sells its own brand of digital cameras. It sells each camera for $32. The company's accountant prepared the following data:

| Manufacturing costs | |
| --- | --- |
| Variable | $15 per unit |
| Fixed | $150,000 per year |
| Selling and administrative expenses | |
| Variable | $9 per unit |
| Fixed | $50,000 per year |

**Required**

**a.** Use the per-unit contribution margin approach to determine the break-even point in units and dollars.

**b.** Use the per-unit contribution margin approach to determine the level of sales in units and dollars required to obtain a $60,000 profit.

**c.** Suppose that variable selling and administrative costs could be eliminated by employing a salaried sales force. If the company could sell 32,000 units, how much could it pay in salaries for the salespeople and still have a profit of $60,000? (*Hint:* Use the equation method.)

**Problem 3-20B**  *Analyzing change in sales price using the contribution margin ratio*   LO 3, 6

Kaito Company reported the following data regarding the one product it sells:

| | |
|---|---|
| Sales price | $16 |
| Contribution margin ratio | 20% |
| Fixed costs | $360,000 per year |

**Required**

Use the contribution margin ratio approach and consider each requirement separately.

a. What is the break-even point in dollars? In units?

b. To obtain a $80,000 profit, what must the sales be in dollars? In units?

c. If the sales price increases to $20 and variable costs do not change, what is the new break-even point in units? In dollars?

**Problem 3-21B**  *Analyzing sales price and fixed cost using the equation method*   LO 1, 6

Salazar Company is analyzing whether its new product will be profitable. The following data are provided for analysis:

| | |
|---|---|
| Expected variable cost of manufacturing | $30 per unit |
| Expected fixed manufacturing costs | $48,000 per year |
| Expected sales commission | $6 per unit |
| Expected fixed administrative costs | $12,000 per year |

The company has decided that any new product must at least break even in the first year.

**Required**

Use the equation method and consider each requirement separately.

a. If the sales price is set at $48, how many units must Salazar sell to break even?

b. Salazar estimates that sales will probably be 6,000 units. What sales price per unit will allow the company to break even?

c. Salazar has decided to advertise the product heavily and has set the sales price at $54. If sales are 9,000 units, how much can the company spend on advertising and still break even?

**Problem 3-22B**  *Margin of safety and operating leverage*   LO 8

Meier Company has three distinctly different options available as it considers adding a new product to its automotive division: engine oil, coolant, or windshield washer. Relevant information and budgeted annual income statements for each product follow:

| Relevant Information | | | |
|---|---|---|---|
| | Engine Oil | Coolant | Windshield Washer |
| Budgeted sales in units (a) | 20,000 | 30,000 | 125,000 |
| Expected sales price (b) | $2.40 | $2.85 | $1.15 |
| Variable costs per unit (c) | $1.00 | $1.25 | $0.35 |
| Income Statements | | | |
| Sales revenue (a × b) | $48,000 | $85,500 | $143,750 |
| Variable costs (a × c) | (20,000) | (37,500) | (43,750) |
| Contribution margin | 28,000 | 48,000 | 100,000 |
| Fixed costs | (21,000) | (32,000) | (50,000) |
| Net income | $ 7,000 | $16,000 | $ 50,000 |

**Required**

a. Determine the margin of safety as a percentage for each product.

b. Prepare revised income statements for each product, assuming 20 percent growth in the budgeted sales volume.

c. For each product, determine the percentage change in net income that results from the 20 percent increase in sales. Which product has the highest operating leverage?

d. Assuming that management is pessimistic and risk averse, which product should the company add? Explain your answer.

e. Assuming that management is optimistic and risk aggressive, which product should the company add? Explain your answer.

**LO 2, 4, 6, 7, 8**    **Problem 3-23B**   *Comprehensive CVP analysis*

Dunlop Company makes a product that it sells for $200. Dunlop incurs annual fixed costs of $250,000 and variable costs of $160 per unit.

**Required**

The following requirements are interdependent. For example, the $50,000 desired profit introduced in Requirement *c* also applies to subsequent requirements. Likewise, the $180 sales price introduced in Requirement *d* applies to the subsequent requirements.

a. Determine the contribution margin per unit.

b. Determine the break-even point in units and in dollars. Confirm your answer by preparing an income statement using the contribution margin format.

c. Suppose that Dunlop desires to earn a $50,000 profit. Determine the sales volume in units and dollars required to earn the desired profit. Confirm your answer by preparing an income statement using the contribution margin format.

d. If the sales price drops to $180 per unit, what level of sales is required to earn the desired profit? Express your answer in units and dollars. Confirm your answer by preparing an income statement using the contribution margin format.

e. If fixed costs drop to $200,000, what level of sales is required to earn the desired profit? Express your answer in units and dollars. Confirm your answer by preparing an income statement using the contribution margin format.

f. If variable costs drop to $130 per unit, what level of sales is required to earn the desired profit? Express your answer in units and dollars. Confirm your answer by preparing an income statement using the contribution margin format.

g. Assume that Dunlop concludes that it can sell 5,000 units of product for $180 each. Recall that variable costs are $130 each and fixed costs are $200,000. Compute the margin of safety in units and dollars and as a percentage.

h. Draw a break-even graph using the cost and price assumptions described in Requirement *g.*

**LO 6, 7, 8, 9**    **Problem 3-24B**   *Assessing simultaneous changes in CVP relationships*

Haas Company sells tennis racquets; variable costs for each are $45, and each is sold for $135. Haas incurs $540,000 of fixed operating expenses annually.

**Required**

a. Determine the sales volume in units and dollars required to attain a $270,000 profit. Verify your answer by preparing an income statement using the contribution margin format.

b. Haas is considering establishing a quality improvement program that will require a $15 increase in the variable cost per unit. To inform its customers of the quality improvements, the company plans to spend an additional $150,000 for advertising. Assuming that the improvement program will increase sales to a level that is 5,000 units above the amount computed in Requirement *a*, should Haas proceed with plans to improve product quality? Support your answer by preparing a budgeted income statement.

c. Determine the new break-even point and the margin of safety percentage, assuming Haas adopts the quality improvement program.

d. Prepare a break-even graph using the cost and price assumptions outlined in Requirement *c.*

**Problem 3-25B**    *Determining the break-even point and margin of safety for a*    **LO 10**
*company with multiple products*

Executive officers of Pena Company have prepared the annual budgets for its two products, Washer and Dryer, as follows.

| | Washer | | | Dryer | | | Total | |
|---|---|---|---|---|---|---|---|---|
| | Budgeted Quantity | Per Unit | Budgeted Amount | Budgeted Quantity | Per Unit | Budgeted Amount | Budgeted Quantity | Budgeted Amount |
| Sales | 400 | @ $540 = | $216,000 | 1,200 | @ $300 = | $360,000 | 1,600 | $576,000 |
| Variable cost | 400 | @  300 = | (120,000) | 1,200 | @  180 = | (216,000) | 1,600 | (336,000) |
| Contribution margin | 400 | @  240 = | 96,000 | 1,200 | @  120 = | 144,000 | 1,600 | 240,000 |
| Fixed costs | | | (34,000) | | | (44,000) | | (78,000) |
| Net income | | | $ 62,000 | | | $100,000 | | $162,000 |

**Required**

a. Based on the number of units budgeted to be sold, determine the relative sales mix between the two products.

b. Determine the weighted-average contribution margin per unit.

c. Calculate the break-even point in total number of units.

d. Determine the number of units of each product Pena must sell to break even.

e. Verify the break-even point by preparing an income statement for each product as well as an income statement for the combined products.

f. Determine the margin of safety based on the combined sales of the two products.

## ANALYZE, THINK, COMMUNICATE

**ATC 3-1    Business Applications    *Cost-volume-profit behavior at Apple Inc.***

In July 2009, Apple Inc. announced that its revenues for the third quarter of its 2009 fiscal year rose 11.7 percent, causing its earnings to increase by 14.6 percent compared with the third quarter of 2008. Sales for this period were $8.34 billion.

In July 2007, the company had announced that a 24 percent increase in revenue had produced a 73 percent increase in earnings, compared to the same quarter of the previous year. Sales for the second quarter of 2007 were $5.41 billion.

**Required**

a. What concept explains how Apple's net income could rise by 14.6 percent when its revenue rose only 11.7 percent?

b. Does the concept identified in Requirement *a* result from fixed costs or variable costs?

c. Notice that in the third quarter of 2007, Apple's percentage increase in earnings was over three times the percentage increase in revenue (73 ÷ 24 = 3.04). In the third quarter of 2009, however, Apple's percentage increase in earnings was only about 1.25 times its increase in revenue (14.6 ÷ 11.7 = 1.25). Explain why the ratio of increase in earnings to increase in revenue was lower in 2009 than in 2007. Assume Apple's general pricing policies and cost structure did not change.

**ATC 3-2    Group Assignment    *Effect of changes in fixed and variable cost on profitability***

In a month when it sold 200 units of product, Queen Manufacturing Company (QMC) produced the following internal income statement:

| Revenue | $8,000 |
|---|---|
| Variable costs | (4,800) |
| Contribution margin | 3,200 |
| Fixed costs | (2,400) |
| Net income | $ 800 |

QMC has the opportunity to alter its operations in one of the following ways:

1. Increasing fixed advertising costs by $1,600, thereby increasing sales by 120 units.
2. Lowering commissions paid to the sales staff by $8 per unit, thereby reducing sales by 10 units.
3. Decreasing fixed inventory holding cost by $800, thereby decreasing sales by 20 units.

### Required

a. The instructor will divide the class into groups and then organize the groups into two sections. For a large class (12 or more groups), four sections may be necessary. At least three groups in each section are needed. Having more groups in one section than another section is acceptable because offsetting advantages and disadvantages exist. Having more groups is advantageous because more people will work on the task but is disadvantageous because having more people complicates communication.

### Group Task

The sections are to compete with each other to see which section can identify the most profitable alternative in the shortest period of time. No instruction is provided regarding how the sections are to proceed with the task. In other words, each section is required to organize itself with respect to how to accomplish the task of selecting the best alternative. A total quality management (TQM) constraint is imposed that requires zero defects. A section that turns in a wrong answer is disqualified. Once an answer has been submitted to the instructor, it cannot be changed. Sections continue to turn in answers until all sections have submitted a response. The first section to submit the correct answer wins the competition.

b. If any section submits a wrong answer, the instructor or a spokesperson from the winning group should explain how the right answer was determined.

c. Discuss the dynamics of group interaction. How was the work organized? How was leadership established?

### ATC 3-3   Research Assignment   *Using real world data from Southwest Airlines*

Use the 2008 Form 10-K for Southwest Airlines to complete the requirements below. To obtain the Form 10-K you can use either the EDGAR system following the instructions in Appendix A, or it can be found under "Investor Relations" which is under the "About Southwest" link on the company's corporate website, www.southwest.com. The company includes its Form 10-K as a part of its 2008 Annual Report. Be sure to read carefully the "Item 6. Selected Financial Data" section of the document.

### Required

a. "Item 6. Selected Financial Data," list data for several measures of activity. List the items from this table that might be used by Southwest as an activity base for CVP analysis.

b. Of the activity bases that you identified for Requirement *a*, which do you think would work best for performing CVP at Southwest? Explain the rationale for your choice.

c. Use the "Operating expense" and the "Revenue passenger miles" data from Item 6, to compute the variable cost and fixed cost components of operating expense using the high-low method presented in Chapter 2. *Warning:* the results you get will not seem reasonable, but perform the calculations and report your results.

d. Try to explain the peculiar results you obtained for Requirement *c.* This will require careful thought, and you may wish to review the *Cost-Volume-Profit Limitations* section of this chapter.

e. "Item 6." reports that in 2008 Southwest's "Load factor" was 71.2%. If this load factor could have been increased by 10% to 78.3%, do you think the company's net earnings would have increased by less than 10%, 10%, or more than 10%? Explain.

**ATC 3-4    Writing Assignment    *Operating leverage, margin of safety, and cost behavior***

In the early years of the 21st century the housing market in the United States was booming. Housing prices were increasing rapidly, new houses were being constructed at a record pace, and companies doing business in the construction and home improvement industry were enjoying rising profits. In 2006 the real estate market had slowed considerably, and the slump continued through 2007.

Home Depot was one major company in the building supplies industry that was adversely affected by the slowdown in the housing market. On August 14, 2007, it announced that its revenues for the first half of the year were 3 percent lower than revenues were for the first six months of 2006. Of even greater concern was the fact that its earnings for the first half of 2007 were 21 percent lower than for the same period in the prior year.

### Required

Write a memorandum that explains how a 3 percent decline in sales could cause a 21 percent decline in profits. Your memo should address the following:

a. An identification of the accounting concept involved.

b. A discussion of how various major types of costs incurred by Home Depot were likely affected by the decline in its sales.

c. The effect of the decline in sales on Home Depot's margin of safety.

**ATC 3-5    Ethical Dilemma    *Opportunity to manipulate earnings***

Sherwin-Williams and PPG Industries are both companies that produce wall coverings, such as paint, among other products. Although they uses similar assets to conduct their businesses, the estimated lives they use to depreciate those assets vary, as shown in the following table:

| | Estimated Useful Lives | |
|---|---|---|
| Asset Category | PPG Industries | Sherwin-Williams |
| Buildings | 20–40 years | 5–40 years |
| Machinery and equipment | 5–25 | 5–20 |
| Other | 3–20 | 3–10 |

Managers have significant flexibility in setting the estimated useful lives of depreciable assets, and as the table shows, PPG Industries uses longer estimated lives for its assets than does Sherwin-Williams.

### Required

a. How does using a longer estimated life for a depreciable asset potentially affect its earnings?

b. Would using a longer estimated life for a depreciable asset be more likely to affect a company's fixed or variable costs?

c. In the past, some companies, not PPG, have been accused of deliberately overestimating the useful lives of their companies' depreciable assets. Speculate as to what would cause them to do this.

d. Review the standards of ethical conduct shown in Exhibit 1.15 of Chapter 1 and comment on which, if any, of the ethical standards are violated by deliberately overestimating the useful lives of depreciable assets.

e. Comment on the provisions of the Sarbanes-Oxley Act that are designed to prevent a company's executives from deliberately overestimating the useful lives of depreciable assets.

**ATC 3-6    Spreadsheet Assignment    *Using Excel***

Bishop Company has provided the estimated data that appear in rows 4 to 8 of the following spreadsheet:

**Required**

Construct a spreadsheet as follows that would allow you to determine net income, break-even in units, and operating leverage for the estimates at the top of the spreadsheet, and to see the effects of changes to the estimates. Set up this spreadsheet so that any change in the estimates will automatically be reflected in the calculation of net income, break-even, and operating leverage.

**Spreadsheet Tip**

To center a heading across several columns, such as the Income Statement title, highlight the area to be centered (Columns B, C, and D), choose Format, then choose Cells, and click on the tab titled Alignment. Near the bottom of the alignment window, place a check mark in the box titled Merge cells. The shortcut method to merge cells is to click on the icon near the middle of the top icons that contains an *a* in a box.

**ATC 3-7    Spreadsheet Assignment    *Mastering Excel***

**Required**

Build the spreadsheet pictured in Exhibit 3.3. Be sure to use formulas that will automatically calculate profitability if fixed cost, variable cost, or sales volume is changed.

**Spreadsheet Tip**

1. The shading in column D and in row 6 can be inserted by first highlighting a section to be shaded, choosing Format from the main menu, then Cells, and then clicking on the tab titled Patterns, and then choosing a color for the shading. The shortcut method to accomplish the shading is to click on the fill color icon (it looks like a tipped bucket and is in the upper right area of the screen).

Microsoft Excel - ch03-mastering1.xls

File Edit View Insert Format Tools Data Window Help

Arial ... 10 ... **B** *I* U ... $ % ...

M30 =

| | A | B | C | D | E | F | G | H | I | J |
|---|---|---|---|---|---|---|---|---|---|---|
| 1 | Selling Price = | $ | 28.00 | | | | | | | |
| 2 | | | | | | | | | | |
| 3 | If | While | | | And Sales Volume is | | | | | |
| 4 | Fixed Cost | Variable Cost | | 2,000 | 3,000 | 4,000 | 5,000 | 6,000 | | |
| 5 | is | is | | | Then Profitability Will Be | | | | | |
| 6 | | | | | | | | | | |
| 7 | $ 20,000 | 11 | | $14,000 | $31,000 | $48,000 | $65,000 | $82,000 | | |
| 8 | 20,000 | 12 | | 12,000 | 28,000 | 44,000 | 60,000 | 76,000 | | |
| 9 | 20,000 | 13 | | 10,000 | 25,000 | 40,000 | 55,000 | 70,000 | | |
| 10 | 30,000 | 11 | | 4,000 | 21,000 | 38,000 | 55,000 | 72,000 | | |
| 11 | 30,000 | 12 | | 2,000 | 18,000 | 34,000 | 50,000 | 66,000 | | |
| 12 | 30,000 | 13 | | - | 15,000 | 30,000 | 45,000 | 60,000 | | |
| 13 | 40,000 | 11 | | (6,000) | 11,000 | 28,000 | 45,000 | 62,000 | | |
| 14 | 40,000 | 12 | | (8,000) | 8,000 | 24,000 | 40,000 | 56,000 | | |
| 15 | 40,000 | 13 | | (10,000) | 5,000 | 20,000 | 35,000 | 50,000 | | |
| 16 | | | | | | | | | | |
| 17 | | | | | | | | | | |

Sheet1 / Sheet2 / Sheet3 /

Ready                                                                                        NUM

2. Similar to basic math rules, the order of calculation within a formula is multiplication and division before addition and subtraction. Therefore, if you wish to subtract variable cost from selling price and multiply the difference by units sold, the formula must be = (28 − C8)*E5.

3. The quickest way to get the correct formulas in the area of E8 to I16 is to place the proper formula in cell E8 and then copy this formula to the entire block of E8:I16. However, the formulas must use the $ around the cell addresses to lock either the row or the column, or both. For example, the formula = 2*$B$8 can be copied to any other cell and the cell reference will remain B8 because the $ symbol locks the row and column. Likewise, $B8 indicates that only the column is locked, and B$8 indicates that only the row is locked.

## COMPREHENSIVE PROBLEM

Use the same transaction data for Magnificant Modems, Inc., as was used in Chapter 1. (See page 52.)

**Required**

a. Use the following partially completed form to prepare an income statement using the contribution margin format.

| | |
|---|---|
| Sales revenue | $600,000 |
| Variable costs: | |
| | |
| | |
| | |
| Contribution margin | 225,000 |
| Fixed costs | |
| | |
| | |
| | |
| Net income | $31,050 |

b. Determine the break-even point in units and in dollars.

c. Assume that next year's sales are budgeted to be the same as the current year's sales. Determine the margin of safety expressed as a percentage.

## CHAPTER 4

# Cost Accumulation, Tracing, and Allocation

## LEARNING OBJECTIVES

**After you have mastered the material in this chapter, you will be able to:**

1  Identify cost objects and cost drivers.

2  Distinguish direct costs from indirect costs.

3  Allocate indirect costs to cost objects.

4  Select appropriate cost drivers for allocating indirect costs.

5  Allocate costs to solve timing problems.

6  Explain the benefits and detriments of allocating pooled costs.

7  Allocate joint product costs.

8  Recognize the effects of cost allocation on employee motivation.

9  Allocate service department costs to operating departments (Appendix).

## CHAPTER OPENING

What does it cost? This is one of the questions most frequently asked by business managers. Managers must have reliable cost estimates to price products, evaluate performance, control operations, and prepare financial statements. As this discussion implies, managers need to know the cost of many different things. The things we are trying to determine the cost of are commonly called **cost objects.** For example, if we are trying to determine the cost of operating a department, that department is the cost object. Cost objects may be products, processes, departments, services, activities, and so on. This chapter explains techniques managerial accountants use to determine the cost of a variety of cost objects.

# The Curious Accountant

A former patient of a California hospital complained about being charged $7 for a single aspirin tablet. After all, an entire bottle of 100 aspirins can be purchased at the local pharmacy store for around $2.

Can you think of any reasons, other than shameless profiteering, that a hospital would need to charge $7 for an aspirin? Remember that the hospital is not just selling the aspirin; it is also delivering it to the patient. (Answer on page 159.)

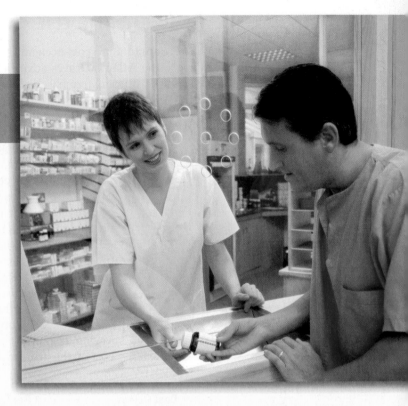

# DETERMINE THE COST OF COST OBJECTS

Identify cost objects and cost drivers.

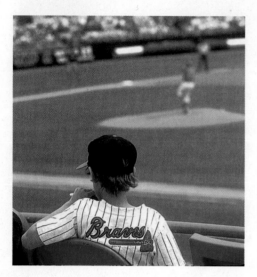

Accountants use **cost accumulation** to determine the cost of a particular object. Suppose the Atlanta Braves advertising manager wants to promote a Tuesday night ball game by offering free baseball caps to all children who attend. What would be the promotion cost? The team's accountant must *accumulate* many individual costs and add them together. For simplicity consider only three cost components: (1) the cost of the caps, (2) the cost of advertising the promotion, and (3) the cost of an employee to work on the promotion.

Cost accumulation begins with identifying the cost objects. The primary cost object is the cost of the promotion. Three secondary cost objects are (1) the cost of caps, (2) the cost of advertising, and (3) the cost of labor. The costs of the secondary cost objects are combined to determine the cost of the primary cost object.

Determining the costs of the secondary cost objects requires identifying what *drives* those costs. A **cost driver** has a *cause-and-effect* relationship with a cost object. For example, the *number of caps* (cost driver) has an effect on the *cost of caps* (cost object). The *number of advertisements* is a cost driver for the *advertising cost* (cost object); the *number of labor hours* worked is a cost driver for the *labor cost* (cost object). Using the following assumptions about unit costs and cost drivers, the accumulated cost of the primary cost object (cost of the cap promotion) is:

| Cost Object | Cost Per Unit | × | Cost Driver | = | Total Cost of Object |
|---|---|---|---|---|---|
| Cost of caps | $2.50 | × | 4,000 Caps | = | $10,000 |
| Cost of advertising | $100.00 | × | 50 Advertisements | = | 5,000 |
| Cost of labor | $8.00 | × | 100 Hours | = | 800 |
| Cost of cap promotion | | | | | $15,800 |

The Atlanta Braves should run the promotion if management expects it to produce additional revenues exceeding $15,800.

## Estimated versus Actual Cost

The accumulated cost of the promotion—$15,800—is an *estimate.* Management cannot know *actual* costs and revenues until after running the promotion. While actual information is more accurate, it is not relevant for deciding whether to run the promotion because the decision must be made before the actual is known. Managers must accept a degree of inaccuracy in exchange for the relevance of timely information. Many business decisions are based on estimated rather than actual costs.

Managers use cost estimates to set prices, bid on contracts, evaluate proposals, distribute resources, plan production, and set goals. Certain circumstances, however, require actual cost data. For example, published financial reports and managerial performance evaluations use actual cost data. Managers frequently accumulate both estimated and actual cost data for the same cost object. For example, companies use cost estimates to establish goals and use actual costs to evaluate management performance in meeting those goals. The following discussion provides a number of business examples that use estimated data, actual data, or a combination of both.

## ASSIGNMENT OF COSTS TO OBJECTS IN A RETAIL BUSINESS

Exhibit 4.1 displays the January income statement for In Style, Inc. (ISI), a retail clothing store. ISI subdivides its operations into women's, men's, and children's departments. To encourage the departmental managers to maximize sales, ISI began

paying the manager of each department a bonus based on a percentage of departmental sales revenue.

Although the bonus incentive increased sales revenue, it also provoked negative consequences. The departmental managers began to argue over floor space; each manager wanted more space to display merchandise. The managers reduced prices; they increased sales commissions. In the drive to maximize sales, the managers ignored the need to control costs. To improve the situation, the store manager decided to base future bonuses on each department's contribution to profitability rather than its sales revenue.

## IDENTIFYING DIRECT AND INDIRECT COSTS

The new bonus strategy requires determining the cost of operating each department. Each department is a separate *cost object.* Assigning costs to the departments (cost objects) requires **cost tracing** and **cost allocation.** *Direct costs* can be easily traced to a cost object. *Indirect costs* cannot be easily traced to a cost object. Whether or not a cost is easily traceable requires *cost/benefit analysis.*

Some of ISI's costs can be easily traced to the cost objects (specific departments). The cost of goods sold is an example of an easily traced cost. Price tags on merchandise can be coded so cash register scanners capture the departmental code for each sale. The cost of goods sold is not only easily traceable but also very useful information. Companies need cost of goods sold information for financial reporting (income statement and balance sheet) and for management decisions (determining inventory reorder points, pricing strategies, and cost control). Because the cost of tracing *cost of goods sold* is small relative to the benefits obtained, cost of goods sold is a *direct cost.*

In contrast, the cost of supplies (shopping bags, sales slips, pens, staples, price tags) used by each department is much more difficult to trace. How could the number of staples used to seal shopping bags be traced to any particular department? The sales staff could count the number of staples used, but doing so would be silly for the benefits obtained. Although tracing the cost of supplies to each department may be possible, it is not worth the effort of doing so. The cost of supplies is therefore an *indirect cost.* Indirect costs are also called **overhead costs.**

Direct and indirect costs can be described as follows:

| Direct costs can be traced to cost objects in a *cost-effective* manner. |
| Indirect costs cannot be traced to objects in a *cost-effective* manner. |

**LO 2**

Distinguish direct costs from indirect costs.

**EXHIBIT 4.1**

**Income Statement**

### IN STYLE, INC.
Income Statement
For the Month Ended January 31

| | |
|---|---:|
| Sales | $360,000 |
| Cost of goods sold | (216,000) |
| Gross margin | 144,000 |
| Sales commissions | (18,000) |
| Dept. managers' salaries | (12,000) |
| Store manager's salary | (9,360) |
| Depreciation | (16,000) |
| Rental fee for store | (18,400) |
| Utilities | (2,300) |
| Advertising | (7,200) |
| Supplies | (900) |
| Net income | $ 59,840 |

By analyzing the accounting records, ISI's accountant classified the costs from the income statement in Exhibit 4.1 as direct or indirect, as shown in Exhibit 4.2. The next paragraph explains the classifications.

All figures represent January costs. Items 1 though 4 are direct costs, traceable to the cost objects in a cost-effective manner. Cost of goods sold is traced to departments at the point of sale using cash register scanners. Sales commissions are based on a percentage of departmental sales and are therefore easy to trace to the departments. Departmental managers' salaries are also easily traceable to the departments. Equipment, furniture, and fixtures are tagged with department codes that permit tracing depreciation charges directly to specific departments. Items 5 through 8 are incurred on behalf of the company as a whole and are therefore not directly traceable to a specific department.

## EXHIBIT 4.2

### Income Statement Classification of Costs

| | Direct Costs | | | Indirect |
| Cost Item | Women's | Men's | Children's | Costs |
|---|---|---|---|---|
| 1.  Cost of goods sold—$216,000 | $120,000 | $58,000 | $38,000 | |
| 2.  Sales commissions—$18,000 | 9,500 | 5,500 | 3,000 | |
| 3.  Dept. managers' salaries—$12,000 | 5,000 | 4,200 | 2,800 | |
| 4.  Depreciation—$16,000 | 7,000 | 5,000 | 4,000 | |
| 5.  Store manager's salary | | | | $ 9,360 |
| 6.  Rental fee for store | | | | 18,400 |
| 7.  Utilities | | | | 2,300 |
| 8.  Advertising | | | | 7,200 |
| 9.  Supplies | | | | 900 |
| Totals | $141,500 | $72,700 | $47,800 | $38,160 |

Although Item 9 could be traced to specific departments, the cost of doing so would exceed the benefits. The cost of supplies is therefore also classified as indirect.

### Cost Classifications—Independent and Context Sensitive

Whether a cost is direct or indirect is independent of whether it is fixed or variable. In the ISI example, both cost of goods sold and the cost of supplies vary relative to sales volume (both are variable costs), but cost of goods sold is direct and the cost of supplies is indirect. Furthermore, the cost of rent and the cost of depreciation are both fixed relative to sales volume, but the cost of rent is indirect and the cost of depreciation is direct. In fact, the very same cost can be classified as direct or indirect, depending on the cost object. The store manager's salary is not directly traceable to a specific department, but it is traceable to a particular store. As these examples demonstrate, cost classification depends on the context in which the costs occur.

## ALLOCATING INDIRECT COSTS TO OBJECTS

Allocate indirect costs to cost objects.

**Common costs** support multiple cost objects, but cannot be directly traced to any specific object. In the case of In Style, Inc., the cost of renting the store (common cost) supports the women's, men's, and children's departments (cost objects). The departmental managers may shirk responsibility for the rental cost by claiming that others higher up the chain of command are responsible. Responsibility can be motivated at the departmental level by assigning (*allocating*) a portion of the total rental cost to each department.

To accomplish appropriate motivation, authority must accompany responsibility. In other words, the departmental managers should be held responsible for a portion of rental cost only if they are able to exercise some degree of control over that cost. For example, if managers are assigned a certain amount of the rental cost for each square foot of space they use, they should have the authority to establish the size of the space used by their departments. **Controllable costs** are costs that can be influenced by a manager's decisions and actions. The controllability concept is discussed in more detail in Chapter 9.

Cost **allocation** involves dividing a total cost into parts and assigning the parts to designated cost objects. How should ISI allocate the $38,160 of indirect costs to each of the three departments? First, identify a cost driver for each cost to be allocated. For example, there is a cause-and-effect relationship between store size and rent cost;

# REALITY BYTES

How does Southwest Airlines know the cost of flying a passenger from Houston, Texas, to Los Angeles, California? The fact is that Southwest does not know the actual cost of flying particular passengers anywhere. There are many indirect costs associated with flying passengers. Some of these include the cost of planes, fuel, pilots, office buildings, and ground personnel. Indeed, besides insignificant food and beverage costs, there are few costs that could be traced directly to customers. Southwest and other airlines are forced to use allocation and averaging to determine the estimated cost of providing transportation services to customers. Estimated rather than actual cost is used for decision-making purposes.

Consider that in its 2008 annual report Southwest reported the average operating expenses of flying one passenger one mile (called a *passenger mile*) were 10.2¢. However, this number was based on 103.3 billion "available passenger miles." In 2008 Southwest operated at 71.2 percent of capacity, not 100 percent, so it was only able to charge passengers for 73.5 billion passenger miles. Thus, its average operating expenses were closer to 14.4¢ for each mile for which they were able to charge. Had they operated at a higher capacity, their average costs would have been lower.

---

the larger the building, the higher the rent cost. This relationship suggests that the more floor space a department occupies, the more rent cost that department should bear. To illustrate, assume ISI's store capacity is 23,000 square feet and the women's, men's, and children's departments occupy 12,000, 7,000, and 4,000 square feet, respectively. ISI can achieve a rational allocation of the rent cost using the following two-step process.[1]

**Step 1.**   Compute the *allocation rate* by dividing the *total cost to be allocated* ($18,400 rental fee) by the *cost driver* (23,000 square feet of store space). *The cost driver is also called the* **allocation base.** This computation produces the **allocation rate,** as follows:

| Total cost to be allocated | ÷ | Cost driver (allocation base) | = | Allocation rate |
|---|---|---|---|---|
| $18,400 rental fee | ÷ | 23,000 square feet | = | $0.80 per square foot |

**Step 2.**   Multiply the *allocation rate* by the *weight of the cost driver* (weight of the base) to determine the allocation *per cost object,* as follows:

| Cost Object | Allocation Rate | × | Number of Square Feet | = | Allocation per Cost Object |
|---|---|---|---|---|---|
| Women's department | $0.80 | × | 12,000 | = | $ 9,600 |
| Men's department | 0.80 | × | 7,000 | = | 5,600 |
| Children's department | 0.80 | × | 4,000 | = | 3,200 |
| Total | | | 23,000 | | $18,400 |

---

[1]Other mathematical approaches achieve the same result. This text consistently uses the two-step method described here. Specifically, the text determines allocations by (1) computing a *rate* and (2) multiplying the *rate* by the *weight of the base* (cost driver).

It is also plausible to presume utilities cost is related to the amount of floor space a department occupies. Larger departments will consume more heating, lighting, air conditioning, and so on than smaller departments. Floor space is a reasonable cost driver for utility cost. Based on square footage, ISI can allocate utility cost to each department as follows:

**Step 1.**  Compute the allocation rate by dividing the total cost to be allocated ($2,300 utility cost) by the cost driver (23,000 square feet of store space):

Total cost to be allocated ÷    Cost driver    =    Allocation rate

$2,300 utility cost    ÷ 23,000 square feet = $0.10 per square foot

**Step 2.**  Multiply the *allocation rate* by the *weight of the cost driver* to determine the allocation *per cost object:*

| Cost Object | Allocation Rate | × | Number of Square Feet | = | Allocation per Cost Object |
|---|---|---|---|---|---|
| Women's department | $0.10 | × | 12,000 | = | $1,200 |
| Men's department | 0.10 | × | 7,000 | = | 700 |
| Children's department | 0.10 | × | 4,000 | = | 400 |
| Total | | | 23,000 | | $2,300 |

---

## ✓ CHECK YOURSELF 4.1

HealthCare, Inc., wants to estimate the cost of operating the three departments (Dermatology, Gynecology, and Pediatrics) that serve patients in its Health Center. Each department performed the following number of patient treatments during the most recent year of operation: Dermatology, 2,600; Gynecology, 3,500; and Pediatrics, 6,200. The annual salary of the Health Center's program administrator is $172,200. How much of the salary cost should HealthCare allocate to the Pediatrics Department?

**Answer**

**Step 1**  Compute the *allocation rate.*

Total cost to be allocated ÷ Cost driver (patient treatments) =    Allocation rate

$172,200 salary cost    ÷    (2,600 + 3,500 + 6,200)    = $14 per patient treatment

**Step 2**  Multiply the *allocation rate* by the *weight of the cost driver* (weight of the base) to determine the allocation per *cost object.*

| Cost Object | Allocation Rate | × | No. of Treatments | = | Allocation per Cost Object |
|---|---|---|---|---|---|
| Pediatrics department | $14 | × | 6,200 | = | $86,800 |

---

## SELECTING A COST DRIVER

**LO 4**

Select appropriate cost drivers for allocating indirect costs.

Companies can frequently identify more than one cost driver for a particular indirect cost. For example, ISI's shopping bag cost is related to both the *number of sales transactions* and the *volume of sales dollars*. As either of these potential cost drivers increases, shopping bag usage also increases. The most useful cost driver is the one with the strongest cause-and-effect relationship.

Consider shopping bag usage for T-shirts sold in the children's department versus T-shirts sold in the men's department. Assume ISI studied T-shirt sales during the first week of June and found the following:

| Department | Children's | Men's |
|---|---|---|
| Number of sales transactions | 120 | 92 |
| Volume of sales dollars | $1,440 | $1,612 |

Given that every sales transaction uses a shopping bag, the children's department uses far more shopping bags than the men's department even though it has a lower volume of sales dollars. A reasonable explanation for this circumstance is that children's T-shirts sell for less than men's T-shirts. The number of sales transactions is the better cost driver because it has a stronger cause-and-effect relationship with shopping bag usage than does the volume of sales dollars. Should ISI therefore use the number of sales transactions to allocate supply cost to the departments? Not necessarily.

The *availability of information* also influences cost driver selection. While the number of sales transactions is the more accurate cost driver, ISI could not use this allocation base unless it maintains records of the number of sales transactions per department. If the store tracks the volume of sales dollars but not the number of transactions, it must use dollar volume even if the number of transactions is the better cost driver. For ISI, sales volume in dollars appears to be the best *available* cost driver for allocating supply cost.

Assuming that sales volume for the women's, men's, and children's departments was $190,000, $110,000, and $60,000, respectively, ISI can allocate the supplies cost as follows:

**Step 1.** Compute the allocation rate by dividing the total cost to be allocated ($900 supplies cost) by the cost driver ($360,000 total sales volume):

| Total cost to be allocated | ÷ | Cost driver | = | Allocation rate |
|---|---|---|---|---|
| $900 supplies cost | ÷ | $360,000 sales volume | = | $0.0025 per sales dollar |

**Step 2.** Multiply the allocation rate by the weight of the cost driver to determine the allocation per cost object:

| Cost Object | Allocation Rate | × | Sales Volume | = | Allocation per Cost Object |
|---|---|---|---|---|---|
| Women's department | $0.0025 | × | $190,000 | = | $475 |
| Men's department | 0.0025 | × | 110,000 | = | 275 |
| Children's department | 0.0025 | × | 60,000 | = | 150 |
| Total | | | $360,000 | | $900 |

ISI believes sales volume is also the appropriate allocation base for advertising cost. The sales generated in each department were likely influenced by the general advertising campaign. ISI can allocate advertising cost as follows:

**Step 1.** Compute the allocation rate by dividing the total cost to be allocated ($7,200 advertising cost) by the cost driver ($360,000 total sales volume):

| Total cost to be allocated | ÷ | Cost driver | = | Allocation rate |
|---|---|---|---|---|
| $7,200 advertising cost | ÷ | $360,000 sales volume | = | $0.02 per sales dollar |

**Step 2.**    Multiply the allocation rate by the weight of the cost driver to determine the allocation per cost object:

| Cost Object | Allocation Rate | × | Sales Volume | = | Allocation per Cost Object |
|---|---|---|---|---|---|
| Women's department | $0.02 | × | $190,000 | = | $3,800 |
| Men's department | 0.02 | × | 110,000 | = | 2,200 |
| Children's department | 0.02 | × | 60,000 | = | 1,200 |
| Total | | | $360,000 | | $7,200 |

There is no strong cause-and-effect relationship between the store manager's salary and the departments. ISI pays the store manager the same salary regardless of sales level, square footage of store space, number of labor hours, or any other identifiable variable. Because no plausible cost driver exists, ISI must allocate the store manager's salary arbitrarily. Here the manager's salary is simply divided equally among the departments as follows:

**Step 1.**    Compute the allocation rate by dividing the total cost to be allocated ($9,360 manager's monthly salary) by the allocation base (number of departments):

Total cost to be allocated    ÷    Cost driver    =    Allocation rate

$9,360 store manager's salary ÷ 3 departments = $3,120 per department

**Step 2.**    Multiply the allocation rate by the weight of the cost driver to determine the allocation per cost object:

| Cost Object | Allocation Rate | × | Number of Departments | = | Allocation per Cost Object |
|---|---|---|---|---|---|
| Women's department | $3,120 | × | 1 | = | $3,120 |
| Men's department | 3,120 | × | 1 | = | 3,120 |
| Children's department | 3,120 | × | 1 | = | 3,120 |
| Total | | | 3 | | $9,360 |

As the allocation of the store manager's salary demonstrates, many allocations are arbitrary or based on a weak relationship between the allocated cost and the allocation base (cost driver). Managers must use care when making decisions using allocated costs.

## Behavioral Implications

Using the indirect cost allocations just discussed, Exhibit 4.4 shows the profit each department generated in January. ISI paid the three departmental managers bonuses based on each department's contribution to profitability. The store manager noticed an immediate change in the behavior of the departmental managers. For example, the manager of the women's department offered to give up 1,000 square feet of floor space because she believed reducing the selection of available products would not reduce sales significantly. Customers would simply buy different brands. Although sales would not decline dramatically, rent and utility cost allocations to the women's department would decline, increasing the profitability of the department.

When we compare the cost that a hospital charges for an aspirin to the price we pay for an aspirin, we are probably not considering the full cost that we incur to purchase aspirin. If someone asks you what you pay for an aspirin, you would probably take the price of a bottle, say $2, and divide it by the number of pills in the bottle, say 100. This would suggest their cost is $0.02 each. Now, consider what it cost to buy the aspirins when all costs are considered. First, there is your time to drive to the store; what do you get paid per hour? Then, there is the cost of operating your automobile. You get the idea; in reality, the cost of an aspirin, from a business perspective, is much more than just the cost of the pills themselves.

Exhibit 4.3 shows the income statement of Hospital Corporation of America (HCA) for three recent years. HCA claims to be " . . . one of the leading health care services companies in the United States." In 2008 it operated 271 facilities in 20 states and England. As you can see, while it generated over $28 billion in revenue, it also incurred a lot of expenses. Look at its first two expense categories. Although it incurred $4.6 billion in supplies expenses, it incurred almost two and a half times this amount in compensation expense. In other words, it cost a lot more to have someone deliver the aspirin to your bed than the aspirin itself costs.

In 2008 HCA earned $673 million from its $28.4 billion in revenues. This is a return on sales percentage of 2.4 percent ($.673 ÷ $28.4). Therefore, on a $7 aspirin, HCA would earn 17 cents of profit, which is still not a bad profit for selling one aspirin. As a comparison, in 2008, Walgreens return on sales was 3.7 percent.

### EXHIBIT 4.3

**HCA, INC.**
Consolidated Income Statements
for the Years Ended December 31, 2008, 2007, and 2006
(Dollars in millions, except per share amounts)

|  | 2008 | 2007 | 2006 |
|---|---|---|---|
| Revenues | $28,374 | $26,858 | $25,477 |
| Salaries and benefits | 11,440 | 10,714 | 10,409 |
| Supplies | 4,620 | 4,395 | 4,322 |
| Other operating expenses | 4,554 | 4,241 | 4,056 |
| Provision for doubtful accounts | 3,409 | 3,130 | 2,660 |
| Gains on investments |  | (8) | (243) |
| Equity in earnings of affiliates | (223) | (206) | (197) |
| Depreciation and amortization | 1,416 | 1,426 | 1,391 |
| Interest expense | 2,021 | 2,215 | 955 |
| Gains on sales of facilities | (97) | (471) | (205) |
| Transaction costs |  |  | 442 |
| Impairment of long-lived assets | 64 | 24 | 24 |
| Total expenses | 27,204 | 25,460 | 23,614 |
| Income before minority interests and income taxes | 1,170 | 1,398 | 1,863 |
| Minority interests in earnings of consolidated entities | 229 | 208 | 201 |
| Income before income taxes | 941 | 1,190 | 1,662 |
| Provision for income taxes | 268 | 316 | 626 |
| Net income | $ 673 | $ 874 | $ 1,036 |

## EXHIBIT 4.4

### Profit Analysis by Department

| | Department | | | |
|---|---|---|---|---|
| | Women's | Men's | Children's | Total |
| Sales | $190,000 | $110,000 | $60,000 | $360,000 |
| Cost of goods sold | (120,000) | (58,000) | (38,000) | (216,000) |
| Sales commissions | (9,500) | (5,500) | (3,000) | (18,000) |
| Dept. managers' salary | (5,000) | (4,200) | (2,800) | (12,000) |
| Depreciation | (7,000) | (5,000) | (4,000) | (16,000) |
| Store manager's salary | (3,120) | (3,120) | (3,120) | (9,360) |
| Rental fee for store | (9,600) | (5,600) | (3,200) | (18,400) |
| Utilities | (1,200) | (700) | (400) | (2,300) |
| Advertising | (3,800) | (2,200) | (1,200) | (7,200) |
| Supplies | (475) | (275) | (150) | (900) |
| Departmental profit | $ 30,305 | $ 25,405 | $ 4,130 | $ 59,840 |

In contrast, the manager of the children's department wanted the extra space. He believed the children's department was losing sales because it did not have enough floor space to display a competitive variety of merchandise. Customers came to the store to shop at the women's department, but they did not come specifically for children's wear. With additional space, the children's department could carry items that would draw customers to the store specifically to buy children's clothing. He believed the extra space would increase sales enough to cover the additional rent and utility cost allocations.

The store manager was pleased with the emphasis on profitability that resulted from tracing and assigning costs to specific departments.

## EFFECTS OF COST BEHAVIOR ON SELECTING THE MOST APPROPRIATE COST DRIVER

Select appropriate cost drivers for allocating indirect costs.

As previously mentioned, indirect costs may exhibit variable or fixed cost behavior patterns. Failing to consider the effects of cost behavior when allocating indirect costs can lead to significant distortions in product cost measurement. We examine the critical relationships between cost behavior and cost allocation in the next section of the text.

### Using Volume Measures to Allocate Variable Overhead Costs

A *causal relationship* exists between variable overhead product costs (indirect materials, indirect labor, inspection costs, utilities, etc.) and the volume of production. For example, the cost of indirect materials such as glue, staples, screws, nails, and varnish will increase or decrease in proportion to the number of desks a furniture manufacturing company makes. *Volume measures are good cost drivers* for allocating variable overhead costs.

Volume can be expressed by such measures as the number of units produced, the number of labor hours worked, or the amount of *direct* materials used in production. Given the variety of possible volume measures, how does management identify the most appropriate cost driver (allocation base) for assigning particular overhead costs? Consider the case of Filmier Furniture Company.

## Using Units as the Cost Driver

During the most recent year, Filmier Furniture Company produced 4,000 chairs and 1,000 desks. It incurred $60,000 of *indirect materials* cost during the period. How much of this cost should Filmier allocate to chairs versus desks? Using number of units as the cost driver produces the following allocation:

**Step 1.**   Compute the allocation rate.

Total cost to be allocated    ÷ Cost driver = Allocation rate

$60,000 indirect materials cost ÷ 5,000 units =  $12 per unit

**Step 2.**   Multiply the allocation rate by the weight of the cost driver to determine the allocation per cost object.

| Product | Allocation Rate | × | Number of Units Produced | = | Allocated Cost |
|---------|-----------------|---|--------------------------|---|----------------|
| Desks   | $12             | × | 1,000                    | = | $12,000        |
| Chairs  | 12              | × | 4,000                    | = | 48,000         |
| Total   |                 |   | 5,000                    | = | $60,000        |

## Using Direct Labor Hours as the Cost Driver

Using the number of units as the cost driver assigns an *equal amount* ($12) of indirect materials cost to each piece of furniture. However, if Filmier uses more indirect materials to make a desk than to make a chair, assigning the same amount of indirect materials cost to each is inaccurate. Assume Filmier incurs the following direct costs to make chairs and desks:

|                      | Desks       | Chairs    | Total       |
|----------------------|-------------|-----------|-------------|
| Direct labor hours   | 3,500 hrs.  | 2,500 hrs.| 6,000 hrs.  |
| Direct materials cost| $1,000,000  | $500,000  | $1,500,000  |

Both direct labor hours and direct materials cost are volume measures that indicate Filmier uses more indirect materials to make a desk than a chair. It makes sense that the amount of direct labor used is related to the amount of indirect materials used. Because production workers use materials to make furniture, it is plausible to assume that the more hours they work, the more materials they use. Using this reasoning, Filmier could assign the indirect materials cost to the chairs and desks as follows:

**Step 1.**   Compute the allocation rate.

Total cost to be allocated    ÷ Cost driver = Allocation rate

$60,000 indirect materials cost ÷ 6,000 hours =  $10 per hour

**Step 2.**   Multiply the allocation rate by the weight of the cost driver.

| Product | Allocation Rate | × | Number of Labor Hours | = | Allocated Cost |
|---------|-----------------|---|-----------------------|---|----------------|
| Desks   | $10.00          | × | 3,500                 | = | $35,000        |
| Chairs  | 10.00           | × | 2,500                 | = | 25,000         |
| Total   |                 |   | 6,000                 | = | $60,000        |

Basing the allocation on labor hours rather than number of units assigns a significantly larger portion of the indirect materials cost to desks ($35,000 versus $12,000). Is this allocation more accurate? Suppose the desks, but not the chairs, require elaborate, labor-intensive carvings. A significant portion of the labor is then not related to consuming indirect materials (glue, staples, screws, nails, and varnish). It would therefore be inappropriate to allocate the indirect materials cost based on direct labor hours.

### Using Direct Material Dollars as the Cost Driver

If labor hours is an inappropriate allocation base, Filmier can consider direct material usage, measured in material dollars, as the allocation base. It is likely that the more lumber (direct material) Filmier uses, the more glue, nails, and so forth (indirect materials) it uses. It is reasonable to presume direct materials usage drives indirect materials usage. Using direct materials dollars as the cost driver for indirect materials produces the following allocation:

**Step 1.** Compute the allocation rate.

Total cost to be allocated ÷ Cost driver = Allocation rate

$60,000 indirect materials cost ÷ $1,500,000 direct material dollars = $0.04 per direct material dollar

**Step 2.** Multiply the allocation rate by the weight of the cost driver.

| Product | Allocation Rate | × | Number of Direct Material Dollars | = | Allocated Cost |
|---------|-----------------|---|-----------------------------------|---|----------------|
| Desks | $0.04 | × | $1,000,000 | = | $40,000 |
| Chairs | 0.04 | × | 500,000 | = | 20,000 |
| Total | | | $1,500,000 | = | $60,000 |

### Selecting the Best Cost Driver

Which of the three volume-based cost drivers (units, labor hours, or direct material dollars) results in the most accurate allocation of the overhead cost? Management must use judgment to decide. In this case, direct material dollars appears to have the most convincing relationship to indirect materials usage. If the cost Filmier was allocating were fringe benefits, however, direct labor hours would be a more appropriate cost driver. If the cost Filmier was allocating were machine maintenance cost, a different volume-based cost driver, machine hours, would be an appropriate base. The most accurate allocations of indirect costs may actually require using multiple cost drivers.

## ✓ CHECK YOURSELF 4.2

Boston Boat Company builds custom sailboats for customers. During the current accounting period, the company built five different-sized boats that ranged in cost from $35,000 to $185,000. The company's manufacturing overhead cost for the period was $118,000. Would you recommend using the number of units (boats) or direct labor hours as the base for allocating the overhead cost to the five boats? Why?

**Answer**   Using the number of units as the allocation base would assign the same amount of overhead cost to each boat. Since larger boats require more overhead cost (supplies, utilities, equipment, etc.) than smaller boats, there is no logical link between the number of boats and the amount of overhead cost required to build a particular boat. In contrast, there is a logical link between direct labor hours used and overhead cost incurred. The more labor used, the more supplies, utilities, equipment, and so on used. Since larger boats require more direct labor than smaller boats, using direct labor hours as the allocation base would allocate more overhead cost to larger boats and less overhead cost to smaller boats, producing a logical overhead allocation. Therefore, Boston should use direct labor hours as the allocation base.

## Allocating Fixed Overhead Costs

Fixed costs present a different cost allocation problem. By definition, the volume of production does not drive fixed costs. Suppose Lednicky Bottling Company rents its manufacturing facility for $28,000 per year. The rental cost is fixed regardless of how much product Lednicky bottles. However, Lednicky may still use a volume-based cost driver as the allocation base. The object of allocating fixed costs to products is to distribute a *rational share* of the overhead cost to each product. Selecting an allocation base that spreads total overhead cost equally over total production often produces a rational distribution. For example, assume Lednicky produced 2,000,000 bottles of apple juice during 2011. If it sold 1,800,000 bottles of the juice during 2011, how much of the $28,000 of rental cost should Lednicky allocate to ending inventory and how much to cost of goods sold? A rational allocation follows:

**Step 1.**   Compute the allocation rate.

Total cost to be allocated ÷ Allocation base (cost driver) =    Allocation rate

$28,000 rental cost    ÷    2,000,000 units    = $0.014 per bottle of juice

   Because the base (number of units) used to allocate the cost does not drive the cost, it is sometimes called an *allocation base* instead of a *cost driver*. However, many managers use the term cost driver in conjunction with fixed cost even though that usage is technically inaccurate. The terms allocation base and cost driver are frequently used interchangeably.

**Step 2.**   Multiply the allocation rate by the weight of the cost driver.

| Financial Statement Item | Allocation Rate | × | Number of Bottles | = | Allocated Cost |
|---|---|---|---|---|---|
| Inventory | $0.014 | × | 200,000 | = | $ 2,800 |
| Cost of goods sold | 0.014 | × | 1,800,000 | = | 25,200 |

Using number of units as the allocation base assigns equal amounts of the rental cost to each unit of product. Equal allocation is appropriate so long as the units are homogeneous. If the units are not identical, however, Lednicky may need to choose a different allocation base to rationally distribute the rental cost. For example, if some of the bottles are significantly larger than others, Lednicky may find using some physical measure, like liters of direct material used, to be a more appropriate allocation base. Whether an indirect cost is fixed or variable, selecting the most appropriate allocation base requires sound reasoning and judgment.

## ALLOCATING COSTS TO SOLVE TIMING PROBLEMS

Allocate costs to solve timing problems.

Under certain circumstances products may be made before or after the costs associated with making them have been incurred. Suppose, for example, premiums for an annual insurance policy are paid in March. The insurance cost benefits the products made in the months before and after March as well as those produced in March. Allocation can be used to spread the insurance cost over products made during the entire accounting period rather than charging the total cost only to products made in March.

Monthly fluctuations in production volume complicate fixed cost allocations. To illustrate, assume Grave Manufacturing pays its production supervisor a monthly salary of $3,000. Furthermore, assume Grave makes 800 units of product in January and 1,875 in February. How much salary cost should Grave assign to the products made in January and February, respectively? The allocation seems simple. Just divide the $3,000 monthly salary cost by the number of units of product made each month as follows:

$$\text{January} \quad \$3,000 \div \quad 800 \text{ units} = \$3.75 \text{ cost per unit}$$

$$\text{February} \quad \$3,000 \div 1,875 \text{ units} = \$1.60 \text{ cost per unit}$$

If Grave Manufacturing based a cost-plus pricing decision on these results, it would price products made in January significantly higher than products made in February. It is likely such price fluctuations would puzzle and drive away customers. Grave needs an allocation base that will spread the annual salary cost evenly over annual production. A timing problem exists, however, because Grave must allocate the salary cost before the end of the year. In order to price its products, Grave needs to know the allocated amount before the actual cost information is available. Grave can manage the timing problem by using estimated rather than actual costs.

Grave Manufacturing can *estimate* the annual cost of the supervisor's salary (indirect labor) as $36,000 ($3,000 × 12 months). The *actual* cost of indirect labor may differ because the supervisor might receive a pay raise or be replaced with a person who earns less. Based on current information, however, $36,000 is a reasonable estimate of the annual indirect labor cost. Grave must also estimate total annual production volume. Suppose Grave produced 18,000 units last year and expects no significant change in the current year. It can allocate indirect labor cost for January and February as follows:

**Step 1.**    Compute the allocation rate.

$$\text{Total cost to be allocated} \div \text{Allocation base} = \text{Allocation rate}$$
$$\text{(cost driver)}$$

$$\$36,000 \qquad \div \quad 18,000 \text{ units} \quad = \$2.00 \text{ per unit}$$

**Step 2.**    Multiply the rate by the weight of the base (number of units per month) to determine how much of the salary cost to allocate to each month's production.

| Month | Allocation Rate | × | Number of Units Produced | = | Allocation per Month |
|-------|-----------------|---|--------------------------|---|----------------------|
| January | $2.00 | × | 800 | = | $1,600 |
| February | 2.00 | × | 1,875 | = | 3,750 |

Grave Manufacturing will add these indirect cost allocations to other product costs to determine the total estimated product cost to use in cost-plus pricing or other managerial decisions.

Because the overhead allocation rate is determined *before* actual cost and volume data are available, it is called the **predetermined overhead rate.** Companies use predetermined overhead rates for product costing estimates and pricing decisions during a year, but they must use actual costs in published year-end financial statements. If necessary, companies adjust their accounting records at year-end when they have used estimated data on an interim basis. The procedures for making such adjustments are discussed in a later chapter.

## AGGREGATING AND DISAGGREGATING INDIVIDUAL COSTS INTO COST POOLS

Allocating *individually* every single indirect cost a company incurs would be tedious and not particularly useful relative to the benefit obtained. Instead, companies frequently accumulate many individual costs into a single **cost pool.** The total of the pooled cost is then allocated to the cost objects. For example, a company may accumulate costs for gas, water, electricity, and telephone service into a single utilities cost pool. It would then allocate the total cost in the utilities cost pool to the cost objects rather than individually allocating each of the four types of utility costs.

Explain the benefits and detriments of allocating pooled costs.

How far should pooling costs go? Why not pool utility costs with indirect labor costs? If the forces driving the utility costs are different from the forces driving the labor costs, pooling the costs will likely reduce the reliability of any associated cost allocations. To promote accuracy, pooling should be limited to costs with common cost drivers.

Costs that have been pooled for one purpose may require disaggregation for a different purpose. Suppose all overhead costs are pooled for the purpose of determining the cost of making a product. Further, suppose that making the product requires two processes that are performed in different departments. A cutting department makes heavy use of machinery to cut raw materials into product parts. An assembly department uses human labor to assemble the parts into a finished product. Now suppose the objective changes from determining the cost of making the product to determining the cost of operating each department. Under these circumstances, it may be necessary to disaggregate the total overhead cost into smaller pools such as a utility cost pool, an indirect labor cost pool, and so on so that different drivers can be used to allocate these costs to the two departments.

## ALLOCATING JOINT COSTS

**Joint costs** are common costs incurred in the process of making two or more **joint products.** The cost of raw milk is a joint cost of producing the joint products cream, whole milk, 2 percent milk, and skim milk. Joint costs include not only materials costs but also the labor and overhead costs of converting the materials into separate products. The point in the production process at which products become separate and identifiable is the **split-off point.** For financial reporting of inventory and cost of goods sold, companies must allocate the joint costs to the separate joint products. Some joint products require additional processing after the split-off point. Any additional materials, labor, or overhead costs incurred after the split-off point are assigned to the specific products to which they relate.

Allocate joint product costs.

To illustrate, assume Westar Chemical Company produces from common raw materials the joint products Compound AK and Compound AL. Compound AL requires further processing before Westar can sell it. The diagram in Exhibit 4.5 illustrates the joint product costs.

## EXHIBIT 4.5

### Allocation of Joint Cost

The joint costs of producing a batch of the two compounds are $48,000, representing $27,000 of materials cost and $21,000 of processing cost. A batch results in 3,000 gallons of Compound AK and 1,000 gallons of Compound AL. Westar allocates joint costs to the products based on the number of gallons produced, as follows:

**Step 1.** Compute the allocation rate.

Total cost to be allocated ÷ Allocation base = Allocation rate

$48,000 joint costs   ÷   4,000 gallons  =  $12 per gallon

**Step 2.** Multiply the allocation rate by the weight of the base.

| Joint Product | Allocation Rate | × | Number of Gallons Produced | = | Allocated Cost |
|---|---|---|---|---|---|
| Compound AK | $12 | × | 3,000 | = | $36,000 |
| Compound AL | 12 | × | 1,000 | = | 12,000 |

Westar sells 3,000 gallons of Compound AK for $50,000, and 1,000 gallons of Compound AL for $13,000. Exhibit 4.5 shows the gross margins for each product using the joint cost allocations computed above.

## Relative Sales Value as the Allocation Base

Because Compound AL shows a $7,000 loss, a manager might mistakenly conclude that Westar should stop making and selling this product. If Westar stops making Compound AL, the total joint cost ($48,000) would be assigned to Compound AK and total gross margin would decline as shown below.

| | | With Compound AL | Without Compound AL |
|---|---|---|---|
| Sales | $63,000 | ($50,000 + $13,000) | $50,000 |
| Cost of goods sold | (56,000) | ($36,000 + $20,000) | (48,000) |
| Gross margin | $ 7,000 | | $ 2,000 |

To avoid the appearance that a product such as Compound AL is producing losses, many companies allocate joint cost to products based on the relative sales value of each product at the split-off point. Westar Chemical would allocate all of the joint costs to Compound AK because Compound AL has no market value at the split-off point. The resulting gross margins follow.

|  | Compound AK | Compound AL |
|---|---|---|
| Sales | $50,000 | $13,000 |
| Cost of goods sold | (48,000) | (8,000) |
| Gross margin | $ 2,000 | $ 5,000 |

Westar's total profit on the joint products is $7,000 whether it allocates the joint costs using gallons or relative market value. However, using market value as the allocation base produces a positive gross margin for both products, reducing the likelihood that a manager will mistakenly eliminate a product that is contributing to profitability.

---

✓ **CHECK YOURSELF 4.3**

What are some logical split-off points for a meat processing company engaged in butchering beef?

**Answer**  The first logical split-off point occurs when processing separates the hide (used to produce leather) from the carcass. Other split-off points occur as further processing produces different cuts of meat (T-bone and New York strip steaks, various roasts, chops, ground chuck, etc.).

---

## COST ALLOCATION: THE HUMAN FACTOR

Cost allocations significantly affect individuals. They may influence managers' performance evaluations and compensation. They may dictate the amount of resources various departments, divisions, and other organizational subunits receive. Control over resources usually offers managers prestige and influence over organization operations. The following scenario illustrates the emotional impact and perceptions of fairness of cost allocation decisions.

Recognize the effects of cost allocation on employee motivation.

### Using Cost Allocations in a Budgeting Decision

Sharon Southport, dean of the School of Business at a major state university, is in dire need of a budgeting plan. Because of cuts in state funding, the money available to the School of Business for copying costs next year will be reduced substantially. Dean Southport supervises four departments: management, marketing, finance, and accounting. The Dean knows the individual department chairpersons will be unhappy and frustrated with the deep cuts they face.

### Using Cost Drivers to Make Allocations

To address the allocation of copying resources, Dean Southport decided to meet with the department chairs. She explained that the total budgeted for copying costs will be $36,000. Based on past usage, department allocations would be as follows: $12,000 for management, $10,000 for accounting, $8,000 for finance, and $6,000 for marketing.

Dr. Bill Thompson, the management department chair, immediately protested that his department could not operate on a $12,000 budget for copy costs. Management has more faculty members than any other department. Dr. Thompson argued that copy costs are directly related to the number of faculty members, so copy funds should be allocated based on the number of faculty members. Dr. Thompson suggested that number of faculty members rather than past usage should be used as the allocation base.

Since the School of Business has 72 faculty members (29 in management, 16 in accounting, 12 in finance, and 15 in marketing), the allocation should be as follows:

**Step 1.**    Compute the allocation rate.

Total cost to be allocated ÷ Cost driver =    Allocation rate

$36,000        ÷    72    = $500 per faculty member

**Step 2.**    Multiply the rate by the weight of the driver (the number of faculty per department) to determine the allocation per object (department).

| Department | Allocation Rate | × | Number of Faculty | = | Allocation per Department | Allocation Based on Past Usage |
|---|---|---|---|---|---|---|
| Management | $500 | × | 29 | | $14,500 | $12,000 |
| Accounting | 500 | × | 16 | | 8,000 | 10,000 |
| Finance | 500 | × | 12 | | 6,000 | 8,000 |
| Marketing | 500 | × | 15 | | 7,500 | 6,000 |
| Total | | | | | $36,000 | $36,000 |

Seeing these figures, Dr. Bob Smethers, chair of the accounting department, questioned the accuracy of using the number of faculty members as the cost driver. Dr. Smethers suggested the number of *students* rather than the number of *faculty members* drives the cost of copying. He argued that most copying results from duplicating syllabi, exams, and handouts. The accounting department teaches mass sections of introductory accounting that have extremely high student/teacher ratios. Because his department teaches more students, it spends more on copying costs even though it has fewer faculty members. Dr. Smethers recomputed the copy cost allocation as follows:

**Step 1.**    Compute the allocation rate based on number of students. University records indicate that the School of Business taught 1,200 students during the most recent academic year. The allocation rate (copy cost per student) follows.

$$\text{Total cost to be allocated} \div \text{Cost driver} = \text{Allocation rate}$$

$$\$36,000 \quad\quad \div \quad 1,200 \quad = \$30 \text{ per student}$$

**Step 2.** Multiply the rate by the weight of the driver (number of students taught by each department) to determine the allocation per object (department).

| Department | Allocation Rate | × | Number of Students | = | Allocation per Department | Allocation Based on Past Usage |
|---|---|---|---|---|---|---|
| Management | $30 | × | 330 | | $ 9,900 | $12,000 |
| Accounting | 30 | × | 360 | | 10,800 | 10,000 |
| Finance | 30 | × | 290 | | 8,700 | 8,000 |
| Marketing | 30 | × | 220 | | 6,600 | 6,000 |
| Total | | | | | $36,000 | $36,000 |

## Choosing the Best Cost Driver

Dr. Thompson objected vigorously to using the number of students as the cost driver. He continued to argue that the size of the faculty is a more appropriate allocation base. The chair of the finance department sided with Dr. Smethers, the chair of the marketing department kept quiet, and the dean had to settle the dispute.

Dean Southport recognized that the views of the chairpersons were influenced by self-interest. The allocation base affects the amount of resources available to each department. Furthermore, the dean recognized that the size of the faculty does drive some of the copying costs. For example, the cost of copying manuscripts that faculty submit for publication relates to faculty size. The more articles faculty submit, the higher the copying cost. Nevertheless, the dean decided the number of students has the most significant impact on copying costs. She also wanted to encourage faculty members to minimize the impact of funding cuts on student services. Dean Southport therefore decided to allocate copying costs based on the number of students taught by each department. Dr. Thompson stormed angrily out of the meeting. The dean developed a budget by assigning the available funds to each department using the number of students as the allocation base.

## Controlling Emotions

Dr. Thompson's behavior may relieve his frustration but it doesn't indicate clear thinking. Dean Southport recognized that Dr. Thompson's contention that copy costs were related to faculty size had some merit. Had Dr. Thompson offered a compromise rather than an emotional outburst, he might have increased his department's share of the funds. Perhaps a portion of the allocation could have been based on the number of faculty members with the balance allocated based on the number of students. Had Dr. Thompson controlled his anger, the others might have agreed to compromise. Technical expertise in computing numbers is of little use without the interpersonal skills to persuade others. Accountants may provide numerical measurements, but they should never forget the impact of their reports on the people in the organization.

# A Look Back

Managers need to know the costs of products, processes, departments, activities, and so on. The target for which accountants attempt to determine cost is a *cost object*. Knowing the cost of specific objects enables management to control costs, evaluate performance, and price products. *Direct costs* can be cost-effectively traced to a cost object. *Indirect costs* cannot be easily traced to designated cost objects.

The same cost can be direct or indirect, depending on the cost object to which it is traced. For example, the salary of a Burger King restaurant manager can be directly traced to a particular store but cannot be traced to particular food items made and sold in the store. Classifying a cost as direct or indirect is independent of whether the cost behaves as fixed or variable; it is also independent of whether the cost is relevant to a given decision. A direct cost could be either fixed or variable or either relevant or irrelevant, depending on the context and the designated cost object.

Indirect costs are assigned to cost objects using *cost allocation*. Allocation divides an indirect cost into parts and distributes the parts among the relevant cost objects. Companies frequently allocate costs to cost objects in proportion to the *cost drivers* that cause the cost to be incurred. The first step in allocating an indirect cost is to determine the allocation rate by dividing the total cost to be allocated by the chosen cost driver. The next step is to multiply the allocation rate by the amount of the cost driver for a particular object. The result is the amount of indirect cost to assign to the cost object.

A particular indirect cost may be related to more than one driver. The best cost driver is the one that most accurately reflects the amount of the resource used by the cost object. Objects that consume the most resources should be allocated a proportionately greater share of the costs. If no suitable cost driver exists, companies may use arbitrary allocations such as dividing a total cost equally among cost objects.

Cost allocations have behavioral implications. Using inappropriate cost drivers can distort allocations and lead managers to make choices that are detrimental to the company's profitability.

The joint costs incurred in the process of making two or more products are allocated among the products at the *split-off point,* the point at which products become separate and identifiable. The allocation base can be the products' relative sales values or some quantity measure of the amount of each product made. If one of the joint products requires additional processing costs to bring it to market, only these additional processing costs are relevant to a decision about whether to undertake further processing. The allocated joint costs are not relevant because they will be incurred whether or not the joint product is processed after the split-off point. By-products share common costs with other products but have an insignificant market value relative to their joint products.

# >> A Look Forward

The failure to accurately allocate indirect costs to cost objects can result in misinformation that impairs decision making. The next chapter explains how increased use of automation in production has caused distortion in allocations determined using traditional approaches. The chapter introduces the allocation of indirect costs using more recently developed activity-based costing and explains how activity-based management can improve efficiency and productivity. Finally, the chapter introduces total quality management, a strategy that seeks to minimize the costs of conforming to a designated standard of quality.

# APPENDIX

## Allocating Service Center Costs

Allocate service department costs to operating departments.

Most organizations establish departments responsible for accomplishing specific tasks. Departments that are assigned tasks leading to the accomplishment of the primary objectives of the organization are called **operating departments.** Those that provide support to operating departments are called **service departments.** For example, the department of accounting at a university is classified as an operating department because its faculty perform the university's primary functions of teaching, research, and service. In contrast, the maintenance department is classified as a service department because its employees provide janitorial services that support primary university functions. Professors are more likely to be motivated to perform university functions when facilities are clean, but the university's primary purpose is not to clean buildings. Similarly, the lending department in a bank is an operating department and the personnel department is a service department. The bank is in the business of making loans. Hiring employees is a secondary function that assists the lending activity.

The costs to produce a product (or a service) include both operating and service department costs. Therefore, service department costs must somehow be allocated to the products produced (or services provided). Service department costs are frequently distributed to products through a two-stage allocation process. First-stage allocations involve the distribution of costs from service center cost pools to operating department cost pools. In the second stage, costs in the operating cost pools are allocated to products. Three different approaches can be used to allocate costs in the first stage of the two-stage costing process: the *direct method,* the *step method,* and the *reciprocal method.*

## Direct Method

The **direct method** is the simplest allocation approach. It allocates service department costs directly to operating department cost pools. To illustrate, assume that Candler & Associates is a law firm that desires to determine the cost of handling each case. The firm has two operating departments, one that represents clients in civil suits and the other that defends clients in criminal cases. The two operating departments are supported by two service departments, personnel and secretarial support. Candler uses a two-stage allocation system to allocate the service centers' costs to the firm's legal cases. In the first stage, the costs to operate each service department are accumulated in separate cost pools. For example, the costs to operate the personnel department are $80,000 in salary, $18,000 in office rental, $12,000 in depreciation, $3,000 in supplies, and $4,000 in miscellaneous costs. These costs are added together in a single services department cost pool amounting to $117,000. Similarly, the costs incurred by the secretarial department are accumulated in a cost pool. We assume that this cost pool contains $156,800 of accumulated costs. The amounts in these cost pools are then allocated to the operating departments' cost pools. The appropriate allocations are described in the following paragraphs.

Assume that Candler's accountant decides that the number of attorneys working in the two operating departments constitutes a rational cost driver for the allocation of the personnel department cost pool and that the number of request forms submitted to the secretarial department constitutes a rational cost driver for the allocation of costs accumulated in the secretarial department cost pool. The total number of attorneys working in the two operating departments is 18, 11 in the civil department and 7 in the criminal department. The secretarial department received 980 work request forms with 380 from the civil department and 600 from the criminal department. Using these cost drivers as the allocation bases, the accountant made the following first-stage allocations.

## Determination of Allocation Rates

$$\text{Allocation rate for personnel department cost pool} = \frac{\$117,000}{18} = \$6,500 \text{ per attorney}$$

$$\text{Allocation rate for secretarial department cost pool} = \frac{\$156,800}{980} = \$160 \text{ per request form}$$

**EXHIBIT 4.6**

**First-Stage Allocations for Candler & Associates—Direct Method**

| Allocated Service Department Overhead | Allocation Rate | × | Weight of Base | = | Civil Department | Criminal Department | Total Service Department Cost Pool |
|---|---|---|---|---|---|---|---|
| Personnel | $6,500 | × | 11 attorneys | = | $ 71,500 | | |
| | 6,500 | × | 7 attorneys | = | | $ 45,500 | |
| Total cost of personnel department | | | | | | | $117,000 |
| Secretarial | 160 | × | 380 requests | = | 60,800 | | |
| | 160 | × | 600 requests | = | | 96,000 | |
| Total cost of secretarial department | | | | | | | 156,800 |
| Total of cost pools after allocation | | | | | 132,300 | 141,500 | $273,800 |
| Other operating department overhead costs | | | | | 785,100 | 464,788 | |
| Total of operating department overhead cost pools | | | | | $917,400 | $606,288 | |

The accountant then multiplied these rates by the weight of the base to determine the amount of each service cost pool to allocate to each operating department cost pool. The appropriate computations are shown in Exhibit 4.6.

As indicated, the allocated service department costs are pooled with other operating department overhead costs to form the operating department cost pools. In the second stage of the costing process, the costs in the operating department cost pools are allocated to the firm's products (cases). To illustrate second-stage allocations, assume that Candler allocates the operating department overhead cost pools on the basis of billable hours. Furthermore, assume that the civil department expects to bill 30,580 hours to its clients and the criminal department expects to bill 25,262 hours. Based on this information, the following predetermined overhead rates are used to allocate operating department cost pools to particular cases.

$$\text{Predetermined overhead rate for the civil department} = \frac{\$917,400}{30,580} = \$30 \text{ per billable hour}$$

$$\text{Predetermined overhead rate for the criminal department} = \frac{\$606,288}{25,262} = \$24 \text{ per billable hour}$$

These rates are used to calculate the amount of operating department cost pools to include in the determination of the cost to litigate specific cases. For example, a case in the civil department that required 300 billable hours of legal service is allocated $9,000 (300 hours × $30 predetermined overhead rate) of overhead cost. Assuming that the direct costs to litigate the case amounted to $25,000, the total cost of this particular case is $34,000 ($25,000 direct cost + $9,000 allocated overhead). This accumulated cost figure could be used as a guide to determine the charge to the client or the profitability of the case.

## Step Method

The direct method of allocating service center costs fails to consider the fact that service departments render assistance to other service departments. A service that is performed by one service department for the benefit of another service department is called an **interdepartmental service.** To illustrate this, we return to the case of Candler & Associates. Suppose that Candler's personnel department works with the employees in the secretarial department as well as the attorneys in the civil and criminal operating departments. Under these circumstances, Candler needs a cost approach that recognizes the

## EXHIBIT 4.7

### Comparison of Direct and Step Allocation Methods

interdepartmental service activity. One such approach is known as the **step method.** The primary difference between the direct method and the step method is depicted graphically in Exhibit 4.7. Focus your attention on the first stage of the allocation process. Notice that the step method includes one additional allocation, specifically from the personnel department cost pool to the secretarial department cost pool. The direct method ignores this interdepartmental service cost allocation. Indeed, the direct method derives its name from the fact that it allocates costs only from service cost pools to operating cost pools.

The fact that the direct method ignores the effect of interdepartmental services may cause distortions in the measurement of cost objects. The primary purpose of the step method is to avoid such distortions, thereby improving the accuracy of product costing. To illustrate this point, consider Candler & Associates. First, note that the interdepartmental portion of the personnel department cost is, in fact, a cost of providing secretarial services. In other words, the personnel service costs could be reduced if the personnel department did not provide service to the secretarial staff. Accordingly, the cost of providing personnel support to the secretarial staff should be included in the secretarial cost pool. Under the direct method, however, the interdepartmental service cost is allocated between the civil and criminal operating departments. This is not a problem in and of itself because the cost of secretarial service is also allocated between the civil and criminal operating departments. Unfortunately, the base used to allocate personnel costs to the operating departments (i.e., number of attorneys) distributes more cost to the civil department than to the criminal department. This is unfortunate because the criminal department uses more secretarial service than the civil department does. In other words, more secretarial cost (i.e., interdepartmental personnel cost) is being allocated to the civil department although the criminal department uses more secretarial services. This means that ultimately the cost to litigate civil cases will be overstated and the cost to litigate criminal cases will be understated.

The step method corrects this distortion by distributing the interdepartmental personnel department cost to the secretarial department cost pool before it is allocated to the operating departments. Because the secretarial cost pool is allocated on the basis of requests for secretarial service, more of the interdepartmental cost will be allocated to the criminal operating deparment. To validate this result, assume that the personnel department cost pool is allocated to the secretarial department cost pool and the two operating department cost pools on the basis of the number of employees in each department. In addition to the 18 attorneys in the firm, assume that two employees work in the secretarial department. Accordingly, the allocation rate for the personnel cost pool is calculated as follows.

$$\text{Allocation rate for personnel department cost pool} = \frac{\$117,000}{20} = \$5,850 \text{ per employee}$$

Based on this rate, the first step in the allocation process distributes the personnel department cost pool as indicated here.

| Personnel Cost Pool Allocated to | Allocation Rate | | Weight of Base | | Allocated Cost |
|---|---|---|---|---|---|
| Secretarial | $5,850 | × | 2 employees | = | $ 11,700 |
| Civil | 5,850 | × | 11 employees | = | 64,350 |
| Criminal | 5,850 | × | 7 employees | = | 40,950 |
| Total | | | 20 employees | | $117,000 |

The result of the distribution of personnel department costs is shown as the Step 1 allocation in Exhibit 4.8. The $11,700 interdepartmental personnel department cost allocated to the secretarial department cost pool is added to the $156,800 existing balance in that cost pool (See Exhibit 4.8). The result is the accumulation of secretarial cost of $168,500. The second step in the costing process allocates this cost pool to the operating departments. Recall that the secretarial cost pool is allocated on the basis of number of work request forms submitted. Furthermore, recall that 980 request forms were submitted to the secretarial department (380 from the civil department and 600 from the criminal department). Accordingly, the allocation rate for the secretarial department cost pool is computed as follows.

$$\text{Allocation rate for secretarial department cost pool} = \frac{\$168,500}{980} = \$171.93878 \text{ per request form}$$

Based on this rate, the second step in the allocation process distributes the secretarial cost pool as indicated here.

| Secretarial Cost Pool Allocated to | Allocation Rate | | Weight of Base | | Allocated Cost |
|---|---|---|---|---|---|
| Civil | $171.93878 | × | 380 requests | = | $ 65,337 |
| Criminal | 171.93878 | × | 600 requests | = | 103,163 |
| Total | | | 980 requests | | $168,500 |

The result of this allocation is shown as the Step 2 allocation in Exhibit 4.8. Notice that the final cost pools for the operating departments reflect the expected shift in the cost distribution between the two departments. Specifically, the cost pool in the criminal department is higher and the cost pool in the civil department is lower than the comparable cost pool amounts computed under the direct method (see Exhibit 4.6 for the appropriate comparison). This distribution of cost is consistent with the fact that more of the interdepartmental service cost should be assigned to the criminal

## EXHIBIT 4.8

### First-Stage Allocations for Candler & Associates—Step Method

| | Personnel Cost Pool | | Secretarial Cost Pool | | Civil Department | | Criminal Department |
|---|---|---|---|---|---|---|---|
| Cost to be allocated | $117,000 | | $156,800 | | | | |
| Step 1 allocation | (117,000) | = | 11,700 | + | $ 64,350 | + | $ 40,950 |
| Step 2 allocation | | | (168,500) | = | 65,337 | + | 103,163 |
| Total in cost pool after allocation | $ 0 | | $ 0 | | 129,687 | | 144,113 |
| Other operating department overhead costs | | | | | 785,100 | | 464,788 |
| Total of operating department overhead cost pool | | | | | $914,787 | | $608,901 |

department because it uses more secretarial services than does the civil department. Accordingly, the step method of allocation more accurately reflects the manner in which the two operating departments consume resources.

The preceding illustration considered a simple two-stage allocation process with only two service departments and two operating departments. In large organizations, the costing process may be significantly more complex. Interdepartmental cost allocations may involve several service departments. For example, a personnel department may provide service to a secretarial department that provides service to an engineering department that provides service to the accounting department that provides service to several operating departments. In addition, general overhead costs may be allocated to both service and operating departments before costs are allocated from service to operating departments. For example, general utility costs may be pooled together and allocated to service and operating departments on the basis of square footage of floor space. These allocated utility costs are then redistributed to other service departments and to operating departments in a sequence of step-down allocations. The step-down process usually begins with the cost pool that represents resources used by the largest number of departments. This constitutes the first step in the costing process. The second step proceeds with allocations from the cost pool that represents resources used by the second largest number of departments and so on, until all overhead costs have been allocated to the operating departments. Accordingly, the first stage of a two-stage costing process may include many allocations (steps) before all costs have been distributed to the operating departments. Regardless of how many allocations are included in the first stage, the second stage begins when costs are allocated from the operating departments to the organization's products.

## Reciprocal Method

Note that the step method is limited to one-way interdepartmental relationships. In practice, many departments have two-way working relationships. For example, the personnel department may provide services to the secretarial department and receive services from it. Two-way associations in which departments provide and receive services from one another are called **reciprocal relationships.** Allocations that recognize reciprocal relationships require complex mathematical manipulation involving the use of simultaneous linear equations. The resultant cost distributions are difficult to interpret. Furthermore, the results attained with the **reciprocal method** are not significantly different from those attained through the step method. As a result, the reciprocal method is rarely used in practice.

**A step-by-step audio-narrated series of slides is provided on the text website at www.mhhe.com/edmonds2011.**

## SELF-STUDY REVIEW PROBLEM

New budget constraints have pressured Body Perfect Gym to control costs. The owner of the gym, Mr. Ripple, has notified division managers that their job performance evaluations will be highly influenced by their ability to minimize costs. The gym has three divisions: weight lifting, aerobics, and spinning. The owner has formulated a report showing how much it cost to operate each of the three divisions last year. In preparing the report, Mr. Ripple identified several indirect costs that must be allocated among the divisions. These indirect costs are $4,200 of laundry expense, $48,000 of supplies, $350,000 of office rent, $50,000 of janitorial services, and $120,000 for administrative salaries. To provide a reasonably accurate cost allocation, Mr. Ripple has identified several potential cost drivers. These drivers and their association with each division follow.

| Cost Driver | Weight Lifting | Aerobics | Spinning | Total |
|---|---|---|---|---|
| Number of participants | 26 | 16 | 14 | 56 |
| Number of instructors | 10 | 8 | 6 | 24 |
| Square feet of gym space | 12,000 | 6,000 | 7,000 | 25,000 |
| Number of staff | 2 | 2 | 1 | 5 |

### Required

**a.** Identify the appropriate cost objects.

**b.** Identify the most appropriate cost driver for each indirect cost, and compute the allocation rate for assigning each indirect cost to the cost objects.

**c.** Determine the amount of supplies expense that should be allocated to each of the three divisions.

**d.** The spinning manager wants to use the number of staff rather than the number of instructors as the allocation base for the supplies expense. Explain why the spinning manager would take this position.

**e.** Identify two cost drivers other than your choice for Requirement *b* that could be used to allocate the cost of the administrative salaries to the three divisions.

### Solution to Requirement a

The objective is to determine the cost of operating each division. Therefore, the cost objects are the three divisions (weight lifting, aerobics, and spinning).

### Solution to Requirement b

The costs, appropriate cost drivers, and allocation rates for assigning the costs to the departments follow:

| Cost | Base | Computation | Allocation Rate |
|---|---|---|---|
| Laundry expense | Number of participants | $ 4,200 ÷ 56 | $75 per participant |
| Supplies | Number of instructors | 48,000 ÷ 24 | $2,000 per instructor |
| Office rent | Square feet | 350,000 ÷ 25,000 | $14 per square foot |
| Janitorial service | Square feet | 50,000 ÷ 25,000 | $2 per square foot |
| Administrative salaries | Number of divisions | 120,000 ÷ 3 | $40,000 per division |

There are other logical cost drivers. For example, the cost of supplies could be allocated based on the number of staff. It is also logical to use a combination of cost drivers. For example, the allocation for the cost of supplies could be based on the combined number of instructors and staff. For this problem, we assumed that Mr. Ripple chose the number of instructors as the base for allocating supplies expense.

## Solution to Requirement c

| Department | Cost to Be Allocated | Allocation Rate | × | Weight of Base | = | Amount Allocated |
|---|---|---|---|---|---|---|
| Weight lifting | Supplies | $2,000 | × | 10 | = | $20,000 |
| Aerobics | Supplies | 2,000 | × | 8 | = | 16,000 |
| Spinning | Supplies | 2,000 | × | 6 | = | 12,000 |
| Total | | | | | | $48,000 |

## Solution to Requirement d

If the number of staff were used as the allocation base, the allocation rate for supplies would be as follows:

$$\$48,000 \div 5 \text{ staff} = \$9,600 \text{ per staff member}$$

Using this rate, the total cost of supplies would be allocated among the three divisions as follows:

| Department | Cost to Be Allocated | Allocation Rate | × | Weight of Base | = | Amount Allocated |
|---|---|---|---|---|---|---|
| Weight lifting | Supplies | $9,600 | × | 2 | = | $19,200 |
| Aerobics | Supplies | 9,600 | × | 2 | = | 19,200 |
| Spinning | Supplies | 9,600 | × | 1 | = | 9,600 |
| Total | | | | | | $48,000 |

By using the number of staff as the allocation base instead of the number of instructors, the amount of overhead cost allocated to the spinning division falls from $12,000 to $9,600. Since managers are evaluated based on minimizing costs, it is clearly in the spinning manager's self-interest to use the number of staff as the allocation base.

## Solution to Requirement e

Among other possibilities, bases for allocating the administrative salaries include the number of participants, the number of lessons, or the number of instructors.

## KEY TERMS

allocation 153
allocation base 155
allocation rate 155
common costs 154
controllable costs 154
cost accumulation 152
cost allocation 153
cost driver 152
cost objects 150

cost pools 165
cost tracing 153
direct cost 153
direct method 171
indirect cost 153
interdepartmental service 172
joint costs 165
joint products 165
operating departments 170

overhead costs 153
predetermined
    overhead rate 165
reciprocal method 175
reciprocal relationships 175
service departments 170
split-off point 165
step method 173

## QUESTIONS

1. What is a cost object? Identify four different cost objects in which an accountant would be interested.

2. Why is cost accumulation imprecise?

3. If the cost object is a manufactured product, what are the three major cost categories to accumulate?

4. What is a direct cost? What criteria are used to determine whether a cost is a direct cost?

5. Why are the terms *direct cost* and *indirect cost* independent of the terms *fixed cost* and *variable cost*? Give an example to illustrate.

6. Give an example of why the statement, "All direct costs are avoidable," is incorrect.

7. What are the important factors in determining the appropriate cost driver to use in allocating a cost?

8. How is an allocation rate determined? How is an allocation made?

9. In a manufacturing environment, which costs are direct and which are indirect in product costing?

10. Why are some manufacturing costs not directly traceable to products?

11. What is the objective of allocating indirect manufacturing overhead costs to the product?

12. On January 31, the managers of Integra, Inc., seek to determine the cost of producing their product during January for product pricing and control purposes. The company can easily determine the costs of direct materials and direct labor used in January production, but many fixed indirect costs are not affected by the level of production activity and have not yet been incurred. The managers can reasonably estimate the overhead costs for the year based on the fixed indirect costs incurred in past periods. Assume the managers decide to allocate an equal amount of these estimated costs to the products produced each month. Explain why this practice may not provide a reasonable estimate of product costs in January.

13. Respond to the following statement: "The allocation base chosen is unimportant. What is important in product costing is that overhead costs be assigned to production in a specific period by an allocation process."

14. Larry Kwang insists that the costs of his school's fund-raising project should be determined after the project is complete. He argues that only after the project is complete can its costs be determined accurately and that it is a waste of time to try to estimate future costs. Georgia Sundum counters that waiting until the project is complete will not provide timely information for planning expenditures. How would you arbitrate this discussion? Explain the trade-offs between accuracy and timeliness.

15. What are the three methods used for allocating service center costs? How do the methods differ? (Appendix)

## MULTIPLE-CHOICE QUESTIONS

**Multiple-choice questions are provided on the text website at www.mhhe.com/edmonds2011.**

## EXERCISES—SERIES A

**All applicable Exercises in Series A are available with McGraw-Hill's *Connect Accounting*.**

**LO 3**

### Exercise 4-1A    *Allocating costs between divisions*

Sims Services Company (SSC) has 50 employees, 38 of whom are assigned to Division A and 12 to Division B. SSC incurred $296,000 of fringe benefits cost during 2011.

**Required**

Determine the amount of the fringe benefits cost to be allocated to Division A and to Division B.

**LO 2**

### Exercise 4-2A    *Direct versus indirect costs*

Jeelani Construction Company is composed of two divisions: (1) Home Construction and (2) Commercial Construction. The Home Construction Division is in the process of building 12 houses and the Commercial Construction Division is working on three projects. Cost items of the company follow:

Company president's salary

Depreciation on crane used in commercial construction

Depreciation on home office building

Salary of corporate office manager

Wages of workers assigned to a specific construction project

Supplies used by the Commercial Construction Division

Labor on a particular house

Salary of the supervisor of commercial construction projects

Supplies, such as glue and nails, used by the Home Construction Division

Cost of building permits

Materials used in commercial construction project

Depreciation on home building equipment (small tools such as hammers or saws)

**Required**

a. Identify each cost as being a direct or indirect cost assuming the cost objects are the individual products (houses or projects).

b. Identify each cost as being a direct or indirect cost, assuming the cost objects are the two divisions.

c. Identify each cost as being a direct or indirect cost assuming the cost object is Jeelani Construction Company as a whole.

### Exercise 4-3A   *Allocating overhead cost among products*

**LO 3, 4**

Dew Hats Corporation manufactures three different models of hats: Vogue, Beauty, and Glamour. Dew expects to incur $576,000 of overhead cost during the next fiscal year. Other budget information follows.

|  | Vogue | Beauty | Glamour | Total |
|---|---|---|---|---|
| Direct labor hours | 2,000 | 4,000 | 6,000 | 12,000 |
| Machine hours | 1,200 | 1,400 | 1,400 | 4,000 |

**Required**

a. Use direct labor hours as the cost driver to compute the allocation rate and the budgeted overhead cost for each product.

b. Use machine hours as the cost driver to compute the allocation rate and the budgeted overhead cost for each product.

c. Describe a set of circumstances where it would be more appropriate to use direct labor hours as the allocation base.

d. Describe a set of circumstances where it would be more appropriate to use machine hours as the allocation base.

### Exercise 4-4A   *Allocating overhead costs among products*

**LO 3, 4**

Nevin Company makes three products in its factory: plastic cups, plastic tablecloths, and plastic bottles. The expected overhead costs for the next fiscal year include the following.

| | |
|---|---|
| Factory manager's salary | $260,000 |
| Factory utility cost | 121,000 |
| Factory supplies | 56,000 |
| Total overhead costs | $437,000 |

Nevin uses machine hours as the cost driver to allocate overhead costs. Budgeted machine hours for the products are as follows:

| | |
|---|---|
| Cups | 420 Hours |
| Tablecloths | 740 |
| Bottles | 1,140 |
| Total machine hours | 2,300 |

**Required**

a. Allocate the budgeted overhead costs to the products.

b. Provide a possible explanation as to why Nevin chose machine hours, instead of labor hours, as the allocation base.

**LO 3, 4**

### Exercise 4-5A   *Allocating costs among products*

Deka Construction Company expects to build three new homes during a specific accounting period. The estimated direct materials and labor costs are as follows.

| Expected Costs | Home 1 | Home 2 | Home 3 |
|---|---|---|---|
| Direct labor | $60,000 | $ 90,000 | $170,000 |
| Direct materials | 90,000 | 130,000 | 180,000 |

Assume Deka needs to allocate two major overhead costs ($40,000 of employee fringe benefits and $20,000 of indirect materials costs) among the three jobs.

**Required**

Choose an appropriate cost driver for each of the overhead costs and determine the total cost of each house.

**LO 3, 5**

### Exercise 4-6A   *Allocating to smooth cost over varying levels of production*

Production workers for Nabors Manufacturing Company provided 280 hours of labor in January and 500 hours in February. Nabors expects to use 4,000 hours of labor during the year. The rental fee for the manufacturing facility is $8,000 per month.

**Required**

Explain why allocation is needed. Based on this information, how much of the rental cost should be allocated to the products made in January and to those made in February?

**LO 3, 5**

### Exercise 4-7A   *Allocating to solve a timing problem*

Production workers for Bianco Manufacturing Company provided 3,600 hours of labor in January and 1,900 hours in February. The company, whose operation is labor intensive, expects to use 32,000 hours of labor during the year. Bianco paid a $96,000 annual premium on July 1 of the prior year for an insurance policy that covers the manufacturing facility for the following 12 months.

**Required**

Explain why allocation is needed. Based on this information, how much of the insurance cost should be allocated to the products made in January and to those made in February?

**LO 3, 5**

### Exercise 4-8A   *Allocating to solve a timing problem*

Stevens Air is a large airline company that pays a customer relations representative $4,000 per month. The representative, who processed 1,000 customer complaints in January and 1,300 complaints in February, is expected to process 24,000 customer complaints during 2012.

**Required**

a.  Determine the total cost of processing customer complaints in January and in February.

b.  Explain why allocating the cost of the customer relations representative would or would not be relevant to decision making.

**LO 3, 5**

### Exercise 4-9A   *Allocating overhead cost to accomplish smoothing*

Woods Corporation expects to incur indirect overhead costs of $60,000 per month and direct manufacturing costs of $11 per unit. The expected production activity for the first four months of 2012 is as follows.

| | January | February | March | April |
|---|---|---|---|---|
| Estimated production in units | 4,000 | 7,000 | 3,000 | 6,000 |

**Required**

a.  Calculate a predetermined overhead rate based on the number of units of product expected to be made during the first four months of the year.

b.  Allocate overhead costs to each month using the overhead rate computed in Requirement *a*.

c.  Calculate the total cost per unit for each month using the overhead allocated in Requirement *b*.

## Exercise 4-10A  *Pooling overhead cost*          LO 3, 5, 6

Jasti Manufacturing Company produced 1,000 units of inventory in January 2011. It expects to produce an additional 8,400 units during the remaining 11 months of the year. In other words, total production for 2011 is estimated to be 9,600 units. Direct materials and direct labor costs are $64 and $52 per unit, respectively. Jasti Company expects to incur the following manufacturing overhead costs during the 2011 accounting period.

| | |
|---|---|
| Production supplies | $ 4,800 |
| Supervisor salary | 192,000 |
| Depreciation on equipment | 144,000 |
| Utilities | 36,000 |
| Rental fee on manufacturing facilities | 96,000 |

**Required**

a. Combine the individual overhead costs into a cost pool and calculate a predetermined overhead rate assuming the cost driver is number of units.

b. Determine the cost of the 1,200 units of product made in January.

c. Is the cost computed in Requirement *a* actual or estimated? Could Jasti improve accuracy by waiting until December to determine the cost of products? Identify two reasons that a manager would want to know the cost of products in January. Discuss the relationship between accuracy and relevance as it pertains to this problem.

## Exercise 4-11A  *How the allocation of fixed cost affects a pricing decision*          LO 3, 5

Mallett Manufacturing Co. expects to make 30,000 chairs during the 2011 accounting period. The company made 3,200 chairs in January. Materials and labor costs for January were $16,000 and $24,000, respectively. Mallett produced 2,500 chairs in February. Material and labor costs for February were $8,000 and $12,000, respectively. The company paid the $240,000 annual rental fee on its manufacturing facility on January 1, 2011.

**Required**

Assuming that Mallett desires to sell its chairs for cost plus 40 percent of cost, what price should be charged for the chairs produced in January and February?

## Exercise 4-12A  *Allocating joint product cost*          LO 3, 7

Turley Chemical Company makes three products, B7, K6, and X9, which are joint products from the same materials. In a standard batch of 300,000 pounds of raw materials, the company generates 70,000 pounds of B7, 150,000 pounds of K6, and 80,000 pounds of X9. A standard batch costs $2,400,000 to produce. The sales prices per pound are $6, $10, and $16 for B7, K6, and X9, respectively.

**Required**

a. Allocate the joint product cost among the three final products using weight as the allocation base.

b. Allocate the joint product cost among the three final products using market value as the allocation base.

## Exercise 4-13A  *Human factor*          LO 8

Dearman Clinics provides medical care in three departments: internal medicine (IM), pediatrics (PD), and obstetrics gynecology (OB). The estimated costs to run each department follow:

| | IM | PD | OB |
|---|---|---|---|
| Physicians | $400,000 | $300,000 | $200,000 |
| Nurses | 80,000 | 120,000 | 160,000 |

Dearman expects to incur $450,000 of indirect (overhead) costs in the next fiscal year.

**Required**

a. Name four allocation bases that could be used to assign the overhead cost to each department.

b. Assume the manager of each department is permitted to recommend how the overhead cost should be allocated to the departments. Which of the allocation bases named in Requirement *a* is the manager of OB most likely to recommend? Explain why. What argument may the manager of OB use to justify his choice of the allocation base?

c. Which of the allocation bases would result in the fairest allocation of the overhead cost from the perspective of the company president?

d. Explain how classifying overhead costs into separate pools could improve the fairness of the allocation of the overhead costs.

## Appendix

**LO 3, 9**

### Exercise 4-14A    *Allocating a service center cost to operating departments*

Fowler Corporation's computer services department assists two operating departments in using the company's information system effectively. The annual cost of computer services is $360,000. The production department employs 22 employees, and the sales department employs 18 employees. Fowler uses the number of employees as the cost driver for allocating the cost of computer services to operating departments.

**Required**

Allocate the cost of computer services to operating departments.

**LO 3, 9**

### Exercise 4-15A    *Allocating costs of service centers to operating departments—step method*

Hardy Health Care Center, Inc., has three clinics servicing the Seattle metropolitan area. The company's legal services department supports the clinics. Moreover, its computer services department supports all of the clinics and the legal services department. The annual cost of operating the legal services department is $217,000. The annual cost of operating the computer services department is $450,000. The company uses the number of patients served as the cost driver for allocating the cost of legal services and the number of computer workstations as the cost driver for allocating the cost of computer services. Other relevant information follows:

|  | Number of Patients | Number of Workstations |
|---|---|---|
| Hoover clinic | 6,000 | 15 |
| Eastwood clinic | 4,200 | 16 |
| Gardendale clinic | 5,800 | 12 |
| Legal services |  | 7 |
| Computer services |  | 10 |

**Required**

a. Allocate the cost of computer services to all of the clinics and the legal services department.

b. After allocating the cost of computer services, allocate the cost of legal services to the three clinics.

c. Compute the total allocated cost of service centers for each clinic.

**LO 3, 9**

### Exercise 4-16A    *Allocating costs of service centers to operating departments—direct method*

Jooste Trust Corporation has two service departments: actuary and economic analysis. Jooste also has three operating departments: annuity, fund management, and employee benefit services. The annual costs of operating the service departments are $440,000 for actuary and $720,000 for economic analysis. Jooste uses the direct method to allocate service center costs to operating departments. Other relevant data follow:

| | Operating Costs* | Revenue |
|---|---|---|
| Annuity | $500,000 | $ 840,000 |
| Fund management | 900,000 | 1,260,000 |
| Employee benefit services | 600,000 | 1,100,000 |
| *The operating costs are measured before allocating service center costs. | | |

## Required

**a.** Use operating costs as the cost driver for allocating service center costs to operating departments.

**b.** Use revenue as the cost driver for allocating service center costs to operating departments.

## PROBLEMS—SERIES A

**All applicable Problems in Series A are available with McGraw-Hill's Connect Accounting.**

### Problem 4-17A  *Cost accumulation and allocation*

Singh Manufacturing Company makes two different products, M and N. The company's two departments are named after the products; for example, Product M is made in Department M. Singh's accountant has identified the following annual costs associated with these two products.

LO 1, 2, 3, 4, 5

CHECK FIGURE
(c) N: $531.65

| Financial data | |
|---|---|
| Salary of vice president of production division | $180,000 |
| Salary of supervisor Department M | 76,000 |
| Salary of supervisor Department N | 56,000 |
| Direct materials cost Department M | 300,000 |
| Direct materials cost Department N | 420,000 |
| Direct labor cost Department M | 240,000 |
| Direct labor cost Department N | 680,000 |
| Direct utilities cost Department M | 120,000 |
| Direct utilities cost Department N | 24,000 |
| General factorywide utilities | 36,000 |
| Production supplies | 36,000 |
| Fringe benefits | 138,000 |
| Depreciation | 720,000 |
| **Nonfinancial data** | |
| Machine hours Department M | 5,000 |
| Machine hours Department N | 1,000 |

## Required

**a.** Identify the costs that are (1) direct costs of Department M, (2) direct costs of Department N, and (3) indirect costs.

**b.** Select the appropriate cost drivers for the indirect costs and allocate these costs to Departments M and N.

**c.** Determine the total estimated cost of the products made in Departments M and N. Assume that Singh produced 2,000 units of Product M and 4,000 units of Product N during the year. If Singh prices its products at cost plus 40 percent of cost, what price per unit must it charge for Product M and for Product N?

LO 1, 3, 4

**Problem 4-18A**   *Selecting an appropriate cost driver (What is the base?)*

The Vest School of Vocational Technology has organized the school training programs into three departments. Each department provides training in a different area as follows: nursing assistant, dental hygiene, and office technology. The school's owner, Wilma Vest, wants to know how much it costs to operate each of the three departments. To accumulate the total cost for each department, the accountant has identified several indirect costs that must be allocated to each. These costs are $10,080 of phone expense, $2,016 of office supplies, $720,000 of office rent, $144,000 of janitorial services, and $150,000 of salary paid to the dean of students. To provide a reasonably accurate allocation of costs, the accountant has identified several possible cost drivers. These drivers and their association with each department follow.

| Cost Driver | Department 1 | Department 2 | Department 3 |
|---|---|---|---|
| Number of telephones | 28 | 32 | 52 |
| Number of faculty members | 20 | 16 | 12 |
| Square footage of office space | 28,800 | 16,800 | 12,000 |
| Number of secretaries | 2 | 2 | 2 |

**Required**

a.  Identify the appropriate cost objects.

b.  Identify the appropriate cost driver for each indirect cost and compute the allocation rate for assigning each indirect cost to the cost objects.

c.  Determine the amount of telephone expense that should be allocated to each of the three departments.

d.  Determine the amount of supplies expense that should be allocated to Department 3.

e.  Determine the amount of office rent that should be allocated to Department 2.

f.  Determine the amount of janitorial services cost that should be allocated to Department 1.

g.  Identify two cost drivers not listed here that could be used to allocate the cost of the dean's salary to the three departments.

LO 1, 2

**Problem 4-19A**   *Cost allocation in a service industry*

Kirby Airlines is a small airline that occasionally carries overload shipments for the overnight delivery company Never-Fail, Inc. Never-Fail is a multimillion-dollar company started by Jack Never immediately after he failed to finish his first accounting course. The company's motto is "We Never-Fail to Deliver Your Package on Time." When Never-Fail has more freight than it can deliver, it pays Kirby to carry the excess. Kirby contracts with independent pilots to fly its planes on a per-trip basis. Kirby recently purchased an airplane that cost the company $5,500,000. The plane has an estimated useful life of 25,000,000 miles and a zero salvage value. During the first week in January, Kirby flew two trips. The first trip was a round trip flight from Chicago to San Francisco, for which Kirby paid $350 for the pilot and $300 for fuel. The second flight was a round trip from Chicago to New York. For this trip, it paid $300 for the pilot and $150 for fuel. The round trip between Chicago and San Francisco is approximately 4,400 miles and the round trip between Chicago and New York is 1,600 miles.

**Required**

a.  Identify the direct and indirect costs that Kirby incurs for each trip.

b.  Determine the total cost of each trip.

c.  In addition to depreciation, identify three other indirect costs that may need to be allocated to determine the cost of each trip.

LO 1, 3, 4

**Problem 4-20A**   *Cost allocation in a manufacturing company*

Hunt Manufacturing Company makes tents that it sells directly to camping enthusiasts through a mail-order marketing program. The company pays a quality control expert $72,000 per year to inspect completed tents before they are shipped to customers. Assume that the company completed 1,600 tents in January and 1,200 tents in February. For the entire year, the company expects to produce 12,000 tents.

**Required**

a. Explain how changes in the cost driver (number of tents inspected) affect the total amount of fixed inspection cost.

b. Explain how changes in the cost driver (number of tents inspected) affect the amount of fixed inspection cost per unit.

c. If the cost objective is to determine the cost per tent, is the expert's salary a direct or an indirect cost?

d. How much of the expert's salary should be allocated to tents produced in January and February?

## Problem 4-21A  *Fairness and cost pool allocations*

LO 1, 4, 6, 8

eXcel

Daniel Manufacturing Company uses two departments to make its products. Department I is a cutting department that is machine intensive and uses very few employees. Machines cut and form parts and then place the finished parts on a conveyor belt that carries them to Department II where they are assembled into finished goods. The assembly department is labor intensive and requires many workers to assemble parts into finished goods. The company's manufacturing facility incurs two significant overhead costs: employee fringe benefits and utility costs. The annual costs of fringe benefits are $252,000 and utility costs are $180,000. The typical consumption patterns for the two departments are as follows.

|  | Department I | Department II | Total |
|---|---|---|---|
| Machine hours used | 16,000 | 4,000 | 20,000 |
| Direct labor hours used | 5,000 | 13,000 | 18,000 |

The supervisor of each department receives a bonus based on how well the department controls costs. The company's current policy requires using a single allocation base (machine hours or labor hours) to allocate the total overhead cost of $432,000.

**Required**

a. Assume that you are the supervisor of Department I. Choose the allocation base that would minimize your department's share of the total overhead cost. Calculate the amount of overhead that would be allocated to both departments using the base that you selected.

b. Assume that you are the supervisor of Department II. Choose the allocation base that would minimize your department's share of the total overhead cost. Calculate the amount of overhead that would be allocated to both departments using the base that you selected.

c. Assume that you are the plant manager and have the authority to change the company's overhead allocation policy. Formulate an overhead allocation policy that would be fair to the supervisors of both Department I and Department II. Compute the overhead allocations for each department using your policy.

d. Explain why it is necessary to disaggregate the overhead cost pool in order to accomplish fairness.

## Problem 4-22A  *Allocation to accomplish smoothing*

LO 1, 3, 5

CHECK FIGURES
a. $4
c. March: $42

O'Hara Corporation estimated its overhead costs would be $24,000 per month except for January when it pays the $72,000 annual insurance premium on the manufacturing facility. Accordingly, the January overhead costs were expected to be $96,000 ($72,000 + $24,000). The company expected to use 7,000 direct labor hours per month except during July, August, and September when the company expected 9,000 hours of direct labor each month to build inventories for high demand that normally occurs during the Christmas season. The company's actual direct labor hours were the same as the estimated hours. The company made 3,500 units of product in each month except July, August, and September in which it produced 4,500 units each month. Direct labor costs were $24 per unit, and direct materials costs were $10 per unit.

**Required**

a. Calculate a predetermined overhead rate based on direct labor hours.

b. Determine the total allocated overhead cost for January, March, and August.

**c.** Determine the cost per unit of product for January, March, and August.

**d.** Determine the selling price for the product, assuming that the company desires to earn a gross margin of $20 per unit.

## Problem 4-23A    *Allocating indirect costs between products*

Erin Tarver is considering expanding her business. She plans to hire a salesperson to cover trade shows. Because of compensation, travel expenses, and booth rental, fixed costs for a trade show are expected to be $12,000. The booth will be open 30 hours during the trade show. Ms. Tarver also plans to add a new product line, ProOffice, which will cost $180 per package. She will continue to sell the existing product, EZRecords, which costs $100 per package. Ms. Tarver believes that the salesperson will spend approximately 20 hours selling EZRecords and 10 hours marketing ProOffice.

**Required**

**a.** Determine the estimated total cost and cost per unit of each product, assuming that the salesperson is able to sell 80 units of EZRecords and 50 units of ProOffice.

**b.** Determine the estimated total cost and cost per unit of each product, assuming that the salesperson is able to sell 200 units of EZRecords and 100 units of ProOffice.

**c.** Explain why the cost per unit figures calculated in Requirement *a* are different from the amounts calculated in Requirement *b*. Also explain how the differences in estimated cost per unit will affect pricing decisions.

## Problem 4-24A    *Cost Pools*

Richter Department Stores, Inc. has three departments: women's, men's, and children's. The following are the indirect costs related to its operations:

Medical insurance
Salaries of secretaries
Water bill
Vacation pay
Sewer bill
Staples
Natural gas bill
Pens
Ink cartridges
Payroll taxes
Paper rolls for cash registers

**Required**

**a.** Organize the costs in the following three pools: indirect materials, indirect labor, and indirect utilities, assuming that each department is a cost object.

**b.** Identify an appropriate cost driver for each pool.

**c.** Explain why accountants use cost pools.

## Problem 4-25A    *Allocating joint product cost*

Koch Chicken Corporation processes and packages chicken for grocery stores. It purchases chickens from farmers and processes them into two different products: chicken drumsticks and chicken steak. From a standard batch of 12,000 pounds of raw chicken that costs $7,000, the company produces two parts: 2,800 pounds of drumsticks and 4,200 pounds of breast for a processing cost of $2,450. The chicken breast is further processed into 3,200 pounds of steak for a processing cost of $2,000. The market price of drumsticks per pound is $1.00 and the market price per pound of chicken steak is $3.40. If Koch decided to sell chicken breast instead of chicken steak, the price per pound would be $2.00.

**Required**

**a.** Allocate the joint cost to the joint products, drumsticks and breasts, using weight as the allocation base. Calculate the net income for each product. Since the drumsticks are producing a net loss, should that product line be eliminated?

**b.** Reallocate the joint cost to the joint products, drumsticks and breasts, using relative market values as the allocation base. Calculate the net income for each product. Compare the total net income (drumsticks + breasts) computed in Requirement *b* with that computed in Requirement *a* above. Explain why the total amount is the same. Comment on which allocation base (weight or market value) is more appropriate.

**c.** Should Koch further process chicken breasts into chicken steak?

## Appendix

### Problem 4-26A *Allocating service center costs—step method and direct method*

Romero Information Services, Inc., has two service departments: human resources and billing. Romero's operating departments, organized according to the special industry each department serves, are health care, retail, and legal services. The billing department supports only the three operating departments, but the human resources department supports all operating departments and the billing department. Other relevant information follows.

**LO 3, 9**

**eXcel**

**CHECK FIGURES**
a. Allocated cost from Billing to Retail: $558,000
b. Allocated cost from HR to LS: $240,000

| | Human Resources | Billing | Health Care | Retail | Legal Services |
|---|---|---|---|---|---|
| Number of employees | 20 | 50 | 190 | 140 | 120 |
| Annual cost* | $900,000 | $1,710,000 | $6,000,000 | $4,800,000 | $2,800,000 |
| Annual revenue | — | — | $9,000,000 | $6,200,000 | $4,800,000 |

*This is the operating cost before allocating service department costs.

### Required

**a.** Allocate service department costs to operating departments, assuming that Romero adopts the step method. The company uses the number of employees as the base for allocating human resources department costs and department annual revenue as the base for allocating the billing department costs.

**b.** Allocate service department costs to operating departments, assuming that Romero adopts the direct method. The company uses the number of employees as the base for allocating the human resources department costs and department annual revenue as the base for allocating the billing department costs.

**c.** Compute the total allocated cost of service centers for each operating department using each allocation method.

## EXERCISES—SERIES B

### Exercise 4-1B *Allocating costs between divisions*

**LO 1, 3**

Smith and Warren, LLP, has three departments: auditing, tax, and information systems. The departments occupy 2,500 square feet, 1,500 square feet, and 1,000 square feet of office space, respectively. The firm pays $6,000 per month to rent its offices.

### Required

How much monthly rent cost should Smith and Warren allocate to each department?

### Exercise 4-2B *Direct versus indirect costs*

**LO 2**

Kenta and Associates, LLP, is an accounting firm that provides two major types of professional services: (1) tax services as provided by the tax department and (2) auditing services as provided by the audit department. Each department has numerous clients. Engagement with each individual client is a separate service (i.e., product) and each department has several engagements in each period. Cost items of the firm follow:

Secretarial labor supporting both departments

Professional labor for an audit engagement

Depreciation of computers used in the audit department

Salary of the partner in charge of the tax department

Travel expenditures for an audit engagement

Salary of the partner in charge of the audit department

Salary of the managing partner of the firm

Cost of office supplies such as paper, pencils, erasers, etc.

Depreciation of computers used in the tax department

License fees of the firm

Professional labor for a tax engagement

**Required**

a. Identify each cost as being a direct or indirect cost assuming the cost objects are the individual engagements (audit engagements or tax engagements).

b. Identify each cost as being a direct or indirect cost assuming the cost objects are the two departments.

c. Identify each cost as being a direct or indirect cost assuming the cost object is Kenta and Associates, LLP, as a whole.

**LO 3, 5**

### Exercise 4-3B   *Allocating overhead costs among products*

Diat Company manufactures three different sizes of automobile sunscreens: large, medium, and small. Diat expects to incur $480,000 of overhead costs during the next fiscal year. Other budget information for the coming year follows:

|                    | Large | Medium | Small | Total  |
|--------------------|-------|--------|-------|--------|
| Direct labor hours | 2,500 | 5,000  | 4,500 | 12,000 |
| Machine hours      | 700   | 1,300  | 1,000 | 3,000  |

**Required**

a. Use direct labor hours as the cost driver to compute the allocation rate and the budgeted overhead cost for each product.

b. Use machine hours as the cost driver to compute the allocation rate and the budgeted overhead cost for each product.

c. Describe a set of circumstances where it would be more appropriate to use direct labor hours as the allocation base.

d. Describe a set of circumstances where it would be more appropriate to use machine hours as the allocation base.

**LO 3, 4**

### Exercise 4-4B   *Allocating overhead costs among products*

Yunan Company makes three models of jump drives in its factory: J512, J1G, and J4G. The expected overhead costs for the next fiscal year are as follows:

| | |
|---|---|
| Payroll for factory managers | $100,000 |
| Factory maintenance costs | 45,000 |
| Factory insurance | 23,000 |
| Total overhead costs | $168,000 |

Yunan uses labor hours as the cost driver to allocate overhead cost. Budgeted labor hours for the products are as follows:

| | |
|---|---|
| J512 | 1,000 hours |
| J1G | 650 |
| J4G | 450 |
| Total labor hours | 2,100 |

**Required**

**a.** Allocate the budgeted overhead costs to the products.

**b.** Provide a possible explanation as to why Yunan chose labor hours, instead of machine hours, as the allocation base.

## Exercise 4-5B     *Allocating costs among products*        LO 3, 4

Blotski Company makes household plastic bags in three different sizes: Snack, Sandwich, and Storage. The estimated direct materials and direct labor costs are as follows.

| Expected Costs | Snack | Sandwich | Storage |
|---|---|---|---|
| Direct materials | $112,000 | $188,000 | $300,000 |
| Direct labor | 60,000 | 116,000 | 224,000 |

Blotski allocates two major overhead costs among the three products: $36,000 of indirect labor cost for workers who move various materials and products to different stations in the factory and $28,000 of employee pension costs.

**Required**

Determine the total cost of each product.

## Exercise 4-6B     *Allocating indirect cost over varying levels of production*        LO 3, 5

Denver Company's annual factory depreciation is $108,000. Denver estimated it would operate the factory a total of 2,400 hours this year. The factory operated 200 hours in November and 150 hours in December.

**Required**

Why would Denver need to allocate factory depreciation cost? How much depreciation cost should Denver allocate to products made in November and those made in December?

## Exercise 4-7B     *Allocating indirect cost over varying levels of production*        LO 3, 5

On January 1, Glaze Corporation paid the annual royalty of $720,000 for rights to use patented technology to make batteries for laptop computers. Glaze plans to use the patented technology to produce five different models of batteries. Glaze uses machine hours as a common cost driver and plans to operate its machines 48,000 hours in the coming year. The company used 3,000 machine hours in June and 3,600 hours in July.

**Required**

Why would Glaze need to allocate the annual royalty payment rather than simply assign it in total to January production? How much of the royalty cost should Glaze allocate to products made in June and those made in July?

## Exercise 4-8B     *Allocating a fixed cost*        LO 3, 5

Last year, Sean Tapper bought an automobile for $24,000 to use in his taxi business. He expected to drive the vehicle for 140,000 miles before disposing of it for $3,000. Sean drove 3,200 miles this week and 2,800 miles last week.

**Required**

**a.** Determine the total cost of vehicle depreciation this week and last week.

**b.** Explain why allocating the vehicle cost would or would not be relevant to decision making.

## Exercise 4-9B     *Allocating overhead cost to accomplish smoothing*        LO 3, 5

In 2012, Pingtung Corporation incurred direct manufacturing costs of $35 per unit and manufacturing overhead costs of $175,000. The production activity for the four quarters of 2012 follows:

| | 1st Quarter | 2nd Quarter | 3rd Quarter | 4th Quarter |
|---|---|---|---|---|
| Number of units produced | 3,300 | 2,700 | 4,500 | 2,000 |

**Required**

a. Calculate a predetermined overhead rate based on the number of units produced during the year.

b. Allocate overhead costs to each quarter using the overhead rate computed in Requirement *a*.

c. Using the overhead allocation determined in Requirement *b*, calculate the total cost per unit for each quarter.

**LO 3, 5, 6**

### Exercise 4-10B    *Pooling overhead cost*

Rosen Manufacturing Company produced 500 units of inventory in January 2011. The company expects to produce an additional 5,500 units of inventory during the remaining 11 months of the year, for total estimated production of 6,000 units in 2011. Direct materials and direct labor costs are $70 and $82 per unit, respectively. Rosen expects to incur the following manufacturing overhead costs during the 2011 accounting period:

| | |
|---|---|
| Indirect materials | $ 6,800 |
| Depreciation on equipment | 24,000 |
| Utilities cost | 10,200 |
| Salaries of plant manager and staff | 96,800 |
| Rental fee on manufacturing facilities | 19,000 |

**Required**

a. Combine the individual overhead costs into a cost pool and calculate a predetermined overhead rate assuming the cost driver is number of units.

b. Determine the estimated cost of the 500 units of product made in January.

c. Is the cost computed in Requirement *a* actual or estimated? Could Rosen improve accuracy by waiting until December to determine the cost of products? Identify two reasons that a manager would want to know the cost of products in January. Discuss the relationship between accuracy and relevance as it pertains to this problem.

**LO 3, 5**

### Exercise 4-11B    *How fixed cost allocation affects a pricing decision*

Neumann Manufacturing Company expects to make 30,000 travel sewing kits during 2012. In January, the company made 1,800 kits. Materials and labor costs for January were $7,200 and $9,000, respectively. In February, Neumann produced 2,200 kits. Material and labor costs for February were $8,800 and $11,000, respectively. The company paid $69,000 for annual factory insurance on January 10, 2012. Ignore other manufacturing overhead costs.

**Required**

Assuming that Neumann desires to sell its sewing kits for cost plus 20 percent of cost, what price should it charge for the kits produced in January and February?

**LO 3, 6**

### Exercise 4-12B    *Allocating joint product cost*

Pannier Food Corporation makes two products from soybeans: cooking oil and cattle feed. From a standard batch of 100,000 pounds of soybeans, Pannier produces 20,000 pounds of cooking oil and 80,000 pounds of cattle feed. Producing a standard batch costs $10,000. The sales prices per pound are $1.00 for cooking oil and $0.75 for cattle feed.

**Required**

a. Allocate the joint product cost to the two products using weight as the allocation base.

b. Allocate the joint product cost to the two products using market value as the allocation base.

**LO 8**

### Exercise 4-13B    *Human factor*

Duddley Company builds custom sailboats. Duddley currently has three boats under construction. The estimated costs to complete each boat are shown below.

| | Boat 1 | Boat 2 | Boat 3 |
|---|---|---|---|
| Direct materials | $25,000 | $32,000 | $12,000 |
| Direct labor | 22,000 | 20,000 | 14,000 |

Duddley expects to incur $48,000 of indirect (overhead) costs in the process of making the boats.

**Required**

a. Based on the information provided, name four allocation bases that could be used to assign the overhead costs to each boat.

b. Assume that the production manager of each boat is permitted to recommend how the overhead costs should be allocated to the boats. Which of the allocation bases named in Requirement *a* is the manager of Boat 2 most likely to recommend? Explain why. What argument may the manager of Boat 2 use to justify his choice of the allocation base?

c. Which of the allocation bases would result in the fairer allocation of the overhead costs from the perspective of the company president?

d. Explain how classifying overhead costs into separate pools could improve the fairness of the allocation of the overhead costs.

## Appendix

**Exercise 4-14B** *Allocating a service center cost to operating departments*    LO 3, 9

The administrative department of Andrews Consulting, LLC, provides office administration and professional support to its two operating departments. Annual administrative costs are $540,000. In 2010, the hours chargeable to clients generated by the information services department and the financial planning department were 24,000 and 36,000, respectively. Andrews uses chargeable hours as the cost driver for allocating administrative costs to operating departments.

**Required**

Allocate the administrative costs to the two operating departments.

**Exercise 4-15B** *Allocating service centers' costs to operating departments—*    LO 3, 9
*step method*

Shepard Consulting, LLP, has three operating departments: tax, estate planning, and small business. The company's internal accounting and maintenance departments support the operating departments. Moreover, the maintenance department also supports the internal accounting department. Other relevant information follows:

| | Annual Cost* | Square Feet | Operating Revenue |
|---|---|---|---|
| Tax | $5,000,000 | 8,000 | $8,000,000 |
| Estate planning | 2,000,000 | 2,000 | 3,500,000 |
| Small business | 3,000,000 | 4,000 | 6,500,000 |
| Internal accounting | 690,000 | 1,000 | 0 |
| Maintenance | 450,000 | 1,000 | 0 |

*The annual cost figures do not include costs allocated from service departments.

Shepard allocates its maintenance cost based on the square footage of each department's office space. The firm allocates the internal accounting cost based on each department's operating revenue.

**Required**

a. Allocate the maintenance cost to the operating and internal accounting departments.

b. After allocating the maintenance cost, allocate the internal accounting cost to the three operating departments.

c. Compute the total allocated cost of the service departments for each operating department.

**Exercise 4-16B** *Allocating service centers' costs to operating departments—*    LO 3, 9
*direct method*

Quebec Corporation, a book publisher, has two service departments: editing and typesetting. Quebec also has three operating departments: children's fiction, youth fiction, and adult fiction. The annual costs of operating the editing department are $240,000 and of operating the typesetting department are $210,000. Quebec uses the direct method to allocate service center costs to operating departments. Other relevant data follow.

| | Number of Pages | Number of Hours |
|---|---|---|
| Children | 15,000 | 5,000 |
| Youth | 10,000 | 8,000 |
| Adult | 5,000 | 7,000 |

**Required**

a. Allocate the service center costs to the operating departments using the number of pages as the cost driver.

b. Allocate the service center costs to the operating departments using the number of hours as the cost driver.

## PROBLEMS—SERIES B

**LO 1, 2, 3, 4, 5**

### Problem 4-17B  *Cost accumulation and allocation*

Otto Tools Company has two production departments in its manufacturing facilities. Home tools specializes in hand tools for individual home users, and professional tools makes sophisticated tools for professional maintenance workers. Otto's accountant has identified the following annual costs associated with these two products:

| Financial data | |
|---|---|
| Salary of vice president of production | $150,000 |
| Salary of manager, home tools | 54,000 |
| Salary of manager, professional tools | 43,500 |
| Direct materials cost, home tools | 300,000 |
| Direct materials cost, professional tools | 375,000 |
| Direct labor cost, home tools | 336,000 |
| Direct labor cost, professional tools | 414,000 |
| Direct utilities cost, home tools | 75,000 |
| Direct utilities cost, professional tools | 30,000 |
| General factorywide utilities | 31,500 |
| Production supplies | 40,500 |
| Fringe benefits | 150,000 |
| Depreciation | 360,000 |
| **Nonfinancial data** | |
| Machine hours, home tools | 4,000 |
| Machine hours, professional tools | 2,000 |

**Required**

a. Identify the costs that are the (1) direct costs of home tools, (2) direct costs of professional tools, and (3) indirect costs.

b. Select the appropriate cost drivers and allocate the indirect costs to home tools and to professional tools.

c. Assume that each department makes only a single product. Home tools produces its Deluxe Drill for home use, and professional tools produces the Professional Drill. The company made 30,000 units of Deluxe Drill and 20,000 units of Professional Drill during the year. Determine the total estimated cost of the products made in each department. If Otto prices its products at cost plus 30 percent of cost, what price per unit must it charge for the Deluxe Drill and the Professional Drill?

## Problem 4-18B  *Selecting an appropriate cost driver (What is the base?)*

LO 1, 3, 4

Letterman Research Institute has three departments: biology, chemistry, and physics. The institute's controller wants to estimate the cost of operating each department. He has identified several indirect costs that must be allocated to each department including $11,200 of phone expense, $2,400 of office supplies, $1,120,000 of office rent, $150,000 of janitorial services, and $150,000 of salary paid to the director. To provide a reasonably accurate allocation of costs, the controller identified several possible cost drivers. These drivers and their association with each department follow.

| Cost Driver | Biology | Chemistry | Physics |
| --- | --- | --- | --- |
| Number of telephones | 10 | 14 | 16 |
| Number of researchers | 8 | 10 | 12 |
| Square footage of office space | 8,000 | 8,000 | 12,000 |
| Number of secretaries | 1 | 1 | 1 |

### Required

a. Identify the appropriate cost objects.

b. Identify the appropriate cost driver for each indirect cost, and compute the allocation rate for assigning each indirect cost to the cost objects.

c. Determine the amount of telephone expense that should be allocated to each of the three departments.

d. Determine the amount of supplies expense that should be allocated to the physics department.

e. Determine the amount of office rent cost that should be allocated to the chemistry department.

f. Determine the amount of janitorial services cost that should be allocated to the biology department.

g. Identify two cost drivers not listed here that could be used to allocate the cost of the director's salary to the three departments.

## Problem 4-19B  *Cost allocation in a service industry*

LO 1, 2

Cook, Newton, and Associates provides legal services for its local community. In addition to its regular attorneys, the firm hires some part-time attorneys to handle small cases. Two secretaries assist all part-time attorneys exclusively. In 2010, the firm paid $48,000 for the two secretaries who worked a total of 4,000 hours. Moreover, the firm paid Jean Sutton $60 per hour and Eric Veasy $50 per hour for their part-time legal services.

In August 2010, Ms. Sutton completed a case that took her 60 hours. Mr. Veasy finished a case on which he worked 30 hours. The firm also paid a private investigator to uncover relevant facts. The investigation fees cost $1,000 for Ms. Sutton's case and $750 for Mr. Veasy's case. Ms. Sutton used 30 hours of secretarial assistance, and Mr. Veasy used 40 hours.

### Required

a. Identify the direct and indirect costs incurred in each case completed in August 2010.

b. Determine the total cost of each case.

c. In addition to secretaries' salaries, identify three other indirect costs that may need to be allocated to determine the cost of the cases.

## Problem 4-20B  *Cost allocation in a manufacturing company*

LO 1, 3, 4

Solid Door Corporation makes a particular type of door. The labor cost is $90 per door and the material cost is $160 per door. Solid rents a factory building for $60,000 a month. Solid plans to produce 24,000 doors annually. In March and April, it made 2,000 and 3,000 doors, respectively.

**Required**

a. Explain how changes in the cost driver (number of doors made) affect the total amount of fixed rental cost.

b. Explain how changes in the cost driver (number of doors made) affect the fixed rental cost per unit.

c. If the cost objective is to determine the cost per door, is the factory rent a direct or an indirect cost?

d. How much of the factory rent should be allocated to doors produced in March and April?

**LO 1, 4, 6, 8**

### Problem 4-21B    *Fairness and cost pool allocations*

Pettway Furniture Company has two production departments. The parts department uses automated machinery to make parts; as a result, it uses very few employees. The assembly department is labor intensive because workers manually assemble parts into finished furniture. Employee fringe benefits and utility costs are the two major overhead costs of the company's production division. The fringe benefits and utility costs for the year are $300,000 and $144,000, respectively. The typical consumption patterns for the two departments follow.

|  | Parts | Assembly | Total |
|---|---|---|---|
| Machine hours used | 26,000 | $ 4,000 | 30,000 |
| Direct labor hours used | 3,500 | 20,500 | 24,000 |

The supervisor of each department receives a bonus based on how well the department controls costs. The company's current policy requires using a single activity base (machine hours or labor hours) to allocate the total overhead cost of $444,000.

**Required**

a. Assume that you are the parts department supervisor. Choose the allocation base that would minimize your department's share of the total overhead cost. Calculate the amount of overhead to allocate to both departments using the base that you selected.

b. Assume that you are the assembly department supervisor. Choose the allocation base that would minimize your department's share of the total overhead cost. Calculate the amount of overhead to allocate to both departments using the base that you selected.

c. Assume that you are the plant manager and that you have the authority to change the company's overhead allocation policy. Formulate an overhead allocation policy that would be fair to the supervisors of both the parts and assembly departments. Compute the overhead allocation for each department using your policy.

d. Explain why it is necessary to disaggregate the overhead cost pool in order to accomplish fairness.

**LO 1, 3, 5**

### Problem 4-22B    *Allocation to accomplish smoothing*

Lagatta Corporation's overhead costs are usually $24,000 per month. However, the company pays $54,000 of real estate tax on the factory facility in March. Thus, the overhead costs for March increase to $78,000. The company normally uses 5,000 direct labor hours per month except for August, September, and October, in which the company requires 9,000 hours of direct labor per month to build inventories for high demand in the Christmas season. Last year, the company's actual direct labor hours were the same as usual. The company made 5,000 units of product in each month except August, September, and October in which it produced 9,000 units per month. Direct labor costs were $8 per unit; direct materials costs were $7 per unit.

**Required**

a. Calculate a predetermined overhead rate based on direct labor hours.

b. Determine the total allocated overhead cost for the months of March, August, and December.

c. Determine the cost per unit of product for the months of March, August, and December.

d. Determine the selling price for the product, assuming that the company desires to earn a gross margin of $7 per unit.

## Problem 4-23B *Allocating indirect cost between products*

LO 1, 3, 5

McCombs Corporation has hired a marketing representative to sell the company's two products: Marvelous and Wonderful. The representative's total salary and fringe benefits are $10,000 monthly. The product cost is $90 per unit for Marvelous and $144 per unit for Wonderful. McCombs expects the representative to spend 48 hours per month marketing Marvelous and 112 hours promoting Wonderful.

### Required

a. Determine the estimated total cost and cost per unit, assuming that the representative is able to sell 100 units of Marvelous and 70 units of Wonderful in a month. Allocate indirect cost on the basis of labor hours.

b. Determine the estimated total cost and cost per unit, assuming that the representative is able to sell 250 units of Marvelous and 140 units of Wonderful. Allocate indirect cost on the basis of labor hours.

c. Explain why the cost per unit figures calculated in Requirement *a* differ from the amounts calculated in Requirement *b*. Also explain how the differences in estimated cost per unit will affect pricing decisions.

## Problem 4-24B *Cost Pools*

LO 1, 6

Esquire Furniture Company incurred the following costs in the process of making tables and chairs.

| | |
|---|---|
| Glue | Paint |
| Supervisor salaries | Water bill |
| Gas bill | Vacation pay |
| Payroll taxes | Sewer bill |
| Cost of nails | Staples |
| Medical insurance | Electric bill |

### Required

a. Organize the costs in the following three pools: indirect materials, indirect labor, and indirect utilities.

b. Identify an appropriate cost driver for each pool.

c. Explain why accountants use cost pools.

## Problem 4-25B *Allocating joint product cost*

LO 3, 9

Mountain Tea Co. makes two products: a high-grade tea branded Wulong and a low-grade tea branded San Tea for the Asian market. Mountain purchases tea leaves from tea firms in mountainous villages of Taiwan and processes the tea leaves into a high-quality product. The tea leaves are dried and baked in the manufacturing process. Mountain pays farmers $600 for 900 kilograms of tea leaves. For 900 kilograms of green leaves, the company can produce 100 kilograms of Wulong and 200 kilograms of tea fragments including dried leave stems and broken dried leaves. The cost of this process is $300 per batch. The tea fragments are packaged into San Tea. The market price for San Tea is $2.00 per kilogram. The market price is $20 per kilogram for Wulong. Mountain has an option of taking an additional process to refine the 100 kilograms of Wulong into 30 kilograms of Donding, a prestigious brand. The market price of Donding is $100 per kilogram. The cost of the additional process is $250 per batch.

### Required

a. Allocate the joint cost to the joint products, Wulong and San Tea, using weight as the allocation base. Calculate the net income for each product. Since the San Tea is sold at a loss, should that product line be eliminated?

b. Allocate the joint cost to the joint products, Wulong and San Tea, using relative market value as the allocation base. Calculate the net income for each product. Compare the total net income (Wulong + San Tea) computed in Requirement *b* with that computed in Requirement *a* above. Explain why the total amount is the same. Comment on which allocation base (weight or relative market value) is more appropriate.

c. Should Mountain Tea further process Wulong into Donding?

## Appendix

**LO 3, 9**

### Problem 4-26B    *Allocating service center costs—step method and direct method*

Dunne Corporation has three production departments: forming, assembly, and packaging. The maintenance department supports only the production departments; the computer services department supports all departments including maintenance. Other relevant information follows.

| | Forming | Assembly | Packaging | Maintenance | Computer Services |
|---|---|---|---|---|---|
| Machine hours | 6,000 | 2,500 | 1,500 | 400 | 0 |
| Number of computers | 14 | 20 | 11 | 15 | 8 |
| Annual cost* | $450,000 | $800,000 | $250,000 | $100,000 | $90,000 |

*This is the annual operating cost before allocating service department costs.

### Required

a. Allocate service department costs to operating departments, assuming that Dunne adopts the step method. The company uses the number of computers as the base for allocating the computer services costs and machine hours as the base for allocating the maintenance costs.

b. Use machine hours as the base for allocating maintenance department costs and the number of computers as the base for allocating computer services cost. Allocate service department costs to operating departments, assuming that Dunne adopts the direct method.

c. Compute the total allocated cost of service centers for each operating department using each allocation method.

## ANALYZE, THINK, COMMUNICATE

### ATC 4-1    Business Applications Case    *Allocating fixed costs at Porsche*

During its fiscal year ending on July 31, 2008, the Dr. Ing. h. c. F. Porsche AG, commonly known as "Porsche," manufactured 105,162 vehicles. During that same year, Porsche recorded depreciation on property, plant and equipment of €281,813,000. (Porsche's financial information is reported in euros, and € is the symbol for the euro.) For the purposes of this problem, assume that all of the depreciation is related to manufacturing activities.

### Required

a. Indicate whether the depreciation charge is a:
   (1) Product cost, or a general, selling and administrative costs.
   (2) Fixed or variable cost relative to the volume of production.
   (3) Direct or indirect if the cost object is the cost of vehicles made in the 2008 fiscal year.

b. Assume that Porsche incurred depreciation of €23,500,000 during each month of the 2008 fiscal year, but that it produced 10,000 vehicles during February and 7,000 vehicles during March. Based on monthly costs and production levels, what was the average amount of depreciation cost per vehicle produced during each of these two months, assuming each vehicle was charged the same amount of depreciation?

**c.** If Porsche had expected to produce 108,000 vehicles during 2008, and had estimated its annual depreciation costs to be €285,000,000, what would have been its predetermined overhead charge per vehicle for depreciation? Explain the advantage of using this amount to determine the cost of manufacturing a car in February and March versus the amounts you computed in Requirement *b*.

**d.** If Porsche's management had estimated the profit per vehicle based on its budgeted production of 108,000 units, would you expect its actual profit per vehicle to be higher or lower than expected? Explain.

## ATC 4-2  Group Assignment  *Selection of the cost driver*

Vulcan College School of Business is divided into three departments: accounting, marketing, and management. Relevant information for each of the departments follows.

| Cost Driver | Accounting | Marketing | Management |
|---|---|---|---|
| Number of students | 1,400 | 800 | 400 |
| Number of classes per semester | 64 | 36 | 28 |
| Number of professors | 20 | 24 | 10 |

Vulcan is a private school that expects each department to generate a profit. It rewards departments for profitability by assigning 20 percent of each department's profits back to that department. Departments have free rein as to how to use these funds. Some departments have used them to supply professors with computer technology. Others have expanded their travel budgets. The practice has been highly successful in motivating the faculty to control costs. The revenues and direct costs for the year 2011 follow:

| | Accounting | Marketing | Management |
|---|---|---|---|
| Revenue | $29,600,000 | $16,600,000 | $8,300,000 |
| Direct costs | 24,600,000 | 13,800,000 | 6,600,000 |

Vulcan allocates to the School of Business $4,492,800 of indirect overhead costs such as administrative salaries and the costs of operating the registrar's office and the bookstore.

### Required

**a.** Divide the class into groups and organize the groups into three sections. Assign each section a department. For example, groups in Section 1 should represent the Accounting Department Groups in Sections 2 and 3 should represent the Marketing Department and Management Department, respectively. Assume that the dean of the school is planning to assign an equal amount of the college overhead to each department. Have the students in each group prepare a response to the dean's plan. Each group should select a spokesperson who is prepared to answer the following questions.

**(1)** Is your group in favor of or opposed to the allocation plan suggested by the dean?

**(2)** Does the plan suggested by the dean provide a fair allocation? Why?

The instructor should lead a discussion designed to assess the appropriateness of the dean's proposed allocation plan.

**b.** Have each group select the cost driver (allocation base) that best serves the self-interest of the department it represents.

**c.** Consensus on Requirement *c* should be achieved before completing Requirement *d*. Each group should determine the amount of the indirect cost to be allocated to each department using the cost driver that best serves the self-interest of the department it represents. Have a spokesperson from each section go to the board and show the income statement that would result for each department.

**d.** Discuss the development of a cost driver(s) that would promote fairness rather than self-interest in allocating the indirect costs.

## ATC 4-3  Research Assignment  *Using real world data from Pepsi Bottling Group*

Use the 2008 Form 10-K for **Pepsi Bottling Group** to complete the requirements below. Pepsi Bottling Group (PBG) is a separate company from PepsiCo, so do not confuse them. To obtain the Form 10-K you can use either the EDGAR system following the instructions in Appendix A, or it can be found under the "Investor Relations" link on the company's corporate website at **www.pbg.com**. The company includes its Form 10-K as a part of its 2008 Annual Report, or it can be found separately under "SEC Filings." Be sure to read carefully the following sections of the document:

> *Under "Item 1. Business," read subsections titled "Introduction," "Principal Products," "Raw Materials and Other Supplies," and "Seasonality."*
>
> *In the footnotes section of the report, under "Note 2—Summary of Significant Accounting Policies," read the subsections titled "Advertising and Marketing Costs" and "Shipping and Handling Costs"*
>
> *"Note 4—Balance Sheet Details," in the footnotes section of the report.*

### Required

**a.** Does PBG consider *shipping and handling costs* and *advertising and marketing costs* to be direct or indirect cost in relation to the manufacturing of its products? Explain.

**b.** Assume that when PBG ships orders of bottled drinks each shipment includes several different products such as Pepsi, Lipton tea, and Starbucks Frappuccino. If PBG wanted to allocate the shipping costs among the various products, what would be an appropriate cost driver? Explain the rationale for your choice.

**c.** Assume that PBG incurs some advertising costs that cannot be directly traced to a single product such as Pepsi or Diet Pepsi. If PBG wanted to allocate the advertising costs among the various products being advertised jointly, what would be an appropriate way of making this allocation? Explain the rationale for your choice.

**d.** As *Note 4* indicates, PBG computes depreciation expense on three separate classes of assets. For which of these classes of assets could its depreciation expense be directly traced to the production of soft drinks? Which class would least likely be traceable to the production of soft drinks? Explain.

**e.** Based on PBG's discussion of the seasonality of its business, should the depreciation of production equipment recorded in a given month be based on the volume of drinks produced that month, or should the depreciation be one-twelfth of the estimated annual depreciation PBG expects to incur? Explain your answer.

## ATC 4-4  Writing Assignment  *Selection of the appropriate cost driver*

Bullions Enterprises, Inc. (BEI), makes gold, silver, and bronze medals used to recognize outstanding athletic performance in regional and national sporting events. The per-unit direct costs of producing the medals follow.

|                  | Gold  | Silver | Bronze |
|------------------|-------|--------|--------|
| Direct materials | $300  | $130   | $ 35   |
| Labor            | 120   | 120    | 120    |

During 2012, BEI made 1,200 units of each type of medal for a total of 3,600 (1,200 × 3) medals. All medals are created through the same production process, and they are packaged and shipped in identical containers. Indirect overhead costs amounted to $324,000. BEI currently uses the number of units as the cost driver for the allocation of overhead cost. As a result, BEI allocated $90 ($324,000 ÷ 3,600 units) of overhead cost to each medal produced.

**Required**

The president of the company has questioned the wisdom of assigning the same amount of overhead to each type of medal. He believes that overhead should be assigned on the basis of the cost to produce the medals. In other words, more overhead should be charged to expensive gold medals, less to silver, and even less to bronze. Assume that you are BEI's chief financial officer. Write a memo responding to the president's suggestion.

## ATC 4-5    Ethical Dilemma    *Allocation to achieve fairness*

The American Acupuncture Association offers continuing professional education courses for its members at its annual meeting. Instructors are paid a fee for each student attending their courses but are charged a fee for overhead costs that is deducted from their compensation. Overhead costs include fees paid to rent instructional equipment such as overhead projectors, provide supplies to participants, and offer refreshments during coffee breaks. The number of courses offered is used as the allocation base for determining the overhead charge. For example, if overhead costs amount to $5,000 and 25 courses are offered, each course is allocated an overhead charge of $200 ($5,000 ÷ 25 courses). Heidi McCarl, who taught one of the courses, received the following statement with her check in payment for her instructional services.

| | |
|---|---|
| Instructional fees (20 students × $50 per student) | $1,000 |
| Less: Overhead charge | (200) |
| Less: Charge for sign language assistant | (240) |
| Amount due instructor | $ 560 |

Although Ms. McCarl was well aware that one of her students was deaf and required a sign language assistant, she was surprised to find that she was required to absorb the cost of this service.

**Required**

a. Given that the Americans with Disabilities Act stipulates that the deaf student cannot be charged for the cost of providing sign language, who should be required to pay the cost of sign language services?

b. Explain how allocation can be used to promote fairness in distributing service costs to the disabled. Describe two ways to treat the $240 cost of providing sign language services that improve fairness.

## ATC 4-6    Spreadsheet Assignment    *Using Excel*

Brook Health Care Center, Inc., has three clinics servicing the Birmingham metropolitan area. The company's legal services department supports the clinics. Moreover, its computer services department supports all of the clinics and the legal services department. The company uses the number of computer workstations as the cost driver for allocating the cost of computer services and the number of patients as the cost driver for allocating the cost of legal services. The annual cost of the Department of Legal Services was $340,000, and the annual cost of the Department of Computer Services was $250,000. Other relevant information follows.

| | Number of Patients | Number of Workstations |
|---|---|---|
| Hoover Clinic | 3,100 | 17 |
| Eastwood Clinic | 2,300 | 13 |
| Gardendale Clinic | 2,800 | 6 |
| Legal Services | 0 | 14 |

**Required**

**a.** Construct a spreadsheet like the following one to allocate the service costs using the step method.

| X Microsoft Excel - ch05-working.xls | | | | | | | | | | | | | |
|---|---|---|---|---|---|---|---|---|---|---|---|---|---|
| File Edit View Insert Format Tools Data Window Help | | | | | | | | | | | | | |

| | A | B | C | D | E | F | G | H | I | J | K | L | M | N |
|---|---|---|---|---|---|---|---|---|---|---|---|---|---|---|
| 1 | Chapter 4 - Working with Excel | | | | | | | | Name: | | | | | |
| 2 | | | | | | | | | | | | | | |
| 3 | | | | | | | | | | | | | | |
| 4 | | | | Computer | | Legal | | Hoover | | Eastwood | | Gardendale | | |
| 5 | | | | Services | | Services | | Clinic | | Clinic | | Clinic | | |
| 6 | | Costs to be allocated | | $250,000 | | $340,000 | | | | | | | | |
| 7 | | Step 1 Allocation | | (250,000) | | 70,000 | | $ 85,000 | | $ 65,000 | | $ 30,000 | | |
| 8 | | Step 2 Allocation | | | | (410,000) | | 155,000 | | 115,000 | | 140,000 | | |
| 9 | | Total in cost pool after allocation | $ | - | | $ - | | $240,000 | | $180,000 | | $170,000 | | |
| 10 | | | | | | | | | | | | | | |
| 11 | | Supporting calculations: | | | | | | | | | | | | |
| 12 | | | | | | | | | | | | | | |
| 13 | a) | Cost to be allocated | | $250,000 | | $410,000 | | | | | | | | |
| 14 | | | | | | | | driver x rate | | driver x rate | | | | |
| 15 | | Hoover Clinic | | 17 | | 3,100 | | $ 85,000 | | $155,000 | | | | |
| 16 | | Eastwood Clinic | | 13 | | 2,300 | | 65,000 | | 115,000 | | | | |
| 17 | | Gardendale Clinic | | 6 | | 2,800 | | 30,000 | | 140,000 | | | | |
| 18 | | Legal Services | | 14 | | | | 70,000 | | | | | | |
| 19 | b) | Total of driver | | 50 | | 8,200 | | | | | | | | |
| 20 | | | | | | | | | | | | | | |
| 21 | | Allocation rate a/b | | $ 5,000 | | $ 50 | | | | | | | | |
| 22 | | | | | | | | | | | | | | |

Sheet1 / Sheet2 / Sheet3 /     Ready     NUM

## Spreadsheet Tips

1. The headings in rows 4 and 5 are right aligned. To right align text, choose Format, then Cells, and then click on the tab titled Alignment, and set the horizontal alignment to Right. The shortcut method to right align text is to click on the right align icon in the middle of the second tool bar.

2. The supporting calculation section must be completed simultaneously with the allocation table. However, most of the supporting calculations can be completed first. The exception is that the value in cell F13 refers to the sum of cells F6 and F7.

## ATC 4-7   Spreadsheet Assignment   *Mastering Excel*

Phillips Paints manufactures three types of paint in a joint process: rubberized paint, rust-proofing paint, and aluminum paint. In a standard batch of 500,000 gallons of raw material, the outputs are 240,000 gallons of rubberized paint, 80,000 gallons of rust-proofing paint, and 180,000 gallons of aluminum paint. The production cost of a batch is $2,700,000. The sales prices per gallon are $15, $18, and $20 for rubberized, rust-proofing, and aluminum paint, respectively.

**Required**

**a.** Construct a spreadsheet to allocate joint costs to the three products using the number of gallons as the allocation base.

**b.** Include formulas in your spreadsheet to calculate the gross margin for each paint.

## COMPREHENSIVE PROBLEM

Magnificent Modems has excess production capacity and is considering the possibility of making and selling paging equipment. The following estimates are based on a production and sales volume of 1,000 pagers.

Unit-level manufacturing costs are expected to be $20. Sales commissions will be established at $1 per unit. The current facility-level costs, including depreciation on manufacturing equipment ($60,000), rent on the manufacturing facility ($50,000), depreciation on the administrative equipment ($12,000), and other fixed administrative expenses ($71,950), will not be affected by the production of the pagers. The chief accountant has decided to allocate the facility-level costs to the existing product (modems) and to the new product (pagers) on the basis of the number of units of product made (i.e., 5,000 modems and 1,000 pagers).

## Required

a. Determine the per-unit cost of making and selling 1,000 pagers.

b. Assuming the pagers could be sold at a price of $34 each, should Magnificent make the pagers?

c. Comment on the validity of using the number of units as an allocation base.

## CHAPTER 5

# Cost Management in an Automated Business Environment

## ABC, ABM, and TQM

## LEARNING OBJECTIVES

**After you have mastered the material in this chapter you will be able to:**

1 Explain how activity-based costing improves accuracy in determining the cost of products and services.

2 Identify cost centers and cost drivers in an activity-based costing system.

3 Use activity-based costing to calculate costs of products and services.

4 Identify the components of quality costs.

5 Prepare and interpret quality cost reports.

## CHAPTER OPENING

Worldwide growth in capitalism has fostered an increasingly competitive global business environment. Companies have responded by using technology to increase productivity. Management accountants have worked with engineers to more accurately measure and control costs. They have eliminated many nonvalue-added activities and have employed quality control procedures that reduce costs and enhance customer satisfaction. These innovative business practices have enabled companies to eliminate unprofitable products and to promote products that maximize profitability. This chapter focuses on newer and emerging business practices employed by world-class companies.

# The Curious Accountant

A vendor incurs a cost when it allows customers to pay using a credit or debit card. Credit card companies, such as **American Express**, charge the vendor either a fixed fee or a percentage of the transaction amount. For example, when the **United States Postal Service (USPS)** allows a customer to pay for $100 of stamps using a credit card, the USPS receives less than $100 from the credit card company, perhaps $97. The actual discount rate the credit card company charges depends on its agreement with the individual vendor. Large customers such as the USPS usually get better rates than smaller customers. Considering that total revenues at the USPS were $74.9 billion in 2008 and that $38.2 billion of these were from first-class mail, the costs of allowing customers to use debit and credit cards to pay for postage can be high.

Most companies that accept credit cards as payment do so believing that customers will spend more money using "plastic" than if forced to pay cash. Also, a company's competitors may be accepting credit cards, leaving the company little choice. However, the USPS has a virtual monopoly on many types of mail services in the United States, so why is it willing to allow customers to pay with credit cards? Why not make everyone pay with cash or checks?

Now consider this: Another large government agency, the **Internal Revenue Service (IRS)** will not accept debit or credit card payments unless the taxpayer pays the credit card fee. If the USPS does not require a surcharge for credit card users, why does the IRS? (Answers on page 215.)

# DEVELOPMENT OF A SINGLE COMPANYWIDE COST DRIVER

Explain how activity-based costing improves accuracy in determining the cost of products and services.

When accountants first developed cost systems, manufacturing processes were labor intensive. Indirect manufacturing costs were relatively minor and highly correlated with labor use; products that used large amounts of labor consumed large amounts of overhead. This link made the number of labor hours a suitable cost driver for allocating overhead costs.

To illustrate, suppose during an eight-hour day Friedman Company production employees worked on two jobs, Job 1 for two hours and Job 2 for six hours. Friedman consumed utilities of $120 during the day. How much of the $120 should the company assign to each job? Friedman cannot trace the utility cost directly to a specific job, but the job that required more labor likely consumed more of the utility cost. The longer employees work the more heat, lights, and water they use. Allocating the utility cost to the two jobs based on *direct labor hours* produces rational results. Friedman could allocate the utility cost at $15 per hour ($120 ÷ 8 hours). It could assign Job 1 $30 of the utility cost ($15 per hour × 2 hours), and Job 2 the remaining $90 ($15 × 6 hours).

In addition to utilities, direct labor drives many other indirect costs. Consider the depreciation cost of tools employees use while working on production jobs. The more time employees work, the more they use the tools. Direct labor hours could be an effective cost driver (allocation base) for allocating tool depreciation costs. The same logic applies to supervisory salaries, production supplies, factory rent expense, and other overhead costs. Many companies applied this reasoning to justify using direct labor hours as the *sole base* for establishing a **companywide allocation rate.** These companies then allocated all overhead costs to their products or other cost objects using the single labor-based, companywide overhead rate. Even though using one base to allocate all overhead costs inaccurately measured some cost objects, in the labor intensive environment that spawned companywide allocation rates, overhead costs were relatively small compared to the costs of labor and materials. Allocation inaccuracies were relatively insignificant in amount.

Automation has changed the nature of manufacturing processes. The number of direct labor hours is no longer an effective allocation base in many modern manufacturing companies. Machines have replaced most human workers. Because they operate technically complex equipment, the remaining workers are highly skilled and not easily replaced. Companies resist laying off these trained workers when production declines. Neither do companies add employees when production increases. Adjusting production volume merely requires turning additional machines on or off. In such circumstances, direct labor is not related to production volume. Direct labor is therefore not an effective base for allocating overhead costs. Former labor-intensive companies that adopt automation usually must develop more sophisticated ways to allocate overhead costs.

When companies replace people with machines, overhead costs such as machinery depreciation and power usage become greater in proportion to total manufacturing costs. In highly automated companies, overhead costs may be greater than direct labor and direct materials costs combined. Although misallocating minor overhead amounts does little harm, misallocating major costs destroys the usefulness of accounting information and leads to poor decisions. Managers must consider how automation affects overhead cost allocation.

## Effects of Automation on Selecting a Cost Driver

In an automated manufacturing environment, robots and sophisticated machinery, rather than human labor, transform raw materials into finished goods. To illustrate the effect of these changes on selecting a cost driver, return to the previous Friedman Company example. Suppose Friedman automates the production process for Job 2, replacing most labor with four hours of machine processing and reducing the number of direct labor hours required from six to one. Assume the new machinery acquired increases utility consumption and depreciation charges, raising daily overhead costs from $120 to $420. Because Job 1 requires two hours of direct labor and Job 2 now requires one hour of direct labor, Friedman's companywide allocation rate increases to $140 per direct labor hour ($420 ÷ 3 hours). The company would allocate $280 ($140 × 2 hours) of the total overhead cost to Job 1 and $140 ($140 × 1 hour) to Job 2. The pre- and postautomation allocations are compared here.

| Product | Preautomation Cost Distribution | Postautomation Cost Distribution |
|---------|---------------------------------|----------------------------------|
| Job 1 | $ 30 | $280 |
| Job 2 | 90 | 140 |
| Total | $120 | $420 |

Using direct labor hours as the cost driver after automating production of Job 2 distorts the overhead cost allocation. Although Friedman did not change the production process for Job 1 at all, Job 1 received a $250 ($280 − $30) increase in its share of allocated overhead cost. This increase should have been assigned to Job 2 because automating production of Job 2 caused overhead costs to increase. The decrease in direct labor hours for Job 2 causes the distortion. Prior to automation, Job 2 used six of eight total direct labor hours and was therefore allocated 75 percent (6 ÷ 8) of the overhead cost. After automation, Job 2 consumed only one of three total direct labor hours, reducing its overhead allocation to only 33 percent of the total. These changes in the allocation base, coupled with the increase in total overhead cost, caused the postautomation overhead cost allocation for Job 1 to be significantly overstated and for Job 2 to be significantly understated.

One way to solve the misallocation problem is to find a more suitable volume-based cost driver. For example, Friedman could allocate utility costs using machine hours instead of direct labor hours. This text illustrated using different **volume-based cost drivers** (such as material dollars and direct labor hours) in Chapter 4. Unfortunately, automated production processes often generate costs which have no cause-and-effect relationship with volume-based cost drivers. Many companies have therefore adopted **activity-based cost drivers** to improve the accuracy of indirect cost allocations. To illustrate, consider the case of Carver Soup Company.

## Activity-Based Cost Drivers

Carver Soup Company (CSC) produces batches of vegetable and tomato soup. Each time CSC switches production from vegetable soup to tomato soup or vice versa, it incurs certain costs. For example, production workers must clean the mixing, blending, and cooking equipment. They must change settings on the equipment to the specifications for the particular soup to be processed. CSC must test each batch for quality to ensure the recipe has been correctly followed. Because these costs are incurred for each new batch, they are called **start-up,** or **setup, costs.** CSC plans to make 180 batches of each type of soup during the coming year. The following table summarizes expected production information:

|                   | Vegetable | Tomato  | Total     |
|-------------------|-----------|---------|-----------|
| Number of cans    | 954,000   | 234,000 | 1,188,000 |
| Number of setups  | 180       | 180     | 360       |

CSC expects each setup will cost $264, for total expected setup costs of $95,040 ($264 × 360 setups). Using number of cans as the cost driver (volume-based driver) produces an allocation rate of $0.08 per can ($95,040 ÷ 1,188,000 cans). Multiplying the allocation rate by the weight of the base (number of cans) produces the following setup cost allocation:

| Product   | Allocation Rate | × | Number of Cans Produced | = | Allocated Setup Cost |
|-----------|-----------------|---|-------------------------|---|----------------------|
| Vegetable | $0.08           | × | 954,000                 | = | $76,320              |
| Tomato    | 0.08            | × | 234,000                 | = | 18,720               |

As expected, the volume-based (number of cans) allocation rate assigns more cost to the high-volume vegetable soup product. However, assigning more setup cost to the vegetable soup makes little sense. Since both products require the *same number* of setups, the setup cost should be distributed equally between them. The volume-based cost driver *overcosts* the high-volume product (vegetable soup) and *undercosts* the low-volume product (tomato soup).

Setup costs are driven by the number of times CSC employees perform the setup activities. The more setups employees undertake, the greater the total setup cost. An *activity-based cost driver* (number of setups) provides a more accurate allocation base for setup costs. Using the allocation rate of $264 ($95,040 ÷ 360 setups) per setup assigns the same amount of setup cost to each product, as follows:

| Product   | Allocation Rate | × | Number of Setups | = | Allocated Setup Cost |
|-----------|-----------------|---|------------------|---|----------------------|
| Vegetable | $264            | × | 180              | = | $47,520              |
| Tomato    | 264             | × | 180              | = | 47,520               |

## Activity-Based Cost Drivers Enhance Relevance

The *activity-based cost driver* produces a better allocation because it distributes the *relevant* costs to the appropriate products. If CSC were to stop producing tomato soup, it could *avoid* spending $47,520 for 180 setups (assuming CSC could eliminate labor, supplies, and other resources used in the setup process). *Avoidable costs are relevant* to decision making. The inaccurate volume-based product cost data could mislead a manager into making a poor decision. Suppose a company specializing in setup activities offered to provide CSC 180 tomato soup setups for $40,000. A manager relying on the volume-based allocated cost of $18,720 would reject the $40,000 offer to outsource as too costly. In fact, CSC should accept the offer because it could avoid $47,520 of cost if the outside company performs the setup activity. In a highly automated environment in which companies produce many different products at varying volume levels, it is little wonder that many companies have turned to activity-based costing to improve the accuracy of cost allocations and the effectiveness of decisions.

Professional Training Services, Inc. (PTSI), offers professional exam review courses for both the certified public accountant (CPA) and the certified management accountant (CMA) exams. Many more students take the CPA review courses than the CMA review courses. PTSI uses the same size and number of classrooms to teach both courses; its CMA courses simply have more empty seats. PTSI is trying to determine the cost of offering the two courses. The company's accountant has decided to allocate classroom rental cost based on the number of students enrolled in the courses. Explain why this allocation base will likely result in an inappropriate assignment of cost to the two cost objects. Identify a more appropriate allocation base.

**Answer**   Using the number of students as the allocation base will assign more of the rental cost to the CPA review courses because those courses have higher enrollments. This allocation is inappropriate because the number of classrooms, not the number of students, drives the amount of rental cost. Since both courses require the same number of classrooms, the rental cost should be allocated equally between them. Several allocation bases would produce an equal allocation, such as the number of classrooms, the number of courses, or a 50/50 percentage split.

## ACTIVITY-BASED COSTING

A company that allocates indirect costs using **activity-based costing (ABC)** follows a two-stage process. In the first stage, costs are assigned to pools based on the activities that cause the costs to be incurred. In the second stage, the costs in the activity cost pools are allocated to products using a variety of cost drivers. The first step in developing an ABC system is to identify essential activities and the costs of performing those activities.

A business undertakes **activities** to accomplish its mission. Typical activities include acquiring raw materials, transforming raw materials into finished products, and delivering products to customers. These broadly defined activities can be divided into subcategories. For example, the activity of acquiring raw materials involves separate subcategory activities such as identifying suppliers, obtaining price quotations, evaluating materials specifications, completing purchase orders, and receiving purchased materials. Each of these subcategories can be subdivided into yet more detailed activities. For instance, identifying suppliers may include such activities as reviewing advertisements, searching Internet sites, and obtaining recommendations from business associates. Further subdivisions are possible. Companies perform thousands of activities.

### Identifying Activity Centers

Maintaining separate cost records for thousands of activities is expensive. To reduce record-keeping costs, companies group related activities into hubs called **activity centers.** The overhead costs of these related activities are combined into a cost pool for each activity center. Because the activities assigned to each center are related, a business can obtain rational cost allocations using a common cost driver for an entire cost pool. Determining the optimal number of activity centers requires *cost/benefit analysis.* Companies will incur the higher record-keeping costs for additional activity centers only to the extent that the additional accuracy improves decision making.

### Comparing ABC with Traditional Cost Allocation

How do ABC systems differ from traditional allocation systems? Traditional allocation systems pool costs by departments, then allocate departmental cost pools to cost objects using volume-based cost drivers. In contrast, ABC systems pool costs

**LO 2**

Identify cost centers and cost drivers in an activity-based costing system.

## EXHIBIT 5.1

by activity centers, then allocate activity center cost pools to cost objects using a variety of volume- and activity-based cost drivers. ABC systems use many more activity centers than the number of departments in a traditional allocation system. As a result, ABC improves cost tracing by using more cause-and-effect relationships in assigning indirect costs to numerous activity centers. Exhibit 5.1 illustrates the primary differences between a traditional two-stage allocation system and an ABC system.

## Types of Production Activities

Many companies organize activities into four hierarchical categories to improve cost tracing. These categories are (1) unit-level activities, (2) batch-level activities, (3) product-level activities, and (4) facility-level activities.[1] The overhead costs in each category are pooled and allocated to products based on how the products benefit from the activities. *The primary objective is to trace the cost of performing activities to the products that are causing the activities to be performed.* To illustrate, consider the overhead costs incurred by Unterman Shirt Company.

Unterman has two product lines, dress shirts and casual shirts. The company expects to incur overhead costs of $5,730,000 in the course of producing 680,000 dress shirts and 120,000 casual shirts during 2011. Currently, Unterman assigns an equal amount of overhead to each shirt, simply dividing the total expected overhead cost by the total expected production ($5,730,000 ÷ 800,000 units = $7.16 per shirt, rounded). Each type of shirt requires approximately the same amount of direct materials, $8.20 per shirt, and the same amount of direct labor, $6.80 per shirt. The total cost per shirt is $22.16 ($7.16 + $8.20 + $6.80). Unterman sells shirts for $31 each, yielding a gross margin of $8.84 per shirt ($31 − $22.16).

Bob Unterman, president and owner of the company, believes the direct materials and direct labor costs are reasonable, but the overhead costs must not be the same for both product lines. Mr. Unterman hired a consultant, Rebecca Lynch, to trace the overhead costs. Ms. Lynch decided to use an *activity-based cost* system. She identified the activities necessary to make shirts and classified them into the following four activity cost centers.

## Unit-Level Activity Center

**Unit-level activities** occur each time a unit of product is made. For example, for every shirt made, Unterman incurs inspection costs, machine-related utility costs, and costs

---

[1]The types of costs in each category will be in Chapter 6.

for production supplies. Total unit-level cost increases with every shirt made and decreases with reductions in production volume. Some costs behave so much like unit-level costs that they may be accounted for as unit-level even though they are not strictly unit-level. For example, suppose Unterman employees lubricate production machinery after every eight hours of continuous operation. Although Unterman does not incur lubrication cost for each shirt produced, the cost behavior pattern is so closely tied to production levels that it may be accounted for as a unit-level cost.

Ms. Lynch identified the following unit-level overhead costs: (1) $300,000 for machine-related utilities, (2) $50,000 for machine maintenance, (3) $450,000 for indirect labor and indirect materials, (4) $200,000 for inspection and quality control, and (5) $296,000 for miscellaneous unit-level costs. She assigned these costs into a single *unit-level activity center* overhead cost pool of $1,296,000. This assignment illustrates the first stage of the two-stage ABC allocation system. Of the total $5,730,000 overhead cost, Ms. Lynch has allocated $1,296,000 to one of the four activity centers. The remaining overhead cost is allocated among the three other activity centers.

The second-stage cost assignment involves allocating the $1,296,000 unit-level cost pool between the two product lines. Because unit-level costs are incurred each time a shirt is produced, they should be allocated using a base correlated to production levels. Ms. Lynch chose direct labor hours as the allocation base. Past performance indicates the dress shirts will require 272,000 direct labor hours and the casual shirts will require 48,000 direct labor hours. Based on this information, Ms. Lynch allocated the unit-level overhead costs and computed the cost per unit as shown in Exhibit 5.2.

## EXHIBIT 5.2

### Allocation of Unit-Level Overhead Costs

| | **Product Lines** | | |
| --- | --- | --- | --- |
| | **Dress Shirts** | **Casual Shirts** | **Total** |
| Number of direct labor hours (a) | 272,000 | 48,000 | 320,000 |
| Cost per labor hour | | | |
| ($1,296,000 ÷ 320,000 hours) (b) | $4.05 | $4.05 | NA |
| Total allocated overhead cost (c = a × b) | $1,101,600 | $194,400 | $1,296,000 |
| Number of shirts (d) | 680,000 | 120,000 | 800,000 |
| Cost per shirt (c ÷ d) | $1.62 | $1.62 | NA |

The unit-level costs exhibit a variable cost behavior pattern. Total cost varies in direct proportion to the number of units produced. Cost per unit is constant. Because production volume does not affect the unit-level overhead cost, the pricing of shirts should not be affected by the fact that the company makes more dress shirts than casual shirts.

## Batch-Level Activity Center

**Batch-level activities** relate to producing groups of products. Batch-level costs are fixed regardless of the number of units produced in a single batch. For example, the costs of setting up machinery to cut fabric for a certain size shirt remain unchanged regardless of the number of shirts cut at that particular machine setting. Similarly, the cost of a first-item batch test is the same whether 200 or 2,000 shirts are made in the batch. Materials handling costs are also commonly classified as batch-level because materials are usually transferred from one department to another in batches. For example, all of the size small casual shirts are cut in the sizing department, then the entire batch of cut fabric is transferred in one operation to the sewing department. The cost of materials handling is the same regardless of whether the batch load is large or small.

Because total batch costs depend on the number of batches produced, more batch costs should be allocated to products that require more batches. Ms. Lynch identified $690,000 of total batch-level overhead costs and assigned this amount to a batch-level cost pool.

For the second-stage allocation, Ms. Lynch determined that the casual-shirt line requires considerably more setups than the dress-shirt line because the casual shirts are subject to frequent style changes. Because customers buy limited amounts of items with short shelf lives, Unterman must produce casual shirts in small batches. Ms. Lynch decided more of the batch-level costs should be allocated to the casual-shirt line than to the dress-shirt line. She chose number of setups as the most rational allocation base. Since casual shirts require 1,280 setups and dress shirts require 1,020 setups, Ms. Lynch allocated the batch-level costs as shown in Exhibit 5.3.

## EXHIBIT 5.3

### Allocation of Batch-Level Overhead Costs

| | Product Lines | | |
| --- | --- | --- | --- |
| | Dress Shirts | Casual Shirts | Total |
| Number of setups performed (a) | 1,020 | 1,280 | 2,300 |
| Cost per setup ($690,000 ÷ 2,300 setups) (b) | $300 | $300 | NA |
| Total allocated overhead cost (c = a × b) | $306,000 | $384,000 | $690,000 |
| Number of shirts (d) | 680,000 | 120,000 | 800,000 |
| Cost per shirt (c ÷ d) | $0.45 | $3.20 | NA |

ABC demonstrates that the per shirt batch-level cost for casual shirts ($3.20 per shirt) is considerably more than for dress shirts ($0.45). One reason is that the casual-shirt line incurs more batch-level costs ($384,000 versus $306,000). The other is that Unterman produces far fewer casual shirts than dress shirts (120,000 units versus 680,000). Because batch-level costs are fixed relative to the number of units in a particular batch, the cost per unit is greater the smaller the batch. For example, if setup costs are $300, the setup cost per unit for a batch of 100 units is $3 ($300 ÷ 100 units). For a batch of only 10 units, however, the setup cost per unit is $30 ($300 ÷ 10 units). When batch-level costs are significant, companies should pursue high-volume products. Low-volume products are more expensive to make because the fixed costs must be spread over fewer units. To the extent that cost affects pricing, Unterman should charge more for casual shirts than dress shirts.

## Product-Level Activity Center

Product-level activities support specific products or product lines. Examples include raw materials inventory holding costs; engineering development costs; and legal fees for patents, copyrights, trademarks, and brand names. Unterman Shirt Company positions itself as a fashion leader. It incurs extensive design costs to ensure that it remains a trendsetter. The company also incurs engineering costs to continually improve the quality of materials used in its shirts and legal fees to protect its brand names. After reviewing Unterman's operations, Ms. Lynch concluded she could trace $1,800,000 of the total overhead cost to the product-level activity center.

The second-stage allocation requires dividing these activities between the dress-shirt line and the casual-shirt line. Interviews with fashion design staff disclosed that they spend more time on casual shirts because of the frequent style changes. Similarly, the engineers spend more of their time developing new fabric, buttons, and zippers for casual shirts. The materials used in dress shirts are fairly stable. Although engineers spend some time improving the quality of dress-shirt materials, they devote far more

## EXHIBIT 5.4

### Allocation of Product-Level Overhead Costs

|  | Product Lines | | |
| --- | :---: | :---: | :---: |
|  | Dress Shirts | Casual Shirts | Total |
| Percent of product-level activity utilization (a) | 30% | 70% | 100% |
| Total allocated overhead cost | | | |
| (b = a × $1,800,000) | $540,000 | $1,260,000 | $1,800,000 |
| Total units produced (c) | 680,000 | 120,000 | 800,000 |
| Cost per unit (b ÷ c) | $0.79* | $10.50 | NA |

*Rounded to the nearest whole cent.

time to the more unusual materials used in the casual shirts. Similarly, the legal department spends more time developing and protecting patents, trademarks, and brand names for the casual-shirt line. Ms. Lynch concluded that 70 percent of the product-level cost pool applied to casual shirts and 30 percent to dress shirts. She allocated product-level costs to the two product lines as shown in Exhibit 5.4.

Product-level costs are frequently distributed unevenly among different product lines. Unterman Shirt Company incurs substantially more costs to sustain its casual-shirt line than its dress-shirt line. Using a single companywide overhead rate in such circumstances distorts cost measurements. Distorted product cost measurements can lead to negative consequences such as irrational pricing policies and rewards for inappropriate decisions. Activity-based costing reduces measurement distortions by more accurately tracing costs to the products that cause their incurrence.

## Facility-Level Activity Center

**Facility-level activities** benefit the production process as a whole and are not related to any specific product, batch, or unit of production. For example, insuring the manufacturing facility against fire losses does not benefit any particular product or product line. Facility-level costs include depreciation on the manufacturing plant, security, landscaping, plant maintenance, general utilities, and property taxes. For Unterman Shirt Company, Ms. Lynch identified $1,944,000 of facility-level overhead costs. Because no cause-and-effect relationship exists between these facility-level manufacturing costs and the two product lines, she must allocate these costs arbitrarily. Basing the arbitrary allocation on the total number of units produced, Ms. Lynch allocated 85 percent (680,000 ÷ 800,000) of the facility-level cost pool to the dress-shirt line and 15 percent (120,000 ÷ 800,000) to the casual-shirt line as shown in Exhibit 5.5.

## EXHIBIT 5.5

### Allocation of Facility-Level Overhead Costs

|  | Product Lines | | |
| --- | :---: | :---: | :---: |
|  | Dress Shirts | Casual Shirts | Total |
| Percent of total units (a) | 85% | 15% | 100% |
| Total allocated overhead cost | | | |
| (b = a × $1,944,000) | $1,652,400 | $291,600 | $1,944,000 |
| Total units produced (c) | 680,000 | 120,000 | 800,000 |
| Cost per unit (b ÷ c) | $2.43 | $2.43 | NA |

## Classification of Activities Not Limited to Four Categories

The number of activity centers a business uses depends on cost/benefit analysis. The four categories illustrated for Unterman Shirt Company represent a useful starting point. Any of the four categories could be further subdivided into more detailed activity centers. Unterman could establish an activity cost center for unit-level labor-related activities and a different activity center for unit-level machine-related activities. Identifying all potential activity centers in a real-world company can be daunting. Paulette Bennett describes the process used in the Material Control Department at Compumotor, Inc., as follows:

> Recognizing that ordinarily the two biggest problems with an ABC project are knowing where to start and how deep to go, we began by analyzing the activities that take place in our procurement process. As the old saying goes, to find the biggest alligators you usually have to wade into the weeds; therefore, we started by writing down all the procurement activities. Creating a real world picture of costs by activity was our aim. But had we used our initial list we would have designed a spreadsheet so large that no human could ever have emerged alive at the other end.[2]

Ms. Bennett's abbreviated list still included 83 separate activities. The list represented the activity centers for only one department of a very large company. Although the Unterman example used only four categories, the real-world equivalent is far more complex.

---

### ✓ CHECK YOURSELF 5.2

Under what circumstances would the number of units produced be an inappropriate allocation base for batch-level costs?

**Answer**   Using the number of units produced as the allocation base would allocate more of the batch-level costs to high-volume products and less of the costs to low-volume products. Since batch-level costs are normally related to the number of batches rather than the number of units made in each batch, allocation of batch-level costs based on units produced would result in poor product cost estimates; the costing system would overcost high-volume products and undercost low-volume products. It would be appropriate to use the number of units produced only when each batch consists of the same number of product units. Even under these circumstances, the number of units merely serves as a proxy for the number of batches. It would still be more appropriate to use the number of batches to allocate batch-level costs.

---

### Context-Sensitive Classification of Activities

Particular activities could fall into any of the four hierarchical categories. For example, inspecting each individual item produced is a unit-level activity. Inspecting the first item of each batch to ensure the setup was correct is a batch-level activity. Inspecting a specific product line is a product-level activity. Finally, inspecting the factory building is a facility-level activity. To properly classify activities, you must learn to analyze the context within which they occur.

### Selecting Cost Drivers

Activity-based costing uses both *volume-based* cost drivers and *activity-based* cost drivers. Volume-based drivers are appropriate for indirect costs that increase or decrease relative to the volume of activity. Using cost drivers such as units, direct labor hours, or

---

[2]Paulette Bennett, "ABM and the Procurement Cost Model," *Management Accounting,* March 1996, pp. 28–32.

machine hours is appropriate for unit-level activities. The flaw in traditional costing systems is that they use a volume-based measure (usually direct labor hours) to allocate all indirect costs. In contrast, the more sophisticated ABC approach uses activity drivers such as number of setups or percentage of utilization for overhead costs that are not influenced by volume. ABC improves the accuracy of allocations by using a combination of volume- and activity-based cost drivers.

## USING ABC INFORMATION TO TRACE COSTS TO PRODUCT LINES

Exhibit 5.6 summarizes the ABC allocations Ms. Lynch prepared. Mr. Unterman was shocked to learn that overhead costs for casual shirts are virtually three times those for dress shirts. Exhibit 5.7 compares the per-unit gross margins for the two product lines using the traditional cost system and using the ABC system. Recall that direct materials and direct labor costs for dress and casual shirts are $8.20 and $6.80, respectively. The difference in the margins is attributable to the overhead allocation. Using a traditional companywide overhead rate allocates an equal amount of overhead to each shirt ($5,730,000 ÷ 800,000 units = $7.16 per shirt). In contrast, the ABC approach assigns $5.29 to each dress shirt and $17.75 to each casual shirt. Total overhead cost is $5,730,000 under both approaches. It is the *allocation* of rather than the *amount* of the overhead cost that differs. ABC shows that making a casual

**LO 3**

Use activity-based costing to calculate costs of products and services.

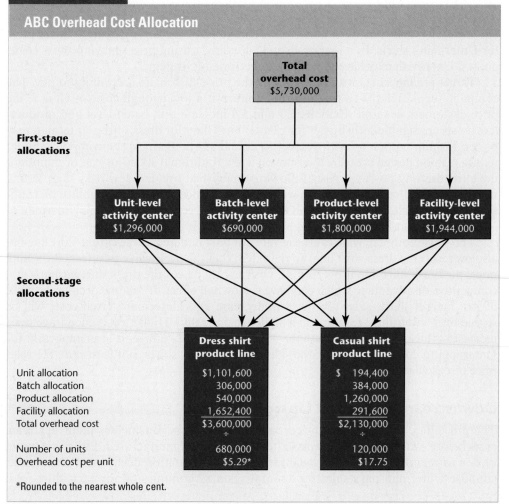

**EXHIBIT 5.6**

**ABC Overhead Cost Allocation**

| | Dress shirt product line | Casual shirt product line |
|---|---|---|
| Unit allocation | $1,101,600 | $   194,400 |
| Batch allocation | 306,000 | 384,000 |
| Product allocation | 540,000 | 1,260,000 |
| Facility allocation | 1,652,400 | 291,600 |
| Total overhead cost | $3,600,000 | $2,130,000 |
| | ÷ | ÷ |
| Number of units | 680,000 | 120,000 |
| Overhead cost per unit | $5.29* | $17.75 |

*Rounded to the nearest whole cent.

## EXHIBIT 5.7

### Gross Margins Using Traditional Versus ABC Costing

| | Gross Margins Traditional System | | Gross Margins ABC Costing | |
|---|---|---|---|---|
| | Dress Shirts | Casual Shirts | Dress Shirts | Casual Shirts |
| Sales price | $31.00 | $31.00 | $31.00 | $31.00 |
| Cost of goods sold | | | | |
| Materials cost | (8.20) | (8.20) | (8.20) | (8.20) |
| Labor cost | (6.80) | (6.80) | (6.80) | (6.80) |
| Overhead | (7.16) | (7.16) | (5.29) | (17.75) |
| Gross margin | $ 8.84 | $ 8.84 | $10.71 | $ (1.75) |

shirt costs more than making a dress shirt. After reviewing the data in Exhibit 5.7, Mr. Unterman realized the company was incurring losses on the casual-shirt line. What options does he have?

## Under- and Overcosting

In using the single companywide overhead rate, Unterman Shirt Company has under-costed its casual line and priced the shirts below cost. The obvious response to the ABC gross margin data in Exhibit 5.7 is to raise the price of casual shirts. Unfortunately, the market may not cooperate. If other companies are selling casual shirts at prices near $31, customers may buy from Unterman's competitors instead of paying a higher price for Unterman's shirts. In a market-driven economy, raising prices may not be a viable option. Unterman may have to adopt a target-pricing strategy.

**Target pricing** starts with determining the price customers are willing to pay. The company then attempts to produce the product at a low enough cost to sell it at the price customers demand. Exhibits 5.3 and 5.4 indicate that batch-level and product-level costs are significantly higher for casual shirts than for dress shirts. Unterman may be too fashion conscious with respect to casual shirts. Perhaps the company should reduce fashion design costs by focusing on a few traditional styles instead of maintaining a trendsetting position. Also, following established trends is less risky than setting new ones. Retail customers may have more confidence in the marketability of traditional casual shirts, which could lead them to place larger orders, enabling Unterman to reduce its per-unit batch costs.

The single companywide overhead rate not only undercosts the casual-shirt line but also overcosts the dress-shirt line. To the extent that the overhead cost affects the selling price, the dress-shirt line is overpriced. Overpricing places the dress shirt business at a competitive disadvantage which can have a snowball effect. If volume declines because of lost market share, sales revenue will decrease and Unterman's fixed costs will be spread over fewer units, resulting in a higher cost per unit. Higher costs encourage price increases, which further aggravate the competitive disadvantage. It is as important for Unterman to consider reducing the sales price of dress shirts as it is to raise the sales price of casual shirts.

## Downstream Costs and Upstream Costs

The preceding paragraph analyzed only product costs. Businesses incur **upstream costs** before—and **downstream costs** after—goods are manufactured. Either upstream or downstream costs may be relevant to product elimination decisions. For example, suppose Unterman pays sales representatives a $2 commission for each shirt sold.

## Answers to The Curious Accountant

The USPS commissioned Coopers & Lybrand (C&L) (now Pricewaterhouse-Coopers), a large accounting firm, to conduct activity-based costing (ABC) studies of its key revenue collection processes. C&L developed an ABC model for USPS's existing cash and check revenue collection and a similar ABC model for debit and credit card activities. The ABC model identified costs associated with unit, batch, and product activities. *Unit-level activity* was defined as the acceptance and processing of a payment by item. *Batch-level activities* involved the closeout at the end of the day, consolidation, and supervisory review. *Product-level activities* included maintenance for bank accounts and deposit reconciliation for the cash and checks model and terminal maintenance and training for the credit and debit card system. A comparison of the cost of the two activity models revealed that a significant cost savings could be achieved in the long term by implementing a debit and credit card system. Some examples of expected cost savings included a decrease in the per-unit transaction cost due to the fact that credit card customers tend to spend more per transaction than do cash customers. In addition, the cost of activities associated with the collection of bad debts falls to virtually zero when debit or credit cards are used and the cost of cash management activities declines. Funds are collected earlier (no check collection float occurs), thereby reducing the need for financing and the resultant interest cost.

Payments received by the IRS are very different from those received by the USPS. The USPS experiences billions of payment transactions each year, many of which are for relatively small amounts; for example, a customer may pay to send one package priority mail for $5.70. The IRS receives fewer payments than the USPS, but most of these payments are for significantly larger amounts. Also, while the USPS has over 36,000 post offices processing payments, the IRS has less than a dozen payment processing centers. In ABC costing terms, the IRS has fewer unit-level activities and batch-level activities associated with processing payments than does the USPS, so the financial analysis used by the USPS is not relevant to the IRS. There is another very good reason the IRS does not accept credit card payments unless the taxpayer pays a surcharge; Congress passed a law stipulating this condition.

Source: Terrel L. Carter, Ali M. Sedghat, and Thomas D. Williams, "How ABC Changed the Post Office," *Management Accounting*, February 1998, pp. 28–36; and the USPS 2008 Annual Report.

Although sales commissions are selling, not product, costs, they are relevant to deciding whether to eliminate the casual-shirt line. Unterman can avoid the commission expense if it sells no casual shirts. Including the sales commission increases the total avoidable cost to $32.32 ($30.32 product costs + $2.00 sales commissions) which is more than the $31 sales price. Unterman would therefore be more profitable if it abandoned the casual-shirt line. Management must also consider upstream costs such as those for research and development. To continue in business, companies must sell products at prices that exceed the *total* cost to develop, make, and sell them.

### Employee Attitudes and the Availability of Data

Activity-based costing can lead management to implement cost-cutting measures, including product and product line eliminations, that can result in the loss of jobs. Employees are therefore sometimes uncooperative with management efforts to adopt an ABC system. Companies must help employees recognize that ABC and other **strategic cost management** techniques frequently result in redirecting workers rather than displacing them. Ultimately, jobs depend on the employer's competitive health. The implementation of an ABC system is more likely to succeed when both managers and rank-and-file employees are convinced their own well-being is tied to the company's well-being.

Even when employees cooperate, implementing an ABC system can be difficult. Frequently, the accounting system is not collecting some of the needed data. For example, suppose a manager wants to allocate inspection costs based on the number of hours job inspections take. Inspectors may not record the time spent on individual jobs. Basing the allocation on inspection hours requires inspectors to begin keeping more detailed time records. The accuracy of the allocation then depends on how conscientiously inspectors complete their time reports. Obtaining employee support and accurate data are two of the more challenging obstacles to successfully implementing ABC.

## TOTAL QUALITY MANAGEMENT

Identify the components of quality costs.

Quality is key to a company's ability to obtain and retain customers. What does *quality* mean? It does not always mean the best. A spoon made of silver is of higher quality than a spoon made of plastic, but customers are perfectly willing to use plastic spoons at fast-food restaurants. **Quality** represents the degree to which products or services *conform* to design specifications. The costs companies incur to ensure quality conformance can be classified into four categories: prevention, appraisal, internal failure, and external failure.

Companies incur **prevention costs** to avoid nonconforming products. They incur **appraisal costs** to identify nonconforming products produced in spite of prevention cost expenditures. **Failure costs** result from correcting defects in nonconforming products produced. **Internal failure costs** pertain to correcting defects before goods reach customers; **external failure costs** result from delivering defective goods to customers.

Because prevention and appraisal costs are a function of managerial discretion, they are often called **voluntary costs.** Management chooses how much to spend on these voluntary costs. In contrast, management does not directly control failure costs. The cost of dissatisfied customers may not be measurable, much less controllable. Even though failure costs may not be directly controllable, they are related to voluntary costs. When management spends additional funds on prevention and appraisal controls, failure costs tend to decline. As the level of control increases, quality conformance increases, reducing failure costs. When control activities are reduced, quality conformance decreases and failure cost increases. *Voluntary costs and failure costs move in opposite directions.*

### Minimizing Total Quality Cost

*Total quality control cost* is the sum of voluntary costs plus failure costs. Because voluntary costs and failure costs are negatively correlated, the minimum amount of *total* quality cost is located at the point on a graph where the marginal voluntary expenditures equal the marginal savings on failure cost as shown in Exhibit 5.8.

**EXHIBIT 5.8**

**Relationships Among Components of Quality Cost**

Exhibit 5.8 indicates that the minimum total quality cost per unit occurs at quality level of less than 100 percent. At very low levels of quality assurance, significant failure costs outweigh any cost savings available by avoiding voluntary costs. In contrast, extremely high levels of quality assurance result in voluntary cost expenditures that are not offset by failure cost savings. Although the goal of zero defects is appealing, it is not a cost-effective strategy. Realistic managers seek to minimize total quality cost rather than to eliminate all defects.

---

### ✓ CHECK YOURSELF 5.3

Is it wiser to spend money on preventing defects or on correcting failures?

**Answer**   The answer depends on where a company's product falls on the "total quality cost" line (see Exhibit 5.8). If the product falls left of the cost minimization point, spending more on preventing defects would produce proportionately greater failure cost savings. In other words, a company would spend less in total by reducing failure costs through increasing prevention costs. Under these circumstances, it would be wise to incur prevention costs. On the other hand, if the product falls right of the cost minimization point line, the company would spend more to prevent additional defects than it would save by reducing failure costs. Under these circumstances, it makes more sense to pay the failure costs than attempt to avoid them by incurring prevention costs.

---

# FOCUS ON INTERNATIONAL ISSUES

## GLOBAL CONSEQUENCES OF EXTERNAL FAILURE COSTS

In late September 2009, Toyota Motor Company announced that it would be conducting a recall related to problems with floor mats in several models of Toyota and Lexus model cars and trucks. In some cases the floor mats had moved, preventing the vehicle's accelerator from moving properly. As an immediate solution, Toyota asked drivers of the affected vehicles to remove the driver's side floor mat, but the company said it would replace the accelerator pedals in the vehicles to prevent the floor mats from causing them to get stuck. The company estimated that 3.8 million vehicles had been sold with the mats under suspicion. A few months later, in February 2010, the company announced further recalls for additional vehicles with faulty accelerator pedals and braking systems.

These are examples of an *external failure cost* since the product made it into costumers' hands before the defect was found. Toyota did not immediately say how much this product failure was estimated to cost the company, but some analysts projected the costs of these recalls, along with lost sales, to be $1.5 to $2.0 billion. First, there is the cost of notifying all affected customers of the potential risk and advising them of what to do. This includes the obvious costs of printing and mailing, but also the costs of lawyers and public-relations consultants. Then there is the replacement cost of the new accelerator pedals. Since some individuals had already been injured and killed in cars that were alleged to have the defects, there will certainly be the costs of lawsuits and settlements. Finally, there is the cost of the potential damage to the company's reputation. Product recalls are nothing unusual in the automobile industry; cars are complex products with thousands of parts. However, Toyota, and particularly its Lexus brand, have reputations for being among the highest quality vehicles. A company can lose its reputation for quality a lot more quickly that it can be developed.

It may cost a little more to make sure your products are made correctly in the first place, but in the long run it is often cheaper than paying the external failure costs.

## Quality Cost Reports

Managing quality costs to achieve the highest level of customer satisfaction is known as **total quality management (TQM).** Accountants support TQM by preparing a **quality cost report,** which typically lists the company's quality costs and analyzes horizontally each item as a percentage of the total cost. Data are normally displayed for two or more accounting periods to disclose the effects of changes over time. Exhibit 5.9 shows a quality cost report for Unterman Shirt Company. The company's accountant prepared the report to assess the effects of a quality control campaign the company recently initiated. Review Exhibit 5.9. What is Unterman's quality control strategy? Is it succeeding?

Exhibit 5.9 indicates Unterman is seeking to control quality costs by focusing on appraisal activities. The total expenditures for prevention activities remained unchanged, but expenditures for appraisal activities increased significantly. The results of this strategy are apparent in the failure cost data. Internal failure costs increased significantly while external failure costs decreased dramatically. The strategy succeeded in lowering total quality costs. The report suggests, however, that more improvement is possible. Notice that 86.13 percent (appraisal 19.63 percent + internal failure 39.01 percent + external failure 27.49 percent) of total quality costs is spent on finding and correcting mistakes. The adage "an ounce of prevention is worth a pound of cure," applied to Unterman, implies spending more on prevention could perhaps eliminate many of the appraisal and failure costs.

### EXHIBIT 5.9

#### Quality Cost Report for Unterman Shirt Company

|  | 2013 | | 2012 | |
| --- | --- | --- | --- | --- |
|  | Amount | Percentage* | Amount | Percentage* |
| **Prevention costs** |  |  |  |  |
| Product design | $ 50,000 | 6.54% | $ 52,000 | 6.60% |
| Preventive equipment (depreciation) | 7,000 | 0.92 | 7,000 | 0.89 |
| Training costs | 27,000 | 3.53 | 25,000 | 3.17 |
| Promotion and awards | 22,000 | 2.88 | 22,000 | 2.79 |
| Total prevention | 106,000 | 13.87 | 106,000 | 13.45 |
| **Appraisal costs** |  |  |  |  |
| Inventory inspection | 75,000 | 9.82 | 25,000 | 3.17 |
| Reliability testing | 43,000 | 5.63 | 15,000 | 1.90 |
| Testing equipment (depreciation) | 20,000 | 2.62 | 12,000 | 1.52 |
| Supplies | 12,000 | 1.57 | 8,000 | 1.02 |
| Total appraisal | 150,000 | 19.63 | 60,000 | 7.61 |
| **Internal failure costs** |  |  |  |  |
| Scrap | 90,000 | 11.78 | 40,000 | 5.08 |
| Repair and rework | 140,000 | 18.32 | 110,000 | 13.96 |
| Downtime | 38,000 | 4.97 | 20,000 | 2.54 |
| Reinspection | 30,000 | 3.93 | 12,000 | 1.52 |
| Total internal failure | 298,000 | 39.01 | 182,000 | 23.10 |
| **External failure costs** |  |  |  |  |
| Warranty repairs and replacement | 120,000 | 15.71 | 260,000 | 32.99 |
| Freight | 20,000 | 2.62 | 50,000 | 6.35 |
| Customer relations | 40,000 | 5.24 | 60,000 | 7.61 |
| Restocking and packaging | 30,000 | 3.93 | 70,000 | 8.88 |
| Total external failure | 210,000 | 27.49 | 440,000 | 55.84 |
| **Grand total** | $764,000 | 100.00% | $788,000 | 100.00% |

*Percentages do not add exactly because of rounding.

# REALITY BYTES

Improving the quality of a product can increase its costs. Are the benefits of the higher quality worth the higher costs? In other words, are companies that spend money to improve the quality of their products rewarded with higher profit margins? This is a difficult question to answer empirically because, among other things, there is not always a definitive, objective measure of the quality of competing products or services.

Nevertheless, we can make some general comparisons based on objective data available for automobile manufactures. Every year JD Power and Associates releases reports on various aspects of quality among auto manufacturers, including the *Vehicle Dependability Study (VDS)*. This study surveys owners who have had their cars for three years, asking what problems they have experienced related to their vehicles' dependability. According to the company, "the study finds that the frequency and severity of component replacement has a potentially strong impact on customer loyalty intentions."

On March 19, JD Power released its 2009 VDS, which looked at the reliability of 2006 model cars. Although Buick came in first as an overall brand-name winner, other GM brands, including Saab, Hummer, Pontiac, and Saturn, came in well below average. Toyota and Lexus, a division of Toyota, were close to Buick at the top of the dependability rankings. Toyota and Lexus are usually near the top of JD Power's VDS as well as its Initial Quality Study, which is based on a survey of owners of new cars. Ford and its Lincoln, Mercury, and Jaguar divisions were also ranked as being above average in the 2009 VDS.

What about these companies' comparative profitability? The table below shows return on assets ratios for the 2008 and 2007 fiscal years of Toyota, Ford, and GM. Although 2008 was not a good year for car manufacturers in general, due to the economic recession, the data show that, generally, car companies with better quality had better financial results. It would certainly be an oversimplification to attribute all of Toyota's financial success to its higher quality evaluations. However, many experts in the automotive business believe Toyota's reputation for building high-quality vehicles has been a significant contributor to its success.

|  | **Return on Assets Ratios** | |
|---|---|---|
|  | **2008** | **2007** |
| Toyota | (1.4)% | 5.3% |
| Ford | (5.9) | (1.0) |
| GM | (33.9) | (26.0) |
| Source: jdpower.com | | |

These data are for years prior to Toyota's recalls for faulty accelerator and braking systems that occurred in late 2009 and early 2010. These widespread recalls had an immediate, negative, effect on the company's sales, and a positive effect on Ford's sales. It is a lot easier to lose customers due to quality problems than it was to attract them in the first place.

# A Look Back

Many traditional cost systems used direct labor hours as the sole base for allocating overhead costs. Labor hours served as an effective *companywide allocation base* because labor was highly correlated with overhead cost incurrence. It made sense to assign more overhead to cost objects that required more labor. Because direct labor was related to production volume, it was frequently called a *volume-based cost driver*. Other volume-based cost drivers included machine hours, number of units, and labor dollars. Companywide, volume-based cost drivers were never perfect measures of overhead consumption. However, misallocation was not a serious problem because overhead costs were relatively small. If a manager misallocated an insignificant cost, it did not matter.

Automation has changed the nature of the manufacturing process. This change may cause significant distortions in the allocation of overhead costs when the allocation base is a companywide, volume-based cost driver. There are two primary reasons for distortions. First, in an automated environment, the same amount of labor (e.g., flipping a switch) may produce a large or a small volume of products. Under these circumstances, labor use is not related to the incurrence of overhead and is not a rational allocation base. Second, the distortions may be significant because overhead costs are much higher relative to the cost of labor and materials. For example, when robots replace people in the production process, depreciation becomes a larger portion of total product cost and labor becomes a smaller portion of the total.

To improve the accuracy of allocations, managerial accountants began to study the wide array of activities required to make a product. Such activities may include acquiring raw materials, materials handling and storage activities, product design activities, legal activities, and traditional production labor activities. Various measures of these activities can be used as bases for numerous overhead allocations related to determining product cost. Using activity measures to allocate overhead costs has become known as *activity-based costing (ABC)*. In an ABC system, costs are allocated in a two-stage process. First, activities are organized into *activity centers* and the related costs of performing these activities are combined into *cost pools*. Second, the pooled costs are allocated to designated cost objects using activity-based cost drivers. Implementing ABC is most likely to succeed when employees understand that it will positively affect their fate and that of the company. Without employee cooperation, collecting data necessary for the system's success may be difficult.

Many ABC systems begin by organizing activities into one of four categories. Total *unit-level activity cost* increases each time a unit of product is made and decreases when production volume declines. Unit-level activity costs can be allocated with a base correlated to the level of production (volume-based cost drivers). *Batch-level activities* are related to producing groups of products. Their costs are fixed regardless of the number of units in a batch. Batch-level costs are assigned so that the products requiring the most batches are assigned the most batch costs. *Product-level activities* support a specific product or product line. Product-level costs are frequently assigned to products based on the product's percentage use of product-level activities. *Facility-level activities* are performed for the benefit of the production process as a whole. The allocation of these costs is often arbitrary.

Accurate allocations prevent the distortions of overcosted or undercosted products. Over-costing can cause a product line to be overpriced. Overpriced products may cause a company to lose market share, and the decline in sales revenue will cause profits to fall. When products are underpriced, revenue is less than it could be, and profitability suffers.

Product costs are frequently distinguished from upstream and downstream costs. *Upstream costs* result from activities that occur *before* goods are manufactured. Examples include research and development, product design, and legal work. *Downstream costs* result from activities that occur *after* goods are manufactured. Examples of downstream costs include selling and administrative expenses. Upstream and downstream costs affect pricing decisions and product elimination decisions.

 **A Look Forward**

The next chapter introduces the concept of cost relevance. Applying the concepts you have learned to real-world business problems can be challenging. Frequently, so much data is available that it is difficult to distinguish important from useless information. The next chapter will help you learn to identify information that is relevant in a variety of short-term decision-making scenarios including special offers, outsourcing, segment elimination, and asset replacement.

**A step-by-step audio-narrated series of slides is provided on the text website at www.mhhe.com/edmonds2011.**

## SELF-STUDY REVIEW PROBLEM

Adventure Luggage Company makes two types of airline carry-on bags. One bag type designed to meet mass-market needs is constructed of durable polyester. The other bag type aimed at the high-end luxury market is made of genuine leather. Sales of the polyester bag have declined recently because of stiff price competition. Indeed, Adventure would have to sell this bag at less than production cost to match the competition. Adventure's president suspects that something is wrong with how the company estimates the bag's cost. He has asked the company's accountant to investigate that possibility. The accountant gathered the following information relevant to estimating the cost of the company's two bag types.

Both bags require the same amount of direct labor. The leather bags have significantly higher materials costs, and they require more inspections and rework because of higher quality standards. Since the leather bags are produced in smaller batches of different colors, they require significantly more setups. Finally, the leather bags generate more legal costs due to patents and more promotion costs because Adventure advertises them more aggressively. Specific cost and activity data follow.

|  | Polyester Bags | Leather Bags |
|---|---|---|
| Per unit direct materials cost | $30 | $90 |
| Per unit direct labor cost | 2 hours @ $14 per hour | 2 hours @ $14 per hour |
| Annual sales volume | 7,000 units | 3,000 units |

Total annual overhead costs are $872,000. Adventure currently allocates overhead costs using a traditional costing system based on direct labor hours.

To reassess the overhead allocation policy and the resulting product cost estimates, the accountant subdivided the overhead into four categories and gathered information about these cost categories and the activities that caused the company to incur the costs. These data follow.

| Category | Estimated Cost | Cost Driver | Amount of Cost Driver Polyester | Leather | Total |
|---|---|---|---|---|---|
| Unit level | $480,000 | Number of machine hours | 20,000 | 60,000 | 80,000 |
| Batch level | 190,000 | Number of machine setups | 1,500 | 3,500 | 5,000 |
| Product level | 152,000 | Number of inspections | 200 | 600 | 800 |
| Facility level | 50,000 | Equal percentage | 50% | 50% | 100% |
| Total | $872,000 | | | | |

### Required

**a.** Determine the total cost and cost per unit for each product line, assuming that Adventure allocates overhead costs to each product line using direct labor hours as a companywide allocation base. Also determine the combined cost of the two product lines.

**b.** Determine the total cost and cost per unit for each product line, assuming that Adventure allocates overhead costs using an ABC system. Determine the combined cost of the two product lines.

**c.** Explain why the total combined cost computed in Requirements *a* and *b* is the same. Given that the combined cost is the same using either system, why is an ABC system with many different allocation rates better than a traditional system with a single companywide overhead rate?

## Solution to Requirement a

### Predetermined Overhead Rate

| Polyester | | Leather | |
|---|---|---|---|
| 2 hr. × 7,000 units | + | 2 hr. × 3,000 units | |
| 14,000 direct labor hours | | 6,000 direct labor hours | = 20,000 hours |

Allocation rate = $872,000 ÷ 20,000 hours = $43.60 per direct labor hour

### Allocated Overhead Costs

| Type of Bag | Allocation Rate | × | Number of Hours | = | Allocated Cost |
|---|---|---|---|---|---|
| Polyester | $43.60 | × | 14,000 | = | $610,400 |
| Leather | 43.60 | × | 6,000 | = | 261,600 |
| Total | | | 20,000 | | $872,000 |

### Total Cost of Each Product Line and Combined Cost

| Type of Bag | Direct Materials* | + | Direct Labor† | + | Allocated Overhead | = | Total |
|---|---|---|---|---|---|---|---|
| Polyester | $210,000 | + | $196,000 | + | $610,400 | = | $1,016,400 |
| Leather | 270,000 | + | 84,000 | + | 261,600 | = | 615,600 |
| Total | $480,000 | + | $280,000 | + | $872,000 | = | $1,632,000 |

*Direct materials
  Polyester  $30 × 7,000 units = $210,000
  Leather  $90 × 3,000 units = $270,000
†Direct labor
  Polyester  $14 × 14,000 hours = $196,000
  Leather  $14 × 6,000 hours = $84,000

### Cost per Unit Computations Using Traditional Cost System

| Type of Bag | Total Cost | ÷ | Units | = | Cost per Unit |
|---|---|---|---|---|---|
| Polyester | $1,016,400 | ÷ | 7,000 | = | $145.20 |
| Leather | 615,600 | ÷ | 3,000 | = | 205.20 |
| Total | $1,632,000 | | | | |

## Solution to Requirement b

### Overhead Cost Allocation Using ABC

| | Unit | Batch | Product | Facility | Total |
|---|---|---|---|---|---|
| Cost pool | $480,000 | $190,000 | $152,000 | $50,000 | $872,000 |
| ÷ Cost drivers | Number of machine hours | Number of setups | Number of inspections | Equally | |
| | 80,000 | 5,000 | 800 | 50% | |
| = Rate | $6 per machine hour | $38 per setup | $190 per inspection | $25,000 | |

### Overhead Allocation for Polyester Bags

| | Unit | Batch | Product | Facility | Total |
|---|---|---|---|---|---|
| Weight | 20,000 | 1,500 | 200 | 1 | |
| × Rate | $ 6 | $ 38 | $ 190 | $25,000 | |
| Allocation | $120,000 | $57,000 | $38,000 | $25,000 | $240,000 |

### Overhead Allocation for Leather Bags

| | Unit | Batch | Product | Facility | Total |
|---|---|---|---|---|---|
| Weight | 60,000 | 3,500 | 600 | 1 | |
| × Rate | $ 6 | $ 38 | $ 190 | $25,000 | |
| Allocation | $360,000 | $133,000 | $114,000 | $25,000 | $632,000 |

## Total Cost of Each Product Line and Combined Cost

| Type of Bag | Direct Materials | + | Direct Labor | + | Allocated Overhead | = | Total |
|---|---|---|---|---|---|---|---|
| Polyester | $210,000 | + | $196,000 | + | $240,000 | = | $ 646,000 |
| Leather | 270,000 | + | 84,000 | + | 632,000 | = | 986,000 |
| Total | $480,000 | + | $280,000 | + | $872,000 | = | $1,632,000 |

## Cost per Unit Computations Under ABC System

| Type of Bag | Total Cost | ÷ | Units | = | Cost per Unit |
|---|---|---|---|---|---|
| Polyester | $ 646,000 | ÷ | 7,000 | = | $ 92.29 |
| Leather | 986,000 | ÷ | 3,000 | = | 328.67 |
| Total | $1,632,000 | | | | |

## Solution to Requirement c

The allocation method (ABC versus traditional costing) does not affect the total amount of cost to be allocated. Therefore, the total cost is the same using either method. However, the allocation method (ABC versus traditional costing) does affect the cost assigned to each product line. Since the ABC system more accurately traces costs to the products that cause the costs to be incurred, it provides a more accurate estimate of the true cost of making the products. The difference in the cost per unit using ABC versus traditional costing is significant. For example, the cost of the polyester bag was determined to be $145.20 using the traditional allocation method and $92.29 using ABC. This difference could have led Adventure to overprice the polyester bag, thereby causing the decline in sales volume. To the extent that ABC is more accurate, using it will improve pricing and other strategic decisions that significantly affect profitability.

## KEY TERMS

Activities 207
Activity-based cost drivers 205
Activity-based costing (ABC) 207
Activity centers 207
Appraisal costs 216
Batch-level activities 209
Companywide allocation rate 204

Downstream costs 214
External failure costs 216
Facility-level activities 211
Failure costs 216
Internal failure costs 216
Prevention costs 216
Product-level activities 210
Quality 216
Quality cost report 218

Start-up (setup) costs 205
Strategic cost management 216
Target pricing 214
Total quality management (TQM) 218
Unit-level activities 208
Upstream costs 214
Volume-based cost drivers 205
Voluntary costs 216

## QUESTIONS

1. Why did traditional costing systems base allocations on a single companywide cost driver?

2. Why are labor hours ineffective as a companywide allocation base in many industries today?

3. What is the difference between volume-based cost drivers and activity-based cost drivers?

4. Why do activity-based cost drivers provide more accurate allocations of overhead in an automated manufacturing environment?

5. When would it be appropriate to use volume-based cost drivers in an activity-based costing system?

6. Martinez Manufacturing makes two products, one of which is produced at a significantly higher volume than the other. The low-volume product consumes more of the company's engineering resources because it is technologically complex. Even so, the company's cost accountant chose to allocate engineering department costs based on the number of units produced. How could selecting this allocation base affect a decision about outsourcing engineering services for the low-volume product?

7. Briefly describe the activity-based costing allocation process.

8. Tom Rehr made the following comment: "Facility-level costs should not be allocated to products because they are irrelevant for decision-making purposes." Do you agree or disagree with this statement? Justify your response.

9. To facilitate cost tracing, a company's activities can be subdivided into four hierarchical categories. What are these four categories? Describe them and give at least two examples of each category.

10. Beth Nelson, who owns and runs a small sporting goods store, buys most of her merchandise directly from manufacturers. Ms. Nelson was shocked at the $7.50 charge for a container of three ping-pong balls. She found it hard to believe that it could have cost more than $1.00 to make the balls. When she complained to Jim Wilson, the marketing manager of the manufacturing company, he tried to explain that the cost also included companywide overhead costs. How could companywide overhead affect the cost of ping-pong balls?

11. If each patient in a hospital is considered a cost object, what are examples of unit-, batch-, product- and facility-level costs that would be allocated to this object using an activity-based costing system?

12. Milken Manufacturing has three product lines. The company's new accountant, Marvin LaSance, is responsible for allocating facility-level costs to these product lines. Mr. LaSance is finding the allocation assignment a daunting task. He knows there have been disagreements among the product managers over the allocation of facility costs, and he fears being asked to defend his method of allocation. Why would the allocation of facility-level costs be subject to disagreements?

13. Why would machine hours be an inappropriate allocation base for batch-level costs?

14. Alisa Kamuf's company has reported losses from operations for several years. Industry standards indicate that prices are normally set at 30 percent above manufacturing cost, which Ms. Kamuf has done. Assuming that her other costs are in line with industry norms, how could she continue to lose money while her competitors earn a profit?

15. Issacs Corporation produces two lines of pocket knives. The Arrowsmith product line involves very complex engineering designs; the Starscore product line involves relatively simple designs. Since its introduction, the low-volume Arrowsmith products have gained market share at the expense of the high-volume Starscore products. This pattern of sales has been accompanied by an overall decline in company profits. Why may the existing cost system be inadequate?

16. What is the relationship between activity-based management and just-in-time inventory?

## MULTIPLE-CHOICE QUESTIONS

**Multiple-choice questions are provided on the text website at www.mhhe.com/edmonds2011.**

### EXERCISES—SERIES A

**All applicable Exercises in Series A are available with McGraw-Hill's *Connect Accounting*.**

LO 3

**Exercise 5-1A    *Classifying the costs of unit-, batch-, product-, or facility-level activities***

Humphrey Manufacturing is developing an activity-based costing system to improve overhead cost allocation. One of the first steps in developing the system is to classify the costs of performing production activities into activity cost pools.

**Required**

Using your knowledge of the four categories of activities, classify the cost of each activity in the following list into unit-, batch-, product-, or facility-level cost pools.

| Cost Activity | Cost Pool |
|---|---|
| a. Engineering product design | |
| b. Supplies | |
| c. Wages of maintenance staff | |
| d. Labeling and packaging | |
| e. Plant security | |
| f. Ordering materials for a specific type of product | |
| g. Wages of workers moving units of work between work stations | |
| h. Factorywide electricity | |
| i. Salary of a manager in charge of a product line | |
| j. Sales commissions | |

## Exercise 5-2A   *Identifying appropriate cost drivers*                    LO 2

**Required**

Provide at least one example of an appropriate cost driver (allocation base) for each of the following activities.

**a.** Maintenance is performed on manufacturing equipment.
**b.** Sales commissions are paid.
**c.** Direct labor is used to change machine configurations.
**d.** Production equipment is set up for new production runs.
**e.** Engineering drawings are produced for design changes.
**f.** Purchase orders are issued.
**g.** Products are labeled, packaged, and shipped.
**h.** Machinists are trained on new computer-controlled machinery.
**i.** Lighting is used for production facilities.
**j.** Materials are unloaded and stored for production.

## Exercise 5-3A   *Classifying costs and identifying the appropriate cost driver*     LO 2, 3

Fairfield Manufacturing incurred the following costs during 2011 to produce its high-quality precision instruments. The company used an activity-based costing system and identified the following activities.

**1.** Inspection of each batch produced.
**2.** Salaries of receiving clerks.
**3.** Setup for each batch produced.
**4.** Insurance on production facilities.
**5.** Depreciation on manufacturing equipment.
**6.** Materials handling.
**7.** Inventory storage.

**Required**

**a.** Classify each activity as a unit-level, batch-level, product-level, or facility-level activity.
**b.** Identify an appropriate cost driver (allocation base) for each activity.

## Exercise 5-4A   *Context-sensitive nature of activity classification*     LO 3

**Required**

Describe a set of circumstances in which the cost of painting could be classified as a unit-level, a batch-level, a product-level, or a facility-level cost.

### Exercise 5-5A   *Context-sensitive nature of activity classification*

Wayne Company makes two types of circuit boards. One is a high-caliber board designed to accomplish the most demanding tasks; the other is a low-caliber board designed to provide limited service at an affordable price. During its most recent accounting period, Wayne incurred $170,000 of inspection cost. When Wayne recently established an activity-based costing system, its activities were classified into four categories. Categories and appropriate cost drivers follow.

|              | Direct Labor Hours | Number of Batches | Number of Inspectors | Number of Square Feet |
|--------------|--------------------|-------------------|----------------------|-----------------------|
| High caliber | 3,000              | 20                | 3                    | 30,000                |
| Low caliber  | 14,000             | 20                | 2                    | 70,000                |
| Total        | 17,000             | 40                | 5                    | 100,000               |

**Required**

Allocate the inspection cost between the two products assuming that it is driven by (a) unit-level activities, (b) batch-level activities, (c) product-level activities, or (d) facility-level activities. Note that each allocation represents a separate alternative. In other words, the $170,000 of inspection cost will be allocated four times, once for each cost driver.

### Exercise 5-6A   *Computing overhead rates based on different cost drivers*

Roebuck Industries produces two electronic decoders, P and Q. Decoder P is more sophisticated and requires more programming and testing than does Decoder Q. Because of these product differences, the company wants to use activity-based costing to allocate overhead costs. It has identified four activity pools. Relevant information follows.

| Activity Pools | Cost Pool Total | Cost Driver |
|----------------|-----------------|-------------|
| Repair and maintenance on assembly machine | $  50,000 | Number of units produced |
| Programming cost | 84,000 | Number of programming hours |
| Software inspections | 6,000 | Number of inspections |
| Product testing | 8,000 | Number of tests |
| Total overhead cost | $148,000 | |

Expected activity for each product follows.

|           | Number of Units | Number of Programming Hours | Number of Inspections | Number of Tests |
|-----------|-----------------|-----------------------------|-----------------------|-----------------|
| Decoder P | 20,000          | 2,000                       | 190                   | 1,400           |
| Decoder Q | 30,000          | 1,500                       | 60                    | 1,100           |
| Total     | 50,000          | 3,500                       | 250                   | 2,500           |

**Required**

a.  Compute the overhead rate for each activity pool.
b.  Determine the overhead cost allocated to each product.

### Exercise 5-7A   *Comparing an ABC system with a traditional costing system*

Use the information in Exercise 5-6A to complete the following requirements. Assume that before shifting to activity-based costing, Roebuck Industries allocated all overhead costs based on direct labor hours. Direct labor data pertaining to the two decoders follow.

|           | Direct Labor Hours |
|-----------|--------------------|
| Decoder P | 15,000             |
| Decoder Q | 22,000             |
| Total     | 37,000             |

**Required**

a. Compute the amount of overhead cost allocated to each type of decoder when using direct labor hours as the allocation base.

b. Determine the cost per unit for overhead when using direct labor hours as the allocation base and when using ABC.

c. Explain why the per unit overhead cost is lower for the high-volume product when using ABC.

## Exercise 5-8A    *Allocating costs with different cost drivers*    LO 1, 3

Wykle Company produces commercial gardening equipment. Since production is highly automated, the company allocates its overhead costs to product lines using activity-based costing. The costs and cost drivers associated with the four overhead activity cost pools follow.

| | Activities | | | |
|---|---|---|---|---|
| | **Unit Level** | **Batch Level** | **Product Level** | **Facility Level** |
| Cost | $50,000 | $20,000 | $10,000 | $120,000 |
| Cost driver | 2,000 labor hrs. | 40 setups | Percentage of use | 12,000 units |

Production of 800 sets of cutting shears, one of the company's 20 products, took 200 labor hours and 6 setups and consumed 15 percent of the product-sustaining activities.

**Required**

a. Had the company used labor hours as a companywide allocation base, how much overhead would it have allocated to the cutting shears?

b. How much overhead is allocated to the cutting shears using activity-based costing?

c. Compute the overhead cost per unit for cutting shears using first activity-based costing and then using direct labor hours for allocation if 800 units are produced. If direct product costs are $100 and the product is priced at 30 percent above cost (rounded to the nearest whole dollar), for what price would the product sell under each allocation system?

d. Assuming that activity-based costing provides a more accurate estimate of cost, indicate whether the cutting shears would be over- or underpriced if direct labor hours are used as an allocation base. Explain how over- or undercosting can affect Wykle's profitability.

e. Comment on the validity of using the allocated facility-level cost in the pricing decision. Should other costs be considered in a cost-plus pricing decision? If so, which ones? What costs would you include if you were trying to decide whether to accept a special order?

## Exercise 5-9A    *Allocating costs with different cost drivers*    LO 2, 3

Swartz Publishing identified the following overhead activities, their respective costs, and their cost drivers to produce the three types of textbooks the company publishes.

| | | Type of Textbook | | |
|---|---|---|---|---|
| **Activity (Cost)** | **Cost Driver** | **Deluxe** | **Moderate** | **Economy** |
| Machine maintenance ($240,000) | Number of machine hours | 250 | 750 | 1,000 |
| Setups ($420,000) | Number of setups | 30 | 15 | 5 |
| Packing ($108,000) | Number of cartons | 10 | 30 | 50 |
| Photo development ($336,000) | Number of pictures | 4,000 | 2,000 | 1,000 |

Deluxe textbooks are made with the finest-quality paper, six-color printing, and many photographs. Moderate texts are made with three colors and a few photographs spread throughout each chapter. Economy books are printed in black and white and include pictures only in chapter openings.

**Required**

a. Swartz currently allocates all overhead costs based on machine hours. The company produced the following number of books during the prior year.

| Deluxe | Moderate | Economy |
|--------|----------|---------|
| 50,000 | 150,000 | 200,000 |

Determine the overhead cost per book for each book type.

b. Determine the overhead cost per book, assuming that the volume-based allocation system described in Requirement *a* is replaced with an activity-based costing system.

c. Explain why the per-unit overhead costs determined in Requirements *a* and *b* differ.

**LO 3**

### Exercise 5-10A    *Computing product cost with given activity allocation rates*

Gamble Manufacturing produces two modems, one for laptop computers and the other for desktop computers. The production process is automated, and the company has found activity-based costing useful in assigning overhead costs to its products. The company has identified five major activities involved in producing the modems.

| Activity | Allocation Base | Allocation Rate |
|----------|-----------------|-----------------|
| Materials receiving & handling | Cost of material | 2% of material cost |
| Production setup | Number of setups | $100.00 per setup |
| Assembly | Number of parts | $5.00 per part |
| Quality inspection | Inspection time | $1.50 per minute |
| Packing and shipping | Number of orders | $10.00 per order |

Activity measures for the two kinds of modems follow.

| | Labor Cost | Material Cost | Number of Setups | Number of Parts | Inspection Time | Number of Orders |
|--|-----------|---------------|------------------|-----------------|-----------------|------------------|
| Laptops | $1,260 | $6,000 | 30 | 42 | 7,200 min. | 65 |
| Desktops | 1,150 | 7,500 | 12 | 24 | 5,100 min. | 20 |

**Required**

a. Compute the cost per unit of laptop and desktop modems, assuming that Gamble made 300 units of each type of modem.

b. Explain why laptop modems cost more to make even though they have less material cost and are smaller than desktop modems.

**LO 3**

### Exercise 5-11A    *Allocating facility-level costs and a product elimination decision*

Jacob Boards produces two kinds of skateboards. Selected unit data for the two boards for the last quarter follow.

| | Basco Boards | Shimano Boards |
|--|--------------|----------------|
| Production costs | | |
| Direct materials | $27 | $36 |
| Direct labor | $39 | $51 |
| Allocated overhead | $15 | $18 |
| Total units produced and sold | 4,000 | 8,000 |
| Total sales revenue | $336,000 | $888,000 |

Jacob allocates production overhead using activity-based costing. It allocates delivery expense and sales commissions, which amount to $54,000 per quarter, to the two products equally.

**Required**

a. Compute the net profit for each product.

b. Assuming that the overhead allocation for Basco boards includes $12,000 of facility-level costs, would you advise Jacob to eliminate these boards? (*Hint:* Consider the method used to allocate the delivery and selling expense.)

### Exercise 5-12A    *Quality cost components and relationships*

**LO 4**

**Required**

The preceding graph depicts the relationships among the components of total quality cost.

a. Label the lines identified as A, B, and C.

b. Explain the relationships depicted in the graph.

## PROBLEMS—SERIES A

**All applicable Problems in Series A are available with McGraw-Hill's *Connect Accounting*.**

### Problem 5-13A    *Comparing an ABC system with a traditional costing system*

**LO 1, 3**

e**X**cel

Peck Electronics produces video games in three market categories, commercial, home, and miniature. Peck has traditionally allocated overhead costs to the three products using the company-wide allocation base of direct labor hours. The company recently implemented an ABC system when it installed computer-controlled assembly stations that rendered the traditional costing system ineffective. In implementing the ABC system, the company identified the following activity cost pools and cost drivers.

| Category | Total Pooled Cost | Types of Costs | Cost Driver |
|---|---|---|---|
| Unit | $720,000 | Indirect labor wages, supplies, depreciation, machine maintenance | Machine hours |
| Batch | 388,800 | Materials handling, inventory storage, labor for setups, packaging, labeling and shipping, scheduling | Number of production orders |
| Product | 211,200 | Research and development | Time spent by research department |
| Facility | 600,000 | Rent, utilities, maintenance, admin. salaries, security | Square footage |

Additional data for each of the product lines follow.

| | Commercial | Home | Miniature | Total |
|---|---|---|---|---|
| Direct materials cost | $36.00/unit | $24.00/unit | $30.00/unit | — |
| Direct labor cost | $14.40/hour | $14.40/hour | $18.00/hour | — |
| Number of labor hours | 6,000 | 12,000 | 2,000 | 20,000 |
| Number of machine hours | 10,000 | 45,000 | 25,000 | 80,000 |
| Number of production orders | 200 | 2,000 | 800 | 3,000 |
| Research and development time | 10% | 20% | 70% | 100% |
| Number of units | 15,000 | 45,000 | 14,000 | 74,000 |
| Square footage | 20,000 | 50,000 | 30,000 | 100,000 |

**Required**

a. Determine the total cost and cost per unit for each product line, assuming that overhead costs are allocated to each product line using direct labor hours as a companywide allocation base. Also determine the combined cost of all three product lines.

b. Determine the total cost and cost per unit for each product line, assuming that an ABC system is used to allocate overhead costs. Determine the combined cost of all three product lines.

c. Explain why the combined total cost computed in Requirements *a* and *b* is the same amount. Given that the combined cost is the same using either allocation method, why is an ABC system with many different allocation rates more accurate than a traditional system with a single companywide overhead rate?

## Problem 5-14A  *Effect of automation on overhead allocation*

Hewitt Rug Company makes two types of rugs, seasonal and all-purpose. Both types of rugs are hand-made, but the seasonal rugs require significantly more labor because of their decorative designs. The annual number of rugs made and the labor hours required to make each type of rug follow.

| | Seasonal | All-Purpose | Totals |
|---|---|---|---|
| Number of rugs | 1,200 | 2,800 | 4,000 |
| Number of direct labor hours | 120,000 | 168,000 | 288,000 |

**Required**

a. Assume that annual overhead costs total $72,000. Select the appropriate cost driver and determine the amount of overhead to allocate to each type of rug.

b. Hewitt automates the seasonal rug line resulting in a dramatic decline in labor usage, to make 1,200 rugs in only 12,000 hours. Hewitt continues to make the all-purpose rugs the same way as before. The number of rugs made and the labor hours required to make them after automation follow.

| | Seasonal | All-Purpose | Totals |
|---|---|---|---|
| Number of rugs | 1,200 | 2,800 | 4,000 |
| Number of direct labor hours | 12,000 | 168,000 | 180,000 |

Overhead costs are expected to increase to $90,000 as a result of the automation. Allocate the increased overhead cost to the two types of rugs using direct labor hours as the allocation base and comment on the appropriateness of the allocation.

## Problem 5-15A  *Using activity-based costing to improve allocation accuracy*

*This problem is an extension of Problem 5-14A, which must be completed first.*
Hewitt's accounting staff has disaggregated the $90,000 of overhead costs into the following items.

| | |
|---|---:|
| (1) Inspection costs | $ 32,000 |
| (2) Setup costs | 21,600 |
| (3) Engineering costs | 32,000 |
| (4) Legal costs related to products | 12,000 |
| (5) Materials movement cost per batch | 4,800 |
| (6) Salaries of production supervisors | 80,000 |
| (7) Fringe benefit costs | 16,000 |
| (8) Utilities costs | 8,000 |
| (9) Plant manager's salary | 48,000 |
| (10) Depreciation on production equipment | 72,000 |
| (11) Depreciation on building | 16,000 |
| (12) Miscellaneous costs | 10,000 |
| (13) Indirect materials costs | 5,600 |
| (14) Production employee incentive costs | 2,000 |
| Total | $360,000 |

### Required

**a.** Each of Hewitt's rug lines operates as a department. The all-purpose department occupies 6,000 square feet of floor space, and the seasonal department occupies 12,000 square feet of space. Comment on the validity of allocating the overhead costs by square footage.

**b.** Assume that the following additional information is available.

(1) Rugs are individually inspected.

(2) Hewitt incurs setup costs each time a new style of seasonal rug is produced. The seasonal rugs were altered nine times during the year. The manual equipment for all-purpose rugs is reset twice each year to ensure accurate weaving. The setup for the technical equipment used to weave seasonal rugs requires more highly skilled workers, but the all-purpose rugs require more manual equipment, thereby resulting in a *per setup* charge that is roughly equal for both types of rugs. Hewitt undertook 22 setups during the year, 18 of which applied to seasonal rugs and 4 that applied to all-purpose rugs.

(3) Ninety percent of the product-level costs can be traced to producing seasonal rugs.

(4) Six supervisors oversee the production of all-purpose rugs. Because seasonal rugs are made in an automated department, only two production supervisors are needed.

(5) Each rug requires an equal amount of indirect materials.

(6) Costs associated with production activities are assigned to six activity cost pools: (1) labor-related activities, (2) unit-level activities, (3) batch-level activities, (4) product-level supervisory activities, (5) other product-level activities, and (6) facility-level activities.

Organize the $360,000 of overhead costs into activity center cost pools and allocate the costs to the two types of rugs.

**c.** Assuming that 90 seasonal and 240 all-purpose rugs were made in January, determine the overhead costs that would be assigned to each of the two rug types for the month of January.

### Problem 5-16A   *Using activity-based costing to improve allocation accuracy*     LO 1, 3

Soloman Academy, is a profit-oriented education business. Soloman provides remedial training for high school students who have fallen behind in their classroom studies. It charges its students $500 per course. During the previous year, Soloman provided instruction for 1,000 students. The income statement for the company follows.

CHECK FIGURES
a. Cost per student:
   Computer-Assisted: $327
   Classroom: $237

| | |
|---|---:|
| Revenue | $ 400,000 |
| Cost of instructors | (170,000) |
| Overhead costs | (85,000) |
| Net income | $ 145,000 |

The company president, Susan Doubleday, indicated in a discussion with the accountant, Merrill Archer, that she was extremely pleased with the growth in the area of computer-assisted instruction. She observed that this department served 200 students using only two part-time instructors. In contrast, the classroom-based instructional department required 32 instructors to teach 800 students. Ms. Doubleday noted that the per-student cost of instruction was dramatically lower for the computer-assisted department. She based her conclusion on the following information.

Soloman pays its part-time instructors an average of $5,000 per year. The total cost of instruction and the cost per student are computed as follows.

| Type of Instruction | Computer-Assisted | Classroom |
|---|---|---|
| Number of instructors (a) | 2 | 32 |
| Number of students (b) | 200 | 800 |
| Total cost (c = a × $5,000) | $10,000 | $160,000 |
| Cost per student (c ÷ b) | $50 | $200 |

Assuming that overhead costs were distributed equally across the student population, Ms. Doubleday concluded that the cost of instructors was the critical variable in the company's capacity to generate profits. Based on her analysis, her strategic plan called for heavily increased use of computer-assisted instruction.

Mr. Archer was not so sure that computer-assisted instruction should be stressed. After attending a seminar on activity-based costing (ABC), he believed that the allocation of overhead cost could be more closely traced to the different types of learning activities. To facilitate an activity-based analysis, he developed the following information about the costs associated with computer-assisted versus classroom instructional activities. He identified $48,000 of overhead costs that were directly traceable to computer-assisted activities, including the costs of computer hardware, software, and technical assistance. He believed the remaining $37,000 of overhead costs should be allocated to the two instructional activities based on the number of students enrolled in each program.

### Required

**a.** Based on the preceding information, determine the total cost and the cost per student to provide courses through computer-assisted instruction versus classroom instruction.

**b.** Comment on the validity of stressing growth in the area of computer-assisted instruction.

**LO 1**

### Problem 5-17A    *Key activity-based costing concepts*

Friar Paint Company makes paint in many different colors; it charges the same price for all of its paint regardless of the color. Recently, Friar's chief competitor cut the price of its white paint, which normally outsells any other color by a margin of 4 to 1. Friar's marketing manager requested permission to match the competitor's price. When Phillip Keaton, Friar's president, discussed the matter with Candice Smalley, the chief accountant, he was told that the competitor's price was below Friar's cost. Mr. Keaton responded, "If that's the case, then there is something wrong with our accounting system. I know the competition wouldn't sell below cost. Prepare a report showing me how you determine our paint cost and get back to me as soon as possible."

The next day, Ms. Smalley returned to Mr. Keaton's office and began by saying, "Determining the cost per gallon is a pretty simple computation. It includes $1.10 of labor, $3.10 of materials, and $4.00 of overhead for a total cost of $8.20 per gallon. The problem is that the competition is selling the stuff for $7.99 per gallon. They've got to be losing money."

Mr. Keaton then asked Ms. Smalley how she determined the overhead cost. She replied, "We take total overhead cost and divide it by total labor hours and then assign it to the products based on the direct labor hours required to make the paint." Mr. Keaton then asked what kinds of costs are included in the total overhead cost. Ms. Smalley said, "It includes the depreciation on the building and equipment, the cost of utilities, supervisory salaries, and interest. Just how detailed do you want me to go with this list?"

Mr. Keaton responded, "Keep going, I'll tell you when I've heard enough."

Ms. Smalley continued, "There is the cost of setups. Every time a color is changed, the machines have to be cleaned, the color release valves reset, a trial batch prepared, and color quality tested. Sometimes mistakes occur and the machines must be reset. In addition, purchasing and handling the color ingredients must be accounted for as well as adjustments in the packaging department to change the paint cans and to mark the boxes to show the color change. Then . . ."

Mr. Keaton interrupted, "I think I've heard enough. We sell so much white paint that we run it through a separate production process. White paint is produced continuously. There are no shutdowns and setups. White uses no color ingredients. So why are these costs being assigned to our white paint production?"

Ms. Smalley replied, "Well, sir, these costs are just a part of the big total that is allocated to all of the paint, no matter what color it happens to be."

Mr. Keaton looked disgusted and said, "As I told you yesterday, Ms. Smalley, something is wrong with our accounting system!"

### Required

a. Explain what the terms *overcost* and *undercost* mean. Is Friar's white paint over- or under-costed?

b. Explain what the term *companywide overhead rate* means. Is Friar using a companywide overhead rate?

c. Explain how Friar could improve the accuracy of its overhead cost allocations.

## Problem 5-18A  *Pricing decisions made with ABC system cost data*

Morello Sporting Goods Corporation makes two types of racquets, tennis and badminton. The company uses the same facility to make both products even though the processes are quite different. The company has recently converted its cost accounting system to activity-based costing. The following are the cost data that June Searight, the cost accountant, prepared for the third quarter of 2011 (during which Morello made 70,000 tennis racquets and 30,000 badminton racquets).

LO 3

CHECK FIGURES
a. Cost per unit:
   Tennis Racquet: $64.71
   Badminton Racquet: $65.67

| Direct Cost | Tennis Racquet (TR) | Badminton Racquet (BR) |
|---|---|---|
| Direct materials | $18 per unit | $14 per unit |
| Direct labor | 32 per unit | 26 per unit |

| Category | Estimated Cost | Cost Driver | Amount of Cost Driver |
|---|---|---|---|
| Unit level | $ 750,000 | Number of inspection hours | TR: 15,000 hours; BR: 10,000 hours |
| Batch level | 250,000 | Number of setups | TR: 80 setups; BR: 45 setups |
| Product level | 150,000 | Number of TV commercials | TR: 4; BR: 1 |
| Facility level | 650,000 | Number of machine hours | TR: 30,000 hours; BR: 35,000 hours |
| Total | $1,800,000 | | |

Inspectors are paid according to the number of actual hours worked, which is determined by the number of racquets inspected. Engineers who set up equipment for both products are paid monthly salaries. TV commercial fees are paid at the beginning of the quarter. Facility-level cost includes depreciation of all production equipment.

### Required

a. Compute the cost per unit for each product.

b. If management wants to price badminton racquets 30 percent above cost, what price should the company set?

c. The market price of tennis racquets has declined substantially because of new competitors entering the market. Management asks you to determine the minimum cost of producing tennis racquets in the short term. Provide that information.

## Problem 5-19A  *Target pricing and target costing with ABC*

LO 3

Heisler Cameras, Inc., manufactures two models of cameras. Model ZM has a zoom lens; Model DS has a fixed lens. Heisler uses an activity-based costing system. The following are the relevant cost data for the previous month.

| Direct Cost per Unit | Model ZM | Model DS |
|---|---|---|
| Direct materials | $20 | $10 |
| Direct labor | 28 | 12 |

| Category | Estimated Cost | Cost Driver | Use of Cost Driver |
|---|---|---|---|
| Unit level | $ 27,000 | Number of units | ZM: 2,400 units; DS: 9,600 units |
| Batch level | 50,000 | Number of setups | ZM: 25 setups; DS: 25 setups |
| Product level | 90,000 | Number of TV commercials | ZM: 15; DS: 10 |
| Facility level | 300,000 | Number of machine hours | ZM: 500 hours; DS: 1,000 hours |
| Total | $467,000 | | |

Heisler's facility has the capacity to operate 4,500 machine hours per month.

**Required**

a. Compute the cost per unit for each product.

b. The current market price for products comparable to Model ZM is $135 and for DS is $47. If Heisler sold all of its products at the market prices, what was its profit or loss for the previous month?

c. A market expert believes that Heisler can sell as many cameras as it can produce by pricing Model ZM at $130 and Model DS at $45. Heisler would like to use those estimates as its target prices and have a profit margin of 20 percent of target prices. What is the target cost for each product?

d. Is there any way for the company to reach its target costs?

## Problem 5-20A  *Cost management with an ABC system*

Fazel Chairs, Inc., makes two types of chairs. Model Diamond is a high-end product designed for professional offices. Model Gold is an economical product designed for family use. Irene Fazel, the president, is worried about cut-throat price competition in the chairs market. Her company suffered a loss last quarter, an unprecedented event in its history. The company's accountant prepared the following cost data for Ms. Fazel.

| Direct Cost per Unit | Model Diamond (D) | Model Gold (G) |
|---|---|---|
| Direct materials | $20 per unit | $10 per unit |
| Direct labor | $18/hour × 2 hours production time | $18/hour × 1 hour production time |

| Category | Estimated Cost | Cost Driver | Use of Cost Driver |
|---|---|---|---|
| Unit level | $ 300,000 | Number of units | D: 15,000 units; G: 35,000 units |
| Batch level | 750,000 | Number of setups | D: 104 setups; G: 146 setups |
| Product level | 450,000 | Number of TV commercials | D: 5; G: 10 |
| Facility level | 500,000 | Number of machine hours | D: 1,500 hours; G: 3,500 hours |
| Total | $2,000,000 | | |

The market price for office chairs comparable to Model Diamond is $118 and to Model Gold is $73.

**Required**

a. Compute the cost per unit for both products.

b. Judson Regland, the chief engineer, told Ms. Fazel that the company is currently making 150 units of Model Diamond per batch and 245 units of Model Gold per batch. He suggests doubling the batch sizes to cut the number of setups in half, thereby reducing the setup cost by 50 percent. Compute the cost per unit for each product if Ms. Fazel adopts his suggestion.

c. Is there any side effect if Ms. Fazel increases the production batch size by 100 percent?

## Problem 5-21A   *Assessing a quality control strategy*

The following quality cost report came from the records of Nelson Company.

|  | 2011 | | 2010 | |
| --- | --- | --- | --- | --- |
|  | Amount | Percentage | Amount | Percentage |
| **Prevention costs** |  |  |  |  |
| Engineering and design | $136,000 | 13.74% | $ 58,000 | 3.86% |
| Training and education | 34,000 | 3.43 | 12,000 | 0.80 |
| Depreciation on prevention equipment | 58,000 | 5.86 | 30,000 | 1.99 |
| Incentives and awards | 88,000 | 8.89 | 40,000 | 2.66 |
| Total prevention | 316,000 | 31.92% | 140,000 | 9.31% |
| **Appraisal costs** |  |  |  |  |
| Inventory inspection | 50,000 | 5.05 | 50,000 | 3.32 |
| Reliability testing | 32,000 | 3.23 | 30,000 | 1.99 |
| Testing equipment (depreciation) | 22,000 | 2.22 | 24,000 | 1.60 |
| Supplies | 14,000 | 1.41 | 16,000 | 1.06 |
| Total appraisal | 118,000 | 11.92% | 120,000 | 7.98% |
| **Internal failure costs** |  |  |  |  |
| Scrap | 48,000 | 4.85 | 80,000 | 5.32 |
| Repair and rework | 98,000 | 9.90 | 220,000 | 14.63 |
| Downtime | 24,000 | 2.42 | 40,000 | 2.66 |
| Reinspection | 8,000 | 0.81 | 24,000 | 1.60 |
| Total internal failure | 178,000 | 17.98% | 364,000 | 24.20% |
| **External failure cost** |  |  |  |  |
| Warranty repairs and replacement | 220,000 | 22.22 | 520,000 | 34.57 |
| Freight | 48,000 | 4.85 | 100,000 | 6.65 |
| Customer relations | 56,000 | 5.66 | 120,000 | 7.98 |
| Restocking and packaging | 54,000 | 5.45 | 140,000 | 9.31 |
| Total external failure | 378,000 | 38.18% | 880,000 | 58.51% |
| Grand total | $990,000 | 100.00% | $1,504,000 | 100.00% |

### Required

a. Explain the strategy that Nelson Company initiated to control its quality costs.

b. Indicate whether the strategy was successful or unsuccessful in reducing quality costs.

c. Explain how the strategy likely affected customer satisfaction.

## EXERCISES—SERIES B

### Exercise 5-1B   *Classifying the costs of unit-, batch-, product-, or facility-level activities*

Tucker Manufacturing is developing an activity-based costing system to improve overhead cost allocation. One of the first steps in developing the system is to classify the costs of performing production activities into activity cost pools.

### Required

Using the four-tier cost hierarchy described in the chapter, classify each of the following costs into unit-level, batch-level, product-level, or facility-level cost pools.

| Cost Activity | Cost Pool |
|---|---|
| a. Wages of assembly line workers | |
| b. Product design costs | |
| c. Materials requisition costs for a particular work order | |
| d. Security guard wages | |
| e. Lubricant for machines | |
| f. Parts used to make a particular product | |
| g. Machine setup cost | |
| h. Salary of the plant manager's secretary | |
| i. Factory depreciation | |
| j. Advertising costs for a particular product | |

**LO 2**

### Exercise 5-2B  *Identifying appropriate cost drivers*

**Required**

Provide at least one example of an appropriate cost driver (allocation base) for each of the following activities.

a.  Workers count completed goods before moving them to a warehouse.
b.  A logistics manager runs a computer program to determine the materials release schedule.
c.  Janitors clean the factory floor after workers have left.
d.  Mechanics apply lubricant to machines.
e.  Engineers design a product production layout.
f.  Engineers set up machines to produce a product.
g.  The production supervisor completes the paperwork initiating a work order.
h.  The production manager prepares materials requisition forms.
i.  Workers move materials from the warehouse to the factory floor.
j.  Assembly line machines are operated.

**LO 2, 3**

### Exercise 5-3B  *Classifying costs and identifying the appropriate cost driver*

Astro Corporation, a furniture manufacturer, uses an activity-based costing system. It has identified the following selected activities:

1.  Incurring property taxes on factory buildings.
2.  Incurring paint cost for furniture produced.
3.  Setting up machines for a particular batch of production.
4.  Inspecting wood prior to using it in production.
5.  Packaging completed furniture in boxes for shipment.
6.  Inspecting completed furniture for quality control.
7.  Purchasing TV time to advertise a particular product.

**Required**

a.  Classify each activity as a unit-level, batch-level, product-level, or facility-level activity.
b.  Identify an appropriate cost driver (allocation base) for each of the activities.

**LO 3**

### Exercise 5-4B  *Understanding the context-sensitive nature of classifying activities*

**Required**

Describe a set of circumstances in which labor cost could be classified as a unit-level, a batch-level, a product-level, or a facility-level cost.

**LO 3**

### Exercise 5-5B  *Understanding the context-sensitive nature of classifying activities*

Mauldin Company makes two types of cell phones. Handy is a thin, pocket-size cell phone that is easy to carry around. Action is a palm-size phone convenient to hold while the user is talking.

During its most recent accounting period, Mauldin incurred $150,000 of quality-control costs. Recently Mauldin established an activity-based costing system, which involved classifying its activities into four categories. The categories and appropriate cost drivers follow.

| | Direct Labor Hours | Number of Batches | Number of Engineers | Number of Square Feet |
|---|---|---|---|---|
| Handy | 26,000 | 38 | 10 | 37,000 |
| Action | 24,000 | 22 | 5 | 83,000 |
| Totals | 50,000 | 60 | 15 | 120,000 |

Mauldin uses direct labors hours to allocate unit-level activities, number of batches to allocate batch-level activities, number of engineers to allocate product-level activities, and number of square feet to allocate facility-level activities.

**Required**

Allocate the quality-control cost between the two products, assuming that it is driven by (a) unit-level activities, (b) batch-level activities, (c) product-level activities, and (d) facility-level activities. Note that each allocation represents a separate allocation. In other words, the $300,000 of quality-control costs will be allocated four times, once for each cost driver.

## Exercise 5-6B    *Computing overhead rates based on different costing drivers*    LO 2, 3

Chase Industries produces two surge protectors: VC620 with six outlets and PH630 with eight outlets and two telephone line connections. Because of these product differences, the company plans to use activity-based costing to allocate overhead costs. The company has identified four activity pools. Relevant information follows.

| Activity Pools | Cost Pool Total | Cost Driver |
|---|---|---|
| Machine setup | $120,000 | Number of setups |
| Machine operation | 300,000 | Number of machine hours |
| Quality control | 48,000 | Number of inspections |
| Packaging | 32,000 | Number of units |
| Total overhead cost | $500,000 | |

Expected activity for each product follows.

| | Number of Setups | Number of Machine Hours | Number of Inspections | Number of Units |
|---|---|---|---|---|
| VC620 | 48 | 1,400 | 78 | 25,000 |
| PH630 | 72 | 2,600 | 172 | 15,000 |
| Total | 120 | 4,000 | 250 | 40,000 |

**Required**

a.  Compute the overhead rate for each activity pool.
b.  Determine the overhead cost allocated to each product.

## Exercise 5-7B    *Comparing an ABC system with a traditional cost system*    LO 1, 3

Use the information in Exercise 5-6B to complete the following requirements. Assume that before shifting to activity-based costing, Chase Industries allocated all overhead costs based on direct labor hours. Direct labor data pertaining to the two surge protectors follow.

|  | Direct Labor Hours |
|---|---|
| VC620 | 16,000 |
| PH630 | 9,000 |
| Total | 25,000 |

**Required**

a. Compute the amount of overhead cost allocated to each type of surge protector when using direct labor hours as the allocation base.

b. Determine the cost per unit for overhead when using direct labor hours as the allocation base and when using ABC.

c. Explain why the per unit overhead cost is lower for the higher-volume product when using ABC.

**LO 1, 2, 3**

### Exercise 5-8B  *Allocating costs with different cost drivers*

Rigsby Sporting Goods, Inc., produces indoor treadmills. The company allocates its overhead costs using activity-based costing. The costs and cost drivers associated with the four overhead activity cost pools follow.

| Activities | Unit Level | Batch Level | Product Level | Facility Level |
|---|---|---|---|---|
| Cost | $500,000 | $250,000 | $150,000 | $450,000 |
| Cost driver | 12,500 labor hours | 50 setups | Percentage of use | 15,000 units |

Producing 5,000 units of PFT200, one of the company's five products, took 4,000 labor hours, 25 setups, and consumed 30 percent of the product-sustaining activities.

**Required**

a. Had the company used labor hours as a companywide allocation base, how much overhead would it have allocated to the 5,000 units of PFT200?

b. How much overhead is allocated to the 5,000 PFT200 units using activity-based costing?

c. Compute the overhead cost per unit for PFT200 using activity-based costing and direct labor hours if 5,000 units are produced. If direct product costs are $120 and PFT200 is priced at 20 percent above cost (rounded to the nearest whole dollar), compute the product's selling price under each allocation system.

d. Assuming that activity-based costing provides a more accurate estimate of cost, indicate whether PFT200 would be over- or underpriced if Rigsby uses direct labor hours as the allocation base. Explain how over- or undercosting can affect Rigsby's profitability.

e. Comment on the validity of using the allocated facility-level costs in the pricing decision. Should other costs be considered in a cost-plus pricing decision? If so, which ones? What costs would you include if you were trying to decide whether to accept a special order?

**LO 2, 3**

### Exercise 5-9B  *Allocating costs with different cost drivers*

Talton Shoes Corporation produces three brands of shoes, Brisk, Pro, and Runner. Relevant information about Talton overhead activities, their respective costs, and their cost drivers follows.

| Overhead Costs | Cost Driver | Brisk | Pro | Runner |
|---|---|---|---|---|
| Fringe benefits ($360,000) | Labor hours | 10,000 | 20,000 | 20,000 |
| Setups ($200,000) | Number of setups | 15 | 25 | 10 |
| Packing costs ($40,000) | Number of cartons | 200 | 300 | 300 |
| Quality control ($300,000) | Number of tests | 120 | 200 | 80 |

## Required

**a.** Talton currently allocates all overhead costs based on labor hours. The company produced the following numbers of pairs of shoes during the prior year.

| Brisk | Pro | Runner |
|---|---|---|
| 10,000 | 15,000 | 20,000 |

Determine the overhead cost per pair of shoes for each brand.

**b.** Determine the overhead cost per pair of shoes for each brand, assuming that the volume-based allocation system described in Requirement *a* is replaced with an activity-based costing system.

**c.** Explain why the per pair overhead costs determined in Requirements *a* and *b* differ.

## Exercise 5-10B    *Computing product cost with given activity allocation rates*     **LO 3**

Using automated production processes, Stegall Videos produces two kinds of digital camcorders: N100 for the novice and D200 for the hobbyist. The company has found activity-based costing useful in assigning overhead costs to its products. It has identified the following five major activities involved in producing the camcorders.

| Activity | Allocation Base | Allocation Rate |
|---|---|---|
| Materials receiving and handling | Cost of materials | 3% of materials cost |
| Production setup | Number of setups | $800 per setup |
| Assembly | Number of parts | $10 per part |
| Quality inspection | Inspection time | $25 per minute |
| Packing and shipping | Number of orders | $80 per order |

Activity measures for the two kinds of camcorders follow.

| | Labor Cost* | Materials Cost* | Number of Setups | Number of Parts | Inspection Time | Number of Orders |
|---|---|---|---|---|---|---|
| N100 | $225,000 | $125,000 | 10 | 10,000 | 800 min. | 25 |
| D200 | 150,000 | 150,000 | 25 | 10,000 | 4,800 min. | 50 |

*Both are direct costs.

## Required

**a.** Compute the cost per unit of N100 and D200, assuming that Stegall made 1,000 units of N100 and 500 units of D200.

**b.** Explain why the D200 camcorders cost more to make although their direct costs are less than those for the N100 camcorders.

## Exercise 5-11B    *Allocating facility-level costs and a product elimination decision*     **LO 3**

Adgar Corporation produces two types of juice that it packages in cases of 24 cans per case. Selected per case data for the two products for the last month follow.

| | Orange Juice | Tomato Juice |
|---|---|---|
| Production costs | | |
| Direct material | $2.25 | $1.50 |
| Direct labor | $1.50 | $2.25 |
| Allocated overhead | $2.25 | $3.00 |
| Total cases produced and sold | 25,000 | 15,000 |
| Total sales revenue | $210,000 | $127,500 |

Adgar allocates production overhead using activity-based costing but allocates monthly packaging expense, which amounted to $60,000 last month, to the two products equally.

### Required

a. Compute the net profit for each product.

b. Assuming that the overhead allocation for the tomato juice includes $30,000 of facility-level costs, would you advise Adgar to eliminate this product? (*Hint:* Consider the method used to allocate the monthly packaging expense.)

**LO 4**

### Exercise 5-12B  *Applying concepts of quality cost management*

Lucas Weldon, the president of Easeley Industries, Inc., was beaming when he was reviewing the company's quality cost report. After he had implemented a quality-control program for three years, the company's defect rate had declined from 20 percent to 3 percent. Mr. Weldon patted Kenyata Terry, the production manager, on her back and said: "You have done a great job! I plan to reward you for your hard work. However, I want the defects to disappear completely before I promote you to the position of executive vice president. So, zero-defect is going to be your personal goal for the coming year." Ms. Terry responded wearily, "I'm not sure that's really a good idea."

### Required

Write a memorandum to the president explaining that zero defect is not a practical policy.

## PROBLEMS—SERIES B

**LO 1, 3**

### Problem 5-13B  *Comparing an ABC system with a traditional costing system*

Since its inception, Ray Laboratory, has produced a single product, Product S109. With the advent of automation, the company added the technological capability to begin producing a second product, Product N227. Because of the success of Product N227, manufacturing has been shifting toward its production. Sales of Product N227 are now 50 percent of the total annual sales of 20,000 units, and the company is optimistic about the new product's future sales growth. One reason the company is excited about the sales potential of its new product is that the new product's gross profit margin is higher than that of Product S109. Management is thrilled with the new product's initial success but concerned about the company's declining profits since the product's introduction. Suspecting a problem with the company's costing system, management hires you to investigate.

In reviewing the company's records, product specifications, and manufacturing processes, you discover the following information.

1. The company is in an extremely competitive industry in which markups are low and accurate estimates of cost are critical to success.

2. Product N227 has complex parts that require more labor, machine time, setups, and inspections than Product S109.

3. Budgeted costs for direct materials and labor follow.

| Direct Cost per Unit | Product S109 | Product N227 |
|---|---|---|
| Direct materials | $25 | $25 |
| Direct labor | $10/hour × 2 hours production time | $10/hour × 2.8 hours production time |

4. The company presently allocates overhead costs to its products based on direct labor hours. After carefully studying the company's overhead, you identify four different categories of overhead costs. Using your knowledge of this company and similar companies in the same industry, you estimate the total costs for each of these categories and identify the most appropriate cost driver for measuring each product's overhead consumption. Detailed information for each cost category follows.

| Category | Estimated Cost | Cost Driver | Use of Cost Driver |
|---|---|---|---|
| Unit level | $ 540,000 | Number of machine hours | S109: 20,000 hours; N227: 60,000 hours |
| Batch level | 228,000 | Number of machine setups | S109: 1,500; N227: 3,500 |
| Product level | 180,000 | Number of inspections | S109: 200; N227: 600 |
| Facility level | 60,000 | Equal percentage for products | S109: 50%; N227: 50% |
| Total | $1,008,000 | | |

### Required

**a.** Determine the predetermined overhead rate the company is using.

**b.** Compute the amount of overhead the company assigns to each product using this rate.

**c.** Determine the cost per unit and total cost of each product when overhead is assigned based on direct labor hours.

**d.** To remain competitive, the company prices its products at only 20 percent above cost. Compute the price for each product with this markup.

**e.** Compute the overhead rate for each category of activity.

**f.** Determine the amount of overhead cost, both in total and per unit, that would be assigned to each product if the company switched to activity-based costing.

**g.** Assuming that prices are adjusted to reflect activity-based costs, determine the revised price for each product.

**h.** Based on your results for Requirements *f* and *g*, explain why Product N227 costs more to make than previously apparent and why sales prices therefore need to be adjusted.

### Problem 5-14B  *Using activity-based costing to improve allocation accuracy*

**LO 1, 3**

Kelvin's Commemoratives makes and sells two types of decorative plates. One plate displays a hand-painted image of Princess Diana; the other plate displays a machine-pressed image of Marilyn Monroe. The Diana plates require 25,000 hours of direct labor to make; the Monroe plates require only 5,000 hours of direct labor. Overhead costs are composed of (1) $210,000 machine-related activity costs including indirect labor, utilities, and depreciation and (2) $150,000 labor-related activity costs including overtime pay, fringe benefits, and payroll taxes.

### Required

**a.** Assuming that Kelvin's uses direct labor hours as the allocation base, determine the amount of the total $240,000 overhead cost that would be allocated to each type of plate.

**b.** Explain why using direct labor hours may distort the allocation of overhead cost to the two products.

**c.** Explain how activity-based costing could improve the accuracy of the overhead cost allocation.

### Problem 5-15B  *Using activity-based costing to improve allocation accuracy*

**LO 1, 3**

*This problem is an extension of Problem 5-14B, which must be completed first.*
Assume the same data as in Problem 5-14B with the following additional information. The hours of machine time for processing plates are 1,000 for Diana plates and 2,500 for Monroe plates.

### Required

**a.** Establish two activity centers, one for machine-related activities and the second for labor-related activities. Assign the total overhead costs to the two activity centers.

**b.** Allocate the machine-related overhead costs to each product based on machine hours.

**c.** Allocate the labor-related overhead costs to each product based on direct labor hours.

**d.** Draw a diagram that compares the one-stage allocation method used in Problem 5-14B with the two-stage activity-based costing approach used in this problem.

**Problem 5-16B**   *Using activity-based costing to improve business decisions*

Wattson CPA and Associates is a local accounting firm specializing in bookkeeping and tax services. The firm has four certified public accountants who supervise 20 clerks. The clerks handle basic bookkeeping jobs and prepare tax return drafts. The CPAs review and approve the bookkeeping jobs and tax returns. Each CPA receives a fixed salary of $7,500 per month; the clerks earn an hourly rate of $18. Because the clerks are paid by the hour and their work hours can be directly traced to individual jobs, their wages are considered direct costs. The CPAs' salaries are not traced to individual jobs and are therefore treated as indirect costs. The firm allocates overhead based on direct labor hours. The following is Wattson's income statement for the previous month.

|  | Bookkeeping | Tax | Total |
|---|---|---|---|
| Revenues | $70,000 | $70,000 | $140,000 |
| Direct expenses | (22,500)* | (22,500)* | (45,000) |
| Indirect supervisory expenses | (15,000) | (15,000) | (30,000) |
| Net income | $32,500 | $32,500 | $ 65,000 |

*1,250 clerical hours were used in each category during the previous month.

Loretta Wattson, CPA and chief executive officer, is not sure that the two operations are equally profitable as the income statement indicates. First, she believes that most of the CPAs' time was spent instructing clerks in tax return preparation. The bookkeeping jobs appear to be routine, and most of the clerks can handle them with little supervision. After attending a recent professional development seminar on activity-based costing (ABC), Ms. Wattson believes that the allocation of indirect costs can be more closely traced to different types of services. To facilitate an activity-based analysis, she asked the CPAs to document their work hours on individual jobs for the last week. The results indicate that, on average, 25 percent of the CPAs' hours was spent supervising bookkeeping activities and the remaining 75 percent was spent supervising tax activities.

**Required**

a. Based on the preceding information, reconstruct the income statement for bookkeeping services, tax services, and the total, assuming that Wattson revises its allocation of indirect supervisory costs based on ABC.

b. Comment on the results and recommend a new business strategy.

**Problem 5-17B**   *Key activity-based costing concepts*

Yoder Boot and Shoe Company makes hand-sewn boots and shoes. Yoder uses a companywide overhead rate based on direct labor hours to allocate indirect manufacturing costs to its products. Making a pair of boots normally requires 2.4 hours of direct labor, and making a pair of shoes requires 1.8 hours. The company's shoe division, facing increased competition from international companies that have access to cheap labor, has responded by automating its shoe production. The reengineering process was expensive, requiring the purchase of manufacturing equipment and the restructuring of the plant layout. In addition, utility and maintenance costs increased significantly for operating the new equipment. Even so, labor costs decreased significantly. Now making a pair of shoes requires only 18 minutes of direct labor. As predicted, the labor savings more than offset the increase in overhead cost, thereby reducing the total cost to make a pair of shoes. The company experienced an unexpected side effect, however; according to the company's accounting records, the cost to make a pair of boots increased although the manufacturing process in the boot division was not affected by the reengineering of the shoe division. In other words, the cost of boots increased although Yoder did not change anything about the way it makes them.

**Required**

a. Explain why the accounting records reflected an increase in the cost to make a pair of boots.
b. Explain how the companywide overhead rate could result in the underpricing of shoes.
c. Explain how activity-based costing could improve the accuracy of overhead cost allocations.

## Problem 5-18B   *Pricing decisions made with ABC system cost data*

**LO 3**

Pittman Furniture Corporation makes two types of dining tables, Elegance for formal dining and Comfort for casual dining, at its single factory. With the economy beginning to experience a recession, Justin Pittman, the president, is concerned about whether the company can stay in business as market prices fall. At Mr. Pittman's request, Yamini Sing, the controller, prepared cost data for analysis.

Inspectors are paid according to the number of actual hours worked, determined by the number of tables inspected. Engineers, who set up equipment for both products, are paid monthly salaries. TV commercial fees are paid at the beginning of the quarter.

| Direct Cost | Elegance (E) | Comfort (C) |
|---|---|---|
| Direct materials | $50 per unit | $30 per unit |
| Direct labor | $36 per hour × 1.5 hours production time | $36 per hour × 1 hour production time |

| Category | Estimated Cost | Cost Driver | Use of Cost Driver |
|---|---|---|---|
| Product inspection | $120,000 | Number of units | E: 2,500 units; C: 7,500 units |
| Machine setups | 75,000 | Number of setups | E: 23 setups; C: 27 setups |
| Product advertising | 210,000 | Number of TV commercials | E: 5; C: 9 |
| Facility depreciation | 405,000 | Number of machine hours | E: 5,000 hours; C: 5,000 hours |
| Total | $810,000 | | |

**Required**

a. Compute the cost per unit for each product.
b. If management wants to make 30 percent of cost as a profit margin for Elegance, what price should the company set?
c. The market price of tables in the Comfort class has declined because of the recession. Management asks you to determine the minimum cost of producing Comfort tables in the short term. Provide that information.

## Problem 5-19B   *Target pricing and target costing with ABC*

**LO 3**

Ricardo Corporation manufactures two models of watches. Model Wonder displays cartoon characters and has simple features designed for kids. Model Marvel has sophisticated features such as dual time zones and an attached calculator. Ricardo's product design team has worked with a cost accountant to prepare a budget for the two products for the next fiscal year as follows.

| Direct Cost | Wonder (W) | Marvel (M) |
|---|---|---|
| Direct materials | $10 per unit | $20 per unit |
| Direct labor | $40/hour × 0.3 hour production time | $40/hour × 0.7 hour production time |

| Category | Estimated Cost | Cost Driver | Use of Cost Driver |
|---|---|---|---|
| Materials handling | $366,000 | Number of parts | W: 700,000; M: 520,000 |
| Machine setups | 180,000 | Number of setups | W: 50; M: 40 |
| Product testing | 28,000 | Number of units tested | W: 1,000; M: 400 |
| Facility depreciation | 360,000 | Number of machine hours | W: 3,200; M: 4,000 |
| Total | $934,000 | | |

Wonder watches have 35 parts, and Marvel watches have 65 parts. The budget calls for producing 20,000 units of Wonder and 8,000 units of Marvel. Ricardo tests 5 percent of its products for quality assurance. It sells all its products at market prices.

**Required**

a. Compute the cost per unit for each product.

b. The current market price for products comparable to Wonder is $43 and for products comparable to Marvel is $115. What will Ricardo's profit or loss for the next year be?

c. Ricardo likes to have a 25 percent profit margin based on the current market price for each product. What is the target cost for each product? What is the total target profit?

d. The president of Ricardo has asked the design team to refine the production design to bring down the product cost. After a series of redesigns, the team recommends a new process that requires purchasing a new machine that costs $400,000 and has five years of useful life and no salvage value. With the new process and the new machine, Ricardo can decrease the number of machine setups to four for each product and cut the cost of materials handling in half. The machine hours used will be 4,500 for Wonder and 6,500 for Marvel. Does this new process enable Ricardo to achieve its target costs?

**LO 3**

## Problem 5-20B    *Cost management with an ABC system*

Hayne Corporation manufactures two different coffee makers, Professional for commercial use and Home for family use. Dwight Hayne, the president, recently received complaints from some members of the board of directors about the company's failure to reach the expected profit of $200,000 per month. Mr. Hayne is, therefore, under great pressure to improve the company's bottom line. Under his direction, Alicia Meek, the controller, prepared the following monthly cost data for Mr. Hayne.

| Direct Cost | Professional (P) | Home (H) |
|---|---|---|
| Direct materials | $25 per unit | $9 per unit |
| Direct labor | $16 per hour × 0.8 hour production time | $16 per hour × 0.3 hour production time |

| Category | Estimated Cost | Cost Driver | Use of Cost Driver |
|---|---|---|---|
| Product inspection | $ 60,000 | Number of units | P: 15,000 units; H: 45,000 units |
| Machine setups | 15,000 | Number of setups | P: 30 setups; H: 45 setups |
| Product promotion | 200,000 | Number of TV commercials | P: 10; H: 10 |
| Facility depreciation | 295,000 | Number of machine hours | P: 7,160 hours; H: 4,640 hours |
| Total | $570,000 | | |

The market price for coffee makers comparable to Professional is $65 and to Home is $22. The company's administrative expenses amount to $125,000.

**Required**

a. Compute the cost per unit for both products.

b. Determine the company's profit or loss.

c. Charlie Chen, the marketing manager, recommends that the company implement a focused marketing strategy. He argues that advertisements in trade journals would be more effective for the commercial market than on TV. In addition, the cost of journal ads would be only $21,000. He also proposes sending discount coupons to targeted households to reach a broad market base. The coupons program would cost $72,000. Compute the new cost of each product, assuming that Mr. Hayne replaces TV advertising with Mr. Chen's suggestions.

d. Determine the company's profit or loss using the information in Requirement *c*.

## Problem 5-21B   *Assessing a quality control strategy*                    LO 4, 5

Carl Wallace, the president of Ritch Plastic Company, is a famous cost cutter in the plastics industry. Two years ago, he accepted an offer from Ritch's board of directors to help the company cut costs quickly. In fact, Mr. Wallace's compensation package included a year-end bonus tied to the percentage of cost decrease over the preceding year. On February 12, 2012, Mr. Wallace received comparative financial information for the two preceding years. He was especially interested in the results of his cost-cutting measures on quality control. The quality report shown below was extracted from the company's financial information.

**Required**

a. Explain the strategy that Mr. Wallace initiated to control Ritch's costs.

b. Indicate whether the strategy was successful or unsuccessful in reducing quality costs.

c. Explain how the strategy will likely affect the company's business in the long term.

| | 2011 | | 2010 | |
| --- | --- | --- | --- | --- |
| | Amount | Percentage | Amount | Percentage |
| **Prevention costs** | | | | |
| Engineering and design | $ 65,000 | 6.57% | $ 69,000 | 7.39% |
| Training and education | 26,000 | 2.63 | 76,000 | 8.14 |
| Depreciation on prevention equipment | 15,000 | 1.51 | 15,000 | 1.60 |
| Incentives and awards | 20,000 | 2.02 | 20,000 | 2.14 |
| Total prevention | 126,000 | 12.73% | 180,000 | 19.27% |
| **Appraisal costs** | | | | |
| Product and materials inspection | 33,000 | 3.33 | 73,000 | 7.82 |
| Reliability testing | 27,000 | 2.73 | 67,000 | 7.17 |
| Testing equipment (depreciation) | 38,000 | 3.83 | 38,000 | 4.07 |
| Supplies | 10,000 | 1.01 | 16,000 | 1.71 |
| Total appraisal | 108,000 | 10.90% | 194,000 | 20.77% |
| **Internal failure costs** | | | | |
| Scrap | 52,000 | 5.25 | 120,000 | 12.85 |
| Repair and rework | 46,000 | 4.65 | 150,000 | 16.06 |
| Downtime | 64,000 | 6.46 | 40,000 | 4.28 |
| Reinspection | 8,000 | 0.81 | 24,000 | 2.57 |
| Total internal failure | 170,000 | 17.17% | 334,000 | 35.76% |
| **External failure cost** | | | | |
| Warranty repairs and replacement | 347,000 | 35.05 | 125,000 | 13.38 |
| Freight | 75,000 | 7.58 | 31,000 | 3.32 |
| Customer relations | 45,000 | 4.55 | 28,000 | 3.00 |
| Restocking and packaging | 119,000 | 12.02 | 42,000 | 4.50 |
| Total external failure | 586,000 | 59.20% | 226,000 | 24.20% |
| Grand total | $990,000 | 100.00% | $934,000 | 100.00% |

## ANALYZE, THINK, COMMUNICATE

### ATC 5-1   Business Applications Case   *Using ABC to improve product pricing*

Drilling Innovations, Inc., produces specialized cutting heads used by companies that drill for oil and natural gas. The company has recently implemented an ABC system for three of its products and is interested in evaluating its effectiveness before converting to an ABC system for all products. To perform this evaluation, the company compiled data for the three products using both the traditional system and the new ABC system. The traditional system used a single driver (machine hours). The ABC system uses a variety of cost drivers related to the activities used to produce the cutting heads. The three products involved in the trial run of the ABC system were GS-157, HS-241, and OS-367. The following data relate to these products; unit data have been rounded to the nearest penny.

| Product | Selling Price per Unit | Units Produced | Total Costs Allocated: Traditional Costing | Cost per Unit: Traditional Costing | Total Cost Allocated: ABC | Costs per Unit: ABC |
|---|---|---|---|---|---|---|
| GS-157 | $19.30 | 120,000 | $1,600,000 | $13.33 | $1,500,000 | $12.50 |
| HS-241 | 17.50 | 90,000 | 1,100,000 | 12.22 | 1,050,000 | 11.67 |
| OS-367 | 15.10 | 40,000 | 400,000 | 10.00 | 550,000 | 13.75 |
| Totals | | | $3,100,000 | | $3,100,000 | |

### Required

a. Determine the gross profit margin for each product produced based on the ABC data [(Selling price − ABC cost per unit) × Units produced].

b. Determine the gross profit margin for each product produced based on the traditional costing data [(Selling price − Traditional cost per unit) × Units produced].

c. Provide an explanation as to why the cost of OS-367 may have increased under the ABC system while the cost of GS-157 decreased.

d. Suggest what action management might take with respect to the discoveries resulting from the ABC versus traditional costing analysis. Assume that Drilling Innovations expects to produce a gross profit margin on each product of at least 30 percent of the selling price.

### ATC 5-2   Group Assignment   *Using ABC in a service business*

A dialysis clinic provides two types of treatment for its patients. Hemodialysis (HD), an in-house treatment, requires that patients visit the clinic three times each week for dialysis treatments. Peritoneal dialysis (PD) permits patients to self-administer their treatments at home on a daily basis. On average, the clinic serves 102 HD patients and 62 PD patients. A recent development caused clinic administrators to develop a keen interest in cost measurement for the two separate services. Managed care plans such as HMOs began to pay treatment providers a fixed payment per insured participant regardless of the level of services provided by the clinic. With fixed fee revenues, the clinic was forced to control costs to ensure profitability. As a result, knowing the cost to provide HD versus PD services was critically important for the clinic. It needed accurate cost measurements to answer the following questions. Were both services profitable, or was one service carrying the burden of the other service? Should advertising be directed toward acquiring HD or PD patients? Should the clinic eliminate HMO service?

Management suspected the existing cost allocation system was inaccurate in measuring the true cost of providing the respective services; it had been developed in response to Medicare reporting requirements. It allocated costs between HD and PD based on the ratio of cost to charges (RCC). In other words, RCC allocates indirect costs in proportion to revenues. To illustrate, consider the allocation of $883,280 of indirect nursing services costs, which are allocated to the two treatment groups in relation to the revenue generated by each group.

Given that the clinic generated total revenue of $3,006,775, an allocation rate of 0.2937633 per revenue dollar was established ($883,280 ÷ $3,006,775). This rate was multiplied by the proportionate share of revenue generated by each service category to produce the following allocation.

| Type of Service | Service Revenue | × | Allocation Rate | = | Allocated Cost |
|---|---|---|---|---|---|
| HD | $1,860,287 | × | 0.2937633 | = | $546,484 |
| PD | 1,146,488 | × | 0.2937633 | = | 336,796 |
| Total | $3,006,775 | × | 0.2937633 | = | $883,280 |

To better assess the cost of providing each type of service, the clinic initiated an activity-based costing (ABC) system. The ABC approach divided the nursing service cost into four separate cost pools. A separate cost driver (allocation base) was identified for each cost pool. The cost pools and their respective cost drivers follow.

|  | Total | HD | PD |
|---|---|---|---|
| Nursing services cost pool categories |  |  |  |
| RNs | $239,120 | ? | ? |
| LPNs | 404,064 | ? | ? |
| Nursing administration and support staff | 115,168 | ? | ? |
| Dialysis machine operations (tech. salaries) | 124,928 | ? | ? |
| Total | $883,280 | ? | ? |

|  | Total | HD | PD |
|---|---|---|---|
| Activity cost drivers (corresponding to cost pools) |  |  |  |
| Number of RNs | 7 | 5 | 2 |
| Number of LPNs | 19 | 15 | 4 |
| Number of treatments (nursing administration) | 34,967 | 14,343 | 20,624 |
| Number of dialyzer treatments (machine operations) | 14,343 | 14,343 | 0 |

*Data Source:* T. D. West and D. A. West, "Applying ABC to Healthcare," *Management Accounting,* February 1999, pp. 22–33.

## Required

a. Organize the class into four sections and divide the sections into groups of four or five students each. Assign Task 1 to the first section of groups, Task 2 to the second section, Task 3 to the third section, and Task 4 to the fourth section.

## Group Tasks

(1) Allocate the RN cost pool between the HD and PD service centers.

(2) Allocate the LPN cost pool between the HD and PD service centers.

(3) Allocate the nursing administration and support staff cost pool between the HD and PD service centers.

(4) Allocate the dialysis machine operations cost pool between the HD and PD service centers.

b. Have the class determine the total cost to allocate to the two service centers in the following manner. Select a representative from each section and have the selected person go to the board. Each representative should supply the allocated cost for the cost pool assigned by her respective section. The instructor should total the amounts and compare the ABC cost allocations with those developed through the traditional RCC system.

c. The instructor should lead the class in a discussion that addresses the following questions.

   (1) Assuming that the ABC system provides a more accurate measure of cost, which service center (HD or PD) is overcosted by the traditional allocation system and which is undercosted?

   (2) What is the potential impact on pricing and profitability for both service centers?

   (3) How could management respond to the conditions described in the problem?

## ATC 5-3   Research Assignment   *Evaluating external failure costs with real world data*

The federal government maintains a website devoted to providing information about product recalls. To complete this assignment you will need to obtain information from this site as follows:

Go to recalls.gov

Click on the Consumer Products tab at the top of the screen

Click on CPSC Recalls—Home

Use the "Find Recalls by" month and year options to look up information about the following recalls that occurred in November 2009:

- ■ Maclaren USA Recalls to Repair Strollers Following Fingertip Amputations, and

- ■ Infant Entrapment and Suffocation Prompts Stork Craft to Recall . . .

### Required

For each of these two recalls:

a. Explain why the product was recalled.

b. Who was most responsible for the problem that resulted in the recall?

c. Who will be negatively affected by the faulty product?

d. What are the external failure costs related to the faulty product? Describe the nature of these costs; you will not be able to identify dollar amounts.

e. At what point in the pre-sale process could steps have been taken to prevent the faulty product from being produced and/or sold?

## ATC 5-4   Writing Assignment   *Assessing a strategy to control quality cost*

Lucy Sawyer, who owns and operates Sawyer Toy Company, is a perfectionist. She believes literally in the "zero-defects" approach to quality control. Her favorite saying is, "You can't spend too much on quality." Even so, in 2010 her company experienced an embarrassing breach of quality that required the national recall of a defective product. She vowed never to repeat the experience and instructed her staff to spend whatever it takes to ensure that products are delivered free of defects in 2011. She was somewhat disappointed with the 2011 year-end quality cost report shown here.

|  | 2010 | 2011 |
|---|---|---|
| Prevention costs | $120,000 | $ 80,000 |
| Appraisal costs | 240,000 | 430,000 |
| Internal failure costs | 140,000 | 560,000 |
| External failure cost | 320,000 | 210,000 |
| Total | $820,000 | $1,280,000 |

Although external failure costs had declined, they remained much higher than expected. The increased inspections had identified defects that were corrected, thereby avoiding another recall; however, the external failure costs were still too high. Ms. Sawyer responded by saying, "We will have to double our efforts." She authorized hiring additional inspectors and instructed her production supervisors to become more vigilant in identifying and correcting errors.

### Required

Assume that you are the chief financial officer (CFO) of Sawyer Toy Company. Ms. Sawyer has asked you to review the company's approach to quality control. Prepare a memo to her that evaluates the existing approach, and recommend changes in expenditure patterns that can improve profitability as well as increase the effectiveness of the quality control system.

### ATC 5-5   Ethical Dilemma   *Conflicts between controlling cost and providing social responsibility to patients*

This case examines potential ethical issues faced by the dialysis clinic described in ATC 5-2. It is, however, an independent case that students may study in conjunction with or separately from ATC 5-2. The dialysis clinic provides two types of treatment for its patients. Hemodialysis (HD), an in-house treatment, requires patients to visit the clinic three times each week. Peritoneal dialysis (PD) permits patients to self-administer their treatments at home on a daily basis. The clinic serves a number of HMO patients under a contract that limits collections from the HMO insurer to a fixed amount per patient. As a result, the clinic's profitability is directly related to its ability to control costs. To illustrate, assume that the clinic is paid a fixed annual fee of $15,000 per HMO patient served. Also assume that the current cost to provide health care averages $14,000 a year per patient, resulting in an average profitability of $1,000 per patient ($15,000 − $14,000). Because the revenue base is fixed, the only way the clinic can increase profitability is to lower its average cost of providing services. If the clinic fails to control costs and the average cost of patient care increases, profitability will decline. A recent ABC study suggests that the cost to provide HD service exceeds the amount of revenue generated from providing that service. The clinic is profitable because PD services generate enough profit to more than make up for losses on HD services.

#### Required

Respond to each potential scenario described here. Each scenario is independent of the others.

**a.** Suppose that as a result of the ABC analysis, the chief accountant, a certified management accountant (CMA), recommends that the clinic discontinue treating HD patients referred by the HMO provider. Based on this assumption, answer the following questions.

   **(1)** Assume that the clinic is located in a small town. If it discontinues treating the HD patients, they will be forced to drive 50 miles to the nearest alternative treatment center. Does the clinic have a moral obligation to society to continue to provide HD service although it is not profitable to do so?

   **(2)** The accountant's recommendation places profitability above the needs of HD patients. Does this recommendation violate any of the standards of ethical conduct described in Chapter 1, Exhibit 1.15?

**b.** Assume that the clinic continues to treat HD patients referred by HMOs. However, to compensate for the loss incurred on these patients, the clinic raises prices charged to non-HMO patients. Is it fair to require non-HMO patients to subsidize services provided to the HMO patients?

**c.** Suppose that the clinic administrators respond to the ABC data by cutting costs. The clinic overbooks HMO patients to ensure that downtime is avoided when cancellations occur. It reduces the RN nursing staff and assigns some of the technical work to less-qualified assistants. Ultimately, an overworked, underqualified nurse's aide makes a mistake, and a patient dies. Who is at fault—the HMO, the accountant who conducted the ABC analysis, or the clinic administrators who responded to the ABC information?

### ATC 5-6   Spreadsheet Assignment   *Using Excel*

Tameron Corporation produces video games in three market categories: commercial, home line, and miniature handheld. Tameron has traditionally allocated overhead costs to the three product categories using the companywide base of direct labor hours. The company recently switched to an ABC system when it installed computer-controlled assembly stations that rendered the traditional costing system ineffective. In implementing the ABC system, the company identified the cost pools and drivers shown in the following spreadsheet. The activity in each of the three product lines appears in rows 3 to 9. The pooled costs are shown in cells E11 to E15.

#### Required

Construct a spreadsheet like the following one to compute the total cost and cost per unit for each product line. Cells K4 to K9, G12 to I15, E19 to E28, G19 to G28, I19 to I28, and K26 should all be formulas.

**Microsoft Excel - ch05-working.xls**

File   Edit   View   Insert   Format   Tools   Data   Window   Help

O34

| | | | Commercial | Home Line | Miniature | Total |
|---|---|---|---|---|---|---|
| 1 | Chapter 5 - Working with Excel | | | Name: | | |
| 3 | b) | Driver | Commercial | Home Line | Miniature | Total |
| 4 | | Labor hours | 5,000 | 11,000 | 4,000 | 20,000 |
| 5 | | Machine hours | 13,000 | 44,000 | 23,000 | 80,000 |
| 6 | | # Production orders | 340 | 1,800 | 860 | 3,000 |
| 7 | | R&D time | 15% | 18% | 67% | 100% |
| 8 | | Units | 14,000 | 44,000 | 17,000 | 75,000 |
| 9 | | Sq. footage | 20,000 | 50,000 | 30,000 | 100,000 |

| | Cost type | Pooled Cost | Total Activity | Pool Rate | |
|---|---|---|---|---|---|
| Unit level | $ 620,000 | 80,000 | $ 7.75 | per mh |
| Batch level | 327,000 | 3,000 | $ 109.00 | per order |
| Product level | 185,000 | 100% | $ 185,000 | times % |
| Facility level | 530,000 | 100,000 | $ 5.30 | per sq. ft. |
| | $1,662,000 | | | |

| Product Cost: | | Commercial | | Home Line | | Miniature | Total |
|---|---|---|---|---|---|---|---|
| Direct materials cost | $30 | $ 420,000 | $20 | $ 880,000 | $25 | $ 425,000 | |
| Direct labor cost | 12 | 60,000 | 12 | 132,000 | 15 | 60,000 | |
| Allocated overhead | | | | | | | |
| Unit-level | | 100,750 | | 341,000 | | 178,250 | |
| Batch-level | | 37,060 | | 196,200 | | 93,740 | |
| Product-level | | 27,750 | | 33,300 | | 123,950 | |
| Facility-level | | 106,000 | | 265,000 | | 159,000 | |
| Total cost | | $ 751,560 | | $1,847,500 | | $1,039,940 | $3,639,000 |
| Cost per unit | | $ 53.68 | | $ 41.99 | | $ 61.17 | |

Sheet1   Sheet2   Sheet3

Ready                                                                 NUM

## ATC 5-7   Spreadsheet Assignment   *Mastering Excel*

Beasley Company makes three types of exercise machines. Data have been accumulated for four possible overhead drivers. Data for these four possible drivers are shown in rows 3 to 7 of the following spreadsheet.

### Required

Construct a spreadsheet that will allocate overhead and calculate unit cost for each of these alternative drivers. A screen capture of the spreadsheet and data follows.

**Microsoft Excel - ch05-mastering.xls**

File   Edit   View   Insert   Format   Tools   Data   Window   Help

F25

| | | Standard | Deluxe | Grand | Total |
|---|---|---|---|---|---|
| 1 | Chapter 5 - Mastering Excel | | Name: | | |
| 3 | Possible Drivers | Standard | Deluxe | Grand | Total |
| 4 | 1 Unit | 10,000 | 15,000 | 20,000 | 45,000 |
| 5 | 2 Setup | 100 | 500 | 400 | 1,000 |
| 6 | 3 Machine hour | 20,000 | 45,000 | 60,000 | 125,000 |
| 7 | 4 Labor hour | 4,000 | 9,000 | 16,000 | 29,000 |

9 Determine the effect of different cost drivers on overhead allocated and the resulting cost per unit.
10 To change the cost driver, insert the appropriate number (1-4) from the list above in cell B15.

12   Overhead Rate:

| | Overhead cost | $500,000 | | | |
|---|---|---|---|---|---|
| 1 | Units | = | 45,000 = | $ 11.11 | per unit |

| Cost | Standard | Deluxe | Grand | Total |
|---|---|---|---|---|
| Direct Materials | $ 12,000 | $ 36,000 | $ 80,000 | $ 128,000 |
| Direct Labor | 800 | 4,000 | 3,200 | 8,000 |
| Allocated Overhead | 111,111 | 166,667 | 222,222 | 500,000 |
| Total | $ 123,911 | $ 206,667 | $ 305,422 | $ 636,000 |
| Cost per unit | $ 12.39 | $ 13.78 | $ 15.27 | |

Sheet1   Sheet2   Sheet3

Ready                                                                 NUM

## Spreadsheet Tips

1. This spreadsheet uses a function called *vertical lookup.* This function can pull the appropriate values from a table. The form of this function is =VLOOKUP (value, table, column#). In this example, the table is in cells B4 to K7. Three examples of the use of VLOOKUP follow.

2. Cell C15 is =VLOOKUP (B15, B4:K7, 2). This function operates by using the one (1) in cell B15 to look up a value in the table. Notice that the table is defined as B4:K7 and that the function is looking up the value in the second column, which is Units.

3. Cell E15 is =VLOOKUP (B15, B4:K7, 10). In this case, the function is looking up the value in the tenth column, which is 45,000. Be sure to count empty columns.

4. Cell E20 is =VLOOKUP (B15, B4:K7, 4)*G15. In this case, the function is looking up the value in the fourth column, which is $10,000. Be sure to count empty columns.

5. Cells I15, G20, and I20 also use the VLOOKUP function.

6. After completing the spreadsheet, you can change the value in cell B15 (1-4) to see the effect of choosing a different driver for overhead.

## COMPREHENSIVE PROBLEM

To this point we have assumed the Magnificent Modems produced only one type of modem. Suppose instead we assume the company produces several different kinds of modems. The production process differs for each type of product. Some require more setup time than others, they are produced in different batch sizes, and they require different amounts of indirect labor (supervision). Packaging and delivery to customers also differs for each type of modem. Even so, Magnificent Modems uses a single allocation base (number of units) to allocate overhead costs.

### Required

Write a brief memo that explains how Magnificent Modems could benefit from an ABC costing system.

## CHAPTER 6

# Relevant Information for Special Decisions

## LEARNING OBJECTIVES

**After you have mastered the material in this chapter, you will be able to:**

1 Identify the characteristics of relevant information.

2 Distinguish between unit-level, batch-level, product-level, and facility-level costs and understand how these costs affect decision making.

3 Make appropriate special order decisions.

4 Make appropriate outsourcing decisions.

5 Make appropriate segment elimination decisions.

6 Make appropriate asset replacement decisions.

7 Explain the conflict between short-term and long-term profitability (Appendix).

8 Make decisions about allocating scarce resources (Appendix).

## CHAPTER OPENING

Mary Daniels paid $25,000 to purchase a car that was used in her rental business. After one year the car had a book value of $21,000. Ms. Daniels needs cash and is considering selling the car. After advertising the vehicle for sale, the best offer she received was $19,000. Ms. Daniels really needed the money, but ultimately decided not to sell because she did not want to incur a $2,000 loss ($21,000 market value − $19,000 book value). Did Ms. Daniels make the right decision?

Whether Ms. Daniels will be better off selling the car or keeping it is unknown. However, it is certain that she based her decision on irrelevant data. Ms. Daniels incurred a loss when the market value of the car dropped. She cannot avoid a loss that already exists. Past mistakes should not affect current decisions. The current value of the car is $19,000. Ms. Daniels's decision is whether to take the money or keep the car. The book value of the car is not relevant. This chapter explains how to isolate and focus on the variables that are relevant in the decision-making process.

# The Curious Accountant

In July 2009, the authors compared the prices of 10 of the top selling prescription drugs at two large on-line pharmacies, one in the United States and one in Canada. The analysis showed the Canadian prices for these 10 popular prescription drugs, such as **Lipitor** and **Zocor**, were only 51 percent of prices charged in the United States.

Major pharmaceutical companies have earnings before tax that average around 25 percent of sales, indicating that their costs average around 75 percent of the prices they charge. In other words, it costs approximately $75 to generate $100 of revenue. Given that drugs are sold in Canada for 51 percent of the U.S. sales price, a drug that is sold in the U.S. for $100 would be sold in Canada for only $51.

How can drugs be sold in Canada for less ($51) than cost ($75)? (Answer on page 259.)

# RELEVANT INFORMATION

Identify the characteristics of relevant information.

How can you avoid irrelevant information when making decisions? Two primary characteristics distinguish relevant from useless information. Specifically, **relevant information** (1) differs among the alternatives and (2) is future oriented.

The first characteristic recognizes that relevant information differs for one or more of the alternatives being considered. Suppose the car Ms. Daniels is considering selling is due for a state required safety inspection. Further assume that the inspection must be completed before the car can be sold or driven. Since the inspection fee must be paid regardless of whether Ms. Daniels keeps or sells the car, it does not differ among the alternatives and therefore is not relevant to her decision. In contrast, assume the car is due for an oil change that can be delayed until after the car is sold. Since Ms. Daniels can avoid the cost of the oil change if she sells the car but must pay for the oil change if she keeps the car, the cost of the oil change differs between the alternatives and is relevant to her decision.

The second characteristic of relevant information is that it impacts the future. "Don't cry over spilt milk." "It's water over the dam." These aphorisms remind people they cannot change the past. With regard to business decisions, the principle means you cannot avoid a cost that has already been incurred. In the Daniels example, the historical cost ($25,000) of the car is not relevant to a decision regarding whether to sell the car today. The current market value of $19,000 is relevant to the decision regarding whether to sell the car today.

It is interesting to note that the two characteristics are merely different views of the same concept because historical information does not differ between the alternatives. In other words, we could say that historical costs are not relevant because they do not differ between alternatives associated with current decisions.

## Sunk Cost

Historical costs are frequently called *sunk costs.* Since **sunk costs** have been incurred in past transactions, they cannot be changed and are not relevant for making current decisions. The $25,000 original cost of the car in the Daniels example is a sunk cost.

Why even bother to collect historical information if it is not relevant? Historical information may be useful in predicting the future. A company that earned $5 million last year is more likely to earn $5 million this year than a company that earned $5,000 last year. The predictive capacity is relevant because it provides insight into the future.

## Opportunity Costs

An **opportunity cost** is the sacrifice that is incurred in order to obtain an alternative opportunity. For example, in the above case, Ms. Daniels must give up the opportunity to obtain $19,000 in order to keep the car. So, the opportunity cost of owning the car is $19,000. Since this cost differs between the alternatives of owning the car versus selling it and since it affects the present or future, it is relevant to the decision regarding whether to keep or sell the car.

The best offer that Ms. Daniels received for the car was $19,000. Suppose Ms. Daniels also received the less favorable offer of $18,000. Does this mean that the opportunity cost of keeping the car is $37,000 ($18,000 + $19,000)? No. Opportunity costs are not cumulative. Ms. Daniels really has only one opportunity. If she accepts the $19,000 offer, she must reject the $18,000 offer or vice versa. Accountants normally measure opportunity cost as the highest value of the available alternatives. In this case, the opportunity cost of keeping the car is $19,000.

## ✓ CHECK YOURSELF 6.1

Aqua, Inc., makes statues for use in fountains. On January 1, 2011, the company paid $13,500 for a mold to make a particular type of statue. The mold had an expected useful life of four years and a salvage value of $1,500. On January 1, 2013, the mold had a market value of $3,000 and a salvage value of $1,200. The expected useful life did not change. What is the relevant cost of using the mold during 2013?

**Answer**   The relevant cost of using the mold in 2013 is the opportunity cost [(market value − salvage value) ÷ remaining useful life], in this case, ($3,000 − $1,200) ÷ 2 = $900. The book value of the asset and associated depreciation is based on a sunk cost that cannot be avoided because it has already been incurred and therefore is not relevant to current decisions. In contrast, Aqua could avoid the opportunity cost (market value) by selling the mold.

## Relevance Is an Independent Concept

The concept of relevance is independent from the concept of cost behavior. In a given circumstance, **relevant costs** could be either fixed or variable. Consider the following illustration. Executives of Better Bakery Products are debating whether to add a new product, either cakes or pies, to the company's line. Projected costs for the two options follow.

| Cost of Cakes | | Cost of Pies | |
|---|---|---|---|
| Materials (per unit) | $    1.50 | Materials (per unit) | $    2.00 |
| Direct labor (per unit) | 1.00 | Direct labor (per unit) | 1.00 |
| Supervisor's salary* | 25,000.00 | Supervisor's salary* | 25,000.00 |
| Franchise fee† | 50,000.00 | Advertising‡ | 40,000.00 |

*It will be necessary to hire a new production supervisor at a cost of $25,000 per year.

†Cakes will be distributed under a nationally advertised label. Better Bakery pays an annual franchise fee for the right to use the product label. Because of the established brand name, Better Bakery will not be required to advertise the product.

‡Better Bakery will market the pies under its own name and will advertise the product in the local market in which the product sells.

Which costs are relevant? Fifty cents per unit of the materials can be avoided by choosing cakes instead of pies. A portion of the materials cost is therefore relevant. Labor costs will be one dollar per unit whether Better Bakery makes cakes or pies.

# REALITY BYTES

Determining what price to charge for their company's goods or services is one of the most difficult decisions that business managers make. Charge too much and customers will go elsewhere. Charge less than customers are willing to pay and lose the opportunity to earn profits. This problem is especially difficult when managers are deciding if they should reduce (mark down) the price of aging inventory—for example, flowers that are beginning to wilt, fruit that is beginning to overripen, or clothing that is going out of season.

At first managers may be reluctant to mark down the inventory below its cost because this would cause the company to take a loss on the aging inventory. However, the concept of sunk cost applies here. Since the existing inventory has already been paid for, its cost is sunk. Since the cost is sunk it is not relevant to the decision. Does this mean the merchandise should be sold for any price? Not necessarily. The concept of opportunity cost must also be considered.

If the goods are marked down too far, too quickly, they may be sold for less than is possible. The lost potential revenue is an opportunity cost. To minimize the opportunity cost, the amount of a markdown must be the smallest amount necessary to sell the merchandise. The decision is further complicated by qualitative considerations. If a business develops a reputation for repeated markdowns, customers may hesitate to buy goods, thinking that the price will fall further if they only wait a while. The result is a dilemma as to when and how much to mark down aging inventories.

How do managers address this dilemma? Part of the answer has been the use of technology. For years airlines have used computerized mathematical models to help them decide how many seats on a particular flight should be sold at a discount. More recently, retailers began using this same type of modeling software. Such software allows retailers to take fewer markdowns at more appropriate times, thereby resulting in higher overall gross profit margins.

Labor cost is therefore not relevant. Although both materials and direct labor are variable costs, one is relevant but the other is not.

Since Better Bakery must hire a supervisor under either alternative, the supervisor's salary is not relevant. The franchise fee can be avoided if Better Bakery makes pies and advertising costs can be avoided if it makes cakes. All three of these costs are fixed, but only two are relevant. Finally, all the costs (whether fixed or variable) could be avoided if Better Bakery rejects both products. Whether a cost is fixed or variable has no bearing on its relevance.

## Relevance Is Context Sensitive

A particular cost that is relevant in one context may be irrelevant in another. Consider a store that carries men's, women's, and children's clothing. The store manager's salary could not be avoided by eliminating the children's department, but it could be avoided if the entire store were closed. The salary is not relevant to deciding whether to eliminate the children's department but is relevant with respect to deciding to close the store. In one context, the salary is not relevant. In the other context, it is relevant.

## Relationship between Relevance and Accuracy

Information need not be exact to be relevant. You may decide to delay purchasing a laptop computer you want if you know its price is going to drop even if you don't know exactly how much the price decrease will be. You know part of the cost can be avoided by waiting; you are just not sure of the amount.

The most useful information is both relevant and precise. Totally inaccurate information is useless. Likewise, irrelevant information is useless regardless of its accuracy.

## Quantitative versus Qualitative Characteristics of Decision Making

Relevant information can have both **quantitative** and **qualitative characteristics.** The previous examples focused on quantitative data. Now consider qualitative issues. Suppose you are deciding which of two laptop computers to purchase. Computer A costs $300 more than Computer B. Both computers satisfy your technical requirements; however, Computer A has a more attractive appearance. From a quantitative standpoint, you would select Computer B because you could avoid $300 of cost. However, if the laptop will be used in circumstances where clients need to be impressed, appearance—a qualitative characteristic—may be more important than minimizing cost. You might purchase Computer A even though quantitative factors favor Computer B. Both qualitative and quantitative data are relevant to decision making.

As with quantitative data, qualitative features must *differ* between the alternatives to be relevant. If the two computers were identical in appearance, attractiveness would not be relevant to making the decision.

## Differential Revenue and Avoidable Cost

Since relevant revenue *differs* among the alternatives, it is sometimes called **differential revenue.** To illustrate, assume Pecks Department Stores sells men's, women's, and children's clothing and is considering eliminating the children's line. The revenue generated by the children's department is differential (relevant) revenue because Pecks' total revenue would be different if the children's department were eliminated.

Why would Pecks consider eliminating the children's department and thereby lose the differential (relevant) revenue? Pecks may be able to save more by eliminating the cost of operating the department than it loses in differential revenue. Some but not all of the costs associated with operating the children's department can be saved. For example, if Pecks Department Stores eliminates the children's department, the company can eliminate the cost of the department manager's salary but cannot get rid of the salary of the company president. The costs that stay the same are not relevant. The costs that can be *avoided* by closing the department are relevant. Indeed, relevant costs are frequently called *avoidable costs.*

**Avoidable costs** are the costs managers can eliminate by making specific choices. In the Pecks example, the cost of the department manager's salary is an avoidable (relevant) cost. The cost of the president's salary is not avoidable and is not relevant to the elimination decision.

## RELATIONSHIP OF COST AVOIDANCE TO A COST HIERARCHY

Classifying costs into one of four hierarchical levels helps identify avoidable costs.[1]

Distinguish between unit-level, batch-level, product-level, and facility-level costs and understand how these costs affect decision making.

1.  *Unit-level costs.* Costs incurred each time a company generates one unit of product are **unit-level costs.**[2] Examples include the cost of direct materials, direct labor, inspections, packaging, shipping, and handling. Incremental (additional) unit-level costs increase *with each additional unit of product generated. Unit-level costs can be avoided by eliminating the production of a single unit of product.*

2.  *Batch-level costs.* Many products are generated in batches rather than individual units. For example, a heating and air conditioning technician may service a batch of air conditioners in an apartment complex. Some of the job costs apply only to individual units, and other costs relate to the entire batch. For instance, the labor to service each air conditioner is a unit-level cost, but the cost of driving to the site is a **batch-level cost.**

    Classifying costs as unit- versus batch-level frequently depends on the context rather than the type of cost. For example, shipping and handling costs to send 200 computers to a university are batch-level costs. In contrast, the shipping and handling cost to deliver a single computer to each of a number of individual customers is a unit-level cost. Eliminating a batch of work avoids both batch-level and unit-level costs. Similarly, adding a batch of work increases batch-level and unit-level costs. Increasing the number of units in a particular batch increases unit-level but not batch-level costs. Decreasing the number of units in a batch reduces unit-level costs but not batch-level costs.

3.  *Product-level costs.* Costs incurred to support specific products or services are called **product-level costs.** Product-level costs include quality inspection costs, engineering design costs, the costs of obtaining and defending patents, the costs of regulatory compliance, and inventory holding costs such as interest, insurance, maintenance, and storage. *Product-level costs can be avoided by discontinuing a product line.* For example, suppose the Snapper Company makes the engines used in its lawn mowers. Buying engines from an outside supplier instead of making them would allow Snapper to avoid the product-level costs such as legal fees for patents, manufacturing supervisory costs of producing the engines, and the maintenance and inventory costs of holding engine parts.

4.  *Facility-level costs.* **Facility-level costs** are incurred to support the entire company. They are not related to any specific product, batch, or unit of product. Because these costs maintain the facility as a whole, they are frequently called *facility-sustaining costs.* Facility-level costs include building rent or depreciation, personnel administration and training, property and real estate taxes, insurance, maintenance, administrative salaries, general selling costs, landscaping, utilities,

---

[1]R. Cooper and R. S. Kaplan, *The Design of Cost Management Systems* (Englewood Cliffs, NJ: Prentice-Hall, 1991). Our classifications are broader than those typically presented. They encompass service and merchandising companies as well as manufacturing businesses. The original cost hierarchy was developed as a platform for activity-based costing, a topic introduced in the previous chapter. These classifications are equally useful as a tool for identifying avoidable costs.

[2]Recall that we use the term *product* in a generic sense to represent producing goods or services.

and security. Total facility-level costs cannot be avoided unless the entire company is dissolved. However, eliminating a business segment (such as a division, department, or office) may enable a company to avoid some facility-level costs. For example, if a bank eliminates one of its branches, it can avoid the costs of renting, maintaining, and insuring that particular branch building. In general, *segment-level* facility costs can be avoided when a segment is eliminated. In contrast, *corporate-level* facility costs cannot be avoided unless the corporation is eliminated.

Precise distinctions between the various categories are often difficult to draw. One company may incur sales staff salaries as a facility-level cost while another company may pay sales commissions traceable to product lines or even specific units of a product line. Cost classifications cannot be memorized. Classifying specific cost items into the appropriate categories requires thoughtful judgment.

# RELEVANT INFORMATION AND SPECIAL DECISIONS

Make appropriate special order decisions.

Five types of special decisions are frequently encountered in business practice: (1) special order, (2) outsourcing, (3) segment elimination, (4) asset replacement, and (5) scarce resource allocation. The following sections discuss using relevant information in making the first four types of special decisions. The Appendix to this chapter discusses scarce resource decisions.

## Special Order Decisions

Occasionally, a company receives an offer to sell its goods at a price significantly below its normal selling price. The company must make a **special order decision** to accept or reject the offer.

### EXHIBIT 6.1

**Budgeted Cost for Expected Production of 2,000 Printers**

| | | |
|---|---:|---:|
| Unit-level costs | | |
|   Materials costs (2,000 units × $90) | $180,000 | |
|   Labor costs (2,000 units × $82.50) | 165,000 | |
|   Overhead (2,000 units × $7.50) | 15,000 | |
|   Total unit-level costs (2,000 × $180) | | $360,000 |
| Batch-level costs | | |
|   Assembly setup (10 batches × $1,700) | 17,000 | |
|   Materials handling (10 batches × $500) | 5,000 | |
|   Total batch-level costs (10 batches × $2,200) | | 22,000 |
| Product-level costs | | |
|   Engineering design | 14,000 | |
|   Production manager salary | 63,300 | |
|   Total product-level costs | | 77,300 |
| Facility-level costs | | |
|   Segment-level costs: | | |
|     Division manager's salary | 85,000 | |
|     Administrative costs | 12,700 | |
|   Allocated—corporate-level costs: | | |
|     Company president's salary | 43,200 | |
|     Building rental | 27,300 | |
|     General expenses | 31,000 | |
|   Total facility-level costs | | 199,200 |
| Total expected cost | | $658,500 |
| Cost per unit: $658,500 ÷ 2,000 = $329.25 | | |

### Quantitative Analysis

Assume Premier Office Products manufactures printers. Premier expects to make and sell 2,000 printers in 10 batches of 200 units per batch during the coming year. Expected production costs are summarized in Exhibit 6.1.

Adding its normal markup to the total cost per unit, Premier set the selling price at $360 per printer.

Suppose Premier receives a *special order* from a new customer for 200 printers. If Premier accepts the order, its expected sales would increase from 2,000 units to 2,200 units. But the special order customer is willing to pay only $250 per printer. This price is well below not only Premier's normal selling price of $360 but also the company's expected per unit cost of $329.25. Should Premier accept or reject the special order? At first glance, it seems Premier should reject the special order because the customer's offer is below the expected cost per unit. Analyzing relevant costs and revenue leads, however, to a different conclusion.

The quantitative analysis follows in three steps.

**Step 1.** **Determine the amount of the relevant (differential) revenue Premier will earn by accepting the special order.** Premier's alternatives are (1) to accept or (2) to

## Answers to The Curious Accountant

There are several factors that enable drug companies to reduce their prices to certain customers. One significant factor is the issue of relevant cost.

Pharmaceutical manufacturers have a substantial amount of fixed cost, such as research and development. For example, in 2008 **Pfizer Inc.** had research and development expenses that were 16.5 percent of sales, while its cost of goods sold expense was almost the same at 16.8 percent of sales. With respect to a special order decision, the research and development costs would not change and therefore would not be relevant. In contrast, the unit-level cost of goods sold would increase and therefore would be relevant. Clearly, relevant costs are significantly less than the total cost. If Canadian prices are based on relevant costs, that is, if drug companies view Canadian sales as a special order opportunity, the lower prices may provide a contribution to profitability even though they are significantly less than the prices charged in the United States.

reject the special order. If Premier accepts the special order, additional revenue will be $50,000 ($250 × 200 units). If Premier rejects the special order, additional revenue will be zero. Since the amount of revenue differs between the alternatives, the $50,000 is relevant.

**Step 2.    Determine the amount of the relevant (differential) cost Premier will incur by accepting the special order.** Examine the costs in Exhibit 6.1. If Premier accepts the special order, it will incur additional unit-level costs (materials, labor, and overhead). It will also incur the cost of one additional 200-unit batch. The unit- and batch-level costs are relevant because Premier could avoid them by rejecting the special order. The other costs in Exhibit 6.1 are not relevant because Premier will incur them whether it accepts or rejects the special order.

**Step 3.    Accept the special order if the relevant revenue exceeds the relevant (avoidable) cost. Reject the order if relevant cost exceeds relevant revenue.** Exhibit 6.2 summarizes the relevant figures. Since the relevant revenue exceeds the relevant cost, Premier should accept the special order because profitability will increase by $11,800.

### EXHIBIT 6.2

**Relevant Information for Special Order of 200 Printers**

| | |
|---|---|
| Differential revenue ($250 × 200 units) | $50,000 |
| Avoidable unit-level costs ($180 × 200 units) | (36,000) |
| Avoidable batch-level costs ($2,200 × 1 batch) | (2,200) |
| Contribution to income | $11,800 |

### *Opportunity Costs*

Premier can consider the special order because it has enough excess productive capacity to make the additional units. Suppose Premier has the opportunity to lease its excess capacity (currently unused building and equipment) for $15,000. If Premier uses the excess capacity to make the additional printers, it must forgo the opportunity to lease the excess capacity to a third party. Sacrificing the potential leasing income represents an opportunity cost of accepting the special order. Adding this opportunity cost to the other relevant costs increases the cost of accepting the special order to $53,200 ($38,200 unit-level and batch-level costs + $15,000 opportunity cost). The avoidable costs would then exceed the differential revenue, resulting in a projected loss of $3,200 ($50,000 differential revenue − $53,200 avoidable costs). Under these circumstances Premier would be better off rejecting the special order and leasing the excess capacity.

### Relevance and the Decision Context

Assume Premier does not have the opportunity to lease its excess capacity. Recall the original analysis indicated the company could earn an $11,800 contribution to profit by accepting a special order to sell 200 printers at $250 per unit (see Exhibit 6.2). Because Premier can earn a contribution to profit by selling printers for $250 each, can the company reduce its normal selling price (price charged to existing customers) to $250? The answer is no, as illustrated in Exhibit 6.3.

### EXHIBIT 6.3

**Projections Based on 2,200 Printers at a Sales Price of $250 per Unit**

| | | |
|---|---:|---:|
| Revenue ($250 × 2,200 units) | | $ 550,000 |
| Unit-level supplies and inspection ($180 × 2,200 units) | $396,000 | |
| Batch-level costs ($2,200 × 11 batches) | 24,200 | |
| Product-level costs | 77,300 | |
| Facility-level costs | 199,200 | |
| Total cost | | (696,700) |
| Projected loss | | $(146,700) |

If a company is to be profitable, it must ultimately generate revenue in excess of total costs. Although the facility-level and product-level costs are not relevant to the special order decision, they are relevant to the operation of the business as a whole.

### Qualitative Characteristics

Should a company ever reject a special order if the relevant revenues exceed the relevant costs? Qualitative characteristics may be even more important than quantitative ones. If Premier's regular customers learn the company sold printers to another buyer at $250 per unit, they may demand reduced prices on future purchases. Exhibit 6.3 shows Premier cannot reduce the price for all customers. Special order customers should therefore come from outside Premier's normal sales territory. In addition, special order customers should be advised that the special price does not apply to repeat business. Cutting off a special order customer who has been permitted to establish a continuing relationship is likely to lead to ill-feelings and harsh words. A business's reputation can depend on how management handles such relationships. Finally, at full capacity, Premier should reject any special orders at reduced prices because filling those orders reduces its ability to satisfy customers who pay full price.

## Outsourcing Decisions

Make appropriate outsourcing decisions.

Companies can sometimes purchase products they need for less than it would cost to make them. This circumstance explains why automobile manufacturers purchase rather than make many of the parts in their cars or why a caterer might buy gourmet desserts from a specialty company. Buying goods and services from other companies rather than producing them internally is commonly called **outsourcing.**

## Quantitative Analysis

Assume Premier Office Products is considering whether to outsource production of the printers it currently makes. A supplier has offered to sell an unlimited supply of printers to Premier for $240 each. The estimated cost of making the printers is $329.25 per unit (see Exhibit 6.1). The data suggest that Premier could save money by outsourcing. Analyzing relevant costs proves this presumption wrong.

A two-step quantitative analysis for the outsourcing decision follows:

**Step 1.** **Determine the production costs Premier can avoid if it outsources printer production.** A review of Exhibit 6.1 discloses the costs Premier could avoid by outsourcing. If Premier purchases the printers, it can avoid the unit-level costs (materials, labor, overhead), and the batch-level costs (assembly setup, and materials handling). It can also avoid the product-level costs (engineering design costs and production manager salary). Deciding to outsource will not, however, affect the facility-level costs. Because Premier will incur them whether or not it outsources printer production, the facility-level costs are not relevant to the outsourcing decision. Exhibit 6.4 shows the avoidable (relevant) costs of outsourcing.

**Step 2.** **Compare the avoidable (relevant) production costs with the cost of buying the product and select the lower-cost option.** Because the relevant production cost is less than the purchase price of the printers ($229.65 per unit versus $240.00), the quantitative analysis suggests that Premier should continue to make the printers. Profitability would decline by $20,700 [$459,300 − ($240 × 2,000)] if printer production were outsourced.

That test was so easy. Why is your score so bad?

I outsourced my homework.

## Opportunity Costs

Suppose Premier's accountant determines that the space Premier currently uses to manufacture printers could be leased to a third party for $40,000 per year. By using the space to manufacture printers, Premier is *forgoing the opportunity* to earn $40,000. Because this *opportunity cost* can be avoided by purchasing the printers, it is relevant to the outsourcing decision. After adding the opportunity cost to the other relevant costs, the total relevant cost increases to $499,300 ($459,300 + $40,000) and the relevant cost per unit becomes $249.65 ($499,300 ÷ 2,000). Since Premier can purchase printers for $240, it should outsource printer production. It would be better off buying the printers and leasing the manufacturing space.

### EXHIBIT 6.4

**Relevant Cost for Expected Production for Outsourcing 2,000 Printers**

| | |
|---|---:|
| Unit-level costs ($180 × 2,000 units) | $360,000 |
| Batch-level costs ($2,200 × 10 batches) | 22,000 |
| Product-level costs | 77,300 |
| Total relevant cost | $459,300 |

Cost per unit: $459,300 ÷ 2,000 = $229.65

## Evaluating the Effect of Growth on the Level of Production

The decision to outsource would change if expected production increased from 2,000 to 3,000 units. Because some of the avoidable costs are fixed relative to the level of production, cost per unit decreases as volume increases. For example, the product-level costs (engineering design, production manager's salary, and opportunity cost) are fixed relative to the level of production. Exhibit 6.5 shows the relevant cost per unit if Premier expects to produce 3,000 printers.

At 3,000 units of production, the relevant cost of making printers is less than the cost of outsourcing ($230.10 versus $240.00). If management believes the company is likely to experience growth in the near future, it should reject

### EXHIBIT 6.5

**Relevant Cost for Expected Production for Outsourcing 3,000 Printers**

| | |
|---|---:|
| Unit-level costs ($180 × 3,000 units) | $540,000 |
| Batch-level costs ($2,200 × 15 batches) | 33,000 |
| Product-level costs | 77,300 |
| Opportunity cost | 40,000 |
| Total relevant cost | $690,300 |

Cost per unit: $690,300 ÷ 3,000 units = $230.10

# FOCUS ON INTERNATIONAL ISSUES

## ARE YOU SURE YOUR GERMAN CAR WAS MADE IN GERMANY?

In recent years there has been much discussion about American companies outsourcing work to other workers in other countries. However, some activities that are seldom outsourced by American companies are routinely outsourced by companies in other countries. In fact, sometimes the "foreign country" who provides the outsourcing is the United States.

Consider an example from the automotive industry. While American automobile companies may use parts that were manufactured in another country, the final assembly of cars they sell in the United States is usually performed in their own plants in the United States or Canada. Japanese auto companies also tend to perform the final assembly of their cars in their own plants, which may be located in another country. In contrast, European car makers are more willing to outsource the final assembly, as well as engineering and parts production, to independent companies. For example, most, if not all BMW X3s are not assembled at a **BMW** plant, but by the employees of **Magna Steyr** in Graz, Austria. This company, by the way, is a subsidiary of **Magna International**, which is a Canadian company. And that Porsche Boxster or Cayman you are hoping to receive as a graduation gift—it almost certainly will be built by **Valmet Automotive** in Finland. In fact, Valmet assembled 22,356 of the 105,162 vehicles that Porsche produced in 2008.

Source: Companies' annual reports.

the outsourcing option. Managers must consider potential growth when making outsourcing decisions.

### Qualitative Features

A company that uses **vertical integration** controls the full range of activities from acquiring raw materials to distributing goods and services. Outsourcing reduces the level of vertical integration, passing some of a company's control over its products to outside suppliers. The reliability of the supplier is critical to an outsourcing decision. An unscrupulous supplier may lure an unsuspecting manufacturer into an outsourcing decision using **low-ball pricing.** Once the manufacturer is dependent on the supplier, the supplier raises prices. If a price sounds too good to be true, it probably is too good to be true. Other potential problems include product quality and delivery commitments. If the printers do not work properly or are not delivered on time, Premier's customers will be dissatisfied with Premier, not the supplier. Outsourcing requires that Premier depend on the supplier to deliver quality products at designated prices according to a specified schedule. Any supplier failures will become Premier's failures.

To protect themselves from unscrupulous or incompetent suppliers, many companies establish a select list of reliable **certified suppliers.** These companies seek to become the preferred customers of the suppliers by offering incentives such as guaranteed volume purchases with prompt payments. These incentives motivate the suppliers to ship high-quality products on a timely basis. The purchasing companies recognize that prices ultimately depend on the suppliers' ability to control costs, so the buyers and suppliers work together to minimize costs. For example, buyers may share confidential information about their production plans with suppliers if such information would enable the suppliers to more effectively control costs.

Companies must approach outsourcing decisions cautiously even when relationships with reliable suppliers are ensured. Outsourcing has both internal and external effects. It usually displaces employees. If the supplier experiences difficulties, reestablishing internal production capacity is expensive once a trained workforce has been released. Loyalty and trust are difficult to build but easy to destroy. In fact, companies must consider not only the employees who will be discharged but also the morale of those who remain. Cost reductions achieved through outsourcing are of little benefit if they are acquired at the expense of low morale and reduced productivity.

In spite of the potential pitfalls outsourcing entails, the vast majority of U.S. businesses engage in some form of it. Such widespread acceptance suggests that most companies believe the benefits achieved through outsourcing exceed the potential shortcomings.

---

### ✓ CHECK YOURSELF 6.2

Addison Manufacturing Company pays a production supervisor a salary of $48,000 per year. The supervisor manages the production of sprinkler heads that are used in water irrigation systems. Should the production supervisor's salary be considered a relevant cost to a special order decision? Should the production supervisor's salary be considered a relevant cost to an outsourcing decision?

**Answer**   The production supervisor's salary is not a relevant cost to a special order decision because Addison would pay the salary regardless of whether it accepts or rejects a special order. Since the cost does not differ for the alternatives, it is not relevant. In contrast, the supervisor's salary would be relevant to an outsourcing decision. Addison could dismiss the supervisor if it purchased the sprinkler heads instead of making them. Since the salary could be avoided by purchasing heads instead of making them, the salary is relevant to an outsourcing decision.

---

## Segment Elimination Decisions

Businesses frequently organize their operations into subcomponents called **segments.** Segment data are used to make comparisons among different products, departments, or divisions. For example, in addition to the companywide income statement provided for external users, **JCPenney** may prepare separate income statements for each retail store for internal users. Executives can then evaluate managerial performance by comparing profitability measures among stores. *Segment reports* can be prepared for products, services, departments, branches, centers, offices, or divisions. These reports normally show segment revenues and costs. The primary objective of segment analysis is to determine whether relevant revenues exceed relevant costs.

LO 5

Make appropriate segment elimination decisions.

### Quantitative Analysis

Assume Premier Office Products makes copy equipment and computers as well as printers. Each product line is made in a separate division of the company. Division (segment) operating results for the most recent year are shown in Exhibit 6.6. Initial review of the results suggests the copier division should be eliminated because it is operating at a loss. However, analyzing the relevant revenues and expenses leads to a different conclusion.

A three-step quantitative analysis for the segment elimination decision follows:

**Step 1.    Determine the amount of relevant (differential) revenue that pertains to eliminating the copier division.** The alternatives are (1) to eliminate or (2) to continue to operate the copier division. If Premier eliminates the copier line it will lose the $550,000 of revenue the copier division currently produces. If the division continues to operate, Premier will earn the revenue. Since the revenue differs between the alternatives, it is relevant.

**Step 2.    Determine the amount of cost Premier can avoid if it eliminates the copier division.** If it eliminates copiers, Premier can avoid the unit-level, batch-level,

## EXHIBIT 6.6

### Projected Revenues and Costs by Segment

| | Copiers | Computers | Printers | Total |
|---|---|---|---|---|
| Projected revenue | $550,000 | $850,000 | $720,000 | $2,120,000 |
| Projected costs | | | | |
| Unit-level costs | | | | |
| Materials costs | (120,000) | (178,000) | (180,000) | (478,000) |
| Labor costs | (160,000) | (202,000) | (165,000) | (527,000) |
| Overhead | (30,800) | (20,000) | (15,000) | (65,800) |
| Batch-level costs | | | | |
| Assembly setup | (15,000) | (26,000) | (17,000) | (58,000) |
| Materials handling | (6,000) | (8,000) | (5,000) | (19,000) |
| Product-level costs | | | | |
| Engineering design | (10,000) | (12,000) | (14,000) | (36,000) |
| Production manager salary | (52,000) | (55,800) | (63,300) | (171,100) |
| Facility-level costs | | | | |
| Segment level | | | | |
| Division manager salary | (82,000) | (92,000) | (85,000) | (259,000) |
| Administrative costs | (12,200) | (13,200) | (12,700) | (38,100) |
| Allocated—corporate-level | | | | |
| Company president salary | (34,000) | (46,000) | (43,200) | (123,200) |
| Building rental | (19,250) | (29,750) | (27,300) | (76,300) |
| General facility expenses | (31,000) | (31,000) | (31,000) | (93,000) |
| Projected income (loss) | $(22,250) | $136,250 | $ 61,500 | $ 175,500 |

product-level, and segment-level facility-sustaining costs. The relevant revenue and the avoidable costs are shown in Exhibit 6.7.

Premier will incur the corporate-level facility-sustaining costs whether it eliminates the copier segment or continues to operate it. Since these costs do not differ between the alternatives, they are not relevant to the elimination decision.

**Step 3.** **If the relevant revenue is less than the avoidable cost, eliminate the segment (division). If not, continue to operate it.** Because operating the segment is contributing $62,000 per year to company profitability (see Exhibit 6.7), Premier should not eliminate the copiers division. Exhibit 6.8 shows Premier's estimated revenues and costs if the computers and printers divisions were operated without the copiers division. Projected company profit declines by $62,000 ($175,500 − $113,500) without the copiers segment, confirming that eliminating it would be detrimental to Premier's profitability.

### Qualitative Considerations in Decisions to Eliminate Segments

As with other special decisions, management should consider qualitative factors when determining whether to eliminate segments. Employee lives will be disrupted; some employees may be reassigned elsewhere in the company, but others will be discharged. As with outsourcing decisions, reestablishing internal production capacity is difficult once a trained workforce has been released. Furthermore, employees in other segments, suppliers, customers, and investors may believe that the elimination of a segment implies the company as a whole is experiencing financial difficulty. These individuals may lose confidence in the company and seek business contacts with other companies they perceive to be more stable.

## EXHIBIT 6.7

### Relevant Revenue and Cost Data for Copier Segment

| | |
|---|---|
| Projected revenue | $550,000 |
| Projected costs | |
| Unit-level costs | |
| Materials costs | (120,000) |
| Labor costs | (160,000) |
| Overhead | (30,800) |
| Batch-level costs | |
| Assembly setup | (15,000) |
| Materials handling | (6,000) |
| Product-level costs | |
| Engineering design | (10,000) |
| Production manager salary | (52,000) |
| Facility-level costs | |
| Segment level | |
| Division manager salary | (82,000) |
| Administrative costs | (12,200) |
| Projected income (loss) | $ 62,000 |

## EXHIBIT 6.8

### Projected Revenues and Costs without Copier Division

|  | Computers | Printers | Total |
|---|---|---|---|
| Projected revenue | $850,000 | $720,000 | $1,570,000 |
| Projected costs |  |  |  |
| Unit-level costs |  |  |  |
| Materials costs | (178,000) | (180,000) | (358,000) |
| Labor costs | (202,000) | (165,000) | (367,000) |
| Overhead | (20,000) | (15,000) | (35,000) |
| Batch-level costs |  |  |  |
| Assembly setup | (26,000) | (17,000) | (43,000) |
| Materials handling | (8,000) | (5,000) | (13,000) |
| Product-level costs |  |  |  |
| Engineering design | (12,000) | (14,000) | (26,000) |
| Production manager salary | (55,800) | (63,300) | (119,100) |
| Facility-level costs |  |  |  |
| Segment level |  |  |  |
| Division manager salary | (92,000) | (85,000) | (177,000) |
| Administrative costs | (13,200) | (12,700) | (25,900) |
| Allocated—corporate-level* |  |  |  |
| Company president salary | (63,000) | (60,200) | (123,200) |
| Building rental | (39,375) | (36,925) | (76,300) |
| General facility expenses | (46,500) | (46,500) | (93,000) |
| Projected income (loss) | $ 94,125 | $ 19,375 | $ 113,500 |

*The corporate-level facility costs that were previously *allocated* to the copier division have been reassigned on the basis of one-half to the computer division and one-half to the printer division.

Management must also consider the fact that sales of different product lines are frequently interdependent. Some customers prefer one-stop shopping; they want to buy all their office equipment from one supplier. If Premier no longer sells copiers, customers may stop buying its computers and printers. Eliminating one segment may reduce sales of other segments.

What will happen to the space Premier used to make the copiers? Suppose Premier decides to make telephone systems in the space it previously used for copiers. The contribution to profit of the telephone business would be an *opportunity cost* of operating the copier segment. As demonstrated in previous examples, adding the opportunity cost to the avoidable costs of operating the copier segment could change the decision.

As with outsourcing, volume changes can affect elimination decisions. Because many costs of operating a segment are fixed, the cost per unit decreases as production increases. Growth can transform a segment that is currently producing real losses into a segment that produces real profits. Managers must consider growth potential when making elimination decisions.

## ✓ CHECK YOURSELF 6.3

Capital Corporation is considering eliminating one of its operating segments. Capital employed a real estate broker to determine the marketability of the building that houses the segment. The broker obtained three bids for the building: $250,000, $262,000, and $264,000. The book value of the building is $275,000. Based on this information alone, what is the relevant cost of the building?

**Answer**    The book value of the building is a sunk cost that is not relevant. There are three bids for the building, but only one is relevant because Capital could sell the building only once. The relevant cost of the building is the highest opportunity cost, which in this case is $264,000.

## Summary of Relationships between Avoidable Costs and the Hierarchy of Business Activity

Distinguish between unit-level, batch-level, product-level, and facility-level costs and understand how these costs affect decision making.

A relationship exists between the cost hierarchy and the different types of special decisions just discussed. A special order involves making additional units of an existing product. Deciding to accept a special order affects unit-level and possibly batch-level costs. In contrast, outsourcing a product stops the production of that product. Outsourcing can avoid many product-level as well as unit- and batch-level costs. Finally, if a company eliminates an entire business segment, it can avoid some of the facility-level costs. The more complex the decision level, the more opportunities there are to avoid costs. Moving to a higher category does not mean, however, that all costs at the higher level of activity are avoidable. For example, all product-level costs may not be avoidable if a company chooses to outsource a product. The company may still incur inventory holding costs or advertising costs whether it makes or buys the product. Understanding the relationship between decision type and level of cost hierarchy helps when identifying avoidable costs. The relationships are summarized in Exhibit 6.9. For each type of decision, look for avoidable costs in the categories marked with an X. Remember also that sunk costs cannot be avoided.

### EXHIBIT 6.9

**Relationship between Decision Type and Level of Cost Hierarchy**

| Decision Type | Unit level | Batch level | Product level | Facility level |
|---|---|---|---|---|
| Special order | X | X | | |
| Outsourcing | X | X | X | |
| Elimination | X | X | X | X |

## Equipment Replacement Decisions

Make appropriate asset replacement decisions.

Equipment may become technologically obsolete long before it fails physically. Managers should base **equipment replacement decisions** on profitability analysis rather than physical deterioration. Assume Premier Office Products is considering replacing an existing machine with a new one. The following table summarizes pertinent information about the two machines:

| Old Machine | | New Machine | |
|---|---|---|---|
| Original cost | $ 90,000 | Cost of the new machine | $29,000 |
| Accumulated depreciation | (33,000) | Salvage value (in 5 years) | 4,000 |
| Book value | $ 57,000 | Operating expenses | |
| | | ($4,500 × 5 years) | 22,500 |
| Market value (now) | $ 14,000 | | |
| Salvage value (in 5 years) | 2,000 | | |
| Annual depreciation expense | 11,000 | | |
| Operating expenses | | | |
| ($9,000 × 5 years) | 45,000 | | |

### Quantitative Analysis

First determine what relevant costs Premier will incur if it keeps the *old machine.*

1. The *original cost* ($90,000), *current book value* ($57,000), *accumulated depreciation* ($33,000), and *annual depreciation expense* ($11,000) are different measures of a cost that was incurred in a prior period. They represent irrelevant sunk costs.

2. The $14,000 market value represents the current sacrifice Premier must make if it keeps using the existing machine. In other words, if Premier does not keep the

machine, it can sell it for $14,000. In economic terms, *forgoing the opportunity to sell the machine costs* as much as buying it. The *opportunity cost* is therefore relevant to the replacement decision.

3. The salvage value of the old machine reduces the opportunity cost. Premier can sell the old machine now for $14,000 or use it for five more years and then sell it for $2,000. The opportunity cost of using the old machine for five more years is therefore $12,000 ($14,000 − $2,000).

4. Because the $45,000 ($9,000 × 5) of operating expenses will be incurred if the old machine is used but can be avoided if it is replaced, the operating expenses are relevant costs.

Next, determine what relevant costs will be incurred if Premier purchases and uses the *new machine.*

1. The cost of the new machine represents a future economic sacrifice Premier must incur if it buys the new machine. It is a relevant cost.

2. The salvage value reduces the cost of purchasing the new machine. Part ($4,000) of the $29,000 cost of the new machine will be recovered at the end of five years. The relevant cost of purchasing the new machine is $25,000 ($29,000 − $4,000).

3. The $22,500 ($4,500 × 5) of operating expenses will be incurred if the new machine is purchased; it can be avoided if the new machine is not purchased. The operating expenses are relevant costs.

The relevant costs for the two machines are summarized here:

| Old Machine | | New Machine | |
|---|---|---|---|
| Opportunity cost | $14,000 | Cost of the new machine | $29,000 |
| Salvage value | (2,000) | Salvage value | (4,000) |
| Operating expenses | 45,000 | Operating expenses | 22,500 |
| Total | $57,000 | Total | $47,500 |

The analysis suggests that Premier should acquire the new machine because buying it produces the lower relevant cost. The $57,000 cost of using the old machine can be *avoided* by incurring the $47,500 cost of acquiring and using the new machine. Over the five-year period, Premier would save $9,500 ($57,000 − $47,500) by purchasing the new machine. One caution: this analysis ignores income tax effects and the time value of money, which are explained later. The discussion in this chapter focuses on identifying and using relevant costs in decision making.

## A Look Back «

Decision making requires managers to choose from alternative courses of action. Successful decision making depends on a manager's ability to identify *relevant information.* Information that is relevant for decision making differs among the alternatives and is future oriented. Relevant revenues are sometimes called *differential revenues* because they differ among the alternatives. Relevant costs are sometimes called *avoidable costs* because they can be eliminated or avoided by choosing a specific course of action.

Costs that do not differ among the alternatives are not avoidable and therefore not relevant. *Sunk costs* are not relevant in decision making because they have been incurred in past transactions and therefore cannot be avoided. *Opportunity costs* are relevant because they represent potential benefits that may or may not be realized, depending on the decision maker's choice. In other words, future benefits that differ among the alternatives are relevant. Opportunity costs are not recorded in the financial accounting records.

Cost behavior (fixed or variable) is independent from the concept of relevance. Furthermore, a cost that is relevant in one decision context may be irrelevant in another context. Decision making depends on qualitative as well as quantitative information. *Quantitative information refers to information that can be measured using numbers. Qualitative information* is nonquantitative information such as personal preferences or opportunities.

Classifying costs into one of four hierarchical levels facilitates identifying relevant costs. *Unit-level costs* such as materials and labor are incurred each time a single unit of product is made. These costs can be avoided by eliminating the production of a single unit of product. *Batch-level costs* are associated with producing a group of products. Examples include setup costs and inspection costs related to a batch (group) of work rather than a single unit. Eliminating a batch would avoid both batch-level costs and unit-level costs. *Product-level costs* are incurred to support specific products or services (design and regulatory compliance costs). Product-level costs can be avoided by discontinuing a product line. *Facility-level costs,* like the president's salary, are incurred on behalf of the whole company or a segment of the company. In segment elimination decisions, the facility-level costs related to a particular segment being considered for elimination are relevant and avoidable. Those applying to the company as a whole are not avoidable.

Four types of special decisions that are frequently encountered in business are (1) *special orders,* (2) *outsourcing,* (3) *elimination decisions,* and (4) *asset replacement.* The relevant costs in a special order decision are the unit-level and batch-level costs that will be incurred if the special order is accepted. If the differential revenues from the special order exceed the relevant costs, the order should be accepted. Outsourcing decisions determine whether goods and services should be purchased from other companies. The relevant costs are the unit-level, batch-level, and product-level costs that could be avoided if the company outsources the product or service. If these costs are more than the cost to buy and the qualitative characteristics are satisfactory, the company should outsource. Segment-related unit-level, batch-level, product-level, and facility-level costs that can be avoided when a segment is eliminated are relevant. If the segment's avoidable costs exceed its differential revenues, it should be eliminated, assuming favorable qualitative factors. Asset replacement decisions compare the relevant costs of existing equipment with the relevant costs of new equipment to determine whether replacing the old equipment would be profitable.

 **A Look Forward**

The next chapter introduces planning and cost control, including how to prepare budgets and projected (pro forma) financial statements. In addition to quantitative aspects, it illustrates the effects of the budgeting process on human behavior.

## APPENDIX

### Short-Term versus Long-Term Goals

Explain the conflict between short-term and long-term profitability.

To examine conflicts between short-term versus long-term goals, we return to the equipment replacement decision made by the management team of Premier Office Products (see page 266 for details). Suppose that the final equipment replacement decision is made by a departmental supervisor who is under significant pressure to maximize profitability. She is told that if profitability declines, she will lose her job. Under these circumstances, the supervisor may choose to keep the old machine even though it is to the company's advantage to purchase the new one. This occurs because the beneficial impact of the new machine is realized in the second through fifth years. Indeed, replacing the equipment will result in more expense/loss recognition in the first year. To illustrate, study the following information.

| Year | First | Second | Third | Fourth | Fifth | Totals |
|---|---|---|---|---|---|---|
| **Keep old machine** | | | | | | |
| Depreciation expense* | $11,000 | $11,000 | $11,000 | $11,000 | $11,000 | $ 55,000 |
| Operating expense | 9,000 | 9,000 | 9,000 | 9,000 | 9,000 | 45,000 |
| Total | $20,000 | $20,000 | $20,000 | $20,000 | $20,000 | $100,000 |
| **Replace old machine** | | | | | | |
| Loss on disposal† | $43,000 | $ 0 | $ 0 | $ 0 | $ 0 | $ 43,000 |
| Depreciation expense‡ | 5,000 | 5,000 | 5,000 | 5,000 | 5,000 | 25,000 |
| Operating expense | 4,500 | 4,500 | 4,500 | 4,500 | 4,500 | 22,500 |
| Total | $52,500 | $ 9,500 | $ 9,500 | $ 9,500 | $ 9,500 | $ 90,500 |

\*($57,000 book value − $2,000 salvage) ÷ 5 years = $11,000
†($57,000 book value − $14,000 market value) = $43,000
‡($29,000 cost − $4,000 salvage) ÷ 5 years = $5,000

This analysis verifies that total cost at the end of the five-year period is $9,500 less if the equipment is replaced ($100,000 − $90,500). Notice, however, that total costs at the end of the first year are higher by $32,500 ($52,500 − $20,000) if the old machine is replaced. A decision maker under significant pressure to report higher profitability may be willing to sacrifice tomorrow's profits to look better today. By emphasizing short-term profitability, she may secure a promotion before the long-term effects of her decision become apparent. Even if she stays in the same position, her boss may be replaced by someone not so demanding in terms of reported profitability. The department supervisor's intent is to survive the moment and let the future take care of itself. Misguided reward systems can be as detrimental as threats of punishment. For example, a manager may choose short-term profitability to obtain a bonus that is based on reported profitability. It is the responsibility of upper-level management to establish policies and procedures that motivate subordinates to perform in ways that maximize the company's long-term profitability.

## Decisions Regarding the Allocation of Scarce Resources

Suppose that Premier Office Products makes two types of computers: a high-end network server and an inexpensive personal computer. The relevant sales and variable cost data for each unit follow.

Make decisions about allocating scarce resources.

| Network Server | | Personal Computer | |
|---|---|---|---|
| Sales price | $4,000 | Sales price | $1,500 |
| Less: Variable cost | (3,760) | Less: Variable cost | (1,370) |
| Contribution margin | $ 240 | Contribution margin | $ 130 |

In many circumstances, variable costs act as proxies for *avoidable costs*. For example, by definition, unit-level costs increase and decrease in direct proportion with the number of units of product made and sold. As previously indicated, unit-level costs are avoidable with respect to many special decision scenarios. To the extent that variable costs are proxies for avoidable costs, the contribution margin can be used as a measure of profitability. Other things being equal, higher contribution margins translate into more profitable products. If Premier could sell 1,000 computers, the company would certainly prefer that they be network servers. The contribution to profitability on those machines is almost double the contribution margin on the personal computer.

Even though the contribution margin is higher for network servers, selling personal computers may be more profitable. Why? If Premier can sell considerably more of the personal computers, the volume of activity will make up for the lower margin. In other words, selling three personal computers produces more total margin (3 × $130 = $390) than selling one network server (1 × $240). Many factors could limit the sales of one or both of the products. Factors that limit a business's ability to satisfy the demand for its product are called **constraints.** Suppose that warehouse space is limited (i.e., the warehouse is a scarce resource that constrains sales). Accordingly, Premier cannot warehouse all of the computers that it needs to satisfy its customer orders. If a network server requires considerably more warehouse space than a personal computer, stocking and selling personal computers may be more profitable than stocking and selling network servers. To illustrate, assume that it requires 5 square feet of warehouse space for a network server and 2 square feet for a personal computer. If only 2,100 square feet of warehouse space are available, which computer should Premier stock and sell?

In this case, the warehouse space is considered a scarce resource. The computer that produces the highest contribution margin per unit of scarce resource (i.e., per square foot) is the more profitable product. The per unit computations for each product are shown here.

|  | Network Server | Personal Computer |
|---|---|---|
| Contribution margin per unit (a) | $240 | $130 |
| Divide by warehouse space needed to store one unit (b) | ÷5 | ÷2 |
| Contribution margin per square foot of warehouse space (a ÷ b) | $ 48 | $ 65 |

The data suggest that Premier should focus on the personal computer. Even though the personal computer produces a lower contribution margin per product, its contribution margin per scarce resource is higher. The effect on total profitability is shown as follows.

|  | Network Server | Personal Computer |
|---|---|---|
| Amount of available warehouse space in square feet (a) | 2,100 | 2,100 |
| Divided by warehouse space needed to store one unit (b) | ÷ 5 | ÷ 2 |
| Warehouse capacity in number of units (a ÷ b) = (c) | 420 | 1,050 |
| Times contribution margin per unit (d) | × $ 240 | × $ 130 |
| Total profit potential (c × d) | $100,800 | $136,500 |

Although the quantitative data suggest that Premier will maximize profitability by limiting its inventory to personal computers, qualitative considerations may force the company to maintain a reasonable sales mix between the two products. For example, a business that buys several personal computers may also need a network server. A customer who cannot obtain both products from Premier may choose to buy nothing at all. Instead, the customer will find a supplier who will satisfy all of his needs. In other words, Premier may still need to stock some servers to offer a competitive product line.

The chairman of the board of directors asked Premier's president why company sales had remained level while the company's chief competitor had experienced significant increases. The president replied, "You cannot sell what you do not have. Our warehouse is too small. We stop production when we fill up the warehouse. The products sell out rapidly, and then we have to wait around for the next batch of computers to be made. When we are out of stock, our customers turn to the competition. We are constrained by the size of the warehouse." In business terms, the warehouse is a **bottleneck.** Its size is limiting the company's ability to produce and sell its products.

Many businesses use a management practice known as the **theory of constraints (TOC)** to increase profitability by managing bottlenecks or constrained resources. TOC's primary objective is to identify the bottlenecks restricting the operations of the business and then to open those bottlenecks through a practice known as **relaxing the constraints.** The effect of applying TOC to the Premier case is apparent via contribution margin analysis. According to the preceding computations, a new server and a new personal computer produce a contribution margin of $48 and $65 per square foot of storage space, respectively. So long as additional warehouse space can be purchased for less than these amounts, Premier can increase its profitability by acquiring the space.

**A step-by-step audio-narrated series of slides is provided on the text website at www.mhhe.com/edmonds2011.**

## SELF-STUDY REVIEW PROBLEM

Flying High, Inc. (FHI), is a division of The Master Toy Company. FHI makes remote-controlled airplanes. During 2011, FHI incurred the following costs in the process of making 5,000 planes:

| | |
|---|---:|
| Unit-level materials costs (5,000 units × $80) | $ 400,000 |
| Unit-level labor costs (5,000 units × $90) | 450,000 |
| Unit-level overhead costs (5,000 × $70) | 350,000 |
| Depreciation cost on manufacturing equipment* | 50,000 |
| Other manufacturing overhead† | 140,000 |
| Inventory holding costs | 240,000 |
| Allocated portion of The Master Toy Company's facility-level costs | 600,000 |
| Total costs | $2,230,000 |

*The manufacturing equipment, which originally cost $250,000, has a book value of $200,000, a remaining useful life of four years, and a zero salvage value. If the equipment is not used in the production process, it can be leased for $30,000 per year.

†Includes supervisors' salaries and rent for the manufacturing building.

### Required

a. FHI uses a cost-plus pricing strategy. FHI sets its price at product cost plus $100. Determine the price that FHI should charge for its remote-controlled airplanes.

b. Assume that a potential customer that operates a chain of high-end toy stores has approached FHI. A buyer for this chain has offered to purchase 1,000 planes from FHI at a price of $275 each. Ignoring qualitative considerations, should FHI accept or reject the order?

c. FHI has the opportunity to purchase the planes from Arland Manufacturing Company for $325 each. Arland maintains adequate inventories so that it can supply its customers with planes on demand. Should FHI accept the opportunity to outsource the making of its planes?

d. When completing this requirement use the sales price computed in Requirement *a*. Use the contribution margin format to prepare an income statement based on historical cost data. Prepare a second income statement that reflects the relevant cost data that Master Toy should consider in a segment elimination decision. Based on a comparison of these two statements, indicate whether Master Toy should eliminate the FHI division.

e. FHI is considering replacing the equipment it currently uses to manufacture its planes. It could purchase replacement equipment for $480,000 that has an expected useful life of four years and a salvage value of $40,000. The new equipment would increase productivity substantially, reducing unit-level labor costs by 20 percent. Assume that FHI would maintain its production and sales at 5,000 planes per year. Prepare a schedule that shows the relevant costs of operating the old equipment versus the costs of operating the new equipment. Should FHI replace the equipment?

## Solution to Requirement a

| Product Cost for Remote-Controlled Airplanes | |
| --- | --- |
| Unit-level materials costs (5,000 units × $80) | $ 400,000 |
| Unit-level labor costs (5,000 units × $90) | 450,000 |
| Unit-level overhead costs (5,000 units × $70) | 350,000 |
| Depreciation cost on manufacturing equipment | 50,000 |
| Other manufacturing overhead | 140,000 |
| Total product cost | $1,390,000 |

The cost per unit is $278 ($1,390,000 ÷ 5,000 units). The sales price per unit is $378 ($278 + $100). Depreciation expense is included because cost-plus pricing is usually based on historical cost rather than relevant cost. To be profitable in the long run, a company must ultimately recover the amount it paid for the equipment (the historical cost of the equipment).

## Solution to Requirement b

The incremental (relevant) cost of making 1,000 additional airplanes follows. The depreciation expense is not relevant because it represents a sunk cost. The other manufacturing overhead costs are not relevant because they will be incurred regardless of whether FHI makes the additional planes.

| Per Unit Relevant Product Cost for Airplanes | |
| --- | --- |
| Unit-level materials costs | $ 80 |
| Unit-level labor costs | 90 |
| Unit-level overhead costs | 70 |
| Total relevant product cost | $240 |

Since the relevant (incremental) cost of making the planes is less than the incremental revenue, FHI should accept the special order. Accepting the order will increase profits by $35,000 [($275 incremental revenue − $240 incremental cost) × 1,000 units].

## Solution to Requirement c

Distinguish this decision from the special order opportunity discussed in Requirement b. That special order (Requirement b) decision hinged on the cost of making additional units with the existing production process. In contrast, a make-or-buy decision compares current production with the possibility of making zero units (closing down the entire manufacturing process). If the manufacturing process were shut down, FHI could avoid the unit-level costs, the cost of the lost opportunity to lease the equipment, the other manufacturing overhead costs, and the inventory holding costs. Since the planes can be purchased on demand, there is no need to maintain any inventory. The allocated portion of the facility-level costs is not relevant because it would be incurred regardless of whether FHI manufactured the planes. The relevant cost of making the planes follows.

| Relevant Manufacturing Cost for Airplanes | |
| --- | --- |
| Unit-level materials costs (5,000 units × $80) | $ 400,000 |
| Unit-level labor costs (5,000 units × $90) | 450,000 |
| Unit-level overhead costs (5,000 units × $70) | 350,000 |
| Opportunity cost of leasing the equipment | 30,000 |
| Other manufacturing overhead costs | 140,000 |
| Inventory holding cost | 240,000 |
| Total product cost | $1,610,000 |

The relevant cost per unit is $322 ($1,610,000 ÷ 5,000 units). Since the relevant cost of making the planes ($322) is less than the cost of purchasing them ($325), FHI should continue to make the planes.

## Solution to Requirement d

### Income Statements

| | Historical Cost Data | Relevant Cost Data |
|---|---|---|
| Revenue (5,000 units × $378) | $1,890,000 | $1,890,000 |
| Less variable costs: | | |
| Unit-level materials costs (5,000 units × $80) | (400,000) | (400,000) |
| Unit-level labor costs (5,000 units × $90) | (450,000) | (450,000) |
| Unit-level overhead costs (5,000 units × $70) | (350,000) | (350,000) |
| Contribution margin | 690,000 | 690,000 |
| Depreciation cost on manufacturing equipment | (50,000) | |
| Opportunity cost of leasing manufacturing equipment | | (30,000) |
| Other manufacturing overhead costs | (140,000) | (140,000) |
| Inventory holding costs | (240,000) | (240,000) |
| Allocated facility-level administrative costs | (600,000) | |
| Net loss | $ (340,000) | |
| Contribution to Master Toy's profitability | | $ 280,000 |

Master Toy should not eliminate the segment (FHI). Although it appears to be incurring a loss, the allocated facility-level administrative costs are not relevant because Master Toy would incur these costs regardless of whether it eliminated FHI. Also, the depreciation cost on the manufacturing equipment is not relevant because it is a sunk cost. However, since the company could lease the equipment if the segment were eliminated, the $30,000 potential rental fee represents a relevant opportunity cost. The relevant revenue and cost data show that FHI is contributing $280,000 to the profitability of The Master Toy Company.

## Solution to Requirement e

The relevant costs of using the old equipment versus the new equipment are the costs that differ for the two alternatives. In this case relevant costs include the purchase price of the new equipment, the opportunity cost of the old equipment, and the labor costs. These items are summarized in the following table. The data show the total cost over the four-year useful life of the replacement equipment.

### Relevant Cost Comparison

| | Old Equipment | New Equipment |
|---|---|---|
| Opportunity to lease the old equipment ($30,000 × 4 years) | $ 120,000 | |
| Cost of new equipment ($480,000 − $40,000) | | $ 440,000 |
| Unit-level labor costs (5,000 units × $90 × 4 years) | 1,800,000 | |
| Unit-level labor costs (5,000 units × $90 × 4 years × .80) | | 1,440,000 |
| Total relevant costs | $1,920,000 | $1,880,000 |

Since the relevant cost of operating the new equipment is less than the cost of operating the old equipment, FHI should replace the equipment.

## KEY TERMS

| | | |
|---|---|---|
| Avoidable costs  257 | Facility-level costs  257 | Relevant costs  254 |
| Batch-level costs  257 | Low-ball pricing  262 | Relevant information  254 |
| Bottleneck  270 | Opportunity cost  254 | Segment  263 |
| Certified suppliers  262 | Outsourcing  260 | Special order decisions  258 |
| Constraints  270 | Product-level costs  257 | Sunk costs  254 |
| Differential revenue  256 | Qualitative characteristics  256 | Theory of constraints (TOC)  271 |
| Equipment replacement | Quantitative characteristics  256 | Unit-level costs  257 |
| decisions  266 | Relaxing the constraints  271 | Vertical integration  262 |

## QUESTIONS

1. Identify the primary qualities of revenues and costs that are relevant for decision making.

2. Are variable costs always relevant? Explain.

3. Identify the four hierarchical levels used to classify costs. When can each of these levels of costs be avoided?

4. Describe the relationship between relevance and accuracy.

5. "It all comes down to the bottom line. The numbers never lie." Do you agree with this conclusion? Explain your position.

6. Carmon Company invested $300,000 in the equity securities of Mann Corporation. The current market value of Carmon's investment in Mann is $250,000. Carmon currently needs funds for operating purposes. Although interest rates are high, Carmon's president has decided to borrow the needed funds instead of selling the investment in Mann. He explains that his company cannot afford to take a $50,000 loss on the Mann stock. Evaluate the president's decision based on this information.

7. What is an opportunity cost? How does it differ from a sunk cost?

8. A local bank advertises that it offers a free noninterest-bearing checking account if the depositor maintains a $500 minimum balance in the account. Is the checking account truly free?

9. A manager is faced with deciding whether to replace machine A or machine B. The original cost of machine A was $20,000 and that of machine B was $30,000. Because the two cost figures differ, they are relevant to the manager's decision. Do you agree? Explain your position.

10. Are all fixed costs unavoidable?

11. Identify two qualitative considerations that could be associated with special order decisions.

12. Which of the following would not be relevant to a make-or-buy decision?

    (a) Allocated portion of depreciation expense on existing facilities.

    (b) Variable cost of labor used to produce products currently purchased from suppliers.

    (c) Warehousing costs for inventory of completed products (inventory levels will be constant regardless of whether products are purchased or produced).

    (d) Cost of materials used to produce the items currently purchased from suppliers.

    (e) Property taxes on the factory building.

13. What two factors should be considered in deciding how to allocate shelf space in a retail establishment?

14. What level(s) of costs is(are) relevant in special order decisions?

15. Why would a company consider outsourcing products or services?

16. Chris Sutter, the production manager of Satellite Computers, insists that the floppy drives used in the company's upper-end computers be outsourced since they can be purchased from a supplier at a lower cost per unit than the company is presently incurring to produce the drives. Jane Meyers, his assistant, insists that if sales growth continues at the current levels, the company will be able to produce the drives in the near future at a lower cost because of the company's predominately fixed cost structure. Does Ms. Meyers have a legitimate argument? Explain.

17. Identify some qualitative factors that should be considered in addition to quantitative costs in deciding whether to outsource.

18. The managers of Wilcox, Inc., are suggesting that the company president eliminate one of the company's segments that is operating at a loss. Why may this be a hasty decision?

19. Why would a supervisor choose to continue using a more costly old machine instead of replacing it with a less costly new machine?

20. Identify some of the constraints that limit a business's ability to satisfy the demand for its products or services.

## MULTIPLE-CHOICE QUESTIONS

**Multiple-choice questions are provided on the text website at www.mhhe.com/edmonds2011.**

## EXERCISES—SERIES A

**All applicable Exercises in Series A are available with McGraw-Hill's *Connect Accounting.***

**LO 1**

### Exercise 6-1A    *Distinction between relevance and cost behavior*

Leah Friend is trying to decide which of two different kinds of candy to sell in her retail candy store. One type is a name brand candy that will practically sell itself. The other candy is cheaper to purchase but does not carry an identifiable brand name. Ms. Friend believes that she will have to incur significant advertising costs to sell this candy. Several cost items for the two types of candy are as follows:

| Brandless Candy | | Name Brand Candy | |
|---|---|---|---|
| Cost per box | $   6.00 | Cost per box | $   7.00 |
| Sales commissions per box | 1.00 | Sales commissions per box | 1.00 |
| Rent of display space | 1,500.00 | Rent of display space | 1,500.00 |
| Advertising | 3,000.00 | Advertising | 2,000.00 |

**Required**

Identify each cost as being relevant or irrelevant to Ms. Friend's decision and indicate whether it is fixed or variable relative to the number of boxes sold.

### Exercise 6-2A    *Distinction between relevance and cost behavior*

**LO 1**

Stanley Company makes and sells a single product. Stanley incurred the following costs in its most recent fiscal year.

### Cost Items Appearing on the Income Statement

Materials cost ($10 per unit)
Company president's salary
Depreciation on manufacturing equipment
Customer billing costs (1% of sales)
Rental cost of manufacturing facility
Advertising costs ($200,000 per year)
Labor cost ($8 per unit)

Sales commissions (2% of sales)
Salaries of administrative personnel
Shipping and handling ($0.50 per unit)
Depreciation on office furniture
Manufacturing supplies ($0.25 per unit)
Production supervisor's salary

Stanley could purchase the products that it currently makes. If it purchased the items, the company would continue to sell them using its own logo, advertising program, and sales staff.

**Required**

Identify each cost as relevant or irrelevant to the outsourcing decision and indicate whether the cost is fixed or variable relative to the number of products manufactured and sold.

### Exercise 6-3A    *Distinction between avoidable costs and cost behavior*

**LO 1**

Medallion Company makes fine jewelry that it sells to department stores throughout the United States. Medallion is trying to decide which of two bracelets to manufacture. Cost data pertaining to the two choices follow.

| | Bracelet A | Bracelet B |
|---|---|---|
| Cost of materials per unit | $ 25 | $ 32 |
| Cost of labor per unit | 32 | 32 |
| Advertising cost per year | 8,000 | 6,000 |
| Annual depreciation on existing equip. | 5,000 | 4,000 |

**Required**

**a.** Identify the fixed costs and determine the amount of fixed cost for each product.

**b.** Identify the variable costs and determine the amount of variable cost per unit for each product.

**c.** Identify the avoidable costs and determine the amount of avoidable cost for each product.

**LO 2**

### Exercise 6-4A    *Cost hierarchy*

Costs can be classified into one of four categories including unit-level, batch-level, product-level, or facility-level costs.

**Required**

Classify each of the items listed below into one of the four categories listed above. The first item has been categorized as an example.

| Cost Description | Cost Classification |
|---|---|
| Salary of company president | Facility-level cost |
| Research and development cost | |
| Factory lawn care cost | |
| Cost of patent | |
| Startup cost to change color of a product | |
| Cost of resetting sewing machines to change shirt size | |
| Real estate tax for the factory | |
| Direct labor | |

**LO 2, 3**

### Exercise 6-5A    *Special order decision*

Norman Concrete Company pours concrete slabs for single-family dwellings. Wayne Construction Company, which operates outside Norman's normal sales territory, asks Norman to pour 40 slabs for Wayne's new development of homes. Norman has the capacity to build 300 slabs and is presently working on 250 of them. Wayne is willing to pay only $2,500 per slab. Norman estimates the cost of a typical job to include unit-level materials, $1,000; unit-level labor, $600; and an allocated portion of facility-level overhead, $700.

**Required**

Should Norman accept or reject the special order to pour 40 slabs for $2,500 each? Support your answer with appropriate computations.

**LO 2, 3**

### Exercise 6-6A    *Special order decision*

Issa Company manufactures a personal computer designed for use in schools and markets it under its own label. Issa has the capacity to produce 25,000 units a year but is currently producing and selling only 15,000 units a year. The computer's normal selling price is $1,600 per unit with no volume discounts. The unit-level costs of the computer's production are $600 for direct materials, $300 for direct labor, and $120 for indirect unit-level manufacturing costs. The total product- and facility-level costs incurred by Issa during the year are expected to be $2,100,000 and $800,000, respectively. Assume that Issa receives a special order to produce and sell 3,000 computers at $1,200 each.

**Required**

Should Issa accept or reject the special order? Support your answer with appropriate computations.

**Exercise 6-7A**  *Identifying qualitative factors for a special order decision*    **LO 3**

**Required**

Describe the qualitative factors that Issa should consider before accepting the special order described in Exercise 6-6A.

**Exercise 6-8A**  *Using the contribution margin approach for a special order decision*    **LO 3**

Shenyang Company, which produces and sells a small digital clock, bases its pricing strategy on a 35 percent markup on total cost. Based on annual production costs for 10,000 units of product, computations for the sales price per clock follow.

| | |
|---|---|
| Unit-level costs | $150,000 |
| Fixed costs | 50,000 |
| Total cost (a) | 200,000 |
| Markup (a × 0.35) | 70,000 |
| Total sales (b) | $270,000 |
| Sales price per unit (b ÷ 10,000) | $    27 |

**Required**

a. Shenyang has excess capacity and receives a special order for 4,000 clocks for $17 each. Calculate the contribution margin per unit; based on it, should Shenyang accept the special order?

b. Support your answer by preparing a contribution margin income statement for the special order.

**Exercise 6-9A**  *Outsourcing decision*    **LO 4**

Roaming Bicycle Manufacturing Company currently produces the handlebars used in manufacturing its bicycles, which are high-quality racing bikes with limited sales. Roaming produces and sells only 6,000 bikes each year. Due to the low volume of activity, Roaming is unable to obtain the economies of scale that larger producers achieve. For example, Roaming could buy the handlebars for $35 each; they cost $32 each to make. The following is a detailed breakdown of current production costs.

| Item | Unit Cost | Total |
|---|---|---|
| Unit-level costs | | |
| Materials | $18 | $108,000 |
| Labor | 12 | 72,000 |
| Overhead | 3 | 18,000 |
| Allocated facility-level costs | 5 | 30,000 |
| Total | $38 | $228,000 |

After seeing these figures, Roaming's president remarked that it would be foolish for the company to continue to produce the handlebars at $38 each when it can buy them for $35 each.

**Required**

Do you agree with the president's conclusion? Support your answer with appropriate computations.

**Exercise 6-10A**  *Establishing price for an outsourcing decision*    **LO 4**

Lunn Company makes and sells lawn mowers for which it currently makes the engines. It has an opportunity to purchase the engines from a reliable manufacturer. The annual costs of making the engines are shown here.

| Cost of materials (15,000 Units × $24) | $360,000 |
| Labor (15,000 Units × $26) | 390,000 |
| Depreciation on manufacturing equipment* | 42,000 |
| Salary of supervisor of engine production | 85,000 |
| Rental cost of equipment used to make engines | 23,000 |
| Allocated portion of corporate-level facility-sustaining costs | 80,000 |
| Total cost to make 15,000 engines | $980,000 |

*The equipment has a book value of $90,000 but its market value is zero.

**Required**

a. Determine the maximum price per unit that Lunn would be willing to pay for the engines.

b. Would the price computed in Requirement *a* change if production increased to 18,750 units? Support your answer with appropriate computations.

**LO 4**

### Exercise 6-11A    *Outsourcing decision with qualitative factors*

Nadir Corporation which makes and sells 79,400 radios annually, currently purchases the radio speakers it uses for $12 each. Each radio uses one speaker. The company has idle capacity and is considering the possibility of making the speakers that it needs. Nadir estimates that the cost of materials and labor needed to make speakers would be a total of $10 for each speaker. In addition, the costs of supervisory salaries, rent, and other manufacturing costs would be $168,000. Allocated facility-level costs would be $99,600.

**Required**

a. Determine the change in net income Nadir would experience if it decides to make the speakers.

b. Discuss the qualitative factors that Nadir should consider.

**LO 2, 4**

### Exercise 6-12A    *Outsourcing decision affected by opportunity costs*

Pace Electronics currently produces the shipping containers it uses to deliver the electronics products it sells. The monthly cost of producing 9,000 containers follows.

| Unit-level materials | $ 6,000 |
| Unit-level labor | 6,600 |
| Unit-level overhead | 4,200 |
| Product-level costs* | 10,800 |
| Allocated facility-level costs | 26,400 |

*One-third of these costs can be avoided by purchasing the containers.

Ace Container Company has offered to sell comparable containers to Pace for $2.70 each.

**Required**

a. Should Pace continue to make the containers? Support your answer with appropriate computations.

b. Pace could lease the space it currently uses in the manufacturing process. If leasing would produce $10,800 per month, would your answer to Requirement *a* be different? Explain.

**LO 6**

### Exercise 6-13A    *Opportunity cost*

Lynch Freight Company owns a truck that cost $30,000. Currently, the truck's book value is $18,000, and its expected remaining useful life is four years. Lynch has the opportunity to purchase for $26,000 a replacement truck that is extremely fuel efficient. Fuel cost for the old truck is expected to be $5,000 per year more than fuel cost for the new truck. The old truck is paid for but, in spite of being in good condition, can be sold for only $12,000.

**Required**

Should Lynch replace the old truck with the new fuel-efficient model, or should it continue to use the old truck until it wears out? Explain.

### Exercise 6-14A    *Opportunity costs*

Steve Denmark owns his own taxi, for which he bought an $18,000 permit to operate two years ago. Mr. Denmark earns $36,000 a year operating as an independent but has the opportunity to sell the taxi and permit for $73,000 and take a position as dispatcher for Sartino Taxi Co. The dispatcher position pays $31,000 a year for a 40-hour week. Driving his own taxi, Mr. Denmark works approximately 55 hours per week. If he sells his business, he will invest the $73,000 and can earn a 10 percent return.

**Required**

a. Determine the opportunity cost of owning and operating the independent business.

b. Based solely on financial considerations, should Mr. Denmark sell the taxi and accept the position as dispatcher?

c. Discuss the qualitative as well as quantitative factors that Mr. Denmark should consider.

### Exercise 6-15A    *Segment elimination decision*

Chamberline Company operates three segments. Income statements for the segments imply that profitability could be improved if Segment A were eliminated.

| CHAMBERLINE COMPANY Income Statements for the Year 2011 | | | |
|---|---|---|---|
| **Segment** | **A** | **B** | **C** |
| Sales | $162,000 | $235,000 | $245,000 |
| Cost of goods sold | (121,000) | (92,000) | (95,000) |
| Sales commissions | (15,000) | (22,000) | (22,000) |
| Contribution margin | 26,000 | 121,000 | 128,000 |
| General fixed oper. exp. (allocation of president's salary) | (44,000) | (52,000) | (44,000) |
| Advertising expense (specific to individual divisions) | (3,000) | (10,000) | 0 |
| Net income | $(21,000) | $ 59,000 | $ 84,000 |

**Required**

a. Explain the effect on profitability if Segment A is eliminated.

b. Prepare comparative income statements for the company as a whole under two alternatives: (1) the retention of Segment A and (2) the elimination of Segment A.

### Exercise 6-16A    *Segment elimination decision*

Baich Transport Company divides its operations into four divisions. A recent income statement for Koslov Division follows.

| BAICH TRANSPORT COMPANY Koslov Division Income Statement for the Year 2012 | |
|---|---|
| Revenue | $ 500,000 |
| Salaries for drivers | (350,000) |
| Fuel expenses | (50,000) |
| Insurance | (70,000) |
| Division-level facility-sustaining costs | (40,000) |
| Companywide facility-sustaining costs | (130,000) |
| Net loss | $(140,000) |

**Required**

a. Should Koslov Division be eliminated? Support your answer by explaining how the division's elimination would affect the net income of the company as a whole. By how much would companywide income increase or decrease?

**b.** Assume that Koslov Division is able to increase its revenue to $540,000 by raising its prices. Would this change the decision you made in Requirement *a*? Determine the amount of the increase or decrease that would occur in companywide net income if the segment were eliminated if revenue were $540,000.

**c.** What is the minimum amount of revenue required to justify continuing the operation of Koslov Division?

**LO 5**

### Exercise 6-17A   *Identifying avoidable cost of a segment*

Safar Corporation is considering the elimination of one of its segments. The segment incurs the following fixed costs. If the segment is eliminated, the building it uses will be sold.

| | |
|---|---:|
| Advertising expense | $ 80,000 |
| Supervisory salaries | 160,000 |
| Allocation of companywide facility-level costs | 49,000 |
| Original cost of building | 110,000 |
| Book value of building | 50,000 |
| Market value of building | 80,000 |
| Maintenance costs on equipment | 70,000 |
| Real estate taxes on building | 6,000 |

**Required**

Based on this information, determine the amount of avoidable cost associated with the segment.

**LO 6**

### Exercise 6-18A   *Asset replacement decision*

A machine purchased three years ago for $300,000 has a current book value using straight-line depreciation of $175,000; its operating expenses are $30,000 per year. A replacement machine would cost $240,000, have a useful life of nine years, and would require $13,000 per year in operating expenses. It has an expected salvage value of $57,000 after nine years. The current disposal value of the old machine is $70,000; if it is kept 9 more years, its residual value would be $10,000.

**Required**

Based on this information, should the old machine be replaced? Support your answer.

**LO 6**

### Exercise 6-19A   *Asset replacement decision*

Rainger Company is considering replacement of some of its manufacturing equipment. Information regarding the existing equipment and the potential replacement equipment follows.

| Existing Equipment | | Replacement Equipment | |
|---|---:|---|---:|
| Cost | $120,000 | Cost | $105,000 |
| Operating expenses* | 120,000 | Operating expenses* | 95,000 |
| Salvage value | 30,000 | Salvage value | 20,000 |
| Market value | 60,000 | Useful life | 8 years |
| Book value | 33,000 | | |
| Remaining useful life | 8 years | | |

*The amounts shown for operating expenses are the cumulative total of all such expected expenses to be incurred over the useful life of the equipment.

**Required**

Based on this information, recommend whether to replace the equipment. Support your recommendation with appropriate computations.

**LO 6**

### Exercise 6-20A   *Asset replacement decision*

Hardin Company paid $90,000 to purchase a machine on January 1, 2009. During 2011, a technological breakthrough resulted in the development of a new machine that costs $120,000. The old machine costs $45,000 per year to operate, but the new machine could be operated for only

$15,000 per year. The new machine, which will be available for delivery on January 1, 2012, has an expected useful life of four years. The old machine is more durable and is expected to have a remaining useful life of four years. The current market value of the old machine is $30,000. The expected salvage value of both machines is zero.

**Required**

Based on this information, recommend whether to replace the machine. Support your recommendation with appropriate computations.

**Exercise 6-21A** *Annual versus cumulative data for replacement decision*     LO 6, 7

Because of rapidly advancing technology, Andersen Publications Corporation is considering replacing its existing typesetting machine with leased equipment. The old machine, purchased two years ago, has an expected useful life of six years and is in good condition. Apparently, it will continue to perform as expected for the remaining four years of its expected useful life. A four-year lease for equipment with comparable productivity can be obtained for $14,000 per year. The following data apply to the old machine:

| | |
|---|---|
| Original cost | $160,000 |
| Accumulated depreciation | 55,000 |
| Current market value | 74,000 |
| Estimated salvage value | 10,000 |

**Required**

a. Determine the annual opportunity cost of using the old machine. Based on your computations, recommend whether to replace it.
b. Determine the total cost of the lease over the four-year contract. Based on your computations, recommend whether to replace the old machine.

**Appendix**

**Exercise 6-22A** *Scarce resource decision*     LO 8

Joyful Novelties has the capacity to produce either 30,000 corncob pipes or 14,000 cornhusk dolls per year. The pipes cost $4 each to produce and sell for $7 each. The dolls sell for $11 each and cost $5 to produce.

**Required**

Assuming that Joyful Novelties can sell all it produces of either product, should it produce the corncob pipes or the cornhusk dolls? Show computations to support your answer.

## PROBLEMS—SERIES A

**All applicable Problems in Series A are available with McGraw-Hill's Connect Accounting.**

**Problem 6-23A** *Context-sensitive relevance*     LO 1

**Required**

Respond to each requirement independently.

a. Describe two decision-making contexts, one in which unit-level materials costs are avoidable, and the other in which they are unavoidable.
b. Describe two decision-making contexts, one in which batch-level setup costs are avoidable, and the other in which they are unavoidable.
c. Describe two decision-making contexts, one in which advertising costs are avoidable, and the other in which they are unavoidable.

d. Describe two decision-making contexts, one in which rent paid for a building is avoidable, and the other in which it is unavoidable.

e. Describe two decision-making contexts, one in which depreciation on manufacturing equipment is avoidable, and the other in which it is unavoidable.

### Problem 6-24A    *Context-sensitive relevance*

Chapman Construction Company is a building contractor specializing in small commercial buildings. The company has the opportunity to accept one of two jobs; it cannot accept both because they must be performed at the same time and Chapman does not have the necessary labor force for both jobs. Indeed, it will be necessary to hire a new supervisor if either job is accepted. Furthermore, additional insurance will be required if either job is accepted. The revenue and costs associated with each job follow.

| Cost Category | Job A | Job B |
|---|---|---|
| Contract price | $800,000 | $700,000 |
| Unit-level materials | 243,700 | 223,450 |
| Unit-level labor | 249,150 | 305,000 |
| Unit-level overhead | 18,000 | 12,600 |
| Supervisor's salary | 116,670 | 116,670 |
| Rental equipment costs | 24,900 | 27,300 |
| Depreciation on tools (zero market value) | 19,900 | 19,900 |
| Allocated portion of companywide facility-sustaining costs | 10,400 | 8,600 |
| Insurance cost for job | 18,200 | 18,200 |

**Required**

a. Assume that Chapman has decided to accept one of the two jobs. Identify the information relevant to selecting one job versus the other. Recommend which job to accept and support your answer with appropriate computations.

b. Assume that Job A is no longer available. Chapman's choice is to accept or reject Job B alone. Identify the information relevant to this decision. Recommend whether to accept or reject Job B. Support your answer with appropriate computations.

### Problem 6-25A    *Effect of order quantity on special order decision*

Ellis Quilting Company makes blankets that it markets through a variety of department stores. It makes the blankets in batches of 1,000 units. Ellis made 20,000 blankets during the prior accounting period. The cost of producing the blankets is summarized here.

| | |
|---|---|
| Materials cost ($25 per unit × 20,000) | $ 500,000 |
| Labor cost ($22 per unit × 20,000) | 440,000 |
| Manufacturing supplies ($2 × 20,000) | 40,000 |
| Batch-level costs (20 batches at $4,000 per batch) | 80,000 |
| Product-level costs | 160,000 |
| Facility-level costs | 290,000 |
| Total costs | $1,510,000 |
| Cost per unit = $1,510,000 ÷ 20,000 = $75.50 | |

**Required**

a. Kent Motels has offered to buy a batch of 500 blankets for $56 each. Ellis normal selling price is $90 per unit. Based on the preceding quantitative data, should Ellis accept the special order? Support your answer with appropriate computations.

b. Would your answer to Requirement *a* change if Kent offered to buy a batch of 1,000 blankets for $56 per unit? Support your answer with appropriate computations.

c. Describe the qualitative factors that Ellis Quilting Company should consider before accepting a special order to sell blankets to Kent Motels.

## Problem 6-26A  *Effects of the level of production on an outsourcing decision*

LO 2, 4

Seymour Chemical Company makes a variety of cosmetic products, one of which is a skin cream designed to reduce the signs of aging. Seymour produces a relatively small amount (15,000 units) of the cream and is considering the purchase of the product from an outside supplier for $4.50 each. If Seymour purchases from the outside supplier, it would continue to sell and distribute the cream under its own brand name. Seymour's accountant constructed the following profitability analysis.

| | |
|---|---:|
| Revenue (15,000 units × $10) | $150,000 |
| Unit-level materials costs (15,000 units × $1.40) | (21,000) |
| Unit-level labor costs (15,000 units × $0.50) | (7,500) |
| Unit-level overhead costs (15,000 × $0.10) | (1,500) |
| Unit-level selling expenses (15,000 × $0.20) | (3,000) |
| Contribution margin | 117,000 |
| Skin cream production supervisor's salary | (44,000) |
| Allocated portion of facility-level costs | (11,300) |
| Product-level advertising cost | (34,000) |
| Contribution to companywide income | $ 27,700 |

CHECK FIGURE
a. Total relevant cost: $74,000

### Required

a. Identify the cost items relevant to the make-or-outsource decision.

b. Should Seymour continue to make the product or buy it from the supplier? Support your answer by determining the change in net income if Seymour buys the cream instead of making it.

c. Suppose that Seymour is able to increase sales by 10,000 units (sales will increase to 25,000 units). At this level of production, should Seymour make or buy the cream? Support your answer by explaining how the increase in production affects the cost per unit.

d. Discuss the qualitative factors that Seymour should consider before deciding to outsource the skin cream. How can Seymour minimize the risk of establishing a relationship with an unreliable supplier?

## Problem 6-27A  *Outsourcing decision affected by equipment replacement*

LO 2, 4, 6

Jenkins Bike Company (JBC) makes the frames used to build its bicycles. During 2011, JBC made 20,000 frames; the costs incurred follow.

CHECK FIGURES
a. Avoidable cost per unit:
$123.60
b. Avoidable cost per unit with
new equipment: $30.90

| | |
|---|---:|
| Unit-level materials costs (20,000 units × $45) | $ 900,000 |
| Unit-level labor costs (20,000 units × $51) | 1,020,000 |
| Unit-level overhead costs (20,000 × $9) | 180,000 |
| Depreciation on manufacturing equipment | 90,000 |
| Bike frame production supervisor's salary | 70,000 |
| Inventory holding costs | 290,000 |
| Allocated portion of facility-level costs | 500,000 |
| Total costs | $3,050,000 |

JBC has an opportunity to purchase frames for $110 each.

### Additional Information

1. The manufacturing equipment, which originally cost $550,000, has a book value of $450,000, a remaining useful life of four years, and a zero salvage value. If the equipment is not used to produce bicycle frames, it can be leased for $70,000 per year.

2. JBC has the opportunity to purchase for $910,000 new manufacturing equipment that will have an expected useful life of four years and a salvage value of $70,000. This equipment will increase productivity substantially, reducing unit-level labor costs by 60 percent. Assume that JBC will continue to produce and sell 20,000 frames per year in the future.

3. If JBC outsources the frames, the company can eliminate 80 percent of the inventory holding costs.

**Required**

a. Determine the avoidable cost per unit of making the bike frames, assuming that JBC is considering the alternatives of making the product using the existing equipment or outsourcing the product to the independent contractor. Based on the quantitative data, should JBC outsource the bike frames? Support your answer with appropriate computations.

b. Assuming that JBC is considering whether to replace the old equipment with the new equipment, determine the avoidable cost per unit to produce the bike frames using the new equipment and the avoidable cost per unit to produce the bike frames using the old equipment. Calculate the impact on profitability if the bike frames were made using the old equipment versus the new equipment.

c. Assuming that JBC is considering whether to either purchase the new equipment or outsource the bike frame, calculate the impact on profitability between the two alternatives.

d. Discuss the qualitative factors that JBC should consider before making a decision to outsource the bike frame. How can JBC minimize the risk of establishing a relationship with an unreliable supplier?

**LO 5**

**CHECK FIGURE**
a. Contribution to profit: $14,225

### Problem 6-28A   *Eliminating a segment*

Brandt Boot Co. sells men's, women's, and children's boots. For each type of boot sold, it operates a separate department that has its own manager. The manager of the men's department has a sales staff of nine employees, the manager of the women's department has six employees, and the manager of the children's department has three employees. All departments are housed in a single store. In recent years, the children's department has operated at a net loss and is expected to continue to do so. Last year's income statements follow.

|  | Men's Department | Women's Department | Children's Department |
|---|---|---|---|
| Sales | $ 600,000 | $ 420,000 | $160,000 |
| Cost of goods sold | (265,500) | (176,400) | (96,875) |
| Gross margin | 334,500 | 243,600 | 63,125 |
| Department manager's salary | (52,000) | (41,000) | (21,000) |
| Sales commissions | (106,200) | (75,600) | (27,900) |
| Rent on store lease | (21,000) | (21,000) | (21,000) |
| Store utilities | (4,000) | (4,000) | (4,000) |
| Net income (loss) | $ 151,300 | $ 102,000 | $ (10,775) |

**Required**

a. Determine whether to eliminate the children's department.

b. Confirm the conclusion you reached in Requirement *a* by preparing income statements for the company as a whole with and without the children's department.

c. Eliminating the children's department would increase space available to display men's and women's boots. Suppose management estimates that a wider selection of adult boots would increase the store's net earnings by $32,000. Would this information affect the decision that you made in Requirement *a*? Explain your answer.

**LO 5**

**CHECK FIGURE**
a. Contribution to profit: $(32,500)

### Problem 6-29A   *Effect of activity level and opportunity cost on segment elimination decision*

Levert Manufacturing Co. produces and sells specialized equipment used in the petroleum industry. The company is organized into three separate operating branches: Division A, which manufactures and sells heavy equipment; Division B, which manufactures and sells hand tools; and Division C, which makes and sells electric motors. Each division is housed in a separate manufacturing facility. Company headquarters is located in a separate building. In recent years, Division B has been operating at a net loss and is expected to continue to do so. Income statements for the three divisions for 2010 follow.

| | Division A | Division B | Division C |
|---|---|---|---|
| Sales | $ 3,000,000 | $ 900,000 | $ 3,800,000 |
| Less: Cost of goods sold | | | |
|   Unit-level manufacturing costs | (1,800,000) | (600,000) | (2,280,000) |
|   Rent on manufacturing facility | (410,000) | (225,000) | (300,000) |
| Gross margin | 790,000 | 75,000 | 1,220,000 |
| Less: Operating expenses | | | |
|   Unit-level selling and admin. expenses | (187,500) | (42,500) | (237,500) |
|   Division-level fixed selling and | | | |
|     admin. expenses | (250,000) | (65,000) | (310,000) |
|   Headquarters facility-level costs | (150,000) | (150,000) | (150,000) |
| Net income (loss) | $ 202,500 | $(182,500) | $ 522,500 |

## Required

a. Based on the preceding information, recommend whether to eliminate Division B. Support your answer by preparing companywide income statements before and after eliminating Division B.

b. During 2010, Division B produced and sold 20,000 units of hand tools. Would your recommendation in response to Requirement *a* change if sales and production increase to 30,000 units in 2011? Support your answer by comparing differential revenue and avoidable cost for Division B, assuming that it sells 30,000 units.

c. Suppose that Levert could sublease Division B's manufacturing facility for $475,000. Would you operate the division at a production and sales volume of 30,000 units, or would you close it? Support your answer with appropriate computations.

## Problem 6-30A    *Comprehensive problem including special order, outsourcing, and segment elimination decisions*

LO 3, 4, 5

eXcel

CHECK FIGURE
a. CM: $3,750

Huffman Corporation makes and sells state-of-the-art electronics products. One of its segments produces The Math Machine, an inexpensive calculator. The company's chief accountant recently prepared the following income statement showing annual revenues and expenses associated with the segment's operating activities. The relevant range for the production and sale of the calculators is between 30,000 and 60,000 units per year.

| | |
|---|---|
| Revenue (40,000 units × $8) | $320,000 |
| Unit-level variable costs | |
|   Materials cost (40,000 × $2) | (80,000) |
|   Labor cost (40,000 × $1) | (40,000) |
|   Manufacturing overhead (40,000 × $0.50) | (20,000) |
|   Shipping and handling (40,000 × $0.25) | (10,000) |
|   Sales commissions (40,000 × $1) | (40,000) |
| Contribution margin | 130,000 |
| Fixed expenses | |
|   Advertising costs | (20,000) |
|   Salary of production supervisor | (60,000) |
|   Allocated companywide facility-level expenses | (80,000) |
| Net loss | $ (30,000) |

## Required (Consider each of the requirements independently.)

a. A large discount store has approached the owner of Huffman about buying 5,000 calculators. It would replace The Math Machine's label with its own logo to avoid affecting Huffman's existing customers. Because the offer was made directly to the owner, no sales commissions on the transaction would be involved, but the discount store is willing to pay only $4.50 per calculator. Based on quantitative factors alone, should Huffman accept the special order? Support your answer with appropriate computations. Specifically, by what amount would the special order increase or decrease profitability?

**b.** Huffman has an opportunity to buy the 40,000 calculators it currently makes from a reliable competing manufacturer for $4.90 each. The product meets Huffman's quality standards. Huffman could continue to use its own logo, advertising program, and sales force to distribute the products. Should Huffman buy the calculators or continue to make them? Support your answer with appropriate computations. Specifically, how much more or less would it cost to buy the calculators than to make them? Would your answer change if the volume of sales were increased to 60,000 units?

**c.** Because the calculator division is currently operating at a loss, should it be eliminated from the company's operations? Support your answer with appropriate computations. Specifically, by what amount would the segment's elimination increase or decrease profitability?

**Appendix**

**Problem 6-31A** *Allocating scarce resources*

The following information applies to the products of Kaito Company.

|  | Product A | Product B |
|---|---|---|
| Selling price per unit | $13 | $12 |
| Variable cost per unit | 11 | 9 |

**Required**

Identify the product that should be produced or sold under each of the following constraints. Consider each constraint separately.

**a.** One unit of Product A requires 2 hours of labor to produce, and one unit of Product B requires 4 hours of labor to produce. Due to labor constraints, demand is higher than the company's capacity to make both products.

**b.** The products are sold to the public in retail stores. The company has limited floor space and cannot stock as many products as it would like. Display space is available for only one of the two products. Expected sales of Product A are 10,000 units and of Product B are 8,000 units.

**c.** The maximum number of machine hours available is 40,000. Product A uses 2 machine hours, and Product B uses 5 machine hours. The company can sell all the products it produces.

**Problem 6-32A** *Conflict between short-term and long-term performance*

Julio Sanchez manages the cutting department of Guzman Timber Company. He purchased a tree-cutting machine on January 1, 2011, for $400,000. The machine had an estimated useful life of five years and zero salvage value, and the cost to operate it is $90,000 per year. Technological developments resulted in the development of a more advanced machine available for purchase on January 1, 2012, that would allow a 25 percent reduction in operating costs. The new machine would cost $240,000 and have a four-year useful life and zero salvage value. The current market value of the old machine on January 1, 2012, is $200,000, and its book value is $320,000 on that date. Straight-line depreciation is used for both machines. The company expects to generate $224,000 of revenue per year from the use of either machine.

**Required**

**a.** Recommend whether to replace the old machine on January 1, 2012. Support your answer with appropriate computations.

**b.** Prepare income statements for four years (2012 through 2015) assuming that the old machine is retained.

**c.** Prepare income statements for four years (2012 through 2015) assuming that the old machine is replaced.

**d.** Discuss the potential ethical conflicts that could result from the timing of the loss and expense recognition reported in the two income statements.

# EXERCISES—SERIES B

### Exercise 6-1B    *Distinction between relevance and cost behavior*                    LO 1

Joe Awad is planning to rent a small shop for a new business. He can sell either sandwiches or donuts. The following costs pertain to the two products.

| Sandwiches | | Donuts | |
|---|---|---|---|
| Cost per sandwich | $    2.00 | Cost per dozen donuts | $    1.75 |
| Sales commissions per sandwich | 0.05 | Sales commissions per dozen donuts | 0.07 |
| Monthly shop rental cost | 1,000.00 | Monthly shop rental cost | 1,000.00 |
| Monthly advertising cost | 500.00 | Monthly advertising cost | 300.00 |

**Required**

Identify each cost as relevant or irrelevant to Mr. Awad's product decision and indicate whether the cost is fixed or variable relative to the number of units sold.

### Exercise 6-2B    *Distinction between relevance and cost behavior*                    LO 1

Gromyko Company makes and sells a toy plane. Gromyko incurred the following costs in its most recent fiscal year:

> ### Cost Items Reported on Income Statement
>
> Sales commissions (1% of sales)
> Sales manager's salary
> Shipping and handling costs ($0.75 per unit)
> Cost of renting the administrative building
> Utility costs for the manufacturing plant ($0.25 per unit produced)
> Manufacturing plant manager's salary
> Materials costs ($4 per unit produced)
> Real estate taxes on the manufacturing plant
> Depreciation on manufacturing equipment
> Packaging cost ($1 per unit produced)
> Wages of the plant security guard
> Costs of TV commercials
> Labor costs ($3 per unit)

Gromyko could purchase the toy planes from a supplier. If it did, the company would continue to sell them using its own logo, advertising program, and sales staff.

**Required**

Identify each cost as relevant or irrelevant to the outsourcing decision and indicate whether the cost is fixed or variable relative to the number of toy planes manufactured and sold.

### Exercise 6-3B    *Distinction between avoidable costs and cost behavior*              LO 1

Preston Phones, Inc., makes telephones that it sells to department stores throughout the United States. Preston is trying to decide which of two telephone models to manufacture. The company could produce either telephone with its existing machinery. Cost data pertaining to the two choices follow:

| | Model 90 | Model 30 |
|---|---|---|
| Materials cost per unit | $    57 | $    57 |
| Labor cost per unit | 46 | 27 |
| Product design cost | 12,000 | $7,000 |
| Depreciation on existing manufacturing machinery | 3,000 | 3,000 |

**Required**

a. Identify the fixed costs and determine the amount of fixed cost for each model.
b. Identify the variable costs and determine the amount of variable cost for each model.
c. Identify the avoidable costs.

**LO 2**

## Exercise 6-4B   *Cost hierarchy*

Costs can be classified into one of four categories including unit-level, batch-level, product-level, or facility-level costs.

**Required**

Classify each of the items listed below into one of the four categories listed above. The first item has been categorized as an example.

| Cost Description | Cost Classification |
|---|---|
| Wages of factory janitors | Facility-level cost |
| Machine setup cost for different production jobs | |
| Direct materials | |
| Salary of the manager in charge of making a product | |
| Tires used to assemble a car | |
| Payroll cost for assembly-line workers | |
| Electricity bill of the factory | |
| Product design | |

**LO 2, 3**

## Exercise 6-5B   *Special order decision*

Ragan Textile Company manufactures high-quality bed sheets and sells them in sets to a well-known retail company for $54 a set. Ragan has sufficient capacity to produce 150,000 sets of sheets annually; the retail company currently purchases 90,000 sets each year. Ragan's unit-level cost is $30 per set and its fixed cost is $810,000 per year. A motel chain has offered to purchase 15,000 sheet sets from Ragan for $40 per set. If Ragan accepts the order, the contract will prohibit the motel chain from reselling the bed sheets.

**Required**

Should Ragan accept or reject the special order? Support your answer with appropriate computations.

**LO 2, 3**

## Exercise 6-6B   *Special order decision*

Mansour Automotive Company manufactures an engine designed for motorcycles and markets the product using its own brand name. Although Mansour has the capacity to produce 40,000 engines annually, it currently produces and sells only 30,000 units per year. The engine normally sells for $500 per unit, with no quantity discounts. The unit-level costs to produce the engine are $200 for direct materials, $150 for direct labor, and $30 for indirect manufacturing costs. Mansour expects total annual product- and facility-level costs to be $540,000 and $750,000, respectively. Assume Mansour receives a special order from a new customer seeking to buy 1,000 engines for $370 each.

**Required**

Should Mansour accept or reject the special order? Support your answer with appropriate computations.

**LO 3**

## Exercise 6-7B   *Identifying qualitative factors for a special order decision*

**Required**

Describe the qualitative factors that Mansour should consider before making the decision described in Exercise 6-6B.

**LO 3**

## Exercise 6-8B   *Using the contribution margin approach for a special order decision*

Winchester Company produces and sells a food processor that it prices at a 25 percent markup on total cost. Based on data pertaining to producing and selling 50,000 food processors, Winchester computes the sales price per food processor as follows:

| | |
|---|---|
| Unit-level costs | $ 900,000 |
| Fixed costs | 640,000 |
| Total cost (a) | $1,540,000 |
| Markup (a × .25) | 385,000 |
| Total sales revenue (b) | $1,925,000 |
| Sales price per unit (b ÷ 50,000) | $38.50 |

## Required

**a.** Winchester receives a special order for 7,000 food processors for $20 each. Winchester has excess capacity. Calculate the contribution margin per unit for the special order. Based on the contribution margin per unit, should Winchester accept the special order?

**b.** Support your answer by preparing a contribution margin income statement for the special order.

### Exercise 6-9B    *Making an outsourcing decision*                     LO 4

Upton Boats Company currently produces a battery used in manufacturing its boats. The company annually manufactures and sells 5,000 units of a particular model of fishing boat. Because of the low volume of activity, Upton is unable to obtain the economies of scale that larger producers achieve. For example, the costs associated with producing the batteries it uses are almost 30 percent more than the cost of purchasing comparable batteries. Upton could buy batteries for $86 each; it costs $110 each to make them. A detailed breakdown of current production costs for the batteries follows:

| Item | Unit Cost | Total |
|---|---|---|
| Unit-level costs: | | |
| Materials | $ 40 | $200,000 |
| Labor | 25 | 125,000 |
| Overhead | 5 | 25,000 |
| Allocated facility-level costs | 40 | 200,000 |
| Total | $110 | $550,000 |

Based on these figures, Upton's president asserted that it would be foolish for the company to continue to produce the batteries at $100 each when it can buy them for $86 each.

## Required

Do you agree with the president's conclusion? Support your answer with appropriate computations.

### Exercise 6-10B    *Establishing a price for an outsourcing decision*              LO 4

Romero Corporation makes and sells skateboards. Romero currently makes the 60,000 wheels used annually in its skateboards but has an opportunity to purchase the wheels from a reliable manufacturer. The costs of making the wheels follow.

## Annual Costs Associated with Manufacturing Skateboard Wheels

| | |
|---|---|
| Materials (60,000 units × $5) | $300,000 |
| Labor (60,000 units × $3) | 180,000 |
| Depreciation on manufacturing equipment* | 24,000 |
| Salary of wheel production supervisor | 65,000 |
| Rental cost of equipment used to make wheels | 55,000 |
| Allocated portion of corporate-level facility-sustaining costs | 33,000 |
| Total cost to make 60,000 wheels | $657,000 |

*The equipment has a book value of $74,000 but its market value is zero.

**Required**

**a.** Determine the maximum price per unit that Romero would be willing to pay for the wheels.

**b.** Would the price computed in Requirement *a* change if production were increased to 80,000 units? Support your answer with appropriate computations.

**LO 4**

**Exercise 6-11B**   *Making an outsourcing decision with qualitative factors considered*

Keating Computers currently purchases for $16 each keyboard it uses in the 50,000 computers it makes and sells annually. Each computer uses one keyboard. The company has idle capacity and is considering whether to make the keyboards that it needs. Keating estimates that materials and labor costs for making keyboards would be $10 each. In addition, supervisory salaries, rent, and other manufacturing costs would be $400,000. Allocated facility-level costs would amount to $70,000.

**Required**

**a.** Determine the change in net income that Keating would experience if it decides to make the keyboards.

**b.** Discuss the qualitative factors that Keating should consider.

**LO 2, 4**

**Exercise 6-12B**   *Outsourcing decision affected by opportunity costs*

Oakey Doors Company currently produces the doorknobs for the doors it makes and sells. The monthly cost of producing 5,000 doorknobs is as follows:

| | |
|---|---|
| Unit-level materials | $4,000 |
| Unit-level labor | 7,500 |
| Unit-level overhead | 1,000 |
| Product-level costs* | 8,000 |
| Allocated facility-level costs | 5,000 |

*Twenty percent of these costs can be avoided if the doorknobs are purchased.

Venice Company has offered to sell comparable doorknobs to Oakey for $3.80 each.

**Required**

**a.** Should Oakey continue to make the doorknobs? Support you answer with appropriate computations.

**b.** For $6,000 per month, Oakey could lease the manufacturing space to another company. Would this potential cash inflow affect your response to Requirement *a*? Explain.

**LO 6**

**Exercise 6-13B**   *Asset replacement decision*

Porter Fishing Tours, Inc., owns a boat that originally cost $120,000. Currently, the boat's net book value is $36,000, and its expected remaining useful life is four years. Porter has an opportunity to purchase for $80,000 a replacement boat that is extremely fuel efficient. Fuel costs for the old boat are expected to be $15,000 per year more than fuel costs would be for the replacement boat. Porter could sell the old boat, which is fully paid for and in good condition, for only $32,000.

**Required**

Should Porter replace the old boat with the new fuel-efficient model, or should it continue to use the old one until it wears out? Explain.

**LO 1**

**Exercise 6-14B**   *Opportunity costs*

Two years ago, Victor Baldwin bought a truck for $22,000 to offer delivery services. Victor earns $32,000 a year operating as an independent trucker. He has an opportunity to sell his truck for $15,000 and take a position as an instructor in a truck driving school. The instructor position pays $25,000 a year for working 40 hours per week. Driving his truck, Victor works approximately 60 hours per week. If Victor sells his truck, he will invest the proceeds of the sale in bonds that pay a 12 percent return.

**Required**

a. Determine the opportunity cost of owning and operating the independent delivery business.

b. Based solely on financial considerations, should Victor sell his truck and accept the instructor position?

c. Discuss the qualitative as well as quantitative characteristics that Victor should consider.

### Exercise 6-15B   *Segment elimination decision*

**LO 5**

Evan Company operates three segments. Income statements for the segments imply that Evan could improve profitability if Segment X is eliminated.

| THE EVAN COMPANY<br>Income Statement<br>For the Year 2011 | | | |
|---|---|---|---|
| **Segment** | **X** | **Y** | **Z** |
| Sales | $ 87,000 | $210,000 | $200,000 |
| Cost of goods sold | (67,000) | (82,000) | (85,000) |
| Sales commissions | (14,000) | (22,000) | (20,000) |
| Contribution margin | 6,000 | 106,000 | 95,000 |
| General fixed oper. exp. (allocation of president's salary) | (20,000) | (20,000) | (20,000) |
| Advertising expense (specific to individual segments) | (3,000) | (18,000) | 0 |
| Net income | $(17,000) | $ 68,000 | $ 75,000 |

**Required**

a. Explain the effect on Evan's profitability if Segment X is eliminated.

b. Prepare comparative income statements for the company as a whole under the two alternatives: (1) Segment X is retained or (2) Segment X is eliminated.

### Exercise 6-16B   *Segment elimination decision*

**LO 5**

Jevon Company divides its operations into six divisions. A recent income statement for the Heath Division follows:

| Income Statement | |
|---|---|
| Revenue | $ 700,000 |
| Salaries for employees | (325,000) |
| Operating expenses | (250,000) |
| Insurance | (45,000) |
| Division-level facility-sustaining costs | (90,000) |
| Companywide facility-sustaining costs | (74,000) |
| Net loss | $ (84,000) |

**Required**

a. Should Jevon eliminate the Heath Division? Support your answer by explaining how the division's elimination would affect the net income of the company as a whole. By how much would companywide income increase or decrease?

b. Assume that the Heath Division could increase its revenue to $760,000 by raising prices. Would this change the decision you made in response to Requirement *a*? Assuming Jevon's revenue becomes $760,000, determine the amount of the increase or decrease that would occur in companywide net income if the segment were eliminated.

c. What is the minimum amount of revenue the Heath Division must generate to justify its continued operation?

### Exercise 6-17B   *Identifying avoidable cost of a segment*

**LO 5**

Norton Corporation is considering the elimination of one of its segments. The following fixed costs pertain to the segment. If the segment is eliminated, the building it uses will be sold.

| | |
|---|---:|
| Annual advertising expense | $240,000 |
| Market value of the building | 36,000 |
| Annual depreciation on the building | 18,000 |
| Annual maintenance costs on equipment | 26,000 |
| Annual real estate taxes on the building | 8,000 |
| Annual supervisory salaries | 72,000 |
| Annual allocation of companywide facility-level costs | 30,000 |
| Original cost of the building | 75,000 |
| Current book value of the building | 54,000 |

**Required**

Based on this information, determine the amount of avoidable cost associated with the segment.

**LO 6**

### Exercise 6-18B    *Asset replacement decision*

Quigley Electronics purchased a manufacturing plant four years ago for $7,000,000. The plant costs $1,800,000 per year to operate. Its current book value using straight-line depreciation is $5,000,000. Quigley could purchase a replacement plant for $14,000,000 that would have a useful life of 10 years. Because of new technology, the replacement plant would require only $500,000 per year in operating expenses. It would have an expected salvage value of $3,000,000 after 10 years. The current disposal value of the old plant is $1,200,000, and if Quigley keeps it 10 more years, its residual value would be $300,000.

**Required**

Based on this information, should Quigley replace the old plant? Support your answer with appropriate computations.

**LO 6**

### Exercise 6-19B    *Asset replacement decision*

Fenwick Company is considering whether to replace some of its manufacturing equipment. Information pertaining to the existing equipment and the potential replacement equipment follows:

| Existing Equipment | | Replacement Equipment | |
|---|---:|---|---:|
| Cost | $45,000 | Cost | $42,000 |
| Operating expenses* | 48,000 | Operating expenses* | 8,000 |
| Salvage value | 8,000 | Salvage value | 10,000 |
| Market value | 16,000 | Useful life | 10 years |
| Book value | 21,000 | | |
| Remaining useful life | 10 years | | |

*The amounts shown for operating expenses are the cumulative total of all such expenses expected to be incurred over the useful life of the equipment.

**Required**

Based on this information, recommend whether to replace the equipment. Support your recommendation with appropriate computations.

**LO 6**

### Exercise 6-20B    *Asset replacement decision*

Gilchrist Company, a Texas-based corporation, paid $57,000 to purchase an air conditioner on January 1, 2000. During 2010, surging energy costs prompted management to consider replacing the air conditioner with a more energy-efficient model. The new air conditioner would cost $80,000. Electricity for the existing air conditioner costs the company $30,000 per year; the new model would cost only $20,000 per year. The new model, which has an expected useful life of 10 years, would be installed on January 1, 2011. Because the old air conditioner is more durable, Gilchrist estimates it still has a remaining useful life of 10 years even though it has been used. The current market value of the old air conditioner is $27,000. The expected salvage value of both air conditioners is zero.

**Required**

Based on this information, recommend whether to replace the equipment. Support your recommendation with appropriate computations.

### Exercise 6-21B  *Annual versus cumulative data for replacement decision*                    LO 6, 7

Because their three adult children have all at last left home, Paul and Cindy Bender recently moved to a smaller house. Paul owns a riding lawnmower he bought three years ago to take care of the former house's huge yard; it should last another five years. With the new house's smaller yard, Paul thinks he could hire someone to cut his grass for $400 per year. He wonders if this option is financially sound. Relevant information follows.

| Riding Lawn Mower | Amount |
|---|---|
| Original cost | $2,400 |
| Accumulated depreciation | 900 |
| Current market value | 1,300 |
| Estimated salvage value | 0 |

**Required**

a. What is the annual opportunity cost of using the riding mower? Based on your computations, recommend whether Paul should sell it and hire a lawn service.

b. Determine the total cost of hiring a lawn service for the next five years. Based on your computations, recommend whether Paul should sell the mower and hire a lawn service.

### Appendix

### Exercise 6-22B  *Scarce resource decision*                                                       LO 8

Quantum Technologies has the capacity to annually produce either 50,000 desktop computers or 28,000 laptop computers. Relevant data for each product follow:

|  | Desktop | Laptop |
|---|---|---|
| Sales price | $1,000 | $1,800 |
| Variable costs | 400 | 650 |

**Required**

Assuming that Quantum can sell all it produces of either product, should the company produce the desktop computers or the laptop computers? Provide computations to support your answer.

## PROBLEMS—SERIES B

### Problem 6-23B  *Context-sensitive relevance*                                                     LO 1

**Required**

Respond to each requirement independently.

a. Describe two decision-making contexts, one in which unit-level labor costs are avoidable, and the other in which they are unavoidable.

b. Describe two decision-making contexts, one in which batch-level shipping costs are avoidable, and the other in which they are unavoidable.

c. Describe two decision-making contexts, one in which administrative costs are avoidable, and the other in which they are unavoidable.

d. Describe two decision-making contexts, one in which the insurance premium paid on a building is avoidable, and the other in which it is unavoidable.

e. Describe two decision-making contexts, one in which amortization of a product patent is avoidable, and the other in which it is unavoidable.

**LO 1**

### Problem 6-24B    *Context-sensitive relevance*

Inman Machines Company is evaluating two customer orders from which it can accept only one because of capacity limitations. The data associated with each order follow.

| Cost Category | Order A | Order B |
|---|---|---|
| Contract price | $900,000 | $770,000 |
| Unit-level materials | 350,000 | 286,000 |
| Unit-level labor | 324,000 | 264,800 |
| Unit-level overhead | 106,000 | 98,000 |
| Supervisor's salary | 80,000 | 80,000 |
| Rental equipment costs | 20,000 | 24,000 |
| Depreciation on tools (zero market value) | 28,000 | 28,000 |
| Allocated portion of companywide facility-sustaining costs | 8,000 | 7,200 |
| Insurance coverage | 54,000 | 54,000 |

**Required**

a. Assume that Inman has decided to accept one of the two orders. Identify the information relevant to selecting one order versus the other. Recommend which job to accept, and support your answer with appropriate computations.

b. The customer presenting Order A has withdrawn it because of its financial hardship. Under this circumstance, Inman's choice is to accept or reject Order B alone. Identify the information relevant to this decision. Recommend whether to accept or reject Order B. Support your answer with appropriate computations.

**LO 2, 3**

### Problem 6-25B    *Effect of order quantity on special order decision*

Lang Company made 100,000 electric drills in batches of 1,000 units each during the prior accounting period. Normally, Lang markets its products through a variety of hardware stores. The following is the summarized cost to produce electric drills.

| | |
|---|---|
| Materials cost ($8.00 per unit × 100,000) | $  800,000 |
| Labor cost ($4.00 per unit × 100,000) | 400,000 |
| Manufacturing supplies ($0.50 × 100,000) | 50,000 |
| Batch-level costs (100 batches at $2,000 per batch) | 200,000 |
| Product-level costs | 150,000 |
| Facility-level costs | 180,000 |
| Total costs | $1,780,000 |

Cost per unit = $1,780,000 ÷ 100,000 = $17.80

**Required**

a. Bypassing Lang's regular distribution channel, Chekhol's Home Maintenance Company, has offered to buy a batch of 500 electric drills for $15.50 each directly from Lang. Lang's normal selling price is $23 per unit. Based on the preceding quantitative data, should Lang accept the special order? Support your answer with appropriate computations.

b. Would your answer to Requirement *a* change if Chekhol's offered to buy a batch of 1,000 electric drills for $14.90 each? Support your answer with appropriate computations.

c. Describe the qualitative factors that Lang should consider before accepting a special order to sell electric drills to Chekhol's.

**LO 2, 4**

### Problem 6-26B    *Effects of the level of production on an outsourcing decision*

One of Yamamoto Company's major products is a fuel additive designed to improve fuel efficiency and keep engines clean. Yamamoto, a petrochemical firm, makes and sells 200,000 units of the fuel additive per year. Its management is evaluating the possibility of having an outside supplier manufacture the product for Yamamoto for $2 each. Yamamoto would continue to sell and distribute the fuel additive under its own brand name for either alternative. Yamamoto's accountant constructed the following profitability analysis:

| | |
|---|---:|
| Revenue (100,000 units × $3.50) | $350,000 |
| Unit-level materials costs (100,000 units × $0.80) | (80,000) |
| Unit-level labor costs (100,000 units × $0.12) | (12,000) |
| Unit-level overhead costs (100,000 × $0.38) | (38,000) |
| Unit-level selling expenses (100,000 × $0.20) | (20,000) |
| Contribution margin | 200,000 |
| Fuel additive production supervisor's salary | (80,000) |
| Allocated portion of facility-level costs | (25,000) |
| Product-level advertising cost | (40,000) |
| Contribution to companywide income | $ 55,000 |

## Required

**a.** Identify the cost items relevant to the make-or-outsource decision.

**b.** Should Yamamoto continue to make the fuel additive or buy it from the supplier? Support your answer by determining the change in net income if Yamamoto buys the fuel additive instead of making it.

**c.** Suppose that Yamamoto is able to increase sales by 60,000 units (sales will increase to 160,000 units). At this level of sales, should Yamamoto make or buy the fuel additive? Support your answer by explaining how the increase in production affects the cost per unit.

**d.** Discuss the qualitative factors that Yamamoto should consider before deciding to outsource the fuel additive. How can Yamamoto minimize the risk of establishing a relationship with an unreliable supplier?

## Problem 6-27B    *Outsourcing decision affected by equipment replacement*    LO 2, 5, 6

During 2011, Vance Toy Company made 10,000 units of Model K, the costs of which follow.

| | |
|---|---:|
| Unit-level materials costs (10,000 units × $10) | $100,000 |
| Unit-level labor costs (10,000 units × $40) | 400,000 |
| Unit-level overhead costs (10,000 × $4) | 40,000 |
| Depreciation on manufacturing equipment | 60,000 |
| Model K production supervisor's salary | 60,000 |
| Inventory holding costs | 120,000 |
| Allocated portion of facility-level costs | 80,000 |
| Total costs | $860,000 |

An independent contractor has offered to make the same product for Vance for $50 each.

### Additional Information:

**1.** The manufacturing equipment originally cost $420,000 and has a book value of $240,000, a remaining useful life of four years, and a zero salvage value. If the equipment is not used to produce Model K in the production process, it can be leased for $40,000 per year.

**2.** Vance has the opportunity to purchase for $240,000 new manufacturing equipment that will have an expected useful life of four years and a salvage value of $80,000. This equipment will increase productivity substantially, thereby reducing unit-level labor costs by 20 percent.

**3.** If Vance discontinues the production of Model K, the company can eliminate 50 percent of its inventory holding cost.

### Required

**a.** Determine the avoidable cost per unit to produce Model K assuming that Vance is considering the alternatives between making the product using the existing equipment and outsourcing the product to the independent contractor. Based on the quantitative data, should Vance outsource Model K? Support your answer with appropriate computations.

**b.** Assuming that Vance is considering whether to replace the old equipment with the new equipment, determine the avoidable cost per unit to produce Model K using the new equipment and the avoidable cost per unit to produce Model K using the old equipment. Calculate the impact on profitability if Model K were made using the old equipment versus the new equipment.

c. Assuming that Vance is considering either to purchase the new equipment or to outsource Model K, calculate the impact on profitability between the two alternatives.

d. Discuss the qualitative factors that Vance should consider before making a decision to outsource Model K. How can Vance minimize the risk of establishing a relationship with an unreliable supplier?

**LO 5**

## Problem 6-28B   *Eliminating a segment*

Dexier's Grocery Store has three departments, meat, canned food, and produce, each of which has its own manager. All departments are housed in a single store. Recently, the produce department has been suffering a net loss and is expected to continue doing so. Last year's income statements follow.

|  | Meat Department | Canned Food Department | Produce Department |
|---|---|---|---|
| Sales | $650,000 | $590,000 | $425,000 |
| Cost of goods sold | (270,000) | (330,000) | (245,000) |
| Gross margin | 380,000 | 260,000 | 180,000 |
| Departmental manager's salary | (42,000) | (30,000) | (35,000) |
| Rent on store lease | (80,000) | (80,000) | (80,000) |
| Store utilities | (20,000) | (20,000) | (20,000) |
| Other general expenses | (98,000) | (98,000) | (98,000) |
| Net income (loss) | $140,000 | $ 32,000 | $(53,000) |

### Required

a. Determine whether to eliminate the produce department.

b. Confirm the conclusion you reached in Requirement *a* by preparing a before and an after income statement, assuming that the produce department is eliminated.

c. Eliminating the produce department would allow the meat department to expand. It could add seafood to its products. Suppose that management estimates that offering seafood would increase the store's net earnings by $160,000. Would this information affect the decision that you made in Requirement *a*? Explain your answer.

**LO 2, 5**

## Problem 6-29B   *Effect of activity level and opportunity cost on segment elimination decision*

Aquilar Company has three separate operating branches: Division X, which manufactures utensils; Division Y, which makes plates; and Division Z, which makes cooking pots. Each division operates its own facility. The company's administrative offices are located in a separate building. In recent years, Division Z has experienced a net loss and is expected to continue to do so. Income statements for 2011 follow.

|  | Division X | Division Y | Division Z |
|---|---|---|---|
| Sales | $1,800,000 | $1,400,000 | $1,500,000 |
| Less: Cost of goods sold |  |  |  |
| Unit-level manufacturing costs | (1,100,000) | (580,000) | (400,000) |
| Rent on manufacturing facility | (240,000) | (220,000) | (360,000) |
| Gross margin | 460,000 | 600,000 | 240,000 |
| Less: Operating expenses |  |  |  |
| Unit-level selling and admin. expenses | (60,000) | (45,000) | (90,000) |
| Division-level fixed selling and admin. expenses | (140,000) | (125,000) | (180,000) |
| Administrative facility-level costs | (80,000) | (80,000) | (80,000) |
| Net income (loss) | $ 180,000 | $ 350,000 | $ (110,000) |

**Required**

a.  Based on the preceding information, recommend whether to eliminate Division Z. Support your answer by preparing companywide income statements before and after eliminating Division Z.

b.  During 2011, Division Z produced and sold 30,000 units of product. Would your recommendation in Requirement *a* change if sales and production increase to 45,000 units in 2012? Support your answer by comparing differential revenue and avoidable cost for Division Z, assuming that 45,000 units are sold.

c.  Suppose that Aquilar could sublease Division Z's manufacturing facility for $740,000. Would you operate the division at a production and sales volume of 45,000 units, or would you close it? Support your answer with appropriate computations.

**Problem 6-30B**    *Comprehensive problem including special order, outsourcing, and segment elimination decisions*    **LO 2, 3, 4, 5**

Emerson Company's electronics division produces an MP3 player. The vice president in charge of the division is evaluating the income statement showing annual revenues and expenses associated with the division's operating activities. The relevant range for the production and sale of the radio/cassette player is between 50,000 and 150,000 units per year.

| Income Statement | |
| --- | --- |
| Revenue (60,000 units × $30) | $1,800,000 |
| Unit-level variable costs | |
| Materials cost (60,000 × $15) | (900,000) |
| Labor cost (60,000 × $8) | (480,000) |
| Manufacturing overhead (60,000 × $1.50) | (90,000) |
| Shipping and handling (60,000 × $0.50) | (30,000) |
| Sales commissions (60,000 × $2) | (120,000) |
| Contribution margin | 180,000 |
| Fixed expenses | |
| Advertising costs related to the division | (30,000) |
| Salary of production supervisor | (126,000) |
| Allocated companywide facility-level expenses | (120,000) |
| Net loss | $ (96,000) |

**Required (Consider each of the requirements independently.)**

a.  An international trading firm has approached top management about buying 30,000 MP3 players for $26.50 each. It would sell the product in a foreign country, so that Emerson's existing customers would not be affected. Because the offer was made directly to top management, no sales commissions on the transaction would be involved. Based on quantitative features alone, should Emerson accept the special order? Support your answer with appropriate computations. Specifically, by what amount would profitability increase or decrease if the special order is accepted?

b.  Emerson has an opportunity to buy the 60,000 MP3 players it currently makes from a foreign manufacturer for $26 each. The manufacturer has a good reputation for reliability and quality, and Emerson could continue to use its own logo, advertising program, and sales force to distribute the products. Should Emerson buy the MP3 players or continue to make them? Support your answer with appropriate computations. Specifically, how much more or less would it cost to buy the MP3 players than to make them? Would your answer change if the volume of sales were increased to 140,000 units?

c.  Because the electronics division is currently operating at a loss, should it be eliminated from the company's operations? Support your answer with appropriate computations. Specifically, by what amount would the segment's elimination increase or decrease profitability?

**Appendix**

LO 8

### Problem 6-31B    *Allocating scarce resources*

Minter Company makes two products, M and N. Product information follows.

|  | Product M | Product N |
|---|---|---|
| Selling price per unit | $69 | $84 |
| Variable cost per unit | 45 | 54 |

**Required**

Identify the product that should be produced or sold under each of the following constraints. Consider each constraint separately.

a. One unit of Product M requires 3 hours of labor to produce, and one unit of Product N requires 5 hours of labor to produce. Due to labor constraints, demand is higher than the company's capacity to make both products.

b. The products are sold to the public in retail stores. The company has limited floor space and cannot stock as many products as it would like. Display space is available for only one of the two products. Expected sales of Product M are 8,000 units, and expected sales of Product N are 7,000 units.

c. The maximum number of machine hours available is 24,000. Product M uses 4 machine hours, and Product N uses 6 machine hours. The company can sell all the products it produces.

LO 7

### Problem 6-32B    *Conflict between short-term and long-term performance*

Traywick Construction Components, Inc., purchased a machine on January 1, 2009, for $240,000. The chief engineer estimated the machine's useful life to be six years and its salvage value to be zero. The operating cost of this machine is $120,000 per year. By January 1, 2011, a new machine that requires 30 percent less operating cost than the existing machine has become available for $180,000; it would have a four-year useful life with zero salvage. The current market value of the old machine on January 1, 2011, is $100,000, and its book value is $160,000 on that date. Straight-line depreciation is used for both machines. The company expects to generate $320,000 of revenue per year from the use of either machine.

**Required**

a. Recommend whether to replace the old machine on January 1, 2011. Support your answer with appropriate computations.

b. Prepare income statements for four years (2011 through 2014) assuming that the old machine is retained.

c. Prepare income statements for four years (2011 through 2014) assuming that the old machine is replaced.

d. Discuss the potential ethical conflicts that could result from the timing of the loss and expense recognition reported in the two income statements.

## ANALYZE, THINK, COMMUNICATE

### ACT 6-1    Business Application Case    *Analyzing inventory reductions at Supervalu*

On January 12, 2010, Supervalu, Inc., announced it was planning to reduce the number of different items it carries in its inventory by as much as 25 percent. Supervalu is one of the largest grocery store companies in the United States. It operates more than 2,400 stores under 14 different brand names, including Albertsons, Farm Fresh, Jewel-Osco, and Save-A-Lot. The company also has a segment that provides third-party supply-chain services.

The planned reduction in inventory items was going to be accomplished more by reducing the number of different package sizes than by reducing entire product brands. The new approach was also intended to allow the company to get better prices from its vendors and to put more emphasis on its own store brands.

### Required

**a.** Identify some costs savings Supervalu might realize by reducing the number of items it carries in inventory by 25 percent. Be as specific as possible and use your imagination.

**b.** Consider the additional information presented below, which is hypothetical. All dollar amounts are in thousands; unit amounts are not. Assume that Supervalu decides to eliminate one product line, Sugar-Bits, for one of its segments that currently produces three products. As a result, the following are expected to occur:

(1) The number of units sold for the segment is expected to drop by only 40,000 because of the elimination of Sugar-Bits, since most customers are expected to purchase a Fiber-Treats or Carbo-Crunch product instead. The shift of sales from Sugar-Bits to Fiber-Treats and Carbo-Crunch is expected to be evenly split. In other words, the sales of Fiber-Treats and Carbo-Crunch will each increase by 100,000 units.

(2) Rent is paid for the entire production facility, and the space used by Sugar-Bits cannot be sublet.

(3) Utilities costs are expected to be reduced by $24,000.

(4) The supervisors for Sugar-Bits were all terminated. No new supervisor will be hired for Fiber-Treats or Carbo-Crunch.

(5) The equipment being used to produce Sugar-Bits is also used to produce the other two products. The company believes that as a result of eliminating Sugar-Bits it can eliminate equipment that has a remaining useful life of five years, and a projected salvage value of $20,000. Its current market value is $35,000.

(6) Facility-level costs will continue to be allocated between the product lines based on the number of units produced.

## Product-line Earnings Statements
### (Dollar amounts are in thousands)

| Annual Costs of Operating Each Product Line | Fiber-Treats | Carbo-Crunch | Sugar-Bits | Total |
|---|---|---|---|---|
| Sales in units | 480,000 | 480,000 | 240,000 | 1,200,000 |
| Sales in dollars | $ 480,000 | $ 480,000 | $ 240,000 | $1,200,000 |
| **Unit-level costs:** | | | | |
| Cost of production | 48,000 | 48,000 | 26,400 | 122,400 |
| Sales commissions | 6,000 | 6,000 | 2,400 | 14,400 |
| Shipping and handling | 10,800 | 9,600 | 4,800 | 25,200 |
| Miscellaneous | 3,600 | 2,400 | 2,400 | 8,400 |
| Total unit-level costs | 68,400 | 66,000 | 36,000 | 170,400 |
| **Product-level costs:** | | | | |
| Supervisors salaries | 4,800 | 3,600 | 1,200 | 9,600 |
| **Facility-level costs:** | | | | |
| Rent | 48,000 | 48,000 | 24,000 | 120,000 |
| Utilities | 60,000 | 60,000 | 30,000 | 150,000 |
| Depreciation on equipment | 192,000 | 192,000 | 96,000 | 480,000 |
| Allocated company-wide expenses | 12,000 | 12,000 | 6,000 | 30,000 |
| Total facility-level costs | 312,000 | 312,000 | 156,000 | 780,000 |
| Total product cost | 385,200 | 381,600 | 193,200 | 960,000 |
| Profit on products | $ 94,800 | $ 98,400 | $ 46,800 | $ 240,000 |

Prepare revised product-line earnings statements based on the elimination of Sugar-Bits. It will be necessary to calculate some per-unit data to accomplish this.

### ACT 6-2  Group Assignment  *Relevance and cost behavior*

Maccoa Soft, a division of Zayer Software Company, produces and distributes an automated payroll software system. A contribution margin format income statement for Maccoa Soft for the past year follows.

| | |
|---|---:|
| Revenue (12,000 units × $1,200) | $14,400,000 |
| Unit-level variable costs | |
| Product materials cost (12,000 × $60) | (720,000) |
| Installation labor cost (12,000 × $200) | (2,400,000) |
| Manufacturing overhead (12,000 × $2) | (24,000) |
| Shipping and handling (12,000 × $25) | (300,000) |
| Sales commissions (12,000 × $300) | (3,600,000) |
| Nonmanufacturing miscellaneous costs (12,000 × $5) | (60,000) |
| Contribution margin (12,000 × $608) | 7,296,000 |
| Fixed costs | |
| Research and development | (2,700,000) |
| Legal fees to ensure product protection | (780,000) |
| Advertising costs | (1,200,000) |
| Rental cost of manufacturing facility | (600,000) |
| Depreciation on production equipment (zero market value) | (300,000) |
| Other manufacturing costs (salaries, utilities, etc.) | (744,000) |
| Division-level facility sustaining costs | (1,730,000) |
| Allocated companywide facility-level costs | (1,650,000) |
| Net loss | $ (2,408,000) |

**a.** Divide the class into groups and then organize the groups into three sections. Assign Task 1 to the first section, Task 2 to the second section, and Task 3 to the third section. Each task should be considered independently of the others.

**Group Tasks**

**(1)** Assume that Maccoa has excess capacity. The sales staff has identified a large franchise company with 200 outlets that is interested in Maccoa's software system but is willing to pay only $800 for each system. Ignoring qualitative considerations, should Maccoa accept the special order?

**(2)** Maccoa has the opportunity to purchase a comparable payroll system from a competing vendor for $600 per system. Ignoring qualitative considerations, should Maccoa outsource producing the software? Maccoa would continue to sell and install the software if the manufacturing activities were outsourced.

**(3)** Given that Maccoa is generating a loss, should Zayer eliminate it? Would your answer change if Maccoa could increase sales by 1,000 units?

**b.** Have a representative from each section explain its respective conclusions. Discuss the following:

**(1)** Representatives from Section 1 should respond to the following: The analysis related to the special order (Task 1) suggests that all variable costs are always relevant. Is this conclusion valid? Explain your answer.

**(2)** Representatives from Section 2 should respond to the following: With respect to the outsourcing decision, identify a relevant fixed cost and a nonrelevant fixed cost. Discuss the criteria for determining whether a cost is or is not relevant.

**(3)** Representatives from Section 3 should respond to the following: Why did the segment elimination decision change when the volume of production and sales increased?

### ATC 6-3  Research Assignment  *Using real world data from Pfizer*

On September 20, 2008, *The Wall Street Journal* (WSJ) reported that Pfizer was going to discontinue efforts to develop drugs related to the treatment of heart disease, obesity, and bone health. Pfizer wanted to focus its resources on areas it thought would be more profitable (p. B-1). On January 17, 2009, the WSJ reported that Pfizer planned to lay off as many as 2,400 salespersons, which would be one-third of its sales force. As a part of its efforts to reduce costs, Pfizer had reduced its workforce by 35,000 employees from January 2007 to January 2009 (p. B-5). On July 7, 2009, the WSJ reported that Pfizer, along with other pharmaceutical companies, was increasing its efforts to sell patented durgs (versus generic drugs) to customers in poorer nations. To accomplish this they were offering these customers lower prices. For example, Pfizer sells drugs in Venezuela for 30 percent less than it sells the same drugs in the United States (p. A-1).

### Required

**a.** By stopping the development of drugs related to the treatment of heart disease, obesity, and bone health Pfizer hoped to reduce the amount spend on research and development. Relative to the level of sales, should R&D costs be considered:

- Fixed costs or variable costs
- Marginal costs or not

**b.** Were the R&D costs that Pfizer had spent in past years to develop drugs related to heart disease relevant to its decision to discontinue their future development? If they were not relevant costs, what kind of cost were they?

**c.** Explain how Pfizer can afford to sell drugs in Venezuela for 30 percent lower prices than it sells them for in the United States.

**d.** Obtain Pfizer's annual report for 2008. Pfizer's annual reports can be found at its website: www.pfizer.com. Calculate its operating costs as a percentage of revenue for 2006, 2007, and 2008. (The easiest way to do this is to calculate its "income from continuing operations" as a percentage of revenue, and subtract that amount from 1.0.) Does it appear that Pfizer is accomplishing its goal of reducing its cost? Show supporting computations.

## ATC 6-4    Writing Assignment    *Relevant versus full cost*

State law permits the State Department of Revenue to collect taxes for municipal governments that operate within the state's jurisdiction and allows private companies to collect taxes for municipalities. To promote fairness and to ensure the financial well-being of the state, the law dictates that the Department of Revenue must charge municipalities a fee for collection services that is above the cost of providing such services but does not define the term *cost*. Until recently, Department of Revenue officials have included a proportionate share of all departmental costs such as depreciation on buildings and equipment, supervisory salaries, and other facility-level overhead costs when determining the cost of providing collection services, a measurement approach known as *full costing*. The full costing approach has led to a pricing structure that places the Department of Revenue at a competitive disadvantage relative to private collection companies. Indeed, highly efficient private companies have been able to consistently underbid the Revenue Department for municipal customers. As a result, it has lost 30 percent of its municipal collection business over the last two years. The inability to be price competitive led the revenue commissioner to hire a consulting firm to evaluate the current practice of determining the cost to provide collection services.

The consulting firm concluded that the cost to provide collection services should be limited to the relevant costs associated with providing those services, defined as the difference between the costs that would be incurred if the services were provided and the costs that would be incurred if the services were not provided. According to this definition, the costs of depreciation, supervisory salaries, and other facility-level overhead costs are not included because they are the same regardless of whether the Department of Revenue provides collection services to municipalities. The Revenue Department adopted the relevant cost approach and immediately reduced the price it charges municipalities to collect their taxes and rapidly recovered the collection business it had lost. Indeed, several of the private collection companies were forced into bankruptcy. The private companies joined together and filed suit against the Revenue Department, charging that the new definition of cost violates the intent of the law.

### Required

**a.** Assume that you are an accountant hired as a consultant for the private companies. Write a brief memo explaining why it is inappropriate to limit the definition of the costs of providing collection services to relevant costs.

**b.** Assume that you are an accountant hired as a consultant for the Department of Revenue. Write a brief memo explaining why it is appropriate to limit the definition of the costs of providing collection services to relevant costs.

**c.** Speculate on how the matter will be resolved.

### ATC 6-5  Ethical Dilemma  *Asset replacement clouded by self-interest*

John Dillworth is in charge of buying property used as building sites for branch offices of the National Bank of Commerce. Mr. Dillworth recently paid $110,000 for a site located in a growing section of the city. Shortly after purchasing this lot, Mr. Dillworth had the opportunity to purchase a more desirable lot at a significantly lower price. The traffic count at the new site is virtually twice that of the old site, but the price of the lot is only $80,000. It was immediately apparent that he had overpaid for the previous purchase. The current market value of the purchased property is only $75,000. Mr. Dillworth believes that it would be in the bank's best interest to buy the new lot, but he does not want to report a loss to his boss, Kelly Fullerton. He knows that Ms. Fullerton will severely reprimand him, even though she has made her share of mistakes. In fact, he is aware of a significant bad loan that Ms. Fullerton recently approved. When confronted with the bad debt by the senior vice president in charge of commercial lending, Ms. Fullerton blamed the decision on one of her former subordinates, Ira Sacks. Ms. Fullerton implied that Mr. Sacks had been dismissed for reckless lending decisions when, in fact, he had been an excellent loan officer with an uncanny ability to assess the creditworthiness of his customers. Indeed, Mr. Sacks had voluntarily resigned to accept a better position.

#### Required

a. Determine the amount of the loss that would be recognized on the sale of the existing branch site.

b. Identify the type of cost represented by the $110,000 original purchase price of the land. Also identify the type of cost represented by its current market value of $75,000. Indicate which cost is relevant to a decision as to whether the original site should be replaced with the new site.

c. Is Mr. Dillworth's conclusion that the old site should be replaced supported by quantitative analysis? If not, what facts do justify his conclusion?

d. Assuming that Mr. Dillworth is a certified management accountant (CMA), do you believe the failure to replace the land violates any of the standards of ethical conduct in Exhibit 1.15 in Chapter 1? If so, which standards would be violated?

e. Discuss the ethical dilemma that Mr. Dillworth faces within the context of the fraud triangle that was discussed in Chapter 1.

f. Would Mr. Dillworth be subject to criminal penalties under the Sarbanes-Oxley Act? Explain your answer.

### ATC 6-6  Spreadsheet Assignment  *Using Excel*

Dorina Company makes cases of canned dog food in batches of 1,000 cases and sells each case for $15. The plant capacity is 50,000 cases; the company currently makes 40,000 cases. DoggieMart has offered to buy 1,500 cases for $12 per case. Because product-level and facility-level costs are unaffected by a special order, they are omitted.

#### Required

a. Prepare a spreadsheet like the following one to calculate the contribution to income if the special order is accepted. Construct formulas so that the number of cases or the price could be changed and the new contribution would be automatically calculated.

b. Try different order sizes (such as 2,000) or different prices to see the effect on contribution to profit.

| | Relevant Information for Special Order | | | |
|---|---|---|---|---|
| Differential revenue | 1,500 x $ 12.00 = | | $18,000 | |
| Unit-level costs | | | | |
| Materials | 1,500 x $ 2.40 = | 3,600 | | |
| Labor | 1,500 x $ 3.20 = | 4,800 | | |
| Supplies | 1,500 x $ 1.20 = | 1,800 | | |
| Batch-level costs | 2 x $ 5,000 = | 10,000 | 20,200 | |
| Contribution to income | | | $ (2,200) | |

## Spreadsheet Tips

1. The numbers in cells F7 to F9 should be formulas that refer to F5. This allows the number of cases to be changed in cell F5 with the other cells changing automatically.

2. The formula in cell F10 uses a function named ROUNDUP to calculate the even number of batches. The formula should be = ROUNDUP(F5/1000,0) where the zero refers to rounding up to the nearest whole number.

## ATC 6-7   Spreadsheet Assignment   *Mastering Excel*

Refer to Problem 6-31A.

### Required

a. Prepare a spreadsheet to solve Requirements *a*, *b*, and *c* in Problem 6-31A.

b. While constructing formulas for Requirement *a* of Problem 6-31A, include a formula to calculate contribution margin per labor hour.

c. While constructing formulas for Requirement *b* of Problem 6-31A, include formulas to calculate total contribution margin for each product.

d. While constructing formulas for Requirement *c* of Problem 6-31A, include formulas to calculate contribution margin per machine hour and total contribution margin for each product.

## COMPREHENSIVE PROBLEM

Use the same transaction data for Magnificent Modems, Inc., as was used in Chapter 1. (See page 52.)

### Required

a. One of Magnificent Modems' sales representatives receives a special offer to sell 1,000 modems at a price of $72 each. Should the offer be accepted?

b. Magnificent Modems has the opportunity to purchase the modems that it currently makes. The modems can be purchased at a price of $76 each. Assuming the manufacturing equipment has a zero market value, should Magnificent buy the modems?

c. Assume that Magnificent Modems expects production and sales to grow to 10,000. At this volume of production, should Magnificent buy the modems?

## CHAPTER 7

# Planning for Profit and Cost Control

## LEARNING OBJECTIVES

**After you have mastered the material in this chapter you will be able to:**

**1** Describe the budgeting process and the benefits it provides.

**2** Explain the relationship between budgeting and human behavior.

**3** Prepare a sales budget and related schedule of cash receipts.

**4** Prepare an inventory purchases budget and related schedule of cash payments.

**5** Prepare a selling and administrative expense budget and related schedule of cash payments.

**6** Prepare a cash budget.

**7** Prepare a pro forma income statement, balance sheet, and statement of cash flows.

## CHAPTER OPENING

Planning is crucial to operating a profitable business. Expressing business plans in financial terms is commonly called **budgeting.** The budgeting process involves coordinating the financial plans of all areas of the business. For example, the production department cannot prepare a manufacturing plan until it knows how many units of product to produce. The number of units to produce depends on the marketing department's sales projection. The marketing department cannot project sales volume until it knows what products the company will sell. Product information comes from the research and development department. The point should be clear: a company's master budget results from combining numerous specific plans prepared by different departments.

Master budget preparation is normally supervised by a committee. The budget committee is responsible for settling disputes among various departments over budget matters. The committee also monitors reports on how various segments are progressing toward achieving their budget goals. The budgeting committee is not an accounting committee. It is a high-level committee that normally includes the company president, vice presidents of marketing, purchasing, production, and finance, and the controller.

# The Curious Accountant

People in television commercials often say they shop at a particular store because, "my family is on a budget." The truth is, most families do not have a formal budget. What these people mean is that they need to be sure their spending does not exceed their available cash.

When a family expects to spend more money in a given year than it will earn, it must plan on borrowing funds needed to make up the difference. However, even if a family's income for a year will exceed its spending, it may still need to borrow money because the timing of its cash inflows may not match the timing of its cash outflows. Whether a budget is being prepared for a family or a business, those preparing the budget must understand the specific issues facing that entity if potential financial problems are to be anticipated. There is no such thing as a "one size fits all" budget.

The **United States Olympic Committee (USOC)**, like all large organizations, devotes considerable effort to budget planning.

Think about the Olympic Games, and how the USOC generates revenues and incurs expenditures. Can you identify any unusual circumstances facing the USOC that complicate its budgeting efforts? (Answer on page 319.)

# THE PLANNING PROCESS

Describe the budgeting process and the benefits it provides.

Planning normally addresses short, intermediate, and long-range time horizons. Short-term plans are more specific than long-term plans. Consider, for example, your decision to attend college. Long-term planning requires considering general questions such as:

- Do I want to go to college?
- How do I expect to benefit from the experience?
- Do I want a broad knowledge base, or am I seeking to learn specific job skills?
- In what field do I want to concentrate my studies?

Many students go to college before answering these questions. They discover the disadvantages of poor planning the hard way. While their friends are graduating, they are starting over in a new major.

Intermediate-range planning usually covers three to five years. In this stage, you consider which college to attend, how to support yourself while in school, and whether to live on or off campus.

Short-term planning focuses on the coming year. In this phase you plan specific courses to take, decide which instructors to choose, schedule part-time work, and join a study group. Short-term plans are specific and detailed. Their preparation may seem tedious, but careful planning generally leads to efficient resource use and high levels of productivity.

# THREE LEVELS OF PLANNING FOR BUSINESS ACTIVITY

Businesses describe the three levels of planning as *strategic planning, capital budgeting,* and *operations budgeting.* **Strategic planning** involves making long-term decisions such as defining the scope of the business, determining which products to develop or discontinue, and identifying the most profitable market niche. Upper-level management is responsible for these decisions. Strategic plans are descriptive rather than quantitative. Objectives such as "to have the largest share of the market" or "to be the best-quality producer" result from strategic planning. Although strategic planning is an integral component of managing a business, an in-depth discussion of it is beyond the scope of this text.

**Capital budgeting** focuses on intermediate range planning. It involves such decisions as whether to buy or lease equipment, whether to stimulate sales, or whether to increase the company's asset base. Capital budgeting is discussed in detail in a later chapter.

**Operations budgeting** concentrates on short-term plans. A key component of operations budgeting is the *master budget,* which describes short-term objectives in specific amounts of sales targets, production goals, and financing plans. The master budget describes how management intends to achieve its objectives and directs the company's short-term activities.

The master budget normally covers one year. It is frequently divided into quarterly projections and often subdivides quarterly data by month. Effective managers cannot wait until year-end to know whether operations conform to budget targets. Monthly data provide feedback to permit making necessary corrections promptly.

Many companies use **perpetual,** or **continuous, budgeting** covering a 12-month reporting period. As the current month draws to a close, an additional month is added at the end of the budget period, resulting in a continuous 12-month budget. A perpetual budget offers the advantage of keeping management constantly focused on thinking ahead to the next 12 months. The more traditional annual approach to budgeting invites a frenzied stop-and-go mentality, with managers preparing the budget in a year-end rush that is soon forgotten. Changing conditions may not be discussed until the next year-end budget is due. A perpetual budget overcomes these disadvantages.

## ADVANTAGES OF BUDGETING

Budgeting is costly and time-consuming. The sacrifices, however, are more than offset by the benefits. Budgeting promotes planning and coordination; it enhances performance measurement and corrective action.

### Planning

Almost everyone makes plans. Each morning, most people think about what they will do during the day. Thinking ahead is planning. Most business managers think ahead about how they will direct operations. Unfortunately, planning is frequently as informal as making a few mental notes. Informal planning cannot be effectively communicated. The business manager might know what her objectives are, but neither her superiors nor her subordinates know. Because it serves as a communication tool, budgeting can solve these problems. The budget formalizes and documents managerial plans, clearly communicating objectives to both superiors and subordinates.

### Coordination

Sometimes a choice benefits one department at the expense of another. For example, a purchasing agent may order large quantities of raw materials to obtain discounts from suppliers. But excessive quantities of materials pose a storage problem for the inventory supervisor who must manage warehouse costs. The budgeting process forces coordination among departments to promote decisions in the best interests of the company as a whole.

### Performance Measurement

Budgets are specific, quantitative representations of management's objectives. Comparing actual results to budget expectations provides a way to evaluate performance. For example, if a company budgets sales of $10 million, it can judge the performance of the sales department against that level. If actual sales exceed $10 million, the company should reward the sales department; if actual sales fall below $10 million, the company should seek an explanation for the shortfall from the sales manager.

### Corrective Action

Budgeting provides advance notice of potential shortages, bottlenecks, or other weaknesses in operating plans. For example, a cash budget alerts management to when the company can expect cash shortages during the coming year. The company can make borrowing arrangements well before it needs the money. Without knowing ahead of time, management might be unable to secure necessary financing on short notice, or it may have to pay excessively high interest rates to obtain funds. Budgeting advises managers of potential problems in time for them to carefully devise effective solutions.

## BUDGETING AND HUMAN BEHAVIOR

Effective budgeting requires genuine sensitivity on the part of upper management to the effect on employees of budget expectations. People are often uncomfortable with budgets. Budgets are constraining. They limit individual freedom in favor of an established plan. Many people find evaluation based on budget expectations stressful. Most students experience a similar fear about testing. Like examinations, budgets represent

Explain the relationship between budgeting and human behavior.

standards by which performance is evaluated. Employees worry about whether their performance will meet expectations.

The attitudes of high-level managers significantly impact budget effectiveness. Subordinates are keenly aware of management's expectations. If upper-level managers degrade, make fun of, or ignore the budget, subordinates will follow suit. If management uses budgets to humiliate, embarrass, or punish subordinates, employees will resent the treatment and the budgeting process. Upper-level managers must demonstrate that they view the budget as a sincere effort to express realistic goals employees are expected to meet. An honest, open, respectful atmosphere is essential to budgeting success.

**Participative budgeting** has frequently proved successful in creating a healthy atmosphere. This technique invites participation in the budget process by personnel at all levels of the organization, not just upper-level managers. Information flows from the bottom up as well as from the top down during budget preparation. Because they are directly responsible for meeting budget goals, subordinates can offer more realistic targets. Including them in budget preparation fosters development of a team effort. Participation fosters more cooperation and motivation, and less fear. With participative budgeting, subordinates cannot complain that the budget is management's plan. The budget is instead a self-imposed constraint. Employees can hold no one responsible but themselves if they fail to accomplish the budget objectives they established.

Upper management participates in the process to ensure that employee-generated objectives are consistent with company objectives. Furthermore, if subordinates were granted complete freedom to establish budget standards, they might be tempted to adopt lax standards to ensure they will meet them. Both managers and subordinates must cooperate if the participatory process is to produce an effective budget. If developed carefully, budgets can motivate employees to achieve superior performance. Normal human fears must be overcome, and management must create an honest budget atmosphere.

## THE MASTER BUDGET

Describe the budgeting process and the benefits it provides.

The **master budget** is a group of detailed budgets and schedules representing the company's operating and financial plans for a future accounting period. The master budget usually includes (1) *operating budgets,* (2) *capital budgets,* and (3) *pro forma financial statements.* The budgeting process normally begins with preparing the **operating budgets,** which focus on detailed operating activities. This chapter illustrates operating budgets for Hampton Hams, a retail sales company that uses (1) a sales budget, (2) an inventory purchases budget, (3) a selling and administrative (S&A) expense budget, and (4) a cash budget.

The sales budget includes a schedule of cash receipts from customers. The inventory purchases and S&A expense budgets include schedules of cash payments for inventory and expenses. Preparing the master budget begins with the sales forecast. Based on the sales forecast, the detailed budgets for inventory purchases and operating expenses are developed. The schedules of cash receipts and cash payments provide the foundation for preparing the cash budget.

The **capital budget** describes the company's intermediate-range plans for investments in facilities, equipment, new products, store outlets, and lines of business. The capital budget affects several operating budgets. For example, equipment acquisitions result in additional depreciation expense on the S&A expense budget. The cash flow effects of capital investments influence the cash budget.

The operating budgets are used to prepare *pro forma statements.* **Pro forma financial statements** are based on projected (budgeted) rather than historical information. Hampton Hams prepares a pro forma income statement, balance sheet, and statement of cash flows.

Exhibit 7.1 shows how information flows in a master budget.

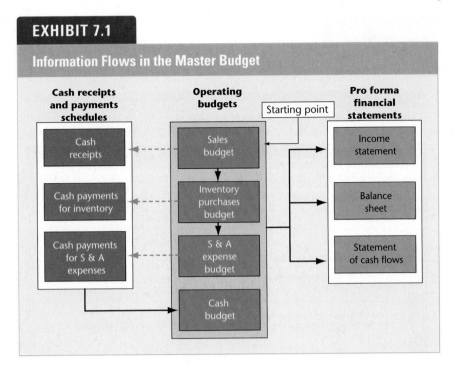

## EXHIBIT 7.1

### Information Flows in the Master Budget

| Cash receipts and payments schedules | Operating budgets | Pro forma financial statements |
| --- | --- | --- |

Starting point

- Cash receipts
- Cash payments for inventory
- Cash payments for S & A expenses

- Sales budget
- Inventory purchases budget
- S & A expense budget
- Cash budget

- Income statement
- Balance sheet
- Statement of cash flows

# HAMPTON HAMS BUDGETING ILLUSTRATION

**HAMPTON** HAMS

Hampton Hams (HH), a major corporation, sells cured hams nationwide through retail outlets in shopping malls. By focusing on a single product and standardized operations, the company controls costs stringently. As a result, it offers high-quality hams at competitive prices.

Hampton Hams has experienced phenomenal growth during the past five years. It opened two new stores in Indianapolis, Indiana, last month and plans to open a third new store in October. Hampton Hams finances new stores by borrowing on a line of credit arranged with National Bank. National's loan officer has requested monthly budgets for each of the first three months of the new store's operations. The accounting department is preparing the new store's master budget for October, November, and December. The first step is developing a sales budget.

## Sales Budget

**LO 3**

Prepare a sales budget and related schedule of cash receipts.

Preparing the master budget begins with the sales forecast. The accuracy of the sales forecast is critical because all the other budgets are derived from the sales budget. Normally, the marketing department coordinates the development of the sales forecast. Sales estimates frequently flow from the bottom up to the higher management levels. Sales personnel prepare sales projections for their products and territories and pass them up the line where they are combined with the estimates of other sales personnel to develop regional and national estimates. Using various information sources, upper-level sales managers adjust the estimates generated by sales personnel. Adjustment information comes from industry periodicals and trade journals, economic analysis, marketing surveys, historical sales figures, and changes in competition. Companies assimilate this data using sophisticated computer programs, statistical techniques, and quantitative methods, or, simply, professional judgment. Regardless of the technique, the senior vice president of sales ultimately develops a sales forecast for which she is held responsible.

To develop the sales forecast for HH's new store, the sales manager studied the sales history of existing stores operating in similar locations. He then adjusted for start-up conditions. October is an opportune time to open a new store because customers will learn the store's location before the holiday season. The sales manager expects significant sales growth in November and December as customers choose the company's hams as the centerpiece for many Thanksgiving and winter holiday dinner tables.

## EXHIBIT 7.2

### Sales Budget

| | A | B | C | D | E | F | G |
|---|---|---|---|---|---|---|---|
| 1 | | Hampton Hams | | | | | |
| 2 | | Sales Budget | | | | | |
| 3 | | | | | | | |
| 4 | | | | | Pro Forma | | |
| 5 | Section 1: Projected Sales | Oct | Nov | Dec | Data | | |
| 6 | Cash Sales | $ 40,000 | $ 48,000 | $ 57,600 | | | |
| 7 | Sales on Account | 120,000 | 144,000 | 172,800 | $172,800 | (a) | |
| 8 | Total Budgeted Sales | $160,000 | $192,000 | $230,400 | $582,400 | (b) | |
| 9 | | | | | | | |
| 10 | Section 2: Schedule of Cash Receipts | | | | | | |
| 11 | Current Cash Sales | $ 40,000 | $ 48,000 | $ 57,600 | | | |
| 12 | Plus Collections of Accounts Receivable | 0 | 120,000 | 144,000 | | | |
| 13 | Total Budgeted Collections | $ 40,000 | $168,000 | $201,600 | | | |
| 14 | | | | | | | |
| 15 | | | | | | | |
| 16 | (a) Quarter-end accounts receivable balance on the balance sheet. | | | | | | |
| 17 | (b) Sales revenue on the income statement (sum of monthly amounts: $160,000 + $192,000 + $230,400). | | | | | | |
| 18 | | | | | | | |
| 19 | | | | | | | |
| 20 | | | | | | | |
| 21 | | | | | | | |
| 22 | | | | | | | |
| 23 | | | | | | | |

The new store's sales are expected to be $160,000 in October ($40,000 in cash and $120,000 on account). Sales are expected to increase 20 percent per month during November and December. Based on these estimates, the sales manager prepared the sales budget in Exhibit 7.2.

### Projected Sales

The sales budget has two sections. Section 1 shows the projected sales for each month. The November sales forecast reflects a 20 percent increase over October sales. For example, November *cash sales* are calculated as $48,000 [$40,000 + ($40,000 × 0.20)] and December *cash sales* as $57,600 [$48,000 + ($48,000 × 0.20)]. *Sales on account* are similarly computed.

### Schedule of Cash Receipts

Section 2 is a schedule of the cash receipts for the projected sales. This schedule is used later to prepare the cash budget. The accountant has assumed in this schedule that Hampton Hams will collect accounts receivable from credit sales *in full* in the month following the sale. In practice, collections may be spread over several months, and some receivables may become bad debts that are never collected. Regardless of additional complexities, the objective is to estimate the amount and timing of expected cash receipts.

In the HH case, *total cash receipts* are determined by adding the current month's *cash sales* to the cash collected from the previous month's *credit sales* (accounts receivable balance). Cash receipts for each month are determined as follows:

■ October receipts are projected to be $40,000. Because the store opens in October, no accounts receivable from September exist to be collected in October. Cash receipts for October equal the amount of October's cash sales.

■ November receipts are projected to be $168,000 ($48,000 November cash sales + $120,000 cash collected from October sales on account).

■ December receipts are projected to be $201,600 ($57,600 December cash sales + $144,000 cash collected from November sales on account).

# FOCUS ON INTERNATIONAL ISSUES

## CASH FLOW PLANNING IN BORDEAUX

The year 2005 was considered a great year for wine in the Bordeaux region of France, and the winemakers could look forward to selling their wines for high prices, but there was one catch; these wines would not be released to consumers until late in 2008. The winemakers had incurred most of their costs in 2005 when the vines were being tended and the grapes were being processed into wine. In many industries this would mean the companies would have to finance their inventory for almost four years—not an insignificant cost. The company must finance the inventory by either borrowing the money, which results in out-of-pocket interest expense, or using its own funds. The second option generates an opportunity cost resulting from the interest revenue that could have been earned if these funds were not being used to finance the inventory.

To address this potential cash flow problem, many of the winemakers in Bordeaux offer some of their wines for sale as "futures." That means the wines are purchased and paid for while they are still aging in barrels in France. Selling wine as futures reduces the time inventory must be financed from four years to only one to two years. Of course there are other types of costs in such deals. For one, the wines must be offered at lower prices than they are expected to sell for upon release. The winemakers have obviously decided this cost is less than the cost of financing inventory through borrowed money, or they would not do it.

Companies in other industries use similar techniques to speed up cash flow, such as factoring of accounts receivable. A major reason entities prepare cash budgets is to be sure they will have enough cash on hand to pay bills as they come due. If the budget indicates a temporary cash flow deficit, action must be taken to avoid the problem, and new budgets must be prepared based on these options. Budgeting is not a static process.

## *Pro Forma Financial Statement Data*

The Pro Forma Data column in the sales budget displays two figures HH will report on the quarter-end (December 31) budgeted financial statements. Since HH expects to collect December credit sales in January, the *accounts receivable balance* will be $172,800 on the December 31, pro forma balance sheet (shown later in Exhibit 7.7).

The $582,400 of *sales revenue* in the Pro Forma Data column will be reported on the budgeted income statement for the quarter (shown later in Exhibit 7.6). The sales revenue represents the sum of October, November, and December sales ($160,000 + $192,000 + $230,400 = $582,400).

## Inventory Purchases Budget

The inventory purchases budget shows the amount of inventory HH must purchase each month to satisfy the demand projected in the sales budget. The *total inventory needed* each month equals the amount of inventory HH plans to sell that month plus the amount of inventory HH wants on hand at month-end. To the extent that total inventory needed exceeds the inventory on hand at the beginning of the month, HH will need to purchase additional inventory. The amount of inventory to purchase is computed as follows:

Prepare an inventory purchases budget and related schedule of cash payments.

| | |
|---|---|
| Cost of budgeted sales | XXX |
| Plus: Desired ending inventory | XXX |
| Total inventory needed | XXX |
| Less: Beginning inventory | (XXX) |
| Required purchases | XXX |

## EXHIBIT 7.3

### Inventory Purchases Budget

| | A | B | C | D | E |
|---|---|---|---|---|---|
| 1 | | Hampton Hams | | | |
| 2 | | Inventory Purchases Budget | | | |
| 3 | | | | | |
| 4 | | | | | Pro Forma |
| 5 | Section 1: Projected Purchases | Oct | Nov | Dec | Data |
| 6 | Budgeted Cost of Goods Sold | $112,000 | 25% $134,400 | 25% $161,280 | $407,680 (a) |
| 7 | Plus Desired Ending Inventory | 33,600 | 40,320 | 35,000 | $35,000 (b) |
| 8 | Total Inventory Needed | 145,600 | 174,720 | 196,280 | |
| 9 | Less Beginning Inventory | 0 | 33,600 | 40,320 | 40% |
| 10 | Required Purchases (on account) | $145,600 | $141,120 | $155,960 | $62,384 (c) |
| 11 | | | | | |
| 12 | Section 2: Schedule of Cash Payments for Inventory Purchases | | | | |
| 13 | Pay 60% of Current Month Accts Pay | $87,360 | $84,672 | $93,576 | |
| 14 | Pay 40% of Prior Month Accts Pay | 0 | 58,240 | 56,448 | |
| 15 | Total Budgeted Disbursements for Inventory | $87,360 | $142,912 | $150,024 | |
| 16 | | | | | |
| 17 | (a) Cost of goods sold reported on pro forma income statement: | | | | |
| 18 | (Sum of monthly amounts $112,000 + $134,400 + $161,280 = $407,680). | | | | |
| 19 | (b) Ending inventory balance reported on pro forma balance sheet. | | | | |
| 20 | (c) Ending accounts payable balance reported on proforma balance sheet ($155,960 x .40) | | | | |
| 21 | | | | | |
| 22 | | | | | |
| 23 | | | | | |

It is HH's policy to maintain an ending inventory equal to 25 percent of the next month's *projected cost of goods sold.* HH's cost of goods sold normally equals 70 percent of *sales.* Using this information and the sales budget, the accounting department prepared the inventory purchases budget shown in Exhibit 7.3.

Section 1 of the inventory purchases budget shows required purchases for each month. HH determined *budgeted cost of goods sold* for October by multiplying October *budgeted sales* by 70 percent ($160,000 × 0.70 = $112,000). Budgeted cost of goods sold for November and December were similarly computed. The October *desired ending inventory* was computed by multiplying November *budgeted cost of goods sold* by 25 percent ($134,400 × 0.25 = $33,600). Desired ending inventory for November is $40,320 ($161,280 × .25). Desired ending inventory for December is based on January projected cost of goods sold (not shown in the exhibit). HH expects ham sales to decline after the winter holidays. Because January projected cost of goods sold is only $140,000, the December desired ending inventory falls to $35,000 ($140,000 × .25).

### Schedule of Cash Payments for Inventory Purchases

Section 2 is the schedule of cash payments for inventory purchases. HH makes all inventory purchases on account. The supplier requires that HH pay for 60 percent of inventory purchases in the month goods are purchased. HH pays the remaining 40 percent the month after purchase.

Cash payments are projected as follows (amounts are rounded to the nearest whole dollar):

- October cash payments for inventory are $87,360. Because the new store opens in October, no accounts payable balance from September remains to be paid in October. Cash payments for October equal 60 percent of October inventory purchases.

- November cash payments for inventory are $142,912 (40 percent of October purchases + 60 percent of November purchases).

- December cash payments for inventory are $150,024 (40 percent of November purchases + 60 percent of December purchases).

## Pro Forma Financial Statement Data

The Pro Forma Data column in the inventory purchases budget displays three figures HH will report on the quarter-end budgeted financial statements. The $407,680 *cost of goods sold* reported on the pro forma income statement (shown later in Exhibit 7.6) is the sum of the monthly cost of goods sold amounts ($112,000 + $134,400 + $161,280 = $407,680).

The $35,000 *ending inventory* as of December 31 is reported on the pro forma balance sheet (shown later in Exhibit 7.7). December 31 is the last day of both the month of December and the three-month quarter represented by October, November, and December.

The $62,384 of *accounts payable* reported on the pro forma balance sheet (shown later in Exhibit 7.7) represents the 40 percent of December inventory purchases HH will pay for in January ($155,960 × .40).

---

## ✓ CHECK YOURSELF 7.1

Main Street Sales Company purchased $80,000 of inventory during June. Purchases are expected to increase by 2 percent per month in each of the next three months. Main Street makes all purchases on account. It normally pays cash to settle 70 percent of its accounts payable during the month of purchase and settles the remaining 30 percent in the month following purchase. Based on this information, determine the accounts payable balance Main Street would report on its July 31 balance sheet.

**Answer** Purchases for the month of July are expected to be $81,600 ($80,000 × 1.02). Main Street will pay 70 percent of the resulting accounts payable in cash during July. The remaining 30 percent represents the expected balance in accounts payable as of July 31. Therefore, the balance would be $24,480 ($81,600 × 0.3).

---

## Selling and Administrative Expense Budget

Section 1 of Exhibit 7.4 shows the selling and administrative (S&A) expense budget for Hampton Hams' new store. Most of the projected expenses are self-explanatory; depreciation and interest, however, merit comment. The depreciation expense is based on projections in the *capital expenditures budget.* Although not presented in this chapter, the capital budget calls for the cash purchase of $130,000 of store fixtures. The fixtures were purchased on October 1. The supplier allows a 30-day inspection period. As a result, payment for the fixtures was made at the end of October. The fixtures are expected to have a useful life of 10 years and a $10,000 salvage value. Using the straight-line method, HH estimates annual depreciation expense at $12,000 ([$130,000 − $10,000] ÷ 10). Monthly depreciation expense is $1,000 ($12,000 annual charge ÷ 12 months).

Interest expense is missing from the S&A expense budget. HH cannot estimate interest expense until it completes its borrowing projections. Expected borrowing (financing activities) and related interest expense are shown in the **cash budget.**

> **LO 5**
>
> Prepare a selling and administrative expense budget and related schedule of cash payments.

### Schedule of Cash Payments for Selling and Administrative Expenses

Section 2 of the S&A expense budget shows the schedule of cash payments. There are several differences between the S&A expenses recognized on the pro forma income statement and the cash payments for S&A expenses. First, Hampton Hams' pays sales commissions and utilities expense the month following their incurrence. Since the store opens in October there are no payments due from September. Cash payments for sales commissions and utilities in October are zero. In November, HH will pay the October expenses for these items and in December it will pay the November sales commissions and utilities expenses. Depreciation expense does not affect the cash payments schedule.

## EXHIBIT 7.4

### Selling and Administrative Expense Budget

| | A | B | C | D | E | F | G | H |
|---|---|---|---|---|---|---|---|---|
| 1 | | **Hampton Hams** | | | | | | |
| 2 | | **Selling and Administrative (S&A) Expense Budget** | | | | | | |
| 3 | | | | | Pro Forma | | | |
| 4 | **Section 1: Projected S&A Expenses** | Oct | Nov | Dec | Data | | | |
| 5 | Salary Expense | $24,000 | $24,000 | $24,000 | | | | |
| 6 | Sales Commissions, 2% of Sales | 3,200 | 3,840 | 4,608 | $ 4,608 (a) | | | |
| 7 | Supplies Expense, 1% of Sales | 1,600 | 1,920 | 2,304 | | | | |
| 8 | Utilities Expense | 1,400 | 1,400 | 1,400 | $ 1,400 (b) | | | |
| 9 | Depreciation Expense on Store Fixtures | 1,000 | 1,000 | 1,000 | $ 3,000 (c) | | | |
| 10 | Rent Expense | 3,600 | 3,600 | 3,600 | | | | |
| 11 | Miscellaneous Expense | 900 | 900 | 900 | | | | |
| 12 | Total S&A Expenses before Interest | $35,700 | $36,660 | $37,812 | $110,172 (d) | | | |
| 13 | | | | | | | | |
| 14 | **Section 2: Schedule of Cash Payments for S&A Expenses** | | | | | | | |
| 15 | Salary Expense | $24,000 | $24,000 | $24,000 | | | | |
| 16 | 100% of Prior Month Sales Commissions | 0 | 3,200 | 3,840 | | | | |
| 17 | Supplies Expense, 1% of Sales | 1,600 | 1,920 | 2,304 | | | | |
| 18 | 100% of Prior Month Utilities Expense | 0 | 1,400 | 1,400 | | | | |
| 19 | Rent Expense | 3,600 | 3,600 | 3,600 | | | | |
| 20 | Miscellaneous Expense | 900 | 900 | 900 | | | | |
| 21 | Total Payments for S&A Expenses | $30,100 | $35,020 | $36,044 | | | | |
| 22 | | | | | | | | |
| 23 | (a) Sales commissions payable in January reported on the pro forma balance sheet. | | | | | | | |
| 24 | (b) Utilities payable in January reported on the pro forma balance sheet. | | | | | | | |
| 25 | (c) Accumulated depreciation on the pro forma balance sheet: sum of monthly amounts ($1,000 + $1,000 + $1,000 = $3,000). | | | | | | | |
| 26 | (d) S&A expense on the pro forma income statement: sum of monthly amounts ($35,700 + $36,660 + $37,812 = $110,172). | | | | | | | |

The cash outflow for the store fixtures occurs when the assets are purchased, not when they are depreciated. The cost of the investment in store fixtures is in the cash budget, not in the cash outflow for S&A expenses.

### Pro Forma Financial Statement Data

The Pro Forma Data column of the S&A expense budget displays four figures HH will report on the quarter-end budgeted financial statements. The first and second figures are the sales commissions payable ($4,608) and utilities payable ($1,400) on the pro forma balance sheet in Exhibit 7.7. Because December sales commissions and utilities expense are not paid until January, these amounts represent liabilities as of December 31. The third figure in the column ($3,000) is the amount of accumulated depreciation on the pro forma balance sheet in Exhibit 7.7. Since depreciation accumulates, the $3,000 balance is the sum of the monthly depreciation amounts ($1,000 + $1,000 + $1,000 = $3,000). The final figure in the Pro Forma Data column ($110,172) is the total S&A expenses reported on the pro forma income statement in Exhibit 7.6. The total S&A expense is the sum of the monthly amounts ($35,700 + $36,660 + 37,812 = $110,172).

## Cash Budget

Little is more important to business success than effective cash management. If a company experiences cash shortages, it will be unable to pay its debts and may be forced into bankruptcy. If excess cash accumulates, a business loses the opportunity to earn investment income or reduce interest costs by repaying debt. Preparing a **cash budget** alerts management to anticipated cash shortages or excess cash balances. Management

**LO 6**

Prepare a cash budget.

## EXHIBIT 7.5

### Cash Budget

| | A | B | C | D | E | F | G | H | I |
|---|---|---|---|---|---|---|---|---|---|
| 1 | | Hampton Hams | | | | | | | |
| 2 | | Cash Budget | | | | | | | |
| 3 | | | | | Pro Forma | | | | |
| 4 | **Section 1:  Cash Receipts** | Oct | Nov | Dec | Data | | | | |
| 5 | Beginning Cash Balance | $ 0 | $ 10,540 | $ 10,428 | | | | | |
| 6 | Add Cash Receipts (Exhibit 7.2) | 40,000 | 168,000 | 201,600 | $409,600 (a) | | | | |
| 7 | Total Cash Available | 40,000 | 178,540 | 212,028 | | | | | |
| 8 | **Section 2:  Cash Payments** | | | | | | | | |
| 9 | For Inventory Purchases (Exhibit 7.3) | 87,360 | 142,912 | 150,024 | $ 380,296 (b) | | | | |
| 10 | For S&A Expenses (Exhibit 7.4) | 30,100 | 35,020 | 36,044 | $ 101,164 (c) | | | | |
| 11 | For Interest Expense | | 2,180 | 2,300 | $  4,480 (d) | | | | |
| 12 | For Purchase of Store Fixtures | 130,000 | 0 | 0 | $ 130,000 (e) | | | | |
| 13 | Total Budgeted Disbursements | 247,460 | 180,112 | 188,368 | | | | | |
| 14 | **Section 3:  Financing Activities** | | | | | | | | |
| 15 | Surplus (Shortage) | (207,460) | (1,572) | 23,660 | | | | | |
| 16 | Borrowing (Repayment) | 218,000 | 12,000 | (13,000) | $ 217,000 (f) | | | | |
| 17 | Ending Cash Balance | $ 10,540 | $ 10,428 | $ 10,660 | $ 10,660 (g) | | | | |
| 18 | | | | | | | | | |
| 19 | Pro forma data items (a) through (d) appear in the operating activities section of the pro forma statement of cash flows. | | | | | | | | |
| 20 | Item (d), interest expense, also appears on the pro forma income statement.  Each of these items is computed by summing | | | | | | | | |
| 21 | the monthly amounts. | | | | | | | | |
| 22 | (a) Cash receipts from customers: $40,000 + $168,000 + $201,600 = $409,600. | | | | | | | | |
| 23 | (b) Cash payments for inventory purchases: $87,360 + $142,912 + $150,024 = $380,296. | | | | | | | | |
| 24 | (c) Cash payments for S&A Expenses: $30,100 + $35,020 + $36,044 = $101,164. | | | | | | | | |
| 25 | (d) Cash payments for interest expense: $0 + $2,180 + $2,300 = $4,480. | | | | | | | | |
| 26 | (e) Investing activities section of the pro forma statement of cash flows. | | | | | | | | |
| 27 | (f) Financing activities section of the pro forma statements of cash flows: $218,000 +12,000 - $13,000 = $217,000. | | | | | | | | |
| 28 | and liabilities section of the pro forma balance sheet. | | | | | | | | |

can plan financing activities, making advance arrangements to cover anticipated shortages by borrowing and planning to repay past borrowings and make appropriate investments when excess cash is expected.

The cash budget is divided into three major sections: (1) a cash receipts section, (2) a cash payments section, and (3) a financing section. Much of the data needed to prepare the cash budget are included in the cash receipts and payments schedules previously discussed; however, further refinements to project financing needs and interest costs are sometimes necessary. The completed cash budget is shown in Exhibit 7.5.

### Cash Receipts Section

The total cash available (Exhibit 7.5, row 7) is determined by adding the beginning cash balance to the cash receipts from customers. There is no beginning cash balance in October because the new store is opening that month. The November beginning cash balance is the October ending cash balance. The December beginning cash balance is the November ending cash balance. Cash receipts from customers comes from the *schedule of cash receipts* in the sales budget (Exhibit 7.2, section 2, row 13).

### Cash Payments Section

Cash payments include expected cash outflows for inventory purchases, S&A expenses, interest expense, and investments. The cash payments for inventory purchases comes from the *schedule of cash payments for inventory purchases* (Exhibit 7.3, section 2, row 15). The cash payments for S&A expenses comes from the *schedule of cash payments for S&A expenses* (Exhibit 7.4, section 2, row 21).

# REALITY BYTES

## BUDGETING IN GOVERNMENTAL ENTITIES

This chapter has presented several reasons organizations should prepare budgets, but for governmental entities, budgets are not simply good planning tools—law requires them. If a manager at a commercial enterprise does not accomplish the budget objectives established for his or her part of the business, the manager may receive a poor performance evaluation. At worst, they may be fired. If managers of governmental agencies spend more than their budgets allow, they may have broken the law. In some cases the manager could be required to personally repay the amount by which the budget was exceeded. Since governmental budgets are enacted by the relevant elected bodies, to violate the budget is to break the law.

Because budgets are so important for governments and are not to be exceeded, government accounting practices require that budgeted amounts be formally entered into the bookkeeping system. As you learned in your first course of accounting, companies do not make formal accounting entries when they order goods; they only make an entry when the goods are received. Governmental accounting systems are different. Each time goods or services are ordered by a government, an "encumbrance" is recorded against the budgeted amount so that agencies do not commit to spend more money than their budgets allow.

HH borrows or repays principal and pays interest on the last day of each month. The cash payments for interest are determined by multiplying the loan balance for the month by the monthly interest rate. Since there is no outstanding debt during October, there is no interest payment at the end of October. HH expects outstanding debt of $218,000 during the month of November. The bank charges interest at the rate of 12 percent per year, or 1 percent per month. The November interest expense and cash payment for interest is $2,180 ($218,000 × .01). The outstanding loan balance during December is $230,000. The December interest expense and cash payment for interest is $2,300 ($230,000 × .01). Determining the amount to borrow or repay at the end of each month is discussed in more detail in the next section of the text.

Finally, the cash payment for the store fixtures comes from the *capital expenditures budget* (not shown in this chapter).

### Financing Section

HH has a line of credit under which it can borrow or repay principal in increments of $1,000 at the end of each month as needed. HH desires to maintain an ending cash balance of at least $10,000 each month. With the $207,460 projected cash shortage in row 15 of the cash budget ($40,000 cash balance in row 7 less $247,460 budgeted cash payments in row 13), HH must borrow $218,000 on October 31 to maintain an ending cash balance of at least $10,000. This $218,000 balance is outstanding during November. On November 30, HH must borrow an additional $12,000 to cover the November projected cash shortage of $1,572 plus the $10,000 desired ending cash balance. HH projects a surplus of $23,660 for the month of December. This surplus will allow HH to repay $13,000 of debt and still maintain the desired $10,000 cash balance.

### Pro Forma Financial Statement Data

Figures in the Pro Forma Data column of the cash budget (Exhibit 7.5) are alphabetically referenced. The cash receipts from customers, item (a), and the cash payment items (b), (c), and (d) are reported in the operating activities section of the pro forma statement of cash flows (Exhibit 7.8). The interest expense, item (d), is also reported on the pro forma income statement (Exhibit 7.6). The figures are determined by summing the monthly amounts. The $130,000 purchase of store fixtures, item (e), is reported in the investing activities section of the pro forma statement of cash flows. The $217,000 net borrowings, item (f), is reported in the financing activities section of the pro forma statement of cash flows (Exhibit 7.8) and also as a liability on the pro forma balance sheet (Exhibit 7.7). The $10,660 ending cash balance, item (g), is reported as the ending balance on the pro forma statement of cash flows and as an asset on the pro forma balance sheet.

---

✓ **CHECK YOURSELF 7.2**

Astor Company expects to incur the following operating expenses during September: Salary Expense, $25,000; Utility Expense, $1,200; Depreciation Expense, $5,400; and Selling Expense, $14,000. In general, it pays operating expenses in cash in the month in which it incurs them. Based on this information alone, determine the total amount of cash outflow Astor would report in the Operating Activities section of the pro forma statement of cash flows.

**Answer**  Depreciation is not included in cash outflows because companies do not pay cash when they recognize depreciation expense. The total cash outflow is $40,200 ($25,000 + $1,200 + $14,000).

---

## Pro Forma Income Statement

Exhibit 7.6 shows the budgeted income statement for Hampton Hams' new store. The figures for this statement come from Exhibits 7.2, 7.3, 7.4, and 7.5. The budgeted income statement provides an advance estimate of the new store's expected profitability. If expected profitability is unsatisfactory, management could decide to abandon the project or modify planned activity. Perhaps HH could lease less costly store space, pay employees a lower rate, or reduce the number of employees hired. The pricing strategy could also be examined for possible changes.

Budgets are usually prepared using spreadsheets or computerized mathematical models that allow managers to easily undertake "what-if" analysis. What if the growth rate differs from expectations? What if interest rates increase or decrease? Exhibits 7.2 through 7.5 in this chapter were prepared using Microsoft Excel. When variables such as growth rate, collection assumptions, or interest rates are changed, the spreadsheet software instantly recalculates the budgets. Although managers remain responsible for data analysis and decision making, computer technology offers powerful tools to assist in those tasks.

**LO 7**

Prepare a pro forma income statement, balance sheet, and statement of cash flows.

**EXHIBIT 7.6**

### HAMPTON HAMS
#### Pro Forma Income Statement
#### For the Quarter Ending December 31

| | | Data Source |
|---|---|---|
| Sales revenue | $ 582,400 | Exhibit 7.2 |
| Cost of goods sold | (407,680) | Exhibit 7.3 |
| Gross margin | 174,720 | |
| Selling and administrative expenses | (110,172) | Exhibit 7.4 |
| Operating income | 64,548 | |
| Interest expense | (4,480) | Exhibit 7.5 |
| Net income | $  60,068 | |

## Pro Forma Balance Sheet

Most of the figures on the pro forma balance sheet in Exhibit 7.7 have been explained. The new store has no contributed capital because its operations will be financed through debt and retained earnings. The amount of retained earnings equals the amount of net income because no earnings from prior periods exist and no distributions are planned.

**EXHIBIT 7.7**

### HAMPTON HAMS
Pro Forma Balance Sheet
As of the Quarter Ending December 31

| | | | Data Source |
|---|---|---|---|
| Assets | | | |
| Cash | | $ 10,660 | Exhibit 7.5 |
| Accounts receivable | | 172,800 | Exhibit 7.2 |
| Inventory | | 35,000 | Exhibit 7.3 |
| Store fixtures | $130,000 | | Exhibit 7.4 Discussion |
| Accumulated depreciation | (3,000) | | Exhibit 7.4 Discussion |
| Book value of store fixtures | | 127,000 | |
| Total assets | | $345,460 | |
| Liabilities | | | |
| Accounts payable | | $ 62,384 | Exhibit 7.3 |
| Sales commissions payable | | 4,608 | Exhibit 7.4 |
| Utilities payable | | 1,400 | Exhibit 7.4 |
| Line of credit borrowings | | 217,000 | Exhibit 7.5 |
| Equity | | | |
| Retained earnings | | 60,068 | |
| Total liabilities and equity | | $345,460 | |

## Pro Forma Statement of Cash Flows

Exhibit 7.8 shows the pro forma statement of cash flows. All information for this statement comes from the cash budget in Exhibit 7.5.

**EXHIBIT 7.8**

### HAMPTON HAMS
Pro Forma Statement of Cash Flows
For the Quarter Ending December 31

| | | |
|---|---|---|
| Cash flow from operating activities | | |
| Cash receipts from customers | $409,600 | |
| Cash payments for inventory | (380,296) | |
| Cash payments for S&A expenses | (101,164) | |
| Cash payments for interest expense | (4,480) | |
| Net cash flow for operating activities | | $ (76,340) |
| Cash flow from investing activities | | |
| Cash outflow to purchase fixtures | | (130,000) |
| Cash flow from financing activities | | |
| Inflow from borrowing on line of credit | | 217,000 |
| Net change in cash | | 10,660 |
| Plus beginning cash balance | | 0 |
| Ending cash balance | | $ 10,660 |

## *Answers to* The Curious Accountant

Budget preparation at the USOC is complicated by the fact that the timing of its revenues does not match the timing of its expenditures. The USOC spends a lot of money helping to train athletes for the United States Olympic team. Training takes place year-round, every year, for many athletes. The USOC's training facilities in Colorado must also be maintained continuously.

Conversely, much of the USOC's revenues are earned in big batches, received every two years. This money comes from fees the USOC receives for the rights to broadcast the Olympic games on television in the United States. Most companies have a one-year budget cycle during which they attempt to anticipate the coming year's revenues and expenses. This model would not work well for the USOC. For example, in 2008, a year of summer Olympics, the USOC reported revenues of $201.7 million and a deficit of $30.6 million. In 2007, a year with no Olympic games, the USOC reported revenues of $146.1 million and a deficit of $35.0 million. In 2006, a year of winter games, the USOC had revenues of $239.7 million and a surplus of $74.9 million.

Every business, like every family, faces its own set of circumstances. Those individuals responsible for preparing an entity's budget must have a thorough understanding of the environment in which the entity operates. This is the reason the budget process must be participatory if it is to be successful. No one person, or small group, can anticipate all the issues that will face a large organization in the coming budget period; they need input from employees at all levels.

Source: Form 990s filed by the USOC with the IRS.

---

### ✓ CHECK YOURSELF 7.3

How do pro forma financial statements differ from the financial statements presented in a company's annual report to stockholders?

**Answer**  Pro forma financial statements are based on estimates and projections about business events that a company expects to occur in the future. The financial statements presented in a company's annual report to stockholders are based on historical events that occurred prior to the preparation of the statements.

---

## A Look Back  **‹‹**

The planning of financial matters is called *budgeting.* The degree of detail in a company's budget depends on the budget period. Generally, the shorter the time period, the more specific the plans. *Strategic planning* involves long-term plans, such as the overall objectives of the business. Examples of strategic planning include which products to manufacture and sell and which market niches to pursue. Strategic plans are stated in broad, descriptive terms. Capital budgeting deals with intermediate investment planning. *Operations budgeting* focuses on short-term plans and is used to create the master budget.

A budgeting committee is responsible for consolidating numerous departmental budgets into a master budget for the whole company. The *master budget* has detailed objectives stated in specific amounts; it describes how management intends to achieve its objectives. The master budget usually covers one year. Budgeting supports planning, coordination, performance measurement, and corrective action.

Employees may be uncomfortable with budgets, which can be constraining. Budgets set standards by which performance is evaluated. To establish an effective budget system, management should recognize the effect on human behavior of budgeting. Upper-level management must set a positive atmosphere by taking budgets seriously and avoiding using them to humiliate subordinates. One way to create the proper atmosphere is to encourage subordinates' participation in the budgeting process; *participative budgeting* can lead to goals that are more realistic about what can be accomplished and to establish a team effort in trying to reach those goals.

The primary components of the master budget are the *operating budgets,* the *capital budgets,* and the *pro forma financial statements.* The budgeting process begins with preparing the operating budgets, which consist of detailed schedules and budgets prepared by various company departments. The first operating budget to be prepared is the sales budget. The detailed operating budgets for inventory purchases and S&A expenses are based on the projected sales from the sales budget. The information in the schedules of cash receipts (prepared in conjunction with the sales budget) and cash payments (prepared in conjunction with the inventory purchases and S&A expense budgets) is used in preparing the cash budget. The cash budget subtracts cash payments from cash receipts; the resulting cash surplus or shortage determines the company's financing activities.

The capital budget describes the company's long-term plans regarding investments in facilities, equipment, new products, or other lines of business. The information from the capital budget is used as input to several of the operating budgets.

The pro forma financial statements are prepared from information in the operating budgets. The operating budgets for sales, inventory purchases, and S&A expenses contain information that is used to prepare the income statement and balance sheet. The cash budget includes the amount of interest expense reported on the income statement, the ending cash balance, the capital acquisitions reported on the balance sheet, and most of the information included in the statement of cash flows.

## >> A Look Forward

Once a company has completed its budget, it has defined its plans. Then the plans must be followed. The next chapter investigates the techniques used to evaluate performance. You will learn to compare actual results to budgets, to calculate variances, and to identify the parties who are normally accountable for deviations from expectations. Finally, you will learn about the human impact management must consider in taking corrective action when employees fail to accomplish budget goals.

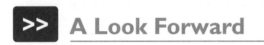

**A step-by-step audio-narrated series of slides is provided on the text website at www.mhhe.com/edmonds2011.**

### SELF-STUDY REVIEW PROBLEM

The Getaway Gift Company operates a chain of small gift shops that are located in prime vacation towns. Getaway is considering opening a new store on January 1, 2012. Getaway's president recently attended a business seminar that explained how formal budgets could be useful in judging the new store's likelihood of succeeding. Assume you are the company's accountant. The president has asked you to explain the budgeting process and to provide sample reports that show the new store's operating expectations for the first three months (January, February, and March). Respond to the following specific requirements:

## Required

a. List the operating budgets and schedules included in a master budget.

b. Explain the difference between pro forma financial statements and the financial statements presented in a company's annual reports to shareholders.

c. Prepare a sample sales budget and a schedule of expected cash receipts using the following assumptions. Getaway estimates January sales will be $400,000 of which $100,000 will be cash and $300,000 will be credit. The ratio of cash sales to sales on account is expected to remain constant over the three-month period. The company expects sales to increase 10 percent per month. The company expects to collect 100 percent of the accounts receivable generated by credit sales in the month following the sale. Use this information to determine the amount of accounts receivable that Getaway would report on the March 31 pro forma balance sheet and the amount of sales it would report on the first quarter pro forma income statement.

d. Prepare a sample inventory purchases budget using the following assumptions. Cost of goods sold is 60 percent of sales. The company desires to maintain a minimum ending inventory equal to 25 percent of the following month's cost of goods sold. Getaway makes all inventory purchases on account. The company pays 70 percent of accounts payable in the month of purchase. It pays the remaining 30 percent in the following month. Prepare a schedule of expected cash payments for inventory purchases. Use this information to determine the amount of cost of goods sold Getaway would report on the first quarter pro forma income statement and the amounts of ending inventory and accounts payable it would report on the March 31 pro forma balance sheet.

## Solution to Requirement a

A master budget would include (1) a sales budget and schedule of cash receipts, (2) an inventory purchases budget and schedule of cash payments for inventory, (3) a general, selling, and administrative expenses budget and a schedule of cash payments related to these expenses, and (4) a cash budget.

## Solution to Requirement b

Pro forma statements result from the operating budgets listed in the response to Requirement a. Pro forma statements describe the results of expected future events. In contrast, the financial statements presented in a company's annual report reflect the results of events that have actually occurred in the past.

## Solution to Requirement c

| General Information | | | | |
|---|---|---|---|---|
| **Sales growth rate 10%** | | | | **Pro Forma Statement Data** |
| Sales Budget | January | February | March | |
| Sales | | | | |
| Cash sales | $100,000 | $110,000 | $121,000 | |
| Sales on account | 300,000 | 330,000 | 363,000 | $ 363,000* |
| Total sales | $400,000 | $440,000 | $484,000 | $1,324,000† |
| **Schedule of Cash Receipts** | | | | |
| Current cash sales | $100,000 | $110,000 | $121,000 | |
| Plus 100% of previous month's credit sales | 0 | 300,000 | 330,000 | |
| Total budgeted collections | $100,000 | $410,000 | $451,000 | |

*Ending accounts receivable balance reported on March 31 pro forma balance sheet.

†Sales revenue reported on first quarter pro forma income statement (sum of monthly sales).

### Solution to Requirement d

| General Information | | | | |
|---|---|---|---|---|
| **Cost of goods sold percentage 60%** | | | | **Pro Forma** |
| **Desired ending inventory percentage of CGS 25%** | | | | **Statement Data** |
| | | | | |
| **Inventory Purchases Budget** | **January** | **February** | **March** | |
| Budgeted cost of goods sold | $240,000 | $264,000 | $290,400 | $794,400* |
| Plus: Desired ending inventory | 66,000 | 72,600 | 79,860 | 79,860† |
| Inventory needed | 306,000 | 336,600 | 370,260 | |
| Less: Beginning inventory | 0 | (66,000) | (72,600) | |
| Required purchases | $306,000 | $270,600 | $297,660 | 89,298‡ |
| **Schedule of Cash Payments for Inventory Purchases** | | | | |
| 70% of current purchases | $214,200 | $189,420 | $208,362 | |
| 30% of prior month's purchases | 0 | 91,800 | 81,180 | |
| Total budgeted payments for inventory | $214,200 | $281,220 | $289,542 | |

*Cost of goods sold reported on first quarter pro forma income statement (sum of monthly amounts).

†Ending inventory balance reported on March 31 pro forma balance sheet.

‡Ending accounts payable balance reported on pro forma balance sheet ($297,660 × 0.3).

## KEY TERMS

Budgeting 304
Capital budget 308
Capital budgeting 306
Cash budget 313
Master budget 308

Operating budgets 306
Operations budgeting 306
Participative budgeting 308
Perpetual (continuous)
    budgeting 306

Pro forma financial
    statements 308
Strategic planning 306

## QUESTIONS

1. Budgets are useful only for small companies that can estimate sales with accuracy. Do you agree with this statement?

2. Why does preparing the master budget require a committee?

3. What are the three levels of planning? Explain each briefly.

4. What is the primary factor that distinguishes the three different levels of planning from each other?

5. What is the advantage of using a perpetual budget instead of the traditional annual budget?

6. What are the advantages of budgeting?

7. How may budgets be used as a measure of performance?

8. Ken Shilov, manager of the marketing department, tells you that "budgeting simply does not work." He says that he made budgets for his employees and when he reprimanded them for failing to accomplish

budget goals, he got unfounded excuses. Suggest how Mr. Shilov could encourage employee cooperation.

9. What is a master budget?

10. What is the normal starting point in developing the master budget?

11. How does the level of inventory affect the production budget? Why is it important to manage the level of inventory?

12. What are the components of the cash budget? Describe each.

13. The primary reason for preparing a cash budget is to determine the amount of cash to include on the budgeted balance sheet. Do you agree or disagree with this statement? Explain.

14. What information does the pro forma income statement provide? How does its preparation depend on the operating budgets?

15. How does the pro forma statement of cash flows differ from the cash budget?

# MULTIPLE-CHOICE QUESTIONS

**Multiple-choice questions are provided on the text website at www.mhhe.com/edmonds2011.**

## EXERCISES—SERIES A

**All applicable Exercises in Series A are available with McGraw-Hill's *Connect Accounting*.**

### Exercise 7-1A    *Budget responsibility*                                    LO 1, 2

Sonya Huffman, the accountant, is a perfectionist. No one can do the job as well as she can. Indeed, she has found budget information provided by the various departments to be worthless. She must change everything they give her. She has to admit that her estimates have not always been accurate, but she shudders to think of what would happen if she used the information supplied by the marketing and operating departments. No one seems to care about accuracy. Indeed, some of the marketing staff have even become insulting. When Ms. Huffman confronted one of the salesmen with the fact that he was behind in meeting his budgeted sales forecast, he responded by saying, "They're your numbers. Why don't you go out and make the sales? It's a heck of a lot easier to sit there in your office and make up numbers than it is to get out and get the real work done." Ms. Huffman reported the incident, but, of course, nothing was done about it.

**Required**

Write a short report suggesting how the budgeting process could be improved.

### Exercise 7-2A    *Preparing a sales budget*                                LO 3, 7

Welch Company, which expects to start operations on January 1, 2011, will sell digital cameras in shopping malls. Welch has budgeted sales as indicated in the following table. The company expects a 10 percent increase in sales per month for February and March. The ratio of cash sales to sales on account will remain stable from January through March.

| Sales | January | February | March |
|---|---|---|---|
| Cash sales | $ 40,000 | ? | ? |
| Sales on account | 100,000 | ? | ? |
| Total budgeted sales | $140,000 | ? | ? |

**Required**

**a.** Complete the sales budget by filling in the missing amounts.

**b.** Determine the amount of sales revenue Welch will report on its first quarter pro forma income statement.

### Exercise 7-3A    *Preparing a schedule of cash receipts*                   LO 3, 7

The budget director of Ginger's Florist has prepared the following sales budget. The company had $300,000 in accounts receivable on July 1. Ginger's Florist normally collects 100 percent of accounts receivable in the month following the month of sale.

| | July | August | September |
|---|---|---|---|
| **Sales Budget** | | | |
| Cash sales | $ 70,000 | $ 75,000 | $ 80,000 |
| Sales on account | 90,000 | 108,000 | 129,600 |
| Total budgeted sales | $160,000 | $183,000 | $209,600 |
| **Schedule of Cash Receipts** | | | |
| Current cash sales | ? | ? | ? |
| Plus: Collections from accounts receivable | ? | ? | ? |
| Total budgeted collections | $370,000 | $165,000 | $188,000 |

**Required**

a. Complete the schedule of cash receipts by filling in the missing amounts.

b. Determine the amount of accounts receivable the company will report on its third quarter pro forma balance sheet.

LO 3

### Exercise 7-4A    *Preparing sales budgets with different assumptions*

Applebaum Corporation, which has three divisions, is preparing its sales budget. Each division expects a different growth rate because economic conditions vary in different regions of the country. The growth expectations per quarter are 4 percent for East Division, 2 percent for West Division, and 6 percent for South Division.

| Division | First Quarter | Second Quarter | Third Quarter | Fourth Quarter |
|---|---|---|---|---|
| East Division | $100,000 | ? | ? | ? |
| West Division | 300,000 | ? | ? | ? |
| South Division | 200,000 | ? | ? | ? |

**Required**

a. Complete the sales budget by filling in the missing amounts. (Round figures to the nearest dollar.)

b. Determine the amount of sales revenue that the company will report on its quarterly pro forma income statements.

LO 3

### Exercise 7-5A    *Determining cash receipts from accounts receivable*

Janice's Dress Delivery operates a mail-order business that sells clothes designed for frequent travelers. It had sales of $560,000 in December. Because Janice's Dress Delivery is in the mail-order business, all sales are made on account. The company expects a 30 percent drop in sales for January. The balance in the Accounts Receivable account on December 31 was $96,400 and is budgeted to be $73,600 as of January 31. Janice's Dress Delivery normally collects accounts receivable in the month following the month of sale.

**Required**

a. Determine the amount of cash Janice's Dress Delivery expects to collect from accounts receivable during January.

b. Is it reasonable to assume that sales will decline in January for this type of business? Why or why not?

LO 3

### Exercise 7-6A    *Using judgment in making a sales forecast*

Contrell Company operates a candy store located in a large shopping mall.

**Required**

Write a brief memo describing the sales pattern that you would expect Contrell to experience during the year. In which months will sales likely be high? In which months will sales likely be low? Explain why.

LO 4

### Exercise 7-7A    *Preparing an inventory purchases budget*

Naftel Company sells lamps and other lighting fixtures. The purchasing department manager prepared the following inventory purchases budget. Naftel's policy is to maintain an ending inventory balance equal to 10 percent of the following month's cost of goods sold. April's budgeted cost of goods sold is $75,000.

| | January | February | March |
|---|---|---|---|
| Budgeted cost of goods sold | $50,000 | $54,000 | $60,000 |
| Plus: Desired ending inventory | 5,400 | ? | ? |
| Inventory needed | 55,400 | ? | ? |
| Less: Beginning inventory | 5,000 | ? | ? |
| Required purchases (on account) | $50,400 | ? | ? |

**Required**

a. Complete the inventory purchases budget by filling in the missing amounts.

b. Determine the amount of cost of goods sold the company will report on its first quarter pro forma income statement.

c. Determine the amount of ending inventory the company will report on its pro forma balance sheet at the end of the first quarter.

### Exercise 7-8A   *Preparing a schedule of cash payments for inventory purchases*

LO 4

Sciara Books buys books and magazines directly from publishers and distributes them to grocery stores. The wholesaler expects to purchase the following inventory.

|  | April | May | June |
|---|---|---|---|
| Required purchases (on account) | $100,000 | $120,000 | $132,000 |

Sciara Books' accountant prepared the following schedule of cash payments for inventory purchases. Sciara Books' suppliers require that 90 percent of purchases on account be paid in the month of purchase; the remaining 10 percent are paid in the month following the month of purchase.

**Schedule of Cash Payments for Inventory Purchases**

|  | April | May | June |
|---|---|---|---|
| Payment for current accounts payable | $90,000 | ? | ? |
| Payment for previous accounts payable | 8,000 | ? | ? |
| Total budgeted payments for inventory | $98,000 | ? | ? |

**Required**

a. Complete the schedule of cash payments for inventory purchases by filling in the missing amounts.

b. Determine the amount of accounts payable the company will report on its pro forma balance sheet at the end of the second quarter.

### Exercise 7-9A   *Determining the amount of expected inventory purchases and cash payments*

LO 4

Tobert Company, which sells electric razors, had $300,000 of cost of goods sold during the month of June. The company projects a 5 percent increase in cost of goods sold during July. The inventory balance as of June 30 is $28,000, and the desired ending inventory balance for July is $29,000. Tobert pays cash to settle 70 percent of its purchases on account during the month of purchase and pays the remaining 30 percent in the month following the purchase. The accounts payable balance as of June 30 was $35,000.

**Required**

a. Determine the amount of purchases budgeted for July.

b. Determine the amount of cash payments budgeted for inventory purchases in July.

### Exercise 7-10A   *Preparing a schedule of cash payments for selling and administrative expenses*

LO 5

The budget director for Metro Cleaning Services prepared the following list of expected selling and administrative expenses. All expenses requiring cash payments are paid for in the month incurred except salary expense and insurance. Salary is paid in the month following the month in which it is incurred. The insurance premium for six months is paid on October 1. October is the first month of operations; accordingly, there are no beginning account balances.

| | October | November | December |
|---|---|---|---|
| **Budgeted S&A Expenses** | | | |
| Equipment lease expense | $ 6,000 | $ 6,000 | $ 6,000 |
| Salary expense | 6,100 | 6,600 | 7,000 |
| Cleaning supplies | 2,800 | 2,730 | 3,066 |
| Insurance expense | 1,200 | 1,200 | 1,200 |
| Depreciation on computer | 1,800 | 1,800 | 1,800 |
| Rent | 1,700 | 1,700 | 1,700 |
| Miscellaneous expenses | 700 | 700 | 700 |
| Total operating expenses | $20,300 | $20,730 | $21,466 |
| **Schedule of Cash Payments for S&A Expenses** | | | |
| Equipment lease expense | ? | ? | ? |
| Prior month's salary expense, 100% | ? | ? | ? |
| Cleaning supplies | ? | ? | ? |
| Insurance premium | ? | ? | ? |
| Depreciation on computer | ? | ? | ? |
| Rent | ? | ? | ? |
| Miscellaneous expenses | ? | ? | ? |
| Total disbursements for operating expenses | $18,400 | $17,230 | $18,066 |

**Required**

a. Complete the schedule of cash payments for S&A expenses by filling in the missing amounts.

b. Determine the amount of salaries payable the company will report on its pro forma balance sheet at the end of the fourth quarter.

c. Determine the amount of prepaid insurance the company will report on its pro forma balance sheet at the end of the fourth quarter.

**LO 4**

**Exercise 7-11A** *Preparing inventory purchases budgets with different assumptions*

Executive officers of Dominick Company are wrestling with their budget for the next year. The following are two different sales estimates provided by two difference sources.

| Source of Estimate | First Quarter | Second Quarter | Third Quarter | Fourth Quarter |
|---|---|---|---|---|
| Sales manager | $380,000 | $310,000 | $280,000 | $480,000 |
| Marketing consultant | 520,000 | 460,000 | 410,000 | 650,000 |

Dominick's past experience indicates that cost of goods sold is about 60 percent of sales revenue. The company tries to maintain 10 percent of the next quarter's expected cost of goods sold as the current quarter's ending inventory. This year's ending inventory is $29,000. Next year's ending inventory is budgeted to be $30,000.

**Required**

a. Prepare an inventory purchases budget using the sales manager's estimate.

b. Prepare an inventory purchases budget using the marketing consultant's estimate.

**LO 5, 7**

**Exercise 7-12A** *Determining the amount of cash payments and pro forma statement data for selling and administrative expenses*

January budgeted selling and administrative expenses for the retail shoe store that Kathy Sibley plans to open on January 1, 2011, are as follows: sales commissions, $25,000; rent, $16,000; utilities, $5,000; depreciation, $4,000; and miscellaneous, $2,000. Utilities are paid in the month after incurrence. Other expenses are expected to be paid in cash in the month in which they are incurred.

**Required**

a. Determine the amount of budgeted cash payments for January selling and administrative expenses.

b. Determine the amount of utilities payable the store will report on the January 31st pro forma balance sheet.

c. Determine the amount of depreciation expense the store will report on the income statement for the year 2011, assuming that monthly depreciation remains the same for the entire year.

### Exercise 7-13A    *Preparing a cash budget*                                   LO 6, 7

The accountant for Teresa's Dress Shop prepared the following cash budget. Teresa's desires to maintain a cash cushion of $14,000 at the end of each month. Funds are assumed to be borrowed and repaid on the last day of each month. Interest is charged at the rate of 2 percent per month.

| Cash Budget | July | August | September |
|---|---|---|---|
| **Section 1: Cash receipts** | | | |
| Beginning cash balance | $ 42,500 | $   ? | $   ? |
| Add cash receipts | 180,000 | 200,000 | 240,600 |
| Total cash available (a) | 222,500 | ? | ? |
| **Section 2: Cash payments** | | | |
| For inventory purchases | 165,526 | 140,230 | 174,152 |
| For S&A expenses | 54,500 | 60,560 | 61,432 |
| For interest expense | 0 | ? | ? |
| Total budgeted disbursements (b) | 220,026 | ? | ? |
| **Section 3: Financing activities** | | | |
| Surplus (shortage) | 2,474 | ? | ? |
| Borrowing (repayments) (c) | 11,526 | ? | ? |
| Ending cash balance (a − b + c) | $ 14,000 | $ 14,000 | $ 14,000 |

**Required**

a. Complete the cash budget by filling in the missing amounts. Round all computations to the nearest whole dollar.

b. Determine the amount of net cash flows from operating activities Teresa's will report on the third quarter pro forma statement of cash flows.

c. Determine the amount of net cash flows from financing activities Teresa's will report on the third quarter pro forma statement of cash flows.

### Exercise 7-14A    *Determining amount to borrow and pro forma statement balances*    LO 6, 7

Athena Sudsberry owns a small restaurant in New York City. Ms. Sudsberry provided her accountant with the following summary information regarding expectations for the month of June. The balance in accounts receivable as of May 31 is $60,000. Budgeted cash and credit sales for June are $150,000 and $600,000, respectively. Credit sales are made through Visa and MasterCard and are collected rapidly. Eighty percent of credit sales is collected in the month of sale, and the remainder is collected in the following month. Ms. Sudsberry's suppliers do not extend credit. Consequently, she pays suppliers on the last day of the month. Cash payments for June are expected to be $700,000. Ms. Sudsberry has a line of credit that enables the restaurant to borrow funds on demand; however, they must be borrowed on the last day of the month. Interest is paid in cash also on the last day of the month. Ms. Sudsberry desires to maintain a $30,000 cash balance before the interest payment. Her annual interest rate is 9 percent.

**Required**

a. Compute the amount of funds Ms. Sudsberry needs to borrow for June.

b. Determine the amount of interest expense the restaurant will report on the June pro forma income statement.

c. What amount will the restaurant report as interest expense on the July pro forma income statement?

### Exercise 7-15A  *Preparing pro forma income statements with different assumptions*

Norman Jelen, the controller of Wing Corporation, is trying to prepare a sales budget for the coming year. The income statements for the last four quarters follow.

|  | First Quarter | Second Quarter | Third Quarter | Fourth Quarter | Total |
|---|---|---|---|---|---|
| Sales revenue | $170,000 | $200,000 | $210,000 | $260,000 | $840,000 |
| Cost of goods sold | 102,000 | 120,000 | 126,000 | 156,000 | 504,000 |
| Gross profit | 68,000 | 80,000 | 84,000 | 104,000 | 336,000 |
| Selling & admin. expenses | 17,000 | 20,000 | 21,000 | 26,000 | 84,000 |
| Net income | $ 51,000 | $ 60,000 | $ 63,000 | $ 78,000 | $252,000 |

Historically, cost of goods sold is about 60 percent of sales revenue. Selling and administrative expenses are about 10 percent of sales revenue.

Sam Wing, the chief executive officer, told Mr. Jelen that he expected sales next year to be 10 percent for each respective quarter above last year's level. However, Glenda Sullivan, the vice president of sales, told Mr. Jelen that she believed sales growth would be only 5 percent.

#### Required

a. Prepare a pro forma income statement including quarterly budgets for the coming year using Mr. Wing's estimate.

b. Prepare a pro forma income statement including quarterly budgets for the coming year using Ms. Sullivan's estimate.

c. Explain why two executive officers in the same company could have different estimates of future growth.

## PROBLEMS—SERIES A

**All applicable Problems in Series A are available with McGraw-Hill's *Connect Accounting.***

### Problem 7-16A  *Preparing a sales budget and schedule of cash receipts*

McCarty Pointers Corporation expects to begin operations on January 1, 2012; it will operate as a specialty sales company that sells laser pointers over the Internet. McCarty expects sales in January 2012 to total $200,000 and to increase 10 percent per month in February and March. All sales are on account. McCarty expects to collect 70 percent of accounts receivable in the month of sale, 20 percent in the month following the sale, and 10 percent in the second month following the sale.

#### Required

a. Prepare a sales budget for the first quarter of 2012.

b. Determine the amount of sales revenue McCarty will report on the first 2012 quarterly pro forma income statement.

c. Prepare a cash receipts schedule for the first quarter of 2012.

d. Determine the amount of accounts receivable as of March 31, 2012.

### Problem 7-17A  *Preparing an inventory purchases budget and schedule of cash payments*

Spratt, Inc., sells fireworks. The company's marketing director developed the following cost of goods sold budget for April, May, June, and July.

|  | April | May | June | July |
|---|---|---|---|---|
| Budgeted cost of goods sold | $60,000 | $70,000 | $80,000 | $86,000 |

Spratt had a beginning inventory balance of $3,600 on April 1 and a beginning balance in accounts payable of $14,800. The company desires to maintain an ending inventory balance equal to 10 percent of the next period's cost of goods sold. Spratt makes all purchases on account. The company pays 60 percent of accounts payable in the month of purchase and the remaining 40 percent in the month following purchase.

### Required

**a.** Prepare an inventory purchases budget for April, May, and June.

**b.** Determine the amount of ending inventory Spratt will report on the end-of-quarter pro forma balance sheet.

**c.** Prepare a schedule of cash payments for inventory for April, May, and June.

**d.** Determine the balance in accounts payable Spratt will report on the end-of-quarter pro forma balance sheet.

**Problem 7-18A**    *Preparing pro forma income statements with different assumptions*

**LO 7**

Top executive officers of Zottoli Company, a merchandising firm, are preparing the next year's budget. The controller has provided everyone with the current year's projected income statement.

**CHECK FIGURE**
a. 12.75%

|  | Current Year |
|---|---|
| Sales revenue | $2,000,000 |
| Cost of goods sold | 1,400,000 |
| Gross profit | 600,000 |
| Selling & admin. expenses | 260,000 |
| Net income | $ 340,000 |

Cost of goods sold is usually 70 percent of sales revenue, and selling and administrative expenses are usually 10 percent of sales plus a fixed cost of $60,000. The president has announced that the company's goal is to increase net income by 15 percent.

### Required

The following items are independent of each other.

**a.** What percentage increase in sales would enable the company to reach its goal? Support your answer with a pro forma income statement.

**b.** The market may become stagnant next year, and the company does not expect an increase in sales revenue. The production manager believes that an improved production procedure can cut cost of goods sold by 2 percent. What else can the company do to reach its goal? Prepare a pro forma income statement illustrating your proposal.

**c.** The company decides to escalate its advertising campaign to boost consumer recognition, which will increase selling and administrative expenses to $340,000. With the increased advertising, the company expects sales revenue to increase by 15 percent. Assume that cost of goods sold remains a constant proportion of sales. Can the company reach its goal?

**Problem 7-19A**    *Preparing a schedule of cash payments for selling and administrative expenses*

**LO 5, 6**

Prestia is a retail company specializing in men's hats. Its budget director prepared the list of expected operating expenses that follows. All items are paid when incurred except sales commissions and utilities, which are paid in the month following their incurrence. July is the first month of operations, so there are no beginning account balances.

**CHECK FIGURE**
a. Sept: $28,510

|  | July | August | September |
|---|---|---|---|
| Salary expense | $18,000 | $18,000 | $18,000 |
| Sales commissions (4 percent of sales) | 1,700 | 1,700 | 1,700 |
| Supplies expense | 360 | 390 | 420 |
| Utilities | 1,100 | 1,100 | 1,100 |
| Depreciation on store equipment | 3,000 | 3,000 | 3,000 |
| Rent | 6,600 | 6,600 | 6,600 |
| Miscellaneous | 690 | 690 | 690 |
| Total S&A expenses before interest | $31,450 | $31,480 | $31,510 |

**Required**

a. Prepare a schedule of cash payments for selling and administrative expenses.

b. Determine the amount of utilities payable as of September 30.

c. Determine the amount of sales commissions payable as of September 30.

### Problem 7-20A   *Preparing a cash budget*

Kinnion Medical Clinic has budgeted the following cash flows.

|  | January | February | March |
|---|---|---|---|
| Cash receipts | $100,000 | $106,000 | $126,000 |
| Cash payments |  |  |  |
| For inventory purchases | 90,000 | 72,000 | 85,000 |
| For S&A expenses | 31,000 | 32,000 | 27,000 |

Kinnion Medical had a cash balance of $8,000 on January 1. The company desires to maintain a cash cushion of $5,000. Funds are assumed to be borrowed, in increments of $1,000, and repaid on the last day of each month; the interest rate is 1 percent per month. Repayments may be made in any amount available. Kinnion pays its vendors on the last day of the month also. The company had a monthly $40,000 beginning balance in its line of credit liability account from this year's quarterly results.

**Required**

Prepare a cash budget. (Round all computations to the nearest whole dollar.)

### Problem 7-21A   *Preparing budgets with multiple products*

Hammond Fruits Corporation wholesales peaches and oranges. Lashanda King is working with the company's accountant to prepare next year's budget. Ms. King estimates that sales will increase 5 percent for peaches and 10 percent for oranges. The current year's sales revenue data follow.

|  | First Quarter | Second Quarter | Third Quarter | Fourth Quarter | Total |
|---|---|---|---|---|---|
| Peaches | $220,000 | $240,000 | $300,000 | $240,000 | $1,000,000 |
| Oranges | 400,000 | 450,000 | 570,000 | 380,000 | 1,800,000 |
| Total | $620,000 | $690,000 | $870,000 | $620,000 | $2,800,000 |

Based on the company's past experience, cost of goods sold is usually 60 percent of sales revenue. Company policy is to keep 10 percent of the next period's estimated cost of goods sold as the current period's ending inventory. (*Hint:* Use the cost of goods sold for the first quarter to determine the beginning inventory for the first quarter.)

**Required**

a. Prepare the company's sales budget for the next year for each quarter by individual product.

b. If the selling and administrative expenses are estimated to be $700,000, prepare the company's budgeted annual income statement.

c. Ms. King estimates next year's ending inventory will be $34,000 for peaches and $56,000 for oranges. Prepare the company's inventory purchases budgets for the next year showing quarterly figures by product.

### Problem 7-22A   *Preparing a master budget for retail company with no beginning account balances*

Patel Company is a retail company that specializes in selling outdoor camping equipment. The company is considering opening a new store on October 1, 2012. The company president formed a planning committee to prepare a master budget for the first three months of operation. As budget coordinator, you have been assigned the following tasks.

**Required**

a. October sales are estimated to be $120,000 of which 40 percent will be cash and 60 percent will be credit. The company expects sales to increase at the rate of 25 percent per month. Prepare a sales budget.

b. The company expects to collect 100 percent of the accounts receivable generated by credit sales in the month following the sale. Prepare a schedule of cash receipts.

c. The cost of goods sold is 60 percent of sales. The company desires to maintain a minimum ending inventory equal to 10 percent of the next month's cost of goods sold. However, ending inventory of December is expected to be $12,000. Assume that all purchases are made on account. Prepare an inventory purchases budget.

d. The company pays 70 percent of accounts payable in the month of purchase and the remaining 30 percent in the following month. Prepare a cash payments budget for inventory purchases.

e. Budgeted selling and administrative expenses per month follow.

| | |
|---|---|
| Salary expense (fixed) | $18,000 |
| Sales commissions | 5 percent of Sales |
| Supplies expense | 2 percent of Sales |
| Utilities (fixed) | $1,400 |
| Depreciation on store fixtures (fixed)* | $4,000 |
| Rent (fixed) | $4,800 |
| Miscellaneous (fixed) | $1,200 |

*The capital expenditures budget indicates that Patel will spend $164,000 on October 1 for store fixtures, which are expected to have a $20,000 salvage value and a three-year (36-month) useful life.

Use this information to prepare a selling and administrative expenses budget.

f. Utilities and sales commissions are paid the month after they are incurred; all other expenses are paid in the month in which they are incurred. Prepare a cash payments budget for selling and administrative expenses.

g. Patel borrows funds, in increments of $1,000, and repays them on the last day of the month. Repayments may be made in any amount available. The company also pays its vendors on the last day of the month. It pays interest of 1 percent per month in cash on the last day of the month. To be prudent, the company desires to maintain a $12,000 cash cushion. Prepare a cash budget.

h. Prepare a pro forma income statement for the quarter.

i. Prepare a pro forma balance sheet at the end of the quarter.

j. Prepare a pro forma statement of cash flows for the quarter.

## Problem 7-23A    *Behavioral impact of budgeting*

Shahid Corporation has three divisions, each operating as a responsibility center. To provide an incentive for divisional executive officers, the company gives divisional management a bonus equal to 15 percent of the excess of actual net income over budgeted net income. The following is Chaudhry Division's current year's performance.

| | Current Year |
|---|---|
| Sales revenue | $4,000,000 |
| Cost of goods sold | 2,500,000 |
| Gross profit | 1,500,000 |
| Selling & admin. expenses | 900,000 |
| Net income | $ 600,000 |

The president has just received next year's budget proposal from the vice president in charge of Chaudhry Division. The proposal budgets a 5 percent increase in sales revenue with an extensive explanation about stiff market competition. The president is puzzled. Chaudhry has enjoyed revenue growth of around 10 percent for each of the past five years. The president had consistently approved the division's budget proposals based on 5 percent growth in the past. This time, the president wants to show that he is not a fool. "I will impose a 15 percent revenue increase to teach them a lesson!" the president says to himself smugly.

Assume that cost of goods sold and selling and administrative expenses remain stable in proportion to sales.

**Required**

a. Prepare the budgeted income statement based on Chaudhry Division's proposal of a 5 percent increase.

b. If growth is actually 10 percent as usual, how much bonus would Chaudhry Division's executive officers receive if the president had approved the division's proposal?

c. Prepare the budgeted income statement based on the 15 percent increase the president imposed.

d. If the actual results turn out to be a 10 percent increase as usual, how much bonus would Chaudhry Division's executive officers receive since the president imposed a 15 percent increase?

e. Propose a better budgeting procedure for Shahid.

## EXERCISES—SERIES B

LO 1, 2

### Exercise 7-1B    *Budget responsibility*

Bennia Judson, the controller of Mullins Industries, is very popular. He is easygoing and does not offend anybody. To develop the company's most recent budget, Mr. Judson first asked all department managers to prepare their own budgets. He then added together the totals from the department budgets to produce the company budget. When Lonnie Morgar, Mullins' president, reviewed the company budget, she sighed and asked, "Is our company a charitable organization?"

**Required**

Write a brief memo describing deficiencies in the budgeting process and suggesting improvements.

LO 3, 7

### Exercise 7-2B    *Preparing a sales budget*

Gardner Restaurant is opening for business in a new shopping center. Ed Rozell, the owner, is preparing a sales budget for the next three months. After consulting friends in the same business, Mr. Rozell estimated July revenues as shown in the following table. He expects revenues to increase 5 percent per month in August and September.

|  | July | August | September |
|---|---|---|---|
| Food sales | $40,000 | ? | ? |
| Beverage and liquor sales | 24,000 | ? | ? |
| Total budgeted revenues | $64,000 | ? | ? |

**Required**

a. Complete the sales budget by filling in the missing amounts.

b. Determine the total amount of revenue Gardner Restaurant will report on its quarterly pro forma income statement.

LO 3, 7

### Exercise 7-3B    *Preparing a schedule of cash receipts*

Brown Imports, Inc., sells goods imported from the Far East. Using the second quarter's sales budget, Mark Yao is trying to complete the schedule of cash receipts for the quarter. The company had accounts receivable of $310,000 on April 1. Brown Imports normally collects 100 percent of accounts receivable in the month following the month of sale.

| Sales | April | May | June |
|---|---|---|---|
| **Sales Budget** | | | |
| Cash sales | $120,000 | $140,000 | $150,000 |
| Sales on account | 480,000 | 568,000 | 500,000 |
| Total budgeted sales | $600,000 | $708,000 | $650,000 |
| **Schedule of Cash Receipts** | | | |
| Current cash sales | ? | ? | ? |
| Plus: Collections from accounts receivable | ? | ? | ? |
| Total budgeted collections | $410,000 | $604,000 | $704,000 |

**Required**

a. Help Mr. Yao complete the schedule of cash receipts by filling in the missing amounts.

b. Determine the amount of accounts receivable the company will report on the quarterly pro forma balance sheet.

### Exercise 7-4B   *Preparing sales budgets with different assumptions*

LO 3

Lagrave International Company has three subsidiaries, Moore Trading Company, Pickrell Medical Supplies Company, and Rice Shipping Company. Because the subsidiaries operate in different industries, Lagrave's corporate budget for the coming year must reflect the different growth potentials of the individual industries. The growth expectations per quarter for the subsidiaries are 4 percent for Moore, 1 percent for Pickrell, and 3 percent for Rice.

| Subsidiary | Current Quarter Sales | First Quarter | Second Quarter | Third Quarter | Fourth Quarter |
|---|---|---|---|---|---|
| Moore | $160,000 | ? | ? | ? | ? |
| Pickrell | 200,000 | ? | ? | ? | ? |
| Rice | 320,000 | ? | ? | ? | ? |

**Required**

a. Complete the sales budget by filling in the missing amounts. (Round the figures to the nearest dollar.)

b. Determine the amount of sales revenue Lagrave will report on the quarterly pro forma income statements.

### Exercise 7-5B   *Determining cash receipts from accounts receivable*

LO 3

Hancock Corporation is about to start a business as an agricultural products distributor. Because its customers will all be retailers, Hancock will sell its products solely on account. The company expects to collect 50 percent of accounts receivable in the month of sale and the remaining 50 percent in the following month. Hancock expects sales revenues of $300,000 in July, the first month of operation, and $280,000 in August.

**Required**

a. Determine the amount of cash Hancock expects to collect in July.

b. Determine the amount of cash Hancock expects to collect in August.

### Exercise 7-6B   *Using judgment in making a sales forecast*

LO 3

Starr Greetings Corporation sells greeting cards for various occasions.

**Required**

Write a brief memo describing the sales pattern that you would expect Starr Greetings to experience during the year. In which months will sales likely be high? Explain why.

**LO 4**

### Exercise 7-7B  *Preparing an inventory purchases budget*

Young Drugstores, Inc., sells prescription drugs, over-the-counter drugs, and some groceries. The purchasing manager prepared the following inventory purchases budget. For this year, Young expects an ending inventory balance equal to 16 percent of the following month's cost of goods sold. April's budgeted cost of goods sold amounts to $63,000.

| Inventory Purchases Budget | January | February | March |
|---|---|---|---|
| Budgeted cost of goods sold | $80,000 | $56,000 | $60,000 |
| Plus: Desired ending inventory | 8,960 | ? | ? |
| Inventory needed | 88,960 | ? | ? |
| Less: Beginning inventory | 12,000 | ? | ? |
| Required purchases (on account) | $76,960 | ? | ? |

**Required**

a. Complete the inventory purchases budget by filling in the missing amounts.
b. Determine the amount of cost of goods sold the company will report on the first quarter pro forma income statement.
c. Determine the amount of ending inventory the company will report on the first quarter pro forma balance sheet.

**LO 4**

### Exercise 7-8B  *Preparing a schedule of cash payments for inventory purchases*

Waldrop Grocery buys and sells groceries in a community far from any major city. Cedric Waldrop, the owner, budgeted the store's purchases as follows:

| | October | November | December |
|---|---|---|---|
| Required purchases (on account) | $40,000 | $30,000 | $36,000 |

Waldrop's suppliers require that 70 percent of accounts payable be paid in the month of purchase. The remaining 30 percent is paid in the month following the month of purchase.

### Schedule of Cash Payments for Inventory Purchases

| | October | November | December |
|---|---|---|---|
| Payment for current accounts payable | $28,000 | ? | ? |
| Payment for previous accounts payable | 9,000 | ? | ? |
| Total budgeted payments for inventory | $37,000 | ? | ? |

**Required**

a. Complete the schedule of cash payments for inventory purchases by filling in the missing amounts.
b. Determine the amount of accounts payable Waldrop will report on the store's quarterly pro forma balance sheet.

**LO 4**

### Exercise 7-9B  *Determining the amount of inventory purchases and cash payments*

Bellaire Oil Corporation, which distributes gasoline products to independent gasoline stations, had $320,000 of cost of goods sold in January. The company expects a 2.5 percent increase in cost of goods sold during February. The ending inventory balance for January is $25,000, and the desired ending inventory for February is $30,000. Bellaire pays cash to settle 60 percent of its purchases on account during the month of purchase and pays the remaining 40 percent in the month following the purchase. The accounts payable balance as of January 31 was $30,000.

**Required**

a. Determine the amount of purchases budgeted for February.

b. Determine the amount of cash payments budgeted for inventory purchases in February.

## Exercise 7-10B    *Preparing a schedule of cash payments for selling and administrative expenses*

LO 5

The controller for Robinson Laundry Services prepared the following list of expected selling and administrative expenses. All expenses requiring cash payments except salary expense and insurance are paid for in the month incurred. Salary is paid in the month following its incursion. The annual insurance premium is paid in advance on January 1. January is the first month of operations. Accordingly, there are no beginning account balances.

|  | January | February | March |
|---|---|---|---|
| **Budgeted Selling and Administrative Expenses** | | | |
| Equipment depreciation | $ 5,000 | $ 5,000 | $ 5,000 |
| Salary expense | 3,400 | 3,200 | 3,600 |
| Cleaning supplies | 1,000 | 940 | 1,100 |
| Insurance expense | 600 | 600 | 600 |
| Equipment maintenance expense | 500 | 500 | 500 |
| Leases expense | 1,600 | 1,600 | 1,600 |
| Miscellaneous expenses | 400 | 400 | 400 |
| Total S&A expenses | $12,500 | $12,240 | $12,800 |
| **Schedule of Cash Payments for Selling and Administrative Expenses** | | | |
| Equipment depreciation | ? | ? | ? |
| Prior month's salary expense, 100% | ? | ? | ? |
| Cleaning supplies | ? | ? | ? |
| Insurance premium | ? | ? | ? |
| Equipment maintenance expense | ? | ? | ? |
| Leases expense | ? | ? | ? |
| Miscellaneous expenses | ? | ? | ? |
| Total payments for S&A expenses | $10,700 | $ 6,840 | $ 6,800 |

**Required**

a. Complete the schedule of cash payments for selling and administrative expenses by filling in the missing amounts.

b. Determine the amount of salaries payable the company will report on its quarterly pro forma balance sheet.

c. Determine the amount of prepaid insurance the company will report on its quarterly pro forma balance sheet.

## Exercise 7-11B    *Preparing inventory purchases budgets with different assumptions*

LO 4

Rachel Khan has been at odds with her brother and business partner, David, since childhood. The sibling rivalry is not all bad, however; their garden shop, Khan Gardens and Gifts, has been very successful. When the partners met to prepare the coming year's budget, their forecasts were different, naturally. Their sales revenue estimates follow.

| Source of Estimate | First Quarter | Second Quarter | Third Quarter | Fourth Quarter |
|---|---|---|---|---|
| Rachel | $360,000 | $400,000 | $300,000 | $420,000 |
| David | 300,000 | 320,000 | 340,000 | 480,000 |

Past experience indicates that cost of goods sold is about 60 percent of sales revenue. The company tries to maintain 15 percent of the next quarter's expected cost of goods sold as the current quarter's ending inventory. The ending inventory this year is $25,000. Next year's ending inventory is budgeted to be $35,000.

**Required**

a. Prepare an inventory purchases budget using Rachel's estimate.
b. Prepare an inventory purchases budget using David's estimate.

**LO 5, 7**

### Exercise 7-12B  *Determining the amount of cash payments for selling and administrative expenses*

Jensi Berger, managing partner of Berger Business Consulting, is preparing a budget for January 2013, the first month of business operations. Jensi estimates the following monthly selling and administrative expenses: office lease, $4,000; utilities, $1,900; office supplies, $2,400; depreciation, $12,000; referral fees, $5,000; and miscellaneous, $1,000. Referral fees will be paid in the month following the month they are incurred. Other expenses will be paid in the month in which they are incurred.

**Required**

a. Determine the amount of budgeted cash payments for January selling and administrative expenses.
b. Determine the amount of referral fees payable the firm will report on the January 31st pro forma balance sheet.
c. Determine the amount of office lease expense the company will report on its 2013 pro forma income statement, assuming that the monthly lease expense remains the same throughout the whole year.

**LO 6, 7**

### Exercise 7-13B  *Preparing a cash budget*

Antonio Kinnard, the accounting manager of Sparks Antique Company, is preparing his company's cash budget for the next quarter. Sparks desires to maintain a cash cushion of $4,000 at the end of each month. As cash flows fluctuate, the company either borrows or repays funds at the end of a month. It pays interest on borrowed funds at the rate of 1 percent per month.

| Cash Budget | July | August | September |
|---|---|---|---|
| **Section 1: Cash Receipts** | | | |
| Beginning cash balance | $ 16,000 | $  ? | $  ? |
| Add cash receipts | 180,000 | 192,000 | 208,000 |
| Total cash available (a) | 196,000 | ? | ? |
| **Section 2: Cash Payments** | | | |
| For inventory purchases | 158,000 | 153,000 | 171,000 |
| For S&A expenses | 37,000 | 36,000 | 39,000 |
| For interest expense | 0 | ? | ? |
| Total budgeted disbursements (b) | 195,000 | ? | ? |
| **Section 3: Financing Activities** | | | |
| Surplus (shortage) | 1,000 | ? | ? |
| Borrowing (repayments) (c) | 3,000 | ? | ? |
| Ending Cash Balance (a − b + c) | $  4,000 | $  4,000 | $  4,000 |

**Required**

a. Complete the cash budget by filling in the missing amounts. Round all computations to the nearest whole dollar.
b. Determine the amount of net cash flows from operating activities Sparks will report on its quarterly pro forma statement of cash flows.
c. Determine the amount of net cash flows from financing activities Sparks will report on its quarterly pro forma statement of cash flows.

**Exercise 7-14B**   *Determining amount to borrow and pro forma statement balances*    **LO 6, 7**

Kerry Norton, the president of Donnelly Corporation, has been working with his controller to manage the company's cash position. The controller provided Kerry the following data.

| | |
|---|---|
| Balance of accounts receivable, June 30 | $ 50,000 |
| Balance of line of credit, June 30 | 0 |
| Budgeted cash sales for July | 70,000 |
| Budgeted credit sales for July | 320,000 |
| Budgeted cash payments for July | 380,000 |

The company typically collects 75 percent of credit sales in the month of sale and the remainder in the month following the sale. Norton's line of credit enables the company to borrow funds readily, with the stipulation that any borrowing must take place on the last day of the month. The company pays its vendors on the last day of the month also. Mr. Norton likes to maintain a $15,000 cash balance before any interest payments. The annual interest rate is 12 percent.

**Required**

a. Compute the amount of funds Mr. Norton needs to borrow on July 31.

b. Determine the amount of interest expense the company will report on the July pro forma income statement.

c. Determine the amount of interest expense the company will report on the August pro forma income statement.

**Exercise 7-15B**   *Preparing pro forma income statements with different assumptions*    **LO 2, 7**

Revell Corporation's budget planning meeting is like a zoo. Millard McFerrin, the credit manager, is naturally conservative and Dorothy Dester, the marketing manager, is the opposite. They have argued back and forth about the effect of various factors that influence the sales growth rate, such as credit policies and market potential. Based on the following current year data provided by Elaine Gann, the controller, Millard expects Revell's revenues to grow 5 percent each quarter above last year's level; Dorothy insists the growth rate will be 8 percent per quarter.

| Current Year | First Quarter | Second Quarter | Third Quarter | Fourth Quarter | Total |
|---|---|---|---|---|---|
| Sales revenue | $240,000 | $200,000 | $216,000 | $314,000 | $970,000 |
| Cost of goods sold | 122,000 | 101,000 | 106,000 | 156,000 | 485,000 |
| Gross margin | 118,000 | 99,000 | 110,000 | 158,000 | 485,000 |
| Selling & admin. expenses | 32,000 | 26,000 | 26,400 | 40,600 | 125,000 |
| Net income | $ 86,000 | $ 73,000 | $ 83,600 | $117,400 | $360,000 |

Historically, cost of goods sold is projected at 50 percent of sales revenue. Selling and administrative expenses are expected to be 12.5 percent of sales revenue.

**Required**

a. Prepare a pro forma income statement for the coming year using the credit manager's growth estimate.

b. Prepare a pro forma income statement for the coming year using the marketing manager's growth estimate.

c. Explain why two executives in the same company could have different estimates of future growth.

## PROBLEMS—SERIES B

**LO 3**

### Problem 7-16B   *Preparing a sales budget and schedule of cash receipts*

Cobb Corporation sells mail-order computers. In December 2011, it has generated $450,000 of sales revenue; the company expects a 20 percent increase in sales in January and 10 percent in February. All sales are on account. Cobb normally collects 80 percent of accounts receivable in the month of sale and 20 percent in the next month.

**Required**

a. Prepare a sales budget for January and February 2012.

b. Determine the amount of sales revenue Cobb would report on the bimonthly pro forma income statement for January and February 2012.

c. Prepare a cash receipts schedule for January and February 2012.

d. Determine the amount of accounts receivable as of February 28, 2012.

**LO 4, 7**

### Problem 7-17B   *Preparing an inventory purchases budget and schedule of cash payments*

Drennan Company's purchasing manager, Neil Grey, is preparing a purchases budget for the next quarter. At his request, Robert Chan, the manager of the sales department, forwarded him the following preliminary sales budget.

|  | October | November | December | January |
|---|---|---|---|---|
| Budgeted sales | $600,000 | $750,000 | $900,000 | $800,000 |

For budgeting purposes, Drennan estimates that cost of goods sold is 75 percent of sales. The company desires to maintain an ending inventory balance equal to 20 percent of the next period's cost of goods sold. The September ending inventory is $90,000. Drennan makes all purchases on account and pays 70 percent of accounts payable in the month of purchase and the remaining 30 percent in the following month. The balance of accounts payable at the end of September is $90,000.

**Required**

a. Prepare an inventory purchases budget for October, November, and December.

b. Determine the amount of ending inventory Drennan will report on the end-of-quarter pro forma balance sheet.

c. Prepare a schedule of cash payments for inventory for October, November, and December.

d. Determine the balance in accounts payable Drennan will report on the end-of-quarter pro forma balance sheet.

**LO 7**

### Problem 7-18B   *Preparing pro forma income statements with different assumptions*

Drexel Morris, a successful entrepreneur, is reviewing the results of his first year in business. His accountant delivered the following income statement just five minutes ago.

|  | Current Year |
|---|---|
| Sales revenue | $500,000 |
| Cost of goods sold | 350,000 |
| Gross profit | 150,000 |
| Selling & admin. expenses | 90,000 |
| Net income | $ 60,000 |

Mr. Morris would like net income to increase 20 percent in the next year. This first year, selling and administrative expenses were 10 percent of sales revenue plus $40,000 of fixed expenses.

## Required

The following questions are independent of each other.

a. Mr. Morris expects that cost of goods sold and variable selling and administrative expenses will remain stable in proportion to sales next year. The fixed selling and administrative expenses will increase to $68,000. What percentage increase in sales would enable the company to reach Mr. Morris's goal? Prepare a pro forma income statement to illustrate.

b. Market competition may become serious next year, and Mr. Morris does not expect an increase in sales revenue. However, he has developed a good relationship with his supplier, who is willing to give him a volume discount that will decrease cost of goods sold by 3 percent. What else can the company do to reach Mr. Morris's goal? Prepare a pro forma income statement illustrating your proposal.

c. If the company escalates its advertising campaign to boost consumer recognition, the selling and administrative expenses will increase to $150,000. With the increased advertising, the company expects sales revenue to increase by 25 percent. Assume that cost of goods sold remains constant in proportion to sales. Can the company reach Mr. Morris's goal?

**Problem 7-19B**  *Preparing a schedule of cash payments for selling and administrative expenses*    LO 5

Redney's Travel Services has prepared its selling and administrative expenses budget for the next quarter. It pays all expenses when they are incurred except sales commissions, advertising expense, and telephone expense. These three items are paid in the month following the one in which they are incurred. January is the first month of operations, so there are no beginning account balances.

|  | January | February | March |
|---|---|---|---|
| Salary expense | $ 9,000 | $ 9,000 | $ 9,000 |
| Sales commissions | 600 | 640 | 800 |
| Advertising expense | 500 | 500 | 600 |
| Telephone expense | 1,000 | 1,080 | 1,100 |
| Depreciation on store equipment | 4,000 | 4,000 | 4,000 |
| Rent | 10,000 | 10,000 | 10,000 |
| Miscellaneous | 800 | 800 | 800 |
| Total S&A expenses before interest | $25,900 | $26,020 | $26,300 |

## Required

a. Prepare a schedule of cash payments for selling and administrative expenses.
b. Determine the amount of telephone expense payable as of March 31.
c. Determine the amount of sales commissions payable as of February 28.

**Problem 7-20B**  *Preparing a cash budget*    LO 6

Pope Company has budgeted the following cash flows:

|  | April | May | June |
|---|---|---|---|
| Cash receipts | $320,000 | $470,000 | $624,000 |
| Cash payments |  |  |  |
| For inventory purchases | 410,000 | 420,000 | 464,000 |
| For S&A expenses | 80,000 | 106,000 | 132,000 |

Pope had a $36,000 cash balance on April 1. The company desires a $60,000 cash cushion before paying interest. Funds are assumed to be borrowed, in increments of $1,000, and repaid on the last day of each month; the interest rate is 1.50 percent per month. Pope also pays its vendors on the last day of the month.

## Required

Prepare a cash budget.

LO 3, 4, 5

### Problem 7-21B   *Preparing budgets with multiple products*

Lowden Enterprises, Inc., has two products, palm-size computers and programmable calculators. Pamela Mason, the chief executive officer, is working with her staff to prepare next year's budget. Ms. Mason estimates that sales will increase at an annual rate of 10 percent for palm-size computers and 4 percent for programmable calculators. The current year sales revenue data follow.

|  | First Quarter | Second Quarter | Third Quarter | Fourth Quarter | Total |
|---|---|---|---|---|---|
| Palm-size computers | $500,000 | $550,000 | $620,000 | $730,000 | $2,400,000 |
| Programmable calculators | 250,000 | 275,000 | 290,000 | 325,000 | 1,140,000 |
| Total | $750,000 | $825,000 | $910,000 | $1,055,000 | $3,540,000 |

Based on the company's past experience, cost of goods sold is usually 75 percent of sales revenue. Company policy is to keep 10 percent of the next period's estimated cost of goods sold as the current period ending inventory.

**Required**

a. Prepare the company's sales budget for the next year for each quarter by individual products.

b. If the selling and administrative expenses are estimated to be $500,000, prepare the company's budgeted annual income statement for the next year.

c. Ms. Mason estimates the current year's ending inventory will be $78,000 for computers and $32,000 for calculators and the ending inventory next year will be $88,000 for computers and $42,000 for calculators. Prepare the company's inventory purchases budget for the next year showing quarterly figures by product.

LO 3, 4, 5

### Problem 7-22B   *Preparing a master budget for a retail company with no beginning account balances*

McGriff Gifts Corporation begins business today, December 31, 2010. Janet Novak, the president, is trying to prepare the company's master budget for the first three months (January, February, and March) of 2011. Since you are her good friend and an accounting student, Ms. Novak asks you to prepare the budget based on the following specifications.

**Required**

a. January sales are estimated to be $250,000 of which 30 percent will be cash and 70 percent will be credit. The company expects sales to increase at the rate of 10 percent per month. Prepare a sales budget.

b. The company expects to collect 100 percent of the accounts receivable generated by credit sales in the month following the sale. Prepare a schedule of cash receipts.

c. The cost of goods sold is 50 percent of sales. The company desires to maintain a minimum ending inventory equal to 20 percent of the next month's cost of goods sold. The ending inventory of March is expected to be $33,000. Assume that all purchases are made on account. Prepare an inventory purchases budget.

d. The company pays 60 percent of accounts payable in the month of purchase and the remaining 40 percent in the following month. Prepare a cash payments budget for inventory purchases.

e. Budgeted selling and administrative expenses per month follow.

| | |
|---|---|
| Salary expense (fixed) | $25,000 |
| Sales commissions | 8 percent of Sales |
| Supplies expense | 4 percent of Sales |
| Utilities (fixed) | $1,800 |
| Depreciation on store fixtures (fixed)* | $5,000 |
| Rent (fixed) | $7,200 |
| Miscellaneous (fixed) | $2,000 |

*The capital expenditures budget indicates that McGriff will spend $350,000 on January 1 for store fixtures. The fixtures are expected to have a $50,000 salvage value and a five-year (60-month) useful life.

Use this information to prepare a selling and administrative expenses budget.

f.  Utilities and sales commissions are paid the month after they are incurred; all other expenses are paid in the month in which they are incurred. Prepare a cash payments budget for selling and administrative expenses.

g.  The company borrows funds, in increments of $1,000, and repays them in any amount available on the last day of the month. It pays interest of 1.5 percent per month in cash on the last day of the month. For safety, the company desires to maintain a $50,000 cash cushion. The company pays its vendors on the last day of the month. Prepare a cash budget.

h.  Prepare a pro forma income statement for the quarter.

i.  Prepare a pro forma balance sheet at the end of the quarter.

j.  Prepare a pro forma statement of cash flows for the quarter.

## Problem 7-23B    *Behavioral impact of budgeting*

LO 2, 7

Geraldin Rollin, the director of Diaz Corporation's Mail-Order Division, is preparing the division's budget proposal for next year. The company's president will review the proposal for approval. Ms. Rollin estimates the current year final operating results will be as follows.

|  | Current Year |
|---|---|
| Sales revenue | $8,000,000 |
| Cost of goods sold | 4,800,000 |
| Gross profit | 3,200,000 |
| Selling & admin. expenses | 1,280,000 |
| Net income | $1,920,000 |

Ms. Rollin believes that the cost of goods sold as well as selling and administrative expenses will continue to be stable in proportion to sales revenue.

Diaz has an incentive policy to reward division managers whose performance exceeds their budget. Division directors receive a 10 percent bonus based on the excess of actual net income over the division's budget. For the last two years, Ms. Rollin has proposed a 4 percent rate of increase, which proved accurate. However, her honesty and accuracy in forecasting caused her to receive no year-end bonus at all. She is pondering whether she should do something differently this time. If she continues to be honest, she should propose an 8 percent growth rate because of robust market demand. Alternatively, she can propose a 4 percent growth rate as usual and thereby expect to receive some bonus at year-end.

### Required

a.  Prepare a pro forma income statement, assuming a 4 percent estimated increase.

b.  Prepare a pro forma income statement, assuming an 8 percent increase.

c.  Assume the president eventually approves the division's proposal with the 4 percent growth rate. If growth actually is 8 percent, how much bonus would Ms. Rollin receive?

d.  Propose a better budgeting procedure for Diaz Corporation.

## ANALYZE, THINK, COMMUNICATE

### ATC 7-1    Business Applications Case    *Preparing and using pro forma statements*

Nancy Pinedo and Justin Johnson recently graduated from the same university. After graduation they decided not to seek jobs at established organizations but, rather, to start their own small business hoping they could have more flexibility in their personal lives for a few years. Nancy's family has operated Mexican restaurants and taco-trucks for the past two generations, and Nancy noticed there were no taco-truck services in the town where their university was located. To reduce the amount they would need for an initial investment, they decided to start a business operating a taco-cart rather than a taco-truck, from which they would cook and serve traditional Mexican styled street food.

They bought a used taco-cart for $15,000. This cost, along with the cost for supplies to get started, a business license, and street vendor license brought their initial expenditures to $20,000.

Five-thousand dollars came from personal savings they had accumulated by working part time during college, and they borrowed $15,000 from Nancy's parents. They agreed to pay interest on the outstanding loan balance each month based on an annual rate of 6 percent. They will repay the principal over the next few years as cash becomes available. They were able to rent space in a parking lot near the campus they had attended, believing that the students would welcome their food as an alternative to the typical fast food that was currently available.

After two months in business, September and October, they had average monthly revenues of $20,000 and out of pocket costs of $16,000 for rent, ingredients, paper supplies, and so on, but not interest. Justin thinks they should repay some of the money they borrowed, but Nancy thinks they should prepare a set of forecasted financial statements for their first year in business before deciding whether or not to repay any principal on the loan. She remembers a bit about budgeting from a survey of accounting course she took and thinks the results from their first two months in business can be extended over the next 10 months to prepare the budget they need. They estimate the cart will last at least five years, after which they expect to sell it for $5,000 and move on to something else in their lives. Nancy agrees to prepare a forecasted (pro forma) income statement, balance sheet, and statement of cash flows for their first year in business, which includes the two months already passed.

### Required

**a.** Prepare the annual pro forma financial statements that you would expect Nancy to prepare based on her comments about her expectations for the business. Assume no principal will be repaid on the loan.

**b.** Review the statements you prepared for the first requirement and prepare a list of reasons why actual results for Justin and Nancy's business probably will not match their budgeted statements.

### ATC 7-2   Group Assignment   *Master budget and pro forma statements*

The following trial balance was drawn from the records of Havel Company as of October 1, 2011.

| | | |
|---|---|---|
| Cash | $ 16,000 | |
| Accounts receivable | 60,000 | |
| Inventory | 40,000 | |
| Store equipment | 200,000 | |
| Accumulated depreciation | | $ 76,800 |
| Accounts payable | | 72,000 |
| Line of credit loan | | 100,000 |
| Common stock | | 50,000 |
| Retained earnings | | 17,200 |
| Totals | $316,000 | $316,000 |

### Required

**a.** Divide the class into groups, each with 4 or 5 students. Organize the groups into three sections. Assign Task 1 to the first section, Task 2 to the second section, and Task 3 to the third section.

### Group Tasks

**(1)** Based on the following information, prepare a sales budget and a schedule of cash receipts for October, November, and December. Sales for October are expected to be $180,000, consisting of $40,000 in cash and $140,000 on credit. The company expects sales to increase at the rate of 10 percent per month. All accounts receivable are collected in the month following the sale.

**(2)** Based on the following information, prepare a purchases budget and a schedule of cash payments for inventory purchases for October, November, and December. The inventory balance as of October 1 was $40,000. Cost of goods sold for October is expected to be $72,000. Cost of goods sold is expected to increase by 10 percent per month. The company expects to maintain a minimum ending inventory equal to 20 percent of the current month cost of goods sold. Seventy-five percent of accounts payable is paid in the month that the purchase occurs; the remaining 25 percent is paid in the following month.

**(3)** Based on the following selling and administrative expenses budgeted for October, prepare a selling and administrative expenses budget for October, November, and December.

| | |
|---|---|
| Sales commissions (10% increase per month) | $ 7,200 |
| Supplies expense (10% increase per month) | 1,800 |
| Utilities (fixed) | 2,200 |
| Depreciation on store equipment (fixed) | 1,600 |
| Salary expense (fixed) | 34,000 |
| Rent (fixed) | 6,000 |
| Miscellaneous (fixed) | 1,000 |

Cash payments for sales commissions and utilities are made in the month following the one in which the expense is incurred. Supplies and other operating expenses are paid in cash in the month in which they are incurred.

**b.** Select a representative from each section. Have the representatives supply the missing information in the following pro forma income statement and balance sheet for the fourth quarter of 2011. The statements are prepared as of December 31, 2011.

| Income Statement | |
|---|---:|
| Sales revenue | $ ? |
| Cost of goods sold | ? |
| Gross margin | 357,480 |
| Operating expenses | ? |
| Operating income | 193,290 |
| Interest expense | (2,530) |
| Net income | $190,760 |

| Balance Sheet | | |
|---|---:|---:|
| **Assets** | | |
| Cash | | $ 9,760 |
| Accounts receivable | | ? |
| Inventory | | ? |
| Store equipment | $200,000 | |
| Accumulated depreciation store equipment | ? | |
| Book value of equipment | | 118,400 |
| Total assets | | $314,984 |
| **Liabilities** | | |
| Accounts payable | | ? |
| Utilities payable | | ? |
| Sales commissions payable | | ? |
| Line of credit | | 23,936 |
| **Equity** | | |
| Common stock | | 50,000 |
| Retained earnings | | ? |
| Total liabilities and equity | | $314,984 |

**c.** Indicate whether Havel will need to borrow money during October.

**ATC 7-3**   Research Assignment   *Analyzing budget data for the United States government*

The annual budget of the United States is very complex, but this case requires that you analyze only a small portion of the historical tables that are presented as a part of each year's budget. The fiscal year of the federal government ends on September 30. Obtain the budget documents needed at www.gpoaccess.gov/usbudget by following these steps:

- Under the "Previous Budgets" heading, click on "Browse"
- Under the Barack H. Obama heading, click on "Fiscal Year 2010"

■ There are two options that can be used on the page that appears next:

- Under the "Budget Documents" heading, you can select the PDF link beside the "Historical Table" subheading.
- Scroll down to the "Spreadsheets" heading and click on the "Historical Tables" subheading. This option provides the data in an Excel compatible format.

■ Under whichever option you choose above, you will need to review Table 1.1, Table 1.2, and Table 4.2 to complete the requirements below.

### Required

**a.** Table 1.2 shows the budget as a *percentage of gross domestic product* (GDP). Using the data in the third column, "Surplus of Deficit," determine how many years since 1960 the budget has shown a surplus and how many times it has shown a deficit. Ignore the "TQ" data between 1976 and 1977. This was a year that the government changed the ending date of its fiscal year.

**b.** Based on the data in Table 1.2, identify the three years with the highest deficits as a percentage of GDP. What were the deficit percentages for these years? Which year had the largest surplus and by what percentage?

**c.** Using your findings for Requirement *b*, regarding the year with the highest deficit as a percentage of GDP, go to Table 1.1 and calculate the deficit for that year as a *percentage of revenues*.

**d.** The president of the United States from 1993 through 2000 was Bill Clinton, a Democrat. The president from 2001 through 2009 was George Bush, a Republican. These men had significant input into the federal budget for the fiscal years 1994–2001 and 2002–2009, respectively. Table 4.2 shows what percentage of the total federal budget was directed toward each department within the government. Compare the data on Table 4.2 for 1994–2001, the Clinton years, to the data for 2002–2009, the Bush years. Identify the five departments that appear to have changed the most from the Clinton years to the Bush years. Ignore "Allowances" and "Undistributed offsetting receipts." Note, if you wish to approach this assignment more accurately, you can compute the average percentage for each department for the eight years each president served, and compare the two averages. The gpoaccess website includes a spreadsheet version of the historical data tables, allowing for a reasonably easy Excel analysis.

## ATC 7-4   Writing Assignment   *Continuous budgeting*

**HON Company** is the largest maker of mid-priced office furniture in the United States and Canada. Its management has expressed dissatisfaction with its *annual* budget system. Fierce competition requires businesses to be flexible and innovative. Unfortunately, building the effects of innovation into an annual budget is difficult because actions and outcomes often are evolutionary. Innovation unfolds as the year progresses. Consequently, HON's management team reached the conclusion that "when production processes undergo continuous change, standards developed annually for static conditions no longer offer meaningful targets for gauging their success."

### Required

Assume that you are HON Company's budget director. Write a memo to the management team explaining how the practice of continuous budgeting could overcome the shortcomings of an annual budget process. (For insight, read the article "Continuous Budgeting at the HON Company," *Management Accounting,* January 1996. This article describes HON's real-world experience with a continuous budget system.)

## ATC 7-5   Ethical Dilemma   *Bad budget system or unethical behavior?*

Clarence Cleaver is the budget director for the Harris County School District. Mr. Cleaver recently sent an urgent E-mail message to Sally Simmons, principal of West Harris County High. The message severely reprimanded Ms. Simmons for failing to spend the funds allocated to her to purchase computer equipment. Ms. Simmons responded that her school already has a sufficient supply of computers; indeed, the computer lab is never filled to capacity and usually is less than half filled. Ms. Simmons suggested that she would rather use the funds for teacher training. She argued that the reason the existing computers are not fully utilized is that the teachers lack sufficient computer literacy necessary to make assignments for their students.

Mr. Cleaver responded that it is not Ms. Simmons's job to decide how the money is to be spent; that is the school board's job. It is the principal's job to spend the money as the board directed. He informed Ms. Simmons that if the money is not spent by the fiscal closing date, the school board would likely reduce next year's budget allotment. To avoid a potential budget cut, Mr. Cleaver reallocated Ms. Simmons's computer funds to Jules Carrington, principal of East Harris County High. Mr. Carrington knows how to buy computers regardless of whether they are needed. Mr. Cleaver's final words were, "Don't blame me if parents of West High students complain that East High has more equipment. If anybody comes to me, I'm telling them that you turned down the money."

### Required

a. Do Mr. Cleaver's actions violate the standards of ethical conduct shown in Exhibit 1.15 of Chapter 1?

b. Does the Sarbanes-Oxley Act apply to this case? Explain your answer.

c. Explain how participative budgeting could improve the allocation of resources for the Harris County School District.

### ATC 7-6   Spreadsheet Assignment   *Using Excel*

The accountant for Nelly's Dress Shop prepared the fourth quarter 2011 cash budget that appears on the following spreadsheet. Nelly's has a policy to maintain a minimum cash balance of $14,000 before the interest payment at the end of each month. The shop borrows and repays funds on the first day of the month. The interest rate is 2 percent per month.

### Required

a. Construct a spreadsheet to model the cash budget as in the following screen capture. Be sure to use formulas where possible so that any changes to the estimates will be automatically reflected in the spreadsheet.

| | October | November | December |
|---|---|---|---|
| Desired cash cushion | $ 14,000 | | |
| Interest rate per month | 2% | | |
| Beginning loan balance | $ 72,806 | $103,152 | $108,615 |
| Beginning cash balance | $ 12,454 | $ 11,937 | $ 11,828 |
| Add cash receipts | 164,000 | 192,000 | 230,000 |
| Cash available before current financing activity (a) | 176,454 | 203,937 | 241,828 |
| Less disbursements | | | |
| For inventory purchases | 150,800 | 139,000 | 162,800 |
| For S&A expenses | 42,000 | 56,400 | 58,400 |
| Total budgeted disbursements (b) | 192,800 | 195,400 | 221,200 |
| Payments minus receipts | | | |
| Suplus (shortage) | (16,346) | 8,537 | 20,628 |
| Needed cash cushion | 14,000 | 14,000 | 14,000 |
| Financing activity | | | |
| Borrowing (repayment) (c) | 30,346 | 5,463 | (6,628) |
| Interest expense (d) | 2,063 | 2,172 | 2,040 |
| Ending cash balance (a-b+c-d) | $ 11,937 | $ 11,828 | $ 11,960 |
| Loan balance | $103,152 | $108,615 | $101,987 |

### Spreadsheet Tips

(1) Rows 11, 15, 17, 18, 20 to 22, and 24 should be based on formulas.

(2) Cells F6, H6, F9, and H9 should be based on formulas also. For example, cell F6 should be = D24.

## ATC 7-7    Spreadsheet Assignment    *Mastering Excel*

Spitzer Company has collected sales forecasts for next year from three people.

| Sources of Sales Estimate | First Quarter | Second Quarter | Third Quarter | Fourth Quarter |
|---|---|---|---|---|
| a. Sales manager | $520,000 | $410,000 | $370,000 | $610,000 |
| b. Marketing consultant | 540,000 | 480,000 | 400,000 | 630,000 |
| c. Production manager | 460,000 | 360,000 | 350,000 | 580,000 |

They have estimated that the cost of goods sold is 70 percent of sales. The company tries to maintain 10 percent of next quarter's expected cost of goods sold as the current quarter's ending inventory. The ending inventory of this year is $25,000. For budgeting, the ending inventory of the next year is expected to be $28,000.

### Required

**a.** Construct a spreadsheet that allows the inventory purchases budget to be prepared for each of the preceding estimates.

### Spreadsheet Tips

The VLOOKUP function can be used to choose one line of the preceding estimates. See the spreadsheet tips in Chapter 6 for an explanation of VLOOKUP.

## COMPREHENSIVE PROBLEM

The management team of Magnificent Modems, Inc. (MMI), wants to investigate the effect of several different growth rates on sales and cash receipts. Cash sales for the month of January are expected to be $10,000. Credit sales for January are expected to be $50,000. MMI collects 100 percent of credit sales in the month following the month of sale. Assume a beginning balance in accounts receivable of $48,000.

### Required

Calculate the amount of sales and cash receipts for the months of February and March assuming a growth rate of 1 percent, 2 percent, and 4 percent.

The results at a growth rate of 1 percent are shown as an example.

### Sales Budget

|  | Jan | Feb | Mar |
|---|---|---|---|
| Cash sales | $10,000 | $10,100 | $10,201 |
| Sales on account | 50,000 | 50,500 | 51,005 |
| Total budgeted sales | $60,000 | $60,600 | $61,206 |

### Schedule of Cash Receipts

|  | Jan | Feb | Mar |
|---|---|---|---|
| Current cash sales | $10,000 | $10,100 | $10,201 |
| Plus collections from accts. rec. | 48,000 | 50,000 | 50,500 |
| Total budgeted collections | $58,000 | $60,100 | $60,701 |

Use the following forms, assuming a growth rate of 2 percent.

### Sales Budget

|  | Jan | Feb | Mar |
|---|---|---|---|
| Cash sales | $10,000 | _____ | _____ |
| Sales on account | 50,000 | _____ | _____ |
| Total budgeted sales | $60,000 | _____ | _____ |

### Schedule of Cash Receipts

|  | Jan | Feb | Mar |
|---|---|---|---|
| Current cash sales | $10,000 | _____ | _____ |
| Plus collections from accts. rec. | 48,000 | _____ | _____ |
| Total budgeted collections | $58,000 | _____ | _____ |

Use the following forms, assuming a growth rate of 4 percent.

### Sales Budget

|  | Jan | Feb | Mar |
|---|---|---|---|
| Cash sales | $10,000 | _____ | _____ |
| Sales on account | 50,000 | _____ | _____ |
| Total budgeted sales | $60,000 | _____ | _____ |

### Schedule of Cash Receipts

|  | Jan | Feb | Mar |
|---|---|---|---|
| Current cash sales | $10,000 | _____ | _____ |
| Plus collections from accts. rec. | 48,000 | _____ | _____ |
| Total budgeted collections | $58,000 | _____ | _____ |

## CHAPTER 8

# Performance Evaluation

## LEARNING OBJECTIVES

**After you have mastered the material in this chapter you will be able to:**

**1** Describe flexible and static budgets.

**2** Classify variances as being favorable or unfavorable.

**3** Compute and interpret sales and variable cost volume variances.

**4** Compute and interpret flexible budget variances.

**5** Calculate and interpret fixed cost variances.

**6** Explain standard cost systems.

**7** Calculate and interpret price and usage variances.

## CHAPTER OPENING

Suppose you are a carpenter who builds picnic tables. You normally build 200 tables each year (the planned volume of activity), but because of unexpected customer demand, you are asked to build 225 tables (the actual volume of activity). You work hard and build the tables. Should management chastise you for using more materials, labor, or overhead than you normally use? Should management criticize the sales staff for selling more tables than expected? Of course not. Management must evaluate performance based on the actual volume of activity, not the planned volume of activity. To help management plan and evaluate performance, managerial accountants frequently prepare flexible budgets based on different levels of volume. Flexible budgets flex, or change, when the volume of activity changes.

# The Curious Accountant

Gourmet Pizzas is located in an affluent section of a major metropolitan area. Its owner worked at a national-chain pizza restaurant while in college. He knew that even though the national pizza chains had a lot of stores, (in 2010 **Domino's**, **Pizza Hut**, and **Papa John's** had approximately 14,000 stores in the United States), more than half of the country's pizzas were sold by other, mostly independently owned, restaurants. Knowing he could not beat the big guys on price, Gourmet Pizzas focuses on quality. Its pizza dough is made from scratch on the premises from organically grown flour, and it offers a wide variety of unusual toppings, such as pancetta.

In order to determine a proper selling price for his pizzas, the owner estimated the cost of making the crusts, among other things. Knowing how much flour, yeast, and so on was needed to make the dough for one pizza and estimating the cost of these ingredients, he determined that the materials for the dough for each pizza should cost him 25 cents. However, after six months in business, he had spent $10,150 on materials for making his dough and had sold 32,750 pizzas. This resulted in an actual price per pizza of 31 cents.

What are two general reasons that may explain why the materials cost for pizza dough was higher than Gourmet Pizzas' owner estimated? (Answer on page 360.)

Sources: Companies' SEC filings and **PMQ.com**.

# PREPARING FLEXIBLE BUDGETS

Describe flexible and static budgets.

A **flexible budget** is an extension of the *master budget* discussed previously. The master budget is based solely on the planned volume of activity. The master budget is frequently called a **static budget** because it remains unchanged even if the actual volume of activity differs from the planned volume. Flexible budgets differ from static budgets in that they show expected revenues and costs at a *variety* of volume levels.

To illustrate the differences between static and flexible budgets, consider Melrose Manufacturing Company, a producer of small, high-quality trophies used in award ceremonies. Melrose plans to make and sell 18,000 trophies during 2011. Management's best estimates of the expected sales price and per unit costs for the trophies are called *standard* prices and costs. The standard price and costs for the 18,000 trophies follow.

| Per unit sales price and variable costs | |
|---|---:|
| Expected sales price | $ 80.00 |
| Standard materials cost | 12.00 |
| Standard labor cost | 16.80 |
| Standard overhead cost | 5.60 |
| Standard general, selling, and administrative cost | 15.00 |
| Total fixed costs | $291,600 |

The static budget is highlighted with red shading in Exhibit 8.1. Sales revenue is determined by multiplying the expected sales price per unit times the planned volume of activity ($80 × 18,000 = $1,440,000). Similarly, the variable costs are calculated by multiplying the standard cost per unit times the planned volume of activity. For example, the manufacturing materials cost is $216,000 ($12 × 18,000). The same computational procedures apply to the other variable costs. The variable costs are subtracted from the sales revenue to produce a contribution margin of $550,800. The fixed costs are subtracted from the contribution margin to produce a budgeted net income of $259,200.

## EXHIBIT 8.1

### Static and Flexible Budgets in Excel Spreadsheet

| | Per Unit Standards | Static Budget | Flexible Budgets | | | | |
|---|---|---|---|---|---|---|---|
| Number of Units | | 18,000 | 16,000 | 17,000 | 18,000 | 19,000 | 20,000 |
| Sales Revenue | $80.00 | $1,440,000 | $1,280,000 | $1,360,000 | $1,440,000 | $1,520,000 | $1,600,000 |
| Variable Manuf. Costs | | | | | | | |
| Materials | $12.00 | 216,000 | 192,000 | 204,000 | 216,000 | 228,000 | 240,000 |
| Labor | 16.80 | 302,400 | 268,800 | 285,600 | 302,400 | 319,200 | 336,000 |
| Overhead | 5.60 | 100,800 | 89,600 | 95,200 | 100,800 | 106,400 | 112,000 |
| Variable G,S,&A | 15.00 | 270,000 | 240,000 | 255,000 | 270,000 | 285,000 | 300,000 |
| Contribution Margin | | 550,800 | 489,600 | 520,200 | 550,800 | 581,400 | 612,000 |
| Fixed Costs | | 291,600 | 291,600 | 291,600 | 291,600 | 291,600 | 291,600 |
| Net Income | | $ 259,200 | $ 198,000 | $ 228,600 | $ 259,200 | $ 289,800 | $ 320,400 |

What happens if the number of units sold is different from the planned volume? In other words, *what* happens to net income *if* Melrose sells more or less than 18,000 units? Managers frequently use flexible budgets to examine such *what if* scenarios. Flexible budget income statements for Melrose at sales volumes of 16,000, 17,000, 18,000, 19,000, and 20,000 are highlighted with blue shading in Exhibit 8.1.

The flexible budgets are prepared with the same per-unit standard amounts and fixed cost data used to produce the static budget. The only difference is the expected number of units sold. For example, the sales revenue at 16,000 units is $1,280,000 ($80 × 16,000), at 17,000 units it is $1,360,000 ($80 × 17,000), and so on. The variable materials cost at 16,000 units is $192,000 ($12 × 16,000), at 17,000 units it is $204,000 ($12 × 17,000), and so on. The other variable costs are computed in the same manner. Note that the fixed costs are the same at all levels of activity because, by definition, they are not affected by changes in volume.

Other flexible budgets are possible. Indeed, a flexible budget can be prepared for any number of units sold. You have probably noticed that Exhibit 8.1 was prepared using an Excel spreadsheet. Excel offers the opportunity to prepare an unlimited number of flexible budgets with minimal effort. For example, formulas can be created with cell references so that new budgets can be created simply by changing the number of units entered in a single cell.

Managers use flexible budgets for both planning and performance evaluation. For example, managers may assess whether the company's cash position is adequate by assuming different levels of volume. They may judge if the number of employees, amounts of materials, and equipment and storage facilities are appropriate for a variety of different potential levels of volume. In addition to helping plan, flexible budgets are critical to implementing an effective performance evaluation system.

---

## ✓ CHECK YOURSELF 8.1

The static (master) budget of Parcel, Inc., called for a production and sales volume of 25,000 units. At that volume, total budgeted fixed costs were $150,000 and total budgeted variable costs were $200,000. Prepare a flexible budget for an expected volume of 26,000 units.

**Answer**   Budgeted fixed costs would remain unchanged at $150,000 because changes in the volume of activity do not affect budgeted fixed costs. Budgeted variable costs would increase to $208,000, computed as follows: Calculate the budgeted variable cost per unit ($200,000 ÷ 25,000 units = $8) and then multiply that variable cost per unit by the expected volume ($8 × 26,000 units = $208,000).

---

# DETERMINING VARIANCES FOR PERFORMANCE EVALUATION

One means of evaluating managerial performance is to compare *standard* amounts with *actual* results. The differences between the standard and actual amounts are called **variances;** variances can be either **favorable** or **unfavorable.** When actual sales revenue is greater than expected (planned) revenue, a company has a favorable sales variance because higher sales increase net income. When actual sales are less than expected, an unfavorable sales variance exists. When actual costs are *less* than standard costs, cost variances are favorable because lower costs increase net income. Unfavorable cost variances exist when actual costs are *more* than standard costs. These relationships are summarized below.

■ When actual sales exceed expected sales, variances are favorable.

■ When actual sales are less than expected sales, variances are unfavorable.

■ When actual costs exceed standard costs, variances are unfavorable.

■ When actual costs are less than standard costs, variances are favorable.

LO 2

Classify variances as being favorable or unfavorable.

# SALES AND VARIABLE COST VOLUME VARIANCES

Compute and interpret sales and variable cost volume variances.

The amount of a **sales volume variance** is the difference between the static budget (which is based on planned volume) and a flexible budget based on actual volume. Likewise, the **variable cost volume variances** are determined by calculating the differences between the static and flexible budget amounts. These variances measure management effectiveness in attaining the planned volume of activity. To illustrate, assume Melrose Manufacturing Company actually makes and sells 19,000 trophies during 2011. The planned volume of activity was 18,000 trophies. Exhibit 8.2 shows Melrose's static budget, flexible budget, and volume variances.

### EXHIBIT 8.2

**Melrose Manufacturing Company's Volume Variances**

| | Static Budget | Flexible Budget | Volume Variances | |
|---|---|---|---|---|
| Number of units | 18,000 | 19,000 | 1,000 | Favorable |
| Sales revenue | $1,440,000 | $1,520,000 | $80,000 | Favorable |
| Variable manufacturing costs | | | | |
| Materials | 216,000 | 228,000 | 12,000 | Unfavorable |
| Labor | 302,400 | 319,200 | 16,800 | Unfavorable |
| Overhead | 100,800 | 106,400 | 5,600 | Unfavorable |
| Variable SG&A | 270,000 | 285,000 | 15,000 | Unfavorable |
| Contribution margin | 550,800 | 581,400 | 30,600 | Favorable |
| Fixed costs | 291,600 | 291,600 | 0 | |
| Net income | $ 259,200 | $ 289,800 | $30,600 | Favorable |

## Interpreting the Sales and Variable Cost Volume Variances

Because the static and flexible budgets are based on the same standard sales price and per-unit variable costs, the variances are solely attributable to the difference between the planned and actual volume of activity. Marketing managers are usually responsible for the volume variances. Because the sales volume drives production levels, production managers have little control over volume. Exceptions occur; for example, if poor production quality control leads to inferior goods that are difficult to sell, the production manager is responsible. The production manager is responsible for production delays that affect product availability, which may restrict sales volume. Under normal circumstances, however, the marketing campaign determines the volume of sales. Upper-level marketing managers develop the promotional program and create the sales plan; they are in the best position to explain why sales goals are or are not met. When marketing managers refer to **making the numbers,** they usually mean reaching the sales volume in the static (master) budget.

In the case of Melrose Manufacturing Company, the marketing manager not only achieved but also exceeded by 1,000 units the planned volume of sales. Exhibit 8.2 shows the activity variances resulting from the extra volume. At the standard price, the additional volume produces a favorable revenue variance of $80,000 (1,000 units × $80 per unit). The increase in volume also produces unfavorable variable cost variances. The net effect of producing and selling the additional 1,000 units is an increase of $30,600 in the contribution margin, a positive result. These preliminary results suggest that the marketing manager is to be commended. The analysis, however, is incomplete. For example, examining market share could reveal whether the manager won customers from competitors or whether the manager simply reaped the benefit of an unexpected industrywide increase in demand. The increase in sales volume could have been attained by reducing the sales price; the success of that strategy will be analyzed further in a later section of this chapter.

Since the variable costs in the flexible budget are higher than the variable costs in the static budget, the variable cost volume variances are *unfavorable*. The unfavorable classification may be misleading because it focuses solely on the cost component of the income statement. While costs are higher than expected, so too may be revenue. Indeed, as shown in Exhibit 8.2, the total of the unfavorable variable cost variances is more than offset by the favorable revenue variance, resulting in a higher contribution margin. Frequently, the assessment of variances requires a holistic perspective.

## Fixed Cost Considerations

At this point, it is important to note that the reason the fixed cost variance shown in Exhibit 8.2 is zero is because we are comparing two budgets (static versus flexible). Variances occur only because the budgets are created using different volumes of activity. Since total fixed cost is not affected by the level of activity, there will be no fixed cost variances associated with static versus flexible budgets.

## FLEXIBLE BUDGET VARIANCES

For performance evaluation, management compares actual results to a flexible budget based on the *actual* volume of activity. Because the actual results and the flexible budget reflect the same volume of activity, any variances in revenues and variable costs result from differences between standard and actual per unit amounts. To illustrate computing and analyzing flexible budget variances, we assume that Melrose's *actual* per unit amounts during 2011 were those shown in the following table. The 2011 per unit *standard* amounts are repeated here for your convenience.

Compute and interpret flexible budget variances.

| | Standard | Actual |
|---|---|---|
| Sales price | $80.00 | $78.00 |
| Variable materials cost | 12.00 | 11.78 |
| Variable labor cost | 16.80 | 17.25 |
| Variable overhead cost | 5.60 | 5.75 |

Actual and budgeted fixed costs are shown in Exhibit 8.3.

Exhibit 8.3 shows Melrose's 2011 flexible budget, actual results, and flexible budget variances. The flexible budget is the same one compared to the static budget in Exhibit 8.2.

### EXHIBIT 8.3

**Flexible Budget Variances for Melrose Manufacturing Company**

| | Flexible Budget | Actual Results | Flexible Budget Variances | |
|---|---|---|---|---|
| Number of units | 19,000 | 19,000 | 0 | |
| Sales revenue | $1,520,000 | $1,482,000 | $38,000 | Unfavorable |
| Variable manufacturing costs | | | | |
| Materials | 228,000 | 223,820 | 4,180 | Favorable |
| Labor | 319,200 | 327,750 | 8,550 | Unfavorable |
| Overhead | 106,400 | 109,250 | 2,850 | Unfavorable |
| Variable SG&A | 285,000 | 283,100 | 1,900 | Favorable |
| Contribution margin | 581,400 | 538,080 | 43,320 | Unfavorable |
| Fixed costs | 291,600 | 295,000 | 3,400 | Unfavorable |
| Net income | $ 289,800 | $ 243,080 | $46,720 | Unfavorable |

Recall the flexible budget amounts come from multiplying the standard per-unit amounts by the actual volume of production. For example, the sales revenue in the flexible budget comes from multiplying the standard sales price by the actual volume ($80 × 19,000). The variable costs are similarly computed. The *actual results* are calculated by multiplying the actual per-unit sales price and cost figures from the preceding table by the actual volume of activity. For example, the sales revenue in the Actual Results column comes from multiplying the actual sales price by the actual volume ($78 × 19,000 = $1,482,000). The actual cost figures are similarly computed. The differences between the flexible budget figures and the actual results are the **flexible budget variances.**

## Calculating the Sales Price Variance

Because both the flexible budget and actual results are based on the actual volume of activity, the flexible budget variance is attributable to sales price, not sales volume. In this case, the actual sales price of $78 per unit is less than the standard price of $80 per unit. Because Melrose sold its product for less than the standard sales price, the **sales price variance** is *unfavorable.* Even though the price variance is unfavorable, however, sales volume was 1,000 units more than expected. It is possible the marketing manager generated the additional volume by reducing the sales price. Whether the combination of lower sales price and higher sales volume is favorable or unfavorable depends on the amount of the unfavorable sales price variance versus the amount of the favorable sales volume variance. The *total* sales variance (price and volume) follows:

| | | |
|---|---|---|
| Actual sales (19,000 units × $78 per unit) | $1,482,000 | |
| Expected sales (18,000 units × $80 per unit) | 1,440,000 | |
| Total sales variance | $   42,000 | Favorable |

Alternatively,

| | | |
|---|---|---|
| Activity variance (sales volume) | $ 80,000 | Favorable |
| Sales price variance | (38,000) | Unfavorable |
| Total sales variance | $ 42,000 | Favorable |

This analysis indicates that reducing the sales price had a favorable impact on *total* contribution margin. Use caution when interpreting variances as good or bad; in this instance, the unfavorable sales price variance was more than offset by the favorable sales volume variance. All unfavorable variances are not bad; all favorable variances are not good. Variances signal the need to investigate.

## ✓ CHECK YOURSELF 8.2

Scott Company's master budget called for a planned sales volume of 30,000 units. Budgeted direct materials cost was $4 per unit. Scott actually produced and sold 32,000 units with an actual materials cost of $131,000. Determine the materials volume variance and identify the organizational unit most likely responsible for this variance. Determine the flexible budget variance and identify the organizational unit most likely responsible for this variance.

**Answer**  The variable cost volume variance is the difference between the expected materials usage at the planned volume of activity and the expected materials usage at the actual volume of activity [($4 × 30,000 units) − ($4 × 32,000) = $8,000]. The variance is unfavorable because expected direct materials cost at actual volume was higher than budgeted direct materials cost at planned volume. The unfavorable variance might not be a bad thing. The variance is due to increased volume, which could be a good thing. The organizational unit most likely responsible for the volume variance is the marketing department.

The flexible budget variance is the difference between the expected materials cost at the actual volume ($4 × 32,000 units = $128,000) and the actual materials cost of $131,000. The $3,000 ($128,000 − $131,000) variance is unfavorable because it cost more than expected to make the 32,000 units. Either the production department or the purchasing department is most likely responsible for this variance.

## The Human Element Associated with Flexible Budget Variances

The flexible budget cost variances offer insight into management efficiency. For example, Melrose Manufacturing Company's favorable materials variance could mean purchasing agents were shrewd in negotiating price concessions, discounts, or delivery terms and therefore reduced the price the company paid for materials. Similarly, production employees may have used materials efficiently, using less than expected. The unfavorable labor variance could mean managers failed to control employee wages or motivate employees to work hard. As with sales variances, cost variances require careful analysis. A favorable variance may, in fact, mask unfavorable conditions. For example, the favorable materials variance might have been caused by paying low prices for inferior goods. Using substandard materials could have required additional labor in the production process, which would explain the unfavorable labor variance. Again, we caution that variances, whether favorable or unfavorable, alert management to investigate further.

## FIXED COST VARIANCES

Because fixed costs do not fluctuate with volume, does not mean that the actual costs will be the same as the budgeted costs. Indeed, there are two fixed cost variances commonly investigated by management. One is called a *fixed cost spending variance;* the other is called a *fixed cost volume variance.*

**LO 5**

Calculate and interpret fixed cost variances.

### Fixed Cost Spending Variance

Companies frequently pay more or less than expected for fixed costs. For example, a supervisor may receive an unplanned raise, causing actual salary cost to be more than the amount budgeted. The difference between the *actual fixed cost* and the *budgeted fixed cost* (amount shown in the static budget) is called a **fixed cost spending variance.** The *fixed cost spending variance* for Melrose is $3,400 (295,000 actual fixed cost − $291,600 budgeted fixed cost). Since actual fixed costs are higher than the budgeted fixed cost, the variance is unfavorable. In other words the company had to pay more than it expected for the fixed costs.

In the Melrose case, there is no way to know who is responsible for the $3,400 unfavorable fixed cost spending variance because all of the costs have been pooled together. To promote accountability, fixed costs that are controllable by a specific manager must be disaggregated and tagged for individual analysis. For example, the plant manager may control the assistant manager's salary cost. If a fixed cost spending variance is associated with the salary cost, the plant manager is responsible for explaining why the variance occurred. Other managers will be held accountable for the specific fixed costs they control.

Uncontrollable fixed costs should also be reported for management oversight. Even if these costs are not controllable in the short term, management should stay abreast of them because they may be controllable in the long term.

## Fixed Cost Volume Variance

Companies frequently need to know the cost of something before the actual cost can be determined. For example, a company may base its selling price on the cost of making and selling a product. Even so, the actual cost of making and selling the product may not be known until after the product has been sold. In order to price the product, the company will be required to use estimated costs rather than actual costs. Likewise it may be necessary to use estimated costs to prepare quarterly financial statements because the actual cost will not be known until after the quarterly statements have been published. To solve such problems, accountants frequently estimate the total annual cost and then apply (allocate) a portion of the estimated annual cost to the products as they are made and sold.

To illustrate, assume that Melrose develops an allocation rate based on its budgeted fixed cost and the planned volume of production as shown below:

Budgeted fixed cost ÷ Planned volume of activity = Allocation rate

$291,600    ÷    18,000 units    = $16.20 per unit

As production proceeds, Melrose would apply $16.20 to the appropriate accounts each time an actual unit of product (trophy) is made and sold. Since the allocation rate is determined *before* the actual cost and volume are known, it is frequently called the *predetermined* allocation rate. Since fixed costs are frequently classified as overhead costs this rate is more frequently called the predetermined *overhead* rate. In summary the **predetermined overhead rate** is calculated as follows:

$$\text{Predetermined overhead rate} = \frac{\text{Budgeted fixed cost from the static budget}}{\text{Planned volume of activity}}$$

The total cost determined by multiplying the *predetermined overhead rate* times the *actual volume* of production is called the **applied fixed cost.** Given that Melrose produced and sold 19,000 units of product during 2011, the amount of applied fixed cost is $307,800 ($16.20 × 19,000 units).

The difference between the *applied fixed cost based on actual volume* and the *budgeted fixed cost based on planned volume* is called the **fixed cost volume variance.** In this case Melrose has a fixed cost volume variance of $16,200 ($307,800 budgeted fixed cost − $291,600 applied fixed cost).

To interpret the fixed cost volume variance, consider the effect that volume changes have on the behavior of fixed cost per unit. As volume increases, fixed cost per unit decreases. In this case, the planned volume was 18,000 units and the actual volume was 19,000 units. Since the higher than expected volume decreases the fixed cost per unit, the volume variance is *favorable.* An *unfavorable* fixed cost volume variance occurs when actual volume is less than planned volume, a condition that increases fixed costs per unit.

The fixed cost volume variance is a measure of facility utilization. If the fixed cost volume variance is unfavorable, the facilities are considered to be underutilized. This is just another way of saying that the company suffered an unfavorable variance because it did not utilize its facilities to make and sell the number of units of product it had planned to make and sell. A favorable fixed cost volume variance suggests that a company utilized its facilities to make and sell *more* than the planned volume of activity. In summary, a fixed cost volume variance indicates over- or underutilization of facilities, not over- or underspending.

For your convenience, the two fixed cost overhead variances are summarized as follows:

> 1. **Fixed cost spending variance = Actual fixed cost − Budgeted fixed cost**
>
> If actual costs are less than the budgeted costs the variance is favorable.
> If actual costs are greater than the budgeted costs the variance is unfavorable.
>
> |   | | Applied fixed cost | Budgeted fixed cost |
> |---|---|---|---|
> | 2. **Fixed cost volume variance =** | | based on | based on |
> |   | | actual volume | planned volume |
>
> 2. **Fixed cost volume variance =** (Applied fixed cost based on actual volume) − (Budgeted fixed cost based on planned volume)
>
> If actual volume is more than the planned volume the variance is favorable.
> If actual volume is less than the planned volume the variance is unfavorable.

### Fixed Cost Volume Variance and Product Pricing

Changes in the fixed cost per unit have important implications for decision making. For example, consider the impact on cost-plus pricing decisions. Because the actual volume is unknown until the end of the accounting period, selling prices must be based on planned volume. Recall that at the planned volume of activity, Melrose's predetermined overhead rate is $16.20 ($291,600 ÷ 18,000 units). Compare this figure with the rate based on actual volume which is $15.35 ($291,600 ÷ 19,000 units). Since the price of the product was based on the predetermined overhead rate ($16.20), instead of the rate based on actual volume ($15.35), the product was overpriced. It follows that if actual volume is less than planned volume, products will be underpriced.

Overpricing can be problematic because it encourages competitors to enter the market. Eventually, these competitors will draw customers away from Melrose by offering lower prices. As Melrose loses customers, its actual fixed cost per unit increases, thereby exacerbating the pricing problem. Underpricing (not encountered by Melrose in this example) can also be detrimental. If planned volume is overstated, the predetermined overhead rate will be understated and prices will be set too low. When the higher amount of actual costs is eventually subtracted from revenues, actual profits will be lower than expected. As this discussion demonstrates, over- or understating the planned volume will cause pricing problems. It is critically important to be as accurate as possible when establishing the planned volume.

### Responsibility for the Fixed Cost Volume Variance

Normally upper-level marketing managers are held accountable for the fixed cost volume variance because they control the volume of sales, which in turn dictates the volume of production. Even so, other possibilities must be considered. For example, goods may not sell because they are poorly constructed, which may be the fault of design engineers or production managers. Likewise, buyers may be at fault for purchasing undesirable products that are difficult to resell. In this case the purchasing department rather than the marketing department would be responsible for the fixed cost volume variance. Determining the amount of the variance is the easy part of performance evaluation; determining responsibility is usually more difficult.

## STANDARD COST SYSTEMS

Standard cost systems help managers plan and also establish benchmarks against which actual performance can be judged. By highlighting differences between standard (expected) and actual performance, standard costing focuses management attention on the areas of greatest need. Because management talent is a valuable and expensive resource, businesses cannot afford to have managers spend large amounts of time on operations that are functioning normally. Instead, managers should concentrate on areas not performing as expected. In other words, management should attend to the exceptions; this management philosophy is known as **management by exception.**

Explain standard cost systems.

Standard costing fosters using the management by exception principle. By reviewing performance reports that show differences between actual and standard costs, management can focus its attention on the items that show significant variances. Areas with only minor variances need little or no review.

## Establishing Standards

Establishing standards is probably the most difficult part of using a standard cost system. A **standard** represents the amount that a price, cost, or quantity *should be* under certain anticipated circumstances. Consider the complexity of establishing the standard cost to produce a pair of blue jeans. Among other things, managers need to know where they can get the best price for materials, who will pay transportation costs, if cash or volume discounts are available, whether the suppliers with the lowest price can reliably supply the quantities needed on a timely basis, how the material should be cut to conserve time and labor, in what order to sew pieces of material together, the wage rates of the relevant production employees, whether overtime will be needed, and how many pairs of jeans will be produced. Obtaining this information requires the combined experience, judgment, and forecasting ability of all personnel who have responsibility for price and usage decisions. Even when a multitalented group of experienced persons is involved in standard setting, the process involves much trial and error. Revising standards is common even with established systems.

Historical data provide a good starting point for establishing standards. These data must be updated for changes in technology, plant layout, new methods of production, and worker productivity. Frequently, changes of this nature result from initiating a standard cost system. Remember that a *standard* represents what *should be* rather than what *is* or *was*. Engineers often help establish standards, recommending the most efficient way to perform required tasks. The engineers undertake time and motion studies and review material utilization in the process of developing standards. Established practices and policies are frequently changed in response to engineers' reports.

Management must consider behavioral implications when developing standards. Managers, supervisors, purchasing agents, and other affected employees should be consulted for two reasons: (1) their experience and expertise provide invaluable input to standard development and (2) persons who are involved in standard setting are more likely to accept and be motivated to reach the resulting standards. Management should also consider how difficult it should be to achieve standard performance. Difficulty levels can be described as follows: (1) ideal standards, (2) practical standards, and (3) lax standards.

**Ideal standards** represent flawless performance; they represent what costs should be under the best possible circumstances. They do not allow for normal materials waste and spoilage or ordinary labor inefficiencies caused by machine downtime, cleanups, breaks, or personal needs. Meeting ideal standards is beyond the capabilities of most, if not all, employees. Ideal standards may motivate some individuals to constantly strive for improvement, but unattainable standards discourage most people. When people consistently fail, they become demotivated and stop trying to succeed. In addition, variances associated with ideal standards lose significance. They reflect deviations that are largely beyond employees' control, and they mask true measures of superior or inferior performance, considerably reducing their usefulness.

**Practical standards** represent reasonable effort; they are attainable for most employees. Practical standards allow for normal levels of inefficiency in materials and labor usage. An average worker performing diligently would be able to achieve standard performance. Practical standards motivate most employees; the feeling of accomplishment attained through earnest effort encourages employees to do their best. Practical standards also produce meaningful variances. Deviations from practical standards usually result from factors employees control. Positive variances normally represent superior performance, and negative variances indicate inferior performance.

**Lax standards** represent easily attainable goals. Employees can achieve standard performance with minimal effort. Lax standards do not motivate most people; continual success with minimal effort leads to boredom and lackluster performance. In addition, variances lose meaning. Deviations caused by superior or inferior performance are obscured by the built-in slack.

Management must consider employee ability levels when establishing standards. Standards that seasoned workers can attain may represent ideal standards to inexperienced workers. Management should routinely monitor standards and adjust them when it is appropriate to do so.

## Selecting Variances to Investigate

Managerial judgment, developed through experience, plays a significant role in deciding which variances to investigate. Managers consider the *materiality* of a variance, the *frequency* with which it occurs, their *capacity to control* the variance, and the *characteristics* of the items behind the variance.

Standard costs are estimates. They cannot perfectly predict actual costs. Most business experience minor variances as part of normal operations. Investigating minor variances is not likely to produce useful information. Many companies therefore establish *materiality* guidelines for selecting variances to analyze. They set dollar or percentage thresholds and ignore variances that fall below these limits, investigating material variances only. A **material variance** is one that could influence management decisions. Material variances should be investigated whether they are favorable or unfavorable. As mentioned earlier, a favorable price variance can result from purchasing substandard materials; the quality of the company's products, however, will suffer from the inferior materials and sales will fall.

How *frequently* a variance occurs impacts materiality. A variance of $20,000 may be immaterial in a single month, but if the same variance occurs repeatedly throughout the year, it can become a material $240,000 variance. Variance reports should highlight frequent as well as large variations.

*Capacity to control* refers to whether management action can influence the variance. If utility rates cause differences between actual and standard overhead costs, management has little control over the resulting variances. Conversely, if actual labor costs exceed standard costs because a supervisor fails to motivate employees, management can take some action. To maximize their value to the firm, managers should concentrate on controllable variances.

The *characteristics* of the items behind the variance may invite management abuse. For example, managers can reduce actual costs in the short term by delaying expenditures for maintenance, research and development, and advertising. Although cost reductions in these areas may produce favorable variances in the current period, they will have a long-term detrimental impact on profitability. Managers under stress may be tempted to focus on short-term benefits. Variances associated with these critical items should be closely analyzed.

The primary advantage of a standard cost system is efficient use of management talent to control costs. Secondary benefits include the following.

1. Standard cost systems quickly alert management to trouble spots. For example, a standard amount of materials may be issued for a particular job. If requisitions of additional materials require supervisory approval, each time a supervisor must grant such approval, she is immediately aware that excess materials are being used and can act before excessive material usage becomes unmanageable.

2. If established and maintained properly, standard cost systems can boost morale and motivate employees. Reward systems can be linked to accomplishments that exceed the established performance standards. Under such circumstances, employees become extremely conscious of the time and materials they use, minimizing waste and reducing costs.

3. Standard cost systems encourage good planning. The failure to plan well leads to overbuying, excessive inventory, wasted time, and so on. A standard cost system forces managers to plan, resulting in more effective operations with less waste.

## Avoiding Gamesmanship

In general, variances should not be used to praise or punish managers. The purpose of identifying variances is to help management improve efficiency and productivity.

If variances are used to assign rewards and blame, managers are likely to respond by withholding or manipulating information. For example, a manager might manipulate the cost standard for a job by deliberately overstating the amount of materials or labor needed to complete it. The manager's performance will later appear positive when the actual cost of materials or labor is less than the inflated standard. This practice is so common it has a name: **budget slack** is the difference between inflated and realistic standards. Sales staff may play a game called *lowballing* in which they deliberately underestimate the amount of expected sales, anticipating a reward when actual sales subsequently exceed the budget.

## Answers to The Curious Accountant

As this chapter demonstrates, there are two primary reasons a company spends more or less to produce a product than it estimated it would.

First, the company may have paid more or less to purchase the inputs needed to produce the product than it estimated. Second, the company used a greater or lesser quantity of these inputs than expected. In the case of Gourmet Pizzas, it may have had to pay more for flour, yeast, cheese, and so on than the owner estimated. Or, it may have used more of these ingredients than expected. For example, if pizza dough sits around too long before being used, it may have to be thrown out. This waste was not anticipated when computing the cost to make only one pizza. Of course, the higher than expected cost could have been a combination of price and quantity factors.

Gourmet Pizza needs to determine if the difference between its expected costs and actual costs was because the estimates were faulty, or because the production process was inefficient. If the estimates were to blame, the owner would need to revise them so he can charge the proper price to his customers. If the production process is inefficient, he needs to correct it if he is to earn an acceptable level of profit.

Gamesmanship can be reduced if superiors and subordinates participate sincerely in setting mutually agreeable, attainable standards. Once standards are established, the evaluation system that uses them must promote long-term respect among superiors and their subordinates. If standards are used solely for punitive purposes, gamesmanship will rapidly degrade the standard costing system.

# PRICE AND USAGE VARIANCES[1]

Under a standard cost system, it is common practice to subdivide the *flexible budget variances* into component parts that more clearly define the cause of these variances. For example, a favorable flexible budget materials cost variance may be the result of paying less than expected for the materials or of using fewer materials than expected, or some combination of *price and usage variances*. To demonstrate, we return to the Melrose Manufacturing Company case that was introduced earlier in the chapter.

Calculate and interpret price and usage variances.

We will limit our discussion to the flexible budget variable manufacturing cost variances shown in Exhibit 8.3. Specifically, there are three of these variances including:

1. Flexible budget materials cost variance: $4,180 Favorable.
2. Flexible budget labor cost variance: $8,550 Unfavorable.
3. Flexible budget variable overhead cost variance: $2,850 Unfavorable.

Recall that these variances were calculated by determining the difference between the flexible budget costs (standard cost per unit times the actual volume) and the actual costs (actual cost per unit times the actual volume). The standard and actual per unit costs for Melrose were shown previously and are repeated here for your convenience.

|  | Standard | Actual |
|---|---|---|
| Variable materials cost per unit of product | $12.00 | $11.78 |
| Variable labor cost per unit of product | 16.80 | 17.25 |
| Variable overhead cost per unit of product | 5.60 | 5.75 |

Using the cost per unit data, the flexible budget manufacturing cost variances can be determined algebraically as shown in Exhibit 8.4. We suggest that you compare the variances shown in the two exhibits to confirm that the algebraic approach in Exhibit 8.4 yields the same result as the variances previously computed in Exhibit 8.3.

Note that the difference between the actual and standard cost is expressed as an absolute value. This mathematical notation suggests that the mathematical sign is not useful in interpreting the condition of the variance. To assess the condition of a variance, you must consider the type of variance being analyzed. With respect to cost

## EXHIBIT 8.4

### Flexible Budget Variances Calculated Algebraically

| Variable Mfg. Costs | Actual Cost Per Unit of Product | − | Standard Cost Per Unit of Product | × | Actual Units | = | Flexible Budget Variance |
|---|---|---|---|---|---|---|---|
| Materials | \| $11.78 | − | $12.00 \| | × | 19,000 | = | $4,180 Favorable |
| Labor | \| 17.25 | − | 16.80 \| | × | 19,000 | = | 8,550 Unfavorable |
| Overhead | \| 5.75 | − | 5.60 \| | × | 19,000 | = | 2,850 Unfavorable |

[1]Businesses use various names for price and usage variances. For example, materials price and usage variances are frequently called materials price and quantity variances; labor price and usage variances are frequently called labor rate and efficiency variances. Regardless of the names, the underlying concepts and computations are the same for all variable price and usage variances.

variances, managers seek to attain actual prices that are lower than standard prices. In this case, the actual price of materials is less than the standard price, so the materials variance is favorable. Since the actual prices for labor and overhead are higher than the standard prices, those variances are unfavorable.

For insight into what caused the flexible budget variances, a separate price and usage variance can be computed for each of the total flexible budget variances. We begin with the $4,180 favorable flexible budget materials cost variance. This variance indicates that Melrose spent less than expected on materials to make 19,000 trophies. Why? The price per unit of material may have been less than expected (price variance), or the company may have used less material than expected (usage variance). To determine what caused the total favorable variance, Melrose must separate the cost per unit of product into two parts, price per unit of material and quantity of material used.

## Calculating Materials Price and Usage Variances

Melrose's accounting records indicate the materials cost per unit of product (trophy) is as follows:

| | Actual Data | Standard Data |
|---|---|---|
| Price **per pound** of material | $ 1.90 | $ 2.00 |
| Quantity of materials per unit of product | × 6.2 pounds | × 6.0 pounds |
| Cost **per unit** of product | $11.78 | $12.00 |

Based on this detail, the total quantity of materials is:

| | Actual Data | Standard Data |
|---|---|---|
| Actual production volume | 19,000 units | 19,000 units |
| Quantity of materials per unit of product | × 6.2 pounds | × 6.0 pounds |
| Total quantity of materials | 117,800 pounds | 114,000 pounds |

Confirm the price and usage components that make up the total flexible budget materials variance, as follows:

| **Actual Cost** | | **Standard Cost** | |
|---|---|---|---|
| Actual quantity used | 117,800 | Standard quantity | 114,000 |
| × | × | × | × |
| Actual price per pound | $1.90 | Standard price per pound | $2.00 |
| | $223,820 | | $228,000 |
| | | Total variance: $4,180 Favorable | |

To isolate the price and usage variances, insert a Variance Dividing column between the Actual Cost and Standard Cost columns. The Variance Dividing column combines standard and actual data, showing the *standard cost* multiplied by the *actual quantity* of materials purchased and used.[2] Exhibit 8.5 shows the result.

---

[2]In practice, raw materials are frequently stored in inventory prior to use. Differences may exist between the amount of materials purchased and the amount of materials used. In such cases, the price variance is based on the quantity of materials *purchased,* and the usage variance is based on the quantity of materials *used.* This text makes the simplifying assumption that the amount of materials purchased equals the amount of materials used during the period.

## EXHIBIT 8.5

### Materials Price and Usage Variances

| Actual Cost | | Variance Dividing Data | | Standard Cost | |
|---|---|---|---|---|---|
| Actual quantity used | 117,800 | Actual quantity used | 117,800 | Standard quantity | 114,000 |
| × | × | × | × | × | × |
| Actual price per pound | $1.90 | Standard price per pound | $2.00 | Standard price per pound | $2.00 |
| | $223,820 | | $235,600 | | $228,000 |

Materials price variance
$11,780 Favorable

Materials usage variance
$7,600 Unfavorable

Total variance: $4,180 Favorable

**Algebraic solution.**    The materials price variance (difference between the Actual Cost column and the Variance Dividing column) can be computed algebraically as follows:

$$\text{Price variance} = |\text{Actual price} - \text{Standard price}| \times \text{Actual quantity}$$
$$= |\$1.90 - \$2.00| \times 117,800$$
$$= \$0.10 \times 117,800$$
$$= \$11,780 \text{ Favorable}$$

Since the actual price ($1.90) is less than the standard price ($2.00), the materials price variance is favorable.

The materials usage variance (difference between the Variance Dividing column and the Standard Cost column) also can be determined algebraically, as follows:

$$\text{Usage variance} = |\text{Actual quantity} - \text{Standard quantity}| \times \text{Standard price}$$
$$= |117,800 - 114,000| \times \$2.00$$
$$= 3,800 \times \$2.00$$
$$= \$7,600 \text{ Unfavorable}$$

**Responsibility for materials variances.**    A purchasing agent is normally responsible for the **materials price variance.** Management establishes the standard materials cost based on a particular grade of material and assumptions about purchasing terms including volume discounts, cash discounts, transportation costs, and supplier services. A diligent purchasing agent places orders that take advantage of positive trading terms. In such circumstances, the company pays less than standard costs, resulting in a favorable price variance. Investigating the favorable price variance could result in identifying purchasing strategies to share with other purchasing agents. Analyzing favorable as well as unfavorable variances can result in efficiencies that benefit the entire production process.

In spite of a purchasing agent's diligence, unfavorable price variances may still occur. Suppliers may raise prices, poor scheduling by the production department may require more costly rush orders, or a truckers' strike may force the company to use a more expensive delivery system. These conditions are beyond a purchasing agent's control. Management must be careful to identify the real causes of unfavorable variances. False accusations and overreactions lead to resentment that will undermine the productive potential of the standard costing system.

The nature of the **materials usage variance** is readily apparent from the quantity data. Because the actual quantity used was more than the standard quantity, the variance is unfavorable. If management seeks to minimize cost, using more materials than expected is unfavorable. The materials usage variance is largely controlled by the production department. Materials waste caused by inexperienced workers, faulty machinery, negligent processing, or poor planning results in unfavorable usage variances.

# REALITY BYTES

Most airlines will allow customers to book a flight approximately one year in advance at a price set on the day the reservation is made. Since the airline does not know what it will actual cost to operate a particular flight a year in advance, the price of the ticket will be based on its estimated costs. This can present a problem if costs rise significantly before the flight occurs.

Imagine that on December 14, 2007, Calvin Haines booked a flight from Boston to Seattle for July 19, 2008, and that the ticket price was $309. Between December 2007 and July 2008 many of the airline's costs would not change unexpectedly; for example the airplane has already been purchased and the salaries of the flight crew have already been set. However, in 2008 approximately 30 percent of the cost of operating an airline was for fuel. In December 2007, the spot price of jet fuel was $2.66 per gallon. The spot price of a commodity is the price it would sell for on a given day to someone who had not placed an advance order at a set price. By July 2008 the spot price for jet fuel had risen to $3.97 per gallon. In standard costing terminology, this would result in an unfavorable price variance. Of course, fuel prices can also rapidly change for the better. By February 2009 the price of jet fuel was down to $1.31 per gallon—one-third of its price just seven months earlier.

How can companies avoid some of the problems of having to set the prices they charge before they know what it will cost them to deliver the promised goods or services? Sometimes they cannot, but jet fuel prices can be hedged. That is, a company can commit to purchase fuel at an agreed-upon price at a future data. As of December 2008 Southwest Airlines had already contracted to buy 10 percent of its fuel needs through 2013, and Delta had hedged 26 percent of its needs through 2010.

Hedging has its own risks. When fuel prices drop the airline will still have had to honor its commitments to buy some of its fuel at a price higher than the spot price.

Sources: Federal government data and the companies' annual reports.

---

Unfavorable variances may also be caused by factors beyond the control of the production department. If the purchasing agent buys substandard materials the inferior materials may lead to more scrap (waste) during production, which would be reflected in unfavorable usage variances.

## Calculating Labor Variances

Labor variances are calculated using the same general formulas as those used to compute materials price and usage variances. To illustrate, assume the labor cost per unit of product (trophy) for Melrose Manufacturing is as follows:

|  | Actual Data | Standard Data |
|---|---|---|
| Price **per hour** | $11.50 | $12.00 |
| Quantity of labor per unit of product | × 1.5 hours | × 1.4 hours |
| Cost **per unit** of product | $17.25 | $16.80 |

Based on this detail, the total quantity of labor is:

|  | Actual Data | Standard Data |
|---|---|---|
| Actual production volume | 19,000 units | 19,000 units |
| Quantity of labor per unit of product | × 1.5 hours | × 1.4 hours |
| Total quantity of labor | 28,500 hours | 26,600 hours |

Using this cost and quantity information, the labor price and usage variances are computed in Exhibit 8.6.

## EXHIBIT 8.6

### Labor Price and Usage Variances

| Actual Cost | | Variance Dividing Data | | Standard Cost | |
|---|---|---|---|---|---|
| Actual hours used | 28,500 | Actual hours used (AHrs) | 28,500 | Standard hours (SHrs) | 26,600 |
| × | × | × | × | × | × |
| Actual price per labor hour (AP) | $11.50 | Standard price per labor hour (SP) | $12.00 | Standard price per labor hour | $12.00 |
| | $327,750 | | $342,000 | | $319,200 |

Labor price variance
$14,250 Favorable

Labor usage variance
$22,800 Unfavorable

Algebraic solution: |AP − SP| × AHrs
|$11.50 − $12.00| × 28,500 = $14,250

Algebraic solution: |AHrs − SHrs| × SP
|28,500 − 26,600| × $12.00 = $22,800

Total variance: $8,550 Unfavorable

**Responsibility for labor variances.** The **labor price variance** is favorable because the actual rate paid for labor is less than the standard rate. The production supervisor is usually responsible for the labor price variance because price variances normally result from labor assignments rather than underpayment or overpayment of the hourly rate. Because labor costs are usually fixed by contracts, paying more or less than established rates is not likely. However, using semiskilled labor to perform highly skilled tasks or vice versa will produce price variances. Similarly, using unanticipated overtime will cause unfavorable variances. Production department supervisors control which workers are assigned to which tasks and are therefore accountable for the resulting labor price variances.

**Labor usage variances** measure the productivity of the labor force. Because Melrose used more labor than expected, the labor usage variance is unfavorable. Unsatisfactory labor performance has many causes; low morale or poor supervision are possibilities. Furthermore, machine breakdowns, inferior materials, and poor planning can waste workers' time and reduce productivity. Production department supervisors generally control and are responsible for labor usage variances.

Price and usage variances may be interrelated. Using less-skilled employees who earned less but took longer to do the work could have caused both the favorable labor price variance and the unfavorable labor usage variance. As mentioned earlier, management must exercise diligence in determining causes of variances before concluding who should be held responsible for them.

## ✓ CHECK YOURSELF 8.3

DogHouse, Inc., expected to build 200 doghouses during July. Each doghouse was expected to require 2 hours of direct labor. Labor cost was expected to be $10 per hour. The company actually built 220 doghouses using an average of 2.1 labor hours per doghouse at an actual labor rate averaging $9.80 per hour. Determine the labor rate and usage variances.

**Answer**

Labor price variance = |Actual rate − Standard rate| × Actual quantity

Labor price variance = |$9.80 − $10.00| × (220 units × 2.1 hours) = $92.40 Favorable

Labor usage variance = |Actual quantity − Standard quantity| × Standard rate

Labor usage variance = |[220 × 2.1] − [220 × 2.0]| × $10 = $220.00 Unfavorable

# REALITY BYTES

Does standard costing apply to service companies as well as manufacturers? Absolutely! If you take your car into an auto dealership to be repaired and the service invoice shows that the repair took one hour to perform, you should not assume that was the actual time the repair required. The time for which you were charged was probably based on the standard time a repair of that type should have taken. The mechanic may have gotten this standard time from a reference manual such as the *Chilton Labor Guide* or the *Real-Time Labor Guide,* which are available in either print or CD versions. Some repair jobs can be completed in less time than the guides suggest, and some jobs will take longer. But since customers are charged based on a standard time allowed, two customers having the same repair performed will be charged the same price.

## Variable Overhead Variances

Variable overhead variances are based on the same general formulas used to compute the materials and labor price and usage variances. Unique characteristics of variable overhead costs, however, require special attention. First, variable overhead represents many inputs such as supplies, utilities, and indirect labor. The variable overhead cost pool is normally assigned to products based on a predetermined variable overhead allocation rate. Using a single rate to assign a mixture of different costs complicates variance interpretation. Suppose the actual variable overhead rate is higher than the predetermined rate. Did the company pay more than expected for supplies, utilities, maintenance, or some other input variable? The cost of some variable overhead items may have been higher than expected while others were lower than expected. Similarly, a variable overhead usage variance provides no clue about which overhead inputs were over- or underused. Because meaningful interpretation of the results is difficult, many companies do not calculate price and usage variances for variable overhead costs. We therefore limit coverage of this subject to the total flexible budget variances shown in Exhibit 8.3.

## Selling, General, and Administrative Cost Variances

Variable selling, general, and administrative (SG&A) costs can have *price and usage* variances. For example, suppose Melrose decides to attach a promotional advertising brochure to each trophy it sells. Melrose may pay more or less than expected for each brochure (a price variance). Melrose also could use more or fewer of the brochures than expected (a usage variance). Businesses frequently compute variances for SG&A costs such as sales commissions, food and entertainment, postage, and supplies. The same algebraic formulas used to compute variances for variable manufacturing costs apply to computing variable SG&A cost variances.

For your convenience the general formulas for determining price and usage variances are shown in Exhibit 8.7.

### EXHIBIT 8.7

**Algebraic Formulas for Variances**

Variable cost variances (materials, labor, and overhead)

a.  Price variance

|Actual price − Standard price| × Actual quantity

b.  Usage variance

|Actual quantity − Standard quantity| × Standard price

# A Look Back <<

The essential topics of this chapter are the master budget, flexible budgets, and variance analysis. The *master budget* is determined by multiplying the standard sales price and per unit variable costs by the planned volume of activity. The master budget is prepared at the beginning of the accounting period for planning purposes. It is not adjusted to reflect differences between the planned and actual volume of activity. Since this budget remains unchanged regardless of actual volume, it is also called a *static budget*. *Flexible budgets* differ from static budgets in that they show the estimated amount of revenue and costs expected at different levels of volume. Both static and flexible budgets are based on the same per unit standard amounts and the same fixed costs. The total amounts of revenue and costs in a static budget differ from those in a flexible budget because they are based on different levels of volume. Flexible budgets are used for planning, cost control, and performance evaluation.

The differences between standard (sometimes called *expected* or *estimated*) and actual amounts are called *variances*. Variances are used to evaluate managerial performance and can be either favorable or unfavorable. *Favorable sales variances* occur when actual sales are greater than expected sales. *Unfavorable sales variances* occur when actual sales are less than expected sales. *Favorable cost variances* occur when actual costs are less than expected costs. *Unfavorable cost variances* occur when actual costs are more than expected costs.

*Volume variances* are caused by the difference between the static and flexible budgets. Since both static and flexible budgets are based on the same standard sales price and costs per unit, the volume variances are attributable solely to differences between the planned and the actual volume of activity. Favorable sales volume variances suggest that the marketing manager has performed well by selling more than was expected. Unfavorable sales volume variances suggest the inverse. Favorable or unfavorable variable cost volume variances are not meaningful for performance evaluation because variable costs are expected to change in proportion to changes in the volume of activity.

*Flexible budget variances* are computed by taking the difference between the amounts of revenue and variable costs that are expected at the actual volume of activity and the actual amounts of revenue and variable costs incurred at the actual volume of activity. Since the volume of activity is the same for the flexible budget and the actual results, variances are caused by the differences between the standard and actual sales price and per unit costs. Flexible budget variances are used for cost control and performance evaluation.

The total fixed cost variance is composed of the following:

a. **Fixed manufacturing overhead cost spending variance**

|Actual fixed overhead costs − Budgeted fixed overhead|

b. **Fixed manufacturing overhead cost volume variance**

|Applied fixed overhead costs − Budgeted fixed overhead costs|

The fixed overhead spending variance occurs because actual costs may be more or less than expected. For example, a production supervisor's salary will remain unchanged regardless of the volume of activity, but the supervisor may receive a raise resulting in higher than expected fixed costs. The fixed overhead volume variance is favorable if the actual volume of production is greater than the expected volume. A higher volume of production results in a lower fixed cost per unit. The volume variance measures how effectively production facilities are being used.

Flexible budget variances can be subdivided into *price and usage variances*. Price and usage variances for materials and labor can be computed with the following formulas. Variable overhead variances are calculated with the same general formulas; interpreting the results is difficult, however, because of the variety of inputs combined in variable overhead.

**Price variance** = |Actual price − Standard price| × Actual quantity

**Usage variance** = |Actual quantity − Standard quantity| × Standard price

The purchasing agent is normally accountable for the material price variance. The production department supervisor is usually responsible for the materials usage variance and the labor price and usage variances.

Management must interpret variances with care. For example, a purchasing agent may produce a favorable price variance by buying inferior materials at a low cost. However, an unfavorable labor usage variance may result because employees have difficulty using the substandard materials. The production supervisor is faced with an unfavorable usage variance for which she is not responsible. In addition, the purchasing agent's undesirable choice produced a favorable price variance. Favorable variances do not necessarily reflect good performance and unfavorable variances do not always suggest poor performance. The underlying causes of variances must be investigated before assigning responsibility for them.

## >> A Look Forward

Chapter 9 introduces other techniques for evaluating managerial performance. The concept of decentralization and its relationship to responsibility accounting will be covered. You will learn how to calculate and interpret return on investment and residual income. Finally, you will study approaches used to establish the price of products that are transferred between divisions of the same company.

**A step-by-step audio-narrated series of slides is provided on the text website at www.mhhe.com/edmonds2011.**

### SELF-STUDY REVIEW PROBLEM

Bugout Pesticides, Inc., established the following standard price and costs for a termite control product that it sells to exterminators.

| Variable price and cost data (per unit) | Standard | Actual |
|---|---|---|
| Sales price | $52.00 | $49.00 |
| Materials cost | 10.00 | 10.66 |
| Labor cost | 12.00 | 11.90 |
| Overhead cost | 7.00 | 7.05 |
| General, selling, and administrative (GS&A) cost | 8.00 | 7.92 |
| **Expected fixed costs (in total)** | | |
| Manufacturing overhead | $150,000 | $140,000 |
| General, selling, and administrative | 60,000 | 64,000 |

The 2010 master budget was established at an expected volume of 25,000 units. Actual production and sales volume for the year was 26,000 units.

### Required

a. Prepare the pro forma income statement for Bugout's 2010 master budget.

b. Prepare a flexible budget income statement at the actual volume.

c. Determine the sales and variable cost volume variances and indicate whether they are favorable or unfavorable. Comment on how Bugout would use the variances to evaluate performance.

**d.** Determine the flexible budget variances and indicate whether they are favorable or unfavorable. Provide another name for the fixed cost flexible budget variances.

**e.** Identify the two variances Bugout is most likely to analyze further. Explain why you chose these two variances. Who is normally responsible for the variances you chose to investigate?

**f.** Each unit of product was expected to require 4 pounds of material, which has a standard price of $2.50 per pound. Actual materials usage was 4.1 pounds per unit at an actual price of $2.60 per pound. Determine the materials price and usage variances.

## Solution to Requirements a, b, and c

| Number of units | | 25,000 | 26,000 | |
|---|---|---|---|---|
| | Per Unit Standards | Master Budget | Flexible Budget | Volume Variances |
| Sales revenue | $52 | $1,300,000 | $1,352,000 | $52,000 F |
| Variable manufacturing costs | | | | |
| Materials | 10 | 250,000 | 260,000 | 10,000 U |
| Labor | 12 | 300,000 | 312,000 | 12,000 U |
| Overhead | 7 | 175,000 | 182,000 | 7,000 U |
| Variable SG&A | 8 | 200,000 | 208,000 | 8,000 U |
| Contribution margin | | 375,000 | 390,000 | 15,000 F |
| Fixed costs | | | | |
| Manufacturing overhead | | 150,000 | 150,000 | 0 |
| SG&A | | 60,000 | 60,000 | 0 |
| Net income | | $ 165,000 | $ 180,000 | $15,000 F |

The sales and variable cost volume variances are useful in determining how changes in sales volume affect revenues and costs. Since the flexible budget is based on standard prices and costs, the variances do not provide insight into differences between standard prices and costs versus actual prices and costs.

## Solution to Requirement d

| Number of units | | 26,000 | 26,000 | |
|---|---|---|---|---|
| | Actual Unit Price/Cost | Flexible Budget* | Actual Results | Flexible Budget Variances |
| Sales revenue | $49.00 | $1,352,000 | $1,274,000 | $78,000 U |
| Variable manufacturing costs | | | | |
| Materials | 10.66 | 260,000 | 277,160 | 17,160 U |
| Labor | 11.90 | 312,000 | 309,400 | 2,600 F |
| Overhead | 7.05 | 182,000 | 183,300 | 1,300 U |
| Variable SG&A | 7.92 | 208,000 | 205,920 | 2,080 F |
| Contribution margin | | 390,000 | 298,220 | 91,780 U |
| Fixed costs | | | | |
| Manufacturing overhead | | 150,000 | 140,000 | 10,000 F[†] |
| SG&A | | 60,000 | 64,000 | 4,000 U[†] |
| Net income | | $ 180,000 | $ 94,220 | $85,780 U |

*The price and cost data for the flexible budget come from the table shown at the beginning of the problem.
[†]The flexible budget variances for the fixed costs are also called *spending variances*.

## Solution to Requirement e

The management by exception doctrine focuses attention on the sales price variance and the materials variance. The two variances are material in size and are generally under the control of management. Upper-level marketing managers are responsible for the sales price variance.

These managers are normally responsible for establishing the sales price. In this case, the actual sales price is less than the planned sales price, resulting in an unfavorable flexible budget variance. Mid-level production supervisors and purchasing agents are normally responsible for the materials cost variance. This variance could have been caused by waste or by paying more for materials than the standard price. Further analysis of the materials cost variance follows in Requirement *f*.

### Solution to Requirement f

(Actual price − Standard price) ×      Actual quantity       = Price variance

($2.60 − $2.50)      × (4.1 pounds × 26,000 units) =   $10,660 U

(Actual quantity − Standard quantity) × Standard price = Usage variance

[(4.1 × 26,000) − (4.0 × 26,000)]      ×      $2.50      =      $6,500 U

The total of the price and usage variances [($10,660 + $6,500) = $17,160] equals the total materials flexible budget variance computed in Requirement *d*.

## KEY TERMS

Applied fixed cost  356
Budget slack  360
Fixed cost spending
    variance  356
Fixed cost volume variance  350
Flexible budget  350
Flexible budget variance  354
Ideal standard  358
Labor price variance  365

Labor usage variance  365
Lax standard  358
Making the numbers  352
Management by
    exception  357
Material variance  359
Materials price variance  363
Materials usage variance  363
Practical standard  358

Predetermined overhead
    rate  356
Sales price variance  354
Sales volume variance  352
Standard  358
Static budget  350
Variable cost volume
    variance  352
Variances  351

## QUESTIONS

1. What is the difference between a static budget and a flexible budget? When is each used?

2. When the operating costs for Bill Smith's production department were released, he was sure that he would be getting a raise. His costs were $20,000 less than the planned cost in the master budget. His supervisor informed him that the results look good but that a more in-depth analysis is necessary before raises can be assigned. What other considerations could Mr. Smith's supervisor be interested in before she rates his performance?

3. When are sales and cost variances favorable and unfavorable?

4. Joan Mason, the marketing manager for a large manufacturing company, believes her unfavorable sales volume variance is the responsibility of the production department. What production circumstances that she does not control could have been responsible for her poor performance?

5. When would variable cost volume variances be expected to be unfavorable? How

should unfavorable variable cost volume variances be interpreted?

6. What factors could lead to an increase in sales revenues that would not merit congratulations to the marketing manager?

7. With respect to fixed costs, what are the consequences of the actual volume of activity exceeding the planned volume?

8. How are flexible budget variances determined? What causes these variances?

9. Minnie Divers, the manager of the marketing department for one of the industry's leading retail businesses, has been notified by the accounting department that her department experienced an unfavorable sales volume variance in the preceding period but a favorable sales price variance. Based on these contradictory results, how would you interpret her overall performance as suggested by her variances?

10. What three attributes are necessary for establishing the best standards? What information and considerations should be taken into account when establishing standards?

11. What are the three ranges of difficulty in standard setting? What level of difficulty normally results in superior employee motivation?

12. "So many variances," exclaimed Carl, a production manager with Bonnyville Manufacturing. "How do I determine the variances that need investigation? I can't possibly investigate all of them." Which variances will lead to useful information?

13. What is the primary benefit associated with using a standard cost system?

14. A processing department of Carmine Corporation experienced a high unfavorable materials quantity variance. The plant manager initially commented, "The best way to solve this problem is to fire the supervisor of the processing department." Do you agree? Explain.

15. Sara Anderson says that she is a busy woman with no time to look at favorable variances. Instead, she concentrates solely on the unfavorable ones. She says that favorable variances imply that employees are doing better than expected and need only quick congratulations. In contrast, unfavorable variances indicate that change is needed to get the substandard performance up to par. Do you agree? Explain.

16. What two factors affect the total materials and labor variances?

17. Who is normally responsible for a materials price variance? Identify two factors that may be beyond this individual's control that could cause an unfavorable price variance.

18. John Jamail says that he doesn't understand why companies have labor price variances because most union contracts or other binding agreements set wage rates that do not normally change in the short term. How could rate variances occur even when binding commitments hold the dollar per hour rate constant?

19. Which individuals are normally held responsible for labor usage variances?

20. What is the primary cause of an unfavorable fixed cost volume variance?

21. What is the primary cause of a favorable fixed cost spending variance?

## MULTIPLE-CHOICE QUESTIONS

**Multiple-choice questions are provided on the text website at www.mhhe.com/edmonds2011.**

## EXERCISES—SERIES A

**All applicable Exercises in Series A are available with McGraw-Hill's *Connect Accounting*.**

**Exercise 8-1A**  *Classifying variances as favorable or unfavorable*                 **LO 2**

**Required**

Indicate whether each of the following variances is favorable or unfavorable. The first one has been done as an example.

| Item to Classify | Standard | Actual | Type of Variance |
|---|---|---|---|
| Labor cost | $10.00 per hour | $9.60 per hour | Favorable |
| Labor usage | 61,000 hours | 61,800 hours | |
| Fixed cost spending | $400,000 | $390,000 | |
| Fixed cost per unit (volume) | $3.20 per unit | $3.16 per unit | |
| Sales volume | 40,000 units | 42,000 units | |
| Sales price | $3.60 per unit | $3.63 per unit | |
| Materials cost | $2.90 per pound | $3.00 per pound | |
| Materials usage | 91,000 pounds | 90,000 pounds | |

**LO 2**

### Exercise 8-2A  *Determining amount and type (favorable vs. unfavorable) of variance*

**Required**

Compute variances for the following items and indicate whether each variance is favorable (F) or unfavorable (U).

| Item | Budget | Actual | Variance | F or U |
|------|--------|--------|----------|--------|
| Sales price | $650 | $525 | | |
| Sales revenue | $580,000 | $600,000 | | |
| Cost of goods sold | $385,000 | $360,000 | | |
| Material purchases at 5,000 pounds | $275,000 | $280,000 | | |
| Materials usage | $180,000 | $178,000 | | |
| Production volume | 950 units | 900 units | | |
| Wages at 4,000 hours | $60,000 | $58,700 | | |
| Labor usage at $16 per hour | $96,000 | $97,000 | | |
| Research and development expense | $22,000 | $25,000 | | |
| Selling and administrative expenses | $49,000 | $40,000 | | |

**LO 1**

### Exercise 8-3A  *Preparing master and flexible budgets*

Sexton Manufacturing Company established the following standard price and cost data.

| | |
|---|---|
| Sales price | $8.00 per unit |
| Variable manufacturing cost | $4 per unit |
| Fixed manufacturing cost | $3,000 total |
| Fixed selling and administrative cost | $1,000 total |

Sexton planned to produce and sell 2,000 units. Actual production and sales amounted to 2,200 units.

**Required**

a. Prepare the pro forma income statement in contribution format that would appear in a master budget.

b. Prepare the pro forma income statement in contribution format that would appear in a flexible budget.

**LO 3**

### Exercise 8-4A  *Determining sales and variable cost volume variances*

**Required**

Use the information provided in Exercise 8-3A.

a. Determine the sales and variable cost volume variances.

b. Classify the variances as favorable (F) or unfavorable (U).

c. Comment on the usefulness of the variances with respect to performance evaluation and identify the member of the management team most likely to be responsible for these variances.

d. Determine the amount of fixed cost that will appear in the flexible budget.

e. Determine the fixed cost per unit based on planned activity and the fixed cost per unit based on actual activity. Assuming Sexton uses information in the master budget to price the company's product, comment on how the fixed cost volume variance could affect the company's profitability.

**LO 4**

### Exercise 8-5A  *Determining flexible budget variances*

Use the standard price and cost data provided in Exercise 8-3A. Assume that the actual sales price is $7.65 per unit and that the actual variable cost is $4.25 per unit. The actual fixed manufacturing cost is $2,500, and the actual selling and administrative costs are $1,025.

**Required**

a. Determine the flexible budget variances.

b. Classify the variances as favorable (F) or unfavorable (U).

c. Provide another name for the fixed cost flexible budget variances.

d. Comment on the usefulness of the variances with respect to performance evaluation and identify the member(s) of the management team who is (are) most likely to be responsible for these variances.

### Exercise 8-6A  *Using a flexible budget to accommodate market uncertainty*

According to its original plan, Darey Consulting Services Company would charge its customers for service at $125 per hour in 2011. The company president expects consulting services provided to customers to reach 45,000 hours at that rate. The marketing manager, however, argues that actual results may range from 40,000 hours to 50,000 hours because of market uncertainty. Darey's standard variable cost is $48 per hour, and its standard fixed cost is $1,500,000.

**Required**

Develop flexible budgets based on the assumptions of service levels at 40,000 hours, 45,000 hours, and 50,000 hours.

### Exercise 8-7A  *Evaluating a decision to increase sales volume by lowering sales price*

Ender Educational Services had budgeted its training service charge at $75 per hour. The company planned to provide 30,000 hours of training services during 2012. By lowering the service charge to $60 per hour, the company was able to increase the actual number of hours to 31,500.

**Required**

a. Determine the sales volume variance, and indicate whether it is favorable (F) or unfavorable (U).

b. Determine the flexible budget variance, and indicate whether it is favorable (F) or unfavorable (U).

c. Did lowering the price of training services increase revenue? Explain.

### Exercise 8-8A  *Responsibility for the fixed cost volume variance*

Ragan Company expected to sell 400,000 of its pagers during 2011. It set the standard sales price for the pager at $30 each. During June, it became obvious that the company would be unable to attain the expected volume of sales. Ragan's chief competitor, Selma Corporation, had lowered prices and was pulling market share from Ragan. To be competitive, Ragan matched Selma's price, lowering its sales price to $28 per pager. Selma responded by lowering its price even further to $24 per pager. In an emergency meeting of key personnel, Ragan's accountant, Suzy Kennedy, stated, "Our cost structure simply won't support a sales price in the $24 range." The production manager, Larry Jones, said, "I don't understand why I'm here. The only unfavorable variance on my report is a fixed manufacturing overhead cost volume variance and that one is not my fault. We shouldn't be making the product if the marketing department isn't selling it."

**Required**

a. Describe a scenario in which the production manager is responsible for the fixed cost volume variance.

b. Describe a scenario in which the marketing manager is responsible for the fixed cost volume variance.

c. Explain how a decline in sales volume would affect Ragan's ability to lower its sales price.

### Exercise 8-9A  *Responsibility for variable manufacturing cost variance*

Goslin Manufacturing Company set its standard variable manufacturing cost at $24 per unit of product. The company planned to make and sell 4,000 units of product during 2012. More specifically, the master budget called for total variable manufacturing cost to be $96,000. Actual production during 2012 was 4,200 units, and actual variable manufacturing costs amounted to

$101,640. The production supervisor was asked to explain the variance between budgeted and actual cost ($101,640 − $96,000 = $5,640). The supervisor responded that she was not responsible for the variance that was caused solely by the increase in sales volume controlled by the marketing department.

**Required**

Do you agree with the production supervisor? Explain.

**LO 7**

### Exercise 8-10A    *Calculating the materials usage variance*

Laura Pierre is the manager of the Roebuck Bagel Shop. The corporate office had budgeted her store to sell 3,000 ham sandwiches during the week beginning July 17. Each sandwich was expected to contain 7 ounces of ham. During the week of July 17, the store actually sold 3,500 sandwiches and used 25,000 ounces of ham. The standard cost of ham is $0.20 per ounce. The variance report from company headquarters showed an unfavorable materials usage variance of $800. Ms. Pierre thought the variance was too high, but she had no accounting background and did not know how to register a proper objection.

**Required**

a.  Is the variance calculated properly? If not, recalculate it.
b.  Provide three independent explanations as to what could have caused the materials usage variance that you determined in Requirement *a*.

**LO 7**

### Exercise 8-11A    *Determining materials price and usage variances*

Gwen's Florals produced a special Mother's Day arrangement that included six roses. The standard and actual costs of the roses used in each arrangement follow.

|  | Standard | Actual |
|---|---|---|
| Average number of roses per arrangement | 6.5 | 7 |
| Price per rose | × $0.36 | × $0.32 |
| Cost of roses per arrangement | $2.34 | $2.24 |

Gwen's Florals planned to make 750 arrangements but actually made 790.

**Required**

a.  Determine the total flexible budget materials variance and indicate whether it is favorable (F) or unfavorable (U).
b.  Determine the materials price variance and indicate whether it is favorable (F) or unfavorable (U).
c.  Determine the materials usage variance and indicate whether it is favorable (F) or unfavorable (U).
d.  Confirm the accuracy of Requirements *a*, *b*, and *c* by showing that the sum of the price and usage variances equals the total variance.

**LO 7**

### Exercise 8-12A    *Responsibility for materials usage variance*

Lehman Fruit Basket Company makes baskets of assorted fruit. The standard and actual costs of oranges used in each basket of fruit follow.

|  | Standard | Actual |
|---|---|---|
| Average number of oranges per basket | 4.50 | 6.30 |
| Price per orange | × $0.28 | × $0.25 |
| Cost of oranges per basket | $1.26 | $1.58 |

Lehman actually produced 25,000 baskets.

**Required**

a. Determine the materials price variance and indicate whether it is favorable (F) or unfavorable (U).

b. Determine the materials usage variance and indicate whether it is favorable (F) or unfavorable (U).

c. Explain why the purchasing agent may have been responsible for the usage variance.

### Exercise 8-13A   *Responsibility for labor price and usage variances*

LO 7

Aman Manufacturing Company incurred a favorable labor price variance and an unfavorable labor usage variance.

**Required**

a. Describe a scenario in which the personnel manager is responsible for the unfavorable usage variance.

b. Describe a scenario in which the production manager is responsible for the unfavorable usage variance.

### Exercise 8-14A   *Calculating and explaining labor price and usage variances*

LO 7

Huber and Sons, a CPA firm, established the following standard labor cost data for completing what the firm referred to as a Class 2 tax return. Huber expected each Class 2 return to require 4.0 hours of labor at a cost of $50 per hour. The firm actually completed 600 returns. Actual labor hours averaged 4.4 hours per return and actual labor cost amounted to $46 per hour.

**Required**

a. Determine the total labor variance and indicate whether it is favorable (F) or unfavorable (U).

b. Determine the labor price variance and indicate whether it is favorable (F) or unfavorable (U).

c. Determine the labor usage variance and indicate whether it is favorable (F) or unfavorable (U).

d. Explain what could have caused these variances.

### Exercise 8-15A   *Determining the standard labor price*

LO 7

Kerensky Car Wash, Inc., expected to wash 1,000 cars during the month of August. Washing each car was expected to require 0.2 hours of labor. The company actually used 210 hours of labor to wash 940 cars. The labor usage variance was $352 unfavorable.

**Required**

a. Determine the standard labor price.

b. If the actual labor rate is $14, indicate whether the labor price variance would be favorable (F) or unfavorable (U).

### Exercise 8-16A   *Calculating the variable overhead variance*

LO 5, 6, 7

Pena Company established a predetermined variable overhead cost rate at $9.40 per direct labor hour. The actual variable overhead cost rate was $8.30 per hour. The planned level of labor activity was 73,000 hours of labor. The company actually used 80,000 hours of labor.

**Required**

a. Determine the total flexible budget variable overhead cost variance.

b. Like many companies, Pena has decided not to separate the total variable overhead cost variance into price and usage components. Explain why Pena made this choice.

### Exercise 8-17A   *Determining and interpreting fixed cost variances*

LO 5, 6, 7

Sloan Company established a predetermined fixed overhead cost rate of $29 per unit of product. The company planned to make 7,000 units of product but actually produced only 6,500 units. Actual fixed overhead costs were $212,000.

**Required**

a. Determine the fixed cost spending variance and indicate whether it is favorable or unfavorable. Explain what this variance means. Identify the manager(s) who is (are) responsible for the variance.

b. Determine the fixed cost volume variance and indicate whether it is favorable or unfavorable. Explain why this variance is important. Identify the manager(s) who is (are) responsible for the variance.

## PROBLEMS—SERIES A

**LO 1, 3**

**CHECK FIGURES**
a. NI = $81,000
b. NI at 29,000 units: $72,000

**All applicable Problems in Series A are available with McGraw-Hill's *Connect Accounting.***

**Problem 8-18A** *Determining sales and variable cost volume variances*

Todhunter Publications established the following standard price and costs for a hardcover picture book that the company produces.

| Standard price and variable costs | |
|---|---|
| Sales price | $36.00 |
| Materials cost | 9.00 |
| Labor cost | 4.50 |
| Overhead cost | 6.30 |
| Selling, general, and administrative costs | 7.20 |
| Planned fixed costs | |
| Manufacturing overhead | $135,000 |
| Selling, general, and administrative | 54,000 |

Todhunter planned to make and sell 30,000 copies of the book.

**Required**

a. Prepare the pro forma income statement that would appear in the master budget.

b. Prepare flexible budget income statements, assuming production volumes of 29,000 and 31,000 units.

c. Determine the sales and variable cost volume variances, assuming volume is actually 31,000 units.

d. Indicate whether the variances are favorable (F) or unfavorable (U).

e. Comment on how Todhunter could use the variances to evaluate performance.

**LO 4**

**CHECK FIGURE**
Flexible budget variance
of NI: $20,450 U

**Problem 8-19A** *Determining and interpreting flexible budget variances*

Use the standard price and cost data supplied in Problem 8-18A. Assume that Todhunter actually produced and sold 31,000 books. The actual sales price and costs incurred follow.

| Actual price and variable costs | |
|---|---|
| Sales price | $35.00 |
| Materials cost | 9.20 |
| Labor cost | 4.40 |
| Overhead cost | 6.35 |
| Selling, general, and administrative costs | 7.00 |
| Actual fixed costs | |
| Manufacturing overhead | $120,000 |
| Selling, general, and administrative | 60,000 |

**Required**

a. Determine the flexible budget variances. Provide another name for the fixed cost flexible budget variances.

b. Indicate whether each variance is favorable (F) or unfavorable (U).

c. Identify the management position responsible for each variance. Explain what could have caused the variance.

## Problem 8-20A    *Flexible budget planning*

Luke Chou, the president of Digitech Computer Services, needs your help. He wonders about the potential effects on the firm's net income if he changes the service rate that the firm charges its customers. The following basic data pertain to fiscal year 2012.

| | |
|---|---|
| Standard rate and variable costs | |
| Service rate per hour | $80.00 |
| Labor cost | 40.00 |
| Overhead cost | 7.20 |
| Selling, general, and administrative cost | 4.30 |
| Expected fixed costs | |
| Facility repair | $525,000.00 |
| Selling, general, and administrative | 150,000.00 |

### Required

a. Prepare the pro forma income statement that would appear in the master budget if the firm expects to provide 30,000 hours of services in 2012.

b. A marketing consultant suggests to Mr. Chou that the service rate may affect the number of service hours that the firm can achieve. According to the consultant's analysis, if Digitech charges customers $75 per hour, the firm can achieve 38,000 hours of services. Prepare a flexible budget using the consultant's assumption.

c. The same consultant also suggests that if the firm raises its rate to $85 per hour, the number of service hours will decline to 25,000. Prepare a flexible budget using the new assumption.

d. Evaluate the three possible outcomes you determined in Requirements *a*, *b*, and *c* and recommend a pricing strategy.

## Problem 8-21A    *Determining materials price and usage variances*

Vacher Fruit Drink Company planned to make 200,000 containers of apple juice. It expected to use two cups of frozen apple concentrate to make each container of juice, thus using 400,000 cups (200,000 containers × 2 cups) of frozen concentrate. The standard price of one cup of apple concentrate is $0.25. Vacher actually paid $110,168.10 to purchase 408,030 cups of concentrate, which was used to make 201,000 containers of apple juice.

### Required

a. Are flexible budget materials variances based on the planned volume of activity (200,000 containers) or actual volume of activity (201,000 containers)?

b. Compute the actual price per cup of concentrate.

c. Compute the standard quantity (number of cups of concentrate) required to produce the containers.

d. Compute the materials price variance and indicate whether it is favorable (F) or unfavorable (U).

e. Compute the materials usage variance and indicate whether it is favorable (F) or unfavorable (U).

## Problem 8-22A    *Determining labor price and usage variances*

Lakesha's Doll Company produces handmade dolls. The standard amount of time spent on each doll is 1.5 hours. The standard cost of labor is $7.72 per hour. The company planned to make 8,000 dolls during the year but actually used 12,500 hours of labor to make 9,000 dolls. The payroll amounted to $98,875.

### Required

a. Should labor variances be based on the planned volume of 8,000 dolls or the actual volume of 9,000 dolls?

b. Prepare a table that shows the standard labor price, the actual labor price, the standard labor hours, and the actual labor hours.

c.  Compute the labor price variance and indicate whether it is favorable (F) or unfavorable (U).

d.  Compute the labor usage variance and indicate whether it is favorable (F) or unfavorable (U).

### Problem 8-23A   *Computing fixed cost variances*

In addition to other costs, Fenwick Telephone Company planned to incur $441,000 of fixed manufacturing overhead in making 350,000 telephones. Fenwick actually produced 359,000 telephones, incurring actual overhead costs of $447,000. Fenwick establishes its predetermined overhead rate based on the planned volume of production (expected number of telephones).

**Required**

a.  Calculate the predetermined overhead rate.

b.  Determine the fixed cost spending variance and indicate whether it is favorable (F) or unfavorable (U).

c.  Determine the fixed cost volume variance and indicate whether it is favorable (F) or unfavorable (U).

### Problem 8-24A   *Computing materials, labor, and cost variances*

The following data were drawn from the records of Inman Corporation.

| | |
|---|---|
| Planned volume for year (static budget) | 4,000 units |
| Standard direct materials cost per unit | 3.1 lbs. @ $1.50 per pound |
| Standard direct labor cost per unit | 2 hours @ $4.00 per hour |
| Total expected fixed overhead costs | $18,800 |
| Actual volume for the year (flexible budget) | 4,200 units |
| Actual direct materials cost per unit | 2.7 lbs. @ $2.00 per pound |
| Actual direct labor cost per unit | 2.3 hrs. @ $3.60 per hour |
| Total actual fixed overhead costs | $15,000 |

**Required**

a.  Prepare a materials variance information table showing the standard price, the actual price, the standard quantity, and the actual quantity.

b.  Calculate the materials price and usage variances. Indicate whether the variances are favorable (F) or unfavorable (U).

c.  Prepare a labor variance information table showing the standard price, the actual price, the standard hours, and the actual hours.

d.  Calculate the labor price and usage variances. Indicate whether the variances are favorable (F) or unfavorable (U).

e.  Calculate the predetermined overhead rate, assuming that Inman uses the number of units as the allocation base.

f.  Calculate the fixed cost spending variance. Indicate whether the variance is favorable (F) or unfavorable (U).

g.  Calculate the fixed cost volume variance. Indicate whether the variance is favorable (F) or unfavorable (U).

### Problem 8-25A   *Computing materials, labor, and fixed cost variances*

Lennox Manufacturing Company produces a component part of a top secret military communication device. Standard production and cost data for the part, Product X, follow.

| | |
|---|---|
| Planned production | 30,000 units |
| Per unit direct materials | 2 lbs. @ $1.80 per lb. |
| Per unit direct labor | 3 hrs. @ $8.00 per hr. |
| Total estimated fixed overhead costs | $702,000 |

Lennox purchased and used 63,345 pounds of material at an average cost of $1.85 per pound. Labor usage amounted to 89,160 hours at an average of $8.10 per hour. Actual production amounted to 30,900 units. Actual fixed overhead costs amounted to $738,000. The company completed and sold all inventory for $1,800,000.

**Required**

a. Prepare a materials variance information table showing the standard price, the actual price, the standard quantity, and the actual quantity.

b. Calculate the materials price and usage variances. Indicate whether the variances are favorable (F) or unfavorable (U).

c. Prepare a labor variance information table showing the standard price, the actual price, the standard hours, and the actual hours.

d. Calculate the labor price and usage variances. Indicate whether the variances are favorable (F) or unfavorable (U).

e. Calculate the predetermined overhead rate, assuming that Lennox uses the number of units as the allocation base.

f. Calculate the fixed cost spending and volume variances and indicate whether they are favorable (F) or unfavorable (U).

g. Determine the amount of gross margin Lennox would report on the year-end income statement.

## Problem 8-26A   *Computing variances*

LO 7

CHECK FIGURES
a. 1,720 lbs.
d. $8.25

Osmond Manufacturing Company produces a single product. The following data apply to the standard cost of materials and labor associated with making the product.

| | |
|---|---|
| Materials quantity per unit | 1 pound |
| Materials price | $5.00 per pound |
| Labor quantity per unit | 2 hours |
| Labor price | $9.00 per hour |

During the year, the company made 1,800 units of product. At the end of the year, the following variances had been calculated.

| | |
|---|---|
| Materials usage variance | $400 Favorable |
| Materials price variance | $352 Unfavorable |
| Labor usage variance | $1,800 Unfavorable |
| Labor price variance | $2,850 Favorable |

**Required**

a. Determine the actual amount of materials used.

b. Determine the actual price paid per pound for materials.

c. Determine the actual labor hours used.

d. Determine the actual labor price per hour.

## Problem 8-27A   *Computing standard cost and analyzing variances*

LO 5, 7

Quilter Company manufactures molded candles that are finished by hand. The company developed the following standards for a new line of drip candles:

| | |
|---|---|
| Amount of direct materials per candle | 1.6 pounds |
| Price of direct materials per pound | $0.60 |
| Quantity of labor per unit | 1 hours |
| Price of direct labor per hour | $8.00/hour |
| Total budgeted fixed overhead | $156,000 |

During 2010, Quilter planned to produce 30,000 drip candles. Production lagged behind expectations, and it actually produced only 24,000 drip candles. At year-end, direct materials purchased and used amounted to 40,000 pounds at a unit price of $0.54 per pound. Direct labor costs were actually $7.50 per hour and 26,400 actual hours were worked to produce the drip candles. Overhead for the year actually amounted to $132,000. Overhead is applied to products using a predetermined overhead rate based on estimated units.

**Required**

(Round all computations to two decimal places.)

**a.** Compute the standard cost per candle for direct materials, direct labor, and overhead.

**b.** Determine the total standard cost for one drip candle.

**c.** Compute the actual cost per candle for direct materials, direct labor, and overhead.

**d.** Compute the total actual cost per candle.

**e.** Compute the price and usage variances for direct materials and direct labor. Identify any variances that Quilter should investigate. Offer possible cause(s) for the variances.

**f.** Compute the fixed cost spending and volume variances. Explain your findings.

**g.** Although the individual variances (price, usage, and overhead) were large, the standard cost per unit and the actual cost per unit differed by only a few cents. Explain why.

**LO 1, 2, 3, 4**

**Problem 8-28A**   *Analyzing not-for-profit entity variances*

The Midwest Management Association held its annual public relations luncheon in April 2012. Based on the previous year's results, the organization allocated $21,360 of its operating budget to cover the cost of the luncheon. To ensure that costs would be appropriately controlled, Michelle Laird, the treasurer, prepared the following budget for the 2012 luncheon.

The budget for the luncheon was based on the following expectations.

**1.** The meal cost per person was expected to be $11.80. The cost driver for meals was attendance, which was expected to be 1,400 individuals.

**2.** Postage was based on $0.44 per invitation and 3,000 invitations were expected to be mailed. The cost driver for postage was number of invitations mailed.

**3.** The facility charge is $1,000 for a room that will accommodate up to 1,600 people; the charge for one to hold more than 1,600 people is $1,500.

**4.** A fixed amount was designated for printing, decorations, the speaker's gift, and publicity.

| MIDWEST MANAGEMENT ASSOCIATION<br>Public Relations Luncheon Budget<br>April 2012 | |
|---|---:|
| Operating funds allocated | $21,360 |
| Expenses | |
| Variable costs | |
| Meals (1,400 × $11.80) | 16,520 |
| Postage (3,000 × 0.44) | 1,320 |
| Fixed costs | |
| Facility | 1,000 |
| Printing | 950 |
| Decorations | 840 |
| Speaker's gift | 130 |
| Publicity | 600 |
| Total expenses | 21,360 |
| Budget surplus (deficit) | $     0 |

Actual results for the luncheon follow.

**MIDWEST MANAGEMENT ASSOCIATION**
Actual Results for Public Relations Luncheon
April 2012

| | |
|---|---:|
| Operating funds allocated | $21,360 |
| Expenses | |
|   Variable costs | |
|   Meals (1,620 × $12.50) | 20,250 |
|   Postage (4,000 × 0.44) | 1,760 |
|   Fixed costs | |
|   Facility | 1,500 |
|   Printing | 950 |
|   Decorations | 840 |
|   Speaker's gift | 130 |
|   Publicity | 600 |
| Total expenses | 26,030 |
| Budget deficit | $ (4,670) |

Reasons for the differences between the budgeted and actual data follow.

1. The president of the organization, Yvonne Davis, increased the invitation list to include 1,000 former members. As a result, 4,000 invitations were mailed.

2. Attendance was 1,620 individuals. Because of higher-than-expected attendance, the luncheon was moved to a larger room, thereby increasing the facility charge to $1,500.

3. At the last minute, Ms. Laird decided to add a dessert to the menu, which increased the meal cost to $12.50 per person.

4. Printing, decorations, the speaker's gift, and publicity costs were as budgeted.

**Required**

a. Prepare a flexible budget and compute the sales and variable cost volume variances based on a comparison between the master budget and the flexible budget.

b. Compute flexible budget variances by comparing the flexible budget with the actual results.

c. Ms. Davis was extremely upset with the budget deficit. She immediately called Ms. Laird to complain about the budget variance for the meal cost. She told Ms. Laird that the added dessert caused the meal cost to be $3,730 ($20,250 − $16,520) over budget. She added, "I could expect a couple hundred dollars one way or the other, but several thousand is totally unacceptable. At the next meeting of the budget committee, I want you to explain what happened." Assume that you are Ms. Laird. What would you tell the members of the budget committee?

d. Since this is a not-for-profit organization, why should anyone be concerned with meeting the budget?

## EXERCISES—SERIES B

**Exercise 8-1B** *Classifying variances as favorable or unfavorable*

LO 2

**Required**

Indicate whether each of the following variances is favorable (F) or unfavorable (U). The first one has been done as an example.

| Item to Classify | Standard | Actual | Type of Variance |
|---|---|---|---|
| Sales volume | 38,000 units | 36,750 units | Unfavorable |
| Sales price | $6.90 per unit | $6.78 per unit | |
| Materials cost | $2.10 per pound | $2.30 per pound | |
| Materials usage | 102,400 pounds | 103,700 pounds | |
| Labor cost | $8.25 per hour | $8.80 per hour | |
| Labor usage | 56,980 hours | 55,790 hours | |
| Fixed cost spending | $249,000 | $244,000 | |
| Fixed cost per unit (volume) | $2.51 per unit | $3.22 per unit | |

**LO 2**

### Exercise 8-2B   *Recognizing favorable vs. unfavorable variances*

Compute variances for the following items and indicate whether each variance is favorable (F) or unfavorable (U).

| Item | Budget | Actual | Variance | F or U |
|---|---|---|---|---|
| Sales price | $550 | $560 | | |
| Sales revenue | $690,000 | $720,000 | | |
| Cost of goods sold | $520,000 | $470,000 | | |
| Materials purchases at 10,000 pounds | $330,000 | $360,000 | | |
| Materials usage | $270,000 | $260,000 | | |
| Production volume | 890 units | 900 units | | |
| Wages at 7,600 hours | $91,200 | $90,800 | | |
| Labor usage | 7,600 hours | 8,000 hours | | |
| Research and development expense | $81,000 | $90,000 | | |
| Selling and administrative expenses | $75,000 | $71,000 | | |

**LO 1**

### Exercise 8-3B   *Preparing master and flexible budgets*

Clyde Manufacturing Company established the following standard price and cost data.

| | |
|---|---|
| Sales price | $20 per unit |
| Variable manufacturing cost | $12 per unit |
| Fixed manufacturing cost | $20,000 total |
| Fixed selling and administrative cost | $18,000 total |

Clyde planned to produce and sell 18,000 units. It actually produced and sold 19,000 units.

**Required**

a. Prepare the pro forma income statement that would appear in a master budget. Use the contribution margin format.

b. Prepare the pro forma income statement that would appear in a flexible budget. Use the contribution margin format.

**LO 3**

### Exercise 8-4B   *Determining sales and variable cost volume variances*

**Required**

Use the information provided in Exercise 8-3B.

a. Determine the sales and variable cost volume variances.

b. Classify the variances as favorable or unfavorable.

c. Comment on the usefulness of the variances with respect to performance evaluation and identify the member of the management team most likely to be responsible for these variances.

d. Determine the amounts of fixed cost that will appear in the flexible budget.

e. Determine the fixed cost per unit based on planned activity and the fixed cost per unit based on actual activity. Assuming Clyde uses information in the master budget to price its product, explain how the fixed cost volume variance could affect the company's profitability.

**Exercise 8-5B**  *Determining flexible budget variances*  **LO 4**

Use the standard price and cost data provided in Exercise 8-3B. Assume the actual sales price was $19.60 per unit and the actual variable cost was $11.80 per unit. The actual fixed manufacturing cost was $21,000, and the actual selling and administrative expenses were $17,300.

**Required**

a. Determine the flexible budget variances.

b. Classify the variances as favorable or unfavorable.

c. Provide another name for the fixed cost flexible budget variances.

d. Comment on the usefulness of the variances with respect to performance evaluation and identify the member(s) of the management team that is (are) most likely to be responsible for these variances.

**Exercise 8-6B**  *Using a flexible budget to accommodate market uncertainty*  **LO 4**

Flemming Cable Installation Services, Inc., is planning to open a new regional office. Based on a market survey Flemming commissioned, the company expects services demand for the new office to be between 30,000 and 40,000 hours annually. The firm normally charges customers $50 per hour for its installation services. Flemming expects the new office to have a standard variable cost of $30 per hour and standard fixed cost of $660,000 per year.

**Required**

a. Develop flexible budgets based on 30,000 hours, 35,000 hours, and 40,000 hours of services.

b. Based on the results for Requirement *a*, comment on the likely success of Flemming's new office.

**Exercise 8-7B**  *Evaluating a decision to increase sales volume by reducing sales price*  **LO 3, 4**

At the beginning of its most recent accounting period, Jackora Company had planned to clean 400 house roofs at an average price of $250 per roof. By reducing the service charge to $225 per roof, the company was able to increase the actual number of roofs cleaned to 450.

**Required**

a. Determine the sales volume variance and indicate whether it is favorable (F) or unfavorable (U).

b. Determine the flexible budget variance and indicate whether it is favorable (F) or unfavorable (U).

c. Did reducing the price charged for cleaning roofs increase revenue? Explain.

**Exercise 8-8B**  *Responsibility for fixed cost volume and spending variances*  **LO 5**

Dill Manufacturing Company had an excellent year. The company hired a new marketing director in January. The new director's great motivational appeal inspired the sales staff, and, as a result, sales were 20 percent higher than expected. In a recent management meeting, the company president, Joe Ezell, congratulated the marketing director and then criticized Gene Hartley, the company's production manager, because of an unfavorable fixed cost spending variance. Mr. Hartley countered that the favorable fixed cost volume variance more than offset the unfavorable fixed cost spending variance. He argued that Mr. Ezell should evaluate the two variances in total and that he should be rewarded rather than criticized.

**Required**

Do you agree with Mr. Hartley's defense of the unfavorable fixed cost spending variance? Explain.

**Exercise 8-9B**  *Assessing responsibility for a labor cost variance*  **LO 4**

Orlov Technologies Company's 2011 master budget called for using 60,000 hours of labor to produce 180,000 units of software. The standard labor rate for the company's employees is $38 per direct labor hour. Demand exceeded expectations, resulting in production and sales of 210,000 software units. Actual direct labor costs were $2,646,000. The year-end variance report showed a total unfavorable labor variance of $366,000.

**Required**

Assume you are the vice president of manufacturing. Should you criticize or praise the production supervisor's performance? Explain.

**LO 7**

### Exercise 8-10B    *Calculating the materials usage variance*

Stella Minten manages the Sweet Candy Shop, which was expected to sell 4,000 servings of its trademark candy during July. Each serving was expected to contain 6 ounces of candy. The standard cost of the candy was $0.60 per ounce. The shop actually sold 3,800 servings and actually used 22,100 ounces of candy.

**Required**

a. Compute the materials usage variance.

b. Explain what could have caused the variance that you computed in Requirement *a*.

**LO 7**

### Exercise 8-11B    *Determining materials price and usage variances*

Howe Company makes paint that it sells in 1-gallon containers to retail home improvement stores. During 2012, the company planned to make 190,000 gallons of paint. It actually produced 198,000 gallons. The standard and actual quantity and cost of the color pigment for 1 gallon of paint follow.

|  | Standard | Actual |
|---|---|---|
| Quantity of materials per gallon | 12 ounces | 13 ounces |
| Price per ounce | × $0.50 | × $0.52 |
| Cost per gallon | $6.00 | $6.76 |

**Required**

a. Determine the total flexible budget materials variance for pigment. Indicate whether the variance is favorable or unfavorable.

b. Determine the materials price variance and indicate whether the variance is favorable (F) or unfavorable (U).

c. Determine the materials usage variance and indicate whether the variance is favorable (F) or unfavorable (U).

d. Confirm your answers to Requirements *a*, *b*, and *c* by showing that the sum of the price and usage variances equals the total variance.

**LO 7**

### Exercise 8-12B    *Responsibility for materials price variance*

Sweer Chill, Inc., makes ice cream that it sells in 5-gallon containers to retail ice cream parlors. During 2011, the company planned to make 100,000 containers of ice cream. It actually produced 97,000 containers. The actual and standard quantity and cost of sugar per container follow.

|  | Standard | Actual |
|---|---|---|
| Quantity of materials per container | 2 pounds | 2.1 pounds |
| Price per pound | × $0.75 | × $0.80 |
| Cost per container | $1.50 | $1.68 |

**Required**

a. Determine the materials price variance and indicate whether the variance is favorable (F) or unfavorable (U).

b. Determine the materials usage variance and indicate whether the variance is favorable (F) or unfavorable (U).

c. Explain how the production manager could have been responsible for the price variance.

**Exercise 8-13B**   *Responsibility for labor price and usage variance*

Newhouse Manufacturing Company incurred an unfavorable labor price variance.

**Required**

a. Describe a scenario in which the personnel manager is responsible for the unfavorable price variance.

b. Describe a scenario in which the production manager is responsible for the unfavorable price variance.

**Exercise 8-14B**   *Calculating and explaining labor price and usage variances*

LO 7

Albertson Landscaping Company established the following standard labor cost data to provide complete lawn care service (cutting, edging, trimming, and blowing) for a small lawn. Albertson planned each lawn to require 2 hours of labor at a cost of $30 per hour. The company actually serviced 500 lawns using an average of 1.75 labor hours per lawn. Actual labor costs were $32 per hour.

**Required**

a. Determine the total labor variance and indicate whether the variance is favorable (F) or unfavorable (U).

b. Determine the labor price variance and indicate whether the variance is favorable (F) or unfavorable (U).

c. Determine the labor usage variance and indicate whether the variance is favorable (F) or unfavorable (U).

d. Explain what could have caused the variances computed in Requirements *b* and *c*.

**Exercise 8-15B**   *Determining standard labor hours*

LO 7

Stylish Hair is a hair salon. It planned to provide 240 hair color treatments during December. Each treatment was planned to require 0.5 hours of labor at the standard labor price of $18 per hour. The salon actually provided 250 treatments. The actual labor price averaged $17.76. The labor price variance was $36 favorable.

**Required**

a. Determine the actual number of labor hours used per treatment.

b. Indicate whether the labor usage variance would be favorable (F) or unfavorable (U).

**Exercise 8-16B**   *Calculating a variable overhead variance*

LO 5, 7

Hahn Manufacturing Company established a predetermined variable overhead cost rate of $40 per direct labor hour. The actual variable overhead cost rate was $38 per direct labor hour. Hahn planned to use 150,000 hours of direct labor. It actually used 152,000 hours of direct labor.

**Required**

a. Determine the total flexible budget variable overhead cost variance.

b. Many companies do not subdivide the total variable overhead cost variance into price and usage components. Under what circumstances would it be appropriate to distinguish between the price and usage components of a variable overhead cost variance? What would be required to accomplish this type of analysis?

**Exercise 8-17B**   *Determining and interpreting fixed cost variances*

LO 5, 7

Smitter Manufacturing Company established a predetermined fixed overhead cost rate of $200 per unit of product. The company planned to make 19,000 units of product but actually produced 20,000 units. Actual fixed overhead costs were $4,000,000.

**Required**

a. Determine the fixed cost spending variance. Indicate whether the variance is favorable (F) or unfavorable (U). Explain what this variance means. Identify the manager(s) who is (are) responsible for the variance.

b. Determine the fixed cost volume variance. Indicate whether the variance is favorable (F) or unfavorable (U). Explain what the designations *favorable* and *unfavorable* mean with respect to the fixed manufacturing overhead cost volume variance.

## PROBLEMS—SERIES B

### Problem 8-18B   *Determining sales and variable cost volume variances*

Vlascenko Food Corporation developed the following standard price and costs for a refrigerated TV dinner that the company produces.

| Standard price and variable costs | |
|---|---|
| Sales price | $25.96 |
| Materials cost | 9.00 |
| Labor cost | 2.60 |
| Overhead cost | 0.56 |
| Selling, general, and administrative costs | 4.20 |
| Planned fixed costs | |
| Manufacturing overhead cost | $500,000 |
| Selling, general, and administrative costs | 360,000 |

Vlascenko plans to make and sell 200,000 TV dinners.

**Required**

a. Prepare the pro forma income statement that would appear in the master budget.

b. Prepare flexible budget income statements, assuming production and sales volumes of 180,000 and 220,000 units.

c. Determine the sales and variable cost volume variances, assuming volume is actually 190,000 units.

d. Indicate whether the variances are favorable (F) or unfavorable (U).

e. Comment on how Vlascenko could use the variances to evaluate performance.

### Problem 8-19B   *Determining and interpreting flexible budget variances*

Use the standard price and cost data supplied in Problem 8-18B. Assume that Vlascenko actually produced and sold 216,000 units. The actual sales price and costs incurred follow.

| Actual price and variable costs | |
|---|---|
| Sales price | $25.80 |
| Materials cost | 8.80 |
| Labor cost | 2.68 |
| Overhead cost | 0.56 |
| Selling, general, and administrative costs | 4.40 |
| Actual fixed costs | |
| Manufacturing overhead | $512,000 |
| Selling, general, and administrative costs | 356,000 |

**Required**

a. Determine the flexible budget variances. Provide another name for the fixed cost flexible budget variances.

b. Indicate whether each variance is favorable (F) or unfavorable (U).

c. Identify the management position responsible for each variance. Explain what could have caused the variance.

### Problem 8-20B   *Flexible budget planning*

Executive officers of Ortiz Seafood Processing Company are holding a planning session for fiscal year 2012. They have already established the following standard price and costs for their canned seafood product.

| Standard price and variable costs | |
|---|---|
| Price per can | $3.00 |
| Materials cost | 1.05 |
| Labor cost | 0.64 |
| Overhead cost | 0.10 |
| Selling, general, and administrative costs | 0.25 |
| Expected fixed costs | |
| Production facility costs | $215,000 |
| Selling, general, and administrative costs | 180,000 |

**Required**

a. Prepare the pro forma income statement that would appear in the master budget if the company expects to produce 600,000 cans of seafood in 2012.

b. A marketing consultant suggests to Ortiz's president that the product's price may affect the number of cans the company can sell. According to the consultant's analysis, if the firm sets its price at $2.70, it could sell 810,000 cans of seafood. Prepare a flexible budget based on the consultant's suggestion.

c. The same consultant also suggests that if the company raises its price to $3.25 per can, the volume of sales would decline to 400,000. Prepare a flexible budget based on this suggestion.

d. Evaluate the three possible outcomes developed in Requirements a, b, and c and recommend a pricing strategy.

## Problem 8-21B   *Determining materials price and usage variances*     LO 7

Tiffany Swimsuit Specialties, Inc., makes fashionable women's swimsuits. Its most popular swimsuit, with the Sarong trade name, uses a standard fabric amount of 6 yards of raw material with a standard price of $5.00 per yard. The company planned to produce 100,000 Sarong swimsuits in 2011. At the end of 2011, the company's cost accountant reported that Tiffany had used 636,000 yards of fabric to make 102,000 swimsuits. Actual cost for the raw material was $3,307,200.

**Required**

a. Are flexible budget material variances based on the planned volume of 100,000 swimsuits or actual volume of 102,000 swimsuits?

b. Compute the actual price per yard of fabric.

c. Compute the standard quantity (yards of fabric) required to produce the swimsuits.

d. Compute the materials price variance and indicate whether it is favorable (F) or unfavorable (U).

e. Compute the materials usage variance and indicate whether it is favorable (F) or unfavorable (U).

## Problem 8-22B   *Determining labor price and usage variances*     LO 7

As noted in Problem 8-21B, Tiffany Swimsuit makes swimsuits. In 2011, Tiffany produced its most popular swimsuit, the Sarong, for a standard labor price of $30 per hour. The standard amount of labor was 1.0 hour per swimsuit. The company had planned to produce 100,000 Sarong swimsuits. At the end of 2011, the company's cost accountant reported that Tiffany had used 107,000 hours of labor to make 102,000 swimsuits. The total labor cost was $3,295,600.

**Required**

a. Should the labor variances be based on the planned volume of 100,000 swimsuits or on the actual volume of 102,000 swimsuits?

b. Prepare a table that shows the standard labor price, the actual labor price, the standard labor hours, and the actual labor hours.

c. Compute the labor price variance and indicate whether it is favorable (F) or unfavorable (U).

d. Compute the labor usage variance and indicate whether it is favorable (F) or unfavorable (U).

**LO 5**

### Problem 8-23B  *Computing fixed cost variances*

Goodwin Sporting Goods Co. manufactures baseballs. According to Goodwin's 2013 budget, the company planned to incur $300,000 of fixed manufacturing overhead costs to make 200,000 baseballs. Goodwin actually produced 187,000 balls, incurring $296,000 of actual fixed manufacturing overhead costs. Goodwin establishes its predetermined overhead rate on the basis of the planned volume of production (expected number of baseballs).

**Required**

a. Calculate the predetermined overhead rate.

b. Determine the fixed cost spending variance and indicate whether it is favorable (F) or unfavorable (U).

c. Determine the fixed cost volume variance and indicate whether it is favorable (F) or unfavorable (U).

**LO 5, 7**

### Problem 8-24B  *Computing materials, labor, and manufacturing overhead cost variances*

Frank Trawick was a new cost accountant at Skoney Plastics Corporation. He was assigned to analyze the following data that his predecessor left him.

| | |
|---|---|
| Planned volume for year (static budget) | 10,000 units |
| Standard direct materials cost per unit | 2 lbs. @ $1.50 per pound |
| Standard direct labor cost per unit | 0.5 hours @ $10.00 per hour |
| Total planned fixed overhead costs | $12,000 |
| Actual volume for the year (flexible budget) | 10,800 units |
| Actual direct materials cost per unit | 1.9 lbs. @ $1.60 per pound |
| Actual direct labor cost per unit | 0.6 hrs. @ $8.00 per hour |
| Total actual fixed overhead costs | $12,400 |

**Required**

a. Prepare a materials variance information table showing the standard price, the actual price, the standard quantity, and the actual quantity.

b. Calculate the materials price and usage variances and indicate whether they are favorable (F) or unfavorable (U).

c. Prepare a labor variance information table showing the standard price, the actual price, the standard hours, and the actual hours.

d. Calculate the labor price and usage variances and indicate whether they are favorable (F) or unfavorable (U).

e. Calculate the predetermined overhead rate, assuming that Skoney Plastics uses the number of units as the allocation base.

f. Calculate the fixed manufacturing overhead cost spending variance and indicate whether it is favorable (F) or unfavorable (U).

g. Calculate the fixed manufacturing overhead cost volume variance and indicate whether it is favorable (F) or unfavorable (U).

**LO 5, 7**

### Problem 8-25B  *Computing materials, labor, and fixed cost variances*

Keedy Corporation makes mouse pads for computer users. After the first year of operation, Diane Keedy, the president and chief executive officer, was eager to determine the efficiency of the company's operation. In her analysis, she used the following standards provided by her assistant.

| | |
|---|---|
| Units of planned production | 400,000 |
| Per-unit direct materials | 1 square foot @ $0.25 per square foot |
| Per-unit direct labor | 0.2 hrs. @ $7.00 per hr. |
| Total estimated fixed overhead costs | $200,000 |

Keedy purchased and used 460,000 square feet of material at an average cost of $0.24 per square foot. Labor usage amounted to 79,200 hours at an average of $6.90 per hour. Actual production amounted to 208,000 units. Actual fixed overhead costs amounted to $204,000. The company completed and sold all inventory for $1,414,400.

### Required

a. Prepare a materials variance information table showing the standard price, the actual price, the standard quantity, and the actual quantity.

b. Calculate the materials price and usage variances and indicate whether they are favorable (F) or unfavorable (U).

c. Prepare a labor variance information table showing the standard price, the actual price, the standard hours, and the actual hours.

d. Calculate the labor price and usage variances and indicate whether they are favorable (F) or unfavorable (U).

e. Calculate the predetermined overhead rate, assuming that Keedy uses the number of units as the allocation base.

f. Calculate the fixed cost spending and volume variances and indicate whether they are favorable (F) or unfavorable (U).

g. Determine the amount of gross margin Keedy would report on the year-end income statement.

## Problem 8-26B  *Computing variances*                                      LO 7

A fire destroyed most of Salazar Products Corporation's records. Rose Penwell, the company's accountant, is trying to piece together the company's operating results from salvaged documents. She discovered the following data.

| | |
|---|---|
| Standard materials quantity per unit | 2.5 pounds |
| Standard materials price | $2 per pound |
| Standard labor quantity per unit | 0.6 hour |
| Standard labor price | $12 per hour |
| Actual number of products produced | 8,000 units |
| Materials price variance | $792 Favorable |
| Materials quantity variance | $400 Favorable |
| Labor price variance | $1,952 Unfavorable |
| Labor usage variance | $960 Unfavorable |

### Required

a. Determine the actual amount of materials used.

b. Determine the actual price per pound paid for materials.

c. Determine the actual labor hours used.

d. Determine the actual labor price per hour.

## Problem 8-27B  *Computing standard cost and analyzing variances*          LO 5, 7

Scofield Manufacturing Company, which makes aluminum alloy wheels for automobiles, recently introduced a new luxury wheel that fits small sports cars. The company developed the following standards for its new product.

| | |
|---|---|
| Amount of direct materials per wheel | 2 pounds |
| Price of direct materials per pound | $5.50 |
| Quantity of labor per wheel | 2.5 hours |
| Price of direct labor per hour | $8.00/hour |
| Total budgeted fixed overhead | $168,000 |

In its first year of operation, Scofield planned to produce 3,000 sets of wheels (four wheels per set). Because of unexpected demand, it actually produced 3,600 sets of wheels. By year-end direct materials purchased and used amounted to 30,000 pounds of aluminum at a cost of $175,500. Direct labor costs were actually $8.40 per hour. Actual hours worked were 2.2 hours per wheel. Overhead for the year actually amounted to $180,000. Overhead is applied to products using a predetermined overhead rate based on the total estimated number of wheels to be produced.

**Required**

(Round all computations to two decimal places.)

**a.** Compute the standard cost per wheel for direct materials, direct labor, and overhead.

**b.** Determine the total standard cost per wheel.

**c.** Compute the actual cost per wheel for direct materials, direct labor, and overhead.

**d.** Compute the actual cost per wheel.

**e.** Compute the price and usage variances for direct materials and direct labor. Identify any variances that Scofield should investigate. Based on your results, offer a possible explanation for the labor usage variance.

**f.** Compute the fixed manufacturing overhead cost spending and volume variances. Explain your findings.

**LO 1, 2, 3, 4**

**Problem 8-28B** *Analyzing not-for-profit organization variances*

The Marketing Department of Hammell State University planned to hold its annual distinguished visiting lecturer (DVL) presentation in October 2012. The secretary of the department prepared the following budget based on costs that had been incurred in the past for the DVL presentation.

### MARKETING DEPARTMENT
#### Distinguished Visiting Lecturer Budget
#### October 2012

| | |
|---|---:|
| Variable costs | |
| Refreshments | $ 375 |
| Postage | 352 |
| Step costs* | |
| Printing | 500 |
| Facility | 250 |
| Fixed costs | |
| Dinner | 200 |
| Speaker's gift | 100 |
| Publicity | 50 |
| Total costs | $1,827 |

*Step costs are costs that change abruptly after a defined range of volume (attendance). They do not change proportionately with unit volume increases (i.e., the cost is fixed within a range of activity but changes to a different fixed cost when the volume changes to a new range). For instance, the facility charge is $250 for from 1 to 400 attendees. From 401 to 500 attendees, the next larger room is needed, and the charge is $350. If more than 500 attended, the room size and cost would increase again.

The budget for the presentation was based on the following expectations:

**1.** Attendance was estimated at 50 faculty from Hammell State and neighboring schools, 125 invited guests from the business community, and 200 students. Refreshments charge per attendee would be $1.00. The cost driver for refreshments is the number of attendees.

**2.** Postage was based on $0.44 per invitation; 800 invitations were expected to be mailed to faculty and finance business executives. The cost driver for postage is the number of invitations mailed.

3. Printing cost was expected to be $500 for 800 invitations and envelopes. Additional invitations and envelopes could be purchased in batches of 100 units with each batch costing $50.

4. The DVL presentation was scheduled at a downtown convention center. The facility charge was $250 for a room that has a capacity of 400 persons; the charge for one to hold more than 400 people was $350.

5. After the presentation, three Hammell State faculty members planned to take the speaker to dinner. The dinner had been prearranged at a local restaurant for $200 for a three-course dinner.

6. A gift for the speaker was budgeted at $100.

7. Publicity would consist of flyers and posters placed at strategic locations around campus and business offices, articles in the business section of the local newspapers, and announcements made in business classes and school newspapers. Printing for the posters and flyers had been prearranged for $50.

8. The speaker lives in the adjoining state and had agreed to drive to the presentation at his own expense.

The actual results of the presentation follow.

1. Attendance consisted of 450 faculty, business executives, and students.

2. An additional 100 invitations were printed and mailed when the Marketing Department decided that selected alumni should also be invited.

3. Based on RSVP responses, the department rented the next size larger room at a cost of $350 for the presentation.

4. The speaker's gift cost was as budgeted.

5. The department chairperson decided to have a four-course dinner, which cost $230.

6. Because of poor planning, the posters and flyers were not distributed as widely as expected. It was decided at the last minute to hire a temporary assistant to make phone calls to alumni. The actual publicity cost was $75.

### Required

a. Prepare a flexible budget and compute sales and variable cost variances based on a comparison between the master budget and the flexible budget. Briefly explain the meaning of the activity variances.

b. Compute flexible budget variances by comparing the flexible budget with the actual results. Briefly explain the meaning of the variable cost flexible budget variances. Discuss the fixed cost variances.

c. Calculate the expected and actual fixed cost per attendee. Discuss the significance of the difference in these amounts.

d. Since the department is a not-for-profit entity, why is it important for it to control the cost of sponsoring the distinguished visiting lecturer presentation?

## ANALYZE, THINK, COMMUNICATE

### ATC 8-1  Business Applications Case   *Static versus flexible budget variances*

Dan Ludwig is the manufacturing production supervisor for Atlantic Lighting Systems. Trying to explain why he did not get the year-end bonus that he had expected, he told his wife, "This is the dumbest place I ever worked. Last year the company set up this budget assuming it would sell 150,000 units. Well, it sold only 140,000. The company lost money and gave me a bonus for not using as much materials and labor as was called for in the budget. This year, the company has the same 150,000 units goal and it sells 160,000. The company's making all kinds of money. You'd think I'd get this big fat bonus. Instead, management tells me I used more materials and labor than was budgeted. They said the company would have made a lot more money if I'd stayed within my budget. I guess I gotta wait for another bad year before I get a bonus. Like I said, this is the dumbest place I ever worked."

Atlantic Lighting Systems's master budget and the actual results for the most recent year of operating activity follow.

| | Master Budget | Actual Results | Variances | F or U |
|---|---|---|---|---|
| Number of units | 150,000 | 160,000 | 10,000 | |
| Sales revenue | $33,000,000 | $35,520,000 | $2,520,000 | F |
| Variable manufacturing costs | | | | |
| Materials | (4,800,000) | (5,300,000) | (500,000) | U |
| Labor | (4,200,000) | (4,400,000) | (200,000) | U |
| Overhead | (2,100,000) | (2,290,000) | (190,000) | U |
| Variable selling, general, | | | | |
| and admin. costs | (5,250,000) | (5,450,000) | (200,000) | U |
| Contribution margin | 16,650,000 | 18,080,000 | 1,430,000 | F |
| Fixed costs | | | | |
| Manufacturing overhead | (7,830,000) | (7,751,000) | 79,000 | F |
| Sellings, general, and admin. costs | (6,980,000) | (7,015,000) | (35,000) | U |
| Net income | $ 1,840,000 | $ 3,314,000 | $1,474,000 | F |

### Required

a. Did Atlantic increase unit sales by cutting prices or by using some other strategy?

b. Is Mr. Ludwig correct in his conclusion that something is wrong with the company's performance evaluation process? If so, what do you suggest be done to improve the system?

c. Prepare a flexible budget and recompute the budget variances.

d. Explain what might have caused the fixed costs to be different from the amount budgeted.

e. Assume that the company's material price variance was favorable and its material usage variance was unfavorable. Explain why Mr. Ludwig may not be responsible for these variances. Now, explain why he may have been responsible for the material usage variance.

f. Assume the labor price variance is unfavorable. Was the labor usage variance favorable or unfavorable?

g. Is the fixed cost volume variance favorable or unfavorable? Explain the effect of this variance on the cost of each unit produced.

### ATC 8-2   Group Assignment   *Variable price and usage variances and fixed manufacturing overhead cost variances*

Kemp Tables, Inc. (KTI), makes picnic tables of 2 × 4 planks of treated pine. It sells the tables to large retail discount stores such as Walmart. After reviewing the following data generated by KTI's chief accountant, the company president, Arianne Darwin, expressed concern that the total manufacturing cost was more than $0.5 million above budget ($7,084,800 − $6,520,000 = $564,800).

| | Actual Results | Master Budget |
|---|---|---|
| Cost of planks per table | $   44.10 | $   40.00 |
| Cost of labor per table | 26.10 | 25.50 |
| Total variable manufacturing cost per table (a) | $   70.20 | $   65.50 |
| Total number of tables produced (b) | 82,000 | 80,000 |
| Total variable manufacturing cost (a × b) | $5,756,400 | $5,240,000 |
| Total fixed manufacturing cost | 1,328,400 | 1,280,000 |
| Total manufacturing cost | $7,084,800 | $6,520,000 |

Ms. Darwin asked Conrad Pearson, KTI's chief accountant, to explain what caused the increase in cost. Mr. Pearson responded that things were not as bad as they seemed. He noted that part of the cost variance resulted from making and selling more tables than had been expected. Making more tables naturally causes the cost of materials and labor to be higher. He explained that the flexible budget cost variance was less than $0.5 million. Specifically, he provided the following comparison.

| | Actual Results | Flexible Budget |
|---|---|---|
| Cost of planks per table | $ 44.10 | $ 40.00 |
| Cost of labor per table | 26.10 | 25.50 |
| Total variable manufacturing cost per table (a) | $ 70.20 | $ 65.50 |
| Total number of tables produced (b) | 82,000 | 82,000 |
| Total variable manufacturing cost (a × b) | $5,756,400 | $5,371,000 |
| Total fixed manufacturing cost | 1,328,400 | 1,280,000 |
| Total manufacturing cost | $7,084,800 | $6,651,000 |

Based on this information, he argued that the relevant variance for performance evaluation was only $433,800 ($7,084,800 − $6,651,000). Ms. Darwin responded, "*Only* $433,800! I consider that a very significant number. By the end of the day, I want a full explanation as to what is causing our costs to increase."

## Required

a. Divide the class into groups of four or five students and divide the groups into three sections. Assign Task 1 to the first section, Task 2 to the second section, and Task 3 to the third section.

## Group Tasks

(1) Based on the following information, determine the total materials cost variance and the price and usage variances. Assuming that the variances are an appropriate indicator of cause, explain what could have caused the variances. Identify the management position responsible.

| | Actual Data | Standard Data |
|---|---|---|
| Number of planks per table | 21 | 20 |
| Price per plank | × $2.10 | × $2.00 |
| Material cost per table | $44.10 | $40.00 |

(2) Based on the following information, determine the total labor cost variance and the price and usage variances. Assuming that the variances are an appropriate indicator of cause, explain what could have caused each variance. Identify the management position responsible.

| | Actual Data | Standard Data |
|---|---|---|
| Number of hours per table | 2.9 | 3.0 |
| Price per hour | × $9.00 | × $8.50 |
| Labor cost per table | $26.10 | $25.50 |

(3) Determine the amount of the fixed cost spending and volume variances. Explain what could have caused these variances. Based on the volume variance, indicate whether the actual fixed cost per unit would be higher or lower than the budgeted fixed cost per unit.

b. Select a spokesperson from each section to report the amount of the variances computed by the group. Reconcile any differences in the variances reported by the sections. Reconcile the individual variances with the total variance. Specifically, show that the total of the materials, labor, and overhead variances equals the total flexible budget variance ($433,800).

c. Discuss how Ms. Darwin should react to the variance information.

### ATC 8-3   Research Assignment   *Using real world data from Papa John's*

Obtain the 2004, 2005, 2006, 2007, and 2008 income statements for Papa John's International, Inc. The 2006–2008 statements are included in Papa John's 2008 annual report and Form 10-Ks. The 2004 and 2005 statements are in its 2005 annual report.

To obtain the Form 10-Ks you can use either the EDGAR system following the instructions in Appendix A, or they can be found under "Investors" link on the company's corporate website; www.papajohns.com. The company's annual reports are also available on its website.

**Required**

**a.** Compute the percentage change for each of the following categories of revenues and expenses for 2004 to 2005, 2005 to 2006, and 2006 to 2007:

> **Domestic revenues:**
>   Company-owned restaurant sales
> **Domestic company-owned restaurant expenses:**
>   Cost of sales
>   Salaries and benefits
>   Advertising and related costs
>   Occupancy costs
>   Other operating expenses

Using an Excel spreadsheet will make this task much easier. Once these averages are obtained, (you should have three averages for each of the six revenue and expense items), calculate an average of the changes for each item. The answer for the "Occupancy coats" item is show as an example:

|  | Percentage Change |
|---|---|
| 2004–2005 | 1.7% |
| 2005–2006 | 3.2 |
| 2006–2007 | 17.0 |
| Average of the changes | 7.3% |

**b.** Prepare a budgeted income statement for 2008 and compare the budgeted data to the actual results for 2008. To calculate budgeted amounts, multiply the average change in each revenue and expense item, from Requirement *b*, by the dollar amount of the corresponding revenue or expense from 2007. This will represent the budgeted amount for that item for 2008. Don't forget to use decimal data and not percentage data. Subtract the actual 2008 results from the budgeted results. Finally, divide the actual versus budgeted difference by the budgeted amount to determine a percentage variance from the budget. Calculate total for "Total domestic company-owned restaurant expenses" by adding the appropriate items. The answer for the "Occupancy costs" item is show as an example: (Dollar amounts are in thousands.)

|  | (1) 2007 Actual | (2) Average 3-year Change | (3) (1 × 2) 2008 Budget | (4) 2008 Actual | (5) (3 − 4) Variance | (5 ÷ 3) Percentage Variance from Budget |
|---|---|---|---|---|---|---|
| Occupancy costs | $31,866 | 1.073 | $34,192 | $34,973 | $(781) | .028 [2.8%] |

### ATC 8-4   Writing Assignment   *Standard costing—The human factor*

Kemp Corporation makes a protein supplement called Power Punch™. Its principal competitor for Power Punch is the protein supplement Superior Strength™, made by Jim Adams Company (JAC). Mr. Adams, a world-renowned weight-lifting champion, founded JAC. The primary market for both products is athletes. Kemp sells Power Punch to wellness stores, which sell it, other supplements, and health foods to the public. In contrast, Superior Strength is advertised in sports magazines and sold through orders generated by the ads.

Mr. Adams's fame is an essential factor in his company's advertising program. He is a dynamic character whose personality motivates people to strive for superior achievement. His demeanor not only stimulates sales but also provides a strong inspirational force for company employees. He is a kind, understanding individual with high expectations who is fond of saying that "mistakes are just opportunities for improvement." Mr. Adams is a strong believer in total quality management.

Mr. Quayle, president of Kemp Corporation, is a stern disciplinarian who believes in teamwork. He takes pride in his company's standard costing system. Managers work as a team to establish standards and then are held accountable for meeting them. Managers who fail to meet expectations are severely chastised, and continued failure leads to dismissal. After several years of rigorous enforcement, managers have fallen in line. Indeed, during the last two years, all managers have met their budget goals.

Even so, costs have risen steadily. These cost increases have been passed on to customers through higher prices. As a result, Power Punch is now priced significantly higher than Superior Strength. In fact, Superior Strength is selling directly to the public at a price that is below the wholesale price that Kemp is charging the wellness stores. The situation has reached a critical juncture. Sales of Power Punch are falling while Superior Strength is experiencing significant growth. Given that industry sales have remained relatively stable, it is obvious that customers are shifting from Power Punch to Superior Strength. Mr. Quayle is perplexed. He wonders how a company with direct marketing expenses can price its products so low.

**Required**

a. Explain why JAC has been able to gain a pricing advantage over Kemp.

b. Assume that you are a consultant whom Kemp's board of directors has asked to recommend how to halt the decline in sales of Power Punch. Provide appropriate recommendations.

### ATC 8-5  Ethical Dilemma  *Budget games*

Melody Lovelady is the most highly rewarded sales representative at Swift Corporation. Her secret to success is always to understate her abilities. Ms. Lovelady is assigned to a territory in which her customer base is increasing at approximately 25 percent per year. Each year she estimates that her budgeted sales will be 10 percent higher than her previous year's sales. With little effort, she is able to double her budgeted sales growth. At Swift's annual sales meeting, she receives an award and a large bonus. Of course, Ms. Lovelady does not disclose her secret to her colleagues. Indeed, she always talks about how hard it is to continue to top her previous performance. She tells herself: "If they are dumb enough to fall for this rubbish, I'll milk it for all it's worth."

**Required**

a. What is the name commonly given to the budget game Ms. Lovelady is playing?

b. Does Ms. Lovelady's behavior violate any of the standards of ethical conduct shown in Exhibit 1.15 of Chapter 1?

c. Recommend how Ms. Lovelady's budget game could be stopped.

### ATC 8-6  Spreadsheet Assignment  *Using Excel*

Irvine Publications established the following standard price and costs for a hardcover picture book that the company produces.

| Standard price and variable costs | |
|---|---|
| Sales price | $ 48.00 |
| Materials cost | 12.00 |
| Labor cost | 6.00 |
| Overhead cost | 8.40 |
| Selling, general, and administrative costs | 9.60 |
| Expected fixed costs | |
| Manufacturing overhead | $180,000 |
| Selling, general, and administrative | 72,000 |

Irvine planned to make and sell 30,000 copies of the book.

**Required**

Construct a spreadsheet like the one shown in Exhibit 8.1 to illustrate a static budget and a flexible budget for production volumes of 28,000, 29,000, 30,000, 31,000, and 32,000.

### ATC 8-7   Spreadsheet Assignment   *Mastering Excel*

Wilkin Fruit Drink Company planned to make 400,000 containers of apple juice. It expected to use two cups of frozen apple concentrate to make each container of juice, thus using 800,000 cups (400,000 containers × 2 cups) of frozen concentrate. The standard price of one cup of apple concentrate is $0.25. Actually, Wilkin produced 404,000 containers of apple juice and purchased and used 820,000 cups of concentrate at $0.26 per cup.

**Required**

a.  Construct a spreadsheet template that could be used to calculate price and usage variances. The template should be constructed so that it could be used for any problem in the chapter that refers to price and usage variances by changing the data in the spreadsheet. The screen capture on this page represents a template for price and usage variances.

**Spreadsheet Tip**

(1) The shaded cells can be changed according to the data in each problem. All other cells are formulas based on the numbers in the shaded cells.

(2) The cells that label the variances as F or U (favorable (F) or unfavorable (U)) are based on a function called IF. The IF function is needed because the variance can be either favorable or unfavorable. The formula must determine whether actual expenditures exceed budgeted expenditures to determine whether the variance is unfavorable or favorable. As an example, the formula in cell D13 is =IF(B11>E11,'U','F'). The formula evaluates the expression B11>E11. If this expression is true (B11 is greater than E11), the text U is inserted in cell D13. The IF function can also be used to place formulas or numbers in a cell based on whether an expression is true or false. For example, the formula =IF(B11>E11,B11−E11,E11−B11) would calculate the amount of the variance as a positive number regardless of which amount is larger.

(3) An easier way to make the variance a positive number regardless of whether it is favorable or unfavorable is to use the absolute value function. The format of the formula in cells C13 and F13 would be =ABS(left number − right number).

(4) The lines around the variances are produced by using the borders in Excel (Format, Cells, Border).

# COMPREHENSIVE PROBLEM

The management of Magnificent Modems, Inc. (MMI), is uncertain as to the volume of sales that will exist in 2011. The president of the company asked the chief accountant to prepare flexible budget income statements assuming that sales activity amounts to 3,000 and 6,000 units. The static budget is shown in the form below.

**Required**

a. Complete the following worksheet to prepare the appropriate flexible budgets.

b. Calculate and show the flexible budget variances for the static budget versus the flexible budget at 6,000 units.

c. Indicate whether each variance is favorable or unfavorable.

## Flexible Budget Income Statements

|  | Cost per Unit | Static Budget | Flexible Budget | Flexible Budget |
|---|---|---|---|---|
| Number of units |  | 5,000 | 3,000 | 6,000 |
| Sales revenue | $120.00 | $600,000 |  |  |
| Variable manuf. costs |  |  |  |  |
| Materials | 40.00 | 200,000 |  |  |
| Labor | 25.00 | 125,000 |  |  |
| Overhead | 4.00 | 20,000 |  |  |
| Variable SG&A | 6.00 | 30,000 | _____ | _____ |
| Contribution margin |  | 225,000 |  |  |
| Fixed costs |  |  |  |  |
| Manufacturing rent |  | 50,000 |  |  |
| Dep. on manu. equip. |  | 60,000 |  |  |
| SG&A expenses |  | 71,950 |  |  |
| Dep. on admin. equip. |  | 12,000 |  |  |
| Net income (loss) |  | $ 31,050 | $(58,950) | $76,050 |

# Responsibility Accounting

## LEARNING OBJECTIVES

**After you have mastered the material in this chapter you will be able to:**

**1** Describe the concept of decentralization.

**2** Describe the differences among cost, profit, and investment centers.

**3** Prepare and use responsibility reports.

**4** Relate management by exception to responsibility reports.

**5** Evaluate investment opportunities using return on investment.

**6** Identify factors that affect return on investment.

**7** Evaluate investment opportunities using residual income.

**8** Describe how transfer prices may be established (Appendix).

## CHAPTER OPENING

Walter Keller, a production manager, complained to the accountant, Kelly Oberson, that the budget system failed to control his department's labor cost. Ms. Oberson responded, "people, not budgets, control costs." Budgeting is one of many tools management uses to control business operations. Managers are responsible for using control tools effectively. **Responsibility accounting** focuses on evaluating the performance of individual managers. For example, expenses controlled by a production department manager are presented in one report and expenses controlled by a marketing department manager are presented in a different report. This chapter discusses the development and use of a responsibility accounting system.

# The Curious Accountant

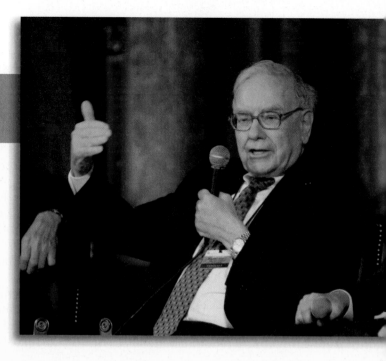

Warren Buffett, often identified as one of the richest men in the world, is the CEO of **Berkshire Hathaway, Inc.** (Berkshire). His company is actually a conglomerate that has major stockholdings in several large companies, including **American Express**, **Anheuser-Bush**, and **The Washington Post**. Additionally, Berkshire wholly owns over 70 other businesses ranging in size and diversity from the insurance giant **GEICO**, to **Fruit of the Loom**, to **See's Candies**. In all, Berkshire has 222,000 employees. How can one person, who is turning 81 in 2011, manage such a large and diverse business? (Answer on page 404.)

# DECENTRALIZATION CONCEPT

Describe the concept of decentralization.

Effective responsibility accounting requires clear lines of authority and responsibility. Divisions of authority and responsibility normally occur as a natural consequence of managing business operations. In a small business, one person can control everything: marketing, production, management, accounting. In contrast, large companies are so complex that authority and control must be divided among many people.

Consider the hiring of employees. A small business usually operates in a limited geographic area. The owner works directly with employees. She knows the job requirements, local wage rates, and the available labor pool. She is in a position to make informed hiring decisions. In contrast, a major corporation may employ thousands of employees throughout the world. The employees may speak different languages and have different social customs. Their jobs may require many different skills and pay a vast array of wage rates. The president of the corporation cannot make informed hiring decisions for the entire company. Instead, he delegates *authority* to a professional personnel manager and holds that manager *responsible* for hiring practices.

Decision-making authority is similarly delegated to individuals responsible for managing specific organization functions such as production, marketing, and accounting. Delegating authority and responsibility is referred to as **decentralization.** Decentralization offers advantages like the following.

1. *Encourages upper-level management to concentrate on strategic decisions.* Because local management makes routine decisions, upper-level management can concentrate on long-term planning, goal setting, and performance evaluation.

2. *Improves the quality of decisions by delegating authority down a chain of command.* Local managers are better informed about local concerns. Furthermore, their proximity to local events allows them to react quickly to changes in local conditions. As a result, local managers can generally make better decisions.

3. *Motivates managers to improve productivity.* The freedom to act coupled with responsibility for the results creates an environment that encourages most individuals to perform at high levels.

4. *Trains lower-level managers for increased responsibilities.* Decision making is a skill. Managers accustomed to making decisions about local issues are generally able to apply their decision-making skills to broader issues when they are promoted to upper management positions.

5. *Improves performance evaluation.* When lines of authority and responsibility are clear, credit or blame can be more accurately assigned.

## Organization Chart

Exhibit 9.1 displays a partial organization chart for Panther Holding Company, a decentralized business. The chart shows five levels of authority and responsibility arranged in a hierarchical order from the top down. Other companies may have more or less complex organizational charts, depending on their decentralization needs and philosophy.

## RESPONSIBILITY CENTERS

Describe the differences among cost, profit, and investment centers.

Decentralized businesses are usually subdivided into distinct reporting units called responsibility centers. A **responsibility center** is an organizational unit that controls identifiable revenue or expense items. The unit may be a division, a department, a subdepartment, or even a single machine. For example, a transportation company may identify a semitrailer truck as a responsibility center. The company holds the truck driver responsible for the revenues and expenses associated with operating the

## EXHIBIT 9.1

### Organization Chart

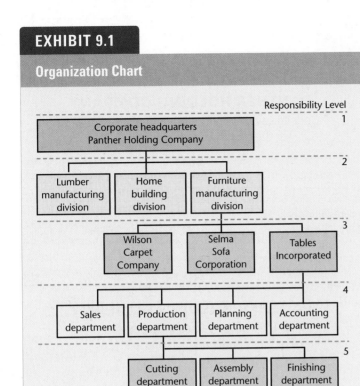

truck. Responsibility centers may be divided into three categories: cost, profit, and investment.

A **cost center** is an organizational unit that incurs expenses but does not generate revenue. In the Panther organization chart (Exhibit 9.1), the finishing department and the production department are cost centers. Cost centers normally fall on the lower levels of an organization chart. The manager of a cost center is judged on his ability to keep costs within budget parameters.

A **profit center** differs from a cost center in that it not only incurs costs but also generates revenue. In the Panther organization chart, the companies at the third level (Wilson Carpet Company, Selma Sofa Corporation, and Tables Incorporated) are considered profit centers. The manager of a profit center is judged on his ability to produce revenue in excess of expenses.

**Investment center** managers are responsible for revenues, expenses, and the investment of capital. Investment centers normally appear at the upper levels of an organization chart. The second-level division managers (managers of the lumber, home, and furniture divisions) in the Panther organization are responsible for investment centers. Managers of investment centers are accountable for assets and liabilities as well as earnings.

## RESPONSIBILITY REPORTS

A **responsibility report** is prepared for each manager who controls a responsibility center. The report compares the expectations for the manager's responsibility center with the center's actual performance. A typical report lists the items under the manager's control, both the budgeted amount and the actual amount spent for each item, and the differences between budgeted and actual amounts (variances).

**LO 3**

Prepare and use responsibility reports.

## EXHIBIT 9.2

**Responsibility Reports**

## PANTHER HOLDING COMPANY
Second Level: Furniture Manufacturing Division
For the Month Ended January 31, 2011

| Controllable expenses | Budget | Actual | Variance |
|---|---|---|---|
| Administrative division expense | $ 20,400 | $ 31,100 | $(10,700) U |
| Company president's salary | 9,600 | 9,200 | 400 F |
| Wilson Carpet Company | 82,100 | 78,400 | 3,700 F |
| Selma Sofa Corporation | 87,200 | 116,700 | (29,500) U |
| Tables Incorporated | 48,600 | 51,250 | (2,650) U |
| Total | $247,900 | $286,650 | $(38,750) U |

## PANTHER HOLDING COMPANY
Third Level: Tables Incorporated
For the Month Ended January 31, 2011

| Controllable expenses | Budget | Actual | Variance |
|---|---|---|---|
| Administrative division expense | $ 3,000 | $ 2,800 | $ 200 F |
| Department managers' salaries | 10,000 | 11,200 | (1,200) U |
| Sales department costs | 9,100 | 8,600 | 500 F |
| Production department costs | 13,500 | 13,750 | (250) U |
| Planning department costs | 4,800 | 7,000 | (2,200) U |
| Accounting department costs | 8,200 | 7,900 | 300 F |
| Total | $ 48,600 | $ 51,250 | $ (2,650) U |

## PANTHER HOLDING COMPANY
Fourth Level: Production Department
For the Month Ended January 31, 2011

| Controllable expenses | Budget | Actual | Variance |
|---|---|---|---|
| Administrative staff expense | $ 900 | $ 1,100 | $ (200) U |
| Supervisory salaries | 2,800 | 2,800 | 0 |
| Cutting department costs | 1,400 | 1,200 | 200 F |
| Assembly department costs | 2,800 | 2,900 | (100) U |
| Finishing department costs | 5,600 | 5,750 | (150) U |
| Total | $ 13,500 | $ 13,750 | $ (250) U |

## PANTHER HOLDING COMPANY
Fifth Level: Finishing Department
For the Month Ended January 31, 2011

| Controllable expenses | Budget | Actual | Variance |
|---|---|---|---|
| Wages expense | $ 3,200 | $ 3,000 | $ 200 F |
| Direct materials | 1,100 | 1,400 | (300) U |
| Supplies | 400 | 500 | (100) U |
| Small tools | 600 | 650 | (50) U |
| Other expenses | 300 | 200 | 100 F |
| Total | $ 5,600 | $ 5,750 | $ (150) U |

# MANAGEMENT BY EXCEPTION

Responsibility reports are arranged to support using the **management by exception** doctrine. Exhibit 9.2 illustrates a partial set of responsibility reports for Panther Holding Company. From the lower level upward, each successive report includes summary data from the preceding report. For example, the detailed information about the finishing department (a level five responsibility center) is summarized as a single line item ($150 unfavorable variance) in the report for the production department (a level four responsibility center).

Relate management by exception to responsibility reports.

The lack of detailed information may appear to hinder the production manager's ability to control costs. In fact, it has the opposite effect. The supervisor of the finishing department should use her responsibility report to identify and correct problems without bothering the production manager. The production manager should become concerned only when one of his supervisors loses control. The summary data in the production manager's report will adequately advise him of such situations. With this format, managers will concentrate only on significant deviations from expectations (management by exception) because the deviations are highlighted in their responsibility reports.

Applying the management by exception doctrine to the variances in her responsibility report, the division manager of the Furniture Manufacturing Division (second level responsibility center) should concentrate her efforts on two areas. First, the $29,500 unfavorable variance for Selma Sofa Corporation indicates Selma's expenditures are out of line. Second, the $10,700 unfavorable variance for the division manager's own administrative expenses indicates those costs are significantly above budget expectations. The division manager should request detailed reports for these two areas. Other responsibility centers seem to be operating within reason and can be left to their respective managers. This reporting format focuses management's attention on the areas where it is most needed.

The complete responsibility accounting report would also include the first responsibility level, corporate headquarters. At the corporate level, responsibility reports normally include year-to-date income statements to inform management of the company's overall performance. To facilitate decision making, these income statements are normally prepared using the contribution margin format. Exhibit 9.3 shows the January 2011 income statement for Panther Holding Company.

## EXHIBIT 9.3

### Panther Income Statement (Contribution Margin Format)

**PANTHER HOLDING COMPANY**
Income Statement for Internal Use
For the Month Ended January 31, 2011

|  | Budget | Actual | Variance |
|---|---|---|---|
| Sales | $984,300 | $962,300 | $22,000 U |
| Variable expenses |  |  |  |
| Variable product costs | 343,100 | 352,250 | 9,150 U |
| Variable selling expenses | 105,000 | 98,000 | 7,000 F |
| Other variable expenses | 42,200 | 51,100 | 8,900 U |
| Total variable expenses | 490,300 | 501,350 | 11,050 U |
| Contribution margin | 494,000 | 460,950 | 33,050 U |
| Fixed expenses |  |  |  |
| Fixed product cost | 54,100 | 62,050 | 7,950 U |
| Fixed selling expense | 148,000 | 146,100 | 1,900 F |
| Other fixed expenses | 23,000 | 25,250 | 2,250 U |
| Total fixed expenses | 225,100 | 233,400 | 8,300 U |
| Net income | $268,900 | $227,550 | $41,350 U |

## Answers to The Curious Accountant

Mr. Buffett oversees the diverse operations of Berkshire by using a very decentralized management structure. According to its 2009 annual report, Berkshire had 222,000 employees and earned $112 billion in revenue. Mr. Buffett managed this empire from his headquarters in Omaha, Nebraska, that consists of 21 employees and occupies only 9,708 square feet, although the company's vice-chairman, Charles Munger, who works out of Los Angeles, occupies another 655 square feet. The total payroll, including benefits, of both locations was only $3,531,978 in 2006, and that amount is *not* in thousands. Mr. Buffett's own description about his and Mr. Munger's management style is, ". . . we delegate almost to the point of abdication." An exaggeration perhaps, but clearly a decentralized style.

Source: Company's annual reports.

### Controllability Concept

The **controllability concept** is crucial to an effective responsibility accounting system. Managers should only be evaluated based on revenues or costs they control. Holding individuals responsible for things they cannot control is demotivating. Isolating control, however, may be difficult, as illustrated in the following case.

Dorothy Pasewark, a buyer for a large department store chain, was criticized when stores could not resell the merchandise she bought at the expected price. Ms. Pasewark countered that the sales staff caused the sluggish sales by not displaying the merchandise properly. The sales staff charged that the merchandise had too little sales potential to justify setting up more enticing displays. The division of influence between the buyer and the sales staff clouds the assignment of responsibility.

Since the exercise of control may be clouded, managers are usually held responsible for items over which they have *predominant* rather than *absolute* control. At times responsibility accounting may be imperfect. Management must strive to ensure that praise or criticism is administered as fairly as possible.

### Qualitative Reporting Features

Responsibility reports should be expressed in simple terms. If they are too complex, managers will ignore them. The reports should include only the budgeted and actual amounts of *controllable* revenues and expenses, with variances highlighted to promote management by exception. Report preparers and report users should communicate regularly to ensure the reports provide relevant information. Furthermore, reports must be timely. A report that presents yesterday's problem is not nearly as useful as one that presents today's problem.

### Managerial Performance Measurement

A primary reason for a responsibility accounting system is to evaluate managerial performance. Managers are assigned responsibility for certain cost, profit, or investment centers. They are then evaluated based on how their centers perform relative to specific goals and objectives. The measurement techniques (standard costs and contribution margin format income reporting) used for cost and profit centers have been discussed in previous chapters. The remainder of this chapter discusses performance measures for investment centers.

# RETURN ON INVESTMENT

Evaluate investment opportunities using return on investment.

Society confers wealth, prestige, and power upon those who have control of assets. Unsurprisingly, managers are motivated to increase the amount of assets employed by the investment centers they control. When companies have additional assets available to invest, how do upper-level managers decide which centers should get them? The additional assets are frequently allotted to the managers who demonstrate the greatest potential for increasing the company's wealth. DuPont pioneered an often-copied approach to assess managerial potential by comparing the return on investment ratios of various investment centers. The **return on investment (ROI)** is the ratio of wealth generated (operating income) to the amount invested (operating assets) to generate the wealth. ROI is commonly expressed with the following equation.

$$\text{ROI} = \frac{\text{Operating income}}{\text{Operating assets}}$$

To illustrate using ROI for comparative evaluations, assume Panther Holding Company's corporate (first level) chief financial officer (CFO) determined the ROIs for the company's three divisions (second level investment centers). The CFO used the following accounting data from the records of each division:

|  | Lumber Manufacturing Division | Home Building Division | Furniture Manufacturing Division |
| --- | --- | --- | --- |
| Operating income | $ 60,000 | $ 46,080 | $ 81,940 |
| Operating assets | 300,000 | 256,000 | 482,000 |

The ROI for each division is:

Lumber manufacturing: $\dfrac{\text{Operating income}}{\text{Operating assets}} = \$60,000 \div \$300,000 = 20\%$

Home building: $\dfrac{\text{Operating income}}{\text{Operating assets}} = \$46,080 \div \$256,000 = 18\%$

Furniture manufacturing: $\dfrac{\text{Operating income}}{\text{Operating assets}} = \$81,940 \div \$482,000 = 17\%$

All other things being equal, higher ROIs indicate better performance. In this case the Lumber Manufacturing Division manager is the best performer. Assume Panther obtains additional funding for expanding the company's operations. Which investment center is most likely to receive the additional funds?

If the manager of the Lumber Manufacturing Division convinces the upper-level management team that his division would continue to outperform the other two divisions, the Lumber Manufacturing Division would most likely get the additional funding. The manager of the lumber division would then invest the funds in additional operating assets, which would in turn increase the division's operating income. As the division prospers, Panther would reward the manager for exceptional performance. Rewarding the manager of the lumber division would likely motivate the other managers to improve their divisional ROIs. Internal competition would improve the performance of the company as a whole.

## Qualitative Considerations

Why do companies compute ROI using operating income and operating assets instead of using net income and total assets? Suppose Panther's corporate headquarters closes a furniture manufacturing plant because an economic downturn temporarily reduces the demand for furniture. It would be inappropriate to include these nonoperating plant assets in the denominator of the ROI computation. Similarly, if Panther sells the

---

### ✓ CHECK YOURSELF 9.1

Green View is a lawn services company whose operations are divided into two districts. The District 1 manager controls $12,600,000 of operating assets. District 1 produced $1,512,000 of operating income during the year. The District 2 manager controls $14,200,000 of operating assets. District 2 reported $1,988,000 of operating income for the same period. Use return on investment to determine which manager is performing better.

**Answer**

District 1

$$\text{ROI} = \text{Operating income} \div \text{Operating assets} = \$1,512,000 \div \$12,600,000 = 12\%$$

District 2

$$\text{ROI} = \text{Operating income} \div \text{Operating assets} = \$1,988,000 \div \$14,200,000 = 14\%$$

Because the higher ROI indicates the better performance, the District 2 manager is the superior performer. This conclusion is based solely on quantitative results. In real-world practice, companies also consider qualitative factors.

---

furniture plant and realizes a large gain on the sale, including the gain in the numerator of the ROI formula would distort the result. Since the manager of the Furniture Manufacturing Division does not control closing the plant or selling it, it is unreasonable to include the effects of these decisions in computing the ROI. These items would, however, be included in computing net income and total assets. Most companies use operating income and operating assets to compute ROI because those variables measure performance more accurately.

## Measuring Operating Assets

The meaning of ROI results is further complicated by the question of how to *value* operating assets. Suppose Echoles Rental Company's two divisions, Northern and Southern, each rent to customers a vending machine that originally cost $5,000. The vending machines have five-year useful lives and no salvage value. The Northern Division purchased its machine one year ago; the Southern Division purchased its machine three years ago. At the end of the current year, the book values of the two machines are as follows:

|  | Northern Division's Vending Machine | Southern Division's Vending Machine |
|---|---|---|
| Original cost | $5,000 | $5,000 |
| Less accumulated depreciation | (1,000) | (3,000) |
| Book value | $4,000 | $2,000 |

Each machine generates operating income averaging $800 per year. The ROI for each machine this year is as follows:

$$\text{Northern Division:} \quad \frac{\text{Operating income}}{\text{Operating assets}} = \$800 \div \$4,000 = 20\%$$

$$\text{Southern Division:} \quad \frac{\text{Operating income}}{\text{Operating assets}} = \$800 \div \$2,000 = 40\%$$

Is the manager of the Southern Division outperforming the manager of the Northern Division? No. The only difference between the two divisions is that Southern is using an older asset than Northern. Using book value as the valuation base can distort the ROI and cause severe motivational problems. Managers will consider comparisons between different investment centers unfair because the ROIs do not accurately reflect performance. Furthermore, managers may avoid replacing obsolete equipment because purchasing new equipment would increase the dollar amount of operating assets, reducing the ROI.

Companies may minimize these problems by using original cost instead of book value in the denominator of the ROI formula. In the vending machine example, using original cost produces an ROI of 16 percent ($800 ÷ $5,000). Using original cost, however, may not entirely solve the valuation problem. As a result of inflation and technological advances, comparable equipment purchased at different times will have different costs. Some accountants advocate using *replacement cost* rather than *historical cost* as the valuation base. This solution is seldom used because determining the amount it would cost to replace particular assets is difficult. For example, imagine trying to determine the replacement cost of all the assets in a steel mill that has been operating for years.

Selecting the asset valuation base is a complex matter. In spite of its shortcomings, most companies use book value as the valuation base. Management must consider those shortcomings when using ROI to evaluate performance.

# FACTORS AFFECTING RETURN ON INVESTMENT

Management can gain insight into performance by dividing the ROI formula into two separate ratios as follows:

$$\text{ROI} = \frac{\text{Operating Income}}{\text{Sales}} \times \frac{\text{Sales}}{\text{Operating assets}}$$

Identify factors that affect return on investment.

The first ratio on the right side of the equation is called the margin. The **margin** is a measure of management's ability to control operating expenses relative to the level of sales. In general, high margins indicate superior performance. Management can increase the margin by reducing the level of operating expenses necessary to generate sales. Decreasing operating expenses increases profitability.

The second ratio in the expanded ROI formula is called turnover. **Turnover** is a measure of the amount of operating assets employed to support the achieved level of sales. Operating assets are scarce resources. To maximize profitability, they must be used wisely. Just as excessive expenses decrease profitability, excessive investments in operating assets also limit profitability.

Both the short and expanded versions of the ROI formula produce the same end result. To illustrate, we will use the ROI for the Lumber Manufacturing Division of Panther Holding Company. Recall that the division employed $300,000 of operating assets to produce $60,000 of operating income, resulting in the following ROI:

$$\text{ROI} = \frac{\text{Operating income}}{\text{Operating assets}} = \frac{\$60,000}{\$300,000} = 20\%$$

Further analysis of the accounting records indicates the Lumber Manufacturing Division had sales of $600,000. The following computation demonstrates that the expanded ROI formula produces the same result as the short formula:

$$\text{ROI} = \text{Margin} \times \text{Turnover}$$

$$= \frac{\text{Operating income}}{\text{Sales}} \times \frac{\text{Sales}}{\text{Operating assets}}$$

$$= \frac{\$60,000}{\$600,000} \times \frac{\$600,000}{\$300,000}$$

$$= .10 \times 2$$

$$= 20\%$$

The expanded formula may seem more complicated. It is generally more useful, however, because it helps managers see a variety of strategies to improve ROI. The expanded formula shows that profitability and ROI can be improved in three ways: *by increasing sales, by reducing expenses,* or *by reducing the investment base.* Each of these possibilities is demonstrated using the Lumber Manufacturing Division (LMD) of Panther Holding Company.

1. *Increase ROI by increasing sales.* Because some expenses are fixed, sales can be increased while those expenses are constant. Managers may even be able to reduce variable expenses by increasing productivity as sales increase. As a result, managers can increase their ROIs by increasing sales while limiting growth in expenses. To illustrate, assume the manager of LMD is able to increase sales from $600,000 to $660,000 while controlling expense growth so that net income increases from $60,000 to $72,600. Assuming investment in operating assets remains constant at $300,000, ROI becomes:

$$\text{ROI} = \text{Margin} \times \text{Turnover}$$
$$= \frac{\text{Operating income}}{\text{Sales}} \times \frac{\text{Sales}}{\text{Operating assets}}$$
$$= \frac{\$72,600}{\$660,000} \times \frac{\$660,000}{\$300,000}$$
$$= .11 \times 2.2$$
$$= 24.2\%$$

2. *Increase ROI by reducing expenses.* Suppose the manager of LMD takes a different approach. He decides to eliminate waste. By analyzing spending, he is able to cut expenses without affecting sales or the investment in operating assets. As a result of controlling expenses, operating income increases from $60,000 to $72,000. Assume the other variables remain the same as in the original example. ROI becomes:

$$\text{ROI} = \text{Margin} \times \text{Turnover}$$
$$= \frac{\text{Operating income}}{\text{Sales}} \times \frac{\text{Sales}}{\text{Operating assets}}$$
$$= \frac{\$72,000}{\$600,000} \times \frac{\$600,000}{\$300,000}$$
$$= .12 \times 2$$
$$= 24\%$$

3. *Increase ROI by reducing the investment base.* Managers who focus too narrowly on income frequently overlook this possibility. Reducing the amount of funds invested in operating assets such as inventory or accounts receivable can increase profitability because the funds released can be invested in other, more productive assets. This effect is reflected in the ROI computation. For example, assume the manager of LMD launches a *just-in-time* inventory system that allows the division to reduce the amount of inventory it carries. The manager also initiates an aggressive campaign to collect receivables which significantly reduces the outstanding receivables balance. As a result of these two initiatives, the assets employed to operate LMD fall from $300,000 to $240,000. All other variables remain the same as in the original example. ROI becomes:

$$\text{ROI} = \text{Margin} \times \text{Turnover}$$
$$= \frac{\text{Operating income}}{\text{Sales}} \times \frac{\text{Sales}}{\text{Operating assets}}$$
$$= \frac{\$60,000}{\$600,000} \times \frac{\$600,000}{\$240,000}$$
$$= .10 \times 2.5$$
$$= 25\%$$

The $60,000 of funds released by reducing the operating assets can be returned to headquarters or be reinvested by LMD depending on the opportunities available.

✓ **CHECK YOURSELF 9.2**

What three actions can a manager take to improve ROI?

**Answer**

1. Increase sales
2. Reduce expenses
3. Reduce the investment base

## RESIDUAL INCOME

Suppose Panther Holding Company evaluates the manager of the Lumber Manufacturing Division (LMD) based on his ability to maximize ROI. The corporation's overall ROI is approximately 18 percent. LMD, however, has consistently outperformed the other investment centers. Its ROI is currently 20 percent. Now suppose the manager has an opportunity to invest additional funds in a project likely to earn a 19 percent ROI. Would the manager accept the investment opportunity?

Evaluate investment opportunities using residual income.

These circumstances place the manager in an awkward position. The corporation would benefit from the project because the expected ROI of 19 percent is higher than the corporate average ROI of 18 percent. Personally, however, the manager would suffer from accepting the project because it would reduce the division ROI to less than the current 20 percent. The manager is forced to choose between his personal best interests and the best interests of the corporation. When faced with decisions such as these, many managers choose to benefit themselves at the expense of their corporations, a condition described as **suboptimization.**

To avoid *suboptimization,* many businesses base managerial evaluation on **residual income.** This approach measures a manager's ability to maximize earnings above some targeted level. The targeted level of earnings is based on a minimum desired ROI. Residual income is calculated as follows:

$$\text{Residual income} = \text{Operating income} - (\text{Operating assets} \times \text{Desired ROI})$$

To illustrate, recall that LMD currently earns $60,000 of operating income with the $300,000 of operating assets it controls. ROI is 20 percent ($60,000 ÷ $300,000). Assume Panther's desired ROI is 18 percent. LMD's residual income is therefore:

$$\text{Residual income} = \text{Operating income} - (\text{Operating assets} \times \text{Desired ROI})$$

$$= \$60,000 - (\$300,000 \times .18)$$

$$= \$60,000 - \$54,000$$

$$= \$6,000$$

Now assume that Panther Holding Company has $50,000 of additional funds available to invest. Because LMD consistently performs at a high level, Panther's corporate management team offers the funds to the LMD manager. The manager believes he could invest the additional $50,000 at a 19 percent rate of return.

If the LMD manager's evaluation is based solely on ROI, he is likely to reject the additional funding because investing the funds at 19 percent would lower his overall ROI. If the LMD manager's evaluation is based on residual income, however, he is likely

# FOCUS ON **INTERNATIONAL ISSUES**

### DO MANAGERS IN DIFFERENT COMPANIES STRESS THE SAME PERFORMANCE MEASURES?

About the only ratio companies are required to disclose in their annual reports to stockholders is the earnings per share ratio. Nevertheless, many companies choose to show their performance as measured by other ratios, as well as providing nonratio data not required by GAAP. The types of ratio data companies choose to include in their annual reports provides a sense of what performance measure they consider most important.

A review of several publicly traded companies from the United Kingdom, Japan, and the United States will show that the most common ratios presented are variations of the return on sales percentage and the return on investment percentage, although they may be called by different names. The country in which the company is located does not seem to determine which ratio it will emphasize.

One nonratio performance measure that is popular with companies in all three countries is free cash flow, and it is usually reported in total pounds, yen, or dollars. Be sure to exercise caution before comparing one company's free cash flow, return on sales, or return on investment to those of other companies. There are no official rules governing how these data are calculated, and different companies make different interpretations about how to compute these measurements.

to accept the funds because an additional investment at 19 percent would increase his residual income as follows:

$$\text{Operating income} = \$50,000 \times .19$$
$$= \$9,500$$

$$\text{Residual income} = \text{Operating income} - (\text{Operating assets} \times \text{Desired ROI})$$
$$= \$9,500 - (\$50,000 \times .18)$$
$$= \$9,500 - \$9,000$$
$$= \$500$$

Accepting the new project would add $500 to LMD's residual income. If the manager of LMD is evaluated based on his ability to maximize residual income, he would benefit by investing in any project that returns an ROI in excess of the desired 18 percent. The reduction in LMD's overall ROI does not enter into the decision. The residual income approach solves the problem of suboptimization.

The primary disadvantage of the residual income approach is that it measures performance in absolute dollars. As a result, a manager's residual income may be larger simply because her investment base is larger rather than because her performance is superior.

To illustrate, return to the example where Panther Holding Company has $50,000 of additional funds to invest. Assume the manager of the Lumber Manufacturing Division (LMD) and the manager of the Furniture Manufacturing Division (FMD) each have investment opportunities expected to earn a 19 percent return. Recall that Panther's desired ROI is 18 percent. If corporate headquarters allots $40,000 of the funds to the manager of LMD and $10,000 to the manager of FMD, the increase in residual income earned by each division is as follows:

$$\text{LMD's Residual income} = (\$40,000 \times .19) - (\$40,000 \times .18) = \$400$$

$$\text{FMD's Residual income} = (\$10,000 \times .19) - (\$10,000 \times .18) = \$100$$

# REALITY BYTES

Thinking about the *investment* in return on investment usually conjures up images of buildings and equipment, but investments typically include a much broader range of expenditures. For example, if Walmart plans to open a new store it has to make an investment in inventory to stock the store that is as permanent as the building. But investment expenditures can be for items much less tangible than inventory. Consider the making of a movie.

While it is true that making a movie can require expenditures for items such as cameras and sets, the single highest cost can often be for actors' salaries. Although movie fans may focus on how much a movie grosses at the box office, from a business perspective it is the movie's ROI that matters.

From an ROI perspective the question is, "which actors are worth the money they are paid?" To this end, BusinessWeek.com created the ROI Award for actors. Calculating ROI for an actor in a movie, rather than for the entire investment in the movie can be tricky and requires several estimates. For example, should the credit for the spectacular success of the Harry Potter movies go to its main actor, Daniel Radcliffe or the special effects, or the author, J. K. Rowling? Nevertheless, BusinessWeek.com reviewed the financial performance of movies starring various actors and actresses over the period of a few years and calculated an ROI for the leading stars.

*And the winner is . . . ?* In 2006 the ROI Award went to Tyler Perry who starred in *Diary of a Mad Black Woman,* and *Madea's Family Reunion.* Mr. Perry's ROI was calculated at 120 percent, suggesting that for every dollar he was paid, the movie earned $2.20 for the movie's producers. As a comparison, Tom Cruise and Will Smith had ROIs of 53 percent. Mr. Perry's movies did not sell the most tickets, but they had the highest ROIs.

Source: *BusinessWeek.com* on MSN Money, July 19, 2006.

Does LMD's higher residual income mean LMD's manager is outperforming FMD's manager? No. It means LMD's manager received more operating assets than FMD's manager received.

## Calculating Multiple ROIs and/or RIs for the Same Company

You may be asked to calculate different ROI and RI measures for the same company. For example, ROI and/or RI may be calculated for the company as a whole, for segments of the company, for specific investment opportunities, and for individual managers. An example is shown in Check Yourself 9.3.

## Responsibility Accounting and the Balanced Scorecard

Throughout the text we have discussed many financial measures companies use to evaluate managerial performance. Examples include standard cost systems to evaluate cost center managers; the contribution margin income statement to evaluate profit center

## ✓ CHECK YOURSELF 9.3

Tambor Incorporated (TI) earned operating income of $4,730,400 on operating assets of $26,280,000 during 2011. The Western Division earned $748,000 on operating assets of $3,400,000. TI has offered the Western Division $1,100,000 of additional operating assets. The manager of the Western Division believes he could use the additional assets to generate operating income amounting to $220,000. TI has a desired return on investment (ROI) of 17 percent. Determine the ROI and RI for TI, the Western Division, and the additional investment opportunity.

*(continued)*

**Answer**

**Return on investment (ROI) = Operating income ÷ Operating assets**
ROI for TI = $4,730,400 ÷ $26,280,000 = 18%
ROI for Western Division = $748,000 ÷ $3,400,000 = 22%
ROI for Investment Opportunity = $220,000 ÷ $1,100,000 = 20%

**Residual income (RI) = Operating income − (Operating assets × Desired ROI)**
RI for TI = $4,730,400 − ($26,280,000 × .17) = $262,800
RI for Western Division = $748,000 − ($3,400,000 × .17) = $170,000
RI for Investment Opportunity = $220,000 − ($1,100,000 × .17) = $33,000

managers; and ROI or residual income to evaluate the performance of investment center managers. Many companies may have goals and objectives such as "satisfaction guaranteed" or "we try harder" that are more suitably evaluated using nonfinancial measures. To assess how well they accomplish the full range of their missions, many companies use a *balanced scorecard.*

A **balanced scorecard** includes financial and nonfinancial performance measures. Standard costs, income measures, ROI, and residual income are common financial measures used in a balanced scorecard. Nonfinancial measures include defect rates, cycle time, on-time deliveries, number of new products or innovations, safety measures, and customer satisfaction surveys. Many companies compose their scorecards to highlight leading versus lagging measures. For example, customer satisfaction survey data is a leading indicator of the sales growth which is a lagging measure. The balanced scorecard is a holistic approach to evaluating managerial performance. It is gaining widespread acceptance among world-class companies.

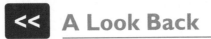 # A Look Back

The practice of delegating authority and responsibility is referred to as *decentralization.* Clear lines of authority and responsibility are essential in establishing a responsibility accounting system. In a responsibility accounting system, segment managers are held accountable for profits based on the amount of control they have over the profits in their segment.

*Responsibility reports* are used to compare actual results with budgets. The reports should be simple with variances highlighted to promote the *management by exception* doctrine. Individual managers should be held responsible only for those revenues or costs they control. Each manager should receive only summary information about the performance of the responsibility centers under her supervision.

A *responsibility center* is the point in an organization where control over revenue or expense is located. *Cost centers* are segments that incur costs but do not generate revenues. *Profit centers* incur costs and also generate revenues, producing a measurable profit. *Investment centers* incur costs, generate revenues, and use identifiable capital investments.

One of the primary purposes of responsibility accounting is to evaluate managerial performance. Comparing actual results with standards and budgets and calculating *return on investment* are used for this purpose. Because return on investment uses revenues, expenses, and investment, problems with measuring these parameters must be considered. The return on investment can be analyzed in terms of the margin earned on sales as well as the turnover (asset utilization) during the period. The *residual income approach* is sometimes used to avoid *suboptimization,* which occurs when managers choose to reject investment projects that would benefit their company's ROI but would reduce their investment center's ROI. The residual income approach evaluates managers based on their ability to generate earnings above some targeted level of earnings.

# A Look Forward

The next chapter expands on the concepts you learned in this chapter. You will see how managers select investment opportunities that will affect their future ROIs. You will learn to use present value techniques that consider the time value of money; specifically, you will learn to compute the net present value and the internal rate of return for potential investment opportunities. You will also learn to use less sophisticated analytical techniques such as payback and the unadjusted rate of return.

# APPENDIX

## Transfer Pricing

In vertically integrated companies, one division commonly sells goods or services to another division. For example, in the case of Panther Holding Company (Exhibit 9.1), the Lumber Manufacturing Division may sell lumber to the Home Building and Furniture Manufacturing Divisions. When such intercompany sales occur, the price to charge is likely to become a heated issue.

Describe how transfer prices may be established.

In a decentralized organization, each division is likely to be defined as an investment center. Division managers are held responsible for profitability. When goods are transferred internally, the sales price charged by the selling division becomes a cost to the buying division. The amount of profit included in the **transfer price** will increase the selling division's earnings and decrease the purchasing division's earnings (via increased expenses). The selling division benefits from getting the highest possible price; the purchasing division seeks the lowest possible price. When managers are competitively evaluated based on profitability measures, the transfer price is the subject of considerable controversy.

Companies use three common approaches to establish transfer prices: (1) price based on market forces; (2) price based on negotiation; and (3) price based on cost. Exhibit 9.4 shows some specific measures and the frequency of their use.

### Market-Based Transfer Prices

The preferred method for establishing transfer prices is to base them on some form of competitive market price. Ideally, selling divisions should be authorized to sell merchandise to outsiders as well as, or in preference to, other divisions. Similarly, purchasing divisions should have the option to buy goods from outsiders if they are able to obtain favorable prices. However, both selling and purchasing divisions would be motivated to deal with each other because of savings in selling, administrative, and transportation costs that arise as a natural result of internal transactions.

**Market-based transfer prices** are preferable because they promote efficiency and fairness. Market forces coupled with the responsibility for profitability motivate managers to use their resources effectively. For example, Jerry Lowe, the manager of the lumber division, may stop producing the high-quality boards the furniture division uses if he finds it is more profitable to produce low-quality lumber. The furniture division can buy its needed material from outside companies that have chosen to operate in the less-profitable, high-quality market sector. The company as a whole benefits from Mr. Lowe's insight. An additional advantage of using market prices is the sense of fairness associated with them. It is difficult for a manager to complain that the price she is being charged is too high when she has the opportunity to seek a lower price elsewhere. The natural justice of the competitive marketplace is firmly implanted in the psyches of most modern managers.

**EXHIBIT 9.4**

**What Companies Actually Use As Transfer Prices**

17% Full cost plus markup

17% Variable cost

24% Full cost

37% Market price

5% Negotiated price

*Source:* R. Tang, "Transfer Pricing in the 1990s," *Management Accounting,* pp. 22–26.

# FOCUS ON INTERNATIONAL ISSUES

The issue of transfer pricing is mostly relevant to performance evaluation of investment centers and their managers. If a company does business in only one country, transfer prices do not affect the overall profit of the company, because the cost that will be recorded as an expense for the company as a whole is the actual cost incurred to produce it, not its transfer price. However, the situation can be different if the producing division is in one country and the acquiring division is in another. This difference occurs because income tax rates are not the same in all countries.

Assume the Global Tool Company manufactures a product in South Korea for the equivalent of $10. The product is transferred to another segment that operates in the United States where it is ultimately sold for $18. Now, assume the income tax rate is 40 percent in South Korea and 30 percent in the United States. Ignoring all other costs, what amount of taxes will the company pay if the transfer price is set at $10? What amount of taxes will the company pay if the transfer price is set at $18?

If a $10 transfer price is used, then all of the company's $8 per unit profit ($18 − $10) will be recognized in the United States. Since the item is assumed to have been "sold" in South Korea at an amount equal to its production cost, there will be no profit for the South Korean division of the company ($10 − $10 = $0). The United States division will pay $2.40 in taxes ($8 × .30 = $2.40). Conversely, if the transfer price is $18, then all of the profit will be reported in South Korea, and $3.20 per unit of taxes will be paid ($8 × .40 = $3.20).

The Internal Revenue Service has rules to prevent companies from setting transfer prices simply for the purpose of reducing taxes, but various companies have been accused of such practices over the years. Remember, it is often impossible to prove exactly what the best transfer price should be. Even though the company in our hypothetical example could not get away with such extreme transfer prices as $10 or $18, it might try to set the price a bit lower than it should be in order to shift more profit to the segment in the United States where the assumed tax rate was lower.

Despite the difficulties of proving what proper transfer prices should be, the IRS does pursue companies it believes are violating the law. In fact, as of 2006, the largest settlement in the history of the IRS involved a transfer pricing case against the British based pharmaceutical company GlaxoSmithKline. The company agreed to pay the IRS $3.4 billion to settle charges that its American unit had improperly overpaid the parent company, thus shifting profits from the United States into the United Kingdom from 1989 through 2005. With respect to the settlement, the commissioner of the IRS stated, "We have consistently said that transfer pricing is one of the most significant challenges for us in the area of corporate tax administration."*

*"IRS Accepts Settlement Offer in Largest Transfer Pricing Dispute," from the IRS website, September 11, 2006.

## Negotiated Transfer Prices

In many instances, a necessary product is not available from outside companies or the market price may not be in the best interest of the company as a whole. Sometimes a division makes a unique product that is used only by one of its company's other divisions; no external market price is available to use as a base for determining the transfer price. Other times, market-based transfer prices may lead to suboptimization, discussed earlier.

Consider the case of Garms Industries. It operates several relatively autonomous divisions. One division, TrueTrust Motors, Inc., makes small electric motors for use in appliances such as refrigerators, washing machines, and fans. Another Garms division, CleanCo, makes and sells approximately 30,000 vacuum cleaners per year. CleanCo currently purchases the motors used in its vacuums from a company that is not part of Garms Industries. The president of Garms asked the TrueTrust division manager to establish a price at which it could make and sell motors to CleanCo. The manager submitted the following cost and price data.

| | |
|---|---:|
| Variable (unit-level) costs | $45 |
| Per-unit fixed cost at a volume of 30,000 units | 15 |
| Allocated corporate level facility-sustaining costs | 20 |
| Total cost | $80 |

*Note:* TrueTrust has enough excess capacity that its existing business will not be affected by a decision to make motors for CleanCo. However, TrueTrust would be required to incur additional fixed costs to purchase equipment and hire a supervisor to make the motors that CleanCo requires.

The TrueTrust manager added a profit margin of $10 per unit and offered to provide motors to CleanCo at a price of $90 per unit. When the offer was presented to the CleanCo division manager, she rejected it. Her division was currently buying motors in the open market for $70 each. Competitive pressures in the vacuum cleaner market would not permit an increase in the sales price of her product. Accepting TrueTrust's offer would significantly increase CleanCo's costs and reduce the division's profitability.

After studying the cost data, Garms's president concluded the company as a whole would suffer from suboptimization if CleanCo were to continue purchasing motors from a third-party vendor. He noted that the allocated corporate level facility-sustaining costs were not relevant to the transfer pricing decision because they would be incurred regardless of whether TrueTrust made the motors for CleanCo. He recognized that both the variable and fixed costs were relevant because they could be avoided if TrueTrust did not make the motors. Since TrueTrust's avoidable cost of $60 ($45 variable cost + $15 fixed cost) per unit was below the $70 price per unit that CleanCo was currently paying, Garms would save $10 per motor, thereby increasing overall company profitability by $300,000 ($10 cost savings per unit × 30,000 units). The president established a reasonable range for a negotiated transfer price.

If the market price were less than the avoidable cost of production, the supplying division (TrueTrust) and the company as a whole (Garms) would be better off to buy the product than to make it. It would therefore be unreasonable to expect TrueTrust to sell a product for less than its avoidable cost of production, thereby establishing the avoidable cost as the bottom point of the reasonable range for the transfer price. On the other hand, it would be unreasonable to expect an acquiring division (CleanCo) to pay more than the price it is currently paying for motors. As a result, the market price becomes the top point of the reasonable range for the transfer price. The reasonable transfer price range can be expressed as follows:

**Market price ≥ Reasonable transfer price ≥ Avoidable product cost**

In the case of Garms Industries, the reasonable range of the transfer price for vacuum cleaner motors is between the market price of $70 per unit and the avoidable production cost of $60.[1] Any transfer price within this range would benefit both divisions and the company as a whole. Garms's president encouraged the two division managers to negotiate a transfer price within the reasonable range that would satisfy both parties.

[1]This discussion assumes the supplying division (TrueTrust) has excess capacity. When the supplying division is operating at full capacity and has external buyers, the minimum price for the reasonable transfer price range would include not only the avoidable cost but also an opportunity cost. An opportunity cost exists when the supplying division must forgo the opportunity to profit from sales it could otherwise make to external buyers. On the other hand, if the supplying division has enough capacity to fill both existing orders and the additional orders on which the transfer price is negotiated, the opportunity cost is zero. In other words, the supplying division does not have to give up anything to accept an order from another division. A full discussion of opportunity cost is complex. It is covered in more advanced courses.

Under the right set of circumstances, a **negotiated transfer price** can be more beneficial than a market-based transfer price. Allowing the managers involved to agree to a negotiated price preserves the notion of fairness. The element of profit remains intact and the evaluation concepts discussed in this chapter can be applied. Negotiated prices may offer many of the same advantages as market prices. They should be the first alternative when a company is unable to use market-based transfer prices.

Suppose the two division managers cannot agree on a negotiated transfer price. Should the president of Garms Industries establish a reasonable price and force the managers to accept it? There is no definitive answer to this question. However, most senior-level executives recognize the motivational importance of maintaining autonomy in a decentralized organization. So long as the negative consequences are not disastrous, division managers are usually permitted to exercise their own judgment. In other words, the long-term benefits derived from autonomous management outweigh the short-term disadvantages of suboptimization.

### Cost-Based Transfer Prices

The least desirable transfer price option is a **cost-based transfer price.** To use cost, it must first be determined. Some companies base the transfer price on *variable cost* (a proxy for avoidable cost). Other companies use *full cost* (variable cost plus an allocated portion of fixed cost) as the transfer price. In either case, basing transfer prices on cost removes the profit motive. Without profitability as a goal, the incentive to control cost is diminished. One department's inefficiency is simply passed on to the next department. The result is low companywide profitability. Despite this potential detrimental effect, many companies base transfer prices on cost because cost represents an objective number that is available. When a company uses cost-based transfer prices, *it should use standard rather than actual costs.* Departments will therefore at least be responsible for the variances they generate which will encourage some degree of cost control.

www.mhhe.com/edmonds2011

**A step-by-step audio-narrated series of slides is provided on the text website at www.mhhe.com/edmonds2011.**

## SELF-STUDY REVIEW PROBLEM

The following financial statements apply to Hola Division, one of three investment centers operated by Costa Corporation. Costa Corporation has a desired rate of return of 15%. Costa Corporation headquarters has $80,000 of additional operating assets to assign to the investment centers.

| HOLA DIVISION<br>Income Statement<br>For the Year Ended December 31, 2011 | |
| --- | --- |
| Sales revenue | $78,695 |
| Cost of goods sold | (50,810) |
| Gross margin | 27,885 |
| Operating expenses | |
| Selling expenses | (1,200) |
| Depreciation expense | (1,125) |
| Operating income | 25,560 |
| Non-operating expense | |
| Loss on sale of land | (3,200) |
| Net income | $22,360 |

### HOLA DIVISION
#### Balance Sheet
#### As of December 31, 2011

| Assets | |
|---|---|
| Cash | $ 8,089 |
| Accounts receivable | 22,870 |
| Merchandise inventory | 33,460 |
| Equipment less acc. dep. | 77,581 |
| Non-operating assets | 8,250 |
| Total assets | $150,250 |
| Liabilities | |
| Accounts payable | $ 5,000 |
| Notes payable | 58,000 |
| Stockholders' equity | |
| Common stock | 55,000 |
| Retained earnings | 32,250 |
| Total liab. and stk. equity | $150,250 |

## Required

a. Should Costa use operating income or net income to determine the rate of return (ROI) for the Hola investment center? Explain.

b. Should Costa use operating assets or total assets to determine the ROI for the Hola investment center? Explain.

c. Calculate the ROI for Hola.

d. The manager of the Hola division has an opportunity to invest the funds at an ROI of 17 percent. The other two divisions have investment opportunities that yield only 16 percent. The manager of Hola rejects the additional funding. Why would the manager of Hola reject the funds under these circumstances?

e. Calculate the residual income from the investment opportunity available to Hola and explain how residual income could be used to encourage the manager to accept the additional funds.

## Solution to Requirement a

Costa should use operating income because net income frequently includes items over which management has no control, such as the loss on sale of land.

## Solution to Requirement b

Costa should use operating assets because total assets frequently includes items over which management has no control, such as assets not currently in use.

## Solution to Requirement c

Operating assets = Total assets − Non-operating assets ($150,250 − $8,250)
ROI = Operating income / Operating assets = $25,560 / $142,000 = 18%

## Solution to Requirement d

Since the rate of return on the investment opportunity (17 percent) is below Hola's current ROI (18 percent), accepting the opportunity would decrease Hola's average ROI, which would have a negative effect on the manager's performance evaluation. While it is to the advantage of the company as a whole for Hola to accept the investment opportunity, it will reflect negatively on the manager to do so. This phenomenon is called *suboptimization*.

### Solution to Requirement e

Operating income from the investment opportunity is $13,600 ($80,000 × .17)

$$\text{Residual income} = \text{Operating income} - (\text{Operating assets} \times \text{Desired ROI})$$

$$\text{Residual income} = \$13,600 - (\$80,000 \times .15)$$

$$\text{Residual income} = \$13,600 - \$12,000$$

$$\text{Residual income} = \$1,600$$

Since the investment opportunity would increase Hola's residual income, the acceptance of the opportunity would improve the manager's performance evaluation, thereby motivating the manager to accept it.

## KEY TERMS

Balanced scorecard  412
Controllability concept  404
Cost-based transfer price  416
Cost center  401
Decentralization  400
Investment center  401
Management by exception  403

Margin  407
Market-based transfer prices  413
Negotiated transfer price  416
Profit center  401
Residual income  409
Responsibility accounting  398

Responsibility center  400
Responsibility report  401
Return on investment  405
Suboptimization  409
Transfer price  413
Turnover  407

## QUESTIONS

1. Pam Kelly says she has no faith in budgets. Her company, Kelly Manufacturing Corporation, spent thousands of dollars to install a sophisticated budget system. One year later the company's expenses are still out of control. She believes budgets simply do not work. How would you respond to Ms. Kelly's beliefs?

2. All travel expenses incurred by Pure Water Pump Corporation are reported only to John Daniels, the company president. Pure Water is a multinational company with five divisions. Are travel expenses reported following the responsibility accounting concept? Explain.

3. What are five potential advantages of decentralization?

4. Who receives responsibility reports? What do the reports include?

5. How does the concept of predominant control as opposed to that of absolute control apply to responsibility accounting?

6. How do responsibility reports promote the management by exception doctrine?

7. What is a responsibility center?

8. What are the three types of responsibility centers? Explain how each differs from the others.

9. Carmen Douglas claims that her company's performance evaluation system is unfair. Her company uses return on investment (ROI) to evaluate performance. Ms. Douglas says that even though her ROI is lower than another manager's, her performance is far superior. Is it possible that Ms. Douglas is correct? Explain your position.

10. What two factors affect the computation of return on investment?

11. What three ways can a manager increase the return on investment?

12. How can a residual income approach to performance evaluation reduce the likelihood of suboptimization?

13. Is it true that the manager with the highest residual income is always the best performer?

14. Why are transfer prices important to managers who are evaluated based on profitability criteria?

15. What are three approaches to establishing transfer prices? List the most desirable approach first and the least desirable last.

16. If cost is the basis for transfer pricing, should actual or standard cost be used? Why?

# MULTIPLE-CHOICE QUESTIONS

**Multiple-choice questions are provided on the text website at www.mhhe.com/edmonds2011.**

## EXERCISES—SERIES A

**All applicable Exercises in Series A are available with McGraw-Hill's *Connect Accounting*.**

**Exercise 9-1A** *Organization chart and responsibilities*　　　　**LO 1**

The production manager is responsible for the assembly, cleaning, and finishing departments. The executive vice president reports directly to the president but is responsible for the activities of the production department, the finance department, and the sales department. The sales manager is responsible for the advertising department.

**Required**

Arrange this information into an organization chart and indicate the responsibility levels involved.

**Exercise 9-2A** *Responsibility report*　　　　**LO 3**

Jenson Department Store is divided into three major departments: Men's Clothing, Women's Clothing, and Home Furnishings. Each of these three departments is supervised by a manager who reports to the general manager. The departments are subdivided into different sections managed by floor supervisors. The Home Furnishings Department has three floor supervisors, one for furniture, one for lamps, and one for housewares. The following items were included in the company's most recent responsibility report.

Travel expenses for the housewares buyer
Seasonal decorations for the furniture section
Revenues for the Home Furnishings Department
Administrative expenses for the Men's Clothing Department
Utility cost allocated to the Home Furnishings Department
Cost of part-time Christmas help for the Women's Department
Delivery expenses for furniture purchases
Salaries for the sales staff in the lamp section
Storewide revenues
Salary of the general manager
Salary of the Men's Clothing Department manager
Allocated companywide advertising expense
Depreciation on the facility

**Required**

Which items are likely to be the responsibility of the Home Furnishings Department manager?

**Exercise 9-3A** *Organization chart and controllable costs*　　　　**LO 1**

Kenta Company has employees with the following job titles.

President of the company
Vice president of marketing
Product manager
Controller
Vice president of manufacturing

Treasurer

Regional sales manager

Personnel manager

Cashier

Vice president of finance

Fringe benefits manager

Board of directors

Production supervisors

Vice president of administration

Sales office manager

**Required**

a. Design an organization chart using these job titles.

b. Identify some possible controllable costs for the person holding each job title.

**LO 4**

### Exercise 9-4A   *Income statement for internal use*

Ladmilla Company has provided the following 2011 data.

| Budget | |
|---|---|
| Sales | $500,000 |
| Variable product costs | 204,000 |
| Variable selling expense | 50,000 |
| Other variable expenses | 3,600 |
| Fixed product costs | 16,600 |
| Fixed selling expense | 24,300 |
| Other fixed expenses | 2,200 |
| Interest expense | 800 |
| Variances | |
| Sales | 8,600 U |
| Variable product costs | 4,000 F |
| Variable selling expense | 2,500 U |
| Other variable expenses | 1,200 U |
| Fixed product costs | 220 F |
| Fixed selling expense | 390 F |
| Other fixed expenses | 150 U |
| Interest expense | 80 F |

**Required**

a. Prepare in good form a budgeted and actual income statement for internal use. Separate operating income from net income in the statements.

b. Calculate variances and identify them as favorable (F) or unfavorable (U).

**LO 3, 4**

### Exercise 9-5A   *Evaluating a cost center including flexible budgeting concepts*

Smiley Medical Equipment Company makes a blood pressure measuring kit. Elbert Jackson is the production manager. The production department's static budget and actual results for 2012 follow.

| | Static Budget | Actual Results |
|---|---|---|
| Production in units | 30,000 kits | 32,000 kits |
| Direct materials | $210,000 | $262,000 |
| Direct labor | 180,000 | 185,600 |
| Variable manufacturing overhead | 48,000 | 54,000 |
| Total variable costs | 438,000 | 501,600 |
| Fixed manufacturing overhead | 210,000 | 205,000 |
| Total manufacturing cost | $648,000 | $706,600 |

**Required**

a. Convert the static budget into a flexible budget.

b. Use the flexible budget to evaluate Mr. Jackson's performance.

c. Explain why Mr. Jackson's performance evaluation does not include sales revenue and net income.

## Exercise 9-6A   *Evaluating a profit center*

LO 2, 3

Virginia Elliott, the president of Lovely Toys Corporation, is trying to determine this year's pay raises for the store managers. Lovely Toys has seven stores in the southwestern United States. Corporate headquarters purchases all toys from different manufacturers globally and distributes them to individual stores. Additionally, headquarters makes decisions regarding location and size of stores. These practices allow Lovely Toys to receive volume discounts from vendors and to implement coherent marketing strategies. Within a set of general guidelines, store managers have the flexibility to adjust product prices and hire local employees. Ms. Elliott is considering three possible performance measures for evaluating the individual stores: cost of goods sold, return on sales (net income divided by sales), and return on investment.

**Required**

a. Using the concept of controllability, advise Ms. Elliott about the best performance measure.

b. Explain how a balanced scorecard can be used to help Ms. Elliott.

## Exercise 9-7A   *Return on investment*

LO 5

An investment center of Aguilar Corporation shows an operating income of $7,500 on total operating assets of $60,000.

**Required**

Compute the return on investment.

## Exercise 9-8A   *Return on investment*

LO 5, 6

Mitchell Company calculated its return on investment as 13 percent. Sales are now $270,000, and the amount of total operating assets is $450,000.

**Required**

a. If expenses are reduced by $27,000 and sales remain unchanged, what return on investment will result?

b. If both sales and expenses cannot be changed, what change in the amount of operating assets is required to achieve the same result?

## Exercise 9-9A   *Residual income*

LO 7

Schiavo Corporation has a desired rate of return of 8 percent. Frank Rodomil is in charge of one of Schiavo's three investment centers. His center controlled operating assets of $2,500,000 that were used to earn $260,000 of operating income.

**Required**

Compute Mr. Rodomil's residual income.

## Exercise 9-10A   *Residual income*

LO 7

Claire Cough Drops operates two divisions. The following information pertains to each division for 2010.

|  | Division A | Division B |
|---|---|---|
| Sales | $200,000 | $72,000 |
| Operating income | $ 15,040 | $ 8,100 |
| Average operating assets | $ 63,000 | $45,000 |
| Company's desired rate of return | 18% | 18% |

**Required**

a. Compute each division's residual income.

b. Which division increased the company's profitability more?

**LO 5, 7**

### Exercise 9-11A    *Return on investment and residual income*

**Required**

Supply the missing information in the following table for Ren Company.

| | |
|---|---|
| Sales | $396,000 |
| ROI | ? |
| Operating assets | ? |
| Operating income | ? |
| Turnover | 2.2 |
| Residual income | ? |
| Operating profit margin | 0.13 |
| Desired rate of return | 18% |

**LO 5, 7**

### Exercise 9-12A    *Comparing return on investment with residual income*

The Wade Division of Geisler Corporation has a current ROI of 20 percent. The company target ROI is 15 percent. The Wade Division has an opportunity to invest $5,000,000 at 18 percent but is reluctant to do so because its ROI will fall to 19.2 percent. The present investment base for the division is $7,500,000.

**Required**

Demonstrate how Geisler can motivate the Wade Division to make the investment by using the residual income method.

**LO 5, 6, 7**

### Exercise 9-13A    *Return on investment and residual income*

McMillan Home Maintenance Company (MHMC) earned operating income of $7,200,000 on operating assets of $60,000,000 during 2011. The Tree Cutting Division earned $1,215,000 on operating assets of $6,750,000. MHMC has offered the Tree Cutting Division $2,050,000 of additional operating assets. The manager of the Tree Cutting Division believes he could use the additional assets to generate operating income amounting to $410,000. MHMC has a desired return on investment (ROI) of 10 percent.

**Required**

a. Calculate the return on investment (ROI) for MHMC, the Tree Cutting Division, and the additional investment opportunity.

b. Calculate the residual income (RI) for MHMC, the Tree Cutting Division, and the additional investment opportunity.

**Appendix**

**LO 8**

### Exercise 9-14A    *Transfer pricing*

Larkey Company has two divisions, A and B. Division A manufactures 6,000 units of product per month. The cost per unit is calculated as follows.

| | |
|---|---|
| Variable costs | $ 8 |
| Fixed costs | 20 |
| Total cost | $28 |

Division B uses the product created by Division A. No outside market for Division A's product exists. The fixed costs incurred by Division A are allocated headquarters-level facility-sustaining costs. The manager of Division A suggests that the product be transferred to Division B at a price of at least $28 per unit. The manager of Division B argues that the same product can be purchased from another company for $18 per unit and requests permission to do so.

**Required**

a. Should Larkey allow the manager of Division B to purchase the product from the outside company for $18 per unit? Explain.

b. Assume you are the president of the company. Write a brief paragraph recommending a resolution of the conflict between the two divisional managers.

### Exercise 9-15A    *Transfer pricing and fixed cost per unit*    LO 8

The Sentry Parts Division of Camden Company plans to set up a facility with the capacity to make 10,000 units annually of an electronic computer part. The avoidable cost of making the part is as follows.

| Costs | Total | Cost per Unit |
|---|---|---|
| Variable cost | $200,000 | $30 |
| Fixed cost | 80,000 | 8 (at capacity) |

**Required**

a. Assume that Camden's Norwood Division is currently purchasing 6,000 of the electronic parts each year from an outside supplier at a market price of $50. What would be the financial consequence to Camden if the Sentry Parts Division makes the part and sells it to the Norwood Division? What range of transfer prices would increase the financial performance of both divisions?

b. Suppose that the Norwood Division increases production so that it could use 10,000 units of the part made by the Sentry Parts Division. How would the change in volume affect the range of transfer prices that would financially benefit both divisions?

## PROBLEMS—SERIES A

**All applicable Problems in Series A are available with McGraw-Hill's *Connect Accounting*.**

### Problem 9-16A    *Determining controllable costs*    LO 3

Wayne Portera is the manager of the production department of Sun Corporation. Sun incurred the following costs during 2011.

| | |
|---|---|
| Production department supplies | $ 6,000 |
| Administrative salaries | 400,000 |
| Production wages | 580,000 |
| Materials used | 529,200 |
| Depreciation on manufacturing equipment | 361,600 |
| Corporate-level rental expense | 240,000 |
| Property taxes | 68,600 |
| Sales salaries | 286,800 |

**Required**

Prepare a list of expenditures that Mr. Portera controls.

### Problem 9-17A    *Controllability, responsibility, and balanced scorecard*    LO 3, 4

Ashley Peek manages the production division of Myrex Corporation. Ms. Peek's responsibility report for the month of August follows.

|  | Budget | Actual | Variance |  |
|---|---|---|---|---|
| **Controllable costs** |  |  |  |  |
| Raw materials | $23,000 | $27,600 | $ 4,600 | U |
| Labor | 10,000 | 15,295 | 5,295 | U |
| Maintenance | 3,200 | 4,600 | 1,400 | U |
| Supplies | 2,350 | 1,100 | 1,250 | F |
| Total | $38,550 | $48,595 | $10,045 | U |

The budget had called for 4,600 pounds of raw materials at $5 per pound, and 4,600 pounds were used during August; however, the purchasing department paid $6 per pound for the materials. The wage rate used to establish the budget was $20 per hour. On August 1, however, it increased to $23 as the result of an inflation index provision in the union contract. Furthermore, the purchasing department did not provide the materials needed in accordance with the production schedule, which forced Ms. Peek to use 110 hours of overtime at a $34.50 rate. The projected 500 hours of labor in the budget would have been sufficient had it not been for the 110 hours of overtime. In other words, 610 hours of labor were used in August.

### Required

a. When confronted with the unfavorable variances in her responsibility report, Ms. Peek argued that the report was unfair because it held her accountable for materials and labor variances that she did *not* control. Is she correct? Comment specifically on the materials and labor variances.

b. Prepare a responsibility report that reflects the cost items that Ms. Peek controlled during August.

c. Will the changes in the revised responsibility report require corresponding changes in the financial statements? Explain.

d. Explain how a balanced scorecard may be used to improve the performance evaluation.

**LO 3, 4**

**CHECK FIGURE**
a. Total controllable costs: $387,510 (actual)

### Problem 9-18A   *Performance reports and evaluation*

Vance Corporation has four divisions: the assembly division, the processing division, the machining division, and the packing division. All four divisions are under the control of the vice president of manufacturing. Each division has a manager and several departments that are directed by supervisors. The chain of command runs downward from vice president to division manager to supervisor. The processing division is composed of the paint and finishing departments. The May responsibility reports for the supervisors of these departments follow.

|  | Budgeted* | Actual | Variance |  |
|---|---|---|---|---|
| **Paint Department** |  |  |  |  |
| Controllable costs |  |  |  |  |
| Raw materials | $30,800 | $ 31,700 | $ 900 | U |
| Labor | 57,700 | 64,000 | 6,300 | U |
| Repairs | 4,800 | 3,870 | 930 | F |
| Maintenance | 2,600 | 2,460 | 140 | F |
| Total | $95,900 | $102,030 | $6,130 | U |
| **Finishing Department** |  |  |  |  |
| Controllable costs |  |  |  |  |
| Raw materials | $22,810 | $ 22,560 | $ 250 | F |
| Labor | 43,300 | 39,900 | 3,400 | F |
| Repairs | 2,830 | 3,170 | 340 | U |
| Maintenance | 1,680 | 2,050 | 370 | U |
| Total | $70,620 | $ 67,680 | $2,940 | F |

*Vance uses flexible budgets for performance evaluation.

Other pertinent cost data for May follow.

| | Budgeted* | Actual |
|---|---|---|
| Cost data of other divisions | | |
| Assembly | $330,000 | $324,300 |
| Machining | 290,000 | 296,400 |
| Packing | 414,950 | 405,700 |
| Other costs associated with | | |
| Processing division manager | 220,000 | 217,800 |
| Vice president of manufacturing | 128,000 | 133,060 |

*Vance uses flexible budgets for performance evaluation.

**Required**

a. Prepare a responsibility report for the manager of the processing division.

b. Prepare a responsibility report for the vice president of manufacturing.

c. Explain where the $6,300 unfavorable labor variance in the paint department supervisor's report is included in the vice president's report.

d. Based on the responsibility report prepared in Requirement *a*, explain where the processing division manager should concentrate his attention.

### Problem 9-19A   *Different types of responsibility centers*

LO 2

Liberty National Bank is a large municipal bank with several branch offices. The bank's computer department handles all data processing for bank operations. In addition, the bank sells the computer department's expertise in systems development and excess machine time to several small business firms, serving them as a service bureau.

The bank currently treats the computer department as a cost center. The manager of the computer department prepares a cost budget annually for senior bank officials to approve. Monthly operating reports compare actual and budgeted expenses. Revenues from the department's service bureau activities are treated as other income by the bank and are not reflected on the computer department's operating reports. The costs of servicing these clients are included in the computer department reports, however.

The manager of the computer department has proposed that bank management convert the computer department to a profit or investment center.

**Required**

a. Describe the characteristics that differentiate a cost center, a profit center, and an investment center from each other.

b. Would the manager of the computer department be likely to conduct the operations of the department differently if the department were classified as a profit center or an investment center rather than as a cost center? Explain.

### Problem 9-20A   *Comparing return on investment and residual income*

LO 5, 7

Wells Corporation operates three investment centers. The following financial statements apply to the investment center named Huber Division.

CHECK FIGURE
c. 21.31%

| HUBER DIVISION | |
|---|---|
| Income Statement | |
| For the Year Ended December 31, 2011 | |
| Sales revenue | $105,480 |
| Cost of goods sold | (60,275) |
| Gross margin | 45,205 |
| Operating expenses | |
| Selling expenses | (2,840) |
| Depreciation expense | (4,205) |
| Operating income | 38,160 |
| Nonoperating item | |
| Gain of sale of land | (5,000) |
| Net income | $ 33,160 |

## HUBER DIVISION
### Balance Sheet
### As of December 31, 2011

| Assets | |
|---|---|
| Cash | $ 12,472 |
| Accounts receivable | 40,266 |
| Merchandise inventory | 36,000 |
| Equipment less accum. dep. | 90,258 |
| Nonoperating assets | 9,000 |
| Total assets | $187,996 |
| Liabilities | |
| Accounts payable | $ 9,637 |
| Notes payable | 72,000 |
| Stockholders' equity | |
| Common stock | 80,000 |
| Retained earnings | 26,359 |
| Total liab. and stk. equity | $187,996 |

**Required**

a. Which should be used to determine the rate of return (ROI) for the Huber investment center, operating income or net income? Explain your answer.

b. Which should be used to determine the ROI for the Huber investment center, operating assets or total assets? Explain your answer.

c. Calculate the ROI for Huber.

d. Wells has a desired ROI of 15 percent. Headquarters has $96,000 of funds to assign to its investment centers. The manager of the Huber Division has an opportunity to invest the funds at an ROI of 17 percent. The other two divisions have investment opportunities that yield only 16 percent. Even so, the manager of Huber rejects the additional funding. Explain why the manager of Huber would reject the funds under these circumstances.

e. Explain how residual income could be used to encourage the manager to accept the additional funds.

**LO 5, 6**

**eXcel**

**CHECK FIGURES**
c. 15%
d. (3) 18.75%

### Problem 9-21A    *Return on investment*

Soto Corporation's balance sheet indicates that the company has $300,000 invested in operating assets. During 2011, Soto earned operating income of $45,000 on $600,000 of sales.

**Required**

a. Compute Soto's profit margin for 2011.

b. Compute Soto's turnover for 2011.

c. Compute Soto's return on investment for 2011.

d. Recompute Soto's ROI under each of the following independent assumptions.

(1) Sales increase from $600,000 to $750,000, thereby resulting in an increase in operating income from $45,000 to $60,000.

(2) Sales remain constant, but Soto reduces expenses, resulting in an increase in operating income from $45,000 to $48,000.

(3) Soto is able to reduce its invested capital from $300,000 to $240,000 without affecting operating income.

**LO 5, 6, 7**

**CHECK FIGURE**
b. Allenby's ROI after the new investment: 13.23%

### Problem 9-22A    *Return on investment and residual income*

Allenby Company has operating assets of $20,000,000. The company's operating income for the most recent accounting period was $2,640,000. The Fisher Division of Allenby controls $7,500,000 of the company's assets and earned $1,170,000 of its operating income. Allenby's desired ROI is 10 percent. Allenby has $900,000 of additional funds to invest. The manager of the Fisher division believes that his division could earn $126,000 on the additional funds. The highest investment opportunity to any of the company's other divisions is 11 percent.

**Required**

**a.** If ROI is used as the sole performance measure, would the manager of the Fisher Division be likely to accept or reject the additional funding? Why or why not?

**b.** Would Allenby Company benefit if the manager of the Fisher Division accepted the additional funds? Why or why not?

**c.** If residual income is used as the sole performance measure would the manager of the Fisher Division be likely to accept or reject the additional funding? Why or why not?

**Problem 9-23A    Return on investment and residual income**

Windom Technologies, Inc. (WTI), has three divisions. WTI has a desired rate of return of 13 percent. The operating assets and income for each division are as follows:

| Divisions | Operating Assets | Operating Income |
|-----------|------------------|------------------|
| Printer | $ 540,000 | $ 96,000 |
| Copier | 810,000 | 90,000 |
| Fax | 360,000 | 54,000 |
| Total | $1,710,000 | $240,000 |

WTI headquarters has $125,000 of additional cash to invest in one of its divisions. The division managers have identified investment opportunities that are expected to yield the following ROIs:

| Divisions | Expected ROIs for Additional Investments |
|-----------|------------------------------------------|
| Printer | 15.5% |
| Copier | 13.5% |
| Fax | 12.0% |

**Required**

**a.** Which division manager is currently producing the highest ROI?

**b.** Based on ROI, which division manager would be most eager to accept the $125,000 of investment funds?

**c.** Based on ROI, which division manager would be least likely to accept the $125,000 of investment funds?

**d.** Which division offers the best investment opportunity for WTI?

**e.** What is the term used to describe the apparent conflict between Requirements *b* and *d*?

**f.** Explain how the residual income performance measure could be used to motivate the managers to act in the best interest of the company.

**g.** Calculate the residual income:

(1) at the corporate (headquarters) level before the additional investment.

(2) at the division level before the additional investment.

(3) at the investment level.

(4) at the division level after the additional investment.

**h.** Based on residual income, which division manager would be most eager to accept the $125,000 investment opportunity?

**Appendix**

**Problem 9-24A    Transfer pricing**

Landry Radio Corporation is a subsidiary of Kandell Companies. Landry makes car radios that it sells to retail outlets. It purchases speakers for the radios from outside suppliers for $28 each. Recently, Kandell acquired the Viola Speaker Corporation, which makes car radio speakers that it sells to manufacturers. Viola produces and sells approximately 200,000 speakers per year, which represents 70 percent of its operating capacity. At the present volume of activity, each

---

**LO 5, 6, 7**

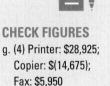

**CHECK FIGURES**
g. (4) Printer: $28,925;
Copier: $(14,675);
Fax: $5,950

**LO 8**

**CHECK FIGURE**
a. The maximum price should be $28.

speaker costs $24 to produce. This cost consists of a $16 variable cost component and an $8 fixed cost component. Viola sells the speakers for $30 each. The managers of Landry and Viola have been asked to consider using Viola's excess capacity to supply Landry with some of the speakers that it currently purchases from unrelated companies. Both managers are evaluated based on return on investment. Viola's manager suggests that the speakers be supplied at a transfer price of $30 each (the current selling price). On the other hand, Landry's manager suggests a $28 transfer price, noting that this amount covers total cost and provides Viola a healthy contribution margin.

### Required

a.  What transfer price would you recommend?

b.  Discuss the effect of the intercompany sales on each manager's return on investment.

c.  Should Viola be required to use more than excess capacity to provide speakers to Landry? In other words, should it sell to Landry some of the 200,000 units that it is currently selling to unrelated companies? Why or why not?

## EXERCISES—SERIES B

**LO 1**

### Exercise 9-1B    *Organizational chart and responsibilities*

Yesterday, Fowler Corporation's board of directors appointed Suzey Cooper as the new president and chief executive officer. This morning, Ms. Cooper presented to the board a list of her management team members. The vice presidents are Joseph Cranston, regional operations; Daniel Invanisevic, research and development; and Iris Ewell, chief financial officer. Reporting to Mr. Cranston are the directors of American, European, and Asian operations. Reporting to Mr. Invanisevic are the directors of the Houston, Seattle, and Charlotte laboratories. Reporting to Ms. Ewell are the controller and the treasurer.

### Required

Arrange the preceding information into an organization chart and indicate the responsibility levels involved.

**LO 3**

### Exercise 9-2B    *Responsibility report*

Fowler Corporation divides its operations into three regions: American, European, and Asian. The following items appear in the company's responsibility report.

European director's salary
Revenues of the French branch
Office expenses of the Japanese branch
Corporation president's salary
Asian director's salary
Revenues of the Taiwanese branch
Revenues of the British branch
Office expenses of the French branch
Revenues of the U.S. branch
Administrative expenses of the corporate headquarters
Office expenses of the Taiwanese branch
Office expenses of the Canadian branch
Revenues of the Japanese branch
Revenues of the Canadian branch
Office expenses of the British branch
Office expenses of the U.S. branch
American director's salary

### Required

Which items should Fowler include in the responsibility report for the director of Asian operations?

## Exercise 9-3B   *Organizational chart and controllable cost*

Daniel Invanisevic, Corporation vice president of research and development, has overall responsibility for employees with the following positions:

Directors of the Houston, Seattle, and Charlotte laboratories
Senior researchers reporting to laboratory directors
A personnel manager in each laboratory
An accounting manager in each laboratory
Research assistants working for senior researchers
Recruiters reporting to a personnel manager
Bookkeepers reporting to an accounting manager

**Required**

a.  Design an organization chart using these job positions.

b.  Identify some possible controllable costs for persons holding each of the job positions.

## Exercise 9-4B   *Income statement for internal use*

McGee Company has provided the following data for 2011:

| | |
|---|---:|
| **Budget** | |
| Sales | $215,000 |
| Variable product costs | 68,000 |
| Variable selling expense | 19,500 |
| Other variable expenses | 4,000 |
| Fixed product costs | 28,000 |
| Fixed selling expense | 10,500 |
| Other fixed expenses | 1,000 |
| Interest expense | 500 |
| **Actual results** | |
| Sales | 230,000 |
| Variable product costs | 70,000 |
| Variable selling expense | 21,000 |
| Other variable expenses | 3,500 |
| Fixed product costs | 30,000 |
| Fixed selling expense | 9,600 |
| Other fixed expenses | 5,000 |
| Interest expense | 525 |

**Required**

a.  Prepare in good form a budgeted and actual income statement for internal use. Separate operating income from net income in the statements.

b.  Calculate variances and identify them as favorable (F) or unfavorable (U).

## Exercise 9-5B   *Evaluating a cost center (including flexible budgeting concepts)*

Doug Oliver, president of Oliver Door Products Company, is evaluating the performance of Gregory Wilson, the plant manager, for the last fiscal year. Mr. Oliver is concerned that production costs exceeded budget by nearly $35,000. He has available the 2011 static budget for the production plant, as well as the actual results, both of which follow:

| | Static Budget | Actual Results |
|---|---:|---:|
| Production in units | 5,000 Doors | 5,250 Doors |
| Direct materials | $ 350,000 | $ 362,000 |
| Direct labor | 200,000 | 222,000 |
| Variable manufacturing overhead | 120,000 | 121,800 |
| Total variable costs | 670,000 | 705,800 |
| Fixed manufacturing overhead | 410,000 | 409,000 |
| Total manufacturing cost | $1,080,000 | $1,114,800 |

**Required**

a. Convert the static budget into a flexible budget.
b. Use the flexible budget to evaluate Mr. Wilson's performance.
c. Explain why Mr. Wilson's performance evaluation doesn't include sales revenue and net income.

**LO 2, 3**

### Exercise 9-6B   *Evaluating a profit center*

Chris Gomez, president of Medina Travel Company, a travel agency, is seeking a method of evaluating her seven branches. Each branch vice president is authorized to hire employees and devise competitive strategies for the branch territory. Ms. Gomez wonders which of the following three different measures would be most suitable: return on investment, operating income, or return on sales (operating income divided by sales).

**Required**

a. Using the concept of controllability, advise Ms. Gomez about the best performance measure.
b. Explain how a balanced scorecard can be used for Ms. Gomez.

**LO 5**

### Exercise 9-7B   *Computing return on investment*

A Layfield Corporation investment center shows an operating income of $78,000 and an investment in operating assets of $890,000.

**Required**

Compute the return on investment.

**LO 5, 6**

### Exercise 9-8B   *Return on investment*

With annual sales of $4,800,000 and operating assets of $3,200,000, Nolan Company achieved a 10 percent ROI.

**Required**

a. If Nolan reduces expenses by $80,000 and sales remain unchanged, what ROI will result?
b. If Nolan cannot change either sales or expenses, what change in the investment base is required to achieve the same result you calculated for Requirement *a*?

**LO 7**

### Exercise 9-9B   *Computing residual income*

Mustafa Corporation's desired rate of return is 12 percent. Leeds Division, one of Mustafa's five investment centers, earned an operating income of $4,000,000 last year. The division controlled $25,000,000 of operational assets.

**Required**

Compute Leeds Division's residual income.

**LO 7**

### Exercise 9-10B   *Computing residual income*

Earl Oil Change operates two divisions. The following pertains to each division for 2011:

|  | New York | New Jersey |
| --- | --- | --- |
| Sales | $1,200,000 | $1,000,000 |
| Operating income | $ 90,000 | $ 60,000 |
| Average operating assets | $300,000 | $240,000 |
| Company's desired rate of return | 15% | 15% |

**Required**

a. Compute each division's residual income.
b. Which division increased the company's profitability more?

**Exercise 9-11B** *Supply missing information regarding return on investment and residual income* LO 5, 7

**Required**

Supply the missing information in the following table for Hansen Company.

| | |
|---|---|
| Sales | ? |
| ROI | 12% |
| Investment in operating assets | $450,000 |
| Operating income | ? |
| Turnover | ? |
| Residual income | ? |
| Operating profit margin | 0.08 |
| Desired rate of return | 11% |

**Exercise 9-12B** *Contrasting return on investment with residual income* LO 5, 7

The Birmingham Division of Alabama Garage Doors, Inc., is currently achieving a 12 percent ROI. The company's target ROI is 8 percent. The division has an opportunity to invest in operating assets an additional $900,000 at 10 percent but is reluctant to do so because its ROI will fall to 11.7 percent. The division's present investment in operating assets is $4,500,000.

**Required**

Explain how management can use the residual income method to motivate the Birmingham Division to make the investment.

**Exercise 9-13B** *Return on investment and residual income* LO 5, 6, 7

Hammod Insurance Company (HIC) earned operating income of $30,000,000 on operating assets of $240,000,000 during 2011. The Automobile Insurance Division earned $6,000,000 on operating assets of $40,000,000. HIC has offered the Automobile Division $3,625,000 of additional operating assets. The manager of the Automobile Insurance Division believes she could use the additional assets to generate operating income amounting to $480,000. HIC has a desired return on investment (ROI) of 10 percent.

**Required**

a. Calculate the return on investment (ROI) for HIC, the Automobile Insurance Division, and the additional investment opportunity.

b. Calculate the residual income (RI) for HIC, the Automobile Insurance Division, and the additional investment opportunity.

**Appendix**

**Exercise 9-14B** *Transfer pricing* LO 8

Oscroft Company makes household water filtration equipment. The Aquafresh Division manufactures filters. The Sweet Water Division then uses the filters as a component of the final product Oscroft sells to consumers. The Aquafresh Division has the capacity to produce 8,000 filters per month at the following cost per unit:

| | |
|---|---|
| Variable costs | $12 |
| Division fixed costs | 10 |
| Allocated corporate-level facility-sustaining costs | 8 |
| Total cost per filter | $30 |

Sweet Water currently uses 6,000 Aquafresh filters per month. Andy Treadway, Sweet Water's manager, is not happy with the $30 transfer price charged by Aquafresh. He points out that Sweet Water could purchase the same filters from outside vendors for a market price of only $24.

Denise Cantor, Aquafresh's manager, refuses to sell the filters to Sweet Water below cost. Mr. Treadway counters that he would be happy to purchase the filters elsewhere. Because Aquafresh does not have other customers for its filters, Ms. Cantor appeals to Jim Volcker, the president of Oscroft, for arbitration.

**Required**

a. Should the president of Oscroft allow Mr. Treadway to purchase filters from outside vendors for $24 per unit? Explain.

b. Write a brief paragraph describing what Mr. Volcker should do to resolve the conflict between the two division managers.

**LO 8**

### Exercise 9-15B    *Transfer pricing and fixed cost per unit*

The Graca Division of Pryor Company currently produces electric fans that desktop computer manufacturers use as cooling components. The Hackney Division, which makes notebook computers, has asked the Graca Division to design and supply 20,000 fans per year for its notebook computers. Hackney currently purchases notebook fans from an outside vendor at the price of $18 each. However, Hackney is not happy with the vendor's unstable delivery pattern. To accept Hackney's order, Graca would have to purchase additional equipment and modify its plant layout. The additional equipment would enable the company to add 35,000 notebook fans to its annual production. Graca's avoidable cost of making 20,000 notebook fans follows:

| Costs | Total | Per Unit |
|---|---|---|
| Variable costs | $120,000 | $6 |
| Fixed cost | $140,000 | 7 |

**Required**

a. What would be the financial consequence to Pryor Company if the Graca Division makes the notebook fans and sells them to the Hackney Division? What range of transfer prices would increase the financial performance of both divisions?

b. Suppose the Hackney Division increases production so that it could use 35,000 Graca Division notebook fans. How would the change in volume affect the range of transfer prices that would financially benefit both divisions?

## PROBLEMS—SERIES B

**LO 3**

### Problem 9-16B    *Determining controllable costs*

At a professional conference just a few days ago, Victor Norman, the president of Alexander Corporation, learned how the concept of controllability relates to performance evaluation. In preparing to put this new knowledge into practice, he reviewed the financial data of the company's sales department.

| | |
|---|---|
| Salaries of salespeople | $    350,000 |
| Cost of goods sold | 22,500,000 |
| Facility-level corporate costs | 410,000 |
| Travel expenses | 32,000 |
| Depreciation on equipment | 100,000 |
| Salary of the sales manager | 60,000 |
| Property taxes | 4,000 |
| Telephone expenses | 39,000 |

**Required**

Help Mr. Norman prepare a list of expenditures that the sales manager controls.

## Problem 9-17B   *Controllability, responsibility, and balanced scorecard*

Dean Ortiz, president of Springfield Corporation, evaluated the performance report of the company's production department. Mr. Ortiz was confused by some arguments presented by Angela Sloan, the production manager. Some relevant data follow.

| Variances | Amount | |
|---|---:|---|
| Materials usage variance | $100,000 | U |
| Materials price variance | 60,000 | F |
| Labor price variance | 19,000 | F |
| Labor usage variance | 69,000 | U |
| Volume variance | 150,000 | U |

Ms. Sloan argues that she had done a great job, noting the favorable materials price variance and labor price variance. She argued that she had had no control over factors causing the unfavorable variances. For example, she argued that the unfavorable materials usage variance was caused by the purchasing department's decision to buy substandard materials that resulted in a substantial amount of spoilage. Moreover, she argued that the unfavorable labor usage variance resulted from the substantial materials spoilage which in turn wasted many labor hours, as did the hiring of underqualified workers by the manager of the personnel department. Finally, she said that the sales department's failure to obtain a sufficient number of customer orders really caused the unfavorable volume variance.

### Required

a. What would you do first if you were Dean Ortiz?
b. Did Ms. Sloan deserve the credit she claimed for the favorable variances? Explain.
c. Was Ms. Sloan responsible for the unfavorable variances? Explain.
d. Explain how a balanced scorecard can be used to improve performance evaluation.

## Problem 9-18B   *Performance reports and evaluation*

The mortgage division of Thorn Financial Services, Inc., is managed by a vice president who supervises three regional operations. Each regional operation has a general manager and several branches directed by branch managers.

The Bronson region has two branches, Gasden and Vance. The March responsibility reports for the managers of these branches follow.

| | Budgeted* | Actual | Variance | |
|---|---:|---:|---:|---|
| **Gasden Branch** | | | | |
| Controllable costs | | | | |
| Employee compensation | $288,000 | $300,800 | $12,800 | U |
| Office supplies | 72,000 | 70,000 | 2,000 | F |
| Promotions | 152,000 | 128,000 | 24,000 | F |
| Maintenance | 16,000 | 21,200 | 5,200 | U |
| Total | $528,000 | $520,000 | $ 8,000 | F |
| **Vance Branch** | | | | |
| Controllable costs | | | | |
| Employee compensation | $260,000 | $250,000 | $10,000 | F |
| Office supplies | 76,000 | 84,000 | 8,000 | U |
| Promotions | 144,000 | 150,000 | 6,000 | U |
| Maintenance | 20,000 | 19,200 | 800 | F |
| Total | $500,000 | $503,200 | $ 3,200 | U |

*Thorn uses flexible budgets for performance evaluation.

Other pertinent cost data for March follow.

|  | Budgeted* | Actual |
|---|---|---|
| Cost data of other regions |  |  |
| Helena | $1,400,000 | $1,452,000 |
| Alabaster | 1,720,000 | 1,688,000 |
| Other costs controllable by |  |  |
| Bronson region general manager | 280,000 | 292,000 |
| Vice president of mortgage | 384,000 | 392,000 |

*Thorn uses flexible budgets for performance evaluation.

**Required**

a. Prepare a responsibility report for the general manager of the Bronson region.

b. Prepare a responsibility report for the vice president of the mortgage division.

c. Explain where the $24,000 favorable promotions variance in the Gasden branch manager's report is included in the vice president's report.

d. Based on the responsibility report prepared in Requirement *a*, explain where the Bronson region's general manager should concentrate her attention.

**LO 2**

### Problem 9-19B  *Different types of responsibility centers*

Kaito Industries, Inc., has five different divisions; each is responsible for producing and marketing a particular product line. The electronics division makes cellular telephones, pagers, and modems. The division also buys and sells other electronic products made by outside companies. Each division maintains sufficient working capital for its own operations. The corporate headquarters, however, makes decisions about long-term capital investments.

**Required**

a. For purposes of performance evaluation, should Kaito classify its electronic division as a cost center, a profit center, or an investment center? Why?

b. Would the manager of the electronics division be likely to conduct the operations of the division differently if the division were classified as a different type of responsibility center than the one you designated in Requirement *a*? Explain.

**LO 5, 7**

### Problem 9-20B  *Comparing return on investment and residual income*

Zimmerman Corporation operates three investment centers. The following financial statements apply to the investment center named Meier Division.

| MEIER DIVISION |  |
|---|---|
| Income Statement |  |
| For the Year Ended December 31, 2011 |  |
| Sales revenue | $250,975 |
| Cost of goods sold | (128,635) |
| Gross margin | 122,340 |
| Operating expenses |  |
| Selling expenses | (13,200) |
| Administrative expense | (2,400) |
| Operating income | 106,740 |
| Nonoperating expense |  |
| Interest expense | (6,800) |
| Net income | $ 99,940 |

**MEIER DIVISION**
Balance Sheet
As of December 31, 2011

| Assets | |
|---|---|
| Cash | $ 68,360 |
| Accounts receivable | 380,290 |
| Merchandise inventory | 53,750 |
| Equipment less accum. dep. | 428,600 |
| Nonoperating assets | 48,000 |
| Total assets | $979,000 |
| Liabilities | |
| Accounts payable | $115,000 |
| Notes payable | 100,000 |
| Stockholders' equity | |
| Common stock | 520,000 |
| Retained earnings | 244,000 |
| Total liab. and stk. equity | $979,000 |

**Required**

a. Should operating income or net income be used to determine the rate of return (ROI) for the Meier investment center? Explain your answer.

b. Should operating assets or total assets be used to determine the ROI for the Meier investment center? Explain your answer.

c. Calculate the ROI for Meier.

d. Zimmerman has a desired ROI of 8 percent. Headquarters has $300,000 of funds to assign to its investment centers. The manager of the Meier Division has an opportunity to invest the funds at an ROI of 10 percent. The other two divisions have investment opportunities that yield only 9 percent. Even so, the manager of Meier rejects the additional funding. Explain why the manager of Meier would reject the funds under these circumstances.

e. Explain how residual income could be used to encourage the manager to accept the additional funds.

## Problem 9-21B  *Return on investment*

LO 5, 6

Clifton Corporation's balance sheet indicates that the company has $100,000 invested in operating assets. During 2011, Clifton earned $16,000 of operating income on $320,000 of sales.

**Required**

a. Compute Clifton's operating profit margin for 2011.

b. Compute Clifton's turnover for 2011.

c. Compute Clifton's return on investment for 2011.

d. Recompute Clifton's ROI under each of the following independent assumptions.

   (1) Sales increase from $320,000 to $360,000, thereby resulting in an increase in operating income from $16,000 to $18,900.

   (2) Sales remain constant, but Clifton reduces expenses, thereby resulting in an increase in income from $16,000 to $16,800.

   (3) Clifton is able to reduce its operating assets from $100,000 to $96,000 without affecting income.

## Problem 9-22B  *Return on investment and residual income*

LO 5, 6, 7

Emery Company has operating assets of $3,600,000. The company's operating income for the most recent accounting period was $407,000. The Lindburg Division of Emery controls $1,200,000 of the company's assets and earned $175,000 of its operating income. Emery's desired ROI is 10 percent. Emery has $300,000 of additional funds to invest. The manager of the Lindburg Division believes that his division could earn $36,000 on the additional funds. The highest investment opportunity to any of the company's other divisions is 11 percent.

**Required**

a. If ROI is used as the sole performance measure, would the manager of the Lindburg Division be likely to accept or reject the additional funding? Why or why not?

b. Would Emery Company benefit if the manager of the Lindburg Division accepted the additional funds? Why or why not?

c. If residual income is used as the sole performance measure, would the manager of the Lindburg Division be likely to accept or reject the additional funding? Why or why not?

**LO 5, 6, 7**

**Problem 9-23B    *Return on investment and residual income***

Otway Trading Company (OTC) has three divisions. OTC has a desired rate of return of 14%. The operating assets and income for each division are as follows:

| Divisions | Operating Assets | Operating Income |
|---|---|---|
| Americas | $1,920,000 | $345,000 |
| Asia | 965,000 | 160,400 |
| Europe | 1,215,000 | 165,000 |
| Total | $4,100,000 | $670,400 |

OTC headquarters has $30,000 of additional cash to invest in one of its divisions. The division managers have identified investment opportunities that are expected to yield the following ROIs.

| Divisions | Expected ROIs for Additional Investments |
|---|---|
| Americas | 16% |
| Asia | 12 |
| Europe | 15 |

**Required**

a. Which division manager is currently producing the highest ROI?

b. Based on ROI, which division manager would be most eager to accept the $30,000 of investment funds?

c. Based on ROI, which division manager would be least likely to accept the $30,000 of investment funds?

d. Which division offers the best investment opportunity for OTC?

e. What is the term used to describe the apparent conflict between Requirements *b* and *d*?

f. Explain how the residual income performance measure could be used to motivate the managers to act in the best interest of the company.

g. Calculate the residual income:

   (1) At the corporate (headquarters) level before the additional investment.

   (2) At the division level before the additional investment.

   (3) At the investment level.

   (4) At the division level after the additional investment.

h. Based on residual income, which division manager would be most eager to accept the $30,000 investment opportunity?

**Appendix**

## Problem 9-24B   *Transfer pricing*

Laya Electronics Corporation makes a modem that it sells to retail stores for $75 each. The variable cost to produce a modem is $35 each; the total fixed cost is $5,000,000. Laya is operating at 80 percent of capacity and is producing 200,000 modems annually. Laya's parent company, Ocean Corporation, notified Laya's president that another subsidiary company, Leap Technologies, has begun making computers and can use Laya's modem as a part. Leap needs 40,000 modems annually and is able to acquire similar modems in the market for $72 each.

Under instructions from the parent company, the presidents of Laya and Leap meet to negotiate a price for the modem. Laya insists that its market price is $75 each and will stand firm on that price. Leap, on the other hand, wonders why it should even talk to Laya when Leap can get modems at a lower price.

**Required**

a.  What transfer price would you recommend?

b.  Discuss the effect of the intercompany sales on each president's return on investment.

c.  Should Laya be required to use more than excess capacity to provide modems to Leap if Leap's demand increases to 60,000 modems? In other words, should it sell some of the 200,000 modems that it currently sells to unrelated companies to Leap instead? Why or why not?

## ANALYZE, THINK, COMMUNICATE

### ATC 9-1   Business Applications Case   *Analyzing segments at Coca-Cola*

The following excerpt is from Coca-Cola Company's 2008 annual report filed with the SEC.

> Management evaluates the performance of our operating segments separately to individually monitor the different factors affecting financial performance. Our Company manages income taxes and financial costs, such as interest income and expense, on a global basis within the Corporate operating segment. We evaluate segment performance based on income or loss before income taxes.

Below are selected segment data for Coca-Cola Company for the 2008 and 2007 fiscal years. Dollar amounts are in millions.

| | Eurasia & Africa | Europe | Latin America | North America | Pacific |
|---|---|---|---|---|---|
| **2008 Fiscal Year** | | | | | |
| Net operating revenues | $2,327 | $5,801 | $3,835 | $ 8,280 | $4,695 |
| Income before taxes | 811 | 3,182 | 2,082 | 1,587 | 1,836 |
| Identifiable operating assets | 956 | 3,012 | 1,849 | 10,845 | 1,444 |
| **2007 Fiscal Year** | | | | | |
| Net operating revenues | $2,109 | $5,292 | $3,244 | $ 7,836 | $4,406 |
| Income before taxes | 696 | 2,796 | 1,752 | 1,665 | 761 |
| Identifiable operating assets | 1,023 | 2,997 | 1,989 | 10,510 | 1,468 |

**Required**

a.  Compute the ROI for each of Coke's geographical segments for each fiscal year. Which segment appears to have the best performance during 2008 based on ROI? Which segment showed the most improvement from 2007 to 2008?

b.  What factor seems most important in explaining why the ROI for North America is so much lower that the ROIs of other segments?

c.  Assuming Coke's management expects a minimum return of 30 percent, calculate the residual income for each segment for each fiscal year. Which segment appears to have the best performance based on residual income? Which segment showed the most improvement from 2007 to 2008?

**d.** Explain why the segment with the highest ROI in 2008 is not the segment with the highest residual income.

**e.** Assume the management of Coke is considering a major expansion effort for the next five years. On which geographic segment would you recommend Coke focus its expansion efforts? Explain the rationale for your answer.

### ATC 9-2   Group Assignment   *Return on investment versus residual income*

Bellco, a division of Becker International Corporation, is operated under the direction of Antoin Sedatt. Bellco is an independent investment center with approximately $72,000,000 of assets that generate approximately $8,640,000 in annual net income. Becker International has additional investment capital of $12,000,000 that is available for the division managers to invest. Mr. Sedatt is aware of an investment opportunity that will provide an 11 percent annual net return. Becker International's desired rate of return is 10 percent.

#### Required

Divide the class into groups of four or five students and then organize the groups into two sections. Assign Task 1 to the first section and Task 2 to the second section.

#### Group Tasks

1. Assume that Mr. Sedatt's performance is evaluated based on his ability to maximize return on investment (ROI). Compute ROI using the following two assumptions: Bellco retains its current asset size and Bellco accepts and invests the additional $12,000,000 of assets. Determine whether Mr. Sedatt should accept the opportunity to invest additional funds. Select a spokesperson to present the decision made by the group.

2. Assume that Mr. Sedatt's performance is evaluated based on his ability to maximize residual income. Compute residual income using the following two assumptions: Bellco retains its current asset base and Bellco accepts and invests the additional $12,000,000 of assets. Determine whether Mr. Sedatt should accept the opportunity to invest additional funds. Select a spokesperson to present the decision made by the group.

3. Have a spokesperson from one of the groups in the first section report the two ROIs and the group's recommendation for Mr. Sedatt. Have the groups in this section reach consensus on the ROI and the recommendation.

4. Have a spokesperson from the second section report the two amounts of residual income and disclose the group's recommendation for Mr. Sedatt. Have this section reach consensus on amounts of residual income.

5. Which technique (ROI or residual income) is more likely to result in suboptimization?

### ATC 9-3   Research Assignment   *Using real-world data from Berkshire Hathaway*

Obtain Berkshire Hathaway's (Berkshire) Form 10-K for the year ended December 31, 2008, and complete the requirements below. To obtain the Form 10-K you can use either the EDGAR system following the instructions in Appendix A, or it can be found under on the company's corporate website www.berkshirehathaway.com. The company's annual reports are also available on its website.

#### Required

**a.** Unlike most companies, Berkshire organizes the revenues and expenses on its earnings statements, and the assets and liabilities on its balance sheets, by major business segments. Calculate the return on investment for each segment of Berkshire's business using the *margin × turnover* method. For segment earnings, use earnings before taxes, which you will have to calculate. Show your computations.

**b.** Rank the segments' performance from best to worst, based on their ROIs.

**c.** Why did the best-performing segment do better than the next best? Was it profitability, the efficiency with which it used its assets, or both?

**ATC 9-4**   Writing Assignment   *Transfer pricing*

Green Lawn Mower, Inc., recently acquired Hallit Engines, a small engine manufacturing company. Green's president believes in decentralization and intends to permit Hallit to continue to operate as an independent entity. However, she has instructed the manager of Green's lawn mower assembly division to investigate the possibility of purchasing engines from Hallit instead of using the current third-party supplier. Hallit has excess capacity. The current full cost to produce each engine is $96. The avoidable cost of making engines is $78 per unit. The assembly division, which currently pays the third-party supplier $90 per engine, offers to purchase engines from Hallit at the $90 price. Hallit's president refuses the offer, stating that his company's engines are superior to those the third-party supplier provides. Hallit's president believes that the transfer price should be based on the market price for independent customers, which is $132 per engine. The manager of the assembly division agrees that Hallit's engines are higher quality than those currently being used but notes that Green's customer base is in the low-end, discount market. Putting more expensive engines on Green mowers would raise the price above the competition and would hurt sales. Green's president tries to negotiate a settlement between the assembly manager and Hallit's president, but the parties are unable to agree on a transfer price.

**Required**

a. Assuming that Green makes and sells 40,000 lawn mowers per year, what is the cost of suboptimization resulting from the failure to establish a transfer price?

b. Assume that you are a consultant asked by the president of Green to recommend whether a transfer price should be arbitrarily imposed. Write a brief memo that includes your recommendation and your justification for making it.

**ATC 9-5**   Ethical Dilemma   *Manipulating return on investment and residual income*

The October 5, 1998, issue of *BusinessWeek* includes the article "Who Can You Trust?" authored by Sarah Bartlett. Among other dubious accounting practices, the article describes a trick known as the "big bath," which occurs when a company makes huge unwarranted asset write-offs that drastically overstate expenses. Outside auditors (CPAs) permit companies to engage in the practice because the assets being written off are of questionable value. Because the true value of the assets cannot be validated, auditors have little recourse but to accept the valuations suggested by management. Recent examples of questionable write-offs include Motorola's $1.8 billion restructuring charge and the multibillion-dollar write-offs for "in-process" research taken by high-tech companies such as Compaq Computer Corp. and WorldCom, Inc.

**Required**

a. Why would managers want their companies to take a big bath? (*Hint:* Consider how a big bath affects return on investment and residual income in the years following the write-off.)

b. Annual reports are financial reports issued to the public. The reports are the responsibility of auditors who are CPAs who operate under the ethical standards promulgated by the American Institute of Certified Public Accountants. As a result, attempts to manipulate annual report data are not restricted by the Institute of Management Accountants Standards of Ethical Conduct shown in Exhibit 1.15 of Chapter 1. Do you agree or disagree with these statements? Explain your position.

**ATC 9-6**   Spreadsheet Assignment   *Using Excel*

Waldon Corporation's balance sheet shows that the company has $600,000 invested in operating assets. During 2010, Waldon earned $120,000 on $960,000 of sales. The company's desired return on investment (ROI) is 12 percent.

**Required**

a. Construct a spreadsheet to calculate ROI and residual income using these data. Build the spreadsheet using formulas so that the spreadsheet could be used as a template for any ROI or residual income problem. The following screen capture shows how to construct the template.

Spreadsheet screen — Microsoft Excel - ch09-working.xls

| | A | B | C | D | E | F | G | H | I | J | K | L | M |
|---|---|---|---|---|---|---|---|---|---|---|---|---|---|
| 1 | Chapter 9 - Working with Excel | | | | | | Name: | | | | | | |
| 3 | | Net Income | = | $ 120,000 | | | | | | | | | |
| 4 | | Sales | = | $ 960,000 | | | | | | | | | |
| 5 | | Investment | = | $ 600,000 | | | | | | | | | |
| 6 | | Desired ROI | = | 12.00% | | | | | | | | | |
| 8 | | ROI | = | Margin | | x | Turnover | | | | | | |
| 10 | | ROI | = | Net Income | | x | Sales | | | | | | |
| 11 | | | | Sales | | | Investment | | | | | | |
| 13 | | ROI | = | $ 120,000 | | x | $ 960,000 | | | | | | |
| 14 | | | | $ 960,000 | | | $ 600,000 | | | | | | |
| 16 | | ROI | = | 12.50% | | x | 1.60 | | | | | | |
| 17 | | ROI | = | 20.00% | | | | | | | | | |
| 20 | | Residual Income | = | Earned Income | | - | ( Investment | | x | Desired ROI ) | | | |
| 21 | | Residual Income | = | $ 120,000 | | - | ( $ 600,000 | | x | 12.00% ) | | | |
| 22 | | Residual Income | = | 120,000 | | - | 72,000 | | | | | | |
| 23 | | Residual Income | = | $ 48,000 | | | | | | | | | |

## Spreadsheet Tips

**(1)** The cells below row 12 that show numbers should all be based on formulas. This allows the results to be automatically recalculated based on changes in the data rows 3 to 6.

**(2)** The parentheses in columns F and J have been entered as text in columns that have a column width of 1.

## ATC 9-7  Spreadsheet Assignment  *Mastering Excel*

The Pillar Manufacturing Company has three identified levels of authority and responsibility. The organization chart as of December 31, 2011, appears as follows:

Pertinent expenses for Level 3 follow:

| | Budget | Actual |
|---|---|---|
| **Finishing Department** | | |
| Wages expense | $6,240 | $6,000 |
| Direct materials | 2,300 | 2,400 |
| Supplies | 840 | 980 |
| Small tools | 1,300 | 1,140 |
| Other | 700 | 820 |

Pertinent expenses for Level 2 follow:

| | Budget | Actual |
|---|---|---|
| Production Department | | |
| Administrative expenses | $ 1,200 | $ 1,400 |
| Supervisory salaries | 5,800 | 5,200 |
| Cutting Department | 6,800 | 6,420 |
| Finishing Department | 11,380 | 11,340 |

Pertinent expenses for Level 1 follow:

| | Budget | Actual |
|---|---|---|
| President's Office Expense | | |
| Supervisory salaries | $ 4,900 | $ 5,100 |
| Clerical staff | 800 | 400 |
| Other expenses | 600 | 700 |
| Production Department | 25,180 | 24,360 |
| Marketing Department | 8,850 | 8,300 |
| Finance Department | 5,900 | 6,220 |

### Required

a. Construct a spreadsheet that shows responsibility reports for the finishing department supervisor, the production vice president, and the president.

b. Include formulas in the responsibility reports that illustrate the interrelationships between these reports. For example, changes in the finishing department report should be automatically reflected in the production department report.

### Spreadsheet Tip

(1) Use the absolute value function [=ABS(value)] in the formulas that calculate the variances.

## COMPREHENSIVE PROBLEM

Assume Magnificent Modems (MM) is a division of Gilmore Business Products (GBP). GBP uses ROI as the primary measure of managerial performance. GBP has a desired return on investment (ROI) of 3 percent. The company has $100,000 of investment funds to be assigned to its divisions. The president of MM is aware of an investment opportunity for these funds that is expected to yield an ROI of 3.5 percent.

### Required

a. Explain why you believe the president of MM will accept or reject the $100,000 investment opportunity. Support your answer by calculating MM's existing ROI. Base your computation on the information contained in the income statement and balance sheet that you prepared in Chapter 1 (page 52).

b. Name the term used to describe the condition that exists in Requirement *a*. Provide a brief definition of this term.

c. If GBP changes its performance measurement criteria from ROI to residual income (RI), will the new evaluation approach affect the President's decision to accept or reject the $100,000 investment opportunity? Support your answer by calculating MM's residual income for the investment opportunity.

## CHAPTER 10

# Planning for Capital Investments

## LEARNING OBJECTIVES

**After you have mastered the material in this chapter you will be able to:**

**1** Explain the time value of money concept and apply it to capital investment decisions.

**2** Determine the present value of future cash flows.

**3** Determine and interpret the net present value of an investment opportunity.

**4** Determine and interpret the internal rate of return of an investment opportunity.

**5** Identify cash flows associated with an investment opportunity.

**6** Compare capital investment alternatives.

**7** Determine the payback period for an investment opportunity.

**8** Determine the unadjusted rate of return for an investment opportunity.

**9** Conduct a postaudit of a completed investment.

## CHAPTER OPENING

The president of EZ Rentals (EZ) is considering expanding the company's rental service business to include LCD projectors that can be used with notebook computers. A marketing study forecasts that renting projectors could generate revenue of $200,000 per year. The possibility of increasing revenue is alluring, but EZ's president has a number of unanswered questions. How much do the projectors cost? What is their expected useful life? Will they have a salvage value? Does EZ have the money to buy them? Does EZ have the technical expertise to support the product? How much will training cost? How long will customer demand last? What if EZ buys the projectors and they become technologically obsolete? How quickly will EZ be able to recover the investment? Are there more profitable ways to invest EZ's funds?

Spending large sums of money that will have long-term effects on company profits makes most managers anxious. What if a cell phone manufacturer spends millions of dollars to build a factory in the United States and its competitors locate their manufacturing facilities in countries that provide cheap labor? The manufacturer's cell phones will be overpriced, but it cannot move overseas because it cannot find a buyer for the factory. What if a pharmaceutical company spends millions of dollars to develop a drug which then fails to receive FDA approval? What if a communications company installs underground cable but satellite transmission steals its market? What if a company buys computer equipment that rapidly becomes technologically obsolete? Although these possibilities may be remote, they can be expensive when they do occur. For example, Wachovia Bank's 1997 annual report discloses a $70 million dollar write-off of computer equipment. This chapter discusses some of the analytical techniques companies use to evaluate major investment opportunities.

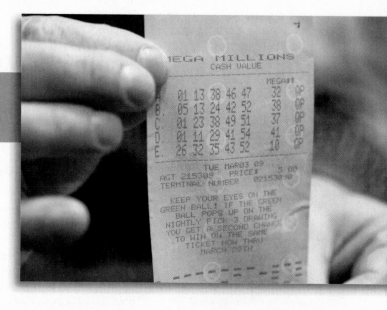

# The Curious Accountant

The August 28, 2009, drawing for the Mega millions multi-state lottery produced two winning tickets. The tickets, which were purchased in California and New York, had an advertised value of $338 million. This amount, however, was based on the assumption that the winners would take their prize as 26 equal annual payments of $14,153,384. If the winnings were taken in this manner, the first payment would be made immediately, and the others would be paid annually over the next 25 years. The winner also had the option of taking an immediate, lump-sum payment of $231 million. With two winning tickets, each winner would receive one-half of these amounts.

Assume that you work as a personal financial planner and that one of your clients held one of the winning lottery tickets. If you think you could invest your client's winnings and earn an annual return of 7 percent, would you advise your client to take the lump-sum payment or the annual payments? Why? (The answer is on page 457.)

# CAPITAL INVESTMENT DECISIONS

Explain the time value of money concept and apply it to capital investment decisions.

Purchases of long-term operational assets are **capital investments.** Capital investments differ from stock and bond investments in an important respect. Investments in stocks and bonds can be sold in organized markets such as the New York Stock Exchange. In contrast, investments in capital assets normally can be recovered only by using those assets. Once a company purchases a capital asset, it is committed to that investment for an extended period of time. If the market turns sour, the company is stuck with the consequences. It may also be unable to seize new opportunities because its capital is committed. Business profitability ultimately hinges, to a large extent, on the quality of a few key capital investment decisions.

A capital investment decision is essentially a decision to exchange current cash outflows for the expectation of receiving future cash inflows. For EZ Rentals, purchasing LCD projectors, cash outflows today, provides the opportunity to collect $200,000 per year in rental revenue, cash inflows in the future. Assuming the projectors have useful lives of four years and no salvage value, how much should EZ be willing to pay for the future cash inflows? If you were EZ's president, would you spend $700,000 today to receive $200,000 each year for the next four years? You would give up $700,000 today for the opportunity to receive $800,000 (4 × $200,000) in the future. What if you collect less than $200,000 per year? If revenue is only $160,000 per year, you would lose $60,000 [$700,000 − (4 × $160,000)]. Is $700,000 too much to pay for the opportunity to receive $200,000 per year for four years? If $700,000 is too much, would you spend $600,000? If not, how about $500,000? There is no one right answer to these questions. However, understanding the *time value of money* concept can help you develop a rational response.

## Time Value of Money

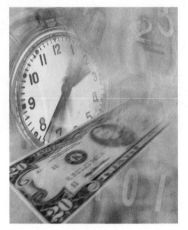

The **time value of money** concept recognizes that *the present value of a dollar received in the future is less than a dollar.* For example, you may be willing to pay only $0.90 today for a promise to receive $1.00 one year from today. The further into the future the receipt is expected to occur, the smaller is its present value. In other words, one dollar to be received two years from today is worth less than one dollar to be received one year from today. Likewise, one dollar to be received three years from today is less valuable than one dollar to be received two years from today, and so on.

The present value of cash inflows decreases as the time until expected receipt increases for several reasons. First, you could deposit today's dollar in a savings account to earn *interest* that increases its total value. If you wait for your money, you lose the opportunity to earn interest. Second, the expectation of receiving a future dollar carries an element of *risk.* Changed conditions may result in the failure to collect. Finally, *inflation* diminishes the buying power of the dollar. In other words, the longer you must wait to receive a dollar, the less you will be able to buy with it.

When a company invests in capital assets, it sacrifices present dollars in exchange for the opportunity to receive future dollars. Since trading current dollars for future dollars is risky, companies expect compensation before they invest in capital assets. The compensation a company expects is called *return on investment (ROI).* As discussed in Chapter 9, ROI is expressed as a percentage of the investment. For example, the ROI for a $1,000 investment that earns annual income of $100 is 10 percent ($100 ÷ $1,000 = 10%).

## Determining the Minimum Rate of Return

To establish the minimum expected *return on investment* before accepting an investment opportunity, most companies consider their cost of capital. To attract capital, companies must provide benefits to their creditors and owners. Creditors expect interest payments; owners expect dividends and increased stock value. Companies that earn lower returns than their cost of capital eventually go bankrupt; they cannot continually pay out more than they collect. *The* **cost of capital** *represents the* **minimum rate of return** *on investments.* Calculating the cost of capital is a complex exercise which is beyond the scope of this text. It is addressed in finance courses. We discuss how management accountants *use* the cost of capital to evaluate investment opportunities. Companies describe the cost of capital in a variety of ways: the *minimum rate of return,* the *desired rate of return,* the *required rate of return,* the *hurdle rate,* the *cutoff rate,* or the *discount rate.* These terms are used interchangeably throughout this chapter.

---

## ✓ CHECK YOURSELF 10.1

Study the following cash inflow streams expected from two different potential investments.

|  | Year 1 | Year 2 | Year 3 | Total |
|---|---|---|---|---|
| Alternative 1 | $2,000 | $3,000 | $4,000 | $9,000 |
| Alternative 2 | 4,000 | 3,000 | 2,000 | 9,000 |

Based on visual observation alone, which alternative has the higher present value? Why?

**Answer**   Alternative 2 has the higher present value. The size of the discount increases as the length of the time period increases. In other words, a dollar received in year 3 has a lower present value than a dollar received in year 1. Since most of the expected cash inflows from Alternative 2 are received earlier than those from Alternative 1, Alternative 2 has a higher present value even though the total expected cash inflows are the same.

---

## CONVERTING FUTURE CASH INFLOWS TO THEIR EQUIVALENT PRESENT VALUES

Given a desired rate of return and the amount of a future cash flow, present value can be determined using algebra. To illustrate, refer to the $200,000 EZ expects to earn the first year it leases LCD projectors.[1] Assuming EZ desires a 12 percent rate of return, what amount of cash would EZ be willing to invest today (present value outflow) to obtain a $200,000 cash inflow at the end of the year (future value)? The answer follows:[2]

Determine the present value of future cash flows.

$$\text{Investment} + (0.12 \times \text{Investment}) = \text{Future cash inflow}$$

$$1.12 \text{ Investment} = \$200,000$$

$$\text{Investment} = \$200,000 \div 1.12$$

$$\text{Investment} = \$178,571$$

If EZ invests $178,571 cash on January 1 and earns a 12 percent return on the investment, EZ will have $200,000 on December 31. An investor who is able to earn a 12 percent return on investment is indifferent between having $178,571 now or receiving

---

[1]The following computations assume the $200,000 cash inflow is received on the last day of each year. In actual practice the timing of cash inflows is less precise and present value computations are recognized to be approximate, not exact.

[2]All computations in this chapter are rounded to the nearest whole dollar.

$200,000 one year from now. The two options are equal, as shown in the following mathematical proof:

$$\text{Investment} + (0.12 \times \text{Investment}) = \$200,000$$

$$\$178,571 + (0.12 \times \$178,571) = \$200,000$$

$$\$178,571 + \$21,429 = \$200,000$$

$$\$200,000 = \$200,000$$

## Present Value Table for Single-Amount Cash Inflows

The algebra illustrated above is used to convert a one-time future receipt of cash to its present value. One-time receipts of cash are frequently called **single-payment,** or **lump-sum,** cash flows. Because EZ desires a 12 percent rate of return, the present value of the first cash inflow is $178,571. We can also determine the present value of a $200,000 single amount (lump sum) at the end of the second, third, and fourth years. Instead of using cumbersome algebraic computations to convert these future values to their present value equivalents, financial analysts frequently use a table of conversion factors to convert future values to their present value equivalents. The table of conversion factors used to convert future values into present values is commonly called a **present value table.**[3] A typical present value table presents columns with different return rates and rows with different periods of time, like Table 1 in the Appendix located at the end of this chapter.

To illustrate using the present value table, locate the conversion factor in Table 1 at the intersection of the 12% column and the one-period row. The conversion factor is 0.892857. Multiplying this factor by the $200,000 expected cash inflow yields $178,571 ($200,000 × 0.892857). This is the same value determined algebraically in the previous section of this chapter. The conversion factors in the present value tables simplify converting future values to present values.

The conversion factors for the second, third, and fourth periods are 0.797194, 0.711780, and 0.635518, respectively. These factors are in the 12% column at rows 2, 3, and 4, respectively. Locate these factors in Table 1 of the Appendix. Multiplying the conversion factors by the future cash inflow for each period produces their present value equivalents, shown in Exhibit 10.1. Exhibit 10.1 indicates that investing $607,470 today at a 12 percent rate of return is equivalent to receiving $200,000 per year for four years. Because EZ Rentals desires to earn (at least) a 12 percent rate of return, the company should be willing to pay up to $607,470 to purchase the LCD projectors.

## Present Value Table for Annuities

The algebra described previously for converting equal lump-sum cash inflows to present value equivalents can be further simplified by adding the present value table factors

---

### EXHIBIT 10.1

**Present Value of a $200,000 Cash Inflow to be Received for Four Years**

| PV | = | FV | × | Present Value Table Factor | = | Present Value Equivalent |
|---|---|---|---|---|---|---|
| Period 1 PV | = | $200,000 | × | 0.892857 | = | $178,571 |
| Period 2 PV | = | 200,000 | × | 0.797194 | = | 159,439 |
| Period 3 PV | = | 200,000 | × | 0.711780 | = | 142,356 |
| Period 4 PV | = | 200,000 | × | 0.635518 | = | 127,104 |
| Total | | | | | | $607,470 |

---

[3]The present value table is based on the formula $[1 \div (1 + r)^n]$ where $r$ equals the rate of return and $n$ equals the number of periods.

together before multiplying them by the cash inflows. The total of the present value table factors in Exhibit 10.1 is 3.037349 (0.892857 + 0.797194 + 0.711780 + 0.635518). Multiplying this **accumulated conversion factor** by the expected annual cash inflow results in the same present value equivalent of $607,470 ($200,000 × 3.037349). As with lump-sum conversion factors, accumulated conversion factors can be calculated and organized in a table with *columns* for different rates of return and *rows* for different periods of time. Table 2 in the Appendix is a present value table of accumulated conversion factors. Locate the conversion factor at the intersection of the 12% column and the fourth time-period row. The factor at this intersection is 3.037349, confirming that the accumulated conversion factors represent the sum of the single-payment conversion factors.

The conversion factors in Table 2 apply to annuities. An **annuity** is a series of cash flows that meets three criteria: (1) equal payment amounts; (2) equal time intervals between payments; and (3) a constant rate of return. For EZ Rentals, the expected cash inflows from renting LCD projectors are all for equivalent amounts ($200,000); the expected intervals between cash inflows are equal lengths of time (one year); and the rate of return for each inflow is constant at 12 percent. The series of expected cash inflows from renting the projectors is therefore an annuity. The present value of an annuity table can be used only if all of these conditions are satisfied.

The present value of an annuity table (Table 2) simplifies converting future cash inflows to their present value equivalents. EZ Rentals can convert the cash inflows as shown in Exhibit 10.1, using four conversion factors, multiplying each conversion factor by the annual cash inflow (four multiplications), and adding the resulting products. In contrast, EZ can recognize that the series of payments is an annuity, which requires multiplying a single conversion factor from Table 2 by the amount of the annuity payment. Regardless of the conversion method, the result is the same (a present value of $607,470). Recall that EZ can also make the conversion using algebra. The table values are derived from algebraic formulas. The present value tables reduce the computations needed to convert future values to present values.

## Software Programs that Calculate Present Values

Software programs offer an even more efficient means of converting future values into present value equivalents. These programs are frequently built into handheld financial calculators and computer spreadsheet programs. As an example, we demonstrate the procedures used in a Microsoft Excel spreadsheet.

An Excel spreadsheet offers a variety of financial functions, one of which converts a future value annuity into its present value equivalent. This present value function uses the syntax *PV(rate,nper,pmt)* in which *rate* is the desired rate of return, *nper* is the number of periods, and *pmt* is the amount of the payment (periodic cash inflow). To convert a future value annuity into its present value equivalent, provide the function with the appropriate amounts for the rate, number of periods, and amount of the annuity (cash inflows) into a spreadsheet cell. Press the Enter key and the present value equivalent appears in the spreadsheet cell.

The power of the spreadsheet to perform computations instantly is extremely useful for answering what-if questions. Exhibit 10.2 demonstrates this power by providing spreadsheet conversions for three different scenarios. The first scenario demonstrates the annuity assumptions for EZ Rentals, providing the present value equivalent ($607,470) of a four-year cash inflow of $200,000 per year at a 12 percent rate of interest. The present value is a *negative* number. This format indicates that an initial $607,470 *cash outflow* is required to obtain the four-year series of cash inflows. The present value equivalent in Scenario 2 shows the present value if the annuity assumptions reflect a 14 percent, rather than 12 percent, desired rate of return. The present value equivalent in Scenario 3 shows the present value if the annuity assumptions under Scenario 1 are changed to reflect annual cash inflows of $300,000, rather than $200,000. A wide range of scenarios could be readily considered by changing any or all the variables in the spreadsheet function. In each case, the computer does the calculations, giving the manager more time to analyze the data rather than compute it.

**EXHIBIT 10.2**

**Microsoft Excel Spreadsheet Present Value Function**

| | A | B | C | D | E | F | G | H | I | J |
|---|---|---|---|---|---|---|---|---|---|---|
| 1 | | | | | | | | | | |
| 2 | | PV(rate,nper,pmt) | | | | | | | | |
| 3 | | | | | | | | | | |
| 4 | | Scenario 1 | | | | | | | | |
| 5 | | PV(0.12,4,200000) | | | | | | | | |
| 6 | | ($607,470) | | | | | | | | |
| 7 | | | | | | | | | | |
| 8 | | Scenario 2 | | | | | | | | |
| 9 | | PV(0.14,4,200000) | | | | | | | | |
| 10 | | ($582,742) | | | | | | | | |
| 11 | | | | | | | | | | |
| 12 | | Scenario 3 | | | | | | | | |
| 13 | | PV(0.12,4,300000) | | | | | | | | |
| 14 | | ($911,205) | | | | | | | | |
| 15 | | | | | | | | | | |

Although software is widely used in business practice, the diversity of interfaces used by different calculators and spreadsheet programs makes it unsuitable for textbook presentations. This text uses the present value tables in the Appendix in the text illustrations and the end-of-chapter exercises and problems. If you use software to solve these problems, your answers will be the same. All these tools—formulas, conversion tables, software—are based on the same mathematical principles and will produce the same results.

## Ordinary Annuity Assumption

All the conversion methods described above assume the cash inflows occur at the *end* of each accounting period. This distribution pattern is called an **ordinary annuity.**[4] In practice, cash inflows are likely to be received throughout the period, not just at the end. For example, EZ Rentals is likely to collect cash revenue from renting projectors each month rather than in a single lump-sum receipt at the end of each of the four years. Companies frequently use the ordinary annuity assumption in practice because it simplifies time value of money computations. Because capital investment decisions are necessarily based on uncertain projections about future cash inflows, the lives of investment opportunities, and the appropriate rates of return, achieving pinpoint accuracy is impossible. Sacrificing precision for simplicity by using the ordinary annuity assumption is a reasonable trade-off in the decision-making process.

## Reinvestment Assumption

The present value computations in the previous sections show that investing $607,470 today at a 12 percent rate of return is equivalent to receiving four individual $200,000 payments at the end of four successive years. Exhibit 10.3 illustrates that a cash inflow of $200,000 per year is equivalent to earning a 12 percent rate of return on a $607,470 investment.[5]

---

[4]When equal cash inflows occur at the *beginning* of each accounting period, the distribution is called an *annuity due.* Although some business transactions are structured as annuities due, they are less common than ordinary annuities. This text focuses on the ordinary annuity assumption.

[5]Exhibit 10.3 is analogous to an amortization table for a long-term note with equal payments of principal and interest.

## EXHIBIT 10.3

### Cash Flow Classifications for EZ's Investment in Projectors

| Time Period | (a) Investment Balance During the Year | (b) Annual Cash Inflow | (c) Return on Investment (a × 0.12) | (d) Recovered Investment (b − c) | (e) Year-End Investment Balance (a − d) |
|---|---|---|---|---|---|
| 1 | $607,470 | $200,000 | $ 72,896 | $127,104 | $480,366 |
| 2 | 480,366 | 200,000 | 57,644 | 142,356 | 338,010 |
| 3 | 338,010 | 200,000 | 40,561 | 159,439 | 178,571 |
| 4 | 178,571 | 200,000 | 21,429 | 178,571 | 0 |
| Totals | | $800,000 | $192,530 | $607,470 | |

It is customary to assume that the desired rate of return includes the effects of *compounding*.[6] Saying an investment is "earning the desired rate of return," assumes the cash inflows generated by the investment are reinvested at the desired rate of return. In this case, we are assuming that EZ will reinvest the $200,000 annual cash inflows in other investments that will earn a 12 percent return.

## TECHNIQUES FOR ANALYZING CAPITAL INVESTMENT PROPOSALS

Managers can choose from among numerous analytical techniques to help them make capital investment decisions. Each technique has advantages and disadvantages. A manager may apply more than one technique to a particular proposal to take advantage of more information. Since most companies have computer capabilities that include a variety of standard capital budgeting programs, applying different techniques to the same proposal normally requires little extra effort. Limiting analysis to only one tool could produce biased results. Obtaining more than one perspective offers substantial benefit.

### Net Present Value

By using the present value conversion techniques described earlier, EZ Rentals' management determined it would be willing to invest $607,470 today (present value) to obtain a four-year, $200,000 future value annuity cash inflow. The $607,470 investment is *not* the cost of the LCD projectors; it is the amount EZ is willing to pay for them. The projectors may cost EZ Rentals more or less than their present value. To determine whether EZ should invest in the projectors, management must compare the present value of the future cash inflows ($607,470) to the cost of the projectors (the current cash outflow required to purchase them). Subtracting the cost of the investment from the present value of the future cash inflows determines the **net present value** of the investment opportunity. A positive net present value indicates the investment will yield a rate of return higher than 12 percent. A negative net present value means the return is less than 12 percent.

**LO 3**

Determine and interpret the net present value of an investment opportunity.

[6]*Compounding* refers to reinvesting investment proceeds so the total amount of invested capital increases, resulting in even higher returns. For example, assume $100 is invested at a 10 percent compounded annual rate of return. At the end of the first year, the investment yields a $10 return ($100 × 0.10). The $10 return plus any recovered investment is reinvested so that the total amount of invested capital at the beginning of the second year is $110. The return for the second year is $11 ($110 × 0.10). All funds are reinvested so that the return for the third year is $12.10 [($110 + $11) × 0.10].

To illustrate, assume EZ can purchase the projectors for $582,742. Assuming the desired rate of return is 12 percent, EZ should buy them. The net present value of the investment opportunity is computed as follows.

| | |
|---|---|
| Present value of future cash inflows | $607,470 |
| Cost of investment (required cash outflow) | (582,742) |
| Net present value | $ 24,728 |

The positive net present value suggests the investment will earn a rate of return in excess of 12 percent (if cash flows are indeed $200,000 each year). Because the projected rate of return is higher than the desired rate of return, this analysis suggests EZ should accept the investment opportunity. Based on the above analysis we are able to establish the following decision rule:

**Net present value decision rule:** If the net present value is equal to or greater than zero, accept the investment opportunity.

---

### ✓ CHECK YOURSELF 10.2

To increase productivity, Wald Corporation is considering the purchase of a new machine that costs $50,000. Wald expects using the machine to increase annual net cash inflows by $12,500 for each of the next five years. Wald desires a minimum annual rate of return of 10 percent on the investment. Determine the net present value of the investment opportunity and recommend whether Wald should acquire the machine.

**Answer**

Present value of future cash flows = Future cash flow × Table 2 factor ($n = 5$, $r = 10\%$)

Present value of future cash flows = $12,500 × 3.790787 = $47,385

Net present value = PV of future cash flows − Cost of machine

Net present value = $47,385 − $50,000 = ($2,615)

The negative net present value indicates the investment will yield a rate of return below the desired rate of return. Wald should not acquire the new machine.

---

## Internal Rate of Return

Determine and interpret the internal rate of return of an investment opportunity.

The net present value method indicates EZ's investment in the projectors will provide a return in excess of the desired rate, but it does not provide the actual rate of return to expect from the investment. If EZ's management team wants to know the rate of return to expect from investing in the projectors, it must use the *internal rate of return method*. The **internal rate of return** is the rate at which the present value of cash inflows equals the cash outflows. It is the rate that will produce a zero net present value. For EZ Rentals, the internal rate of return can be determined as follows. First, compute the *present value table factor* for a $200,000 annuity that would yield a $582,742 present value cash outflow (cost of investment).

Present value table factor × $200,000 = $582,742

Present value table factor = $582,742 ÷ $200,000

Present value table factor = 2.91371

Second, since the expected annual cash inflows represent a four-year annuity, scan Table 2 in the Appendix at period $n = 4$. Try to locate the table factor 2.91371.

The rate listed at the top of the column in which the factor is located is the internal rate of return. Turn to Table 2 and determine the internal rate of return for EZ Rentals before you read further. The above factor is in the 14 percent column. The difference in the table value (2.913712) and the value computed here (2.91371) is not significant. If EZ invests $582,742 in the projectors and they produce a $200,000 annual cash flow for four years, EZ will earn a 14 percent rate of return on the investment.

The *internal rate of return* may be compared with a *desired rate of return* to determine whether to accept or reject a particular investment project. Assuming EZ desires to earn a minimum rate of return of 12 percent, the preceding analysis suggests it should accept the investment opportunity because the internal rate of return (14 percent) is higher than the desired rate of return (12 percent). An internal rate of return below the desired rate suggests management should reject a particular proposal. The desired rate of return is sometimes called the *cutoff rate* or the *hurdle rate*. To be accepted, an investment proposal must provide an internal rate of return higher than the hurdle rate, cutoff rate, or desired rate of return. These terms are merely alternatives for the *cost of capital*. Ultimately, to be accepted, an investment must provide an internal rate of return higher than a company's cost of capital. Based on the above analysis we are able to establish the following decision rule:

**Internal rate of return decision rule:** If the internal rate of return is equal to or greater than the desired rate of return, accept the investment opportunity.

## TECHNIQUES FOR MEASURING INVESTMENT CASH FLOWS

The EZ Rentals example represents a simple capital investment analysis. The investment option involved only one cash outflow and a single annuity inflow. Investment opportunities often involve a greater variety of cash outflows and inflows. The following section of this chapter discusses different types of cash flows encountered in business practice.

Identify cash flows associated with an investment opportunity.

### Cash Inflows

*Cash inflows* generated from capital investments come from *four basic sources.* As in the case of EZ Rentals, the most common source of cash inflows is incremental revenue. **Incremental revenue** refers to the *additional* cash inflows from operating activities generated by using additional capital assets. For example, a taxi company expects revenues from taxi fares to increase if it purchases additional taxicabs. Similarly, investing in new apartments should increase rent revenue; opening a new store should result in additional sales revenue.

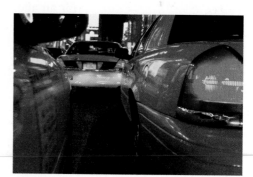

A second type of cash inflow results from *cost savings.* Decreases in cash outflows have the same beneficial effect as increases in cash inflows. Either way, a firm's cash position improves. For example, purchasing an automated computer system may enable a company to reduce cash outflows for salaries. Similarly, relocating a manufacturing facility closer to its raw materials source can reduce cash outflows for transportation costs.

An investment's *salvage value* provides a third source of cash inflows. Even when one company has finished using an asset, the asset may still be useful to another company. Many assets are sold after a company no longer wishes to use them. The salvage value represents a one-time cash inflow obtained when a company terminates an investment.

Companies can also experience a cash inflow through a *reduction in the amount of* **working capital** needed to support an investment. A certain level of working capital is required to support most business investments. For example, a new retail store outlet requires cash, receivables, and inventory to operate. When an investment is terminated, the decrease in the working capital commitment associated with the investment normally results in a cash inflow.

## Cash Outflows

*Cash outflows* fall into *three primary categories.* One category consists of outflows for the *initial investment.* Managers must be alert to all the cash outflows connected with purchasing a capital asset. The purchase price, transportation costs, installation costs, and training costs are examples of typical cash outflows related to an initial investment.

A second category of cash outflows may result from *increases in operating expenses.* If a company increases output capacity by investing in additional equipment, it may experience higher utility bills, labor costs, and maintenance expenses when it places the equipment into service. These expenditures increase cash outflows.

Third, *increases in working capital* commitments result in cash outflows. Frequently, investments in new assets must be supported by a certain level of working capital. For example, investing in a copy machine requires spending cash to maintain a supply of paper and toner. Managers should treat an increased working capital commitment as a cash outflow in the period the commitment occurs.

Exhibit 10.4 lists the cash inflows and outflows discussed above. The list is not exhaustive but does summarize the most common cash flows businesses experience.

---

**EXHIBIT 10.4**

**Typical Cash Flows Associated With Capital Investments**

| Inflows | Outflows |
|---|---|
| 1. Incremental revenue | 1. Initial investment |
| 2. Cost savings | 2. Incremental expenses |
| 3. Salvage values | 3. Working capital commitments |
| 4. Recovery of working capital | |

---

## TECHNIQUES FOR COMPARING ALTERNATIVE CAPITAL INVESTMENT OPPORTUNITIES

**LO 6**

Compare capital investment alternatives.

The management of Torres Transfer Company is considering two investment opportunities. One alternative, involving the purchase of new equipment for $80,000, would enable Torres to modernize its maintenance facility. The equipment has an expected useful life of five years and a $4,000 salvage value. It would replace existing equipment that had originally cost $45,000. The existing equipment has a current book value of $15,000 and a trade-in value of $5,000. The old equipment is technologically obsolete but can operate for an additional five years. On the day Torres purchases the new equipment, it would also pay the equipment manufacturer $3,000 for training costs to teach employees to operate the new equipment. The modernization has two primary advantages. One, it will improve management of the small parts inventory. The company's accountant believes that by the end of the first year, the carrying value of the small parts inventory could be reduced by $12,000. Second, the modernization is expected to increase efficiency, resulting in a $21,500 reduction in annual operating expenses.

The other investment alternative available to Torres is purchasing a truck. Adding another truck would enable Torres to expand its delivery area and increase revenue. The truck costs $115,000. It has a useful life of five years and a $30,000 salvage value. Operating the truck will require the company to increase its inventory of supplies, its petty cash account, and its accounts receivable and payable balances. These changes would add $5,000 to the company's working capital base immediately upon buying the truck. The working capital cash outflow is expected to be recovered at the end of the truck's useful life. The truck is expected to produce $69,000 per year in additional revenues. The driver's salary and other operating expenses are expected to be $32,000 per year. A major overhaul costing $20,000 is expected to be required at the end of the third year of operation. Assuming Torres desires to earn a rate of return of 14 percent, which of the two investment alternatives should it choose?

### Net Present Value

Begin the analysis by calculating the net present value of the two investment alternatives. Exhibit 10.5 shows the computations. Study this exhibit. Each alternative is analyzed using three steps. Step 1 requires identifying all cash inflows; some may be annuities, and others may be lump-sum receipts. In the case of Alternative 1, the cost

## EXHIBIT 10.5

### Net Present Value Analysis

| | Amount | × | Conversion Factor | = | Present Value |
|---|---:|:---:|:---:|:---:|---:|
| **Alternative 1: Modernize Maintenance Facility** | | | | | |
| Step 1: Cash inflows | | | | | |
| 1. Cost savings | $21,500 | × | 3.433081* | = | $ 73,811 |
| 2. Salvage value | 4,000 | × | 0.519369† | = | 2,077 |
| 3. Working capital recovery | 12,000 | × | 0.877193‡ | = | 10,526 |
| Total | | | | | $ 86,414 |
| Step 2: Cash outflows | | | | | |
| 1. Cost of equipment | | | | | |
| ($80,000 cost—$5,000 trade-in) | $75,000 | × | 1.000000§ | = | $ 75,000 |
| 2. Training costs | 3,000 | × | 1.000000§ | = | 3,000 |
| Total | | | | | $ 78,000 |
| Step 3: Net present value | | | | | |
| Total present value of cash inflows | | | | | $ 86,414 |
| Total present value of cash outflows | | | | | (78,000) |
| Net present value | | | | | $  8,414 |
| **Alternative 2: Purchase Delivery Truck** | | | | | |
| Step 1: Cash inflows | | | | | |
| 1. Incremental revenue | $69,000 | × | 3.433081* | = | $236,883 |
| 2. Salvage value | 30,000 | × | 0.519369† | = | 15,581 |
| 3. Working capital recovery | 5,000 | × | 0.519369† | = | 2,597 |
| Total | | | | | $255,061 |
| Step 2: Cash outflows | | | | | |
| 1. Cost of truck | $115,000 | × | 1.000000§ | = | $115,000 |
| 2. Working capital increase | 5,000 | × | 1.000000§ | = | 5,000 |
| 3. Increased operating expense | 32,000 | × | 3.433081§§ | = | 109,859 |
| 4. Major overhaul | 20,000 | × | 0.674972§§ | = | 13,499 |
| Total | | | | | $243,358 |
| Step 3: Net present value | | | | | |
| Total present value of cash inflows | | | | | $255,061 |
| Total present value of cash outflows | | | | | (243,358) |
| Net present value | | | | | $ 11,703 |

*Present value of annuity table 2, $n = 5$, $r = 14\%$.
†Present value of single payment table 1, $n = 5$, $r = 14\%$.
‡Present value of single payment table 1, $n = 1$, $r = 14\%$.
§Present value at beginning of period 1.
§§Present value of single payment table 1, $n = 3$, $r = 14\%$.

saving is an annuity, and the inflow from the salvage value is a lump-sum receipt. Once the cash inflows have been identified, the appropriate conversion factors are identified and the cash inflows are converted to their equivalent present values. Step 2 follows the same process to determine the present value of the cash outflows. Step 3 subtracts the present value of the outflows from the present value of the inflows to determine the net present value. The same three-step approach is used to determine the net present value of Alternative 2.

With respect to Alternative 1, the original cost and the book value of the existing equipment are ignored. As indicated in a previous chapter, these measures represent *sunk costs;* they are not relevant to the decision. The concept of relevance applies to long-term capital investment decisions just as it applies to the short-term special decisions that were discussed in Chapter 5. To be relevant to a capital investment decision, costs or revenues must involve different present and future cash flows for each alternative. Since the historical cost of the old equipment does not differ between the alternatives, it is not relevant.

Since the *net present value* of each investment alternative is *positive,* either investment will generate a return in excess of 14 percent. Which investment is the more favorable? The data could mislead a careless manager. Alternative 2 might seem the better choice because it has a greater present value than Alternative 1 ($11,703 vs. $8,414). Net present value, however, is expressed in *absolute dollars.* The net present value of a more costly capital investment can be greater than the net present value of a smaller investment even though the smaller investment earns a higher rate of return.

To compare different size investment alternatives, management can compute a **present value index** by dividing the present value of cash inflows by the present value of cash outflows. *The higher the ratio, the higher the rate of return per dollar invested in the proposed project.* The present value indices for the two alternatives Torres Transfer Company is considering are as follows.

$$\text{Present value index for Alternative 1} = \frac{\text{Present value of cash inflows}}{\text{Present value of cash outflows}} = \frac{\$86,414}{\$78,000} = 1.108$$

$$\text{Present value index for Alternative 2} = \frac{\text{Present value of cash inflows}}{\text{Present value of cash outflows}} = \frac{\$255,061}{\$243,358} = 1.048$$

Management can use the present value indices to rank the investment alternatives. In this case, Alternative 1 yields a higher return than Alternative 2.

## Internal Rate of Return

Management can also rank investment alternatives using the internal rate of return for each investment. Generally, *the higher the internal rate of return, the more profitable the investment.* We previously demonstrated how to calculate the internal rate of return for an investment that generates a simple cash inflow annuity. The computations are significantly more complex for investments with uneven cash flows. Recall that the internal rate of return is the rate that produces a zero net present value. Manually computing the rate that produces a zero net present value is a tedious trial-and-error process. You must first estimate the rate of return for a particular investment, then calculate the net present value. If the calculation produces a negative net present value, you try a lower estimated rate of return and recalculate. If this calculation produces a positive net present value, the actual internal rate of return lies between the first and second estimates. Make a third estimate and once again recalculate the net present value, and so on. Eventually you will determine the rate of return that produces a net present value of zero.

Many calculators and spreadsheet programs are designed to make these computations. We illustrate the process with a Microsoft Excel spreadsheet. Excel uses the syntax *IRR (values, guess)* in which *values* refers to cells that specify the cash flows for which you want to calculate the internal rate of return and *guess* is a number you estimate is close to the actual internal rate of return (IRR). The IRRs for the two investment alternatives available to Torres Transfer Company are shown in Exhibit 10.6. Study this exhibit. Excel requires netting cash outflows against cash inflows for each period in which both outflows and inflows are expected. For your convenience, we have labeled the net cash flows in the spreadsheet. Labeling is not necessary to execute the IRR function. The entire function, including values and guess, can be entered into a single cell of the spreadsheet. Persons familiar with spreadsheet programs learn to significantly simplify the input required.

The IRR results in Exhibit 10.6 confirm the ranking determined using the present value index. Alternative 1 (modernize maintenance facility), with an internal rate of return of 18.69 percent, ranks above Alternative 2 (purchase a truck) with an internal rate of return of 17.61 percent, even though Alternative 2 has a higher net present value (see Exhibit 10.5). Alternative 2, however, still may be the better investment option, depending on the amount available to invest. Suppose Torres has $120,000 of available funds to invest. Because Alternative 1 requires an initial investment of only $78,000, $42,000 ($120,000 − $78,000) of capital will not be invested. If Torres has

# REALITY BYTES

Developing proficiency with present value mathematics is usually the most difficult aspect of capital budgeting for students taking their first managerial accounting course. In real-world companies, the most difficult aspect of capital budgeting is forecasting cash flows for several years into the future. Consider the following capital budgeting project.

In 1965 representatives from the Georgia Power Company visited Ms. Taylor's fifth grade class to tell her students about the Edwin I. Hatch Nuclear Plant that was going to be built nearby. One of the authors of this text was a student in that class.

In 1966 construction began on the first unit of the plant, and the plant started producing electricity in 1975. The next year, 10 years after hearing the presentation in his fifth grade class, the author worked on construction of the second unit of the plant during the summer before his senior year of college. This second unit began operations in 1978.

In its 2009 annual report, the Southern Company, which is now the major owner of the plant, stated that the Hatch plant is expected to operate until 2038, and that decommissioning of the plant will continue until 2061. The cost to construct both units of the plant was $934 million. The estimated cost to dismantle and decommission the plant is over $1 billion.

It seems safe to assume that the students in Ms. Taylor's fifth grade class were not among the first to hear about the power company's plans for the Hatch plant. Thus, we can reasonably conclude that the life of this capital project will be over 100 years, from around 1960 until 2061.

Try to imagine that you were assigned the task of predicting the cost inflows and outflows for a project that was expected to last 100 years. Clearly, mastering present value mathematics would not be your biggest worry.

## EXHIBIT 10.6

### Microsoft Excel Spreadsheet Internal Rate of Return Function

| | A | B | C | D | E | F | G | H | I | J | K | L |
|---|---|---|---|---|---|---|---|---|---|---|---|---|
| 1 | | | | | | | | | | | | |
| 2 | | Internal Rate of Return for Alternative 1 | | | | | | | | | | |
| 3 | | IRR (Values, Guess) | | | | | | | | | | |
| 4 | | IRR (B6:B11, 10%) = | 18.6932% | | | | | | | | | |
| 5 | | | | | | | | | | | | |
| 6 | | −78000 | ($80,000 Cost of Equipment − $5,000 Trade-In + $3,000 Training Cost) | | | | | | | | | |
| 7 | | 33500 | ($21,500 Cost Savings + $12,000 Working Capital Recovery) | | | | | | | | | |
| 8 | | 21500 | (Cost Savings) | | | | | | | | | |
| 9 | | 21500 | (Cost Savings) | | | | | | | | | |
| 10 | | 21500 | (Cost Savings) | | | | | | | | | |
| 11 | | 25500 | ($21,500 Cost Savings + $4,000 Salvage Value) | | | | | | | | | |
| 12 | | | | | | | | | | | | |
| 13 | | | | | | | | | | | | |
| 14 | | Internal Rate of Return for Alternative 2 | | | | | | | | | | |
| 15 | | IRR (Values, Guess) | | | | | | | | | | |
| 16 | | IRR (B18:B23, 10%) = | 17.6083% | | | | | | | | | |
| 17 | | | | | | | | | | | | |
| 18 | | −120000 | ($115,000 Cost of Truck + $5,000 Working Capital Increase) | | | | | | | | | |
| 19 | | 37000 | ($69,000 Revenue − $32,000 Operating Expense) | | | | | | | | | |
| 20 | | 37000 | ($69,000 Revenue − $32,000 Operating Expense) | | | | | | | | | |
| 21 | | 17000 | ($69,000 Revenue − $32,000 Operating Expense − $20,000 Overhaul) | | | | | | | | | |
| 22 | | 37000 | ($69,000 Revenue − $32,000 Operating Expense) | | | | | | | | | |
| 23 | | 72000 | ($69,000 Revenue − $32,000 Operating Expense + $30,000 Salvage + 5,000 Working Capital Recovery) | | | | | | | | | |

no other investment opportunities for this $42,000, the company would be better off investing the entire $120,000 in Alternative 2 ($115,000 cost of truck + $5,000 working capital increase). Earning 17.61 percent on a $120,000 investment is better than earning 18.69 percent on a $78,000 investment with no return on the remaining $42,000. Management accounting requires exercising judgment when making decisions.

## Relevance and the Time Value of Money

Suppose you have the opportunity to invest in one of two capital projects. Both projects require an immediate cash outflow of $6,000 and will produce future cash inflows of $8,000. The only difference between the two projects is the timing of the inflows. The receipt schedule for both projects follows.

| Year | Project 1 | Project 2 |
|------|-----------|-----------|
| 1 | $3,500 | $2,000 |
| 2 | 3,000 | 2,000 |
| 3 | 1,000 | 2,000 |
| 4 | 500 | 2,000 |
| Total | $8,000 | $8,000 |

Because both projects cost the same and produce the same total cash inflows, they may appear to be equal. Whether you select Project 1 or Project 2, you pay $6,000 and receive $8,000. Because of the time value of money, however, Project 1 is preferable to Project 2. To see why, determine the net present value of both projects, assuming a 10 percent desired rate of return.

### Computation of Net Present Value for Project 1 and Project 2

#### Net Present Value for Project 1

| Period | Cash Inflow | × | Conversion Factor Table 1, $r = 10\%$ | = | Present Value |
|--------|-------------|---|----------------------------------------|---|---------------|
| 1 | $3,500 | × | 0.909091 | = | $3,182 |
| 2 | 3,000 | × | 0.826446 | = | 2,479 |
| 3 | 1,000 | × | 0.751315 | = | 751 |
| 4 | 500 | × | 0.683013 | = | 342 |
| Present value of future cash inflows | | | | | 6,754 |
| Present value of cash outflow | | | | | (6,000) |
| Net present value Project 1 | | | | | $ 754 |

#### Net Present Value for Project 2

| | Cash Inflow Annuity | × | Conversion Factor Table 2, $r = 10\%$, $n = 4$ | | |
|---|---------------------|---|-----------------------------------------------|---|---|
| Present value of cash inflow | $2,000 | × | 3.169865 | | $6,340 |
| Present value of cash outflow | | | | | (6,000) |
| Net present value Project 2 | | | | | $ 340 |

The net present value of Project 1 ($754) exceeds the net present value of Project 2 ($340). The timing as well as the amount of cash flows has a significant impact on capital investment returns. Recall that to be relevant, costs or revenues must differ between alternatives. Differences in the timing of cash flow payments or receipts are also relevant for decision-making purposes.

## Answers to The Curious Accountant

One way to answer your client's question is to determine which option has the highest net present value. The present value of the lump-sum payment option is simple; it is the $115.5 [$231 ÷ 2] million the lottery is prepared to pay them now. The present value of the annuity option must be calculated, and it consists of two parts. The first of the 26 payments of $7,076,692 will be paid immediately, so it is worth $7,076,692 today. The remaining 25 payments will occur at one-year intervals, so their present value is computed as:

$$\$7,076,692 \times 11.653583^* = \$82,468,818$$

Adding $7,076,692 to $82,468,818 yields a present value of $89,545,510, which is a lot less than $115.5 million. This suggests your client should take the lump-sum payment. Of course, the risk of the lottery not making its annual payments is very low. There is a greater risk that a financial planner may not find investments to earn a 7% annual return, so the winner would have to consider his or her tolerance for risk before making a final decision.

In the case of these particular lottery winners, one chose the lump-sum payment and the other chose the annuity.

*This factor is not included in the tables at the end of the chapter, so it is provided here for the purposes of this illustration.

## Tax Considerations

The previous examples have ignored the effect of income taxes on capital investment decisions. Taxes affect the amount of cash flows generated by investments. To illustrate, assume Wu Company purchases an asset that costs $240,000. The asset has a four-year useful life, no salvage value, and is depreciated on a straight-line basis. The asset generates cash revenue of $90,000 per year. Assume Wu's income tax rate is 40 percent. What is the net present value of the asset, assuming Wu's management desires to earn a 10 percent rate of return after taxes? The first step in answering this question is to calculate the annual cash flow generated by the asset, as shown in Exhibit 10.7.

### EXHIBIT 10.7

**Determining Cash Flow from Investment**

|  | Period 1 | Period 2 | Period 3 | Period 4 |
|---|---|---|---|---|
| Cash revenue | $ 90,000 | $ 90,000 | $ 90,000 | $ 90,000 |
| Depreciation expense (noncash) | (60,000) | (60,000) | (60,000) | (60,000) |
| Income before taxes | 30,000 | 30,000 | 30,000 | 30,000 |
| Income tax at 40% | (12,000) | (12,000) | (12,000) | (12,000) |
| Income after tax | 18,000 | 18,000 | 18,000 | 18,000 |
| Depreciation add back | 60,000 | 60,000 | 60,000 | 60,000 |
| Annual cash inflow | $ 78,000 | $ 78,000 | $ 78,000 | $ 78,000 |

Because recognizing depreciation expense does not require a cash payment (cash is paid when assets are purchased, not when depreciation is recognized), depreciation expense must be added back to after-tax income to determine the annual cash inflow. Once the cash flow is determined, the net present value is computed as shown here.

| Cash flow annuity | × | Conversion factor Table 2, $r = 10\%$, $n = 4$ | = | Present value cash inflows | − | Present value cash outflows | = | Net present value |
|---|---|---|---|---|---|---|---|---|
| $78,000 | × | 3.169865 | = | $247,249 | − | $240,000 | = | $7,249 |

The depreciation sheltered some of the income from taxation. Income taxes apply to income after deducting depreciation expense. Without depreciation expense, income taxes each year would have been $36,000 ($90,000 × 0.40) instead of $12,000 ($30,000 × 0.40). The $24,000 difference ($36,000 − $12,000) is known as a *depreciation tax shield.* The amount of the depreciation tax shield can also be computed by multiplying the depreciation expense by the tax rate ($60,000 × 0.40 = $24,000).

Because of the time value of money, companies benefit by maximizing the depreciation tax shield early in the life of an asset. For this reason, most companies calculate depreciation expense for tax purposes using the *modified accelerated cost recovery system (MACRS)* permitted by tax law rather than using straight-line depreciation. MACRS recognizes depreciation on an accelerated basis, assigning larger amounts of depreciation in the early years of an asset's useful life. The higher depreciation charges result in lower amounts of taxable income and lower income taxes. In the later years of an asset's useful life, the reverse is true, and lower depreciation charges result in higher taxes. Accelerated depreciation does not allow companies to avoid paying taxes but to delay them. The longer companies can delay paying taxes, the more cash they have available to invest.

## TECHNIQUES THAT IGNORE THE TIME VALUE OF MONEY

Determine the payback period for an investment opportunity.

Several techniques for evaluating capital investment proposals ignore the time value of money. Although these techniques are less accurate, they are quick and simple. When investments are small or the returns are expected within a short time, these techniques are likely to result in the same decisions that more sophisticated techniques produce.

### Payback Method

The **payback method** is simple to apply and easy to understand. It shows how long it will take to recover the initial cash outflow (the cost) of an investment. The formula for computing the payback period, measured in years, is as follows.

**Payback period = Net cost of investment ÷ Annual net cash inflow**

To illustrate, assume Winston Cleaners can purchase a new ironing machine that will press shirts in half the time of the one currently used. The new machine costs $100,000 and will reduce labor cost by $40,000 per year over a four-year useful life. The payback period is computed as follows.

**Payback period = $100,000 ÷ $40,000 = 2.5 years**

*Interpreting Payback*

Generally, investments with shorter payback periods are considered better. Because the payback method measures only investment recovery, not profitability, however, this conclusion can be invalid when considering investment alternatives. To illustrate, assume Winston Cleaners also has the opportunity to purchase a different machine that costs $100,000 and provides an annual labor savings of $40,000. However, the second machine will last for five instead of four years. The payback period is still 2.5 years ($100,000 ÷ $40,000), but the second machine is a better investment because it improves profitability by providing an additional year of cost savings. The payback analysis does not measure this difference between the alternatives.

## Unequal Cash Flows

The preceding illustration assumed Winston's labor cost reduction saved the same amount of cash each year for the life of the new machine. The payback method requires adjustment when cash flow benefits are unequal. Suppose a company purchases a machine for $6,000. The machine will be used erratically and is expected to provide incremental revenue over the next five years as follows.

| 2007 | 2008 | 2009 | 2010 | 2011 |
|------|------|------|------|------|
| $3,000 | $1,000 | $2,000 | $1,000 | $500 |

Based on this cash inflow pattern, what is the payback period? There are two acceptable solutions. One accumulates the incremental revenue until the sum equals the amount of the original investment.

| Year | Annual Amount | Cumulative Total |
|------|---------------|------------------|
| 2007 | $3,000 | $3,000 |
| 2008 | 1,000 | 4,000 |
| 2009 | 2,000 | 6,000 |

This approach indicates the payback period is three years.

A second solution uses an averaging concept. The average annual cash inflow is determined. This figure is then used in the denominator of the payback equation. Using the preceding data, the payback period is computed as follows.

1.  Compute the average annual cash inflow.

    $$2007 + 2008 + 2009 + 2010 + 2011 = \text{Total} \div 5 = \text{Average}$$

    $$\$3,000 + \$1,000 + \$2,000 + \$1,000 + \$500 = \$7,500 \div 5 = \$1,500$$

2.  Compute the payback period.

    $$\frac{\text{Net cost of investment}} {} \div \frac{\text{Average annual net cash inflow}}{} = 6,000 \div 1,500 = 4 \text{ years}$$

The average method is useful when a company purchases a number of similar assets with differing cash return patterns.

## Unadjusted Rate of Return

The **unadjusted rate of return** method is another common evaluation technique. Investment cash flows are not adjusted to reflect the time value of money. The unadjusted rate of return is sometimes called the *simple rate of return*. It is computed as follows.

$$\frac{\text{Unadjusted}}{\text{rate of return}} = \frac{\text{Average incremental increase in annual net income}}{\text{Net cost of original investment}}$$

**LO 8**

Determine the unadjusted rate of return for an investment opportunity.

To illustrate computing the unadjusted rate of return, assume The Dining Table, Inc., is considering establishing a new restaurant that will require a $2,000,000 original investment. Management anticipates operating the restaurant for 10 years before significant renovations will be required. The restaurant is expected to provide an average after-tax return of $280,000 per year. The unadjusted rate of return is computed as follows.

$$\text{Unadjusted rate of return} = \$280,000 \div \$2,000,000 = 14\% \text{ per year}$$

The accuracy of the unadjusted rate of return suffers from the failure to recognize the recovery of invested capital. With respect to a depreciable asset, the capital investment is normally recovered through revenue over the life of the asset. To illustrate, assume we purchase a $1,000 asset with a two-year life and a zero salvage value. For simplicity, ignore income taxes. Assume the asset produces $600 of cash revenue per year. The income statement for the first year of operation appears as follows.

| | |
|---|---|
| Revenue | $ 600 |
| Depreciation expense | (500) |
| Net income | $ 100 |

What is the amount of invested capital during the first year? First, a $1,000 cash outflow was used to purchase the asset (the original investment). Next, we collected $600 of cash revenue of which $100 was a *return on investment* (net income) and $500 was a **recovery of investment.** As a result, $1,000 was invested in the asset at the beginning of the year and $500 was invested at the end of the year. Similarly, we will recover an additional $500 of capital during the second year of operation, leaving zero invested capital at the end of the second year. Given that the cash inflows from revenue are collected somewhat evenly over the life of the investment, the amount of invested capital will range from a beginning balance of $1,000 to an ending balance of zero. On average, we will have $500 invested in the asset (the midpoint between $1,000 and zero). The average investment can be determined by dividing the total original investment by 2 ($1,000 ÷ 2 = $500). The unadjusted rate of return based on average invested capital can be calculated as follows.

$$\frac{\text{Unadjusted rate of return}}{\text{(Based on average investment)}} = \frac{\text{Average incremental increase in annual net income}}{\text{Net cost of original investment} \div 2}$$

$$= \frac{\$100}{\$1,000 \div 2} = 20\%$$

To avoid distortions caused by the failure to recognize the recovery of invested capital, the unadjusted rate of return should be based on the *average investment* when working with investments in depreciable assets.

---

## ✓ CHECK YOURSELF 10.3

EZ Rentals can purchase a van that costs $24,000. The van has an expected useful life of three years and no salvage value. EZ expects rental revenue from the van to be $12,000 per year. Determine the payback period and the unadjusted rate of return.

**Answer**

Payback = Cost of the investment ÷ Annual cash inflow

Payback = $24,000 ÷ $12,000 = 2 years

Unadjusted rate of return = Net income ÷ Average cost of the investment

| | | |
|---|---|---|
| Revenue | $12,000 | |
| Depreciation expense | (8,000) | [$24,000 ÷ 3 years] |
| Net income | $ 4,000 | |

Unadjusted rate of return = $4,000 ÷ ($24,000 ÷ 2) = 33.33%

---

## REAL-WORLD REPORTING PRACTICES

In a study, researchers found that companies in the forest products industry use discounted cash flow techniques more frequently when the capital project being considered is a long-term timber investment. The use of techniques that ignore the time value of money increased when other shorter-term capital investment projects were being considered. Exhibit 10.8 shows the researchers' findings.

**EXHIBIT 10.8**

**Forestry Industry Investments**

**Long-term investments in timber**

Net present value **38%**

**9%** Unadjusted rate of return

Internal rate of return **38%**

**15%** Payback period

**Investments in other assets**

Net present value **22%**

**13%** Unadjusted rate of return

Internal rate of return **33%**

**32%** Payback period

Data Source: J. Bailes, J. Nielsen, and S. Lawton, "How Forest Product Companies Analyze Capital Budgets," *Management Accounting,* October 1998, pp. 24–30.

## POSTAUDITS

The analytical techniques for evaluating capital investment proposals depend highly on estimates of future cash flows. Although predictions cannot be perfectly accurate, gross miscalculations can threaten the existence of an organization. For example, optimistic projections of future cash inflows that do not materialize will lead to investments that do not return the cost of capital. Managers must take their projections seriously. A postaudit policy can encourage managers to carefully consider their capital investment decisions. A **postaudit** is conducted at the completion of a capital investment project, using the same analytical technique that was used to justify the original investment. For example, if an internal rate of return was used to justify approving an investment project, the internal rate of return should be computed in the postaudit. In the postaudit computation, *actual* rather than estimated cash flows are used. Postaudits determine whether the expected results were achieved.

Postaudits should focus on continuous improvement rather than punishment. Managers who are chastised for failing to achieve expected results might become overly cautious when asked to provide estimates for future projects. Being too conservative can create problems as serious as those caused by being too optimistic. Managers can err two ways with respect to capital investment decisions. First, a manager might accept a project that should have been rejected. This mistake usually stems from excessively optimistic future cash flow projections. Second, a manager might reject a project that should have been accepted. These missed opportunities are usually the result of underestimating future cash flows. A too cautious manager can become unable to locate enough projects to fully invest the firm's funds.

Idle cash earns no return. If projects continue to outperform expectations, managers are probably estimating future cash flows too conservatively. If projects consistently fail to live up to expectations, managers are probably being too optimistic in their projections of future cash flows. Either way, the company suffers. The goal of a postaudit is to provide feedback that will help managers improve the accuracy of future cash flow projections, maximizing the quality of the firm's capital investments.

**LO 9**

Conduct a postaudit of a completed investment.

# A Look Back

Capital expenditures have a significant, long-term effect on profitability. They usually involve major cash outflows that are recovered through future cash inflows. The most common cash inflows include incremental revenue, operating cost savings, salvage value, and working capital releases. The most common outflows are the initial investment, increases in operating expenses, and working capital commitments.

Several techniques for analyzing the cash flows associated with capital investments are available. The techniques can be divided into two categories: (1) techniques that use time value of money concepts and (2) techniques that ignore the time value of money. Generally, techniques that ignore the time value of money are less accurate but simpler and easier to understand. These techniques include the *payback method* and the *unadjusted rate of return method.*

The techniques that use time value of money concepts are the *net present value method* and the *internal rate of return method.* These methods offer significant improvements in accuracy but are more difficult to understand. They may involve tedious computations and require using experienced judgment. Computer software and programmed calculators that ease the tedious computational burden are readily available to most managers. Furthermore, the superiority of the techniques justifies learning how to use them. These methods should be used when investment expenditures are larger or when cash flows extend over a prolonged time period.

## >> A Look Forward

The next chapter moves into unexplored territory. It introduces the concept of inventory cost flow. It discusses how costs move through the inventory accounts Raw Materials, Work in Process, and Finished Goods. It presents techniques for assigning overhead costs to inventory as the inventory is produced. It identifies differences in product costing for service and manufacturing companies. Finally, it contrasts two approaches used to value inventory, variable costing versus full-absorption costing.

## APPENDIX

### TABLE 1 — Present Value of $1

| n | 4% | 5% | 6% | 7% | 8% | 9% | 10% | 12% | 14% | 16% | 20% |
|---|---|---|---|---|---|---|---|---|---|---|---|
| 1 | 0.961538 | 0.952381 | 0.943396 | 0.934579 | 0.925926 | 0.917431 | 0.909091 | 0.892857 | 0.877193 | 0.862069 | 0.833333 |
| 2 | 0.924556 | 0.907029 | 0.889996 | 0.873439 | 0.857339 | 0.841680 | 0.826446 | 0.797194 | 0.769468 | 0.743163 | 0.694444 |
| 3 | 0.888996 | 0.863838 | 0.839619 | 0.816298 | 0.793832 | 0.772183 | 0.751315 | 0.711780 | 0.674972 | 0.640658 | 0.578704 |
| 4 | 0.854804 | 0.822702 | 0.792094 | 0.762895 | 0.735030 | 0.708425 | 0.683013 | 0.635518 | 0.592080 | 0.552291 | 0.482253 |
| 5 | 0.821927 | 0.783526 | 0.747258 | 0.712986 | 0.680583 | 0.649931 | 0.620921 | 0.567427 | 0.519369 | 0.476113 | 0.401878 |
| 6 | 0.790315 | 0.746215 | 0.704961 | 0.666342 | 0.630170 | 0.596267 | 0.564474 | 0.506631 | 0.455587 | 0.410442 | 0.334898 |
| 7 | 0.759918 | 0.710681 | 0.665057 | 0.622750 | 0.583490 | 0.547034 | 0.513158 | 0.452349 | 0.399637 | 0.353830 | 0.279082 |
| 8 | 0.730690 | 0.676839 | 0.627412 | 0.582009 | 0.540269 | 0.501866 | 0.466507 | 0.403883 | 0.350559 | 0.305025 | 0.232568 |
| 9 | 0.702587 | 0.644609 | 0.591898 | 0.543934 | 0.500249 | 0.460428 | 0.424098 | 0.360610 | 0.307508 | 0.262953 | 0.193807 |
| 10 | 0.675564 | 0.613913 | 0.558395 | 0.508349 | 0.463193 | 0.422411 | 0.385543 | 0.321973 | 0.269744 | 0.226684 | 0.161506 |
| 11 | 0.649581 | 0.584679 | 0.526788 | 0.475093 | 0.428883 | 0.387533 | 0.350494 | 0.287476 | 0.236617 | 0.195417 | 0.134588 |
| 12 | 0.624597 | 0.556837 | 0.496969 | 0.444012 | 0.397114 | 0.355535 | 0.318631 | 0.256675 | 0.207559 | 0.168463 | 0.112157 |
| 13 | 0.600574 | 0.530321 | 0.468839 | 0.414964 | 0.367698 | 0.326179 | 0.289664 | 0.229174 | 0.182069 | 0.145227 | 0.093464 |
| 14 | 0.577475 | 0.505068 | 0.442301 | 0.387817 | 0.340461 | 0.299246 | 0.263331 | 0.204620 | 0.159710 | 0.125195 | 0.077887 |
| 15 | 0.555265 | 0.481017 | 0.417265 | 0.362446 | 0.315242 | 0.274538 | 0.239392 | 0.182696 | 0.140096 | 0.107927 | 0.064905 |
| 16 | 0.533908 | 0.458112 | 0.393646 | 0.338735 | 0.291890 | 0.251870 | 0.217629 | 0.163122 | 0.122892 | 0.093041 | 0.054088 |
| 17 | 0.513373 | 0.436297 | 0.371364 | 0.316574 | 0.270269 | 0.231073 | 0.197845 | 0.145644 | 0.107800 | 0.080207 | 0.045073 |
| 18 | 0.493628 | 0.415521 | 0.350344 | 0.295864 | 0.250249 | 0.211994 | 0.179859 | 0.130040 | 0.094561 | 0.069144 | 0.037561 |
| 19 | 0.474642 | 0.395734 | 0.330513 | 0.276508 | 0.231712 | 0.194490 | 0.163508 | 0.116107 | 0.082948 | 0.059607 | 0.031301 |
| 20 | 0.456387 | 0.376889 | 0.311805 | 0.258419 | 0.214548 | 0.178431 | 0.148644 | 0.103667 | 0.072762 | 0.051385 | 0.026084 |

### TABLE 2    Present Value of an Annuity of $1

| n | 4% | 5% | 6% | 7% | 8% | 9% | 10% | 12% | 14% | 16% | 20% |
|---|---|---|---|---|---|---|---|---|---|---|---|
| 1 | 0.961538 | 0.952381 | 0.943396 | 0.934579 | 0.925926 | 0.917431 | 0.909091 | 0.892857 | 0.877193 | 0.862069 | 0.833333 |
| 2 | 1.886095 | 1.859410 | 1.833393 | 1.808018 | 1.783265 | 1.759111 | 1.735537 | 1.690051 | 1.646661 | 1.605232 | 1.527778 |
| 3 | 2.775091 | 2.723248 | 2.673012 | 2.624316 | 2.577097 | 2.531295 | 2.486852 | 2.401831 | 2.321632 | 2.245890 | 2.106481 |
| 4 | 3.629895 | 3.545951 | 3.465106 | 3.387211 | 3.312127 | 3.239720 | 3.169865 | 3.037349 | 2.913712 | 2.798181 | 2.588735 |
| 5 | 4.451822 | 4.329477 | 4.212364 | 4.100197 | 3.992710 | 3.889651 | 3.790787 | 3.604776 | 3.433081 | 3.274294 | 2.990612 |
| 6 | 5.242137 | 5.075692 | 4.917324 | 4.766540 | 4.622880 | 4.485919 | 4.355261 | 4.111407 | 3.888668 | 3.684736 | 3.325510 |
| 7 | 6.002055 | 5.786373 | 5.582381 | 5.389289 | 5.206370 | 5.032953 | 4.868419 | 4.563757 | 4.288305 | 4.038565 | 3.604592 |
| 8 | 6.732745 | 6.463213 | 6.209794 | 5.971299 | 5.746639 | 5.534819 | 5.334926 | 4.967640 | 4.638864 | 4.343591 | 3.837160 |
| 9 | 7.435332 | 7.107822 | 6.801692 | 6.515232 | 6.246888 | 5.995247 | 5.759024 | 5.328250 | 4.946372 | 4.606544 | 4.030967 |
| 10 | 8.110896 | 7.721735 | 7.360087 | 7.023582 | 6.710081 | 6.417658 | 6.144567 | 5.650223 | 5.216116 | 4.833227 | 4.192472 |
| 11 | 8.760477 | 8.306414 | 7.886875 | 7.498674 | 7.138964 | 6.805191 | 6.495061 | 5.937699 | 5.452733 | 5.028644 | 4.327060 |
| 12 | 9.385074 | 8.863252 | 8.383844 | 7.942686 | 7.536078 | 7.160725 | 6.813692 | 6.194374 | 5.660292 | 5.197107 | 4.439217 |
| 13 | 9.985648 | 9.393573 | 8.852683 | 8.357651 | 7.903776 | 7.486904 | 7.103356 | 6.423548 | 5.842362 | 5.342334 | 4.532681 |
| 14 | 10.563123 | 9.898641 | 9.294984 | 8.745468 | 8.244237 | 7.786150 | 7.366687 | 6.628168 | 6.002072 | 5.467529 | 4.610567 |
| 15 | 11.118387 | 10.379658 | 9.712249 | 9.107914 | 8.559479 | 8.060688 | 7.606080 | 6.810864 | 6.142168 | 5.575456 | 4.675473 |
| 16 | 11.652296 | 10.837770 | 10.105895 | 9.446649 | 8.851369 | 8.312558 | 7.823709 | 6.973986 | 6.265060 | 5.668497 | 4.729561 |
| 17 | 12.165669 | 11.274066 | 10.477260 | 9.763223 | 9.121638 | 8.543631 | 8.021553 | 7.119630 | 6.372859 | 5.748704 | 4.774634 |
| 18 | 12.659297 | 11.689587 | 10.827603 | 10.059087 | 9.371887 | 8.755625 | 8.201412 | 7.249670 | 6.467420 | 5.817848 | 4.812195 |
| 19 | 13.133939 | 12.085321 | 11.158116 | 10.335595 | 9.603599 | 8.905115 | 8.364920 | 7.365777 | 6.550369 | 5.877455 | 4.843496 |
| 20 | 13.590326 | 12.462210 | 11.469921 | 10.594014 | 9.818147 | 9.128546 | 8.513564 | 7.469444 | 6.623131 | 5.928841 | 4.869580 |

**A step-by-step audio-narrated series of slides is provided on the text website at www.mhhe.com/edmonds2011.**

## SELF-STUDY REVIEW PROBLEM

The CFO of Advo Corporation is considering two investment opportunities. The expected future cash inflows for each opportunity follow:

|  | Year 1 | Year 2 | Year 3 | Year 4 |
|---|---|---|---|---|
| Project 1 | $144,000 | $147,000 | $160,000 | $178,000 |
| Project 2 | 204,000 | 199,000 | 114,000 | 112,000 |

Both investments require an initial payment of $400,000. Advo's desired rate of return is 16 percent.

### Required

**a.** Compute the net present value of each project. Which project should Advo adopt based on the net present value approach?

**b.** Use the incremental revenue summation method to compute the payback period for each project. Which project should Advo adopt based on the payback approach?

### Solution to Requirement a

| Project 1 | | | | | |
|---|---|---|---|---|---|
| | **Cash Inflows** | | **Table Factor*** | | **Present Value** |
| Year 1 | $144,000 | × | 0.862069 | = | $124,138 |
| Year 2 | 147,000 | × | 0.743163 | = | 109,245 |
| Year 3 | 160,000 | × | 0.640658 | = | 102,505 |
| Year 4 | 178,000 | × | 0.552291 | = | 98,308 |
| PV of cash inflows | | | | | 434,196 |
| Cost of investment | | | | | (400,000) |
| Net present value | | | | | $ 34,196 |

*Table 1, $n = 1$ through 4, $r = 16\%$

| Project 2 | | | | | |
|---|---|---|---|---|---|
| | **Cash Inflows** | | **Table Factor*** | | **Present Value** |
| Year 1 | $204,000 | × | 0.862069 | = | $175,862 |
| Year 2 | 199,000 | × | 0.743163 | = | 147,889 |
| Year 3 | 114,000 | × | 0.640658 | = | 73,035 |
| Year 4 | 112,000 | × | 0.552291 | = | 61,857 |
| PV of cash inflows | | | | | 458,643 |
| Cost of investment | | | | | (400,000) |
| Net present value | | | | | $ 58,643 |

*Table 1, $n = 1$ through 4, $r = 16\%$

Advo should adopt Project 2 since it has a greater net present value.

### Solution to Requirement b

| Cash Inflows | Project 1 | Project 2 |
|---|---|---|
| Year 1 | $144,000 | $204,000 |
| Year 2 | 147,000 | 199,000 |
| Total | $291,000 | $403,000 |

By the end of the second year, Project 2's cash inflows have more than paid for the cost of the investment. In contrast, Project 1 still falls short of investment recovery by $109,000 ($400,000 − $291,000). Advo should adopt Project 2 since it has a shorter payback period.

## KEY TERMS

Accumulated conversion factor 447
Annuity 447
Capital investments 444
Cost of capital 445
Incremental revenue 451
Internal rate of return 450

Minimum rate of return 445
Net present value 449
Ordinary annuity 448
Payback method 458
Postaudit 461
Present value index 454
Present value table 446

Recovery of investment 460
Single-payment (lump-sum) 446
Time value of money 444
Unadjusted rate of return 449
Working capital 451

## QUESTIONS

**1.** What is a capital investment? How does it differ from an investment in stocks or bonds?

**2.** What are three reasons that cash is worth more today than cash to be received in the future?

3. "A dollar today is worth more than a dollar in the future." "The present value of a future dollar is worth less than one dollar." Are these two statements synonymous? Explain.

4. Define the term *return on investment*. How is the return normally expressed? Give an example of a capital investment return.

5. How does a company establish its minimum acceptable rate of return on investments?

6. If you wanted to have $500,000 one year from today and desired to earn a 10 percent return, what amount would you need to invest today? Which amount has more value, the amount today or the $500,000 a year from today?

7. Why are present value tables frequently used to convert future values to present values?

8. Define the term *annuity*. What is one example of an annuity receipt?

9. How can present value "what-if" analysis be enhanced by using software programs?

10. Receiving $100,000 per year for five years is equivalent to investing what amount today at 14 percent? Provide a mathematical formula to solve this problem, assuming use of a present value annuity table to convert the future cash flows to their present value equivalents. Provide the expression for the Excel spreadsheet function that would perform the present value conversion.

11. Maria Espinosa borrowed $15,000 from the bank and agreed to repay the loan at 8 percent annual interest over four years, making payments of $4,529 per year. Because part of the bank's payment from Ms. Espinosa is a recovery of the original investment, what assumption must the bank make to earn its desired 8 percent compounded annual return?

12. Two investment opportunities have positive net present values. Investment A's net present value amounts to $40,000 while B's is only $30,000. Does this mean that A is the better investment opportunity? Explain.

13. What criteria determine whether a project is acceptable under the net present value method?

14. Does the net present value method provide a measure of the rate of return on capital investments?

15. Which is the best capital investment evaluation technique for ranking investment opportunities?

16. Paul Henderson is a manager for Spark Company. He tells you that his company always maximizes profitability by accepting the investment opportunity with the highest internal rate of return. Explain to Mr. Henderson how his company may improve profitability by sometimes selecting investment opportunities with lower internal rates of return.

17. What is the relationship between desired rate of return and internal rate of return?

18. What typical cash inflow and outflow items are associated with capital investments?

19. "I always go for the investment with the shortest payback period." Is this a sound strategy? Why or why not?

20. "The payback method cannot be used if the cash inflows occur in unequal patterns." Do you agree or disagree? Explain.

21. What are the advantages and disadvantages associated with the unadjusted rate of return method for evaluating capital investments?

22. How do capital investments affect profitability?

23. What is a postaudit? How is it useful in capital budgeting?

## MULTIPLE-CHOICE QUESTIONS

**Multiple-choice questions are provided on the text website at www.mhhe.com/edmonds2011.**

## EXERCISES—SERIES A

**All applicable Exercises in Series A are available with McGraw-Hill's *Connect Accounting*.**

### Exercise 10-1A   *Identifying cash inflows and outflows*

LO 1, 5

**Required**

Indicate which of the following items will result in cash inflows and which will result in cash outflows. The first one is shown as an example.

| Item | Type of Cash Flow |
|---|---|
| a. Initial investment | Outflow |
| b. Salvage values | |
| c. Recovery of working capital | |
| d. Incremental expenses | |
| e. Working capital commitments | |
| f. Cost savings | |
| g. Incremental revenue | |

**LO 1, 2**

### Exercise 10-2A   *Determining the present value of a lump-sum future cash receipt*

Stan Sweeney turned 20 years old today. His grandfather had established a trust fund that will pay him $80,000 on his next birthday. However, Stan needs money today to start his college education, and his father is willing to help. Mr. Sweeney has agreed to give Stan the present value of the $80,000 future cash inflow, assuming a 10 percent rate of return.

**Required**

a. Use a present value table to determine the amount of cash that Stan Sweeney's father should give him.

b. Use an algebraic formula to prove that the present value of the trust fund (the amount of cash computed in Requirement *a*) is equal to its $80,000 future value.

**LO 1, 2**

### Exercise 10-3A   *Determining the present value of a lump-sum future cash receipt*

Marsha Bittner expects to receive a $600,000 cash benefit when she retires five years from today. Ms. Bittner's employer has offered an early retirement incentive by agreeing to pay her $360,000 today if she agrees to retire immediately. Ms. Bittner desires to earn a rate of return of 12 percent.

**Required**

a. Assuming that the retirement benefit is the only consideration in making the retirement decision, should Ms. Bittner accept her employer's offer?

b. Identify the factors that cause the present value of the retirement benefit to be less than $600,000.

**LO 1, 2**

### Exercise 10-4A   *Determining the present value of an annuity*

The dean of the School of Natural Science is trying to decide whether to purchase a copy machine to place in the lobby of the building. The machine would add to student convenience, but the dean feels compelled to earn an 8 percent return on the investment of funds. Estimates of cash inflows from copy machines that have been placed in other university buildings indicate that the copy machine would probably produce incremental cash inflows of approximately $15,000 per year. The machine is expected to have a three-year useful life with a zero salvage value.

**Required**

a. Use Present Value Table 1 in the Appendix to determine the maximum amount of cash the dean should be willing to pay for a copy machine.

b. Use Present Value Table 2 in the Appendix to determine the maximum amount of cash the dean should be willing to pay for a copy machine.

c. Explain the consistency or lack of consistency in the answers to Requirements *a* and *b*.

**LO 3**

### Exercise 10-5A   *Determining net present value*

Metro Shuttle Company is considering investing in two new vans that are expected to generate combined cash inflows of $28,000 per year. The vans' combined purchase price is $91,000. The expected life and salvage value of each are four years and $21,000, respectively. Metro Shuttle has an average cost of capital of 14 percent.

**Required**

a. Calculate the net present value of the investment opportunity.

b. Indicate whether the investment opportunity is expected to earn a return that is above or below the cost of capital and whether it should be accepted.

## Exercise 10-6A  *Determining net present value*

LO 3

Dimitry Chernitsky is seeking part-time employment while he attends school. He is considering purchasing technical equipment that will enable him to start a small training services company that will offer tutorial services over the Internet. Dimitry expects demand for the service to grow rapidly in the first two years of operation as customers learn about the availability of the Internet assistance. Thereafter, he expects demand to stabilize. The following table presents the expected cash flows.

| Year of Operation | Cash Inflow | Cash Outflow |
|---|---|---|
| 2012 | $13,500 | $ 9,000 |
| 2013 | 19,500 | 12,000 |
| 2014 | 21,000 | 12,600 |
| 2015 | 21,000 | 12,600 |

In addition to these cash flows, Mr. Chernitsky expects to pay $21,000 for the equipment. He also expects to pay $3,600 for a major overhaul and updating of the equipment at the end of the second year of operation. The equipment is expected to have a $1,500 salvage value and a four-year useful life. Mr. Chernitsky desires to earn a rate of return of 8 percent.

**Required**

(Round computations to the nearest whole penny.)

**a.** Calculate the net present value of the investment opportunity.

**b.** Indicate whether the investment opportunity is expected to earn a return that is above or below the desired rate of return and whether it should be accepted.

## Exercise 10-7A  *Using the present value index*

LO 3, 6

Alonso Company has a choice of two investment alternatives. The present value of cash inflows and outflows for the first alternative is $90,000 and $84,000, respectively. The present value of cash inflows and outflows for the second alternative is $220,000 and $213,000, respectively.

**Required**

**a.** Calculate the net present value of each investment opportunity.

**b.** Calculate the present value index for each investment opportunity.

**c.** Indicate which investment will produce the higher rate of return.

## Exercise 10-8A  *Determining the internal rate of return*

LO 4

Irving Manufacturing Company has an opportunity to purchase some technologically advanced equipment that will reduce the company's cash outflow for operating expenses by $1,280,000 per year. The cost of the equipment is $6,186,530.56. Irving expects it to have a 10-year useful life and a zero salvage value. The company has established an investment opportunity hurdle rate of 15 percent and uses the straight-line method for depreciation.

**Required**

**a.** Calculate the internal rate of return of the investment opportunity.

**b.** Indicate whether the investment opportunity should be accepted.

## Exercise 10-9A  *Using the internal rate of return to compare investment opportunities*

LO 4, 6

Hulsey and Wright (H&W) is a partnership that owns a small company. It is considering two alternative investment opportunities. The first investment opportunity will have a five-year useful life, will cost $9,335.16, and will generate expected cash inflows of $2,400 per year. The second investment is expected to have a useful life of three years, will cost $6,217.13, and will generate expected cash inflows of $2,500 per year. Assume that H&W has the funds available to accept only one of the opportunities.

**Required**

a. Calculate the internal rate of return of each investment opportunity.

b. Based on the internal rates of return, which opportunity should H&W select?

c. Discuss other factors that H&W should consider in the investment decision.

**LO 1, 2, 5, 6**

### Exercise 10-10A   *Determining the cash flow annuity with income tax considerations*

To open a new store, Alpha Tire Company plans to invest $240,000 in equipment expected to have a four-year useful life and no salvage value. Alpha expects the new store to generate annual cash revenues of $315,000 and to incur annual cash operating expenses of $195,000. Alpha's average income tax rate is 30 percent. The company uses straight-line depreciation.

**Required**

Determine the expected annual net cash inflow from operations for each of the first four years after Alpha opens the new store.

**LO 9**

### Exercise 10-11A   *Evaluating discounted cash flow techniques*

Rita Hendrix is angry with Bill Shaw. He is behind schedule developing supporting material for tomorrow's capital budget committee meeting. When she approached him about his apparent lacka-daisical attitude in general and his tardiness in particular, he responded, "I don't see why we do this stuff in the first place. It's all a bunch of estimates. Who knows what future cash flows will really be? I certainly don't. I've been doing this job for five years, and no one has ever checked to see if I even came close at these guesses. I've been waiting for marketing to provide the estimated cash inflows on the projects being considered tomorrow. But, if you want my report now, I'll have it in a couple of hours. I can make up the marketing data as well as they can."

**Required**

Does Mr. Shaw have a point? Is there something wrong with the company's capital budgeting system? Write a brief response explaining how to improve the investment evaluation system.

**LO 7**

### Exercise 10-12A   *Determining the payback period*

Sky Airline Company is considering expanding its territory. The company has the opportunity to purchase one of two different used airplanes. The first airplane is expected to cost $18,000,000; it will enable the company to increase its annual cash inflow by $6,000,000 per year. The plane is expected to have a useful life of five years and no salvage value. The second plane costs $36,000,000; it will enable the company to increase annual cash flow by $9,000,000 per year. This plane has an eight-year useful life and a zero salvage value.

**Required**

a. Determine the payback period for each investment alternative and identify the alternative Sky should accept if the decision is based on the payback approach.

b. Discuss the shortcomings of using the payback method to evaluate investment opportunities.

**LO 5, 7**

### Exercise 10-13A   *Determining the payback period with uneven cash flows*

Melton Company has an opportunity to purchase a forklift to use in its heavy equipment rental business. The forklift would be leased on an annual basis during its first two years of operation. Thereafter, it would be leased to the general public on demand. Melton would sell it at the end of the fifth year of its useful life. The expected cash inflows and outflows follow.

| Year | Nature of Item | Cash Inflow | Cash Outflow |
|------|----------------|-------------|--------------|
| 2012 | Purchase price |             | $72,000      |
| 2012 | Revenue        | $30,000     |              |
| 2013 | Revenue        | 30,000      |              |
| 2014 | Revenue        | 21,000      |              |
| 2014 | Major overhaul |             | 9,000        |
| 2015 | Revenue        | 18,000      |              |
| 2016 | Revenue        | 14,400      |              |
| 2016 | Salvage value  | 9,600       |              |

**Required**

**a.** Determine the payback period using the accumulated cash flows approach.

**b.** Determine the payback period using the average cash flows approach.

### Exercise 10-14A  *Determining the unadjusted rate of return*

LO 8

Lilly Painting Company is considering whether to purchase a new spray paint machine that costs $4,000. The machine is expected to save labor, increasing net income by $600 per year. The effective life of the machine is 15 years according to the manufacturer's estimate.

**Required**

**a.** Determine the unadjusted rate of return based on the average cost of the investment.

**b.** What is the predominant shortcoming of using the unadjusted rate of return to evaluate investment opportunities?

### Exercise 10-15A  *Computing the payback period and unadjusted rate of return for the same investment opportunity*

LO 7, 8

Foy Rentals can purchase a van that costs $60,000; it has an expected useful life of three years and no salvage value. Foy uses straight-line depreciation. Expected revenue is $30,000 per year. Assume that depreciation is the only expense associated with this investment.

**Required**

**a.** Determine the payback period.

**b.** Determine the unadjusted rate of return based on the average cost of the investment.

## PROBLEMS—SERIES A

**All Problems in Series A are available with McGraw-Hill's**
***Connect Accounting.***

### Problem 10-16A  *Using present value techniques to evaluate alternative investment opportunities*

LO 3, 5, 6

e**X**cel

**CHECK FIGURES**
a. NPV of the vans
   investment: $100,811.42
b. NPV index of the trucks
   investment: 1.126

Fast Delivery is a small company that transports business packages between New York and Chicago. It operates a fleet of small vans that moves packages to and from a central depot within each city and uses a common carrier to deliver the packages between the depots in the two cities. Fast Delivery recently acquired approximately $6 million of cash capital from its owners, and its president, Don Keenon, is trying to identify the most profitable way to invest these funds.

Clarence Roy, the company's operations manager, believes that the money should be used to expand the fleet of city vans at a cost of $720,000. He argues that more vans would enable the company to expand its services into new markets, thereby increasing the revenue base. More specifically, he expects cash inflows to increase by $280,000 per year. The additional vans are expected to have an average useful life of four years and a combined salvage value of $100,000. Operating the vans will require additional working capital of $40,000, which will be recovered at the end of the fourth year.

In contrast, Patricia Lipa, the company's chief accountant, believes that the funds should be used to purchase large trucks to deliver the packages between the depots in the two cities. The conversion process would produce continuing improvement in operating savings with reductions in cash outflows as the following:

| Year 1 | Year 2 | Year 3 | Year 4 |
|---|---|---|---|
| $160,000 | $320,000 | $400,000 | $440,000 |

The large trucks are expected to cost $800,000 and to have a four-year useful life and a $80,000 salvage value. In addition to the purchase price of the trucks, up-front training costs are expected to amount to $16,000. Fast Delivery's management has established a 16 percent desired rate of return.

**Required**

a. Determine the net present value of the two investment alternatives.

b. Calculate the present value index for each alternative.

c. Indicate which investment alternative you would recommend. Explain your choice.

**Problem 10-17A**  *Using the payback period and unadjusted rate of return to evaluate alternative investment opportunities*

Louis Gallo owns a small retail ice cream parlor. He is considering expanding the business and has identified two attractive alternatives. One involves purchasing a machine that would enable Mr. Gallo to offer frozen yogurt to customers. The machine would cost $8,100 and has an expected useful life of three years with no salvage value. Additional annual cash revenues and cash operating expenses associated with selling yogurt are expected to be $5,940 and $900, respectively.

Alternatively, Mr. Gallo could purchase for $10,080 the equipment necessary to serve cappuccino. That equipment has an expected useful life of four years and no salvage value. Additional annual cash revenues and cash operating expenses associated with selling cappuccino are expected to be $8,280 and $2,430, respectively.

Income before taxes earned by the ice cream parlor is taxed at an effective rate of 20 percent.

**Required**

a. Determine the payback period and unadjusted rate of return (use average investment) for each alternative.

b. Indicate which investment alternative you would recommend. Explain your choice.

**Problem 10-18A**  *Using net present value and internal rate of return to evaluate investment opportunities*

Veronica Tanner, the president of Tanner Enterprises, is considering two investment opportunities. Because of limited resources, she will be able to invest in only one of them. Project A is to purchase a machine that will enable factory automation; the machine is expected to have a useful life of four years and no salvage value. Project B supports a training program that will improve the skills of employees operating the current equipment. Initial cash expenditures for Project A are $100,000 and for Project B are $40,000. The annual expected cash inflows are $31,487 for Project A and $13,169 for Project B. Both investments are expected to provide cash flow benefits for the next four years. Tanner Enterprise's cost of capital is 8 percent.

**Required**

a. Compute the net present value of each project. Which project should be adopted based on the net present value approach?

b. Compute the approximate internal rate of return of each project. Which one should be adopted based on the internal rate of return approach?

c. Compare the net present value approach with the internal rate of return approach. Which method is better in the given circumstances? Why?

**Problem 10-19A**  *Using net present value and payback period to evaluate investment opportunities*

Bruce Graham saved $250,000 during the 25 years that he worked for a major corporation. Now he has retired at the age of 50 and has begun to draw a comfortable pension check every month. He wants to ensure the financial security of his retirement by investing his savings wisely and is currently considering two investment opportunities. Both investments require an initial payment of $187,500. The following table presents the estimated cash inflows for the two alternatives.

|  | Year 1 | Year 2 | Year 3 | Year 4 |
|---|---|---|---|---|
| Opportunity #1 | $ 55,625 | $ 58,750 | $78,750 | $101,250 |
| Opportunity #2 | 102,500 | 108,750 | 17,500 | 15,000 |

Mr. Graham decides to use his past average return on mutual fund investments as the discount rate; it is 8 percent.

**Required**

a. Compute the net present value of each opportunity. Which should Mr. Graham adopt based on the net present value approach?

b. Compute the payback period for each project. Which should Mr. Graham adopt based on the payback approach?

c. Compare the net present value approach with the payback approach. Which method is better in the given circumstances?

**Problem 10-20A    Effects of straight-line versus accelerated depreciation on an investment decision**

LO 3, 6, 7, 8

CHECK FIGURES
a. NPV = $71,810
d. Payback period: 2.32 years

Zito Electronics is considering investing in manufacturing equipment expected to cost $184,000. The equipment has an estimated useful life of four years and a salvage value of $24,000. It is expected to produce incremental cash revenues of $96,000 per year. Zito has an effective income tax rate of 30 percent and a desired rate of return of 12 percent.

**Required**

a. Determine the net present value and the present value index of the investment, assuming that Zito uses straight-line depreciation for financial and income tax reporting.

b. Determine the net present value and the present value index of the investment, assuming that Zito uses double-declining-balance depreciation for financial and income tax reporting.

c. Why do the net present values computed in Requirements *a* and *b* differ?

d. Determine the payback period and unadjusted rate of return (use average investment), assuming that Zito uses straight-line depreciation.

e. Determine the payback period and unadjusted rate of return (use average investment), assuming that Zito uses double-declining-balance depreciation. (*Note:* Use average annual cash flow when computing the payback period and average annual income when determining the unadjusted rate of return.)

f. Why are there no differences in the payback periods or unadjusted rates of return computed in Requirements *d* and *e*?

**Problem 10-21A    Applying the net present value approach with and without tax considerations**

LO 3, 5, 6

CHECK FIGURE
a. $(46,120.48)

Paxton Kingsley, the chief executive officer of Kingsley Corporation, has assembled his top advisers to evaluate an investment opportunity. The advisers expect the company to pay $150,000 cash at the beginning of the investment and the cash inflow for each of the following four years to be the following.

| Year 1 | Year 2 | Year 3 | Year 4 |
|--------|--------|--------|--------|
| $84,000 | $96,000 | $120,000 | $184,000 |

Mr. Kingsley agrees with his advisers that the company should use the discount rate (required rate of return) of 12 percent to compute net present value to evaluate the viability of the proposed project.

**Required**

a. Compute the net present value of the proposed project. Should Mr. Kingsley approve the project?

b. Wilma Pate, one of the advisers, is wary of the cash flow forecast and she points out that the advisers failed to consider that the depreciation on equipment used in this project will be tax deductible. The depreciation is expected to be $80,000 per year for the four-year period. The company's income tax rate is 30 percent per year. Use this information to revise the company's expected cash flow from this project.

c. Compute the net present value of the project based on the revised cash flow forecast. Should Mr. Kingsley approve the project?

## Problem 10-22A  *Comparing internal rate of return with unadjusted rate of return*

Walker Auto Repair, Inc., is evaluating a project to purchase equipment that will not only expand the company's capacity but also improve the quality of its repair services. The board of directors requires all capital investments to meet or exceed the minimum requirement of a 10 percent rate of return. However, the board has not clearly defined the rate of return. The president and controller are pondering two different rates of return: unadjusted rate of return and internal rate of return. The equipment, which costs $100,000, has a life expectancy of five years. The increased net profit per year will be approximately $7,000, and the increased cash inflow per year will be approximately $27,700.

### Required

a. If it uses the unadjusted rate of return (use average investment) to evaluate this project, should the company invest in the equipment?

b. If it uses the internal rate of return to evaluate this project, should the company invest in the equipment?

c. Which method is better for this capital investment decision?

## Problem 10-23A  *Postaudit evaluation*

Ernest Jones is reviewing his company's investment in a cement plant. The company paid $15,000,000 five years ago to acquire the plant. Now top management is considering an opportunity to sell it. The president wants to know whether the plant has met original expectations before he decides its fate. The company's discount rate for present value computations is 8 percent. Expected and actual cash flows follow.

|          | Year 1      | Year 2      | Year 3      | Year 4      | Year 5      |
|----------|-------------|-------------|-------------|-------------|-------------|
| Expected | $3,300,000  | $4,920,000  | $4,560,000  | $4,980,000  | $4,200,000  |
| Actual   | 2,700,000   | 3,060,000   | 4,920,000   | 3,900,000   | 3,600,000   |

### Required

a. Compute the net present value of the expected cash flows as of the beginning of the investment.

b. Compute the net present value of the actual cash flows as of the beginning of the investment.

c. What do you conclude from this postaudit?

## EXERCISES—SERIES B

### Exercise 10-1B  *Identifying cash inflows and outflows*

### Required

Barry Nance is considering whether to invest in a dump truck. Mr. Nance would hire a driver and use the truck to haul trash for customers. He wants to use present value techniques to evaluate the investment opportunity. List sources of potential cash inflows and cash outflows Mr. Nance could expect if he invests in the truck.

### Exercise 10-2B  *Determining the present value of a lump-sum future cash receipt*

One year from today Bernice Smyth is scheduled to receive a $60,000 payment from a trust fund her father established. She wants to buy a car today but does not have the money. A friend has agreed to give Bernice the present value of the $60,000 today if she agrees to give him the full $60,000 when she collects it one year from now. They agree that 8 percent reflects a fair discount rate.

### Required

a. You have been asked to determine the present value of the future cash flow. Use a present value table to determine the amount of cash that Bernice's friend should give her.

b. Use an algebraic formula to verify the result you determined in Requirement *a*.

## Exercise 10-3B    *Determining the present value of a lump-sum future cash receipt*

Cornelius Toran has a terminal illness. His doctors have estimated his remaining life expectancy as three years. Cornelius has a $1,000,000 life insurance policy but no close relative to list as the beneficiary. He is considering canceling the policy because he needs the money he is currently paying for the premiums to buy medical supplies. A wealthy close friend has advised Cornelius not to cancel the policy. The friend has proposed instead giving Cornelius $500,000 to use for his medical needs while keeping the policy in force. In exchange, Cornelius would designate the friend as the policy beneficiary. Cornelius is reluctant to take the $500,000 because he believes that his friend is offering charity. His friend has tried to convince Cornelius that the offer is a legitimate business deal.

**Required**

a. Determine the present value of the $1,000,000 life insurance benefit. Assume a 10 percent discount rate.

b. Assuming 10 percent represents a fair rate of return, is Cornelius' friend offering charity or is he seeking to profit financially from Cornelius' misfortune?

## Exercise 10-4B    *Determining the present value of an annuity*

Julia Rainy is considering whether to install a drink machine at the gas station she owns. Julia is convinced that providing a drink machine at the station would increase customer convenience. However, she is not convinced that buying the machine would be a profitable investment. Friends who have installed drink machines at their stations have estimated that she could expect to receive net cash inflows of approximately $4,000 per year from the machine. Julia believes that she should earn 10 percent on her investments. The drink machine is expected to have a two-year life and zero salvage value.

**Required**

a. Use Present Value Table 1 to determine the maximum amount of cash Julia should be willing to pay for a drink machine.

b. Use Present Value Table 2 to determine the maximum amount of cash Julia should be willing to pay for a drink machine.

c. Explain the consistency or lack of consistency in the answers to Requirement *a* versus Requirement *b*.

## Exercise 10-5B    *Determining the net present value*

Rafael Ortega, manager of the Pena Music Hall, is considering the opportunity to expand the company's concession revenues. Specifically, she is considering whether to install a popcorn machine. Based on market research, she believes that the machine could produce incremental cash inflows of $2,400 per year. The purchase price of the machine is $7,500. It is expected to have a useful life of three years and a $1,500 salvage value. Ms. Ortega has established a desired rate of return of 16 percent.

**Required**

a. Calculate the net present value of the investment opportunity.

b. Should the company buy the popcorn machine?

## Exercise 10-6B    *Determining the net present value*

Howard Parmer has decided to start a small delivery business to help support himself while attending school. Mr. Parmer expects demand for delivery services to grow steadily as customers discover their availability. Annual cash outflows are expected to increase only slightly because many of the business operating costs are fixed. Cash inflows and outflows expected from operating the delivery business follow:

| Year of Operation | Cash Inflow | Cash Outflow |
|---|---|---|
| 2012 | $6,800 | $3,200 |
| 2013 | 7,600 | 3,600 |
| 2014 | 8,400 | 3,840 |
| 2015 | 9,200 | 4,000 |

The used delivery van Mr. Parmer plans to buy is expected to cost $13,200. It has an expected useful life of four years and a salvage value of $2,400. At the end of 2013, Mr. Parmer expects to pay additional costs of approximately $540 for maintenance and new tires. Mr. Parmer's desired rate of return is 12 percent.

**Required**

(Round computations to the nearest whole penny.)

a. Calculate the net present value of the investment opportunity.
b. Indicate whether the investment opportunity is expected to earn a return above or below the desired rate of return. Should Mr. Parmer start the delivery business?

**LO 3**

### Exercise 10-7B    *Using the present value index*

Two alternative investment opportunities are available to Claude Reyna, president of Reyna Enterprises. For the first alternative, the present value of cash inflows is $133,000, and the present value of cash outflows is $127,000. For the second alternative, the present value of cash inflows is $230,000, and the present value of cash outflows is $223,000.

**Required**

a. Calculate the net present value of each investment opportunity.
b. Calculate the present value index for each investment opportunity.
c. Indicate which investment will produce the higher rate of return.

**LO 4**

### Exercise 10-8B    *Determining the internal rate of return*

Sam Eatmon, CFO of Chaiston Enterprises, is evaluating an opportunity to invest in additional manufacturing equipment that will enable the company to increase its net cash inflows by $150,000 per year. The equipment costs $448,591.80. It is expected to have a five-year useful life and a zero salvage value. Chaiston's cost of capital is 18 percent.

**Required**

a. Calculate the internal rate of return of the investment opportunity.
b. Indicate whether Chaiston should purchase the equipment.

**LO 4, 6**

### Exercise 10-9B    *Using the internal rate of return to compare investment opportunities*

Yvonne Tower has two alternative investment opportunities to evaluate. The first opportunity would cost $149,512.23 and generate expected cash inflows of $21,000 per year for 17 years. The second opportunity would cost $136,909.44 and generate expected cash inflows of $18,000 per year for 15 years. Ms. Tower has sufficient funds available to accept only one opportunity.

**Required**

a. Calculate the internal rate of return of each investment opportunity.
b. Based on the internal rate of return criteria, which opportunity should Ms. Tower select?
c. Identify two other evaluation techniques Ms. Tower could use to compare the investment opportunities.

**LO 1, 2, 5**

### Exercise 10-10B    *Determining a cash flow annuity with income tax considerations*

Jay Welch is considering whether to invest in a computer game machine that he would place in a hotel his brother owns. The machine would cost $14,000 and has an expected useful life of three years and a salvage value of $2,000. Mr. Welch estimates the machine would generate revenue of $7,000 per year and cost $1,200 per year to operate. He uses the straight-line method for depreciation. His income tax rate is 30 percent.

**Required**

What amount of net cash inflow from operations would Mr. Welch expect for the first year if he invests in the machine?

**Exercise 10-11B**   *Evaluating discounted cash flow techniques*                  **LO 9**

Four years ago Jeanne Nolen decided to invest in a project. At that time she had projected annual net cash inflows would be $54,000. Over its expected four-year useful life, the project had produced significantly higher cash inflows than anticipated. The actual average annual cash inflow from the project was $63,000. Nolen breathed a sigh of relief. She always worried that projects would not live up to expectations. To avoid this potential disappointment she tried always to underestimate the projected cash inflows of potential investments. She commented, "I prefer pleasant rather than unpleasant surprises." Indeed, no investment approved by Ms. Nolen had ever failed a postaudit review. Her investments consistently exceeded expectations.

**Required**

Explain the purpose of a postaudit and comment on Ms. Nolen's investment record.

**Exercise 10-12B**   *Determining the payback period*                              **LO 7**

The management team at Rawden Manufacturing Company has decided to modernize the manufacturing facility. The company can replace an existing, outdated machine with one of two technologically advanced machines. One replacement machine would cost $50,000. Management estimates that it would reduce cash outflows for manufacturing expenses by $20,000 per year. This machine is expected to have an eight-year useful life and a $1,250 salvage value. The other replacement machine would cost $63,000 and would reduce annual cash outflows by an estimated $22,500. This machine has an expected 10-year useful life and an $6,250 salvage value.

**Required**

a. Determine the payback period for each investment alternative and identify which replacement machine Rawden should buy if it bases the decision on the payback approach.

b. Discuss the shortcomings of the payback method of evaluating investment opportunities.

**Exercise 10-13B**   *Determining the payback period with uneven cash flows*      **LO 5, 7**

Cascade Snowmobile Company is considering whether to invest in a particular new snowmobile model. The model is top-of-the-line equipment for which Cascade expects high demand during the first year it is available for rent. However, as the snowmobile ages, it will become less desirable and its rental revenues are expected to decline. The expected cash inflows and outflows follow.

| Year | Nature of Cash Flow | Cash Inflow | Cash Outflow |
|------|--------------------|-------------|--------------|
| 2013 | Purchase price     | —           | $35,000      |
| 2013 | Revenue            | $20,000     | —            |
| 2014 | Revenue            | 15,000      | —            |
| 2015 | Revenue            | 13,750      | —            |
| 2016 | Major overhaul     | —           | 5,000        |
| 2017 | Revenue            | 7,500       | —            |
| 2018 | Revenue            | 5,000       | —            |
| 2019 | Salvage value      | 4,000       | —            |

**Required**

a. Determine the payback period using the accumulated cash flows approach.

b. Determine the payback period using the average cash flows approach.

**Exercise 10-14B**   *Determining the unadjusted rate of return*                    **LO 8**

Intercity Shuttle Service, Inc., is considering whether to purchase an additional shuttle van. The van would cost $36,000 and have a zero salvage value. It would enable the company to increase net income by $6,030 per year. The manufacturer estimates the van's effective life as five years.

**Required**

a. Determine the unadjusted rate of return based on the average cost of the investment.

b. What is the shortcoming of using the unadjusted rate of return to evaluate investment opportunities?

**LO 7, 8**

### Exercise 10-15B  *Computing the payback period and unadjusted rate of return for the same investment opportunity*

Gunter Marina (Guntersville) rents pontoon boats to customers. It has the opportunity to purchase an additional pontoon boat for $30,000; it has an expected useful life of four years and no salvage value. Guntersville uses straight-line depreciation. Expected rental revenue for the boat is $10,000 per year.

**Required**

a. Determine the payback period.

b. Determine the unadjusted rate of return based on the average cost of the investment.

c. Assume that the company's desired rate of return is 30 percent. Should Guntersville purchase the additional boat?

## PROBLEMS—SERIES B

**LO 3, 5, 6**

### Problem 10-16B  *Using present value techniques to evaluate alternative investment opportunities*

Porter Automobile Repair, Inc., currently has three repair shops in Boston. Vincent Porter, the president and chief executive officer, is facing a pleasant dilemma: the business has continued to grow rapidly and major shareholders are arguing about different ways to capture more business opportunities. The company requires a 12 percent rate of return for its investment projects and uses the straight-line method of depreciation for all fixed assets.

One group of shareholders wants to open another shop in a newly developed suburban community. This project would require an initial investment of $480,000 to acquire all the necessary equipment, which has a useful life of five years with a salvage value of $160,000. Once the shop begins to operate, another $120,000 of working capital would be required; it would be recovered at the end of the fifth year. The expected net cash inflow from the new shop follows.

| Year 1 | Year 2 | Year 3 | Year 4 | Year 5 |
|--------|--------|--------|--------|--------|
| $48,000 | $96,000 | $152,000 | $192,000 | $240,000 |

A second group of shareholders prefers to invest $400,000 to acquire new computerized diagnostic equipment for the existing shops. The equipment is expected to have a useful life of five years with a salvage value of $80,000. Using this state-of-the-art equipment, mechanics would be able to pinpoint automobile problems more quickly and accurately. Consequently, it would allow the existing shops to increase their service capacity and revenue by $120,000 per year. The company would need to train mechanics to use the equipment, which would cost $40,000 at the beginning of the first year.

**Required**

a. Determine the net present value of the two investment alternatives.

b. Calculate the present value index for each alternative.

c. Indicate which investment alternative you would recommend. Explain your choice.

**LO 7, 8**

### Problem 10-17B  *Using the payback period and unadjusted rate of return to evaluate alternative investment opportunities*

Jessica and Victor Services is planning a new business venture. With $100,000 of available funds to invest, it is investigating two options. One is to acquire an exclusive contract to operate vending machines in civic and recreation centers in a small suburban city for four years. The contract requires the firm to pay the city $40,000 cash at the beginning. The firm expects the cash revenue from the operation to be $50,000 per year and the cash expenses to be $28,000 per year.

The second option is to operate a printing shop in an office complex. This option would require the company to spend $72,000 for printing equipment that has a useful life of four years with a zero salvage value. The cash revenue is expected to be $85,000 per year and cash expenses are expected to be $47,000 per year. The firm uses the straight-line method of depreciation. Its effective income tax rate is expected to be 20 percent.

**Required**

a. Determine the payback period and unadjusted rate of return (use average investment) for each alternative.

b. Indicate which investment alternative you would recommend. Explain your choice.

**Problem 10-18B**   *Using net present value and internal rate of return to evaluate*                **LO 3, 4, 5, 6**
*investment opportunities*

Kerry Wood's rich uncle gave him $60,000 cash as a gift for his 40th birthday. Unlike his spoiled cousins who spend money carelessly, Mr. Wood wants to invest the money for his future retirement. After an extensive search, he is considering one of two investment opportunities. Project 1 would require an immediate cash payment of $52,800; Project 2 needs only a $24,000 cash payment at the beginning. The expected cash inflows are $17,280 per year for Project 1 and $8,400 per year for Project 2. Both projects are expected to provide cash flow benefits for the next four years. Mr. Wood found that the interest rate for a four-year certificate of deposit is about 7 percent. He decided that this is his required rate of return.

**Required**

a. Compute the net present value of each project. Which project should Mr. Wood adopt based on the net present value approach?

b. Compute the approximate internal rate of return of each project. Which project should Mr. Wood adopt based on the internal rate of return approach?

c. Compare the net present value approach with the internal rate of return approach. Which method is better in the given circumstances?

**Problem 10-19B**   *Using net present value and payback period to evaluate investment*                **LO 3, 6, 7**
*opportunities*

Margaret Hubbard just won a lottery and received a cash award of $800,000 net of tax. She is 61 years old and would like to retire in four years. Weighing this important fact, she has found two possible investments, both of which require an immediate cash payment of $640,000. The expected cash inflows from the two investment opportunities are as follows.

|               | Year 1   | Year 2   | Year 3   | Year 4   |
|---------------|----------|----------|----------|----------|
| Opportunity A | $364,800 | $208,000 | $118,400 | $134,400 |
| Opportunity B | 91,200   | 107,200  | 236,800  | 540,800  |

Ms. Hubbard decided that her required rate of return should be 10 percent.

**Required**

a. Compute the net present value of each opportunity. Which should Ms. Hubbard choose based on the net present value approach?

b. Compute the payback period for each opportunity. Which should Ms. Hubbard choose based on the payback approach?

c. Compare the net present value approach with the payback approach. Which method is better in the given circumstances?

**Problem 10-20B**   *Effects of straight-line versus accelerated depreciation on an*                **LO 3, 6, 7, 8**
*investment decision*

Pacific Steel Company decided to spend $160,000 to purchase new state-of-the-art equipment for its manufacturing plant. The equipment has a five-year useful life and a salvage value of $40,000. It is expected to generate additional cash revenue of $64,000 per year. Pacific Steel required rate of return is 10 percent; its effective income tax rate is 25 percent.

**Required**

a. Determine the net present value and the present value index of the investment, assuming that Pacific Steel uses straight-line depreciation for financial and income tax reporting.

b. Determine the net present value and the present value index of the investment, assuming that Pacific Steel uses double-declining-balance depreciation for financial and income tax reporting.

c. Why are there differences in the net present values computed in Requirements a and b?

d. Determine the payback period and unadjusted rate of return (use average investment), assuming that Pacific Steel uses straight-line depreciation.

e. Determine the payback period and unadjusted rate of return (use average investment), assuming that Pacific Steel uses double-declining-balance depreciation. (*Note:* Use average annual cash flow when computing the payback period and average annual income when computing the unadjusted rate of return.)

f. Why are there no differences in the payback period or unadjusted rate of return computed in Requirements d and e?

**LO 3, 5, 6**

**Problem 10-21B** *Applying the net present value approach with and without tax considerations*

Luther Currie, the president of Luther's Moving Services, Inc., is planning to spend $625,000 for new trucks. He expects the trucks to increase the company's cash inflow as follows.

| Year 1 | Year 2 | Year 3 | Year 4 |
|--------|--------|--------|--------|
| $163,500 | $178,215 | $194,255 | $211,735 |

The company's policy stipulates that all investments must earn a minimum rate of return of 10 percent.

**Required**

a. Compute the net present value of the proposed purchase. Should Mr. Currie purchase the trucks?

b. Cheryl Percy, the controller, is wary of the cash flow forecast and points out that Mr. Currie failed to consider that the depreciation on trucks used in this project will be tax deductible. The depreciation is expected to be $150,000 per year for the four-year period. The company's income tax rate is 30 percent per year. Use this information to revise the company's expected cash flow from this purchase.

c. Compute the net present value of the purchase based on the revised cash flow forecast. Should Mr. Currie purchase the trucks?

**LO 4, 8**

**Problem 10-22B** *Comparing internal rate of return with unadjusted rate of return*

Ledlow Corporation faces stiff market competition. Top management is considering the replacement of its current production facility. The board of directors requires all capital investments to meet or exceed a 9 percent rate of return. However, the board has not clearly defined the rate of return. The president and controller are pondering two different rates of return: unadjusted rate of return and internal rate of return. To purchase a new facility with a life expectancy of four years, the company must pay $90,000. The increased net profit per year resulting from improved conditions would be approximately $10,000; the increased cash inflow per year would be approximately $27,500.

**Required**

a. If it uses the unadjusted rate of return (use average investment) to evaluate this project, should the company invest in the new facility?

b. If it uses the internal rate of return to evaluate this project, should the company invest in the new facility?

c. Which method is better for this capital investment decision?

**LO 9**

**Problem 10-23B** *Postaudit evaluation*

Max Baldwin is wondering whether he made the right decision four years ago. As the president of Baldwin Health Care Services, he acquired a hospital specializing in elder care with an initial cash investment of $2,800,000. Mr. Baldwin would like to know whether the hospital's financial performance has met the original investment objective. The company's discount rate (required rate of return) for present value computations is 14 percent. Expected and actual cash flows follow.

|  | Year 1 | Year 2 | Year 3 | Year 4 |
|---|---|---|---|---|
| Expected | $920,000 | $960,000 | $1,000,000 | $1,200,000 |
| Actual | 800,000 | 760,000 | 1,280,000 | 1,400,000 |

**Required**

a. Compute the net present value of the expected cash flows as of the beginning of the investment.

b. Compute the net present value of the actual cash flows as of the beginning of the investment.

c. What do you conclude from this postaudit?

## ANALYZE, THINK, COMMUNICATE

### ATC 10-1    Business Application Case    *Home remodeling decision*

Karen and Steve Catrow want to replace the windows in the older house they purchased recently. The company they have talked to about doing the work claims that new windows will reduce the couple's heating and cooling costs by around 30 percent. The Catrows have heard from real estate agents that they will get back 70 percent of the cost of the new windows when they sell their house. The new windows will cost $30,000.

The heating and cooling costs for the Catrows' house average around $5,000 per year, and they expect to stay in this house for 10 years. To pay for the windows they would have to withdraw the money from a mutual fund that has earned an average annual return of 3 percent over the past few years.

**Required**

a. From a financial planning perspective alone, determine whether or not the Catrows should purchase the replacement windows. Show supporting computations.

b. (Requirement *b* can only be solved with Excel, or similar software, or with a financial calculator.) Karen and Steve are not sure their mutual fund will continue to earn 3 percent annually over the next 10 years; therefore, they want to know the minimum return their fund would need to earn to make the new windows financially acceptable. Compute the internal rate of return for the replacement windows.

c. Identify some of the nonfinancial factors the couple may wish to consider in addition to the financial aspects of the decision above.

### ATC 10-2    Group Assignment    *Net present value*

Espada Real Estate Investment Company (EREIC) purchases new apartment complexes, establishes a stable group of residents, and then sells the complexes to apartment management companies. The average holding time is three years. EREIC is currently investigating two alternatives.

1. EREIC can purchase Harding Properties for $4,500,000. The complex is expected to produce net cash inflows of $360,000, $502,500, and $865,000 for the first, second, and third years of operation, respectively. The market value of the complex at the end of the third year is expected to be $5,175,000.

2. EREIC can purchase Summit Apartments for $3,450,000. The complex is expected to produce net cash inflows of $290,000, $435,000, and $600,000 for the first, second, and third years of operation, respectively. The market value of the complex at the end of the third year is expected to be $4,050,000.

EREIC has a desired rate of return of 12 percent.

## Required

a. Divide the class into groups of four or five students per group and then divide the groups into two sections. Assign Task 1 to the first section and Task 2 to the second section.

## Group Tasks

(1) Calculate the net present value and the present value index for Harding Properties.

(2) Calculate the net present value and the present value index for Summit Apartments.

b. Have a spokesperson from one group in the first section report the amounts calculated by the group. Make sure that all groups in the section have the same result. Repeat the process for the second section. Have the class as a whole select the investment opportunity that EREIC should accept given that the objective is to produce the higher rate of return.

c. Assume that EREIC has $4,500,000 to invest and that any funds not invested in real estate properties must be invested in a certificate of deposit earning a 5 percent return. Would this information alter the decision made in Requirement *b*?

d. This requirement is independent of Requirement *c*. Assume there is a 10 percent chance that the Harding project will be annexed by the city of Hoover, which has an outstanding school district. The annexation would likely increase net cash flows by $37,500 per year and would increase the market value at the end of year 3 by $300,000. Would this information change the decision reached in Requirement *b*?

## ATC 10-3  Research Assignment  *Capital Expenditures at the Archer Daniels Midland Company*

Obtain Archer Daniels Midland Company's (ADM) Form 10-Ks for the fiscal year ending on June 30, 2006 and 2009. To obtain the Form 10-Ks you can use either the EDGAR system following the instructions in Appendix A, or it can be found under the "Investor Relations" link on the company's website at www.admworld.com/naen. Read the "General Development of Business" under the "Item I. Business" section of the 2006 10-K, and the Statement of Cash Flows and Note 15 of the 2009 10-K.

## Required

a. What major plant expansions did ADM announce during 2006? How much does ADM estimate these expansions will cost?

b. How much did ADM spend on investing activities in its 2009 and 2008 fiscal years?

c. Where did ADM get the cash used to make these investments?

d. How much of ADM's investments in new property, plant, and equipment was related to its "corn processing" segment in 2009 and 2008?

## ATC 10-4  Writing Assignment  *Limitations of capital investment techniques*

Webb Publishing Company is evaluating two investment opportunities. One is to purchase an Internet company with the capacity to open new marketing channels through which Webb can sell its books. This opportunity offers a high potential for growth but involves significant risk. Indeed, losses are projected for the first three years of operation. The second opportunity is to purchase a printing company that would enable Webb to better control costs by printing its own books. The potential savings are clearly predictable but would make a significant change in the company's long-term profitability.

## Required

Write a response discussing the usefulness of capital investment techniques (net present value, internal rate of return, payback, and unadjusted rate of return) in making a choice between these two alternative investment opportunities. Your response should discuss the strengths and weaknesses of capital budgeting techniques in general. Furthermore, it should include a comparison between techniques based on the time value of money versus those that are not.

## ATC 10-5  Ethical Dilemma  *Postaudit*

Gaines Company recently initiated a postaudit program. To motivate employees to take the program seriously, Gaines established a bonus program. Managers receive a bonus equal to 10 percent of the amount by which actual net present value exceeds the projected net present value. Victor Holt, manager of the North Western Division, had an investment proposal on his desk when the new system was implemented. The investment opportunity required a $250,000 initial cash outflow and was expected to return cash inflows of $90,000 per year for the next five years. Gaines' desired rate of return is 10 percent. Mr. Holt immediately reduced the estimated cash inflows to $70,000 per year and recommended accepting the project.

**Required**

a. Assume that actual cash inflows turn out to be $91,000 per year. Determine the amount of Mr. Holt's bonus if the original computation of net present value were based on $90,000 versus $70,000.

b. Is Mr. Holt's behavior in violation of any of the standards of ethical conduct in Exhibit 1.15 of Chapter 1?

c. Speculate about the long-term effect the bonus plan is likely to have on the company.

d. Recommend how to compensate managers in a way that discourages gamesmanship.

## ATC 10-6   Spreadsheet Assignment   *Using Excel*

Kilby Company is considering the purchase of new automated manufacturing equipment that would cost $150,000. The equipment would save $42,500 in labor costs per year over its six-year life. At the end of the fourth year, the equipment would require an overhaul that would cost $25,000. The equipment would have a $7,500 salvage value at the end of its life. Kilby's cost of capital is 12 percent.

**Required**

a. Prepare a spreadsheet similar to the one following to calculate net present value, the present value index, and the internal rate of return.

## Spreadsheet Tips

Spreadsheets have built-in financial functions that make net present value and internal rate of return calculations very easy. The formats of these formulas are as follows.

1. *Net Present Value:* =NPV(rate,value1,value2,value3 . . . value29) where up to 29 values are allowed. The values must be at the end of the period, and each period must be equal in time (one year, for example). The formula is =NPV(D3,D7,D8,D9,D10,D11,D12) + D6.

2. *Internal Rate of Return:* =IRR (values,guess) where *values* is the range that includes the cash flows (D6 to D12) and *guess* is an estimate of the rate. Use the cost of capital as the guess.

3. *Percentage:* Rather than entering 12% in the formulas, refer to cell D3. This will allow you to change the rate and see the effect on the NPV and present value index.

4. *Present Value Index:* You must construct a formula because no built-in function calculates it.

## ATC 10-7   Spreadsheet Assignment   *Mastering Excel*

ASAP Delivery is a small company that transports business packages between San Francisco and Los Angeles. It operates a fleet of small vans that moves packages to and from a central depot within each city and uses a common carrier to deliver the packages between the depots in the two cities. ASAP recently acquired approximately $4 million of cash capital from its owners, and its president, Alex Cade, is trying to identify the most profitable way to invest these funds.

Phil Duvall, the company's operations manager, believes that the money should be used to expand the fleet of city vans at a cost of $3,600,000. He argues that more vans would enable the company to expand its services into new markets, thereby increasing the revenue base. More specifically, he expects cash inflows to increase by $1,400,000 per year. The additional vans are expected to have an average useful life of four years and a combined salvage value of $500,000. Operating the vans will require additional working capital of $200,000, which will be recovered at the end of the fourth year.

In contrast, Amber Gomez, the company's chief accountant, believes that the funds should be used to purchase large trucks to deliver the packages between the depots in the two cities. The conversion process would produce continuing improvement in operating savings with reductions in cash outflows as the following:

| Year 1 | Year 2 | Year 3 | Year 4 |
|--------|--------|--------|--------|
| $800,000 | $1,600,000 | $2,000,000 | $2,200,000 |

The large trucks are expected to cost $4,000,000 and to have a four-year useful life and a $400,000 salvage value. In addition to the purchase price of the trucks, up-front training costs are expected to amount to $80,000. ASAP Delivery's management has established a 16 percent desired rate of return.

### Required

a. Prepare a spreadsheet similar to the preceding one that calculates the net present value and the present value index for the two investments.

b. Include formulas in your spreadsheet to calculate the internal rate of return for each investment alternative.

## COMPREHENSIVE PROBLEM

Magnificent Modems, Inc. (MMI), has several capital investment opportunities. The term, expected annual cash inflows, and the cost of each opportunity are outlined in the following table. MMI has established a desired rate of return of 16 percent for these investment opportunities.

| Opportunity | A | B | C | D |
|-------------|---|---|---|---|
| Investment term | 4 years | 5 years | 3 years | 5 years |
| Expected cash inflow | $ 6,000 | $ 5,000 | $ 8,000 | $ 4,800 |
| Cost of investment | $16,000 | $15,000 | $18,000 | $16,000 |

### Required

a. Compute the net present value of each investment opportunity manually using the present value tables. Record your answers in the following table. The results for Investment Opportunity A have been recorded in the table as an example.

| Opportunity | A | B | C | D |
|---|---|---|---|---|
| Cash inflow | $6,000.00 | $5,000.00 | $8,000.00 | $4,800.00 |
| Times present value factor | 2.798181 | | | |
| Present value of cash flows | $16,789.09 | | | |
| Minus cost of investment | ($16,000.00) | ($15,000.00) | ($18,000.00) | ($16,000.00) |
| Net present value | $789.09 | | | |

**b.** Use Excel spreadsheet software or a financial calculator to determine the net present value and the internal rate of return for each investment opportunity. Record the results in the following table. The results for investment Opportunity A have been recorded in the following table as an example. Note that the manual computation yields the same net present value amounts as the financial function routines of Excel or a financial calculator.

| Opportunity | A | B | C | D |
|---|---|---|---|---|
| Net present value | $789.09 | | | |
| Internal rate of return | 18.45% | | | |

## CHAPTER 11

# Product Costing in Service and Manufacturing Entities

## LEARNING OBJECTIVES

**After you have mastered the material in this chapter you will be able to:**

**1** Describe the nature and treatment of product cost information for manufacturing and service companies.

**2** Demonstrate the flow of materials and labor costs for a manufacturing company.

**3** Assign estimated overhead costs to inventory and cost of goods sold.

**4** Account for completion and sale of products.

**5** Prepare a schedule of cost of goods manufactured and sold.

**6** Prepare financial statements for a manufacturing company.

**7** Distinguish between absorption and variable costing.

## CHAPTER OPENING

*Service* and *product costing systems* supply information about the cost of providing services or making products. Organizations need service and product cost information for financial reporting, managerial accounting, and contract negotiations.

For *financial reporting,* companies are required by generally accepted accounting principles (GAAP) to report service and product costs in their published financial statements. For example, product costs for manufacturing companies must be allocated between inventory (reported on the balance sheet) and cost of goods sold (reported on the income statement). Similarly, service companies must match on their income statements the costs of providing services with the revenues generated from the services provided.

For *managerial accounting,* managers need to know the cost of providing services or making products so they can plan company operations. For example, companies could not prepare budgets without knowing the cost of services or products. Service and product costing is also needed for cost control. Managers compare expected costs with actual costs to identify problems that need correcting. Service and product cost information may be used for pricing and other short-term decisions. For example, the cost of a service or product may be used in special order, outsourcing, or product elimination decisions.

Service and product costing information may be used by governmental agencies to regulate rates for public service entities such as utility companies or hospitals. Service and product costs are also used in determining the amount due on contracts that compensate companies for the costs they incur plus a reasonable profit (cost-plus contracts). For example, many governmental defense contracts are negotiated on a cost-plus basis. Cost-plus pricing may also be used by private companies. For example, many builders of custom homes charge customers based on cost-plus contracts. Cost information is therefore necessary for contract negotiations. This chapter shows how manufacturing companies determine the cost of the products they make.

# The Curious Accountant

Northwestern Aviation is a small company in Kotzebue, Alaska, that provides bush flying services to persons wanting to travel into the arctic to go fishing, canoeing, hiking, or who wish to do flight-seeing trips to wilderness areas such as Kobuk Valley National Park. Given the climate, the company does most of its business during the summer months.

Northwestern incurs a variety of costs. Some of these costs, such as the cost of aviation gasoline, vary with the number and type of trips. Recently, when aviation fuel was selling for around $5 per gallon in the lower 48 states, it was priced at $7 per gallon in Kotzebue, due to its remote location. The Cessna 206 airplane that Northwestern uses consumes around 15 gallons of fuel per hour, creating a fuel cost of $105 for each hour flown. Other cost go up with increased activity but may not be incurred on a per trip basis. For example, the Cessna 206 needs a major engine overhaul about every 1,400 operating hours. Finally, there are costs that are fixed; they must be paid for regardless of the number of trips the company flies each year. For example, a new Cessna 206 cost around $500,000 and payments on airplanes must be made regardless of the amount of revenue they earn. Costs for facilities, such as airport space, also do not depend of how much, or how little, business is done in a given season. As you have learned in earlier chapters, the higher the level of activity, the lower the fixed cost per unit of activity will be.

These cost behaviors present a problem for Northwestern. Potential clients contact the company months in advance to book trips, and they want to know the price they will be charged. The company, however, does not know what it will actually cost to provide the trip in question since the final cost depends on its level of activity, and it does not know how many trips it will provide in the upcoming season until the season is over. Nevertheless, prices must be quoted, in advance, on a per hour basis.

How can a company with significant fixed costs, such as Northwestern Aviation, know what to charge customers when it will not know the real cost of any one trip until the season is over? (Answer on page 494.)

# COST FLOW IN MANUFACTURING COMPANIES

Describe the nature and treatment of product cost information for manufacturing and service companies.

In previous chapters, we assumed all inventory started during an accounting period was also completed during that accounting period. All product costs (materials, labor, and manufacturing overhead) were either in inventory or expensed as cost of goods sold. At the end of an accounting period, however, most real-world companies have raw materials on hand, and manufacturing companies are likely to have in inventory items that have been started but are not completed. Most manufacturing companies accumulate product costs in three distinct inventory accounts: (1) **Raw Materials Inventory,** which includes lumber, metals, paints, and chemicals that will be used to make the company's products; (2) **Work in Process Inventory,** which includes partially completed products; and (3) **Finished Goods Inventory,** which includes completed products that are ready for sale.

The cost of materials is first recorded in the Raw Materials Inventory account. The cost of materials placed in production is then transferred from the Raw Materials Inventory account to the Work in Process Inventory account. The costs of labor and overhead are added to the Work in Process Inventory account. The cost of the goods completed during the period is transferred from the Work in Process Inventory account to the Finished Goods Inventory account. The cost of the goods that are sold during the accounting period is transferred from the Finished Goods Inventory account to the Cost of Goods Sold account. The balances that remain in the Raw Materials, Work in Process, and Finished Goods Inventory accounts are reported on the balance sheet. The amount of product cost transferred to the Cost of Goods Sold account is expensed on the income statement. Exhibit 11.1 shows the flow of manufacturing costs through the accounting records.

**EXHIBIT 11.1**

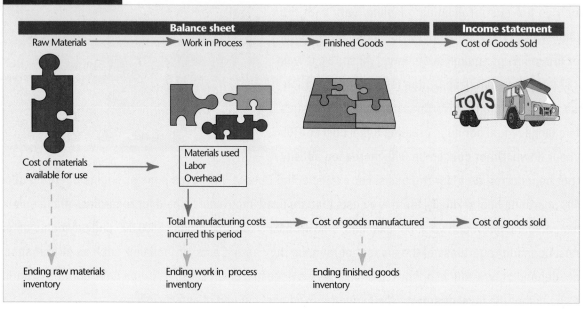

# COST FLOW IN SERVICE COMPANIES

Like manufacturing companies, many service companies purchase raw materials and transform them through production stages such as work in process, finished goods, and cost of goods sold. For example, a **McDonald's** hamburger starts with raw materials (meat, bun, and condiments), goes through work in process (is cooked, assembled, and wrapped), becomes a finished product, and is sold to a customer. Why then is McDonald's considered a *service* rather than a *manufacturing* company? The distinguishing feature is that products from McDonald's are consumed immediately. In general, services cannot be stored and sold later. Service companies do not have Work in Process and Finished Goods Inventory accounts for collecting costs before transferring them to a Cost of Goods Sold account. At the end of the day, McDonald's has no work in process or finished goods inventory.

Is a retail company such as Toys "R" Us a service company or a manufacturing company? Because wholesale and retail companies have large inventories, it may seem odd to think of them as service companies. Consider, however, what employees of a wholesale or retail company do. Their efforts cannot be stored and used later. The services of a salesperson are consumed as customers are assisted. Other service organizations include insurance companies, banks, cleaning establishments, airlines, law firms, hospitals, hotels, and governmental agencies.

Even though service companies do not collect costs in inventory accounts for financial reporting purposes, they do accumulate cost information for decision making. For example, a hotel manager needs to know the cost of providing a room to assess whether the pricing policy is appropriate. A private school may compare the expected and actual cost of offering a course to ensure that costs are controlled. Airline executives need to know the cost of serving a specific route to decide whether to maintain or eliminate the route. Measuring the cost of providing services is just as necessary as measuring the cost of making products whether the cost is collected in an inventory account or charged directly to the income statement.

## MANUFACTURING COST FLOW ILLUSTRATED

To illustrate how manufacturing costs flow through ledger accounts, consider Ventra Manufacturing Company, which makes mahogany jewelry boxes that it sells to department stores. The account balances in Exhibit 11.2 were drawn from the company's accounting records as of January 1, 2012.

Ventra Manufacturing's 2012 accounting events are explained here. The effects of the events are summarized in the T-accounts in Exhibit 11.4 on page 495. Study the entries in Exhibit 11.4 as you read the event descriptions in the following section of this chapter. The illustration assumes Ventra determines the cost of making its jewelry boxes on a monthly basis. Accounting events for January are described next.

Demonstrate the flow of materials and labor costs for a manufacturing company.

VENTRA

### EXHIBIT 11.2

| Trial Balance as of January 1, 2012 | | |
|---|---:|---:|
| Cash | $ 64,500 | |
| Raw materials inventory | 500 | |
| Work in process inventory | 0 | |
| Finished goods inventory | 836 | |
| Manufacturing equipment | 40,000 | |
| Accumulated depreciation | | $ 10,000 |
| Common stock | | 76,000 |
| Retained earnings | | 19,836 |
| Totals | $105,836 | $105,836 |

## Events Affecting Manufacturing Cost Flow in January

**EVENT 1**   Ventra Manufacturing paid $26,500 cash to purchase raw materials.

The effects of the materials purchase on the company's financial statements are shown in the following horizontal financial statements model.[1]

| Assets | | | = | Liabilities | + | Equity | Revenue | − | Expenses | = | Net Income |
|---|---|---|---|---|---|---|---|---|---|---|---|
| Cash | + | Raw Materials Inventory | | | | | | | | | |
| (26,500) | + | 26,500 | = | NA | + | NA | NA | − | NA | = | NA |

This event is an asset exchange. One asset—cash—decreases, and another asset—raw materials inventory—increases. Neither total assets reported on the balance sheet nor any revenues or expenses on the income statement are affected. Raw materials costs are only one component of total manufacturing (product) costs. The raw materials costs will be included in the cost of goods sold (expense) recognized when completed jewelry boxes are sold to customers.

### EVENT 2    Ventra placed $1,100 of raw materials into production in the process of making jewelry boxes.

This event is also an asset exchange. One asset—raw materials inventory—decreases, and another asset—work in process inventory—increases. Total assets reported on the balance sheet are not affected. The income statement is not affected. The effects on the company's financial statements of using the raw materials follow.

| Assets | | | = | Liabilities | + | Equity | Revenue | − | Expenses | = | Net Income |
|---|---|---|---|---|---|---|---|---|---|---|---|
| Raw Materials Inventory | + | Work in Process Inventory | | | | | | | | | |
| (1,100) | + | 1,100 | = | NA | + | NA | NA | − | NA | = | NA |

Ventra's raw materials are *direct* inputs to the production process. They are accounted for using the *perpetual inventory method.* Because the raw materials are traced directly to products, it is easy to match the cost flow with the physical flow. Every time direct raw materials are moved from storage to work in process, their cost is transferred in the accounting records as well.

### EVENT 3    Ventra paid $2,000 cash to purchase production supplies (glue, nails, sandpaper).

This event is also an asset exchange. One asset—cash—decreases, and another asset—production supplies—increases. Total assets reported on the balance sheet are not affected. Net income is not affected. The effects of this event on the company's financial statements follow.

| Assets | | | = | Liabilities | + | Equity | Revenue | − | Expenses | = | Net Income |
|---|---|---|---|---|---|---|---|---|---|---|---|
| Cash | + | Production Supplies | | | | | | | | | |
| (2,000) | + | 2,000 | = | NA | + | NA | NA | − | NA | = | NA |

---

[1]The horizontal model arranges the major financial statement elements horizontally across a single page. Reading from left to right, balance sheet elements are presented first, followed by income statement elements.

The production supplies are recorded in a separate asset account because Ventra finds it more practical to account for them using the *periodic inventory method*. Production supplies are *indirect* inputs. Such small quantities are used on each jewelry box that it is not worth the trouble to track the actual costs as the materials are used. Nobody wants to stop to make a journal entry every time several drops of glue are used. *Instead of recognizing production supplies usage as it occurs (perpetually), Ventra determines at the end of the accounting period (periodically) the cost of supplies used.* The record-keeping procedures for including the cost of production supplies in the flow of manufacturing costs are described in the explanation of the Manufacturing Overhead account described shortly.

**EVENT 4    Ventra paid production workers $1,400 cash.**

These wages are *not* classified as salary expense. Because the labor was used to make jewelry boxes, the cost is added to the Work in Process Inventory account. This event is yet another asset exchange. Ventra exchanged cash for the value added by making the inventory. One asset—cash—decreases, and another asset—work in process inventory—increases. Total assets reported on the balance sheet are not affected. The income statement is not affected. The effects on the company's financial statements of incurring production labor costs follow.

| Assets | | | = | Liabilities | + | Equity | Revenue | − | Expenses | = | Net Income |
|---|---|---|---|---|---|---|---|---|---|---|---|
| Cash | + | Work in Process Inventory | | | | | | | | | |
| (1,400) | + | 1,400 | = | NA | + | NA | NA | − | NA | = | NA |

# REALITY BYTES

Like manufacturing companies, service companies must use predetermined overhead rates to make timely decisions, such as determining what price to charge customers. Consider **National Technical Systems, Inc.**, a large technical services company headquartered in Calabasas, California. In its 2009 fiscal year, the E&E segment generated over $120 million in revenues.

According to the company's 2009 annual report, it "provides highly trained technical personnel for product certification, product safety testing, and product evaluation . . ." including ". . . performing structural testing and analysis . . . of large articles such as entire airframes." Fixed pricing is one method the company uses to price its goods.

Since the company has a lot of fixed overhead costs that include, among other things, depreciation of its testing facilities and equipment, it does not know the actual cost of completing a job until the end of the year. However, it cannot wait until then to give the customer a price for a test to be performed in March. How does it determine the price to charge? According to the company's annual report, "At the time the Company enters into a contract that

includes multiple tasks, the Company **estimates** the amount of actual labor *and other costs* that will be required to complete each task based on historical experience." (Emphasis supplied.) These cost estimates are used to establish a price to be charged.

The company also notes, "To the extent management does not accurately forecast the level of effort required to complete a contract, or individual tasks within a contract . . . the Company may incur losses on individual contracts."

Source: the Company's annual report.

## Flow of Overhead Costs

Assume Ventra made 500 jewelry boxes during January. What is the cost per jewelry box? Why does management need to know this cost? If Ventra uses a cost-plus pricing strategy, management must know the cost per jewelry box to determine what price to charge for each one. Product cost information is also used to control costs and evaluate managerial performance. By comparing current production costs with historical or standard costs, management can evaluate whether performance meets expectations and take appropriate action to ensure the company accomplishes its goals. Ventra has many reasons for needing to know in January the cost of products made in January.

The *direct costs* of making the 500 jewelry boxes in January are $1,100 for materials and $1,400 for labor. The *actual indirect overhead costs* are unknown. Ventra will not know the exact amount of some of these indirect costs until the end of the year. For example, Ventra uses the periodic inventory method to determine the cost of production supplies consumed. The actual cost of supplies consumed is unknown until the end of the year when Ventra counts any unused supplies. Similarly, the actual cost for 2012 of taxes, insurance, landscaping, supervisory bonuses, and other indirect costs may be unknown in January. Ventra cannot delay making managerial decisions until actual cost data become available. Ventra needs information on January 31 that will not be available until December 31. This dilemma is depicted in the following graphic.

To solve the problem of needing cost information before it is available, Ventra records *estimated costs* in its accounting system *during the accounting period.* To illustrate, assume the accountant estimated Ventra will incur total indirect overhead costs of $40,320 during 2012. This *estimate* of overhead cost includes $1,600 for the cost of production supplies Ventra will use, $10,000 of depreciation cost, and $28,720 of other costs such as supervisory salaries, rent on the manufacturing facility, utilities, and maintenance. How much of the $40,320 *estimated* overhead cost should Ventra allocate to the units produced in January? Ventra must first identify the most appropriate allocation base. Assuming the goods (jewelry boxes) are homogeneous (the jewelry boxes are identical), it makes sense to use number of units as the allocation base, assigning an equal amount of overhead cost to each box.

Suppose Ventra's accountant expected Ventra to produce 12,000 jewelry boxes during the year. Based on this estimate, the allocation rate is $3.36 per unit ($40,320 expected cost ÷ 12,000 units). Because the overhead allocation rate is determined before the actual overhead costs are known, it is called a **predetermined overhead rate.** Using the $3.36 predetermined overhead rate, Ventra allocated $1,680 of overhead cost to the 500 jewelry boxes made in January ($3.36 × 500 boxes).

## Manufacturing Overhead Account

How are overhead costs recorded in the accounting records? Estimated overhead costs are *applied* (assigned) to work in process inventory *at the time goods are produced.* As shown in Event 5, for January Ventra Manufacturing would apply (transfer) $1,680 of overhead cost to the Work in Process Inventory account. Actual overhead costs may be incurred at different times from when goods are made. For example, Ventra may recognize depreciation or supplies use at year-end. Actual and estimated overhead costs are therefore recorded at different times during the accounting period.

At the time estimated overhead is added (a debit) to the Work in Process Inventory account, a corresponding entry is recorded on the credit side of a *temporary* account called *Manufacturing Overhead.* This credit entry in the Manufacturing Overhead account is **applied overhead.** Think of the **Manufacturing Overhead account** as a temporary asset account. Recognizing estimated overhead can be viewed as an asset exchange transaction. When estimated overhead is recognized, the temporary account, Manufacturing Overhead, decreases and the Work in Process Inventory account increases.

Actual overhead costs are recorded as increases (debits) in the Manufacturing Overhead account. For example, at the end of the year, Ventra will reduce the Production Supplies account and increase the Manufacturing Overhead account by the actual amount of supplies used. The balance in the Production Supplies account will be decreased and the balance in the Manufacturing Overhead account will be increased. When Ventra pays monthly rent cost for the manufacturing facilities, it will increase Manufacturing Overhead and decrease cash. Other actual overhead costs are recorded the same way.

Since differences normally exist between estimated and actual overhead costs, the Manufacturing Overhead account is likely to have a balance at the end of the year. If more overhead has been applied than was actually incurred, the account balance represents the amount of **overapplied overhead.** If less overhead was applied than was incurred, the account balance is **underapplied overhead.** Overapplied overhead means the amount of estimated overhead cost recorded in the Work in Process Inventory account exceeded the actual overhead cost incurred. Underapplied overhead means the amount of estimated overhead cost recorded in the Work in Process Inventory account was less than the actual overhead cost incurred.

Because costs flow from Work in Process Inventory to Finished Goods Inventory and then to Cost of Goods Sold, these accounts will also be overstated or understated relative to actual costs. If the amount of overapplied or underapplied overhead is significant, it must be allocated proportionately at the end of the year to the Work in Process Inventory, Finished Goods Inventory, and Cost of Goods Sold accounts so these accounts will reflect actual, rather than estimated, amounts for financial reporting.

In most cases, over- or underapplied overhead is not significant and companies may allocate it in any convenient manner. In these circumstances, companies normally assign the total amount of the overhead correction directly to Cost of Goods Sold. We have adopted this simplifying practice throughout the text and in the end-of-chapter exercises and problems. Exhibit 11.3 shows the flow of product costs, including actual and applied overhead. To illustrate using a Manufacturing Overhead account, return to Ventra Manufacturing Company.

## EXHIBIT 11.3

### Flow of Product Costs

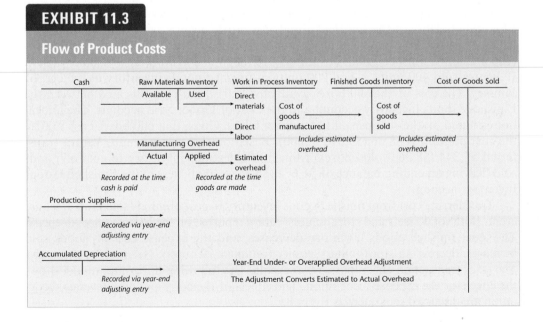

**EVENT 5**    Ventra recognized $1,680 of estimated manufacturing overhead costs at the end of January (see previous section entitled Flow of Overhead Costs to review computing this amount).

This event is another asset exchange. Total assets reported on the balance sheet, net income, and cash flow are not affected. The temporary asset account Manufacturing Overhead decreases, and the asset account Work in Process Inventory increases. The effects of this event on the company's financial statements follow.

| Assets | | | = | Liabilities | + | Equity | Revenue | − | Expenses | = | Net Income |
|---|---|---|---|---|---|---|---|---|---|---|---|
| Manufacturing Overhead | + | Work in Process Inventory | | | | | | | | | |
| (1,680) | + | 1,680 | = | NA | + | NA | NA | − | NA | = | NA |

**LO 4**

Account for completion and sale of products.

**EVENT 6**    Ventra transferred the total cost of the 500 jewelry boxes made in January ($1,100 materials + $1,400 labor + $1,680 estimated overhead = $4,180 cost of goods manufactured) from work in process to finished goods.

This event is an asset exchange. Total assets reported on the balance sheet, net income, and cash flow are not affected. The asset account Work in Process Inventory decreases, and the asset account Finished Goods Inventory increases. The effects of this event on the company's financial statements follow.

| Assets | | | = | Liabilities | + | Equity | Revenue | − | Expenses | = | Net Income |
|---|---|---|---|---|---|---|---|---|---|---|---|
| Work in Process Inventory | + | Finished Goods Inventory | | | | | | | | | |
| (4,180) | + | 4,180 | = | NA | + | NA | NA | − | NA | = | NA |

**EVENT 7**    Ventra transferred the cost of 400 sold jewelry boxes from finished goods inventory to cost of goods sold.

Recall that Ventra made 500 jewelry boxes costing $4,180 during January. Also, the beginning balance in the Finished Goods Inventory account was $836. Assume this balance represented 100 jewelry boxes that had been made in 2011. Therefore, 600 units (100 + 500) of finished goods costing $5,016 ($836 + $4,180) were available for sale. If Ventra sold 400 units, it had 200 units in finished goods inventory at the end of January. The cost of the 600 boxes available ($5,016) must be allocated between the Finished Goods Inventory account and the Cost of Goods Sold account. The allocation is based on the cost per unit of jewelry boxes. Given that 600 boxes cost $5,016, the cost per unit is $8.36 ($5,016 ÷ 600). Based on this cost per unit, Ventra transferred $3,344 ($8.36 × 400 boxes) from finished goods inventory to cost of goods sold, leaving an ending balance of $1,672 ($8.36 × 200 boxes) in the Finished Goods Inventory account.

Transferring cost from finished goods inventory to cost of goods sold is an asset use event. Both total assets and stockholders' equity reported on the balance sheet decrease. The asset finished goods inventory decreases, and the expense cost of goods sold increases, decreasing stockholders' equity (retained earnings). Net income decreases. The sales transaction encompasses two events. The following horizontal model shows the effects of the expense recognition. The effects of the corresponding revenue recognition are discussed separately as Event 8.

| Assets | = | Liabilities | + | Equity | Revenue | − | Expenses | = | Net Income |
|---|---|---|---|---|---|---|---|---|---|
| Finished Goods Inventory | | | | Retained Earnings | | | | | |
| (3,344) | = | NA | + | (3,344) | NA | − | 3,344 | = | (3,344) |

Knowing the cost per jewelry box is useful for many purposes. For example, the amount of the allocation between the ending Finished Goods Inventory and the Cost of Goods Sold accounts is needed for the financial statements. Ventra must compute the cost per unit data if it wishes to prepare interim (monthly or quarterly) financial reports. The cost per unit for the month of January also could be compared to the cost per unit for the previous accounting period or to standard cost data to evaluate cost control and managerial performance. Finally, the cost per unit data are needed for setting the price under a cost-plus pricing strategy. Assume Ventra desires to earn a gross margin of $5.64 per jewelry box. It would therefore charge $14 ($8.36 cost + $5.64 gross margin) per unit for each jewelry box. When recording the effects of recognizing revenue for the 400 boxes sold, we assume that Ventra charges its customers $14 per unit.

**EVENT 8   Ventra recognized $5,600 ($14 per unit × 400 units) of sales revenue for the cash sale of 400 jewelry boxes.**

Recognizing revenue is an asset source transaction. The asset cash increases and stockholders' equity (retained earnings) increases. Net income increases. These effects are shown here.

| Assets | = | Liabilities | + | Equity | Revenue | − | Expenses | = | Net Income |
|---|---|---|---|---|---|---|---|---|---|
| 5,600 | = | NA | + | 5,600 | 5,600 | − | NA | = | 5,600 |

**EVENT 9   Ventra paid $1,200 cash for manufacturing overhead costs including indirect labor, utilities, and rent.**

Paying for actual overhead costs is an asset exchange event. Ventra transfers cost from the asset account Cash to the temporary asset account Manufacturing Overhead. Total assets on the balance sheet and net income are unaffected. These effects follow.

| Assets | | | = | Liabilities | + | Equity | Revenue | − | Expenses | = | Net Income |
|---|---|---|---|---|---|---|---|---|---|---|---|
| Cash | + | Manufacturing Overhead | | | | | | | | | |
| (1,200) | + | 1,200 | = | NA | + | NA | NA | − | NA | = | NA |

Recall that $1,680 of overhead cost was applied to the January work in process inventory. This amount is significantly more than the $1,200 of actual overhead costs paid for above. These amounts differ because the estimated (applied) overhead includes several costs that have not yet been recognized. For example, the amount of supplies used and depreciation expense are not recognized until Ventra records adjusting entries on December 31. Although these costs are not recognized until December, a portion of them must be included in the cost of products made in January. Otherwise, all of the supplies cost and depreciation cost would be assigned to products made in December.

## *Answers to* The Curious Accountant

Obviously, an enterprise such as Northwest Aviction cannot stay in business if it cannot give customers a price for the services it is selling. As the chapter has explained, manufacturers estimate the overhead cost of a job based on a predetermined overhead rate. Although these estimates will not be perfect, they do allow the companies to price their goods or services before they are produced. If the company does not do a reasonably good job of estimating the costs it will incur to complete a job, then it will suffer by either pricing its goods too high, which will cause it to lose business to its competitors, or pricing its goods too low, which will cause it to not make a profit adequate to stay in business.

The manufacturing equipment and supplies are actually used throughout the year. Assigning the total cost of these resources to December alone would overstate the cost of December production and understate the cost of production during other months. Such distortions in measuring product cost could mislead managers making decisions based on the reported costs. By using *estimated* overhead costs during the accounting period, management reduces the distortions that using actual monthly costs would create. The difference between actual and estimated overhead is corrected in a *year-end adjusting entry*. Companies do not adjust for these differences on an interim basis.

---

### ✓ CHECK YOURSELF 11.1

Candy Manufacturing Company had a beginning balance of $24,850 in its Work in Process Inventory account. Candy added the following costs to work in process during the accounting period: direct materials, $32,000; direct labor, $46,000; manufacturing overhead, $39,900. If the ending balance in the Work in Process Inventory account was $22,100, what was the amount of the Cost of Goods Manufactured (cost of goods transferred to Finished Goods Inventory)?

**Answer**

| | |
|---|---:|
| Beginning work in process inventory | $ 24,850 |
| Manufacturing costs added | |
| Direct materials | 32,000 |
| Direct labor | 46,000 |
| Manufacturing overhead | 39,900 |
| Total work in process | 142,750 |
| Less: Ending work in process inventory | (22,100) |
| Cost of goods manufactured | $120,650 |

---

### Summary of January Events

Exhibit 11.4 summarizes the events that occurred during January. The upper section of the exhibit illustrates the *physical flow* of the resources used to make the jewelry boxes. The lower section shows the product *cost flow* through Ventra's ledger accounts. The exhibit illustrates Events 1 through 9. The January balances in the Finished

## EXHIBIT 11.4

### Flow of Product Costs for Ventra Manufacturing Company's January Production

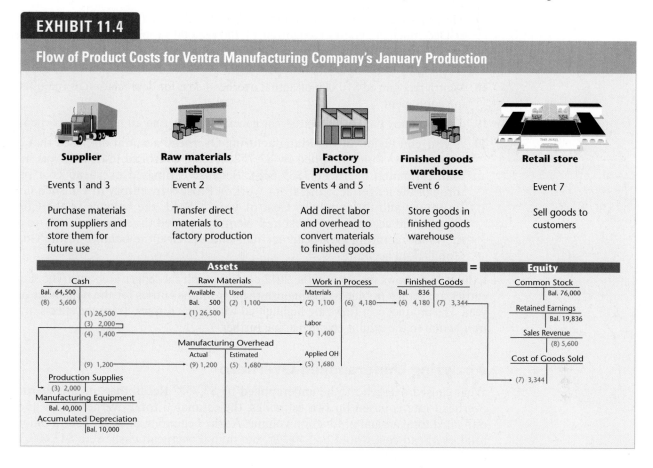

Goods Inventory and Cost of Goods Sold accounts include the cost of materials, labor, and an *estimated* amount of overhead. Estimated overhead cost is applied to work in process inventory throughout the year. Actual overhead costs are accumulated in the Manufacturing Overhead account as they are incurred. The accounts are adjusted at year-end to reconcile the difference between the estimated and actual overhead costs.

## Manufacturing Cost Flow Events for February through December

Ventra Manufacturing Company's accounting events for February through December are summarized here. The sequence of events continues from the January activity. Since nine events occurred in January, the first February event is Event 10. The events for the remainder of 2012 follow.

10. Ventra used $24,860 of raw materials.

11. The company paid production workers $31,640 cash.

12. Ventra started production of an additional 11,300 jewelry boxes. Ventra applied overhead of $37,968 (11,300 units × the predetermined overhead rate of $3.36 per unit) to work in process inventory.

13. The company completed 10,300 units and transferred $86,108 of cost of goods manufactured from work in process inventory to finished goods inventory.

14. Ventra sold 9,600 units and recorded $80,256 of cost of goods sold.

15. The company recognized $134,400 of cash revenue for the products sold in Event 14.

16. The company paid $30,500 cash for overhead costs including indirect labor, rent, and utilities.

17. The year-end count of production supplies indicated $300 of supplies were on hand at December 31. Ventra recognized $1,700 ($2,000 supplies available − $300 ending balance) of indirect materials cost for supplies used during the year. This entry reflects year-end recognition of an actual overhead cost.

18. Ventra recognized $10,000 of actual overhead cost for depreciation of manufacturing equipment.

19. The company paid $31,400 cash for general, selling, and administrative expenses.

20. A year-end review of the Manufacturing Overhead account disclosed that overhead cost was underapplied by $3,752. Actual overhead ($43,400) was higher than estimated overhead ($39,648). Because estimated overhead cost passes through the ledger accounts from Work in Process Inventory to Finished Goods Inventory and ultimately to Cost of Goods Sold, the balance in the Cost of Goods Sold account is understated. Ventra recorded the adjusting entry to close the Manufacturing Overhead account and increase the balance in the Cost of Goods Sold account.

Exhibit 11.5 shows the flow of the 2012 costs through the ledger accounts. The January entries are shown in blue to distinguish them from the entries for the remainder of the year. The product cost flows are highlighted with black arrows. Trace the effects of each transaction to the exhibit before reading further.

## Analyzing Underapplied Overhead

What caused overhead to be underapplied by $3,752? Recall that the predetermined overhead rate is based on two estimates, the estimated total overhead cost and the estimated total annual production volume. At the beginning of 2012, Ventra estimated total overhead cost would be $40,320, but actual overhead costs were $43,400, indicating Ventra spent $3,080 more than expected for overhead cost. This $3,080 is a *spending variance.* The remaining $672 of the underapplied overhead ($3,752 − $3,080) results from the difference between the actual and estimated volume of activity; it is called a *volume variance.* Recall that Ventra estimated production volume would be 12,000 units, but actual volume was only 11,800 units (500 units made in January + 11,300 units made from February through December).[2] The predetermined overhead rate of $3.36 per unit was applied to 200 fewer units (12,000 units − 11,800 units) than expected, resulting in a volume variance of $672 ($3.36 predetermined overhead rate × 200 units). The combination of the spending and volume variances[3] explains the total underapplied overhead ($3,080 + $672 = $3,752).

Because the actual cost is higher than the expected cost, the spending variance is unfavorable. The volume variance is also unfavorable because actual volume is less than expected, suggesting the manufacturing facilities were not utilized to the extent anticipated. In other words, fixed costs such as depreciation, rent, and supervisory salaries were spread over fewer units of product than expected, thereby increasing the cost per unit of product. If the variances are significant, estimated product costs could have been understated enough to have distorted decisions using the data. For example, products may have been underpriced, adversely affecting profitability. Making estimates as accurately as possible is critically important. Nevertheless, some degree of inaccuracy is inevitable. No one knows precisely what the future will bring. Managers seek to improve decision making. Although managers cannot make exact predictions, the more careful the estimates, the more useful will be the resulting information for timely decision making.

---

[2]There were 11,800 units placed into production. There were 10,800 units completed, leaving an ending work in process inventory balance of 1,000 units.

[3]The predetermined overhead rate in this chapter represents the standard cost and quantity of both variable and fixed inputs. As discussed in Chapter 8, companies may establish separate standards for variable costs and fixed costs. In this chapter, we assume the variable cost variances are insignificant and focus the discussion on the effects of fixed cost variances only.

# EXHIBIT 11.5

## Product Cost Flow for Ventra Manufacturing Company's 2012 Accounting Period

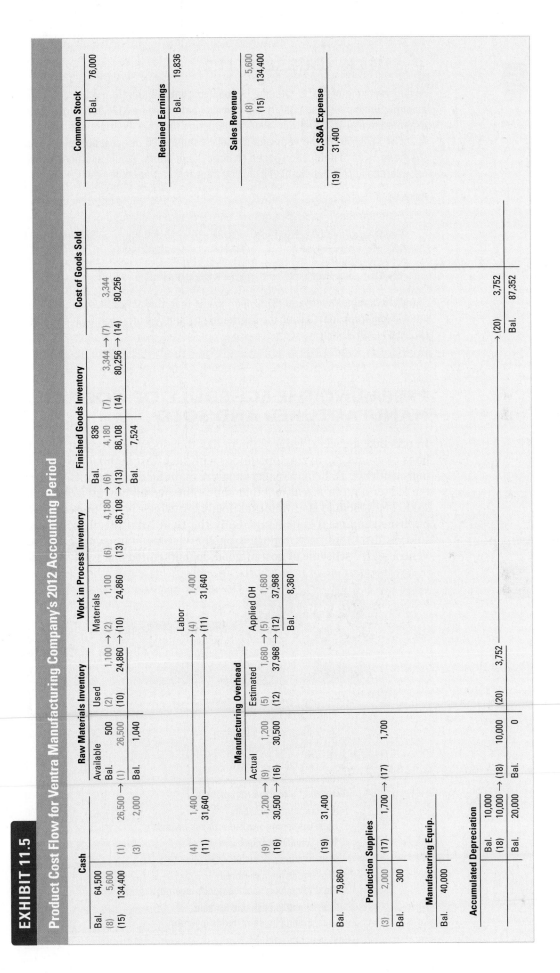

## ✓ CHECK YOURSELF 11.2

At the beginning of the accounting period, Nutrient Manufacturing Company estimated its total manufacturing overhead cost for the coming year would be $124,000. Furthermore, the company expected to use 15,500 direct labor hours during the year. Nutrient actually incurred overhead costs of $128,500 for the year and actually used 15,800 direct labor hours. Nutrient allocates overhead costs to production based on direct labor hours. Would overhead costs be overapplied or underapplied? What effect will closing the overhead account have on cost of goods sold?

**Answer**

Predetermined overhead rate = Total expected overhead cost ÷ Allocation base
Predetermined overhead rate = $124,000 ÷ 15,500 hours = $8 per direct labor hour

Applied overhead = Predetermined overhead rate × Actual direct labor hours
Applied overhead = $8 × 15,800 = $126,400

Since the applied overhead ($126,400) is less than the actual overhead ($128,500), the overhead is underapplied. Closing the overhead account will increase Cost of Goods Sold by $2,100 ($128,500 − $126,400).

## PREPARING THE SCHEDULE OF COST OF GOODS MANUFACTURED AND SOLD

Prepare a schedule of cost of goods manufactured and sold.

In practice, a general ledger system like that shown in Exhibit 11.5 may capture millions of events. Analyzing operations with such vast numbers of transactions is exceedingly difficult. To help managers analyze manufacturing results, companies summarize the ledger data in a *schedule* that shows the overall cost of goods manufactured and sold. The schedule is an internal document which is not presented with a company's published financial statements. Only the final total on the schedule (cost of goods sold) is disclosed; it is reported on the income statement. Exhibit 11.6 illustrates Ventra's 2012 **schedule of cost of goods manufactured and sold.**

### EXHIBIT 11.6

**VENTRA MANUFACTURING COMPANY**
Schedule of Cost of Goods Manufactured and Sold
For the Year Ended December 31, 2012

| | |
|---|---:|
| Beginning raw materials inventory | $    500 |
| Plus: Purchases | 26,500 |
| Raw materials available for use | 27,000 |
| Less: Ending raw materials inventory | (1,040) |
| Direct raw materials used | 25,960 |
| Direct labor | 33,040 |
| Overhead (actual overhead cost) | 43,400 |
| Total manufacturing costs | 102,400 |
| Plus: Beginning work in process inventory | 0 |
| Total work in process inventory | 102,400 |
| Less: Ending work in process inventory | (8,360) |
| Cost of goods manufactured | 94,040 |
| Plus: Beginning finished goods inventory | 836 |
| Cost of goods available for sale | 94,876 |
| Less: Ending finished goods inventory | (7,524) |
| Cost of goods sold | $ 87,352 |

The schedule in Exhibit 11.6 reflects the transaction data in the ledger accounts. Confirm this relationship by comparing the information in the Raw Materials Inventory account in Exhibit 11.5 with the computation of the cost of direct raw materials used in the schedule in Exhibit 11.6. The beginning raw materials inventory, purchases, and ending raw materials inventory amounts in the ledger account agree with the schedule. The schedule, however, presents various amounts in summary form. For example, in the schedule the amount of direct raw materials used is $25,960. In Exhibit 11.5 this same amount is shown as two separate entries ($1,100 + $24,860) in the T-account. Similarly, the $33,040 shown as direct labor in the schedule represents the total of the two amounts ($1,400 + $31,640) of labor cost entered in the Work in Process Inventory account in Exhibit 11.5. In practice, one number in the schedule may represent thousands of individual events captured in the ledger accounts. The schedule simplifies analyzing manufacturing cost flow data for decision-making purposes.

The schedule of cost of goods manufactured and sold includes the *actual* amount of overhead cost. Data for financial statement reports are summarized at the end of the year when actual cost data are available. Although companies use estimated costs for internal records and decision making during the year, they use actual historical cost data in this schedule prepared at the end of the year.

# FINANCIAL STATEMENTS

Prepare financial statements for a manufacturing company.

The final total on the schedule of cost of goods manufactured and sold is reported as the single line item *cost of goods sold* on the company's income statement. Cost of goods sold is subtracted from sales revenue to determine gross margin. Selling and administrative expenses are subtracted from gross margin to reach net income. Exhibit 11.7 shows Ventra Manufacturing's 2012 income statement; Exhibit 11.8 shows the year-end balance sheet. In Exhibit 11.8 we show the three inventory accounts (Raw Materials, Work in Process, and Finished Goods) separately for teaching purposes. In practice, these accounts are frequently combined and reported as a single amount (Inventories) on the balance sheet. Study each statement, tracing the information from the T-accounts in Exhibit 11.5 to the exhibits to see how companies gather the information they report to the public in their published financial statements.

**EXHIBIT 11.7**

### VENTRA MANUFACTURING COMPANY
#### Income Statement
#### For the Year Ended December 31, 2012

| | |
|---|---:|
| Sales revenue | $140,000 |
| Cost of goods sold | (87,352) |
| Gross margin | 52,648 |
| Selling and administrative expenses | (31,400) |
| Net income | $ 21,248 |

**EXHIBIT 11.8**

### VENTRA MANUFACTURING COMPANY
#### Balance Sheet
#### As of December 31, 2012

| | |
|---|---:|
| **Assets** | |
| Cash | $ 79,860 |
| Raw materials inventory | 1,040 |
| Work in process inventory | 8,360 |
| Finished goods inventory | 7,524 |
| Production supplies | 300 |
| Manufacturing equipment | 40,000 |
| Accumulated depreciation—manufac. equip. | (20,000) |
| Total assets | $117,084 |
| **Stockholders' equity** | |
| Common stock | $ 76,000 |
| Retained earnings | 41,084 |
| Total stockholders' equity | $117,084 |

# MOTIVE TO OVERPRODUCE

Distinguish between absorption and variable costing.

## Absorption Costing versus Variable Costing

As discussed previously, managers frequently separate product manufacturing costs into variable and fixed categories based on how the costs behave. For example, the cost of materials, labor, and supplies usually increases and decreases in direct proportion to the number of units produced. Other product costs, such as rent, depreciation, and supervisory salaries are fixed; they remain constant regardless of the number of products made. Generally accepted accounting principles require that *all* product costs, both variable and fixed, be reported as inventory until the products are sold, when the product costs are expensed as cost of goods sold. This practice is called **absorption (full) costing.**[4] To illustrate, assume Hokai Manufacturing Company incurs the following costs to produce 2,000 units of inventory.

| Inventory Costs | Cost per Unit | × | Units | = | Total |
|---|---|---|---|---|---|
| Variable manufacturing costs | $9 | × | 2,000 | = | $18,000 |
| Fixed overhead | | | | = | 12,000 |
| Total (full absorption product cost) | | | | = | $30,000 |

Suppose Hokai sells all 2,000 units of inventory for $20 per unit (sales = 2,000 × $20 = $40,000). Gross margin is therefore $10,000 ($40,000 sales − $30,000 cost of goods sold). What happens to reported profitability if Hokai increases production without also increasing sales? Profitability increases because cost of goods sold decreases. Overproducing spreads the fixed cost over more units, thereby reducing the cost per unit and the amount charged to cost of goods sold. Exhibit 11.9 illustrates this effect; it shows the cost per unit at production levels of 2,000, 3,000, and 4,000 units.

## EXHIBIT 11.9

### Cost per Unit Absorption Costing

| Inventory Costs | | | |
|---|---|---|---|
| Fixed overhead (a) | $12,000 | $12,000 | $12,000 |
| Number of units (b) | 2,000 | 3,000 | 4,000 |
| Fixed overhead per unit (a ÷ b) | $ 6 | $ 4 | $ 3 |
| Variable manufacturing costs | 9 | 9 | 9 |
| Full absorption product cost per unit | $ 15 | $ 13 | $ 12 |

Exhibit 11.10 illustrates for Hokai alternate income statements assuming sales of 2,000 units and production levels of 2,000, 3,000, and 4,000 units, the first using absorption costing and the second using variable costing.

Suppose Hokai's management is under pressure to increase profitability but cannot control sales because customers make buying decisions. Management may

---

[4]Since all manufacturing costs are classified as product costs under absorption costing, absorption costing is also called *full costing*.

## EXHIBIT 11.10

**Absorption Costing Income Statements at Different Levels of Production with Sales Held Constant at 2,000 Units**

| Level of Production | 2,000 | | 3,000 | | 4,000 |
|---|---|---|---|---|---|
| Sales ($20 per unit × 2,000 units) | $40,000 | | $40,000 | | $40,000 |
| Cost of goods sold ($15 × 2,000) = | 30,000 | ($13 × 2,000) = | 26,000 | ($12 × 2,000) = | 24,000 |
| Gross margin | $10,000 | | $14,000 | | $16,000 |

be tempted to increase reported profitability by increasing production. What is wrong with increasing production without also increasing sales? The problem lies in inventory accumulation. Notice inventory increases 1,000 units when 3,000 units are produced but only 2,000 are sold. Likewise, inventory rises 2,000 units when 4,000 are produced but 2,000 are sold. Holding excess inventory entails considerable risks and costs. Inventory is subject to obsolescence, damage, theft, or destruction by fire, weather, or other disasters. Furthermore, holding inventory requires expenditures for warehouse space, employee handling, financing, and insurance coverage. These risks and costs reduce a company's profitability. Overproducing inventory is a poor business practice. To motivate managers to increase profitability without tempting them to overproduce, many companies use *variable costing* for internal reporting.

## Variable Costing

Under **variable costing,** inventory includes only *variable* product costs. The income statement is presented using the contribution margin approach, with variable product costs subtracted from sales revenue to determine the contribution margin. Fixed costs are then subtracted from the contribution margin to determine net income.

Fixed manufacturing costs are expensed in the period in which they are incurred (the period in which the resource is used) regardless of when inventory is sold. Using variable costing, increases in production have no effect on the amount of reported profit, as shown in the income statements in Exhibit 11.11.

Although managers may still overproduce under variable costing, at least they are not tempted to do so by the lure of reporting higher profits. The variable costing reporting format encourages management to make business decisions that have a more favorable impact on long-term profitability. Variable costing can be used only for internal reporting because generally accepted accounting principles prohibit its use in external financial statements.

## EXHIBIT 11.11

**Variable Costing Income Statements at Different Levels of Production with Sales Held Constant at 2,000 Units**

| Level of Production | 2,000 | | 3,000 | | 4,000 |
|---|---|---|---|---|---|
| Sales ($20 per unit × 2,000 units) | $40,000 | | $40,000 | | $40,000 |
| Variable cost of goods sold ($9 × 2,000) = | (18,000) | ($9 × 2,000) = | (18,000) | ($9 × 2,000) = | (18,000) |
| Contribution margin | 22,000 | | 22,000 | | 22,000 |
| Fixed manufacturing costs | (12,000) | | (12,000) | | (12,000) |
| Net income | $10,000 | | $10,000 | | $10,000 |

# CHECK YOURSELF 11.3

If production exceeds sales, will absorption or variable costing produce the higher amount of net income? Which method (absorption or variable costing) is required for external financial reporting?

**Answer**   Absorption costing produces a higher amount of net income when production exceeds sales. With absorption costing, fixed manufacturing costs are treated as inventory and remain in inventory accounts until the inventory is sold. In contrast, all fixed manufacturing costs are expensed with variable costing. Therefore, with absorption costing, some fixed manufacturing costs will be in inventory rather than in expense accounts, so expenses will be lower and net income will be higher than with variable costing (when production exceeds sales). Generally accepted accounting principles require companies to use absorption costing for external financial reporting purposes.

## ◄◄   A Look Back

Most manufacturing companies accumulate product costs in three inventory accounts. The *Raw Materials Inventory account* is used to accumulate the cost of direct *raw materials* purchased for use in production. The *Work in Process Inventory account* includes the cost of partially completed products. Finally, the *Finished Goods Inventory account* contains the costs of fully completed products that are ready for sale. When direct materials are purchased, their costs are first recorded in raw materials inventory. The costs of the materials used in production are transferred from raw materials inventory to work in process inventory. The cost of direct labor and overhead are added to work in process inventory. As goods are completed, their costs are transferred from work in process inventory to finished goods inventory. When goods are sold, their cost is transferred from finished goods inventory to cost of goods sold. The ending balances in the Raw Materials, Work in Process, and Finished Goods Inventory accounts are reported in the balance sheet. The product cost in the Cost of Goods Sold account is subtracted from sales revenue on the income statement to determine gross margin.

The actual amounts of many indirect overhead costs incurred to make products are unknown until the end of the accounting period. Examples of such costs include the cost of rent, supplies, utilities, indirect materials, and indirect labor. Because many managerial decisions require product cost information before year-end, companies frequently estimate the amount of overhead cost. The estimated overhead costs are assigned to products using a *predetermined overhead rate.*

Actual and applied overhead costs are accumulated in the temporary asset account *Manufacturing Overhead.* Differences between actual and applied overhead result in a balance in the Manufacturing Overhead account at the end of the accounting period. If actual overhead exceeds applied overhead, the account balance represents *underapplied overhead.* If actual overhead is less than applied overhead, the balance represents *overapplied overhead.* If the amount of over- or underapplied overhead is insignificant, it is closed directly to cost of goods sold through a year-end adjusting entry.

Manufacturing cost information is summarized in a report known as a *schedule of cost of goods manufactured and sold.* This schedule shows how the amount of cost of goods sold reported on the income statement was determined. Actual, rather than applied, overhead cost is used in the schedule.

Generally accepted accounting principles require all product costs (fixed and variable) to be included in inventory until the products are sold. This practice is called *absorption costing.* Results reported under absorption costing may tempt management to increase profitability by producing more units than the company can sell (overproducing). Overproducing spreads fixed costs over more units, reducing the cost per unit and the amount charged to cost of goods sold. Overproducing has the adverse effect of reducing profitability in the long term by increasing the risks and costs of inventory accumulation. To eliminate the temptation to overproduce, for internal reporting many companies determine product cost using *variable costing.* Under variable costing, only the variable product costs are included in inventory. Fixed product costs are expensed in the period they are incurred, regardless of when products are sold. As a result, overproduction does not decrease the product cost per unit and managers are not tempted to overproduce to increase profitability.

## A Look Forward  >>

Would you use the same product cost system to determine the cost of a bottle of Pepsi as to determine the cost of a stealth bomber? We answer this question in the next chapter, which expands on the basic cost flow concepts introduced in this chapter. You will be introduced to job-order, process, and hybrid cost systems. You will learn to identify the types of services and products that are most appropriate for each type of cost system.

**A step-by-step audio-narrated series of slides is provided on the text website at www.mhhe.com/edmonds2011.**

## SELF-STUDY REVIEW PROBLEM

Tavia Manufacturing Company's first year of operation is summarized in the following list. All transactions are cash transactions unless otherwise indicated.

1. Acquired cash by issuing common stock.
2. Purchased administrative equipment.
3. Purchased manufacturing equipment.
4. Purchased direct raw materials.
5. Purchased indirect materials (production supplies).
6. Used direct raw materials in making products.
7. Paid direct labor wages to manufacturing workers.
8. Applied overhead costs to Work in Process Inventory.
9. Paid indirect labor salaries (production supervisors).
10. Paid administrative and sales staff salaries.
11. Paid rent and utilities on the manufacturing facilities.
12. Completed work on products.
13. Sold completed inventory for cash (revenue event only).
14. Recognized cost of goods sold.
15. Recognized depreciation on manufacturing equipment.
16. Recognized depreciation on administrative equipment.
17. Recognized the amount of production supplies that had been used during the year.
18. Closed the Manufacturing Overhead account. Overhead had been underapplied during the year.

**Required**

a. Use the horizontal statements model to show how each event affects the balance sheet and the income statement.

b. Identify the accounts affected by each event and indicate whether they increased or decreased as a result of the event.

## Solution to Requirement a

| Event No. | Assets | = Liab. | + Equity | Rev. | − Exp. | = Net Inc. |
|---|---|---|---|---|---|---|
| 1 | + | n/a | + | n/a | n/a | n/a |
| 2 | − + | n/a | n/a | n/a | n/a | n/a |
| 3 | − + | n/a | n/a | n/a | n/a | n/a |
| 4 | − + | n/a | n/a | n/a | n/a | n/a |
| 5 | − + | n/a | n/a | n/a | n/a | n/a |
| 6 | − + | n/a | n/a | n/a | n/a | n/a |
| 7 | − + | n/a | n/a | n/a | n/a | n/a |
| 8 | − + | n/a | n/a | n/a | n/a | n/a |
| 9 | − + | n/a | n/a | n/a | n/a | n/a |
| 10 | − | n/a | − | n/a | + | − |
| 11 | − + | n/a | n/a | n/a | n/a | n/a |
| 12 | − + | n/a | n/a | n/a | n/a | n/a |
| 13 | + | n/a | + | + | n/a | + |
| 14 | − | n/a | − | n/a | + | − |
| 15 | − + | n/a | n/a | n/a | n/a | n/a |
| 16 | − | n/a | − | n/a | + | − |
| 17 | − + | n/a | n/a | n/a | n/a | n/a |
| 18 | − | n/a | − | n/a | + | − |

## Solution to Requirement b

| Event No. | Account Title | Increase/ Decrease | Account Title | Increase/ Decrease |
|---|---|---|---|---|
| 1 | Cash | + | Common Stock | + |
| 2 | Administrative Equipment | + | Cash | − |
| 3 | Manufacturing Equipment | + | Cash | − |
| 4 | Raw Materials Inventory | + | Cash | − |
| 5 | Production Supplies | + | Cash | − |
| 6 | Work in Process Inventory | + | Raw Materials Inventory | − |
| 7 | Work in Process Inventory | + | Cash | − |
| 8 | Work in Process Inventory | + | Manufacturing Overhead | − |
| 9 | Manufacturing Overhead | + | Cash | − |
| 10 | Salary Expense | + | Cash | − |
| 11 | Manufacturing Overhead | + | Cash | − |
| 12 | Finished Goods Inventory | + | Work in Process Inventory | − |
| 13 | Cash | + | Sales Revenue | + |
| 14 | Cost of Goods Sold | + | Finished Goods Inventory | − |
| 15 | Manufacturing Overhead | + | Accumulated Depreciation | + |
| 16 | Depreciation Expense | + | Accumulated Depreciation | + |
| 17 | Manufacturing Overhead | + | Production Supplies | − |
| 18 | Cost of Goods Sold | + | Manufacturing Overhead | − |

## KEY TERMS

Absorption (full) costing  500
Applied overhead  491
Finished Goods Inventory  486
Manufacturing Overhead
   account  491
Overapplied overhead  491

Predetermined overhead
   rate  490
Raw Materials Inventory  486
Schedule of cost of goods
   manufactured
   and sold  498

Underapplied
   overhead  491
Variable costing  501
Work in Process
   Inventory  486

## QUESTIONS

1. What is the difference between direct and indirect raw materials costs?

2. Direct raw materials were purchased on account, and the costs were subsequently transferred to Work in Process Inventory. How would the transfer affect assets, liabilities, equity, and cash flows? What is the effect on the income statement? Would your answers change if the materials had originally been purchased for cash?

3. How do manufacturing costs flow through inventory accounts?

4. Goods that cost $2,000 to make were sold for $3,000 on account. How does their sale affect assets, liabilities, and equity? What is the effect on the income statement?

5. At the end of the accounting period, an adjusting entry is made for the accrued wages of production workers. How would this entry affect assets, liabilities, and equity? What is the effect on the income statement?

6. X Company recorded the payment for utilities used by the manufacturing facility by crediting Cash and debiting Manufacturing Overhead. Why was the debit made to Manufacturing Overhead instead of Work in Process Inventory?

7. Why is the salary of a production worker capitalized while the salary of a marketing manager expensed?

8. Al Carmon says that his company has a difficult time establishing a predetermined overhead rate because the number of units of product produced during a period is difficult to measure. What are two measures of production other than the number of units of product that Mr. Carmon could use to establish a predetermined overhead rate?

9. What do the terms *overapplied overhead* and *underapplied overhead* mean?

10. What are *product costs* and *selling, general, and administrative costs?* Give examples of product costs and of selling, general, and administrative costs.

11. How does the entry to close an insignificant amount of overapplied overhead to the Cost of Goods Sold account affect net income?

12. Why are actual overhead costs not used in determining periodic product cost?

13. Because of seasonal fluctuations, Buresch Corporation has a problem determining the unit cost of its products. For example, high heating costs during the winter months cause the cost per unit to be higher than the per-unit cost in the summer months even when the same number of units of product is produced. Suggest how Buresch can improve the computation of per-unit cost.

14. What is the purpose of the Manufacturing Overhead account?

15. For what purpose is the schedule of cost of goods manufactured and sold prepared? Do all companies use the statement?

16. How does the variable costing approach differ from the absorption costing approach? Explain the different income statement formats used with each approach.

17. How is profitability affected by increases in productivity under the variable and absorption costing approaches?

18. Under what circumstance is a variable costing statement format used? What potential problem could it eliminate?

 ## MULTIPLE-CHOICE QUESTIONS

**Multiple-choice questions are provided on the text website at www.mhhe.com/edmonds2011.**

## EXERCISES—SERIES A

**All applicable Exercises in Series A are available with McGraw-Hill's**
***Connect Accounting.***

**LO 2, 3, 4, 5**

### Exercise 11-1A  *Product cost flow and financial statements*

Joiner Manufacturing Company was started on January 1, 2011. The company was affected by the following events during its first year of operation.

1. Acquired $1,600 cash from the issue of common stock.
2. Paid $500 cash for direct raw materials.
3. Transferred $400 of direct raw materials to work in process.
4. Paid production employees $600 cash.
5. Paid $300 cash for manufacturing overhead costs.
6. Applied $245 of manufacturing overhead costs to work in process.
7. Completed work on products that cost $1,000.
8. Sold products that cost $800 for $1,400 cash.
9. Paid $400 cash for selling and administrative expenses.
10. Made a $50 cash distribution to the owners.
11. Closed the Manufacturing Overhead account.

**Required**

a.  Record these events in a horizontal statements model. The first event is shown as an example.

| Assets | | | | | = | Equity | | | | | | |
|---|---|---|---|---|---|---|---|---|---|---|---|---|
| Cash | + MOH | + Raw M. | + WIP | + F. Goods | = | C. Stk. | + Ret. Ear. | | Rev. | − Exp. | = | Net Inc. |
| 1,600 | + NA | + NA | + NA | + NA | = | 1,600 | + NA | | NA | − NA | = | NA |

b.  Prepare a schedule of cost of goods manufactured and sold.

**LO 2, 3, 4, 5, 6**

### Exercise 11-2A  *Recording events in T-accounts and preparing financial statements*

Pruitt Manufacturing Company was started on January 1, 2011, when it acquired $2,000 cash from the issue of common stock. During the first year of operation, $800 of direct raw materials was purchased with cash, and $600 of the materials was used to make products. Direct labor costs of $1,000 were paid in cash. Pruitt applied $640 of overhead cost to the Work in Process account. Cash payments of $640 were made for actual overhead costs. The company completed products that cost $1,600 and sold goods that had cost $1,200 for $2,000 cash. Selling and administrative expenses of $480 were paid in cash.

**Required**

a.  Open T-accounts and record the events affecting Pruitt Manufacturing. Include closing entries.
b.  Prepare a schedule of cost of goods manufactured and sold, an income statement, and a balance sheet.
c.  Explain the difference between net income and cash flow from operating activities.

**LO 2, 3, 4**

### Exercise 11-3A  *Effect of accounting events on financial statements*

**Required**

Use a horizontal statements model to indicate how each of the following independent accounting events affects the elements of the balance sheet and the income statement. Indicate whether the event increases (I), decreases (D), or does not affect (NA) each element of the statements. The first two transactions are shown as examples.

a.  Paid cash to purchase raw materials.
b.  Recorded cash sales revenue.
c.  Paid cash for actual manufacturing overhead cost.

**d.** Closed the Manufacturing Overhead account when overhead was overapplied.

**e.** Transferred cost of completed inventory to finished goods.

**f.** Paid cash for wages of production workers.

**g.** Paid cash for salaries of selling and administrative personnel.

**h.** Recorded adjusting entry to recognize amount of manufacturing supplies used (the company uses the periodic inventory method to account for manufacturing supplies).

| Event No. | Balance Sheet | | | | Income Statement | | |
|---|---|---|---|---|---|---|---|
| | Assets | = Liab. + | C. Stk + | Ret Ear. | Rev. − | Exp. = | Net Inc. |
| a. | ID | NA | NA | NA | NA | NA | NA |
| b. | I | NA | NA | I | I | NA | I |

## Exercise 11-4A  *Preparing financial statements*

**LO 2, 3, 4, 5, 6**

Cooper Corporation began fiscal year 2011 with the following balances in its inventory accounts.

| | |
|---|---|
| Raw Materials | $56,000 |
| Work in Process | 84,000 |
| Finished Goods | 28,000 |

During the accounting period, Cooper purchased $240,000 of raw materials and issued $248,000 of materials to the production department. Direct labor costs for the period amounted to $324,000, and manufacturing overhead of $48,000 was applied to Work in Process Inventory. Assume that there was no over- or underapplied overhead. Goods costing $612,000 to produce were completed and transferred to Finished Goods Inventory. Goods costing $602,000 were sold for $800,000 during the period. Selling and administrative expenses amounted to $72,000.

**Required**

**a.** Determine the ending balance of each of the three inventory accounts that would appear on the year-end balance sheet.

**b.** Prepare a schedule of cost of goods manufactured and sold and an income statement.

## Exercise 11-5A  *Missing information in a schedule of cost of goods manufactured*

**LO 5**

**Required**

Supply the missing information on the following schedule of cost of goods manufactured.

### DEWBERRY CORPORATION
Schedule of Cost of Goods Manufactured
For the Year Ended December 31, 2011

| | | |
|---|---|---|
| Raw materials | | |
| Beginning inventory | $    ? | |
| Plus: Purchases | 120,000 | |
| Raw materials available for use | $148,000 | |
| Minus: Ending raw materials inventory | ? | |
| Cost of direct raw materials used | | $124,000 |
| Direct labor | | ? |
| Manufacturing overhead | | 24,000 |
| Total manufacturing costs | | 310,000 |
| Plus: Beginning work in process inventory | | ? |
| Total work in process | | ? |
| Minus: Ending work in process inventory | | 46,000 |
| Cost of goods manufactured | | $306,000 |

**LO 5**

### Exercise 11-6A    *Cost of goods manufactured and sold*

The following information pertains to Pandey Manufacturing Company for March 2012. Assume actual overhead equaled applied overhead.

| March 1 | |
|---|---|
| Inventory balances | |
| Raw materials | $125,000 |
| Work in process | 120,000 |
| Finished goods | 78,000 |
| **March 31** | |
| Inventory balances | |
| Raw materials | $ 85,000 |
| Work in process | 145,000 |
| Finished goods | 80,000 |
| **During March** | |
| Costs of raw materials purchased | $120,000 |
| Costs of direct labor | 100,000 |
| Costs of manufacturing overhead | 63,000 |
| Sales revenues | 350,000 |

**Required**

a. Prepare a schedule of cost of goods manufactured and sold.

b. Calculate the amount of gross margin on the income statement.

**LO 3**

### Exercise 11-7A    *Calculating applied overhead*

Avery, Inc., estimates manufacturing overhead costs for the 2012 accounting period as follows.

| | |
|---|---|
| Equipment depreciation | $192,000 |
| Supplies | 21,000 |
| Materials handling | 34,000 |
| Property taxes | 15,000 |
| Production setup | 21,000 |
| Rent | 45,000 |
| Maintenance | 40,000 |
| Supervisory salaries | 132,000 |

The company uses a predetermined overhead rate based on machine hours. Estimated hours for labor in 2012 were 200,000 and for machines were 125,000.

**Required**

a. Calculate the predetermined overhead rate.

b. Determine the amount of manufacturing overhead applied to Work in Process Inventory during the 2012 period if actual machine hours were 140,000.

**LO 3**

### Exercise 11-8A    *Treatment of over- or underapplied overhead*

Lindburg Company estimates that its overhead costs for 2011 will be $270,000 and output in units of product will be 300,000 units.

**Required**

a. Calculate Lindburg's predetermined overhead rate based on expected production.

b. If 24,000 units of product were made in March 2011, how much overhead cost would be allocated to the Work in Process Inventory account during the month?

c. If actual overhead costs in March were $21,000, would overhead be overapplied or underapplied and by how much?

## Exercise 11-9A    *Recording overhead costs in T-accounts*                    LO 3

Kent Company and Trent Company both apply overhead to the Work in Process Inventory account using direct labor hours. The following information is available for both companies for the year.

|                                | Kent Company | Trent Company |
|--------------------------------|--------------|---------------|
| Actual manufacturing overhead  | $120,000     | $240,000      |
| Actual direct labor hours      | 20,000       | 24,000        |
| Underapplied overhead          |              | 12,000        |
| Overapplied overhead           | 24,000       |               |

**Required**

a. Compute the predetermined overhead rate for each company.

b. Using T-accounts, record the entry to close the overapplied or underapplied overhead at the end of the accounting period for each company, assuming the amounts are immaterial.

## Exercise 11-10A    *Treatment of over- or underapplied overhead*                LO 3

Belmont Company and Delmont Company assign manufacturing overhead to Work in Process Inventory using direct labor cost. The following information is available for the companies for the year:

|                                     | Belmont Company | Delmont Company |
|-------------------------------------|-----------------|-----------------|
| Actual direct labor cost            | $145,000        | $120,000        |
| Estimated direct labor cost         | 150,000         | 100,000         |
| Actual manufacturing overhead cost  | 56,000          | 92,000          |
| Estimated manufacturing overhead cost | 60,000        | 80,000          |

**Required**

a. Compute the predetermined overhead rate for each company.

b. Determine the amount of overhead cost that would be applied to Work in Process Inventory for each company.

c. Compute the amount of overapplied or underapplied manufacturing overhead cost for each company.

## Exercise 11-11A    *Recording manufacturing overhead costs in T-accounts*       LO 3

Gill Corporation manufactures model airplanes. The company purchased for $170,000 automated production equipment that can make the model parts. The equipment has a $10,000 salvage value and a 10-year useful life.

**Required**

a. Assuming that the equipment was purchased on January 1, record in T-accounts the adjusting entry that the company would make on December 31 to record depreciation on equipment.

b. In which month would the depreciation costs be assigned to units produced?

**LO 2, 3, 4**

### Exercise 11-12A    *Missing information in T-accounts*

Kline Manufacturing recorded the following amounts in its inventory accounts in 2011.

| Raw Materials Inventory | | Work in Process Inventory | |
|---|---|---|---|
| 30,000 | (a) | | 8,000 |
| 8,000 | | 16,000 | |
| | | 12,000 | |
| **Finished Goods Inventory** | | (c) | |
| 8,000 | (d) | **Cost of Goods Sold** | |
| 1,000 | | | |
| **Manufacturing Overhead** | | (e) | |
| (b) | 12,000 | | |
| 1,000 | | | |

**Required**

Determine the dollar amounts for (a), (b), (c), (d), and (e). Assume that underapplied and over-applied overhead is closed to Cost of Goods Sold.

**LO 7**

### Exercise 11-13A    *Variable costing versus absorption costing*

Lange Company incurred manufacturing overhead cost for the year as follows.

| | |
|---|---|
| Direct materials | $40/unit |
| Direct labor | $28/unit |
| Manufacturing overhead | |
| Variable | $ 12/unit |
| Fixed ($20/unit for 1,500 units) | $ 30,000 |
| Variable selling and admin. expenses | $  8,000 |
| Fixed selling and admin. expenses | $1 6,000 |

The company produced 1,500 units and sold 1,000 of them at $180 per unit. Assume that the production manager is paid a 2 percent bonus based on the company's net income.

**Required**

a.  Prepare an income statement using absorption costing.
b.  Prepare an income statement using variable costing.
c.  Determine the manager's bonus using each approach. Which approach would you recommend for internal reporting and why?

**LO 1, 2, 3**

### Exercise 11-14A    *Smoothed unit cost*

Wagner Manufacturing estimated its product costs and volume of production for 2012 by quarter as follows.

| | First Quarter | Second Quarter | Third Quarter | Fourth Quarter |
|---|---|---|---|---|
| Direct raw materials | $ 80,000 | $ 40,000 | $120,000 | $ 60,000 |
| Direct labor | 48,000 | 24,000 | 72,000 | 36,000 |
| Manufacturing overhead | 80,000 | 124,000 | 160,000 | 92,000 |
| Total production costs | $208,000 | $188,000 | $352,000 | $188,000 |
| Expected units produced | 16,000 | 8,000 | 24,000 | 12,000 |

Wagner Company sells a souvenir item at various resorts across the country. Its management uses the product's estimated quarterly cost to determine the selling price of its product. The company expects a large variance in demand for the product between quarters due to its seasonal nature. The company does not expect overhead costs, which are predominately fixed, to vary significantly as to production volume or with amounts for previous years. Prices are established by using a cost-plus pricing strategy. The company finds variations in short-term unit cost confusing to use. Unit cost variations complicate pricing decisions and many other decisions for which cost is a consideration.

### Required

**a.** Based on estimated total production cost, determine the expected quarterly cost per unit for Wagner's product.

**b.** How could overhead costs be estimated each quarter to solve the company's unit cost problem? Calculate the unit cost per quarter based on your recommendation.

## PROBLEMS—SERIES A

**All applicable Problems in Series A are available with McGraw-Hill's *Connect Accounting.***

■ connect
|ACCOUNTING

### Problem 11-15A   *Manufacturing cost flow across three accounting cycles*

LO 2, 3, 4, 5, 6

The following accounting events affected Massey Manufacturing Company during its first three years of operation. Assume that all transactions are cash transactions.

CHECK FIGURE
b. Cost of goods sold for 2010: $578;
NI for 2010: $152

#### Transactions for 2010

1. Started manufacturing company by issuing common stock for $3,000.
2. Purchased $1,200 of direct raw materials.
3. Used $800 of direct raw materials to produce inventory.
4. Paid $400 of direct labor wages to employees to make inventory.
5. Applied $250 of manufacturing overhead cost to Work in Process Inventory.
6. Finished work on inventory that cost $900.
7. Sold goods that cost $600 for $1,100.
8. Paid $370 for selling and administrative expenses.
9. Actual manufacturing overhead cost amounted to $228 for the year.

#### Transactions for 2011

1. Acquired additional $800 of cash from common stock.
2. Purchased $1,200 of direct raw materials.
3. Used $1,300 of direct raw materials to produce inventory.
4. Paid $600 of direct labor wages to employees to make inventory.
5. Applied $320 of manufacturing overhead cost to Work in Process Inventory.
6. Finished work on inventory that cost $1,800.
7. Sold goods that cost $1,600 for $2,800.
8. Paid $500 for selling and administrative expenses.
9. Actual manufacturing overhead cost amounted to $330 for the year.

#### Transactions for 2012

1. Paid a cash dividend of $700.
2. Purchased $1,400 of direct raw materials.
3. Used $1,200 of direct raw materials to produce inventory.
4. Paid $440 of direct labor wages to employees to make inventory.
5. Applied $290 of manufacturing overhead cost to work in process.
6. Finished work on inventory that cost $2,000.
7. Sold goods that cost $2,200 for $3,500.
8. Paid $710 for selling and administrative expenses.
9. Annual manufacturing overhead costs were $280 for the year.

**Required**

a. Record the preceding events in a horizontal statements model. Close overapplied or underapplied overhead to Cost of Goods Sold. The first event is shown as an example.

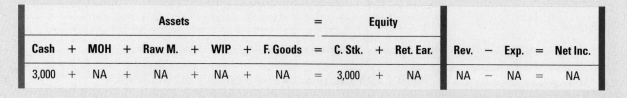

| Assets | | | | | = | Equity | | | | | |
|---|---|---|---|---|---|---|---|---|---|---|---|
| Cash | + MOH | + Raw M. | + WIP | + F. Goods | = | C. Stk. | + Ret. Ear. | Rev. | − Exp. | = Net Inc. |
| 3,000 | + NA | + NA | + NA | + NA | = | 3,000 | + NA | NA | − NA | = NA |

b. Prepare a schedule of cost of goods manufactured and sold, an income statement, and a balance sheet as of the close of business on December 31, 2010.

c. Close appropriate accounts.

d. Repeat Requirements *a* through *c* for years 2011 and 2012.

**LO 2, 3, 4, 5, 6**

**Problem 11-16A**   *Manufacturing cost flow for monthly and annual accounting periods*

Dorothy Huddle started Huddle Manufacturing Company to make a universal television remote control device that she had invented. The company's labor force consisted of part-time employees. The following accounting events affected Huddle Manufacturing Company during its first year of operation. (Assume that all transactions are cash transactions unless otherwise stated.)

**Transactions for January 2011, First Month of Operation**

1. Issued common stock for $10,000.
2. Purchased $420 of direct raw materials and $60 of production supplies.
3. Used $240 of direct raw materials.
4. Used 80 direct labor hours; production workers were paid $9.60 per hour.
5. Expected total overhead costs for the year to be $3,300, and direct labor hours used during the year to be 1,000. Calculate an overhead rate and apply the appropriate amount of overhead costs to Work in Process Inventory.
6. Paid $144 for salaries to administrative and sales staff.
7. Paid $24 for indirect manufacturing labor.
8. Paid $210 for rent and utilities on the manufacturing facilities.
9. Started and completed 100 remote controls during the month; all costs were transferred from the Work in Process Inventory account to the Finished Goods Inventory account.
10. Sold 75 remote controls at a price of $21.60 each.

**Transactions for Remainder of 2011**

11. Acquired an additional $18,000 by issuing common stock.
12. Purchased $3,900 of direct raw materials and $900 of production supplies.
13. Used $3,000 of direct raw materials.
14. Paid production workers $9.60 per hour for 900 hours of work.
15. Applied the appropriate overhead cost to Work in Process Inventory.
16. Paid $1,560 for salaries of administrative and sales staff.
17. Paid $240 of indirect manufacturing labor cost.
18. Paid $2,400 for rental and utility costs on the manufacturing facilities.
19. Transferred 950 additional remote controls that cost $12.72 each from the Work in Process Inventory account to the Finished Goods Inventory account.
20. Determined that $168 of production supplies was on hand at the end of the accounting period.
21. Sold 850 remote controls for $21.60 each.
22. Determine whether the overhead is over- or underapplied. Close the Manufacturing Overhead account to the Cost of Goods Sold account.
23. Close the revenue and expense accounts.

**Required**

a. Open T-accounts and post transactions to the accounts.

b. Prepare a schedule of cost of goods manufactured and sold, an income statement, and a balance sheet for 2011.

## Problem 11-17A  *Manufacturing cost flow for one-year period*

**LO 2, 3, 4, 5, 6**

**CHECK FIGURE**
b. NI: $538

Fulton Manufacturing started 2011 with the following account balances.

| | |
|---|---|
| Cash | $5,000 |
| Common stock | 4,500 |
| Retained earnings | 4,500 |
| Raw materials inventory | 1,200 |
| Work in process inventory | 800 |
| Finished goods inventory (320 units @$6.25) | 2,000 |

### Transactions during 2010

1. Purchased $2,880 of raw materials with cash.
2. Transferred $3,750 of raw materials to the production department.
3. Incurred and paid cash for 180 hours of direct labor @ $16 per hour.
4. Applied overhead costs to the Work in Process Inventory account. The predetermined overhead rate is $16.50 per direct labor hour.
5. Incurred actual overhead costs of $3,000 cash.
6. Completed work on 1,200 units for $6.40 per unit.
7. Paid $1,400 in selling and administrative expenses in cash.
8. Sold 1,200 units for $9,600 cash revenue (assume FIFO cost flow).

Fulton charges overapplied or underapplied overhead directly to Cost of Goods Sold.

**Required**

a. Record the preceding events in a horizontal statements model. The beginning balances are shown as an example.

| Assets | | | | | = | Equity | | | | | | |
|---|---|---|---|---|---|---|---|---|---|---|---|---|
| Cash | + MOH | + Raw M. | + WIP | + F. Goods | = | C. Stk. | + Ret. Ear. | | Rev. | − Exp. | = | Net Inc. |
| 5,000 | + NA | + 1,200 | + 800 | + 2,000 | = | 4,500 | + 4,500 | | NA | − NA | = | NA |

b. Prepare a schedule of cost of goods manufactured and sold, an income statement, and a balance sheet for 2011.

## Problem 11-18A  *Manufacturing cost for one accounting cycle*

**LO 2, 3, 4, 5, 6**

**CHECK FIGURE**
b. NI: $3,974

The following trial balance was taken from the records of Wheaton Manufacturing Company at the beginning of 2012.

| | | |
|---|---|---|
| Cash | $ 9,400 | |
| Raw materials inventory | 750 | |
| Work in process inventory | 1,200 | |
| Finished goods inventory | 2,100 | |
| Property, plant, and equipment | 7,500 | |
| Accumulated depreciation | | $ 3,000 |
| Common stock | | 7,800 |
| Retained earnings | | 10,150 |
| Total | $20,950 | $20,950 |

### Transactions for the Accounting Period

1. Wheaton purchased $5,700 of direct raw materials and $300 of indirect raw materials on account. The indirect materials are capitalized in the Production Supplies account. Materials requisitions showed that $5,400 of direct raw materials had been used for production during the period. The use of indirect materials is determined at the end of the year by physically counting the supplies on hand.

2. By the end of the year, $5,250 of the accounts payable had been paid in cash.

3. During the year, direct labor amounted to 950 hours recorded in the Wages Payable account at $10.50 per hour.

4. By the end of the year, $9,000 of wages payable had been paid in cash.

5. At the beginning of the year, the company expected overhead cost for the period to be $6,300 and 1,000 direct labor hours to be worked. Overhead is allocated based on direct labor hours, which, as indicated in Event 3, amounted to 950 for the year.

6. Selling and administrative expenses for the year amounted to $900 paid in cash.

7. Utilities and rent for production facilities amounted to $4,650 paid in cash.

8. Depreciation on the plant and equipment used in production amounted to $1,500.

9. There was $12,000 of goods completed during the year.

10. There was $12,750 of finished goods inventory sold for $18,000 cash.

11. A count of the production supplies revealed a balance of $89 on hand at the end of the year.

12. Any over- or underapplied overhead is considered to be insignificant.

### Required

a. Open T-accounts with the beginning balances shown in the preceding list and record all transactions for the year including closing entries in the T-accounts. (*Note:* Open new T-accounts as needed.)

b. Prepare a schedule of cost of goods manufactured and sold, an income statement, and a balance sheet.

**LO 2, 3, 4, 5, 6**

**CHECK FIGURES**
b. NI for 2010: $22,860
   NI for 2011: $33,040

### Problem 11-19A    *Manufacturing cost flow for multiple accounting cycles*

The following events apply to Caldwell Manufacturing Company. Assume that all transactions are cash transactions unless otherwise indicated.

### Transactions for the 2010 Accounting Period

1. The company was started on January 1, 2010, when it acquired $162,000 cash by issuing common stock.

2. The company purchased $36,000 of direct raw materials with cash and used $2,430 of these materials to make its products in January.

3. Employees provided 900 hours of labor at $5.70 per hour during January. Wages are paid in cash.

4. The estimated manufacturing overhead costs for 2010 were $64,800. Overhead is applied on the basis of direct labor hours. The company expected to use 12,000 direct labor hours during 2010. Calculate an overhead rate and apply the overhead for January to work in process inventory.

5. The employees completed work on all inventory items started in January. The cost of this production was transferred to the Finished Goods Inventory account. Determine the cost per unit of product produced in January, assuming that a total of 1,800 units of product were started and completed during the month.

6. The company used an additional $31,050 of direct raw materials and 11,500 hours of direct labor at $5.70 per hour during the remainder of 2010. Overhead was allocated on the basis of direct labor hours.

7. The company completed work on inventory items started between February 1 and December 31, and the cost of the completed inventory was transferred to the Finished Goods Inventory account. Determine the cost per unit for goods produced between February 1 and December 31, assuming that 23,000 units of inventory were produced. If the company desires to earn a gross profit of $2.70 per unit, what price per unit must it charge for the merchandise sold?

8. The company sold 22,000 units of inventory for cash at $9.60 per unit. Determine the number of units in ending inventory and the cost per unit incurred for this inventory.

9. Actual manufacturing overhead costs paid in cash were $65,700.

10. The company paid $37,800 cash for selling and administrative expenses.

11. Close the Manufacturing Overhead account.

12. Close the revenue and expense accounts.

## Transactions for the 2011 Accounting Period

1. The company purchased $40,500 of direct raw materials with cash and used $2,280 of these materials to make products in January.

2. Employees provided 950 hours of labor at $5.70 per hour during January.

3. On January 1, 2011, Caldwell hired a production supervisor at an expected cost of $1,080 cash per month. The company paid cash to purchase $4,500 of manufacturing supplies; it anticipated that $4,140 of these supplies would be used by year-end. Other manufacturing overhead costs were expected to total $64,800. Overhead is applied on the basis of direct labor hours. Caldwell expected to use 14,000 hours of direct labor during 2011. Based on this information, determine the total expected overhead cost for 2011. Calculate the predetermined overhead rate and apply the overhead cost for the January production.

4. The company recorded a $1,080 cash payment to the production supervisor.

5. The employees completed work on all inventory items started in January. The cost of this production was transferred to the Finished Goods Inventory account. Determine the cost per unit of product produced in January, assuming that 1,900 units of product were started and completed during the month.

6. During February 2011, the company used $2,850 of raw materials and 1,000 hours of labor at $5.70 per hour. Overhead was allocated on the basis of direct labor hours.

7. The company recorded a $1,080 cash payment to the production supervisor for February.

8. The employees completed work on all inventory items started in February; the cost of this production was transferred to the Finished Goods Inventory account. Determine the cost per unit of product produced in February, assuming that 2,000 units of product were started and completed during the month.

9. The company used an additional $34,200 of direct raw materials and 12,000 hours of direct labor at $5.70 per hour during the remainder of 2011. Overhead was allocated on the basis of direct labor hours.

10. The company recorded $10,800 of cash payments to the production supervisor for work performed between March 1 and December 31.

11. The company completed work on inventory items started between March 1 and December 31. The cost of the completed goods was transferred to the Finished Goods Inventory account. Compute the cost per unit of this inventory, assuming that there were 24,000 units of inventory produced.

12. The company sold 26,000 units of product for $9.90 cash per unit. Assume that the company uses the FIFO inventory cost flow method to determine the cost of goods sold.

13. The company paid $38,700 cash for selling and administrative expenses.

14. As of December 31, 2011, $450 of production supplies was on hand.

15. Actual cost of other manufacturing overhead was $63,020 cash.

16. Close the Manufacturing Overhead account.

17. Close the revenue and expense accounts.

## Required

a. Open T-accounts and record the effects of the preceding events.

b. Prepare a schedule of cost of goods manufactured and sold, an income statement, and a balance sheet for each year.

## Problem 11-20A   *Comprehensive review problem*                    LO 1, 2, 3, 4

During their senior year at Quentin College, two business students, Josh Tanner and Christy Chase, began a part-time business making personal computers. They bought the various components from a local supplier and assembled the machines in the basement of a friend's house. Their only cost was $360 for parts; they sold each computer for $630. They were able to make three machines per week and to sell them to fellow students. The activity was appropriately called Tanner Chase Computers (TCC). The product quality was good, and as graduation approached, orders were coming in much faster than TCC could fill them.

A national CPA firm made Ms. Chase an attractive offer of employment, and a large electronics company was ready to hire Mr. Tanner. Students and faculty at Quentin College, however, encouraged the two to make TCC a full-time venture. The college administration had decided to require all students in the schools of business and engineering to buy their own computers beginning in the coming fall term. It was believed that the quality and price of the TCC machines would attract the college bookstore to sign a contract to buy a minimum of 1,000 units the first year for $500 each. The bookstore sales were likely to reach 2,000 units per year, but the manager would not make an initial commitment beyond 1,000.

The prospect of $500,000 in annual sales for TCC caused the two young entrepreneurs to wonder about the wisdom of accepting their job offers. Before making a decision, they decided to investigate the implications of making TCC a full-time operation. Their study provided the following information relating to the production of their computers.

| | |
|---|---|
| Components from wholesaler | $ 240 per computer |
| Assembly labor | 15 per hour |
| Manufacturing space rent | 2,250 per month |
| Utilities | 450 per month |
| Janitorial services | 360 per month |
| Depreciation of equipment | 2,880 per year |
| Labor | 2 hours per computer |

The two owners expected to devote their time to the sales and administrative aspects of the business.

**Required**

a. Classify each cost item into the categories of direct materials, direct labor, and manufacturing overhead.

b. Classify each cost item as either variable or fixed.

c. What is the cost per computer if TCC produces 1,000 units per year? What is the cost per unit if TCC produces 2,000 units per year?

d. If the job offers for Mr. Tanner and Ms. Chase totaled $96,000, would you recommend that they accept the offers or proceed with plans to make TCC a full-time venture?

**LO 7**

eXcel

**Problem 11-21A**  *Absorption versus variable costing*

Ellis Manufacturing Company makes a product that sells for $74 per unit. Manufacturing costs for the product amount to $26 per unit variable, and $80,000 fixed. During the current accounting period, Ellis made 4,000 units of the product and sold 3,500 units. Selling and administrative expenses were zero.

**Required**

a. Prepare an absorption costing income statement.

b. Prepare a variable costing income statement.

c. Explain why the amount of net income on the absorption costing income statement differs from the amount of net income on the variable costing income statement. Your answer should include the amount of the inventory balance that would exist under the two costing approaches.

**LO 7**

**Problem 11-22A**  *Absorption versus variable costing*

Stowe Glass Company makes stained glass lamps. Each lamp that it sells for $315 per lamp requires $18 of direct materials and $72 of direct labor. Fixed overhead costs are expected to be $202,500 per year. Stowe Glass expects to sell 1,000 lamps during the coming year. Selling and administrative expenses were zero.

**Required**

a. Prepare income statements using absorption costing, assuming that Stowe Glass makes 1,000, 1,250, and 1,500 lamps during the year.

b. Prepare income statements using variable costing, assuming that Stowe Glass makes 1,000, 1,250, and 1,500 lamps during the year.

c. Explain why Stowe Glass may produce income statements under both absorption and variable costing formats. Your answer should include an explanation of the advantages and disadvantages associated with the use of the two reporting formats.

**CHECK FIGURES**
a. NI when 1,000 lamps
   were produced: $22,500
b. NI when 1,500 lamps
   were produced: $22,500

### Problem 11-23A  *Absorption and variable costing*

Thornell Manufacturing pays its production managers a bonus based on the company's profitability. During the two most recent years, the company maintained the same cost structure to manufacture its products.

**LO 7**

e**X**cel

**CHECK FIGURES**
a. NI for 2011: $24,000
d. $138,000

| Year | Units Produced | Units Sold |
|---|---|---|
| **Production and Sales** | | |
| 2011 | 4,000 | 4,000 |
| 2012 | 6,000 | 4,000 |
| | | |
| **Cost Data** | | |
| Direct materials | | $15 per unit |
| Direct labor | | $24 per unit |
| Manufacturing overhead—variable | | $12 per unit |
| Manufacturing overhead—fixed | | $108,000 |
| Variable selling and administrative expenses | | $9 per unit sold |
| Fixed selling and administrative expenses | | $60,000 |

(Assume that selling & administrative expenses are associated with goods sold.)

Thornell sells its products for $108 a unit.

**Required**

a. Prepare income statements based on absorption costing for 2011 and 2012.

b. Since Thornell sold the same number of units in 2011 and 2012, why did net income increase in 2012?

c. Discuss management's possible motivation for increasing production in 2012.

d. Determine the costs of ending inventory for 2012. Comment on the risks and costs associated with the accumulation of inventory.

e. Based on your answers to Requirements *b* and *c*, suggest a different income statement format. Prepare income statements for 2011 and 2012 using your suggested format.

## EXERCISES—SERIES B

### Exercise 11-1B  *Product cost flow and financial statements*

**LO 2, 3, 4, 5**

Murray Manufacturing began business on January 1, 2012. The following events pertain to its first year of operation.

1. Acquired $3,000 cash by issuing common stock.
2. Paid $600 cash for direct raw materials.
3. Transferred $500 of direct raw materials to Work in Process Inventory.
4. Paid production employees $700 cash.
5. Applied $325 of manufacturing overhead costs to Work in Process Inventory.
6. Completed work on products that cost $1,100.
7. Sold products for $1,600 cash.
8. Recognized cost of goods sold from Event No. 7 of $875.

9. Paid $450 cash for selling and administrative expenses.
10. Paid $350 cash for actual manufacturing overhead costs.
11. Made a $200 cash distribution to owners.
12. Closed the Manufacturing Overhead account.

**Required**

a. Record the preceding events in a horizontal statements model. The first event is shown as an example.

| Assets | | | | | = | Equity | | | | | |
|---|---|---|---|---|---|---|---|---|---|---|---|
| Cash | + MOH | + Raw M. | + WIP | + F. Goods | = | C. Stk. | + Ret. Ear. | Rev. | − Exp. | = | Net Inc. |
| 3,000 | + NA | + NA | + NA | + NA | = | 3,000 | + NA | NA | − NA | = | NA |

b. Prepare a schedule of cost of goods manufactured and sold.

**LO 2, 3, 4, 5, 6**   **Exercise 11-2B** *Recording events in T-accounts and preparing financial statements*

Hinnop Manufacturing Company was started on January 1, 2012, when it acquired $1,500 cash by issuing common stock. During its first year of operation, it purchased $480 of direct raw materials with cash and used $360 of the materials to make products. Hinnop paid $640 of direct labor costs in cash. The company applied $464 of overhead costs to Work in Process Inventory. It made cash payments of $464 for actual overhead costs. The company completed products that cost $1,040 to make. It sold goods that had cost $824 to make for $1,360 cash. It paid $320 of selling and administrative expenses in cash.

**Required**

a. Open the necessary T-accounts and record the 2012 events in the accounts. Include closing entries.

b. Prepare a schedule of cost of goods manufactured and sold, an income statement, and a balance sheet.

**LO 2, 3, 4**   **Exercise 11-3B** *Effect of accounting events on financial statements*

**Required**

Use a horizontal statements model to show how each of the following independent accounting events affects the elements of the balance sheet and the income statement. Indicate whether the event increases (I), decreases (D), or does not affect (NA) each element of the financial statements. The first two transactions are shown as examples.

a. Paid cash to purchase raw materials.
b. Recorded cash sales revenue.
c. Applied overhead to Work in Process Inventory based on the predetermined overhead rate.
d. Closed the Manufacturing Overhead account when overhead was underapplied.
e. Recognized cost of goods sold.
f. Recognized depreciation expense on manufacturing equipment.
g. Purchased manufacturing supplies on account.
h. Sold fully depreciated manufacturing equipment for the exact amount of its salvage value.

| Event No. | Balance Sheet | | | | Income Statement | | |
|---|---|---|---|---|---|---|---|
| | Assets | = Liab. | + C. Stk | + Ret Ear. | Rev. | − Exp. | = Net Inc. |
| a. | I D | NA | NA | NA | NA | NA | NA |
| b. | I | NA | NA | I | I | NA | I |

**Exercise 11-4B**  *Preparing financial statements*

Morris Manufacturing Company started 2011 with the following balances in its inventory accounts: Raw Materials, $2,800; Work in Process, $2,800; Finished Goods, $3,300. During 2011 Morris purchased $17,000 of raw materials and issued $16,500 of materials to the production department. It incurred $19,000 of direct labor costs and applied manufacturing overhead of $18,700 to Work in Process Inventory. Assume there was no over- or underapplied overhead at the end of the year. Morris completed goods costing $52,500 to produce and transferred them to finished goods inventory. During the year, Morris sold goods costing $50,700 for $76,900. Selling and administrative expenses for 2011 were $18,000.

**Required**

a.  Using T-accounts, determine the ending balance Morris would report for each of the three inventory accounts that would appear on the December 31, 2011, balance sheet.

b.  Prepare the 2011 schedule of cost of goods manufactured and sold and the 2011 income statement.

**Exercise 11-5B**  *Missing information in a schedule of cost of goods manufactured and sold*

**Required**

Supply the missing information on the following schedule of cost of goods manufactured and sold.

### TORBERT CORPORATION
#### Schedule of Cost of Goods Manufactured and Sold
#### For the Year Ended December 31, 2011

| | |
|---|---:|
| Raw materials | |
| Beginning inventory | $ 20,000 |
| Plus: Purchases | ? |
| Raw materials available for use | 160,000 |
| Minus: Ending raw materials inventory | ? |
| Cost of direct raw materials used | 145,000 |
| Direct labor | 120,000 |
| Manufacturing overhead | ? |
| Total manufacturing costs | 375,000 |
| Plus: Beginning work in process inventory | ? |
| Total work in process during the year | 393,000 |
| Minus: Ending work in process inventory | (20,500) |
| Cost of goods manufactured | ? |
| Plus: Beginning finished goods inventory | ? |
| Finished goods available for sale | 399,000 |
| Minus: Ending finished goods inventory | ? |
| Cost of goods sold | $378,000 |

**Exercise 11-6B**  *Cost of goods manufactured and sold*

The following information was drawn from the accounting records of Connor Manufacturing Company.

| | Beginning | Ending |
|---|---:|---:|
| Raw materials inventory | $4,000 | $4,600 |
| Work in process inventory | 6,200 | 5,000 |
| Finished goods inventory | 6,800 | 5,800 |

During the accounting period, Connor paid $16,000 to purchase raw materials, $15,000 for direct labor, and $11,000 for overhead costs. Assume that actual overhead equaled applied overhead.

**Required**

a.  Determine the amount of raw materials used.

b.  Determine the amount of cost of goods manufactured (the amount transferred from Work in Process Inventory to Finished Goods Inventory).

c.  Assuming sales revenue of $76,800, determine the amount of gross margin.

**LO 3**

### Exercise 11-7B    *Calculating applied overhead*

Salazar Enterprises' budget included the following estimated costs for the 2012 accounting period.

| | |
|---|---:|
| Depreciation on manufacturing equipment | $17,200 |
| Cost of manufacturing supplies | 3,000 |
| Direct labor cost | 86,400 |
| Rent on manufacturing facility | 7,600 |
| Direct materials cost | 74,000 |
| Manufacturing utilities cost | 6,000 |
| Maintenance cost for manufacturing facility | 5,200 |
| Administrative salaries cost | 30,500 |

The company uses a predetermined overhead rate based on machine hours. It estimated machine hour usage for 2012 would be 30,000 hours.

**Required**

a.  Identify the manufacturing overhead costs Salazar would use to calculate the predetermined overhead rate.

b.  Calculate the predetermined overhead rate.

c.  Explain why the rate is called "predetermined."

d.  Assuming Salazar actually used 29,200 machine hours during 2012, determine the amount of manufacturing overhead it would have applied to Work in Process Inventory during the period.

**LO 3**

### Exercise 11-8B    *Treatment of over- or underapplied overhead*

On January 1, 2011, Grey Company estimated that its total overhead costs for the coming year would be $306,000 and that it would make 34,000 units of product. Grey actually produced 34,600 units of product and incurred actual overhead costs of $303,200 during 2011.

**Required**

a.  Calculate Grey's predetermined overhead rate based on expected costs and production.

b.  Determine whether overhead was overapplied or underapplied during 2011.

c.  Explain how the entry to close the Manufacturing Overhead account will affect the Cost of Goods Sold account.

**LO 3**

### Exercise 11-9B    *Recording overhead costs in a T-account*

Gann Manufacturing Company incurred actual overhead costs of $149,000 during 2011. It uses direct labor dollars as the allocation base for overhead costs. In 2011, actual direct labor costs were $210,000, and overhead costs were underapplied by $2,000.

**Required**

a.  Calculate the predetermined overhead rate for 2011.

b.  Open T-accounts for Manufacturing Overhead and Cost of Goods Sold. Record the overhead costs and the adjusting entry to close Manufacturing Overhead in these accounts.

c.  Explain how the entry to close the Manufacturing Overhead account at the end of 2011 would affect the amount of net income reported on the 2011 income statement.

## Exercise 11-10B  *Treatment of over- or underapplied overhead*

**LO 3**

Kay Company and Way Company base their predetermined overhead rates on machine hours. The following information pertains to the companies' most recent accounting periods.

|  | Kay | Way |
|---|---|---|
| Actual machine hours | 12,300 | 19,500 |
| Estimated machine hours | 12,000 | 20,000 |
| Actual manufacturing overhead costs | $68,000 | $138,000 |
| Estimated manufacturing overhead costs | $67,200 | $139,200 |

### Required

a. Compute the predetermined overhead rate for each company.

b. Determine the amount of overhead cost that would be applied to work in process for each company and compute the amount of overapplied or underapplied manufacturing overhead cost for each company.

c. Explain how closing the Manufacturing Overhead account would affect the Cost of Goods Sold account for each company.

## Exercise 11-11B  *Recording manufacturing overhead costs*

**LO 3**

DeCastro Manufacturing Company incurred the following actual manufacturing overhead costs: (1) cash paid for plant supervisor's salary, $58,000; (2) depreciation on manufacturing equipment, $27,000; and (3) manufacturing supplies used, $2,300 (DeCastro uses the periodic inventory method for manufacturing supplies). Applied overhead amounted to $88,000.

### Required

a. Open the appropriate T-accounts and record the manufacturing overhead costs described.

b. Record the entry DeCastro would make to close the Manufacturing Overhead account to Cost of Goods Sold.

## Exercise 11-12B  *Missing information in inventory T-accounts*

**LO 2, 3, 4**

The following incomplete T-accounts were drawn from the records of Chilton Manufacturing Company:

| Raw Materials Inventory | | Work in Process Inventory | |
|---|---|---|---|
| 25,000 | (a) | | 52,000 |
| 1,200 | | 15,600 | |
| | | (b) | |
| **Finished Goods Inventory** | | | |
| (c) | | **Cost of Goods Sold** | |
| 5,000 | | | |
| | | (d) | |
| **Manufacturing Overhead** | | | |
| 17,000 | (e) | | |
| 800 | | | |

### Required

Determine the dollar amounts for (a), (b), (c), (d), and (e). Assume that underapplied and overapplied overhead is closed to Cost of Goods Sold.

**LO 7**

### Exercise 11-13B   *Variable costing versus absorption costing*

The following information was drawn from the records of Daffin Company:

| Variable costs (per unit) | | Fixed costs (in total) | |
|---|---|---|---|
| Direct materials | $16 | Manufacturing overhead | $48,000 |
| Direct labor | 20 | Selling and administrative | 49,600 |
| Manufacturing overhead | 6 | | |
| Selling and administrative | 14 | | |

During the most recent month Daffin produced 4,000 units of product and sold 3,800 units of product at a sales price of $98 per unit.

#### Required

a. Prepare an income statement for the month using absorption costing.

b. Prepare an income statement for the month using variable costing.

c. Explain why a company might use one type of income statement for external reporting and a different type for internal reporting.

**LO 1, 2, 3**

### Exercise 11-14B   *Smoothing unit cost*

Unit-level (variable) manufacturing costs for Dunmyer Manufacturing Company amount to $4. Fixed manufacturing costs are $4,500 per month. Production workers provided 800 hours of direct labor in January and 1,400 hours in February. Dunmyer expects to use 12,000 hours of labor during the year. It actually produced 1,200 units of product in January and 2,100 units of product in February.

#### Required

a. For each month, determine the total product cost and the per-unit product cost, assuming that actual fixed overhead costs are charged to monthly production.

b. Use a predetermined overhead rate based on direct labor hours to allocate the fixed overhead costs to each month's production. For each month, calculate the total product cost and the per-unit product cost.

c. Dunmyer employs a cost-plus pricing strategy. Would you recommend charging production with actual or allocated fixed overhead costs? Explain.

## PROBLEMS—SERIES B

**LO 2, 3, 4, 5, 6**

### Problem 11-15B   *Manufacturing cost flow across three accounting cycles*

The following accounting events affected Gitau Manufacturing Company during its first three years of operation. Assume that all transactions are cash transactions.

#### Transactions for 2010

1. Started manufacturing company by issuing common stock for $1,440.
2. Purchased $576 of direct raw materials.
3. Used $432 of direct raw materials to produce inventory.
4. Paid $360 of direct labor wages to employees to make inventory.
5. Applied $360 of manufacturing overhead to Work in Process Inventory.
6. Actual manufacturing overhead costs amounted to $366.
7. Finished work on inventory that cost $648.
8. Sold goods that cost $432 for $576.
9. Paid $36 for selling and administrative expenses.

#### Transactions for 2011

1. Acquired additional $720 of cash from issuance of common stock.
2. Purchased $576 of direct raw materials.
3. Used $504 of direct raw materials to produce inventory.

4. Paid $432 of direct labor wages to employees to make inventory.
5. Applied $384 of manufacturing overhead to Work in Process Inventory.
6. Actual manufacturing overhead costs amounted to $378.
7. Finished work on inventory that cost $1,080.
8. Sold goods that cost $1,008 for $1,152.
9. Paid $72 for selling and administrative expenses.

### Transactions for 2012

1. Purchased $360 of direct raw materials.
2. Used $576 of direct raw materials to produce inventory.
3. Paid $216 of direct labor wages to employees to make inventory.
4. Applied $300 of manufacturing overhead to Work in Process Inventory.
5. Actual manufacturing overhead costs amounted to $312.
6. Finished work on inventory that cost $1,188.
7. Sold goods that cost $1,296 for $1,584.
8. Paid $144 for selling and administrative expenses.
9. Paid a cash dividend of $288.

### Required

a. Record the preceding events in a horizontal statements model. Close overapplied or under-applied overhead to Cost of Goods Sold. The first event is shown as an example.

| Assets | | | | | = | Equity | | | | | | |
|---|---|---|---|---|---|---|---|---|---|---|---|---|
| Cash | + MOH | + Raw M. | + WIP | + F. Goods | = | C. Stk. | + Ret. Ear. | Rev. | − Exp. | = | Net Inc. | | |
| 1,440 | + NA | + NA | + NA | + NA | = | 1,440 | + NA | NA | − NA | = | NA | | |

b. Prepare a schedule of cost of goods manufactured and sold, an income statement, and a balance sheet as of the close of business on December 31, 2010.
c. Close appropriate accounts to the Retained Earnings account.
d. Repeat Requirements a through c for years 2011 and 2012.

### Problem 11-16B   *Manufacturing cost for one accounting cycle*    LO 2, 3, 4, 5, 6

The following trial balance was taken from the records of Jemison Manufacturing Company at the beginning of 2011.

| | | |
|---|---|---|
| Cash | $ 5,000 | |
| Raw materials inventory | 200 | |
| Work in process inventory | 600 | |
| Finished goods inventory | 400 | |
| Property, plant, and equipment | 7,000 | |
| Accumulated depreciation | | $ 2,000 |
| Common stock | | 5,000 |
| Retained earnings | | 6,200 |
| Total | $13,200 | $13,200 |

### Transactions for the Accounting Period

1. Jemison purchased $4,600 of direct raw materials and $500 of indirect raw materials on account. The indirect materials are capitalized in the Production Supplies account. Materials requisitions showed that $4,000 of direct raw materials had been used for production during the period. The use of indirect materials is determined at the end of the period by physically counting the supplies on hand at the end of the year.
2. By the end of the accounting period, $3,500 of the accounts payable had been paid in cash.
3. During the year, direct labor amounted to 1,200 hours recorded in the Wages Payable account at $6 per hour.

4. By the end of the accounting period, $6,500 of the Wages Payable account had been paid in cash.

5. At the beginning of the accounting period, the company expected overhead cost for the period to be $5,500 and 1,250 direct labor hours to be worked. Overhead is applied based on direct labor hours, which, as indicated in Event 3, amounted to 1,200 for the year.

6. Administrative and sales expenses for the period amounted to $1,400 paid in cash.

7. Utilities and rent for production facilities amounted to $3,000 paid in cash.

8. Depreciation on the plant and equipment used in production amounted to $2,000.

9. Assume that $15,000 of goods were completed during the period.

10. Assume that $10,000 of finished goods inventory was sold for $14,000 cash.

11. A count of the production supplies revealed a balance of $150 on hand at the end of the accounting period.

12. Any over- or underapplied overhead is considered to be insignificant.

**Required**

a. Open T-accounts with the beginning balances shown in the preceding list and record all transactions for the period including closing entries in the T-accounts. (*Note:* Open new T-accounts as needed.)

b. Prepare a schedule of cost of goods manufactured and sold, an income statement, and a balance sheet.

**LO 2, 3, 4, 5, 6**    **Problem 11-17B**    *Manufacturing cost flow for one-year period*

Burnside Manufacturing started 2011 with the following account balances.

| | |
|---|---|
| Cash | $3,000 |
| Common stock | 2,500 |
| Retained earnings | 1,200 |
| Raw materials inventory | 300 |
| Work in process inventory | 220 |
| Finished goods inventory (50 units @ $3.60/unit) | 180 |

**Transactions during 2011**

1. Purchased $750 of raw materials with cash.
2. Transferred $500 of raw materials to the production department.
3. Incurred and paid cash for 80 hours of direct labor at $7.50 per hour.
4. Applied overhead costs to Work in Process Inventory. The predetermined overhead rate is $7.50 per direct labor hour.
5. Incurred actual overhead costs of $650 cash.
6. Completed work on 300 units for $3.60 per unit.
7. Paid $200 in selling and administrative expenses in cash.
8. Sold 200 units for $1,500 cash revenues. (Assume LIFO cost flow.)

Burnside charges overapplied or underapplied overhead directly to Cost of Goods Sold.

**Required**

a. Record the preceding events in a horizontal statements model. The beginning balances are shown as an example.

| Assets | | | | | = | Equity | | | | | |
|---|---|---|---|---|---|---|---|---|---|---|---|
| Cash + | Raw M. + | MOH + | WIP + | F. Goods | = | C. Stk. + | Ret. Ear. | | Rev. − | Exp. = | Net Inc. |
| 3,000 + | 300 + | NA + | 220 + | 180 | = | 2,500 + | 1,200 | | NA − | NA = | NA |

b. Prepare a schedule of cost of goods manufactured and sold, an income statement, and a balance sheet for 2011.

## Problem 11-18B   *Manufacturing cost flow for monthly and annual accounting periods*    LO 2, 3, 4, 5, 6

York Manufacturing Company manufactures puzzles that depict the works of famous artists. The company rents a small factory and uses local labor on a part-time basis. The following accounting events affected York during its first year of operation. (Assume that all transactions are cash transactions unless otherwise stated.)

### Transactions for First Month of Operation 2011

1. Issued common stock for $45,000.

2. Purchased $5,000 of direct raw materials and $600 of indirect raw materials. Indirect materials are recorded in a Production Supplies account.

3. Used $3,896 of direct raw materials.

4. Used 700 direct labor hours; production workers were paid $6 per hour.

5. Expected total overhead costs for the year to be $16,800 and direct labor hours used during the year to be 9,600. Calculate an overhead rate and apply the appropriate amount of overhead costs to Work in Process.

6. Paid $800 for salaries to administrative and sales staff.

7. Paid $700 for indirect manufacturing labor.

8. Paid $600 for rent and utilities on the manufacturing facilities.

9. Started and completed 956 puzzles; all costs were transferred from the Work in Process Inventory account to the Finished Goods Inventory account.

10. Sold 800 puzzles at a price of $12 each.

### Transactions for Remainder of 2011

11. Acquired an additional $150,000 by issuing common stock.

12. Purchased $46,000 of direct raw materials and $4,000 of indirect raw materials.

13. Used $41,050 of direct raw materials.

14. Paid production workers $6 per hour for 9,800 hours of work.

15. Applied the appropriate overhead cost to Work in Process Inventory.

16. Paid $8,800 for salaries of administrative and sales staff.

17. Paid $7,700 for the salary of the production supervisor.

18. Paid $6,600 for rental and utility costs on the manufacturing facilities.

19. Transferred 12,000 additional puzzles that cost $9.75 each from Work in Process Inventory to Finished Goods Inventory accounts.

20. Determined that $3,200 of production supplies was on hand at the end of the accounting period.

21. Sold 8,000 puzzles for $12 each.

22. Determine whether overhead is over- or underapplied. Close the Manufacturing Overhead account to Cost of Goods Sold.

23. Close the revenue and expense accounts.

### Required

a. Open T-accounts and post transactions to the accounts.

b. Prepare a schedule of cost of goods manufactured and sold, an income statement, and a balance sheet for 2011.

## Problem 11-19B   *Manufacturing cost flow for multiple accounting cycles*    LO 2, 3, 4, 5, 6

The following events apply to Wilkinson Manufacturing Company. Assume that all transactions are cash transactions unless otherwise indicated.

### Transactions for the 2011 Accounting Period

1. The company was started on January 1, 2011, when it acquired $700,000 cash by issuing common stock.

2. The company purchased $300,000 of direct raw materials with cash and used $26,000 of these materials to make its products in January.

3. Employees provided 1,500 hours of labor at $8 per hour during January. Wages are paid in cash.

4. The estimated manufacturing overhead costs for 2011 are $650,000. Overhead is applied on the basis of direct labor costs. The company expected $130,000 of direct labor costs during 2011. Record applied overhead for January.

5. By the end of January, the employees completed work on all inventory items started in January. The cost of this production was transferred to the Finished Goods Inventory account. Determine the cost per unit of product produced in January, assuming that a total of 10,000 units of product were started and completed during the month.

6. The company used an additional $234,000 of direct raw materials and 13,500 hours of direct labor at $8 per hour during the remainder of 2011. Overhead was allocated on the basis of direct labor cost.

7. The company completed work on inventory items started between February 1 and December 31, and the cost of the completed inventory was transferred to the Finished Goods Inventory account. Determine the cost per unit for goods produced between February 1 and December 31, assuming that 90,000 units of inventory were produced. If the company desires to earn a gross profit of $6 per unit, what price per unit must it charge for the merchandise sold?

8. The company sold 60,000 units of inventory for cash at $12.80 per unit. Determine the number of units in ending inventory and the cost per unit of this inventory.

9. Actual manufacturing overhead costs paid in cash were $610,000.

10. The company paid $150,000 cash for selling and administrative expenses.

11. Close the Manufacturing Overhead account.

12. Close the revenue and expense accounts.

## Transactions for the 2012 Accounting Period

1. The company acquired $350,000 cash from the owners.

2. The company purchased $200,000 of direct raw materials with cash and used $20,800 of these materials to make products in January.

3. Employees provided 1,200 hours of labor at $8 per hour during January.

4. On January 1, 2012, Wilkinson expected the production facilities to cost $1,500 cash per month. The company paid cash to purchase $7,000 of manufacturing supplies, and it anticipated that $7,000 of these supplies would be used by year-end. Other manufacturing overhead costs were expected to total $455,000. Overhead is applied on the basis of direct labor costs. Wilkinson expects direct labor costs of $80,000 during 2012. Based on this information, determine the total expected overhead cost for 2012. Calculate the predetermined overhead rate and apply the overhead cost for the January production. Also, record the purchase of manufacturing supplies.

5. The company recorded a $1,500 cash payment for production facilities in January.

6. On January, the employees completed work on all inventory items started in January. The cost of this production was transferred to the Finished Goods Inventory account. Determine the cost per unit of product produced in January assuming that a total of 8,000 units of product was started and completed during the month.

7. During February 2012, the company used $15,600 of raw materials and 900 hours of labor at $8 per hour. Overhead was allocated on the basis of direct labor cost.

8. The company recorded a $1,500 cash payment for production facilities in February.

9. In February, the employees completed work on all inventory items started in February; the cost of this production was transferred to the Finished Goods Inventory account. Determine the cost per unit of product produced in February, assuming that 6,000 units of product were started and completed during the month.

10. The company used an additional $143,000 of direct raw materials and 8,250 hours of direct labor at $8 per hour during the remainder of 2012. Overhead was allocated on the basis of direct labor cost.

11. The company recorded $15,000 of cash payments for production facilities for the period between March 1 and December 31.

12. The company completed work on inventory items started between March 1 and December 31. The cost of the completed goods was transferred to the Finished Goods Inventory account. Compute the cost per unit of this inventory, assuming that 55,000 units of inventory were produced.

**13.** The company sold 90,000 units of product for $14 per unit cash. Assume that the company uses the FIFO inventory cost flow method to determine the cost of goods sold.

**14.** The company paid $130,000 cash for selling and administrative expenses.

**15.** As of December 31, 2012, $1,200 of production supplies was on hand.

**16.** Actual cost of other manufacturing overhead was $461,000 cash.

**17.** Close the Manufacturing Overhead account.

**18.** Close the revenue and expense accounts.

**Required**

**a.** Open T-accounts and record the effects of the preceding events.

**b.** Prepare a schedule of cost of goods manufactured and sold, an income statement, and a balance sheet for each year.

## Problem 11-20B  *Comprehensive review problem*

LO 1, 2, 3, 4

Anita Rowley has worked as the plant manager of Gambrell Corporation, a large manufacturing company, for 10 years. The company produces stereo CD players for automotive vehicles and sells them to some of the largest car manufacturers in the country. Ms. Rowley has always toyed with the idea of starting her own car stereo manufacturing business. With her experience and knowledge, she is certain that she can produce a superior stereo at a low cost. Ms. Rowley's business strategy would be to market the product to smaller, more specialized car manufacturers. Her potential market is car manufacturers who sell at a lower volume to discriminating customers. She is confident that she could compete in this market that values low-cost quality production. She would not compete with Gambrell or the other large stereo producers that dominate the market made up of the largest automotive producers.

Ms. Rowley already has firm orders for 800 stereos from several automotive producers. Based on the contacts that she has made working for Gambrell, Ms. Rowley is confident that she can make and sell 2,000 stereos during the first year of operation. However, before making a final decision, she decides to investigate the profitability of starting her own business. Relevant information follows.

| | |
|---|---|
| Components from wholesaler | $36.00 per stereo |
| Assembly labor | $8.40 per hour |
| Rent of manufacturing buildings | $9,600.00 per year |
| Utilities | $240.00 per month |
| Sales salaries | $480.00 per month |
| Depreciation of equipment | $1,600.00 per year |
| Labor | 3 hours per stereo |

During the first year, Ms. Rowley expects to be able to produce the stereos with only two production workers and a part-time salesperson to market the product. Ms. Rowley expects to devote her time to the administrative aspects of the business and to provide back-up support in the production work. She has decided not to pay herself a salary but to live off the profits of the business.

**Required**

**a.** Classify each cost item into the categories of direct materials, direct labor, and manufacturing overhead.

**b.** Classify each cost item as either variable or fixed.

**c.** What is the cost per stereo if Ms. Rowley's company produces 800 units per year? What is the unit cost if the company produces 2,000 units per year?

**d.** If Ms. Rowley's job presently pays her $12,000 a year, would you recommend that she proceed with the plans to start the new company if she could sell stereos for $96 each?

## Problem 11-21B  *Absorption versus variable costing*

LO 7

Hattaway Manufacturing Company makes a product that sells for $50 per unit. Manufacturing costs for the product amount to $24 per unit variable, and $160,000 fixed. During the current accounting period, Hattaway made 8,000 units of the product and sold 7,600 units. Selling and administrative expenses were zero.

**Required**

a. Prepare an absorption costing income statement.

b. Prepare a variable costing income statement.

c. Explain why the amount of net income on the absorption costing income statement differs from the amount of net income on the variable costing income statement. Your answer should include the amount of the inventory balance that would exist under the two costing approaches.

**LO 7**

## Problem 11-22B   *Absorption versus variable costing*

Alvarez Company makes leather chairs that it sells for $200 per chair. Each chair requires $28 of direct materials and $72 of direct labor. Fixed overhead costs are expected to be $120,000 per year. Alvarez expects to sell 1,500 chairs during the coming year. Selling and administrative expenses were zero.

**Required**

a. Prepare income statements using absorption costing, assuming that Alvarez makes 1,500, 2,000, and 2,500 chairs during the year.

b. Prepare income statements using variable costing, assuming that Alvarez makes 1,500, 2,000, and 2,500 chairs during the year.

c. Explain why Alvarez may produce income statements under both absorption and variable costing formats. Your answer should include an explanation of the advantages or disadvantages associated with the use of the two reporting formats.

**LO 7**

## Problem 11-23B   *Absorption and variable costing*

Moncier Manufacturing pays its production managers a bonus based on the company's profitability. During the two most recent years, the company maintained the same cost structure to manufacture its products.

| Year | Units Produced | Units Sold |
|---|---|---|
| **Production and Sales** | | |
| 2011 | 4,000 | 4,000 |
| 2012 | 6,000 | 4,000 |
| | | |
| **Cost Data** | | |
| Direct materials | | $8 per unit |
| Direct labor | | $12 per unit |
| Manufacturing overhead—variable | | $4 per unit |
| Manufacturing overhead—fixed | | $72,000 |
| Variable selling and administrative expenses | | $4 per unit sold |
| Fixed selling and administrative expenses | | $30,000 |

(Assume that selling and administrative expenses are associated with goods sold.)

Moncier's sales revenue for both years was $230,000.

**Required**

a. Prepare income statements based on absorption costing for the years 2011 and 2012.

b. Since Moncier sold the same amount in 2011 and 2012, why did net income increase in 2012?

c. Discuss management's possible motivation for increasing production in 2012.

d. Determine the costs of ending inventory for 2012. Comment on the risks and costs associated with the accumulation of inventory.

e. Based on your answers to Requirements *b* and *c*, suggest a different income statement format and prepare income statements for 2011 and 2012 using your suggested format.

# ANALYZE, THINK, COMMUNICATE

**ATC 11-1** Business Applications Case *Predetermined overhead rate*

Airline Meal Services (AMS) makes prepared meals that it sells to regional airlines. The average materials cost per meal is $3.90, and the average labor cost is $2.40. AMS incurs approximately $720,000 of fixed manufacturing overhead costs annually. The marketing department estimated that AMS would sell approximately 300,000 meals during the coming year. Unfortunately, AMS has experienced a steady decline in sales even though the airline industry has had a steady increase in the number of meals sold. The chief accountant, Michelle Winters, was overheard saying that when she calculated the predetermined overhead rate, she deliberately lowered the estimated number of meals expected to be sold because she had lost faith in the marketing department's ability to deliver on its estimated sales numbers. Ms. Winters explained, "This way, our actual cost is always below the estimated cost. It is about the only way we continue to make a profit." Indeed, the company had a significant amount of overapplied overhead at the end of each year.

### Required

a. Explain how the overapplied overhead affects the determination of year-end net income.

b. Assume that Ms. Winters used 280,000 meals as the estimated sales to calculate the predetermined overhead rate. Determine the difference in expected cost per meals she calculated and the cost per meals that would result if the marketing department's estimate (300,000 units) had been used.

c. Assuming that AMS uses a cost-plus pricing policy, speculate how Ms. Winters' behavior could be contributing to the decline in sales.

**ATC 11-2** Group Assignment *Schedule of cost of goods manufactured and sold*

The following information is from the accounts of Depree Manufacturing Company for 2010.

### Required

a. Divide the class into groups of four or five students per group and organize the groups into three sections. Assign Task 1 to the first section of groups, Task 2 to the second section, and Task 3 to the third section.

### Group Tasks

(1) The ending balance in the Raw Materials Inventory account was $208,000. During the accounting period, Depree used $2,348,900 of raw materials inventory and purchased $2,200,000 of raw materials. Determine the beginning raw materials inventory balance.

(2) During the accounting period, Depree used $2,348,900 of raw materials inventory and $2,780,200 of direct labor. Actual overhead costs were $3,300,000. Ending work in process inventory amounted to $450,000, and cost of goods manufactured amounted to $8,389,100. Determine the beginning balance in the Work in Process Inventory account.

(3) The cost of goods manufactured was $8,389,100, and the cost of goods sold was $8,419,100. Ending finished goods inventory amounted to $360,000. Determine the beginning balance in the Finished Goods Inventory account.

b. Select a spokesperson from each section. Use input from the three spokespersons to prepare a schedule of cost of goods manufactured and sold. The spokesperson from the first section should provide information for the computation of the beginning balance in the raw materials account. The spokesperson from the second section should provide information for the determination of the beginning balance in the Work-in-Process Inventory account. The spokesperson from the third section should provide information for the determination of the beginning balance in the Finished Goods Inventory account.

**ATC 11-3** Research Assignment *Distinction between service and manufacturing companies*

**Electronic Arts, Inc.**, more commonly known as EA Sports, develops and markets games for Sony's PlayStation 3 and Microsoft's Xbox. Using either the company's March 31, 2009, Form 10-K or its annual report, answer the following questions. Access the company's website to obtain the Form 10-K or use the EDGAR system by following the instructions in Appendix A. An interactive version of the company's annual report is available on its website.

**Required**

a. Read the "Overview" subsection of the "Business" section of the company's 10-K or annual report. The business section is near the beginning of the documents. Based on this information, is EA Sports a service or a manufacturing business? Explain.

b. Based on your response to Requirement *a*, what types of inventory do you expect EA Sports to have? Review the information in Note (9) of the company's financial statements. Does the company have any inventory? If so, what is (are) the type(s) and dollar amounts of any inventory that EA Sports has? Does the information in Note (9) lead you to rethink your answer to Requirement *a*?

c. What are some cost drivers EA Sports might use to allocate common costs to the various games it markets?

### ATC 11-4   Writing Assignment   *Inventory cost flow in manufacturing environment*

Barret Cameron, a student in Professor Wagner's managerial accounting course, asked the following question. "In the first accounting course, the teacher said inventory costs flow on a FIFO, LIFO, or weighted average pattern. Now you are telling us inventory costs flow through raw materials, to work in process, and then to finished goods. Is this manufacturing stuff a new cost flow method or what?"

**Required**

Assume that you are Professor Wagner. Write a brief memo responding to Mr. Cameron's question.

### ATC 11-5   Ethical Dilemma   *Absorption costing*

Cliff Dennis may become a rich man. He is the creative force behind Amazing Drives, a new company. Amazing makes external drives that permit computer users to store large amounts of information on small floppy diskettes. Amazing has experienced tremendous growth since its inception three years ago. Investors have recognized the company's potential, and its stock is currently selling at 60 times projected earnings. More specifically, the company's 2009 earnings forecast shows estimated income to be $0.30 per share and the current market price is $18 per share ($0.30 × 60). Mr. Dennis has stock options permitting him to buy 2,000,000 shares of stock for $12 per share on January 1, 2010. This means that he could earn $6 per share on the options. In other words, he would buy the stock at $12 per share and sell it at $18 per share. As a result, Mr. Dennis would earn $12,000,000 ($6 × 2,000,000 shares).

Unfortunately, weak economies in foreign countries have caused low demand for Amazing's products in international markets. Company insiders are painfully aware that Amazing Drives is going to be unable to meet its projected income numbers. If actual earnings fall short of the projected earnings, the market will manifest its disappointment by discounting the stock price. Mr. Dennis is concerned that the value of his stock options could plummet.

At its inception three years ago, Amazing invested heavily in manufacturing equipment. Indeed, expecting dramatic growth, the company purchased a significant amount of excess capacity. As a result, the company incurs approximately $28,800,000 in fixed manufacturing costs annually. If Amazing continues to produce at its current level, it will make and sell approximately 800,000 drives during 2009. In the face of declining sales, Mr. Dennis has issued a puzzling order to his production manager. Specifically, he has told the production manager to increase production so that 1,200,000 drives will be completed during 2009. Mr. Dennis explained that he believes the economies in foreign countries will surge ahead in 2010 and that he wants Amazing to have the inventory necessary to satisfy the demand.

**Required**

a. Suppose that actual earnings for 2009 are $0.18 per share. The market becomes disappointed, and the price-earnings ratio falls to 40 times earnings. What is the value of Mr. Dennis's stock options under these circumstances?

b. Determine the impact on income reported in 2009 if production is 800,000 units versus 1,200,000 units.

c. Why would Mr. Dennis order the increase in production?

d. Does Mr. Dennis's behavior violate any of the standards of ethical conduct in Exhibit 1.15 of Chapter 1?

e. Identify the features described in this case that could motivate criminal and ethical misconduct. (It may be helpful to reread the fraud triangle in Chapter 1 before attempting to satisfy this requirement.)

## ATC 11-6    Spreadsheet Assignment    *Using Excel*

Manning Cassey Computers (MCC) plans to produce and sell 1,600 computers for $720 each in the next fiscal year. The company's cost data follow.

| | |
|---|---|
| Components from wholesaler | $480 per computer |
| Assembly labor | $15 per hour |
| Manufacturing space rent | $3,000 per month |
| Utilities | $600 per month |
| Janitorial services | $480 per month |
| Depreciation of equipment | $3,840 per year |
| Labor time per computer | 2 hours |

### Required

a. Construct a spreadsheet to calculate the cost of goods manufactured and the cost per unit for MCC. Use formulas in the schedule so that the cost of goods manufactured will automatically be calculated as you change the number of units sold.

b. Add an abbreviated income statement to your spreadsheet that incorporates the cost from Requirement *a*.

### Spreadsheet Tip

Build the spreadsheet so that the number of units in cell E3 can be changed and cost of goods manufactured and net income will be recalculated automatically.

## ATC 11-7    Spreadsheet Assignment    *Mastering Excel*

Stanley Manufacturing Company, which sold 16,000 units of product at $20 per unit, collected the following information regarding three different levels of production.

**Inventory Costs**

| | | | |
|---|---|---|---|
| Fixed overhead | $100,000 | $100,000 | $100,000 |
| Number of units produced | 16,000 | 20,000 | 25,000 |
| Fixed overhead per unit | $6.25 | $5.00 | $4.00 |
| Variable manufacturing costs | $12.00 | $12.00 | $12.00 |
| Full absorption cost per unit | $18.25 | $17.00 | $16.00 |

**Required**

a. Construct a spreadsheet that includes the preceding data in the top of the spreadsheet. The rows for fixed overhead per unit and full absorption cost per unit should be based on formulas.

b. Include absorption costing income statements at these three levels of production like those in Exhibit 11.10. Use formulas so that the number of units produced in the preceding table can be changed and net income will be recalculated automatically.

c. Include variable costing income statements at these three levels of production like those in Exhibit 11.11. Use formulas so that the number of units produced in the preceding table can be changed and net income will be recalculated automatically.

## COMPREHENSIVE PROBLEM

Magnificent Modems, Inc., acquired a subsidiary named Anywhere, Inc. (AI). AI manufactures a wireless modem that enables users to access the Internet through cell phones. The following trial balance was drawn from the accounts of the subsidiary.

| | | |
|---|---|---|
| Cash | $200,000 | |
| Raw materials inventory | 4,000 | |
| Work in process inventory | 6,000 | |
| Finished goods inventory | 7,000 | |
| Common stock | | $129,000 |
| Retained earnings | | 88,000 |
| Totals | $217,000 | $217,000 |

The subsidiary completed the following transactions during 2011.

1. Paid $60,000 cash for direct raw materials.
2. Transferred $50,000 of direct raw materials to work in process.
3. Paid production employees $80,000 cash.
4. Applied $53,000 of manufacturing overhead costs to work in process.
5. Completed work on products that cost $163,000.
6. Sold products that cost $143,000 for $182,000 cash. Record the recognition of revenue in a row labeled 6a and the cost of goods sold in a row labeled 6b.
7. Paid $20,000 cash for selling and administrative expenses.
8. Actual overhead costs paid in cash amounted to $55,000.
9. Closed the Manufacturing Overhead account. The amount of over- or underapplied overhead was insignificant (immaterial).
10. Made a $5,000 cash distribution to the owners.

**Required**

a. For Anywhere, Inc., record the events in the financial statements model like the one shown below.

| Assets | | | | | | = | Equity | | | | | | |
|---|---|---|---|---|---|---|---|---|---|---|---|---|---|
| Cash | + MOH | + Raw M. | + WIP | + F. Goods | | = | C. Stk. | + Ret. Ear. | | Rev. | − Exp. | = | Net Inc. |
| 200,000 | + 0 | + 4,000 | + 6,000 | + 7,000 | | = | 129,000 | + 88,000 | | NA | − NA | = | NA |

b. Prepare a schedule of cost of goods manufactured and sold.

c. Prepare an income statement and a balance sheet.

## CHAPTER 12

# Job-Order, Process, and Hybrid Costing Systems

## LEARNING OBJECTIVES

**After you have mastered the material in this chapter you will be able to:**

1 Distinguish between job-order and process costing systems.

2 Identify documentation used in a job-order costing system.

3 Explain how events in a job-order costing system affect financial statements.

4 Explain how events in a process costing system affect financial statements.

5 Calculate equivalent units and prepare a cost of production report.

## CHAPTER OPENING

Benchmore Boat Company built five boats during the current year. Each boat has unique characteristics that affect its cost. For example, an 80-foot yacht required more labor and materials than a 30-foot sailboat. Because different boats cost different amounts, Benchmore needs a cost system that traces product costs to individual inventory items (specific boats).

In contrast, Janis Juice Company produced 500,000 cans of apple juice during the same year. Each can of juice is identical to the others. Determining the cost of a boat built by Benchmore requires a different costing system than the system Janis needs to determine the cost of a can of juice. Benchmore needs a costing system that captures the unique cost of each individual inventory item. Janis needs a costing system that distributes costs evenly across total production (number of cans of juice produced during an accounting period).

# The Curious Accountant

Consider the following two situations:

First, imagine you worked at **Kellogg's**, a company that produces breakfast cereals. Assume that during the past year your company produced 70 million, 24-ounce boxes of Corn Flakes, and incurred manufacturing costs of $115 million related to this one product.

Next, imagine you worked for **Bechtel**, a private company that is one of the world's largest construction companies. During 2009 it was constructing such diverse projects as a plant to produce liquefied natural gas (LNG) in Angola, off the coast of West Africa, and a plant in Hanford, Washington, to treat nuclear waste materials. Assume that during 2009 Bechtel worked on 40 different projects and incurred manufacturing costs of $20 billion.

How would you determine the cost of one box of cereal? How would you determine the cost incurred to construct the LNG project in Angola? Which of the two questions asked above do you think would be the most difficult to answer for real world companies? (Answers on page 552.)

# COSTING SYSTEMS

Distinguish between job-order and process costing systems.

The type of product a company produces affects the type of accounting system needed to determine product cost. The two most common types of costing systems are job-order costing and process costing. Some companies use hybrid costing systems that combine features of both job-order and process systems. The following section of the text discusses the types of products most suited to each costing system and the accounting procedures used in each type of costing system.

## Costing Systems and Type of Product

**Job-order costing systems** accumulate costs by individual products. The boats Benchmore builds are suited to job-order costing. Other products for which job-order costing is suitable include movies made by **Walt Disney Productions**, office buildings constructed by **Rust Engineering**, and airplanes made by **Boeing**. Job-order costing systems apply not only to individual inventory items but also to batches of inventory items. For example, **Hernandes Shirt Company** may account for producing a special order of 20,000 shirts sold to the United States Army as a single job. Companies use job-order costing systems when they need to know the costs of individual products or batches of products.

**Process costing systems** allocate costs evenly to homogeneous products. In addition to beverage companies such as Janis Juice, oil refiners such as **Texaco**, chemical producers such as **Dow Chemical**, food processors such as **General Mills**, and paint manufacturers such as **Sherwin-Williams** use process costing. These companies normally make products in mass quantities using continuous processes. The *per-unit product cost* is determined by dividing the *total* product cost by the number of units produced during the accounting period. Process costing systems provide *average* product costs.

To a lesser extent, job-order costing systems also use average costs. It is either not possible or not cost effective to trace costs of indirect materials, indirect labor, utilities, rent, and depreciation directly to particular jobs. Companies normally combine these costs and allocate them to individual products using an average overhead rate based on a common measure of production such as labor hours, machine hours, or square footage. When jobs are produced in batches of a number of similar products, the cost per unit is determined by dividing the total cost of the job by the number of units in the batch. Although more costs are traced to specific products under a job-order system than a process system, *both* systems require *some* form of *cost averaging.*

## Job-Order Cost Flow

Job-order and process costing systems are patterned after the physical flow of products moving through production. For example, consider how Benchmore Boat Company builds custom boats. Each boat is a separate project. Benchmore starts a project by requisitioning raw materials from materials storage. It assigns specific employees to work on specific boats. Finally, it assigns indirect (overhead) costs to each boat based on the number of direct labor hours required to build the boat.

Benchmore's *job-order costing system* accumulates cost in a manner parallel to physical boat construction. Benchmore assigns each boat a specific job identification number. It records transactions in inventory accounts on a perpetual basis. Product costs are accumulated separately for each job identification number. The costs of each boat move through the Work in Process Inventory account to the Finished Goods Inventory account and finally to the Cost of Goods Sold account as the boat is produced and sold. Exhibit 12.1 shows the flow of product costs for the five boats Benchmore plans to build in 2012. In a job-order system, the amount recorded in the Work in Process Inventory account is the total cost to date of distinct jobs. Each distinct job

## EXHIBIT 12.1

### Cost Flow in a Job-Order Costing System

**Balance sheet**

Product costs → Work in process inventory → Finished goods inventory → Income statement

Materials / Labor / Overhead →

Boat 104 — Materials / Labor / Overhead

Boat 105 — Materials / Labor / Overhead

Boat 103 — Materials / Labor / Overhead

Boat 101 — Materials / Labor / Overhead

Boat 102 — Materials / Labor / Overhead

Cost of goods available for sale maintained separately for

Boat 101
Boat 102
Boat 103
Boat 104
Boat 105

→ Cost of goods sold

represents the costs of materials, labor, and overhead accumulated for that specific inventory project. The Work in Process Inventory account is a *control* account supported by numerous *subsidiary* accounts (the records for individual jobs). The Finished Goods Inventory account is also a control account. It is supported by subsidiary accounts in which are recorded the separate costs of each completed, but not yet sold, boat.

## Process Cost Flow

*Process costing systems* use the same general ledger accounts as job-order costing systems. Product costs flow from Raw Materials Inventory to Work in Process Inventory to Finished Goods Inventory to Cost of Goods Sold. The primary difference between the two systems centers on accounting for the work in process inventory. The physical products move continuously through a series of processing centers. Instead of accumulating product costs by jobs that add up to a single Work in Process Inventory control account, process costing systems accumulate product costs by processing centers, or *departments*. Each department has its own separate Work in Process Inventory account. For example, Janis Juice Company uses three distinct processes to produce cans of apple juice. Raw apples enter the extraction department where juice concentrate is pressed from whole fruit. The concentrate moves to the mixing department where Janis adds water, sugar, food coloring, and preservatives. The resulting juice mixture moves to the packaging department where it is canned and boxed. The materials, labor, and overhead costs incurred as products move through a processing center (department) are charged to that center's Work in Process Inventory account.

Parallel to the physical flow of product through the manufacturing process, cost accumulations pass from one department to the next. The end products of one department become the raw materials of the next department. The costs transferred from one department to the next are **transferred-in costs.** Transferred-in costs are combined with the additional materials, labor, and overhead costs incurred by each succeeding department. When goods are complete, the total product cost transferred to the Finished Goods Inventory account represents the sum of product costs from all the departments. Exhibit 12.2 illustrates cost flow for the process costing system used by Janis Juice Company. Compare the cost flow patterns in Exhibits 12.1 and 12.2 to clarify the distinction between job-order and process costing systems.

JANIS

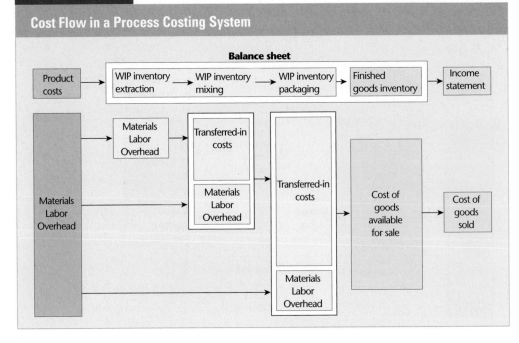

**EXHIBIT 12.2**

**Cost Flow in a Process Costing System**

## Hybrid Accounting Systems

Many companies use **hybrid costing systems.** Hybrid systems combine features of both process and job-order costing systems. For example, Gateway 2000 makes thousands of identical computers using a continuous assembly line that is compatible with process costing. Each unit requires the same amount of labor to assemble a standard set of parts into a finished computer ready for immediate sale. Gateway also builds custom computers with unique features. Customers can order larger monitors, more memory, or faster processors than Gateway's standard model has. Gateway meets these requests by customizing the computers as they move through production. The costs of customized features must be traced to products with a job-order type of system. Gateway charges customers a premium for the custom items.

## DOCUMENTATION IN A JOB-ORDER COSTING SYSTEM

Identify documentation used in a job-order costing system.

In a job-order costing system, product costs for each individual job are accumulated on a **job cost sheet,** also called a *job-order cost sheet* or a *job record.* As each job moves through production, detailed cost information for materials, labor, and overhead is recorded on the job cost sheet. When a job is finished, the job cost sheet summarizes all costs incurred to complete that job.

Two primary source documents, materials requisition forms and work tickets, provide the information recorded on the job cost sheet. Before starting a job, the job supervisor prepares a **materials requisition form** which lists the materials needed to begin work. The materials requisition represents the authorization for raw materials to be released from storage to production. Some companies deliver hard-copy forms to and from the different departments, but most modern businesses deliver requests electronically through a computer network. Whether recorded on paper documents or in electronic files, the information from material requisitions for each job is sent to the accounting department to be summarized on the job cost sheet.

The **work ticket,** sometimes called a *time card,* provides space for the job number, employee identification, and work description. Employees record on the work ticket the amount of time they spend on each job. This information is forwarded to the accounting department. Using wage rate records, the accounting department computes the

**EXHIBIT 12.3**

**Job-Order Cost Sheet and Source Documents**

### Job Cost Sheet

Job Order No. __Boat 101__    Customer Name: __Arturo Martinez__

Due Date: __10/31/2011__    Date Started: __08/01/2011__    Date Finished: __11/30/2011__

| Direct materials | | Direct labor | | | Applied overhead | | |
|---|---|---|---|---|---|---|---|
| Req. No. | Cost | Ticket | Hours | Cost | Rate | Hours | Cost |
| 24585 | 7,100 | 367 | 1,400 | 9,100 | 3.90 | 1,400 | 5,460 |
| 24600 | 5,600 | 360 | 1,600 | 10,400 | 3.90 | 1,600 | 6,240 |
| 24609 | 6,100 | | | | | | |
| Total | 18,800 | Total | | 19,500 | Total | | 11,700 |

Cost summary

| Direct materials | $18,800 |
|---|---|
| Direct labor | 19,500 |
| Overhead | 11,700 |
| Total | $50,000 |

| Material requisitions | | |
|---|---|---|
| | Date | Quantity |
| Package K | 8/1 | Mixed |
| Package R | 9/1 | Mixed |
| Package T | 10/1 | Mixed |
| Information transferred electronically | | |

| Work tickets | | |
|---|---|---|
| | Date | Hours |
| Process 1 | 9/30 | 1,400 |
| Process 2 | 11/30 | 1,600 |
| Information transferred electronically | | |

amount of labor cost and records it on the job cost sheet. The data can be gathered manually or electronically.

Finally, each job cost sheet provides space for applied overhead. Companies maintain job cost sheet records perpetually, adding additional cost data as work on jobs progresses. Using predetermined overhead rates, estimated overhead costs are regularly added to job cost sheets. Exhibit 12.3 illustrates a job cost sheet along with materials requisition forms and work tickets for Benchmore Boat Company's job-order number Boat 101.

## REALITY BYTES

Job-order, process, and hybrid costing systems apply to service businesses as well as manufacturing concerns. Consider a local franchisee of Lawn Doctor who is pricing lawn maintenance contracts for a variety of residential customers. A separate price will be quoted for each lawn, and this price will be based on what the company believes it will cost to maintain that particular lawn. Some customers have larger lawns than others, which cost more to service. Some customers want less lawn care service than others, which costs less. This type of service business will use a job-order system.

Now, consider a company in the clothes laundering business. The price the company charges to wash, press, and hang a man's shirt is the same for all shirts because the cost of servicing each shirt, whether large or small, is about the same. This business will use a process costing system to determine the cost of laundering one shirt.

However, to determine the cost of one specific customer's job a hybrid system would be used, because different customers bring in different numbers of shirts to be cleaned. While process costing is used to determine the cost to clean one shirt, job order costing is used to calculate the cost of the entire job.

# JOB-ORDER COSTING SYSTEM ILLUSTRATED

Explain how events in a job-order costing system affect financial statements.

To illustrate how a job-order costing system works, we follow the operations of Benchmore Boat Company during 2012. Exhibit 12.4 shows the company's 2012 beginning account balances.

Entries for Benchmore's 2012 accounting events, described next, are shown in ledger T-accounts in Exhibit 12.5 on page 542. As you study each event, trace it to the T-accounts. The entries in Exhibit 12.5 are cross-referenced to sequential event numbers. The individual effect of each event on the financial statements is shown and discussed in the following section.

**EXHIBIT 12.4**

**BENCHMORE BOAT COMPANY**
Trial Balance
As of January 1, 2012

| | Debit | Credit |
|---|---|---|
| Cash | $ 73,000 | |
| Raw materials inventory | 7,000 | |
| Work in process inventory | 34,000 | |
| Finished goods inventory | 85,000 | |
| Production supplies | 300 | |
| Manufacturing equipment | 90,000 | |
| Accumulated depreciation | | $ 32,000 |
| Common stock | | 200,000 |
| Retained earnings | | 57,300 |
| Total | $289,300 | $289,300 |

**EXHIBIT 12.4**

*continued*

**Subsidiary Account Balances**

| Work in Process Inventory | | Finished Goods Inventory | |
|---|---|---|---|
| Boat 103 | $14,000 | Boat 101 | $50,000 |
| Boat 104 | 8,000 | Boat 102 | 35,000 |
| Boat 105 | 12,000 | | |
| Total | $34,000 | Total | $85,000 |

**EVENT 1   Benchmore paid $14,000 cash to purchase raw materials.**

The effects of this event on the company's financial statements follow.

| Assets | | | = | Liabilities | + | Equity | Revenue | − | Expenses | = | Net Income |
|---|---|---|---|---|---|---|---|---|---|---|---|
| Cash | + | Raw Materials Inventory | | | | | | | | | |
| (14,000) | + | 14,000 | = | NA | + | NA | NA | − | NA | = | NA |

Event 1 is an asset exchange; it does not affect total assets reported on the balance sheet. The asset cash decreases and the asset raw materials inventory increases. The income statement is not affected.

**EVENT 2   Benchmore used $17,000 of direct raw materials in the process of making boats.**

The amounts used for Boat 103, Boat 104, and Boat 105 were $8,000, $3,400, and $5,600, respectively. The effects of this event on the financial statements follow.

| Assets | | | = | Liabilities | + | Equity | Revenue | − | Expenses | = | Net Income |
|---|---|---|---|---|---|---|---|---|---|---|---|
| Raw Materials Inventory | + | Work in Process Inventory | | | | | | | | | |
| (17,000) | + | 17,000 | = | NA | + | NA | NA | − | NA | = | NA |

This event is an asset exchange. It does not affect total assets reported on the balance sheet. The asset raw materials inventory decreases and the asset work in process inventory increases. The income statement is not affected. In addition to recording the effects in the Work in Process Inventory control account, Benchmore adjusted the individual job cost sheets to reflect the raw materials used on each job, as shown in Exhibit 12.5.

**EVENT 3    Benchmore paid $1,200 cash to purchase production supplies.**

The effects of this event on the company's financial statements are shown here.

| Assets | | | = | Liabilities | + | Equity | Revenue | – | Expenses | = | Net Income |
|---|---|---|---|---|---|---|---|---|---|---|---|
| Cash | + | Production Supplies | | | | | | | | | |
| (1,200) | + | 1,200 | = | NA | + | NA | NA | – | NA | = | NA |

This event is also an asset exchange. It does not affect total assets reported on the balance sheet. One asset, cash, decreases and another asset, production supplies, increases. Purchasing production supplies does not affect the income statement. The cost of supplies is allocated to work in process inventory as part of overhead and is expensed as part of cost of goods sold.

**EVENT 4    Benchmore paid $8,000 cash to production employees who worked on Boat 103.**

The effects of this event on the company's financial statements follow.

| Assets | | | = | Liabilities | + | Equity | Revenue | – | Expenses | = | Net Income |
|---|---|---|---|---|---|---|---|---|---|---|---|
| Cash | + | Work in Process Inventory | | | | | | | | | |
| (8,000) | + | 8,000 | = | NA | + | NA | NA | – | NA | = | NA |

These wages are *not* salary expense. Because the employees worked to make inventory, the cost of their labor is added to work in process inventory. This event is an asset exchange. The asset cash decreases, and the asset work in process inventory increases. Neither total assets reported on the balance sheet nor any revenues or expenses on the income statement are affected. In addition to recording the effects in the Work in Process Inventory control account, Benchmore adjusted the Boat 103 job cost sheet to reflect the labor used on the job. Refer to Exhibit 12.5; the $8,000 labor cost is entered in both the Work in Process Inventory control account and on the job cost sheet for Boat 103.

**EVENT 5    Benchmore applied manufacturing overhead costs of $6,240 to the Boat 103 job.**

Production employees completed Boat 103. When the boat was finished, the actual amount of many costs to make it were not then known. During the year, Benchmore sells boats before knowing the exact costs of making them. Although a portion of the total production supplies, depreciation, supervisory salaries, rental cost, and utilities were used while Boat 103 was under construction, the actual cost of these resources is not known until the end of the year. To make timely decisions, such as setting the selling prices for boats, Benchmore must assign estimated overhead costs to boats as they are completed.

To estimate overhead as accurately as possible, Benchmore first reviewed the previous year's actual overhead costs. It adjusted those amounts for expected changes. Assume Benchmore estimated total overhead costs for 2012 to be as follows: production supplies, $1,400; depreciation, $4,000; utilities and other indirect costs, $10,590, for a total of $15,990 ($1,400 + $4,000 + $10,590).

# EXHIBIT 12.5

## Ledger T-Accounts for Benchmore Boat Company

### Cash

| | | | |
|---|---|---|---|
| Bal. | 73,000 | (1) | 14,000 |
| (13) | 91,000 | (3) | 1,200 |
| | | (4) | 8,000 |
| | | (7) | 24,500 |
| | | (8) | 12,000 |
| | | (10) | 10,100 |
| Bal. | 94,200 | | |

### Production Supplies

| | | | |
|---|---|---|---|
| Bal. | 300 | (12) | 1,100 |
| (3) | 1,200 | | |
| Bal. | 400 | | |

### Manufacturing Equipment

| | |
|---|---|
| Bal. | 90,000 |

### Accumulated Dep.

| | | | |
|---|---|---|---|
| | | Bal. | 32,000 |
| | | (11) | 4,000 |
| | | Bal. | 36,000 |

### Raw Materials Inventory

| | | | |
|---|---|---|---|
| Bal. | 7,000 | (2) | 17,000 |
| (1) | 14,000 | | |
| Bal. | 4,000 | | |

### Manufacturing Overhead

| | | | |
|---|---|---|---|
| (10) | 10,100 | (5) | 6,240 |
| (11) | 4,000 | (9) | 9,360 |
| (12) | 1,100 | | |
| (15) | 400 | | |
| Bal. | 0 | | |

### Work in Process Inventory

| | | | |
|---|---|---|---|
| Bal. | 34,000 | (6) | 36,240 |
| (2) | 17,000 | | |
| (4) | 8,000 | | |
| (5) | 6,240 | | |
| (8) | 12,000 | | |
| (9) | 9,360 | | |
| Bal. | 50,360 | | |

### Job Cost Sheets (Subsidiary accounts)

**Boat 103**

| | |
|---|---|
| Beginning balance | 14,000 |
| Materials | 8,000 |
| Labor | 8,000 |
| Overhead | 6,240 |
| Product cost | 36,240 |
| To finish goods | (36,240) |
| Ending balance | 0 |

**Boat 104**

| | |
|---|---|
| Beginning balance | 8,000 |
| Materials | 3,400 |
| Labor | 5,000 |
| Overhead | 3,900 |
| Ending balance | 20,300 |

**Boat 105**

| | |
|---|---|
| Beginning balance | 12,000 |
| Materials | 5,600 |
| Labor | 7,000 |
| Overhead | 5,460 |
| Ending balance | 30,060 |

### Finished Goods Inventory

| | | | |
|---|---|---|---|
| Bal. | 85,000 | (14) | 50,000 |
| (6) | 36,240 | | |
| Bal. | 71,240 | | |

**Boat 101**

| | |
|---|---|
| Balance | 50,000 |
| Sold | (50,000) |
| Balance | 0 |

**Boat 102**

| | |
|---|---|
| Balance | 35,000 |
| Cost transferred | 0 |
| Balance | 35,000 |

**Boat 103**

| | |
|---|---|
| Balance | 0 |
| Cost transferred | 36,240 |
| Balance | 36,240 |

### Common Stock

| | | | |
|---|---|---|---|
| | | Bal. | 200,000 |

### Retained Earnings

| | | | |
|---|---|---|---|
| | | Bal. | 57,300 |

### Sales Revenue

| | | | |
|---|---|---|---|
| | | (13) | 91,000 |

### Cost of Goods Sold

| | | | |
|---|---|---|---|
| (14) | 50,000 | (15) | 400 |
| Bal. | 49,600 | | |

### Selling and Admin. Exp.

| | |
|---|---|
| (7) | 24,500 |

**Boat 101**

Cost sheet data transferred to permanent storage

Benchmore has identified a cause and effect relationship between direct labor time and overhead cost. Boats that require more labor also require more overhead. For example, the more hours production employees work, the more supplies they use. Similarly, more labor hours translates into more equipment use, causing more utilities and depreciation costs. Because of the relationship between labor and indirect costs, Benchmore uses *direct labor hours* as the allocation base for overhead costs. Benchmore estimated it would use a total of 4,100 labor hours during 2012. It established a *predetermined overhead rate* as follows:

$$\text{Predetermined overhead rate} = \text{Total estimated overhead costs} \div \text{Total estimated direct labor hours}$$

$$\text{Predetermined overhead rate} = \$15,990 \div 4,100$$

$$= \$3.90 \text{ per direct labor hour}$$

Boat 103 required 1,600 actual direct labor hours. Benchmore applied $6,240 (1,600 hours × $3.90) of overhead to that job. The effects of the overhead application on the company's financial statements follow.

| Assets | | | = | Liabilities | + | Equity | Revenue | − | Expenses | = | Net Income |
|---|---|---|---|---|---|---|---|---|---|---|---|
| Manufacturing Overhead | + | Work in Process Inventory | | | | | | | | | |
| (6,240) | + | 6,240 | = | NA | + | NA | NA | − | NA | = | NA |

The event is an asset exchange. One asset, work in process inventory, increases and a temporary asset, manufacturing overhead, decreases. Applying overhead costs to work in process inventory does not affect the income statement. When finished goods are sold, overhead costs affect the income statement through cost of goods sold. The job cost sheet for Boat 103 reflects the applied (estimated) overhead cost. The T-accounts in Exhibit 12.5 also show the overhead application.

**EVENT 6**    **Benchmore transferred $36,240 of product costs for completed Boat 103 from work in process inventory to finished goods inventory.**

The effects of this transfer on the company's financial statements follow.

| Assets | | | = | Liabilities | + | Equity | Revenue | − | Expenses | = | Net Income |
|---|---|---|---|---|---|---|---|---|---|---|---|
| Work in Process Inventory | + | Finished Goods Inventory | | | | | | | | | |
| (36,240) | + | 36,240 | = | NA | + | NA | NA | − | NA | = | NA |

This event is an asset exchange. Benchmore transferred cost from the Work in Process Inventory control account to the Finished Goods Inventory control account. The transfer does not affect total assets reported on the balance sheet, nor does it affect the income statement. The job cost sheet is moved to the finished goods file folder. Exhibit 12.5 illustrates these effects.

**EVENT 7**    **Benchmore paid $24,500 cash for selling and administrative expenses.**

The effects of this transaction on the financial statements follow.

| Assets | = | Liabilities | + | Equity | Revenue | − | Expenses | = | Net Income |
|---|---|---|---|---|---|---|---|---|---|---|
| (24,500) | = | NA | + | (24,500) | NA | − | 24,500 | = | (24,500) |

This is an asset use transaction. Cash and stockholders' equity (retained earnings) decrease. Recognizing the expense decreases net income.

**EVENT 8**  **Benchmore paid $12,000 cash to production employees for work on Boats 104 and 105.**

The cost of direct labor used was $5,000 for Boat 104 and $7,000 for Boat 105. These jobs were still incomplete at the end of 2012. The effects of this event on the financial statements follow.

| Assets | | | = | Liabilities | + | Equity | Revenue | − | Expenses | = | Net Income |
|---|---|---|---|---|---|---|---|---|---|---|---|
| Cash | + | Work in Process Inventory | | | | | | | | | |
| (12,000) | + | 12,000 | = | NA | + | NA | NA | − | NA | = | NA |

This event is an asset exchange. It does not affect total assets reported on the balance sheet. It does not affect the income statement. In addition to the effects on the Work in Process Inventory control account, Benchmore adjusted the individual job cost sheets to reflect the labor used on each job. Exhibit 12.5 illustrates these effects.

**EVENT 9**  **Benchmore applied estimated manufacturing overhead costs to the Boat 104 and Boat 105 jobs.**

As previously explained, the predetermined overhead rate was $3.90 per direct labor hour (see Event 5). Assume the work described in Event 8 represented 1,000 direct labor hours for Boat 104 and 1,400 direct labor hours for Boat 105. The amount of estimated overhead cost Benchmore applied to the two jobs is calculated as follows:

| Job Number | Predetermined Overhead Rate | × | Actual Labor Hours Used | = | Amount of Applied Overhead |
|---|---|---|---|---|---|
| Boat 104 | $3.90 | × | 1,000 | = | $3,900 |
| Boat 105 | 3.90 | × | 1,400 | = | 5,460 |
| Total | | | | | $9,360 |

The effects on the company's financial statements of applying the overhead follow.

| Assets | | | = | Liabilities | + | Equity | Revenue | − | Expenses | = | Net Income |
|---|---|---|---|---|---|---|---|---|---|---|---|
| Manufacturing Overhead | + | Work in Process Inventory | | | | | | | | | |
| (9,360) | + | 9,360 | = | NA | + | NA | NA | − | NA | = | NA |

Applying overhead is an asset exchange. Total assets and net income, are not affected. Overhead costs of $3,900 for Boat 104 and $5,460 for Boat 105 are recorded on the job cost sheets. The total, $9,360, is recorded in the Work in Process Inventory control account. Trace these allocations to Exhibit 12.5.

**EVENT 10**  **Benchmore paid $10,100 cash for utilities and other indirect product costs.**

The effects of this event on the financial statements are shown here.

| Assets | | | = | Liabilities | + | Equity | Revenue | − | Expenses | = | Net Income |
|---|---|---|---|---|---|---|---|---|---|---|---|
| Cash | + | Manufacturing Overhead | | | | | | | | | |
| (10,100) | + | 10,100 | = | NA | + | NA | NA | − | NA | = | NA |

Paying for *actual* overhead costs is an asset exchange. Total assets, net income, and job cost sheets are not affected. Recall that estimated overhead costs were previously recorded in work in process inventory and on the job cost sheets (Events 5 and 9).

**EVENT 11   Benchmore recognized $4,000 of actual manufacturing equipment depreciation.**

The effects of this event on the financial statements follow.

| Assets | | | = | Liabilities | + | Equity | Revenue | − | Expenses | = | Net Income |
|---|---|---|---|---|---|---|---|---|---|---|---|
| Book Value of Manufacturing Equipment | + | Manufacturing Overhead | | | | | | | | | |
| (4,000) | + | 4,000 | = | NA | + | NA | NA | − | NA | = | NA |

Depreciation of manufacturing equipment represents an *actual* indirect product cost (overhead), *not* an expense (even though the *amount* of depreciation is an estimate). Recognizing this depreciation is an asset exchange. The book value of the manufacturing equipment decreases and the Manufacturing Overhead account increases. Neither the total amount of assets reported on the balance sheet nor the income statement are affected. The job cost sheets are also not affected when *actual* overhead cost (depreciation) is recognized. The inventory accounts and job cost sheets reflect *estimated* overhead.

**EVENT 12   Benchmore counted the production supplies on hand at year-end and recognized actual overhead cost for the supplies used.**

During 2012, Benchmore had available for use $1,500 of production supplies ($300 beginning balance + $1,200 supplies purchased). A physical count disclosed there were $400 of supplies on hand at the end of 2012. Benchmore therefore must have used $1,100 of supplies ($1,500 − $400). The effects on the company's financial statements of recognizing supplies used follow.

| Assets | | | = | Liabilities | + | Equity | Revenue | − | Expenses | = | Net Income |
|---|---|---|---|---|---|---|---|---|---|---|---|
| Production Supplies | + | Manufacturing Overhead | | | | | | | | | |
| (1,100) | + | 1,100 | = | NA | + | NA | NA | − | NA | = | NA |

The event is an asset exchange. Total assets and net income are not affected. The job cost sheets are not affected. Remember that estimated overhead costs were previously recorded on the job cost sheets.

**EVENT 13   Benchmore sold Boat 101 for $91,000 cash.**

The effects of this event on the financial statements follow.

| Assets | = | Liabilities | + | Equity | Revenue | − | Expenses | = | Net Income |
|---|---|---|---|---|---|---|---|---|---|---|
| 91,000 | = | NA | + | 91,000 | 91,000 | − | NA | = | 91,000 |

Recognizing revenue from selling inventory is an asset source event. Both assets (cash) and stockholders' equity (retained earnings) increase. Revenue recognition also increases the net income reported on the income statement.

**EVENT 14   Benchmore recognized cost of goods sold for Boat 101.**

The effects of this event on the financial statements follow.

| Assets | = | Liabilities | + | Equity | Revenue | − | Expenses | = | Net Income |
|---|---|---|---|---|---|---|---|---|---|
| (50,000) | = | NA | + | (50,000) | NA | − | 50,000 | = | (50,000) |

Recognizing cost of goods sold is an asset use transaction. It decreases assets (finished goods inventory) and stockholders' equity (retained earnings). The expense recognition decreases net income. The job cost sheet for Boat 101 is transferred to the permanent files. The cost sheet is retained because information from it could be useful for estimating costs of future jobs.

**EVENT 15 Benchmore closed the Manufacturing Overhead account, reducing cost of goods sold by $400.**

During 2012, Benchmore applied $15,600 of estimated overhead cost to production. Actual overhead costs were $15,200. Overhead was therefore overapplied by $400 ($15,600 − $15,200), meaning too much overhead was transferred to the Work in Process Inventory, Finished Goods Inventory, and Cost of Goods Sold accounts. If the amount of overapplied overhead were significant, Benchmore would have to allocate it proportionately among the inventory and Cost of Goods Sold accounts. In this case, the amount is insignificant and Benchmore assigned it entirely to cost of goods sold. The effects of this event on the company's financial statements follow.

| Assets | = | Liabilities | + | Equity | Revenue | − | Expenses | = | Net Income |
|---|---|---|---|---|---|---|---|---|---|
| 400 | = | NA | + | 400 | NA | − | (400) | = | 400 |

Overapplied overhead indicates the estimated cost transferred from the asset accounts to cost of goods sold was too high. The entry to close manufacturing overhead corrects the overstatement. Recording $400 in the overhead account increases total assets. The increase in assets is matched by a decrease in cost of goods sold, which reduces expenses, increases net income, and increases stockholders' equity (retained earnings). After this adjustment, the total increases in the overhead account (actual costs) equal the total decreases (estimated costs). Manufacturing Overhead is a temporary account. It is closed at year-end and does not appear in the financial statements. Exhibit 12.6 displays Benchmore Boat Company's preclosing trial balance at the end of 2012.

---

**EXHIBIT 12.6**

## BENCHMORE BOAT COMPANY
### Trial Balance
### As of December 31, 2012

| | Debit | Credit |
|---|---|---|
| Cash | $ 94,200 | |
| Raw materials inventory | 4,000 | |
| Work in process inventory | 50,360 | |
| Finished goods inventory | 71,240 | |
| Production supplies | 400 | |
| Manufacturing equipment | 90,000 | |
| Accumulated depreciation | | $ 36,000 |
| Common stock | | 200,000 |
| Retained earnings | | 57,300 |
| Sales revenue | | 91,000 |
| Cost of goods sold | 49,600 | |
| Selling and administrative expense | 24,500 | |
| Total | $384,300 | $384,300 |

## ✓ CHECK YOURSELF 12.1

Wilson Cabinets makes custom cabinets for home builders. It incurred the following costs during the most recent month.

| Inventory | Materials | Labor |
|---|---|---|
| Job 1 | $4,200 | $2,700 |
| Job 2 | 2,300 | 5,000 |
| Job 3 | 1,700 | 800 |

Wilson's predetermined overhead rate is $0.80 per direct labor dollar. Actual overhead costs were $7,100. Wilson completed and sold Jobs 1 and 2 during the month, but Job 3 was not complete at month-end. The selling prices for Jobs 1 and 2 were $14,900 and $16,600, respectively. What amount of gross margin would Wilson report on the income statement for the month?

**Answer**    Cost accumulated in the Work in Process account:

| Inventory | Materials | Labor | Overhead* | Total |
|---|---|---|---|---|
| Job 1 | $4,200 | $2,700 | $2,160 | $ 9,060 |
| Job 2 | 2,300 | 5,000 | 4,000 | 11,300 |
| Job 3 | 1,700 | 800 | 640 | 3,140 |

*80% of direct labor cost.

Total allocated overhead is $6,800 ($2,160 + $4,000 + $640). Since actual overhead is $7,100, overhead is underapplied by $300 ($7,100 − $6,800).

| | |
|---|---|
| Sales revenue ($14,900 + $16,600) | $31,500 |
| Cost of goods sold (Job 1, $9,060 + Job 2, $11,300 + Underapplied overhead, $300) | (20,660) |
| Gross margin | $10,840 |

## PROCESS COSTING SYSTEM ILLUSTRATED

**LO 4**

Explain how events in a process costing system affect financial statements.

In process costing systems, product costs flow through the same general ledger accounts as in job-order costing systems: Raw Materials Inventory, Work in Process Inventory, Finished Goods Inventory, and ultimately Cost of Goods Sold. Accounting for work in process inventory, however, differs between the two systems. Instead of accumulating work in process costs by jobs, process costing systems accumulate product costs by departments. The cost of all goods that move through a processing department during a given accounting period is charged to that department. Work in process subsidiary documents (job cost sheets) are not needed. Process costing systems are easier to use than job-order systems. They do not, however, distinguish the cost of one product from another. Process systems are therefore not appropriate for manufacturers of distinctly different products; they are suited to account for continuous mass production of uniform products. Process costing systems produce the same cost per unit for all products.

To illustrate how a process costing system operates, we analyze the operations of Janis Juice Company during 2012. Recall that Janis uses three distinct processes to produce cans of apple juice. Raw materials (whole apples) enter the *extraction department* where

## EXHIBIT 12.7

### JANIS JUICE COMPANY
Trial Balance
As of January 1, 2012

| | Debit | Credit |
|---|---|---|
| Cash | $320,000 | |
| Raw materials—fruit | 7,800 | |
| Raw materials—additives | 3,100 | |
| Raw materials—containers | 9,500 | |
| Work in process—extraction | 22,360 | |
| Work in process—mixing | 7,960 | |
| Work in process—packaging | 21,130 | |
| Finished goods inventory | 20,700 | |
| Common stock | | $180,000 |
| Retained earnings | | 232,550 |
| Total | $412,550 | $412,550 |

juice concentrate is extracted from whole fruit. The juice extract passes to the *mixing department* where Janis adds water, sugar, food coloring, and preservatives. The juice mixture then moves to the *packaging department* where it is canned and boxed for shipment. Exhibit 12.7 shows the company's 2012 beginning account balances.

The entries for Janis Juice Company's 2012 accounting events, discussed individually in the following sections, are shown in ledger T-accounts in Exhibit 12.9 on page 556. The T-account entries are cross-referenced to sequential event numbers. As you study each event, trace it to the T-accounts.

**EVENT 1** Janis paid $84,000 cash to purchase raw materials.

The effects of this event on the company's financial statements follow.

| Assets | | | = | Liabilities | + | Equity | Revenue | − | Expenses | = | Net Income |
|---|---|---|---|---|---|---|---|---|---|---|---|
| Cash | + | Raw Materials Inventory | | | | | | | | | |
| (84,000) | + | 84,000 | = | NA | + | NA | NA | − | NA | = | NA |

This event is an asset exchange. Total assets and net income are not affected. The total purchase was for $25,000 of whole fruit, $30,000 of additives, and $29,000 of containers. Janis maintains separate inventory accounts for each category of raw material. Trace the entries for this event to the ledger accounts in Exhibit 12.9.

**EVENT 2** Janis processed $26,720 of whole fruit to produce juice extract.

The effects of this event on the financial statements follow.

| Assets | | | = | Liabilities | + | Equity | Revenue | − | Expenses | = | Net Income |
|---|---|---|---|---|---|---|---|---|---|---|---|
| Raw Materials—Fruit | + | WIP—Extraction | | | | | | | | | |
| (26,720) | + | 26,720 | = | NA | + | NA | NA | − | NA | = | NA |

This event is an asset exchange. It does not affect total assets or net income. Janis assigns the cost of the materials used to the extraction department rather than to any particular product or batch of products. The extraction department adds the same amount of value to each can of juice.

**EVENT 3** Janis paid $38,000 cash to production employees who worked in the extraction department.

The effects of this event on the financial statements follow.

| Assets | | | = | Liabilities | + | Equity | Revenue | − | Expenses | = | Net Income |
|---|---|---|---|---|---|---|---|---|---|---|---|
| Cash | + | WIP—Extraction | | | | | | | | | |
| (38,000) | + | 38,000 | = | NA | + | NA | NA | − | NA | = | NA |

This event is also an asset exchange. Production labor cost is not salary expense. Total assets and net income are not affected. Like the raw materials, the labor cost is assigned to the department rather than to individual products.

**EVENT 4   Janis applied estimated manufacturing overhead costs to the extraction department work in process inventory.**

Janis has identified a relationship between labor dollars and indirect overhead costs. The more labor dollars paid, the more indirect resources consumed. Janis estimated total indirect costs in 2012 would be $96,000 and that it would pay $120,000 to production employees. Using these estimates, Janis established a *predetermined overhead rate* as follows.

$$\frac{\text{Predetermined}}{\text{overhead rate}} = \frac{\text{Total estimated}}{\text{overhead costs}} \div \frac{\text{Total estimated}}{\text{direct labor dollars}}$$

$$\frac{\text{Predetermined}}{\text{overhead rate}} = \$96,000 \div \$120,000$$

$$= \$0.80 \text{ per direct labor dollar}$$

Since the extraction department incurred $38,000 of labor cost (see Event 3), Janis applied $30,400 ($38,000 × $0.80) of overhead to that department. The effects of the overhead application on the financial statements follow.

| Assets | | | = | Liabilities | + | Equity | Revenue | − | Expenses | = | Net Income |
|---|---|---|---|---|---|---|---|---|---|---|---|
| Manufacturing Overhead | + | WIP— Extraction | | | | | | | | | |
| (30,400) | + | 30,400 | = | NA | + | NA | NA | − | NA | = | NA |

The event is an asset exchange. Total assets and net income are not affected.

**EVENT 5   Janis finished processing some of the whole fruit and transferred the related cost from the extraction department Work in Process Inventory account to the mixing department Work in Process Inventory account.**

Total product costs in the extraction department Work in Process Inventory account amounted to $117,480 ($22,360 beginning balance + $26,720 materials + $38,000 labor + $30,400 applied overhead). The beginning inventory represented 100,000 units of product (cans) and the fruit Janis added started an additional 485,000 cans. The amount of fruit placed into production therefore represented 585,000 (100,000 + 485,000) units. Assume the extract transferred to the mixing department represented 500,000 cans of juice. The extraction department therefore had 85,000 (585,000 − 500,000) units in ending inventory that were *started but not completed.*

LO 5

Calculate equivalent units and prepare a cost of production report.

Janis had to allocate the total $117,480 product cost between the 85,000 partially completed units in ending inventory and the 500,000 completed units it transferred to the mixing department. A rational allocation requires converting the 85,000 partially completed units into *equivalent whole units*. The logic behind **equivalent whole units** relies on basic arithmetic. For example, 2 units that are 50 percent complete are equivalent to 1 whole (100 percent complete) unit (2 × 0.5 = 1). Similarly, 4 units that are 25 percent complete are equivalent to 1 whole unit (4 × 0.25 = 1). Further, 100 units that are 30 percent complete are equivalent to 30 whole units (100 units × 0.30 = 30).

An engineer estimated the 85,000 units in the extraction department's ending inventory were 40 percent complete. The equivalent whole units in ending inventory was therefore 34,000 (85,000 × 0.4). The *total* equivalent units processed by the extraction department during 2012 was 534,000 (500,000 units finished and transferred to the mixing department plus 34,000 equivalent whole units in ending inventory). Janis determined the average **cost per equivalent unit** as follows:

$$\text{Cost per equivalent unit} = \text{Total cost} \div \text{Number of equivalent whole units}$$

$$\text{Cost per equivalent unit} = \$117,480 \div \phantom{xxxx} 534,000$$

$$= \$0.22 \text{ per equivalent unit}$$

Janis used the *cost per equivalent unit* to allocate the total cost incurred in the extraction department between the amount transferred to the mixing department and the amount in the extraction department's ending work in process inventory as follows.

| | Equivalent Units | × | Cost per Unit | Cost to Be Allocated |
|---|---|---|---|---|
| Transferred-out costs | 500,000 | × | $0.22 | $110,000 |
| Ending inventory | 34,000 | × | 0.22 | 7,480 |
| Total | | | | $117,480 |

The effects of transferring $110,000 from the extraction department's work in process inventory to the mixing department's work in process inventory follow.

| Assets | | | = | Liabilities | + | Equity | Revenue | − | Expenses | = | Net Income |
|---|---|---|---|---|---|---|---|---|---|---|---|
| WIP— Extraction | + | WIP— Mixing | | | | | | | | | |
| (110,000) | + | 110,000 | = | NA | + | NA | NA | − | NA | = | NA |

This event is an asset exchange. Total assets and net income are unaffected.

The allocation of costs between units transferred out and ending inventory is frequently summarized in a *cost of production report*. Cost of production reports usually provide details for three categories: the computation of equivalent units; the determination of cost per equivalent unit; and the allocation of total production cost between the units transferred out and the units in ending inventory. Exhibit 12.8 illustrates Janis's 2012 cost of production report for the extraction department.

The method used here to determine equivalent units is the **weighted average method.** The weighted average method does not account for the state of completion of units in *beginning* inventory. Equivalent units are computed for *ending* inventory only. Failing to account for equivalent units in beginning as well as ending inventories can distort the accuracy of the cost assigned to goods transferred out and goods in inventory accounts at the end of the period. Managers frequently tolerate some inaccuracy because the weighted average method is relatively easy to use. If accuracy is of paramount importance, however, a company might use the **first-in, first-out (FIFO) method.** The FIFO method accounts for the degree of completion of both beginning and ending inventories, but it is more complex to apply. Applying the FIFO method in process costing applications is explained in upper-level accounting courses. It is beyond the scope of this text.

### EVENT 6  Janis mixed (used) $24,400 of additives with the extract transferred from the extraction department.

Conceptually, the juice extract transferred from the extraction department is a raw material to the mixing department. The mixing department adds other materials to the juice extract, such as sweetener, food coloring, and preservatives. Although both *transferred-in costs* and *additives* represent raw materials, they are traditionally classified separately.

**EXHIBIT 12.8**

### JANIS JUICE COMPANY
#### Cost of Production Report
#### Extraction Department
#### For the Year Ended December 31, 2012

|  | Actual |  | Equivalent |
|---|---|---|---|
| **Determination of Equivalent Units** |  |  |  |
| Beginning inventory | 100,000 |  |  |
| Units added to production | 485,000 |  |  |
| Total | 585,000 |  |  |
| Transferred to finished goods | 500,000 | 100% Complete | 500,000 |
| Ending inventory | 85,000 | 40% Complete | 34,000 |
| Total | 585,000 |  | 534,000 |
| **Determination of Cost per Unit** |  |  |  |
| Cost accumulation |  |  |  |
| Beginning inventory | $ 22,360 |  |  |
| Materials | 26,720 |  |  |
| Labor | 38,000 |  |  |
| Overhead | 30,400 |  |  |
| Total | $117,480 |  |  |
| Divided by | ÷ |  |  |
| equivalent units | 534,000 |  |  |
| Cost per equivalent unit (i.e., per can) | $ 0.22 |  |  |
| **Cost Allocation** |  |  |  |
| To work in process inventory, mixing dept. |  |  |  |
| (500,000 × $0.22) | $110,000 |  |  |
| To ending inventory (34,000 × $0.22) | 7,480 |  |  |
| Total | $117,480 |  |  |

Review the mixing department's Work in Process account in Exhibit 12.9 to see these costs. The effects of using additional materials in the mixing department follow.

| Assets |  |  | = | Liabilities | + | Equity | Revenue | − | Expenses | = | Net Income |
|---|---|---|---|---|---|---|---|---|---|---|---|
| Raw Materials— Additives | + | WIP— Mixing |  |  |  |  |  |  |  |  |  |
| (24,400) | + | 24,400 | = | NA | + | NA | NA | − | NA | = | NA |

This event is an asset exchange. Total assets and net income are not affected.

**EVENT 7    Janis paid $48,000 cash to production employees who worked in the mixing department.**

The effects of this event on the financial statements follow.

| Assets |  |  | = | Liabilities | + | Equity | Revenue | − | Expenses | = | Net Income |
|---|---|---|---|---|---|---|---|---|---|---|---|
| Cash | + | WIP— Mixing |  |  |  |  |  |  |  |  |  |
| (48,000) | + | 48,000 | = | NA | + | NA | NA | − | NA | = | NA |

This is an asset exchange. Total assets and net income are not affected.

## Answers to The Curious Accountant

The company that produces breakfast cereal should use a process costing system. This system is conceptually very simple, especially when there is no beginning or ending work in process inventory. In the situation described in the Curious Accountant, the cost of one box of Corn Flakes would be calculated by dividing $115 million by 70 million boxes, yielding a cost of $1.64 per box.

The construction company should use a job-order costing system. This system, as you have seen, requires extensive recordkeeping. The cost of each item of material that goes into the LNG project and the wages of each worker who helps build the project must be tracked to the specific job in question. These costs, along with the appropriate amount of overhead, will comprise the cost of that particular job.

**EVENT 8    Janis applied estimated manufacturing overhead costs to the mixing department work in process inventory.**

Using the *predetermined overhead rate* calculated in Event 4, Janis determined it should apply $38,400 ($48,000 labor × 0.80 overhead rate) of overhead costs to the mixing department's work in process inventory. The effects of the overhead application on the financial statements follow.

| Assets | | | = | Liabilities | + | Equity | Revenue | − | Expenses | = | Net Income |
|---|---|---|---|---|---|---|---|---|---|---|---|
| Manufacturing Overhead | + | WIP— Mixing | | | | | | | | | |
| (38,400) | + | 38,400 | = | NA | + | NA | NA | − | NA | = | NA |

The event is an asset exchange. Total assets and net income are not affected.

**EVENT 9    Janis finished mixing some of the juice extract with additives and transferred the related cost from the mixing department Work in Process Inventory account to the packaging department Work in Process Inventory account.**

Total product costs in the mixing department were $228,760 ($7,960 beginning balance + $110,000 transferred-in cost + $24,400 materials + $48,000 labor + $38,400 overhead). An engineer estimated that Janis transferred 510,000 units of mixed juice from the mixing department to the packaging department and that the 88,000 units of juice in the mixing department ending inventory were 25 percent complete.

The mixing department ending inventory therefore represented 22,000 (88,000 × 0.25) *equivalent whole units.* The total equivalent whole units produced by the mixing department was 532,000 (510,000 + 22,000). The average *cost per equivalent unit* was therefore $0.43 ($228,760 ÷ 532,000). Janis allocated the total product costs incurred in the mixing department between the amount transferred to the packaging department and the amount in the mixing department's *ending* work in process inventory as follows.

| | Equivalent Units | × | Cost per Unit | Cost to Be Allocated |
|---|---|---|---|---|
| Transferred-out costs | 510,000 | × | $0.43 | $219,300 |
| Ending inventory | 22,000 | × | 0.43 | 9,460 |
| Total | | | | $228,760 |

The effects of transferring $219,300 from the mixing department work in process inventory to the packaging department work in process inventory are as follows.

| Assets | | | = | Liabilities | + | Equity | Revenue | − | Expenses | = | Net Income |
|---|---|---|---|---|---|---|---|---|---|---|---|
| WIP—Mixing | + | WIP—Packaging | | | | | | | | | |
| (219,300) | + | 219,300 | = | NA | + | NA | NA | − | NA | = | NA |

This event is an asset exchange. Total assets and net income are unaffected. Find the ending balance in the mixing department's Work in Process Inventory account in Exhibit 12.9. Also find the entry that transfers $219,300 of product cost from the mixing department's Work in Process Inventory account to the packaging department's Work in Process Inventory account.

**EVENT 10   Janis added containers and other packaging materials costing $32,000 to work in process in the packaging department.**

The effects of this event on the financial statements follow:

| Assets | | | = | Liabilities | + | Equity | Revenue | − | Expenses | = | Net Income |
|---|---|---|---|---|---|---|---|---|---|---|---|
| Raw Materials—Containers | + | WIP—Packaging | | | | | | | | | |
| (32,000) | + | 32,000 | = | NA | + | NA | NA | − | NA | = | NA |

This event is an asset exchange. Total assets and net income are not affected.

**EVENT 11   Janis paid $43,000 cash to production employees who worked in the packaging department.**

The effects of this event on the financial statements follow.

| Assets | | | = | Liabilities | + | Equity | Revenue | − | Expenses | = | Net Income |
|---|---|---|---|---|---|---|---|---|---|---|---|
| Cash | + | WIP—Packaging | | | | | | | | | |
| (43,000) | + | 43,000 | = | NA | + | NA | NA | − | NA | = | NA |

This is an asset exchange. Total assets and net income are not affected.

**EVENT 12   Janis applied estimated manufacturing overhead costs to the packaging department work in process inventory.**

Using the *predetermined overhead rate* calculated in Event 4, Janis determined it should apply $34,400 ($43,000 labor × 0.80 overhead rate) of overhead costs to the packaging department's work in process inventory. The effects of the overhead application on the financial statements follow.

| Assets | | | = | Liabilities | + | Equity | Revenue | − | Expenses | = | Net Income |
|---|---|---|---|---|---|---|---|---|---|---|---|
| Manufacturing Overhead | + | WIP—Packaging | | | | | | | | | |
| (34,400) | + | 34,400 | = | NA | + | NA | NA | − | NA | = | NA |

The event is an asset exchange. Total assets and net income are not affected.

**EVENT 13** **Janis finished packaging some of the juice and transferred the related cost from the packaging department Work in Process Inventory account to the Finished Goods Inventory account.**

Total product costs in the packaging department were $349,830 ($21,130 beginning balance + $219,300 transferred-in cost + $32,000 materials + $43,000 labor + $34,400 overhead). An engineer estimated that Janis transferred 480,000 units of packaged juice from the packaging department to finished goods inventory and that the 90,000 units of juice in the packaging department ending inventory were 30 percent complete.

The packaging department ending inventory therefore represented 27,000 (90,000 × 0.30) *equivalent whole units.* The total equivalent whole units produced by the packaging department was 507,000 (480,000 + 27,000). The average *cost per equivalent unit* was therefore $0.69 ($349,830 ÷ 507,000). Janis allocated the total product costs incurred in the packaging department between the amount transferred to finished goods inventory and the amount in the packaging department's ending work in process inventory as follows.

| | Equivalent Units | × | Cost per Unit | Cost to Be Allocated |
|---|---|---|---|---|
| Transferred-out costs | 480,000 | × | $0.69 | $331,200 |
| Ending inventory | 27,000 | × | 0.69 | 18,630 |
| Total | | | | $349,830 |

The effects of transferring $331,200 from the packaging department work in process inventory to the finished goods inventory follow.

| Assets | | | = | Liabilities | + | Equity | Revenue | − | Expenses | = | Net Income |
|---|---|---|---|---|---|---|---|---|---|---|---|
| WIP— Packaging | + | Finished Goods | | | | | | | | | |
| (331,200) | + | 331,200 | = | NA | + | NA | NA | − | NA | = | NA |

This event is an asset exchange. Total assets and net income are unaffected. Find the ending balance in the packaging department's Work in Process Inventory account in Exhibit 12.9. Also find the entry that transfers $331,200 of product cost from the packaging department's Work in Process Inventory account to the Finished Goods Inventory account.

**EVENT 14** **Janis paid $106,330 cash for actual overhead costs.**

The effects of this event on the financial statements follow.

| Assets | | | = | Liabilities | + | Equity | Revenue | − | Expenses | = | Net Income |
|---|---|---|---|---|---|---|---|---|---|---|---|
| Cash | + | Manufacturing Overhead | | | | | | | | | |
| (106,330) | + | 106,330 | = | NA | + | NA | NA | − | NA | = | NA |

Incurring *actual overhead costs* is an asset exchange event. Total assets and net income are not affected.

**EVENT 15** **Janis sold 490,000 cans of juice for $1 per can.**

The effects of this event on the financial statements follow.

| Assets | = | Liabilities | + | Equity | Revenue | − | Expenses | = | Net Income |
|--------|---|-------------|---|--------|---------|---|----------|---|------------|
| 490,000 | = | NA | + | 490,000 | 490,000 | − | NA | = | 490,000 |

Recognizing revenue from the sale of inventory is an asset source event. Assets (cash) and stockholders' equity (retained earnings) both increase, as do revenue and net income reported on the income statement.

**EVENT 16    Janis recognized cost of goods sold for the 490,000 cans of juice sold in Event 15.**

The average cost per finished can of juice was $0.69 (see Event 13). Cost of goods sold was therefore $338,100 (490,000 units × $0.69). The effects of this event on the financial statements follow.

| Assets | = | Liabilities | + | Equity | Revenue | − | Expenses | = | Net Income |
|--------|---|-------------|---|--------|---------|---|----------|---|------------|
| (338,100) | = | NA | + | (338,100) | NA | − | 338,100 | = | (338,100) |

Recognizing cost of goods sold is an asset use transaction. Both assets (finished goods inventory), and stockholders' equity (retained earnings), decrease. The increase in the expense, cost of goods sold, decreases net income.

**EVENT 17    Janis paid $78,200 cash for selling and administrative expenses.**

The effects of this event on the financial statements follow.

| Assets | = | Liabilities | + | Equity | Revenue | − | Expenses | = | Net Income |
|--------|---|-------------|---|--------|---------|---|----------|---|------------|
| (78,200) | = | NA | + | (78,200) | NA | − | 78,200 | = | (78,200) |

Recognizing selling and administrative expense is an asset use transaction. It decreases assets (cash) and stockholders' equity (retained earnings). Recognizing the expense decreases net income.

**EVENT 18    Janis closed the Manufacturing Overhead account and increased the Cost of Goods Sold account by $3,130.**

During 2012, Janis applied $103,200 of overhead cost to production. Actual overhead costs were $106,330. Overhead was therefore underapplied by $3,130 ($106,330 − $103,200), indicating that too little overhead was transferred to work in process inventory, finished goods inventory, and cost of goods sold. Janis considered the underapplied amount insignificant and assigned it directly to cost of goods sold. The effects of this event on the financial statements follow.

| Assets | = | Liabilities | + | Equity | Revenue | − | Expenses | = | Net Income |
|--------|---|-------------|---|--------|---------|---|----------|---|------------|
| (3,130) | = | NA | + | (3,130) | NA | − | 3,130 | = | (3,130) |

Since underapplied overhead means too little estimated cost was transferred from the asset accounts to the Cost of Goods Sold account, closing the Manufacturing Overhead account to cost of goods sold corrects the understatement. The additional overhead costs of $3,130 increase cost of goods sold and decrease net income. After this adjustment, the total increases in the overhead account (actual costs) equal the total decreases (estimated costs). The ending balance in the Manufacturing Overhead account is zero. Manufacturing overhead is not reported on any financial statement.

Exhibit 12.10 shows the year-end adjusted trial balance for Janis Juice Company.

# EXHIBIT 12.9

## Ledger T-Accounts for Janis Juice Company

**Cash**

| | | | |
|---|---|---|---|
| Bal. | 320,000 | (1) | 84,000 |
| (15) | 490,000 | (3) | 38,000 |
| | | (7) | 48,000 |
| | | (11) | 43,000 |
| | | (14) | 106,330 |
| | | (17) | 78,200 |
| Bal. | 412,470 | | |

**Raw Materials—Fruit**

| | | | |
|---|---|---|---|
| Bal. | 7,800 | (2) | 26,720 |
| (1) | 25,000 | | |
| Bal. | 6,080 | | |

**Raw Materials—Additives**

| | | | |
|---|---|---|---|
| Bal. | 3,100 | (6) | 24,400 |
| (1) | 30,000 | | |
| Bal. | 8,700 | | |

**Raw Materials—Containers**

| | | | |
|---|---|---|---|
| Bal. | 9,500 | (10) | 32,000 |
| (1) | 29,000 | | |
| Bal. | 6,500 | | |

**Manufacturing Overhead**

| | | | |
|---|---|---|---|
| (14) | 106,330 | (4) | 30,400 |
| | | (8) | 38,400 |
| | | (12) | 34,400 |
| | | (18) | 3,130 |
| Bal. | 0 | | |

**Work in Process—Extraction**

| | | | |
|---|---|---|---|
| Bal. | 22,360 | (5) | 110,000 |
| (2) | 26,720 | | |
| (3) | 38,000 | | |
| (4) | 30,400 | | |
| Bal. | 7,480 | | |

**Work in Process—Mixing**

| | | | |
|---|---|---|---|
| Bal. | 7,960 | (9) | 219,300 |
| (5) | 110,000 | | |
| (6) | 24,400 | | |
| (7) | 48,000 | | |
| (8) | 38,400 | | |
| Bal. | 9,460 | | |

**Work in Process—Packaging**

| | | | |
|---|---|---|---|
| Bal. | 21,130 | (13) | 331,200 |
| (9) | 219,300 | | |
| (10) | 32,000 | | |
| (11) | 43,000 | | |
| (12) | 34,400 | | |
| Bal. | 18,630 | | |

**Finished Goods Inventory**

| | | | |
|---|---|---|---|
| Bal. | 20,700 | (16) | 338,100 |
| (13) | 331,200 | | |
| Bal. | 13,800 | | |

**Common Stock**

| | | | |
|---|---|---|---|
| | | Bal. | 180,000 |

**Retained Earnings**

| | | | |
|---|---|---|---|
| | | Bal. | 232,550 |

**Sales Revenue**

| | | | |
|---|---|---|---|
| | | (15) | 490,000 |

**Cost of Goods Sold**

| | | | |
|---|---|---|---|
| (16) | 338,100 | | |
| (18) | 3,130 | | |
| Bal. | 341,230 | | |

**Selling and Admin. Exp.**

| | | | |
|---|---|---|---|
| (17) | 78,200 | | |

**EXHIBIT 12.10**

## JANIS JUICE COMPANY
### Adjusted Trial Balance
### As of December 31, 2012

|  | Debit | Credit |
|---|---|---|
| Cash | $412,470 | |
| Raw materials—fruit | 6,080 | |
| Raw materials—additives | 8,700 | |
| Raw materials—containers | 6,500 | |
| Work in process—extraction | 7,480 | |
| Work in process—mixing | 9,460 | |
| Work in process—packaging | 18,630 | |
| Finished goods inventory | 13,800 | |
| Common stock | | $180,000 |
| Retained earnings | | 232,550 |
| Sales revenue | | 490,000 |
| Cost of goods sold | 341,230 | |
| Selling and administrative expenses | 78,200 | |
| Total | $902,550 | $902,550 |

## ✓ CHECK YOURSELF 12.2

Western Manufacturing Company uses a process costing system. Its products pass through two departments. Beginning inventory in Department I's Work in Process (WIP) account was $5,000. During the month the department added $13,200 of product costs to the WIP account. There were 200 units of product in beginning inventory, and 500 units were started during the month. Ending inventory consisted of 300 units 40 percent complete. Prepare a cost of production report showing the cost of goods transferred from Department I to Department II and the cost of Department I's ending work in process inventory.

**Answer**

### Cost of Production Report

|  | Actual |  | Equivalent Units |
|---|---|---|---|
| **Determination of Equivalent Units** | | | |
| Beginning inventory | 200 | | |
| Units added to production | 500 | | |
| Total | 700 | | |
| Transferred to finished goods | 400 | 100% Complete | 400 |
| Ending inventory | 300 | 40% Complete | 120 |
| Total | 700 | | 520 |
| **Determination of Cost per Unit** | | | |
| Cost accumulation | | | |
| Beginning inventory | $ 5,000 | | |
| Product costs added | 13,200 | | |
| Total product costs | $18,200 | | |
| Divide by | ÷ | | |
| equivalent units | 520 | | |
| Cost per equivalent unit | $    35 | | |
| **Cost Allocation** | | | |
| Transferred to Department II (400 × $35) | $14,000 | | |
| Ending WIP inventory (120 × $35) | 4,200 | | |
| Total | $18,200 | | |

# FOCUS ON INTERNATIONAL ISSUES

**JOB-ORDER, PROCESS, AND HYBRID COSTING SYSTEMS CROSS INTERNATIONAL BORDERS**

Companies throughout the world use job-order, process, and hybrid costing systems. **Nestlé Group**, a Swiss company, makes chocolate candy bars, among many other products. A homogeneous product like candy bars requires the use of a process cost system. In contrast, **Airbus** is an aircraft manufacturing company headquartered in Toulouse, France. When it completes an order for five A320 airplanes for Air New Zealand, the cost of this order will be determined using a job-order costing system.

 ## ◄◄ A Look Back

*Job-order* and *process costing systems* represent the two primary methods of accounting for product cost flows in manufacturing companies. In both systems, entries in the accounting records parallel the physical flow of products as they move through production. Job-order costing systems are used by manufacturers that produce distinct products or distinct batches of products. Products suited to job-order systems include buildings, ships, airplanes, and special-order batches. A job-order costing system accumulates costs for individual products or batches of products. Each product or batch has a job identification number. Costs are accumulated separately by job number. A job-order costing system requires detailed accounting information. The total cost of all jobs is accumulated in one Work in Process Inventory control account; details of the cost of materials, labor, and overhead for each job are kept in subsidiary records called *job-order cost sheets*. Process costing systems are used by manufacturers that make homogeneous products in a continuous production process. Products suited to a process costing system include paint, gasoline, and soft drinks. A process costing system accumulates product costs for each processing department (cutting, processing, assembling, packaging). Because the units are homogeneous, the cost per unit can be determined by dividing the total processing cost by the number of units (cost averaging). Any units that are partially complete at the end of an accounting period must be converted into equivalent whole units prior to determining the average cost per unit. The cost per equivalent whole unit is used to allocate the total processing cost among departments and ending inventories.

 ## ►► A Look Forward

The remaining two chapters are transitional chapters. Chapter 13 discusses financial statement analysis. Chapter 14 discusses advanced topics relating to the statement of cash flows. Some instructors include these subjects in the financial accounting course, and other instructors cover them in the managerial accounting course.

**A step-by-step audio-narrated series of slides is provided on the text website at www.mhhe.com/edmonds2011.**

## SELF-STUDY REVIEW PROBLEM 1

Hill Construction Company uses a job-order costing system. The company had three jobs in process at the beginning of the month. The beginning balance in the Work in Process control account was $145,400, made up of $42,400, $65,100, and $37,900 shown on the job cost sheets for Jobs 302, 303, and 304, respectively. During the month, Hill added the following materials and labor costs to each job:

| Inventory | Materials | Labor |
|---|---|---|
| Job 302 | $10,200 | $32,000 |
| Job 303 | 12,400 | 18,000 |
| Job 304 | 16,500 | 10,000 |
| Total | $39,100 | $60,000 |

Overhead cost is applied at the predetermined rate of $0.60 per direct labor dollar. Actual overhead costs for the month were $36,800. Hill completed Job 303 and sold it for $129,000 cash during the month.

### Required

a. Determine the balance in the Work in Process account at the end of the month.

b. Explain how the entry to close the Manufacturing Overhead account would affect the Cost of Goods Sold account.

c. Determine the amount of gross margin Hill would report on its income statement for the month.

### Solution to Requirement a

Cost accumulated in the Work in Process account:

| Inventory | Beg. Bal. | + | Materials | + | Labor | + | Overhead* | = | Total |
|---|---|---|---|---|---|---|---|---|---|
| Job 302 | $42,400 | | $10,200 | | $32,000 | | $19,200 | | $103,800 |
| Job 303 | 65,100 | | 12,400 | | 18,000 | | 10,800 | | 106,300 |
| Job 304 | 37,900 | | 16,500 | | 10,000 | | 6,000 | | 70,400 |

*60% of direct labor cost.

Since Hill has sold Job 303, work in process at the end of the month is the sum of costs assigned to Jobs 302 and 304, $174,200 ($103,800 + $70,400).

### Solution to Requirement b

Total applied overhead is $36,000 ($19,200 + $10,800 + $6,000). Since actual overhead is $36,800, overhead is underapplied by $800 ($36,800 − $36,000). Since the overhead is underapplied, cost of goods sold is understated. The entry to close the overhead account would increase the amount of cost of goods sold by $800.

### Solution to Requirement c

| | |
|---|---|
| Sales revenue | $129,000 |
| Cost of goods sold (Job 303, $106,300 + Underapplied overhead, $800) | (107,100) |
| Gross margin | $ 21,900 |

A step-by-step audio-narrated series of slides is provided on the text website at
www.mhhe.com/edmonds2011.

## SELF-STUDY REVIEW PROBLEM 2

United Technology Manufacturing Company (UTMC) uses a process costing system. Products
pass through two departments. The following information applies to the Assembly Department.
Beginning inventory in the department's Work in Process (WIP) account was $18,400. During
the month UTMC added $200,273 of product costs to the WIP account. There were 5,700 units
of product in the beginning inventory and 45,300 units started during the month. The ending
inventory consisted of 4,200 units, which were 30 percent complete.

### Required

Prepare a cost of production report for the month.

### Solution

### Cost of Production Report

|  | Actual |  | Equivalent Units |
|---|---|---|---|
| **Determination of Equivalent Units** |  |  |  |
| Beginning inventory | 5,700 |  |  |
| Units added to production | 45,300 |  |  |
| Total | 51,000 |  |  |
| Transferred to finished goods | 46,800 | 100% Complete | 46,800 |
| Ending inventory | 4,200 | 30% Complete | 1,260 |
| Total | 51,000 |  | 48,060 |
| **Determination of Cost per Unit** |  |  |  |
| Cost accumulation |  |  |  |
| Beginning inventory | $ 18,400 |  |  |
| Product costs added | 200,273 |  |  |
| Total product costs | $218,673 |  |  |
| Divide by | ÷ |  |  |
| equivalent units | 48,060 |  |  |
| Cost per equivalent unit | $    4.55 |  |  |
| **Cost Allocation** |  |  |  |
| Transferred out (46,800 × $4.55) | $212,940 |  |  |
| Ending WIP inventory (1,260 × $4.55) | 5,733 |  |  |
| Total | $218,673 |  |  |

## KEY TERMS

Cost per equivalent unit  550
Equivalent whole units  549
First-in, first-out (FIFO)
  method  550
Hybrid costing system  538

Job cost sheet  538
Job-order costing
  system  536
Materials requisition
  form  538

Process costing system  536
Transferred-in costs  537
Weighted average
  method  550
Work ticket  538

## QUESTIONS

1. To what types of products is a job-order
   costing system best suited? Provide examples.

2. To what types of products is a process costing system best suited? Provide examples.

3. Why do both job-order and process costing require some form of cost averaging?

4. How is the unit cost of a product determined in a process costing system?

5. Ludwig Company, which normally operates a process costing system to account for the cost of the computers that it produces, has received a special order from a corporate client to produce and sell 5,000 computers. Can Ludwig use a job-order costing system to account for the costs associated with the special order even though it uses a process costing system for its normal operations?

6. Which system, a job-order or a process costing system, requires more documentation?

7. How do source documents help accountants operate a costing system?

8. In a job-order costing system, what are the Work in Process Inventory subsidiary records called? What information is included in these subsidiary records?

9. How is indirect labor recorded in ledger accounts? How is this labor eventually assigned to the items produced in a job-order costing system?

10. How is depreciation on manufacturing equipment recorded in ledger accounts? How is this depreciation assigned to the items produced in a job-order costing system and in a process costing system?

11. Why is a process costing system not appropriate for companies that produce items that are distinctly different from one another?

12. The president of Videl Corporation tells you that her company has a difficult time determining the cost per unit of product that it makes. It seems that some units are always partially complete. Counting these units as complete understates the cost per unit because all of the units but only part of the cost is included in the unit cost computation. Conversely, ignoring the number of partially completed products overstates the cost per unit because all of the costs are included but some of the number of units are omitted from the per-unit computation. How can Videl obtain a more accurate cost per unit figure?

13. Bindon Furniture Manufacturing has completed its monthly inventory count for dining room chairs and recorded the following information for ending inventory: 600 units 100 percent complete, 300 units 60 percent complete, and 100 units 20 percent complete. The company uses a process costing system to determine unit cost. Why would unit cost be inaccurate if 1,000 units were used to determine unit cost?

14. What is the weighted average method of determining equivalent units? Why is it used? What are its weaknesses?

15. What is the purpose of each of the three primary steps in a process costing system? Describe each.

16. In a process costing system, what does the term *transferred-in costs* mean? How is the amount of transferred-in costs determined?

17. The finishing department is the last of four sequential production departments for Kowalski Graphics, Inc. The company's other production departments are design, layout, and printing. The finishing department incurred the following costs in March 2012: direct materials, $40,000; direct labor, $80,000; applied overhead, $90,000; and transferred-in costs, $120,000. Which department incurred the transferred-in costs? In what month were the transferred-in costs incurred?

## MULTIPLE-CHOICE QUESTIONS

**Multiple-choice questions are provided on the text website at www.mhhe.com/edmonds2011.**

## EXERCISES—SERIES A

**All applicable Exercises in Series A are available with McGraw-Hill's *Connect Accounting*.**

**Exercise 12-1A**  *Matching products with appropriate costing systems*

LO 1

**Required**

Indicate which costing system (job-order, process, or hybrid) would be most appropriate for the type of product listed in the left-hand column. The first item is shown as an example.

| Type of Product | Type of Costing System |
|---|---|
| a. Hollywood movie | job-order |
| b. Airplane | |
| c. Personal computer with special features | |
| d. Coffee table | |
| e. Plastic storage containers | |
| f. TV set | |
| g. Ship | |
| h. Potato chips | |
| i. House | |
| j. Custom-made suit | |
| k. Van with custom features | |
| l. CPA review course | |
| m. Shirts | |
| n. Pots and pans | |
| o. Apartment building | |
| p. Automobile | |

**LO 1**

### Exercise 12-2A    *Identifying the appropriate costing system*

Flagg Company makes small aluminum storage bins that it sells through a direct marketing mail-order business. The typical bin measures 6 × 8 feet. The bins are normally used to store garden tools or other small household items. Flagg customizes bins for special-order customers by adding shelving; occasionally, it makes large bins following the unique specifications of commercial customers.

#### Required

Recommend the type of costing system (job-order, process, or hybrid) that Flagg should use. Explain your recommendation.

**LO 1, 2**

### Exercise 12-3A    *Job-order or process costing system and a pricing decision*

Sam Wu, a tailor in his home country, recently immigrated to the United States. He is interested in starting a business making custom suits for men. Mr. Wu is trying to determine the cost of making a suit so he can set an appropriate selling price. He estimates that his materials cost will range from $100 to $160 per suit. Because he will make the suits himself, he assumes there will be no labor cost. Some suits will require more time than others, but Mr. Wu considers this fact to be irrelevant because he is personally supplying the labor, which costs him nothing. Finally, Mr. Wu knows that he will incur some overhead costs such as rent, utilities, advertising, packaging, delivery, and so on; however, he is uncertain as to the exact cost of these items.

#### Required

a.  Should Mr. Wu use a job-order or a process costing system?

b.  How can Mr. Wu determine the cost of suits he makes during the year when he does not know what the total overhead cost will be until the end of the year?

c.  Is it appropriate for Mr. Wu to consider labor cost to be zero?

d.  With respect to the overhead costs mentioned in the problem, distinguish the *manufacturing overhead* costs from the *selling and administrative* expenses. Comment on whether Mr. Wu should include the selling and administrative expenses in determining the product cost if he uses cost-plus pricing. Comment on whether the selling and administrative expenses should be included in determining the product cost for financial reporting purposes.

**LO 3**

### Exercise 12-4A    *Job-order costing in a manufacturing company*

Ferguson Corporation builds sailboats. On January 1, 2012, the company had the following account balances: $65,000 for both cash and common stock. Boat 25 was started on February 10 and finished on May 31. To build the boat, Ferguson had incurred cash costs of $5,100 for labor and $4,350 for materials. During the same period, Ferguson paid $6,600 cash for actual manufacturing overhead costs. The company expects to incur $175,500 of indirect overhead cost during 2012. The overhead is allocated to jobs based on direct labor cost. The expected total labor cost for the year is $135,000.

Ferguson uses a just-in-time inventory management system. Consequently, it does not have raw materials inventory. Raw materials purchases are recorded directly in the Work in Process Inventory account.

**Required**

a. Use the horizontal financial statements model, as illustrated here, to record Ferguson's business events. The first row shows beginning balances.

| Assets | | | | | = | Equity | | | | | | |
|---|---|---|---|---|---|---|---|---|---|---|---|---|
| Cash | + | Work in Process | + | Finished Goods | + | Manuf. Overhead | = | Com. Stock | + | Ret. Ear. | Rev. − Exp. = Net Inc. | | |
| 65,000 | + | NA | + | NA | + | NA | = | 65,000 | + | NA | NA − NA = NA | | |

b. If Ferguson desires to earn a profit equal to 20 percent of cost, for what price should it sell the boat?

c. If the boat is not sold by year-end, what amount would appear in the Work in Process Inventory and Finished Goods Inventory on the balance sheet for Boat 25?

d. Is the amount of inventory you calculated in Requirement *c* the actual or the estimated cost of the boat?

e. When is it appropriate to use estimated inventory cost on a year-end balance sheet?

## Exercise 12-5A  *Job-order costing in a manufacturing company*

LO 3

Keeney Corporation makes custom-order furniture to meet the needs of disabled persons. On January 1, 2011, the company had the following account balances: $90,000 for both cash and common stock. In 2011, Keeney worked on three jobs. The relevant direct operating costs follow.

| | Direct Labor | Direct Materials |
|---|---|---|
| Job 1 | $ 4,000 | $4,500 |
| Job 2 | 2,800 | 1,400 |
| Job 3 | 8,200 | 3,600 |
| Total | $15,000 | $9,500 |

Keeney's predetermined manufacturing overhead rate was $0.40 per direct labor dollar. Actual manufacturing overhead costs amounted to $5,758. Keeney paid cash for all costs. The company completed and delivered Jobs 1 and 2 to customers during the year. Job 3 was incomplete at the end of the year. The company sold Job 1 for $16,000 cash and Job 2 for $7,800 cash. Keeney also paid $3,000 cash for selling and administrative expenses for the year.

Keeney uses a just-in-time inventory management system. Consequently, it does not have raw materials inventory. Raw materials purchases are recorded directly in the Work in Process Inventory account.

**Required**

a. Record the preceding events in a horizontal statements model. The first row shows beginning balances.

| Assets | | | | | = | Equity | | | | | | |
|---|---|---|---|---|---|---|---|---|---|---|---|---|
| Cash | + | Work in Process | + | Finished Goods | + | Manuf. Overhead | = | Com. Stock | + | Ret. Ear. | Rev. − Exp. = Net Inc. | | |
| 90,000 | + | NA | + | NA | + | NA | = | 90,000 | + | NA | NA − NA = NA | | |

b. Record the entry to close the amount of underapplied or overapplied overhead for the year to Cost of Goods Sold (in the expense category) in the horizontal financial statements model.

c. Determine the gross margin for the year.

**LO 3**

### Exercise 12-6A    *Job-order costing in a service company*

Bailes Condos Corporation is a small company owned by Ray Miller. It leases three condos of differing sizes to customers as vacation facilities. Labor costs for each condo consist of maid service and maintenance cost. Other direct operating costs consist of interest and depreciation. The direct operating costs for each condo follow.

|  | Direct Labor | Other Direct Operating Costs |
|---|---|---|
| Condo 1 | $16,200 | $37,800 |
| Condo 2 | 18,600 | 42,000 |
| Condo 3 | 22,500 | 57,000 |
| Total | $ 5,730 | $13,680 |

Indirect operating expenses, which amounted to $41,040, are allocated to the condos in proportion to the amount of other direct operating costs incurred for each.

**Required**

a. Assuming that the amount of rent revenue from Condo 2 is $96,000, what amount of income did it earn?

b. Based on the preceding information, will the company show finished goods inventory on its balance sheet? If so, what is the amount of this inventory? If not, explain why not.

**LO 3**

### Exercise 12-7A    *Job-order costing system*

The following information applies to Job 730 completed by Porthro Manufacturing Company during October 2010. The amount of labor cost for the job was $81,000. Applied overhead amounted to $102,400. The project was completed and delivered to Rodewald Company at a contract price of $314,000. Porthro recognized a gross profit of $54,400 on the job.

**Required**

Determine the amount of raw materials used to complete Job 730.

**LO 5**

### Exercise 12-8A    *Process costing system—determine equivalent units*

Sheridan Furniture Company's cutting department had 400 units in its beginning work in process inventory. During the accounting period it began work on 1,200 units of product and had 600 partially complete units in its ending inventory.

**Required**

(Each requirement is independent of the others.)

a. Assuming the ending inventory units were 60 percent complete, determine the total number of equivalent whole units (number transferred out plus number in ending inventory) accounted for by the cutting department.

b. Assuming that the total number of equivalent whole units (number transferred out plus number in ending inventory) accounted for by the cutting department was 1,240, what was the ending inventory percentage of completion?

**LO 5**

### Exercise 12-9A    *Cost allocation in a process system*

McAlister Watches, Inc., makes watches. Its assembly department started the accounting period with a beginning inventory balance of $22,000. During the accounting period, the department incurred $43,500 of transferred-in cost, $21,000 of materials cost, $60,000 of labor cost, and $67,000 of applied overhead cost. The department processed 6,100 total equivalent units of product during the accounting period.

**Required**

(Each requirement is independent of the others.)

a.  Assuming that 1,200 equivalent units of product were in the ending work in process inventory, determine the amount of cost transferred out of the Work in Process Inventory account of the assembly department to the Finished Goods Inventory account. What was the assembly department's cost of ending work in process inventory?

b.  Assuming that 5,600 units of product were transferred out of the assembly department's work in process inventory to finished goods inventory, determine the amount of the assembly department's cost of ending work in process inventory. What was the cost of the finished goods inventory transferred out of the assembly department?

### Exercise 12-10A  *Process costing system—determine equivalent units and allocate costs*

**LO 5**

Milwaukee Ski Company manufactures snow skis. During the most recent accounting period, the company's finishing department transferred 4,200 sets of skis to finished goods. At the end of the accounting period, 450 sets of skis were estimated to be 40 percent complete. Total product costs for the finishing department amounted to $219,000.

**Required**

a.  Determine the cost per equivalent.

b.  Determine the cost of the goods transferred out of the finishing department.

c.  Determine the cost of the finishing department's ending work in process inventory.

### Exercise 12-11A  *Process costing system*

**LO 5**

Fancher Company is a cosmetics manufacturer. Its assembly department receives raw cosmetics from the molding department. The assembly department places the raw cosmetics into decorative containers and transfers them to the packaging department. The assembly department's Work in Process Inventory account had a $62,000 balance as of August 1. During August, the department incurred raw materials, labor, and overhead costs amounting to $72,000, $85,000, and $80,000, respectively. The department transferred products that cost $342,000 to the packaging department. The balance in the assembly department's Work in Process Inventory account as of August 31 was $83,000.

**Required**

Determine the cost of raw cosmetics transferred from the molding department to the assembly department during August.

### Exercise 12-12A  *Selecting the appropriate costing system*

**LO 1**

Larry's Car Wash (LCW) offers customers three cleaning options. Under Option 1, only the exterior is cleaned. With Option 2, the exterior and interior are cleaned. Option 3 provides exterior waxing as well as exterior and interior cleaning. LCW completed 4,000 Option 1 cleanings, 5,200 Option 2 cleanings, and 3,200 Option 3 cleanings during 2012. The average cost of completing each cleaning option and the price charged for it are shown here.

|  | Option 1 | Option 2 | Option 3 |
|---|---|---|---|
| Price charged | $10 | $12 | $21 |
| Costs of completing task | 4 | 5 | 15 |

**Required**

a.  Is LCW a manufacturing or a service company? Explain.

b.  Which costing system, job-order or process, is most appropriate for LCW? Why?

c.  What is the balance in LCW's Work in Process and Finished Goods Inventory accounts on the December 31 balance sheet?

d.  Speculate as to the major costs that LCW incurs to complete a cleaning job.

## PROBLEMS—SERIES A

**All Problems in Series A are available with McGraw-Hill's**
*Connect Accounting.*

**Problem 12-13A** *Job-order costing system*

Baucom Manufacturing Corporation was started with the issuance of common stock for $50,000. It purchased $7,000 of raw materials and worked on three job orders during 2012 for which data follow. (Assume that all transactions are for cash unless otherwise indicated.)

|       | Direct Raw Materials Used | Direct Labor |
|-------|---------------------------|--------------|
| Job 1 | $1,000                    | $2,000       |
| Job 2 | 2,000                     | 4,000        |
| Job 3 | 3,000                     | 2,000        |
| Total | $6,000                    | $8,000       |

Factory overhead is applied using a predetermined overhead rate of $0.60 per direct labor dollar. Jobs 2 and 3 were completed during the period and Job 3 was sold for $10,000 cash. Baucom paid $400 for selling and administrative expenses. Actual factory overhead was $4,300.

**Required**

a. Record the preceding events in a horizontal statements model. The first event for 2012 has been recorded as an example.

| Assets | | | | | = | Equity | | | | | |
|--------|--|--|--|--|---|--------|--|--|--|--|--|
| Cash | + Raw M. | + MOH | + WIP | + F. Goods | = | C. Stk. | + Ret. Ear. | Rev. | − Exp. | = | Net Inc. |
| $50,000 + | NA | + NA | + NA | + NA | = | $50,000 + | NA | NA | − NA | = | NA |

b. Reconcile all subsidiary accounts with their respective control accounts.
c. Record the closing entry for over- or underapplied manufacturing overhead in the horizontal statements model, assuming that the amount is insignificant.
d. Prepare a schedule of cost of goods manufactured and sold, an income statement, and a balance sheet for 2012.

**Problem 12-14A** *Job-order costing system*

Fenske Construction Company began operations on January 1, 2012, when it acquired $10,000 cash from the issuance of common stock. During the year, Fenske purchased $2,600 of direct raw materials and used $2,400 of the direct materials. There were 108 hours of direct labor worked at an average rate of $8 per hour paid in cash. The predetermined overhead rate was $3.00 per direct labor hour. The company started construction on three prefabricated buildings. The job cost sheets reflected the following allocations of costs to each building.

|       | Direct Materials | Direct Labor Hours |
|-------|------------------|--------------------|
| Job 1 | $ 600            | 30                 |
| Job 2 | 1,000            | 50                 |
| Job 3 | 800              | 28                 |

The company paid $100 cash for indirect labor costs. Actual overhead cost paid in cash other than indirect labor was $240. Fenske completed Jobs 1 and 2 and sold Job 1 for $1,600 cash. The company incurred $150 of selling and administrative expenses that were paid in cash. Over- or underapplied overhead is closed to Cost of Goods Sold.

**Required**

a. Record the preceding events in a horizontal statements model. The first event for 2012 has been recorded as an example.

| Assets | | | | | = | Equity | | | | | | |
|---|---|---|---|---|---|---|---|---|---|---|---|---|
| Cash | + Raw M. | + MOH | + WIP | + F. Goods | = | C. Stk. | + Ret. Ear. | | Rev. | − Exp. | = | Net Inc. |
| 10,000 | + NA | + NA | + NA | + NA | = | 10,000 | + NA | | NA | − NA | = | NA |

b. Reconcile all subsidiary accounts with their respective control accounts.

c. Record the closing entry for over- or underapplied manufacturing overhead in the horizontal statements model, assuming that the amount is insignificant.

d. Prepare a schedule of cost of goods manufactured and sold, an income statement, and a balance sheet for 2012.

## Problem 12-15A  *Process costing system*

LO 4, 5

CHECK FIGURES
d. COGS: $36,800
Cash: $54,000

Alston Corporation makes rocking chairs. The chairs move through two departments during production. Lumber is cut into chair parts in the cutting department, which transfers the parts to the assembly department for completion. The company sells the unfinished chairs to hobby shops. The following transactions apply to Alston's operations for its first year, 2011. (Assume that all transactions are for cash unless otherwise stated.)

1. The company was started when it acquired a $100,000 cash contribution from the owners.

2. The company purchased $30,000 of direct raw materials and $800 of indirect materials. Indirect materials are capitalized in the Production Supplies account.

3. Direct materials totaling $12,000 were issued to the cutting department.

4. Labor cost was $56,400. Direct labor for the cutting and assembly departments was $20,000 and $26,000, respectively. Indirect labor costs were $10,400.

5. The predetermined overhead rate was $0.50 per direct labor dollar in each department.

6. Actual overhead costs other than indirect materials and indirect labor were $12,800 for the year.

7. The cutting department transferred $24,000 of inventory to the assembly department.

8. The assembly department transferred $40,000 of inventory to finished goods.

9. The company sold inventory costing $36,000 for $60,000.

10. Selling and administrative expenses were $6,000.

11. A physical count revealed $200 of production supplies on hand at the end of 2011.

12. Assume that over- or underapplied overhead is insignificant.

**Required**

a. Record the data in T-accounts.

b. Record the closing entry for over- or underapplied manufacturing overhead, assuming that the amount is insignificant.

c. Close the revenue and expense accounts.

d. Prepare a schedule of cost of goods manufactured and sold, an income statement, and a balance sheet for 2011.

## Problem 12-16A  *Process costing system*

LO 4, 5

CHECK FIGURES
d. NI: $21,800
Cash: $6,700

Use the ending balances from Problem 12-15A as the beginning balances for this problem. The transactions for the second year of operation (2012) are described here. (Assume that all transactions are cash transactions unless otherwise indicated.)

1. The company purchased $40,000 of direct raw materials and $1,300 of indirect materials. Indirect materials are capitalized in the Production Supplies account.

2. Materials totaling $13,400 were issued to the cutting department.

3. Labor cost was $47,000. Direct labor for the cutting and assembly departments was $22,000 and $20,000, respectively. Indirect labor costs were $5,000. (*Note:* Assume that sufficient cash is available when periodic payments are made. These amounts represent summary data for the entire year and are not presented in exact order of collection and payment.)

4. The predetermined overhead rate was $0.50 per direct labor dollar in each department.

5. Actual overhead costs other than indirect materials and indirect labor for the month were $14,600.

6. The cutting department transferred $30,000 of inventory to the assembly department.

7. The assembly department transferred $60,000 of inventory to finished goods.

8. The company sold inventory costing $34,000 for $64,000.

9. Selling and administrative expenses were $8,400.

10. At the end of 2012, $300 of production supplies was on hand.

11. Assume that over- or underapplied overhead is insignificant.

**Required**

a. Record the data in T-accounts.

b. Record the closing entry for over- or underapplied manufacturing overhead, assuming that the amount is insignificant.

c. Close the revenue and expense accounts.

d. Prepare a schedule of cost of goods manufactured and sold, an income statement, and a balance sheet for 2012.

**LO 5**

**eXcel**

**CHECK FIGURE**
b. $33.80

### Problem 12-17A    *Process costing system cost of production report*

Burris Company had 250 units of product in its work in process inventory at the beginning of the period and started 2,000 additional units during the period. At the end of the period, 750 units were in work in process inventory. The ending work in process inventory was estimated to be 40 percent complete. The cost of work in process inventory at the beginning of the period was $6,840, and $54,000 of product costs was added during the period.

**Required**

Prepare a cost of production report showing the following.

a. The number of equivalent units of production.

b. The product cost per equivalent unit.

c. The total cost allocated between the ending Work in Process Inventory and Finished Goods Inventory accounts.

**LO 5**

**CHECK FIGURE**
b. $60

### Problem 12-18A    *Determining inventory cost using a process costing system*

Espinoza Company had 200 units of product in work in process inventory at the beginning of the period. It started 1,400 units during the period and transferred 1,200 units to finished goods inventory. The ending work in process inventory was estimated to be 70 percent complete. Cost data for the period follow.

| | Product Costs |
|---|---|
| Beginning balance | $31,600 |
| Added during period | 57,200 |
| Total | $88,800 |

**Required**

Prepare a cost of production report showing the following.

a. The number of equivalent units of production.

b. The product cost per equivalent unit.

c. The total cost allocated between ending work in process inventory and finished goods inventory.

## Problem 12-19A  *Process costing system*

**LO 5**

Rockwall Plastic Products Company makes a plastic toy using two departments, parts and assembly. The following data pertain to the parts department's transactions in 2011.

1. The beginning balance in the Work in Process Inventory account was $11,400. This inventory consisted of parts for 1,000 toys. The beginning balances in the Raw Materials Inventory, Production Supplies, and Cash accounts were $128,000, $2,000, and $400,000, respectively.

2. Direct materials costing $104,000 were issued to the parts department. The materials were sufficient to make 5,000 additional toys.

3. Direct labor cost was $94,000, and indirect labor costs are $9,200. All labor costs were paid in cash.

4. The predetermined overhead rate was $0.30 per direct labor dollar.

5. Actual overhead costs other than indirect materials and indirect labor for the year were $19,000, which was paid in cash.

6. The parts department completed work for 4,500 toys. The remaining toy parts were 20 percent complete. The completed parts were transferred to the assembly department.

7. All of the production supplies had been used by the end of 2011.

8. Over- or underapplied overhead was closed to the Cost of Goods Sold account.

### Required

a. Determine the number of equivalent units of production.

b. Determine the product cost per equivalent unit.

c. Allocate the total cost between the ending work in process inventory and parts transferred to the assembly department.

d. Record the transactions in a partial set of T-accounts.

## Problem 12-20A  *Process costing system*

**LO 5**

Zest Cola Corporation produces a new soft drink brand, Sweet Spring, using two production departments, mixing and bottling. Zest's beginning balances and data pertinent to the mixing department's activities for 2011 follow.

| Accounts | Beginning Balances |
|---|---|
| Cash | $ 45,000 |
| Raw materials inventory | 14,800 |
| Production supplies | 100 |
| Work in process inventory (400,000 units) | 48,000 |
| Common stock | 107,900 |

1. Zest Cola issued additional common stock for $54,000 cash.

2. The company purchased raw materials and production supplies for $29,600 and $800, respectively, in cash.

3. The company issued $32,360 of raw materials to the mixing department for the production of 800,000 units of Sweet Spring that were started in 2011. A unit of soft drink is the amount needed to fill a bottle.

4. The mixing department used 2,400 hours of labor during 2011, consisting of 2,200 hours for direct labor and 200 hours for indirect labor. The average wage was $9.60 per hour. All wages were paid in 2011 in cash.

5. The predetermined overhead rate was $1.60 per direct labor hour.

6. Actual overhead costs other than indirect materials and indirect labor for the year amounted to $1,260, which was paid in cash.

7. The mixing department completed 600,000 units of Sweet Spring. The remaining inventory was 25 percent complete.

8. The completed soft drink was transferred to the bottling department.

9. The ending balance in the Production Supplies account was $560.

**Required**

a. Determine the number of equivalent units of production.

b. Determine the product cost per equivalent unit.

c. Allocate the total cost between the ending work in process inventory and units transferred to the bottling department.

d. Record the transactions in T-accounts.

**LO 4, 5**

**CHECK FIGURES**
a. Cost/unit: $1.00
b. Cost/unit: $1.60

### Problem 12-21A   *Process costing system with second department*

Reed Corporation makes a health beverage named Reed that is manufactured in a two-stage production process. The drink is first created in the Conversion Department where material ingredients (natural juices, supplements, preservatives, etc.) are combined. On July 1, 2011, the company had a sufficient quantity of partially completed beverage mix in the Conversion Department to make 40,000 containers of Reed. This beginning inventory had a cost of $30,000. During July, the company added ingredients necessary to make 160,000 containers of Reed. The cost of these ingredients was $154,000. During July, liquid mix representing 180,000 containers of the beverage was transferred to the Finishing Department. The beverage mix is poured into containers and packaged for shipment in the Finishing Department. Beverage that remained in the Conversion Department at the end of July was 20 percent complete. At the beginning of July the Finishing Department had 10,000 containers of beverage mix. The cost of this mix was $24,000. The department added $44,000 of manufacturing costs (materials, labor and overhead) during July. During July, 120,000 containers of Reed were completed. The ending inventory for this department was 50 percent complete at the end of July.

**Required**

a. Prepare a Cost of Production Report for the Conversion Department for July.

b. Prepare a Cost of Production Report for the Finishing Department for July.

c. If 100,000 containers of Reed are sold in July for $240,000, determine the company's gross margin for July.

## EXERCISES—SERIES B

**LO 1**

### Exercise 12-1B   *Matching products with appropriate costing systems*

**Required**

Indicate which costing system (job-order, process, or hybrid) would be most appropriate for the type of product listed in the left-hand column. The first item is shown as an example.

| Type of Product | Type of Costing System |
|---|---|
| a. Shoes | Process |
| b. Treadmill | |
| c. Textbook | |
| d. House | |
| e. Oil | |
| f. Luxury yacht | |
| g. Special-order personal computer | |
| h. Over-the-counter personal computer | |
| i. Mouse pad for a computer | |
| j. Aircraft carrier | |
| k. Makeup sponge | |
| l. Handheld video game player | |
| m. Generic coffee mug | |
| n. Personalized coffee mug | |
| o. Surgery | |
| p. Audit engagement | |

## Exercise 12-2B  *Identifying the appropriate costing system*

Dahl Corporation's Morgan Plant in Jacksoville, Florida, produces the company's weed-control chemical solution, Weed Terminator. Production begins with pure water from a controlled stream to which the plant adds different chemicals in the production process. Finally, the plant bottles the resulting chemical solution. The process is highly automated with different computer-controlled maneuvers and testing to ensure the quality of the end product. With only 15 employees, the plant can produce up to 6,000 bottles per day.

### Required

Recommend the type of costing system (job-order, process, or hybrid) Morgan Plant should use. Explain your recommendation.

## Exercise 12-3B  *Job-order or process costing*

Jayne Allen, an artist, plans to make her living drawing customer portraits at a stand in Underground Atlanta. She will carry her drawing equipment and supplies to work each day in bags. By displaying two of her best hand-drawn portraits on either side of her stand, she expects to attract tourists' attention. Ms. Allen can usually draw a customer's portrait in 30 minutes. Her materials cost is minimal, about $2 for a portrait. Her most significant cost will be leasing the stand for $1,200 per month. She estimates she can replace supplies and worn out equipment for $50 per month. She plans to work 20 days each month from noon to 9:00 P.M. After surveying her planned work environment before beginning the business, she observed that six other artists were providing customer portraits in that section of Underground Atlanta. Their portrait prices ranged from $25 to $45 per portrait. They also offered to frame portraits for customers at $15 per frame. Ms. Allen found that she could obtain comparable frames for $5 each and that properly framing a portrait takes about 10 minutes. The biggest challenge, Ms. Allen observed, was attracting tourists' interest. If she could draw portraits continuously during her workdays, she could earn quite a respectable income. But she noticed several of the artists were reading magazines as she walked by.

### Required

a. Should Ms. Allen use a job-order or process costing system for her art business?
b. List the individual types of costs Ms. Allen will likely incur in providing portraits.
c. How could Ms. Allen estimate her overhead rate per portrait when she does not know the number of portraits she will draw in a month?
d. Ms. Allen will not hire any employees. Will she have labor cost? Explain.

## Exercise 12-4B  *Job-order costing in a manufacturing company*

Popejoy Drapery, Inc., specializes in making custom draperies for both commercial and residential customers. It began business on August 1, 2011, by acquiring $48,000 cash through issuing common stock. In August 2011, Popejoy accepted drapery orders, Jobs 801 and 802, for two new commercial buildings. The company paid cash for the following costs related to the orders:

| Job 801 | |
|---|---|
| Raw materials | $ 8,000 |
| Direct labor (512 hours at $20 per hour) | 10,240 |
| **Job 802** | |
| Raw materials | 6,000 |
| Direct labor (340 hours at $20 per hour) | 6,800 |

During the same month, Popejoy paid $14,400 for various indirect costs such as utilities, equipment leases, and factory-related insurance. The company estimated its annual manufacturing overhead cost would be $240,000 and expected to use 20,000 direct labor hours in its first year of operation. It planned to allocate overhead based on direct labor hours. On August 31, 2011, Popejoy completed Job 801 and collected the contract price of $28,000. Job 802 was still in process.

Popejoy uses a just-in-time inventory management system. Consequently, it has no raw materials inventory. Raw materials purchases are recorded directly in the Work in Process Inventory account.

**Required**

a. Use a horizontal financial statements model as follows to record Popejoy's accounting events for August 2011. The first event is shown as an example.

| | | Assets | | | | | | = | Equity | | | | | | | |
|---|---|---|---|---|---|---|---|---|---|---|---|---|---|---|---|---|
| Cash | + | Work in Process | + | Finished Goods | + | Manuf. Overhead | = | Com. Stock | + | Ret. Ear. | | Rev. | − | Exp. | = | Net Inc. |
| 48,000 | + | NA | + | NA | + | NA | = | 48,000 | + | NA | | NA | − | NA | = | NA |

b. What was Popejoy's ending inventory on August 31, 2011? Is this amount the actual or the estimated inventory cost?

c. When is it appropriate to use estimated inventory cost on a year-end balance sheet?

**LO 3**

**Exercise 12-5B** *Job-order costing in a manufacturing company*

Agu Advertisements Corporation designs and produces television commercials for clients. On March 1, 2012, the company issued common stock for $75,000 cash. During March, Agu worked on three jobs. Pertinent data follow.

| Special Orders | Materials | Labor |
|---|---|---|
| Job 301 | $3,600 | 450 hours @ $32 per hour |
| Job 302 | 6,480 | 360 hours @ $60 per hour |
| Job 303 | 5,840 | 680 hours @ $28 per hour |

Actual production overhead cost: $24,080

Predetermined overhead rate: $16 per direct labor hour

Agu paid these costs in cash. Jobs 301 and 302 were completed and sold for cash to customers during March. Job 303 was incomplete at month end. Job 301 sold for $32,000, and Job 302 sold for $45,000. Agu also paid $8,000 cash in March for selling and administrative expenses.

Agu uses a just-in-time inventory management system. Consequently, it has no raw materials inventory. Raw materials purchases are recorded directly in the Work in Process Inventory account.

**Required**

a. Use a horizontal financial statements model, as follows, to record Agu's accounting events for March 2012. The first event is shown as an example.

| | | Assets | | | | | | = | Equity | | | | | | | |
|---|---|---|---|---|---|---|---|---|---|---|---|---|---|---|---|---|
| Cash | + | Work in Process | + | Finished Goods | + | Manuf. Overhead | = | Com. Stock | + | Ret. Ear. | | Rev. | − | Exp. | = | Net Inc. |
| 75,000 | + | NA | + | NA | + | NA | = | 75,000 | + | NA | | NA | − | NA | = | NA |

**b.** Record the entry to close the amount of underapplied or overapplied manufacturing overhead to Cost of Goods Sold (in the expense category) in the horizontal financial statements model.

**c.** Determine the gross margin for March.

## Exercise 12-6B   *Job-order costing in a service company*

LO 3

Navasota Consulting provides financial and estate planning services on a retainer basis for the executive officers of its corporate clients. It incurred the following labor costs on services for three corporate clients during March 2011.

|  | Direct Labor |
|---|---|
| Contract 1 | $14,000 |
| Contract 2 | 7,200 |
| Contract 3 | 28,800 |
| Total | $50,000 |

Navasota allocated March overhead costs of $22,000 to the contracts based on the amount of direct labor costs incurred on each contract.

**Required**

**a.** Assuming the revenue from Contract 3 was $70,000, what amount of income did Navasota earn from this contract?

**b.** Based on the preceding information, will Navasota report finished goods inventory on its balance sheet for Contract 1? If so, what is the amount of this inventory? If not, explain why not.

## Exercise 12-7B   *Determine missing information for a job order*

LO 3

The following information pertains to Job 712 that Gillman Manufacturing Company completed during January 2011. Materials and labor costs for the job were $70,000 and $38,000, respectively. Applied overhead costs were $44,000. Gillman completed and delivered the job to its customer and earned a $54,000 gross profit.

**Required**

Determine the contract price for the job.

## Exercise 12-8B   *Process costing: determining equivalent units*

LO 5

In March 2011, Rite Corporation's battery plant had 2,000 units in its beginning work in process inventory. During March, the company added 18,000 units to production. At the end of the month, 6,000 units of product were in process.

**Required**

(Each requirement is independent of the other.)

**a.** Assuming the ending inventory units were 60 percent complete, determine the total number of equivalent units (number transferred out plus number in ending inventory) processed by the battery plant.

**b.** Assuming the total number of equivalent units (number transferred out plus number in ending inventory) processed by the battery plant was 15,500, what was the ending inventory percentage of completion?

## Exercise 12-9B   *Allocating costs in a process costing system*

LO 5

Duval Corporation, a manufacturer of diabetic testing kits, started November production with $60,000 in beginning inventory. During the month, the company incurred $360,000 of materials cost and $240,000 of labor cost. It applied $165,000 of overhead cost to inventory. The company processed 15,000 total equivalent units of product.

**Required**

(Each requirement is independent of the other.)

**a.** Assuming 4,000 equivalent units of product were in ending work in process inventory, determine the amount of cost transferred from the Work in Process Inventory account to the Finished Goods Inventory account. What was the cost of the ending work in process inventory?

**b.** Assuming 12,000 equivalent units of product were transferred from work in process inventory to finished goods inventory, determine the cost of the ending work in process inventory. What was the cost of the finished goods inventory transferred from work in process?

**LO 5**

### Exercise 12-10B   *Process costing: determining equivalent units and allocating costs*

Bell Corporation, which makes suitcases, completed 30,000 suitcases in August 2011. At the end of August, work in process inventory consisted of 5,000 suitcases estimated to be 40 percent complete. Total product costs for August amounted to $480,000.

**Required**

**a.** Determine the cost per equivalent unit.
**b.** Determine the cost of the goods transferred to finished goods.
**c.** Determine the cost of the ending work in process inventory.

**LO 5**

### Exercise 12-11B   *Process costing: supply missing information*

Gospel Publications, Inc., produces Bibles in volume. It printed and sold 120,000 Bibles last year. Demand is sufficient to support producing a particular edition continuously throughout the year. For this operation, Gospel uses two departments, printing and binding. The printing department prints all pages and transfers them to the binding department, where it binds the pages into books. The binding department's Work in Process Inventory account had a $20,000 balance on September 1. During September, the binding department incurred raw materials, labor, and overhead costs of $5,500, $19,000, and $35,500, respectively. During the month, the binding department transferred Bibles that cost $175,000 to finished goods. The balance in the binding department's Work in Process Inventory account as of September 30 was $30,000.

**Required**

Determine the cost of pages transferred from the printing department to the binding department during the month of September.

**LO 1**

### Exercise 12-12B   *Selecting the appropriate costing system*

Schroeder Automotive Specialties, Inc., has a successful market niche. It customizes automobile interiors to fit the various needs of disabled customers. Some customers need special equipment to accommodate disabled drivers. Others need modified entrance and seating arrangements for disabled passengers. Customer vehicles vary according to different brands and models of sedans, minivans, sport utility vehicles, and full-size vans. Schroeder's engineers interview customers directly to ascertain their special needs. The engineers then propose a design, explaining it and its cost for the customer's approval. Customers have the opportunity to request changes. Once the company and customer agree on an engineering design and its price, they sign a contract, and the customer's vehicle is delivered to Schroeder's factory. The factory manager directs mechanics to customize the vehicle according to the engineering design.

**Required**

**a.** Is Schroeder a manufacturing company or a service company? Explain.
**b.** Which costing system, job-order or process, would be most appropriate for Schroeder? Why?
**c.** Does Schroeder have work in process and finished goods inventories?
**d.** Should Schroeder classify engineering design costs as materials, labor, or overhead? Why?

# PROBLEMS—SERIES B

## Problem 12-13B   *Job-order costing system*     LO 3

Plano Corporation was created on January 1, 2011, when it received a stockholder's contribution of $65,000. It purchased $7,900 of raw materials and worked on three job orders during the year. Data about these jobs follow. (Assume all transactions are for cash unless otherwise indicated.)

|  | Direct Raw Materials Used | Direct Labor |
|---|---|---|
| Job 1 | $2,500 | $ 3,200 |
| Job 2 | 1,800 | 4,800 |
| Job 3 | 3,200 | 4,480 |
| Total | $7,500 | $12,480 |

The average wage rate is $16 per hour. Manufacturing overhead is applied using a predetermined overhead rate of $7.50 per direct labor hour. Jobs 1 and 3 were completed during the year, and Job 1 was sold for $10,000. Plano paid $1,400 for selling and administrative expenses. Actual factory overhead was $6,000.

### Required

a. Record the preceding events in a horizontal statements model. The first event for 2011 has been recorded as an example.

| | | Assets | | | | = | Equity | | | | | |
|---|---|---|---|---|---|---|---|---|---|---|---|---|
| Cash | + | Raw M. | + MOH + | WIP + | F. Goods | = | C. Stk. | + Ret. Ear. | Rev. | − Exp. | = | Net Inc. |
| 65,000 | + | NA | + NA + | NA + | NA | = | 65,000 | + NA | NA | − NA | = | NA |

b. Reconcile all subsidiary accounts with their respective control accounts.

c. Record the closing entry for over- or underapplied manufacturing overhead, assuming that the amount is insignificant.

d. Prepare a schedule of cost of goods manufactured and sold, an income statement, and a balance sheet for 2011.

## Problem 12-14B   *Job-order costing system*     LO 3

Presley Roofing Corporation was founded on January 1, 2012, when stockholders contributed $5,000 for common stock. During the year, Presley purchased $2,400 of direct raw materials and used $2,160 of direct materials. There were 80 hours of direct labor worked at an average rate of $8 per hour paid in cash. The predetermined overhead rate was $6.50 per direct labor hour. The company started three custom roofing jobs. The job cost sheets reflected the following allocations of costs to each.

|  | Direct Materials | Direct Labor Hours |
|---|---|---|
| Roof 1 | $800 | 20 |
| Roof 2 | 400 | 12 |
| Roof 3 | 960 | 48 |

The company paid $176 cash for indirect labor costs and $240 cash for production supplies, which were all used during 2012. Actual overhead cost paid in cash other than indirect materials and indirect labor was $144. Presley completed Roofs 1 and 2 and collected the contract price for Roof 1 of $2,160 cash. The company incurred $496 of selling and administrative expenses that were paid with cash. Over- or underapplied overhead is closed to Cost of Goods Sold.

**Required**

a. Record the preceding events in a horizontal statements model. The first event for 2012 has been recorded as an example.

| Assets | | | | | = | Equity | | | | | |
|---|---|---|---|---|---|---|---|---|---|---|---|
| Cash | + Raw M. | + MOH | + WIP | + F. Goods | = | C. Stk. | + Ret. Ear. | Rev. | − Exp. | = | Net Inc. |
| 5,000 | + NA | + NA | + NA | + NA | = | 5,000 | + NA | NA | − NA | = | NA |

b. Reconcile all subsidiary accounts with their respective control accounts.

c. Record the closing entry for over- or underapplied manufacturing overhead in the horizontal statements model, assuming that the amount is insignificant.

d. Prepare a schedule of cost of goods manufactured and sold, an income statement, and a balance sheet for 2012.

**LO 4, 5**

## Problem 12-15B   *Process costing system*

Whitaker Food Company makes frozen vegetables. Production involves two departments, processing and packaging. Raw materials are cleaned and cut in the processing department and then transferred to the packaging department where they are packaged and frozen. The following transactions apply to Whitaker's first year (2011) of operations. (Assume that all transactions are for cash unless otherwise stated.)

1. The company was started when it acquired $100,000 cash from the issue of common stock.
2. Whitaker purchased $48,000 of direct raw materials and $8,000 of indirect materials. Indirect materials are capitalized in the Production Supplies account.
3. Direct materials totaling $38,000 were issued to the processing department.
4. Labor cost was $77,000. Direct labor for the processing and packaging departments was $32,500 and $25,500, respectively. Indirect labor costs were $19,000.
5. The predetermined overhead rate was $0.80 per direct labor dollar in each department.
6. Actual overhead costs other than indirect materials and indirect labor were $22,500 for the year.
7. The processing department transferred $60,500 of inventory to the packaging department.
8. The packaging department transferred $70,000 of inventory to finished goods.
9. The company sold inventory costing $63,000 for $117,500.
10. Selling and administrative expenses were $23,500.
11. A physical count revealed $3,000 of production supplies on hand at the end of 2011.
12. Assume that over- or underapplied overhead is insignificant.

**Required**

a. Record the data in T-accounts.

b. Record the closing entry for over- or underapplied manufacturing overhead, assuming that the amount is insignificant.

c. Close the revenue and expense accounts.

d. Prepare a schedule of cost of goods manufactured and sold, an income statement, and a balance sheet for 2011.

## Problem 12-16B    *Process costing system*    LO 4, 5

Use the ending balances from Problem 12-15B as the beginning balances for this problem. The transactions for the second year of operation (2012) are described here. (Assume that all transactions are cash transactions unless otherwise indicated.)

1. The company purchased $51,000 of direct raw materials and $9,000 of indirect materials. Indirect materials are capitalized in the Production Supplies account.
2. Materials costing $41,000 were issued to the processing department.
3. Labor cost was $89,500. Direct labor for the processing and packaging departments was $36,000 and $29,500, respectively. Indirect labor costs were $24,000. (*Note:* Assume that sufficient cash is available when periodic payments are made. These amounts represent summary data for the entire year and are not presented in exact order of collection and payment.)
4. The predetermined overhead rate was $0.80 per direct labor dollar.
5. Actual overhead costs other than indirect materials and indirect labor for the year were $25,000.
6. The processing department transferred $125,000 of inventory to the packaging department.
7. The packaging department transferred $175,000 of inventory to finished goods.
8. The company sold inventory costing $171,000 for $325,000.
9. Selling and administrative expenses amounted to $32,000.
10. At the end of the year, $2,500 of production supplies was on hand.
11. Assume that over- or underapplied overhead is insignificant.

### Required

a. Record the data in T-accounts.
b. Record the closing entry for over- or underapplied manufacturing overhead, assuming that the amount is insignificant.
c. Close the revenue and expense accounts.
d. Prepare a schedule of cost of goods manufactured and sold, an income statement, and a balance sheet for 2012.

## Problem 12-17B    *Process costing system cost of production report*    LO 5

At the beginning of 2012, Lingua Company had 2,500 units of product in its work in process inventory, and it started 22,500 additional units of product during the year. At the end of the year, 6,000 units of product were in the work in process inventory. The ending work in process inventory was estimated to be 25 percent complete. The cost of work in process inventory at the beginning of the period was $10,000, and $154,000 of product costs was added during the period.

### Required

Prepare a cost of production report showing the following.

a. The number of equivalent units of production.
b. The product cost per equivalent unit.
c. The total cost allocated between the ending Work in Process Inventory and Finished Goods Inventory accounts.

## Problem 12-18B    *Determining inventory cost using process costing*    LO 5

Ash Company's beginning work in process inventory consisted of 6,000 units of product on January 1, 2011. During 2011, the company started 24,000 units of product and transferred 25,000 units to finished goods inventory. The ending work in process inventory was estimated to be 40 percent complete. Cost data for 2011 follow.

|  | Product Costs |
| --- | --- |
| Beginning balance | $ 12,000 |
| Added during period | 123,000 |
| Total | $135,000 |

**Required**

Prepare a cost of production report showing the following.

a. The number of equivalent units of production.

b. The product cost per equivalent unit.

c. The total cost allocated between ending work in process inventory and finished goods inventory.

**LO 5**

## Problem 12-19B  *Process costing system*

Burdorf Corporation makes blue jeans. Its process involves two departments, cutting and sewing. The following data pertain to the cutting department's transactions in 2011.

1. The beginning balance in work in process inventory was $8,772. This inventory consisted of fabric for 6,000 pairs of jeans. The beginning balances in raw materials inventory, production supplies, and cash were $45,000, $2,100, and $135,600, respectively.

2. Direct materials costing $28,068 were issued to the cutting department; this amount of materials was sufficient to start work on 15,000 pairs of jeans.

3. Direct labor cost was $33,600, and indirect labor cost was $2,700. All labor costs were paid in cash.

4. The predetermined overhead rate was $0.25 per direct labor dollar.

5. Actual overhead costs other than indirect materials and indirect labor for the year amounted to $3,840, which was paid in cash.

6. The cutting department completed cutting 16,000 pairs of jeans. The remaining jeans were 40 percent complete.

7. The completed units of cut fabric were transferred to the sewing department.

8. All of the production supplies had been used by the end of the year.

9. Over- or underapplied overhead was closed to the Cost of Goods Sold account.

**Required**

a. Determine the number of equivalent units of production.

b. Determine the product cost per equivalent unit.

c. Allocate the total cost between ending work in process inventory and units transferred to the sewing department.

d. Record the transactions in a partial set of T-accounts.

**LO 5**

## Problem 12-20B  *Process costing system*

Seguin Paper Products Corporation produces paper cups using two production departments, printing and forming. Beginning balances and printing department data for 2011 follow.

| Accounts | Beginning Balances |
|---|---|
| Cash | $50,000 |
| Raw materials | 22,000 |
| Production supplies | 1,500 |
| Work in process inventory (300,000 units) | 17,000 |
| Common stock | 90,500 |

1. Seguin Paper Products issued additional common stock for $110,000 cash.

2. The company purchased raw materials and production supplies for $40,000 and $3,500, respectively, in cash.

3. The company issued $57,000 of raw materials and $3,600 of production supplies to the printing department for the production of 800,000 paper cups.

4. The printing department used 6,200 hours of labor during 2011, consisting of 5,600 hours for direct labor and 600 hours for indirect labor. The average wage was $10 per hour. All the wages were paid in 2011 in cash.

5. The predetermined overhead rate was $0.25 per direct labor dollar.

6. Actual overhead costs other than indirect materials and indirect labor for the year amounted to $4,400, which was paid in cash.

7. The printing department completed 700,000 paper cups. The remaining cups were 50 percent complete.

8. The completed paper cups were transferred to the forming department.

9. The ending balance in the Production Supplies account was $1,400.

**Required**

a. Determine the number of equivalent units of production.

b. Determine the product cost per equivalent unit.

c. Allocate the total cost between the ending work in process inventory and units transferred to the forming department.

d. Record the transactions in T-accounts.

## Problem 12-21B  *Process costing system with second department*          LO 4, 5

Shin Gifts makes unique western gifts that are sold at souvenir shops. One of the company's more popular products is a ceramic eagle that is produced in a mass production process that entails two manufacturing stages. In the first production stage ceramic glass is heated and molded into the shape of the eagle by the Compression Department. Finally, color and artistic detail is applied to the eagle by the Finishing Department. The company has just hired a new accountant who will be responsible for preparing the Cost of Production Report for June 2011. The accountant is given the following information from which to prepare his report.

Departmental Cost Information for June:

|  | Compression | Finishing |
| --- | --- | --- |
| Costs in beginning inventory | $ 3,000 | $14,400 |
| Costs added during June: |  |  |
| Materials | 42,000 | 18,120 |
| Labor | 20,000 | 13,200 |
| Overhead | 90,000 | 62,000 |

Departmental Product Information for June:

|  | Compression | Finishing |
| --- | --- | --- |
| Units in beginning inventory | 10,000 | 3,600 |
| Units started | 52,000 | 46,000 |
| Units in ending inventory | 16,000 (25% complete) | 9,600 (80% complete) |

**Required**

a. Prepare a Cost of Production Report for the Compression Department for June.

b. Prepare a Cost of Production Report for the Finishing Department for June.

c. If 24,000 units are sold in June for $160,000, determine the company's gross margin for June.

## ANALYZE, THINK, COMMUNICATE

### ATC 12-1  Business Application Case  *Comprehensive job-order costing problem*

This problem covers concepts that were presented in Chapters 11 and 12 concerning job-order costing systems.

Mid-Life Motorcycles (MLM) is a small shop that builds customized motorcycles, mostly for middle-aged men with significant discretionary income, who are hoping to fulfill a high-school dream. Since it works with high-end clients, all of its work is custom, and it makes many of the bike parts, including the frames, in-house. Other parts, such as the engine, are purchased from outside suppliers and then modified in-house. Although most of its bikes are created to-order for a specific individual, the shop occasionally builds a bike with no prearranged buyer. These bikes are sometimes intended to be entered in custom-bike contest and then sold afterwards.

The shop has been in existence for 10 years, but for the sake of simplicity, assume it has no beginning inventories for 2011. Five motorcycle projects were worked on during 2011. By the end of the year, four of these projects were completed and three of these four were sold.

The following selected data are from MLM's 2011 *budget:*

| | |
|---|---:|
| Advertising | $ 5,000 |
| Direct materials | 150,000 |
| Direct labor | 130,000 |
| Rent on office space | 6,000 |
| Rent on factory space | 20,000 |
| Indirect materials | 11,000 |
| Maintenance costs for factory equipment | 3,000 |
| Utilities costs for office space | 1,000 |
| Utilities costs for factory space | 2,000 |
| Depreciation on factory equipment | 8,000 |
| Machine hours expected to be worked | 4,000 |
| Direct labor hours expected to be worked | 6,500 |

The following information relates to production events during 2011.

■ Raw materials were purchased for $155,000.

■ Materials used in production totaled $150,800; $11,500 of these were considered indirect materials costs. The remaining $139,300 of direct materials costs related to individual restoration jobs as follows:

| Job Number | Direct Materials Cost |
|:---:|:---:|
| 115 | $28,200 |
| 116 | 32,100 |
| 117 | 25,800 |
| 118 | 31,700 |
| 119 | 21,500 |

■ Labor costs incurred for production totaled $133,100. The workers are highly skilled craftsmen who require little supervision. Therefore all of these were considered direct labor costs and related to individual restoration jobs as follows:

| Job Number | Direct Labor Cost |
|:---:|:---:|
| 115 | $30,900 |
| 116 | 29,300 |
| 117 | 22,100 |
| 118 | 36,600 |
| 119 | 14,200 |

■ Paid factory rent of $18,000.

■ Recorded depreciation on factory equipment of $8,500.

■ Made $2,500 of payments to outside vendors for maintenance of factory equipment.

■ Paid factory utilities costs of $2,400.

■ Applied manufacturing overhead using a predetermined rate of $11.00 per machine hour. The 3,750 machine hours that were used relate to each job as follows:

| Job Number | Machine Hours Worked |
|------------|----------------------|
| 115 | 850 |
| 116 | 720 |
| 117 | 870 |
| 118 | 900 |
| 119 | 410 |

■ Completed all restoration jobs except 119 and transferred the projects to finished goods.

■ Sold three jobs for the following amounts:

| Job Number | Sales Price |
|------------|-------------|
| 115 | $88,900 |
| 116 | $93,000 |
| 117 | $74,800 |

■ Closed the Manufacturing Overhead account to transfer any overapplied or underapplied overhead to the Cost of Goods Sold account.

### Required

**a.** Assume MLM had used direct labor hours (versus machine hours) as its cost driver. Compute its predetermined overhead rate.

**b.** Determine the ending balance in Raw Materials Inventory.

**c.** Determine the ending balance in Finished Goods Inventory.

**d.** Determine the ending balance in Work in Process Inventory.

**e.** Determine the costs of goods manufactured.

**f.** Determine the amount of Cost of Goods Sold.

**g.** Determine the amount of gross margin that was earned on Jobs 115, 116, and 117.

**h.** Determine the amount of overapplied or underapplied overhead the existed at the end of the year.

*Hint:* Though not required, you might find it helpful to organize the data using a horizontal financial statements model, although it will still be necessary to prepare job cost sheet for each individual job.

## ATC 12-2   Group Assignment   *Job-order costing system*

Bowen Bridge Company constructs bridges for the State of Kentucky. During 2010, Bowen started work on three bridges. The cost of materials and labor for each bridge follows.

| Special Orders | Materials | Labor |
|----------------|-----------|-------|
| Bridge 305 | $407,200 | $352,700 |
| Bridge 306 | 362,300 | 375,000 |
| Bridge 307 | 801,700 | 922,800 |

The predetermined overhead rate is $1.20 per direct labor dollar. Actual overhead costs were $2,170,800. Bridge 306 was completed for a contract price of $1,357,000 and was turned over to the state. Construction on Bridge 305 was also completed but the state had not yet finished its inspection process. General selling and administrative expenses amounted to $210,000. Over- or underapplied overhead is closed directly to the Cost of Goods Sold account. The company recognizes revenue when it turns over a completed bridge to a customer.

**Required**

a. Divide the class into groups of four or five students each and organize the groups into three sections. Assign Task 1 to the first section of groups, Task 2 to the second section, and Task 3 to the third section.

**Group Tasks**

(1) Determine the cost of construction for Bridge 305.

(2) Determine the cost of construction for Bridge 306.

(3) Determine the cost of construction for Bridge 307.

b. Select a spokesperson from each section. Use input from the three spokespersons to prepare an income statement and the asset section of the balance sheet.

c. Does the net income accurately reflect the profitability associated with Bridge 306? Explain.

d. Would converting to a process costing system improve the accuracy of the amount of reported net income? Explain.

### ATC 12-3    Research Assignment    *Identifying appropriate product costing systems for three real world companies*

Obtain the Form 10-Ks for these three companies: AGCO Corporation, Crown Holdings, Inc., and Noble Corporation. To obtain the Form 10-Ks you can use either the EDGAR system following the instructions in Appendix A, or they can be found on the companies' websites: www.agcocorp.com (Investors), www.crowncork.com (For Investors), and www.noblecorp.com (Investor Relations). Read the "Item 1. Business" sections of their 10-Ks in order to understand the nature of these companies' businesses.

**Required**

For each company, determine if it primarily uses a job-order or process costing system to compute the cost of the products or services it sells. Explain the rationale for your answer. If you believe a company uses elements of both job-order and process costing systems, a hybrid system, explain the rationale for that conclusion.

### ATC 12-4    Writing Assignment    *Determining the proper costing system*

Professor Julia Silverman received the following e-mail message.

"I don't know if you remember me. I am Tim Wallace. I was in your introductory accounting class a couple of years ago. I recently graduated and have just started my first real job. I remember you talking about job-order and process costing systems. I even looked the subject up in the textbook you wrote. In that book, you say that a process costing system is used when a company produces a single, homogeneous, high-volume, low-cost product. Well, the company I am working for makes T-shirts. All of the shirts are the same. They don't cost much, and we make nearly a million of them every year. The only difference in any of the shirts is the label we sew in them. We make the shirts for about 20 different companies. It seems to me that we should be using a process costing system. Even so, our accounting people are using a job-order costing system. Unfortunately, you didn't tell us what to do when the company we work for is screwed up. I need some advice. Should I tell them they are using the wrong accounting system? I know I am new around here, and I don't want to offend anybody, but if your book is right, the company would be better off if it started using a process costing system. Some of these people around here didn't go to college, and I'm afraid they don't know what they are doing. I guess that's why they hired someone with a degree. Am I right about this or what?"

**Required**

Assume that you are Professor Silverman. Write a return e-mail responding to Mr. Wallace's inquiry.

## ATC 12-5    Ethical Dilemma    *Amount of equivalent units*

René Alverez knew she was in over her head soon after she took the job. Even so, the opportunity for promotion comes along rarely and she believed that she would grow into it. Ms. Alverez is the cost accounting specialist assigned to the finishing department of Standard Tool Company. Bill Sawyer, the manager of the finishing department, knows exactly what he is doing. In each of the three years he has managed the department, the cost per unit of product transferred out of his Work in Process Inventory account has declined. His ability to control cost is highly valued, and it is widely believed that he will be the successor to the plant manager, who is being promoted to manufacturing vice president. One more good year would surely seal the deal for Mr. Sawyer. It was little wonder that Ms. Alverez was uncomfortable in challenging Mr. Sawyer's estimate of the percentage of completion of the department's ending inventory. He contended that the inventory was 60 percent complete, but she believed that it was only about 40 percent complete.

After a brief altercation, Ms. Alverez agreed to sign off on Mr. Sawyer's estimate. The truth was that although she believed she was right, she did not know how to support her position. Besides, Mr. Sawyer was about to be named plant manager, and she felt it unwise to challenge such an important person.

The department had beginning inventory of 5,500 units of product and it started 94,500 units during the period. It transferred out 90,000 units during the period. Total transferred-in and production cost for the period was $902,400. This amount included the cost in beginning inventory plus additional costs incurred during the period. The target (standard) cost per unit is $9.45.

**Required**

a.  Determine the equivalent cost per unit, assuming that the ending inventory is considered to be 40 percent complete.

b.  Determine the equivalent cost per unit, assuming that the ending inventory is considered to be 60 percent complete.

c.  Comment on Mr. Sawyer's motives for establishing the percentage of completion at 60 percent rather than 40 percent.

d.  Assuming that Ms. Alverez is a certified management accountant, would informing the chief accountant of her dispute with Mr. Sawyer violate the confidentiality standards of ethical conduct in Exhibit 1.15 of Chapter 1?

e.  Did Ms. Alverez violate any of the standards of ethical conduct in Exhibit 1.15 of Chapter 1? If so, which ones?

f.  Discuss the components of the fraud triangle that affected Ms. Alverez's behavior.

## ATC 12-6    Spreadsheet Assignment    *Using Excel*

Lewis Company had 8,000 units of product in work in process inventory at the beginning of the period and started 16,000 units during the period. At the end of the period, 4,000 units remained in work in process. The ending work in process inventory was estimated to be 40 percent complete. The cost of the units in beginning work in process inventory was $22,080. During the period, $38,400 of product costs were added.

**Required**

a.  Construct a spreadsheet that incorporates the preceding data into a table. The following screen capture is an example.

b.  Insert a section into the spreadsheet to calculate total manufacturing costs.

c.  Insert a section into the spreadsheet to calculate equivalent units and cost per equivalent unit.

**d.** Insert a section into the spreadsheet to allocate the manufacturing costs between finished goods and ending work in process.

**Spreadsheet Tip**

(1) The cells that contain numbers below row 7 should all be formulas so that changes to the data in rows 3 to 6 will automatically be reflected in the rest of the spreadsheet.

**ATC 12-7**   Spreadsheet Assignment   *Mastering Excel*

Refer to the job cost sheet in Exhibit 12.3.

**Required**

Construct a spreadsheet that recreates the job cost sheet in Exhibit 12.3. Use formulas wherever possible, such as in the total row.

**Spreadsheet Tips**

(1) Center the headings for direct materials, direct labor, and applied overhead across two or three columns by choosing Format and Cells and checking the Merge box under the alignment tab. A shortcut to center these is to click on the Merge and Center icon in the formatting tool bar.

(2) All lines in the job cost sheet can be drawn using Format and Cells and then choosing the border tab.

## COMPREHENSIVE PROBLEM

This is a continuation of the comprehensive problem in Chapter 11. During 2012, Anywhere, Inc. (AI), incurred the following product costs.

| | |
|---|---|
| Raw materials | $62,000 |
| Labor | 89,422 |
| Overhead | 58,000 |

Recall that the 2011 ending balance in the Work in Process (WIP) account was $26,000. Accordingly, this is the beginning WIP balance for 2012. There were 110 units of product in beginning WIP inventory. AI started 1,840 units of product during 2012. Ending WIP inventory consisted of 90 units that were 60 percent complete.

## Required

Prepare a cost of production report by filling in the cells that contain question marks.

---

### Equivalent Unit Computations

| | Units | % Complete | Equivalent Units |
|---|---|---|---|
| Beginning inventory | 110 | | |
| Units started | 1,840 | | |
| Total units available for completion | ? | | |
| Units in ending inventory | (90) | ? | ? |
| Units complete | 1,860 | 100% | ? |
| Total equivalent units | | | 1,914 |

### Cost per Equivalent Unit

| | Cost | ÷ | Units | = | Cost Per Unit |
|---|---|---|---|---|---|
| Beginning inventory | $26,000 | | | | |
| Raw materials | ? | | | | |
| Labor | ? | | | | |
| Overhead | 58,000 | | | | |
| Total product cost | ? | ÷ | 1,914 | = | ? |

### Allocation of Product Cost

| | |
|---|---|
| Cost transferred to finished goods | ? |
| Cost in ending inventory | ? |
| Total product cost | $235,422 |

## CHAPTER 13

# Financial Statement Analysis

## LEARNING OBJECTIVES

**After you have mastered the material in this chapter you will be able to:**

1 Describe factors associated with communicating useful information.

2 Differentiate between horizontal and vertical analysis.

3 Explain ratio analysis.

4 Calculate ratios for assessing a company's liquidity.

5 Calculate ratios for assessing a company's solvency.

6 Calculate ratios for assessing company management's effectiveness.

7 Calculate ratios for assessing a company's position in the stock market.

8 Explain the limitations of financial statement analysis.

## CHAPTER OPENING

Expressing financial statement information in the form of ratios enhances its usefulness. Ratios permit comparisons over time and among companies, highlighting similarities, differences, and trends. Proficiency with common financial statement analysis techniques benefits both internal and external users. Before beginning detailed explanations of numerous ratios and percentages, however, we consider factors relevant to communicating useful information.

# The Curious Accountant

On September 7, 2009, Kraft Foods, Inc., announced that it had made an offer to the board of directors of **Cadbury PLC** to purchase their company for $16.7 billion in cash and stock. The CEO of Cadbury promptly rejected the offer, and a four month war of words began. Among other things, Cadbury's CEO described Kraft as an "unfocused conglomerate," with "unappealing categories," and hav-ing "a management that underperforms." He said that Kraft's offer greatly undervalued Cadbury. Meanwhile, the CEO of Kraft said its offer for Cadbury was "full and fair." Upon making its offer to Cadbury's board, Kraft also stipulated that if the board did not accept the offer by January 20, 2010, Kraft would make its offer to buy the company's stock directly to Cadbury's shareholders.

When a company makes a bid for one of its competitors, it often causes other companies to enter the bidding process. Analysts predicted that **Hershey** and **Nestle** would soon make their own offers for Cadbury. These offers did not materialize, although there were rumors that Hershey was preparing to make an offer of $18.8 billion.

On the morning of January 19, 2010, the last day before Kraft planned to take its offer directly to Cadbury's shareholders, the two companies announced they had reached an agreement. Kraft would buy Cadbury for $19.4 billion.

If after four months of waiting for Cadbury to accept its offer no other company was willing to make a compet-ing bid for Cadbury, why whould Kraft agree to buy it at a price that was 16 percent higher than its original offer? (Answer on page 591.)

Describe factors associated with communicating useful information.

# FACTORS IN COMMUNICATING USEFUL INFORMATION

The primary objective of accounting is to provide information useful for decision making. To provide information that supports this objective, accountants must consider the intended users, the types of decisions users make with financial statement information, and available means of analyzing the information.

## The Users

Users of financial statement information include managers, creditors, stockholders, potential investors, and regulatory agencies. These individuals and organizations use financial statements for different purposes and bring varying levels of sophistication to understanding business activities. For example, investors range from private individuals who know little about financial statements to large investment brokers and institutional investors capable of using complex statistical analysis techniques. At what level of user knowledge should financial statements be aimed? Condensing and reporting complex business transactions at a level easily understood by nonprofessional investors is increasingly difficult. Current reporting standards target users that have a reasonably informed knowledge of business, though that level of sophistication is difficult to define.

## The Types of Decisions

Just as the knowledge level of potential users varies, the information needs of users varies, depending on the decision at hand. A supplier considering whether or not to sell goods on account to a particular company wants to evaluate the likelihood of getting paid; a potential investor in that company wants to predict the likelihood of increases in the market value of the company's common stock. Financial statements, however, are designed for general purposes; they are not aimed at any specific user group. Some disclosed information, therefore, may be irrelevant to some users but vital to others. Users must employ different forms of analysis to identify information most relevant to a particular decision.

Financial statements can provide only highly summarized economic information. The costs to a company of providing excessively detailed information would be prohibitive. In addition, too much detail leads to **information overload,** the problem of having so much data that important information becomes obscured by trivial information. Users faced with reams of data may become so frustrated attempting to use it that they lose the value of *key* information that is provided.

## Information Analysis

Because of the diversity of users, their different levels of knowledge, the varying information needs for particular decisions, and the general nature of financial statements, a variety of analysis techniques has been developed. In the following sections, we explain several common methods of analysis. The choice of method depends on which technique appears to provide the most relevant information in a given situation.

# METHODS OF ANALYSIS

Differentiate between horizontal and vertical analysis.

Financial statement analysis should focus primarily on isolating information useful for making a particular decision. The information required can take many forms but usually involves comparisons, such as comparing changes in the same item for the same company over a number of years, comparing key relationships within the same year, or comparing the operations of several different companies in the same industry. This chapter discusses three categories of analysis methods: horizontal, vertical, and ratio. Exhibits 13.1 and 13.2 present comparative financial statements for Milavec Company. We refer to these statements in the examples of analysis techniques.

## EXHIBIT 13.1

### MILAVEC COMPANY
Income Statements and Statements of
Retained Earnings
For the Years Ending December 31

|  | 2012 | 2011 |
|---|---|---|
| Sales | $900,000 | $800,000 |
| Cost of goods sold |  |  |
| Beginning inventory | 43,000 | 40,000 |
| Purchases | 637,000 | 483,000 |
| Goods available for sale | 680,000 | 523,000 |
| Ending inventory | 70,000 | 43,000 |
| Cost of goods sold | 610,000 | 480,000 |
| Gross margin | 290,000 | 320,000 |
| Operating expenses | 248,000 | 280,000 |
| Income before taxes | 42,000 | 40,000 |
| Income taxes | 17,000 | 18,000 |
| Net income | 25,000 | 22,000 |
| Plus: Retained earnings, |  |  |
| beginning balance | 137,000 | 130,000 |
| Less: Dividends | 0 | 15,000 |
| Retained earnings, |  |  |
| ending balance | $162,000 | $137,000 |

## EXHIBIT 13.2

### MILAVEC COMPANY
Balance Sheets
As of December 31

|  | 2012 | 2011 |
|---|---|---|
| **Assets** |  |  |
| Cash | $ 20,000 | $ 17,000 |
| Marketable securities | 20,000 | 22,000 |
| Notes receivable | 4,000 | 3,000 |
| Accounts receivable | 50,000 | 56,000 |
| Merchandise inventory | 70,000 | 43,000 |
| Prepaid expenses | 4,000 | 4,000 |
| Property, plant, and |  |  |
| equipment (net) | 340,000 | 310,000 |
| Total assets | $508,000 | $455,000 |
| **Liabilities and Stockholders' Equity** |  |  |
| Accounts payable | $ 40,000 | $ 38,000 |
| Salaries payable | 2,000 | 3,000 |
| Taxes payable | 4,000 | 2,000 |
| Bonds payable, 8% | 100,000 | 100,000 |
| Preferred stock, 6%, |  |  |
| $100 par, cumulative | 50,000 | 50,000 |
| Common stock, $10 par | 150,000 | 125,000 |
| Retained earnings | 162,000 | 137,000 |
| Total liabilities and |  |  |
| stockholders' equity | $508,000 | $455,000 |

## Horizontal Analysis

**Horizontal analysis,** also called **trend analysis,** refers to studying the behavior of individual financial statement items over several accounting periods. These periods may be several quarters within the same fiscal year or they may be several different years. The analysis of a given item may focus on trends in the absolute dollar amount of the item or trends in percentages. For example, a user may observe that revenue increased from one period to the next by $42 million (an absolute dollar amount) or that it increased by a percentage such as 15 percent.

### Absolute Amounts

The **absolute amounts** of particular financial statement items have many uses. Various national economic statistics, such as gross domestic product and the amount spent to replace productive capacity, are derived by combining absolute amounts reported by businesses. Financial statement users with expertise in particular industries might evaluate amounts reported for research and development costs to judge whether a company is spending excessively or conservatively. Users are particularly concerned with how amounts change over time. For example, a user might compare a pharmaceutical company's revenue before and after the patent expired on one of its drugs.

Comparing only absolute amounts has drawbacks, however, because *materiality* levels differ from company to company or even from year to year for a given company. The **materiality** of information refers to its relative importance. An item is considered material if knowledge of it would influence the decision of a reasonably informed user. Generally accepted accounting principles permit companies to account for *immaterial* items in the most convenient way, regardless of technical accounting rules. For example, companies may expense, rather than capitalize and depreciate, relatively inexpensive long-term assets like pencil sharpeners or waste baskets even if the assets have useful lives of many years. The concept of materiality, which has both quantitative and qualitative aspects, underlies all accounting principles.

It is difficult to judge the materiality of an absolute financial statement amount without considering the size of the company reporting it. For reporting purposes, **Exxon Corporation**'s financial statements are rounded to the nearest million dollars. For Exxon, a $400,000 increase in sales is not material. For a small company, however, $400,000 could represent total sales, a highly material amount. Meaningful comparisons between the two companies' operating performance are impossible using only absolute amounts. Users can surmount these difficulties with percentage analysis.

### Percentage Analysis

**Percentage analysis** involves computing the percentage relationship between two amounts. In horizontal percentage analysis, a financial statement item is expressed as a percentage of the previous balance for the same item. Percentage analysis sidesteps the materiality problems of comparing different size companies by measuring changes in percentages rather than absolute amounts. Each change is converted to a percentage of the base year. Exhibit 13.3 presents a condensed version of Milavec's income statement with horizontal percentages for each item.

The percentage changes disclose that, even though Milavec's net income increased slightly more than sales, products may be underpriced. Cost of goods sold increased much more than sales, resulting in a lower gross margin. Users would also want to investigate why operating expenses decreased substantially despite the increase in sales.

Whether basing their analyses on absolute amounts, percentages, or ratios, users must avoid drawing overly simplistic conclusions about the reasons for the results. Numerical relationships flag conditions requiring further study. Recall that a change that appears favorable on the surface may not necessarily be a good sign. Users must evaluate the underlying reasons for the change.

**EXHIBIT 13.3**

## MILAVEC COMPANY
### Comparative Income Statements
### For the Years Ending December 31

|  | 2012 | 2011 | Percentage Difference |
|---|---|---|---|
| Sales | $900,000 | $800,000 | +12.5%* |
| Cost of goods sold | 610,000 | 480,000 | +27.1 |
| Gross margin | 290,000 | 320,000 | −9.4 |
| Operating expenses | 248,000 | 280,000 | −11.4 |
| Income before taxes | 42,000 | 40,000 | +5.0 |
| Income taxes | 17,000 | 18,000 | −5.6 |
| Net income | $ 25,000 | $ 22,000 | +13.6 |

*($900,000 − $800,000) ÷ $800,000; all changes expressed as percentages of previous totals.

---

## ✓ CHECK YOURSELF 13.1

The following information was drawn from the annual reports of two retail companies (amounts are shown in millions). One company is an upscale department store; the other is a discount store. Based on this limited information, identify which company is the upscale department store.

|  | Jenkins Co. | Horn's, Inc. |
|---|---|---|
| Sales | $325 | $680 |
| Cost of goods sold | 130 | 408 |
| Gross margin | $195 | $272 |

**Answer**   Jenkins' gross margin represents 60 percent ($195 ÷ $325) of sales. Horn's gross margin represents 40 percent ($272 ÷ $680) of sales. Since an upscale department store would have higher margins than a discount store, the data suggest that Jenkins is the upscale department store.

## Answers to The Curious Accountant

Obviously Kraft agreed to acquire Cadbury because it believed it could make a profit on the investment. Two major reasons were discussed as to why Kraft would want Cadbury. First, Cadbury was a bigger player than Kraft in important markets outside of the United States. Owning Cadbury would make it easier for Kraft to expand globally, especially in several rapidly developing markets, including Egypt, India, Mexico, and Thailand. Second, in 2008, Mars, Inc. had acquired the giant chewing gum company, Wm. Wrigley Jr. Company, making it a much larger confectionary company. By purchasing Cadbury, Kraft felt it could better compete with Mars.

Kraft's optimism about its purchase of Cadbury does not guarantee that the investment will be successful. In the late 1980s and early 1990s Hershey's purchased several Dutch, German, and Italian confectionary companies that, a few years later, it sold at losses. How do companies decide what another company is worth, and how can such successful companies as Hershey, Nestlé, Kraft, and Cadbury have such different opinions about the value of an investment? Valuing a potential investment is the result of extensive financial analysis, as discussed in this chapter, and capital budgeting techniques, discussed in Chapter 10. As you have seen in these chapters, such decision making is based on estimates about future events. Predicting the future is imperfect, no matter how well trained the forecaster might be.

Does this mean that financial analysis is useless? No. Consider someone planning to drive across the United States. Would they prefer to take the trip with a map or without? Obviously they would prefer to have a map or GPS, even though they know neither device is perfect. Similarly, just as five different financial analysts may reach five different amounts they think a company is worth; five individuals planning a trip from Key West, Florida, to Anchorage Alaska, could look at the same map and decide on five different ways to get there. Only after the trips have been completed can we say which person made the best decision.

Sources: "Cadbury Sour on Kraft Bid," *The Wall Street Journal*, September 8, 2009, pp. A–1 and A–17, "Nestlé's Undercooked Deal Making," *The Wall Street Journal*, January 9 & 10, 2010, pp. B–10, "Kraft Near Deal for Cadbury," *The Wall Street Journal*, January 19, 2010, pp. A–1 and A–6, "Kraft Wins a Reluctant Cadbury with Help of Clock, Hedge Funds," *The Wall Street Journal*, January 20, 2010, pp. B–1 and B–6, and "Hershey, On Its Own, Has Limited Options," *The Wall Street Journal*, January 20, 2010, p. B–6.

When comparing more than two periods, analysts use either of two basic approaches: (1) choosing one base year from which to calculate all increases or decreases or (2) calculating each period's percentage change from the preceding figure. For example, assume Milavec's sales for 2009 and 2010 were $600,000 and $750,000, respectively.

|  | 2012 | 2011 | 2010 | 2009 |
|---|---|---|---|---|
| Sales | $900,000 | $800,000 | $750,000 | $600,000 |
| Increase over 2009 sales | 50.0% | 33.3% | 25.0% | — |
| Increase over preceding year | 12.5% | 6.7% | 25.0% | — |

Analysis discloses that Milavec's 2012 sales represented a 50 percent increase over 2009 sales, and a large increase (25 percent) occurred in 2010. From 2010 to 2011, sales increased only 6.7 percent but in the following year increased much more (12.5 percent).

## Vertical Analysis

**Vertical analysis** uses percentages to compare individual components of financial statements to a key statement figure. Horizontal analysis compares items over many time periods; vertical analysis compares many items within the same time period.

### Vertical Analysis of the Income Statement

Vertical analysis of an income statement (also called a *common size* income statement) involves converting each income statement component to a percentage of sales. Although vertical analysis suggests examining only one period, it is useful to compare common size income statements for several years. Exhibit 13.4 presents Milavec's income statements, along with vertical percentages, for 2012 and 2011. This analysis discloses that cost of goods sold increased significantly as a percentage of sales. Operating expenses and income taxes, however, decreased in relation to sales. Each of these observations indicates a need for more analysis regarding possible trends for future profits.

### EXHIBIT 13.4

**MILAVEC COMPANY**
Vertical Analysis of Comparative Income Statements

|  | 2012 | | 2011 | |
|  | Amount | Percentage* of Sales | Amount | Percentage* of Sales |
|---|---|---|---|---|
| Sales | $900,000 | 100.0% | $800,000 | 100.0% |
| Cost of goods sold | 610,000 | 67.8 | 480,000 | 60.0 |
| Gross margin | 290,000 | 32.2 | 320,000 | 40.0 |
| Operating expenses | 248,000 | 27.6 | 280,000 | 35.0 |
| Income before taxes | 42,000 | 4.7 | 40,000 | 5.0 |
| Income taxes | 17,000 | 1.9 | 18,000 | 2.3 |
| Net income | $ 25,000 | 2.8% | $ 22,000 | 2.8% |

*Percentages may not add exactly due to rounding.

### Vertical Analysis of the Balance Sheet

Vertical analysis of the balance sheet involves converting each balance sheet component to a percentage of total assets. The vertical analysis of Milavec's balance sheets in Exhibit 13.5 discloses few large percentage changes from the preceding year. Even small individual percentage changes, however, may represent substantial dollar increases. For example, inventory constituted 9.5% of total assets in 2011 and 13.8% in 2012. While this appears to be a small increase, it actually represents a 62.8% increase in the inventory account balance [($70,000 − $43,000) ÷ $43,000] from 2011 to 2012. Careful analysis requires considering changes in both percentages *and* absolute amounts.

## RATIO ANALYSIS

**LO 3**

Explain ratio analysis.

**Ratio analysis** involves studying various relationships between different items reported in a set of financial statements. For example, net earnings (net income) reported on the income statement may be compared to total assets reported on the balance sheet. Analysts calculate many different ratios for a wide variety of purposes. The remainder of this chapter is devoted to discussing some of the more commonly used ratios.

**EXHIBIT 13.5**

### MILAVEC COMPANY
#### Vertical Analysis of Comparative Balance Sheets

|  | 2012 | Percentage* of Total | 2011 | Percentage* of Total |
|---|---|---|---|---|
| **Assets** | | | | |
| Cash | $ 20,000 | 3.9% | $ 17,000 | 3.7% |
| Marketable securities | 20,000 | 3.9 | 22,000 | 4.8 |
| Notes receivable | 4,000 | 0.8 | 3,000 | 0.7 |
| Accounts receivable | 50,000 | 9.8 | 56,000 | 12.3 |
| Merchandise inventory | 70,000 | 13.8 | 43,000 | 9.5 |
| Prepaid expenses | 4,000 | 0.8 | 4,000 | 0.9 |
| Total current assets | 168,000 | 33.1 | 145,000 | 31.9 |
| Property, plant, and equipment | 340,000 | 66.9 | 310,000 | 68.1 |
| Total assets | $508,000 | 100.0% | $455,000 | 100.0% |
| **Liabilities and Stockholders' Equity** | | | | |
| Accounts payable | $ 40,000 | 7.9% | $ 38,000 | 8.4% |
| Salaries payable | 2,000 | 0.4 | 3,000 | 0.7 |
| Taxes payable | 4,000 | 0.8 | 2,000 | 0.4 |
| Total current liabilities | 46,000 | 9.1 | 43,000 | 9.5 |
| Bonds payable, 8% | 100,000 | 19.7 | 100,000 | 22.0 |
| Total liabilities | 146,000 | 28.7 | 143,000 | 31.4 |
| Preferred stock 6%, $100 par | 50,000 | 9.8 | 50,000 | 11.0 |
| Common stock, $10 par | 150,000 | 29.5 | 125,000 | 27.5 |
| Retained earnings | 162,000 | 31.9 | 137,000 | 30.1 |
| Total stockholders' equity | 362,000 | 71.3 | 312,000 | 68.6 |
| Total liabilities and stockholders' equity | $508,000 | 100.0% | $455,000 | 100.0% |

*Percentages may not add exactly due to rounding.

## Objectives of Ratio Analysis

As suggested earlier, various users approach financial statement analysis with many different objectives. Creditors are interested in whether a company will be able to repay its debts on time. Both creditors and stockholders are concerned with how the company is financed, whether through debt, equity, or earnings. Stockholders and potential investors analyze past earnings performance and dividend policy for clues to the future value of their investments. In addition to using internally generated data to analyze operations, company managers find much information prepared for external purposes useful for examining past operations and planning future policies. Although many of these objectives are interrelated, it is convenient to group ratios into categories such as measures of debt-paying ability and measures of profitability.

## MEASURES OF DEBT-PAYING ABILITY

### Liquidity Ratios

**Liquidity ratios** indicate a company's ability to pay short-term debts. They focus on current assets and current liabilities. The examples in the following section use the financial statement information reported by Milavec Company.

LO 4

Calculate ratios for assessing a company's liquidity.

## *Working Capital*

**Working capital** is current assets minus current liabilities. Current assets include assets most likely to be converted into cash in the current operating period. Current liabilities represent debts that must be satisfied in the current period. Working capital therefore measures the excess funds the company will have available for operations, excluding any new funds it generates during the year. Think of working capital as the cushion against short-term debt-paying problems. Working capital at the end of 2012 and 2011 for Milavec Company was as follows.

|  | 2012 | 2011 |
|---|---|---|
| Current assets | $168,000 | $145,000 |
| − Current liabilities | 46,000 | 43,000 |
| Working capital | $122,000 | $102,000 |

Milavec's working capital increased from 2011 to 2012, but the numbers themselves say little. Whether $122,000 is sufficient or not depends on such factors as the industry in which Milavec operates, its size, and the maturity dates of its current obligations. We can see, however, that the increase in working capital is primarily due to the increase in inventories.

## *Current Ratio*

Working capital is an absolute amount. Its usefulness is limited by the materiality difficulties discussed earlier. It is hard to draw meaningful conclusions from comparing Milavec's working capital of $122,000 with another company that also has working capital of $122,000. By expressing the relationship between current assets and current liabilities as a ratio, however, we have a more useful measure of the company's debt-paying ability relative to other companies. The **current ratio,** also called the **working capital ratio,** is calculated as follows.

$$\text{Current ratio} = \frac{\text{Current assets}}{\text{Current liabilities}}$$

To illustrate using the current ratio for comparisons, consider Milavec's current position relative to Laroque's, a larger firm with current assets of $500,000 and current liabilities of $378,000.

|  | Milavec | Laroque |
|---|---|---|
| Current assets (a) | $168,000 | $500,000 |
| − Current liabilities (b) | 46,000 | 378,000 |
| Working capital | $122,000 | $122,000 |
| Current ratio (a ÷ b) | 3.65:1 | 1.32:1 |

The current ratio is expressed as the number of dollars of current assets for each dollar of current liabilities. In the above example, both companies have the same amount of working capital. Milavec, however, appears to have a much stronger working capital position. Any conclusions from this analysis must take into account the circumstances of the particular companies; there is no single ideal current ratio that suits all companies. In recent years the average current ratio of the nonfinancial companies that constitute the Dow Jones Industrial Average was around 1.29:1. The individual company ratios, however, ranged from .33:1 to 3.24:1. A current ratio can be too high. Money invested in factories and developing new products is usually more profitable than money held as large cash balances or invested in inventory.

## Quick Ratio

The **quick ratio,** also known as the **acid-test ratio,** is a conservative variation of the current ratio. The quick ratio measures a company's *immediate* debt-paying ability. Only cash, receivables, and current marketable securities (*quick assets*) are included in the numerator. Less liquid current assets, such as inventories and prepaid expenses, are omitted. Inventories may take several months to sell; prepaid expenses reduce otherwise necessary expenditures but do not lead eventually to cash receipts. The quick ratio is computed as follows.

$$\text{Quick ratio} = \frac{\text{Quick assets}}{\text{Current liabilities}}$$

Milavec Company's current ratios and quick ratios for 2012 and 2011 follow.

|  | **2012** | **2011** |
|---|---|---|
| Current ratio | 168,000 ÷ 46,000 | 145,000 ÷ 43,000 |
|  | 3.65:1 | 3.37:1 |
| Quick ratio | 94,000 ÷ 46,000 | 98,000 ÷ 43,000 |
|  | 2.04:1 | 2.28:1 |

The decrease in the quick ratio from 2011 to 2012 reflects both a decrease in quick assets and an increase in current liabilities. The result indicates that the company is less liquid (has less ability to pay its short-term debt) in 2012 than it was in 2011.

## Accounts Receivable Ratios

Offering customers credit plays an enormous role in generating revenue, but it also increases expenses and delays cash receipts. To minimize bad debts expense and collect cash for use in current operations, companies want to collect receivables as quickly as possible without losing customers. Two relationships are often examined to assess a company's collection record: *accounts receivable turnover* and *average days to collect receivables (average collection period)*.

**Accounts receivable turnover** is calculated as follows.

$$\text{Accounts receivable turnover} = \frac{\text{Net credit sales}}{\text{Average accounts receivable}}$$

*Net credit sales* refers to total sales on account less sales discounts and returns. When most sales are credit sales or when a breakdown of total sales between cash sales and credit sales is not available, the analyst must use total sales in the numerator. The denominator is based on *net accounts receivable* (receivables after subtracting the allowance for doubtful accounts). Since the numerator represents a whole period, it is preferable to use average receivables in the denominator if possible. When comparative statements are available, the average can be based on the beginning and ending balances. Milavec Company's accounts receivable turnover is computed as follows.

|  | **2012** | **2011** |
|---|---|---|
| Net sales (assume all on account) (a) | $900,000 | $800,000 |
| Beginning receivables (b) | $ 56,000 | $ 55,000* |
| Ending receivables (c) | 50,000 | 56,000 |
| Average receivables (d) = (b + c) ÷ 2 | $ 53,000 | $ 55,500 |
| Accounts receivable turnover (a ÷ d) | 16.98 | 14.41 |

*The beginning receivables balance was drawn from the 2010 financial statements, which are not included in the illustration.

The 2012 accounts receivable turnover of 16.98 indicates Milavec collected its average receivables almost 17 times that year. The higher the turnover, the faster the collections. A company can have cash flow problems and lose substantial purchasing power if resources are tied up in receivables for long periods.

**Average days to collect receivables** is calculated as follows.

$$\text{Average days to collect receivables} = \frac{365 \text{ days}}{\text{Accounts receivable turnover}}$$

This ratio offers another way to look at turnover by showing the number of days, on average, it takes to collect a receivable. If receivables were collected 16.98 times in 2012, the average collection period was 21 days, 365 ÷ 16.98 (the number of days in the year divided by accounts receivable turnover). For 2011, it took an average of 25 days (365 ÷ 14.41) to collect a receivable.

Although the collection period improved, no other conclusions can be reached without considering the industry, Milavec's past performance, and the general economic environment. In recent years the average time to collect accounts receivable for the 26 nonfinancial companies that make up the Dow Jones Industrial Average was around 39 days. (Financial firms are excluded because, by the nature of their business, they have very long collection periods.)

### Inventory Ratios

A fine line exists between having too much and too little inventory in stock. Too little inventory can result in lost sales and costly production delays. Too much inventory can use needed space, increase financing and insurance costs, and become obsolete. To help analyze how efficiently a company manages inventory, we use two ratios similar to those used in analyzing accounts receivable.

**Inventory turnover** indicates the number of times, on average, that inventory is totally replaced during the year. The relationship is computed as follows.

$$\text{Inventory turnover} = \frac{\text{Cost of goods sold}}{\text{Average inventory}}$$

The average inventory is usually based on the beginning and ending balances that are shown in the financial statements. Inventory turnover for Milavec was as follows.

| | 2012 | 2011 |
|---|---|---|
| Cost of goods sold (a) | $610,000 | $480,000 |
| Beginning inventory (b) | $ 43,000 | $ 40,000* |
| Ending inventory (c) | 70,000 | 43,000 |
| Average inventory (d) = (b + c) ÷ 2 | $ 56,500 | $ 41,500 |
| Inventory turnover (a ÷ d) | 10.80 | 11.57 |

*The beginning inventory balance was drawn from the company's 2010 financial statements, which are not included in the illustration.

Generally, a higher turnover indicates that merchandise is being handled more efficiently. Trying to compare firms in different industries, however, can be misleading. Inventory turnover for grocery stores and many retail outlets is high. Because of the nature of the goods being sold, inventory turnover is much lower for appliance and jewelry stores. We look at this issue in more detail when we discuss return on investment.

**Average days to sell inventory** is determined by dividing the number of days in the year by the inventory turnover as follows.

$$\text{Average days to sell inventory} = \frac{365 \text{ days}}{\text{inventory turnover}}$$

The result approximates the number of days the firm could sell inventory without purchasing more. For Milavec, this figure was 34 days in 2012 (365 ÷ 10.80) and 32 days in 2011 (365 ÷ 11.57). In recent years it took around 70 days, on average, for the companies in the Dow Jones Industrial Average that have inventory to sell their inventory. The time it took individual companies to sell their inventory varied by industry, ranging from 7 days to 198 days.

## Solvency Ratios

**Solvency ratios** are used to analyze a company's long-term debt-paying ability and its financing structure. Creditors are concerned with a company's ability to satisfy outstanding obligations. The larger a company's liability percentage, the greater the risk that the company could fall behind or default on debt payments. Stockholders, too, are concerned about a company's solvency. If a company is unable to pay its debts, the owners could lose their investment. Each user group desires that company financing choices minimize its investment risk, whether the investment is in debt or stockholders' equity.

LO 5

Calculate ratios for assessing a company's solvency.

### Debt Ratios

The following ratios represent two different ways to express the same relationship. Both are frequently used.

**Debt to assets ratio.**    This ratio measures the percentage of a company's assets that are financed by debt.

**Debt to equity ratio.**    As used in this ratio, *equity* means stockholders' equity. The debt to equity ratio compares creditor financing to owner financing. It is expressed as the dollar amount of liabilities for each dollar of stockholders' equity.

These ratios are calculated as follows.

$$\text{Debt to assets} = \frac{\text{Total liabilities}}{\text{Total assets}}$$

$$\text{Debt to equity} = \frac{\text{Total liabilities}}{\text{Total stockholders' equity}}$$

Applying these formulas to Milavec Company's results produces the following.

|  | 2012 | 2011 |
|---|---|---|
| Total liabilities (a) | $146,000 | $143,000 |
| Total stockholders' equity (b) | 362,000 | 312,000 |
| Total equities (liabilities + stockholders' equity) (c) | $508,000 | $455,000 |
| Debt to assets (a ÷ c) | 29% | 31% |
| Debt to equity ratio (a ÷ b) | 0.40:1 | 0.46:1 |

Each year less than one-third of the company's assets were financed with debt. The amount of liabilities per dollar of stockholders' equity declined by 0.06. It is difficult to judge whether the reduced percentage of liabilities is favorable. In general, a lower level of liabilities provides greater security because the likelihood of bankruptcy is reduced. Perhaps, however, the company is financially strong enough to incur more liabilities and benefit from financial leverage. The 26 nonfinancial companies that make up the Dow Jones Industrial Average report around 38 percent of their assets, on average, are financed through borrowing. The debt to asset ratios of these companies ranged from 5 percent to 85 percent.

### Number of Times Interest Is Earned

This ratio measures the burden a company's interest payments represent. Users often consider times interest is earned along with the debt ratios when evaluating financial risk. The numerator of this ratio uses *earnings before interest and taxes (EBIT),* rather than net earnings, because the amount of earnings *before* interest and income taxes is available for paying interest.

$$\frac{\text{Number of times}}{\text{interest is earned}} = \frac{\text{Earnings before interest and taxes expense}}{\text{Interest expense}}$$

Dividing EBIT by interest expense indicates how many times the company could have made its interest payments. Obviously, interest is paid only once, but the more times it *could* be paid, the bigger the company's safety net. Although interest is paid from cash, not accrual earnings, it is standard practice to base this ratio on accrual-based EBIT, not a cash-based amount. For Milavec, this calculation is as follows.

|  | 2012 | 2011 |
|---|---|---|
| Income before taxes | $42,000 | $40,000 |
| Interest expense (b) | 8,000 | 8,000* |
| Income before taxes and interest (a) | $50,000 | $48,000 |
| Times interest earned (a ÷ b) | 6.25 times | 6 times |

*Interest on bonds: $100,000 × .08 = $8,000.

Any expense or dividend payment can be analyzed this way. Another frequently used calculation is the number of times the preferred dividend is earned. In that case, the numerator is net income (after taxes) and the denominator is the amount of the annual preferred dividend.

---

## ✓ CHECK YOURSELF 13.2

Selected data for Riverside Corporation and Academy Company follow (amounts are shown in millions).

|  | Riverside Corporation | Academy Company |
|---|---|---|
| Total liabilities (a) | $650 | $450 |
| Stockholders' equity (b) | 300 | 400 |
| Total liabilities + stockholders' equity (c) | $950 | $850 |
| Interest expense (d) | $ 65 | $ 45 |
| Income before taxes (e) | 140 | 130 |
| Income before taxes and interest (f) | $205 | $175 |

Based on this information alone, which company would likely obtain the less favorable interest rate on additional debt financing?

**Answer**   Interest rates vary with risk levels. Companies with less solvency (long-term debt-paying ability) generally must pay higher interest rates to obtain financing. Two solvency measures for the two companies follow. Recall:

Total assets = Liabilities + Stockholders' equity

|  | Riverside Corporation | Academy Company |
|---|---|---|
| Debt to assets ratio (a ÷ c) | 68.4% | 52.9% |
| Times interest earned (f ÷ d) | 3.15 times | 3.89 times |

Since Riverside has a higher percentage of debt and a lower times interest earned ratio, the data suggest that Riverside is less solvent than Academy. Riverside would therefore likely have to pay a higher interest rate to obtain additional financing.

*Plant Assets to Long-Term Liabilities*

Companies often pledge plant assets as collateral for long-term liabilities. Financial statement users may analyze a firm's ability to obtain long-term financing on the strength of its asset base. Effective financial management principles dictate that asset purchases should be financed over a time span about equal to the expected lives of the assets. Short-term assets should be financed with short-term liabilities; the current ratio, introduced earlier, indicates how well a company manages current debt. Long-lived assets should be financed with long-term liabilities, and the *plant assets to long-term liabilities* ratio suggests how well long-term debt is managed. It is calculated as follows.

$$\text{Plant assets to long-term liabilities} = \frac{\text{Net plant assets}}{\text{Long-term liabilities}}$$

For Milavec Company, these ratios follow.

|                                              | 2012      | 2011      |
|----------------------------------------------|-----------|-----------|
| Net plant assets (a)                         | $340,000  | $310,000  |
| Bonds payable (b)                            | 100,000   | 100,000   |
| Plant assets to long-term liabilities (a ÷ b)| 3.4:1     | 3.1:1     |

# MEASURES OF PROFITABILITY

*Profitability* refers to a company's ability to generate earnings. Both management and external users employ **profitability ratios** to assess a company's success in generating profits and how these profits are used to reward investors. Some of the many ratios available to measure different aspects of profitability are discussed in the following two sections.

## Measures of Managerial Effectiveness

The most common ratios used to evaluate managerial effectiveness measure what percentage of sales results in earnings and how productive assets are in generating those sales. As mentioned earlier, the *absolute amount* of sales or earnings means little without also considering company size.

**LO 6**

Calculate ratios for assessing company management's effectiveness.

*Net Margin (or Return on Sales)*

*Gross margin* and *gross profit* are alternate terms for the amount remaining after subtracting the expense cost of goods sold from sales. **Net margin,** sometimes called *operating margin, profit margin,* or the *return on sales ratio,* describes the percent remaining of each sales dollar after subtracting other expenses as well as cost of goods sold. Net margin can be calculated in several ways; some of the more common methods only subtract normal operating expenses or all expenses other than income tax expense. For simplicity, our calculation uses net income (we subtract all expenses). Net income divided by net sales expresses net income (earnings) as a percentage of sales, as follows.

$$\text{Net margin} = \frac{\text{Net income}}{\text{Net sales}}$$

For Milavec Company, the net margins for 2012 and 2011 were as follows.

|                        | 2012      | 2011      |
|------------------------|-----------|-----------|
| Net income (a)         | $ 25,000  | $ 22,000  |
| Net sales (b)          | 900,000   | 800,000   |
| Net margin (a ÷ b)     | 2.78%     | 2.75%     |

Milavec has maintained approximately the same net margin. Obviously, the larger the percentage, the better; a meaningful interpretation, however, requires analyzing the company's history and comparing the net margin to other companies in the same industry. The average net margin for the 26 nonfinancial companies that make up the Dow Jones Industrial Average has been around 12 percent in recent years; some companies, such as Merck & Co. with 33 percent, have been much higher than the average. Of course, if a company has a net loss, its net margin for that year will be negative.

### Asset Turnover Ratio

The **asset turnover ratio** (sometimes called *turnover of assets ratio*) measures how many sales dollars were generated for each dollar of assets invested. As with many ratios used in financial statement analysis, users may define the numerator and denominator of this ratio in different ways. For example, they may use total assets or only include operating assets. Since the numerator represents a whole period, it is preferable to use average assets in the denominator if possible, especially if the amount of assets changed significantly during the year. We use average total assets in our illustration.

$$\text{Asset turnover} = \frac{\text{Net sales}}{\text{Average total assets}}$$

For Milavec, the asset turnover ratios were as follows.

|  | 2012 | 2011 |
|---|---|---|
| Net sales (a) | $900,000 | $800,000 |
| Beginning assets (b) | $455,000 | $420,000* |
| Ending assets (c) | 508,000 | 455,000 |
| Average assets (d) = (b + c) ÷ 2 | $481,500 | $437,500 |
| Asset turnover (a ÷ d) | 1.87 | 1.83 |

*The beginning asset balance was drawn from the 2010 financial statements, which are not included in the illustration.

As with most ratios, the implications of a given asset turnover ratio are affected by other considerations. Asset turnover will be high in an industry that requires only minimal investment to operate, such as real estate sales companies. On the other hand, industries that require large investments in plant and machinery, like the auto industry, are likely to have lower asset turnover ratios. The asset turnover ratios of the nonfinancial companies that make up the Dow Jones Industrial Average have averaged around 0.91 in recent years. This means that annual sales have averaged 91 percent of their assets.

### Return on Investment

**Return on investment (ROI),** also called **return on assets** or *earning power,* is the ratio of wealth generated (net income) to the amount invested (average total assets) to generate the wealth. ROI can be calculated as follows.[1]

$$\text{ROI} = \frac{\text{Net income}}{\text{Average total assets}}$$

[1]Detailed coverage of the return on investment ratio is provided in Chapter 9. As discussed in that chapter, companies frequently manipulate the formula to improve managerial motivation and performance. For example, instead of using net income, companies frequently use operating income because net income may be affected by items that are not controllable by management such as loss on a plant closing, storm damage, and so on.

For Milavec, ROI was as follows.

2012

$25,000 ÷ $481,500* = 5.19%

2011

$22,000 ÷ $437,500* = 5.03%

*The computation of average assets is shown above.

In general, higher ROIs suggest better performance. The ROI of the large non-financial companies that make up the Dow Jones Industrial Average had averaged around 9 percent in recent years. These data suggest that Milavec is performing below average, and therefore signals a need for further evaluation that would lead to improved performance.

### Return on Equity

**Return on equity (ROE)** is often used to measure the profitability of the stockholders' investment. ROE is usually higher than ROI because of financial leverage. Financial leverage refers to using debt financing to increase the assets available to a business beyond the amount of assets financed by owners. As long as a company's ROI exceeds its cost of borrowing (interest expense), the owners will earn a higher return on their investment in the company by using borrowed money. For example, if a company borrows money at 8 percent and invests it at 10 percent, the owners will enjoy a return that is higher than 10 percent. ROE is computed as follows.

$$ROE = \frac{\text{Net income}}{\text{Average total stockholders' equity}}$$

If the amount of stockholders' equity changes significantly during the year, it is desirable to use average equity rather than year-end equity in the denominator. The ROE figures for Milavec Company were as follows.

|  | 2012 | 2011 |
|---|---|---|
| Net income (a) | $ 25,000 | $ 22,000 |
| Preferred stock, 6%, $100 par, cumulative | 50,000 | 50,000 |
| Common stock, $10 par | 150,000 | 125,000 |
| Retained earnings | 162,000 | 137,000 |
| Total stockholders' equity (b) | $362,000 | $312,000 |
| ROE (a ÷ b) | 6.9% | 7.1% |

The slight decrease in ROE is due primarily to the increase in common stock. The effect of the increase in total stockholders' equity offsets the effect of the increase in earnings. This information does not disclose whether Milavec had the use of the additional stockholder investment for all or part of the year. If the data are available, calculating a weighted average amount of stockholders' equity provides more meaningful results.

We mentioned earlier the companies that make up the Dow Jones Industrial Average had an average ROI of 9 percent. The average ROE for the companies in the Dow was 26 percent, indicating effective use of financial leverage.

## Stock Market Ratios

Existing and potential investors in a company's stock use many common ratios to analyze and compare the earnings and dividends of different size companies in different industries. Purchasers of stock can profit in two ways: through receiving dividends and through increases in stock value. Investors consider both dividends and overall earnings performance as indicators of the value of the stock they own.

LO 7

Calculate ratios for assessing a company's position in the stock market.

*Earnings per Share*

Perhaps the most frequently quoted measure of earnings performance is **earnings per share (EPS).** EPS calculations are among the most complex in accounting, and more advanced textbooks devote entire chapters to the subject. At this level, we use the following basic formula.

$$\text{Earnings per share} = \frac{\text{Net earnings available for common stock}}{\text{Average number of outstanding common shares}}$$

EPS pertains to shares of *common stock.* Limiting the numerator to earnings available for common stock eliminates the annual preferred dividend (0.06 × $50,000 = $3,000) from the calculation. Exhibit 13.1 shows that Milavec did not pay the preferred dividends in 2012. Since the preferred stock is cumulative, however, the preferred dividend is in arrears and not available to the common stockholders. The number of common shares outstanding is determined by dividing the book value of the common stock by its par value per share ($150,000 ÷ $10 = 15,000 for 2012 and $125,000 ÷ $10 = 12,500 for 2011). Using these data, Milavec's 2012 EPS is calculated as follows.

$$\frac{\$25,000 \text{ (net income)} - \$3,000 \text{ (preferred dividend)}}{(15,000 + 12,500)/2 \text{ (average outstanding common shares)}} = \$1.60 \text{ per share}$$

Investors attribute a great deal of importance to EPS figures. The amounts used in calculating EPS, however, have limitations. Many accounting choices, assumptions, and estimates underlie net income computations, including alternative depreciation methods, different inventory cost flow assumptions, and estimates of future bad debt or warranty expenses, to name only a few. The denominator is also inexact because various factors (discussed in advanced accounting courses) affect the number of shares to include. Numerous opportunities therefore exist to manipulate EPS figures. Prudent investors consider these variables in deciding how much weight to attach to earnings per share.

*Book Value*

**Book value per share** is another frequently quoted measure of a share of stock. It is calculated as follows.

$$\text{Book value per share} = \frac{\text{Stockholders' equity} - \text{Preferred rights}}{\text{Outstanding common shares}}$$

Instead of describing the numerator as stockholders' equity, we could have used assets minus liabilities, the algebraic computation of a company's "net worth." Net worth is a misnomer. A company's accounting records reflect book values, not worth. Because assets are recorded at historical costs and different methods are used to transfer asset costs to expense, the book value of assets after deducting liabilities means little if anything. Nevertheless, investors use the term *book value per share* frequently.

*Preferred rights* represents the amount of money required to satisfy the claims of preferred stockholders. If the preferred stock has a call premium, the call premium amount is subtracted. In our example, we assume the preferred stock can be retired at par. Book value per share for 2012 was therefore as follows.

$$\frac{\$362,000 - \$50,000}{15,000 \text{ shares}} = \$20.80 \text{ per share}$$

*Price-earnings Ratio*

The **price-earnings ratio,** or *P/E ratio,* compares the earnings per share of a company to the market price for a share of the company's stock. Assume Avalanche Company and Brushfire Company each report earnings per share of $3.60. For the same year, Cyclone Company reports EPS of $4.10. Based on these data alone, Cyclone stock may seem to be the best investment. Suppose, however, that the price for one share of stock in each company is $43.20, $36.00, and $51.25, respectively. Which stock would you buy? Cyclone's stock price is the highest, but so is its EPS. The P/E ratio provides a common base of comparison.

$$\text{Price-earnings ratio} = \frac{\text{Market price per share}}{\text{Earnings per share}}$$

The P/E ratios for the three companies are:

| Avalanche | Brushfire | Cyclone |
|---|---|---|
| 12.0 | 10.0 | 12.5 |

Brushfire might initially seem to be the best buy for your money. Yet there must be some reason that Cyclone's stock is selling at 12½ times earnings. In general, a higher P/E ratio indicates the market is more optimistic about a company's growth potential than it is about a company with a lower P/E ratio. The market price of a company's stock reflects judgments about both the company's current results and expectations about future results. Investors cannot make informed use of these ratios for investment decisions without examining the reasons behind the ratios. In October 2009, when the Dow Jones Industrial Average was around 9,000 points, the average P/E ratio for the companies in the Dow Jones Industrial Average was around 17.

## Dividend Yield

There are two ways to profit from a stock investment. One, investors can sell the stock for more than they paid to purchase it (if the stock price rises). Two, the company that issued the stock can pay cash dividends to the shareholders. Most investors view rising stock prices as the primary reward for investing in stock. The importance of receiving dividends, however, should not be overlooked. Evaluating dividend payments is more complex than simply comparing the dividends per share paid by one company to the dividends per share paid by another company. Receiving a $1 dividend on a share purchased for $10 is a much better return than receiving a $1.50 dividend on stock bought for $100. Computing the **dividend yield** simplifies comparing dividend payments. Dividend yield measures dividends received as a percentage of a stock's market price.

$$\text{Dividend yield} = \frac{\text{Dividends per share}}{\text{Market price per share}}$$

To illustrate, consider Dragonfly, Inc., and Elk Company. The information for calculating dividend yield follows.

|  | Dragonfly | Elk |
|---|---|---|
| Dividends per share (a) | $ 1.80 | $ 3.00 |
| Market price per share (b) | 40.00 | 75.00 |
| Dividend yield (a ÷ b) | 4.5% | 4.0% |

Even though the dividend per share paid by Elk Company is higher, the yield is lower (4.5 percent versus 4.0 percent) because Elk's stock price is so high. The dividend yields for the companies included in the Dow Jones Industrial Average were averaging around 1.4 percent in October of 2009.

## Other Ratios

Investors can also use a wide array of other ratios to analyze profitability. Most *profitability ratios* use the same reasoning. For example, you can calculate the *yield* of a variety of financial investments. Yield represents the percentage the amount received is of the amount invested. The dividend yield explained above could be calculated for either common or preferred stock. Investors could measure the earnings yield by calculating earnings per share as a percentage of market price. Yield on a bond can be calculated the same way: interest received divided by the price of the bond.

The specific ratios presented in this chapter are summarized in Exhibit 13.6.

## EXHIBIT 13.6

### Summary of Key Relationships

| | | |
|---|---|---|
| **Liquidity Ratios** | 1. Working capital | Current assets − Current liabilities |
| | 2. Current ratio | Current assets ÷ Current liabilities |
| | 3. Quick (acid-test) ratio | (Current assets − Inventory − Prepaids) ÷ Current liabilities |
| | 4. Accounts receivable turnover | Net credit sales ÷ Average receivables |
| | 5. Average days to collect receivables | 365 ÷ Accounts receivable turnover |
| | 6. Inventory turnover | Cost of goods sold ÷ Average inventory |
| | 7. Average days to sell inventory | 365 ÷ Inventory turnover |
| **Solvency Ratios** | 8. Debt to assets ratio | Total liabilities ÷ Total assets |
| | 9. Debt to equity ratio | Total liabilities ÷ Total stockholders' equity |
| | 10. Number of times interest is earned | Earnings before interest and taxes ÷ Interest expense |
| | 11. Plant assets to long-term liabilities | Net plant assets ÷ Long-term liabilities |
| **Profitability Ratios** | 12. Net margin | Net income ÷ Net sales |
| | 13. Asset turnover | Net sales ÷ Average total assets |
| | 14. Return on investment (also: return on assets) | Net income ÷ Average total assets |
| | 15. Return on equity | Net income ÷ Average total stockholders' equity |
| **Stock Market Ratios** | 16. Earnings per share | Net earnings available for common stock ÷ Average outstanding common shares |
| | 17. Book value per share | (Stockholders' equity − Preferred rights) ÷ Outstanding common shares |
| | 18. Price-earnings ratio | Market price per share ÷ Earnings per share |
| | 19. Dividend yield | Dividends per share ÷ Market price per share |

## LIMITATIONS OF FINANCIAL STATEMENT ANALYSIS

Explain the limitations of financial statement analysis.

Analyzing financial statements is analogous to choosing a new car. Each car is different, and prospective buyers must evaluate and weigh a myriad of features: gas mileage, engine size, manufacturer's reputation, color, accessories, and price, to name a few. Just as it is difficult to compare a Toyota minivan to a Ferrari sports car, so it is difficult to compare a small textile firm to a giant oil company. To make a meaningful assessment, the potential car buyer must focus on key data that can be comparably expressed for each car, such as gas mileage. The superior gas mileage of the minivan may pale in comparison to the thrill of driving the sports car, but the price of buying and operating the sports car may be the characteristic that determines the ultimate choice.

External users can rely on financial statement analysis only as a general guide to the potential of a business. They should resist placing too much weight on any particular figure or trend. Many factors must be considered simultaneously before making any judgments. Furthermore, the analysis techniques discussed in this chapter are all based on historical information. Future events and unanticipated changes in conditions will also influence a company's operating results.

### Different Industries

Different industries may be affected by unique social policies, special accounting procedures, or other individual industry attributes. Ratios of companies in different industries are not comparable without considering industry characteristics. A high debt to assets ratio is more acceptable in some industries than others. Even within an

# REALITY BYTES

The single most important source of financial information is a company's annual report, but decision makers should also consider other sources. Interested persons can access quarterly and annual reports through the SEC's EDGAR database, and often from company websites. Many companies will provide printed versions of these reports upon request. Companies also post information on their websites that is not included in their annual reports. For example, some automobile companies provide very detailed production data through their corporate websites.

Users can frequently obtain information useful in analyzing a particular company from independent sources as well as from the company itself. For example, the websites of popular news services, such as CNN (www.money.cnn.com) and CNBC (www.moneycentral. msn.com) provide archived news stories and independent financial information about many companies. The websites of brokerage houses like www.schwab.com offer free financial information about companies. Finally, libraries often subscribe to independent services that evaluate companies as potential investments. One example worth reviewing is *Value Line Investment Survey*.

industry, a particular business may require more or less working capital than the industry average. If so, the working capital and quick ratios would mean little compared to those of other firms, but may still be useful for trend analysis.

Because of industry-specific factors, most professional analysts specialize in one, or only a few, industries. Financial institutions such as brokerage houses, banks, and insurance companies typically employ financial analysts who specialize in areas such as mineral or oil extraction, chemicals, banking, retail, insurance, bond markets, or automobile manufacturing.

## Changing Economic Environment

When comparing firms, analysts must be alert to changes in general economic trends from year to year. Significant changes in fuel costs and interest rates in recent years make old rule-of-thumb guidelines for evaluating these factors obsolete. In addition, the presence or absence of inflation affects business prospects.

## Accounting Principles

Financial statement analysis is only as reliable as the data on which it is based. Although most firms follow generally accepted accounting principles, a wide variety of acceptable accounting methods is available from which to choose, including different inventory and depreciation methods, different schedules for recognizing revenue, and different ways to account for oil and gas exploration costs. Analyzing statements of companies that seem identical may produce noncomparable ratios if the companies used different accounting methods. Analysts may seek to improve comparability by trying to recast different companies' financial statements as if the same accounting methods had been applied.

Accrual accounting requires the use of many estimates; bad debt expense, warranty expense, asset lives, and salvage value are just a few. The reliability of the resulting financial reports depends on the expertise and integrity of the persons who make the estimates.

The quality and usefulness of accounting information are influenced by underlying accounting concepts. Two particular concepts, *conservatism* and *historical cost,* have a tremendous impact on financial reporting. Conservatism dictates recognizing estimated losses as soon as they occur, but gain recognition is almost always deferred until the gains are actually realized. Conservatism produces a negative bias in financial statements. There are persuasive arguments for the conservatism principle, but users should be alert to distortions it may cause in accounting information.

The pervasive use of the historical cost concept is probably the greatest single cause of distorted financial statement analysis results. The historical cost of an asset does not represent its current value. The asset purchased in 2001 for $10,000 is not comparable in value to the asset purchased in 2010 for $10,000 because of changes in the value of the dollar. Using historical cost produces financial statements that report dollars with differing purchasing power in the same statement. Combining these differing dollar values is akin to adding miles to kilometers. To get the most from analyzing financial statements, users should be cognizant of these limitations.

## ✓ CHECK YOURSELF 13.3

The return on equity for Gup Company is 23.4 percent and for Hunn Company is 17 percent. Does this mean Gup Company is better managed than Hunn Company?

**Answer**   No single ratio can adequately measure management performance. Even analyzing a wide range of ratios provides only limited insight. Any useful interpretation requires the analyst to recognize the limitations of ratio analysis. For example, ratio norms typically differ between industries and may be affected by temporary economic factors. In addition, companies' use of different accounting practices and procedures produces different ratio results even when underlying circumstances are comparable.

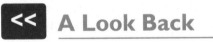

## ◀◀ A Look Back

Financial statement analysis involves many factors, among them user characteristics, information needs for particular types of decisions, and how financial information is analyzed. Analytical techniques include *horizontal, vertical,* and *ratio analysis.* Users commonly calculate ratios to measure a company's liquidity, solvency, and profitability. The specific ratios presented in this chapter are summarized in Exhibit 13.6. Although ratios are easy to calculate and provide useful insights into business operations, when interpreting analytical results, users should consider limitations resulting from differing industry characteristics, differing economic conditions, and the fundamental accounting principles used to produce reported financial information.

## ▶▶ A Look Forward

The next chapter presents a detailed explanation of the statement of cash flows. In that chapter, you will learn how to classify cash receipts and payments as financing activities, investing activities, or operating activities. The chapter explains how to use the T-account method to prepare a statement of cash flows and the difference between the direct method of presenting cash flows from operating activities and the indirect method of presenting cash flows from operating activities. The depth and timing of statement of cash flows coverage varies among colleges. Your instructor may or may not cover this chapter.

**A step-by-step audio-narrated series of slides is provided on the text website at www.mhhe.com/edmonds2011.**

## SELF-STUDY REVIEW PROBLEM

Financial statements for Stallings Company follow.

| Income Statements for the Years Ended December 31 | | |
|---|---|---|
| | **2012** | **2011** |
| Revenues | | |
| Net sales | $ 315,000 | $ 259,000 |
| Expenses | | |
| Cost of goods sold | (189,000) | (154,000) |
| Selling, general, and administrative expenses | (54,000) | (46,000) |
| Interest expense | (4,000) | (4,500) |
| Income before taxes | 68,000 | 54,500 |
| Income tax expense (40%) | (27,200) | (21,800) |
| Net income | $ 40,800 | $ 32,700 |

| Balance Sheets As of December 31 | | |
|---|---|---|
| | **2012** | **2011** |
| **Assets** | | |
| Current assets | | |
| Cash | $ 6,500 | $ 11,500 |
| Accounts receivable | 51,000 | 49,000 |
| Inventories | 155,000 | 147,500 |
| Total current assets | 212,500 | 208,000 |
| Plant and equipment (net) | 187,500 | 177,000 |
| Total assets | $400,000 | $385,000 |
| **Liabilities and Stockholders' Equity** | | |
| Liabilities | | |
| Current liabilities | | |
| Accounts payable | $ 60,000 | $ 81,500 |
| Other | 25,000 | 22,500 |
| Total current liabilities | 85,000 | 104,000 |
| Bonds payable | 100,000 | 100,000 |
| Total liabilities | 185,000 | 204,000 |
| Stockholders' equity | | |
| Common stock (50,000 shares, $3 par) | 150,000 | 150,000 |
| Paid-In capital in excess of par | 20,000 | 20,000 |
| Retained earnings | 45,000 | 11,000 |
| Total stockholders' equity | 215,000 | 181,000 |
| Total liabilities and stockholders' equity | $400,000 | $385,000 |

**Required**

**a.** Use horizontal analysis to determine which expense item increased by the highest percentage from 2011 to 2012.

**b.** Use vertical analysis to determine whether the inventory balance is a higher percentage of total assets in 2011 or 2012.

**c.** Calculate the following ratios for 2011 and 2012. When data limitations prohibit computing averages, use year-end balances in your calculations.

    (1)  Net margin

    (2)  Return on investment

    (3)  Return on equity

    (4)  Earnings per share

    (5)  Price-earnings ratio (market price per share at the end of 2012 and 2011 was $12.04 and $8.86, respectively)

    (6)  Book value per share of common stock

    (7)  Times interest earned

    (8)  Working capital

    (9)  Current ratio

    (10)  Acid-test ratio

    (11)  Accounts receivable turnover

    (12)  Inventory turnover

    (13)  Debt to equity

### Solution to Requirement a

Income tax expense increased by the greatest percentage. Computations follow.

Cost of goods sold ($189,000 − $154,000) ÷ $154,000 = 22.73%

General, selling, and administrative ($54,000 − $46,000) ÷ $46,000 = 17.39%

Interest expense decreased.

Income tax expense ($27,200 − $21,800) ÷ $21,800 = 24.77%

### Solution to Requirement b

2011: $147,500 ÷ $385,000 = 38.31%

2012: $155,000 ÷ $400,000 = 38.75%

Inventory is slightly larger relative to total assets in 2012.

### Solution to Requirement c

| | | 2012 | 2011 |
|---|---|---|---|
| 1. | $\dfrac{\text{Net income}}{\text{Net sales}}$ | $\dfrac{\$40,800}{\$315,000} = 12.95\%$ | $\dfrac{\$32,700}{\$259,000} = 12.63\%$ |
| 2. | $\dfrac{\text{Net income}}{\text{Average total assets}}$ | $\dfrac{\$40,800}{\$392,500} = 10.39\%$ | $\dfrac{\$32,700}{\$385,000} = 8.49\%$ |
| 3. | $\dfrac{\text{Net income}}{\text{Average total stockholders' equity}}$ | $\dfrac{\$40,800}{\$198,000} = 20.61\%$ | $\dfrac{\$32,700}{\$181,000} = 18.07\%$ |
| 4. | $\dfrac{\text{Net income}}{\text{Average common shares outstanding}}$ | $\dfrac{\$40,800}{50,000 \text{ shares}} = \$0.816$ | $\dfrac{\$32,700}{50,000 \text{ shares}} = \$0.654$ |
| 5. | $\dfrac{\text{Market price per share}}{\text{Earnings per share}}$ | $\dfrac{\$12.04}{\$0.816} = 14.75 \text{ times}$ | $\dfrac{\$8.86}{\$0.654} = 13.55 \text{ times}$ |
| 6. | $\dfrac{\text{Stockholders' equity} - \text{Preferred rights}}{\text{Outstanding common shares}}$ | $\dfrac{\$215,000}{50,000 \text{ shares}} = \$4.30$ | $\dfrac{\$181,000}{50,000 \text{ shares}} = \$3.62$ |
| 7. | $\dfrac{\text{Net income} + \text{Taxes} + \text{Interest expense}}{\text{Interest expense}}$ | $\dfrac{\$40,800 + \$27,200 + \$4,000}{\$4,000} = 18 \text{ times}$ | $\dfrac{\$32,700 + \$21,800 + \$4,500}{\$4,500} = 13.1 \text{ times}$ |
| 8. | Current assets − Current liabilities | $\$212,500 - \$85,000 = \$127,500$ | $\$208,000 - \$104,000 = \$104,000$ |
| 9. | $\dfrac{\text{Current assets}}{\text{Current liabilities}}$ | $\dfrac{\$212,500}{\$85,000} = 2.5:1$ | $\dfrac{\$208,000}{\$104,000} = 2:1$ |
| 10. | $\dfrac{\text{Quick assets}}{\text{Current liabilities}}$ | $\dfrac{\$57,500}{\$85,000} = 0.68:1$ | $\dfrac{\$60,500}{\$104,000} = 0.58:1$ |
| 11. | $\dfrac{\text{Net credit sales}}{\text{Average accounts receivable}}$ | $\dfrac{\$315,000}{\$50,000} = 6.3 \text{ times}$ | $\dfrac{\$259,000}{\$49,000} = 5.29 \text{ times}$ |
| 12. | $\dfrac{\text{Cost of goods sold}}{\text{Average inventory}}$ | $\dfrac{\$189,000}{\$151,250} = 1.25 \text{ times}$ | $\dfrac{\$154,000}{\$147,500} = 1.04 \text{ times}$ |
| 13. | $\dfrac{\text{Total liabilities}}{\text{Total stockholders' equity}}$ | $\dfrac{\$185,000}{\$215,000} = 86.05\%$ | $\dfrac{\$204,000}{\$181,000} = 112.71\%$ |

## KEY TERMS

| | | |
|---|---|---|
| Absolute amounts 589 | Debt to equity ratio 597 | Profitability ratios 599 |
| Accounts receivable turnover 595 | Dividend yield 603 | Quick ratio 595 |
| Acid-test ratio 595 | Earnings per share 602 | Ratio analysis 592 |
| Asset turnover ratio 600 | Horizontal analysis 589 | Return on assets 600 |
| Average days to collect receivables 596 | Information overload 588 | Return on equity 601 |
| Average days to sell inventory 596 | Inventory turnover 598 | Return on investment 600 |
| Book value per share 602 | Liquidity ratios 593 | Solvency ratios 597 |
| Current ratio 594 | Materiality 589 | Trend analysis 589 |
| Debt to assets ratio 597 | Net margin 599 | Vertical analysis 592 |
| | Percentage analysis 590 | Working capital 594 |
| | Price-earnings ratio 602 | Working capital ratio 594 |

## QUESTIONS

1. Why are ratios and trends used in financial analysis?

2. What do the terms *liquidity* and *solvency* mean?

3. What is apparent from a horizontal presentation of financial statement information? A vertical presentation?

4. What is the significance of inventory turnover, and how is it calculated?

5. What is the difference between the current ratio and the quick ratio? What does each measure?

6. Why are absolute amounts of limited use when comparing companies?

7. What is the difference between return on investment and return on equity?

8. Which ratios are used to measure long-term debt-paying ability? How is each calculated?

9. What are some limitations of the earnings per share figure?

10. What is the formula for calculating return on investment (ROI)?

11. What is information overload?

12. What is the price-earnings ratio? Explain the difference between it and the dividend yield.

13. What environmental factors must be considered in analyzing companies?

14. How do accounting principles affect financial statement analysis?

## MULTIPLE-CHOICE QUESTIONS

**Multiple-choice questions are provided on the text website at www.mhhe.com/edmonds2011.**

## EXERCISES—SERIES A

**All applicable Exercises in Series A are available with McGraw-Hill's *Connect Accounting*.**

### Exercise 13-1A   *Inventory turnover*

LO 4

Selected financial information for Feemster Company for 2012 follows.

| | |
|---|---|
| Sales | $2,000,000 |
| Cost of goods sold | 1,400,000 |
| Merchandise inventory | |
| Beginning of year | 155,000 |
| End of year | 195,000 |

**Required**

Assuming that the merchandise inventory buildup was relatively constant, how many times did the merchandise inventory turn over during 2012?

**LO 5**

### Exercise 13-2A   *Number of times interest earned*

The following data come from the financial records of Bynum Corporation for 2011.

| | |
|---|---|
| Sales | $840,000 |
| Interest expense | 5,000 |
| Income tax expense | 27,000 |
| Net income | 28,000 |

**Required**

How many times was interest earned in 2011?

**LO 4**

### Exercise 13-3A   *Current ratio*

Meador Corporation wrote off a $1,000 uncollectible account receivable against the $12,000 balance in its allowance account.

**Required**

Explain the effect of the write-off on Meador's current ratio.

**LO 4**

### Exercise 13-4A   *Working capital and current ratio*

On June 30, 2011, Weslaco Company's total current assets were $500,000 and its total current liabilities were $275,000. On July 1, 2011, Weslaco issued a short-term note to a bank for $40,000 cash.

**Required**

a. Compute Weslaco's working capital before and after issuing the note.

b. Compute Weslaco's current ratio before and after issuing the note.

**LO 4**

### Exercise 13-5A   *Working capital and current ratio*

On June 30, 2011, Weslaco Company's total current assets were $500,000 and its total current liabilities were $275,000. On July 1, 2011, Weslaco issued a long-term note to a bank for $40,000 cash.

**Required**

a. Compute Weslaco's working capital before and after issuing the note.

b. Compute Weslaco's current ratio before and after issuing the note.

**LO 2, 3**

### Exercise 13-6A   *Horizontal analysis*

Pettit Corporation reported the following operating results for two consecutive years.

| | 2011 | 2010 | Percentage Change |
|---|---|---|---|
| Sales | $1,300,000 | $1,000,000 | |
| Cost of goods sold | 800,000 | 600,000 | |
| Gross margin | 500,000 | $ 400,000 | |
| Operating expenses | 300,000 | 200,000 | |
| Income before taxes | 200,000 | $ 200,000 | |
| Income taxes | 61,000 | 53,000 | |
| Net income | $ 139,000 | $ 147,000 | |

**Required**

a. Compute the percentage changes in Pettit Corporation's income statement components between the two years.

b. Comment on apparent trends revealed by the percentage changes computed in Requirement *a*.

**Exercise 13-7A**    *Vertical analysis*

Conroe Company reported the following operating results for two consecutive years.

| 2011 | Amount | Percent of Sales |
|---|---|---|
| Sales | $1,000,000 | |
| Cost of goods sold | 550,000 | |
| Gross margin on sales | 450,000 | |
| Operating expenses | 130,000 | |
| Income before taxes | 320,000 | |
| Income taxes | 80,000 | |
| Net income | $ 240,000 | |

| 2012 | Amount | Percent of Sales |
|---|---|---|
| Sales | $1,080,000 | |
| Cost of goods sold | 600,000 | |
| Gross margin on sales | 480,000 | |
| Operating expenses | 150,000 | |
| Income before taxes | 330,000 | |
| Income taxes | 82,000 | |
| Net income | $ 248,000 | |

**Required**

Express each income statement component for each of the two years as a percent of sales.

**Exercise 13-8A**    *Ratio analysis*

The balance sheet for Kamel Corporation follows.

| | |
|---|---|
| Current assets | $ 240,000 |
| Long-term assets (net) | 760,000 |
| Total assets | $1,000,000 |
| Current liabilities | $ 150,000 |
| Long-term liabilities | 450,000 |
| Total liabilities | 600,000 |
| Common stock and retained earnings | 400,000 |
| Total liabilities and stockholders' equity | $1,000,000 |

**Required**

Compute the following.

| | |
|---|---|
| Working capital | _____ |
| Current ratio | _____ |
| Debt to assets ratio | _____ |
| Debt to equity ratio | _____ |

**Exercise 13-9A**    *Ratio analysis*

During 2011, Stanton Corporation reported after-tax net income of $3,600,000. During the year, the number of shares of stock outstanding remained constant at 10,000 of $100 par, 9 percent preferred stock and 400,000 shares of common stock. The company's total stockholders' equity is $20,000,000 at December 31, 2011. Stanton Corporation's common stock was selling at $52 per share at the end of its fiscal year. All dividends for the year have been paid, including $4.80 per share to common stockholders.

**Required**

Compute the following:

a. Earnings per share
b. Book value per share of common stock
c. Price-earnings ratio
d. Dividend yield

**LO 4, 5, 6, 7**

### Exercise 13-10A    *Ratio analysis*

**Required**

Match each of the following ratios with the formula used to compute it.

| | |
|---|---|
| _____ 1. Working capital | a. Net income ÷ Average total stockholders' equity |
| _____ 2. Current ratio | b. Cost of goods sold ÷ Average inventory |
| _____ 3. Quick ratio | c. Current assets − Current liabilities |
| _____ 4. Accounts receivable turnover | d. 365 ÷ Inventory turnover |
| _____ 5. Average days to collect | e. Net income ÷ Average total assets |
| _____ 6. Inventory turnover | f. (Net income − Preferred dividends) ÷ Average outstanding common shares |
| _____ 7. Average days to sell inventory | g. (Current assets − Inventory − Prepaid expenses) ÷ Current liabilities |
| _____ 8. Debt to assets ratio | h. Total liabilities ÷ Total assets |
| _____ 9. Debt to equity ratio | i. 365 ÷ Accounts receivable turnover |
| _____ 10. Return on investment | j. Total liabilities ÷ Total stockholders' equity |
| _____ 11. Return on equity | k. Net credit sales ÷ Average accounts receivables |
| _____ 12. Earnings per share | l. Current assets ÷ Current liabilities |

**LO 2**

### Exercise 13-11A    *Horizontal and vertical analysis*

Income statements for Thompson Company for 2011 and 2012 follow.

| | 2012 | 2011 |
|---|---|---|
| Sales | $200,000 | $180,000 |
| Cost of goods sold | 142,000 | 120,000 |
| Selling expenses | 20,000 | 18,000 |
| Administrative expenses | 12,000 | 14,000 |
| Interest expense | 3,000 | 5,000 |
| Total expenses | $177,000 | 157,000 |
| Income before taxes | 23,000 | 23,000 |
| Income taxes expense | 5,000 | 3,000 |
| Net income | $ 18,000 | $20,000 |

**Required**

a. Perform a horizontal analysis, showing the percentage change in each income statement component between 2011 and 2012.
b. Perform a vertical analysis, showing each income statement component as a percent of sales for each year.

**Exercise 13-12A**    *Ratio analysis*                    LO 4, 5, 6, 7

Compute the specified ratios using Hilda Company's balance sheet for 2011.

| Assets | |
|---|---:|
| Cash | $ 15,000 |
| Marketable securities | 8,000 |
| Accounts receivable | 13,000 |
| Inventory | 11,000 |
| Property and equipment | 170,000 |
| Accumulated depreciation | (12,500) |
| Total assets | $204,500 |
| **Liabilities and Stockholders' Equity** | |
| Accounts payable | $ 8,500 |
| Current notes payable | 3,500 |
| Mortgage payable | 4,500 |
| Bonds payable | 21,500 |
| Common stock | 114,000 |
| Retained earnings | 52,500 |
| Total liabilities and stockholders' equity | $204,500 |

The average number of common stock shares outstanding during 2011 was 880 shares. Net income for the year was $15,000.

**Required**

Compute each of the following:

a. Current ratio.
b. Earnings per share.
c. Quick (acid-test) ratio.
d. Return on investment.
e. Return on equity.
f. Debt to equity ratio.

**Exercise 13-13A**    *Comprehensive analysis*            LO 4, 5, 6, 7

**Required**

Indicate the effect of each of the following transactions on (1) the current ratio, (2) working capital, (3) stockholders' equity, (4) book value per share of common stock, (5) retained earnings. Assume that the current ratio is greater than 1:1.

a. Collected account receivable.
b. Wrote off account receivable.
c. Converted a short-term note payable to a long-term payable.
d. Purchased inventory on account.
e. Declared cash dividend.
f. Sold merchandise on account at a profit.
g. Issued stock dividend.
h. Paid account payable.
i. Sold building at a loss.

**Exercise 13-14A**    *Accounts receivable turnover, inventory turnover, and net margin*            LO 4, 6

Selected data from Warren Company follow.

| Balance Sheet As of December 31 | | |
| --- | --- | --- |
| | **2011** | **2010** |
| Accounts receivable | $400,000 | $376,000 |
| Allowance for doubtful accounts | (20,000) | (16,000) |
| Net accounts receivable | $380,000 | $360,000 |
| Inventories, lower of cost or market | $480,000 | $440,000 |

| Income Statement for the Years Ended December 31 | | |
| --- | --- | --- |
| | **2011** | **2010** |
| Net credit sales | $2,000,000 | $1,760,000 |
| Net cash sales | 400,000 | 320,000 |
| Net sales | 2,400,000 | 2,080,000 |
| Cost of goods sold | 1,600,000 | 1,440,000 |
| Selling, general, and administrative expenses | 240,000 | 216,000 |
| Other expenses | 40,000 | 24,000 |
| Total operating expenses | $1,880,000 | $1,680,000 |

**Required**

Compute the following:

a.  The accounts receivable turnover for 2011.

b.  The inventory turnover for 2011.

c.  The net margin for 2010.

**LO 4, 5**

### Exercise 13-15A  *Comprehensive analysis*

The December 31, 2012, balance sheet for Kessler Corporation is presented here. These are the only accounts on Kessler's balance sheet. Amounts indicated by question marks (?) can be calculated using the following additional information.

| **Assets** | |
| --- | --- |
| Cash | $ 25,000 |
| Accounts receivable (net) | ? |
| Inventory | ? |
| Property, plant, and equipment (net) | 294,000 |
| | $432,000 |
| **Liabilities and Stockholders' Equity** | |
| Accounts payable (trade) | $    ? |
| Income taxes payable (current) | 25,000 |
| Long-term debt | ? |
| Common stock | 300,000 |
| Retained earnings | ? |
| | $    ? |

*continued*

**Additional Information**

| | |
|---|---|
| Current ratio (at year end) | 1.5 to 1.0 |
| Total liabilities ÷ Total stockholders' equity | 80% |
| Gross margin percent | 30% |
| Inventory turnover (Cost of goods sold ÷ Ending inventory) | 10.5 times |
| Gross margin for 2012 | $ 315,000 |

**Required**

Determine the following.

**a.** The balance in trade accounts payable as of December 31, 2012.

**b.** The balance in retained earnings as of December 31, 2012.

**c.** The balance in the inventory account as of December 31, 2012. (Assume that the level of inventory did not change from last year.)

## PROBLEMS—SERIES A

**All applicable Problems in Series A are available with McGraw-Hill's *Connect Accounting.***

**Problem 13-16A**   *Vertical analysis*                                           **LO 2**

The following percentages apply to Lowther Company for 2011 and 2012.

| | 2012 | 2011 |
|---|---|---|
| Sales | 100.0% | 100.0% |
| Cost of goods sold | 61.0 | 64.0 |
| Gross margin | 39.0 | 36.0 |
| Selling and administrative expense | 26.5 | 20.5 |
| Interest expense | 2.5 | 2.0 |
| Total expenses | 29.0 | 22.5 |
| Income before taxes | 10.0 | 13.5 |
| Income tax expense | 5.5 | 7.0 |
| Net income | 4.5% | 6.5% |

**CHECK FIGURES**
NI of 2012: $27,000
Total Expenses of 2011: $112,500

**Required**

Assuming that sales were $500,000 in 2011 and $600,000 in 2012, prepare income statements for the two years.

**Problem 13-17A**   *Ratio analysis*                                           **LO 5, 6, 7**

Weimar Company's income statement information follows.

| | 2011 | 2010 |
|---|---|---|
| Net sales | $420,000 | $260,000 |
| Income before interest and taxes | 110,000 | 85,000 |
| Net income after taxes | 55,500 | 63,000 |
| Interest expense | 9,000 | 8,000 |
| Stockholders' equity, December 31 (2009: $200,000) | 305,000 | 235,000 |
| Common stock, par $50, December 31 | 206,000 | 230,000 |

**CHECK FIGURES**
a. 2011: 12.22 times
c. 2010: 8.5 times

The average number of shares outstanding was 7,800 for 2011 and 6,900 for 2010.

**Required**

Compute the following ratios for Weimar for 2011 and 2010.

**a.** Number of times interest was earned.

**b.** Earnings per share based on the average number of shares outstanding.

**c.** Price-earnings ratio (market prices: 2011, $64 per share; 2010, $78 per share).

**d.** Return on average equity.

**e.** Net margin.

**LO 4**

## Problem 13-18A   *Effect of transactions on current ratio and working capital*

Sherman Manufacturing has a current ratio of 3:1 on December 31, 2011. Indicate whether each of the following transactions would increase (+), decrease (−), or have no effect (NA) on Sherman's current ratio and its working capital.

**Required**

**a.** Paid cash for a trademark.

**b.** Wrote off an uncollectible account receivable.

**c.** Sold equipment for cash.

**d.** Sold merchandise at a profit (cash).

**e.** Declared a cash dividend.

**f.** Purchased inventory on account.

**g.** Scrapped a fully depreciated machine (no gain or loss).

**h.** Issued a stock dividend.

**i.** Purchased a machine with a long-term note.

**j.** Paid a previously declared cash dividend.

**k.** Collected accounts receivable.

**l.** Invested in current marketable securities.

**LO 7**

## Problem 13-19A   *Ratio analysis*

Selected data for Richmond Company for 2011 and additional information on industry averages follow.

**CHECK FIGURE**
a. Earnings per share: $3.50

| | | |
|---|---:|---:|
| Earnings (net income) | | $ 174,000 |
| Preferred stock (13,200 shares at $50 par, 4%) | | $ 660,000 |
| Common stock (45,000 shares no par, market value $56) | | 510,000 |
| Retained earnings | | 562,500 |
| | | $1,732,500 |
| Less: Treasury stock | | |
| Preferred (1,800 shares) | $54,000 | |
| Common (1,800 shares) | 24,000 | 78,000 |
| Total stockholders' equity | | $1,654,500 |

| Industry averages | |
|---|---:|
| Earnings per share | $ 5.20 |
| Price-earnings ratio | 9.50 |
| Return on equity | 11.20% |

**Required**

**a.** Calculate and compare Richmond Company's ratios with the industry averages.

**b.** Discuss factors you would consider in deciding whether to invest in the company.

## Problem 13-20A  *Supply missing balance sheet numbers*

The bookkeeper for Lowell's Country Music Bar left this incomplete balance sheet. Lowell's working capital is $90,000 and its debt to assets ratio is 40 percent.

**Assets**

| | |
|---|---:|
| Current assets | |
| Cash | $ 21,000 |
| Accounts receivable | 42,000 |
| Inventory | (A) |
| Prepaid expenses | 9,000 |
| Total current assets | (B) |
| Long-term assets | |
| Building | (C) |
| Less: Accumulated depreciation | (39,000) |
| Total long-term assets | 210,000 |
| Total assets | $    (D) |

**Liabilities and Stockholders' Equity**

| | |
|---|---:|
| Liabilities | |
| Current liabilities | |
| Accounts payable | $    (E) |
| Notes payable | 12,000 |
| Income tax payable | 10,500 |
| Total current liabilities | 37,500 |
| Long-term liabilities | |
| Mortgage payable | (F) |
| Total liabilities | (G) |
| Stockholders' equity | |
| Common stock | 105,000 |
| Retained earnings | (H) |
| Total stockholders' equity | (I) |
| Total liabilities and stockholders' equity | $    (J) |

### Required

Complete the balance sheet by supplying the missing amounts.

## Problem 13-21A  *Ratio analysis*

The following financial statements apply to Bassie Company.

| | 2012 | 2011 |
|---|---:|---:|
| Revenues | | |
| Net sales | $210,000 | $175,000 |
| Other revenues | 4,000 | 5,000 |
| Total revenues | 214,000 | 180,000 |
| Expenses | | |
| Cost of goods sold | 126,000 | 103,000 |
| Selling expenses | 21,000 | 19,000 |
| General and administrative expenses | 11,000 | 10,000 |
| Interest expense | 3,000 | 3,000 |
| Income tax expense | 21,000 | 18,000 |
| Total expenses | 182,000 | 153,000 |
| | | *continued* |

| | 2012 | 2011 |
|---|---|---|
| Earnings from continuing operations before extraordinary items | 32,000 | 27,000 |
| Extraordinary gain (net of $3,000 tax) | 4,000 | 0 |
| Net income | $ 36,000 | $ 27,000 |
| **Assets** | | |
| Current assets | | |
|   Cash | $ 4,000 | $ 8,000 |
|   Marketable securities | 1,000 | 1,000 |
|   Accounts receivable | 35,000 | 32,000 |
|   Inventories | 100,000 | 96,000 |
|   Prepaid expenses | 3,000 | 2,000 |
|     Total current assets | 143,000 | 139,000 |
| Plant and equipment (net) | 105,000 | 105,000 |
| Intangibles | 20,000 | 0 |
| Total assets | $268,000 | $244,000 |
| **Liabilities and Stockholders' Equity** | | |
| Liabilities | | |
|   Current liabilities | | |
|     Accounts payable | $ 40,000 | $ 54,000 |
|     Other | 17,000 | 15,000 |
|       Total current liabilities | 57,000 | 69,000 |
|   Bonds payable | 66,000 | 67,000 |
|   Total liabilities | 123,000 | 136,000 |
| Stockholders' equity | | |
|   Common stock (50,000 shares) | 115,000 | 115,000 |
|   Retained earnings | 30,000 | (7,000) |
|     Total stockholders' equity | 145,000 | 108,000 |
| Total liabilities and stockholders' equity | $268,000 | $244,000 |

**Required**

Calculate the following ratios for 2011 and 2012. When data limitations prohibit computing averages, use year-end balances in your calculations.

a. Net margin

b. Return on investment

c. Return on equity

d. Earnings per share

e. Price-earnings ratio (market prices at the end of 2011 and 2012 were $5.94 and $4.77, respectively)

f. Book value per share of common stock

g. Times interest earned

h. Working capital

i. Current ratio

j. Quick (acid-test) ratio

k. Accounts receivable turnover

l. Inventory turnover

m. Debt to equity ratio

n. Debt to assets ratio

## Problem 13-22A    *Horizontal analysis*

Financial statements for Bernard Company follow.

**LO 2**

**CHECK FIGURES**
Total Assets: +11.6%
Total Liabilities: +14.4%

### BERNARD COMPANY
### Balance Sheets
### As of December 31

| | 2012 | 2011 |
|---|---|---|
| **Assets** | | |
| Current assets | | |
| Cash | $ 16,000 | $ 12,000 |
| Marketable securities | 20,000 | 6,000 |
| Accounts receivable (net) | 54,000 | 46,000 |
| Inventories | 135,000 | 143,000 |
| Prepaid items | 25,000 | 10,000 |
| Total current assets | 250,000 | 217,000 |
| Investments | 27,000 | 20,000 |
| Plant (net) | 270,000 | 255,000 |
| Land | 29,000 | 24,000 |
| Total assets | $576,000 | $516,000 |
| **Liabilities and Stockholders' Equity** | | |
| Liabilities | | |
| Current liabilities | | |
| Notes payable | $ 17,000 | $ 6,000 |
| Accounts payable | 113,800 | 100,000 |
| Salaries payable | 21,000 | 15,000 |
| Total current liabilities | 151,800 | 121,000 |
| Noncurrent liabilities | | |
| Bonds payable | 100,000 | 100,000 |
| Other | 32,000 | 27,000 |
| Total noncurrent liabilities | 132,000 | 127,000 |
| Total liabilities | 283,800 | 248,000 |
| Stockholders' equity | | |
| Preferred stock, (par value $10, 4% cumulative, non-participating; 8,000 shares authorized and issued) | 80,000 | 80,000 |
| Common stock (No par; 50,000 shares authorized; 10,000 shares issued) | 80,000 | 80,000 |
| Retained earnings | 132,200 | 108,000 |
| Total stockholders' equity | 292,200 | 268,000 |
| Total liabilities and stockholders' equity | $576,000 | $516,000 |

### BERNARD COMPANY
### Statements of Income and Retained Earnings
### For the Years Ended December 31

| | 2012 | 2011 |
|---|---|---|
| Revenues | | |
| Sales (net) | $230,000 | $210,000 |
| Other revenues | 8,000 | 5,000 |
| Total revenues | 238,000 | 215,000 |

*continued*

| | 2012 | 2011 |
|---|---|---|
| Expenses | | |
| Cost of goods sold | 120,000 | 103,000 |
| Selling, general, and administrative | 55,000 | 50,000 |
| Interest expense | 8,000 | 7,200 |
| Income tax expense | 23,000 | 22,000 |
| Total expenses | 206,000 | 182,200 |
| Net earnings (net income) | 32,000 | 32,800 |
| Retained earnings, January 1 | 108,000 | 83,000 |
| Less: Preferred stock dividends | 2,800 | 2,800 |
| Common stock dividends | 5,000 | 5,000 |
| Retained earnings, December 31 | $132,200 | $108,000 |

**Required**

Prepare a horizontal analysis of both the balance sheet and income statement.

LO 4, 5, 6, 7

**eXcel**

## Problem 13-23A    *Ratio analysis*

**Required**

Use the financial statements for Bernard Company from Problem 13-22A to calculate the following ratios for 2012 and 2011:

a. Working capital

b. Current ratio

c. Quick ratio

d. Receivables turnover (beginning receivables at January 1, 2011, were $47,000.)

e. Average days to collect accounts receivable

f. Inventory turnover (beginning inventory at January 1, 2011, was $140,000.)

g. Number of days to sell inventory

h. Debt to assets ratio

i. Debt to equity ratio

j. Number of times interest was earned

k. Plant assets to long-term debt

l. Net margin

m. Turnover of assets

n. Return on investment

o. Return on equity

p. Earnings per share

q. Book value per share of common stock

r. Price-earnings ratio (market price per share: 2011, $11.75; 2012, $12.50)

s. Dividend yield on common stock

LO 2

**eXcel**

## Problem 13-24A    *Vertical analysis*

**Required**

Use the financial statements for Bernard Company from Problem 13-22A to perform a vertical analysis of both the balance sheets and income statements for 2012 and 2011.

# EXERCISES—SERIES B

### Exercise 13-1B    *Inventory turnover*

**LO 4**

Selected financial information for Dulock Company for 2012 follows.

| | |
|---|---:|
| Sales | $4,000,000 |
| Cost of goods sold | 3,200,000 |
| Merchandise inventory | |
|   Beginning of year | 380,000 |
|   End of year | 620,000 |

**Required**

Assuming that the merchandise inventory buildup was relatively constant, how many times did the merchandise inventory turn over during 2012?

### Exercise 13-2B    *Number of times interest earned*

**LO 5**

The following data come from the financial records of the Midland Corporation for 2011.

| | |
|---|---:|
| Sales | $2,000,000 |
| Interest expense | 100,000 |
| Income tax | 280,000 |
| Net income | 640,000 |

**Required**

How many times was interest earned in 2011?

### Exercise 13-3B    *Current ratio*

**LO 4**

Camp Corporation purchased $350 of merchandise on account.

**Required**

Explain the effect of the purchase on Camp's current ratio.

### Exercise 13-4B    *Working capital and current ratio*

**LO 4**

On October 31, 2012, Henderson Company's total current assets were $65,000 and its total current liabilities were $20,000. On November 1, 2012, Henderson purchased marketable securities for $10,000 cash.

**Required**

a.  Compute Henderson's working capital before and after the securities purchase.
b.  Compute Henderson's current ratio before and after the securities purchase.

### Exercise 13-5B    *Working capital and current ratio*

**LO 4**

On October 31, 2012, Henderson Company's total current assets were $65,000 and its total current liabilities were $20,000. On November 1, 2012, Henderson bought manufacturing equipment for $10,000 cash.

**Required**

a.  Compute Henderson's working capital before and after the equipment purchase.
b.  Compute Henderson's current ratio before and after the equipment purchase.

**LO 2, 3**

### Exercise 13-6B    *Horizontal analysis*

Everett Corporation reported the following operating results for two consecutive years.

|  | 2012 | 2011 | Percentage Change |
|---|---|---|---|
| Sales | $440,000 | $400,000 | |
| Cost of goods sold | 264,000 | 254,000 | |
| Gross margin | 176,000 | 146,000 | |
| Operating expenses | 75,000 | 65,000 | |
| Income before taxes | 101,000 | 81,000 | |
| Income taxes | 45,000 | 31,600 | |
| Net income | $ 56,000 | $ 49,400 | |

**Required**

a. Compute the percentage changes in Everrett Corporation's income statement components for the two years.

b. Comment on apparent trends revealed by the percentage changes computed in Requirement *a*.

**LO 2**

### Exercise 13-7B    *Vertical analysis*

Wallace Company reported the following operating results for two consecutive years.

| 2011 | Amount | Percentage of Sales |
|---|---|---|
| Sales | $100,000 | |
| Cost of goods sold | 64,000 | |
| Gross margin | 36,000 | |
| Operating expenses | 19,000 | |
| Income before taxes | 57,000 | |
| Income taxes | 5,400 | |
| Net income | $ 11,600 | |

| 2012 | Amount | Percentage of Sales |
|---|---|---|
| Sales | $128,000 | |
| Cost of goods sold | 81,600 | |
| Gross margin | 46,400 | |
| Operating expenses | 23,000 | |
| Income before taxes | 23,400 | |
| Income taxes | 6,200 | |
| Net income | $ 17,200 | |

**Required**

Express each income statement component for each of the two years as a percentage of sales.

**LO 4, 5**

### Exercise 13-8B    *Ratio analysis*

Balance sheet data for the Lawrence Corporation follows.

| | |
|---|---|
| Current assets | $ 20,000 |
| Long-term assets (net) | 140,000 |
| Total assets | $160,000 |
| Current liabilities | $ 15,000 |
| Long-term liabilities | 45,000 |
| Total liabilities | 60,000 |
| Common stock and retained earnings | 100,000 |
| Total liabilities and stockholders' equity | $160,000 |

**Required**

Compute the following:

**a.** Working capital

**b.** Current ratio

**c.** Debt to assets ratio

**d.** Debt to equity ratio

## Exercise 13-9B    *Ratio analysis*                                LO 7

During 2012, Carl Corporation reported net income after taxes of $1,080,000. During the year, the number of shares of stock outstanding remained constant at 20,000 shares of $100 par 8 percent preferred stock and 200,000 shares of common stock. The company's total equities at December 31, 2012, were $3,500,000, which included $640,000 of liabilities. The common stock was selling for $40 per share at the end of the year. All dividends for the year were declared and paid, including $3.60 per share to common stockholders.

**Required**

Compute the following.

**a.** Earnings per share

**b.** Book value per share

**c.** Price-earnings ratio

**d.** Dividend yield

## Exercise 13-10B    *Ratio analysis*                         LO 2, 3, 4, 5, 6, 7

Match each of the following ratios with its formula.

| | |
|---|---|
| _____ **1.** Price-earnings ratio | **a.** Total liabilities ÷ Total stockholders' equity |
| _____ **2.** Dividend yield | **b.** Current assets ÷ Current liabilities |
| _____ **3.** Book value per share | **c.** 365 ÷ Accounts receivable turnover |
| _____ **4.** Plant assets to long-term liabilities | **d.** (Net income − Preferred dividends) ÷ Average outstanding common shares |
| _____ **5.** Times interest earned | **e.** (Stockholders' equity − Preferred rights) ÷ Outstanding common shares |
| _____ **6.** Earnings per share | **f.** 365 ÷ Inventory turnover |
| _____ **7.** Net margin | **g.** Dividends per share ÷ Market price per share |
| _____ **8.** Debt to equity ratio | **h.** Net plant assets ÷ Long-term liabilities |
| _____ **9.** Current ratio | **i.** Market price per share ÷ Earnings per share |
| _____ **10.** Turnover of assets | **j.** Net income ÷ Net sales |
| _____ **11.** Days to collect A/R | **k.** Net sales ÷ Average total assets |
| _____ **12.** Number of days to sell inventory | **l.** Income before taxes and interest expense ÷ Interest expense |

## Exercise 13-11B    *Horizontal and vertical analysis*                LO 2

McAllen Company reported the following operating results for 2012 and 2011.

| | 2012 | 2011 |
|---|---|---|
| Sales | $480,000 | $420,000 |
| Cost of goods sold | 246,000 | 225,000 |
| Selling expenses | 28,000 | 24,000 |
| Administrative expenses | 52,000 | 49,000 |
| Interest expense | 8,000 | 10,000 |
| Total expenses | 334,000 | 308,000 |
| Income before taxes | 146,000 | 112,000 |
| Income taxes expense | 25,000 | 21,000 |
| Net income | $121,000 | $ 91,000 |

**Required**

a. Perform a horizontal analysis, showing the percentage change in each income statement component between 2012 and 2011.

b. Perform a vertical analysis, showing each income statement component as a percent of sales for each year.

**LO 4, 5, 6, 7**    **Exercise 13-12B**    *Ratio analysis*

Compute the specified ratios using the following December 31, 2011, statement of financial position for Geofferey Company.

| Assets | |
|---|---:|
| Cash | $ 40,000 |
| Marketable securities | 9,000 |
| Accounts receivable | 72,800 |
| Inventory | 112,200 |
| Property and equipment | 150,000 |
| Accumulated depreciation | (24,000) |
| Total assets | $360,000 |
| **Liabilities and Stockholders' Equity** | |
| Accounts payable | $ 39,200 |
| Current notes payable | 6,800 |
| Mortgage payable | 62,000 |
| Bonds payable | 42,000 |
| Common stock | 128,000 |
| Retained earnings | 82,000 |
| Total liabilities and stockholders' equity | $360,000 |

The average number of common shares outstanding during 2011 was 1,500. Net income for the year was $60,000.

**Required**

Compute each of the following:

a. Current ratio
b. Earnings per share
c. Acid-test ratio
d. Return on investment
e. Return on equity
f. Debt to equity ratio

**LO 4, 5, 6, 7**    **Exercise 13-13B**    *Comprehensive analysis*

The following is a list of transactions.

a. Paid cash for short-term marketable securities.
b. Purchased a computer, issuing a short-term note for the purchase price.
c. Purchased factory equipment, issuing a long-term note for the purchase price.
d. Sold merchandise on account at a profit.
e. Paid cash on accounts payable.
f. Received cash from issuing common stock.
g. Sold a factory for cash at a profit.
h. Purchased raw materials on account.
i. Paid cash for property taxes on administrative buildings.

**Required**

Indicate the effect of each of the preceding transactions on (a) the quick ratio, (b) working capital, (c) stockholders' equity, (d) the debt/equity ratio, (e) retained earnings. Assume that the current ratio is greater than 1:1.

**Exercise 13-14B**   *Accounts receivable turnover, inventory turnover, and net margin*     **LO 4, 6**

Selected data from Magnolia Company follow.

| Balance Sheet Data As of December 31 | | |
|---|---|---|
| | **2012** | **2011** |
| Accounts receivable | $640,000 | $600,000 |
| Allowance for doubtful accounts | (32,000) | (28,000) |
| Net accounts receivable | $608,000 | $572,000 |
| Inventories, lower of cost or market | $400,000 | $420,000 |

| Income Statement Data Year Ended December 31 | | |
|---|---|---|
| | **2012** | **2011** |
| Net credit sales | $5,000,000 | $3,600,000 |
| Net cash sales | 1,000,000 | 800,000 |
| Net sales | $6,000,000 | $4,400,000 |
| Cost of goods sold | $3,500,000 | $2,600,000 |
| Selling, general, and administrative expenses | 600,000 | 320,000 |
| Other expenses | 300,000 | 240,000 |
| Total operating expenses | $4,400,000 | $3,160,000 |

**Required**

Compute the following.

a.  The accounts receivable turnover for 2012.

b.  The inventory turnover for 2012.

c.  The net margin for 2011.

**Exercise 13-15B**   *Comprehensive analysis*     **LO 4, 5**

December 31, 2012, balance sheet data for Brady Company follow. All accounts are represented. Amounts indicated by question marks (?) can be calculated using the following additional information.

| Assets | |
|---|---|
| Cash | $ 30,000 |
| Accounts receivable (net) | ? |
| Inventory | ? |
| Property, plant, and equipment (net) | 556,000 |
| | $    ? |
| **Liabilities and Stockholders' Equity** | |
| Accounts payable (trade) | $ 52,000 |
| Income taxes payable (current) | 28,000 |
| Long-term debt | ? |
| Common stock | 320,000 |
| Retained earnings | ? |
| | $    ? |
| | *continued* |

**Additional Information**

| | |
|---|---|
| Quick ratio (at year end) | 1.3 to 1 |
| Working capital | $84,000 |
| Inventory turnover (cost of goods sold ÷ ending inventory) | 12 times |
| Debt/Equity ratio | 80% |
| Gross margin for 2012 | $252,000 |

**Required**

Determine the following.

a. The balance in accounts receivable as of December 31, 2012.
b. The turnover of assets for 2012.
c. The balance of long-term debt as of December 31, 2012.
d. The balance in retained earnings as of December 2012.

## PROBLEMS—SERIES B

**LO 2**

### Problem 13-16B    *Vertical analysis*

Willrick Corporation's controller has prepared the following vertical analysis for the president.

| | 2012 | 2011 |
|---|---|---|
| Sales | 100.0% | 100.0% |
| Cost of goods sold | 57.0 | 54.0 |
| Gross margin | 43.0 | 46.0 |
| Selling and administrative expense | 18.0 | 20.0 |
| Interest expense | 2.8 | 4.0 |
| Total expenses | 20.8 | 24.0 |
| Income before taxes | 22.2 | 22.0 |
| Income tax expense | 10.0 | 8.0 |
| Net income | 12.2% | 14.0% |

**Required**

Sales were $600,000 in 2011 and $750,000 in 2012. Convert the analysis to income statements for the two years.

**LO 5, 6, 7**

### Problem 13-17B    *Ratio analysis*

Information from Snelling Company's financial statements follows.

| | 2011 | 2010 |
|---|---|---|
| Net sales | $1,440,000 | $1,000,000 |
| Income before interest and taxes | 320,000 | 260,000 |
| Net income after taxes | 148,000 | 96,000 |
| Bond interest expense | 36,000 | 24,000 |
| Stockholders' equity, December 31 (2009: $480,000) | 720,000 | 600,000 |
| Common stock, par $24, December 31 | 420,000 | 360,000 |

Average number of shares outstanding was 16,000 for 2011 and 15,000 for 2010.

**Required**

Compute the following ratios for Snelling Company for 2011 and 2010.

a. Number of times interest was earned.

b. Earnings per share based on the average number of shares outstanding.

c. Price-earnings ratio (market prices: 2011, $60 per share; 2010, $48 per share).

d. Return on equity.

e. Net margin.

### Problem 13-18B    *Effect of transactions on current ratio and working capital*    LO 4

Lennox Company has a current ratio of 2:1 on June 30, 2011. Indicate whether each of the following transactions would increase (+), decrease (−), or not affect (NA) Lennox's current ratio and its working capital.

**Required**

a. Issued 10-year bonds for $100,000 cash.

b. Paid cash to settle an account payable.

c. Sold merchandise for more than cost.

d. Recognized depreciation on plant equipment.

e. Purchased a machine by issuing a long-term note payable.

f. Purchased merchandise inventory on account.

g. Received customer payment on account receivable.

h. Paid cash for federal income tax expense (assume that the expense has not been previously accrued).

i. Declared cash dividend payable in one month.

j. Received cash for interest on a long-term note receivable (assume that interest has not been previously accrued).

k. Received cash from issuing a short-term note payable.

l. Traded a truck for a sedan.

### Problem 13-19B    *Ratio analysis*    LO 7

Selected data for Ernsmeyer Company for 2011 and additional information on industry averages follow.

| | |
|---|---:|
| Earnings (net income) | $ 168,000 |
| Preferred stock (16,000 shares at $35 par, 6%) | $ 560,000 |
| Common stock (40,500 shares no par, market value $52) | 684,000 |
| Retained earnings | 480,000 |
| | 1,724,000 |
| Less: Treasury stock | |
| Preferred (1,000 shares) | $28,800 |
| Common (500 shares) | 12,800        41,600 |
| Total stockholders' equity | $1,682,400 |

| Industry averages | |
|---|---:|
| Earnings per share | $2.00 |
| Price-earnings ratio | 8.00 |
| Return on equity | 7.30% |

**Required**

a. Calculate and compare Ernsmeyer Company's ratios with the industry averages.

b. Discuss factors you would consider in deciding whether to invest in the company.

LO 4, 5    **Problem 13-20B**    *Supply missing balance sheet numbers*

Cathy Sand discovered a piece of wet and partially burned balance sheet after her office was destroyed by fire. She could recall a current ratio of 1.75 and a debt to assets ratio of 45 percent.

| Assets | |
| --- | --- |
| **Current assets** | |
| Cash | $ 37,500 |
| Accounts receivable | (A) |
| Inventory | 63,000 |
| Prepaid expenses | 13,500 |
| Total current assets | (B) |
| **Long-term assets** | |
| Building | (C) |
| Less: Accumulated depreciation | (45,000) |
| Total long-term assets | 270,000 |
| **Total assets** | $      (D) |
| **Liabilities and Stockholders' Equity** | |
| **Liabilities** | |
| Current liabilities | |
| Accounts payable | $ 63,000 |
| Notes payable | (E) |
| Income tax payable | 27,000 |
| Total current liabilities | 120,000 |
| Long-term liabilities | |
| Bonds payable | 67,500 |
| Mortgage payable | (F) |
| Total liabilities | (G) |
| Stockholders' equity | |
| Common stock | 135,000 |
| Retained earnings | (H) |
| Total stockholders' equity | (I) |
| Total liabilities and stockholders' equity | $      (J) |

**Required**

Complete the balance sheet by supplying the missing amounts.

LO 4, 5, 6, 7    **Problem 13-21B**    *Ratio analysis*

The following financial statements apply to Boyd Appliances, Inc.

### BOYD APPLIANCES, INC.
#### Balance Sheets
#### As of December 31

| | 2012 | 2011 |
| --- | --- | --- |
| **Assets** | | |
| Current assets | | |
| Cash | $118,000 | $ 91,000 |
| Marketable securities | 24,000 | 18,000 |
| Accounts receivable (net) | 112,000 | 108,000 |
| Inventories | 180,000 | 192,000 |
| Prepaid expenses | 27,000 | 14,000 |
| Total current assets | 461,000 | 423,000 |
| | | *continued* |

|  | 2012 | 2011 |
|---|---|---|
| Investments | 120,000 | 120,000 |
| Plant (net) | 260,000 | 254,000 |
| Other | 81,000 | 74,000 |
| Total assets | $922,000 | $871,000 |
| **Liabilities and Stockholders' Equity** | | |
| Liabilities | | |
| Current liabilities | | |
| Notes payable | $ 20,000 | $ 15,000 |
| Accounts payable | 80,000 | 38,000 |
| Other | 66,000 | 9,000 |
| Total current liabilities | 166,000 | 62,000 |
| Noncurrent liabilities | | |
| Bonds payable | 110,000 | 210,000 |
| Other | 26,000 | 12,000 |
| Total noncurrent liabilities | 136,000 | 222,000 |
| Total liabilities | 302,000 | 284,000 |
| Stockholders' equity | | |
| Preferred stock ($100 par, 4% cumulative, non-participating; $100 liquidating value; 1,000 shares authorized and issued; no dividends in arrears) | 100,000 | 100,000 |
| Common stock (no par; 50,000 shares authorized; 12,000 shares issued) | 240,000 | 240,000 |
| Retained earnings | 280,000 | 247,000 |
| Total stockholders' equity | 620,000 | 587,000 |
| Total liabilities and stockholders' equity | $922,000 | $871,000 |

## BOYD APPLIANCES, INC.
### Statements of Income and Retained Earnings
### For the Years Ended December 31

|  | 2012 | 2011 |
|---|---|---|
| Revenues | | |
| Sales (net) | $240,000 | $230,000 |
| Other revenues | 7,000 | 4,000 |
| Total revenues | 247,000 | 234,000 |
| Expenses | | |
| Cost of goods sold | 143,000 | 130,000 |
| Selling, general, and administrative | 46,000 | 57,000 |
| Bond interest expense | 7,000 | 10,000 |
| Income tax expense | 8,000 | 14,000 |
| Total expenses | 204,000 | 211,000 |
| Net income | 43,000 | 23,000 |
| Retained earnings, January 1 | 247,000 | 234,000 |
| Less: Preferred stock dividends | 4,000 | 4,000 |
| Common stock dividends | 6,000 | 6,000 |
| Retained earnings, December 31 | $280,000 | $247,000 |

**Required**

Calculate the following ratios for 2012.

a. Working capital
b. Current ratio
c. Quick ratio

**d.** Accounts receivable turnover

**e.** Average days to collect accounts receivable

**f.** Inventory turnover

**g.** Avg. days to sell inventory

**h.** Debt to assets ratio

**i.** Debt to equity ratio

**j.** Times interest was earned

**k.** Plant assets to long-term debt

**l.** Net margin

**m.** Turnover of assets

**n.** Return on investment

**o.** Return on equity

**p.** Earnings per share

**q.** Book value per share

**r.** Price-earnings ratio (market price: $13.26)

**s.** Dividend yield on common stock

**LO 4, 5, 6, 7**

**eXcel**

### Problem 13-22B    *Ratio analysis*

Addison Company's stock is quoted at $16 per share at December 31, 2012 and 2011. Addison's financial statements follow.

| ADDISON COMPANY | | |
|---|---|---|
| Balance Sheets | | |
| As of December 31 | | |
| (In thousands) | | |
| | **2012** | **2011** |
| **Assets** | | |
| Current assets | | |
| Cash | $ 3,000 | $ 2,000 |
| Marketable securities at cost which approximates market | 5,000 | 4,000 |
| Accounts receivable, net of allowance for doubtful accounts | 47,000 | 44,000 |
| Inventories, lower of cost or market | 50,000 | 60,000 |
| Prepaid expenses | 2,000 | 1,000 |
| Total current assets | 107,000 | 111,000 |
| Property, plant, and equipment, net of accumulated depreciation | 100,000 | 105,000 |
| Investments | 1,000 | 1,000 |
| Long-term receivables | 3,000 | 2,000 |
| Goodwill and patents, net of accumulated amortization | 2,000 | 4,000 |
| Other assets | 2,000 | 3,000 |
| Total assets | $215,000 | $226,000 |
| **Liabilities and Stockholders' Equity** | | |
| Current liabilities | | |
| Notes payable | $ 3,000 | $ 5,000 |
| Accounts payable | 12,000 | 16,000 |
| Accrued expenses | 9,000 | 11,000 |
| Income taxes payable | 1,000 | 1,000 |
| Payments due within one year | 3,000 | 2,000 |
| Total current liabilities | 28,000 | 35,000 |
| Long-term debt | 50,000 | 60,000 |
| Deferred income taxes | 30,000 | 27,000 |
| Other liabilities | 5,000 | 4,000 |
| Total liabilities | 113,000 | 126,000 |

*continued*

|  | 2012 | 2011 |
|---|---|---|
| Stockholders' equity | | |
| 5% cumulative preferred stock, par value $100 per share; | | |
| $100 liquidating value; authorized 250,000 shares; issued | | |
| and outstanding 200,000 shares | 20,000 | 20,000 |
| Common stock, no par; 10,000,000 shares authorized | | |
| and 5,000,000 shares issued and outstanding | 40,000 | 40,000 |
| Retained earnings | 42,000 | 40,000 |
| Total stockholders' equity | 102,000 | 100,000 |
| Total liabilities and stockholders' equity | $215,000 | $226,000 |

## ADDISON COMPANY
### Statements of Income and Retained Earnings
### For the Years Ended December 31
### (In thousands)

|  | 2012 | 2011 |
|---|---|---|
| Net sales | $180,000 | $150,000 |
| Expenses | | |
| Cost of goods sold | 147,000 | 120,000 |
| Selling, general, and administrative expenses | 20,000 | 18,000 |
| Other | 2,000 | 2,000 |
| Total expenses | 169,000 | 140,000 |
| Income before income taxes | 11,000 | 10,000 |
| Income taxes | 5,000 | 4,000 |
| Net income | 6,000 | 6,000 |
| Retained earnings at beginning of period | 40,000 | 38,000 |
| Less: Dividends on common stock | 3,000 | 3,000 |
| Dividends on preferred stock | 1,000 | 1,000 |
| Retained earnings at end of period | $ 42,000 | $ 40,000 |

**Required**

Based on the preceding information, compute the following for 2012 only.

a.  Current ratio
b.  Quick (acid-test) ratio
c.  Average days to collect accounts receivable, assuming all sales on account
d.  Inventory turnover
e.  Book value per share of common stock
f.  Earnings per share on common stock
g.  Price-earnings ratio on common stock
h.  Debt to assets ratio
i.  Return on investment
j.  Return on equity

## Problem 13-23B    *Horizontal analysis*    LO 2

**Required**

Use the financial statements for Addison Company from Problem 13-22B to perform a horizontal analysis of both the balance sheet and income statement for 2012 and 2011.

**LO 2**

### Problem 13-24B    *Vertical analysis*

**Required**

Use the financial statements for Addison Company from Problem 13-22B to perform a vertical analysis (based on total assets, total equities, and sales) of both the balance sheets and income statements for 2012 and 2011.

## ANALYZE, THINK, COMMUNICATE

### ATC 13-1    Business Applications Case    *Analyzing the Kroger Company and Whole Foods Market*

The following information relates to The Kroger Company and Whole Foods Market, Inc. for their 2009 and 2008 fiscal years.

| THE KROGER COMPANY<br>Selected Financial Information<br>(Amounts in millions, except per share amounts) | | |
|---|---|---|
| | January 31,<br>2009 | February 2,<br>2008 |
| Total current assets | $ 7,206 | $ 7,114 |
| Merchandise inventories | 6,459 | 6,063 |
| Property and equipment, net of depreciation | 13,161 | 12,498 |
| Total assets | 23,211 | 22,299 |
| Total current liabilities | 7,629 | 8,689 |
| Total long-term liabilities | 10,311 | 8,696 |
| Total liabilities | 17,940 | 17,385 |
| Total shareholders equity | 5,271 | 4,914 |
| Revenue | 76,000 | 70,235 |
| Cost of goods sold | 58,564 | 53,779 |
| Gross profit | 17,436 | 16,456 |
| Operating income | 2,451 | 2,301 |
| Earnings from continuing operations<br>before income tax expense | 1,966 | 1,827 |
| Income tax expense | 717 | 646 |
| Net earnings | 1,249 | 1,181 |
| Basic earnings per share | $ 1.92 | $ 1.71 |

| WHOLE FOODS MARKET, INC.<br>Selected Financial Information<br>(Amounts in millions except per share data) | | |
|---|---|---|
| | September 27,<br>2009 | September 28,<br>2008 |
| Total current assets | $1,055 | $ 623 |
| Merchandise inventory | 311 | 327 |
| Property and equipment, net of depreciation | 1,898 | 1,900 |
| Total assets | 3,783 | 3,381 |
| Total current liabilities | 684 | 666 |
| Total long-term liabilities | 1,058 | 1,209 |
| Total liabilities | 1,742 | 1,875 |
| Total stockholders' equity | 2,041 | 1,506 |

*continued*

| | September 27, 2009 | September 28, 2008 |
|---|---|---|
| Revenues | $8,032 | $7,954 |
| Cost of goods sold | 5,277 | 5,247 |
| Gross profit | 2,754 | 2,707 |
| Operating income | 284 | 236 |
| Earnings from continuing operations before income taxes | 251 | 207 |
| Income tax expense | 104 | 92 |
| Net earnings | 147 | 115 |
| Basic earnings per share | $ 0.85 | $ 0.82 |

## Required

**a.** Compute the following ratios for the companies' 2009 fiscal years:

    **(1)** Current ratio.

    **(2)** Average days to sell inventory. (Use average inventory.)

    **(3)** Debt to assets ratio.

    **(4)** Return on investment. (Use average assets and use "earnings from continuing operations" rather than "net earnings.")

    **(5)** Gross margin percentage.

    **(6)** Asset turnover. (Use average assets.)

    **(7)** Return on sales. (Use "earnings from continuing operations" rather than "net earnings.")

    **(8)** Plant assets to long-term debt ratio.

**b.** Which company appears to be more profitable? Explain your answer and identify which of the ratio(s) from Requirement *a* you used to reach your conclusion.

**c.** Which company appears to have the higher level of financial risk? Explain your answer and identify which of the ratio(s) from Requirement *a* you used to reach your conclusion.

**d.** Which company appears to be charging higher prices for its goods? Explain your answer and identify which of the ratio(s) from Requirement *a* you used to reach your conclusion.

**e.** Which company appears to be the more efficient at using its assets? Explain your answer and identify which of the ratio(s) from Requirement *a* you used to reach your conclusion.

## ATC 13-2   Group Assignment   *Ratio analysis and logic*

Presented here are selected data from the 10-K reports of four companies. The four companies, in alphabetical order, are

**BellSouth Corporation**, a telephone company that operates in the southeastern United States.

**Caterpillar, Inc.**, a manufacturer of heavy machinery.

**Dollar General Corporation**, a company that owns Dollar General Stores discount stores.

**Tiffany & Company**, a company that operates high-end jewelry stores.

The data, presented in the order of the amount of sales, are as follows. Dollar amounts are in millions.

| | A | B | C | D |
|---|---|---|---|---|
| Sales | $20,561 | $18,110 | $2,627.3 | $1,017.6 |
| Cost of goods sold | 6,254 | 13,374 | 1,885.2 | 453.4 |
| Net earnings | 3,261 | 1,665 | 144.6 | 72.8 |
| Inventory or NA | 2,603 | 632.0 | 386.4 | NA |
| Materials and supplies | 398 | NA | NA | NA |
| Accounts receivable | 4,750 | 3,331 | 0 | 99.5 |
| Total assets | 36,301 | 20,756 | 914.8 | 827.1 |

## Required

**a.** Divide the class into groups of four or five students per group and then organize the groups into four sections. Assign Task 1 to the first section of groups, Task 2 to the second section, Task 3 to the third section, and Task 4 to the fourth section.

### Group Tasks

**(1)** Assume that you represent BellSouth Corporation. Identify the set of financial data (Column A, B, C, or D) that relates to your company.

**(2)** Assume that you represent Caterpillar, Inc. Identify the set of financial data (Column A, B, C, or D) that relates to your company.

**(3)** Assume that you represent Dollar General Corporation. Identify the set of financial data (Column A, B, C, or D) that relates to your company.

**(4)** Assume that you represent Tiffany & Company. Identify the set of financial data (Column A, B, C, or D) that relates to your company.

*Hint:* Use a gross margin ratio (gross margin ÷ sales), a net margin ratio (net income ÷ sales), and return on assets (net income ÷ total assets) to facilitate identifying the financial data related to your particular company.

**b.** Select a representative from each section. Have the representatives explain the rationale for the group's selection. The explanation should include a set of ratios that support the group's conclusion.

### ATC 13-3   Research Assignment   *Analyzing Whirlpool's acquisition of Maytag*

To complete the requirements below you will need to obtain Whirlpool's income statements for 2005, 2007 and 2008, and its balance sheets for 2004 through 2008. The easiest way to obtain these financial statements is to retrieve the company's 2005 and 2008 Form 10-Ks. To obtain the Form 10-Ks you can use either the EDGAR system following the instructions in Appendix A, or they can be found under the "Investors" link on the company's corporate website at www.whirlpoolcorp.com. On March 31, 2006, Whirlpool Corporation acquired Maytag, another manufacturer of home appliances. The company's 2006, 2007 and 2008 financial statements include the activities of Maytag; its 2005 and 2004 statements do not.

### Required

**a.** Compute the following ratios for 2005, 2007 and 2008. Show your calculations.

| | |
|---|---|
| Gross margin percentage | Net margin |
| Return on investment | Return on equity |
| Current ratio | Debt to assets ratio |

**b.** Based on the ratios computed in Requirement *a*, comment on the apparent effects of Whirlpool's acquisition of Maytag. Assume any significant change in these ratios was the result of the acquisition.

**c.** Based on this limited analysis, does it appear that the short-term effects of the acquisition were good or bad for Whirlpool?

### ATC 13-4   Writing Assignment   *Inentifying companies based on financial statement information*

The following ratios are for four companies in different industries. Some of these ratios have been discussed in the textbook, others have not, but their names explain how the ratio was computed. These data are for the companies' 2008 fiscal years. The four sets of ratios, presented randomly are:

| | Company 1 | Company 2 | Company 3 | Company 4 |
|---|---|---|---|---|
| Current assets ÷ Total assets | 47% | 11% | 15% | 20% |
| Average days to sell inventory | 33 | 138 | 7 | 9 |
| Average days to collect receivables | 25 | 83 | 3 | 21 |
| Return on assets | 5% | 4% | 4% | 18% |
| Gross profit ÷ Sales | 20% | 40% | 20% | 54% |
| Asset turnover | 0.46 | 0.71 | 2.19 | 1.39 |
| Sales ÷ Number of full-time employees | $453,407 | $341,958 | $49,865 | $29,057 |

The four companies to which these ratios relate, listed in alphabetical order, are:

**Caterpillar, Inc.** is a company that manufactures heavy construction equipment.

**Denny's Corporation** operated over 1,541 restaurants as of December 31, 2008.

**Molson Coors Brewing, Inc.** is a company that produces beer and related products.

**Weight Watchers International, Inc.** is a company that provides weight loss services and products.

**Required**

Determine which company should be matched with each set of ratios. Write a memorandum explaining the rationale for your decisions.

### ATC 13-5    Ethical Dilemma    *Making the ratios look good*

J. Talbot is the accounting manager for Kolla Waste Disposal Corporation. Kolla is having its worst financial year since its inception. The company is expected to report a net loss. In the midst of such bad news, Ms. Talbot surprised the company president, Mr. Winston, by suggesting that the company write off approximately 25 percent of its garbage trucks. Mr. Winston responded by noting that the trucks could still be operated for another two or three years. Ms. Talbot replied, "We may use them for two or three more years, but you couldn't sell them on the street if you had to. Who wants to buy a bunch of old garbage trucks and besides, it will make next year's financials so sweet. No one will care about the additional write-off this year. We are already showing a loss. Who will care if we lose a little bit more?"

**Required**

a. How will the write-off affect the following year's return on assets ratio?

b. How will the write-off affect the asset and income growth percentages?

c. Would writing off the garbage trucks violate any of the standards of ethical conduct shown in Exhibit 1.15 of Chapter 1?

d. Explain how the components of the fraud triangle relate to this case.

### ATC 13-6    Spreadsheet Assignment    *Using Excel*

Tomkung Corporation's 2010 income statements are presented in the following spreadsheet.

**Required**

Construct a spreadsheet to conduct horizontal analysis of the income statements for 2010 and 2009.

| | | 2010 | 2009 | Percentage Change |
|---|---|---|---|---|
| 6 | Sales | $1,025,000 | $987,000 | 3.9% |
| 7 | Cost of Goods Sold | 795,000 | 732,000 | 8.6% |
| 8 | Gross Margin | 230,000 | 255,000 | -9.8% |
| 9 | Operating Expenses | 200,000 | 205,000 | -2.4% |
| 10 | Income before Taxes | 30,000 | 50,000 | -40.0% |
| 11 | Income Taxes | 10,000 | 17,100 | -41.5% |
| 12 | Net Income | $20,000 | $32,900 | -39.2% |

*Chapter 13 - Working with Excel    Name:*

### ATC 13-7    Spreadsheet Assignment    *Mastering Excel*

Refer to the data in ATC 13-6.

**Required**

Construct a spreadsheet to conduct vertical analysis for both years, 2010 and 2009.

## CHAPTER 14

# Statement of Cash Flows

## LEARNING OBJECTIVES

**After you have mastered the material in this chapter, you will be able to:**

**1** Prepare the operating activities section of a statement of cash flows using the indirect method.

**2** Prepare the operating activities section of a statement of cash flows using the direct method.

**3** Prepare the investing activities section of a statement of cash flows.

**4** Prepare the financing activities section of a statement of cash flows.

## CHAPTER OPENING

To make informed investment and credit decisions, financial statement users need information to help them assess the amounts, timing, and uncertainty of a company's prospective cash flows. This chapter explains more about the items reported on the statement of cash flows and describes a more practical way to prepare the statement than analyzing every entry in the cash account. As previously shown, the statement of cash flows reports how a company obtained and spent cash during an accounting period. Sources of cash are *cash inflows,* and uses are *cash outflows.* Cash receipts (inflows) and payments (outflows) are reported as either operating activities, investing activities, or financing activities.

# The Curious Accountant

**Sirius XM Radio, Inc.**, was created by a merger between Sirius Radio and XM Radio, in July 2008. Sirius Radio was formed in 1990, and XM Radio began in 1992, although these companies did not generate any significant amounts of revenue in the early years of their existence. Even though their revenues grew steadily over the years, neither XM, Sirius, nor the combined company, Sirius XM Radio, has ever earned a profit. Its cumulative net losses totaled $9.7 billion by the end of 2008, with $5.5 billion of that coming in 2008 alone.

How could Sirius XM lose so much money and still be able to pay its bills? (Answer on page 643.)

# AN OVERVIEW OF THE STATEMENT OF CASH FLOWS

The statement of cash flows provides information about cash coming into and going out of a business during an accounting period. Cash flows are classified into one of three categories: operating activities, investing activities, or financing activities. A separate section also displays any significant noncash investing and financing activities. Descriptions of these categories and how they are presented in the statement of cash flows follow.

## Operating Activities

Routine cash inflows and outflows resulting from running (operating) a business are reported in the **operating activities** section of the statement of cash flows. Cash flows reported as operating activities include:

1. Cash receipts from revenues including interest and dividend revenue.
2. Cash payments for expenses including interest expense. Recall that dividend payments are not expenses. Dividend payments are reported in the financing activities section.

**EXHIBIT 14.1**

**Operating Activities—Direct Method**

| Cash Flows from Operating Activities | |
|---|---|
| Cash receipts from customers | $400 |
| Cash payments for expenses | (350) |
| Net cash flow from operating activities | $ 50 |

Under generally accepted accounting principles, the operating activities section of the statement of cash flows can be presented using either the *direct* or the *indirect* method. The **direct method** explicitly (*directly*) identifies the major *sources* and *uses* of cash. To illustrate, assume that during 2011 New South Company earns revenue on account of $500 and collects $400 cash from customers. Further assume the company incurs $390 of expenses on account and pays $350 cash to settle accounts payable. Exhibit 14.1 shows the operating activities section of the statement of cash flows using the *direct method.*

In contrast, the **indirect method** starts with net income as reported on the income statement followed by the adjustments necessary to convert the accrual-based net income figure to a cash-basis equivalent. To illustrate, begin with New South Company's income statement based on the above assumptions.

| Revenues | $500 |
|---|---|
| Expenses | (390) |
| Net income | $110 |

Converting the net income of $110 to the net cash flow from operating activities of $50 requires the following adjustments.

1. New South earned $500 of revenue but collected only $400 in cash. The remaining $100 will be collected in the next accounting period. This $100 *increase in accounts receivable* must be *subtracted* from net income to determine cash flow because it increased net income but did not increase cash.
2. New South incurred $390 of expense but paid only $350 in cash. The remaining $40 will be paid in the next accounting period. This $40 *increase in accounts payable* must be *added* back to net income to determine cash flow because it decreased net income but did not use cash.

**EXHIBIT 14.2**

**Operating Activities—Indirect Method**

| Cash Flows from Operating Activities | |
|---|---|
| Net income | $110 |
| Subtract: Increase in accounts receivable | (100) |
| Add: Increase in accounts payable | 40 |
| Net cash flow from operating activities | $ 50 |

Exhibit 14.2 shows the operating activities section of the statement of cash flows using the indirect method.

Compare the direct method presented in Exhibit 14.1 with the indirect method presented in Exhibit 14.2. Both methods report $50 of net cash flow from operating activities. They represent two different approaches to computing the same amount.

Because people typically find the direct method easier to understand, the Financial Accounting Standards Board (FASB) recommends it. Most companies, however, use the indirect method. Why? Back when the FASB adopted a requirement for companies to include a statement of cash flows in their annual reports, most companies used accounting systems that were compatible with the indirect method. It was therefore easier to prepare the new statement under the indirect method using existing systems than to create new record-keeping systems compatible with the direct method.

The FASB continues to advocate the direct method and a growing number of companies use it. Since the majority of companies continue to use the indirect method, however, financial statement users should understand both methods.

---

## ✓ CHECK YOURSELF 14.1

Hammer, Inc., had a beginning balance of $22,400 in its Accounts Receivable account. During the accounting period, Hammer earned $234,700 of net income. The ending balance in the Accounts Receivable account was $18,200. Based on this information alone, determine the amount of cash flow from operating activities.

**Answer**

| Account Title | Ending | Beginning | Change |
|---|---|---|---|
| Accounts receivable | $18,200 | $22,400 | $(4,200) |

| Applicable Rule | Cash Flow from Operating Activities | Amount |
|---|---|---|
|  | Net income | $234,700 |
| Rule 1 | Add: Decrease in accounts receivable | 4,200 |
|  | Cash flow from operating activities | $238,900 |

---

## Investing Activities

For a business, long-term assets are investments. Cash flows related to acquiring or disposing of long-term assets are therefore reported in the **investing activities** section of the statement of cash flows. Cash flows reported as investing activities include:

1. Cash receipts (inflows) from selling property, plant, equipment, or marketable securities as well as collections from nonoperating credit instruments such as notes or mortgages receivable.
2. Cash payments (outflows) for purchasing property, plant, equipment, or marketable securities as well as nonoperating loans to borrowers.

## Financing Activities

Cash flows related to borrowing (short- or long-term) and stockholders' equity are reported in the **financing activities** section of the statement of cash flows. Cash flows reported as financing activities include:

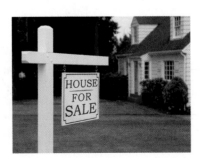

1. Cash receipts (inflows) from borrowing money and issuing stock.
2. Cash payments (outflows) to repay debt, purchase treasury stock, and pay dividends.

The classification of cash flows is based on the type of activity, not the type of account. For example, buying another company's common stock is an investing activity, but issuing a company's own common stock is a financing activity. Receiving dividends from a common stock investment is an operating activity, and paying dividends to a company's own stockholders is a financing activity. Similarly, loaning money is an investing activity, although borrowing it is a financing activity. Focus on the type of activity rather than the type of account when classifying cash flows as operating, investing, or financing activities.

## Noncash Investing and Financing Activities

Companies sometimes undertake significant **noncash investing and financing activities** such as acquiring a long-term asset in exchange for common stock. Since these types of transactions do not involve exchanging cash they are not reported in the main body of the statement of cash flows. However, because the FASB requires that all material investing and financing activities be disclosed, whether or not they involve exchanging cash, companies must include with the statement of cash flows a separate schedule of any noncash investing and financing activities.

## Reporting Format for the Statement of Cash Flows

Cash flow categories are reported in the following order: (1) operating activities; (2) investing activities; and (3) financing activities. In each category, the difference between the inflows and outflows is presented as a net cash inflow or outflow for the category. These net amounts are combined to determine the net change (increase or decrease) in the company's cash for the period. The net change in cash is combined with the beginning cash balance to determine the ending cash balance. The ending cash balance on the statement of cash flows is the same as the cash balance reported on the balance sheet. The schedule of noncash investing and financing activities is typically presented at the bottom of the statement of cash flows. Exhibit 14.3 outlines this format.

| EXHIBIT 14.3 | Format for Statement of Cash Flows |
| --- | --- |

**WESTERN COMPANY**
Statement of Cash Flows
For the Year Ended December 31, 2011

| | |
| --- | --- |
| Cash flows from operating activities | |
| Net increase (decrease) from operating activities | XXX |
| Cash flows from investing activities | |
| Net increase (decrease) from investing activities | XXX |
| Cash flows from financing activities | |
| Net increase (decrease) from financing activities | XXX |
| Net increase (decrease) in cash | XXX |
| Plus: Beginning cash balance | XXX |
| Ending cash balance | XXX |
| **Schedule of Noncash Investing and Financing Activities** | |
| List of significant noncash transactions | XXX |

As indicated in Exhibit 14.4, most companies present the statement of cash flows as the last of the four primary financial statements. However, a sizable number of companies present it after the income statement and balance sheet but before the statement of changes in stockholders' equity. Some companies place the statement of cash flows first, before the other three statements.

## EXHIBIT 14.4

**Placement of Statement of Cash Flows Relative to Other Financial Statements**

First statement
**7%**

After income statement and balance sheet
**39%**

Final statement
**54%**

Data Source: AICPA, *Accounting Trends and Techniques.*

## PREPARING A STATEMENT OF CASH FLOWS

Most of the data needed to construct a statement of cash flows can be obtained from two successive balance sheets and the intervening income statement. Certain information from the long-term asset records is also usually required. To illustrate, refer to the financial statements for New South Company presented in Exhibit 14.5. Notice that cash decreased from $400 at the end of 2011 to $300 at the end of 2012. The statement of cash flows explains what caused this $100 decrease.

## EXHIBIT 14.5  Financial Statements for New South Company

### NEW SOUTH COMPANY
Balance Sheets
As of December 31

|  | 2012 | 2011 |
|---|---|---|
| Current assets: |  |  |
| Cash | $   300 | $   400 |
| Accounts receivable | 1,000 | 1,200 |
| Interest receivable | 400 | 300 |
| Inventory | 8,900 | 8,200 |
| Prepaid insurance | 1,100 | 1,400 |
| Total current assets | 11,700 | $11,500 |
| Long-term assets |  |  |
| Investment securities | 5,100 | 3,500 |
| Store fixtures | 5,400 | 4,800 |
| Accumulated depreciation | (900) | (1,200) |
| Land | 8,200 | 6,000 |
| Total long-term assets | 17,800 | 13,100 |
| Total assets | $29,500 | $24,600 |
| Current liabilities: |  |  |
| Accounts payable—inventory purchases | $   800 | $ 1,100 |
| Salaries payable | 1,000 | 900 |
| Other operating expenses payable | 1,500 | 1,300 |
| Interest payable | 300 | 500 |
| Unearned rent revenue | 600 | 1,600 |
| Total current liabilities | 4,200 | 5,400 |

*continued*

| EXHIBIT 14.5 | *concluded* |
| --- | --- |

## NEW SOUTH COMPANY
### Balance Sheets
### As of December 31

| | 2012 | 2011 |
| --- | --- | --- |
| Long-term liabilities | | |
| Mortgage payable | 2,200 | 0 |
| Bonds payable | 1,000 | 4,000 |
| Total long-term liabilities | 3,200 | 4,000 |
| Stockholders' equity | | |
| Common stock | 10,000 | 8,000 |
| Retained earnings | 12,700 | 7,200 |
| Treasury stock | (600) | 0 |
| Total stockholders' equity | 22,100 | 15,200 |
| Total liabilities and stockholders' equity | $29,500 | $24,600 |

## NEW SOUTH COMPANY
### Income Statement
### For the Year Ended December 31, 2012

| | | |
| --- | --- | --- |
| Sales revenue | | $20,600 |
| Cost of goods sold | | (10,500) |
| Gross margin | | 10,100 |
| Operating expenses | | |
| Depreciation expense | $(1,000) | |
| Salaries expense | (2,700) | |
| Insurance expense | (1,300) | |
| Other operating expenses | (1,400) | |
| Total operating expenses | | (6,400) |
| Income from sales business | | 3,700 |
| Other income—rent revenue | | 2,400 |
| Operating income | | 6,100 |
| Nonoperating revenue and expense | | |
| Interest revenue | 700 | |
| Interest expense | (400) | |
| Gain on sale of store fixtures | 600 | |
| Total nonoperating items | | 900 |
| Net income | | $ 7,000 |

Note 1: No investment securities were sold during 2012.
Note 2: During 2012, New South sold store fixtures that had originally cost $1,700. At the time of
sale, accumulated depreciation on the fixtures was $1,300.
Note 3: Land was acquireds during 2012 by issuing a mortgage note payable. No land sales
occurred during 2012.

## PREPARING THE OPERATING ACTIVITIES SECTION OF A STATEMENT OF CASH FLOWS USING THE INDIRECT METHOD

Prepare the operating activities
section of a statement of cash flows
using the indirect method.

Recall that the indirect approach begins with the amount of net income. Many aspects of accrual accounting, such as recognizing revenues and expenses on account, can cause differences between the amount of net income reported on a company's income statement and the amount of net cash flow it reports from operating activities. Most of the differences between revenue and expense recognition and cash flows are related to changes in the balances of the noncash current assets and current liabilities.

## Answers to The Curious Accountant

First, it should be remembered that GAAP requires earnings and losses to be computed on an accrual basis. A company can have negative earnings and still have positive cash flows from operating activities. This was not the case at Sirius XM Radio (Sirius). From 2005 through 2008 the company's cash flows from operating activities totaled a negative $1 billion. Although this is much less than the $7.8 billion of cumulative net losses the company incurred during the same period, negative cash flows do not pay the bills.

In its early years of operations, Sirius, like many new companies, was able to stay in business because of the cash it raised through financing activities. In the most recent years, however, it has raised cash primarily through its investing activities, most notably, through the cash it received in 2008 as a part of the merger. Obviously, a company cannot operate indefinitely without generating cash from operating activities. Individuals and institutions who are willing to buy a company's stock or loan it cash in its early years will disappear if they do not believe the company will eventually begin earning profits and positive cash flows from operations. Exhibit 14.6 presents Sirius's statements of cash flows from 2005 through 2008.

### EXHIBIT 14.6

**SIRIUS XM RADIO INC. AND SUBSIDIARIES**
Consolidated Statements of Cash Flows
(dollar amounts in thousands)

| | For the Years Ended December 31 | | | |
|---|---|---|---|---|
| | 2008 | 2007 | 2006 | 2005 |
| **Cash Flows from Operating Activities:** | | | | |
| Net loss | $(5,313,288) | $(565,252) | $(1,104,867) | $(862,997) |
| Adjustments to reconcile net loss to net cash used in operating activities: | | | | |
| Depreciation and amortization | 203,752 | 106,780 | 105,749 | 98,555 |
| Impairment of goodwill | 4,766,190 | — | — | — |
| Noncash interest expense, net of amortization of premium | (6,311) | 4,269 | 3,107 | 3,169 |
| Provision for doubtful accounts | 21,589 | 9,002 | 9,370 | 4,311 |
| Noncash income (expense) from affiliate | — | — | — | 3,192 |
| Noncash loss from redemption of debt | 98,203 | — | — | 712 |
| Amortization of deferred income related to equity method investment | (1,156) | — | — | — |
| Loss on disposal of assets | 4,879 | (428) | 1,661 | 1,028 |
| Equity granted to third parties and employees | — | — | — | 163,078 |
| Impairment loss | — | — | 10,917 | — |
| Loss on investments, net | 28,999 | — | 4,445 | — |
| Shared-based payment expense | 87,405 | 78,900 | 437,918 | — |
| Deferred income taxes | 2,476 | 2,435 | 2,065 | 2,311 |
| Other noncash purchase price adjustments | (68,330) | — | — | — |
| Other | 1,643 | — | — | — |

*continued*

| EXHIBIT 14.6 | *concluded* |
| --- | --- |

### SIRIUS XM RADIO INC. AND SUBSIDIARIES
Consolidated Statements of Cash Flows
(dollar amounts in thousands)

| | For the Years Ended December 31 | | | |
| --- | --- | --- | --- | --- |
| | **2008** | **2007** | **2006** | **2005** |
| Changes in operating assets and liabilities, net of assets and liabilities acquired: | | | | |
| Marketable securities | — | — | — | 16 |
| Accounts receivable | (32,121) | (28,881) | (1,871) | (28,440) |
| Inventory | 8,291 | 4,965 | (20,246) | (6,329) |
| Receivables from distributors | 14,401 | (13,179) | (20,312) | — |
| Related party assets | (22,249) | (1,241) | (1,189) | — |
| Prepaid expenses and other current assets | (19,953) | 11,118 | (42,132) | (29,129) |
| Other long-term assets | (5,490) | 13,691 | (18,377) | 6,476 |
| Accounts payable and accrued expenses | (65,481) | 66,169 | 26,366 | 145,052 |
| Accrued interest | 23,081 | (8,920) | 1,239 | 17,813 |
| Deferred revenue | 55,778 | 169,905 | 181,003 | 210,947 |
| Related party liabilities | 34,646 | — | — | — |
| Other long-term liabilities | 30,249 | 1,901 | 3,452 | (3,505) |
| Net cash used in operating activities | (152,797) | (148,766) | (421,702) | (273,740) |
| **Cash Flows from Investing Activities:** | | | | |
| Additions to property and equipment | (130,551) | (65,264) | (92,674) | (49,888) |
| Sales of property and equipment | 105 | 641 | 127 | 72 |
| Purchases of restricted and other investments | (3,000) | (310) | (12,339) | (21,291) |
| Release of restricted investments | — | — | — | 10,997 |
| Acquisition of acquired entity cash | 819,521 | — | — | — |
| Merger related costs | (23,519) | (29,444) | — | — |
| Purchase of available-for-sale securities | — | — | (123,500) | (148,900) |
| Sale of restricted and other investments | 65,869 | 40,191 | 255,715 | 31,850 |
| Maturities of available-for-sale securities | — | — | — | 5,085 |
| Net cash provided by (used in) investing activities | 728,425 | (54,186) | 27,329 | (172,075) |
| **Cash Flows from Financing Activities:** | | | | |
| Proceeds from exercise of warrants and stock options and from share borrow arrangement | 471 | 4,097 | 25,787 | 18,543 |
| Long-term borrowings, net of related costs | 531,743 | 244,879 | — | 493,005 |
| Redemption of debt | — | — | — | (57,609) |
| Payment of premiums on redemption of debt | (18,693) | — | — | — |
| Payments to minority interest holder | (1,479) | — | — | — |
| Repayment of long-term borrowings | (1,146,044) | (625) | — | — |
| Other | — | — | — | (8) |
| Net cash (used in) provided by financing activities | (634,002) | (248,351) | 25,787 | 453,931 |
| Net (decrease) increase in cash and cash equivalents | (58,374) | 45,399 | (368,586) | 8,116 |
| Cash and cash equivalents at beginning of period | 438,820 | 393,421 | 762,007 | 753,891 |
| Cash and cash equivalents at end of period | $ 380,446 | $438,820 | $393,421 | $762,007 |

## Indirect Method—Reconciliation Approach

The following section of this chapter examines the relationships between items reported on the income statement and the related assets and liabilities. Begin by reconciling the *noncash* current asset and current liability amounts shown on the balance sheets in Exhibit 14.5. *Do not include Cash in this analysis.* The amount of the change in the cash balance is the result of not only operating activities but also investing and financing activities.

## Reconciliation of Accounts Receivable

Use the information in Exhibit 14.5 to prepare the following reconciliation of Accounts Receivable. The beginning and ending balances appear on the balance sheets. The *increase due to revenue recognized on account* is the sales revenue reported on the income statement.

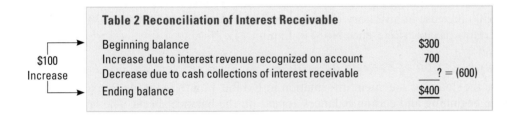

| Table 1 Reconciliation of Accounts Receivable | |
|---|---|
| Beginning balance | $ 1,200 |
| Increase due to revenue recognized on account | 20,600 |
| Decrease due to cash collections from customers | ? = (20,800) |
| Ending balance | $ 1,000 |

$200 Decrease

To balance Accounts Receivable, the *decrease due to cash collections from customers* must be $20,800.[1]

The reconciliation shows that the $200 decrease in the accounts receivable balance occurred because *cash collections from customers* were $200 more than the amount of *revenue recognized on account* ($20,800 versus $20,600). Since the amount of cash collected is more than the amount of revenue recognized, we add $200 to the amount of net income to determine net cash flow from operating activities (Reference No. 1 in Exhibit 14.7).

## Reconciliation of Interest Receivable

The beginning and ending balances appear on the balance sheets in Exhibit 14.5. The *increase due to interest revenue recognized on account* is the interest revenue reported on the income statement.

| Table 2 Reconciliation of Interest Receivable | |
|---|---|
| Beginning balance | $300 |
| Increase due to interest revenue recognized on account | 700 |
| Decrease due to cash collections of interest receivable | ? = (600) |
| Ending balance | $400 |

$100 Increase

To balance Interest Receivable, the *decrease due to cash collections of interest receivable* must be $600.

The reconciliation shows that the $100 increase in the interest receivable balance occurred because *cash collections of interest* were $100 less than the *interest revenue recognized on account* ($600 versus $700). Since the amount of cash collected is less than the amount of revenue recognized, we subtract the $100 from the amount of net income to determine net cash flow from operating activities (Reference No. 2 in Exhibit 14.7).

## Reconciliation of Inventory and Accounts Payable

To simplify computing the amount of cash paid for inventory purchases, assume that all inventory purchases are made on account. The computation requires two steps. First, Inventory must be analyzed to determine the amount of inventory purchased. Second, Accounts Payable must be analyzed to determine the amount of cash paid to purchase inventory.

Use the financial statement information in Exhibit 14.5 to prepare the following Inventory reconciliation. The beginning and ending balances appear on the balance sheets. The *decrease due to recognizing cost of goods sold* is the cost of goods sold reported on the income statement.

[1]This text uses the simplifying assumption that all sales occur on account.

Table 3 Reconciliation of Inventory

| | |
|---|---|
| Beginning balance | $ 8,200 |
| Increase due to inventory purchases | ? = 11,200 |
| Decrease due to recognizing cost of goods sold | (10,500) |
| Ending balance | $ 8,900 |

$700 Increase

To balance Inventory, the *increase due to inventory purchases* must be $11,200.

Assuming the inventory was purchased on account, the $11,200 of inventory purchases determined above equals the *increase due to inventory purchases* used in the reconciliation of Accounts Payable below. The beginning and ending balances appear on the balance sheets in Exhibit 14.5.

Table 4 Reconciliation of Accounts Payable*

| | |
|---|---|
| Beginning balance | $ 1,100 |
| Increase due to inventory purchases | 11,200 |
| Decrease due to cash settlements of accounts payable—inv. | ? = (11,500) |
| Ending balance | $ 800 |

$300 Decrease

*Assume that Accounts Payable is used for purchases of inventory only.

To balance Accounts Payable, the *decrease due to cash settlements of accounts payable—inventory* (cash paid to purchase inventory) must be $11,500.

Since the amount of *cash paid to purchase inventory* is $1,000 more than the amount of *cost of goods sold* recognized on the income statement ($11,500 versus $10,500), we subtract the $1,000 difference from the amount of net income to determine net cash flow from operating activities. In Exhibit 14.7 the $1,000 subtraction is divided between a $700 increase in inventory (Reference No. 3 in Exhibit 14.7) and a $300 decrease in accounts payable (Reference No. 4 in Exhibit 14.7).

### Reconciliation of Prepaid Insurance

Use the financial statement information in Exhibit 14.5 to reconcile Prepaid Insurance. The beginning and ending balances appear on the balance sheets. The *decrease due to recognizing insurance expense* is the insurance expense reported on the income statement.

Table 5 Reconciliation of Prepaid Insurance

| | |
|---|---|
| Beginning balance | $1,400 |
| Increase due to the cash purchase of insurance | ? = 1,000 |
| Decrease due to recognizing insurance expense | (1,300) |
| Ending balance | $1,100 |

$300 Decrease

To balance Prepaid Insurance, the amount of the *increase due to the cash purchase of insurance* must be $1,000.

The reconciliation shows that the $300 decrease in the prepaid insurance balance occurred because *cash paid to purchase insurance* was $300 less than the amount of *insurance expense recognized* ($1,000 versus $1,300). Since the amount of cash paid is less than the amount of expense recognized, we add $300 to the amount of net income to determine the net cash flow from operating activities (Reference No. 5 in Exhibit 14.7).

### Reconciliation of Salaries Payable

Use the financial statement information in Exhibit 14.5 to reconcile Salaries Payable. The beginning and ending balance appear on the balance sheets. The *increase due to recognizing salary expense on account* is the salaries expense reported on the income statement.

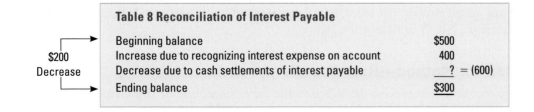

**Table 6 Reconciliation of Salaries Payable**

| | |
|---|---|
| Beginning balance | $ 900 |
| Increase due to recognizing salary expense on account | 2,700 |
| Decrease due to cash settlements of salaries payable | ? = (2,600) |
| Ending balance | $1,000 |

$100 Increase

To balance Salaries Payable, the amount of the *decrease due to cash settlements of salaries payable* (cash paid for salaries expense) must be $2,600. The reconciliation shows that the $100 increase in the salaries payable balance occurred because the *cash paid for salary expense* is $100 less than the amount of *salary expense recognized on account* ($2,600 versus $2,700). Since the amount of cash paid is less than the amount of expense recognized, we add $100 to the amount of net income to determine the cash flow from operating activities (Reference No. 6 in Exhibit 14.7).

### Reconciliation of Other Operating Expenses Payable

Use the financial statement information in Exhibit 14.5 to reconcile Other Operating Expenses Payable. The beginning and ending balances appear on the balance sheets. The *increase due to recognizing other operating expenses on account* is the other operating expenses amount reported on the income statement.

**Table 7 Reconciliation of Other Operating Expenses Payable**

| | |
|---|---|
| Beginning balance | $1,300 |
| Increase due to recognizing other operating expenses on account | 1,400 |
| Decrease due to cash settlements of other operating expenses pay. | ? = (1,200) |
| Ending balance | $1,500 |

$200 Increase

To balance Other Operating Expenses Payable, the amount of the *decrease due to cash settlements of other operating expenses payable* must be $1,200.

The reconciliation shows that the $200 increase in the other operating expenses payable balance occurred because the *cash paid for other operating expenses* was $200 less than the amount of *other operating expenses recognized on account* ($1,200 versus $1,400). Since the amount of cash paid is less than the amount of expense recognized, we add $200 to the amount of net income to determine the net cash flow from operating activities (Reference No. 7 in Exhibit 14.7).

### Reconciliation of Interest Payable

Use the financial statement information in Exhibit 14.5 to reconcile Interest Payable. The beginning and ending balances appear on the balance sheets. The *increase due to recognizing interest expense on account* is the interest expense reported on the income statement.

**Table 8 Reconciliation of Interest Payable**

| | |
|---|---|
| Beginning balance | $500 |
| Increase due to recognizing interest expense on account | 400 |
| Decrease due to cash settlements of interest payable | ? = (600) |
| Ending balance | $300 |

$200 Decrease

To balance Interest Payable, the amount of the *decrease due to cash settlements of interest payable* (cash paid for interest expense) must be $600.

The reconciliation shows that the $200 decrease in the interest payable balance occurred because the amount of *cash paid for interest expense* is $200 more than the amount of *interest expense recognized on account* ($600 versus $400). Since the amount of cash paid is more than the amount of interest expense recognized, we subtract $200 from the amount of net income to determine the net cash flow from operating activities (Reference No. 8 in Exhibit 14.7).

### Reconciliation of Unearned Rent Revenue

Use the financial statement information in Exhibit 14.5 to reconcile Unearned Rent Revenue. The beginning and ending balances appear on the balance sheets. The *decrease due to recognizing other income—rent revenue* is the other income—rent revenue reported on the income statement.

| Table 9 Reconciliation of Unearned Rent Revenue | |
| --- | --- |
| Beginning balance | $ 1,600 |
| Increase due to collecting cash in advance of providing rental services | ? = 1,400 |
| Decrease due to recognizing other income—rent revenue | (2,400) |
| Ending balance | $ 600 |

$1,000 Decrease

To balance Unearned Rent Revenue, the amount of the *increase due to collecting cash in advance of providing rental services* must be $1,400.

The reconciliation shows that the $1,000 decrease in the unearned rent revenue balance occurred because the amount of *cash collected in advance of providing rental services* is $1,000 less than the amount of *rent revenue recognized* ($1,400 versus $2,400). Since the amount of cash collected is less than the amount of revenue recognized, we subtract $1,000 from the amount of net income to determine the net cash flow from operating activities (Reference No. 9 in Exhibit 14.7).

### Noncash Expenses

The calculation of accrual-based net income frequently includes noncash expenses such as depreciation expense. Since noncash expenses are deducted in determining net income, they must be added back to the amount of net income when computing net cash flow from operating activities (Reference No. 10 in Exhibit 14.7).

### Gains and Losses

When a company retires a long-term asset, the company may receive cash from the sale of the asset being retired. If the asset is sold for more than book value (cost − accumulated depreciation), the gain increases net income; if the asset is sold for less than book value, the loss decreases net income. In either case, the cash inflow is the total amount of cash collected from selling the asset, not the amount of the gain or loss, and this cash inflow is reported in the investing activities section of the statement of cash flows. Since gains increase net income and losses decrease net income, but neither represents the amount of cash received from an asset sale, gains must be subtracted from and losses added back to net income to determine net cash flow from operating activities (Reference No. 11 in Exhibit 14.7).

## Indirect Method—Rule-Based Approach

The reconciliation process described in the previous section of this chapter leads to a set of rules that can be used to convert accrual-based revenues and expenses to their cash flow equivalents. These rules are summarized in Exhibit 14.8.

Although the rule-based approach offers less insight, it is easy to apply. To illustrate, return to the financial statement data in Exhibit 14.5. The *noncash* current assets

## EXHIBIT 14.7

### Cash Flows from Operating Activities—Indirect Method

| Reference No. | Cash Flows from Operating Activities | |
|---|---|---|
| | Net income | $7,000 |
| | Adjustments to reconcile net income to net cash flow from operating activities: | |
| 1 | Decrease in accounts receivable | 200 |
| 2 | Increase in interest receivable | (100) |
| 3 | Increase in inventory | (700) |
| 4 | Decrease in accounts payable for inventory purchases | (300) |
| 5 | Decrease in prepaid insurance | 300 |
| 6 | Increase in salaries payable | 100 |
| 7 | Increase in other operating expenses payable | 200 |
| 8 | Decrease in interest payable | (200) |
| 9 | Decrease in unearned rent revenue | (1,000) |
| 10 | Depreciation expense | 1,000 |
| 11 | Gain on sale of store fixtures | (600) |
| | Net cash flow from operating activities | $5,900 |

## EXHIBIT 14.8

### Cash Flows from Operating Activities—Indirect Method

| | | |
|---|---|---|
| | Net income | XXX |
| Rule 1 | Add decreases and subtract increases in noncash current assets | XXX |
| Rule 2 | Add increases and subtract decreases in noncash current liabilities | XXX |
| Rule 3 | Add noncash expenses (e.g., depreciation) | XXX |
| Rule 4 | Add losses and subtract gains | XXX |
| | Net cash flow from operating activities | XXX |

and current liabilities reported on the balance sheets are summarized in Exhibit 14.9 for your convenience. The amount of the change in each balance is shown in the *Change* column.

Refer to the income statement to identify the amounts of net income, noncash expenses, gains, and losses. The income statement for New South Company in Exhibit 14.5 includes three relevant figures: net income of $7,000; depreciation expense of $1,000;

## EXHIBIT 14.9

### Noncash Current Assets and Current Liabilities

| Account Title | 2012 | 2011 | Change |
|---|---|---|---|
| Accounts receivable | $1,000 | $1,200 | $ (200) |
| Interest receivable | 400 | 300 | 100 |
| Inventory | 8,900 | 8,200 | 700 |
| Prepaid insurance | 1,100 | 1,400 | (300) |
| Accounts payable—inventory purchases | 800 | 1,100 | (300) |
| Salaries payable | 1,000 | 900 | 100 |
| Other operating expenses payable | 1,500 | 1,300 | 200 |
| Interest payable | 300 | 500 | (200) |
| Unearned rent revenue | 600 | 1,600 | (1,000) |

| EXHIBIT 14.10 | Cash Flows from Operating Activities—Indirect Method, Operating Activities |
|---|---|

**NEW SOUTH COMPANY**
Statement of Cash Flows
For the Year Ended December 31, 2012

| Applicable Rule | Cash Flows from Operating Activities | |
|---|---|---|
| | Net income | $7,000 |
| | Adjustments to reconcile net income to net cash flow from operating activities: | |
| Rule 1 | Decrease in accounts receivable | 200 |
| Rule 1 | Increase in interest receivable | (100) |
| Rule 1 | Increase in inventory | (700) |
| Rule 2 | Decrease in accounts payable for inventory purchases | (300) |
| Rule 1 | Decrease in prepaid insurance | 300 |
| Rule 2 | Increase in salaries payable | 100 |
| Rule 2 | Increase in other operating expenses payable | 200 |
| Rule 2 | Decrease in interest payable | (200) |
| Rule 2 | Decrease in unearned rent revenue | (1,000) |
| Rule 3 | Depreciation expense | 1,000 |
| Rule 4 | Gain on sale of store fixtures | (600) |
| | Net cash flow from operating activities | $5,900 |

and a $600 gain on sale of store fixtures. Applying the rules in Exhibit 14.8 produces the operating activities section of the statement of cash flows shown in Exhibit 14.10. The applicable rule for each item is referenced in the first column of the exhibit.

The operating activities section of the statements of cash flows shown in Exhibits 14.10 and 14.7 are identical. The rule-based approach is an alternative way to prepare this section when using the indirect method.

## ✓ CHECK YOURSELF 14.2

Q Magazine, Inc., reported $369,000 of net income for the month. At the beginning of the month, its Unearned Revenue account had a balance of $78,000. At the end of the month, the account had a balance of $67,000. Based on this information alone, determine the amount of net cash flow from operating activities.

**Answer**

| Account Title | Ending | Beginning | Change |
|---|---|---|---|
| Unearned revenue | $67,000 | $78,000 | $(11,000) |

| Applicable Rule | Cash Flows from Operating Activities | Amount |
|---|---|---|
| | Net income | $369,000 |
| Rule 2 | Deduct: Decrease in unearned revenue | (11,000) |
| | Net cash flow from operating activities | $358,000 |

## ✓ CHECK YOURSELF 14.3

The following account balances were drawn from the accounting records of Loeb, Inc.

| Account Title | Ending Balance | Beginning Balance |
|---|---|---|
| Prepaid rent | $3,000 | $4,200 |
| Interest payable | 2,650 | 2,900 |

Loeb reported $7,400 of net income during the accounting period. Based on this information alone, determine the amount of net cash flow from operating activities.

**Answer**    Based on Rule 1, the $1,200 decrease ($3,000 − $4,200) in Prepaid Rent (current asset) must be added to net income to determine the amount of net cash flow from operating activities. Rule 2 requires that the $250 decrease ($2,650 − $2,900) in interest Payable (current liability) must be deducted from net income. Accordingly, the cash flow from operating activities is $8,350 ($7,400 + $1,200 − $250). Note that paying interest is defined as an operating activity and should not be confused with dividend payments, which are classified as financing activities.

## ✓ CHECK YOURSELF 14.4

Arley Company's income statement reported net income (all amounts are in millions) of $326 for the year. The income statement included depreciation expense of $45 and a net loss on the sale of long-term assets of $22. Based on this information alone, determine the net cash flow from operating activities.

**Answer**    Based on Rule 3 and Rule 4, both the depreciation expense and the loss would have to be added to net income to determine net cash flow from operating activities. Net cash flow from operating activities would be $393 million ($326 + $45 + $22).

## PREPARING THE OPERATING ACTIVITIES SECTION OF A STATEMENT OF CASH FLOWS USING THE DIRECT METHOD

The reconciliation tables developed earlier to determine net cash flow from operating activities under the *indirect method* also disclose the information needed to present the amount of net cash flow from operating activities under the *direct method*. Remember that the amount of net cash flow from operating activities is the same whether it is presented using the indirect or the direct method.

The direct method shows the specific sources and uses of cash that are associated with operating activities. It does not show adjustments to net income. To illustrate, examine Exhibit 14.11. The information in the reference column identifies the reconciliation table from which the cash flow amounts were drawn. The page number indicates where the reconciliation table is located in this chapter.

Table 3 is not included above because it does not directly involve a cash flow. Also, noncash expenses, gains, and losses are not used in the determination of net cash flow from operating activities when using the direct method.

**LO 2**

Prepare the operating activities section of a statement of cash flows using the direct method.

## EXHIBIT 14.11

### Cash Flows from Operating Activities—Direct Method

| Reference | Cash Flows from Operating Activities | |
|---|---|---|
| Table 1, page 645 | Inflow from customers | $ 20,800 |
| Table 2, page 645 | Inflow from interest revenue | 600 |
| Table 4, page 646 | Outflow for inventory purchases | (11,500) |
| Table 5, page 646 | Outflow to purchase insurance | (1,000) |
| Table 6, page 647 | Outflow to pay salary expense | (2,600) |
| Table 7, page 647 | Outflow for other operating expenses | (1,200) |
| Table 8, page 647 | Outflow to pay interest expense | (600) |
| Table 9, page 648 | Inflow from rent revenue | 1,400 |
| | Net cash flow from operating activities | $ 5,900 |

# PREPARING THE INVESTING ACTIVITIES SECTION OF A STATEMENT OF CASH FLOWS

**LO 3**

Prepare the investing activities section of a statement of cash flows.

The direct and indirect methods discussed above pertain only to the presentation of operating activities. The *investing activities* section of the statement of cash flows is the same regardless of whether the direct or indirect method is used for operating activities. The information necessary to identify cash inflows and outflows from investing activities is obtained by reconciling changes in a company's long-term assets. In general:

■ Increases in long-term asset balances suggest cash outflows to purchase assets.

■ Decreases in long-term asset balances suggest cash inflows from selling assets.

It is usually necessary to analyze data from the long-term asset records to determine details about long-term asset purchases and sales. In the New South Company example, these details are presented as notes at the bottom of the balance sheets.

To illustrate, return to the financial statements in Exhibit 14.5. New South Company reports the following three long-term assets on its balance sheets. *It is not necessary to reconcile accumulated depreciation since it does not affect cash flow.*

| Long-term Assets | 2012 | 2011 |
|---|---|---|
| Investment securities | $5,100 | $3,500 |
| Store fixtures | 5,400 | 4,800 |
| Land | 8,200 | 6,000 |

For each long-term asset, reconcile the beginning and ending balances by identifying purchases and sales affecting it. Review the notes for additional relevant information. Begin with investment securities.

## Reconciliation of Investment Securities

| Reconciliation of Investment Securities | |
|---|---|
| Beginning balance in investment securities | $3,500 |
| Increase due to purchase of investment securities | ? = 1,600 |
| Decrease due to sale of investment securities | 0 |
| Ending balance in investment securities | $5,100 |

Because Note 1 below the balance sheets indicates no investment securities were sold during 2012, the *decrease due to sale of investment securities* is zero. To balance Investment Securities, the *increase due to purchase of investment securities* must be $1,600. In the absence of contrary information, assume New South used cash to purchase the investment securities. This cash outflow is reported in the investing activities section of the statement of cash flows in Exhibit 14.12.

## Reconciliation of Store Fixtures

| Reconciliation of Store Fixtures | | |
| --- | --- | --- |
| Beginning balance in store fixtures | $4,800 | |
| Increase due to purchase of store fixtures | ? | = 2,300 |
| Decrease due to sale of store fixtures | (1,700) | |
| Ending balance in store fixtures | $5,400 | |

Note 2 below the balance sheets indicates that the *decrease due to sale of store fixtures* is $1,700. What is the cash flow from this sale? The book value of these fixtures was $400 ($1,700 cost − $1,300 accumulated depreciation). Since the income statement reports a $600 gain on the sale of store fixtures, the cash collected from the sale was more than the book value of the store fixtures. Compute the amount of cash collected from the sale of store fixtures as follows:

$$\text{Cash inflow} = \text{book value} + \text{gain} = \$400 + \$600 = \$1,000$$

The $1,000 cash inflow from the sale of store fixtures is reported in the investing activities section of the statement of cash flows in Exhibit 14.12.

To balance Store Fixtures, the *increase due to purchase of store fixtures* must be $2,300. In the absence of contrary information, assume New South used cash to purchase store fixtures. The cash outflow is reported in the investing activities section of the statement of cash flows in Exhibit 14.12.

## Reconciliation of Land

| Reconciliation of Land | | |
| --- | --- | --- |
| Beginning balance in land | $6,000 | |
| Increase due to purchase of land | ? | = 2,200 |
| Decrease due to sale of land | 0 | |
| Ending balance in land | $8,200 | |

Because Note 3 below the balance sheets indicates no land was sold during 2012, the *decrease due to sale of land* is zero. To balance Land, the *increase due to purchase of land* must be $2,200. Since the land was acquired by issuing a mortgage note payable, New South did not use cash for the purchase. This type of transaction is reported in the *noncash investing and financing activities* section of the statement of cash flows, discussed in more detail later in the chapter. The cash inflows and outflows from investing activities are summarized in Exhibit 14.12.

### EXHIBIT 14.12

**Cash Flows from Investing Activities**

**Cash Flows from Investing Activities**

| | |
|---|---:|
| Cash outflow to purchase investment securities | $(1,600) |
| Cash inflow from the sale of store fixtures | 1,000 |
| Cash outflow to purchase store fixtures | (2,300) |
| Net cash outflow from investing activities | $(2,900) |

---

## ✓ CHECK YOURSELF 14.5

On January 1, 2011, Wyatt Company had an Equipment balance of $124,000. During 2011, Wyatt purchased equipment that cost $50,000. The balance in Equipment on December 31, 2011, was $90,000. The 2011 income statement included a $7,000 loss from the sale of equipment. On the date of sale, accumulated depreciation on the equipment sold was $49,000.

**Required**

**a.** Determine the cost of the equipment sold during 2011.

**b.** Determine the amount of cash flow from the sale of equipment that should be reported in the investing activities section of the 2011 statement of cash flows.

**Solution**

**a.**

**Reconciliation of Equipment**

| | |
|---|---:|
| Beginning balance | $124,000 |
| Increase due to the purchase of equipment | 50,000 |
| Decrease due to sale of equipment | ? = (84,000) |
| Ending balance | $ 90,000 |

To balance Equipment, *decrease due to sale of equipment* must be $84,000.

**b.** The book value of the equipment sold was $35,000 ($84,000 − $49,000 accumulated depreciation). Since Wyatt recognized a loss on the equipment sale, the amount of cash collected from the sale was less than the book value of the equipment. The cash collected from the sale of the equipment was $28,000 ($35,000 book value − $7,000 loss on sale).

## PREPARING THE FINANCING ACTIVITIES SECTION OF A STATEMENT OF CASH FLOWS

**LO 4**

Prepare the financing activities section of a statement of cash flows.

Because the differences between the direct and the indirect methods of presenting the statement of cash flows pertain only to operating activities, the *financing activities* section is the same under either approach. The information necessary to identify cash inflows and outflows from financing activities is obtained by reconciling changes in short-term notes payable, long-term liabilities, and stockholders' equity. In general:

■ Increases in short-term notes payable or long-term debt balances suggest cash inflows occurred from issuing debt instruments (notes or bonds).

■ Decreases in short-term notes payable or long-term debt balances suggest cash outflows occurred for payment of debt (notes or bonds).

- Increases in contributed capital (common stock, preferred stock, or paid-in capital) suggest cash inflows occurred from issuing equity instruments.

- Increases or decreases in treasury stock suggest cash outflows or inflows occurred to purchase or sell a company's own stock.

- Decreases in retained earnings from cash dividends suggest cash outflows occurred to pay dividends.

To illustrate, return to the financial statements of the New South Company in Exhibit 14.5. The following long-term liability and stockholders' equity balances are reported on the New South balance sheets.

| Account Title | 2012 | 2011 |
|---|---|---|
| Mortgage payable | $ 2,200 | $ 0 |
| Bonds payable | 1,000 | 4,000 |
| Common stock | 10,000 | 8,000 |
| Retained earnings | 12,700 | 7,200 |
| Treasury stock | 600 | 0 |

For each account, reconcile the beginning and ending balances by identifying the increases and decreases affecting it. Review the notes for additional relevant information. Begin with the mortgage payable liability.

## Reconciliation of Mortgage Payable

| Reconciliation of Mortgage Payable | |
|---|---|
| Beginning balance in mortgage payable | $ 0 |
| Increase due to issuing mortgage payable | 2,200 |
| Decrease due to payment of mortgage payable | 0 |
| Ending balance in mortgage payable | $2,200 |

As previously discussed, Note 3 indicates a mortgage payable was issued to acquire land. The *increase due to issuing mortgage payable* is $2,200. Since New South received land, not cash, by issuing the mortgage, the transaction is reported in the noncash investing and financing activities section of the statement of cash flows.

## Reconciliation of Bonds Payable

| Bonds Payable | |
|---|---|
| Beginning balance in bonds payable | $4,000 |
| Increase due to issuing bonds payable | 0 |
| Decrease due to payment of bonds payable | ? = (3,000) |
| Ending balance in bonds payable | $1,000 |

Since there is no indication that New South issued bonds during 2012, assume the *increase due to issuing bonds payable* is zero. To balance Bonds Payable, the *decrease due to payment of bonds payable* must be $3,000. The cash outflow is reported in the financing activities section in Exhibit 14.13.

## Reconciliation of Common Stock

| Reconciliation of Common Stock | |
| --- | --- |
| Beginning balance in common stock | $ 8,000 |
| Increase due to issuing common stock | ? = 2,000 |
| Ending balance in common stock | $10,000 |

To balance Common Stock, the *increase due to issuing common stock* has to be $2,000. The cash inflow is reported in the financing activities section in Exhibit 14.13.

## Reconciliation of Retained Earnings

| Reconciliation of Retained Earnings | |
| --- | --- |
| Beginning balance in retained earnings | $ 7,200 |
| Increase due to net income | 7,000 |
| Decrease due to of dividends | ? = (1,500) |
| Ending balance in retained earnings | $12,700 |

The *increase due to net income* comes from the income statement. To balance Retained Earnings, the decrease due to of dividends must be $1,500. In the absence of information to the contrary, assume the decrease is due to the cash payment of dividends. The cash outflow for payment of dividends is reported in the financing activities section of the statement of cash flows in Exhibit 14.13.

## Reconciliation of Treasury Stock

| Reconciliation of Treasury Stock | |
| --- | --- |
| Beginning balance in treasury stock | $ 0 |
| Increase due to purchasing treasury stock | ? = 600 |
| Decrease due to reissuing treasury stock | 0 |
| Ending balance in treasury stock | $600 |

Since there is no indication that New South reissued treasury stock during 2012, the *decrease due to reissuing treasury stock* is zero. To balance Treasury Stock, the increase due to purchasing treasury stock must be $600. The cash outflow is reported in the financing activities section in Exhibit 14.13.

**EXHIBIT 14.13**

### Cash Flows from Financing Activities

| Cash Flows from Financing Activities | |
| --- | --- |
| Cash outflow to reduce bonds payable | $(3,000) |
| Cash inflow from issuing common stock | 2,000 |
| Cash outflow to pay dividends | (1,500) |
| Cash outflow to purchase treasury stock | (600) |
| Net cash outflow from financing activities | $(3,100) |

Exhibits 14.14 and 14.15 illustrate the complete statement of cash flows for New South Company under the two alternative methods. Exhibit 14.14 presents operating activities using the indirect method. Exhibit 14.15 presents operating activities using the direct method. The investing and financing activities do not differ between methods. Under either method the combined effects of operating, investing, and financing activities result in a net decrease in cash of $100 for 2012. This $100 decrease is necessarily consistent with the difference between the December 31, 2012, and the December 31, 2011, cash balances shown in the balance sheets in Exhibit 14.5.

**EXHIBIT 14.14** Statement of Cash Flows—Indirect Method

## NEW SOUTH COMPANY
### Statement of Cash Flows
### For the Year Ended December 31, 2012

**Cash Flows from Operating Activities**

| | | |
|---|---:|---:|
| Net income | | $ 7,000 |
| Adjustments to reconcile net income to net cash flow from operating activities: | | |
| Decrease in accounts receivable | 200 | |
| Increase in interest receivable | (100) | |
| Increase in inventory | (700) | |
| Decrease in accounts payable for inventory purchases | (300) | |
| Decrease in prepaid insurance | 300 | |
| Increase in salaries payable | 100 | |
| Increase in other operating expenses payable | 200 | |
| Decrease in interest payable | (200) | |
| Decrease in unearned rent revenue | (1,000) | |
| Depreciation expense | 1,000 | |
| Gain on sale of store fixtures | (600) | |
| Net cash flow from operating activities | | $5,900 |
| **Cash Flows from Investing Activities** | | |
| Cash outflow to purchase investment securities | (1,600) | |
| Cash inflow from the sale of store fixtures | 1,000 | |
| Cash outflow to purchase store fixtures | (2,300) | |
| Net cash outflow from investing activities | | (2,900) |
| **Cash Flows from Financing Activities** | | |
| Cash outflow to reduce bonds payable | (3,000) | |
| Cash inflow from issuing common stock | 2,000 | |
| Cash outflow to pay dividends | (1,500) | |
| Cash outflow to purchase treasury stock | (600) | |
| Net cash outflow from financing activities | | (3,100) |
| Net decrease in cash | | (100) |
| Plus: Beginning cash balance | | 400 |
| Ending cash balance | | $ 300 |
| **Schedule of Noncash Investing and Financing Activities** | | |
| Issue mortgage for land | | $2,200 |

**EXHIBIT 14.15** Statement of Cash Flows—Direct Method

## NEW SOUTH COMPANY
### Statement of Cash Flows
### For the Year Ended December 31, 2012

**Cash Flows from Operating Activities**

| | | |
|---|---:|---:|
| Inflow from customers | $ 20,800 | |
| Inflow from interest revenue | 600 | |
| Outflow for inventory purchases | (11,500) | |
| Outflow to purchase insurance | (1,000) | |
| Outflow to pay salary expense | (2,600) | |
| Outflow for other operating expenses | (1,200) | |
| Outflow to pay interest expense | (600) | |
| Inflow from rent revenue | 1,400 | |
| Net cash flow from operating activities | | $5,900 |

*continued*

**EXHIBIT 14.15**    *concluded*

## NEW SOUTH COMPANY
### Statement of Cash Flows
### For the Year Ended December 31, 2012

| | | |
|---|---:|---:|
| **Cash Flows from Investing Activities** | | |
| Cash outflow to purchase investment securities | (1,600) | |
| Cash inflow from the sale of store fixtures | 1,000 | |
| Cash outflow to purchase store fixtures | (2,300) | |
| Net cash outflow from investing activities | | (2,900) |
| **Cash Flows from Financing Activities** | | |
| Cash outflow to reduce bonds payable | (3,000) | |
| Cash inflow from issuing common stock | 2,000 | |
| Cash outflow to pay dividends | (1,500) | |
| Cash outflow to purchase treasury stock | (600) | |
| Net cash outflow from financing activities | | (3,100) |
| Net decrease in cash | | (100) |
| Plus: Beginning cash balance | | 400 |
| Ending cash balance | | $ 300 |
| **Schedule of Noncash Investing and Financing Activities** | | |
| Issue mortgage for land | | $2,200 |

---

## ✓ CHECK YOURSELF 14.6

On January 1, 2011, Sterling Company had a balance of $250,000 in Bonds Payable. During 2011, Sterling issued bonds with a $75,000 face value. The bonds were issued at face value. The balance in Bonds Payable on December 31, 2011, was $150,000.

**Required**

**a.** Determine the cash outflow for repayment of bond liabilities assuming the bonds were retired at face value.

**b.** Prepare the financing activities section of the 2011 statement of cash flows.

**Solution**

**a.**

| Reconciliation of Bonds Payable | |
|---|---:|
| Beginning balance | $250,000 |
| Increase due to issuing bonds payable | 75,000 |
| Decrease due to payment of bonds payable | ? = (175,000) |
| Ending balance | $150,000 |

In order to balance Bonds Payable, the decrease due to payment of bonds payable must be $175,000. In the absence of information to the contrary, assume cash was used to pay the bond liabilities.

**b.**

| Cash Flows from Financing Activities | |
|---|---:|
| Inflow from issuing bond liabilities | $ 75,000 |
| Outflow for reduction of bond liabilities | (175,000) |
| Net cash outflow from financing activities | $(100,000) |

## PREPARING THE SCHEDULE OF NONCASH INVESTING AND FINANCING ACTIVITIES

As mentioned earlier, companies may engage in significant noncash investing and financing activities. For example, New South Company acquired land by issuing a $2,200 mortgage note. Since these types of transactions do not involve exchanging cash, they are not reported in the main body of the statement of cash flows. However, the Financial Accounting Standards Board (FASB) requires disclosure of all material investing and financing activities whether or not they involve exchanging cash. Companies must therefore include with the statement of cash flows a separate schedule that reports noncash investing and financing activities. See the *Schedule of Noncash Investing and Financing Activities* at the bottom of Exhibits 14.14 and 14.15 for an example.

## REALITY BYTES

How did **Dillard's, Inc.**, the department store chain, acquire $22 million of property, plant, and equipment in its 2006 fiscal year *without* spending any cash? Oddly enough, the answer can be found on its statement of cash flows.

The supplemental "noncash transactions" information included at the bottom of Dillard's statement of cash flows revealed that it acquired the assets by exchanging debt directly for assets. Capital lease transactions, a form of borrowing, were responsible for $19.5 million of these purchases. The remaining $2.5 million was purchased through "accrued capital transactions."

Had Dillard's borrowed $22 million from a bank and then used this cash to purchase $22 million of assets, it would have reported two separate cash events in the body of its statement of cash flows. A cash inflow would have been reported in the financing activities for the borrowing transaction, and a cash outflow would have been reported in the investing activities section for the purchase transaction. Acquiring large amounts of assets is considered important, even if there is no immediate exchange of cash, so generally accepted accounting principles require such events to be reported as a part of the statement of cash flows.

## INTERPRETING THE STATEMENT OF CASH FLOWS

Why are financial analysts interested in the statement of cash flows? Understanding the cash flows of a business is essential because cash is used to pay the bills. A company, especially one experiencing rapid growth, can be short of cash in spite of earning substantial net income. To illustrate, assume you start a computer sales business. You borrow $2,000 and spend the money to purchase two computers for $1,000 each. You sell one of the computers on account for $1,500. If your loan required a payment at this time, you could not make it. Even though you have net income of $500 ($1,500 sales − $1,000 cost of goods sold), you have no cash until you collect the $1,500 account receivable. A business cannot survive without managing cash flow carefully. It is little wonder that financial analysts are keenly interested in cash flow.

### Real-World Data

The statement of cash flows frequently provides a picture of business activity that would otherwise be lost in the complexities of accrual accounting. For example, **IBM Corporation**'s combined operating losses (before taxes) for 1991, 1992, and 1993 were more than $17.9 *billion*. During this same period, IBM reported "restructuring charges"

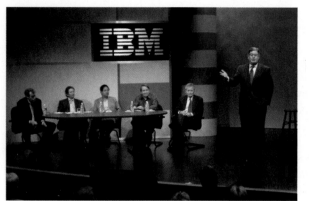

of more than $24 billion. Restructuring costs relate to reorganizing a company. They may include the costs of closing facilities and losses on asset disposals. Without the restructuring charges, IBM would have reported operating *profits* of about $6 billion (before taxes). Do restructuring charges signal positive or negative changes? Different financial analysts have different opinions about this issue. However, one aspect of IBM's performance during these years is easily understood. The company produced over $21 billion in positive cash flow from operating activities. It had no trouble paying its bills.

Investors consider cash flow information so important that they are willing to pay for it, even when the FASB discourages its use. The FASB *prohibits* companies from disclosing *cash flow per share* in audited financial statements. However, one prominent stock analysis service, *Value Line Investment Survey,* sells this information to a significant customer base. Clearly, Value Line's customers value information about cash flows.

Exhibit 14.16 compares income from operations to cash flows from operating activities for six real-world companies for 2003 through 2005 and 2007 and 2008. These first three years were a time of economic expansion in the United States, but the economy had slowed and eventually entered into a recession in 2007 and 2008.

Several things are apparent from Exhibit 14.16. The cash flow from operating activities exceeds income from operations for all but four of the 30 comparisons, and three of these four are for one company, Pulte Homes. Cash flows often exceed income because depreciation, a noncash expense, is usually significant. Excluding Pulte Homes, which will be discussed separately, the most dramatic example of the differences between cash flow and income is Alaska Air Group, the company that owns Alaska Airlines. For the five years shown in Exhibit 14.16, its net income totals $71.8 million, but its cash flows from operations were $1.6 billion. The difference between cash flow from operating activities and operating income helps explain how

## EXHIBIT 14.16

### Operating Income versus Cash Flow from Operations (Amounts in $000)

|  | 2008 | 2007 | 2005 | 2004 | 2003 |
|---|---|---|---|---|---|
| **Alaska Air Group** | | | | | |
| Operating income | $ (135,900) | $ 125,000 | $ 84,500 | $ (15,300) | $ 13,500 |
| Cash flow—operations | 164,300 | 482,000 | 271,900 | 334,000 | 355,200 |
| **Boeing** | | | | | |
| Operating income | 2,654,000 | 4,058,000 | 2,562,000 | 1,820,000 | 718,000 |
| Cash flow—operations | (401,000) | 9,584,000 | 7,000,000 | 3,458,000 | 3,881,000 |
| **Johnson & Johnson** | | | | | |
| Operating income | 12,949,000 | 10,576,000 | 10,411,000 | 8,509,000 | 7,197,000 |
| Cash flow—operations | 14,972,000 | 15,249,000 | 11,877,000 | 11,131,000 | 10,595,000 |
| **McAfee** | | | | | |
| Operating income | 172,209 | 166,980 | 138,828 | 225,065 | 70,242 |
| Cash flow—operations | 308,322 | 393,415 | 419,457 | 358,913 | 156,304 |
| **McDonalds** | | | | | |
| Operating income | 4,313,200 | 2,335,000 | 2,602,200 | 2,278,500 | 1,508,200 |
| Cash flow—operations | 5,917,200 | 4,876,300 | 4,336,800 | 3,903,600 | 3,268,800 |
| **Pulte Homes, Inc.** | | | | | |
| Operating income | (1,473,113) | (2,274,417) | 1,436,888 | 998,008 | 617,322 |
| Cash flow—operations | 1,220,392 | 1,218,255 | 18,704 | (698,280) | (301,848) |

some companies can have significant losses over a few years and continue to stay in business and pay their bills.

The exhibit also shows that cash flow from operating activities can be more stable than operating income. Results for Alaska Air Group also demonstrate this clearly. For the five years presented, Alaska Air earned a profit in three years, but had a loss in two years. However, its operating cash flows were not only positive for all five years, but they were never lower than $164.3 million.

What could explain why Pulte Homes had *less* cash flow from operating activities than operating income in 2003, 2004, and 2005, but not in 2007 and 2008? In the early years, when the housing market was strong, Pulte was experiencing the kind of growth described earlier for your computer business. Its cash outflows were supporting growth in inventory. Pulte is one of the nation's largest new-home construction companies. Its growth rates, based on sales of new homes, were 25%, 31%, and 28% for 2003, 2004, and 2005, but sales declined by 35% and 33% in 2007 and 2008. Notice that in the years of declining sales, its cash flows from operating activities *exceeded* its net income.

Finally, why did Boeing have negative cash flow from operations in 2008 even though its revenue and operating income were also declining? It was because of a growth in inventory, but not due to revenue growth. This situation was significant enough that Boeing explained it in the footnotes of its 2008 annual report, as follows.

> *In 2008 inventory grew at a faster rate than customer advances. The 2008 increase in inventories was driven by continued spending on production materials, airplane engines, and supplier advances during the IAM strike, lower commercial airplane deliveries and the continued ramp-up of the 787 program. We expect to generate positive operating cash flows in 2009.*

The Pulte Homes situation highlights a potential weakness in the format of the statement of cash flows. Some accountants consider it misleading to classify all increases in long-term assets as *investing activities* and all changes in inventory as affecting cash flow from operating activities. They argue that the increase in inventory at Pulte that results from building more houses should be classified as an investing activity, just as the cost of a new building is. Although inventory is classified as a current asset and buildings are classified as long-term assets, in reality there is a certain level of inventory a company must permanently maintain to stay in business. The GAAP format of the statement of cash flows penalizes cash flow from operating activities for increases in inventory that are really a permanent investment in assets.

Conversely, the same critics might argue that some purchases of long-term assets are not actually *investments* but merely replacements of old, existing property, plant, and equipment. In other words, the *investing activities* section of the statement of cash flows makes no distinction between expenditures that expand the business and those that simply replace old equipment (sometimes called *capital maintenance* expenditures).

Users of the statement of cash flows must exercise the same care interpreting it as when they use the balance sheet or the income statement. Numbers alone are insufficient. Users must evaluate numbers based on knowledge of the particular business and industry they are analyzing.

Accounting information alone cannot guide a businessperson to a sound decision. Making good business decisions requires an understanding of the business in question, the environmental and economic factors affecting the operation of that business, and the accounting concepts on which the financial statements of that business are based.

# A Look Back

This chapter examined in detail only one financial statement, the statement of cash flows. The chapter provided a more comprehensive discussion of how accrual accounting relates to cash-based accounting. Effective use of financial statements requires understanding not only accrual and cash-based accounting systems but also how they relate to each other. That relationship is why a statement of cash flows can begin with a reconciliation of net income, an accrual measurement, to net cash flow from operating activities, a cash measurement. Finally, this chapter explained how the conventions for classifying cash flows as operating, investing, or financing activities require analysis and understanding to make informed decisions with the financial information.

**A step-by-step audio-narrated series of slides is provided on the text website at www.mhhe.com/edmonds2011.**

## SELF-STUDY REVIEW PROBLEM

The following financial statements pertain to Schlemmer Company.

| Balance Sheets As of December 31 | | |
|---|---|---|
| | **2012** | **2011** |
| Cash | $48,400 | $ 2,800 |
| Accounts receivable | 2,200 | 1,200 |
| Inventory | 5,600 | 6,000 |
| Equipment | 18,000 | 22,000 |
| Accumulated depreciation—equip. | (13,650) | (17,400) |
| Land | 17,200 | 10,400 |
| Total assets | $77,750 | $25,000 |
| Accounts payable (inventory) | $ 5,200 | $ 4,200 |
| Long-term debt | 5,600 | 6,400 |
| Common stock | 19,400 | 10,000 |
| Retained earnings | 47,550 | 4,400 |
| Total liabilities and equity | $77,750 | $25,000 |

| Income Statement For the Year Ended December 31, 2012 | |
|---|---|
| Sales revenue | $67,300 |
| Cost of goods sold | (24,100) |
| Gross margin | 43,200 |
| Depreciation expense | (1,250) |
| Operating income | 41,950 |
| Gain on sale of equipment | 2,900 |
| Loss on disposal of land | (100) |
| Net income | $44,750 |

### Additional Data

1. During 2012 equipment that had originally cost $11,000 was sold. Accumulated depreciation on this equipment was $5,000 at the time of sale.

2. Common stock was issued in exchange for land valued at $9,400 at the time of the exchange.

### Required

Using the indirect method, prepare in good form a statement of cash flows for the year ended December 31, 2012.

**Solution**

## SCHLEMMER COMPANY
### Statement of Cash Flows
### For the Year Ended December 31, 2012

| | | |
|---|---:|---:|
| **Cash Flows from Operating Activities** | | |
| Net income | $44,750 | |
| Add: | | |
| Decrease in inventory (1) | 400 | |
| Increase in accounts payable (2) | 1,000 | |
| Depreciation expense (3) | 1,250 | |
| Loss on disposal of land (4) | 100 | |
| Subtract: | | |
| Increase in accounts receivable (1) | (1,000) | |
| Gain on sale of equipment (4) | (2,900) | |
| Net cash inflow from operating activities | | $43,600 |
| **Cash Flows from Investing Activities** | | |
| Cash inflow from the sale of equipment (5) | 8,900 | |
| Cash outflow for the purchase of equipment (5) | (7,000) | |
| Cash inflow from sale of land (6) | 2,500 | |
| Net cash outflow from investing activities | | 4,400 |
| **Cash Flows from Financing Activities** | | |
| Cash outflow to repay long-term debt (7) | (800) | |
| Cash outflow to pay dividends (8) | (1,600) | |
| Net cash outflow from financing activities | | (2,400) |
| **Net Increase in Cash** | | 45,600 |
| Plus: Beginning cash balance | | 2,800 |
| Ending cash balance | | $48,400 |
| **Schedule of Noncash Investing and Financing Activities** | | |
| Issue of common stock for land (9) | | $ 9,400 |

**(1)** Add decreases and subtract increases in current asset account balances to net income.

**(2)** Add increases and subtract decreases in current liability account balances to net income.

**(3)** Add noncash expenses (depreciation) to net income.

**(4)** Add losses on the sale of noncurrent assets to net income and subtract gains on the sale of long-term assets from net income.

**(5)** Information regarding the Equipment account is summarized in the following table.

| Equipment Account Information | |
|---|---:|
| Beginning balance in equipment | $22,000 |
| Purchases of equipment (cash outflows) | ? |
| Sales of equipment (cash inflows) | (11,000) |
| Ending balance in equipment | $18,000 |

To balance the account, equipment costing $7,000 must have been purchased. In the absence of information to the contrary, we assume cash was used to make the purchase.

Note 1 to the financial statement shows that equipment sold had a book value of $6,000 ($11,000 cost − $5,000 accumulated depreciation). The amount of the cash inflow from this sale is computed as follows:

$$\text{Cash inflow} = \text{book value} + \text{gain} = \$6,000 + \$2,900 = \$8,900$$

**(6)** The information regarding the Land account is as follows:

| Land Account Information | |
| --- | --- |
| Beginning balance in land | $10,400 |
| Purchase of land (issue of common stock) | 9,400 |
| Sale of land (cash inflows) | ? |
| Ending balance in land | $17,200 |

Note 2 indicates that land valued at $9,400 was acquired by issuing common stock. Since there was no cash flow associated with this purchase, the event is shown in the *noncash investing and financing activities* section of the statement of cash flows.

To balance the account, the cost (book value) of land sold had to be $2,600. Since the income statement shows a $100 loss on the sale of land, the cash collected from the sale is computed as follows:

$$\text{Cash inflow} = \text{book value} - \text{less} = \$2,600 - \$100 = \$2,500$$

**(7)** The information regarding the Long-term Debt account is as follows:

| Long-term Debt Information | |
| --- | --- |
| Beginning balance in long-term debt | $6,400 |
| Issue of long-term debt instruments (cash inflow) | 0 |
| Payment of long-term debt (cash outflow) | ? |
| Ending balance in long-term debt | $5,600 |

There is no information in the financial statements that suggest that long-term debt was issued. Therefore, to balance the account, $800 of long-term debt had to be paid off, thereby resulting in a cash outflow.

**(8)** The information regarding the Retained Earnings account is as follows:

| Retained Earnings Information | |
| --- | --- |
| Beginning balance in retained earnings | $ 4,400 |
| Net income | 44,750 |
| Dividends (cash outflow) | ? |
| Ending balance in retained earnings | $47,550 |

To balance the account, $1,600 of dividends had to be paid, thereby resulting in a cash outflow.

**(9)** Note 2 states that common stock was issue to acquire land valued at $9,400. This is a non-cash investing and financing activity.

## KEY TERMS

| | | |
| --- | --- | --- |
| Cash inflows  636 | Financing activities  639 | Noncash investing and |
| Cash outflows  636 | Indirect method  638 | financing activities  640 |
| Direct method  638 | Investing activities  639 | Operating activities  638 |

## QUESTIONS

**1.** What is the purpose of the statement of cash flows?

**2.** What are the three categories of cash flows reported on the cash flow statement?

Discuss each and give an example of an inflow and an outflow for each category.

**3.** What are noncash investing and financing activities? Provide an example. How are such transactions shown on the statement of cash flows?

4. Albring Company had a beginning balance in accounts receivable of $12,000 and an ending balance of $14,000. Net income amounted to $110,000. Based on this information alone, determine the amount of net cash flow from operating activities.

5. Forsyth Company had a beginning balance in utilities payable of $3,300 and an ending balance of $5,200. Net income amounted to $87,000. Based on this information alone, determine the amount of net cash flow from operating activities.

6. Clover Company had a beginning balance in unearned revenue of $4,300 and an ending balance of $3,200. Net income amounted to $54,000. Based on this information alone, determine the amount of net cash flow from operating activities.

7. Which of the following activities are financing activities?

   (a) Payment of accounts payable.
   (b) Payment of interest on bonds payable.
   (c) Sale of common stock.
   (d) Sale of preferred stock at a premium.
   (e) Payment of a cash dividend.

8. Does depreciation expense affect net cash flow? Explain.

9. If Best Company sold land that cost $4,200 at a $500 gain, how much cash did it collect from the sale of land?

10. If Best Company sold office equipment that originally cost $7,500 and had $7,200 of accumulated depreciation at a $100 loss, what was the selling price for the office equipment?

11. In which section of the statement of cash flows would the following transactions be reported?

   (a) The amount of the change in the balance of accounts receivable.
   (b) Cash purchase of investment securities.
   (c) Cash purchase of equipment.
   (d) Cash sale of merchandise.
   (e) Cash sale of common stock.
   (f) The amount of net income.
   (g) Cash proceeds from loan.
   (h) Cash payment on bonds payable.
   (i) Cash receipt from sale of old equipment.
   (j) The amount of the change in the balance of accounts payable.

12. What is the difference between preparing the statement of cash flows using the direct method and using the indirect method?

13. Which method (direct or indirect) of presenting the statement of cash flows is more intuitively logical? Why?

14. What is the major advantage of using the indirect method to present the statement of cash flows?

15. What is the advantage of using the direct method to present the statement of cash flows?

16. How would Best Company report the following transactions on the statement of cash flows?

   (a) Purchased new equipment for $46,000 cash.
   (b) Sold old equipment for $8,700 cash. The equipment had a book value of $4,900.

17. Can a company report negative net cash flows from operating activities for the year on the statement of cash flows but still have positive net income on the income statement? Explain.

## MULTIPLE-CHOICE QUESTIONS

**Multiple-choice questions are provided on the text website at www.mhhe.com/edmonds2011.**

## EXERCISES—SERIES A

**All applicable Exercises in Series A are available with McGraw-Hill's *Connect Accounting.***

**Exercise 14-1A** *Use the indirect method to determine cash flows from operating activities*

LO 1

An accountant for Golden Enterprise Companies (GEC) computed the following information by making comparisons between GEC's 2011 and 2012 balance sheets. Further information was determined by examining the company's 2011 income statement.

1. The amount of an increase in the balance of the Accounts Receivable account.
2. The amount of a loss arising from the sale of land.
3. The amount of an increase in the balance of the Other Operating Expenses Payable account.
4. The amount of a decrease in the balance of the Bonds Payable account.
5. The amount of depreciation expense shown on the income statement.
6. The amount of cash dividends paid to the stockholders.
7. The amount of a decrease in the balance of an Unearned Revenue account.
8. The amount of an increase in the balance of an Inventory account.
9. The amount of an increase in the balance of a Land account.
10. The amount of a decrease in the balance of a Prepaid Rent account.
11. The amount of an increase in the balance of a Treasury Stock account.

**Required**

For each item described above indicate whether the amount should be added to or subtracted from the amount of net income when determining the amount of net cash flow from operating activities. If an item does not affect net cash flow from operating activities, identify it as being not affected.

LO 1

**Exercise 14-2A    Use the indirect method to determine cash flows from operating activities**

Mendez Incorporated presents its statement of cash flows using the indirect method. The following accounts and corresponding balances were drawn from the company's 2012 and 2011 year-end balance sheets.

| Account Title | 2012 | 2011 |
|---|---|---|
| Accounts receivable | $15,200 | $16,500 |
| Accounts payable | 8,800 | 9,200 |

The 2012 income statement showed net income of $27,200.

**Required**

a. Prepare the operating activities section of the statement of cash flows.
b. Explain why the change in the balance in accounts receivable was added to or subtracted from the amount of net income when you completed Requirement *a*.
c. Explain why the change in the balance in accounts payable was added to or subtracted from the amount of net income when you completed Requirement *a*.

LO 1

**Exercise 14-3A    Use the indirect method to determine cash flows from operating activities**

Chang Company presents its statement of cash flows using the indirect method. The following accounts and corresponding balances were drawn from Chang's 2012 and 2011 year-end balance sheets.

| Account Title | 2012 | 2011 |
|---|---|---|
| Accounts receivable | $28,000 | $32,000 |
| Prepaid rent | 1,800 | 1,500 |
| Interest receivable | 700 | 500 |
| Accounts payable | 8,500 | 9,800 |
| Salaries payable | 3,600 | 3,200 |
| Unearned revenue | 4,000 | 6,000 |

The income statement contained a $1,200 gain on the sale of equipment, a $900 loss on the sale of land, and $2,500 of depreciation expense. Net income for the period was $52,000.

**Required**

Prepare the operating activities section of the statement of cash flows.

**Exercise 14-4A** *Use the direct method to determine cash flows from operating activities*

LO 2

The following accounts and corresponding balances were drawn from Widjaja Company's 2012 and 2011 year-end balance sheets.

| Account Title | 2012 | 2011 |
|---|---|---|
| Unearned revenue | $6,500 | $5,000 |
| Prepaid rent | 1,800 | 2,400 |

During the year, $68,000 of unearned revenue was recognized as having been earned. Rent expense for 2012 was $15,000.

**Required**

Based on this information alone, prepare the operating activities section of the statement of cash flows assuming the direct approach is used.

**Exercise 14-5A** *Use the direct method to determine cash flows from operating activities*

LO 2

The following accounts and corresponding balances were drawn from Berry Company's 2012 and 2011 year-end balance sheets.

| Account Title | 2012 | 2011 |
|---|---|---|
| Accounts receivable | $46,000 | $42,000 |
| Interest receivable | 5,000 | 6,000 |
| Other operating expenses payable | 27,000 | 22,000 |
| Salaries payable | 12,000 | 15,000 |

The 2012 income statement is shown below:

| Income Statement | |
|---|---|
| Sales | $680,000 |
| Salary expense | (172,000) |
| Other operating expenses | (270,000) |
| Operating income | 238,000 |
| Nonoperating items: Interest revenue | 24,000 |
| Net income | $262,000 |

**Required**

a. Use the direct method to compute the amount of cash inflows from operating activities.

b. Use the direct method to compute the amount of cash outflows from operating activities.

**Exercise 14-6A** *Direct versus indirect method of determining cash flows from operating activities*

LO 1, 2

Master Mechanics, Inc. (MMI), recognized $1,200 of sales revenue on account and collected $1,100 of cash from accounts receivable. Further, MMI recognized $700 of operating expenses on account and paid $500 cash as partial settlement of operating expenses payable.

**Required**

Based on this information alone:

a. Prepare the operating activities section of the statement of cash flows under the direct method.

b. Prepare the operating activities section of the statement of cash flows under the indirect method.

**Exercise 14-7A**    *The direct versus the indirect method of determining cash flows from operating activities*

The following accounts and corresponding balances were drawn from Larry Company's 2012 and 2011 year-end balance sheets.

| Account Title | 2012 | 2011 |
|---|---|---|
| Accounts receivable | $78,000 | $75,000 |
| Prepaid rent | 800 | 900 |
| Utilities payable | 1,500 | 1,200 |
| Other operating expenses payable | 34,000 | 33,000 |

The 2012 income statement is shown below:

| Income Statement | |
|---|---|
| Sales | $272,000 |
| Rent expense | (24,000) |
| Utilities expense | (36,400) |
| Other operating expenses | (168,000) |
| Net Income | $ 43,600 |

**Required**

a. Prepare the operating activities section of the statement of cash flows using the direct method.

b. Prepare the operating activities section of the statement of cash flows using the indirect method.

**Exercise 14-8A**    *Determining cash flow from investing activities*

On January 1, 2011, Webber Company had a balance of $278,000 in its Land account. During 2011, Webber sold land that had cost $94,000 for $120,000 cash. The balance in the Land account on December 31, 2011, was $300,000.

**Required**

a. Determine the cash outflow for the purchase of land during 2011.

b. Prepare the investing activities section of the 2011 statement of cash flows.

**Exercise 14-9A**    *Determining cash flows from investing activities*

On January 1, 2011, Duncan Company had a balance of $59,600 in its Delivery Equipment account. During 2011, Duncan purchased delivery equipment that cost $18,500. The balance in the Delivery Equipment account on December 31, 2011, was $60,000. The 2011 income statement reported a gain from the sale of equipment for $3,000. On the date of sale, accumulated depreciation on the equipment sold amounted to $10,000.

**Required**

a. Determine the cost of the equipment that was sold during 2011.

b. Determine the amount of cash flow from the sale of delivery equipment that should be shown in the investing activities section of the 2011 statement of cash flows.

**Exercise 14-10A**    *Determining cash flows from investing activities*

The following accounts and corresponding balances were drawn from Winston Company's 2012 and 2011 year-end balance sheets.

| Account Title | 2012 | 2011 |
|---|---|---|
| Investment securities | $102,000 | $112,000 |
| Machinery | 520,000 | 425,000 |
| Land | 140,000 | 90,000 |

Other information drawn from the accounting records:

1. Winston incurred a $2,000 loss on the sale of investment securities during 2012.
2. Old machinery with a book value of $5,000 (cost of $25,000 minus accumulated depreciation of $20,000) was sold. The income statement showed a gain on the sale of machinery of
   $4,000.
3. Winston did not sell land during the year.

**Required**

a. Compute the amount of cash flow associated with the sale of investment securities.
b. Compute the amount of cash flow associated with the purchase of machinery.
c. Compute the amount of cash flow associated with the sale of machinery.
d. Compute the amount of cash flow associated with the purchase of land.
e. Prepare the investing activities section of the statement of cash flows.

## Exercise 14-11A   *Determining cash flows from financing activities*

LO 4

On January 1, 2011, BGA Company had a balance of $500,000 in its Bonds Payable account.
During 2011, BGA issued bonds with a $150,000 face value. There was no premium or discount
associated with the bond issue. The balance in the Bonds Payable account on December 31,
2011, was $300,000.

**Required**

a. Determine the cash outflow for the repayment of bond liabilities assuming that the bonds
   were retired at face value.
b. Prepare the financing activities section of the 2011 statement of cash flows.

## Exercise 14-12A   *Determining cash flows from financing activities*

LO 4

On January 1, 2011, Parker Company had a balance of $120,000 in its Common Stock account.
During 2011, Parker paid $18,000 to purchase treasury stock. Treasury stock is accounted for
using the cost method. The balance in the Common Stock account on December 31, 2011, was
$130,000. Assume that the common stock is no par stock.

**Required**

a. Determine the cash inflow from the issue of common stock.
b. Prepare the financing activities section of the 2011 statement of cash flows.

## Exercise 14-13A   *Determining cash flows from financing activities*

LO 4

The following accounts and corresponding balances were drawn from Berry Company's 2012
and 2011 year-end balance sheets.

| Account Title | 2012 | 2011 |
|---|---|---|
| Bonds payable | $210,000 | $300,000 |
| Common stock | 370,000 | 275,000 |

Other information drawn from the accounting records:

1. Dividends paid during the period amounted to $30,000.
2. There were no bond liabilities issued during the period.

**Required**

a. Compute the amount of cash flow associated with the repayment of bond liabilities.
b. Compute the amount of cash flow associated with the issue of common stock.
c. Prepare the financing activities section of the statement of cash flows.

## PROBLEMS—SERIES A

ACCOUNTING

**All applicable Problems in Series A are available with McGraw-Hill's**
*Connect Accounting.*

**LO 1, 2**

eXcel

**CHECK FIGURE**
Net cash flow from operating
activities: $28,700

**Problem 14-14A**    *The direct versus the indirect method to determine cash flow from operating activities*

Top Brands, Inc. (TBI), presents its statement of cash flows using the indirect method. The following accounts and corresponding balances were drawn from TBI's 2012 and 2011 year-end balance sheets.

| Account Title | 2012 | 2011 |
|---|---|---|
| Accounts receivable | $24,000 | $26,000 |
| Merchandise inventory | 56,000 | 52,000 |
| Prepaid insurance | 19,000 | 24,000 |
| Accounts payable | 23,000 | 20,000 |
| Salaries payable | 4,600 | 4,200 |
| Unearned service revenue | 1,000 | 2,700 |

The 2012 income statement is shown below:

| Income Statement | |
|---|---|
| Sales | $ 603,000 |
| Cost of goods sold | (383,000) |
| Gross margin | 220,000 |
| Service revenue | 4,000 |
| Insurance expense | (40,000) |
| Salaries expense | (160,000) |
| Depreciation expense | (6,000) |
| Operating income | 18,000 |
| Gain on sale of equipment | 3,000 |
| Net income | $ 21,000 |

**Required**

**a.** Prepare the operating activities section of the statement of cash flows using the direct method.

**b.** Prepare the operating activities section of the statement of cash flows using the indirect method.

**LO 3**

**CHECK FIGURES**
b. $5,000
c. $35,000

**Problem 14-15A**    *Determining cash flows from investing activities*

The following information was drawn from the year-end balance sheets of Desoto Company:

| Account Title | 2012 | 2011 |
|---|---|---|
| Investment securities | $ 33,500 | $ 30,000 |
| Equipment | 235,000 | 220,000 |
| Buildings | 845,000 | 962,000 |
| Land | 80,000 | 69,000 |

Additional information regarding transactions occurring during 2012:

**1.** Investment securities that had cost $5,600 were sold. The 2012 income statement contained a loss on the sale of investment securities of $600.

**2.** Equipment with a cost of $50,000 was purchased.

3. The income statement showed a gain on the sale of equipment of $6,000. On the date of sale, accumulated depreciation on the equipment sold amounted to $8,000.
4. A building that had originally cost $158,000 was demolished.
5. Land that had cost $25,000 was sold for $22,000.

**Required**

a. Determine the amount of cash flow for the purchase of investment securities during 2012.
b. Determine the amount of cash flow from the sale of investment securities during 2012.
c. Determine the cost of the equipment that was sold during 2012.
d. Determine the amount of cash flow from the sale of equipment during 2012.
e. Determine the amount of cash flow for the purchase of buildings during 2012.
f. Determine the amount of cash flow for the purchase of land during 2012.
g. Prepare the investing activities section of the 2012 statement of cash flows.

**Problem 14-16A** *Determining cash flows from financing activities*

LO 4

The following information was drawn from the year-end balance sheets of Pet Doors, Inc.:

CHECK FIGURES
c. $15,000
e. Net cash flow from financing
activities: ($74,000) outflow

| Account Title | 2012 | 2011 |
|---|---|---|
| Bonds payable | $800,000 | $900,000 |
| Common stock | 197,000 | 140,000 |
| Treasury stock | 25,000 | 10,000 |
| Retained earnings | 80,000 | 69,000 |

Additional information regarding transactions occurring during 2012:

1. Pet Doors, Inc., issued $50,000 of bonds during 2012. The bonds were issued at face value. All bonds retired were retired at face value.
2. Common stock did not have a par value.
3. Pet Doors, Inc., uses the cost method to account for treasury stock.
4. The amount of net income shown on the 2012 income statement was $27,000.

**Required**

a. Determine the amount of cash flow for the retirement of bonds that should appear on the 2012 statement of cash flows.
b. Determine the amount of cash flow from the issue of common stock that should appear on the 2012 statement of cash flows.
c. Determine the amount of cash flow for the purchase of treasury stock that should appear on the 2012 statement of cash flows.
d. Determine the amount of cash flow for the payment of dividends that should appear on the 2012 statement of cash flows.
e. Prepare the financing activities section of the 2012 statement of cash flows.

**Problem 14-17A** *Preparing a statement of cash flows*

LO 1, 3, 4

The following information can be obtained by examining a company's balance sheet and income statement information.

a. Decreases in noncash current asset account balances.
b. Cash outflows to repay long-term debt.
c. Increases in noncash current asset account balances.
d. Cash outflows made to purchase long-term assets.
e. Decreases in current liability account balances.
f. Noncash expenses (depreciation).
g. Cash outflows to purchase treasury stock.
h. Gains recognized on the sale of long-term assets.

i. Cash outflows to pay dividends.

j. Cash inflows from the issue of common stock.

k. Cash inflows from the sale of long-term assets.

l. Increases in current liability account balances.

m. Cash inflows from the issue of long-term debt.

n. Losses incurred from the sale of long-term assets.

**Required**

Construct a table like the one shown below. For each item, indicate whether it would be used in the computation of net cash flows from operating, investing, or financing activities. Also, indicate whether the item would be added or subtracted when determining the net cash flow from operating, investing, or financing activities. Assume the indirect method is used to prepare the operating activities section of the statement of cash flows. The first item has been completed as an example.

| Item | Type of Activity | Add or Subtract |
|------|-----------------|-----------------|
| a. | Operating | Add |
| b. | | |
| c. | | |
| d. | | |
| e. | | |
| f. | | |
| g. | | |
| h. | | |
| i. | | |
| j. | | |
| k. | | |
| l. | | |
| m. | | |
| n. | | |

**LO 1, 3, 4**

**Problem 14-18A**  *Using financial statements to prepare a statements of cash flows—Indirect method*

The comparative balance sheets and income statements for Pacific Company follow.

| Balance Sheets As of December 31 | | |
|---|---|---|
| | **2012** | **2011** |
| **Assets** | | |
| Cash | $24,200 | $ 2,800 |
| Accounts receivable | 2,000 | 1,200 |
| Inventory | 6,400 | 6,000 |
| Equipment | 19,000 | 42,000 |
| Accumulated depreciation—equipment | (9,000) | (17,400) |
| Land | 18,400 | 10,400 |
| Total assets | $61,000 | $45,000 |
| **Liabilities and equity** | | |
| Accounts payable (inventory) | $ 2,600 | $ 4,200 |
| Long-term debt | 2,800 | 6,400 |
| Common stock | 22,000 | 10,000 |
| Retained earnings | 33,600 | 24,400 |
| Total liabilities and equity | $61,000 | $45,000 |

| Income Statement For the Year Ended December 31, 2012 | |
|---|---|
| Sales revenue | $35,700 |
| Cost of goods sold | (14,150) |
| Gross margin | 21,550 |
| Depreciation expense | (3,600) |
| Operating income | 17,950 |
| Gain on sale of equipment | 500 |
| Loss on disposal of land | (50) |
| Net income | $18,400 |

## Additional Data

1. During 2012, the company sold equipment for $18,500; it had originally cost $30,000. Accumulated depreciation on this equipment was $12,000 at the time of the sale. Also, the company purchased equipment for $7,000 cash.

2. The company sold land that had cost $4,000. This land was sold for $3,950, resulting in the recognition of a $50 loss. Also, common stock was issued in exchange for title to land that was valued at $12,000 at the time of exchange.

3. Paid dividends of $9,200.

## Required

Prepare a statement of cash flows using the indirect method.

**Problem 14-19A**   *Using financial statements to prepare a statement of cash flows—Indirect method*

The comparative balance sheets and an income statement for Redwood Corporation follow.

LO 1, 3, 4

**CHECK FIGURES**
Net cash flow from operating activities: $170,200
Net increase in cash: $28,200

| Balance Sheets As of December 31 | | |
|---|---|---|
| | **2012** | **2011** |
| **Assets** | | |
| Cash | $ 68,800 | $ 40,600 |
| Accounts receivable | 30,000 | 22,000 |
| Merchandise inventory | 160,000 | 176,000 |
| Prepaid rent | 2,400 | 4,800 |
| Equipment | 256,000 | 288,000 |
| Accumulated depreciation | (146,800) | (236,000) |
| Land | 192,000 | 80,000 |
| Total assets | $562,400 | $375,400 |
| **Liabilities** | | |
| Accounts payable (inventory) | $ 67,000 | $ 76,000 |
| Salaries payable | 28,000 | 24,000 |
| **Stockholders' equity** | | |
| Common stock, $25 par value | 250,000 | 200,000 |
| Retained earnings | 217,400 | 75,400 |
| Total liabilities and stockholders' equity | $562,400 | $375,400 |

| Income Statement | |
|---|---|
| For the Year Ended December 31, 2012 | |
| Sales | $1,500,000 |
| Cost of goods sold | (797,200) |
| Gross profit | 702,800 |
| Operating expenses | |
| Depreciation expense | (22,800) |
| Rent expense | (24,000) |
| Salaries expense | (256,000) |
| Other operating expenses | (258,000) |
| Net income | $ 142,000 |

**Other Information**

1. Purchased land for $112,000.
2. Purchased new equipment for $100,000.
3. Sold old equipment that cost $132,000 with accumulated depreciation of $112,000 for $20,000 cash.
4. Issued common stock for $50,000.

**Required**

Prepare the statement of cash flows for 2012 using the indirect method.

**LO 2, 3, 4**

**CHECK FIGURE**
Net Cash Flow from Operating
Activities: $(110,775)

**Problem 14-20A**  *Using transaction data to prepare a statement of cash flows— Direct method*

Store Company engaged in the following transactions during the 2011 accounting period. The beginning cash balance was $28,600 and ending cash balance was $6,025.

1. Sales on account were $250,000. The beginning Accounts Receivable balance was $87,000 and the ending balance was $83,000.
2. Salaries expense for the period was $56,000. The beginning Salaries Payable balance was $3,500 and the ending balance was $2,000.
3. Other operating expenses for the period were $125,000. The beginning Other Operating Expenses Payable balance was $4,500 and the ending balance was $8,500.
4. Recorded $19,500 of depreciation expense. The beginning and ending balances in the Accumulated Depreciation account were $14,000 and $33,500, respectively.
5. The Equipment account had beginning and ending balances of $210,000 and $240,000 respectively. There were no sales of equipment during the period.
6. The beginning and ending balances in the Notes Payable account were $50,000 and $150,000, respectively. There were no payoffs of notes during the period.
7. There was $6,000 of interest expense reported on the income statement. The beginning and ending balances in the Interest Payable account were $1,500 and $1,000, respectively.
8. The beginning and ending Merchandise Inventory account balances were $90,000 and $108,000, respectively. The company sold merchandise with a cost of $156,000 (cost of goods sold for the period was $156,000). The beginning and ending balances of Accounts Payable were $9,500 and $11,500, respectively.
9. The beginning and ending balances of Notes Receivable were $5,000 and $10,000, respectively. Notes receivable result from long-term loans made to employees. There were no collections from employees during the period.
10. The beginning and ending balances of the Common Stock account were $100,000 and $120,000, respectively. The increase was caused by the issue of common stock for cash.
11. Land had beginning and ending balances of $50,000 and $41,000, respectively. Land that cost $9,000 was sold for $12,200, resulting in a gain of $3,200.

12. The tax expense for the period was $7,700. The Taxes Payable account had a $950 beginning balance and an $875 ending balance.

13. The Investments account had beginning and ending balances of $25,000 and $29,000, respectively. The company purchased investments for $18,000 cash during the period, and investments that cost $14,000 were sold for $9,000, resulting in a $5,000 loss.

**Required**

a. Determine the amount of cash flow for each item and indicate whether the item should appear in the operating, investing, or financing activities section of a statement of cash flows. If an item does not affect the cash flow statement, make a statement indicating that the cash flow statement will not be affected. Assume Store Company uses the direct method for showing net cash flow from operating activities.

b. Prepare a statement of cash flows based on the information you developed in Requirement *a*.

**Problem 14-21A**  *Using financial statements to prepare a statement of cash flows—*
*Direct method*

LO 2, 3, 4

The following financial statements were drawn from the records of Raceway Sports:

| Balance Sheets As of December 31 | | |
|---|---|---|
| | **2012** | **2011** |
| Assets | | |
| Cash | $123,600 | $ 28,200 |
| Accounts receivable | 57,000 | 66,000 |
| Inventory | 126,000 | 114,000 |
| Notes receivable (long-term) | 0 | 30,000 |
| Equipment | 147,000 | 255,000 |
| Accumulated depreciation-equipment | (74,740) | (141,000) |
| Land | 82,500 | 52,500 |
| Total assets | $461,360 | $404,700 |
| Liabilities and equity | | |
| Accounts payable (inventory) | $ 42,000 | $ 48,600 |
| Salaries payable | 30,000 | 24,000 |
| Utilities payable | 600 | 1,200 |
| Interest payable | 0 | 1,800 |
| Notes payable (long-term) | 0 | 60,000 |
| Common stock | 300,000 | 240,000 |
| Retained earnings | 88,760 | 29,100 |
| Total liabilities and equity | $461,360 | $404,700 |

| Income Statement For the Year Ended December 31, 2012 | |
|---|---|
| Sales revenue | $580,000 |
| Cost of goods sold | (288,000) |
| Gross margin | 292,000 |
| Operating expenses | |
| Salary expense | (184,000) |
| Depreciation expense | (17,740) |
| Utilities expense | (12,200) |
| Operating income | 78,060 |
| Nonoperating items | |
| Interest expense | (3,000) |
| Loss on the sale of equipment | (1,800) |
| Net income | $ 73,260 |

**Additional Information**

1. Sold equipment costing $108,000 with accumulated depreciation of $84,000 for $22,200 cash.
2. Paid a $13,600 cash dividend to owners.

**Required**

Analyze the data and prepare a statement of cash flows using the direct method.

## EXERCISES—SERIES B

**LO 1**

### Exercise 14-1B   *Use the indirect method to determine cash flows from operating activities*

An accountant for Farve Enterprise Companies (FEC) computed the following information by making comparisons between FEC's 2012 and 2011 balance sheets. Further information was determined by examining the company's 2012 income statement.

1. The amount of cash dividends paid to the stockholders.
2. The amount of an increase in the balance of an Unearned Revenue account.
3. The amount of a decrease in the balance of an Inventory account.
4. The amount of a decrease in the balance of a Land account.
5. The amount of an increase in the balance of a Prepaid Rent account.
6. The amount of an increase in the balance of a Treasury Stock account.
7. The amount of a decrease in the balance of the Accounts Receivable account.
8. The amount of a gain arising from the sale of land.
9. The amount of an increase in the balance of the Salaries Payable account.
10. The amount of an increase in the balance of the Bonds Payable account.
11. The amount of depreciation expense shown on the income statement.

**Required**

For each item described above, indicate whether the amount should be added to or subtracted from the amount of net income when determining the amount of net cash flow from operating activities using the indirect method. If an item does not affect net cash flow from operating activities, identify it as being not affected.

**LO 1**

### Exercise 14-2B   *Use the indirect method to determine cash flows from operating activities*

Haughton Incorporated presents its statement of cash flows using the indirect method. The following accounts and corresponding balances were drawn from the company's 2012 and 2011 year-end balance sheets:

| Account Title | 2012 | 2011 |
|---|---|---|
| Accounts receivable | $26,200 | $21,400 |
| Accounts payable | 9,700 | 9,300 |

The 2012 income statement showed net income of $36,300.

**Required**

a. Prepare the operating activities section of the statement of cash flows.
b. Explain why the change in the balance in accounts receivable was added to or subtracted from the amount of net income when you completed Requirement *a*.
c. Explain why the change in the balance in accounts payable was added to or subtracted from the amount of net income when you completed Requirement *a*.

**Exercise 14-3B**   *Use the indirect method to determine cash flows from operating activities*

LO 1

Hong Company presents its statement of cash flows using the indirect method. The following accounts and corresponding balances were drawn from Hong's 2012 and 2011 year-end balance sheets:

| Account Title | 2012 | 2011 |
|---|---|---|
| Accounts receivable | $46,000 | $38,000 |
| Prepaid rent | 2,400 | 2,800 |
| Interest receivable | 900 | 1,000 |
| Accounts payable | 10,500 | 9,000 |
| Salaries payable | 4,200 | 4,800 |
| Unearned revenue | 5,000 | 4,500 |

The income statement contained a $500 loss on the sale of equipment, a $700 gain on the sale of land, and $3,200 of depreciation expense. Net income for the period was $47,000.

**Required**

Prepare the operating activities section of the statement of cash flows.

**Exercise 14-4B**   *Use the direct method to determine cash flows from operating activities*

LO 2

The following accounts and corresponding balances were drawn from Pizzazz Company's 2012 and 2011 year-end balance sheets:

| Account Title | 2012 | 2011 |
|---|---|---|
| Unearned revenue | $5,000 | $6,500 |
| Prepaid rent | 2,400 | 1,800 |

During the year, $72,000 of unearned revenue was recognized as having been earned. Rent expense for 2012 was $20,000.

**Required**

Based on this information alone, prepare the operating activities section of the statement of cash flows assuming the direct approach is used.

**Exercise 14-5B**   *Use the direct method to determine cash flows from operating activities*

LO 2

The following accounts and corresponding balances were drawn from Hughes Company's 2012 and 2011 year-end balance sheets:

| Account Title | 2012 | 2011 |
|---|---|---|
| Accounts receivable | $56,000 | $41,000 |
| Interest receivable | 6,000 | 5,000 |
| Other operating expenses payable | 22,000 | 28,000 |
| Salaries payable | 15,000 | 13,000 |

The 2012 income statement is shown below:

| Income Statement | |
|---|---|
| Sales | $725,000 |
| Salary expense | (180,000) |
| Other operating expenses | (310,000) |
| Operating income | 235,000 |
| Nonoperating items: Interest revenue | 18,000 |
| Net income | $253,000 |

**Required**

a. Use the direct method to compute the amount of cash inflows from operating activities.

b. Use the direct method to compute the amount of cash outflows from operating activities.

LO 1, 2

### Exercise 14-6B *Direct versus indirect method of determining cash flows from operating activities*

Security Services, Inc. (SSI), recognized $2,400 of sales revenue on account and collected $1,900 of cash from accounts receivable. Further, SSI recognized $900 of operating expenses on account and paid $400 cash as partial settlement of accounts payable.

**Required**

Based on this information alone:

a. Prepare the operating activities section of the statement of cash flows under the direct method.

b. Prepare the operating activities section of the statement of cash flows under the indirect method.

LO 1, 2

### Exercise 14-7B *The direct versus the indirect method of determining cash flows from operating activities*

The following accounts and corresponding balances were drawn from Littlejohn Company's 2012 and 2011 year-end balance sheets:

| Account Title | 2012 | 2011 |
|---|---|---|
| Accounts receivable | $89,000 | $92,000 |
| Prepaid rent | 1,100 | 1,500 |
| Utilities payable | 2,100 | 2,600 |
| Other operating expenses payable | 42,000 | 49,000 |

The 2012 income statement is shown below:

| Income Statement | |
|---|---|
| Sales | $312,000 |
| Rent expense | (36,000) |
| Utilities expense | (41,900) |
| Other operating expenses | (189,000) |
| Net income | $ 45,100 |

**Required**

a. Prepare the operating activities section of the statement of cash flows using the direct method.

b. Prepare the operating activities section of the statement of cash flows using the indirect method.

LO 3

### Exercise 14-8B *Determining cash flow from investing activities*

On January 1, 2011, Oswalt Company had a balance of $156,000 in its Land account. During 2011, Oswalt sold land that had cost $66,000 for $98,000 cash. The balance in the Land account on December 31, 2011, was $220,000.

**Required**

a. Determine the cash outflow for the purchase of land during 2011.

b. Prepare the investing activities section of the 2011 statement of cash flows.

### Exercise 14-9B  *Determining cash flow from investing activities*

LO 3

On January 1, 2011, Artex Company had a balance of $65,600 in its Office Equipment account. During 2011, Artex purchased office equipment that cost $21,600. The balance in the Office Equipment account on December 31, 2011, was $65,000. The 2011 income statement contained a gain from the sale of equipment for $5,000. On the date of sale, accumulated depreciation on the equipment sold amounted to $8,300.

**Required**

a.  Determine the cost of the equipment that was sold during 2011.

b.  Determine the amount of cash flow from the sale of office equipment that should be shown in the investing activities section of the 2011 statement of cash flows.

### Exercise 14-10B  *Determining cash flows from investing activities*

LO 3

The following accounts and corresponding balances were drawn from Callon Company's 2012 and 2011 year-end balance sheets:

| Account Title | 2012 | 2011 |
|---|---|---|
| Investment securities | $ 98,000 | $106,000 |
| Machinery | 565,000 | 520,000 |
| Land | 90,000 | 140,000 |

Other information drawn from the accounting records:

1.  Callon incurred a $4,000 loss on the sale of investment securities during 2012.

2.  Old machinery with a book value of $7,000 (cost of $32,000 minus accumulated depreciation of $25,000) was sold. The income statement showed a gain on the sale of machinery of $5,500.

3.  Callon incurred a loss of $2,500 on the sale of land in 2012.

**Required**

a.  Compute the amount of cash flow associated with the sale of investment securities.

b.  Compute the amount of cash flow associated with the purchase of machinery.

c.  Compute the amount of cash flow associated with the sale of machinery.

d.  Compute the amount of cash flow associated with the sale of land.

e.  Prepare the investing activities section of the statement of cash flows.

### Exercise 14-11B  *Determining cash flows from financing activities*

LO 4

On January 1, 2011, MMC Company had a balance of $700,000 in its Bonds Payable account. During 2011, MMC issued bonds with a $200,000 face value. There was no premium or discount associated with the bond issue. The balance in the Bonds Payable account on December 31, 2011, was $400,000.

**Required**

a.  Determine the cash outflow for the repayment of bond liabilities assuming that the bonds were retired at face value.

b.  Prepare the financing activities section of the 2011 statement of cash flows.

### Exercise 14-12B  *Determining cash flows from financing activities*

LO 4

On January 1, 2011, Graves Company had a balance of $200,000 in its Common Stock account. During 2011, Graves paid $15,000 to purchase treasury stock. Treasury stock is accounted for using the cost method. The balance in the Common Stock account on December 31, 2011, was $240,000. Assume that the common stock is no par stock.

**Required**

a.  Determine the cash inflow from the issue of common stock.

b.  Prepare the financing activities section of the 2011 statement of cash flows.

**LO 4**

### Exercise 14-13B   *Determining cash flows from financing activities*

The following accounts and corresponding balances were drawn from Poole Company's 2012 and 2011 year-end balance sheets:

| Account Title | 2012 | 2011 |
|---|---|---|
| Bonds payable | $300,000 | $210,000 |
| Common stock | 550,000 | 450,000 |

Other information drawn from the accounting records:

1. Dividends paid during the period amounted to $40,000.
2. There were no bond liabilities repaid during the period.

**Required**

a. Compute the amount of cash flow associated with the issue of bond liabilities.
b. Compute the amount of cash flow associated with the issue of common stock.
c. Prepare the financing activities section of the statement of cash flows.

## PROBLEMS—SERIES B

**LO 1, 2**

### Problem 14-14B   *The direct versus the indirect method to determine cash flows from operating activities*

The following accounts and corresponding balances were drawn from Bryan Sports, Inc.'s 2012 and 2011 year-end balance sheets:

| Account Title | 2012 | 2011 |
|---|---|---|
| Accounts receivable | $36,000 | $45,000 |
| Merchandise inventory | 65,000 | 62,000 |
| Prepaid insurance | 24,000 | 20,000 |
| Accounts payable | 20,000 | 25,000 |
| Salaries payable | 4,500 | 3,900 |
| Unearned service revenue | 9,500 | 8,600 |

The 2012 income statement is shown below:

| Income Statement | |
|---|---|
| Sales | $651,500 |
| Cost of goods sold | (402,000) |
| Gross margin | 249,500 |
| Service revenue | 15,000 |
| Insurance expense | (38,000) |
| Salaries expense | (175,000) |
| Depreciation expense | (8,000) |
| Operating income | 43,500 |
| Gain on sale of equipment | 2,500 |
| Net income | $ 46,000 |

**Required**

a. Prepare the operating activities section of the statement of cash flows using the direct method.
b. Prepare the operating activities section of the statement of cash flows using the indirect method.

## Problem 14-15B  *Determining cash flows from investing activities*

The following information was drawn from the year-end balance sheets of Madison Company:

| Account Title | 2012 | 2011 |
|---|---|---|
| Investment securities | $ 46,500 | $ 50,000 |
| Equipment | 275,000 | 260,000 |
| Buildings | 950,000 | 920,000 |
| Land | 110,000 | 90,000 |

Additional information regarding transactions occurring during 2012:

1. Investment securities that had cost $7,800 were sold. The 2012 income statement contained a loss on the sale of investment securities of $1,200.
2. Equipment with a cost of $75,000 was purchased.
3. The income statement showed a gain on the sale of equipment of $10,000. On the date of sale, accumulated depreciation on the equipment sold amounted to $52,000.
4. A building that had originally cost $70,000 was demolished.
5. Land that had cost $15,000 was sold for $20,000.

**Required**

a. Determine the amount of cash flow for the purchase of investment securities during 2012.
b. Determine the amount of cash flow from the sale of investment securities during 2012.
c. Determine the cost of the equipment that was sold during 2012.
d. Determine the amount of cash flow from the sale of equipment during 2012.
e. Determine the amount of cash flow for the purchase of buildings during 2012.
f. Determine the amount of cash flow for the purchase of land during 2012.
g. Prepare the investing activities section of the 2012 statement of cash flows.

## Problem 14-16B  *Determining cash flows from financing activities*

The following information was drawn from the year-end balance sheets of Sports Supply, Inc.:

| Account Title | 2012 | 2011 |
|---|---|---|
| Bonds payable | $700,000 | $800,000 |
| Common stock | 180,000 | 140,000 |
| Treasury stock | 40,000 | 25,000 |
| Retained earnings | 96,000 | 80,000 |

Additional information regarding transactions occurring during 2012:

1. Sports Supply, Inc., issued $70,000 of bonds during 2012. The bonds were issued at face value. All bonds retired were retired at face value.
2. Common stock did not have a par value.
3. Sports Supply, Inc., uses the cost method to account for treasury stock. Sports Supply, Inc., did not resell any treasury stock in 2012.
4. The amount of net income shown on the 2012 income statement was $36,000.

**Required**

a. Determine the amount of cash flow for the retirement of bonds that should appear on the 2012 statement of cash flows.
b. Determine the amount of cash flow from the issue of common stock that should appear on the 2012 statement of cash flows.

c. Determine the amount of cash flow for the purchase of treasury stock that should appear on the 2012 statement of cash flows.

d. Determine the amount of cash flow for the payment of dividends that should appear on the 2012 statement of cash flows.

e. Prepare the financing activities section of the 2012 statement of cash flows.

**LO 1, 3, 4**    **Problem 14-17B    *Preparing a statement of cash flows***

The following information can be obtained by examining a company's balance sheet and income statement information.

**a.** Gains recognized on the sale of noncurrent assets.
**b.** Cash outflows to pay dividends.
**c.** Cash inflows from the issue of common stock.
**d.** Cash inflows from the sale of noncurrent assets.
**e.** Increases in current liability account balances.
**f.** Cash inflows from the issue of noncurrent debt.
**g.** Losses incurred from the sale of noncurrent assets.
**h.** Decreases in noncash current asset account balances.
**i.** Cash outflows to repay noncurrent debt.
**j.** Increases in noncash current asset account balances.
**k.** Cash outflows made to purchase noncurrent assets.
**l.** Decreases in current liability account balances.
**m.** Noncash expenses (e.g., depreciation).
**n.** Cash outflows to purchase treasury stock.

**Required**

Construct a table like the one shown below. For each item, indicate whether it would be used in the computation of net cash flows from operating, investing, or financing activities. Also, indicate whether the item would be added or subtracted when determining the net cash flow from operating, investing, or financing activities. Assume the indirect method is used to prepare the operating activities section of the statement of cash flows. The first item has been completed as an example.

| Item | Type of Activity | Add or Subtract |
|------|------------------|-----------------|
| a. | Operating | Subtract |
| b. | | |
| c. | | |
| d. | | |
| e. | | |
| f. | | |
| g. | | |
| h. | | |
| i. | | |
| j. | | |
| k. | | |
| l. | | |
| m. | | |
| n. | | |

**Problem 14-18B**    *Using financial statements to prepare a statement of cash flows—*    LO 1, 3, 4
*Indirect method*

The following financial statements were drawn from the records of Healthy Products Co.

| Balance Sheets As of December 31 | | |
|---|---|---|
| | **2012** | **2011** |
| Assets | | |
| Cash | $16,120 | $ 1,940 |
| Accounts receivable | 2,400 | 2,000 |
| Inventory | 2,000 | 2,600 |
| Equipment | 13,700 | 17,100 |
| Accumulated depreciation—equipment | (11,300) | (12,950) |
| Land | 13,000 | 8,000 |
| Total assets | $35,920 | $18,690 |
| Liabilities and stockholders' equity | | |
| Accounts payable (inventory) | $ 3,600 | $ 2,400 |
| Long-term debt | 3,200 | 4,000 |
| Common stock | 17,000 | 10,000 |
| Retained earnings | 12,120 | 2,290 |
| Total liabilities and stockholders' equity | $35,920 | $18,690 |

| Income Statement For the Year Ended December 31, 2012 | |
|---|---|
| Sales revenue | $17,480 |
| Cost of goods sold | (6,200) |
| Gross margin | 11,280 |
| Depreciation expense | (1,750) |
| Operating income | 9,530 |
| Gain on sale of equipment | 1,800 |
| Loss on disposal of land | (600) |
| Net income | $10,730 |

**Additional Data**

1. During 2012, the company sold equipment for $6,800; it had originally cost $8,400. Accumulated depreciation on this equipment was $3,400 at the time of the sale. Also, the company purchased equipment for $5,000 cash.

2. The company sold land that had cost $2,000. This land was sold for $1,400, resulting in the recognition of a $600 loss. Also, common stock was issued in exchange for title to land that was valued at $7,000 at the time of exchange.

3. Paid dividends of $900.

**Required**

Prepare a statement of cash flows using the indirect method.

**Problem 14-19B**    *Using financial statements to prepare a statement of cash flows—*    LO 1, 3, 4
*Indirect method*

The comparative balance sheets and an income statement for Lind Beauty Products, Inc., are shown on the next page.

| Balance Sheets As of December 31 | | |
| --- | --- | --- |
| | 2012 | 2011 |
| Assets | | |
| Cash | $ 6,300 | $ 48,400 |
| Accounts receivable | 10,200 | 7,260 |
| Merchandise inventory | 45,200 | 56,000 |
| Prepaid rent | 700 | 2,140 |
| Equipment | 140,000 | 144,000 |
| Accumulated depreciation | (73,400) | (118,000) |
| Land | 116,000 | 50,000 |
| Total assets | $245,000 | $189,800 |
| Liabilities and equity | | |
| Accounts payable (inventory) | $ 37,200 | $ 40,000 |
| Salaries payable | 12,200 | 10,600 |
| Stockholders' equity | | |
| Common stock, $50 par value | 150,000 | 120,000 |
| Retained earnings | 45,600 | 19,200 |
| Total liabilities and equity | $245,000 | $189,800 |

| Income Statement For the Year Ended December 31, 2012 | |
| --- | --- |
| Sales | $480,000 |
| Cost of goods sold | (264,000) |
| Gross profit | 216,000 |
| Operating expenses | |
| Depreciation expense | (11,400) |
| Rent expense | (7,000) |
| Salaries expense | (95,200) |
| Other operating expenses | (76,000) |
| Net income | $ 26,400 |

**Other Information**

1. Purchased land for $66,000.
2. Purchased new equipment for $62,000.
3. Sold old equipment that cost $66,000 with accumulated depreciation of $56,000 for $10,000 cash.
4. Issued common stock for $30,000.

**Required**

Prepare the statement of cash flows for 2012 using the indirect method.

LO 2, 3, 4

**Problem 14-20B**    *Using transaction data to prepare a statement of cash flows— Direct method*

Greenstein Company engaged in the following transactions during 2012. The beginning cash balance was $86,000 and ending cash balance was $123,100.

1. Sales on account were $548,000. The beginning Accounts Receivable balance was $128,000 and the ending balance was $90,000.
2. Salaries expense was $232,000. The beginning Salaries Payable balance was $16,000 and the ending balance was $8,000.
3. Other operating expenses were $236,000. The beginning Other Operating Expenses Payable balance was $16,000 and the ending balance was $10,000.
4. Recorded $30,000 of depreciation expense. The beginning and ending balances in the Accumulated Depreciation account were $12,000 and $42,000, respectively.

5. The Equipment account had beginning and ending balances of $44,000 and $56,000, respectively. There were no sales of equipment during the period.

6. The beginning and ending balances in the Notes Payable account were $44,000 and $36,000, respectively. There were no notes payable issued during the period.

7. There was $4,600 of interest expense reported on the income statement. The beginning and ending balances in the Interest Payable account were $8,400 and $7,500, respectively.

8. The beginning and ending Merchandise Inventory account balances were $22,000 and $29,400, respectively. The company sold merchandise with a cost of $83,600. The beginning and ending balances of Accounts Payable were $8,000 and $6,400, respectively.

9. The beginning and ending balances of Notes Receivable were $100,000 and $60,000, respectively. Notes receivable result from long-term loans made to creditors. There were no loans made to creditors during the period.

10. The beginning and ending balances of the Common Stock account were $120,000 and $160,000, respectively. The increase was caused by the issue of common stock for cash.

11. Land had beginning and ending balances of $24,000 and $14,000, respectively. Land that cost $10,000 was sold for $6,000, resulting in a loss of $4,000.

12. The tax expense for the period was $6,600. The Tax Payable account had a $2,400 beginning balance and a $2,200 ending balance.

13. The Investments account had beginning and ending balances of $20,000 and $60,000, respectively. The company purchased investments for $50,000 cash during the period, and investments that cost $10,000 were sold for $22,000, resulting in a $12,000 gain.

### Required

a. Determine the amount of cash flow for each item and indicate whether the item should appear in the operating, investing, or financing activities section of a statement of cash flows. If an item does not affect the cash flow statement, make a statement indicating that the cash flow statement will not be affected. Assume Greenstein Company uses the direct method for showing net cash flow from operating activities.

b. Prepare a statement of cash flows based on the information you developed in Requirement *a*.

**Problem 14-21B**    *Using financial statements to prepare a statement of cash flows—*    LO 2, 3, 4
                      *Direct method*

The following financial statements were drawn from the records of Norton Materials, Inc.

| Balance Sheets As of December 31 | | |
|---|---|---|
| | **2012** | **2011** |
| Assets | | |
| Cash | $ 94,300 | $ 14,100 |
| Accounts receivable | 36,000 | 40,000 |
| Inventory | 72,000 | 64,000 |
| Notes receivable (long-term) | 0 | 16,000 |
| Equipment | 98,000 | 170,000 |
| Accumulated depreciation—equipment | (47,800) | (94,000) |
| Land | 46,000 | 30,000 |
| Total assets | $298,500 | $240,100 |
| Liabilities and equity | | |
| Accounts payable | $ 24,000 | $ 26,400 |
| Salaries payable | 15,000 | 10,000 |
| Utilities payable | 800 | 1,400 |
| Interest payable | 0 | 1,000 |
| Notes payable (long-term) | 0 | 24,000 |
| Common stock | 150,000 | 110,000 |
| Retained earnings | 108,700 | 67,300 |
| Total liabilities and equity | $298,500 | $240,100 |

| Income Statement For the Year Ended December 31, 2012 | |
|---|---|
| Sales revenue | $300,000 |
| Cost of goods sold | (144,000) |
| Gross margin | 156,000 |
| Operating expenses | |
| Salary expense | (88,000) |
| Depreciation expense | (9,800) |
| Utilities expense | (6,400) |
| Operating income | 51,800 |
| Nonoperating items | |
| Interest expense | (2,400) |
| Loss on sale of equipment | (800) |
| Net income | $ 48,600 |

**Additional Information**

1.  Sold equipment costing $72,000 with accumulated depreciation of $56,000 for $15,200 cash.
2.  Paid a $7,200 cash dividend to owners.

**Required**

Analyze the data and prepare a statement of cash flows using the direct method.

## ANALYZE, THINK, COMMUNICATE

### ATC 14-1   Real-World Case   *Following the cash*

Vonage Holding Corporation provides telecommunication services using voice over Internet technology. It began operations in 2002 and has never made a profit. By the end of 2008 it had cumulative losses of $1 billion. Vonage's statements of cash flows for 2006, 2007, and 2008 follow.

## VONAGE HOLDINGS CORP.
### Statements of Cash Flows
### (amounts in thousands)

| | For the Years Ended | | |
|---|---|---|---|
| | 2008 | 2007 | 2006 |
| **Cash Flows from Operating Activities** | | | |
| Net income (loss) | $ (64,576) | $(267,428) | $(338,573) |
| Depreciation and amortization and impairment charges | 45,796 | 33,574 | 22,709 |
| Amortization of intangibles | 2,816 | 2,144 | 968 |
| Loss on early extinguishment of notes | 30,570 | — | — |
| Beneficial conversion on interest in kind on convertible notes | 108 | 42 | 32 |
| Amortization of discount on debt | 882 | — | — |
| Accrued interest | 3,014 | 846 | 4,002 |
| Allowance for doubtful accounts | 207 | 1,852 | 266 |
| Allowance for obsolete inventory | 1,519 | 2,799 | 1,441 |
| Amortization of deferred financing costs | — | 4,689 | 1,999 |
| Amortization of debt-related costs | 3,237 | — | — |

*continued*

| | **For the Years Ended** | | |
|---|---|---|---|
| | **2008** | **2007** | **2006** |
| Loss (gain) on disposal of fixed assets | 12 | 283 | 320 |
| Share-based expense | 12,238 | 7,542 | 26,980 |
| Other adjustments | — | — | (49) |
| Accounts receivable | 2,028 | (5,296) | (10,196) |
| Inventory | 7,472 | 2,196 | (10,133) |
| Prepaid expenses and other current assets | (282) | (6,185) | (6,218) |
| Deferred customer acquisition costs | 13,322 | (10,796) | (21,053) |
| Due from related parties | 2 | 74 | 32 |
| Other assets | (7,498) | (81) | (294) |
| Accounts payable | (22,029) | (2,966) | 42,407 |
| Accrued expenses | (12,738) | (77,770) | 62,281 |
| Deferred revenue | (10,124) | 20,509 | 34,181 |
| Other liability | (5,321) | 23,046 | — |
| Net cash flows from operating activities | 655 | (270,926) | (188,898) |
| **Cash Flows from Investing Activities** | | | |
| Capital expenditures | (11,386) | (20,386) | (45,336) |
| Purchase of intangible assets | (560) | (5,500) | (5,268) |
| Purchase of marketable securities | (21,375) | (236,875) | (639,707) |
| Maturities and sales of marketable securities | 101,317 | 446,949 | 484,116 |
| Acquisition and development of software assets | (26,530) | (21,346) | (4,060) |
| Decrease (increase) in restricted cash | (980) | (31,385) | (543) |
| Net cash flows from investing activities | 40,486 | 131,457 | (210,798) |
| **Cash Flows from Financing Activities** | | | |
| Principal payments on capital lease obligations | (1,036) | (1,020) | (826) |
| Principal payments on debt | (326) | — | — |
| Proceeds from issuance of debt | 223,200 | — | 2,047 |
| Discount on notes payable | (7,167) | — | — |
| Early extinguishment of notes | (253,460) | — | — |
| Debt-related costs | (26,799) | — | (283) |
| Proceeds from subscription receivable, net | 9 | 279 | 169 |
| Proceeds from common stock issuance, net | — | — | 493,040 |
| Purchase of treasury stock | — | — | (11,723) |
| Proceeds (payments) for directed-share program, net | 62 | 169 | (5,426) |
| Proceeds from exercise of stock options | 47 | 817 | 431 |
| Net cash flows from financing activities | (65,470) | 245 | 477,429 |
| Effect of exchange rate changes on cash | (1,079) | 513 | (29) |
| Net change in cash and cash equivalents | (25,408) | (138,711) | 77,704 |
| Cash and cash equivalents, beginning of period | 71,542 | 210,253 | 132,549 |
| Cash and cash equivalents, end of period | $ 46,134 | $ 71,542 | $ 210,253 |

## Required

a. This chapter explained that many companies that report net losses on their earnings statements report positive cash flows from operating activities. How does Vonage's net income for each year compare to its cash flows from operating activities?

b. Based only on the information in the statements of cash flows, does Vonage appear to be improving its position in the telecommunications business? Explain.

c. In 2008 Vonage paid off over $250 million in debt. Where did it get the funds to repay this debt?

d. All things considered, based on the information in its statements of cash flows, did Vonage's cash position appear to be improving or deteriorating?

### ATC 14-2    Group Assignment    *Preparing a statement of cash flows*

The following financial statements and information are available for Blythe Industries Inc.

| Balance Sheets As of December 31 | | |
|---|---|---|
| | **2011** | **2012** |
| **Assets** | | |
| Cash | $120,600 | $ 160,200 |
| Accounts receivable | 85,000 | 103,200 |
| Inventory | 171,800 | 186,400 |
| Marketable securities (available for sale) | 220,000 | 284,000 |
| Equipment | 490,000 | 650,000 |
| Accumulated depreciation | (240,000) | (310,000) |
| Land | 120,000 | 80,000 |
| Total assets | $967,400 | $1,153,800 |
| **Liabilities and equity** | | |
| **Liabilities** | | |
| Accounts payable (inventory) | $ 66,200 | $ 36,400 |
| Notes payable—Long-term | 250,000 | 230,000 |
| Bonds payable | 100,000 | 200,000 |
| Total liabilities | 416,200 | 466,400 |
| **Stockholders' equity** | | |
| Common stock, no par | 200,000 | 240,000 |
| Preferred stock, $50 par | 100,000 | 110,000 |
| Paid-in capital in excess of par—Preferred stock | 26,800 | 34,400 |
| Total paid-In capital | 326,800 | 384,400 |
| Retained earnings | 264,400 | 333,000 |
| Less: Treasury stock | (40,000) | (30,000) |
| Total stockholders' equity | 551,200 | 687,400 |
| Total liabilities and stockholders' equity | $967,400 | $1,153,800 |

| Income Statement For the Year Ended December 31, 2012 | | |
|---|---|---|
| Sales revenue | | $1,050,000 |
| Cost of goods sold | | (766,500) |
| Gross profit | | 283,500 |
| Operating expenses | | |
| Supplies expense | $20,400 | |
| Salaries expense | 92,000 | |
| Depreciation expense | 90,000 | |
| Total operating expenses | | (202,400) |
| Operating income | | 81,100 |
| Nonoperating items | | |
| Interest expense | | (16,000) |
| Gain from the sale of marketable securities | | 30,000 |
| Gain from the sale of land and equipment | | 12,000 |
| Net income | | $ 107,100 |

### Additional Information

1. Sold land that cost $40,000 for $44,000.
2. Sold equipment that cost $30,000 and had accumulated depreciation of $20,000 for $18,000.

3. Purchased new equipment for $190,000.

4. Sold marketable securities, classified as available-for-sale, that cost $40,000 for $70,000.

5. Purchased new marketable securities, classified as available-for-sale, for $104,000.

6. Paid $20,000 on the principal of the long-term note.

7. Paid off a $100,000 bond issue and issued new bonds for $200,000.

8. Sold 100 shares of treasury stock at its cost.

9. Issued some new common stock.

10. Issued some new $50 par preferred stock.

11. Paid dividends. (*Note:* The only transactions to affect retained earnings were net income and dividends.)

### Required

Organize the class into three sections, and divide each section into groups of three to five students. Assign each section of groups an activity section of the statement of cash flows (operating activities, investing activities, or financing activities).

### Group Task

Prepare your assigned portion of the statement of cash flows. Have a representative of your section put your activity section of the statement of cash flows on the board. As each section adds its information on the board, the full statement of cash flows will be presented.

### Class Discussion

Have the class finish the statement of cash flows by computing the net change in cash. Also have the class answer the following questions:

a.  What is the cost per share of the treasury stock?

b.  What was the issue price per share of the preferred stock?

c.  What was the book value of the equipment sold?

### ATC 14-3 Business Applications Case *Identifying different presentation formats*

In *Statement of Financial Accounting Standards No. 95,* the Financial Accounting Standards Board (FASB) recommended but did not require that companies use the direct method. In Appendix B, Paragraphs 106–121, of the standard, the FASB discussed its reasons for this recommendation.

### Required

Obtain a copy of *Standard No. 95* and read Appendix B Paragraphs 106–121. Write a brief response summarizing the issues that the FASB considered and its specific reaction to those issues. Your response should draw heavily on paragraphs 119–121.

### ATC 14-4 Writing Assignment *Explaining discrepancies between cash flow and operating income*

The following selected information was drawn from the records of Fleming Company:

| Assets | 2011 | 2012 |
|---|---|---|
| Accounts receivable | $ 400,000 | $ 840,200 |
| Merchandise inventory | 720,000 | 1,480,000 |
| Equipment | 1,484,000 | 1,861,200 |
| Accumulated depreciation | (312,000) | (402,400) |

Fleming is experiencing cash flow problems. Despite the fact that it reported significant increases in operating income, operating activities produced a net cash outflow. Recent financial forecasts predict that Fleming will have insufficient cash to pay its current liabilities within three months.

**Required**

Write an explanation of Fleming's cash shortage. Include a recommendation to remedy the problem.

**ATC 14-5**    Ethical Dilemma    *Would I lie to you, baby?*

Andy and Jean Crocket are involved in divorce proceedings. When discussing a property settlement, Andy told Jean that he should take over their investment in an apartment complex because she would be unable to absorb the loss that the apartments are generating. Jean was somewhat distrustful and asked Andy to support his contention. He produced the following income statement, which was supported by a CPA's unqualified opinion that the statement was prepared in accordance with generally accepted accounting principles.

| CROCKET APARTMENTS | | |
|---|---|---|
| Income Statement | | |
| For the Year Ended December 31, 2011 | | |
| Rent revenue | | $580,000 |
| Less: Expenses | | |
| Depreciation expense | $280,000 | |
| Interest expense | 184,000 | |
| Operating expense | 88,000 | |
| Management fees | 56,000 | |
| Total expenses | | (608,000) |
| Net loss | | $ (28,000) |

All revenue is earned on account. Interest and operating expenses are incurred on account. Management fees are paid in cash. The following accounts and balances were drawn from the 2010 and 2011 year-end balance sheets.

| Account Title | 2010 | 2011 |
|---|---|---|
| Rent receivable | $40,000 | $44,000 |
| Interest payable | 12,000 | 18,000 |
| Accounts payable (oper. exp.) | 6,000 | 4,000 |

Jean is reluctant to give up the apartments but feels that she must do so because her present salary is only $40,000 per year. She says that if she takes the apartments, the $28,000 loss would absorb a significant portion of her salary, leaving her only $12,000 with which to support herself. She tells you that while the figures seem to support her husband's arguments, she believes that she is failing to see something. She knows that she and her husband collected a $20,000 distribution from the business on December 1, 2011. Also, $150,000 cash was paid in 2011 to reduce the principal balance on a mortgage that was taken out to finance the purchase of the apartments two years ago. Finally, $24,000 cash was paid during 2011 to purchase a computer system used in the business. She wonders, "If the apartments are losing money, where is my husband getting all the cash to make these payments?"

**Required**

a. Prepare a statement of cash flows for the 2011 accounting period.

b. Compare the cash flow statement prepared in Requirement *a* with the income statement and provide Jean Crocket with recommendations.

c. Comment on the value of an unqualified audit opinion when using financial statements for decision-making purposes.

## ATC 14-6 Research Assignment *Analyzing cash flow information*

In 2008 Time Warner, Inc., reported a net loss of $13.4 billion. This loss occurred predominantly because Time Warner took a charge for "asset impairments" of $24,309 million, ($24.3 billion). (These amounts do not include tax benefits.) Without these special charges, Time Warner's net income would have been a positive $10.9 billion. Using the company's 2008 Form 10-K, complete the requirements below. Be sure to use the Form 10-K for *Time Warner, Inc.,* not *Time Warner Cable, Inc.* The Form 10-K can be found on the company's website. It can also be obtained using the EDGAR system following the instructions in Appendix A.

### Required

**a.** How much cash flow from operating activities did Time Warner generate?

**b.** Based on the statement of cash flows, how much cash did the company pay out as a result of the asset impairments?

**c.** How much cash did Time Warner spend on investing activities (net)?

**d.** How much cash did the company use the repay debt? Where did it get the cash to make these payments?

## APPENDIX A

# Accessing the EDGAR Database through the Internet

Successful business managers need many different skills, including communication, interpersonal, computer, and analytical. Most business students become very aware of the data analysis skills used in accounting, but they may not be as aware of the importance of "data-finding" skills. There are many sources of accounting and financial data. The more sources you are able to use, the better.

One very important source of accounting information is the EDGAR database. Others are probably available at your school through the library or business school network. Your accounting instructor will be able to identify these for you and make suggestions regarding their use. By making the effort to learn to use electronic databases, you will enhance your abilities as a future manager and your marketability as a business graduate.

These instructions assume that you know how to access and use an Internet browser. Follow the instructions to retrieve data from the Securities and Exchange Commission's EDGAR database. Be aware that the SEC may have changed its interface since this appendix was written. Accordingly, be prepared for slight differences between the following instructions and what appears on your computer screen. Take comfort in the fact that changes are normally designed to simplify user access. If you encounter a conflict between the following instructions and the instructions provided in the SEC interface, remember that the SEC interface is more current and should take precedence over the following instructions.

Most companies provide links to their SEC filings from their corporate website. These links are often simpler to use and provide more choices regarding file formats than SEC's EDGAR site. On company websites, links to their SEC filings are usually found under one of the following links: "Investor Relations," "Company Info," or "About Us."

1. Connect to the EDGAR database through the following address: **http://www.sec.gov/.**
2. After the SEC homepage appears, under the heading **Filings and Forms,** click on **Search for Company Filings.**
3. On the screen that appears, click on **Company or Fund Name. . . .**
4. On the screen that appears, enter the name of the company whose file you wish to retrieve and click on the **Find Companies** button.
5. The following screen will present a list of companies that have the same, or similar, names to the one you entered. Identify the company you want and click on the CIK number beside it.
6. Enter the SEC form number that you want to retrieve in the window titled **Filling Type** that appears in the upper left portion of the screen. For example, if you want Form 10-K, which will usually be the case, enter **10-K** and click on the **Search** button.
7. A list of the forms you requested will be presented, along with the date they were filed. Click on the **Document** button next to the file you wish to retrieve.
8. You will be presented with a list of documents from which to select; usually you will want to choose the file **form10k.htm.**
9. Once the 10-K has been retrieved, you can search it online or save it on your computer.
10. Often the 10-K will have a table of contents that can help locate the part of the report you need. The financial statements are seldom located at the beginning of the Form 10-K. They are usually in either Section 8 or Section 15.

**absolute amounts**    Dollar totals reported on financial statements; using them in financial analysis comparisons can be misleading because they do not reflect materiality levels of the underlying companies. *p. 589*

**absorption (full) costing**    Reporting method in which all product costs, including fixed manufacturing costs, are initially capitalized in inventory and then expensed when goods are sold. (Contrast with *variable costing*.) *p. 500*

**accounts receivable turnover**    Financial ratio that measures how quickly accounts receivable are converted to cash; computed by dividing net credit sales by average net accounts receivable. *p. 595*

**accrual accounting**    Accounting system that recognizes revenues when earned and expenses when incurred regardless of when the related cash is exchanged.

**accumulated conversion factor**    Factor used to convert a series of future cash flows into their present value equivalent when applied to cash flows of equal amounts spread over equal interval time periods; this factor can be computed by adding the individual single factors applicable to each period. *p. 47*

**acid-test ratio**    See *quick ratio. p. 595*

**activities**    Measures an organization undertakes to accomplish its mission. *p. 207*

**activity base**    Factor that causes changes in total variable cost; usually some measure of volume when used to explain cost behavior. *p. 65*

**activity-based cost drivers**    Measures of activities that cause costs to be incurred, such as number of setups, percentage of use, and pounds of material delivered; using such measures as allocation bases can improve the accuracy of cost allocations in business environments where overhead costs are not driven by volume. *p. 205*

**activity-based costing (ABC)**    A two-stage cost allocation process. First, costs associated with specific business activities are allocated or assigned to activity cost pools. Second, these pooled costs are allocated to designated cost objects by using a variety of appropriate cost drivers. The cost drivers chosen for each cost pool are those that most accurately reflect the demand placed on that cost pool by the cost object. *p. 207*

**activity-based management (ABM)**    Managing organization activities to add the greatest value by developing products that satisfy the needs of the organization's customers. *p. 23*

**activity centers**    Cost centers composed of operating activities with similar characteristics; pooling indirect costs into activity centers reduces record-keeping costs by allowing allocations based on a common cost driver for each center. *p. 207*

**allocation**    Process of dividing a total cost into parts and assigning the parts to the relevant cost objects. *p. 153*

**allocation base**    The factor used as the base for cost allocation; when possible, a driver of the allocated cost. *p. 155*

**allocation rate**    The mathematical factor used to allocate or assign costs to a cost object, determined by dividing the total cost to be allocated by the appropriate cost driver or allocation base. *p. 155*

**annuity**    Series of equal cash flows received or paid over equal time intervals at a constant rate of return. *p. 447*

**applied fixed cost**    Total cost determined by multiplying the predetermined overhead rate times the actual volume of production. *p. 356*

**applied overhead**    Amount of overhead costs assigned during the period to work in process using a predetermined overhead rate. *p. 491*

**appraisal costs**    Costs of identifying nonconforming products produced regardless of prevention cost expenditures. *p. 216*

**asset turnover ratio**    A measure of revenue dollars generated by the assets invested; calculated as net sales divided by average total assets. *p. 600*

**average cost (per unit)**    The total cost of making products divided by the total number of products made. *p. 26*

**average days to collect receivables (average collection period)**    Measure of how quickly, on average, a business collects its accounts receivable; calculated as 365 divided by the accounts receivable turnover. *p. 596*

**average days to sell inventory (average days in inventory)**    Measure of how quickly, on average, a business sells its inventory; calculated as 365 divided by the inventory turnover ratio. *p. 596*

**avoidable costs**    Potential future costs an organization can circumvent by choosing a particular course of action. To be avoidable, costs must differ among decision alternatives. For example, if materials cost for two different products is the same for each product, materials cost could not be avoided by choosing to produce one product instead of the other. The materials cost would therefore not be an avoidable cost. *p. 257*

**balanced scorecard**    A management evaluation tool that uses both financial and nonfinancial measures to assess how well an organization is meeting its objectives. *p. 412*

**batch-level activities**    Actions taken (e.g., materials handling, production setups) to produce groups of products, the cost of which is fixed regardless of the number of units produced in a batch. *p. 209*

**batch-level costs**    The costs associated with producing a batch of products, most accurately allocated using cost drivers that measure activity levels. For example, the cost of setting up a press to print 500 copies of an engraved invitation is a batch-level cost. Classifying costs as batch-level is context sensitive. The postage to mail a single product would be classified as a unit-level cost. In contrast, the postage to mail a large number of products in a single shipment would be classified as a batch-level cost. *p. 257*

**benchmarking**    Identifying best practices used by world-class competitors in a given industry. *p. 24*

**best practices** Identifiable procedures used by world-class companies. *p. 24*

**book value per share** An accounting measure of a share of common stock, computed by dividing total stockholders' equity less preferred rights by the number of common shares outstanding. *p. 602*

**bottleneck** A constraint that limits a company's capacity to produce or sell its products, such as a piece of equipment that cannot produce enough component parts to fully occupy employees in the assembly department. *p. 270*

**break-even point** Sales volume at which total revenue equals total cost; can be expressed in units or sales dollars. *p. 108*

**budgeting** Form of planning that formalizes a company's goals and objectives in financial terms. *p. 304*

**budget slack** Difference between inflated and realistic standards. *p. 360*

**by-products** Products that share common inputs with other joint products but have insignificant market values relative to the other joint products.

**capital budget** Budget detailing the company's plans to invest in operational assets, new products, or lines of business for the coming year; influences many of the operating budgets and is a formal part of the master budget. *p. 308*

**capital budgeting** Financial planning for the intermediate time range involving decisions such as whether to buy or lease equipment, purchase additional assets, or increase operating expenses to stimulate sales. *p. 306*

**capital investments** Purchases of operational assets involving a long-term commitment of funds that can be critically important to the company's ultimate success; costs normally recovered through using the assets. *p. 444*

**cash budget** A budget detailing expected future cash receipts and payments. *p. 313*

**cash inflows** Cash receipts including cash generated from operating activities such as cash revenues or collections of accounts receivable; cash collected from investing activities such as selling investments; and cash collected from financing activities such as borrowing money or issuing stock. *p. 636*

**cash outflows** Cash disbursements including cash paid for operating activities such as cash expenses or payments to settle accounts payable; cash paid for investing activities such as buying investments; and cash paid for financing activities such as repaying long-term debt or purchasing treasury stock. *p. 636*

**certified suppliers** Suppliers who have demonstrated reliability by providing the buyer with quality goods and services at desirable prices, usually in accord with strict delivery specifications; frequently offer the buyer preferred customer status in exchange for guaranteed purchase quantities and prompt payment schedules. *p. 262*

**common costs** Costs that are incurred to support more than one cost object but cannot be traced to any specific object. *p. 154*

**companywide allocation rate** Factor based on a single measure of volume, such as direct labor-hours, used to allocate all overhead cost to the company's products or other cost objects. *p. 204*

**constraints** Conditions that limit a business's ability to satisfy the demand for its products. *p. 270*

**continuous improvement** An ongoing process through which employees learn to eliminate waste, reduce response time, minimize defects, and simplify the design and delivery of products and services to customers; a feature of total quality management (TQM). *p. 24*

**contribution margin** The difference between sales revenue and variable cost; the amount available to pay for fixed cost and thereafter to provide a profit. *p. 61*

**contribution margin per unit** The sales price per unit minus the variable cost per unit. *p. 109*

**contribution margin ratio** The contribution margin per unit divided by the sales price per unit; can be used in cost-volume-profit analysis to calculate in dollars the break-even sales volume or the level of sales required to attain a desired profit. *p. 110*

**controllable costs** Costs that can be influenced by a particular manager's decisions and actions. *p. 154*

**controllability concept** Evaluating managerial performance based only on revenue and costs under the manager's direct control. *p. 404*

**cost** Measure of resources used to acquire an asset or to produce revenue.

**cost accumulation** Measuring the cost of a particular object by combining many individual costs into a single total cost. *p. 152*

**cost allocation** Process of dividing a total cost into parts and assigning the parts to relevant objects. *pp. 12, 153*

**cost averaging** Measuring the cost per unit of a product or service by dividing the total production cost by the total activity base to which the cost pertains; average cost is often more relevant to pricing, performance evaluation, and control than actual cost. *p. 66*

**cost-based transfer price** Transfer price based on the historical or standard cost incurred by the supplying segment. *p. 416*

**cost behavior** How a cost changes (increase, decrease, remain constant) relative to changes in some measure of activity (e.g., the behavior of raw materials cost is to increase as the number of units of product made increases). *p. 54*

**cost center** A responsibility center that incurs costs but does not generate revenue. *p. 401*

**cost driver** Any factor, usually a volume measure, that causes cost to be incurred; sometimes described as *activity base* or *allocation base*. Changes in cost drivers, such as labor-hours or machine-hours, cause corresponding changes in cost. *p. 152*

**cost objects** Items for which managers need to measure cost; can be products, processes, departments, services, activities, and so on. *p. 150*

**cost of capital** Return paid to investors and creditors for supplying assets (capital); usually represents a company's minimum rate of return. *p. 445*

**cost per equivalent unit** Unit cost of product determined by dividing total production costs by the number of equivalent whole units; used to allocate product costs between processing departments (amount of ending inventory and amount of costs transferred to the subsequent department). *p. 550*

**cost per unit of input**  Cost of material, labor, or overhead for one unit; determined by multiplying the price paid for one unit of material, labor, or overhead input by the usage of that input for one unit of product or service.

**cost-plus pricing**  Strategy that sets the selling price at cost plus a markup equal to a percentage of the cost. *p. 112*

**cost pool**  A collection of costs organized around a common cost driver. The cost pool, as opposed to individual costs, is allocated to cost objects using the common cost driver, thereby promoting efficiency in the allocation process. *p. 165*

**cost structure**  The relative proportion of a company's variable and fixed costs to total cost. The percentage change in net income a company experiences for a given percentage change in sales volume is directly related to the company's cost structure. The greater a company's percentage of fixed to total costs, the more its net income will fluctuate with changes in sales. *p. 59*

**cost tracing**  Assigning specific costs to the objects that cause their incurrence. *p. 153*

**cost-volume-profit (CVP) analysis**  Management tool that reflects the interrelationships among sales prices, volume, fixed costs, and variable costs; used in determining the break-even point or the most profitable combination of these variables. *p. 107*

**current ratio (working capital ratio)**  Measure of liquidity; calculated by dividing current assets by current liabilities. *p. 594*

**decentralization**  Delegating authority and responsibility for business segment operation to lower-level managers. *p. 400*

**deferral transactions**  Accounting transactions in which cash payments or receipts occur before the related expense or revenue is recognized.

**differential costs**  Costs that differ among alternative business opportunities; usually relevant for decision making. Some differential costs, however, are not relevant. For example, although depreciation may differ between the alternatives, it is an unavoidable sunk cost and is therefore not relevant for decision making. *p. 259*

**differential revenue**  Revenues that are relevant to decision-making because they differ among alternative courses of action. *p. 256*

**direct cost**  Cost that is easily traceable to a cost object and for which it is economically feasible to do so. *p. 153*

**direct labor**  Wages paid to production workers whose efforts can be easily and conveniently traced to products. *p. 9*

**direct method**  (1) Allocation method that allocates service center costs directly to operating department cost pools; does not account for any relationships among service centers. (2) Method of reporting cash flows from operating activities on the statement of cash flows that shows individual categories of cash receipts from and cash payments for major activities (collections from customers, payments to suppliers, etc.). *pp. 171, 638*

**direct raw materials**  Costs of raw materials used to make products that can be easily and conveniently traced to those products. *p. 9*

**dividend yield**  Ratio for comparing stock dividends paid relative to the market price; calculated as dividends per share divided by market price per share. *p. 603*

**downstream costs**  Costs incurred after the manufacturing process is complete, such as delivery costs and sales commissions. *pp. 14, 214*

**earnings per share**  Measure of the value of a share of common stock based on company earnings; calculated as net income available to common stockholders divided by the average number of outstanding common shares. *p. 602*

**economies of scale**  Reducing the unit cost of production by increasing an operation's size. Increasing size usually increases the volume of activity, reducing the per unit fixed cost and resulting in a lower total production cost.

**efficient market hypothesis**  The proposition that creditors and investors evaluate the underlying substance of business events regardless of how those events are reported in financial reports.

**equation method**  Cost-volume-profit analysis technique that uses the algebraic relationship among sales, variable costs, fixed costs, and desired net income before taxes to solve for required sales volume. *p. 108*

**equipment replacement decisions**  Deciding whether to replace existing equipment with newer equipment based on comparing the avoidable costs of keeping the old or purchasing new equipment to determine which choice is more profitable. *p. 266*

**equivalent whole units**  A quantity of partially completed goods expressed as an equivalent number of fully completed goods. *p. 549*

**expense transactions**  Business events that decrease assets or increase liabilities in order to produce revenue in the course of operating a business.

**external failure costs**  Costs resulting from delivering defective goods to customers. *p. 216*

**facility-level activities**  Actions taken (e.g., insuring the facility, providing plant maintenance, employing a company president) that benefit the production process as a whole. *p. 211*

**facility-level costs**  Costs incurred to support the whole company or a segment thereof, not related to any specific product, batch, or unit of production or service and unavoidable unless the entire company or segment is eliminated; they are so indirect that any allocation of facility-level costs is necessarily arbitrary. *p. 211*

**failure costs**  Costs resulting from producing or providing nonconforming products or services. *p. 316*

**favorable variance**  Variance indicating that actual costs are less than standard costs or actual sales exceed budgeted sales. *p. 351*

**financial accounting**  Branch of accounting focused on the business information needs of external users (creditors, investors, governmental agencies, financial analysts, etc.); its objective is to classify and record business events and transactions to produce external financial reports (income statement, balance sheet, statement of cash flows, and statement of changes in equity). *p. 2*

**Financial Accounting Standards Board (FASB)**  Private, independent standard-setting body established by the accounting profession that has been delegated the authority by the SEC to establish most of the accounting rules and regulations for public financial reporting. *p. 5*

**financing activities** Cash inflows and outflows from transactions with investors and creditors (except interest), including cash receipts from issuing stock, borrowing activities, and cash disbursements to pay dividends. *p. 639*

**finished goods** Completed products resulting from the manufacturing process; measured by the accumulated cost of raw materials, labor, and overhead. *p. 6*

**Finished Goods Inventory** Asset account used to accumulate the product costs (direct materials, direct labor, and overhead) associated with completed products that have not yet been sold. *p. 486*

**first-in, first-out (FIFO) method** Means of computing equivalent units in a process cost system that accounts for the degree of completion of both beginning and ending inventories; more complex than the weighted average method, and used when greater accuracy is desired.

**fixed cost** Cost that remains constant in total regardless of changes in the volume of activity; per unit amount varies inversely with changes in the volume of activity. *p. 550*

**fixed cost spending variance** The difference between the *actual* fixed manufacturing overhead costs and the *budgeted* fixed manufacturing overhead costs. *p. 356*

**fixed cost volume variance** The difference between the *budgeted* fixed manufacturing overhead costs and the *applied* fixed manufacturing overhead costs. *p. 350*

**flexible budgets** Budgets that show expected revenues and costs at a variety of different activity levels. *p. 350*

**flexible budget variances** Differences between budgets based on standard amounts at the actual level of activity and actual results; caused by differences between standard unit cost and actual unit cost at the volume of activity achieved.

**full costing** See *absorption costing. p. 500*

**generally accepted accounting principles (GAAP)** Rules and practices that accountants agree to follow in financial reports prepared for public distribution. *p. 5*

**high-low method** Method of estimating the fixed and variable components of a mixed cost; the variable cost per unit is the difference between the total cost at the high- and low-volume points divided by the difference between the corresponding high and low volumes. The fixed cost component is determined by subtracting the variable cost from the total cost at either the high- or low-volume level. *p. 68*

**horizontal analysis** Financial analysis technique of comparing amounts of the same item over several time periods. *p. 589*

**hybrid costing systems** Cost systems that blend some features of a job-order costing system with some features of a process costing system. *p. 538*

**ideal standard** A measure of the highest level of efficiency attainable; assumes all input factors interact perfectly under ideal or optimum conditions. *p. 358*

**incremental revenue** Additional cash inflows from operating activities generated by using an additional capital asset. *p. 451*

**indirect cost** Cost that either cannot be easily traced to a cost object or for which it is not economically feasible to do so. See also *overhead. pp. 11, 153*

**indirect method** Method of reporting cash flows from operating activities on the statement of cash flows that starts with the net income from the income statement, followed by adjustments necessary to convert accrual-based net income to a cash-basis equivalent. *p. 638*

**information overload** Condition where so much information is presented that it confuses the user of the information. *p. 588*

**interdepartmental service** Service performed by one service department for the benefit of another service department. *p. 172*

**internal failure costs** Costs incurred to correct defects before goods reach the customer. *p. 216*

**internal rate of return** Rate at which the present value of an investment's future cash inflows equals the cash outflows required to acquire the investment; the rate that produces a net present value of zero. *p. 450*

**inventory holding costs** Costs associated with acquiring and retaining inventory including cost of storage space; lost, stolen, or damaged merchandise; insurance; personnel and management costs; and interest. *p. 14*

**inventory turnover** A measure of sales volume relative to inventory levels; calculated as the cost of goods sold divided by average inventory. *p. 598*

**investing activities** Cash inflows and outflows associated with buying or selling long-term assets and cash inflows and outflows associated with lending activities (loans to others— cash outflows; collecting loans to others—cash inflows). *p. 639*

**investment center** Type of responsibility center for which revenue, expense, and capital investments can be measured. *p. 401*

**job cost sheet** Record used in a job-order costing system to accumulate the materials, labor, and overhead costs of a job during production; at job completion, it summarizes all costs that were incurred to complete that job; also known as a *job-order cost sheet* or *job record. p. 538*

**job-order costing system** System in which costs are traced to products that are produced individually (e.g., custom-designed building) or in batches (e.g., an order for 100 wedding invitations); used to determine the costs of distinct, one-of-a-kind products. *p. 536*

**joint costs** Common costs incurred in the process of making two or more products. *p. 165*

**joint products** Separate products derived from common inputs. *p. 165*

**just in time (JIT)** Inventory management system that minimizes the amount of inventory on hand by avoiding inventory acquisition until products are demanded by customers, therefore eliminating the need to store inventory. The system reduces inventory holding costs including financing, warehouse storage, supervision, theft, damage, and obsolescence. It can also eliminate opportunity costs such as lost revenue due to the lack of availability of inventory. *p. 14*

**labor efficiency variance** Standard cost variance that indicates how the actual amount of direct labor used differs from the standard amount required.

**labor price variance** Standard cost variance that indicates how the actual pay rate for direct labor differs from the standard pay rate. *p. 365*

**lax standards**    Easily attainable goals that can be reached with minimal effort. *p. 358*

**least-squares regression**    A technique used to draw a line through a data set by minimizing the sum of the squared deviations between the line and the points in the data set. *p. 72*

**liquidity ratios**    Measures of a company's capacity to pay short-term debt. *p. 593*

**low-ball pricing**    Supplier practice of pricing a product below competitors' prices to attract customers and then raising the price once customers depend on the supplier for the product. *p. 262*

**making the numbers**    Expression that indicates marketing managers attained the planned master budget sales volume. *p. 352*

**management by exception**    The philosophy of focusing management attention and resources only on those operations where performance deviates significantly from expectations. *pp. 357, 403*

**managerial accounting**    Branch of accounting focused on the information needs of managers and others working within the business. Its objective is to gather and report information that adds value to the business. Managerial accounting information is not regulated or reported to the public. *p. 2*

**manufacturing overhead**    Production costs that cannot be easily or economically traced directly to products. *p. 11*

**Manufacturing Overhead account**    Temporary account used during an accounting period to accumulate the actual overhead costs incurred and the amount of overhead applied to production. A debit balance in the account at the end of the period means overhead has been underapplied and a credit balance means overhead has been overapplied. The account is closed at year-end in an adjusting entry to the Work in Process and Finished Goods Inventory accounts and the Cost of Goods Sold account. If the balance is insignificant, it is closed only to Cost of Goods Sold. *p. 491*

**margin**    Ratio that measures control of operating expenses relative to sales; computed as operating income divided by sales. Along with *turnover*, a component of return on investment. *p. 401*

**margin of safety**    Difference between break-even sales and budgeted sales expressed in units, dollars, or as a percentage; the amount by which actual sales can fall below budgeted sales before incurring losses. *p. 119*

**market-based transfer price**    Transfer price based on the external market price less any cost savings; it offers the closest approximation to an arm's-length price possible for intersegment transactions. *p. 413*

**master budget**    The combination of the numerous separate but interdependent departmental budgets that detail a wide range of operating and financing plans including sales, production, manufacturing expenses, and administrative expenses. See also *static budget. p. 308*

**material variance**    A variance sufficiently significant that its investigation could influence decision making. *p. 359*

**materiality**    The point at which knowledge of information would influence a user's decision; can be measured in absolute, percentage, quantitative, or qualitative terms. *p. 589*

**materials price variance**    Standard cost variance that indicates how the actual price paid for raw materials differs from the standard price for the materials. *p. 363*

**materials quantity variance**    Standard cost variance that indicates the actual amount of raw materials used to make products differs from the standard amount required.

**materials requisition form**    A form, either paper or electronic, used to request the materials needed for a specified job. The accounting department summarizes all materials requisitioned for a job on a job cost sheet. *p. 538*

**minimum rate of return**    Minimum rate of profitability required for a company to accept an investment opportunity; also called *desired rate of return, required rate of return, hurdle rate, cutoff rate,* and *discount rate. p. 445*

**mixed costs (semivariable costs)**    Costs that have both fixed and variable components. *p. 64*

**multiple regression analysis**    A statistical tool that permits analysis of how a number of independent variables simultaneously affect a dependent variable.

**negotiated transfer price**    Transfer price established through mutual agreement of the selling and buying segments. *p. 416*

**net margin**    Profitability ratio that measures the percentage of sales dollars resulting in profit; calculated as net income divided by net sales. *p. 599*

**net present value**    Capital budgeting evaluation technique in which future cash flows are discounted, using a desired rate of return, to their present value equivalents and then the cost of the investment is subtracted from the present value equivalents to determine the net present value. A zero or positive net present value (present value of cash inflows equals or exceeds the present value of cash outflows) means the investment opportunity provides an acceptable rate of return. *p. 449*

**noncash investing and financing activities**    Certain business transactions, usually long-term, that do not involve cash, such as exchanging stock for land or purchasing property by using debt; reported separately on the statement of cash flows. *p. 640*

**nonvalue-added activities**    Tasks undertaken that do not contribute to a product's ability to satisfy customer needs. *p. 15*

**operating activities**    Cash inflows from and outflows for routine, everyday business operations, normally resulting from revenue and expense transactions including interest.

**operating budgets**    Departmental budgets that become a part of the company's master budget; typically include a sales budget, an inventory purchases budget, a selling and administrative expense budget, and a cash budget. *p. 638*

**operating departments**    Departments that perform tasks directly related to accomplishing the organization's objectives. (Contrast with *service departments.*) *p. 170*

**operating leverage**    Cost structure condition that produces a proportionately larger percentage change in net income for a given percentage change in revenue; measured by dividing the contribution margin by net income. The higher the proportion of fixed cost to total costs, the greater the operating leverage. *p. 56*

**operations budgeting**    Short-range planning activities such as the development and implementation of the master budget. *p. 306*

**opportunity cost**    Cost of lost opportunities such as revenue forgone because of insufficient inventory. *pp. 15, 254*

**ordinary annuity**  Annuity in which cash flows occur at the end of each accounting period. *p. 448*

**outsourcing**  Buying goods and services from an outside company rather than producing them internally. *p. 260*

**overapplied or underapplied overhead**  The difference between the amount of overhead costs actually incurred and the amount of overhead costs allocated to work in process. *p. 491*

**overhead**  Costs associated with producing products or providing services that cannot be traced directly to those products or services in a cost-effective manner; includes indirect costs such as indirect materials, indirect labor, utilities, rent, depreciation on manufacturing facilities and equipment, and planning, design, and setup costs related to the product or service. *p. 6*

**overhead costs**  Indirect costs of operating a business that cannot be directly traced to a product, department, process, or service, such as depreciation. *p. 153*

**participative budgeting**  Technique in which upper-level managers involve subordinates in setting budget objectives, thereby encouraging employee cooperation and support in attaining the company's goals. *p. 308*

**payback method**  Capital budgeting evaluation technique in which the length of time necessary to recover the initial net investment through incremental revenue or cost savings is determined; the shorter the period, the better the investment opportunity. *p. 458*

**percentage analysis**  Financial analysis technique of comparing numerical relationships between two different financial statement items to draw conclusions; circumvents difficulties caused by differing materiality levels. *p. 590*

**period costs**  General, selling, and administrative costs that are expensed in the period in which the economic sacrifice is incurred. (Contrast with *product costs.*) *p. 10*

**perpetual (continuous) budgeting**  Maintaining a budget that always reflects plans for the coming 12 months by adding a new monthly budget to the end as the current month's expires; keeps management constantly involved in the budget process to allow timely recognition of changing conditions. *p. 306*

**postaudit**  After-the-fact evaluation of an investment project; the capital budgeting techniques employed in originally deciding to accept the project are used to calculate the results of the project using actual data; provides feedback regarding whether the expected results were actually achieved. *p. 461*

**practical standard**  A measure of efficiency in which the ideal standard has been modified to allow for normal tolerable inefficiencies. *p. 358*

**predetermined overhead rate**  Allocation rate calculated before actual costs or activity are known; determined by dividing the estimated overhead costs for the coming period by some measure of estimated total production activity for the period, such as the number of labor-hours or machine-hours. The base should relate rationally to overhead use. The rate is used throughout the accounting period to allocate overhead costs to work in process inventory based on actual production activity. *pp. 356, 490*

**present value index**  Present value of cash inflows divided by the present value of cash outflows. Higher index numbers indicate higher rates of return. *p. 454*

**present value table**  Matrix of factors to use in converting future values into their present value equivalents; composed of columns that represent alternative rates of return and rows that represent alternative time periods. *p. 446*

**prestige pricing**  Strategy that sets the selling price at a premium (more than average markup above cost) under the assumption that customers will pay more for the product because of its prestigious brand name, media attention, or some other reason that has piqued the interest of the public. *p. 112*

**prevention costs**  Costs incurred to avoid making nonconforming products. *p. 216*

**price-earnings ratio**  Measure that reflects the values of different stocks in terms of earnings; calculated as market price per share divided by earnings (net income) per share. *p. 602*

**pro forma financial statements**  Budgeted financial statements that reflect the master budget plans. *p. 308*

**process costing system**  System in which costs are distributed evenly across total production of homogeneous products, such as chemicals, foods, or paints; the average cost per unit is determined by dividing the total product costs of each production department by the number of units of product made in that department during the accounting period. The total costs in the last production department include all costs incurred in preceding departments so that the unit cost determined for the last department reflects the final unit cost of the product. *p. 536*

**product costs**  All costs related to obtaining or manufacturing a product intended for sale to customers; accumulated in inventory accounts and expensed as cost of goods sold at the point of sale. For a manufacturing company, product costs are direct materials, direct labor, and manufacturing overhead. (Contrast with *period costs.*) *p. 5*

**product costing**  Classifying and accumulating the costs of individual inputs (materials, labor, and overhead) to determine the cost of making a product or providing a service. *p. 5*

**product-level activities**  Actions taken (e.g., holding inventory, developmental engineering) that support a specific product or product line. *p. 210*

**product-level costs**  Costs incurred to support specific products or services; allocated based on the extent to which they sustain the product or service, and avoidable by eliminating the product line or type of service. *p. 257*

**productive assets**  Assets used to operate the business. May also be called *long-term assets.*

**profit center**  Responsibility center for which both revenues and costs can be identified. *p. 401*

**profitability ratios**  Measures of a company's capacity to generate earnings. *p. 599*

**qualitative characteristics**  Features of information such as company reputation, employee welfare, and customer satisfaction that cannot be quantified but may be relevant to decision making. *p. 256*

**quality**  The degree to which products or services conform to their design specifications. *p. 216*

**quality cost report**  Accounting report that typically lists the company's quality costs both in absolute dollars and as a percentage of total quality cost. *p. 218*

**quantitative characteristics** Features of information that can be mathematically measured, such as the dollar amounts of revenues and expenses, often relevant to decision making. *p. 256*

**quick ratio (acid-test ratio)** Measure of immediate debt-paying ability; calculated by dividing highly liquid assets (cash, receivables, and marketable securities) by current liabilities. *p. 592*

**ratio analysis** Same as *percentage analysis. p. 592*

**raw materials** Physical commodities (e.g., wood, metal, paint) transformed into products through the manufacturing process. *p. 9*

**Raw Materials Inventory** Asset account used to accumulate the costs of materials (such as lumber, metals, paints, chemicals) that will be used to make the company's products. *p. 486*

**reciprocal method** Allocation method that uses simultaneous linear equations to account for two-way relationships among service centers (service centers both provide services to and receive services from other service centers); the resultant cost distributions are difficult to interpret. *p. 175*

**reciprocal relationships** Two-way relationships in which departments provide services to and receive services from one another. *p. 175*

**recovery of investment** Recovery of the funds used to acquire the original investment. *p. 460*

**reengineering** Business practices companies design to improve competitiveness in world markets by eliminating or minimizing waste, errors, and costs in production and delivery systems. *p. 24*

**regression analysis** See *least-squares regression. p. 73*

**relaxing the constraints** Opening bottlenecks that limit the profitable operations of a business. *p. 271*

**relevant costs** Future-oriented costs that differ among alternative business decisions; also known as *avoidable costs. p. 254*

**relevant information** Decision-making information about costs, cost savings, or revenues that: (1) is future-oriented and (2) differs among the available alternatives; decision specific (information relevant to one decision may not be relevant to another decision). *Relevant costs* are also called *avoidable* or *incremental costs* and *relevant revenues* are also called *differential* or *incremental revenues. p. 254*

**relevant range** Range of activity over which the definitions of fixed and variable costs are valid. *p. 65*

**residual income** Performance measure that evaluates managers based on how well they maximize the dollar value of earnings above some targeted level of earnings. *p. 409*

**responsibility accounting** Performance evaluation system in which accountability for results is assigned to a segment manager of the business based on the amount of control or influence the manager has over those results. *p. 398*

**responsibility center** Identifiable part of an organization where control over revenues or expenses can be assigned. *p. 400*

**responsibility reports** Performance reports for the various company responsibility centers that highlight controllable items; show variances between budgeted and actual controllable items. *p. 401*

**retained earnings** Portion of stockholders' equity that represents the amount of net income kept in the business since inception (revenues minus expenses and distributions for all accounting periods). *p. 656*

**return on assets** The ratio of net income divided by average total assets. See also *return on investment. p. 600*

**return on equity** Profitability measure based on earnings a company generates relative to its stockholders' equity; calculated as net income divided by average stockholders' equity. *p. 601*

**return on investment** Profitability measure based on earnings a company generates relative to its asset base; calculated as net income divided by average total assets. ROI can be viewed as the product of net margin and asset turnover. Also called *return on assets* or *earning power. pp. 405, 600*

**revenue transactions** Business events that increase assets or decrease liabilities by providing services or products to customers in the course of operating a business.

**R Square ($R^2$) statistic** The $R^2$ Statistic represents the percentage of change in a dependent variable that is explained by a change in an independent variable. *p. 73*

**sales price variance** Variance attributable to the actual sales price differing from the standard sales price; calculated as the difference between actual sales revenue and flexible budget sales revenue (the standard sales price per unit times the actual number of units sold). *p. 354*

**sales volume variance** Variance attributable to the actual volume of sales differing from the budgeted volume of sales; calculated as the difference between the static budget (standard sales price times standard level of activity) and the flexible budget (standard sales price times actual level of activity). *p. 352*

**Sarbanes-Oxley Act of 2002** A federal law that regulates corporate governance. *p. 21*

**scattergraph** Method of estimating the variable and fixed components of a mixed cost by plotting cost data on a graph and visually drawing a regression line through the data points so that the total distance between the points and the line is minimized. *p. 69*

**schedule of cost of goods manufactured and sold** Internal accounting report that summarizes the manufacturing product costs for the period; its result, cost of goods sold, is reported as a single line item on the company's income statement. *p. 499*

**Securities and Exchange Commission (SEC)** Government agency authorized by Congress to regulate financial reporting practices of public companies; requires companies that issue securities to the public to file audited financial statements with the government annually. *p. 5*

**segment** Component part of an organization that is designated as a reporting entity. *p. 263*

**selling, general, and administrative costs (SG&A)** All costs not associated with obtaining or manufacturing a product; sometimes called *period costs* because they are normally expensed in the period in which the economic sacrifice is incurred. *p. 5*

**semivariable costs** See *mixed costs. p. 54*

**sensitivity analysis** Spreadsheet tool used to answer "what-if" questions to assess the sensitivity of profits to simultaneous changes in fixed cost, variable cost, and sales volume. *p. 121*

**service departments** Departments such as quality control, repair and maintenance, personnel, and accounting that provide support to other departments. (Contrast with *operating departments.*) *p. 170*

**single-payment (lump-sum)**   A one-time future cash flow that can be converted to its present value using a conversion factor. *p. 446*

**solvency ratios**   Measures of a company's capacity to pay long-term debt. *p. 597*

**special order decisions**   Deciding whether to accept orders from customers who offer to buy goods or services at prices significantly below selling prices regular customers pay. If the order's differential revenues exceed its avoidable costs, the order should be accepted unless qualitative factors, such as the order's effect on the existing customer base, could lead to unfavorable consequences. *p. 258*

**split-off point**   Stage in the production process where products made from common inputs become separate and identifiable. *p. 165*

**standards**   Budgeted per-unit selling prices or costs that are based on anticipated circumstances; multiplying the per-unit standards for cost and quantity produces the per-unit standard cost. *p. 358*

**start-up (setup) costs**   Costs of activities performed to prepare to make a different product or batch of products, such as resetting machinery, changing the production configuration, and conducting inspection. *p. 205*

**statement of cash flows**   The financial statement that classifies and reports a company's sources and uses of cash during an accounting period. *p. 636*

**static budget**   A budget based solely on the planned level of activity, such as the master budget; not adjusted for changes in activity volume. *p. 350*

**step method**   Two-step allocation method that accounts for one-way interdepartmental service center relationships by allocating costs from service centers to service centers as well as from service centers to operating departments; does not account for reciprocal relationships between service centers. *p. 173*

**strategic cost management**   Newer techniques managers can use to more accurately measure and control costs; implemented as a response to the complex modern automated business environment. These strategies include eliminating nonvalue-added activities, designing more efficient manufacturing processes, and developing more effective ways, like activity-based costing, to trace overhead costs to cost objects. *p. 216*

**strategic planning**   Long-range planning activities such as defining the scope of the business, determining which products to develop, deciding whether to discontinue a business segment, and determining which market niche would be most profitable. *p. 306*

**suboptimization**   Condition in which the best interests of the organization as a whole are in conflict with managers' own self-interests. *p. 409*

**sunk costs**   Costs that have been previously incurred; not relevant for decision making. For example, in an equipment replacement decision, the cost paid for the existing machine presently in use is a nonavoidable sunk cost because it has already been incurred. *p. 254*

**T-account method**   Technique for determining the cash inflows and outflows for the period by analyzing changes in balance sheet accounts from the beginning to the end of the period; infers the period's transactions from income statement and other data.

**target pricing (target costing)**   Strategy that sets the selling price by determining the price at which a product that will satisfy market demands will sell and then developing that product at a cost that results in a profit. *pp. 112, 214*

**theory of constraints (TOC)**   A management practice used to increase profitability by identifying bottlenecks or resource limitations that restrict operations and then removing them by relaxing the constraints. *p. 271*

**time value of money**   The concept that the present value of one dollar to be exchanged in the future is less than one dollar because of interest, risk, and inflation factors. *p. 444*

**times interest earned**   Ratio that measures a company's ability to make its interest payments; calculated by dividing the amount of earnings available for interest payments (net income before interest and income taxes) by the amount of the interest payments. *p. 497*

**total quality management (TQM)**   Management strategy that focuses on (1) continuous systematic problem-solving by personnel at all levels of the organization to eliminate waste, defects, and nonvalue-added activities; and (2) managing quality costs in a manner that leads to the highest level of customer satisfaction. *pp. 24, 218*

**transferred-in costs**   Costs transferred from one department to the next; combined with the materials, labor, and overhead costs incurred in the subsequent department so that when goods are complete, the total product cost of all departments is transferred to the Finished Goods Inventory account. *p. 537*

**transfer price**   Price at which products or services are transferred between divisions or other segments of an organization. *p. 413*

**trend analysis**   Study of business performance over a period of time. *p. 589*

**turnover**   Measure of sales in relation to operating assets; calculated as sales divided by operating assets. Along with *margin*, a component of return on investment. *p. 407*

**turnover of assets ratio**   See *asset turnover ratio*. *p. 407*

**unadjusted rate of return (simple rate of return)**   Measure of profitability computed by dividing the average incremental increase in annual net income by the average cost of the original investment (original cost divided by 2); does not account for the *time value of money*. *p. 449*

**unfavorable variance**   Variance indicating that actual costs exceed standard costs or actual sales are less than budgeted sales. *p. 351*

**unit-level activities**   Actions taken (e.g., using direct materials or direct labor) each time a unit of product is produced. *p. 208*

**unit-level costs**   Costs incurred with each unit of product made or single service performed; exhibit variable cost behavior; avoidable by not producing the unit of product or providing the service. Similarly, unit-level costs increase with each additional product produced or service provided. *p. 257*

**upstream costs**   Costs incurred before beginning the manufacturing process, such as research and development costs. *pp. 13, 214*

**value-added activity**   Any part of business operations that contributes to a product's ability to satisfy customer needs. *p. 24*

**value-added principle**   The benefits attained (value added) from a process should exceed the cost of the process. *p. 5*

**value chain** Linked sequence of activities that create value for the customer. *p. 24*

**variable cost** Cost that in total changes in direct proportion to changes in volume of activity; remains constant per unit regardless of changes in activity volume. *p. 54*

**variable cost volume variance** The difference between a variable cost calculated at the planned volume of activity and the same variable cost calculated at the actual volume of activity. *p. 352*

**variable costing** Costing method in which only variable manufacturing costs are capitalized in inventory; all fixed costs, including fixed manufacturing overhead, are expensed in the period incurred. On a variable costing income statement, all variable costs are subtracted from revenue to determine contribution margin, then all fixed costs are subtracted from the contribution margin to determine net income. Under variable costing, production volume has no effect on the amount of net income. (Contrast with *absorption costing*.) *p. 501*

**variances** Differences between standard (budgeted) and actual amounts. *p. 351*

**vertical analysis** Financial analysis technique of comparing items within financial statements to significant totals. *p. 592*

**vertical integration** Maintaining control over the entire continuum of business activity from production to selling, such as a company owning both a grocery store and a farm. *p. 262*

**visual fit line** Line drawn by visual inspection on a scatter-graph of data points to minimize the total distance between the data points and the line; used to estimate fixed and variable cost. *p. 70*

**volume-based cost drivers** Measures of volume such as labor-hours, machine-hours, or quantities of materials that are highly correlated with unit-level overhead cost; serve as appropriate bases for allocating unit-level overhead costs. *p. 204*

**voluntary costs** Discretionary quality costs incurred for prevention and appraisal activities. *p. 216*

**weighted average method** Means of computing equivalent units in a process cost system that accounts for the degree of completion of ending inventory only; ignores the state of completion of items in beginning inventory, accounting for them as if complete. *p. 550*

**Work in Process Inventory** Asset account used to accumulate the product costs (direct materials, direct labor, and overhead) associated with incomplete products that have been started but are not yet completed. *p. 486*

**work ticket** Mechanism (paper or electronic) used to accumulate the time spent on a job by each employee; sometimes called a *time card*. It is sent to the accounting department where wage rates are recorded and labor costs determined. The amount of labor costs for each ticket is summarized on the appropriate job-order cost sheet. *p. 538*

**working capital** A measure of the adequacy of short-term assets; computed as current assets minus current liabilities. *pp. 451, 594*

**working capital ratio** See *current ratio*. *p. 594*

# PHOTO CREDITS

**Chapter 1**

p. 3 © Schwinn via Getty Images, p. 5 © AP Photo/Susan Walsh, p. 15 Courtesy of Ford Motor Company, p. 20 © Alex L. Fradkin/Getty Images, p. 22 © Adam Roundtree/Bloomberg via Getty Images

**Chapter 2**

p. 55 © AP Photo/Phil Coale, p. 57 © Author's Image/Punchstock, p. 67 © AP Photo/Ted S. Warren, p. 71 © Beawiharta/Reuters/Corbis

**Chapter 3**

p. 107 © AP Photo/Mark Lennihan, p. 114 © Peter Morgan/Reuters/Corbis, p. 118 © Bill Pugliano/Getty Images, p. 127 © Ryan McVay/Getty Images

**Chapter 4**

p. 151 © Stockbyte/PunchStock, p. 152 © Lynn Seldon, p. 155 Courtesy of Southwest Airlines, p. 163 © John A. Rizzo/Getty Images

**Chapter 5**

p. 203 © AP Photo/Kathy Willens, p. 204 © Digital Vision/PunchStock, p. 217 © Press Association via AP Images, p. 219 Courtesy of J. D. Power and Associates

**Chapter 6**

p. 253 © Scott Olsen/Getty Images, p. 255 Blend Images/Getty Images, p. 257 © Ryan Pyle/Corbis, p. 262 © AP Photo/Markus Leodolter

**Chapter 7**

p. 305 © Kyodo via AP Images, p. 307 © 2007 Getty Images, Inc., p. 311 © F. Schussler/PhotoLink/Getty Images, p. 316 © AP Photo/J. Scott Applewhite

**Chapter 8**

p. 349 © Brand X Pictures/PunchStock, p. 352 © Thomas Barwick/Getty Images, p. 358 © AP Photo/William Foreman, p. 364 © PhotoLink/Photodisc/Getty Images, p. 366 © ColorBlind Images/Getty Images

**Chapter 9**

p. 399 © AP Photo/Gerald Herbert, p. 401 © Chris Kerrigan, p. 410 © Stockbyte/PunchStock, p. 411 © AP Photo/Kevork Djansezian, p. 414 © Steve Allen/Getty Images

**Chapter 10**

p. 443 © AP Photo/Mike Derer, p. 444 © Don Bishop/Getty Images, p. 451 © Image 100/Corbis, p. 455 © Creatas/PunchStock

**Chapter 11**

p. 485 © William W. Bacon/Alaska Stock LLC/Alamy, p. 487 © AP Photo, p. 489 © Allan H. Shoemake/Getty Images

**Chapter 12**

p. 535 © Peter Yates/Corbis, p. 536 © Walt Disney Co./courtesy Everett Collection, p. 539 © Radius Images/Corbis, p. 558 © Christophe Bosset/Bloomberg via Getty Images

**Chapter 13**

p. 587 © AP Photo/Paul Sakuma, p. 588 © Susan Van Etten/PhotoEdit, p. 600 © Hannelore Foerster/Bloomberg via Getty Images

**Chapter 14**

p. 637 © Jason Reed/Reuters/Landov, p. 639 © Ryan McVay/Getty Images, p. 655 © Royalty-Free/Corbis, p. 659 © The McGraw-Hill Companies, Inc./Lars A. Niki, photographer, p. 660 Courtesy of International Business Machines Corporation. Unauthorized use not permitted.

Page numbers followed by n refer to notes.